Derivatives Markets

Third Edition

ROBERT L. McDONALD

PEARSON

All trademarks used herein are the property of their respective owners. The use of any trademark in this text does not vest in the author or publisher any trademark ownership rights in such trademarks, nor does the use of such trademarks imply any affiliation with or endorsement of this book by such owners.

Authorized Licensed Edition of the original UK edition, entitled Derivatives Markets*: Pearson New International Edition: Third Edition* by Mcdonald, Robert L, published by Pearson Education Limited,
© 2013 Pearson Education Limited

All rights reserved. This book is sold subject to the condition that it shall not, by way of trade or otherwise, be lent, resold, hired out, or otherwise circulated without the publisher's prior written consent in any form of binding or cover other than that in which it is published and without a similar condition including this condition being imposed on the subsequent purchaser and without limiting the rights under copyright reserved above, no part of this publication may be reproduced, stored in or introduced into a retrieval system, or transmitted in any form or by any means (electronic, mechanical, photocopying, recording or otherwise), without the prior written permission of both the copyright owner and the above-mentioned publisher of this book.

Indian edition published by Dorling Kindersley India Pvt. Ltd. Copyright © 2014

ISBN 978-93-325-3674-6

First Impression, 2014

This edition is manufactured in India and is authorized for sale only in India, Bangladesh, Bhutan, Pakistan, Nepal, Sri Lanka and the Maldives. Circulation of this edition outside of these territories is UNAUTHORIZED.

Published by Pearson India Education Services Pvt.Ltd,CIN:U72200TN2005PTC057128.
Formerly known as TutorVista Global Pvt Ltd, licensees of Pearson Education in South Asia

Head Office: 7th Floor, knowledge Boulevard, A-8(A) Sector-62, Noida (U.P) 201309, India

Registered Office: Module G4, Ground Floor, Elnet Software City, TS -140,Block 2 & 9
Rajiv Gandhi Salai, Taramani, Chennai, Tamil Nadu 600113.,Fax: 080-30461003,
Phone: 080-30461060, www.pearson.co.in email id: companysecretary.india@pearson.com

Digitally Printed in India by Repro India Ltd. in the year of 2015.

Table of Contents

Glossary

Absolute priority A procedure for a firm in bankruptcy in which junior creditors are not paid unless more senior creditors have been fully repaid.

Accreting swap A swap where the notional amount increases over the life of the swap.

Accrued interest The pro-rated portion of a bond's coupon since the previous coupon date.

Affine function A function $A(x)$ is affine if $A(x) = a + bL(x)$, where $L(x)$ is a linear function of x. Note that $f(x) = a + bx$ is affine but not linear.

Alpha-porting Using a futures overlay to transfer a portfolio alpha (a measure of superior performance) from one asset class to another.

American option An option that may be exercised at any time during its life.

Amortizing swap A swap where the notional amount declines over the life of the swap.

Antithetic variate method A technique used in Monte Carlo valuation, in which each random draw is used to create two simulated prices from opposite tails of the asset price distribution.

Arbitrage A transaction generating a positive cash flow either today or in the future by simultaneously buying and selling related assets, with no net investment of funds, and with no risk.

Arithmetic Brownian motion A continuous stochastic process, $x(t)$, in which the increments are given as $dx(t) = \alpha\, dt + \sigma\, dZ$, where dZ is the increment to a Brownian process.

Asian option An option in which the payoff at maturity depends upon an average of the asset prices over the life of the option.

Asian tail A reference price that is computed as an average of recent prices. For example, an equity-linked note may have a payoff based on the average daily stock price over the last 20 days (the Asian tail).

Ask price The price at which a dealer or market-maker offers to sell a security. Also called the *offer price*.

Asset swap A swap, typically involving a bond, in which fixed bond payments are swapped for payments based on a floating rate.

Asset-backed security A financial claim to the cash flows from a pool of assets. The regulatory definition of an ABS in the United States is in 17 C.F.R. §229.1101(c)(1).

Asset-or-nothing call An option that pays a unit of the asset if the asset price exceeds the strike price at expiration or zero otherwise.

Asset-or-nothing option An option that pays a unit of the asset if the option is in-the-money or zero otherwise.

Asset-or-nothing put An option that pays a unit of the asset if the asset price is less than the strike price at expiration or zero otherwise.

Asymmetric butterfly spread A butterfly spread in which the distance between strike prices is not equal.

At-the-money An option for which the price of the underlying asset approximately equals the strike price.

Back-to-back transaction A transaction where a dealer enters into offsetting transactions with different parties, effectively serving as a go-between.

Backward equation See *Kolmogorov backward equation.*

Backwardation A forward curve in which the futures prices are falling with time to expiration.

Barrel A unit of volume commonly used in quoting oil prices, equal to 42 gallons.

From *Derivatives Markets*, Third Edition, Robert McDonald. Copyright © 2013 by Pearson Education, Inc. Published by Pearson Prentice Hall. All rights reserved.

Barrier option An option that has a payoff depending upon whether, at some point during the life of the option, the price of the underlying asset has moved past a reference price (the barrier). Examples are knock-in and knock-out options.

Basis The difference between the cash price of the underlying asset and the futures price.

Basis point 1/100th of 1%, i.e., one ten-thousandth (0.0001).

Basis risk The possibility of unexpected changes in the difference between the price of an asset and the price of the contract hedging the asset.

Bear spread The sale of a call (or put) together with the purchase of an otherwise identical higher-strike call (or put).

Bermudan option An option that can only be exercised at specified times during its life.

Beta A Greek letter commonly used to denote the slope coefficient from regressing the return on an asset against the return on the return on a broad market index, such as the S&P 500. Beta thus measures the extent to which a particular asset moves together with the index. Because beta measures comovement, it is a measure of systematic risk—risk that cannot be diversified in a portfolio.

Bid price The price at which a dealer or market-maker buys a security.

Bid-ask spread The difference between the bid price and the ask price.

Binary option An option that has a payoff that is a discrete amount—for example, $1 or one share. Also called a *digital option*.

Binomial tree A representation of possible asset price movements over time, in which the asset price is modeled as moving up or down by a given amount each period.

Black formula A version of the Black-Scholes formula in which the underlying asset is a futures price and the dividend yield is replaced with the risk-free rate.

Black-Scholes equation The partial differential equation relating price, delta, gamma, and theta, that must be satisfied by derivatives. The Black-Scholes *formula* solves the Black-Scholes *equation*.

Black-Scholes formula The formula giving the price of a European call option as a function of the stock price, strike price, time to expiration, interest rate, volatility, and dividend yield.

Bootstrapping This term has two meanings. First, it refers to the procedure where coupon bonds are used to generate the set of zero-coupon bond prices. Second, it means the use of historical returns to create an empirical probability distribution for returns.

Boundary condition The value of a derivative claim at a certain time, or at a particular price of the underlying asset. For example, a boundary condition for a zero-coupon bond is that the bond at maturity is worth its promised maturity value.

Box spread An option position in which the stock is synthetically purchased (buy call, sell put) at one price and sold (sell call, buy put) at a different price. When constructed with European options, the box spread is equivalent to a zero-coupon bond.

Brownian motion A stochastic process in which the random variable moves continuously and follows a random walk with normally distributed, independent increments. Named after the Scottish botanist Robert Brown, who in 1827 noticed that pollen grains suspended in water exhibited continual movement. Brownian motion is also called a *Wiener process*.

Bull spread The purchase of a call (or put) together with the sale of an otherwise identical higher-strike call (or put).

Bushel A unit of dry measure commonly used in quoting grain prices. A bushel is 4 pecks, equal to approximately 2150 cubic inches. By comparison, a cubic foot is 1728 cubic inches.

Butterfly spread A position created by buying a call, selling two calls at a higher strike price, and buying a fourth call at a still higher strike price, with an equal distance between strike prices. The butterfly spread can also be created using puts alone, or by buying a straddle and insuring it with the purchase of out-of-the-money calls and puts, or in a variety of other ways.

Calendar spread A spread position in which the bought and sold options or futures have the same underlying asset but different times to maturity.

Call option A contract giving the buyer the right, but not the obligation, to buy the underlying asset at a prespecified price.

Call protection A period during which a callable bond cannot be called.

Call schedule A contractual feature of a callable bond, specifying the price at which the company can buy the bond back from bondholders at different points in time.

Callable bond A bond where the issuer has the right to buy the bond back from bondholders by paying a prespecified amount.

Cap An options contract that serves as insurance against a high price. (See also *Interest rate cap*.)

Caplet A contract that insures a borrower against a high interest rate on a single date. A collection of caplets is an *interest rate cap*.

Capped option An option with a maximum payoff, where the option is automatically exercised if the underlying asset reaches the price at which the maximum payoff is attained.

Carry Another term for owning an asset, typically used to refer to commodities. (See also *Carry market* and *Cost of carry*.)

Carry market A situation where the forward price is such that the return on a cash-and-carry is the risk-free rate.

Carry trade A risky strategy in which an investor borrows at a low rate of interest and lends at a high rate of interest. Common carry trades are borrowing in one currency and lending in another, or in fixed income, borrowing short-term and lending long-term.

Cash flow mapping A procedure in which the cash flows of a given claim are assigned—or mapped—to a set of benchmark claims. This provides a way to approximate the claim in terms of the benchmark claims.

Cash settlement A procedure where settlement entails a cash payment from one party to the other, instead of delivery of an asset.

Cash-and-carry The simultaneous spot purchase and forward sale of an asset or commodity.

Cash-and-carry arbitrage The use of a cash-and-carry to effect an arbitrage.

Cash-or-nothing call An option that pays a fixed amount of cash if the asset price exceeds the strike price at expiration or zero otherwise.

Cash-or-nothing option An option that pays a fixed amount of cash if the option is in-the-money or zero otherwise.

Cash-or-nothing put An option that pays a fixed amount of cash if the asset price is less than the strike price at expiration or zero otherwise.

CDO See *collateralized debt obligation*.

CDO-squared A collateralized debt obligation in which the underlying asset pool consists of tranches from a set of different collateralized debt obligations.

Central limit theorem One of the most important results in statistics, which states that the sum of independent and identically distributed random variables has a limiting distribution that is normal.

Cheapest to deliver When a futures contract gives the seller a choice of asset to deliver to the buyer, the asset that is most profitable for the short to deliver.

Cholesky decomposition A formula used to construct a set of correlated random variables from a set of uncorrelated random variables.

Clean price The present value of a bond's future cash flows less accrued interest.

Clearinghouse A financial organization, typically associated with one or more exchanges, that matches the buy and sell orders that take place during the day and keeps track of the obligations and payments required of the members of the clearinghouse.

Collar The purchase of a put and sale of a call at a higher strike price.

Collar width The difference between the strike prices of the two options in a collar.

Collateralized debt obligation A financial structure that consists of a pool of assets, financed by issuing financial claims that reapportion the return on the asset pool.

Collect-on-delivery option An option where the premium is paid only when the option is exercised.

Commodity spread Offsetting long and short positions in closely related commodities. (See also *Crack spread* and *Crush spread*.)

Compound option An option that has an option as the underlying asset.

Concave Shaped like the cross-section of an upside-down bowl.

Conditional VaR (CVaR) The expected loss conditional upon the VaR loss being exceeded. Another name for tail VaR.

Constructive sale A term in tax law describing the owner of an asset entering into an offsetting position that largely eliminates the risk of holding the asset.

Contango A forward curve in which futures prices are rising with time to expiration.

Contingent convertible bond A bond that becomes convertible once a contingency (for example, the share price is greater than $100 for 30 days) has occurred.

Continuation value The value of leaving an option unexercised. You make an exercise decision by comparing the continuation value to the value of immediate exercise.

Continuously compounded interest rate A way of quoting an interest rate such that if $1 is invested at a continuously compounded rate of r, the payoff in 1 year is e^r.

Control variate method A technique used in Monte Carlo valuation in which simulated asset prices are used to compute two derivatives prices: the price of the derivative that is being valued, and the price of a related derivative for which the value is known. The error in valuing the derivative with a known price is used as a control for that with the unknown price.

Convenience yield A nonmonetary return to ownership of an asset or commodity.

Conversion A risk-free position consisting of an asset, a purchased put, and a written call.

Convertible bond A bond which, at the option of the bondholder, can be surrendered for a specified number of shares of stock.

Convex Shaped like the cross-section of a bowl.

Convexity The second derivative of a bond's price with respect to a change in the interest rate, divided by the bond price.

Cooling degree-day The greater of (i) the average daily temperature minus 65 degrees Fahrenheit, and (ii) zero.

Cost of carry The interest cost of owning an asset, less lease or dividend payments received as a result of ownership; the net cash flow resulting from borrowing to buy an asset.

Covered call A long position in an asset together with a written call on the same asset.

Covered interest arbitrage A zero-investment strategy with simultaneous borrowing in one currency, lending in another, and entering into a forward contract to guarantee the exchange rate when the loans mature.

Covered write A long position in an asset coupled with sale of a call option on the same asset.

Crack spread The difference between the price of crude oil futures and that of equivalent amounts of heating oil and gasoline.

Credit derivative A claim where the payoff depends upon the credit rating or default status of a firm.

Credit risk Risk resulting from the possibility that a counterparty will be financially unable to meet its contractual obligations.

Credit spread The difference between the yields on a bond that can default and on an otherwise equivalent default-free bond.

Credit-linked note A bond that has payments determined at least in part by credit events (e.g., default) at a different firm.

Cross-hedging The use of a derivative on one underlying asset to hedge the risk of another underlying asset.

Crush spread The difference between the price of a quantity of soybeans and that of the soybean meal and oil that can be produced by those soybeans.

Cumulative distribution function A function giving the probability that a value drawn from a distribution will be less than or equal to some specified value.

Cumulative normal distribution function The cumulative distribution function for the normal distribution; $N(x)$ in the Black-Scholes equation.

Currency swap A swap in which the parties make payments based on the difference in debt payments in different currencies.

Currency-translated index An investment in an index denominated in a foreign currency, where the buyer bears both currency and asset risk.

Debenture A bond for which payments are secured only by the general credit of the issuer.

Debt capacity The maximum amount of debt that can be issued by a firm or secured by a specific asset.

Default Generally, the failure to make a promised payment on a bond or a loan. The term *technical default* typically means that a debtor has violated a covenant (i.e., a requirement of the indebtedness contract).

Default premium The difference between the yield on a bond and that on an otherwise equivalent default-free bond.

Default swap A contract in which the swap buyer pays a regular premium; in exchange, if a default in a specified bond occurs, the swap seller pays the buyer the loss due to the default.

Deferred down rebate option A deferred rebate option for which the current stock price is above the rebate barrier.

Deferred rebate option A claim that pays $1 at expiration if the price of the underlying asset has reached a barrier prior to expiration.

Deferred swap A swap with terms specified today, but for which swap payments begin at a later date than for an ordinary swap.

Deferred up rebate option A deferred rebate option for which the current stock price is below the rebate barrier.

Deflator A value used to express prices in alternative units. A numeraire serves as a deflator. For example, if we divide asset prices by the share price of XYZ, XYZ serves as a deflator. When deflated in this way, other asset prices rise or fall depending on whether the asset has a return greater or less than XYZ.

Delivery The act of the seller (e.g., of a forward contract) supplying the underlying asset to the buyer.

Delta The change in the price of a derivative due to a change in the price of the underlying asset.

Delta-gamma approximation A formula using the delta and gamma to approximate the change in the derivative price due to a change in the price of the underlying asset.

Delta-gamma-theta approximation A formula using the delta, gamma, and theta to approximate the change in the derivative price due to a change in the price of the underlying asset and the passage of time.

Delta-hedging Hedging a derivative position using the underlying asset, with the amount of the underlying asset determined by the derivative's sensitivity (*delta*) to the price of the underlying asset.

Derivative A financial instrument that has a value determined by the price of something else.

Diff swap A swap in which payments are based on the difference in floating interest rates on a given notional amount denominated in a single currency.

Differential equation An equation relating a variable to its derivatives and one or more independent variables.

Diffusion process Generally, a continuous stochastic process in which uncertainty increases with time. Also used to describe the Brownian (random) part of an Itô process.

Digital option Another name for a binary option.

Dirty price The present value of a bond's future cash flows (this implicitly includes accrued interest).

Distance to default The distance between the current firm asset value and the level at which default occurs, measured in standard deviations.

Diversifiable risk Risk that is, in the limit, eliminated by combining a large number of assets in a portfolio.

Dividend forward contract A forward contract that pays $FV_{0,T}(D) - F_{0,T}$, where $FV_{0,T}(D)$ is the future value of dividends paid over the period and $F_{0,T}$ is the forward price.

Dividend swap A swap that makes regular payments of $FV_{t,t+h}(D) - R$ where $FV_{t,t+h}(D)$ is the future value of dividends paid between t and $t + h$ and R is the swap price. In the United States, firms pay dividends quarterly, so h would naturally be three months.

Down-and-in A knock-in option for which the barrier is less than the current price of the underlying asset.

Down-and-out A knock-out option for which the barrier is less than the current price of the underlying asset.

Drift The expected change per unit time in an asset price.

Duration Generally, the weighted average life of the bond, which also provides a measure of the bond's sensitivity to interest rate changes. Two common duration measures are *modified duration* and *Macaulay duration*.

DV01 Dollar value of an "01"; the change in a bond price when the yield moves one basis point. Also known as the price value of a basis point (PVBP).

Effective annual interest rate A way of quoting an interest rate such that the quoted rate is the annual percentage increase in an amount invested at this rate. If \$1 is invested at an effective annual rate of r, the payoff in one year is $\$1 + r$.

Elasticity The percent change in an option price for a 1% change in the price of the underlying asset.

Equity-linked forward A forward contract (e.g., for currency) where the quantity to be bought or sold depends upon the performance of a stock or stock index.

European option An option that can only be exercised at expiration.

Exchange option An option permitting the holder to obtain one asset by giving up another. Standard calls and puts are exchange options in which one of the two assets is cash.

Exercise The exchange of the strike price (or strike asset) for the underlying asset at the terms specified in the option contract.

Exercise price Under the terms of an option contract, the amount that can be exchanged for the underlying asset.

Exercise style The circumstances under which an option holder has the right to exercise an option. "European" and "American" are exercise styles.

Exotic option A derivatives contract in which an ordinary derivative has been altered to change the characteristics of the derivative in a meaningful way. Also called a *nonstandard option*.

Expectations hypothesis A term with multiple meanings, one of which is that the expected future interest rate equals the implied forward rate.

Expected tail loss The expected loss conditional upon the VaR loss being exceeded. Another name for tail VaR.

Expiration The date beyond which an unexercised option is worthless.

Extractive commodity A commodity that occurs naturally underground and that is obtained by mining or pumping. Examples include metals (gold, silver, copper), oil, and natural gas.

Fair value Another name for the theoretical forward price: spot price plus interest less the future value of dividends.

Fed funds rate The interest rate in the U.S. at which banks lend money to one another overnight.

Financial engineering Creating new financial instruments by combining other derivatives, or more generally, by using derivatives pricing techniques.

Floor An option position that guarantees a minimum price.

Forward contract An agreement that sets today the terms—including price and quantity—at which you buy or sell an asset or commodity at a specific time in the future.

Forward curve The set of forward or futures prices with different expiration dates on a given date for a given asset.

Forward measure The probability distribution under which $S_i(t)/P_t(t, T)$ is a martingale, where $S_i(t)$ is the price of a risky asset and $P_t(t, T)$ is the time t price of a zero-coupon bond maturing at time T.

Forward premium The annualized percentage difference between the forward price and the spot price.

Forward rate agreement A forward contract for an interest rate.

Forward strip Another name for the *forward curve*.

Funded A position that is paid for in full at the outset. A prepaid forward, for example, is a funded position in a stock. See also *unfunded*.

Futures contract An agreement that is similar to a forward contract except that the buyer and seller post margin and the contract is marked-to-market periodically. Futures are typically exchange-traded.

Futures overlay Converting an investment in asset A into the economic equivalent of an investment in asset B by entering into a short futures position on asset A and a long futures position on asset B.

Gamma The change in delta when the price of the underlying asset changes by one unit.

Gap option An option where the option owner has the right to exercise the option at strike K_1 if the stock price exceeds (or, depending on the option, is less than) the price K_2. For an ordinary option, $K_1 = K_2$.

Geometric Brownian motion A continuous stochastic process, $x(t)$, in which the increments are given as $dx(t)/x(t) = \alpha dt + \sigma dZ$, where dZ is the increment to a Brownian process.

Girsanov's theorem A result that permits a change in the drift of an Itô process accompanied by a change in the probability distribution of the Brownian motion driving the process.

Greeks A term generally referring to delta, gamma, vega, theta, and rho, all of which measure the change in the price of a derivative when there is a change in an input to the pricing formula.

Haircut The collateral, over and above the market value of the security, required by the lender when a security is borrowed.

Heat rate A measure of the efficiency with which heat can be used to produce electricity. Specifically, it is the number of British Thermal Units required to produce 1 kilowatt/hour of electricity.

Heating degree-day The greater of (i) 65 degrees Fahrenheit minus the average daily temperature, and (ii) zero.

Hedge ratio In a hedging transaction, the ratio of the quantity of the forward or futures position to the quantity of the underlying asset.

Hedging An action—such as entering into a derivatives position—that reduces the risk of loss.

Heston model An option pricing model in which the instantaneous variance of the stock return follows a mean-reverting square root process.

Heteroskedasticity Data that is characterized by variances that are not equal, either over time or across different observations at a point in time.

Historical volatility The standard deviation of the continuously compounded return on an asset, measured using historical prices.

Homoskedasticity Data that is characterized by variances that are equal over time or across different observations at a point in time.

Hysteresis The failure of an effect to reverse itself as the underlying cause is reversed.

Implied forward rate The forward interest rate between time t_1 and time t_2 ($t_1 < t_2$) that makes an investor indifferent between, on the one hand, buying a bond maturing at t_2, and, on the other hand, buying a bond maturing at t_1 and reinvesting the proceeds at this forward interest rate.

Implied repo rate The rate of return on a cash-and-carry.

Implied volatility The volatility for which the theoretical option price (typically computed using the Black-Scholes formula) equals the observed market price of the option.

Interest rate cap A contract that periodically pays the difference between the market interest rate and a guaranteed rate, if the difference is positive.

In-the-money An option that would have value if exercised. For an in-the-money call, the stock price exceeds the strike price. For an in-the-money put, the stock price is less than the strike price.

Investment trigger price The price of an investment project (or the price of the good to be produced) at which it is optimal to invest in the project.

Itô process A continuous stochastic process that can be written in the form $dX(t) = \alpha[X(t), t]\,dt + \sigma[X(t), t]\,dZ(t)$, where $dZ(t)$ is the increment to a Brownian process.

Itô's Lemma If x follows an Itô process, Itô's Lemma describes the process followed by $f(x)$. For example, if x is a stock price and $f(x)$ an option price, Itô's Lemma characterizes the behavior of the option price in terms of the process for the stock.

Jensen's inequality If x is a random variable and $f(x)$ is convex, Jensen's inequality states that $E[f(x)] \geq f[E(x)]$. The inequality is reversed if $f(x)$ is concave.

Jump-diffusion model A process for an asset price in which the asset most of the time follows an Itô process but can also jump discretely, with occurrence of the jump controlled by a Poisson process.

Kappa Another name for *vega*.

Knock-in option An option in which there can only be a final payoff if, during a specified period of time, the price of the underlying asset has reached a specified level.

Knock-out option An option in which there can only be a final payoff if, during a specified period of time, the price of the underlying asset has *not* reached a specified level.

Kolmogorov backward equation A partial differential equation that is related to the Black-Scholes equation and that is satisfied by probability distributions for the underlying asset.

Kurtosis A measure of the peakedness of a probability distribution. For a random variable x with mean μ and standard deviation σ, kurtosis is the fourth central moment divided by the squared variance, $E(x-\mu)^4/\sigma^4$. For a normal random variable, kurtosis is 3.

Ladder option If the barrier $L > K$ is reached over the life of the option, a ladder option at expiration pays $\max(0, L-K, S_T-K)$. If the barrier is not reached, the option pays $\max(0, S_T-K)$.

Lambda Another name for *vega*.

Lattice A binomial tree in which an up move followed by a down move leads to the same price as a down move followed by an up move. Also called a *recombining tree*.

Law of one price The assertion that two portfolios generating exactly the same return must have the same price.

Lease rate The annualized payment required to borrow an asset, or equivalently, the annualized payment received in exchange for lending an asset.

Leverage effect A rise in the stock price volatility when the stock price declines.

LIBID London Interbank Bid Rate. See *LIBOR*.

LIBOR London Interbank Offer Rate. A measure of the borrowing rate for large international banks. The British Banker's Association determines LIBOR daily for different currencies by surveying at least eight banks, asking at what rate they could borrow, dropping the top and bottom quartiles of the responses, and computing an arithmetic average of the remaining quotes. Since LIBOR is an average, there may be no actual transactions at that rate. Confusingly, LIBOR is also sometimes referred to as a lending rate. This is because a bank serving as a market-maker in the interbank market will offer to lend money at a high interest rate (LIBOR) and borrow money at a low interest rate (LIBID). (The difference between LIBOR and LIBID is the bid-ask spread in the interbank market.) A bank needing to borrow will thus pay LIBOR, and a bank with excess funds will receive LIBID.

Linear function A function $L(x)$ is linear if $L(x_1 + x_2) = L(x_1) + L(x_2)$ and $L(\lambda x) = \lambda L(x)$. See also *affine function*.

Log contract A derivative contract that, at maturity, pays the natural log of an asset price.

Lognormal distribution A probability distribution in which the natural logarithm of the random variable is normally distributed.

Long A position is long with respect to a price if the position profits from an increase in that price. An owner of a stock profits from an increase in the stock price and, hence, is long the stock. An owner of an option profits from an increase in volatility and, hence, is long volatility.

Long forward The party to a forward contract who has an obligation to buy the underlying asset.

Lookback call See *Lookback option*.

Lookback option An option that, at maturity, pays off based on the maximum ($\overline{S}_T$) or minimum ($\underline{S}_T$) stock price over the life of the option. A *lookback call* has the payoff $S_T - \underline{S}_T$ and a *lookback put* has the payoff $\overline{S}_T - S_T$.

Lookback put See *Lookback option*.

Macaulay duration The percent change in a bond's price for a given percent change in one plus the bond's yield. This calculation can be interpreted as the weighted average life of the bond, with the weights being the percentage of the bond's value due to each payment.

Maintenance margin The level of margin at which the contract holder is required to add cash or securities to the margin account.

Mandatorily convertible bond A bond that makes payments in shares instead of cash, with the number of shares paid to the bondholder typically dependent upon the share price.

Margin A deposit required for both buyers and sellers of a futures contract, which indemnifies the counterparty against the failure of the buyer or seller to meet the obligations of the contract.

Margin call The requirement that the owner of a margined position add funds to the margin account. This can result from a loss on the position or an increase in the margin requirement.

Market corner Owning a large percentage of the available supply of an asset or commodity that is required for delivery under the terms of a derivatives contract.

Market-maker A trader in an asset, commodity, or derivative who simultaneously offers to buy at one price (the bid price) or to sell at a higher price (the offer price), thereby "making a market."

Market-timing The allocation of assets between stocks and bonds in an attempt to invest in whichever asset is going to have a higher return.

Mark-to-market The procedure of revaluing a portfolio or position to reflect current market prices.

Martingale A stochastic process for which $E[X(t+s)|\Phi(t)] = X(t)$, where $\Phi(t)$ is information available at time t.

Modified duration The percent change in a bond's price for a unit change in the yield. Modified duration is also Macaulay duration divided by one plus the bond's yield per payment period.

Monte Carlo valuation A procedure for pricing derivative claims by discounting expected payoffs, where the expected payoff is computed using simulated prices for the underlying asset.

Naked writing Selling options without an offsetting position in the underlying asset.

Net payoff Another term for *profit*.

Nondiversifiable risk Risk that remains after a large number of assets are combined in a portfolio.

Nonrecombining tree A binomial tree describing asset price moves in which an up move followed by a down move yields a different price than a down move followed by an up move.

Nonstandard option See *Exotic option*.

Nontraded asset A cash flow stream that cannot be purchased directly in financial markets. Many corporate investment projects are non-traded because they can only be acquired by buying the entire company.

Normal distribution A bell-shaped, symmetric, continuous probability distribution that assigns positive probability to all values from $-\infty$ to $+\infty$. Sometimes called the "bell curve." (See also *Central limit theorem*.)

Notional amount The dollar amount used as a scale factor in calculating payments for a forward contract, futures contract, or swap.

Notional principal The notional amount for an interest rate swap.

Notional value The amount used to calculate gains and losses on a contract. When the contract provides leverage, the notional value can differ from the market value. For example, an S&P 500 futures contract has zero value (like any futures contract), but gains and losses are computed on $250 times the S&P 500 index value, which is the notional value.

Novation The process in derivatives markets where one party (typically a clearinghouse) interposes itself between a buyer and seller, becoming the counterparty for each.

Numeraire The units in which a payoff is denominated.

Offer price The same as the *ask price*.

Off-market forward A forward contract in which the forward price is set so that the value of the contract is not zero.

Off-the-run A government bond that is not one of the recently issued bonds.

On-the-run The most recently auctioned government bonds at the government's specific auction maturities.

Open interest The quantity of a derivatives contract that is outstanding at a point in time. (One long and one short position count as one unit outstanding.)

Open outcry A system of trading in which buyers and sellers in one physical location convey offers to buy and sell by gesturing and shouting.

Option backdating The practice of retrospectively selecting the low stock price when granting at-the-money options.

Option elasticity The percent change in an option price for a 1% change in the price of the underlying asset.

Option overwriting Selling a call option against a long position in the underlying asset.

Option writer The party with a short position in the option.

Order statistics The n draws of a random variable sorted in ascending order.

Out-of-the-money An option that would be exercised at a loss. An out-of-the-money call has the stock price less than the strike price. An out-of-the-money put has the stock price greater than the strike price.

Outperformance option An option in which the payoff is determined by the extent to which one asset price is greater than another asset price.

Over-the-counter market A term used generally to refer to transactions (e.g., purchases and sales of securities or derivatives contracts) that occur without the involvement of a regulated exchange.

Par bond A bond for which the price at issue equals the maturity value.

Par coupon The coupon rate on a par bond.

Partial expectation The sum (or integral) of a set of outcomes times the probability of those outcomes.

Path-dependent A derivative where the final payoff depends upon the path taken by the stock price, instead of just the final stock price.

Payer swaption A swaption giving the holder the right to be the fixed-rate payer in a swap.

Paylater strategy Generally used to refer to option strategies in which the position buyer makes no payments unless the option moves more into the money.

Payoff The value of a position at a point in time. The term often implicitly refers to a payoff at expiration or maturity.

Payoff diagram A graph in which the value of a derivative or other claim at a point in time is plotted against the price of the underlying asset.

Payout protected A characteristic of a derivative where a change in the dividend payout on the underlying asset does not change the value of the derivative.

Perpetual option An option that never expires.

Physical probability The observed probability of an event in the real world.

Poisson distribution A probability distribution that counts the number of events occurring in an interval of time, assuming that the occurrence of events is independent.

Positive-definite An $n \times n$ matrix with elements $a_{i,j}$ is positive-definite if, for every $\omega_i \neq 0$, $i = 1, \ldots, n$, $\sum_{i=1}^{n} \sum_{j=1}^{n} \omega_i \omega_j a_{i,j} > 0$. A covariance matrix is positive-definite.

Power option An option where the payoff is based on the price of an asset raised to a power.

Premium The initial price one party pays to enter into a contract. The premium for a forward contract or swap is zero, while the premium to buy an option is positive. There are related but distinct terms, including *risk premium* and *forward premium*.

Prepaid forward contract A contract calling for payment today and delivery of the asset or commodity at a time in the future.

Prepaid forward price The price the buyer pays today for a prepaid forward contract.

Prepaid swap A contract calling for payment today and delivery of the asset or commodity at multiple specified times in the future.

Prepaid variable forward See *Variable prepaid forward.*

Price limit In futures markets, the size of a futures price move such that trading is halted temporarily.

Price participation The extent to which an equity-linked note benefits from an increase in the price of the stock or index to which it is linked.

Price value of a basis point The change in a bond price due to a 1-basis-point change in the yield of the bond. Frequently abbreviated PVBP.

Primary commodity An unprocessed commodity, directly extracted by mining or drilling, or produced by agriculture.

Profit The payoff less the future value of the original cost to acquire the position.

Profit diagram A graph plotting the *profit* on a position against a range of prices for the underlying asset.

Proprietary trading Taking positions in an asset or derivative to express a view—for example, that a stock price will rise or that implied volatility will fall.

Psi The change in the price of a derivative due to a change in the dividend yield.

Purchased call A long position in a call.

Purchased put A long position in a put.

Put option A contract giving the buyer the right, but not the obligation, to sell the underlying asset at a prespecified price.

Put-call parity A relationship stating that the difference between the premiums of a call and a put with the same strike price and time to expiration equals the difference between the present value of the forward price and the present value of the strike price.

Puttable bond A bond that the investor can sell back to the issuer at a predetermined price schedule.

PVBP See *Price value of a basis point.*

Quadratic variation The sum of squared increments to a Brownian motion.

Quantile A data point is the xth quantile if $x\%$ of the data lies below that point.

Quanto A derivatives contract with a payoff in which foreign-currency-denominated quantities are treated as if they were denominated in the domestic currency.

Quasi-arbitrage The replacement of one asset or position with another that has equivalent risk and a higher expected rate of return.

Rainbow option An option that has a payoff based on the maximum or minimum of two (or more) risky assets and cash. For example, the payoff to a rainbow call is $\max(S_T, Q_T, K)$, where S_T and Q_T are risky asset prices.

Random walk A stochastic process, $X(t)$, in which increments, $\epsilon(t)$, are independent and identically distributed: $X(t) = X(t-h) + \epsilon(t)$.

Ratings transition A change in the credit rating of a bond from one value to another.

Ratio spread Buying m of an option at one strike and selling n of an otherwise identical option at a different strike.

Real options The applications of derivatives theory to the operation and valuation of real (physical) investment projects.

Realized quadratic variation The sum of squared continuously compounded asset returns, typically measured at a high frequency.

Realized volatility Another term for realized quadratic variation.

Rebate option A claim that pays \$1 at the time the price of the underlying asset reaches a barrier.

Receiver swaption A swaption giving the holder the right to receive the fixed rate in a swap.

Recombining tree A binomial tree describing asset price moves in which an up move followed by a down move yields the same price as a down move followed by an up move. Also called a *lattice*.

Recovery rate The percentage of par value received by a bond holder in a bankruptcy.

Reference price A market price or rate used to determine the payoff on a derivatives contract.

Rehypothecation The reuse of collateral to collateralize an additional borrowing transaction.

Renewable commodity A commodity that is not depleted by production or extraction. Examples include agricultural products and energy from wind, sunlight, and hydroelectricity.

Repo Another name for a *repurchase agreement*.

Repo rate The annualized percentage difference between the original sale price and final repurchase price in a repurchase agreement.

Repricing The replacement of an out-of-the-money compensation option with an at-the-money compensation option.

Repurchase agreement The sale of a security coupled with an agreement to buy it back at a later date.

Reverse cash-and-carry The simultaneous short-sale and forward purchase of an asset or commodity.

Reverse conversion A short position in an asset coupled with a purchased call and written put, both with the same strike price and time to expiration. The position is equivalent to a short bond.

Reverse convertible bond A bond that converts to an asset at low asset prices.

Reverse repo Another name for *reverse repurchase agreement*.

Reverse repurchase agreement The purchase of a security coupled with an agreement to sell it at a later date. The opposite of a repurchase agreement.

Rho The change in value of a derivative due to a change in the interest rate.

Risk averse A term describing an investor who prefers x to taking a risky bet with an expected value equal to x.

Risk management The active use of derivatives and other techniques to alter risk and protect profitability.

Risk neutral A term describing an investor who is indifferent between receiving x and taking a risky bet with an expected value equal to x.

Risk premium The difference between the expected return on an asset and the risk-free rate; the expected return differential that compensates investors for risk.

Risk reversal This term has two meanings. First, a risk reversal is another name for a collar in which the call and put have similar deltas (in absolute value) or are by some other measure equally distant from the forward price. Second, "risk reversal" refers to the difference in the implied volatilities of a call and a put with equal deltas (in absolute value). Commonly a delta of 0.25 is used for this calculation. Risk reversals are frequently quoted in currency markets.

Risk-neutral measure The probability distribution for an asset transformed so that the expected return on the asset is the risk-free rate.

Risk-neutral probability In the binomial model, the probability of an up move in the asset price such that the expected return on the asset is the risk-free rate.

Risk-neutral valuation A valuation procedure in which the expected payoff is computed using risk-neutral probabilities and this result is then discounted at the risk-free rate.

Secondary commodity A commodity created by processing a primary commodity. Examples include soybean meal and oil (created from soybeans), and gasoline and heating oil (created from crude oil).

Securitization The process of creating financial claims (securities) based on the returns of a pool of assets.

Self-financing portfolio A portfolio that retains specified characteristics (e.g., it is zero-investment and risk-free) without the need for additional investments in the portfolio.

Settlement The time in a transaction at which all obligations of both the buyer and the seller are fulfilled.

Share-equivalent The position in shares that has equivalent dollar risk to a derivative. (See also *Delta*.)

Sharpe ratio For an asset, the ratio of the risk premium to the return standard deviation.

Short A position is short with respect to a price if the position profits from a decrease in that price. A short-seller of a stock profits from a decrease in the stock price and, hence, is short the stock. A seller of an option profits from a decrease in volatility and, hence, is short volatility.

Short call A call that has been sold.

Short forward The party to a forward contract who has an obligation to sell the underlying asset.

Short put A put that has been sold.

Short rebate The rate of return paid on collateral when shares are borrowed.

Short-against-the-box The short-sale of a stock that the short-seller owns. The result of a short-against-the-box is that the short-seller has both a long and short position and, hence, bears no risk from the stock yet receives the value of the shares from the short sale.

Short-sale A transaction in which an investor borrows a security, sells it, and then returns it at a later date to the lender. If the security makes payments, the short-seller must make the same payments to the lender.

Shout option A shout call option expiring at time T has the payoff $\max(0, S_{\hat{t}} - K, S_T - K)$, where $\hat{t}$ is the time and $S_{\hat{t}}$ is the price at which the option holder "shouted," thereby guaranteeing an expiration payoff at least as great as $S_{\hat{t}} - K$.

Skewness A measure of the symmetry of a probability distribution. For a random variable x with mean μ and standard deviation σ, skewness is the third central moment divided by the cubed standard deviation, $\mathrm{E}(x - \mu)^3/\sigma^3$. For a normal variable, skewness is 0. (See also *Volatility skew*.)

Spark spread The difference between the price of electricity and that of the quantity of natural gas required to produce the electricity.

Spot curve The set of zero-coupon bond prices with different maturities, usually inferred from government bond prices.

Spot price The current market price of an asset.

Spread Simultaneously buying and selling closely related derivatives. A spread in options is a position in which some options are bought and some are sold, and all options in the position are calls or all are puts. (See also *Calendar spread* and *Commodity spread*.)

Spread option An option with a payoff where a spread (the difference between prices) takes the place of the underlying asset.

Stable distribution A probability distribution for which sums of random variables have the same distribution as the original random variable. The normal distribution is stable because sums of normally distributed random variables are normally distributed.

Stack and roll A hedging strategy in which an existing stack hedge with maturing futures contracts is replaced by a new stack hedge with longer dated futures contracts.

Stack hedge Hedging a stream of obligations by entering futures contracts with a *single* maturity, with the number of contracts selected so that changes in the *present value* of the future obligations are offset by changes in the value of this "stack" of futures contracts.

State One of a set of possible economic outcomes that affects the utility of investors. For example, the outcome where the dollar/euro exchange rate is $1.25 and the S&P index is 1300 is a particular economic state. More generally, it is common to speak loosely of good and bad states or high and low states.

State price The price of a claim that pays $1 if a given future state occurs.

Static NPV The net present value of a project at a point in time, ignoring the possibility of postponing adoption of the project.

Static option replication The use of options to hedge options, with the goal of creating a hedging portfolio that has a delta that naturally moves in tandem with the delta of the option being hedged.

Stochastic differential equation An equation characterizing the change in a variable in which one or more of the differential terms are increments to a stochastic process.

Stochastic process A mathematical model for a random process as a function of time.

Stochastic volatility A process in which the instantaneous volatility can vary randomly, either as a function of the stock price or other variables.

Stock index An average of the prices of a group of stocks. A stock index can be a simple average of stock prices, in which case it is *equally weighted*, or it can be a weighted average, with the weights proportional to market capitalization, in which case it is *value-weighted*.

Straddle The purchase of a call and a put with the same strike price and time to expiration.

Straddle rules Tax regulations controlling the circumstances in which a loss on a claim can be realized when a taxpayer continues to own related securities or derivatives.

Strangle The purchase of a put and a higher-strike call with the same time to expiration.

Stratified sampling A technique used in Monte Carlo valuation in which random numbers are drawn from each percentile (or other regular interval) of the distribution.

Stressed value-at-risk A value-at-risk calculation that relies on distributional assumptions from a period of market stress, such as the financial crisis in 2008.

Strike price Another term for *exercise price*.

Strip hedge Hedging a stream of obligations by offsetting each individual obligation with a futures contract matching the maturity and quantity of the obligation.

STRIPS Acronym for *Separate Trading of Registered Interest and Principal of Securities*. STRIPS are the interest and principal payments from Treasury bonds and notes traded as individual securities.

Structured note A bond that makes payments that, at least in part, are contingent on some variable such as a stock price, interest rates, or exchange rates.

Supershare A claim to a portfolio that pays the holder a portion of the portfolio only if a particular event occurs. (An example of an event would be the asset losing between 25% and 26% of its value.)

Swap A contract calling for the exchange of payments over time. Often one payment is fixed in advance and the other is floating, based upon the realization of a price or interest rate.

Swap spread The difference between the fixed rate on an interest rate swap and the yield on a Treasury bond with the same maturity.

Swap tenor The lifetime of a swap.

Swap term Another name for *swap tenor*.

Swaption An option to enter into a swap.

Synthetic CDO A derivative that has the same payoff as a leveraged position in a CDO tranche

T+3 Settlement The convention under which a securities market transaction is settled three days after the trade. The buyer pays and the seller supplies the security simultaneously, a practice known as "delivery vs. payment."

Tail VaR The expected loss conditional upon the VaR loss being exceeded.

Tailing A reduction in the quantity of an asset held in order to offset future income received by the asset.

Tenor Time to maturity or expiration of a contract, frequently used when referring to swaps.

Term repo A repurchase agreement lasting for a specified period of time longer than 1 day.

Theta The change in the value of a derivative due solely to the passage of time.

Time decay Another term for *theta*.

Total return swap A swap in which one party pays the total return (dividends plus capital gains) on a reference asset, and the other party pays a floating rate such as LIBOR.

Traded present value The value an investment project would have once the investment was made; also called *twin security*.

Twin security See *Traded present value*.

Tranched payoff A claim for which the payoff is senstive to the underlying asset over a range of returns.

Tri-party repo A repurchase agreement in which a dealer, who is not a party to the transaction, serves as an intermediary and assists with collateral management, pricing, and other details.

Troy ounce A unit of weight commonly used for precious metals, equal to 480 grains or 31.103 grams, approximately 9% greater than the more familiar avoirdupois ounce, which is about 28.349 grams.

Underlying asset The asset whose price determines the profitability of a derivative. For example, the underlying asset for a purchased call is the asset that the call owner can buy by paying the strike price.

Unfunded A position that is not paid for at the outset, and for which cash inflows and outflows can later occur. A forward contract, for example, is an unfunded position in a stock. See also *Funded*.

Up-and-in A knock-in option for which the barrier exceeds the current price of the underlying asset.

Up-and-out A knock-out option for which the barrier exceeds the current price of the underlying asset.

Value at risk The level of loss that will be exceeded a given percentage of the time over a given horizon.

Vanilla A standard option or other derivative. For example, ordinary puts and calls are "vanilla" options.

Variable prepaid forward A financial structure with a payoff that is contingent on the future price of a stock or other asset. Commonly, the VPF payoff resembles that of a collared stock.

Variance swap A forward contract that settles based on cumulative squared asset returns.

Vega The change in the price of a derivative due to a change in volatility. Also sometimes called *kappa* or *lambda*.

Vertical spread The sale of an option at one strike and purchase of an option of the same type (call or put) at a different strike, both having the same underlying asset and time to expiration.

Volatility The standard deviation of the continuously compounded return on an asset.

Volatility clustering The tendency of high volatility days to be followed by high volatility days.

Volatility skew Generally, implied volatility as a function of the strike price. Volatility skew refers to a difference in premiums as reflected in differences in implied volatility. Skew is sometimes used more precisely to refer to a difference in implied volatilities between in-the-money and out-of-the-money options.

Volatility smile A volatility skew in which both in-the-money and out-of-the-money options have a higher volatility than at-the-money options (i.e., when you plot implied volatility against the strike price, the curve looks like a smile).

Volatility surface A three-dimensional graph in which volatility is plotted against strike price and time to maturity.

Volatility swap A forward contract that settles based on some measure of the standard deviation of returns on an asset.

Warrant An option issued by a firm with its own stock as the underlying asset. This term also refers more generally to an option issued in fixed supply.

Weather derivative A derivative contract with a payment based on a weather-related measurement, such as heating or cooling degree-days.

Wiener process See *Brownian motion*.

Written call A call that has been sold; a short call.

Written put A put that has been sold; a short put.

Written straddle The simultaneous sale of a call and sale of a put, with the same strike price and time to expiration.

Yield curve The set of yields to maturity for bonds with different times to maturity.

Yield to maturity The single discount factor for which the present value of a bond's payments is equal to the observed bond price.

Zero-cost collar The purchase of a put and sale of a call where the strikes are chosen so that the premiums of the two options are the same.

Zero-coupon bond A bond that makes only a single payment, at maturity.

Zero-coupon yield curve The set of yields to maturity for zero-coupon bonds with different times to maturity.

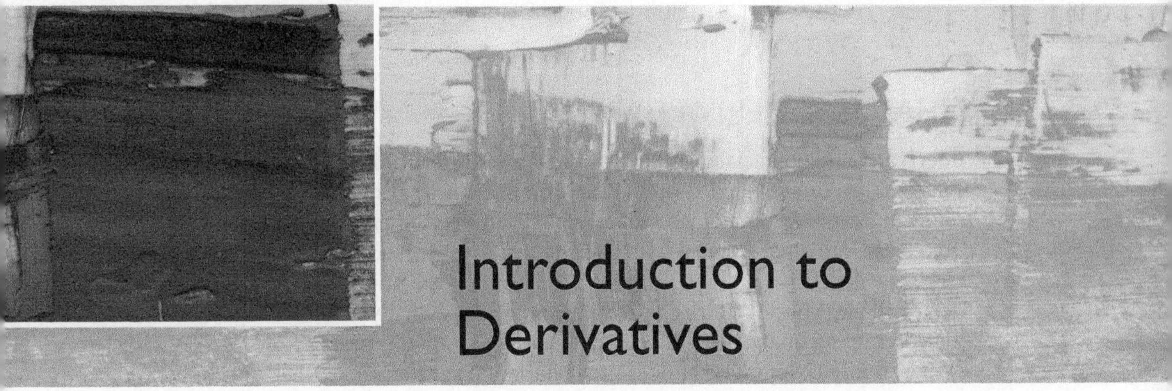

Introduction to Derivatives

The world of finance has changed dramatically in recent decades. Electronic processing, globalization, and deregulation have all transformed markets, with many of the most important changes involving derivatives. The set of financial claims traded today is quite different than it was in 1970. In addition to ordinary stocks and bonds, there is now a wide array of products collectively referred to as financial derivatives: futures, options, swaps, credit default swaps, and many more exotic claims.

Derivatives sometimes make headlines. Prior to the financial crisis in 2008, there were a number of well-known derivatives-related losses: Procter & Gamble lost $150 million in 1994, Barings Bank lost $1.3 billion in 1995, Long-Term Capital Management lost $3.5 billion in 1998, the hedge fund Amaranth lost $6 billion in 2006, Société Générale lost €5 billion in 2008. During the crisis in 2008 the Federal Reserve loaned $85 billion to AIG in conjunction with AIG's losses on credit default swaps. In the wake of the financial crisis, a significant portion of the Dodd-Frank Wall Street Reform and Consumer Protection Act of 2010 pertained to derivatives.

What is *not* in the headlines is the fact that, most of the time, for most companies and most users, these financial products are a useful and everyday part of business. Just as companies routinely issue debt and equity, they also routinely use swaps to fix the cost of production inputs, futures contracts to hedge foreign exchange risk, and options to compensate employees, to mention just a few examples.

Besides their widespread use, another important reason to understand derivatives is that the theory underlying financial derivatives provides a language and a set of analytical techniques that is fundamental for thinking about risk and valuation. It is almost impossible to discuss or perform asset management, risk management, credit evaluation, or capital budgeting without some understanding of derivatives and derivatives pricing.

In this chapter, we introduce some important concepts underlying derivatives and provide some background to place derivatives in context. We begin by defining a derivative. We will then briefly examine financial markets, and see that derivatives markets have become increasingly important in recent years. The size of these markets may leave you wondering exactly what functions they serve. We next discuss the role of financial markets in our lives, and the importance of risk sharing. We also discuss different perspectives on derivatives. Finally, we will discuss how trading occurs, providing some basic concepts.

From Chapter 1 of *Derivatives Markets*, Third Edition, Robert McDonald. Copyright © 2013 by Pearson Education, Inc. Published by Pearson Prentice Hall. All rights reserved.

1. WHAT IS A DERIVATIVE?

A **derivative** is a financial instrument that has a value determined by the price of something else. Options, futures, and swaps are all examples of derivatives. A bushel of corn is not a derivative; it is a commodity with a value determined in the corn market. However, you could enter into an agreement with a friend that says: If the price of a bushel of corn in 1 year is greater than $3, you will pay the friend $1. If the price of corn is less than $3, the friend will pay you $1. This is a derivative in the sense that you have an agreement with a value depending on the price of something else (corn, in this case).

You might think: "That doesn't sound like it's a derivative; that's just a bet on the price of corn." Derivatives can be thought of as bets on the price of something, but the term "bet" is not necessarily pejorative. Suppose your family grows corn and your friend's family buys corn to mill into cornmeal. The bet provides insurance: You earn $1 if your family's corn sells for a low price; this supplements your income. Your friend earns $1 if the corn his family buys is expensive; this offsets the high cost of corn. Viewed in this light, the bet hedges you both against unfavorable outcomes. The contract has reduced risk for both of you.

Investors who do not make a living growing or processing corn could also use this kind of contract simply to speculate on the price of corn. In this case the contract does not serve as insurance; it is simply a bet. This example illustrates a key point: *It is not the contract itself, but how it is used, and who uses it, that determines whether or not it is risk-reducing.* Context is everything.

2. AN OVERVIEW OF FINANCIAL MARKETS

In this section we will discuss the variety of markets and financial instruments that exist. You should bear in mind that financial markets are rapidly evolving and that any specific description today may soon be out-of-date. Nevertheless, though the specific details may change, the basic economic functions associated with trading will continue to be necessary.

Trading of Financial Assets

The trading of a financial asset—i.e., the process by which an asset acquires a new owner—is more complicated than you might guess and involves at least four discrete steps. To understand the steps, consider the trade of a stock:

1. The buyer and seller must locate one another and agree on a price. This process is what most people mean by "trading" and is the most visible step. Stock exchanges, derivatives exchanges, and dealers all facilitate trading, providing buyers and sellers a means to find one another.

2. Once the buyer and seller agree on a price, the trade must be *cleared*, i.e., the obligations of each party are specified. In the case of a stock transaction, the buyer

will be required to deliver cash and the seller to deliver the stock. In the case of some derivatives transactions, both parties must post collateral.[1]

3. The trade must be *settled*, that is, the buyer and seller must deliver in the required period of time the cash or securities necessary to satisfy their obligations.
4. Once the trade is complete, ownership records are updated.

To summarize, trading involves striking a deal, clearing, settling, and maintaining records. Different entities can be involved in these different steps.

Much trading of financial claims takes place on organized exchanges. An exchange is an organization that provides a venue for trading, and that sets rules governing what is traded and how trading occurs. A given exchange will trade a particular set of financial instruments. The New York Stock Exchange, for example, lists several thousand firms, both U.S. and non-U.S., for which it provides a trading venue. Once upon a time, the exchange was solely a physical location where traders would stand in groups, buying and selling by talking, shouting, and gesturing. However, such in-person trading venues have largely been replaced by electronic networks that provide a virtual trading venue.[2]

After a trade has taken place, a **clearinghouse** matches the buyers and sellers, keeping track of their obligations and payments. The traders who deal directly with a clearinghouse are called *clearing members*. If you buy a share of stock as an individual, your transaction ultimately is cleared through the account of a clearing member.

For publicly traded securities in the United States, the Depository Trust and Clearing Corporation (DTCC) and its subsidiary, the National Securities Clearing Corporation (NSCC), play key roles in clearing and settling virtually every stock and bond trade that occurs in the U.S. Other countries have similar institutions. Derivatives exchanges are always associated with a clearing organization because such trades must also be cleared and settled. Examples of derivatives clearinghouses are CME Clearing, which is associated with the CME Group (formerly the Chicago Mercantile Exchange), and ICE Clear U.S., which is associated with the Intercontinental Exchange (ICE).

With stock and bond trades, after the trade has cleared and settled, the buyer and seller have no continuing obligations to one another. However, with derivatives trades, one party may have to pay another in the future. To facilitate these payments and to help manage credit risk, a derivatives clearinghouse typically interposes itself in the transaction, becoming the buyer to all sellers and the seller to all buyers. This substitution of one counterparty for another is known as **novation**.

It is possible for large traders to trade many financial claims directly with a dealer, bypassing organized exchanges. Such trading is said to occur in the **over-the-counter** (OTC)

1. A party "posting collateral" is turning assets over to someone else to ensure that they will be able to meet their obligations. The posting of collateral is a common practice in financial markets.

2. When trading occurs in person, it is valuable for a trader to be physically close to other traders. With certain kinds of automated electronic trading, it is valuable for a trader's *computer* to be physically close to the computers of an exchange. Traders make large investments to gain such speed advantages. One group is spending $300 million for an undersea cable in order to reduce communication time between New York and London by 5 milliseconds (Philips, 2012).

market.[3] There are several reasons why buyers and sellers might transact directly with dealers rather than on an exchange. First, it can be easier to trade a large quantity directly with another party. A seller of fifty thousand shares of IBM may negotiate a single price with a dealer, avoiding exchange fees as well as the market tumult and uncertainty about price that might result from simply announcing a fifty-thousand-share sale. Second, we might wish to trade a custom financial claim that is not available on an exchange. Third, we might wish to trade a number of different financial claims at once. A dealer could execute the entire trade as a single transaction, compared to the alternative of executing individual orders on a variety of different markets.

Most of the trading volume numbers you see reported in the newspaper pertain to exchange-based trading. Exchange activity is public and highly regulated. Over-the-counter trading is not easy to observe or measure and is generally less regulated. For many categories of financial claims, the value of OTC trading is greater than the value traded on exchanges.

Financial institutions are rapidly evolving and consolidating, so any description of the industry is at best a snapshot. Familiar names have melded into single entities. In recent years, for example, the New York Stock Exchange merged with Euronext, a group of European exchanges, to form NYSE Euronext, which in turn bought the American Stock Exchange (AMEX). The Chicago Mercantile Exchange merged with the Chicago Board of Trade and subsequently acquired the New York Mercantile Exchange, forming CME Group.

Measures of Market Size and Activity

Before we discuss specific markets, it will be helpful to explain some ways in which the size of a market and its activity can be measured. There are at least four different measures that you will see mentioned in the press and on financial websites. No one measure is "correct" or best, but some are more applicable to stock and bond markets, others to derivatives markets. The different measures count the number of transactions that occur daily (trading volume), the number of positions that exist at the end of a day (open interest), and the value (market value) and size (notional value) of these positions. Here are more detailed definitions:

Trading volume. This measure counts the number of financial claims that change hands daily or annually. Trading volume is the number commonly emphasized in press coverage, but it is a somewhat arbitrary measure because it is possible to redefine the meaning of a financial claim. For example, on a stock exchange, trading volume refers to the number of shares traded. On an options exchange, trading volume refers to the number of options traded, but each option on an individual stock covers 100 shares of stock.[4]

Market value. The market value (or "market cap") of the listed financial claims on an exchange is the sum of the market value of the claims that *could* be traded, without

3. In an OTC trade, the dealer serves the economic function of a clearinghouse, effectively serving as counterparty to a large number of investors. Partly because of concerns about the fragility of a system where dealers also play the role of clearinghouses, the Dodd-Frank Act in 2010 required that, where feasible, derivatives transactions be cleared through designated clearinghouses. Duffie and Zhu (2011) discuss the costs and benefits of such a central clearing mandate.

4. When there are stock splits or mergers, individual stock options will sometimes cover a different number of shares.

regard to whether they have traded. A firm with 1 million shares and a share price of $50 has a market value of $50 million.[5] Some derivative claims can have a zero market value; for such claims, this measure tells us nothing about activity at an exchange.

Notional value. Notional value measures the *scale* of a position, usually with reference to some underlying asset. Suppose the price of a stock is $100 and that you have a derivative contract giving you the right to buy 100 shares at a future date. We would then say that the notional value of one such contract is 100 shares, or $10,000. The concept of notional value is especially important in derivatives markets. Derivatives exchanges frequently report the notional value of contracts traded during a period of time.

Open interest. Open interest measures the total number of contracts for which counterparties have a future obligation to perform. Each contract will have two counterparties. Open interest measures contracts, not counterparties. Open interest is an important statistic in derivatives markets.

Stock and Bond Markets

Companies often raise funds for purposes such as financing investments. Typically they do so either by selling ownership claims on the company (common stock) or by borrowing money (obtaining a bank loan or issuing a bond). Such financing activity is a routine part of operating a business. Virtually every developed country has a market in which investors can trade with each other the stocks that firms have issued.

Securities exchanges facilitate the exchange of ownership of a financial asset from one party to another. Some exchanges, such as the NYSE, designate market-makers, who stand ready to buy or sell to meet customer demand. Other exchanges, such as NASDAQ, rely on a competitive market among many traders to provide fair prices. In practice, most investors will not notice these distinctions.

The bond market is similar in size to the stock market, but bonds generally trade through dealers rather than on an exchange. Most bonds also trade much less frequently than stocks.

Table 1 shows the market capitalization of stocks traded on the six largest stock exchanges in the world in 2011. To provide some perspective, the aggregate value of publicly traded common stock in the U.S. was about $20 trillion at the end of 2011. Total corporate debt was about $10 trillion, and borrowings of federal, state, and local governments in the U.S. was about $18 trillion. By way of comparison, the gross domestic product (GDP) of the U.S. in 2011 was $15.3 trillion.[6]

5. For example, in early 2012 IBM had a share price of about $180 and about 1.15 billion shares outstanding. The market value was thus about $180 × 1.15 billion = $207 billion. Market value changes with the price of the underlying shares.

6. To be clear about the comparison: The values of securities represent the outstanding amount at the end of the year, irrespective of the year in which the securities were first issued. GDP, by contrast, represents output produced in the U.S. during the year. The market value and GDP numbers are therefore not directly comparable. The comparison is nonetheless frequently made.

TABLE 1 The six largest stock exchanges in the world, by market capitalization (in billions of US dollars) in 2011.

Rank	Exchange	Market Cap (Billions of U.S. $)
1	NYSE Euronext (U.S.)	11,796
3	Nasdaq OMX	3,845
2	Tokyo Stock Exchange	3,325
4	London Stock Exchange	3,266
5	NYSE Euronext (Europe)	2,447
6	Shanghai Stock Exchange	2,357

Source: http://www.world-exchanges.org/.

Derivatives Markets

Because a derivative is a financial instrument with a value determined by the price of something else, there is potentially an unlimited variety of derivative products. Derivatives exchanges trade products based on a wide variety of stock indexes, interest rates, commodity prices, exchange rates, and even nonfinancial items such as weather. A given exchange may trade futures, options, or both. The distinction between exchanges that trade physical stocks and bonds, as opposed to derivatives, has largely been due to regulation and custom, and is eroding.

The introduction and use of derivatives in a market often coincides with an increase in price risk in that market. Currencies were permitted to float in 1971 when the gold standard was officially abandoned. The modern market in financial derivatives began in 1972, when the Chicago Mercantile Exchange (CME) started trading futures on seven currencies. OPEC's 1973 reduction in the supply of oil was followed by high and variable oil prices. U.S. interest rates became more volatile following inflation and recessions in the 1970s. The market for natural gas has been deregulated gradually since 1978, resulting in a volatile market and the introduction of futures in 1990. The deregulation of electricity began during the 1990s.

To illustrate the increase in variability since the early 1970s, panels (a)–(c) in Figure 1 show monthly changes for the 3-month Treasury bill rate, the dollar-pound exchange rate, and a benchmark spot oil price. The link between price variability and the development of derivatives markets is natural—there is no need to manage risk when there is no risk.[7] When risk does exist, we would expect that markets will develop to permit efficient risk-sharing. Investors who have the most tolerance for risk will bear more of it, and risk-bearing will be widely spread among investors.

7. It is sometimes argued that the existence of derivatives markets can increase the price variability of the underlying asset or commodity. However, the introduction of derivatives can also be a response to increased price variability.

FIGURE 1

(a) The monthly change in the 3-month Treasury bill rate, 1947–2011. (b) The monthly percentage change in the dollar-pound exchange rate, 1947–2011. (c) The monthly percentage change in the West Texas Intermediate (WTI) spot oil price, 1947–2011. (d) Millions of futures contracts traded annually at the Chicago Board of Trade (CBT), Chicago Mercantile Exchange (CME), and the New York Mercantile Exchange (NYMEX), 1970–2011.

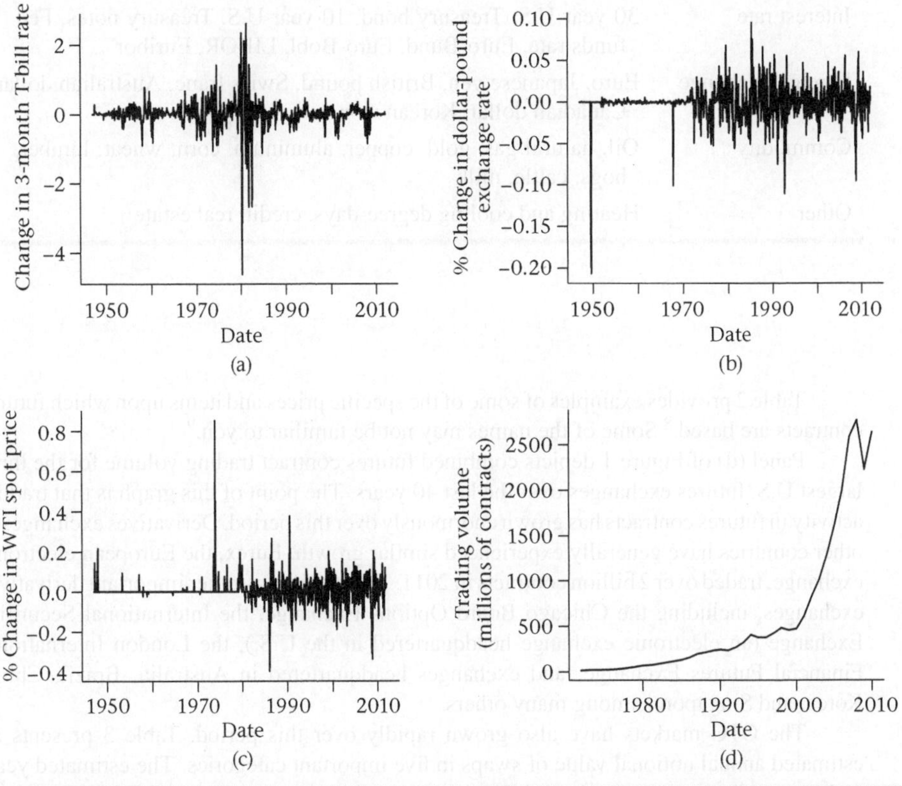

Sources: (a) St. Louis Fed; (b) DRI and St. Louis Fed; (c) St. Louis Fed; (d) CRB Yearbook.

TABLE 2 Examples of underlying assets on which futures contracts are traded.

Category	Description
Stock index	S&P 500 index, Euro Stoxx 50 index, Nikkei 225, Dow-Jones Industrials, Dax, NASDAQ, Russell 2000, S&P Sectors (healthcare, utilities, technology, etc.)
Interest rate	30-year U.S. Treasury bond, 10-year U.S. Treasury notes, Fed funds rate, Euro-Bund, Euro-Bobl, LIBOR, Euribor
Foreign exchange	Euro, Japanese yen, British pound, Swiss franc, Australian dollar, Canadian dollar, Korean won
Commodity	Oil, natural gas, gold, copper, aluminum, corn, wheat, lumber, hogs, cattle, milk
Other	Heating and cooling degree-days, credit, real estate

Table 2 provides examples of some of the specific prices and items upon which futures contracts are based.[8] Some of the names may not be familiar to you.[9]

Panel (d) of Figure 1 depicts combined futures contract trading volume for the three largest U.S. futures exchanges over the last 40 years. The point of this graph is that trading activity in futures contracts has grown enormously over this period. Derivatives exchanges in other countries have generally experienced similar growth. Eurex, the European electronic exchange, traded over 2 billion contracts in 2011. There are many other important derivatives exchanges, including the Chicago Board Options Exchange, the International Securities Exchange (an electronic exchange headquartered in the U.S.), the London International Financial Futures Exchange, and exchanges headquartered in Australia, Brazil, China, Korea, and Singapore, among many others.

The OTC markets have also grown rapidly over this period. Table 3 presents an estimated annual notional value of swaps in five important categories. The estimated year-end outstanding notional value of interest rate and currency swaps in 2010 was an eye-popping $523 trillion. For a variety of reasons the notional value number can be difficult to interpret, but the enormous growth in these contracts in recent years is unmistakable.

8. It is instructive to browse the websites of derivatives exchanges. For example, the CME Group open interest report for April 2012 reports positive open interest for 16 different interest rate futures contracts, 26 different equity index contracts, 15 metals, hundreds of different energy futures contracts, and over 40 currencies. Many of these contracts exist to handle specialized requirements.

9. German government bonds are known as "Bubills" (bonds with maturity of less than 1 year), "Schaetze" (maturity of 2 years), "Bobls" (5 years), and "Bunds" (10 and 30 years). Futures contracts also trade on Japanese and UK government bonds ("gilt").

TABLE 3 Estimated year-end notional value of outstanding derivative contracts, by category, in billions of dollars.

	Foreign Exchange	Interest Rate	Equity	Commodity	Credit Default	Total
1998	18011	50014	1488	408	—	80309
1999	14344	60090	1809	548	—	88201
2000	15665	64667	1890	662	—	95199
2001	16747	77567	1880	598	—	111177
2002	18447	101657	2308	923	—	141665
2003	24475	141990	3787	1405	—	197166
2004	29288	190501	4384	1443	6395	258627
2005	31360	211970	5793	5434	13908	299260
2006	40270	291581	7487	7115	28650	418131
2007	56238	393138	8469	8455	58243	585932
2008	50042	432657	6471	4427	41882	598147
2009	49181	449874	5937	2944	32692	603899
2010	57795	465259	5634	2921	29897	601046

Source: Bank of International Settlements.

3. THE ROLE OF FINANCIAL MARKETS

Stock, bond, and derivatives markets are large and active, but what role do financial markets play in the economy and in our lives? We routinely see headlines stating that the Dow Jones Industrial Average has gone up 100 points, the dollar has fallen against the euro, and interest rates have risen. But why do we care about these things? In this section we will examine how financial markets affect our lives.

Financial Markets and the Averages

To understand how financial markets affect us, consider the Average family, living in Anytown. Joe and Sarah Average have children and both work for the XYZ Co., the dominant employer in Anytown. Their income pays for their mortgage, transportation, food, clothing, and medical care. Remaining income goes into savings earmarked for their children's college tuition and their own retirement.

The Averages are largely unaware of the ways in which global financial markets affect their lives. Here are a few:

- The Averages invest their savings in mutual funds that own stocks and bonds from companies around the world. The transaction cost of buying stocks and bonds in this way is low. Moreover, the Averages selected mutual funds that provide diversified investments. As a result, the Averages are not heavily exposed to any one company.[10]

- The Averages live in an area susceptible to tornadoes and insure their home. The local insurance company reinsures tornado risk in global markets, effectively pooling Anytown tornado risk with Japan earthquake risk and Florida hurricane risk. This pooling makes insurance available at lower rates and protects the Anytown insurance company.
- The Averages financed their home with a mortgage from Anytown bank. The bank in turn sold the mortgage to other investors, freeing itself from interest rate and default risk associated with the mortgage. Because the risks of their mortgage is borne by those willing to pay the highest price for it, the Averages get the lowest possible mortgage rate.
- The Average's employer, XYZ Co., can access global markets to raise money. Investors in Asia, for example, may thereby finance an improvement to the Anytown factory.
- XYZ Co. insures itself against certain risks. In addition to having property and casualty insurance for its buildings, it uses global derivatives markets to protect itself against adverse currency, interest rate, and commodity price changes. By being able to manage these risks, XYZ is less likely to go into bankruptcy, and the Averages are less likely to become unemployed.

In all of these examples, particular financial functions and risks have been split up and parceled out to others. A bank that sells a mortgage does not have to bear the risk of the mortgage. A single insurance company does not bear the entire risk of a regional disaster. Risk-sharing is one of the most important functions of financial markets.

Risk-Sharing

Risk is an inevitable part of our lives and all economic activity. As we've seen in the example of the Averages, financial markets enable at least some of these risks to be shared. Risk arises from natural events, such as earthquakes, floods, and hurricanes, and from unnatural events such as wars and political conflicts. Drought and pestilence destroy agriculture every year in some part of the world. Some economies boom as others falter. On a more personal scale, people are born, die, retire, find jobs, lose jobs, marry, divorce, and become ill.

Given that risk exists, it is natural to have arrangements where the lucky share with the unlucky. There are both formal and informal risk-sharing arrangements. On the formal level, the insurance market is a way to share risk. Buyers pay a premium to obtain various kinds of insurance, such as homeowner's insurance. Total collected premiums are then available to help those whose houses burn down. The lucky, meanwhile, did not need insurance and have lost their premium. This market makes it possible for the lucky to help the unlucky. On the informal level, risk-sharing also occurs in families and communities, where those encountering misfortune are helped by others.

10. There is one important risk that the Averages cannot easily avoid. Since both Averages work at XYZ, they run the risk that if XYZ falls on hard times they will lose their jobs. This could be an important reason for the Averages to *avoid* investing in XYZ.

In the business world, changes in commodity prices, exchange rates, and interest rates can be the financial equivalent of a house burning down. If the dollar becomes expensive relative to the yen, some companies are helped and others are hurt. It makes sense for there to be a mechanism enabling companies to exchange this risk, so that the lucky can, in effect, help the unlucky.

Even insurers need to share risk. Consider an insurance company that provides earthquake insurance for California residents. A large earthquake could generate claims sufficient to bankrupt a stand-alone insurance company. Thus, insurance companies often use the *reinsurance market* to buy, from reinsurers, insurance against large claims. Reinsurers pool different kinds of risks, thereby enabling insurance risks to become more widely held.

In some cases, reinsurers further share risks by issuing **catastrophe bonds**—bonds that the issuer need not repay if there is a specified event, such as a large earthquake, causing large insurance claims. Bondholders willing to accept earthquake risk can buy these bonds, in exchange for greater interest payments on the bond if there is no earthquake. An earthquake bond allows earthquake risk to be borne by exactly those investors who wish to bear it.

You might be wondering what this discussion has to do with the notions of diversifiable and nondiversifiable risk familiar from portfolio theory. Risk is **diversifiable risk** if it is unrelated to other risks. The risk that a lightning strike will cause a factory to burn down, for example, is idiosyncratic and hence diversifiable. If many investors share a small piece of this risk, it has no significant effect on anyone. Risk that does not vanish when spread across many investors is **nondiversifiable risk**. The risk of a stock market crash, for example, is nondiversifiable.

Financial markets in theory serve two purposes. Markets permit diversifiable risk to be widely shared. This is efficient: By definition, diversifiable risk vanishes when it is widely shared. At the same time, financial markets permit nondiversifiable risk, which does not vanish when shared, to be held by those most willing to hold it. Thus, *the fundamental economic idea underlying the concepts and markets is that the existence of risk-sharing mechanisms benefits everyone*.

Derivatives markets continue to evolve. A recent development has been the growth in **prediction markets**, discussed in Box 1.

4. THE USES OF DERIVATIVES

We can think about derivatives and other financial claims in different ways. One is a functional perspective: Who uses them and why? Another is an analytical perspective: When we look at financial markets, how do we interpret the activity that we see? In this section, we discuss these different perspectives.

Uses of Derivatives

What are reasons someone might use derivatives? Here are some motives:

Risk management. Derivatives are a tool for companies and other users to reduce risks. With derivatives, a farmer—a seller of corn—can enter into a contract that makes a payment when the price of corn is low. This contract reduces the risk of loss for the farmer, who we therefore say is **hedging**. Every form of insurance is a derivative: For

BOX 1: Prediction Markets

Prediction markets are derivatives markets in which the value of traded claims depends on the outcome of events. With one common contract, an investor can own a claim that receives $1 if the event occurs, or sell a claim that requires the investor to pay $1 if the event occurs. Such markets can be used to speculate on presidential elections, the winner of an Olympic event, the occurrence of a natural disaster, or the value of a government statistic such as employment or the consumer price index.

Much of the interest in prediction markets stems from the idea that the price of a contract will aggregate individual information that could not otherwise be observed. For years, the Iowa Electronic Markets (http://tippie.uiowa.edu/iem/markets/) has permitted speculation on the outcome of presidential and other elections. The "vote share" contracts pay in cents the percentage of the popular vote received by the official candidate of a party. For example, if the Republican were to receive 48% of the vote, the Republican vote share contract on election day would be worth $0.48. The Democratic and Republican "winner-take-all" contracts pay $1 if that party wins the election, and zero otherwise. There are also party nomination contracts that allow an investor to bet on a specific candidate winning the party nomination. (See Box 2.)

Intrade.com allows political bets along with a wide variety of others. One contract stated its event as "Higgs Boson Particle to be observed on/before 31 Dec 2014," while another stated "Highest Marginal Single-Filer Fed Income Tax Rate to be Equal or Greater than 34% in 2012."

Prediction markets face significant regulatory hurdles in the U.S. As of this writing, a 2006 law prohibiting unauthorized internet gambling made it illegal for U.S. investors to use any prediction market not authorized by the Commodity Futures Trading Commission.

example, automobile insurance pays if you have an accident. If you destroy your car in an accident, your insurance is valuable; if the car remains undamaged, it is not.

Speculation. Derivatives can serve as investment vehicles. Derivatives can provide a way to make bets that are highly leveraged (that is, the potential gain or loss on the bet can be large relative to the initial cost of making the bet) and tailored to a specific view. For example, if you want to bet that the S&P 500 stock index will be between 1300 and 1400 1 year from today, derivatives can be constructed to let you do that.

Reduced transaction costs. Sometimes derivatives provide a lower-cost way to undertake a particular financial transaction. For example, the manager of a mutual fund may wish to sell stocks and buy bonds. Doing this entails paying fees to brokers and paying other trading costs, such as the bid-ask spread, which we will discuss later. It is possible to trade derivatives instead and achieve the same economic effect as if stocks had actually been sold and replaced by bonds. Using the derivative might result in lower transaction costs than actually selling stocks and buying bonds.

Regulatory arbitrage. It is sometimes possible to circumvent regulatory restrictions, taxes, and accounting rules by trading derivatives. Derivatives are often used, for example, to achieve the economic sale of stock (receive cash and eliminate the risk of holding the stock) while still maintaining physical possession of the stock. This transaction may allow the owner to defer taxes on the sale of the stock, or retain voting rights, without the risk of holding the stock.

These are common reasons for using derivatives. The general point is that derivatives provide an alternative to a simple sale or purchase, and thus increase the range of possibilities for an investor or manager seeking to accomplish some goal. Obviously, for society as a whole, hedging may be desirable while regulatory arbitrage is not. But it is difficult to control trading on the basis of motive.

In recent years the U.S. Securities and Exchange Commission (SEC), the Financial Accounting Standards Board (FASB), and the International Accounting Standard Board (IASB) have increased the requirements for corporations to report on their use of derivatives. Nevertheless, surprisingly little is known about how companies actually use derivatives to manage risk. The basic strategies companies use are well-understood, but it is not known, for example, what fraction of perceived risk is hedged by a given company, or by all companies in the aggregate. We frequently do not know a company's specific rationale for hedging or not hedging.

We would expect the use of derivatives to vary by type of firm. For example, financial firms, such as banks, are highly regulated and have capital requirements. They may have assets and liabilities in different currencies, with different maturities, and with different credit risks. Hence banks could be expected to use interest rate derivatives, currency derivatives, and credit derivatives to manage risks in those areas. Manufacturing firms that buy raw materials and sell in global markets might use commodity and currency derivatives, but their incentives to manage risk are less clear-cut because they are not regulated in the same ways as financial firms.

Perspectives on Derivatives

How you think about derivatives depends on who you are. The following are three distinct perspectives on derivatives:

The end-user perspective. End-users are the corporations, investment managers, and investors who enter into derivative contracts for the reasons listed in the previous section: to manage risk, speculate, reduce costs, or avoid a rule or regulation. End-users have a goal (for example, risk reduction) and care about how a derivative helps to meet that goal.

The market-maker perspective. Market-makers are intermediaries, traders who will buy derivatives from customers who wish to sell, and sell derivatives to customers who wish to buy. In order to make money, market-makers charge a spread: They buy at a low price and sell at a high price. In this respect market-makers are like grocers, who buy at the low wholesale price and sell at the higher retail price. Market-makers are also like grocers in that their inventory reflects customer demands rather than their own preferences: As long as shoppers buy paper towels, the grocer doesn't care whether they buy the decorative or super-absorbent style. After dealing with customers, market-makers are left with whatever position results from accommodating customer demands. Market-makers typically hedge this risk and thus are deeply concerned about the mathematical details of pricing and hedging.

The economic observer. Finally, we can look at the use of derivatives, the activities of the market-makers, the organization of the markets, and the logic of the pricing models and try to make sense of everything. This is the activity of the economic observer. Regulators must often don their economic observer hats when deciding whether and how to regulate a certain activity or market participant.

These three perspectives are intertwined with different degrees of emphasis.

Financial Engineering and Security Design

One of the major ideas in derivatives—perhaps *the* major idea—is that it is generally possible to create a given payoff in multiple ways. The construction of a given financial product from other products is sometimes called **financial engineering**. The fact that this is possible has several implications. First, since market-makers need to hedge their positions, this idea is central in understanding how market-making works. The market-maker sells a contract to an end-user, and then creates an offsetting position that pays him if it is necessary to pay the customer. This creates a hedged position.

Second, the idea that a given contract can be replicated often suggests how it can be customized. The market-maker can, in effect, turn dials to change the risk, initial premium, and payment characteristics of a derivative. These changes permit the creation of a product that is more appropriate for a given situation.

Third, it is often possible to improve intuition about a given derivative by realizing that it is equivalent to something we already understand.

Finally, because there are multiple ways to create a payoff, the regulatory arbitrage discussed above can be difficult to stop. Distinctions existing in the tax code, or in regulations, may not be enforceable, since a particular security or derivative that is regulated or taxed may be easily replaced by one that is treated differently but has the same economic profile.

5. BUYING AND SHORT-SELLING FINANCIAL ASSETS

Let's talk about buying, selling, and short-selling assets such as stocks. These basic transactions are so important that it is worth describing the details. First, it is important to understand the costs associated with buying and selling. Second, it is helpful to understand the mechanisms one can use to buy or sell. Third, a very important idea in transactions is that of short-sales. The concept of short-selling seems as if it should be intuitive—a short-sale is just the opposite of a purchase—but for almost everyone it is hard to grasp at first. Even if you are familiar with short-sales, you should spend a few minutes reading this section.

Although we will use shares of stock to illustrate the mechanics of buying and selling, there are similar issues associated with buying any asset.

Transaction Costs and the Bid-Ask Spread

Suppose you want to buy shares of XYZ stock. We can calculate the cost to own 100 shares: If the price to buy the stock is \$50, 100 shares will cost $\$50 \times 100 = \$5000$. However, we must also account for transaction costs.

First, there is a commission, which is a transaction fee you pay your broker. A commission for the above order could be \$15, or 0.3% of the purchase price.

Second, the term "stock price" is, surprisingly, imprecise. There are in fact two prices, a price at which you can buy, and a price at which you can sell. The price at which you can buy is called the **offer price** or **ask price**, and the price at which you can sell is called the **bid price**. To understand these terms, consider the position of the broker.

To buy stock, you contact a broker. Suppose that you wish to buy immediately at the best available price. If the stock is not too obscure and your order is not too large, your purchase will probably be completed in a matter of seconds. Where does the stock that you have just bought come from? It is possible that at the exact same moment, another customer called the broker and put in an order to sell. More likely, however, a market-maker sold you the stock. As their name implies, market-makers make markets. If you want to buy, they sell, and if you want to sell, they buy. In order to earn a living, market-makers sell for a high price and buy for a low price. If you deal with a market-maker, therefore, you buy for a high price and sell for a low price. This difference between the price at which you can buy and the price at which you can sell is called the **bid-ask spread**.[11] In practice, the bid-ask spread on the stock you are buying may be \$49.75 to \$50. This means that you can buy for \$50/share and sell for \$49.75/share. If you were to buy immediately and then sell, you would pay the commission twice, and you would pay the bid-ask spread.

Example 1. Suppose XYZ is bid at \$49.75 and offered at \$50, and the commission is \$15. If you buy 100 shares of the stock you pay $(\$50 \times 100) + \$15 = \$5015$. If you immediately sell them again, you receive $(\$49.75 \times 100) - \$15 = \$4960$. Your round-trip transaction cost—the difference between what you pay and what you receive from a sale, not counting changes in the bid and ask prices—is $\$5015 - \$4960 = \$55$. ■

This discussion reveals where the terms "bid" and "ask" come from. The terminology seems backward, but rather than the price you pay, the bid price is what the *market-maker* pays; hence it is the price at which you sell. The offer price is what the market-maker will sell for; hence it is what you have to pay. The terminology reflects the perspective of the market-maker.

What happens to your shares after you buy them? Unless you make other arrangements, shares are typically held in a central depository (in the U.S., at the DTCC) in the name of your broker. Such securities are said to be held in *street name*.

Ways to Buy or Sell

A buyer or seller of an asset can employ different strategies in trading the asset. You implement these different strategies by telling the broker (or the electronic trading system) what kind of order you are submitting.

A **market order** is an instruction to trade a specific quantity of the asset immediately, at the best price that is currently available. The advantage of a market order is that the trade

11. If you think a bid-ask spread is unreasonable, ask what a world without dealers would be like. Every buyer would have to find a seller, and vice versa. The search would be costly and take time. Dealers, because they maintain inventory, offer an immediate transaction, a service called *immediacy*.

is executed as soon as possible. The disadvantage of a market order is that you might have been able to get a better price had you been more patient.

A **limit order** is an instruction to trade a specific quantity of the asset at a specified or better price. A limit order to buy 100 shares at $47.50 can be filled at $47.50 or below. A limit order to sell at $50.25 can be filled at $50.25 or above. Having your limit order filled depends upon whether or not anyone else is willing to trade at that price. As time passes, your order may or may not be filled. Thus, the advantage of a limit order is obtaining a better price. The disadvantage is the possibility that the order is never filled.

There are other kinds of orders. For example, suppose you own 100 shares of XYZ. If you enter a *stop-loss order* at $45, then your order becomes a market order to sell once the price falls to $45. Because your order is a market order, you may end up selling for less than $45.

In the earlier example we supposed that the bid and ask prices for XYZ were $49.75 and $50. You can think of those prices as limit orders—someone has offered to buy at $49.75 and (possibly someone different) to sell at $50.

Box 2 illustrates bid and offer prices for one prediction market.

Short-Selling

The sale of a stock you do not already own is called a **short-sale**. In order to understand short-sales, we first need to understand the terms "long" and "short."

When we buy something, we are said to have a *long* position in that thing. For example, if we buy the stock of XYZ, we pay cash and receive the stock. Some time later, we sell the stock and receive cash. This transaction is a form of *lending*, in that we pay money today and receive money back in the future. For many assets the rate of return we receive is not known in advance (the return depends upon whether the stock price goes up or down), but it is a loan nonetheless.

The opposite of a long position is a short position. A short-sale of XYZ entails borrowing shares of XYZ from an owner, and then selling them, receiving the cash.[12] Some time later, we buy back the XYZ stock, paying cash for it, and return it to the lender. A short-sale can be viewed as a way of borrowing money. With ordinary borrowing, you receive money today and repay it later, paying a rate of interest set in advance. This also happens with a short-sale, except that typically you don't know in advance the rate you will pay.

There are at least three reasons to short-sell:

1. **Speculation:** A short-sale, considered by itself, makes money if the price of the stock goes down. The idea is to first sell high and then buy low. (With a long position, the idea is to first buy low and then sell high.)
2. **Financing:** A short-sale is a way to borrow money, and it is frequently used as a form of financing. This is very common in the bond market, for example.
3. **Hedging:** You can undertake a short-sale to offset the risk of owning the stock or a derivative on the stock. This is frequently done by market-makers and traders.

12. Most brokerage agreements give your broker the right to lend your shares to another investor. The broker earns fees from doing this. You generally do not know if your shares have been loaned.

BOX 2: Bid and Ask Prices in a Prediction Market

In Box 1 we discussed prediction markets. These markets have bid-ask spreads, as you would expect. Here is a table showing the bid-ask spreads in the U.S. presidential market from the Iowa Presidential Nomination Market on May 24, 2012. The "vote share" contract pays the percentage of the popular vote received by that party's candidate, while the "winner take all" contract pays $1 if the candidate wins and zero otherwise.

Share of Vote			Winner Takes All		
Party	Bid	Ask	Party	Bid	Ask
Democratic	0.512	0.527	Democratic	0.592	0.600
Republican	0.470	0.484	Republican	0.400	0.409
Total	0.982	1.011	Total	0.992	1.009

If you wished to buy the Democratic winner-take-all contract, you would pay $0.600 per contract. An immediate sale would earn you $0.592. If you bought both the Democratic and Republican contracts, you would be guaranteed to earn $1 by the end of the convention, but the cost would be $1.009. Similarly, if you sold all four, you would have to pay $1 at the end of the convention but you would receive only $0.992.

The prices in the table are limit orders placed by other traders. What you cannot see in the table is how many contracts you can trade at those prices (this is called *market depth*). You also cannot see any additional buy limit orders below the bid price and additional sell limit orders above the ask price.

These reasons are not mutually exclusive. For example, a market-maker might use a short-sale to simultaneously hedge and finance a position.

Example: Short-Selling Wine. Because short-sales can seem confusing, here is a detailed example that illustrates how short-sales work.

There are markets for many collectible items, such as fine wines. If you believe prices will rise, you would buy the wine on the market and plan to sell after the price rises. However, suppose there is a wine from a particular vintage and producer that you believe to be overpriced and you expect the price to fall. How could you speculate based on this belief? The answer is that you can engage in a short-sale.

In order to short-sell, you must first obtain wine. You can do this by borrowing a case from a collector. The collector, of course, will want a promise that you will return the wine at some point; suppose you agree to return it 1 week later. Having reached agreement, you borrow the wine and then sell it at the market price. After 1 week, you acquire a replacement case on the market, then return it to the collector from whom you originally borrowed the wine. If the price has fallen, you will have bought the replacement wine for less than the price at which you sold the original, so you make money. If the price has risen, you have lost money. Either way, you have just completed a *short-sale* of wine. The act of buying replacement wine and returning it to the lender is said to be *closing* or *covering* the short position.

Note that short-selling is a way to borrow money. Initially, you received money from selling the wine. A week later you paid the money back (you had to buy a replacement case to return to the lender). The rate of interest you paid was low if the price of the replacement case was low, and high if the price of the replacement case was high.

This example is obviously simplified. We have assumed several points:

TABLE 4 Cash flows associated with short-selling a share of IBM for 90 days. S_0 and S_{90} are the share prices on days 0 and 90. Note that the short-seller must pay the dividend, D, to the share-lender.

	Day 0	Dividend Ex-Day	Day 90
Action	Borrow shares	—	Return shares
Security	Sell shares	—	Purchase shares
Cash	$+S_0$	$-D$	$-S_{90}$

- It is easy to find a lender of wine.
- It is easy to buy, at a fair price, satisfactory wine to return to the lender: The wine you buy after 1 week is a perfect substitute for the wine you borrowed.
- The collector from whom you borrowed is not concerned that you will fail to return the borrowed wine.

Example: Short-Selling Stock. Now consider a short-sale of stock. As with wine, when you short-sell stock you borrow the stock and sell it, receiving cash today. At some future date you buy the stock in the market and return it to the original owner.

Suppose you want to short-sell IBM stock for 90 days. Table 4 depicts the cash flows. Observe in particular that if the share pays dividends, the short-seller must in turn make dividend payments to the share-lender. This issue did not arise with wine! This dividend payment is taxed to the recipient, just like an ordinary dividend payment, and it is tax-deductible to the short-seller.

Notice that the cash flows in Table 4 are exactly the opposite of the cash flows from purchasing the stock. Thus, *short-selling is literally the opposite of buying.*

The Lease Rate of an Asset

We have seen that when you borrow an asset it may be necessary to make payments to the lender. Dividends on short-sold stock are an example of this. We will refer to the payment required by the lender as the **lease rate** of the asset. This concept will arise frequently, and, as we will see, it provides a unifying concept for our later discussions of derivatives.

The wine example did not have a lease payment. But under some circumstances it might be necessary to make a payment to borrow wine. Wine does not pay an explicit dividend but does pay an implicit dividend if the owner enjoys seeing bottles in the cellar. The owner might thus require a payment in order to lend a bottle. This would be a lease rate for wine.

Risk and Scarcity in Short-Selling

The preceding examples were simple illustrations of the mechanics and economics of short-selling, and they demonstrate the ideas you will need to understand our discussions of derivatives. It turns out, however, that some of the complexities we skipped over are easy to understand and are important in practice. In this section we use the wine example to illustrate some of these practical issues.

Credit Risk. As the short-seller, you have an obligation to the lender to return the wine. The lender fears that you will renege on this obligation. This concern can be addressed with collateral: After you sell the wine, the lender can hold the money you received from selling the wine. You have an obligation to return the wine; the lender keeps the money in the event that you don't.

Holding on to the money will help the lender feel more secure, but after thinking the matter over, the lender will likely want more from you than just the current value of the wine. Suppose you borrow $5000 worth of wine. What happens, the lender will think, if the price of that particular wine rises 1 week later to $6000? This is a $1000 loss on your short-sale. In order to return the wine, you will have to pay $6000 for wine you just sold for $5000. Perhaps you cannot afford the extra $1000 and you will fail to return the borrowed wine. The lender, thinking ahead, will be worried at the outset about this possibility and will ask you to provide *more* than the $5000 the wine is worth—say, an extra $1000. This extra amount is called a **haircut** and serves to protect the lender against your failure to return the wine when the price rises.[13] In practice, short-sellers must have funds—called *capital*—to be able to pay haircuts. The amount of capital places a limit on their ability to short-sell.

Scarcity. As the short-seller, do you need to worry about the short-sale proceeds? The lender is going to have $6000 of your money. Most of this, however, simply reflects your obligation, and we could ask a trustworthy third party, such as a bank, to hold the money so the lender cannot abscond with it. However, when you return the wine, you are going to want your money back, *plus interest*. This raises the question: What rate of interest will the lender pay you? Over the course of the short-sale, the lender can invest your money, earning, say, 6%. The lender could offer to pay you 4% on the funds, thinking to keep as a fee the 2% difference between the 6% earned on the money and the 4% paid to you. What happens if the lender and borrower negotiate?

Here is the interesting point: The rate of interest the lender pays on the collateral is going to depend on how many people want to borrow wine from the particular vintage and producer, and how many are willing to lend it! As a practical matter, it may not be easy to find a lender; the wine may be "hard to locate." If there is high demand for borrowed wine, the lender will offer a low rate of interest, essentially earning a fee for being willing to lend something that is scarce. However, if no one else wants to borrow the wine, the lender might conclude that a small fee is better than nothing and offer you a rate of interest close to the market rate.

The rate paid on collateral is called different things in different markets: the **repo rate** in bond markets and the **short rebate** in the stock market. Whatever it is called, the difference between this rate and the market rate of interest is another cost to your short-sale.

---

13. Note that the lender is not concerned about your failure to perform when the price goes down because the lender has the money!

CHAPTER SUMMARY

Derivatives are financial instruments with a payoff determined by the price of something else. They can be used as a tool for risk management and speculation, and to reduce transaction costs or avoid taxes and regulation.

One important function of financial markets is to facilitate optimal risk-sharing. There are different ways to measure the size and activity of stock, bond, and derivatives markets, but these markets are by any measure large and growing. The growth of derivatives markets over the last 50 years has coincided with an increase in the risks evident in various markets. Events such as the 1973 oil shock, the abandonment of fixed exchange rates, and the deregulation of energy markets have created a new role for derivatives.

There are costs to trading an asset, one of which is the bid-ask spread. The bid-ask spread is a key means by which those traders who make markets are compensated for doing so. In markets without explicit market-makers, limit orders create a bid-ask spread.

An important transaction is a short-sale, which entails borrowing a security, selling it, making dividend (or other cash) payments to the security lender, and then returning it. A short-sale is conceptually the opposite of a purchase. Short-sales can be used for speculation, as a form of financing, or as a way to hedge. Many of the details of short-selling in practice can be understood as a response to credit risk of the short-seller and scarcity of shares that can be borrowed. Short-sellers typically leave the short-sale proceeds on deposit with lenders, along with additional capital called a haircut. The rate paid on this collateral is called the short rebate, and is less than the interest rate.

FURTHER READING

The derivatives exchanges have websites that list their contracts and provide further details. Because the web addresses can change (e.g., due to mergers), the easiest way to find them is with a web search.

Jorion (2006) discusses a number of derivatives disasters, and Jorion (1995) examines in detail one famous episode: Orange County in California. Bernstein (1992) presents a history of the development of financial markets, and Bernstein (1996) discusses the concept of risk measurement and how it evolved over the last 800 years. Miller (1986) discusses origins of past financial innovation, while Merton (1999) and Shiller (2003) provide a stimulating look at possible *future* developments in financial markets. Finally, Lewis (1989) is a classic, funny, insider's account of investment banking, offering a different (to say the least) perspective on the mechanics of global risk-sharing.

The financial crisis spawned dozens of books. Lo (2012) reviews 21 of them. Informative and entertaining books aimed at a popular audience include Cohan (2009), Tett (2010), Sorkin (2010), and Lewis (2011). Gorton (2010) provides a more detailed and technical perspective.

PROBLEMS

1. Heating degree-day and cooling degree-day futures contracts make payments based on whether the temperature is abnormally hot or cold. Explain why the following businesses might be interested in such a contract:

a. Soft-drink manufacturers.

b. Ski-resort operators.

c. Electric utilities.

d. Amusement park operators.

2. Suppose the businesses in the previous problem use futures contracts to hedge their temperature-related risk. Who do you think might accept the opposite risk?

3. ABC stock has a bid price of $40.95 and an ask price of $41.05. Assume there is a $20 brokerage commission.

a. What amount will you pay to buy 100 shares?

b. What amount will you receive for selling 100 shares?

c. Suppose you buy 100 shares, then immediately sell 100 shares with the bid and ask prices being the same in both cases. What is your round-trip transaction cost?

4. Repeat the previous problem supposing that the brokerage fee is quoted as 0.3% of the bid or ask price.

5. Suppose a security has a bid price of $100 and an ask price of $100.12. At what price can the market-maker purchase a security? At what price can a market-maker sell a security? What is the spread in dollar terms when 100 shares are traded?

6. Suppose you short-sell 300 shares of XYZ stock at $30.19 with a commission charge of 0.5%. Supposing you pay commission charges for purchasing the security to cover the short-sale, how much profit have you made if you close the short-sale at a price of $29.87?

7. Suppose you desire to short-sell 400 shares of JKI stock, which has a bid price of $25.12 and an ask price of $25.31. You cover the short position 180 days later when the bid price is $22.87 and the ask price is $23.06.

a. Taking into account only the bid and ask prices (ignoring commissions and interest), what profit did you earn?

b. Suppose that there is a 0.3% commission to engage in the short-sale (this is the commission to sell the stock) and a 0.3% commission to close the short-sale (this is the commission to buy the stock back). How do these commissions change the profit in the previous answer?

c. Suppose the 6-month interest rate is 3% and that you are paid nothing on the short-sale proceeds. How much interest do you lose during the 6 months in which you have the short position?

8. When you open a brokerage account, you typically sign an agreement giving the broker the right to lend your shares without notifying or compensating you. Why do brokers want you to sign this agreement?

9. Suppose a stock pays a quarterly dividend of $3. You plan to hold a short position in the stock across the dividend ex-date. What is your obligation on that date? If you are a taxable investor, what would you guess is the tax consequence of the payment?

(In particular, would you expect the dividend to be tax deductible?) Suppose the company announces instead that the dividend is $5. Should you care that the dividend is different from what you expected?

10. Short interest is a measure of the aggregate short positions on a stock. Check an online brokerage or other financial service for the short interest on several stocks of your choice. Can you guess which stocks have high short interest and which have low? Is it theoretically possible for short interest to exceed 100% of shares outstanding?

11. Suppose that you go to a bank and borrow $100. You promise to repay the loan in 90 days for $102. Explain this transaction using the terminology of short-sales.

12. Suppose your bank's loan officer tells you that if you take out a mortgage (i.e., you borrow money to buy a house), you will be permitted to borrow no more than 80% of the value of the house. Describe this transaction using the terminology of short-sales.

13. Pick a derivatives exchange such as CME Group, Eurex, or the Chicago Board Options Exchange. Go to that exchange's website and try to determine the following:

a. What products the exchange trades.

b. The trading volume in the various products.

c. The notional value traded.

What do you predict would happen to these measures if the notional value of a popular contract were cut in half? (For example, instead of an option being based on 100 shares of stock, suppose it were based on 50 shares of stock.)

14. Consider the widget exchange. Suppose that each widget contract has a market value of $0 and a notional value of $100. There are three traders, A, B, and C. Over one day, the following trades occur:

- A long, B short, 5 contracts.
- A long, C short, 15 contract.
- B long, C short, 10 contracts.
- C long, A short, 20 contracts.

a. What is each trader's net position in the contract at the end of the day? (Calculate long positions minus short positions.)

b. What are trading volume, open interest, and the notional values of trading volume and open interest? (Calculate open interest as the sum of the net *long positions*, from your previous answer.)

c. How would your answers have been different if there were an additional trade: C long, B short, 5 contracts?

d. How would you expect the measures in part (b) to be different if each contract had a notional value of $20?

Insurance, Hedging, and Simple Strategies

Basic derivatives contracts include: forward contracts, futures contracts, call options, and put options. All of these are contracts between two parties, with a payoff at some future date based on the price of an underlying asset (this is why they are called derivatives).

There are a number of things we want to understand about these instruments. What are they? How do they work and what do they cost? If you enter into a forward contract, futures contract, or option, what obligations or rights have you acquired? Payoff and profit diagrams provide an important graphical tool to summarize the risk of these contracts.

Once we understand what the basic derivatives contracts are, what can we do with them? Among other things, they can be used to provide insurance, to convert a stock investment into a risk-free investment and vice versa, and to speculate in a

From *Derivatives Markets*, Third Edition, Robert McDonald. Copyright © 2013 by Pearson Education, Inc. Published by Pearson Prentice Hall. All rights reserved.

variety of ways. Derivatives can often be customized for a particular purpose. It is interesting to see how corporate risk managers can use derivatives, and some reasons for doing so.

An Introduction to Forwards and Options

This chapter introduces the basic derivatives contracts: forward contracts, call options, and put options. These fundamental contracts are widely used, and serve as building blocks for more complicated derivatives. We explain here how the contracts work and how to think about their risk. We also introduce an extremely important tool for analyzing derivatives positions—namely, payoff and profit diagrams. The terminology and concepts introduced in this chapter are fundamental.

1. FORWARD CONTRACTS

To understand a forward contract, it is helpful to first consider the process of buying or selling stock. Such a transaction entails at least three separate steps: (1) the buyer and seller agree to transact and set the price to be paid, (2) cash is transferred from the buyer to the seller, and (3) shares are transferred from the seller to the buyer. Typically, steps 2 and 3 occur shortly after the buyer and seller agree to transact.[1] However, as a logical matter, a price could be set today and the transfer of shares and cash could then occur at a specified date in the future.

This is in fact the definition of a **forward contract**: It sets today the terms at which you buy or sell an asset or commodity at a specific time in the future. A forward contract does the following:

- Specifies the quantity and exact type of the asset or commodity the seller must deliver.
- Specifies delivery logistics, such as time, date, and place.
- Specifies the price the buyer will pay at the time of delivery.
- Obligates the seller to sell and the buyer to buy, subject to the above specifications.

The time at which the contract settles is called the **expiration date**. The asset or commodity on which the forward contract is based is called the **underlying asset**. Apart from commissions and bid-ask spreads, a forward contract requires no initial payment or **premium**. The contractual forward price simply represents the price at which consenting adults agree today

1. The current industry standard is for steps 2 and 3 to occur no later than three days after the agreement to transact. This is called **T+3 settlement**.

From Chapter 2 of *Derivatives Markets*, Third Edition, Robert McDonald. Copyright © 2013 by Pearson Education, Inc. Published by Pearson Prentice Hall. All rights reserved.

FIGURE 1

Index futures price listings.

	Open	Contract High	hilo	Low	Settle	Chg	Open Interest
Index Futures							
DJ Industrial Average (CBT)—$10 x index							
June	10981	11070	▲	10977	**11065**	102	6,972
Sept	10977	10977	▲	10977	**11002**	103	13
Mini DJ Industrial Average (CBT)—$5 x index							
June	10979	11072	▲	10975	**11065**	102	84,086
S&P 500 Index (CME)—$250 x index							
June	1195.30	1207.00		1194.50	**1206.60**	13.50	313,917
Dec	1193.00	1197.60	▲	1192.00	**1197.10**	13.50	3,301
Mini S&P 500 (CME)—$50 x index							
June	1195.50	1207.25	▲	1194.50	**1206.50**	13.50	2,412,904
Sept	1190.50	1202.00	▲	1190.00	**1201.75**	13.50	11,460
Nasdaq 100 (CME)—$100 x index							
June	2010.00	2027.00	▲	2007.25	**2026.50**	25.25	16,139
Mini Nasdaq 100 (CME)—$20 x index							
June	2009.8	2026.8	▲	2006.8	**2026.5**	25.3	308,163
Sept	2005.8	2024.0	▲	2005.0	**2024.3**	25.5	377
Mini Russell 2000 (ICE-US)—$100 x index							
June	706.50	721.00	▲	705.80	**720.10**	15.40	373,776
Sept	706.70	718.00	▲	706.30	**717.70**	15.40	2,835
Mini Russell 1000 (ICE-US)—$100 x index							
June	661.50	665.70	▲	659.50	**665.30**	7.50	19,004
U.S. Dollar Index (ICE-US)—$1,000 x index							
June	80.56	80.52	▲	80.14	**80.29**	–.33	44,534
Sept	80.81	80.86	▲	80.51	**80.57**	–.34	2,231

Data from the *Wall Street Journal*, April 15, 2010, p. C-7.

to transact in the future, at which time the buyer pays the seller the forward price and the seller delivers the asset.

Futures contracts are similar to forward contracts in that they create an obligation to buy or sell at a predetermined price at a future date. We can think of them as interchangeable.

Figure 1 shows futures price listings from the *Wall Street Journal* for futures contracts on several stock indices, including the Dow Jones Industrial Average (DJ 30) and the Standard and Poor's 500 (S&P 500). The indices are the underlying assets for the contracts. (A **stock index** is the average price of a group of stocks. In these examples we work with this group price rather than the price of just one stock.) The first column of the listing gives the expiration month. The columns that follow show the price at the beginning of the day (the open), the high and low during the day, and the settlement price, which reflects the last transactions of the day.

The listing also gives the price change from the previous day and open interest, which measures the number of contracts outstanding. (Since each trade of a contract has both a buyer and a seller, a buyer-seller pair counts as one contract.) Finally, the head of the listing tells us where the contracts trade (the Chicago Board of Trade [CBT], Chicago Mercantile Exchange [CME] and the Intercontinental Exchange[ICE]), and the size of the contract, which for the S&P 500, for example, is $250 times the index value. Note that there is also an S&P 500 "mini" contract. This is the same as the S&P 500 contract except for scale: The Mini S&P 500 futures contract is one-fifth the size of the regular S&P 500 futures contract. The mini contracts were introduced to make index futures more appealing to ordinary investors. There are many more exchange-traded stock index futures contracts than

TABLE 1 Some indexes on which futures contracts are traded.

Index	Exchange	Weights	Description
S&P 500 Index	CME	Market	500 large U.S. stocks
DJ Industrial Average	CME	Price	30 large U.S. stocks
NASDAQ 100	CME	Market	100 large global non-financial firms listed on Nasdaq
S&P Midcap 400	CME	Market	400 mid-cap U.S. stocks
Russell 1000	ICE	Market	Largest 1000 U.S. companies
Russell 2000	ICE	Market	2000 small-cap U.S. companies
MSCI World	LIFFE	Market	1500 stocks from 23 developed countries
MSCI EAFE (Europe, Australasia, Far East)	LIFFE, CME	Market	Stocks from 21 developed countries, excluding Canada and the U.S.
Euro Stoxx 50	Eurex	Market	50 blue-chip Eurozone stocks
Nikkei 225	SGX, OSE, CME	Price	225 stocks listed on the Tokyo Stock Exchange
Hang Seng	HKEx	Market	43 of the largest companies on the Hong Kong Stock Exchange
DAX	Eurex	Market	30 large German companies listed on the Frankfurt Stock Exchange
S&P Goldman Sachs Commodity Index	CME	Production	Wide range of commodities on which futures contracts are traded

Abbreviations: CME = Chicago Mercantile Exchange, ICE = Intercontinental Exchange, LIFFE = London International Financial Futures Exchange, SGX = Singapore Exchange, OSE = Osaka Stock Exchange, HKEx = Hong Kong Exchange and Clearing. For the weights, "market" means weights are proportional to market capitalization, "price" means weights are proportional to the stock price, "production" means weights are proporational to global production.

those in Figure 1, both in the United States and around the world. Table 1 is a non-exhaustive list of global stock indexes.

The price quotes in Figure 1 are from April. The prices are therefore set in April for purchase of the index in later months. For example, the December futures settlement price for the S&P 500 index is \$1197.10.[2] By contrast, the current S&P index price that day (not in Figure 1) is \$1210.65. This is the **spot price** for the index—the market price for immediate delivery of the index.

There are also futures contracts on interest rates and commodities. Futures are widely used in risk management and as an alternative way to invest in the underlying asset.

---

2. The use and nonuse of dollar signs for futures prices can be confusing. Many futures prices, in particular those for index futures, are in practice quoted without dollar signs, and multiplied by a dollar amount to determine the value of the contract. In this chapter, we will depart from this convention and use dollar signs for index futures prices.

Agricultural futures (such as corn and soybeans) can be used by farmers and others to hedge crop prices. Box 1 discusses an unsuccessful proposal for a new futures contract that was in the news in 2003.

In this chapter we take prices as given and examine profit and loss on a forward contract. We will also see how a position in a forward contract is similar to and different from alternative investments, such as a direct investment in the underlying index.

BOX 1: Terrorism Futures?

Newspaper readers in July 2003 were undoubtedly startled to see the headline "Pentagon Prepares a Futures Market on Terror Attacks" (*New York Times*, July 29, 2003, p. A1). The article continued:

> Traders bullish on a biological attack on Israel or bearish on the chances of a North Korean missile strike would have the opportunity to bet on the likelihood of such events on a new Internet site established by the Defense Advanced Research Projects Agency.
>
> The Pentagon called its latest idea a new way of predicting events and part of its search for the "broadest possible set of new ways to prevent terrorist attacks."

Critics immediately attacked the plan:

> Two Democratic senators who reported the plan called it morally repugnant and grotesque. . . . One of the two senators, Byron L. Dorgan of North Dakota, said the idea seemed so preposterous that he had trouble persuading people it was not a hoax. "Can you imagine," Mr. Dorgan asked, "if another country set up a betting parlor so that people could go in . . . and bet on the assassination of an American political figure?"

The other critic, Senator Ron Wyden of Oregon, described the plan:

> You may think early on that Prime Minister X is going to be assassinated. So you buy the futures contracts for 5 cents each. As more people begin to think the person's going to be assassinated, the cost of the contract could go up, to 50 cents. The payoff if he's assassinated is \$1 per future. So if it comes to pass, and those who bought at 5 cents make 95 cents. Those who bought at 50 cents make 50 cents.

Later the same day (July 29), this headline appeared on the *New York Times* website: "Pentagon Abandons Plan for Futures Market on Terror."

Before dropping the plan, Defense officials defended it: "Research indicates that markets are extremely efficient, effective, and timely aggregators of dispersed and even hidden information. Futures markets have proven themselves to be good at predicting such things as elections results; they are often better than expert opinions."

A common concern about futures markets is the possibility that markets can be manipulated by better informed traders. The possibility of manipulation in this case was described as a "technical challenge and uncertainty." The natural worry was that terrorists would use the futures market to make money from attacks, or to mislead authorities about where they would attack.

TABLE 2

Payoff after 6 months from a long S&R forward contract and a short S&R forward contract at a forward price of $1020. If the index price in 6 months is $1020, both the long and short have a 0 payoff. If the index price is greater than $1020, the long makes money and the short loses money. If the index price is less than $1020, the long loses money and the short makes money.

S&R Index	S&R Forward	
in 6 Months	Long	Short
900	−$120	$120
950	−70	70
1000	−20	20
1020	0	0
1050	30	−30
1100	80	−80

The Payoff on a Forward Contract

Every forward contract has both a party agreeing to buy and one agreeing to sell. The term **long** is used to describe the buyer and **short** is used to describe the seller. Generally, a long position is one that makes money when the price goes up and a short is one that makes money when the price goes down. Because the long has agreed to buy at the fixed forward price, a long position profits if prices rise.

The **payoff** to a contract is the value of the position at expiration. The payoff to a long forward contract is

$$\text{Payoff to long forward} = \text{Spot price at expiration} - \text{forward price} \tag{1}$$

Because the short has agreed to sell at the fixed forward price, the short profits if prices fall. The payoff to a short forward contract is

$$\text{Payoff to short forward} = \text{Forward price} - \text{spot price at expiration} \tag{2}$$

To illustrate these calculations, consider a forward contract on a hypothetical stock index. Suppose the non-dividend-paying S&R ("Special and Rich") 500 index has a current price of $1000 and the 6-month forward price is $1020.[3] The holder of a long position in the S&R forward contract is obligated to pay $1020 in 6 months for one unit of the index. The holder of the short position is obligated to sell one unit of the index for $1020. Table 2 lists the payoff on the position for various possible future values of the index.

3. We use a hypothetical stock index—the S&R—in order to avoid complications associated with dividends.

FIGURE 2

Long and short forward positions on the S&R 500 index.

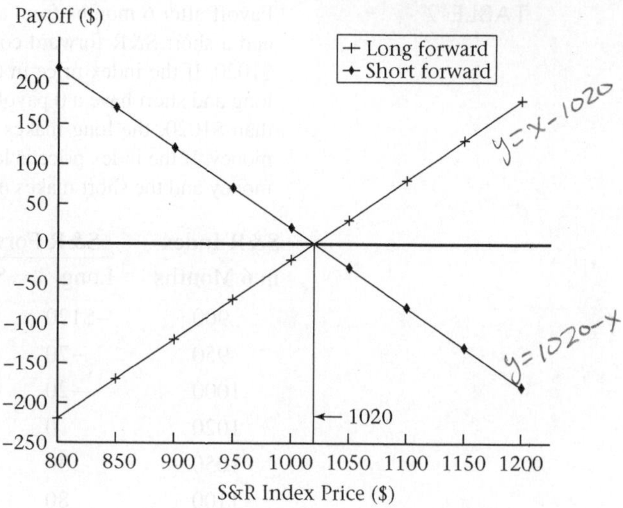

Example 1. Suppose the index price is \$1050 in 6 months. A holder who entered a long position at a forward price of \$1020 is obligated to pay \$1020 to acquire the index, and hence earns $\$1050 - \$1020 = \$30$ per unit of the index. The short is likewise obligated to sell for \$1020, and thus loses \$30. ■

This example illustrates the mechanics of a forward contract, showing why the long makes money when the price rises and the short makes money when the price falls.

Graphing the Payoff on a Forward Contract

We can graph the information in Table 2 to show the payoff in 6 months on the forward contract as a function of the index. Figure 2 graphs the long and short positions, with the index price at the expiration of the forward contract on the horizontal axis and payoff on the vertical axis. As you would expect, the two positions have a zero payoff when the index price in 6 months equals the forward price of \$1020. The graph for the short forward is a mirror image (about the x-axis) of the graph for the long forward. For a given value of the index, the payoff to the short is exactly the opposite of the payoff to the long. In other words, the gain to one party is the loss to the other.

This kind of graph is widely used because it summarizes the risk of the position at a glance.

Comparing a Forward and Outright Purchase

The S&R forward contract is a way to acquire the index by paying \$1020 after 6 months. An alternative way to acquire the index is to purchase it outright at time 0, paying \$1000. Is

FIGURE 3

Comparison of payoff after 6 months of a long position in the S&R index versus a forward contract in the S&R index.

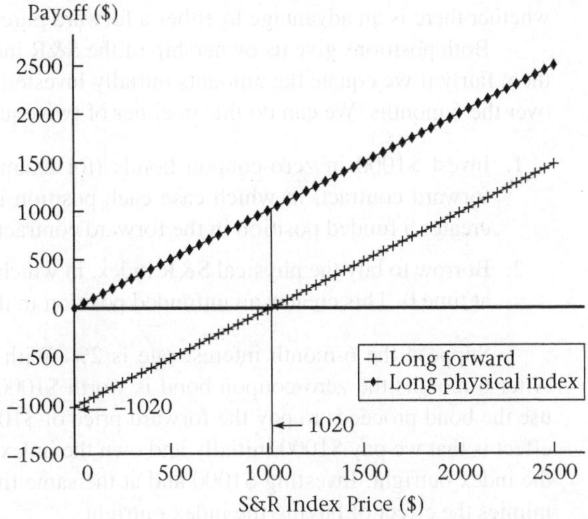

there any advantage to using the forward contract to buy the index, as opposed to purchasing it outright?

If we buy the S&R index today, it costs us \$1000. The value of the position in 6 months is the value of the S&R index. The payoff to a long position in the physical S&R index is graphed in Figure 3. For comparison, the payoff to the long forward position, is graphed as well. Note that the axes have different scales in Figures 3 and 2.

To see how Figure 3 is constructed, suppose the S&R index price is \$0 after 6 months. If the index price is \$0, the physical index will be worth \$0; hence we plot a 0 on the y-axis against 0 on the x-axis. Similarly, for all other prices of the S&R index, the payoff equals the value of the S&R index. For example, if we own the index and the price in 6 months is \$750, the value of the position is \$750.

If the index price in 6 months is \$0, the payoff to the forward contract, using equation (1), is

$$\text{Payoff to long forward} = 0 - \$1020 = -\$1020$$

If instead the index price is \$1020, the long index position will be worth \$1020 and the forward contract will be worth \$0.

With both positions, we own the index after 6 months. What the figure does not reflect, however, is the different *initial* investments required for the two positions. With the cash index, we invest \$1000 initially and then we own the index. With the forward contract, we invest \$0 initially and \$1020 after 6 months; then we own the index. The financing of the two positions is different. The payoff graph tells us how much money we end up with after 6 months, but does not account for the initial \$1000 investment with the outright purchase. We will refer to a position that has been paid in full as **funded**, and one for which payment is deferred as **unfunded**. In this example, the index position is funded and the forward contract is unfunded. Figure 3 is accurate, but it does not answer our question—namely, whether there is an advantage to either a forward purchase or an outright purchase.

Both positions give us ownership of the S&R index after 6 months. We can compare them fairly if we equate the amounts initially invested and then account for interest earned over the 6 months. We can do this in either of two equivalent ways:

1. Invest $1000 in zero-coupon bonds (for example, Treasury bills) along with the forward contract, in which case each position initially costs $1000 at time 0. This creates a funded position in the forward contract.
2. Borrow to buy the physical S&R index, in which case each position initially costs $0 at time 0. This creates an unfunded position in the index.

Suppose the 6-month interest rate is 2%. With alternative 1, we pay $1000 today. After 6 months the zero-coupon bond is worth $\$1000 \times 1.02 = \$1020$. At that point, we use the bond proceeds to pay the forward price of $1020. We then own the index. The net effect is that we pay $1000 initially and own the index after 6 months, just as if we bought the index outright. Investing $1000 and at the same time entering a long forward contract mimics the effect of buying the index outright.

With alternative 2, we borrow $1000 to buy the index, which costs $1000. Hence we make no net cash payment at time 0. After 6 months we owe $1000 plus interest. At that time we repay $\$1000 \times 1.02 = \$1020$ for the borrowed money. The net effect is that we invest nothing initially, and after six months pay $1020. We also own the index. Borrowing to buy the stock therefore mimics the effect of entering into a long forward contract.[4]

We conclude that when the index pays no dividends, the only difference between the forward contract and the cash index investment is the timing of a payment that will be made for certain. Therefore, we can compare the two positions by using the interest rate to shift the timing of payments. In the above example, we conclude that the forward contract and the cash index are equivalent investments, differing only in the timing of the cash flows. Neither form of investing has an advantage over the other.

This analysis suggests a way to systematically compare positions that require different initial investments. We can assume that we borrow any required initial payment. At expiration, we receive the payoff from the contract, and repay any borrowed amounts. We will call this the **net payoff** or **profit**. Because this calculation accounts for differing initial investments in a simple fashion, we will primarily use profit rather than payoff diagrams.[5] Note that the payoff and profit diagrams are the same for a forward contract because it requires no initial investment.

To summarize, a **payoff diagram** graphs the cash value of a position at a point in time. A **profit diagram** subtracts from the payoff the future value of the investment in the position.

This discussion raises a question: Given our assumptions, should we really expect the forward price to equal $1020, which is the future value of the index? The answer in this case is yes.

4. If the index paid a dividend in this example, then we would receive the dividend by holding the physical index, but not when we entered into the forward contract.

5. The term "profit" is defined variously by accountants and economists. All of our profit calculations are for the purpose of *comparing* one position with another, not computing profit in any absolute sense.

FIGURE 4

Payoff diagram for a long S&R forward contract, together with a zero-coupon bond that pays \$1020 at maturity. Summing the value of the long forward plus the bond at each S&R Index price gives the line labeled "Forward + bond."

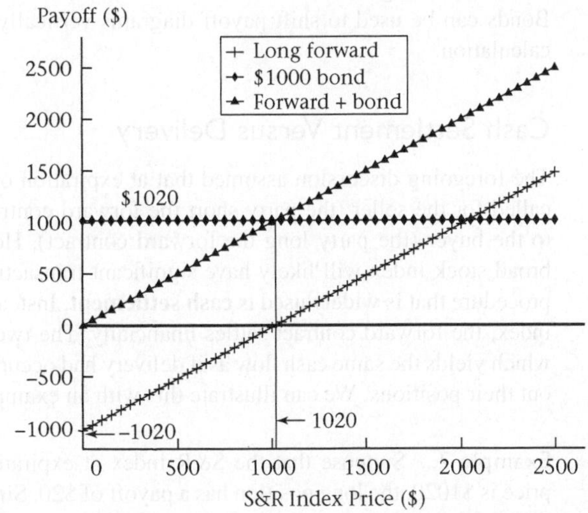

Zero-Coupon Bonds in Payoff and Profit Diagrams

The preceding discussion showed that the long forward contract and outright purchase of the physical S&R index are essentially the same once we take time value of money into account. Buying the physical index is like entering into the forward contract and simultaneously investing \$1000 in a zero-coupon bond. We can see this same point graphically by using a payoff diagram where we include a zero-coupon bond.

Suppose we enter into a long S&R index forward position, and at the same time purchase a \$1000 zero-coupon bond, which will pay \$1020 after 6 months. (This was alternative 1 in the previous section.) Algebraically, the payoff to the forward plus the bond is

$$\text{Forward} + \text{bond} = \underbrace{\text{Spot price at expiration} - \$1020}_{\text{Forward payoff}} + \underbrace{\$1020}_{\text{Bond payoff}}$$
$$= \text{Spot price at expiration}$$

This is the same as the payoff to investing in the physical index.

The payoff diagram for this position is an easy modification of Figure 3. We simply add a line representing the value of the bond after 6 months (\$1000 × 1.02 = \$1020), and then add the bond payoff to the forward payoff. This is graphed in Figure 4. The forward plus bond looks exactly like the physical index in Figure 3.

What is the profit diagram corresponding to this payoff diagram? For the forward contract, profit is the same as the payoff because there is no initial investment. Profit for the forward plus bond is obtained by subtracting the future value of the initial investment. The initial investment was the cost of the bond, \$1000. Its future value is, by definition, \$1020, the value of the bond after 6 months. Thus, the profit diagram for a forward contract plus a bond is obtained by *ignoring* the bond! Put differently, adding a bond to a position leaves a profit diagram unaffected.

Depending on the context, it can be helpful to draw either payoff or profit diagrams. Bonds can be used to shift payoff diagrams vertically, but they do not change the profit calculation.

Cash Settlement Versus Delivery

The foregoing discussion assumed that at expiration of the forward contract, the contract called for the seller (the party short the forward contract) to deliver the cash S&R index to the buyer (the party long the forward contract). However, a physical transaction in a broad stock index will likely have significant transaction costs. An alternative settlement procedure that is widely used is **cash settlement**. Instead of requiring delivery of the actual index, the forward contract settles financially. The two parties make a net cash payment, which yields the same cash flow as if delivery had occurred and both parties had then closed out their positions. We can illustrate this with an example.

Example 2. Suppose that the S&R index at expiration is \$1040. Because the forward price is \$1020, the long position has a payoff of \$20. Similarly, the short position loses \$20. With cash settlement, the short simply pays \$20 to the long, with no transfer of the physical asset, and hence no transaction costs. It is as if the long paid \$1020, acquired the index worth \$1040, and then immediately sold it with no transaction costs.

If the S&R index price at expiration had instead been \$960, the long position would have a payoff of −\$60 and the short would have a payoff of \$60. Cash settlement in this case entails the long paying \$60 to the short. ■

Cash settlement is feasible only when there is an accepted reference price upon which the settlement can be based. Cash settlement is not limited to forward contracts—virtually any financial contract can be settled using cash rather than delivery.

Credit Risk

Any forward or futures contract—indeed, any derivatives contract—has **credit risk**, which means there is a possibility that the counterparty who owes money fails to make a payment. If you agree to sell the index in one year at a fixed price and the spot price turns out to be lower than the forward price, the counterparty is obligated to buy the index for more than it is worth. You face the risk that the counterparty will for some reason fail to pay the forward price for the index. Similarly, the counterparty faces the risk that you will not fulfill the contract if the spot price in 1 year turns out to be higher than the forward price.

With exchange-traded contracts, the exchange goes to great lengths to minimize this risk by requiring collateral of all participants and being the ultimate counterparty in all transactions. With over-the-counter contracts, the fact that the contracts are transacted directly between two parties means that each counterparty bears the credit risk of the other.[6]

6. Of course, credit risk also exists in exchange-traded contracts. The specific details of how exchanges are structured to minimize credit risk is a complicated and fascinating subject (see Edwards and Ma (1992), ch. 3, for details). In practice, exchanges are regarded by participants as good credit risks.

Credit risk is an important problem with all derivatives, but it is also quite complicated. Credit checks of counterparties and credit protections such as collateral and bank letters of credit are commonly employed to guard against losses from counterparty default.

2. CALL OPTIONS

We have seen that a forward contract obligates the buyer (the holder of the long position) to pay the forward price at expiration, even if the value of the underlying asset at expiration is less than the forward price. Because losses are possible with a forward contract, it is natural to wonder: Could there be a contract where the buyer has the right to walk away from the deal?

The answer is yes; a **call option** is a contract where the buyer has the right to buy, but not the obligation to buy. Here is an example illustrating how a call option works at expiration.

Example 3. Suppose that the call buyer agrees to pay $1020 for the S&R index in 6 months but is not obligated to do so. (The buyer has purchased a call option.) If in 6 months the S&R price is $1100, the buyer will pay $1020 and receive the index. This is a payoff of $80 per unit of the index. If the S&R price is $900, the buyer walks away. ■

Now think about this transaction from the seller's point of view. The buyer is in control of the option, deciding when to buy the index by paying $1020. Thus, the rights of the option buyer are obligations for the option seller.

Example 4. If in 6 months the S&R price is $1100, the seller will receive $1020 and give up an index worth more, for a loss of $80 per unit of the index. If the S&R price is less than $1020, the buyer will not buy, so the seller has no obligation. Thus, at expiration, the seller will have a payoff that is zero (if the S&R price is less than $1020) or negative (if the S&R price is greater than $1020). ■

Does it seem as if something is wrong here? Because the buyer can decide whether to buy, the seller *cannot* make money at expiration. This situation suggests that the seller must, in effect, be "bribed" to enter into the contract in the first place. At the time the buyer and seller agree to the contract, the buyer must pay the seller an initial price, the premium. This initial payment compensates the seller for being at a disadvantage at expiration. Contrast this with a forward contract, for which the initial premium is zero.

Option Terminology

Here are some key terms used to describe options:

Strike price. The **strike price**, or **exercise price**, of a call option is what the buyer pays for the asset. In the example above, the strike price was $1020. The strike price can be set at any value.

Exercise. The **exercise** of a call option is the act of paying the strike price to receive the asset. In Example 3, the buyer decided after 6 months whether to exercise the option—that is, whether to pay $1020 (the strike price) to receive the S&R index.

Expiration. The **expiration** of the option is the date by which the option must either be exercised or it becomes worthless. The option in Example 3 had an expiration of 6 months.

Exercise style. The **exercise style** of the option governs the time at which exercise can occur. In the above example, exercise could occur only at expiration. Such an option is said to be a **European-style option**. If the buyer has the right to exercise at any time during the life of the option, it is an **American-style option**. If the buyer can only exercise during specified periods, but not for the entire life of the option, the option is a **Bermudan-style option**. (The terms "European" and "American," by the way, have nothing to do with geography. European, American, and Bermudan options are bought and sold worldwide.)

To summarize, a European call option gives the owner of the call the right, but not the obligation, to buy the underlying asset on the expiration date by paying the strike price. The option described in Examples 3 and 4 is a *6-month European-style S&R call with a strike price of \$1020*. The buyer of the call can also be described as having a *long position* in the call.

For the time being, we will discuss European-style options exclusively. We do this because European options are the simplest to discuss and are also quite common in practice. Most exchange-traded options are American.

Payoff and Profit for a Purchased Call Option

We can graph call options as we did forward contracts. The buyer is not obligated to buy the index, and hence will only exercise the option if the payoff is greater than zero. The algebraic expression for the *payoff* to a purchased call is therefore

$$\text{Purchased call payoff} = \max[0, \text{spot price at expiration} - \text{strike price}] \tag{3}$$

The expression $\max[a, b]$ means take the greater of the two values a and b. (Spreadsheets contain a max function, so it is easy to compute option payoffs in a spreadsheet.)

Example 5. Consider a call option on the S&R index with 6 months to expiration and a strike price of \$1000. Suppose the index in 6 months is \$1100. Clearly it is worthwhile to pay the \$1000 strike price to acquire the index worth \$1100. Using equation (3), the call payoff is

$$\max[0, \$1100 - \$1000] = \$100$$

If the index is 900 at expiration, it is not worthwhile paying the \$1000 strike price to buy the index worth \$900. The payoff is then

$$\max[0, \$900 - \$1000] = \$0 \quad ■$$

As discussed before, the payoff does not take account of the initial cost of acquiring the position. For a purchased option, the premium is paid at the time the option is acquired. In computing profit at expiration, suppose we defer the premium payment; then by the time of expiration we accrue 6 months' interest on the premium. The option *profit* is computed as

$$\begin{aligned}\text{Purchased call profit} = {} & \max[0, \text{spot price at expiration} - \text{strike price}] \\ & - \text{future value of option premium}\end{aligned} \tag{4}$$

BOX 2: How Do You Buy an Option?

How would you actually buy an option? The quick answer is that buying an option is just like buying a stock. Option premiums are quoted just like stock prices. Figure 5 provides an example. (For current quotes see, for example, http://www.cboe.com; you can find bid and ask prices at the Chicago Board Options Exchange.) Using either an online or flesh-and-blood broker, you can enter an order to buy an option. As with stocks, in addition to the option premium, you pay a commission, and there is a bid-ask spread.

Options on numerous stocks are traded on exchanges, and for any given stock or index, there can be over a hundred options available, differing in strike price and expiration date. (In July 2012, a quick count at the Chicago Board Options Exchange website showed over 1200 options, with differing strikes and maturities, both puts and calls, with the S&P 500 index as the underlying asset.) Options may be either American or European. If you buy an American option, you have to be aware that exercising the option prior to expiration may be optimal. Thus, you need to have some understanding of why and when exercise might make sense.

You can also sell, or write, options. In this case, you have to post collateral (called margin) to protect others against the possibility you will default. See Appendix A for a discussion of this and other issues.

The following example illustrates the computation of the profit.

Example 6. Use the same option as in Example 5, and suppose that the risk-free rate is 2% over 6 months. Assume that the index spot price is \$1000 and that the premium for this call is \$93.81.[7] Hence, the future value of the call premium is $\$93.81 \times 1.02 = \$95.68$. If the S&R index price at expiration is \$1100, the owner will exercise the option. Using equation (4), the call profit is

$$\max[0, \$1100 - \$1000] - \$95.68 = \$4.32$$

If the index is 900 at expiration, the owner does not exercise the option. It is not worthwhile paying the \$1000 strike price to buy the index worth \$900. Profit is then

$$\max[0, \$900 - \$1000] - \$95.68 = -\$95.68$$

reflecting the loss of the premium. ■

We graph the call *payoff* by computing, for any index price at expiration, the payoff on the option position as a function of the price. We graph the call *profit* by subtracting from this the future value of the option premium. Table 3 computes the payoff and profit at different index values, computed as in Examples 5 and 6. Note that because the strike price is fixed, a higher market price at expiration of the S&R index benefits the call buyer.

---

7. It is not important at this point how we compute this price, but if you wish to replicate the option premiums, they are computed using the Black-Scholes formula. Using the BSCall spreadsheet function, the call price is computed as $\text{BSCall}(1000, 1000, 0.3, 2 \times \ln(1.02), 0.5, 0) = 93.81$.

TABLE 3 Payoff and profit after 6 months from a purchased 1000-strike S&R call option with a future value of premium of $95.68. The option premium is assumed to be $93.81 and the effective interest rate is 2% over 6 months. The payoff is computed using equation (3), and the profit using equation (4).

S&R Index in 6 Months	Call Payoff	Future Value of Premium	Call Profit
800	$0	−$95.68	−$95.68
850	0	−95.68	−95.68
900	0	−95.68	−95.68
950	0	−95.68	−95.68
1000	0	−95.68	−95.68
1050	50	−95.68	−45.68
1100	100	−95.68	4.32
1150	150	−95.68	54.32
1200	200	−95.68	104.32

Figure 5 graphs the call payoff that is computed in Table 3. The graph clearly shows the "optionality" of the option: Below the strike price of $1000, the payoff is zero, while it is positive and increasing above $1000.

The last column in Table 3 computes the call profit at different index values. Because a purchased call and a forward contract are both ways to buy the index, it is interesting to contrast the two. Thus, Figure 6 plots the profit on both a purchased call and a long forward contract. Note that profit and payoff diagrams for an option differ by the future value of the premium, whereas for a forward contract they are the same.

If the index rises, the forward contract is more profitable than the option because it does not entail paying a premium. If the index falls sufficiently, however, the option is more profitable because the most the option buyer loses is the future value of the premium. This difference suggests that we can think of the call option as an *insured* position in the index. Insurance protects against losses, and the call option does the same. Carrying the analogy a bit further, we can think of the option premium as, in part, reflecting the cost of that insurance. The forward, which is free, has no such insurance, and potentially has losses larger than those on the call.

This discussion highlights the important point that there are always trade-offs in selecting a position. The forward contract outperforms the call if the index rises and underperforms the call if the index falls sufficiently. When all contracts are fairly priced, you will not find a contract that has higher profits for all possible index market prices.

Payoff and Profit for a Written Call Option

Now let's look at the option from the point of view of the seller. The seller is said to be the **option writer**, or to have a short position in a call option. The option writer is the

FIGURE 5

The payoff at expiration of a purchased S&R call with a \$1000 strike price.

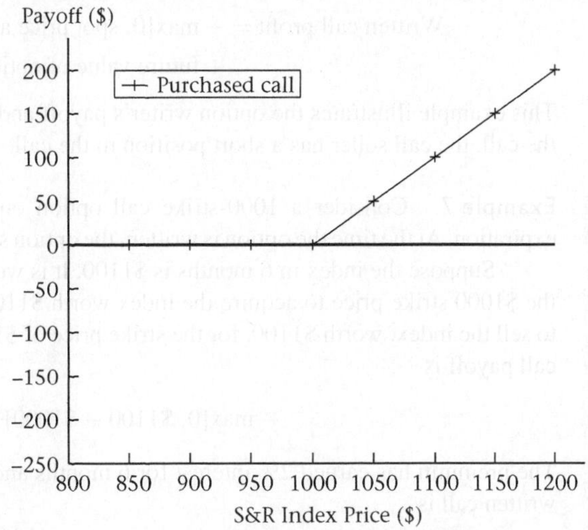

FIGURE 6

Profit at expiration for purchase of a 6-month S&R index call with a strike price of \$1000 versus profit on a long S&R index forward position.

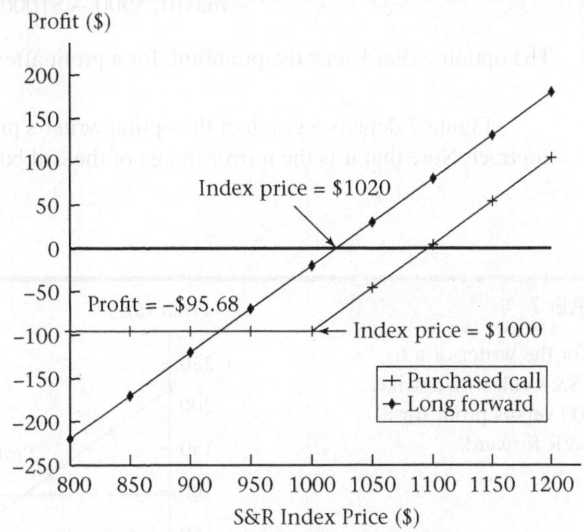

counterparty to the option buyer. The writer receives the premium for the option and then has an obligation to sell the underlying security in exchange for the strike price if the option buyer exercises the option.

The payoff and profit to a written call are just the opposite of those for a purchased call:

$$\text{Written call payoff} = -\max[0, \text{spot price at expiration} - \text{strike price}] \quad (5)$$

$$\text{Written call profit} = -\max[0, \text{spot price at expiration} - \text{strike price}] + \text{future value of option premium} \quad (6)$$

This example illustrates the option writer's payoff and profit. Just as a call buyer is long in the call, the call seller has a short position in the call.

Example 7. Consider a 1000-strike call option on the S&R index with 6 months to expiration. At the time the option is written, the option seller receives the premium of $93.81.

Suppose the index in 6 months is $1100. It is worthwhile for the option buyer to pay the $1000 strike price to acquire the index worth $1100. Thus, the option writer will have to sell the index, worth $1100, for the strike price of $1000. Using equation (5), the written call payoff is

$$-\max[0, \$1100 - \$1000] = -\$100$$

The premium has earned 2% interest for 6 months and is now worth $95.68. Profit for the written call is

$$-\$100 + \$95.68 = -\$4.32$$

If the index is 900 at expiration, it is not worthwhile for the option buyer to pay the $1000 strike price to buy the index worth $900. The payoff is then

$$-\max[0, \$900 - \$1000] = \$0.$$

The option writer keeps the premium, for a profit after 6 months of $95.68. ■

Figure 7 depicts a graph of the option writer's profit, graphed against a short forward contract. Note that it is the mirror image of the call buyer's profit in Figure 6.

FIGURE 7

Profit for the writer of a 6-month S&R call with a strike of $1000 versus profit for a short S&R forward.

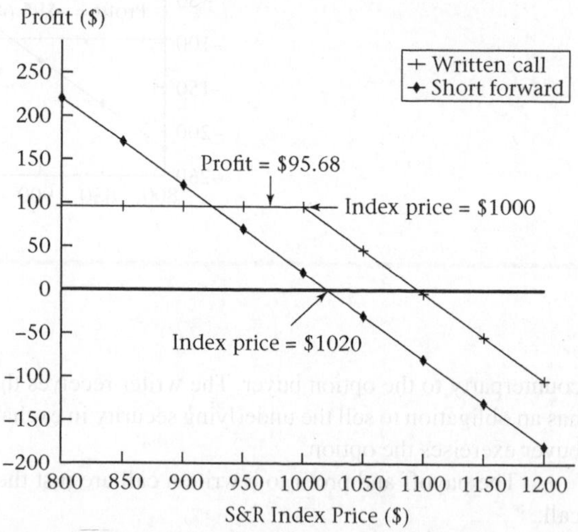

3. PUT OPTIONS

We introduced a call option by comparing it to a forward contract in which the buyer need not buy the underlying asset if it is worth less than the agreed-to purchase price. Perhaps you wondered if there could also be a contract in which the *seller* could walk away if it is not in his or her interest to sell. The answer is yes. A **put option** is a contract where the seller has the right to sell, but not the obligation. Here is an example to illustrate how a put option works.

Example 8. Suppose that the seller agrees to sell the S&R index for \$1020 in 6 months but is not obligated to do so. (The seller has purchased a put option.) If in 6 months the S&R price is \$1100, the seller will not sell for \$1020 and will walk away. If the S&R price is \$900, the seller *will* sell for \$1020 and will earn \$120 at that time. ■

A put must have a premium for the same reason a call has a premium. The buyer of the put controls exercise; hence the seller of the put will never have a positive payoff at expiration. A premium paid by the put buyer at the time the option is purchased compensates the put seller for this no-win position.

It is important to be crystal clear about the use of the terms "buyer" and "seller" in the above example, because there is potential for confusion. The buyer of the put owns a contract giving the right to sell the index at a set price. Thus, *the buyer of the put is a seller of the index!* Similarly, the seller of the put is obligated to *buy* the index, should the put buyer decide to sell. Thus, the buyer of the put is potentially a seller of the index, and the seller of the put is potentially a buyer of the index. (If thinking through these transactions isn't automatic for you now, don't worry. It will become second nature as you continue to think about options.)

Other terminology for a put option is the same as for a call option, with the obvious change that "buy" becomes "sell." In particular, the strike price is the agreed-upon selling price (\$1020 in Example 8), exercising the option means selling the underlying asset in exchange for the strike price, and the expiration date is that on which you must exercise the option or it is valueless. As with call options, there are European, American, and Bermudan put options.

Payoff and Profit for a Purchased Put Option

We now see how to compute payoff and profit for a purchased put option. The put option gives the put buyer the right to sell the underlying asset for the strike price. The buyer does this only if the asset is less valuable than the strike price. Thus, the payoff on the put option is

$$\text{Put option payoff} = \max[0, \text{strike price} - \text{spot price at expiration}] \quad (7)$$

The put buyer has a long position in the put. Here is an example.

Example 9. Consider a put option on the S&R index with 6 months to expiration and a strike price of \$1000.

Suppose the index in 6 months is \$1100. It is not worthwhile to sell the index worth \$1100 for the \$1000 strike price. Using equation (7), the put payoff is

$$\max[0, \$1000 - \$1100] = \$0$$

If the index were 900 at expiration, it *is* worthwhile selling the index for \$1000. The payoff is then

$$\max[0, \$1000 - \$900] = \$100 \quad ■$$

As with the call, the payoff does not take account of the initial cost of acquiring the position. At the time the option is acquired, the put buyer pays the option premium to the put seller; we need to account for this in computing profit. If we borrow the premium amount, we must pay 6 months' interest. The option *profit* is computed as

$$\begin{aligned}\text{Purchased put profit} &= \max[0, \text{strike price} - \text{spot price at expiration}] \\ &\quad - \text{future value of option premium}\end{aligned} \tag{8}$$

The following example illustrates the computation of profit on the put.

Example 10. Use the same option as in Example 9, and suppose that the risk-free rate is 2% over 6 months. Assume that the premium for this put is \$74.20.[8] The future value of the put premium is $\$74.20 \times 1.02 = \$75.68$.

If the S&R index price at expiration is \$1100, the put buyer will not exercise the option. Using equation (8), profit is

$$\max[0, \$1000 - \$1100] - \$75.68 = -\$75.68$$

reflecting the loss of the premium.

If the index is \$900 at expiration, the put buyer exercises the put, selling the index for \$1000. Profit is then

$$\max[0, \$1000 - \$900] - \$75.68 = \$24.32 \quad ■$$

Table 4 computes the payoff and profit on a purchased put for a range of index values at expiration. Whereas call profit increases as the value of the underlying asset *increases*, put profit increases as the value of the underlying asset *decreases*.

Because a put is a way to sell an asset, we can compare it to a short forward position, which is a mandatory sale. Figure 8 graphs profit from the purchased put described in Table 4 against the profit on a short forward.

We can see from the graph that if the S&R index goes down, the short forward, which has no premium, has a higher profit than the purchased put. If the index goes up sufficiently, the put outperforms the short forward. As with the call, the put is like an insured forward contract. With the put, losses are limited should the index go up. With the short forward, losses are potentially unlimited.

Payoff and Profit for a Written Put Option

Now we examine the put from the perspective of the put writer. The put writer is the counterparty to the buyer. Thus, when the contract is written, the put writer receives the premium. At expiration, if the put buyer elects to sell the underlying asset, the put writer must buy it.

---

8. This price is computed using the Black-Scholes formula for the price of a put: BSPut(1000, 1000, 0.3, $2 \times \ln(1.02)$, 0.5, 0) = 74.20.

TABLE 4 Profit after 6 months from a purchased 1000-strike S&R put option with a future value of premium of $75.68.

S&R Index in 6 Months	Put Payoff	Future Value of Premium	Put Profit
$800	$200	−$75.68	$124.32
850	150	−75.68	74.32
900	100	−75.68	24.32
950	50	−75.68	−25.68
1000	0	−75.68	−75.68
1050	0	−75.68	−75.68
1100	0	−75.68	−75.68
1150	0	−75.68	−75.68
1200	0	−75.68	−75.68

FIGURE 8

Profit on a purchased S&R index put with a strike price of $1000 versus a short S&R index forward.

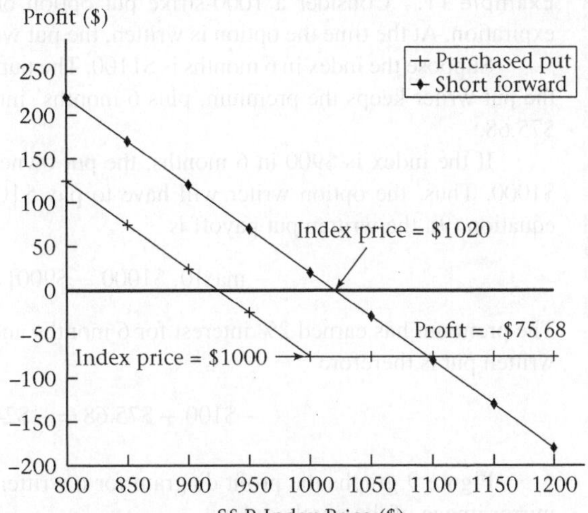

The payoff and profit for a written put are the opposite of those for the purchased put:

$$\text{Written put payoff} = -\max[0, \text{strike price} - \text{spot price at expiration}] \tag{9}$$

$$\text{Written put profit} = -\max[0, \text{strike price} - \text{spot price at expiration}] + \text{future value of option premium} \tag{10}$$

The put seller has a short position in the put.

FIGURE 9

Written S&R index put option with a strike of $1000 versus a long S&R index forward contract.

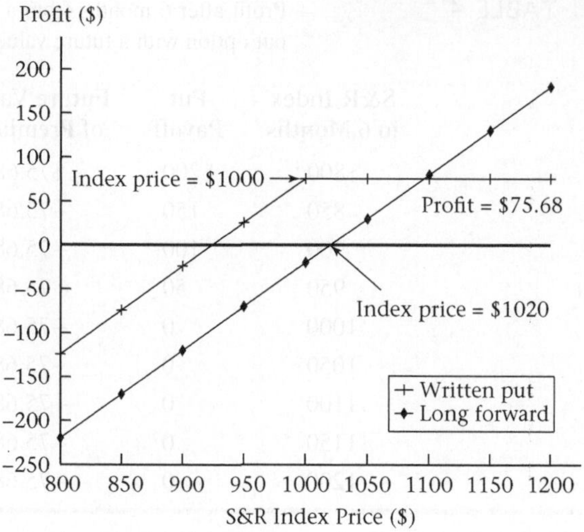

Example 11. Consider a 1000-strike put option on the S&R index with 6 months to expiration. At the time the option is written, the put writer receives the premium of $74.20.

Suppose the index in 6 months is $1100. The put buyer will not exercise the put. Thus, the put writer keeps the premium, plus 6 months' interest, for a payoff of 0 and profit of $75.68.

If the index is $900 in 6 months, the put owner will exercise, selling the index for $1000. Thus, the option writer will have to pay $1000 for an index worth $900. Using equation (9), the written put payoff is

$$-\max[0, \$1000 - \$900] = -\$100$$

The premium has earned 2% interest for 6 months and is now worth $75.68. Profit for the written put is therefore

$$-\$100 + \$75.68 = -\$24.32 \quad ■$$

Figure 9 graphs the profit diagram for a written put. As you would expect, it is the mirror image of the purchased put.

The "Moneyness" of an Option

Options are often described by their degree of *moneyness*. This term describes whether the option payoff would be positive if the option were exercised immediately. (The term is used to describe both American and European options even though European options cannot be exercised until expiration.) An **in-the-money option** is one which would have a positive payoff (but not necessarily positive profit) if exercised immediately. A call with a strike price less than the asset price and a put with a strike price greater than the asset price are both in-the-money.

An **out-of-the-money option** is one that would have a negative payoff if exercised immediately. A call with a strike price greater than the asset price and a put with a strike price less than the asset price are both out-of-the-money.

An **at-the-money option** is one for which the strike price is approximately equal to the asset price.

4. SUMMARY OF FORWARD AND OPTION POSITIONS

We have now examined six different positions: short and long forwards, and purchased and written calls and puts. There are different ways to categorize these positions. One way is by their potential for gain and loss. Table 5 summarizes the maximum possible gain and loss at maturity for forwards and European options.

Another way to categorize the positions is by whether the positions represent buying or selling the underlying asset. Those that represent buying are fundamentally *long* with respect to the underlying asset, while those that represent selling are fundamentally *short* with respect to the underlying asset. If you find yourself confused by "long" and "short," you can consult Box 3.

Positions Long with Respect to the Index

The following positions are long in the sense that there are circumstances in which they represent either a right or an obligation to *buy* the underlying asset:

Long forward: An *obligation* to buy at a fixed price.

Purchased call: The *right* to buy at a fixed price if it is advantageous to do so.

Written put: An obligation of the put writer to buy the underlying asset at a fixed price if it is advantageous to the option buyer to sell at that price. (Recall that the option *buyer* decides whether or not to exercise.)

TABLE 5 Maximum possible profit and loss at maturity for long and short forwards and purchased and written calls and puts. FV(*premium*) denotes the future value of the option premium.

Position	Maximum Loss	Maximum Gain
Long forward	−Forward price	Unlimited
Short forward	Unlimited	Forward price
Long call	−FV(*premium*)	Unlimited
Short call	Unlimited	FV(*premium*)
Long put	−FV(*premium*)	Strike price − FV(*premium*)
Short put	FV(*premium*) − Strike price	FV(*premium*)

BOX 3: "Long" and "Short" Revisited

When you purchase an option you are said to have a long position in that option. Thus, a call that you purchase is a "long call" and a put that you purchase is a "long put." In both cases, you make money if the price of the option you purchased goes up. Similarly, any option that you sell is a short position in that option. A call that you sell is a "short call" and a put that you sell is a "short put."

The terms "long" and "short" can be confusing, however, because they are often used more generally. In this more general usage, a position is long with respect to x if the value of the position goes up when x goes up, and it is short with respect to x if the value of the position goes down when x goes up.

A purchased call is therefore *long* with respect to the stock, because the call becomes more valuable when the stock price goes up. Similarly, a purchased put is *short* with respect to the stock, because the put becomes more valuable when the stock price goes down. The case of a purchased put illustrates that a position can be simultaneously long with respect to one thing (its own price) and short with respect to something else (the price of the underlying asset).

Finally, a written put is a "short put" because you lose money if the put price goes up. However, the written put is long with respect to the stock, because the put price goes down, and hence the written put makes money, when the stock price goes up.

You may find that it takes a while to become comfortable with the long and short terminology. A position can be simultaneously long with respect to one thing and short with respect to something else, so you must always be clear about what you are long or short with respect to.

Figure 10 compares these three positions. Note that the purchased call is long when the asset price is greater than the strike price, and the written put is long when the asset price is less than the strike price. *All three of these positions benefit from a higher index price.*

Positions Short with Respect to the Index

The following positions are short in the sense that there are circumstances in which they represent either a right or an obligation to *sell* the underlying asset:

Short forward: An *obligation* to sell at a fixed price.

Written call: An obligation of the call writer to sell the underlying asset at a fixed price if it is advantageous to the option holder to buy at that price (recall that the option *buyer* decides whether to exercise).

Purchased put: The *right* to sell at a fixed price if it is advantageous to do so.

Figure 11 compares these three positions. Note that the written call is short when the asset price is greater than the strike price, and the purchased put is short when the asset price is less than the strike price. *All three of these positions benefit from a lower price of the index.*

FIGURE 10

Profit diagrams for the three basic long positions: long forward, purchased call, and written put.

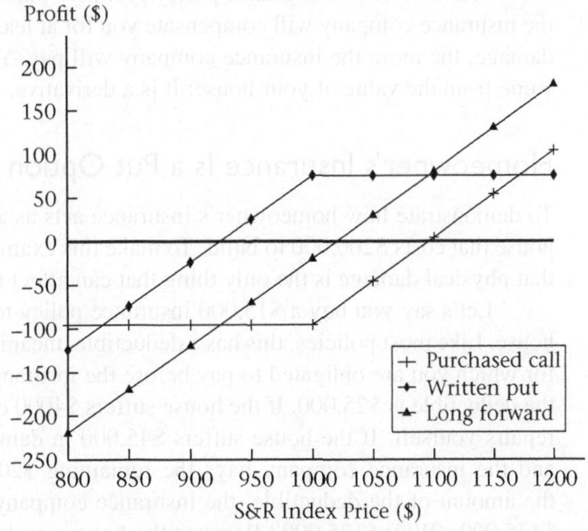

FIGURE 11

Profit diagrams for the three basic short positions: short forward, written call, and purchased put.

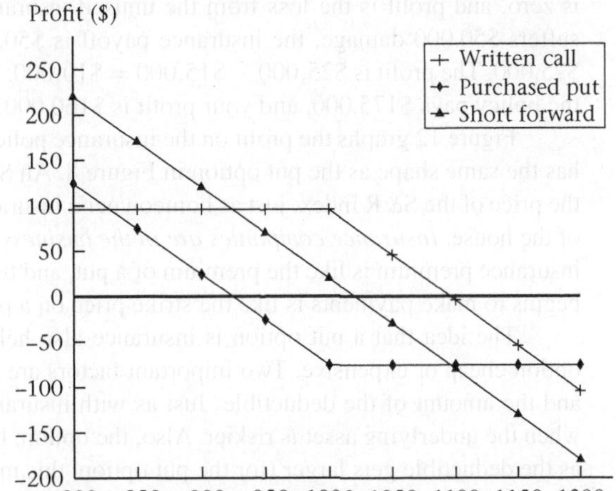

5. OPTIONS ARE INSURANCE

In many investment strategies using options, we will see that options serve as insurance against a loss. In what sense are options the same as insurance? In this section we answer this question by considering homeowner's insurance. You will see that options are literally insurance, and insurance is an option.

A homeowner's insurance policy promises that in the event of damage to your house, the insurance company will compensate you for at least part of the damage. The greater the damage, the more the insurance company will pay. Your insurance policy thus derives its value from the value of your house: It is a derivative.

Homeowner's Insurance Is a Put Option

To demonstrate how homeowner's insurance acts as a put option, suppose that you own a house that costs \$200,000 to build. To make this example as simple as possible, we assume that physical damage is the only thing that can affect the market value of the house.

Let's say you buy a \$15,000 insurance policy to compensate you for damage to the house. Like most policies, this has a deductible, meaning that there is an amount of damage for which you are obligated to pay before the insurance company pays anything. Suppose the deductible is \$25,000. If the house suffers \$4000 damage from a storm, you pay for all repairs yourself. If the house suffers \$45,000 in damage from a storm, you pay \$25,000 and the insurance company pays the remaining \$20,000. Once damage occurs beyond the amount of the deductible, the insurance company pays for all further damage, up to \$175,000. (Why \$175,000? Because the house can be rebuilt for \$200,000, and you pay \$25,000 of that—the deductible—yourself.)

Let's graph the profit to you for this insurance policy. On the vertical axis is the profit on the insurance policy—the payoff less the insurance premium—and on the horizontal axis, the value of the house. If the house is undamaged (the house value is \$200,000) the payoff is zero, and profit is the loss from the unused insurance premium, \$15,000. If the house suffers \$50,000 damage, the insurance payoff is \$50,000 less the \$25,000 deductible, or \$25,000. The profit is \$25,000 − \$15,000 = \$10,000. If the house is completely destroyed, the policy pays \$175,000, and your profit is \$160,000.

Figure 12 graphs the profit on the insurance policy. The insurance policy in Figure 12 has the same shape as the put option in Figure 8. An S&R put is insurance against a fall in the price of the S&R index, just as homeowner's insurance insures against a fall in the price of the house. *Insurance companies are in the business of writing put options*! The \$15,000 insurance premium is like the premium of a put, and the \$175,000 level at which insurance begins to make payments is like the strike price on a put.

The idea that a put option is insurance also helps us understand what makes a put option cheap or expensive. Two important factors are the riskiness of the underlying asset and the amount of the deductible. Just as with insurance, options will be more expensive when the underlying asset is riskier. Also, the option, like insurance, will be less expensive as the deductible gets larger (for the put option, this means lowering the strike price).

You have probably recognized that there are some practical differences between a financial put option and homeowner's insurance. One important difference is that the S&R put pays off no matter why the index price declines. Homeowner's insurance, on the other hand, pays off only if the house declines in value for specified reasons. In particular, a simple decline in real estate prices is not covered by typical homeowner's insurance policies. We avoided this complication by assuming at the outset that only damage could affect the value of the house.

But I Thought Insurance Is Prudent and Put Options Are Risky . . .

If we accept that insurance and put options are the same thing, how do we reconcile this with the common idea that buying insurance is prudent and buying put options is risky?

FIGURE 12

Profit from insurance policy on a $200,000 house.

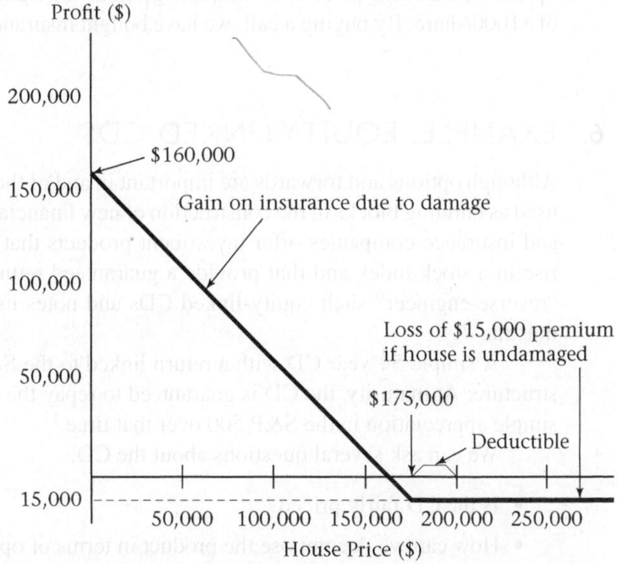

The risk of a derivative or any other asset or security can only be evaluated in context. Figure 12 depicts the risk of an insurance contract *without considering the risk of the insured asset*. This would be like owning insurance on your neighbor's house. It would be "risky" because you would buy the insurance policy, and you would lose your entire investment if there were no insurance claim.[9] We do not normally think of insurance like this, but it illustrates the point that an insurance policy is a put option on the insured asset.

In the same way, Figure 8 depicts the risk of a put option without considering the risk of any other positions an investor might be holding. In contrast to homeowner's insurance, many investors *do* own put options without owning the underlying asset. This is why options have a reputation for being risky while homeowner's insurance does not. With stock options it is possible to own the insurance without the asset. Of course, many investors who own put options also own the stock. For these investors, the risk is like that of insurance, which we normally think of as risk-reducing rather than risk-increasing.

Call Options Are Also Insurance

Call options can also be insurance. Whereas a put option is insurance for an asset we already own, a call option is insurance for an asset we plan to own in the future. Put differently, a put option is insurance for a *long* position while a call option is insurance for a *short* position.

Return to the earlier example of the S&R index. Suppose that the current price of the S&R index is $1000 and that we plan to buy the index in the future. If we buy an S&R call

9. Of course, in real life no insurance company will sell you insurance on your neighbor's house. The reason is that you will then be tempted to cause damage in order to make your policy valuable. Insurance companies call this "moral hazard."

option with a strike price of \$1000, this gives us the right to buy S&R for a maximum cost of \$1000/share. By buying a call, we have bought insurance against an *increase* in the price.

6. EXAMPLE: EQUITY-LINKED CDS

Although options and forwards are important in and of themselves, they are also commonly used as building blocks in the construction of new financial instruments. For example, banks and insurance companies offer investment products that allow investors to benefit from a rise in a stock index and that provide a guaranteed return if the market declines. We can "reverse-engineer" such equity-linked CDs and notes using the tools we have developed thus far.[10]

A simple $5\frac{1}{2}$ year CD with a return linked to the S&P 500 might have the following structure: At maturity, the CD is guaranteed to repay the invested amount, plus 70% of the simple appreciation in the S&P 500 over that time.[11]

We can ask several questions about the CD:

- Is the CD fairly priced?
- How can we decompose the product in terms of options and bonds?
- How does the issuing bank hedge the risk associated with issuing the product?
- How does the issuing bank make a profit?

To understand this product, suppose the S&P index is 1300 initially and an investor invests \$10,000. If the index is below 1300 after 5.5 years, the CD returns to the investor the original \$10,000 investment. If the index is above 1300 after 5.5 years, the investor receives \$10,000 plus 70% of the percentage gain on the index. For example, if the index is 2200, the investor receives

$$\$10{,}000 \times [1 + (2200/1300 - 1) \times 70\%] = \$14{,}846$$

At first glance this product *appears* to permit gains but no losses. However, by now you are probably skeptical of a phrase like "gains but no losses"; the investor *must* pay something for an investment like this.

Graphing the Payoff on the CD

As a first step in analyzing the CD, we will draw a payoff diagram. If we invest \$10,000, we receive at least \$10,000. If the index rises to $S_{\text{final}} > 1300$, we also receive on our investment 70% of the rate of return

$$\frac{S_{\text{final}}}{1300} - 1$$

10. A CD (certificate of deposit) is a kind of interest-bearing bank account. You can think of a CD as being the same as a note or a bond.

11. This is the structure of a CD issued in 1999 by First Union National Bank.

FIGURE 13

Payoff at expiration to \$10,000 investment in an equity-linked CD that repays the initial investment at expiration plus 70% of the rate of appreciation of the market above 1300.

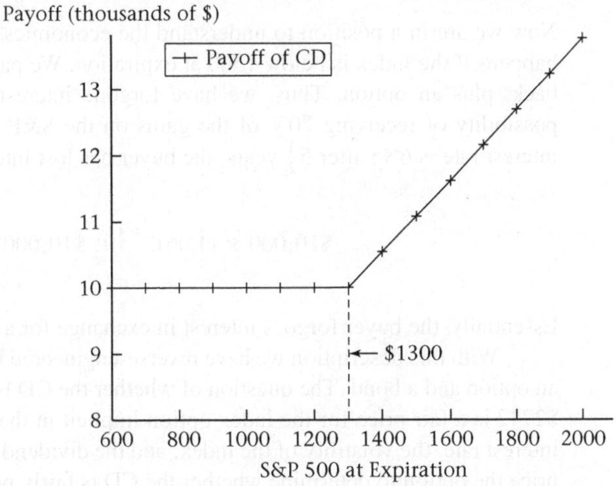

TABLE 6 Payoff of equity-linked CD at expiration.

S&P Index After 5.5 Years	CD Payoff
500	\$10,000.00
1000	10,000.00
1500	11,076.92
2000	13,769.23
2500	16,461.54
3000	19,153.85

Thus, the CD pays

$$\$10{,}000 \times \left(1 + 0.7 \times \max\left[0, \frac{S_{\text{final}}}{1300} - 1\right]\right) \tag{11}$$

Figure 13 graphs the payoff at expiration to this investment in the CD.

Recall the discussion in Section 1 of incorporating a zero-coupon bond into a payoff diagram. Per unit of the index (there are 10,000/1300 = 7.69 units of the index in a \$10,000 investment), the CD buyer receives 0.7 of an index call option, plus a zero-coupon bond paying \$1300 at expiration.

Table 6 computes the payoff to the equity-linked CD for different values of the index.

Economics of the CD

Now we are in a position to understand the economics of this product. Think about what happens if the index is below 1300 at expiration. We pay \$10,000 and we receive \$10,000 back, plus an option. Thus, we have forgone interest on \$10,000 in exchange for the possibility of receiving 70% of the gains on the S&P. Suppose that the effective annual interest rate is 6%; after $5\frac{1}{2}$ years, the buyer has lost interest with a present value of

$$\$10,000 \times (1.06)^{-5.5} - \$10,000 = -\$2,742$$

Essentially, the buyer forgoes interest in exchange for a call option on the index.

With this description we have reverse-engineered the CD, decomposing it in terms of an option and a bond. The question of whether the CD is fairly priced turns on whether the \$2742 is a fair price for the index option implicit in the CD. Given information about the interest rate, the volatility of the index, and the dividend yield on the index, it is possible to price the option to determine whether the CD is fairly priced.

Why Equity-Linked CDs?

With reverse-engineering, we see that an investor could create the equivalent of an equity-linked CD by buying a zero-coupon bond and 0.7 call options. Why, then, do products like this exist?

Consider what must be done to replicate the payoff. If a retail investor were to insure an index investment using options, the investor would have to learn about options, decide what maturity, strike price, and quantity to buy, and pay transaction costs. Exchange-traded options have at most 3 years to maturity, so obtaining longer-term protection requires rolling over the position at some point.

An equity-linked CD provides a prepackaged solution. It may provide a pattern of market exposure that many investors could not otherwise obtain at such low transaction costs.

The idea that a prepackaged deal may be attractive should be familiar to you. Supermarkets sell whole heads of lettuce—salad building blocks, as it were—and they also sell, at a premium price, lettuce already washed, torn into bite-sized pieces, and mixed as a salad. The transaction cost of salad preparation leads some consumers to prefer the prepackaged salads.

What does the financial institution get out of this? Just as the supermarket earns profit on prepackaged salads, the issuing bank wants to earn a transaction fee on the CD. When it sells a CD, the issuing bank borrows money (the zero-coupon bond portion of the CD) and receives the premium for writing a call option. The cost of the CD to the bank is the cost of the zero-coupon bond plus the cost of the call option. Obviously the bank would not issue the equity-linked CD in the first place unless it was less expensive than alternative ways to attract deposits, such as standard CDs. The equity-linked CD is risky because the bank has written a call, but the bank can manage this risk in several ways, one of which is to purchase call options from a dealer to offset the risk of having written calls. Using data from the early 1990s, Baubonis et al. (1993) estimated that issuers of equity-linked CDs

TABLE 7 Forwards, calls, and puts at a glance: A summary of forward and option positions.

Derivative Position	Position with Respect to Underlying Asset	Asset Price Contingency	Strategy
Long forward	Long (buy)	Always	Guaranteed purchase price
Short forward	Short (sell)	Always	Guaranteed sale price
Long call	Long (buy)	> Strike	Insures against high price
Short call	Short (sell)	> Strike	Sells insurance against high price
Long put	Short (sell)	< Strike	Insures against low price
Short put	Long (buy)	< Strike	Sells insurance against low price

earned about 3.5% of the value of the CD as a fee, with about 1% as the transaction cost of hedging the written call.[12]

In this discussion we have viewed the equity-linked CD from several perspectives. The end-user is interested in the product and whether it meets a financial need at a fair cost. The market-maker (the bank in this case) is interested in making a profit without bearing risk from having issued the CD. And the economic observer is interested in knowing why equity-linked CDs exist. The three perspectives overlap, and a full explanation of the product touches on all of them.

CHAPTER SUMMARY

Forward contracts and put and call options are the basic derivative instruments that can be used directly and that serve as building blocks for other instruments. A long forward contract represents an obligation to buy the underlying asset at a fixed price, a call option gives its owner the right (but not the obligation) to buy the underlying asset at a fixed price, and a put option gives its owner the right (but not the obligation) to sell the underlying asset at a fixed price. Payoff and profit diagrams are commonly used tools for evaluating the risk of these contracts. Payoff diagrams show the gross value of a position at expiration, and profit diagrams subtract from the payoff the future value of the cost of the position.

Table 7 summarizes the characteristics of forwards, calls, and puts, showing which are long or short with respect to the underlying asset. The table describes the strategy associated with each: Forward contracts guarantee a price, purchased options are insurance, and written options are selling insurance. Figure 14 provides a graphical summary of these positions.

12. A back-of-the-envelope calculation suggests the issuer fees for this product are in the neighborhood of 4% to 5%.

FIGURE 14

The basic profit diagrams: long and short forward, long and short call, and long and short put.

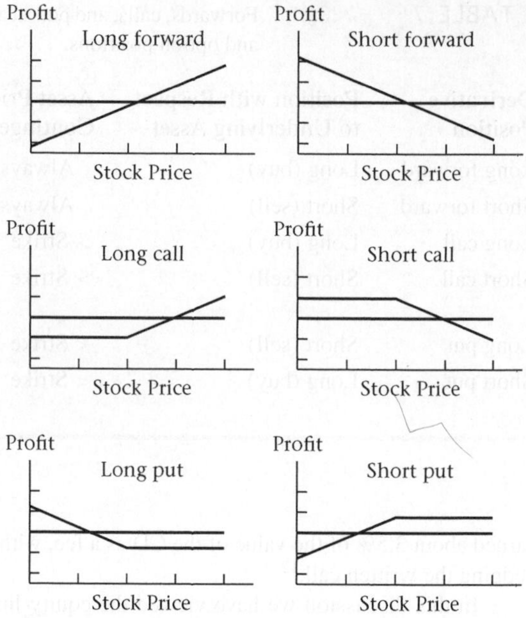

Options can also be viewed as insurance. A put option gives the owner the right to sell if the price declines, just as insurance gives the insured the right to sell (put) a damaged asset to the insurance company.

FURTHER READING

Brokerages routinely supply options customers with an introductory pamphlet about options entitled *Characteristics and Risks of Standardized Options*. This is available online from http://www.optionsclearing.com. You can also obtain current option prices from websites such as the CBOE's and various brokerage sites.

The notion that options are insurance has been applied in practice. Sharpe (1976), for example, analyzed optimal pension funding policy taking into account pension insurance provided by the Pension Benefit Guaranty Corporation. Merton (1977a) observed that bank deposit insurance and in fact any loan guarantee can be modeled as a put option. Baubonis et al. (1993) discuss equity-linked CDs.

PROBLEMS

In the following problems, if the "effective annual interest rate" is r, a \$1 investment yields $1 + r$ after 1 year.

1. Suppose XYZ stock has a price of $50 and pays no dividends. The effective annual interest rate is 10%. Draw payoff and profit diagrams for a long position in the stock. Verify that profit is 0 at a price in 1 year of $55.

2. Using the same information as the previous question, draw payoff and profit diagrams for a short position in the stock. Verify that profit is 0 at a price in 1 year of $55.

3. What position is the opposite of a purchased call? The opposite of a purchased put?

4. **a.** Suppose you enter into a long 6-month forward position at a forward price of $50. What is the payoff in 6 months for prices of $40, $45, $50, $55, and $60?

b. Suppose you buy a 6-month call option with a strike price of $50. What is the payoff in 6 months at the same prices for the underlying asset?

c. Comparing the payoffs of parts (a) and (b), which contract should be more expensive (i.e., the long call or long forward)? Why?

5. **a.** Suppose you enter into a short 6-month forward position at a forward price of $50. What is the payoff in 6 months for prices of $40, $45, $50, $55, and $60?

b. Suppose you buy a 6-month put option with a strike price of $50. What is the payoff in 6 months at the same prices for the underlying asset?

c. Comparing the payoffs of parts (a) and (b), which contract should be more expensive (i.e., the long put or short forward)? Why?

6. A default-free zero-coupon bond costs $91 and will pay $100 at maturity in 1 year. What is the effective annual interest rate? What is the payoff diagram for the bond? The profit diagram?

7. Suppose XYZ stock pays no dividends and has a current price of $50. The forward price for delivery in 1 year is $55. Suppose the 1-year effective annual interest rate is 10%.

a. Graph the payoff and profit diagrams for a forward contract on XYZ stock with a forward price of $55.

b. Is there any advantage to investing in the stock or the forward contract? Why?

c. Suppose XYZ paid a dividend of $2 per year and everything else stayed the same. Now is there any advantage to investing in the stock or the forward contract? Why?

8. Suppose XYZ stock pays no dividends and has a current price of $50. The forward price for delivery in one year is $53. *If* there is no advantage to buying either the stock or the forward contract, what is the 1-year effective interest rate?

9. An *off-market* forward contract is a forward where either you have to pay a premium or you receive a premium for entering into the contract. (With a standard forward contract, the premium is zero.) Suppose the effective annual interest rate is 10% and the S&R index is 1000. Consider 1-year forward contracts.

a. Verify that if the forward price is $1100, the profit diagrams for the index and the 1-year forward are the same.

b. Suppose you are offered a long forward contract at a forward price of $1200. How much would you need to be paid to enter into this contract?

c. Suppose you are offered a long forward contract at $1000. What would you be willing to pay to enter into this forward contract?

10. For Figure 6, verify the following:

a. The S&R index price at which the call option diagram intersects the x-axis is $1095.68.

b. The S&R index price at which the call option and forward contract have the same profit is $924.32.

11. For Figure 8, verify the following:

a. The S&R index price at which the put option diagram intersects the x-axis is $924.32.

b. The S&R index price at which the put option and forward contract have the same profit is $1095.68.

12. For each entry in Table 5, explain the circumstances in which the maximum gain or loss occurs.

13. Suppose the stock price is $40 and the effective annual interest rate is 8%.

a. Draw on a single graph payoff and profit diagrams for the following options:

(i) 35-strike call with a premium of $9.12.

(ii) 40-strike call with a premium of $6.22.

(iii) 45-strike call with a premium of $4.08.

b. Consider your payoff diagram with all three options graphed together. Intuitively, why should the option premium decrease with the strike price?

14. Suppose the stock price is $40 and the effective annual interest rate is 8%. Draw payoff and profit diagrams for the following options:

a. 35-strike put with a premium of $1.53.

b. 40-strike put with a premium of $3.26.

c. 45-strike put with a premium of $5.75.

Consider your payoff diagram with all three options graphed together. Intuitively, why should the option premium increase with the strike price?

15. The profit calculation in the chapter assumes that you borrow at a fixed interest rate to finance investments. An alternative way to borrow is to short-sell stock. What complications would arise in calculating profit if you financed a $1000 S&R index investment by shorting IBM stock, rather than by borrowing $1000?

16. Construct a spreadsheet that permits you to compute payoff and profit for a short and long stock, a short and long forward, and purchased and written puts and calls.

The spreadsheet should let you specify the stock price, forward price, interest rate, option strikes, and option premiums. Use the spreadsheet's max function to compute option payoffs.

Appendix A MORE ON BUYING A STOCK OPTION

Box 2 discusses buying options. There are at least four practical issues that an option buyer should be aware of: dividends, exercise, margins, and taxes. In this section we will focus on retail investors and exchange-traded stock options. Be aware that specific rules regarding margins and taxes change frequently. This section is intended to help you identify issues and is not intended as a substitute for professional brokerage, accounting, or legal advice.

Dividends

The owner of a standard call option has the right to buy a fixed number of shares of stock at a fixed price, but has no right to receive dividends paid on the underlying stock over the life of the option. When a stock pays a dividend, the stock price declines by approximately the amount of the dividend. This decline in the price lowers the return to the owner of a call option.

For exchange-traded options in the United States, there is typically no adjustment in the terms of the option if the stock pays an "ordinary" dividend (one that is typical for the stock). However, if the stock pays an unusual dividend, then officials at the Options Clearing Corporation (OCC) decide whether or not to make an adjustment.

In June 2003, Iomega Corporation declared a \$5 dividend, payable on October 1. At the time of the declaration, Iomega's share price was \$11.40. Since the dividend was 44% of the share price, the OCC reduced all Iomega option strike prices by \$5, effective October 2.[13]

When we discuss option pricing, we will see that it is necessary to take dividends into account when pricing an option.

Exercise

Some options, for example those that are cash-settled, are automatically exercised at maturity; the option owner need not take any action. Suppose you own a traded option that is not cash-settled and not automatically exercised. In this case you must provide exercise instructions prior to the broker's deadline. If you fail to do so, the option will expire worthless. When you exercise the option, you generally pay a commission. If you do not wish to own the stock, exercising the option would require that you pay a commission to exercise and then a commission to sell the shares. It might be preferable to sell the option instead of exercising it. If you do wish to own the underlying asset, you can exercise the option. The option writer who is obligated to fulfill the option exercise (delivering the shares for a

13. Reducing the strike price by the amount of the dividend leaves call holders worse off, albeit better off than if no adjustment had been made. If S is the cum-dividend stock price and $S - D$ the ex-dividend stock price, Merton (1973b, p. 152) shows that to leave the value of a call position unchanged, it is necessary to reduce the strike price by the factor $(S - D)/S$, and give the option holder $S/(S - D) - 1$ additional options. An option with a value protected against dividends is said to be **payout-protected.**

call or buying the shares for a put) is said to have been *assigned*. Assignment can involve paying a commission.

American-style options can be exercised prior to expiration. If you own an option and fail to exercise when you should, you will lose money relative to following the optimal exercise strategy. If you write the option, and it is exercised (you are assigned), you will be required to sell the stock (if you sold a call) or buy the stock (if you sold a put). Therefore, if you buy or sell an American option, you need to understand the circumstances under which exercise might be optimal. Dividends are one factor that can affect the exercise decision.

Margins for Written Options

Purchased options for which you fully pay require no margin, as there is no counterparty risk. With written option positions, however, you can incur a large loss if the stock moves against you. When you write an option, therefore, you are required to post collateral to insure against the possibility that you will default. This collateral is called *margin.*

Margin rules are beyond the scope of this text and change over time. Moreover, different option positions have different margin rules. Both brokers and exchanges can provide information about current margin requirements.

Taxes

Tax rules for derivatives in general can be complicated, and they change frequently as the tax law changes. The taxation of simple option transactions is straightforward.

If you purchase a call option or stock and then sell it, gain or loss on the position is treated like gain or loss on a stock, and accorded long-term or short-term capital gains treatment depending on the length of time for which the position has been held. If you purchase a call option and then exercise it, the cost basis of the resulting stock position is the exercise price plus the option premium plus commissions. The holding period for the resulting stock position begins the day after the option is exercised. The time the option is held does not contribute to the holding period.

The rules become more intricate when forwards and options are held in tandem with the underlying asset. The reasons for this complexity are not hard to understand. Tax laws in the United States accord different tax treatment to different kinds of income. The tax code views interest income, dividend income, and capital gains income as distinct and subject to different tax rules. Futures also have special rules. However, using derivatives, one kind of income can be turned into another. We saw in this chapter, for example, that buying zero-coupon bonds and a forward contract mimics a stock investment.

One category of special rules governs a **constructive sale**. If you own a stock, entering into certain option or forward positions can trigger a constructive sale, meaning that even if you continue to own the stock, for tax purposes you are deemed to have sold it at the time you enter into the forward or option positions. By shorting a forward against the stock, for example, the stock position is transformed into a bond position. When you have no risk stemming from stock ownership, tax law deems you to no longer be an owner.

The so-called **straddle rules** are tax rules intended to control the recognition of losses for tax purposes when there are offsetting risks as with constructive sales. Such positions often arise when investors are undertaking tax arbitrage, which is why the positions are accorded special treatment. A stock owned together with a put is a tax straddle.[14] Generally, the straddle rules prevent loss recognition on only a part of the entire position. A straddle for tax purposes is not the same thing as an option straddle.

It is probably obvious to you that if you are taxable and transact in options, and especially if you have both stock and offsetting option positions, you should be prepared to seek professional tax advice.

14. For an illustration of the complexity, in this particular case, an exception to the straddle rules occurs if the stock and put are a "married put," meaning that the two are purchased together and the stock is delivered to settle the put.

Insurance, Collars, and Other Strategies

In this chapter we discuss forwards, calls, and puts. We elaborate on the idea that options are insurance. We also examine the link between forward prices and option prices, including the important concept of put-call parity. Finally, we look at some common option strategies, such as spreads, straddles, and collars. Among your goals in this chapter should be to become familiar with drawing and interpreting profit and loss diagrams for option positions.

1. BASIC INSURANCE STRATEGIES

There are an infinity of ways to combine options to create different payoffs. In this section we examine two important kinds of strategies in which the option is combined with a position in the underlying asset. First, options can be used to insure long or short asset positions. Second, options can be written against an asset position, in which case the option writer is selling insurance. We consider four positions: being long the asset coupled with a purchased put or written call, and being short the asset coupled with a purchased call or written put.

In this section we use S&R index examples. We assume an index price of \$1000, a 2% effective 6-month interest rate, and premiums of \$93.809 for the 1000-strike 6-month call and \$74.201 for the 1000-strike 6-month put.

Insuring a Long Position: Floors

An analysis has demonstrated that put options are insurance against a fall in the price of an asset. Thus, if we own the S&R index, we can insure the position by buying an S&R put option. The purchase of a put option is also called a **floor**, because we are guaranteeing a minimum sale price for the value of the index.

To examine this strategy, we want to look at the *combined* payoff of the index position and put. We add them together to see the net effect of holding both positions at the same time.

Table 1 summarizes the result of buying a 1000-strike put with 6 months to expiration, in conjunction with holding an index position with a current value of \$1000. The table computes the payoff for each position and sums them to obtain the total payoff. The final column takes account of financing cost by subtracting cost plus interest from the payoff

From Chapter 3 of *Derivatives Markets*, Third Edition, Robert McDonald. Copyright © 2013 by Pearson Education, Inc. Published by Pearson Prentice Hall. All rights reserved.

TABLE 1 Payoff and profit at expiration from purchasing the S&R index and a 1000-strike put option. Payoff is the sum of the first two columns. Cost plus interest for the position is ($1000 + $74.201) × 1.02 = $1095.68. Profit is payoff less $1095.68.

Payoff at Expiration				
S&R Index	S&R Put	Payoff	−(Cost + Interest)	Profit
$900	$100	$1000	−$1095.68	−$95.68
950	50	1000	−1095.68	−95.68
1000	0	1000	−1095.68	−95.68
1050	0	1050	−1095.68	−45.68
1100	0	1100	−1095.68	4.32
1150	0	1150	−1095.68	54.32
1200	0	1200	−1095.68	104.32

to obtain profit. "Cost" here means the initial cash required to establish the position. This is positive when payment is required, and negative when cash is received. We could also have computed profit separately for the put and index. For example, if the index is $900 at expiration, we have

$$\underbrace{\$900 - (\$1000 \times 1.02)}_{\text{Profit on S\&R Index}} + \underbrace{\$100 - (\$74.201 \times 1.02)}_{\text{Profit on Put}} = -\$95.68$$

This gives the same result as the calculation performed in Table 1. The level of the floor is −$95.68, which is the lowest possible profit.

Figure 1 graphs the components of Table 1. Panels (c) and (d) show the payoff and profit for the combined index and put positions. The combined payoff graph in panel (c) is created by adding at each index price the value of the index and put positions; this is equivalent to summing columns 1 and 2 in Table 1.

Notice in Figure 1 that the combined position created by adding the index and the put looks like a call. Intuitively this equivalence makes sense. A call has a limited loss—the premium—and benefits from gains in the index above the strike price. Similarly, when we own the index and buy a put, the put limits losses, but it permits us to benefit from gains in the index. Thus, the call on the one hand and the insured index position on the other have similar characteristics.

Panel (c), however, illustrates that the payoff to the combined position (index plus put) is *not* identical to the payoff from buying a call. The difference stems from the fact that buying a call entails paying only the option premium, while buying the index and put entails paying for *both* the index and the put option, which together are more expensive than buying a call. The profit diagram in panel (d) of Figure 1, however, does look like a call.

FIGURE 1

Panel (a) shows the payoff diagram for a long position in the index (column 1 in Table 1). Panel (b) shows the payoff diagram for a purchased index put with a strike price of $1000 (column 2 in Table 1). Panel (c) shows the combined payoff diagram for the index and put (column 3 in Table 1). Panel (d) shows the combined profit diagram for the index and put, obtained by subtracting $1095.68 from the payoff diagram in panel (c) (column 5 in Table 1).

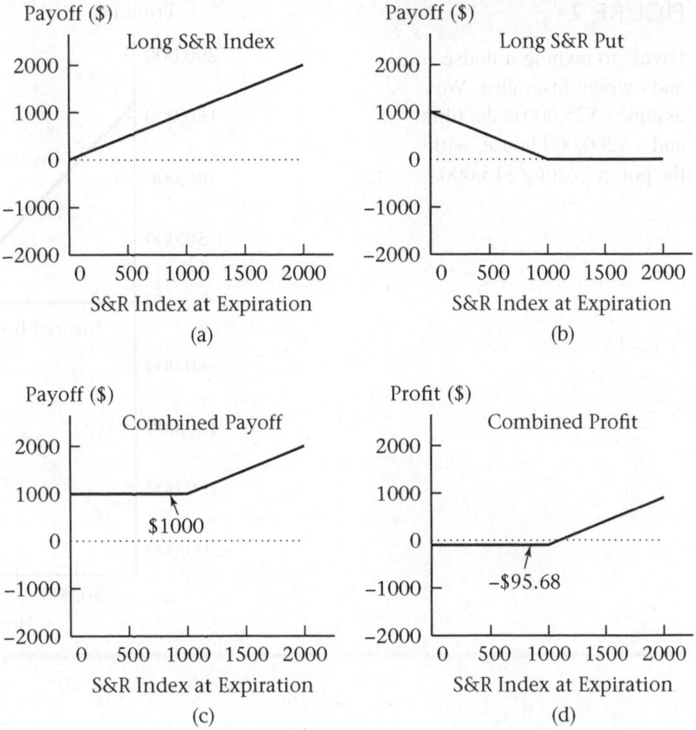

In fact, it is identical to the profit diagram for buying an S&R index call with a strike price of $1000. The profit of −$95.68 for prices below $1000 is exactly the future value of the 1000-strike 6-month to expiration call premium above.

Adding a bond to a payoff diagram shifts it vertically but leaves the corresponding profit diagram unaffected. The combined position of index plus put in panel (c) is therefore equivalent to buying a 1000-strike call—depicted by itself in panel (d)—and buying a zero-coupon bond that pays $1000 at expiration of the option.

In practice, a buyer of homeowner's insurance also owns the insured asset (the house). Owning a home is analogous to owning the stock index, and insuring the house is like owning a put. Thus, owning a home plus insurance is like owning the index and owning a put. Figure 2 depicts an insurance policy, together with the uninsured house and the combined position. Interpreting the house as the S&R index and insurance as the put, Figure 2 looks exactly like Figure 1. *An insured house has a profit diagram that looks like a call option.*

FIGURE 2

Payoff to owning a house and owning insurance. We assume a $25,000 deductible and a $200,000 house, with the policy costing $15,000.

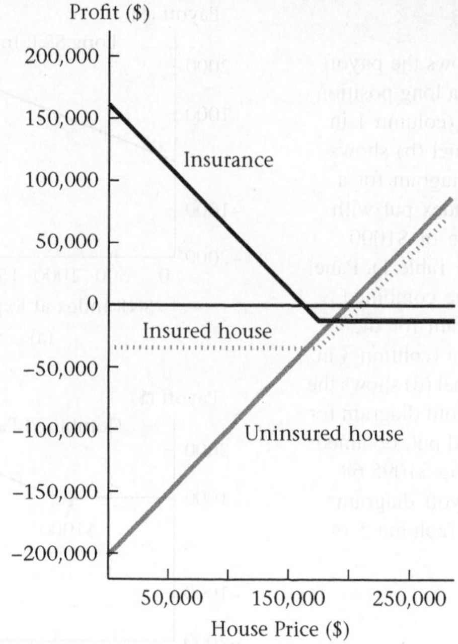

Insuring a Short Position: Caps

If we have a short position in the S&R index, we experience a loss when the index rises. We can insure a short position by purchasing a call option to protect against a higher price of repurchasing the index.[1] Buying a call option is also called a **cap**.

Table 2 presents the payoff and profit for a short position in the index coupled with a purchased call option. Because we short the index, we earn interest on the short proceeds less the cost of the call option, giving −$924.32 as the future value of the cost.

Figure 3 graphs the columns of Table 2. The payoff and profit diagrams resemble those of a purchased put. As with the insured index position in Figure 1, we have to be careful in dealing with cash flows. The *payoff* in panel (c) of Figure 3 is like that of a purchased put coupled with borrowing. In this case, the payoff diagram for shorting the index and buying a call is equivalent to that from buying a put and borrowing the present value of $1000 ($980.39). Since profit diagrams are unaffected by borrowing, however, the profit diagram in panel (d) is exactly the same as that for a purchased S&R index put. Not only does the insured short position look like a put, it has the same loss as a purchased put if the price is above $1000: $75.68, which is the future value of the $74.201 put premium.

1. Keep in mind that if you have an obligation to buy the index in the future but the price is not fixed, then you have an *implicit* short position (if the price goes up, you will have to pay more). A call is insurance for both explicit and implicit short-sellers.

TABLE 2 Payoff and profit at expiration from short-selling the S&R index and buying a 1000-strike call option at a premium of \$93.809. The payoff is the sum of the first two columns. Cost plus interest for the position is (−\$1000 + \$93.809) × 1.02 = −\$924.32. Profit is payoff plus \$924.32.

Payoff at Expiration				
Short S&R Index	S&R Call	Payoff	−(Cost + Interest)	Profit
−\$900	\$0	−\$900	\$924.32	\$24.32
−950	0	−950	924.32	−25.68
−1000	0	−1000	924.32	−75.68
−1050	50	−1000	924.32	−75.68
−1100	100	−1000	924.32	−75.68
−1150	150	−1000	924.32	−75.68
−1200	200	−1000	924.32	−75.68

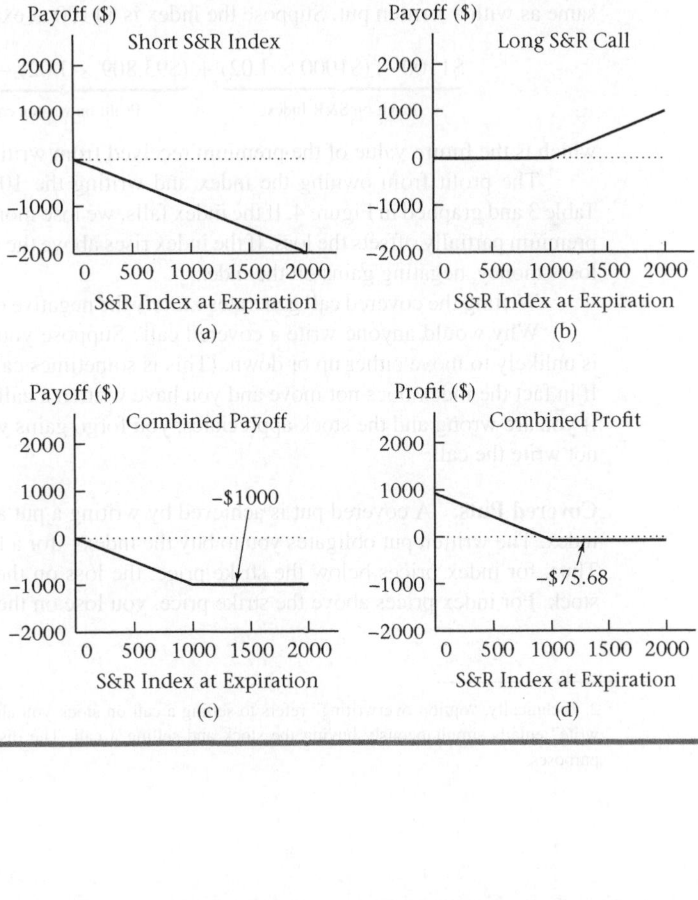

FIGURE 3 Panel (a) shows the payoff diagram for a short position in the index (column 1 in Table 2). Panel (b) shows the payoff diagram for a purchased index call with a strike price of \$1000 (column 2 in Table 2). Panel (c) shows the combined payoff diagram for the short index and long call (column 3 in Table 2). Panel (d) shows the combined profit diagram for the short index and long call, obtained by adding \$924.32 to the payoff diagram in panel (c) (column 5 in Table 2).

Selling Insurance

We can expect that some investors want to purchase insurance. However, for every insurance buyer there must be an insurance seller. In this section we examine strategies in which investors *sell* insurance.

It is possible, of course, for an investor to simply sell calls and puts. Often, however, investors also have a position in the asset when they sell insurance. Writing an option when there is a corresponding long position in the underlying asset is called **covered writing**, **option overwriting**, or selling a covered call. All three terms mean essentially the same thing.[2] In contrast, **naked writing** occurs when the writer of an option does not have a position in the asset.

In addition to the covered writing strategies we will discuss here, there are other insurance-selling strategies, such as delta-hedging, which are less risky than naked writing and are used in practice by market-makers.

Covered Call Writing. If we own the S&R index and simultaneously sell a call option, we have written a **covered call**. A covered call will have limited profitability if the index increases, because an option writer is obligated to sell the index for the strike price. Should the index decrease, the loss on the index is offset by the premium earned from selling the call. A payoff with limited profit for price increases and potentially large losses for price decreases sounds like a written put.

The covered call looks exactly like a written put, and the maximum profit will be the same as with a written put. Suppose the index is \$1100 at expiration. The profit is

$$\underbrace{\$1100 - (\$1000 \times 1.02)}_{\text{Profit on S\&R Index}} + \underbrace{(\$93.809 \times 1.02) - \$100}_{\text{Profit on written call}} = \$75.68$$

which is the future value of the premium received from writing a 1000-strike put.

The profit from owning the index and writing the 1000-strike call is computed in Table 3 and graphed in Figure 4. If the index falls, we lose money on the index but the option premium partially offsets the loss. If the index rises above the strike price, the written option loses money, negating gains on the index.

Writing the covered call generates *exactly* the negative of the profit from buying a put.

Why would anyone write a covered call? Suppose you have the view that the index is unlikely to move either up or down. (This is sometimes called a "neutral" market view.) If in fact the index does not move and you have written a call, then you keep the premium. If you are wrong and the stock appreciates, you forgo gains you would have had if you did not write the call.

Covered Puts. A covered put is achieved by writing a put against a short position on the index. The written put obligates you to buy the index—for a loss—if it goes down in price. Thus, for index prices below the strike price, the loss on the written put offsets the short stock. For index prices above the strike price, you lose on the short stock.

2. Technically, "option overwriting" refers to selling a call on stock you already own, while a "covered write" entails simultaneously buying the stock and selling a call. The distinction is irrelevant for our purposes.

TABLE 3 Payoff and profit at expiration from purchasing the S&R index and selling a 1000-strike call option. The payoff column is the sum of the first two columns. Cost plus interest for the position is ($1000 − $93.809) × 1.02 = $924.32. Profit is payoff less $924.32.

Payoff at Expiration				
S&R Index	Short S&R Call	Payoff	−(Cost + Interest)	Profit
$900	$0	$900	−$924.32	−$24.32
950	0	950	−924.32	25.68
1000	0	1000	−924.32	75.68
1050	−50	1000	−924.32	75.68
1100	−100	1000	−924.32	75.68
1150	−150	1000	−924.32	75.68
1200	−200	1000	−924.32	75.68

FIGURE 4 Payoff and profit diagrams for writing a covered S&R call. Panel (a) is the payoff to a long S&R position. Panel (b) is the payoff to a short S&R call with strike price of 1000. Panel (c) is the combined payoff for the S&R index and written call. Panel (d) is the combined profit, obtained by subtracting ($1000 − $93.809) × 1.02 = $924.32 from the payoff in panel (c).

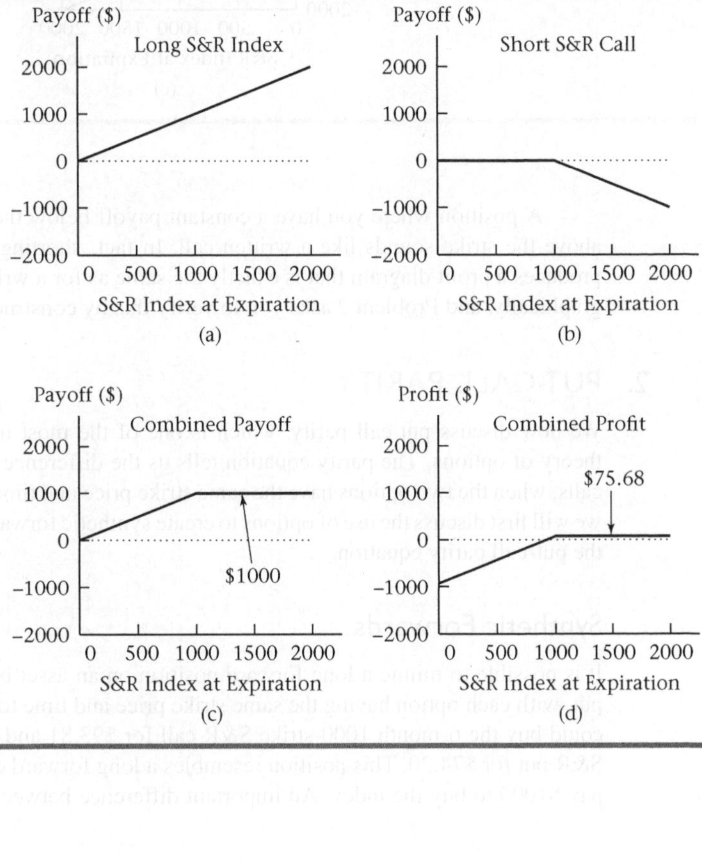

FIGURE 5

Payoff and profit diagrams for writing a covered S&R put. Panel (a) is the payoff to a short S&R position. Panel (b) is the payoff to a short S&R put with a strike price of $1000. Panel (c) is the combined payoff for the short S&R index and written put. Panel (d) is the combined profit, obtained by adding ($1000 + $74.201) × 1.02 = $1095.68 to the payoff in panel (c).

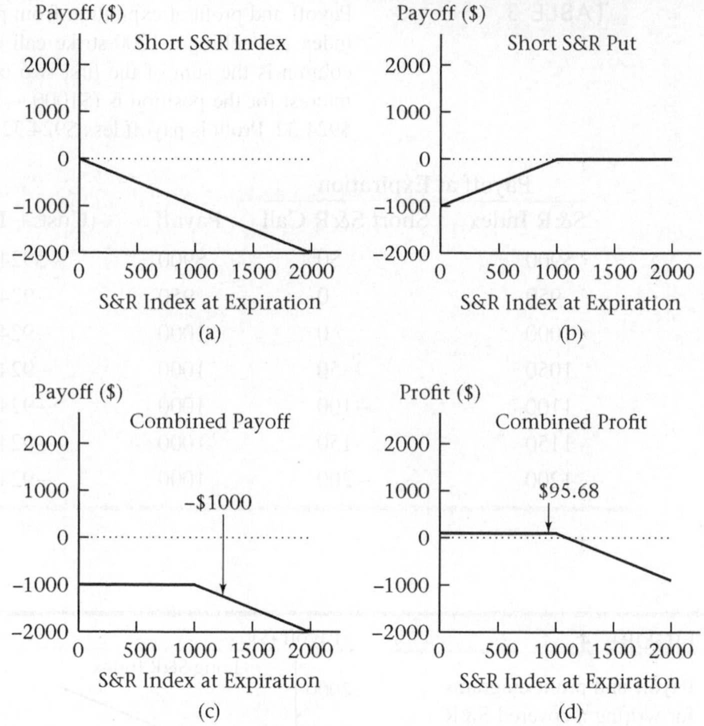

A position where you have a constant payoff below the strike and increasing losses above the strike sounds like a written call. In fact, shorting the index and writing a put produces a profit diagram that is exactly the same as for a written call. Figure 5 shows this graphically, and Problem 2 asks you to verify this by constructing a payoff table.

2. PUT-CALL PARITY

We now discuss put-call parity, which is one of the most important relationships in the theory of options. The parity equation tells us the difference in the premiums of puts and calls, when the two options have the same strike price and time to expiration. In this section we will first discuss the use of options to create synthetic forward contracts. We then develop the put-call parity equation.

Synthetic Forwards

It is possible to mimic a long forward position on an asset by buying a call and selling a put, with each option having the same strike price and time to expiration. For example, we could buy the 6-month 1000-strike S&R call for $93.81 and sell the 6-month 1000-strike S&R put for $74.20. This position resembles a long forward contract: In 6 months we will pay $1000 to buy the index. An important difference between the forward and the option

FIGURE 6

Purchase of a 1000-strike S&R call, sale of a 1000-strike S&R put, and the combined position. The combined position resembles the profit on a long forward contract.

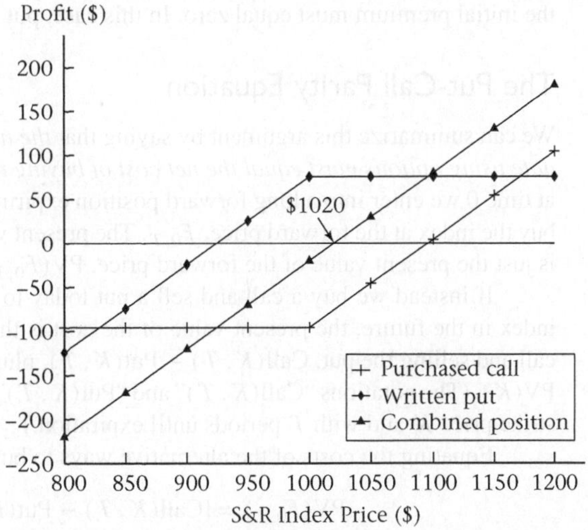

position is that the forward contract has no premium, but the options have a net cost of \$93.81 − \$74.20 = \$19.61.

To better understand this position, suppose that the index in 6 months is at 900. We will not exercise the call, but we have written a put. The put buyer will exercise the right to sell the index for \$1000; therefore we are obligated to buy the index at \$1000. If instead the index is at \$1100, the put is not exercised, but we exercise the call, buying the index for \$1000. Thus, whether the index rises or falls, when the options expire we buy the index for the strike price of the options, \$1000.

The purchased call, written put, and combined positions are shown in Figure 6. The purchase of a call and sale of a put creates a *synthetic* long forward contract, which has two minor differences from the actual forward:

1. The forward contract has a zero premium, while the synthetic forward requires that we pay the net option premium.
2. With the forward contract we pay the forward price, while with the synthetic forward we pay the strike price.

If you think about it, these two considerations must be related. If we set the strike price low, we are obligated to buy the index at a discount relative to the forward price. Buying at a lower price than the forward price is a benefit. In order to obtain this benefit we have to pay the positive net option premium, which stems from the call being more expensive than the put. In fact, in Figure 6, the implicit cost of the synthetic forward—the price at which the profit on the combined call-put position is zero—is \$1020, which is the S&R forward price.

Similarly, if we set the strike price high, we are obligated to buy the index at a high price relative to the forward price. To offset the extra cost of acquiring the index using the high strike options, it makes sense that we would receive payment initially. This would occur if the put that we sell is more expensive than the call we buy.

Finally, if we set the strike price equal to the forward price, then to mimic the forward the initial premium must equal zero. In this case, put and call premiums must be equal.

The Put-Call Parity Equation

We can summarize this argument by saying that *the net cost of buying the index at a future date using options must equal the net cost of buying the index using a forward contract*. If at time 0 we enter into a long forward position expiring at time T, we obligate ourselves to buy the index at the forward price, $F_{0,T}$. The present value of buying the index in the future is just the present value of the forward price, $\text{PV}(F_{0,T})$.

If instead we buy a call and sell a put today to guarantee the purchase price for the index in the future, the present value of the cost is the net option premium for buying the call and selling the put, $\text{Call}(K, T) - \text{Put}(K, T)$, plus the present value of the strike price, $\text{PV}(K)$. (The notations "$\text{Call}(K, T)$" and "$\text{Put}(K, T)$" denote the premiums of options with strike price K and with T periods until expiration.)

Equating the costs of the alternative ways to buy the index at time t gives us

$$\text{PV}(F_{0,T}) = [\text{Call}(K, T) - \text{Put}(K, T)] + \text{PV}(K)$$

We can rewrite this as

$$\boxed{\text{Call}(K, T) - \text{Put}(K, T) = \text{PV}(F_{0,T} - K)} \qquad (1)$$

In words, the present value of the bargain element from buying the index at the strike price [the right-hand side of equation (1)] must equal the initial net option premium [the left-hand side of equation (1)]. Equation (1) is known as **put-call parity**.

Example 1. As an example of equation (1), consider buying the 6-month 1000-strike S&R call for a premium of \$93.809 and selling the 6-month 1000-strike put for a premium of \$74.201. These transactions create a synthetic forward permitting us to buy the index in 6 months for \$1000. Because the actual forward price is \$1020, this synthetic forward permits us to buy the index at a bargain of \$20, the present value of which is \$20/1.02 = \$19.61. The difference in option premiums is also \$19.61 (\$93.809 − \$74.201 = \$19.61). This result is exactly what we get with equation (1):

$$\$93.809 - \$74.201 = \text{PV}(\$1020 - \$1000) \quad \blacksquare$$

A forward contract for which the premium is not zero is sometimes called an **off-market forward**. This terminology arises since a true forward by definition has a zero premium. Therefore, a forward contract with a nonzero premium must have a forward price that is "off the market (forward) price." Unless the strike price equals the forward price, buying a call and selling a put creates an off-market forward.

Equivalence of Different Positions. We have seen earlier that buying the index and buying a put generates the same profit as buying a call. Similarly, selling a covered call (buying the index and selling a call) generates the same profit as selling a put. Equation (1) explains why this happens.

Consider buying the index and buying a put, as in Section 1. Recall that, in this example, we have the forward price equal to \$1020 and the index price equal to \$1000.

Thus, the present value of the forward price equals the index price. Rewriting equation (1) gives

$$\text{PV}(F_{0,T}) + \text{Put}(K, T) = \text{Call}(K, T) + \text{PV}(K)$$
$$\$1000 + \$74.201 = \$93.809 + \$980.39$$

That is, buying the index and buying the put cost the same, and generate the same payoff, as buying the call and buying a zero-coupon bond costing $\text{PV}(K)$.

Similarly, in the case of writing a covered call, we have

$$\text{PV}(F_{0,T}) - \text{Call}(K, T) = \text{PV}(K) - \text{Put}(K, T)$$

That is, writing a covered call has the same profit as lending $\text{PV}(K)$ and selling a put. Equation (1) provides a tool for constructing equivalent positions.

No Arbitrage. In deriving equation (1), and in some earlier discussions, we relied on the idea that if two different investments generate the same payoff, they must have the same cost. If equation (1) did not hold, there would be both low-cost and high-cost ways to acquire the index at time T. We could simultaneously buy the index at low cost and sell the index at high cost. This transaction has no risk (since we both buy and sell the index) and generates a positive cash flow (because of the difference in costs). Taking advantage of such an opportunity is called arbitrage, and the idea that prices should not permit arbitrage is called "no-arbitrage pricing." We implicitly illustrated this idea earlier in showing how owning the index and buying a put has the same profit as a call, etc.[3]

3. SPREADS AND COLLARS

There are many well-known, commonly used strategies that combine two or more options. In this section we discuss some of these strategies and explain the motivation for using them. The underlying theme in this section is that there are always trade-offs in designing a position: It is always possible to lower the cost of a position by reducing its payoff. Thus there are many variations on each particular strategy.

All the examples in this section will use the set of option prices in Table 4. We will assume the continuously compounded interest rate is 8%.

Bull and Bear Spreads

An option **spread** is a position consisting of only calls or only puts, in which some options are purchased and some written. Spreads are a common strategy. In this section we define some typical spread strategies and explain why you might use a spread.

Suppose you believe a stock will appreciate. Let's compare two ways to speculate on this belief: entering into a long forward contract or buying a call option with the strike price equal to the forward price. The forward contract has a zero premium and the call has a positive premium. A difference in payoffs explains the difference in premiums. If the stock

3. Another way to express the principle of no arbitrage is using profit diagrams. Given two profit diagrams, there is an arbitrage opportunity if one diagram is nowhere below and somewhere above the other.

TABLE 4 Black-Scholes option prices assuming stock price = $40, volatility = 30%, effective annual risk-free rate = 8.33% (8%, continuously compounded), dividend yield = $0, and 91 days to expiration.

Strike	Call	Put
35	6.13	0.44
40	2.78	1.99
45	0.97	5.08

price at expiration is greater than the forward price, the forward contract and call have the same payoff. If the stock price is less than the forward price, however, the forward contract has a loss and the call is worth zero. Put-call parity tells us that the call is equivalent to the forward contract plus a put option. Thus, the call premium equals the cost of the put, which is insurance against the stock price being less than the forward price.

You might ask: Is there a lower-cost way to speculate that the stock price will rise, that still has the insurance implicit in the call? The answer is yes: You can lower the cost of your strategy if you are willing to reduce your profit should the stock appreciate. You can do this by selling a call at a higher strike price. The owner of this second call buys appreciation above the higher strike price and pays you a premium. You achieve a lower cost by giving up some portion of profit. A position in which you buy a call and sell an otherwise identical call with a higher strike price is an example of a **bull spread**.

Bull spreads can also be constructed using puts. Perhaps surprisingly, you can achieve the same result either by buying a low-strike call and selling a high-strike call, or by buying a low-strike put and selling a high-strike put.

Spreads constructed with either calls or puts are sometimes called **vertical spreads**. The terminology stems from the way option prices are typically presented, with strikes arrayed vertically (as in Table 4).

Example 2. To see how a bull spread arises, suppose we want to speculate on the stock price increasing. Consider buying a 40-strike call with 3 months to expiration. From Table 4, the premium for this call is $2.78. We can reduce the cost of the position—and also the potential profit—by selling the 45-strike call.

An easy way to construct the graph for this position is to emulate a spreadsheet: For each price, compute the profit of each option position and add up the profits for the individual positions. It is worth working through one example in detail to see how this is done.

The initial net cost of the two options is $\$2.78 - \$0.97 = \$1.81$. With 3 months interest, the total cost at expiration is $\$1.81 \times (1.0833)^{0.25} = \$1.85$. Table 5 computes the cash flow at expiration for both options and computes profit on the position by subtracting the future value of the net premium.

Figure 7 graphs the position in Table 5. You should verify that if you buy the 40-strike put and sell the 45-strike put, you obtain exactly the same graph. ■

TABLE 5 Profit at expiration from purchase of 40-strike call and sale of 45-strike call.

Stock Price at Expiration	Purchased 40-Call	Written 45-Call	Premium Plus Interest	Total
\$35.0	\$0.0	\$0.0	−\$1.85	−\$1.85
37.5	0.0	0.0	−1.85	−1.85
40.0	0.0	0.0	−1.85	−1.85
42.5	2.5	0.0	−1.85	0.65
45.0	5.0	0.0	−1.85	3.15
47.5	7.5	−2.5	−1.85	3.15
50.0	10.0	−5.0	−1.85	3.15

FIGURE 7

Profit diagram for a 40–45 bull spread: buying a 40-strike call and selling a 45-strike call.

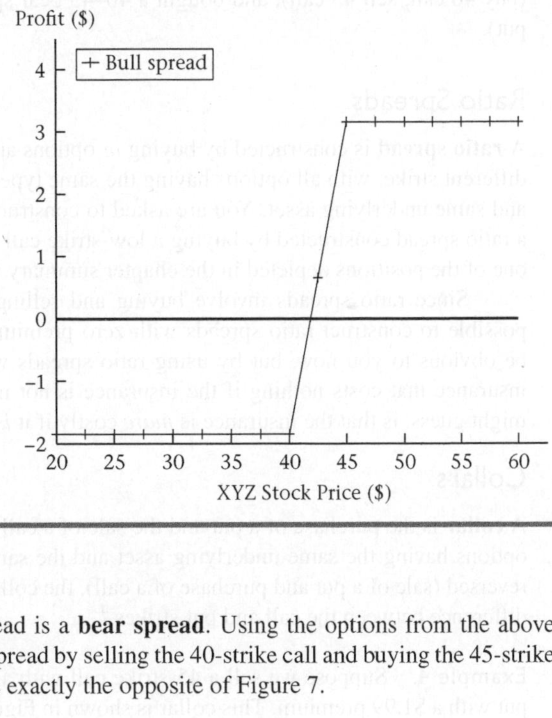

The opposite of a bull spread is a **bear spread**. Using the options from the above example, we could create a bear spread by selling the 40-strike call and buying the 45-strike call. The profit diagram would be exactly the opposite of Figure 7.

Box Spreads

A **box spread** is accomplished by using options to create a synthetic long forward at one price and a synthetic short forward at a different price. This strategy guarantees a cash flow in the future. Hence, it is an option spread that is purely a means of borrowing or lending money: It is costly but has no stock price risk. The reasons for using a box spread are discussed in Box 1.

Example 3. Suppose we simultaneously enter into the following two transactions:

1. Buy a 40-strike call and sell a 40-strike put.
2. Sell a 45-strike call and buy a 45-strike put.

The first transaction is a synthetic forward purchase of a stock for \$40, while the second transaction is the synthetic forward sale of the stock for \$45. Clearly the payoff at expiration will be \$5; hence, the transaction has no stock price risk. Using the assumptions in Table 4, the cost of the strategy should be

$$5 \times (1.0833)^{-0.25} = \$4.90$$

In fact, using the premiums in Table 4, the initial cash flow is

$$(\$1.99 - \$2.78) + (\$0.97 - \$5.08) = -\$4.90$$

Another way to view this transaction is that we have bought a 40–45 bull spread using calls (buy 40 call, sell 45 call), and bought a 40–45 bear spread using puts (sell 40 put, buy 45 put). ■

Ratio Spreads

A **ratio spread** is constructed by buying m options at one strike and selling n options at a different strike, with all options having the same type (call or put), same time to maturity, and same underlying asset. You are asked to construct ratio spreads in Problem 15. Also, a ratio spread constructed by buying a low-strike call and selling two higher-strike calls is one of the positions depicted in the chapter summary in Figure 16.

Since ratio spreads involve buying and selling unequal numbers of options, it is possible to construct ratio spreads with zero premium. The significance of this may not be obvious to you now, but by using ratio spreads we can construct paylater strategies: insurance that costs nothing if the insurance is not needed. The trade-off to this, as you might guess, is that the insurance is *more* costly if it *is* needed.

Collars

A **collar** is the purchase of a put and the sale of a call with a higher strike price, with both options having the same underlying asset and the same expiration date. If the position is reversed (sale of a put and purchase of a call), the collar is written. The **collar width** is the difference between the call and put strikes.[4]

Example 4. Suppose we sell a 45-strike call with a \$0.97 premium and buy a 40-strike put with a \$1.99 premium. This collar is shown in Figure 8. Because the purchased put has a higher premium than the written call, the position requires investment of \$1.02. ■

4. Collars in which call and put strikes are equidistant from the forward price are sometimes called **risk reversals**. This term also has a different but related meaning.

BOX 1: The Use of Box Spreads

A box spread is an alternative to buying a bond. Option market-makers in particular have low transaction costs and can sell box spreads, which is equivalent to borrowing. Box spreads can therefore be a source of funds. In the past, box spreads also provided a tax benefit for some investors. Although a change in the tax law in 1993 ostensibly eliminated this use of box spreads, the issue provides an illustration of why derivatives create problems for the tax authorities.

Consider a taxable investor who has sold stock investments at a loss. This loss is classified for tax purposes as a capital loss. In the United States, capital gains are always taxed, but capital losses are only deductible against capital gains. (The exception to this is that individual investors are allowed to deduct a limited amount of capital losses against ordinary income.) Thus, a taxable investor with large capital losses would like to find a mechanism to generate income which can be labeled as capital gains. This is not as easy as it sounds. A risk-free zero-coupon bond—which is certain to appreciate over its life—generates interest income, which cannot be used to offset capital losses. A stock held to generate gains could instead go down in price, generating additional losses.

A box spread sounds as if it should enable investors to generate capital gains as needed: It is a synthetic bond, guaranteed to appreciate in value just like a bond. Moreover, the gain or loss on an option is a capital gain or loss. *If* the change in value of a box spread were taxed as a capital gain, box spreads could be used to create risk-free capital gains income, against which capital losses could be offset.

Lawmakers in the United States have anticipated strategies like this. Section 1258 of the U.S. Tax Code, enacted in 1993, explicitly states that capital income should be taxed as ordinary income if all expected return is due to time value of money on the investment (in other words, if the investment is equivalent to a bond). This would seem to eliminate the tax motive for entering into box spreads. The problem for the tax authorities, however, is how to identify taxpayers using box spreads for this purpose. There is nothing wrong with entering into a box spread; the law is only violated if the taxpayer reports the resulting income as a capital gain. This is difficult to detect. Tax rules may also differ internationally. In *Griffin* v. *Citibank Investments Ltd.* (2000), for example, British courts ruled that a box spread was not necessarily equivalent to a loan.

The fundamental problem is that the tax code calls for different taxation of bonds and options, but options can be used to create bonds. There are many similar illustrations of this problem.

In Figure 8, the collar resembles a short forward contract. Economically, it *is* like a short forward contract in that it is fundamentally a short position: The position benefits from price decreases in the underlying asset and suffers losses from price increases. A collar differs from a short forward contract in having a range between the strikes in which the expiration payoff is unaffected by changes in the value of the underlying asset.

In practice, collars are frequently used to implement insurance strategies—for example, by buying a collar when we own the stock. This position, which we will call a *collared stock*, entails buying the stock, buying a put, and selling a call. It is an insured position because we own the asset and buy a put. The sale of a call helps to pay for the purchase of the put. The collared stock looks like a bull spread; however, it arises from a different set

FIGURE 8

Profit diagram of a purchased collar constructed by selling a 45-strike call and buying a 40-strike put.

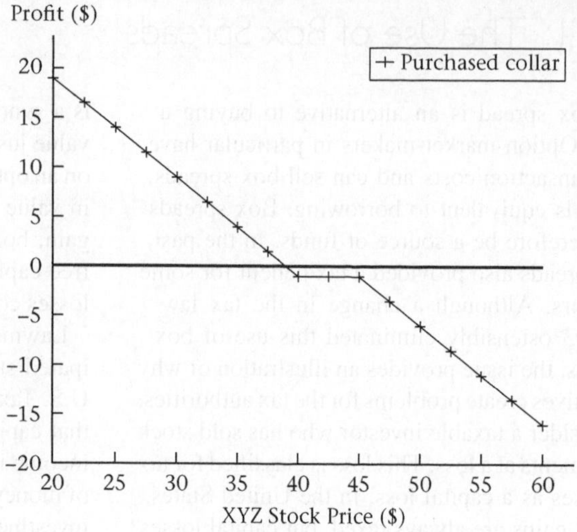

of transactions. The bull spread is created by buying one option and selling another. The collared stock begins with a position in the underlying asset that is coupled with a collar.

Example 5. Suppose that you own shares of XYZ for which the current price is \$40, and you wish to buy insurance. You do this by purchasing a put option. A way to reduce the cost of the insurance is to sell an out-of-the-money call. The profit calculations for this set of transactions—buy the stock, buy a 40-strike put, sell a 45-strike call—are shown in Table 6. Comparing this table to Table 5 demonstrates that profit on the collared stock position is identical to profit on the bull spread. Note that it is essential to account for interest as a cost of holding the stock. ■

If you have a short position in the stock, you can collar the position by buying a call for insurance and selling an out-of-the-money put to partially fund the call purchase. The result looks like a bear spread.

Zero-Cost Collars. The collar depicted in Table 6 entails paying a net premium of \$1.02: \$1.99 for the purchased put, against \$0.97 for the written call. It is possible to find strike prices for the put and call such that the two premiums exactly offset one another. This position is called a **zero-cost collar**.

To illustrate a zero-cost collar, suppose you buy the stock and buy the 40-strike put that has a premium of \$1.99. Trial and error with the Black-Scholes formula reveals that a call with a strike of \$41.72 also has a premium of \$1.99. Thus, you can buy a 40-strike put and sell a 41.72-strike call without paying any premium. The result is depicted in Figure 9. At expiration, the collar exposes you to stock price movements between \$40 and \$41.72, coupled with downside protection below \$40. You pay for this protection by giving up gains should the stock move above \$41.72.

TABLE 6 Profit at expiration from purchase of 40-strike put and sale of 45-strike call.

Stock Price at Expiration	Purchased 40-Put	Written 45-Call	Premium Plus Interest	Profit on Stock	Total
$35.00	$5.00	$0.00	−$1.04	−$5.81	−$1.85
37.50	2.50	0.00	−1.04	−3.31	−1.85
40.00	0.00	0.00	−1.04	−0.81	−1.85
42.50	0.00	0.00	−1.04	1.69	0.65
45.00	0.00	0.00	−1.04	4.19	3.15
47.50	0.00	−2.50	−1.04	6.69	3.15
50.00	0.00	−5.00	−1.04	9.19	3.15

FIGURE 9

Zero-cost collar on XYZ, created by buying XYZ at $40, buying a 40-strike put with a premium of $1.99, and selling a 41.72-strike call with a premium of $1.99.

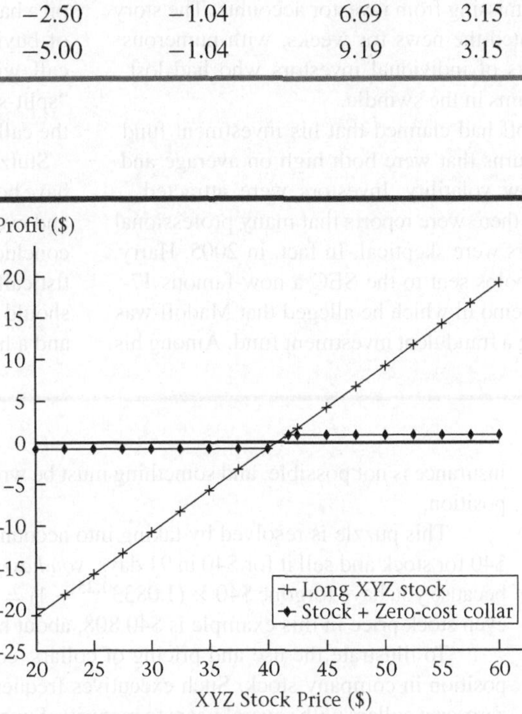

For any given stock there is an infinite number of zero-cost collars. One way to see this is to first pick the desired put strike below the forward price. It is then possible to find a strike above the forward price such that a call has the same premium.

Understanding Collars. One aspect of the zero-cost collar that may seem puzzling is that you can finance the purchase of an at-the-money put by selling an out-of-the-money call. In the above example, with the stock at $40, you were able to costlessly buy a 40-strike put by also selling a 41.72-strike call. This makes it seem as if you have free insurance with some possibility of gain. Even if you are puzzled by this, you probably realize that "free"

BOX 2: Bernard Madoff: A Collar by Any Other Name

In 2009, Bernard L. Madoff confessed to having run a Ponzi scheme in his investment fund, Bernard L. Madoff Investment Securities, LLC. A Ponzi scheme (named after Charles Ponzi) is a fraudulent investment vehicle in which funds paid in by late investors are used to pay off early investors. The sheer scale of Madoff's fraud was astonishing: There was an estimated $65 ***billion*** missing from investor accounts. The story dominated the news for weeks, with numerous accounts of individual investors who had lost huge sums in the swindle.

Madoff had claimed that his investment fund had returns that were both high on average and with low volatility. Investors were attracted, though there were reports that many professional investors were skeptical. In fact, in 2005, Harry Markopolos sent to the SEC a now-famous 17-page memo in which he alleged that Madoff was running a fraudulent investment fund. Among his assertions were that Madoff's returns reported to clients were too great to be real, and that the correlation of his returns to the S&P 500 index was too low.

Madoff claimed to be using collars to achieve his stable high returns. According to Markopolos, Madoff claimed to investors that he achieved his returns using a "split-strike conversion" strategy on a basket of large stocks. A conversion consists of buying a stock, buying a put, and selling a call, with the options having the same strike. In a "split-strike" conversion, the put strike is below the call strike—in other words, it's a collar.

Stutzer (2010) and Bernard and Boyle (2009) have both examined Madoff's investment strategy and evaluated Markopolos's claims. Both papers conclude that Madoff's reported returns are statistically implausible. In particular, the strategy should have exhibited a greater return volatility and a higher correlation with the index.

insurance is not possible, and something must be wrong with this way of thinking about the position.

This puzzle is resolved by taking into account financing cost. Recall that if you pay $40 for stock and sell it for $40 in 91 days, *you have not broken even.* You have lost money, because you have forgone $\$40 \times (1.0833^{0.25} - 1) = \$0.808$ in interest. Thus, the true break-even stock price in this example is $40.808, about halfway between $40 and $41.72.

To illustrate the use and pricing of collars, consider an executive who owns a large position in company stock. Such executives frequently hedge their stock positions, using zero-cost collars with several years to maturity. Suppose, for example, that a firm has a price of $30/share and an executive wishes to hedge 1 million shares. If the executive buys a 30-strike put with 3 years to maturity, what 3-year call will have the same premium? Assuming an effective annual risk-free rate of 6%, a zero dividend yield, and a 40% volatility, the Black-Scholes price is $5.298 for a 30-strike put with 3 years to maturity. Using trial and error (or a numerical solver), a call option with a strike of $47.39 has the same premium. Once again, the zero-cost collar seems highly asymmetric. However, this comparison does not take into account financing cost. The executive selling stock in 3 years for $30/share will in fact have lost 3 years' worth of interest: $\$30 \times [(1.06)^3 - 1] = \$5.73$.

Box 2 discusses another example of how collars were (or were not) used.

The Cost of the Collar and the Forward Price. Suppose you try to construct a zero-cost collar in which you set the strike of the put option at the stock price plus financing cost—

i.e., the future value of the stock price. In the 91-day example above, this would require that you set the put strike equal to $40.808, which gives a premium of $2.39. The call premium at this strike is also $2.39! *If you try to insure against all losses on the stock, including interest, then a zero-cost collar has zero width.*

This is an implication of put-call parity, equation (1). It turns out that $40.808 is also the theoretical forward price. If we set the strike equal to the forward price, the call premium equals the put premium.

4. SPECULATING ON VOLATILITY

The positions we have just considered are all directional: A bull spread or a collared stock is a bet that the price of the underlying asset will increase. Options can also be used to create positions that are nondirectional with respect to the underlying asset. With a nondirectional position, the holder does not care whether the stock goes up or down, but only how much it moves. We now examine straddles, strangles, and butterfly spreads, which are examples of nondirectional speculations.

Straddles

Consider the strategy of buying a call and a put with the same strike price and time to expiration: This strategy is called a **straddle**. The general idea of a straddle is simple: If the stock price rises, there will be a profit on the purchased call, and if the stock price declines, there will be a profit on the purchased put. Thus, the advantage of a straddle is that it can profit from stock price moves in both directions. The disadvantage to a straddle is that it has a high premium because it requires purchasing two options. If the stock price at expiration is near the strike price, the two premiums are lost. The profit diagram for a 40-strike straddle is graphed in Figure 10. The initial cost of the straddle at a stock price of $40 is $4.77: $2.78 for the call and $1.99 for the put.

Figure 10 demonstrates that a straddle is a bet that volatility will be high: The buyer of an at-the-money straddle is hoping that the stock price will move but does not care about the direction of the move. Because option prices reflect the market's estimate of volatility, the cost of a straddle will be greater when the market's perception is that volatility is greater. If at a given set of option prices all investors found it desirable to buy straddles, then option prices would increase. Thus, purchasing a straddle is really a bet that volatility is greater than the market's assessment of volatility, as reflected in option prices.

Strangle. The disadvantage of a straddle is the high premium cost. To reduce the premium, you can buy out-of-the-money options rather than at-the-money options. Such a position is called a **strangle**. For example, consider buying a 35-strike put and a 45-strike call, for a total premium of $1.41, with a future value of $1.44. These transactions reduce your maximum loss if the options expire with the stock near $40, but they also increase the stock-price move required for a profit.

Figure 11 shows the 40-strike straddle graphed against the 35–45 strangle. This comparison illustrates a key point: In comparing any two fairly priced option positions, there will always be a region where each outperforms the other. Indeed, this is necessary to have a fairly priced position.

FIGURE 10

Combined profit diagram for a purchased 40-strike straddle—i.e., purchase of one 40-strike call option and one 40-strike put option.

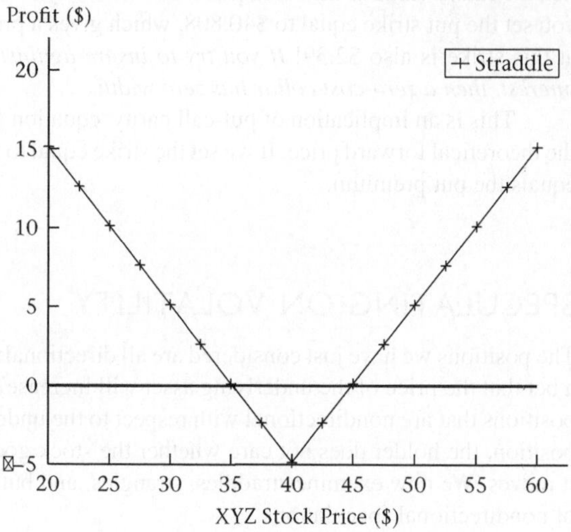

In Figure 11, the strangle outperforms the straddle roughly when the stock price at expiration is between \$36.57 and \$43.43. Obviously, there is a much broader range in which the straddle outperforms the strangle. How can you decide which is the better investment? The answer is that unless you have a particular view on the stock's performance, you cannot say that one position is preferable to the other. An option pricing model implicitly evaluates the likelihood that one strategy will outperform the other, and it computes option prices so that the two strategies are equivalently fair deals. An investor might have a preference for one strategy over the other due to subjective probabilities that differ from the market's.

Written Straddle. What if an investor believes that volatility is *lower* than the market's assessment? Because a purchased straddle is a bet that volatility is high (relative to the market's assessment), a **written straddle**—selling a call and put with the same strike price and time to expiration—is a bet that volatility is low (relative to the market's assessment).

Figure 12 depicts a written straddle, which is exactly the opposite of Figure 10, the purchased straddle. The written straddle is most profitable if the stock price is \$40 at expiration, and in this sense it is a bet on low volatility. What is striking about Figure 12, however, is the potential for loss. A large change in the stock price in either direction leads to a large, potentially unlimited, loss.

It might occur to you that an investor wishing to bet that volatility will be low could write a straddle and acquire insurance against extreme negative outcomes. That intuition is correct and leads to our next strategy.

Butterfly Spreads

The straddle writer can insure against large losses on the straddle by buying options to protect against losses on both the upside and downside. Buying an out-of-the-money put provides insurance on the downside, protecting against losses on the at-the-money written

FIGURE 11

40-strike straddle and strangle composed of 35-strike put and 45-strike call.

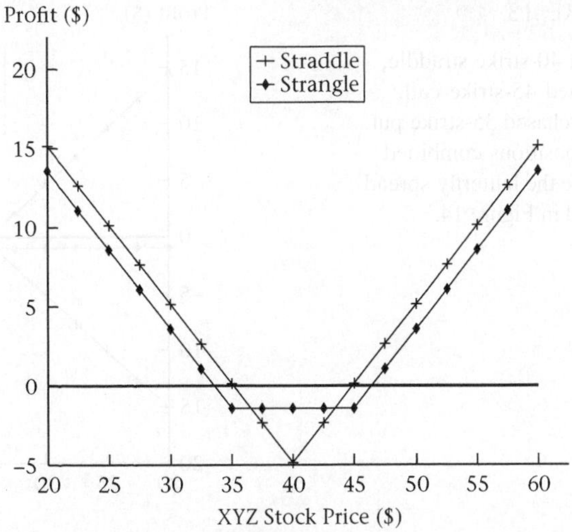

FIGURE 12

Profit at expiration from a written straddle—i.e., selling a 40-strike call and a 40-strike put.

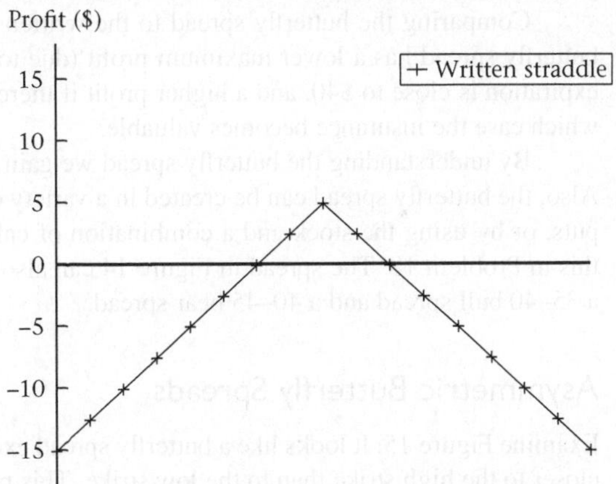

put. Buying an out-of-the-money call provides insurance on the upside, protecting against losses on the written at-the-money call.

Figure 13 displays the straddle written at a strike price of $40, along with the options to safeguard the position: a 35-strike put and a 45-strike call. The net result of combining these three strategies is an insured written straddle, which is called a **butterfly spread**,

FIGURE 13

Written 40-strike straddle, purchased 45-strike call, and purchased 35-strike put. These positions combined generate the butterfly spread graphed in Figure 14.

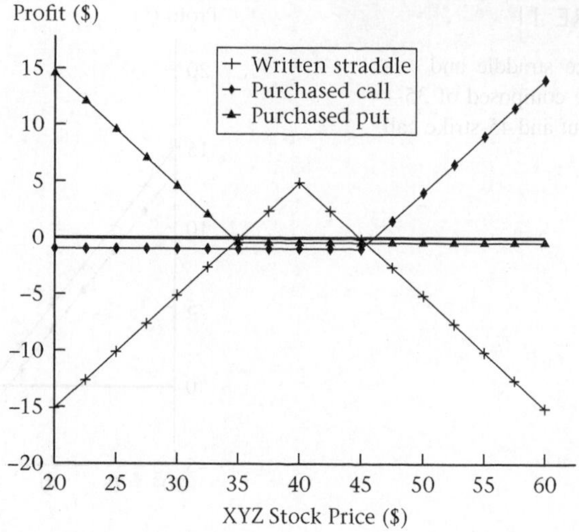

graphed in Figure 14. It can be thought of as a written straddle for the timid (or for the prudent!).

Comparing the butterfly spread to the written straddle (Figure 14), we see that the butterfly spread has a lower maximum profit (due to the cost of insurance) if the stock at expiration is close to $40, and a higher profit if there is a large move in the stock price, in which case the insurance becomes valuable.

By understanding the butterfly spread we gain important insights into option prices. Also, the butterfly spread can be created in a variety of ways: solely with calls, solely with puts, or by using the stock and a combination of calls and puts.[5] You are asked to verify this in Problem 18. The spread in Figure 14 can also be created by simultaneously buying a 35–40 bull spread and a 40–45 bear spread.

Asymmetric Butterfly Spreads

Examine Figure 15. It looks like a butterfly spread except that it is asymmetric: The peak is closer to the high strike than to the low strike. This picture was created by buying two 35-strike calls, selling ten 43-strike calls (with a premium of $1.525, using the assumptions in Table 4), and buying eight 45-strike calls. The position is like a butterfly in that it earns a profit if the stock stays within a small range, and the loss is the same for high and low stock prices. However, the profit diagram is now tilted to the right, rather than being symmetric.

Suppose you knew that you wanted a position that looks like Figure 15. How would you know how many options to buy and sell to construct this position? In order to obtain

5. Technically, a true butterfly spread is created solely with calls or solely with puts. A butterfly spread created by selling a straddle and buying a strangle is called an "iron butterfly."

FIGURE 14

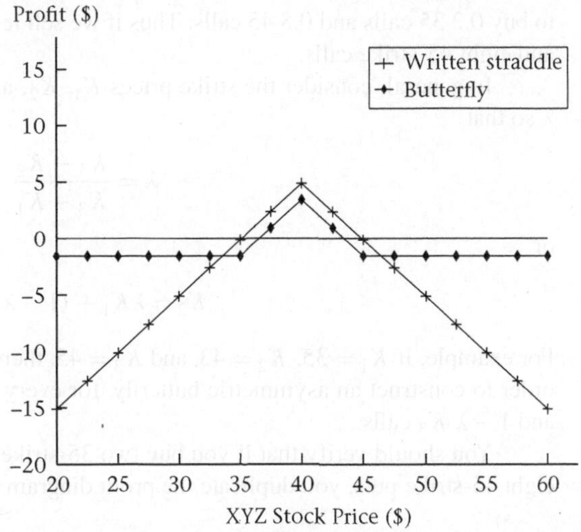

Comparison of the 35–40–45 butterfly spread, obtained by adding the profit diagrams in Figure 13, with the written 40-strike straddle.

FIGURE 15

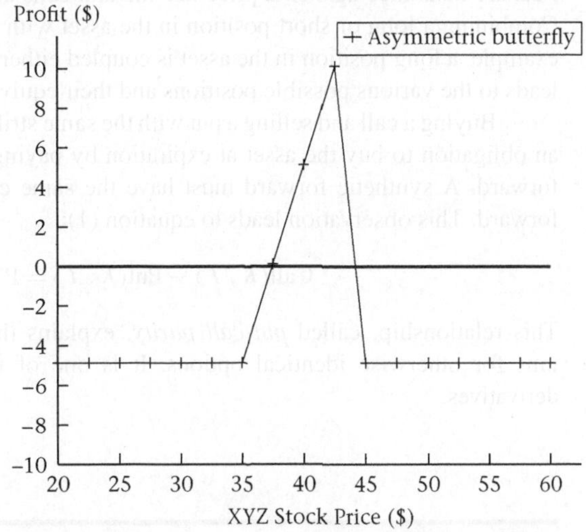

Asymmetric butterfly, created by buying two 35-strike calls and eight 45-strike calls and selling ten 43-strike calls.

this position, the strikes clearly have to be at 35, 43, and 45. The total distance between 35 and 45 is 10. The number 43 is 80% ($= \frac{43-35}{10}$) of the way from 35 to 45. In fact, we can write 43 as

$$43 = (0.2 \times 35) + (0.8 \times 45)$$

This way of writing 43 tells us our call position: For every written 43-strike call, we want to buy 0.2 35 calls and 0.8 45 calls. Thus if we sell ten 43-strike calls, we buy two 35 calls and eight 45-strike calls.

In general, consider the strike prices K_1, K_2, and K_3, where $K_1 < K_2 < K_3$. Define λ so that

$$\lambda = \frac{K_3 - K_2}{K_3 - K_1}$$

or

$$K_2 = \lambda K_1 + (1 - \lambda) K_3$$

For example, if $K_1 = 35$, $K_2 = 43$, and $K_3 = 45$, then $\lambda = 0.2$, as in the above example. In order to construct an asymmetric butterfly, for every K_2 call we write, we buy λ K_1 calls and $1 - \lambda$ K_3 calls.

You should verify that if you buy two 35-strike puts, sell ten 43-strike puts, and buy eight 45-strike puts, you duplicate the profit diagram in Figure 15.

CHAPTER SUMMARY

Puts are insurance against a price decline and calls are insurance against a price increase. Combining a long or short position in the asset with an offsetting position in options (for example, a long position in the asset is coupled either with a purchased put or written call) leads to the various possible positions and their equivalents in Table 7.

Buying a call and selling a put with the same strike price and time to expiration creates an obligation to buy the asset at expiration by paying the strike price. This is a synthetic forward. A synthetic forward must have the same cost in present value terms as a true forward. This observation leads to equation (1):

$$\text{Call}(K, T) - \text{Put}(K, T) = \text{PV}(F_{0,T} - K) \tag{1}$$

This relationship, called *put-call parity*, explains the difference in call and put premiums for otherwise identical options. It is one of the most important relationships in derivatives.

TABLE 7 Summary of equivalent positions from Section 1.

Position	Is Equivalent To	And Is Called
Index + Put	Zero-Coupon Bond + Call	Insured Asset (floor)
Index − Call	Zero-Coupon Bond − Put	Covered Written Call
−Index + Call	−Zero-Coupon Bond + Put	Insured Short (cap)
−Index − Put	−Zero-Coupon Bond − Call	Covered Written Put

FIGURE 16

Profit diagrams for positions discussed in the chapter: bull spread, collar, straddle, strangle, butterfly, and 2:1 ratio spread.

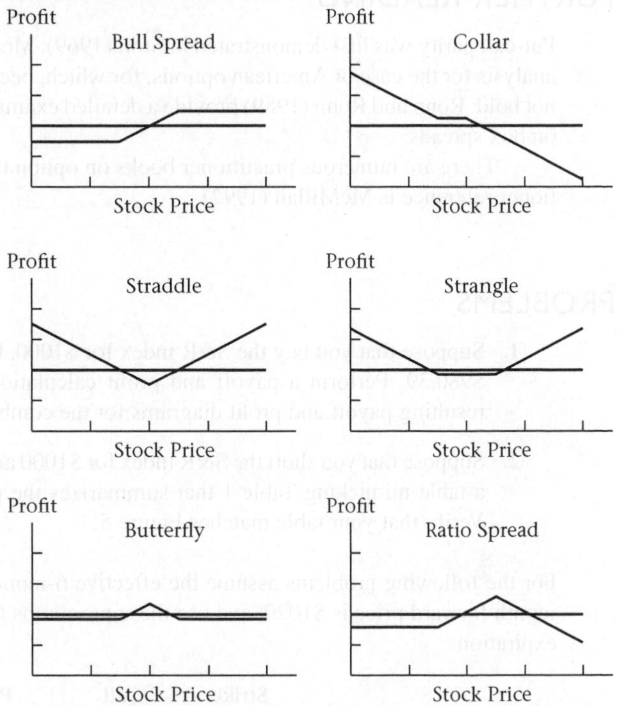

TABLE 8

Positions consistent with different views on the stock price and volatility direction.

	Volatility Will Increase	No Volatility View	Volatility Will Fall
Price will fall	Buy puts	Sell underlying	Sell calls
No price view	Buy straddle	Do nothing	Sell straddle
Price will increase	Buy calls	Buy underlying	Sell puts

There are numerous strategies that permit speculating on the direction of the stock or on the size of stock price moves (volatility). Some of these positions are summarized graphically in Figure 16. We also categorize in Table 8 various strategies according to whether they reflect bullish or bearish views on the stock price direction or volatility.[6]

6. Table 8 was suggested by David Shimko.

FURTHER READING

Put-call parity was first demonstrated in Stoll (1969). Merton (1973a) corrected the original analysis for the case of American options, for which, because of early exercise, parity need not hold. Ronn and Ronn (1989) provide a detailed examination of price bounds and returns on box spreads.

There are numerous practitioner books on option trading strategies. A classic practitioner reference is McMillan (1992).

PROBLEMS

1. Suppose that you buy the S&R index for $1000, buy a 1000-strike put, and borrow $980.39. Perform a payoff and profit calculation mimicking Table 1. Graph the resulting payoff and profit diagrams for the combined position.

2. Suppose that you short the S&R index for $1000 and sell a 1000-strike put. Construct a table mimicking Table 1 that summarizes the payoff and profit of this position. Verify that your table matches Figure 5.

For the following problems assume the effective 6-month interest rate is 2%, the S&R 6-month forward price is $1020, and use these premiums for S&R options with 6 months to expiration:

Strike	Call	Put
$950	$120.405	$51.777
1000	93.809	74.201
1020	84.470	84.470
1050	71.802	101.214
1107	51.873	137.167

3. Suppose you buy the S&R index for $1000 and buy a 950-strike put. Construct payoff and profit diagrams for this position. Verify that you obtain the same payoff and profit diagram by investing $931.37 in zero-coupon bonds and buying a 950-strike call.

4. Suppose you short the S&R index for $1000 and buy a 950-strike call. Construct payoff and profit diagrams for this position. Verify that you obtain the same payoff and profit diagram by borrowing $931.37 and buying a 950-strike put.

5. Suppose you short the S&R index for $1000 and buy a 1050-strike call. Construct payoff and profit diagrams for this position. Verify that you obtain the same payoff and profit diagram by borrowing $1029.41 and buying a 1050-strike put.

6. Verify that you earn the same profit and payoff by (a) buying the S&R index for $1000 and (b) buying a 950-strike S&R call, selling a 950-strike S&R put, and lending $931.37.

7. Verify that you earn the same profit and payoff by (a) shorting the S&R index for $1000 and (b) selling a 1050-strike S&R call, buying a 1050-strike put, and borrowing $1029.41.

8. Suppose the premium on a 6-month S&R call is $109.20 and the premium on a put with the same strike price is $60.18. What is the strike price?

9. Construct payoff and profit diagrams for the purchase of a 950-strike S&R call and sale of a 1000-strike S&R call. Verify that you obtain exactly the same *profit* diagram for the purchase of a 950-strike S&R put and sale of a 1000-strike S&R put. What is the difference in the payoff diagrams for the call and put spreads? Why is there a difference?

10. Construct payoff and profit diagrams for the purchase of a 1050-strike S&R call and sale of a 950-strike S&R call. Verify that you obtain exactly the same *profit* diagram for the purchase of a 1050-strike S&R put and sale of a 950-strike S&R put. What is the difference in the initial cost of these positions?

11. Suppose you invest in the S&R index for $1000, buy a 950-strike put, and sell a 1050-strike call. Draw a profit diagram for this position. What is the net option premium? If you wanted to construct a zero-cost collar keeping the put strike equal to $950, in what direction would you have to change the call strike?

12. Suppose you invest in the S&R index for $1000, buy a 950-strike put, and sell a 1107-strike call. Draw a profit diagram for this position. How close is this to a zero-cost collar?

13. Draw profit diagrams for the following positions:

a. 1050-strike S&R straddle.

b. Written 950-strike S&R straddle.

c. Simultaneous purchase of a 1050-strike straddle and sale of a 950-strike S&R straddle.

14. Suppose you buy a 950-strike S&R call, sell a 1000-strike S&R call, sell a 950-strike S&R put, and buy a 1000-strike S&R put.

a. Verify that there is no S&R price risk in this transaction.

b. What is the initial cost of the position?

c. What is the value of the position after 6 months?

d. Verify that the implicit interest rate in these cash flows is 2% over 6 months.

15. Compute profit diagrams for the following ratio spreads:

a. Buy 950-strike call, sell two 1050-strike calls.

b. Buy two 950-strike calls, sell three 1050-strike calls.

c. Consider buying n 950-strike calls and selling m 1050-strike calls so that the premium of the position is zero. Considering your analysis in (a) and (b), what can you say about n/m? What exact ratio gives you a zero premium?

16. In the previous problem we saw that a ratio spread can have zero initial premium. Can a bull spread or bear spread have zero initial premium? A butterfly spread? Why or why not?

17. Construct an asymmetric butterfly using the 950-, 1020-, and 1050-strike options. How many of each option do you hold? Draw a profit diagram for the position.

18. Verify that the butterfly spread in Figure 14 can be duplicated by the following transactions (use the option prices in Table 4):

a. Buy 35 call, sell two 40 calls, buy 45 call.

b. Buy 35 put, sell two 40 puts, buy 45 put.

c. Buy stock, buy 35 put, sell two 40 calls, buy 45 call.

19. Here is a quote from an investment website about an investment strategy using options:

> One strategy investors are applying to the XYZ options is using "synthetic stock." A synthetic stock is created when an investor simultaneously purchases a call option and sells a put option on the same stock. The end result is that the synthetic stock has the same value, in terms of capital gain potential, as the underlying stock itself. Provided the premiums on the options are the same, they cancel each other out so the transaction fees are a wash.

Suppose, to be concrete, that the premium on the call you buy is the same as the premium on the put you sell, and both have the same strikes and times to expiration.

a. What can you say about the strike price?

b. What term best describes the position you have created?

c. Suppose the options have a bid-ask spread. If you are creating a synthetic purchased stock and the net premium is zero *inclusive of the bid-ask spread*, where will the strike price be relative to the forward price?

d. If you create a synthetic short stock with zero premium inclusive of the bid-ask spread, where will the strike price be relative to the forward price?

e. Do you consider the "transaction fees" to really be "a wash"? Why or why not?

20. Construct a spreadsheet for which you can input up to five strike prices and quantities of put and call options bought or sold at those strikes, and which will automatically construct the total expiration payoff diagram for that position. Modify the spreadsheet to permit you to choose whether to graph a payoff or profit function.

Introduction to Risk Management

Business, like life, is inherently risky. Firms convert inputs such as labor, raw materials, and machines into goods and services. A firm is profitable if the cost of what it produces exceeds the cost of the inputs. Prices can change, however, and what appears to be a profitable activity today may not be profitable tomorrow. Many instruments are available that permit firms to hedge various risks, ranging from commodity prices to weather. A firm that actively uses derivatives and other techniques to alter its risk and protect its profitability is engaging in **risk management**. In this chapter we take a look at how derivatives—such as forwards, calls, and puts—are used in practice to manage risk.

We begin by examining two hypothetical firms—Golddiggers, a gold-mining firm, and Auric Enterprises, a manufacturer using gold as an input—to see what risks they face and to demonstrate the use of derivatives strategies to manage those risks. After looking at these examples, we will explore some reasons firms seek to manage risk in the first place.

1. BASIC RISK MANAGEMENT: THE PRODUCER'S PERSPECTIVE

Golddiggers is a gold-mining firm planning to mine and sell 100,000 ounces of gold over the next year. For simplicity, we will assume that they sell all of the next year's production precisely 1 year from today, receiving whatever the gold price is that day. The price of gold today is \$405/oz. We will ignore production beyond the next year.

Obviously Golddiggers—like any producer—hopes that the gold price will rise over the next year. However, Golddiggers's management computes estimated net income for a range of possible prices of gold in 1 year (Table 1). The net income calculation shows that Golddiggers's profit is affected by gold prices.

Should Golddiggers simply shut the mine if gold prices fall enough to make net income negative? The answer depends on the extent to which costs are fixed. The firm incurs the fixed cost whether or not it produces gold. Variable costs are incurred only if the mine operates. Thus, for any gold price above the variable cost of \$50/oz, it will make sense to produce gold.[1]

---

1. Suppose that the gold price is \$350/oz. If Golddiggers produces no gold, the firm loses its fixed cost, which we assume to be \$33,000,000. With production of 100,000 ounces, this is an average cost of \$330/oz.

From Chapter 4 of *Derivatives Markets*, Third Edition, Robert McDonald. Copyright © 2013 by Pearson Education, Inc. Published by Pearson Prentice Hall. All rights reserved.

TABLE 1 Golddiggers's estimated net income 1 year from today, unhedged.

Gold Price in One Year	Fixed Cost	Variable Cost	Net Income
\$350	−\$330	−\$50	−\$30
\$400	−\$330	−\$50	\$20
\$450	−\$330	−\$50	\$70
\$500	−\$330	−\$50	\$120

TABLE 2 Golddiggers's net income 1 year from today, hedged with a forward sale of gold.

Gold Price in One Year	Fixed Cost	Variable Cost	Profit on Short Forward	Net Income on Hedged Position
\$350	−\$330	−\$50	\$70	\$40
\$400	−\$330	−\$50	\$20	\$40
\$450	−\$330	−\$50	−\$30	\$40
\$500	−\$330	−\$50	−\$80	\$40

Hedging with a Forward Contract

Golddiggers can lock in a price for gold in 1 year by entering into a short forward contract, agreeing today to sell its gold for delivery in 1 year. Suppose that gold to be delivered in 1 year can be sold today for \$420/oz and that Golddiggers agrees to sell forward all of its gold production. We will assume in all examples that the forward contract settles financially. As noted earlier, the payoff to a forward is the same with physical or financial settlement.

Profit calculations when Golddiggers is hedged are summarized in Table 2. This table adds the profit on the forward contract to net income from Table 1. Figure 1 contains three curves showing the following:

- **Unhedged profit:** Since cost is \$380/oz, the line labeled "unhedged seller" shows zero profit at \$380, a loss at lower prices, and profit at higher prices. For example, at

---

If Golddiggers produces gold, the firm has a variable cost of \$50/oz in addition to the fixed cost. If the price is \$350/oz, the firm loses \$350 − (\$330 + \$50) = −\$30/oz. It is better to lose \$30/oz instead of \$330/oz, so Golddiggers will produce even when they have negative net income. If the gold price were to fall below the variable cost of \$50/oz, then it would make sense for Golddiggers to stop producing. For convenience we will refer to \$330/oz as the fixed cost, but note that this presumes a production level, in this case, 100,000 ounces.

FIGURE 1

Producer profit in 1 year, assuming hedging with a short forward contract at a forward price of $420/oz.

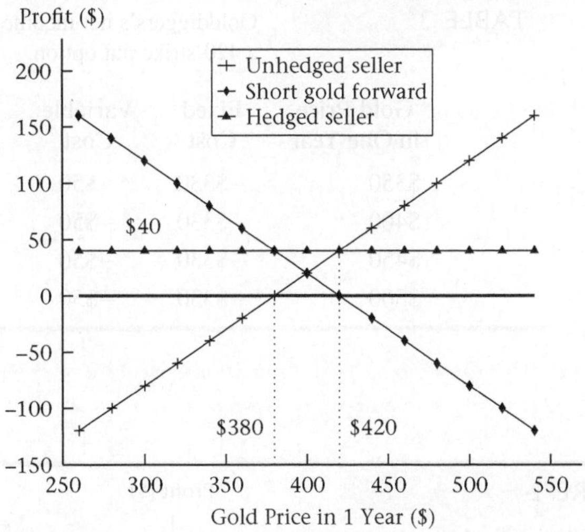

$420, profit is $40/oz. Since it has gold in the ground, Golddiggers has a long position in gold.

- **Profit on the short forward position:** The "short gold forward" line represents the profit from going short the gold forward contract at a forward price of $420/oz. We profit from locking in the price if prices are lower than $420, and we lose if prices are higher.
- **Hedged profit:** The line labeled "hedged seller" is the sum of the other two lines, adding them vertically at every gold price. It is flat at $40/oz, as we would expect from Table 2. A quick way to add the lines together is to notice that the "unhedged seller" graph has a positive slope of 1, and the "short gold forward" graph has a slope of −1. Added together vertically, the two graphs will have a slope of 0, so the only question is the height of the line. A profit calculation at a single point tells us that it must be at $40/oz.

Insurance: Guaranteeing a Minimum Price with a Put Option

A possible objection to hedging with a forward contract is that if gold prices do rise, Golddiggers will still receive only $420/oz; there is no prospect for greater profit. Gold insurance—i.e., a put option—provides a way to have higher profits at high gold prices while still being protected against low prices. Suppose that the market price for a 420-strike put is $8.77/oz.[2] This put provides a *floor* on the price.

2. This uses the Black-Scholes formula for the put price with inputs $S = 420$, $K = 420$, $r = 4.879\%$, $\sigma = 5.5\%$, $\delta = 4.879\%$, and $t = 1$ (year).

TABLE 3 Golddiggers's net income 1 year from today, hedged with a 420-strike put option.

Gold Price in One Year	Fixed Cost	Variable Cost	Profit on Put Option	Net Income
\$350	−\$330	−\$50	\$60.79	\$30.79
\$400	−\$330	−\$50	\$10.79	\$30.79
\$450	−\$330	−\$50	−\$9.21	\$60.79
\$500	−\$330	−\$50	−\$9.21	\$110.79

FIGURE 2

Comparison of unhedged position, 420-strike put option, and unhedged position plus 420-strike put.

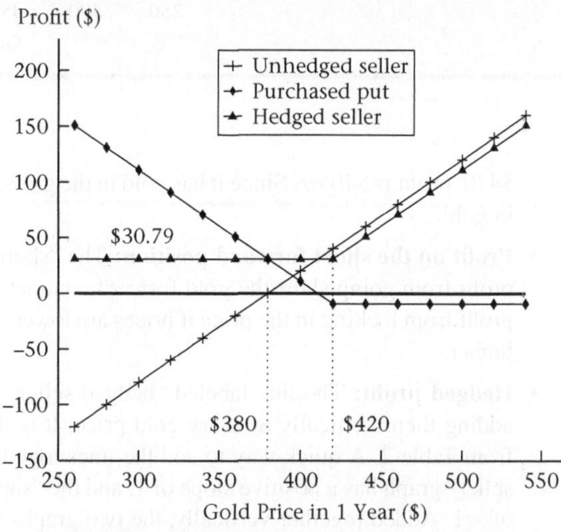

Since the put premium is paid 1 year prior to the option payoff, we must take into account interest cost when we compute profit in 1 year. The future value of the premium is $\$8.77 \times 1.05 = \$9.21$. As with the forward contract, we assume financial settlement, although physical settlement would yield the same net income.

Table 3 shows the result of buying this put. If the price is less than \$420, the put is exercised and Golddiggers sells gold for \$420/oz. less the cost of the put. This gives net income of \$30.79. If the price is greater than \$420, Golddiggers sells gold at the market price.

The insurance strategy—buying the put—performs better than shorting the forward if the price of gold in 1 year is more than \$429.21. Otherwise the short forward outperforms insurance. Figure 2 shows the unhedged position, profit from the put by itself, and the result of hedging with the put.

FIGURE 3

Comparison of payoffs for Golddiggers hedged with a forward contract and hedged with a put option.

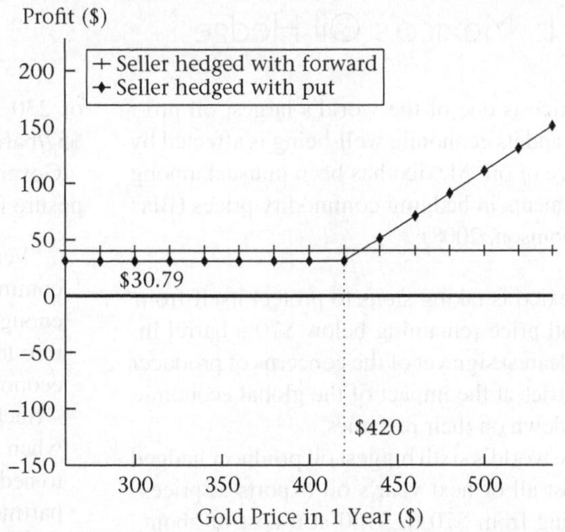

What this analysis does not address is the *probability* that the gold price in 1 year will be in different regions; that is, how likely is it that the gold price will exceed \$429.21? The price of the put option implicitly contains information about the likelihood that the gold price will exceed \$420, and by how much. The *probability distribution* of the gold price is a key factor determining the pricing of the put.

Figure 3 compares the profit from the two protective strategies we have examined: Selling a forward contract and buying a put. As you would expect, neither strategy is clearly preferable; rather, there are trade-offs, with each contract outperforming the other for some range of prices.

The fact that no hedging strategy always outperforms the other will be true of all fairly priced strategies. In practice, considerations such as transaction costs and market views are likely to govern the choice of a strategy. Box 1 discusses oil hedging by Mexico, and the attendant political risks of such a strategy.

Insuring by Selling a Call

With the sale of a call, Golddiggers receives a premium, which reduces losses, but the written call limits possible profits. One can debate whether this really constitutes insurance, but our goal is to see how the sale of a call affects the potential profit and loss for Golddiggers.

Suppose that instead of buying a put, Golddiggers sells a 420-strike call and receives an \$8.77 premium. Golddiggers in this case would be said to have sold a *cap*.

Figure 4 shows the profit to this strategy. If we compute the actual profit 1 year from today, we see that if the gold price in 1 year exceeds \$420, Golddiggers will show profits of

$$\$420 + \$9.21 - \$380 = \$49.21$$

That is, Golddiggers sells gold for \$420 (since the written call is exercised by the holder), receives the future value of the premium, and has a cost of \$380. If the price of

BOX 1: Mexico's Oil Hedge

Mexico is one of the world's largest oil producers and its economic well-being is affected by the price of oil. Mexico has been unusual among governments in hedging commodity prices (Blas and Thomson, 2008):

> Mexico is taking steps to protect itself from the oil price remaining below $70 a barrel in the clearest sign yet of the concerns of producer countries at the impact of the global economic slowdown on their revenues.
>
> The world's sixth biggest oil producer hedged almost all of next year's oil exports at prices ranging from $70 to $100 at a cost of about $1.5bn through derivatives contracts, according to bankers familiar with the deal.
>
> The cover is far higher than the country—which relies on oil for up to 40 per cent of government revenue—usually seeks. Last year, Mexico hedged 20–30 per cent of its exports.
>
> Mexico's finance ministry declined to comment but said in its latest quarterly report that its oil income stabilisation fund spent about $1.5bn on "financial investments, as part of the measures taken for risk management."
>
> Oil prices hit an all-time high of $147.27 a barrel in July but have since fallen to less than $65 as the global economy cools.

Global investment banks were counterparties for Mexico's trades, which earned it $5 billion. In 2009 Mexico also hedged its 2010 net exposure of 230 million barrels at an average price of $57/barrel (Williams, 2009).

Governments that hedge commodity price exposure face political risk (Blas, 2009):

> "Very few government officials of commodity-exporting countries are secure enough in their jobs to place a bet on the future level of commodity prices," wrote the oil economist Philip K. Verleger . . .
>
> Such political fears were plainly exposed when the state of Alaska discussed whether to hedge its oil income in 2002. The state's department of revenues warned that policymakers would "be reluctant to take the political risks" of a hedging programme.
>
> "If a programme succeeded, it is unlikely the policymakers who took the initiative to create the programme would be rewarded with public congratulations," the report said. "On the other hand, if the state lost significant sums . . . the conventional wisdom is that public criticism would be harsh," it concluded.
>
> The political risk also explains why the few countries or states that have launched sovereign oil hedging including Mexico and, in the past, Ecuador, Colombia, Algeria, Texas and Louisiana, have made use of put options—an insurance policy that sets a price floor without giving away any potential upside—rather than futures that fix a price.

Based on Blas & Thomas 2008, Williams 2009

gold is less than $420, Golddiggers will make

$$P_g + \$9.21 - \$380$$

On the downside, Golddiggers has exposure to gold but keeps the option premium.

By writing the call, Golddiggers keeps the $8.77 call premium and 1 year later makes $9.21 more than an unhedged gold seller. On the other hand, if the gold price exceeds $420, the call is exercised and the price Golddiggers receives is capped at $420. Thus, for gold prices above $429.21, an unhedged strategy has a higher payoff than that of writing a 420-

FIGURE 4

Comparison of Golddiggers hedging with sale of 420-strike call versus unhedged.

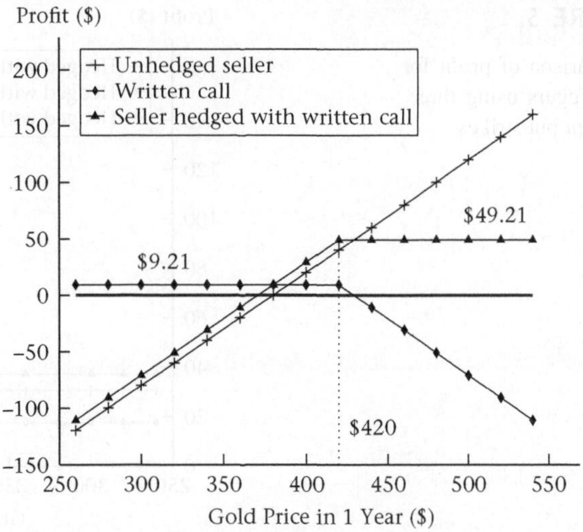

strike call. Also, for prices below $410.79, being fully hedged is preferable to having sold the call.

Adjusting the Amount of Insurance

Consider again Golddiggers's strategy of obtaining insurance against a price decline by purchasing a put option. A common objection to the purchase of insurance is that it is expensive. Insurance has a premium because it eliminates the risk of a large loss, while allowing a profit if prices increase. The cost of insurance reflects this asymmetry.

There are at least two ways to reduce the cost of insurance:

- Reduce the insured amount by lowering the strike price of the put option.
- Sell some of the gain.

Both of these strategies reduce the asymmetry between gains and losses, and hence lower the cost of insurance. The first strategy, lowering the strike price, permits some additional loss, while the second, selling some of the gain, puts a cap on the potential gain.

Reducing the strike price lowers the amount of insurance; therefore, the put option will have a lower premium. Figure 5 compares profit diagrams for Golddiggers's hedging using put options with strikes of $400 (premium = $2.21), $420 (premium = $8.77), and $440 (premium = $21.54). The 400-strike, low-premium option yields the highest profit if insurance is not needed (the price is high) and the lowest profit if insurance is needed (the price is low). The 440-strike, high-premium option yields the lowest profit if insurance is not needed, and the highest profit if insurance is needed.

The manager's view of the market and willingness to absorb risk will undoubtedly influence the choice among these alternatives. Managers optimistic about the price of gold will opt for low-strike-price puts, whereas pessimistic managers will more likely choose high-strike puts. While corporations *per se* may not be risk-averse, managers may be. Also,

FIGURE 5

Comparison of profit for Golddiggers using three different put strikes.

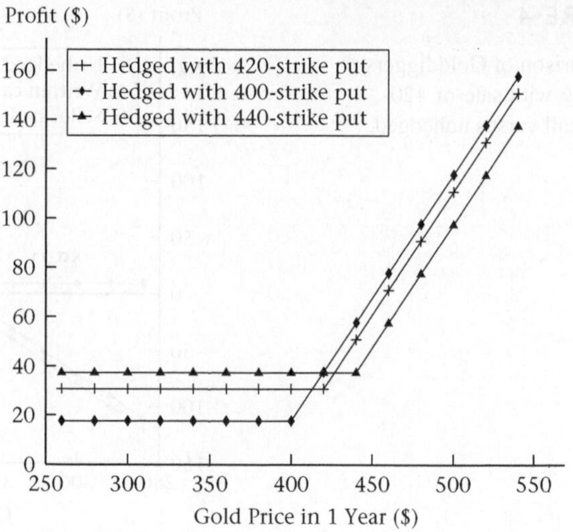

some managers may perceive losses to be costly in terms of the public's perception of the firm or the boss's perception of them.

This problem of choosing the appropriate strike price is not unique to corporate risk management. Safe drivers and more careful homeowners often reduce premiums by purchasing auto and homeowner's insurance with larger deductibles. This reflects their proprietary view of the likelihood that the insurance will be used. One important difference between gold insurance and property insurance, however, is that poor drivers would like smaller deductibles for their auto insurance; this differential demand by the quality of the insured is called *adverse selection* and is reflected in the premiums for different deductibles. A driver known to be good would face a lower premium for any deductible than a driver known to be bad. With gold, however, the price of the put is independent of who is doing the buying.[3]

2. BASIC RISK MANAGEMENT: THE BUYER'S PERSPECTIVE

Auric Enterprises is a manufacturer of widgets, a product that uses gold as an input. We will suppose for simplicity that the price of gold is the only uncertainty Auric faces. In particular, we assume that

- Auric sells each widget for a fixed price of $800, a price known in advance.
- The fixed cost per widget is $340.

3. You might think that a dealer would charge a higher price for a purchased option if the dealer knew that an option buyer had superior information about the market for gold. However, in general the dealer will quickly hedge the risk from the option and therefore has less concern than an ordinary investor about future movements in the price of gold.

TABLE 4 Auric estimated net income, unhedged, 1 year from today.

Revenue per Widget	Gold Price in 1 Year	Fixed Cost	Variable Cost	Net Income
\$800	\$350	\$340	\$0	\$110
\$800	\$400	\$340	\$0	\$60
\$800	\$450	\$340	\$0	\$10
\$800	\$500	\$340	\$0	−\$40

- The manufacture of each widget requires 1 oz of gold as an input.
- The nongold variable cost per widget is zero.
- The quantity of widgets to be sold is known in advance.

Because Auric makes a greater profit if the price of gold falls, Auric's gold position is implicitly short. As with Golddiggers, we will examine various risk-management strategies for Auric. The pro forma net income calculation for Auric is shown in Table 4.

Hedging with a Forward Contract

The forward price is \$420 as before. Auric can lock in a profit by entering into a long forward contract. Auric thereby guarantees a profit of

$$\text{Profit} = \$800 - \$340 - \$420 = \$40$$

Note that whereas Golddiggers was *selling* in the forward market, Auric is *buying* in the forward market. Thus, Golddiggers and Auric are natural *counterparties* in an economic sense. In practice, they need not be direct counterparties since they can enter into forward contracts through dealers or on exchanges. But in an economic sense, one firm's desire to sell forward has a counterpart in the other's desire to buy forward.

Figure 6 compares the profit diagrams for the unhedged buyer and a long forward position in gold. It also shows the profit for the hedged buyer, which is generated by summing up the forward position and the unhedged payoff. We see graphically that the buyer can lock in a profit of \$40/oz.

Insurance: Guaranteeing a Maximum Price with a Call Option

Rather than lock in a price unconditionally, Auric might like to pay \$420/oz if the gold price is greater than \$420/oz but pay the market price if it is less. Auric can accomplish this by buying a call option. As a future buyer, Auric is naturally short; hence, a call is insurance. Suppose the call has a premium of \$8.77/oz (recall that this is the same as the premium on the put with the same strike price). The future value of the premium is $\$8.77 \times 1.05 = \$9.21$.

If Auric buys the insurance contract, net income on the hedged position will be as shown in Table 5. If the price is less than \$420, the call is worthless at expiration and Auric

FIGURE 6

Profit diagrams for unhedged buyer, long forward, and buyer hedged with long forward.

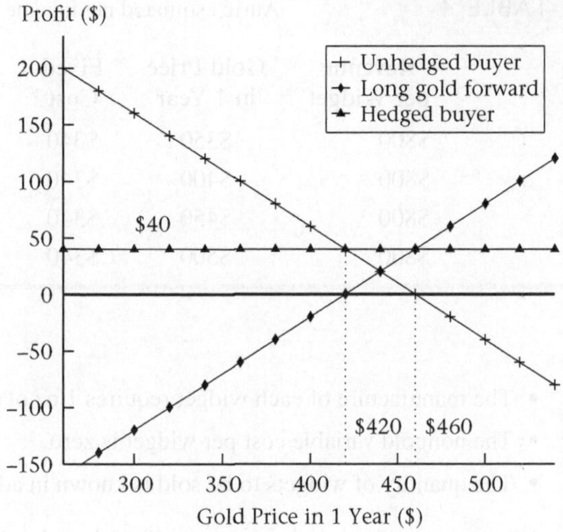

TABLE 5

Auric net income 1 year from today, hedged with 420-strike call option.

Gold Price in 1 Year	Unhedged Net Income from Table 4	Profit on Call Option	Net Income
$350	$110	−$9.21	$100.79
$400	$60	−$9.21	$50.79
$450	$10	$20.79	$30.79
$500	−$40	$70.79	$30.79

buys gold at the market price. If the price is greater than $420, the call is exercised and Auric buys gold for $420/oz, less the cost of the call. This gives a profit of $30.79.

If the price of gold in 1 year is less than $410.79, insuring the price by buying the call performs better than locking in a price of $420. At low prices, the option permits us to take advantage of lower gold prices. If the price of gold in 1 year is greater than $410.79, insuring the price by buying the call performs worse than locking in a price of $420 since we have paid the call premium.

Figure 7 shows the profit from the call by itself, along with the results of hedging with the call. As before, the graph does not show the *probability* that the gold price in 1 year will be in different regions; hence, we cannot evaluate the likelihood of different outcomes.

FIGURE 7

Comparison of profit for unhedged gold buyer, gold buyer hedged with call, and stand-alone call.

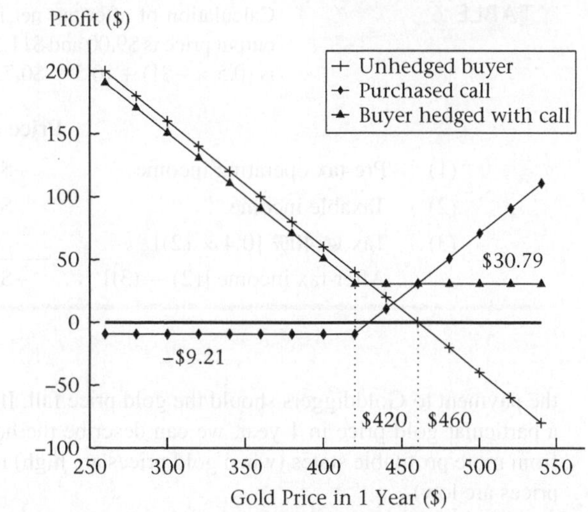

3. WHY DO FIRMS MANAGE RISK?

The Golddiggers and Auric examples illustrate how the two companies can use forwards, calls, and puts to reduce losses in case of an adverse gold price move, essentially insuring their future cash flows. Why would a firm use these strategies?

There are four reasons that firms might use derivatives: to hedge, to speculate, to reduce transaction costs, and to effect regulatory arbitrage. In practice, more than one of these considerations may be important. We have already discussed the fact that market views—for example, opinions about the future price of gold—can affect the choice of a hedging strategy. Thus, the choice of a hedging strategy can have a speculative component. Managers often cite the accounting treatment of a transaction as important, and transaction costs are obviously a consideration.

In this section we discuss why firms might hedge, ignoring speculation, transaction costs, and regulation (but we do consider taxes). It seems obvious that managers would want to reduce risk. However, in a world with fairly priced derivatives, no transaction costs, and no other market imperfections such as taxes, derivatives change the *distribution* of cash flows but do not increase the value of cash flows. Moreover, large publicly held firms are owned by diverse shareholders. These shareholders can, in theory, configure their own portfolios to bear risk optimally, suiting their own taste. In order to hedge, the firm must pay commissions and bid-ask spreads, and bear counterparty credit risk. Why incur these costs?

There are several reasons that firms might seek to manage risk. Before discussing them, let's think about what derivatives accomplish. To be concrete, suppose that Golddiggers sells gold forward at $420/oz. As we saw, this guarantees a net income of $40/oz.

When hedged with the forward, Golddiggers will have a profit of $40 whatever the price in 1 year. In effect, the value of the reduced profits, should the gold price rise, subsidizes

TABLE 6 Calculation of after-tax net income in states where the output price is \$9.00 and \$11.20. Expected after-tax income is $(0.5 \times -\$1) + (0.5 \times \$0.72) = -\$0.14$.

		Price = \$9	Price = \$11.20
(1)	Pre-tax operating income	−\$1	\$1.20
(2)	Taxable income	\$0	\$1.20
(3)	Tax @ 40% [0.4 × (2)]	0	\$0.48
	After-tax income [(2) − (3)]	−\$1	\$0.72

the payment to Golddiggers should the gold price fall. If we use the term "state" to denote a particular gold price in 1 year, we can describe the hedging strategy as shifting dollars from more profitable states (when gold prices are high) to less profitable states (when gold prices are low).

This shifting of dollars from high gold price states to low gold price states will have value for the firm *if the firm values the dollar more in a low gold price state than in a high gold price state*. Why might a firm value a dollar differently in different states?

An Example Where Hedging Adds Value

Consider a firm that produces one unit per year of a good costing \$10. Immediately after production, the firm receives a payment of either \$11.20 or \$9, with 50% probability. Thus, the firm has either a \$1.20 profit or a \$1 loss. On a pre-tax basis, the firm has an expected profit of

$$[0.5 \times (\$9 - \$10)] + [0.5 \times (\$11.20 - \$10)] = \$0.10$$

However, on an after-tax basis, the firm could have an expected loss.

For example, suppose that when the firm reports a profit, 40% of the profit is taxed, but when the firm reports a loss, it pays no taxes and receives no tax refund. Table 6 computes expected after-tax profit under these circumstances. The taxation of profits converts an expected \$0.10 pre-tax gain into an after-tax \$0.14 loss.[4] Because of taxes, the firm values a dollar of profit at \$0.60 (\$0.40 goes to the government), but values a dollar of loss at \$1. In this situation, it is desirable for the firm to trade pre-tax profits for pre-tax losses.

Suppose that there is a forward market for the firm's output, and that the forward price is \$10.10. If the firm sells forward, profit is computed as in Table 7. Instead of an expected loss of \$0.14, we obtain a certain profit of \$0.06. Hedging with a forward transfers net income from a less-valued to a more highly valued state, raising the expected value of cash flows.

Figure 8 depicts how the nondeductibility of losses affects after-tax cash flows. First, observe that after-tax profit (line ACB) is a concave function of the output price. (A **concave**

4. Problem 15 asks you to compute profit when losses are deductible.

TABLE 7 Calculation of hedged after-tax net income in states where the output price is \$9.00 and \$11.20. Expected after-tax income is \$0.06.

		Price = \$9	Price = \$11.20
(1)	Pre-tax operating income	−\$1.00	\$1.20
(2)	Income from short forward	\$1.10	−\$1.10
(3)	Taxable income [(1) + (2)]	\$0.10	\$0.10
(4)	Tax @ 40% [0.4 × (3)]	\$0.04	\$0.04
	After-tax income [(3) − (4)]	\$0.06	\$0.06

FIGURE 8

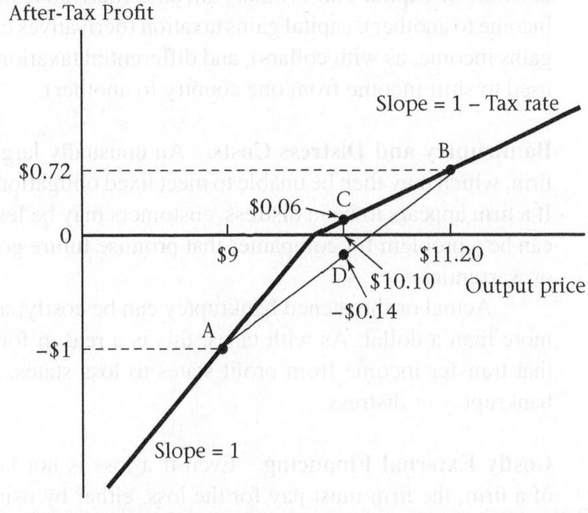

After-tax profit as a function of pre-tax profit. Point A is profit at a price of \$9 (−\$1.00), point B is profit at \$11.20 (\$0.72), point C is profit at \$10.10 (\$0.06), and point D is expected profit if price is \$9 or \$11.20 with one-half probability, −\$0.14.

function is one shaped like the cross section of an upside-down bowl.) When profits are concave, the expected value of profits is increased by reducing uncertainty. We can see this in the graph. If the price is certain to be \$10.10, then profit will be given by point C. However, if price can be either \$9 or \$11.20, expected profit is at point D, on the line ADB at the expected price of \$10.10. *Because ACB is concave, point D lies below point C, and hedging increases expected profits.*[5]

5. This is an illustration of *Jensen's inequality*.

Some of the hedging rationales we discuss hinge on there being concave profits, so that value is increased by reducing uncertainty.

Reasons to Hedge

There are in fact a number of reasons why losses might be more harmful than profits are beneficial. We now discuss some of those reasons.[6]

Taxes. The previous example illustrating the effect of taxes was oversimplified in assuming that losses are completely untaxed, but it *is* typically the case that governments tax profits but do not give full credits for losses. Tax systems usually permit a loss to be offset against a profit from a different year. However, in present value terms, the loss will have a lower effective tax rate than that applied to profits, which still generates a motive to hedge.

There are other aspects of the tax code that can encourage firms to shift income using derivatives; such uses may or may not appear to be hedging and may or may not be approved of by tax authorities. Tax rules that may entice firms to use derivatives include the separate taxation of capital and ordinary income (derivatives can be used to convert one form of income to another), capital gains taxation (derivatives can be used to defer taxation of capital gains income, as with collars), and differential taxation across countries (derivatives can be used to shift income from one country to another).

Bankruptcy and Distress Costs. An unusually large loss can threaten the survival of a firm, which may then be unable to meet fixed obligations, such as debt payments and wages. If a firm appears to be in distress, customers may be less willing to purchase its goods. This can be a problem for companies that promise future goods or services, such as airline seats or warranties.

Actual or threatened bankruptcy can be costly; a dollar of loss can cost the company more than a dollar. As with taxes, this is a reason for firms to enter derivatives contracts that transfer income from profit states to loss states, thereby reducing the probability of bankruptcy or distress.

Costly External Financing. Even if a loss is not large enough to threaten the survival of a firm, the firm must pay for the loss, either by using cash reserves or by raising funds externally (for example, by borrowing or issuing new securities).

Raising funds externally can be costly. There are explicit costs, such as bank and underwriting fees. There can also be implicit costs. If you borrow money, the lender may worry that you need to borrow because you are in decline, which increases the probability that you will not repay the loan. The lender will therefore raise the interest rate on the loan. For the same reason, you may be able to issue equity only at a reduced price.

At the same time, cash reserves are valuable because they reduce a firm's need to raise funds externally in the future. So if the firm uses cash to pay for a loss, the reduction in cash increases the probability that the firm will need costly external financing in the future.

The fact that external financing is costly can even lead the firm to forgo investment projects it would have taken had cash been available to use for financing.

6. The following are discussed in Smith and Stulz (1985) and Froot et al. (1994).

Thus, however the firm pays for the loss, a dollar of loss may actually cost the firm more than a dollar. Hedging can safeguard cash reserves and reduce the probability of costly external financing.

Increase Debt Capacity. Because of the deductibility of interest expense for tax purposes, firms may find debt to be a tax-advantaged way to raise funds.[7] However, lenders, fearful of bankruptcy, may be unwilling to lend to firms with risky cash flows. The amount that a firm can borrow is its **debt capacity**.

A firm that credibly reduces the riskiness of its cash flows should be able to borrow more, since for any given level of debt, bankruptcy is less likely. Such a firm is said to have raised its debt capacity. To the extent debt has a tax advantage, such a firm will also be more valuable.

Managerial Risk Aversion. While large, public firms are owned by well-diversified investors, firm managers are typically *not* well-diversified. Salary, bonus, and compensation options are all tied to the performance of the firm.

An individual who is unwilling to take a fair bet (i.e., one with an expected payoff equal to the money at stake) is said to be **risk-averse**. Risk-averse persons are harmed by a dollar of loss more than they are helped by a dollar of gain. Thus, they benefit from reducing uncertainty. The effect is analogous to that shown in Figure 8.

If managers are risk-averse and have wealth that is tied to the company, we might expect that they will try to reduce uncertainty. However, matters are not this simple: Managers are often compensated in ways that encourage them to take more risk. For example, options given to managers as compensation are more valuable, other things equal, when the firm's stock price is riskier. Thus, a manager's risk aversion may be offset by compensation that is more valuable if the firm is riskier.

Nonfinancial Risk Management. Firms make risk-management decisions when they organize and design a business. For example, suppose you plan to sell widgets in Europe. You can construct a plant in the United States and export to Europe, or you can construct the plant in Europe, in which case costs of construction, labor, interest rates, and other inputs will be denominated in the same currency as the widgets you sell. Exchange rate hedging, to take one example, would be unnecessary.

Of course, if you build in a foreign country, you will encounter the costs of doing business abroad, including dealing with different tax codes and regulatory regimes.

Risk can also be affected by such decisions as leasing versus buying equipment, which determines the extent to which costs are fixed. Firms can choose flexible production technologies that may be more expensive at the outset but which can be reconfigured at low cost. Risk is also affected by the decision to enter a particular line of business in the first place. Firms making computer mice and keyboards, for example, have to consider the possibility of lawsuits for repetitive stress injuries.

The point is that risk management is not a simple matter of hedging or not hedging using financial derivatives, but rather a series of decisions that start when the business is first conceived.

7. For a discussion of this issue, see Brealey et al. (2011, ch. 17).

Reasons *Not* to Hedge

There are also reasons why firms might elect not to hedge:

- Transacting in derivatives entails paying transaction costs, such as commissions and the bid-ask spread.
- The firm must assess costs and benefits of a given strategy; this can require costly expertise.
- The firm must monitor transactions and have managerial controls in place to prevent unauthorized trading.
- The firm must be prepared for tax and accounting consequences of their transactions. In particular, this may complicate reporting.

Thus, while there are reasons to hedge, there are also costs. When thinking about costs and benefits, keep in mind that some of what firms do could be called risk management but may not obviously involve derivatives. For example, suppose Auric enters into a 2-year agreement with a supplier to buy gold at a fixed price. Will management think of this as a derivative? In fact this is a derivative under current accounting standards (it is a swap), but it is exempt from derivatives accounting.[8] Finally, firms can face collateral requirements (the need to post extra cash with their counterparty) if their derivatives position loses money.

Periodically, firms appears in the news for their hedging successes or, more commonly, failures. Boxes 2 and 3 illustrate the challenges of managing corporate hedging programs.

Empirical Evidence on Hedging

We know surprisingly little about the risk-management practice and derivatives use of firms in real life. It is difficult to tell, from publicly available information, the extent to which firms use derivatives. Beginning in 2000, Statement of Financial Accounting Standards (SFAS) 133 required firms to recognize derivatives as assets or liabilities on the balance sheet, to measure them at fair value, and to report changes in their market value.[9] This reporting does not necessarily reveal a firm's hedging position (forward contracts have zero value, for example). Prior to 2000, firms had to report notional exposure; hence, much existing evidence relies on data from the 1990s.

Research tries to address two questions: How much do firms use derivatives and why? *Financial* firms—commercial banks, investment banks, broker-dealers, and other financial institutions—transact in derivatives frequently. Risks are identifiable, and regulators encourage risk management. The more open question is the extent to which *nonfinancial* firms use derivatives. We can summarize research findings as follows:

- Roughly half of nonfinancial firms report using derivatives, with usage greater among large firms (Bodnar et al., 1998; Bartram et al., 2004).

---

8. Current derivatives accounting rules contain a "normal purchases and sales" exemption. Firms need not use derivatives accounting for forward contracts with physical delivery, for quantities likely to be used or sold over a reasonable period in the normal course of business.

9. See Gastineau et al. (2001) for a discussion of SFAS 133 and previous accounting rules.

BOX 2: Ford: A Hedge Too Far

Ford Motor Co. stunned investors in January 2002 when it announced a $1 billion write-off on stockpiles of palladium, a precious metal Ford used in catalytic converters (devices that reduce polluting emissions from cars and trucks). Ironically, Ford sustained the loss while attempting to actively manage palladium risk.

According to the *Wall Street Journal* (see Gregory L. White, "A Mismanaged Palladium Stockpile Was Catalyst for Ford's Write-Off," February 6, 2002, p. A1), Ford in the late 1980s had begun to use palladium as a replacement for platinum. Palladium prices were steady until 1997, when Russia, a major supplier with a large stockpile of palladium, withheld supply from the market. Prices more than doubled to $350/oz at a time when Ford was planning to increase its use of the metal. By early 2000, prices had doubled again, to $700. While GM had begun work several years earlier to reduce reliance on palladium, Ford continued to rely heavily on the metal.

In 2000, Ford management agreed to allow the purchasing staff to stockpile palladium. The purchasing staff evidently did not communicate with Ford's treasury department, which had hedging experience. Thus, for example, Ford did not buy puts to protect against a drop in palladium prices. The purchasing staff also did not communicate with Ford's research department, which was working to reduce reliance on palladium. Ford continued to buy palladium in 2001 as prices exceeded $1000. However, by the middle of the year, palladium prices had fallen to $350.

By the end of 2001, Ford had developed technology that would eventually reduce the need for palladium by 50%. The year-end price of palladium was $440/oz.

As a result of this experience, "Ford has instituted new procedures to ensure that treasury-department staffers with experience in hedging are involved in any major commodities purchases in the future, [Ford Chief Financial Officer Martin] Inglis says."

- Among firms that do use derivatives, less than 25% of perceived risk is hedged, with firms likelier to hedge short-term risks (Bodnar et al., 1998).
- Firms with more investment opportunities are likelier to hedge (Géczy et al., 1997).
- Firms that use derivatives may have a higher market value (Allayannis and Weston, 2001; Allayannis et al., 2004; Bartram et al., 2004; Carter et al., 2006; MacKay and Moeller, 2007), more leverage (Graham and Rogers, 2002; Haushalter, 2000), and lower interest costs (Campello et al., 2010).[10] Jin and Jorion (2006), however, find that hedging firms do not have a higher market value.

Guay and Kothari (2003) obtain many similar results but conclude that for most firms, derivatives use is of minor economic significance. In their sample of large firms, slightly more than half report derivatives usage. Among derivatives users, the authors estimate that the *median* firm hedges only about 3% to 6% of exposure to interest rates and exchange rates. Bartram et al. (2009) examine annual reports from over 7000 international companies to link

10. Graham and Smith (1999) find that after-tax profits are concave for a majority of firms, as in Figure 8. However, Graham and Rogers (2002) are unable to find a link between hedging and tax-induced concavity.

BOX 3: Hedging Jet Fuel: Southwest Airlines

Southwest Airlines is well known for systematically hedging the cost of jet fuel. In the 1990s, fuel on average accounted for 10–15% of Southwest's operating costs (Carter et al., 2004). In recent years, fuel costs have been as much as a quarter of operating expenses. Since fuel costs have risen over the last decade, Southwest has benefited from hedging. In its 2005 quarterly financial reports, for example, Southwest reported savings from its hedge program of $155, $196, $295, and $258 million, against net income of $75, $159, $227, and $86 million. Clearly, fuel hedging was important for Southwest's profitability.

Southwest uses cross-hedges to hedge jet fuel, and hedges a significant portion of its future projected fuel needs. Here is what Southwest said about its hedging program in its 3rd quarter 2006 financial statement:

> The Company endeavors to acquire jet fuel at the lowest possible cost. Because jet fuel is not traded on an organized futures exchange, liquidity for hedging is limited. However, the Company has found commodities for hedging of jet fuel costs, primarily crude oil, and refined products such as heating oil and unleaded gasoline. . . . The Company currently has a mixture of purchased call options, collar structures, and fixed price swap agreements in place to protect against over 85 percent of its remaining 2006 total anticipated jet fuel requirements . . .

Southwest also stated that it had hedged 85% of expected fuel purchases for 2007, over 43% for 2008, with smaller positions as far out as 2012.

A company that hedges the price of inputs can lose if prices fall. From the *New York Times*, October 17, 2008:

> Southwest Airlines said Thursday that it lost $120 million in the third quarter, its first quarterly loss in more than 17 years, because of a noncash charge to write down the declining value of its hedging contracts.
>
> The airline took a one-time charge of $247 million, reflecting the decline in oil prices, which hit record high levels in July. The last time Southwest lost money was in the first quarter of 1991.
>
> Without the charge, Southwest said it would have earned $69 million. . . .
>
> "It's like you can't win," said Betsy J. Snyder, an industry analyst with Standard & Poor's Ratings Services. "People bother you when you don't hedge, and when you do, and prices go down, you get hit."

Excerpts from New York Times Oct 17, 2008 and Southwest's 2006 Financial Statement.

firm characteristics and derivatives usage. They argue that it is hard to test specific hedging theories because derivatives use is only one of many firm decisions that affect financial risk.

Because data are hard to obtain, some studies have focused on particular industries and even firms. Tufano (1996), Petersen and Thiagarajan (2000), and Brown et al. (2003) have examined hedging behavior by gold-mining firms. Using a uniquely detailed data set, Tufano found that most gold firms use some derivatives, with the median firm in his sample (North American firms) selling forward about 25% of 3-year production. Fifteen percent of firms used no derivatives. Brown et al. found substantial variation over time in the amount of hedging by gold firms. Firms tended to increase hedging as the price rose, and managers reported that they adjusted hedges based on their views about gold prices.

TABLE 8 Call and put premiums for gold options.

Strike Price	Put Premium	Call Premium
440	21.54	2.49
420	8.77	8.77
400	2.21	21.26

Note: These prices are computed using the Black formula for options on futures, with a futures price of \$420, effective annual interest rate of 5%, volatility of 5.5%, and 1 year to expiration.

The currency-hedging operations of a U.S.-based manufacturing firm are examined in detail by Brown (2001), who finds that foreign exchange hedging is an integral part of firm operations, but the company has no clear rationale for hedging. For example, Brown reports one manager saying, "We do not take speculative positions, but the extent we are hedged depends on our views." Bartram (2008) investigates in depth one large German firm and also finds that hedging reduces currency exposure. Faulkender (2005) finds consistent evidence for interest-rate hedging in the chemical industry. These firms increase exposure to short-term interest rates as the yield curve becomes more upward-sloping,[11] but correlations between cash flows and interest rates do not affect behavior.

The varied evidence suggests that some use of derivatives is common, especially at large firms, but the evidence is weak that economic theories explain hedging.

4. GOLDDIGGERS REVISITED

We have looked at simple hedging and insurance strategies for buyers and sellers. We now examine some additional strategies that permit tailoring the amount and cost of insurance. For simplicity we will focus primarily on Golddiggers; however, in every case there are analogous strategies for Auric.

Table 8 lists premiums for three calls and puts on gold with 1 year to expiration and three different strikes. The examples use these values.

Selling the Gain: Collars

As discussed earlier, we can reduce the cost of insurance by reducing potential profit, i.e., by selling our right to profit from high gold prices. We can do this by selling a call. If the gold price is above the strike on the call, we are contractually obligated to sell at the strike. This caps our profits, in exchange for an initial premium payment.

A 420–440 Collar. Suppose that Golddiggers buys a 420-strike put option for \$8.77 and sells a 440-strike call option for a premium of \$2.49. If the price of gold in 1 year is \$450/oz,

11. An upward-sloping yield curve means that long-term bond yields are greater than short-term bond yields. This appears to make short-term financing less expensive. However, if a company hedges all of its future short-term financing costs, long-term and short-term financing will cost the same.

FIGURE 9

Net profit at expiration resulting from buying a 420-strike put with premium of \$8.77 and selling a 440-strike call with premium of \$2.49. The profit for gold prices between \$420 and \$440 is (\$2.49 − \$8.77) × 1.05 = −\$6.60.

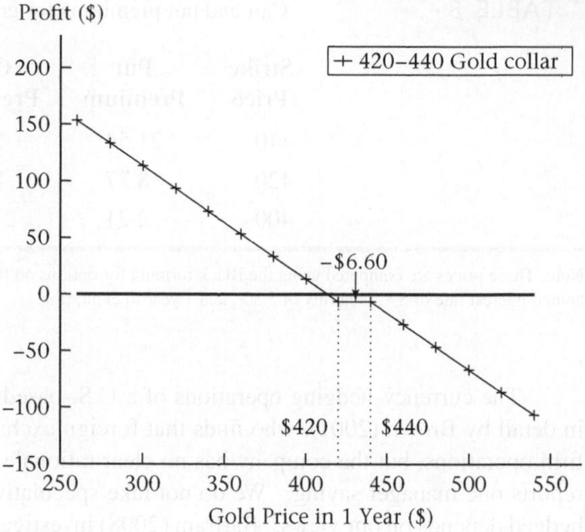

the call owner will exercise and Golddiggers is obligated to sell gold at the strike price of \$440, rather than the market price of \$450. The \$2.49 premium Golddiggers received initially compensates them for the possibility that this will happen.

Figure 9 depicts the combination of the purchased put and written call, while Figure 10 shows the two profit diagrams for Golddiggers hedged with a 420-strike put, as opposed to hedged with a 420-strike put plus writing a 440-strike call.

Note that the 420–440 collar still entails paying a premium. The 420 put costs \$8.77, and the 440 call yields a premium of only \$2.49. Thus, there is a net expenditure of \$6.28. It is probably apparent, though, that we can tinker with the strike prices and pay a still lower net premium, including zero premium, if we wish. The trade-off is that the payoff on the collar becomes less attractive as we lower the required premium.

A Zero-Cost Collar. To construct a zero-cost collar, we could argue as follows: A 400-strike put and a 440-strike call are equally distant from the forward price of \$420. This equivalence suggests that the options should have approximately the same premium. As we can see from the table of premiums for different strike options, the 400-strike put has a premium of \$2.21, while the 440-strike call has a premium of \$2.49. The net premium we would *receive* from buying this collar is thus \$0.28. We can construct a true zero-cost collar by slightly changing the strike prices, making the put more expensive (raising the strike) and the call less expensive (also raising the strike). With strikes of \$400.78 for the put and \$440.78 for the call, we obtain a premium of \$2.355 for both options.

In reality this zero-cost collar of width 40 would be sold at lower strike prices than \$400.78 and \$440.78. The reason is that there is a bid-ask spread: Dealers are willing to buy a given option at a low price and sell it at a high price.

The purchased put will be bought at the dealer's offer price and the call will be sold at the bid. The dealer can earn this spread in either of two ways: selling the 400.78–440.78 collar and charging an explicit transaction fee, or lowering the strike prices appropriately

FIGURE 10

Comparison of Golddiggers hedged with 420-strike put versus hedged with 420-strike put and written 440-strike call (420–440 collar).

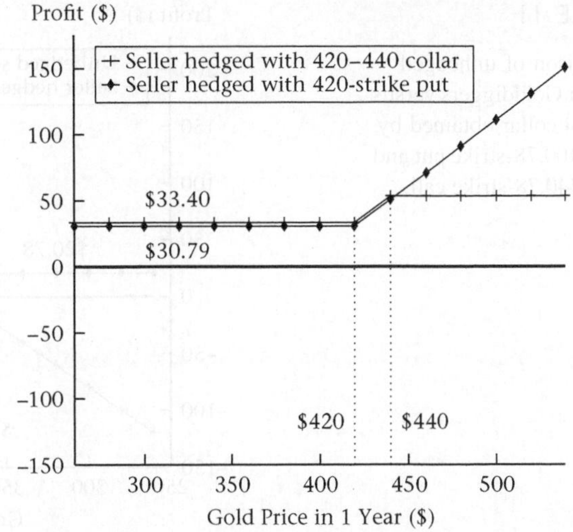

and charging a zero transaction fee. Either way, the dealer earns the fee. One of the tricky aspects of the more complicated derivatives is that it is relatively easy for dealers to embed fees that are invisible to the buyer. Of course a buyer can mitigate this problem by always seeking quotes from different dealers.

We can examine the payoffs by considering separately the three interesting regions of gold prices:

Price of gold < $400.78: In this region, Golddiggers can sell gold for $400.78 by exercising the put option.

Price of gold between $400.78 and $440.78: In this region, Golddiggers can sell gold at the market price.

Price of gold > $440.78: In this region, Golddiggers sells gold at $440.78. It has sold a call, so the owner of the call will exercise. This forces Golddiggers to sell gold to the call owner for the strike price of $440.78.

Figure 11 graphs the zero-cost collar against the unhedged position. Notice that between $400.78 and $440.78, the zero-cost collar graph is coincident with the unhedged profit. Above the 440.78-strike the collar provides profit of $60.78, and below the 400.78-strike, the collar provides profit of $20.78.

The Forward Contract as a Zero-Cost Collar. Because the put and call with strike prices of $420 have the same premiums, we could also construct a zero-cost collar by buying the $420-strike put and selling the $420-strike call. If we do this, here is what happens:

Price of gold < $420: Golddiggers will exercise the put option, selling gold at the price of $420.

Price of gold > $420: Golddiggers has sold a 420-strike call. The owner of that call will exercise, obligating Golddiggers to sell gold for $420.

FIGURE 11

Comparison of unhedged profit for Golddiggers versus zero-cost collar obtained by buying 400.78-strike put and selling 440.78-strike call.

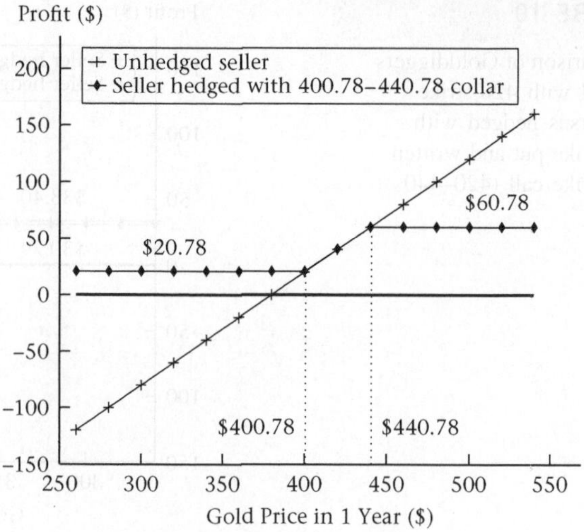

In either case, Golddiggers sells gold at $420. Thus, the "420–420 collar" is exactly like a forward contract. By buying the put and selling the call at the same strike price, Golddiggers has synthetically created a short position in a forward contract. Since a short forward and 420–420 collar have the same payoff, they must cost the same. *This is why the premiums on the 420-strike options are the same.*

Synthetic Forwards at Prices Other Than $420. We can easily extend this example to understand the relationship between option premiums at other strike prices. In the previous example, Golddiggers created a synthetic forward sale at $420. You might think that you could benefit by creating a synthetic forward contract at a higher price such as $440. Other things being equal, you would rather sell at $440 than $420. To accomplish this you buy the 440 put and sell the 440 call. However, there is a catch: The 440-strike put is in-the-money and the 440-strike call is out-of-the-money. Since we would be buying the expensive option and selling the inexpensive option, we have to pay a premium.

How much is it worth to Golddiggers to be able to lock in a selling price of $440 instead of $420? Obviously, it is worth $20 1 year from today, or $20 ÷ (1.05) = $19.05 in present value terms. Since locking in a $420 price is free, it should therefore be the case that we pay $19.05 in net premium in order to lock in a $440 price. In fact, looking at the prices of the 440-strike put and call in Table 8, we have premiums of $21.54 for the put and $2.49 for the call. This gives us

$$\text{Net premium} = \$21.54 - \$2.49 = \$19.05$$

Similarly, suppose Golddiggers explored the possibility of locking in a $400 price for gold in 1 year. Obviously, Golddiggers would require compensation to accept a lower price. In fact, they would need to be paid $19.05—the present value of $20—today.

Again we compute the option premiums and see that the 400-strike call sells for $21.26 while the 400-strike put sells for $2.21. Again we have

$$\text{Net premium} = \$2.21 - \$21.26 = -\$19.05$$

Golddiggers in this case receives the net premium for accepting a lower price.

Other Collar Strategies

Collar-type strategies are quite flexible. We have focused on the case where the firm buys one put and sells one call. However, it is also possible to deal with fractional options. For example, consider the 400.78–440.78 collar above. We could buy one put to obtain full downside protection, and we could vary the strike price of the call by selling fractional calls at strike prices other than $440.78. For example, we could lower the call strike price below $440.78, in which case we would obtain a higher premium per call. To offset the higher premium, we could sell less than one call. The trade-off is that we cap the gold price on part of production at a lower level, but we maintain some participation at any price above the strike.

Alternatively, we could raise the cap level (the strike price on the call) and sell more than one call. This would increase participation in gold price increases up to the cap level, but also have the effect of generating a net short position in gold if prices rose above the cap.

Paylater Strategies

A disadvantage to buying a put option is that Golddiggers pays the premium even when the gold price is high and insurance was, after the fact, unnecessary. One strategy to avoid this problem is a **paylater** strategy, where the premium is paid only when the insurance is needed. While it is possible to construct exotic options in which the premium is paid only at expiration and only if the option is in the money, the strategy we discuss here is a ratio spread using ordinary put options. The goal is to find a strategy where if the gold price is high, there is no net option premium. If the gold price is low, there is insurance, but the effective premium is greater than with an ordinary insurance strategy.

If there is no premium when the gold price is high, we must have no initial premium. This means that we must sell at least one option. Consider the following strategy for Golddiggers: Sell a 434.6-strike put and buy two 420-strike puts. Using our assumptions, the premium on the 434.6-strike put is $17.55, while the premium on the 420-strike put is $8.77. Thus, the net option premium from this strategy is $\$17.55 - (2 \times \$8.775) = 0$.

Figure 12 depicts the result of Golddiggers's hedging with a paylater strategy. When the price of gold is greater than $434.60, neither put is exercised, and Golddiggers's profit is the same as if it were unhedged. When the price of gold is between $420 and $434.60, because of the written $434.60 put, the firm loses $2 of profit for every $1 decline in the price of gold. Below $420 the purchased 420-strike puts are exercised, and profit becomes constant. The net result is an insurance policy that is not paid for unless it is needed.

Also depicted in Figure 12 is the familiar result from a conventional insurance strategy of hedging by purchasing a single 420-strike put. When the gold price is high, the paylater strategy with a zero premium outperforms the single put. When the gold price is low, the paylater strategy does worse because it offers less insurance. Thus, the premium is paid later, if insurance is needed.

FIGURE 12

Depiction of "paylater" strategy, in which Golddiggers sells a 434.6-strike put and buys two 420-strike puts, compared to the conventional insurance strategy of buying a 420-strike put.

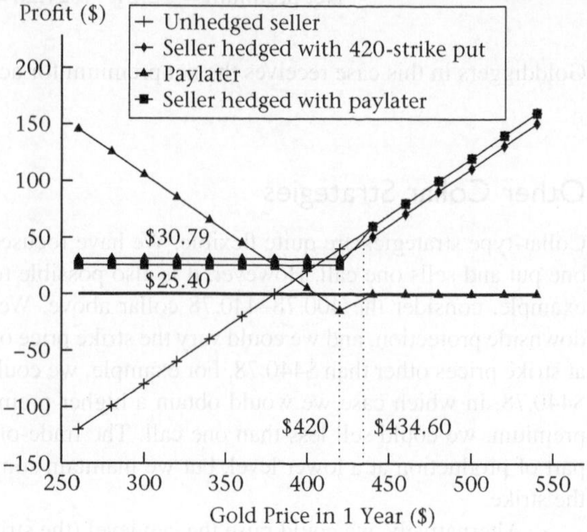

5. SELECTING THE HEDGE RATIO

In the Golddiggers and Auric examples, we performed all calculations in terms of one unit of gold and made two important assumptions. First, we assumed perfect correlation between the price of gold and the price of what each company wants to hedge. Second, we assumed that the companies knew for certain the quantity of gold they would sell and buy. As a result of these assumptions, we effectively assumed that the hedge ratio is 1, where the **hedge ratio** is defined as the ratio of the forward position to the underlying asset.

In practice, neither assumption may be valid. We first examine the effect of widget price uncertainty on hedging, and discuss *cross-hedging*. We then examine *quantity uncertainty* using an agricultural example.

Cross-Hedging

In the Auric example we assumed that widget prices are fixed. However, since gold is used to produce widgets, widget prices might vary with gold prices. If widget and gold prices vary one-for-one, Auric's profits would be independent of the price of gold and Auric would have no need to hedge.[12]

More realistically, the price of widgets could change with the price of gold, but not one-for-one; other factors could affect widget prices as well. In this case, Auric might find it helpful to use gold derivatives to hedge the price of the widgets it sells as well as the price of the gold it buys. Using gold to hedge widgets would be an example of **cross-hedging**: the use of a derivative on one asset to hedge another asset. Cross-hedging arises in many different contexts.

12. "One-for-one" in this context means that if the price of gold rises by $1, the price of a widget rises by $1 times the amount of gold used to make the widget.

The hedging problem for Auric is to hedge the *difference* in the price of widgets and gold. Conceptually, we can think of hedging widgets and gold separately, and then combining those separate hedges into one net hedge.

We now generalize the Auric example. Suppose that we can produce one widget with λ ounces of gold. If we produce N_w widgets at a price of P_w and do not hedge, profit is

$$\text{Profit} = N_w P_w - \lambda N_w P_g \tag{1}$$

where P_g is the future spot price of gold.

Now suppose that we hedge by going long H gold futures contracts, with each contract covering q oz of gold. If F is the gold forward price, the profit on the hedged position is

$$\begin{aligned}\text{Hedged profit} &= N_w P_w - \lambda N_w P_g + Hq(P_g - F)\\ &= N_w P_w + (Hq - \lambda N_w) P_g - HqF\end{aligned}$$

The variance of hedged profit is

$$\sigma^2_{\text{hedged}} = N_w^2 \sigma_w^2 + (Hq - \lambda N_w)^2 \sigma_g^2 + 2N_w(Hq - \lambda N_w)\rho\sigma_w\sigma_g \tag{2}$$

where σ_w is the standard deviation of the widget price, σ_g is the standard deviation of the gold price, and ρ is the price correlation between widgets and gold. The covariance between widget and gold prices is $\rho\sigma_w\sigma_g$.

We can select H in equation (2) so as to minimize the variance of hedged profit. The variance-minimizing hedge position, H^*, satisfies[13]

$$qH^* = \lambda N_w - N_w \frac{\rho\sigma_w}{\sigma_g} \tag{3}$$

Equation (3) has a straightforward interpretation. The first term on the right-hand side hedges the cost of buying gold: To produce N_w widgets, we must purchase λN_w ounces of gold. We go long this amount. However, if the price of widgets varies with the price of gold we need to take this into account. The second term on the right-hand side, $N_w\rho\sigma_w/\sigma_g$, measures the comovement between widget revenue and gold. The term $\rho\sigma_w/\sigma_g$ would typically be referred to as the hedge ratio for hedging widgets with gold.[14] The hedge ratio times the number of widgets, N_w, gives us the number of gold contracts to short for the purpose of hedging widget price risk. The net number of gold futures, H^*, is the difference in the number of contracts needed to hedge gold inputs and widget outputs.

13. This can be derived by differentiating equation (2) with respect to H.

14. The term $\rho\sigma_w/\sigma_g$ is often measured as the slope coefficient, β, in a linear regression. A common approach is to regress price changes on price changes:

$$P_{w,t} - P_{w,t-1} = \alpha + \beta(P_{g,t} - P_{g,t-1}) + u_t$$

where the subscript t denotes the value at time t. Other specifications, including the use of percentage changes, or regressing levels on levels, are possible. The correct regression to use depends on context. In general, regressions using changes are more likely to give a correct hedge coefficient since the goal of the hedge is to have changes in the price of the asset matched by changes in futures price. Regressions of level on level are problematic in many contexts. For example, in the case of stocks, asset pricing models tell us that stock *returns* are related, but we would not expect a stable relationship between two *prices*. The appropriate regression is returns on returns. A comprehensive discussion is Siegel and Siegel (1990, pp. 114–135).

Example 1. Suppose that a firm produces $N_w = 350$ widgets; that each widget requires as an input $\lambda = 0.5$ oz of gold; and that $\sigma_w = 0.15$, $\sigma_g = 0.25$, and $\rho = 0.8$. Suppose further that a gold futures contract calls for delivery of $q = 5$ oz of gold. Applying equation (3), we have

$$5H^* = 0.5 \times 350 - 350\frac{0.8 \times 0.15}{0.25} = 7$$

We go long 7 oz of gold, or $H = 1.4$ contracts. ■

We can parse Example 1 to understand the hedge calculation. Producing 350 widgets requires 175 ($= 0.5 \times 350$) oz of gold. If widget prices were uncorrelated with gold ($\rho = 0$), we would go long 175 oz, which is a long position in 35 contracts (each contract covering 5 oz). However, with $\rho = 0.8$, if the price of gold rises, we pay more for gold but we also receive a higher price for widgets. The second term on the right-hand side of equation (3) tells us that this offsetting effect of higher widget prices reduces the required position by 168 oz. The net result is that we go long 7 oz of gold to hedge profit.

When we hedge with H^* futures, σ^2_{hedged} is obtained by substituting H^* into equation (2):

$$\sigma^2_{\text{hedged}} = N_w^2 \sigma_w^2 \left(1 - \rho^2\right) \tag{4}$$

The uncertainty remaining in the hedged position is due to **basis risk**, which is risk due to the hedging instrument (gold) and the hedged price (widgets) not moving as predicted. The variance of profits ultimately depends upon the ability to hedge the price of widgets, which, since we are using gold to hedge, depends on the correlation, ρ, between widgets and gold. The larger that ρ is, the less is basis risk.

You can see in equation (4) that if $|\rho| = 1$, $\sigma^2_{\text{hedged}} = 0$. However, if $|\rho| \neq 1$, variance will be positive. The optimal hedge strategy will then depend upon how the hedger evaluates the residual risk and return from the imperfectly hedged position. In this case a common benchmark is the hedge that minimizes σ^2_{hedged}. Many other hedging strategies are possible, however. For a discussion of the different strategies and a review of the literature, see (Chen et al., 2003).

In this section we have shown that the ability to cross-hedge depends upon the correlation between the hedging instrument and the asset being hedged, and that we can determine the hedging amount as a regression coefficient. The same analysis obtains when we use stock index futures contracts to cross-hedge a stock portfolio.

Quantity Uncertainty

The quantity a firm produces and sells may vary with the prices of inputs or outputs. When this happens, using the "obvious" hedge ratio (for example, by hedging the expected quantity of an input) can increase rather than decrease risk. In this section we examine quantity uncertainty.

Agricultural producers commonly face quantity uncertainty because crop size is affected by factors such as weather and disease. Moreover, we expect there to be a correlation between quantity and price, because good weather gives rise to bountiful harvests. What

TABLE 9 Three scenarios illustrating different correlations between price and quantity for an agricultural producer. Each row is equally likely. In scenario A, there is no quantity uncertainty. In scenario B, quantity is negatively correlated with price, and in scenario C, quantity is positively correlated with price.

	Production Scenario		
Corn Price ($)	A (Uncorrelated)	B (Negative correlation)	C (Positive correlation)
3	1.0m	1.0m	1.5m
3	1.0m	0.6m	0.8m
2	1.0m	1.5m	1.0m
2	1.0m	0.8m	0.6m

quantity of forward contracts should a corn producer enter into to minimize the variability of revenue?

We will look at three examples of different relationships between price and quantity: the benchmark case where quantity is certain, an example where quantity and price are negatively correlated, and an example where quantity and price are positively correlated.[15]

In all the examples, we suppose that the corn forward price is \$2.50/bu and that there is a 50% probability that in 1 year the corn price will be \$2/bu or \$3/bu. In addition, for each possible price of corn there are two equally likely quantities, for a total of four possible price-quantity pairs. Table 9 illustrates the three scenarios. Note that in scenario B, average quantity is low when price is high (negative correlation), whereas in scenario C, average quantity is high when price is high (positive correlation).

First, consider scenario A, where quantity is certain: The producer always produces 1m bushels. Let S and Q denote the price and quantity in 1 year. Revenue is SQ. Without hedging, revenue will be either \$3m (if the corn price is \$3) or \$2m (if the corn price is \$2).

On the other hand, if the producer sells forward 1m bushels at the forward price $F = 2.50$, revenue is

$$\text{Revenue} = (S \times 1\text{m}) - [1\text{m} \times (S - 2.50)] = 2.5\text{m}$$

We have guaranteed revenue in this case. The calculation is illustrated explicitly in Table 10.

In general, if the producer enters into forward contracts on H units, hedged revenue, $R(H)$, will be

$$\text{Hedged revenue} = R(H) = (S \times Q) + [H \times (S - F)] \tag{5}$$

15. There are futures contracts intended to mitigate the problem of quantity uncertainty in an agricultural context. Corn yield futures, for example, traded at the Chicago Board of Trade, permit farmers to hedge variations in regional production quantity, and provide an agricultural example of a "quanto" contract.

TABLE 10 When the producer is sure to produce 1m bushels (Scenario A), revenue of \$2.5m is assured by selling forward 1m bushels.

Corn Price	Quantity	Revenue: Unhedged	Revenue: Sell Forward 1m bu
3	1.0m	3.0m	2.5m
2	1.0m	2.0m	2.5m

TABLE 11 Results in Scenario B (negative correlation between the price of corn and the quantity of production) from shorting 975,000 corn forwards (columns 4 and 5) and from selling forward 100,000 bushels (columns 6 and 7). Each price-quantity combination is equally likely, with a probability of 0.25. Standard deviations are computed using the population estimate of standard deviation.

Price	Quantity	Unhedged Revenue	Sell Forward 0.975m bu: Futures Gain	Sell Forward 0.975m bu: Total	Sell Forward 0.100m bu: Futures Gain	Sell Forward 0.100m bu: Total
\$3	1.0m	\$3.0m	−\$0.488m	\$2.512m	−\$0.050m	\$2.95m
\$3	0.6m	\$1.8m	−\$0.488m	\$1.312m	−\$0.050m	\$1.75m
\$2	1.5m	\$3.0m	\$0.488m	\$3.488m	\$0.050m	\$3.05m
\$2	0.8m	\$1.6m	\$0.488m	\$2.088m	\$0.050m	\$1.65m
	$\sigma_{\text{totalrevenue}}$	\$0.654m		\$0.814m		\$0.652m

Using equation (5), when there is uncertainty, the variability of hedged revenue, $\sigma^2_{R(H)}$, is

$$\sigma^2_{R(H)} = \sigma^2_{SQ} + H^2\sigma^2_S + 2H\rho_{SQ,S}\sigma_{SQ}\sigma_S \tag{6}$$

The standard deviation of total revenue, SQ, is σ_{SQ}, and the correlation of total revenue with price is $\rho_{SQ,S}$. As in the preceding discussion of cross-hedging, the H that minimizes the variance of hedged revenue will be

$$H = -\frac{\rho_{SQ,S}\sigma_{SQ}}{\sigma_S} \tag{7}$$

This is the same as the second term in equation (3). The formula for the variance-minimizing hedge ratio in equation (7) is the negative of the coefficient from a regression of unhedged revenue on price. We can therefore determine the variance-minimizing hedge ratios for the negative- and positive-correlation scenarios (scenarios B and C) in Table 9 either by using equation (7) directly or by running a regression of revenue on price.

First, consider what happens in Scenario B if we hedge by shorting the expected quantity of production. As a benchmark, column 3 of Table 11 shows that unhedged revenue has variability of \$0.654m. From Table 9, expected production in the negative correlation scenario, B, is

$$0.25 \times (1 + 0.6 + 1.5 + 0.8) = 0.975$$

If we short this quantity of corn, column 5 of Table 11 shows that there is still variability in hedged revenue. Perhaps more surprising, the variability of total revenue actually *increases*. The reason is that price decreases when quantity increases, so nature already provides a degree of hedging: The increase in quantity partially offsets the decrease in price. Hedging by shorting the full expected quantity leaves us *overhedged*, with a commensurate increase in variability.

The variance-minimizing hedge can be obtained using equation (7). By direct calculation, we have $\rho_{SQ,S} = 0.07647$, $\sigma_S = \$0.5$, and $\sigma_{SQ} = \$0.654\text{m}$.[16] Thus, we have

$$H = -\frac{0.07647 \times \$0.654\text{m}}{\$0.5} = -0.100\text{m}$$

Column (7) of Table 11 shows that variability is reduced to \$0.652m when hedging this amount. The optimal hedge quantity is closer to no hedging than to full hedging. In fact, we gain little by hedging optimally, but we increase the standard deviation of revenue by 25% if we adopt the plausible but incorrect hedging strategy of shorting 975,000 bushels. Problem 21 asks you to verify that you obtain the same answer by running a regression of revenue on price.

You might guess by now that when correlation is positive (Scenario C), the optimal hedge quantity exceeds expected quantity. The fact that quantity goes up when price goes up makes revenue that much more variable than when price alone varies, and a correspondingly larger hedge position is required. Problem 23 asks you to compute the optimal hedge in scenario C. The answer is to short almost 2 million bushels even though production is never that large.

CHAPTER SUMMARY

A producer selling a risky commodity, such as gold, has an inherent long position in the commodity. Assuming costs are fixed, the firm's profit increases when the price of the commodity increases. Such a firm can hedge profit with a variety of strategies, including selling forward, buying puts, and buying collars. A firm that faces price risk on inputs has an inherent short position in the commodity, with profit that decreases when the price of the input increases. Hedging strategies for such a firm include buying forward, buying calls, and selling collars. All of the strategies involving options can be customized by changing the option strike prices. Strategies such as a paylater can provide insurance with no initial premium but on which the company has greater losses should the insurance be needed.

16. Because Table 11 presents the complete population of outcomes, which are equally likely, it is appropriate to use the population estimate of the standard deviation. In Excel, this is STDEVP as opposed to STDEV. The calculation for σ_{SQ} is obtained as STDEVP(3, 1.8, 3, 1.6) = 0.6538.

Hedging can be optimal for a company when an extra dollar of income received in times of high profits is worth less than an extra dollar of income received in times of low profits. Profits for such a firm are concave, in which case hedging can increase expected cash flow. Concave profits can arise from taxes, bankruptcy costs, costly external finance, preservation of debt capacity, and managerial risk aversion. Such a firm can increase expected cash flow by hedging. Nevertheless, firms may elect not to hedge for reasons including transaction costs of dealing in derivatives, the requirement for expertise, the need to monitor and control the hedging process, and complications from tax and accounting considerations.

FURTHER READING

In this chapter we have examined uses of forwards and options, taking for granted the pricing of those contracts. Two big unanswered questions are: How are those prices determined? How does the market for them work?

Wharton and CIBC regularly survey nonfinancial firms to assess their hedging. A recent survey is summarized in Bodnar et al. (1998). Bartram et al. (2004) examine hedging behavior in an international sample of over 7000 firms. Tufano (1996, 1998), Petersen and Thiagarajan (2000), and Brown et al. (2003) have studied hedging practices in the gold-mining industry. Other papers examining hedging include Géczy et al. (1997), Allayannis and Weston (2001), Allayannis et al. (2003), and Allayannis et al. (2004). Guay and Kothari (2003) attempt to quantify derivatives usage using information in firm annual reports from 1997. Brown (2001) provides an interesting and detailed description of the hedging decisions by one (anonymous) firm, and Faulkender (2005) examines interest rate hedging in the chemical industry.

Gastineau et al. (2001) discuss Statement of Financial Accounting Standards 133, which currently governs accounting for derivatives.

Finally, Fleming (1997) relates some of the history of (the fictitious) Auric Enterprises.

PROBLEMS

For the following problems consider the following three firms:

- *XYZ* mines copper, with fixed costs of \$0.50/lb and variable cost of \$0.40/lb.
- *Wirco* produces wire. It buys copper and manufactures wire. One pound of copper can be used to produce one unit of wire, which sells for the price of copper plus \$5. Fixed cost per unit is \$3 and noncopper variable cost is \$1.50.
- *Telco* installs telecommunications equipment and uses copper wire from Wirco as an input. For planning purposes, Telco assigns a fixed revenue of \$6.20 for each unit of wire it uses.

The 1-year forward price of copper is \$1/lb. The 1-year continuously compounded interest rate is 6%. One-year option prices for copper are shown in the table below.[17]

17. These are option prices from the Black formula assuming that the risk-free rate is 0.06, volatility is 0.1, and time to expiration is 1 year.

Strike	Call	Put
0.9500	\$0.0649	\$0.0178
0.9750	0.0500	0.0265
1.0000	0.0376	0.0376
1.0250	0.0274	0.0509
1.0340	0.0243	0.0563
1.0500	0.0194	0.0665

In your answers, at a minimum consider copper prices in 1 year of \$0.80, \$0.90, \$1.00, \$1.10, and \$1.20.

1. If XYZ does nothing to manage copper price risk, what is its profit 1 year from now, per pound of copper? If on the other hand XYZ sells forward its expected copper production, what is its estimated profit 1 year from now? Construct graphs illustrating both unhedged and hedged profit.

2. Suppose the 1-year copper forward price were \$0.80 instead of \$1. If XYZ were to sell forward its expected copper production, what is its estimated profit 1 year from now? Should XYZ produce copper? What if the forward copper price is \$0.45?

3. Compute estimated profit in 1 year if XYZ buys a put option with a strike of \$0.95, \$1.00, or \$1.05. Draw a graph of profit in each case.

4. Compute estimated profit in 1 year if XYZ sells a call option with a strike of \$0.95, \$1.00, or \$1.05. Draw a graph of profit in each case.

5. Compute estimated profit in 1 year if XYZ buys collars with the following strikes:

a. \$0.95 for the put and \$1.00 for the call.

b. \$0.975 for the put and \$1.025 for the call.

c. \$1.05 for the put and \$1.05 for the call.

Draw a graph of profit in each case.

6. Compute estimated profit in 1 year if XYZ buys paylater *puts* as follows (the net premium may not be exactly zero):

a. Sell one 1.025-strike put and buy two 0.975-strike puts.

b. Sell two 1.034-strike puts and buy three 1.00-strike puts.

Draw a graph of profit in each case.

7. If Telco does nothing to manage copper price risk, what is its profit 1 year from now, per pound of copper that it buys? If it hedges the price of wire by buying copper forward, what is its estimated profit 1 year from now? Construct graphs illustrating both unhedged and hedged profit.

8. Compute estimated profit in 1 year if Telco buys a call option with a strike of \$0.95, \$1.00, or \$1.05. Draw a graph of profit in each case.

9. Compute estimated profit in 1 year if Telco sells a put option with a strike of \$0.95, \$1.00, or \$1.05. Draw a graph of profit in each case.

10. Compute estimated profit in 1 year if Telco sells collars with the following strikes:

a. \$0.95 for the put and \$1.00 for the call.

b. \$0.975 for the put and \$1.025 for the call.

c. \$0.95 for the put and \$0.95 for the call.

Draw a graph of profit in each case.

11. Compute estimated profit in 1 year if Telco buys paylater *calls* as follows (the net premium may not be exactly zero):

a. Sell one 0.975-strike call and buy two 1.034-strike calls.

b. Sell two 1.00-strike calls and buy three 1.034-strike calls.

Draw a graph of profit in each case.

12. Suppose that Wirco does nothing to manage the risk of copper price changes. What is its profit 1 year from now, per pound of copper? Suppose that Wirco buys copper forward at \$1. What is its profit 1 year from now?

13. What happens to the variability of Wirco's profit if Wirco undertakes any strategy (buying calls, selling puts, collars, etc.) to lock in the price of copper next year? You can use your answer to the previous question to illustrate your response.

14. Golddiggers has zero net income if it sells gold for a price of \$380. However, by shorting a forward contract it is possible to guarantee a profit of \$40/oz. Suppose a manager decides not to hedge and the gold price in 1 year is \$390/oz. Did the firm earn \$10 in profit (relative to accounting break-even) or lose \$30 in profit (relative to the profit that could be obtained by hedging)? Would your answer be different if the manager did hedge and the gold price had been \$450?

15. Consider the example in Table 6. Suppose that losses are fully tax-deductible. What is the expected after-tax profit in this case?

16. Suppose that firms face a 40% income tax rate on all profits. In particular, losses receive full credit. Firm A has a 50% probability of a \$1000 profit and a 50% probability of a \$600 loss each year. Firm B has a 50% probability of a \$300 profit and a 50% probability of a \$100 profit each year.

a. What is the expected pre-tax profit next year for firms A and B?

b. What is the expected after-tax profit next year for firms A and B?

17. Suppose that firms face a 40% income tax rate on positive profits and that net losses receive no credit. (Thus, if profits are positive, after-tax income is $(1 - 0.4) \times$ *profit*, while if there is a loss, after-tax income is the amount lost.) Firms A and B have the same cash flow distribution as in the previous problem. Suppose the appropriate effective annual discount rate for both firms is 10%.

a. What is the expected pre-tax profit for A and B?

b. What is the expected after-tax profit for A and B?

c. What would Firms A and B pay today to receive next year's expected cash flow for sure, instead of the variable cash flows described above?

For the following problems use the BSCall option pricing function with a stock price of \$420 (the forward price), volatility of 5.5%, continuously compounded interest rate of 4.879%, dividend yield of 4.879%, and time to expiration of 1 year. The problems require you to vary the strike prices.

18. Consider the example of Auric.

   a. Suppose that Auric insures against a price increase by purchasing a 440-strike call. Verify by drawing a profit diagram that simultaneously selling a 400-strike put will generate a collar. What is the cost of this collar to Auric?

   b. Find the strike prices for a zero-cost collar (buy high-strike call, sell low-strike put) for which the strikes differ by \$30.

19. Suppose that LMN Investment Bank wishes to sell Auric a zero-cost collar of width 30 without explicit premium (i.e., there will be no cash payment from Auric to LMN). Also suppose that on every option the bid price is \$0.25 below the Black-Scholes price and the offer price is \$0.25 above the Black-Scholes price. LMN wishes to earn their spread (\$0.25 per option) without any explicit charge to Auric. What should the strike prices on the collar be? (*Note*: Since the collar involves two options, LMN is looking to make \$0.50 on the deal. You need to find strike prices that differ by 30 such that LMN makes \$0.50.)

20. Use the same assumptions as in the preceding problem, without the bid-ask spread. Suppose that we want to construct a paylater strategy using a ratio spread. Instead of buying a 440-strike call, Auric will sell one 440-strike call and use the premium to buy two higher-strike calls, such that the net option premium is zero.

   a. What higher strike for the purchased calls will generate a zero net option premium?

   b. Graph the profit for Auric resulting from this strategy.

21. Using the information in Table 11, verify that a regression of revenue on price gives a regression slope coefficient of about 100,000.

22. Using the information in Table 9 about Scenario C:

   a. Compute $\sigma_{\text{total revenue}}$ when correlation between price and quantity is positive.

   b. What is the correlation between price and revenue?

23. Using the information in Table 9 about Scenario C:

   a. Using your answer to the previous question, use equation (7) to compute the variance-minimizing hedge ratio.

   b. Run a regression of revenue on price to compute the variance-minimizing hedge ratio.

   c. What is the variability of optimally hedged revenue?

24. Using the information in Table 9 about Scenario C:

   a. What is the expected quantity of production?

   b. Suppose you short the expected quantity of corn. What is the standard deviation of hedged revenue?

25. Suppose that price and quantity are positively correlated as in this table:

Price	Quantity	Revenue
$2	0.6m bu	$1.2m
$3	0.934m bu	$2.8m

There is a 50% chance of either price. The futures price is $2.50. Demonstrate the effect of hedging if we do the following:

a. Short the expected quantity.

b. Short the minimum quantity.

c. Short the maximum quantity.

d. What is the hedge position that eliminates variability in revenue? Why?

Forwards, Futures, and Swaps

Forward contracts permit the purchase of an asset in the future at terms that are set today. The pricing of forward and futures contracts can be explored on a wide variety of underlying assets: financial assets (such as stocks, currencies, and bonds) and commodities (such as gold, corn, and natural gas). Swaps have multiple future settlement dates, as opposed to forward contracts, which settle on a single date. Swaps are in effect a bundle of forward contracts combined with borrowing and lending. As such, swaps are a natural generalization of forward contracts.

Forward contracts involve deferring receipt of, and payment for, the underlying asset. Thus, computing the forward price requires you to determine the costs and benefits of this deferral.

From *Derivatives Markets*, Third Edition, Robert McDonald. Copyright © 2013 by Pearson Education, Inc. Published by Pearson Prentice Hall. All rights reserved.

Commodity Forwards and Futures

Tolstoy observed that happy families are all alike; each unhappy family is unhappy in its own way. An analogous idea in financial markets is that financial forwards are all alike; each commodity, however, has unique economic characteristics that determine forward pricing in that market. In this chapter we will see the extent to which commodity forwards on different assets differ from each other, and also how they differ from financial forwards and futures. We first discuss the pricing of commodity contracts, and then examine specific contracts, including gold, corn, natural gas, and oil. Finally, we discuss hedging.

You might wonder about the definition of a commodity. Gerard Debreu, who won the Nobel Prize in economics, said this (Debreu, 1959, p. 28):

> A commodity is characterized by its physical properties, the date at which it will be available, and the location at which it will be available. The price of a commodity is the amount which has to be paid *now* for the (future) availability of one unit of that commodity.

Notice that with this definition, corn in July and corn in September, for example, are different commodities: They are available on different dates. With a financial asset, such as a stock, we think of the stock as being fundamentally the same asset over time.[1] The same is not necessarily true of a commodity, since it can be costly or impossible to transform a commodity on one date into a commodity on another date. This observation will be important.

The price of a financial asset today is the present value of the asset at time T, less the value of dividends to be received between now and time T. It follows that the difference between the forward price and spot price of a financial asset reflects the costs and benefits of delaying payment for, and receipt of, the asset. Specifically, the forward price on a financial asset is given by

$$F_{0,T} = S_0 e^{(r-\delta)T} \tag{1}$$

1. When there are dividends, however, a share of stock received on different dates can be materially different.

From Chapter 6 of *Derivatives Markets*, Third Edition, Robert McDonald. Copyright © 2013 by Pearson Education, Inc. Published by Pearson Prentice Hall. All rights reserved.

where S_0 is the spot price of the asset, r is the continuously compounded interest rate, and δ is the continuous dividend yield on the asset. We will explore the extent to which equation (1) also holds for commodities.

1. INTRODUCTION TO COMMODITY FORWARDS

This section provides an overview of some issues that arise in discussing commodity forward and futures contracts. We begin by looking at some commodity futures prices. We then discuss some terms and concepts that will be important for commodities.

Examples of Commodity Futures Prices

For many commodities there are futures contracts available that expire at different dates in the future. Table 1 provides illustrative examples; we can examine these prices to see what issues might arise with commodity forward pricing.

First, consider corn. From May to July, the corn futures price rises from 646.50 to 653.75. This is a 2-month increase of $653.75/646.50 - 1 = 1.12\%$, an annual rate of approximately 7%. As a reference interest rate, 3-month LIBOR on March 17, 2011, was 0.31%, or about 0.077% for 3 months. Assuming that $\delta \geq 0$, this futures price is greater than that implied by equation (1). An arbitrage strategy would be: Buy May corn and sell July corn. However, storing corn for 2 months will be costly, a consideration that did not arise with financial futures. Another issue arises with the December price: The price of corn falls 74.5 cents between July and December. It seems unlikely that this could be explained by a dividend. An alternative, intuitive explanation would be that the fall harvest causes the price of corn to drop, and hence the December futures price is low. But how is this explanation consistent with our results about no-arbitrage pricing of financial forwards?

TABLE 1 Futures prices for various commodities, March 17, 2011.

Expiration Month	Corn (cents/ bushel)	Soybeans (cents/ bushel)	Gasoline (cents/ gallon)	Oil (Brent) (dollars/ barrel)	Gold (dollars/ ounce)
April	—	—	2.9506	—	1404.20
May	646.50	1335.25	2.9563	114.90	1404.90
June	—	—	2.9491	114.65	1405.60
July	653.75	1343.50	2.9361	114.38	—
August	—	—	2.8172	114.11	1406.90
September	613.00	1321.00	2.8958	113.79	—
October	—	—	2.7775	113.49	1408.20
November	—	1302.25	2.7522	113.17	—
December	579.25	—	2.6444	112.85	1409.70

Data from CME Group.

If you examine the other commodities, you will see similar patterns for soybeans, gasoline, and oil. Only gold, with the forward price rising at approximately \$0.70 per month (about 0.6% annually), has behavior resembling that of a financial contract.

The prices in Table 1 suggest that commodities are different than financial contracts. The challenge is to reconcile the patterns with our understanding of financial forwards, in which explicit expectations of future prices (and harvests!) do not enter the forward price formula.

There are *many* more commodities with traded futures than just those in Table 1. You might think that a futures contract could be written on anything, but it is an interesting bit of trivia, discussed in the box below, that Federal law in the United States prohibits trading on two commodities.

BOX 1: Forbidden Futures

In the United States, futures contracts on two items are explicitly prohibited by statute: onions and box office receipts for movies. Title 7, Chapter 1, §13-1 of the United States Code is titled "Violations, prohibition against dealings in onion futures; punishment" and states

> (a) No contract for the sale of onions for future delivery shall be made on or subject to the rules of any board of trade in the United States. The terms used in this section shall have the same meaning as when used in this chapter.
>
> (b) Any person who shall violate the provisions of this section shall be deemed guilty of a misdemeanor and upon conviction thereof be fined not more than \$5,000.

Along similar lines, Title VII of the Dodd-Frank Wall Street Reform and Consumer Protection Act of 2010 bans trading in "motion picture box office receipts (or any index, measure, value, or data related to such receipts), and all services, rights, and interests . . . in which contracts for future delivery are presently or in the future dealt in."

These bans exist because of lobbying by special interests. The onion futures ban was passed in 1959 when Michigan onion growers lobbied their new congressman, Gerald Ford, to ban such trading, believing that it depressed prices. Today, some regret the law:

> Onion prices soared 400% between October 2006 and April 2007, when weather reduced crops, according to the U.S. Department of Agriculture, only to crash 96% by March 2008 on overproduction and then rebound 300% by this past April.
>
> The volatility has been so extreme that the son of one of the original onion growers who lobbied Congress for the trading ban now thinks the onion market would operate more smoothly if a futures contract were in place.
>
> "There probably has been more volatility since the ban," says Bob Debruyn of Debruyn Produce, a Michigan-based grower and wholesaler. "I would think that a futures market for onions would make some sense today, even though my father was very much involved in getting rid of it."
>
> *Source:* Fortune magazine on-line, June 27, 2008.

Similarly, futures on movie box office receipts had been approved early in 2010 by the Commodity Futures Trading Commission. After lobbying by Hollywood interests, the ban on such trading was inserted into the Dodd-Frank financial reform bill.

Differences Between Commodities and Financial Assets

In discussing the commodity prices in Table 1, we invoked considerations that did not arise with financial assets, but that will arise repeatedly when we discuss commodities. Among these are:

Storage costs. The cost of storing a physical item such as corn or copper can be large relative to its value. Moreover, some commodities deteriorate over time, which is also a cost of storage. By comparison, financial securities are inexpensive to store. Consequently, we did not mention storage costs when discussing financial assets.

Carry markets. A commodity for which the forward price compensates a commodity owner for costs of storage is called a **carry market**. (In such a market, the return on a cash-and-carry, net of all costs, is the risk-free rate.) Storage of a commodity is an economic decision that varies across commodities and that can vary over time for a given commodity. Some commodities are at times stored for later use (we will see that this is the case for natural gas and corn), others are more typically used as they are produced (oil, copper). By contrast, financial markets are always carry markets: Assets are always "stored" (owned), and forward prices always compensate owners for storage.

Lease rate. The short-seller of an item may have to compensate the owner of the item for lending. In the case of financial assets, short-sellers have to compensate lenders for missed dividends or other payments accruing to the asset. For commodities, a short-seller may have to make a payment, called a lease payment, to the commodity lender. The lease payment typically would not correspond to dividends in the usual sense of the word.

Convenience yield. The owner of a commodity in a commodity-related business may receive nonmonetary benefits from physical possession of the commodity. Such benefits may be reflected in forward prices and are generically referred to as a **convenience yield**.

We will discuss all of these concepts in more depth later in the chapter. For now, the important thing to keep in mind is that commodities differ in important respects from financial assets.

Commodity Terminology

There are many terms that are particular to commodities and thus often unfamiliar even to those well acquainted with financial markets. These terms deal with the properties of the forward curve and the physical characteristics of commodities.

Table 1 illustrates two terms often used by commodity traders in talking about forward curves: **contango** and **backwardation**. If the forward curve is upward sloping—i.e., forward prices more distant in time are higher—then we say the market is in contango. We observe this pattern with near-term corn and soybeans, and with gold. If the forward curve is downward sloping, we say the market is in backwardation. We observe this with medium-term corn and soybeans, with gasoline (after 2 months), and with crude oil.

Commodities can be broadly classified as **extractive** and **renewable.** Extractive commodities occur naturally in the ground and are obtained by mining and drilling. Examples include metals (silver, gold, and copper) and hydrocarbons, including oil and natural gas. Renewable commodities are obtained through agriculture and include grains (corn, soybeans, wheat), livestock (cattle, pork bellies), dairy (cheese, milk), and lumber.

Commodities can be further classified as **primary** and **secondary**. Primary commodities are unprocessed; corn, soybeans, oil, and gold are all primary. Secondary commodities have been processed. In Table 1, gasoline is a secondary commodity.

Finally, commodities are measured in uncommon units for which you may not know precise definitions. Table 1 has several examples. A **barrel** of oil is 42 gallons. A **bushel** is a dry measure containing approximately 2150 cubic inches. The ounce used to weigh precious metals, such as gold, is a **troy ounce**, which is approximately 9.7% greater in weight than the customary avoirdupois ounce.[2]

Entire books are devoted to commodities (e.g., see Geman, 2005). Our goal here is to understand the *logic* of forward pricing for commodities and where it differs from the logic of forward pricing for financial assets. We will see that understanding a forward curve generally requires that we understand something about the underlying commodity.

2. EQUILIBRIUM PRICING OF COMMODITY FORWARDS

In this section we present definitions relating the prepaid forward price, forward price, and present value of a future commodity price. These ideas are important for understanding commodities.

The prepaid forward price for a commodity is the price today to receive a unit of the commodity on a future date. The prepaid forward price is therefore by definition the present value of the commodity on the future date. Hence, the prepaid forward price is

$$F_{0,T}^{P} = e^{-\alpha T} E_0[S_T] \tag{2}$$

where α is the discount rate for the commodity.

The forward price is the future value of the prepaid forward price, with the future value computed using the risk-free rate:

$$F_{0,T} = e^{rT} F_{0,T}^{P} \tag{3}$$

Substituting equation (2) into equation (3), we see that the commodity forward price is the expected spot price, discounted at the risk premium:

$$F_{0,T} = E_0(S_T)e^{-(\alpha-r)T} \tag{4}$$

We can rewrite equation (4) to obtain

$$e^{-rT} F_{0,T} = E_0(S_T)e^{-\alpha T} \tag{5}$$

Equation (5) deserves emphasis: *The time-T forward price discounted at the risk-free rate is the present value of a unit of commodity received at time T*. This equation implies that, for example, an industrial producer who buys oil can calculate the present value of future

2. A troy ounce is 480 grains and the more familiar avoirdupois ounce is 437.5 grains. Twelve troy ounces make 1 troy pound, which weighs approximately 0.37 kg.

oil costs by discounting oil forward prices at the risk-free rate. This calculation does not depend upon whether the producer hedges. We will see an example of this calculation later in the chapter.

3. PRICING COMMODITY FORWARDS BY ARBITRAGE

We now investigate no-arbitrage pricing for commodity forward contracts. We begin by using copper as an example. Copper is durable and can be stored, but it is typically not stored except as needed for production. The primary goal in this section will be to understand the issues that distinguish forward pricing for commodities from forward pricing for financial assets.

Figure 1 shows specifications for the CME Group copper contract and Figure 2 shows forward curves for copper on four dates. The copper forward curve lacks drama: For three of the four curves, the forward price in 1 year is approximately equal to the forward price in the current month. For the fourth curve, the 1-year price is below the current price (the curve exhibits backwardation).

We saw that for non-dividend-paying financial assets, the forward price rises at the interest rate. How can the forward price of copper on a future date equal the current forward price? At an intuitive level, it is reasonable to expect the price of copper in 1 year to equal the price today. Suppose, for example, that the extraction and other costs of copper production are \$3/pound and are expected to remain \$3. If demand is not expected to change, or if it is easy for producers to alter production, it would be reasonable to expect that on average the price of copper would remain at \$3. The question is how to reconcile this intuition with the behavior of forward prices for financial assets.

While it is reasonable to think that the price of copper will be expected to remain the same over the next year, it is important to recognize that a constant price would *not* be a reasonable assumption about the price of a non-dividend-paying stock. Investors must expect that a stock will on average pay a positive return, or no one would own it. In equilibrium, stocks and other financial assets must be held by investors, or *stored*. The stock price appreciates on average so that investors will willingly store the stock. There is no such requirement for copper, which can be extracted and then used in production. The equilibrium condition for copper relates to extraction, not to storage above ground. This distinction between a storage and production equilibrium is a central concept in our discussion of commodities. At the outset, then, there is an obvious difference between copper and a financial asset. It is not necessarily obvious, however, what bearing this difference has on pricing forward contracts.

An Apparent Arbitrage

Suppose that you observe that both the current price and 1-year forward price for copper are \$3.00 and that the effective annual interest rate is 10%. For the reasons we have just discussed, market participants could rationally believe that the copper price in 1 year will be \$3.00. From our discussion of financial forwards, however, you might think that the forward price should be $1.10 \times \$3.00 = \$3.30$, the future value of the current copper price.

FIGURE 1

Specifications for the CME Group/COMEX high-grade copper contract.

Underlying	High-grade (Grade 1) copper
Where traded	CME Group/COMEX
Size	25,000 pounds
Months	24 consecutive months
Trading ends	Third-to-last business day of the maturing month
Delivery	Exchange-designated warehouse within the United States

Data from Datastream.

FIGURE 2

Forward curves for four dates for the CME Group high-grade copper futures contract.

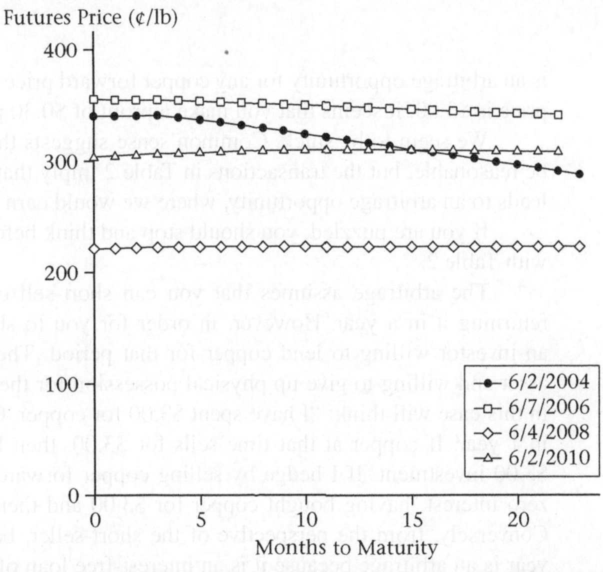

Data from Datastream.

The $3.00 forward price would therefore create an arbitrage opportunity.[3] If the forward price were $3.00 you could buy copper forward and short-sell copper today. Table 2 depicts the cash flows in this reverse cash-and-carry arbitrage. The result seems to show that there

3. We will discuss arbitrage in this section focusing on the forward price relative to the spot price. However, the difference between any forward prices at different dates must also reflect no-arbitrage conditions. So you can apply the discussions in this section to any two points on the forward curve.

TABLE 2 Apparent reverse cash-and-carry arbitrage for copper if the copper forward price is $F_{0,1} < \$3.30$. These calculations *appear* to demonstrate that there is an arbitrage opportunity if the copper forward price is below \$3.30. S_1 is the spot price of copper in 1 year, and $F_{0,1}$ is the copper forward price. There is a logical error in the table.

Transaction	Cash Flows Time 0	Time 1
Long forward @ $F_{0,1}$	0	$S_1 - F_{0,1}$
Short-sell copper	+\$3.00	$-S_1$
Lend short-sale proceeds @ 10%	−\$3.00	\$3.30
Total	0	$\$3.30 - F_{0,1}$

is an arbitrage opportunity for any copper forward price below \$3.30. If the copper forward price is \$3.00, it seems that you make a profit of \$0.30 per pound of copper.

We seem to be stuck. Common sense suggests that a forward price of \$3.00 would be reasonable, but the transactions in Table 2 imply that any forward price less than \$3.30 leads to an arbitrage opportunity, where we would earn $\$3.30 - F_{0,1}$ per pound of copper.

If you are puzzled, you should stop and think before proceeding. There is a problem with Table 2.

The arbitrage assumes that you can short-sell copper by borrowing it today and returning it in a year. However, in order for you to short-sell for a year, there must be an investor willing to lend copper for that period. The lender must both be holding the asset and willing to give up physical possession for the period of the short-sale. A lender in this case will think: "I have spent \$3.00 for copper. Copper that I lend will be returned in 1 year. If copper at that time sells for \$3.00, then I have earned zero interest on my \$3.00 investment. If I hedge by selling copper forward for \$3.00, I will for certain earn zero interest, having bought copper for \$3.00 and then selling it for \$3.00 a year later." Conversely, from the perspective of the short-seller, borrowing a pound of copper for a year is an arbitrage because it is an interest-free loan of \$3.00. The borrower benefits and the lender loses, so *no one will lend copper without charging an additional fee*. While it is straightforward to borrow a financial asset, borrowing copper appears to be a different matter.

To summarize: The apparent arbitrage in Table 2 has nothing to do with mispriced forward contracts on copper. The issue is that the copper loan is equivalent to an interest-free loan, and thus generates an arbitrage profit.

Short-selling and the Lease Rate

How do we correct the arbitrage analysis in Table 2? We have to recognize that the copper lender has invested \$3.00 in copper and must expect to earn a satisfactory return on that investment. *The copper lender will require us to make a lease payment so that the commodity loan is a fair deal*. The actual payment the lender requires will depend on the forward price.

TABLE 3 Reverse cash-and-carry arbitrage for copper. This table demonstrates that there is no arbitrage opportunity if the commodity lender requires an appropriate lease payment.

	Cash Flows	
Transaction	**Time 0**	**Time 1**
Long forward @ $F_{0,1}$	0	$S_1 - F_{0,1}$
Short-sell copper	+\$3.00	$-S_1$
Lease payment	0	$-(\$3.30 - F_{0,1})$
Lend short-sale proceeds @ 10%	−\$3.00	\$3.30
Total	0	0

The lender will recognize that it is possible to use the forward market to lock in a selling price for the copper in 1 year, and will reason that copper bought for \$3.00 today can be sold for $F_{0,1}$ in 1 year. A copper borrower must therefore be prepared to make an extra payment—a lease payment—of

$$\text{Lease payment} = 1.1 \times \$3.00 - F_{0,1}$$

With the lender requiring this extra payment, we can correct the analysis in Table 2. Table 3 incorporates the lease payment and shows that the apparent arbitrage vanishes.

We can also interpret a lease payment in terms of discounted cash flow. Let α denote the equilibrium discount rate for an asset with the same risk as the commodity. The lender is buying the commodity for S_0. One unit returned at time T is worth S_T, with a present value of $E_0(S_T)e^{-\alpha T}$. If there is a proportional continuous lease payment of δ_l, the NPV of buying the commodity and lending it is

$$\text{NPV} = E_0(S_T)e^{-\alpha T}e^{\delta_l T} - S_0 \tag{6}$$

The lease rate that makes NPV zero is then

$$\delta_l = \alpha - \frac{1}{T}\ln\left[E_0(S_T)/S_0\right]$$

The lease rate is the difference between the discount rate for the commodity and the expected price appreciation. From substituting equation (5) into this expression, an equivalent way to write the continuous lease rate is

$$\delta_l = r - \frac{1}{T}\ln\left[F_{0,T}/S_0\right] \tag{7}$$

It is important to be clear about the reason a lease payment is required for a commodity and not for a financial asset. For a non-dividend-paying financial asset, the price is the present value of the future price, so that $S_0 = E(S_T)e^{-\alpha T}$. This implies that the lease payment is zero. For most commodities, the current price is not the present value of the expected future price, so there is no presumption that the lease rate would be zero.

No-Arbitrage Pricing Incorporating Storage Costs

We now consider the effects of storage costs. Storage is not always feasible (for example, fresh strawberries are perishable), and when technically feasible, storage for commodities is almost always costly. If storage is feasible, how do storage costs affect forward pricing? The intuitive answer is that if it is optimal to store the commodity, then the forward price must be high enough so that the returns on a cash-and-carry compensate for both financing and storage costs. However, if storage is not optimal, storage costs are irrelevant. We will examine both cash-and-carry and reverse cash-and-carry arbitrages to see how they are affected by storage costs.

Cash-and-Carry Arbitrage. Put yourself in the position of a commodity merchant who owns one unit of the commodity, and ask whether you would be willing to store it until time T. You face the choice of selling it today, receiving S_0, or selling it at time T. If you guarantee your selling price by selling forward, you will receive $F_{0,T}$.

It is common sense that *you will store only if the present value of selling at time T is at least as great as that of selling today*. Denote the future value of storage costs for one unit of the commodity from time 0 to T as $\lambda(0, T)$. Table 4 summarizes the cash flows for a cash-and-carry with storage costs. The table shows that the cash-and-carry arbitrage is not profitable if

$$F_{0,1} < (1 + R)S_0 + \lambda(0, 1) \tag{8}$$

If inequality (8) is violated, storage will occur because the forward premium is great enough that sale proceeds in the future compensate for the financial costs of storage (RS_0) and the physical costs of storage ($\lambda(0, 1)$). If there is to be both storage and no arbitrage, then equation (8) holds with equality. An implication of equation (8) is that when costly storage occurs, the forward curve can rise faster than the interest rate. We can view storage costs as a negative dividend: Instead of receiving cash flow for holding the asset, you have to pay to hold the asset. If there is storage, storage costs increase the upper bound for the forward price. Storage costs can include depreciation of the commodity, which is less a problem for metals such as copper than for commodities such as strawberries and electricity.

TABLE 4 Cash-and-carry for copper for 1 year, assuming that there is a 1-year storage cost of $\lambda(0, 1)$ payable at time 1, and an effective interest rate of R.

	Cash Flows	
Transaction	Time 0	Time 1
Buy copper	$-S_0$	S_1
Pay storage cost	0	$-\lambda(0, 1)$
Short forward	0	$F_{0,1} - S_1$
Borrow @ R	$+S_0$	$-(1 + R)S_0$
Total	0	$F_{0,1} - [(1 + R)S_0 + \lambda(0, 1)]$

In the special case where continuous storage costs of λ are paid continuously and are proportional to the value of the commodity, storage cost is like a continuous negative dividend. If storage occurs and there is no arbitrage, we have[4]

$$F_{0,T} = S_0 e^{(r+\lambda)T} \tag{9}$$

This would be the forward price in a carry market, where the commodity is stored.

Example 1. Suppose that the November price of corn is \$2.50/bushel, the effective monthly interest rate is 1%, and storage costs per bushel are \$0.05/month. Assuming that corn is stored from November to February, the February forward price must compensate owners for interest and storage. The future value of storage costs is

$$\$0.05 + (\$0.05 \times 1.01) + (\$0.05 \times 1.01^2) = (\$0.05/.01) \times \left[(1 + 0.01)^3 - 1\right]$$
$$= \$0.1515$$

Thus, the February forward price will be

$$2.50 \times (1.01)^3 + 0.1515 = 2.7273$$

Problem 9 asks you to verify that this is a no-arbitrage price. ■

Keep in mind that just because a commodity *can* be stored does not mean that it *should* (or will) be stored. Copper is typically not stored for long periods, because storage is not economically necessary: A constant new supply of copper is available to meet demand. Thus, equation (8) describes the forward price *when storage occurs*. We now consider a reverse cash-and-carry arbitrage to see what happens when the forward price is lower than in equation (8).

Reverse Cash-and-Carry Arbitrage. Suppose an arbitrageur buys the commodity forward and short-sells it. We have seen that the commodity lender likely requires a lease payment and that the payment *should* be equal to $(1 + R)S_0 - F_{0,1}$. The results of this transaction are in Table 5. Note first that storage costs do not affect profit because neither the arbitrageur nor the lender is actually storing the commodity. The reverse cash-and-carry is profitable if the lender requires a lease payment below $(1 + R)S_0 - F_{0,1}$. Otherwise, arbitrage is not profitable. If the commodity lender uses the forward price to determine the lease rate, then the resulting circularity guarantees that profit is zero. This is evident in Table 5, where profit is zero if $L = (1 + R)S_0 - F_{0,1}$.

This analysis has the important implication that the ability to engage in a reverse cash-and-carry arbitrage does not put a lower bound on the forward price. We conclude that a forward price that is too high can give rise to arbitrage, but a forward price that is too low need not.

Of course there are economic pressures inducing the forward price to reach the "correct" level. If the forward price is too low, there will be an incentive for arbitrageurs

4. You might be puzzled by the different ways of representing quantities such as costs and dividends. In some cases we have used discrete values; in others, we have used continuous approximations. All of these represent the same conceptual amount (a present or future value of a cost of cash flow). You should be familiar with different ways of writing the formulas.

TABLE 5 Reverse cash-and-carry for copper for 1 year, assuming that the commodity lender requires a lease payment of L.

	Cash Flows	
Transaction	Time 0	Time 1
Short-sell copper	S_0	$-S_1$
Lease payment	0	$-L$
Long forward	0	$S_1 - F_{0,1}$
Invest @ R	$-S_0$	$(1+R)S_0$
Total	0	$[(1+R)S_0 - F_{0,1}] - L$

to buy the commodity forward. If it is too high, there is an incentive for traders to sell the commodity, whether or not arbitrage is feasible. Leasing and storage costs complicate arbitrage, however.

Convenience Yields

The discussion of commodities has so far ignored business reasons for holding commodities. For example, if you are a food producer for whom corn is an essential input, you will hold corn in inventory. If you hold too much corn, you can sell the excess. However, if you hold too little, you may run out of corn, halting production and idling workers and machines. The physical inventory of corn in this case has value: It provides insurance that you can keep producing in case there is a disruption in the supply of corn.

In this situation, corn holdings provide an extra nonmonetary return called the convenience yield.[5] You will be willing to store corn with a lower rate of return than if you did not earn the convenience yield. What are the implications of the convenience yield for the forward price?

The convenience yield is only relevant when the commodity is stored. In order to store the commodity, an owner will require that the forward price compensate for the financial and physical costs of storing, but the owner will accept a lower forward price to the extent there is a convenience yield. Specifically, if the continuously compounded convenience yield is c, proportional to the value of the commodity, the owner will earn an acceptable return from storage if the forward price is

$$F_{0,T} \geq S_0 e^{(r+\lambda-c)T}$$

Because we saw that low commodity forward prices cannot easily be arbitraged, this price would not yield an arbitrage opportunity.

5. The term *convenience yield* is defined differently by different authors. Convenience yield generally means a return to physical ownership of the commodity. In practice it is sometimes used to mean what we call the lease rate. The lease rate of a commodity can be inferred from the forward price using equation (7).

What is the commodity lease rate in this case? An owner lending the commodity saves λ and loses c from not storing the commodity. Hence, the commodity borrower would need to pay $\delta_l = c - \lambda$ in order to compensate the lender for convenience yield less storage cost.

The difficulty with the convenience yield in practice is that convenience is hard to observe. The concept of the convenience yield serves two purposes. First, it explains patterns in storage—for example, why a commercial user might store a commodity when the average investor will not. Second, it provides an additional parameter to better explain the forward curve. You might object that we can invoke the convenience yield to explain *any* forward curve, and therefore the concept of the convenience yield is vacuous. While convenience yield can be tautological, it is a meaningful economic concept and it would be just as arbitrary to assume that there is never convenience. Moreover, the upper bound in equation (8) depends on storage costs but not the convenience yield. Thus, the convenience yield only explains anomalously low forward prices, and only when there is storage.

Summary

Much of the discussion in this section was aimed at explaining the differences between commodities and financial assets. The main conclusions are intuitive:

- The forward price, $F_{0,T}$, should not exceed $S_0 e^{(r+\lambda)T}$. If the forward price were greater, you could undertake a simple cash-and-carry and earn a profit after paying both storage costs and interest on the position. Storage costs here includes deterioration of the commodity, so fragile commodities could have large (or infinite) storage costs.
- In a carry market, the forward price should equal $S_0 e^{(r-c+\lambda)T}$. A user who buys and stores the commodity will then be compensated for interest and physical storage costs less a convenience yield.
- In any kind of market, a reverse cash-and-carry arbitrage (attempting to arbitrage too low a forward price) will be difficult, because the terms at which a lender will lend the commodity will likely reflect the forward price, making profitable arbitrage difficult.

4. GOLD

Of all commodities, gold is most like a financial asset. Gold is durable, nonreactive, noncorrosive, relatively inexpensive to store (compared to its value), widely held, and actively produced through gold mining. Because of transportation costs and purity concerns, gold often trades in certificate form, as a claim to physical gold at a specific location. There are exchange-traded gold futures, specifications for which are in Figure 3.

Figure 4 graphs futures prices for all available gold futures contracts—the forward curve—for four different dates. The forward curves all show the forward price steadily increasing with time to maturity.

FIGURE 3

Specifications for the CME Group gold futures contract.

Underlying	Refined gold bearing approved refiner stamp
Where traded	CME Group/NYMEX
Size	100 troy ounces
Months	February, April, August, October, out 2 years. June, December, out 5 years
Trading ends	Third-to-last business day of maturity month
Delivery	Any business day of the delivery month

FIGURE 4

The forward curve for gold on four dates, from NYMEX gold futures prices.

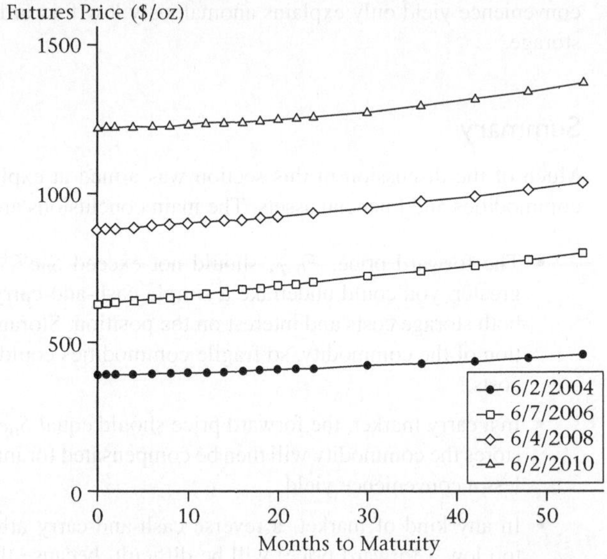

Data from Datastream.

Gold Leasing

From our discussion in Section 3, the forward price implies a lease rate for gold. Short-sales and loans of gold are in fact common in the gold market. On the lending side, large gold holders (including some central banks) put gold on deposit with brokers, in order that it may be loaned to short-sellers. The gold lenders earn the lease rate.

The lease rate for gold, silver, and other commodities is typically reported using equation (7), with LIBOR as the interest rate. In recent years the lease rate has often been negative, especially for periods of 6 months or less.

As an example of the lease rate computation, consider gold prices on June 2, 2010. The June, December, and June 2011 futures settlement prices that day were 1220.6, 1226.8, and 1234.3. The return from buying June gold and selling December gold would have been

$$\text{Return}_{6\text{ months}} = \frac{1226.8}{1220.6} - 1 = 0.00508$$

At the same time, June LIBOR was 99.432 and September LIBOR was 99.2, so the implied 6-month interest rate was $(1 + 0.00568/4) \times (1 + 0.008/4)$, a 6-month interest rate of 0.00342. Because the (nonannualized) implied 6-month gold appreciation rate exceeds (nonannualized) 6-month LIBOR, the lease rate is negative. The annualized lease rate in this calculation is

$$2 \times (0.00342 - 0.00508) = -0.003313$$

The negative lease rate seems to imply that gold owners would pay to lend gold. With significant demand in recent years for gold storage, the negative lease rate could be measuring increased marginal storage costs. It is also possible that LIBOR is not the correct interest rate to use in computing the lease rate. Whatever the reason for negative lease rates, gold in recent years has been trading at close to full carry.

Evaluation of Gold Production

Suppose we wish to compute the present value of future production for a proposed gold mine. As discussed in Section 2, the present value of a unit of commodity received in the future is simply the present value of the forward price, with discounting performed at the risk-free rate. We can thus use the forward curve for gold to compute the value of an operating gold mine.

Suppose that at times t_i, $i = 1, \ldots, n$, we expect to extract n_{t_i} ounces of gold by paying a per-unit extraction cost of $x(t_i)$. We have a set of n forward prices, F_{0,t_i}. If the continuously compounded annual risk-free rate from time 0 to t_i is $r(0, t_i)$, the value of the gold mine is

$$\text{PV gold production} = \sum_{i=1}^{n} n_{t_i} \left[F_{0,t_i} - x(t_i) \right] e^{-r(0,t_i)t_i} \tag{10}$$

This equation assumes that the gold mine is certain to operate the entire time and that the quantity of production is known. Only price is uncertain. Note that in equation (10), by computing the present value of the forward price, we compute the prepaid forward price.

Example 2. Suppose we have a mining project that will produce 1 ounce of gold every year for 6 years. The cost of this project is \$1100 today, the marginal cost per ounce at the time of extraction is \$100, and the continuously compounded interest rate is 6%.

We observe the gold forward prices in the second column of Table 6, with implied prepaid forward prices in the third column. Using equation (10), we can use these prices to perform the necessary present value calculations.

$$\text{Net present value} = \sum_{i=1}^{6} \left[F_{0,i} - 100 \right] e^{-0.06\times i} - \$1100 = \$119.56 \quad ■ \tag{11}$$

TABLE 6 Gold forward and prepaid forward prices on 1 day for gold delivered at 1-year intervals, out to 6 years. The continuously compounded interest rate is 6% and the lease rate is assumed to be a constant 1.5%.

Expiration Year	Forward Price ($)	Prepaid Forward Price ($)
1	313.81	295.53
2	328.25	291.13
3	343.36	286.80
4	359.17	282.53
5	375.70	278.32
6	392.99	274.18

FIGURE 5

Specifications for the CME Group/CBOT corn futures contract.

Underlying	#2 Yellow, with #1 Yellow deliverable at a $0.015 premium and #3 Yellow at a $0.015 discount.
Where traded	CME Group/CBOT
Size	5000 bushels (∼127 metric tons)
Months	March, May, July, September, and December, out 2 years
Trading ends	Business day prior to the 15th day of the month.
Delivery	Second business day following the last trading day of the delivery month

5. CORN

Important grain futures in the United States include corn, soybeans, and wheat. In this section we discuss corn as an example of an agricultural product. Corn is harvested primarily in the fall, from September through November. The United States is a leading corn producer, generally exporting rather than importing corn. Figure 5 presents specifications for the CME Group corn futures contract.

Given seasonality in production, what should the forward curve for corn look like? Corn is produced at one time of the year, but consumed throughout the year. In order to be consumed when it is not being produced, corn must be stored.

As discussed in Section 3, storage is an economic decision in which there is a trade-off between selling today and selling tomorrow. If we can sell corn today for $2/bu and in 2 months for $2.25/bu, the storage decision entails comparing the price we can get today with the present value of the price we can get in 2 months. In addition to interest, we need to include storage costs in our analysis.

An equilibrium with some current selling and some storage requires that corn prices be expected to rise at the interest rate plus storage costs, which implies that there will be an

FIGURE 6

Forward curves for corn for four years.

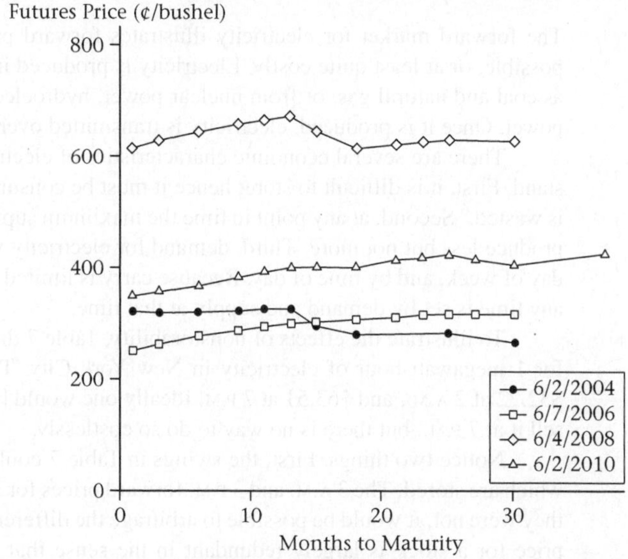

Data from Datastream.

upward trend in the price between harvests. While corn is being stored, the forward price should behave as in equation (9), rising at interest plus storage costs.

In a typical year, once the harvest begins, storage is no longer necessary; if supply and demand remain constant from year to year, the harvest price will be the same every year. Those storing corn will plan to deplete inventory as harvest approaches and to replenish inventory from the new harvest. The corn price will fall at harvest, only to begin rising again after the harvest.

The behavior of the corn forward price, graphed in Figure 6, largely conforms with this description. In three of the four forward curves, the forward price of corn rises to reward storage between harvests, and it falls at harvest. An important caveat is that the supply of corn varies from year to year. When there is an unusually large crop, producers will expect corn to be stored not just over the current year but into the next year as well. If there is a large harvest, therefore, we might see the forward curve rise continuously until year 2. This might explain the low price and steady rise in 2006.

Although corn prices vary throughout the year, farmers will plant in anticipation of receiving the harvest price. It is therefore the harvest price that guides production decisions. The price during the rest of the year should approximately equal the harvest price plus storage, less convenience.

6. ENERGY MARKETS

One of the most important and heavily traded commodity sectors is energy. This sector includes oil, oil products (heating oil and gasoline), natural gas, and electricity. These products represent different points on the spectrum of storage costs and carry.

Electricity

The forward market for electricity illustrates forward pricing when storage is often not possible, or at least quite costly. Electricity is produced in different ways: from fuels such as coal and natural gas, or from nuclear power, hydroelectric power, wind power, or solar power. Once it is produced, electricity is transmitted over the power grid to end-users.

There are several economic characteristics of electricity that are important to understand. First, it is difficult to store; hence it must be consumed when it is produced or else it is wasted.[6] Second, at any point in time the maximum supply of electricity is fixed. You can produce less but not more. Third, demand for electricity varies substantially by season, by day of week, and by time of day. Because carry is limited and costly, the electricity price at any time is set by demand and supply at that time.

To illustrate the effects of nonstorability, Table 7 displays 1-day-ahead hourly prices for 1 megawatt-hour of electricity in New York City. The 1-day-ahead forward price is $32.22 at 2 A.M., and $63.51 at 7 P.M. Ideally one would buy 2 A.M. electricity, store it, and sell it at 7 P.M., but there is no way to do so costlessly.

Notice two things. First, the swings in Table 7 could not occur with financial assets, which are stored. The 3 A.M. and 3 P.M. forward prices for a stock will be almost identical; if they were not, it would be possible to arbitrage the difference. Second, whereas the forward price for a stock is largely redundant in the sense that it reflects information about the current stock price, interest, and the dividend yield, the forward prices in Table 7 provide **price discovery**, revealing otherwise unobtainable information about the future price of the commodity. The prices in Table 7 are best interpreted using equation (4).

Just as intraday arbitrage is difficult, there is no costless way to buy winter electricity and sell it in the summer, so there are seasonal variations as well as intraday variations. Peak-load power plants operate only when prices are high, temporarily increasing the supply of electricity. However, expectations about supply, storage, and peak-load power generation should already be reflected in the forward price.

Natural Gas

Natural gas is a market in which seasonality and storage costs are important. The natural gas futures contract, introduced in 1990, has become one of the most heavily traded futures contracts in the United States. The asset underlying one contract is 10,000 MMBtu, delivered over one month at a specific location (different gas contracts call for delivery at different locations). Figure 7 details the specifications for the Henry Hub contract.

Natural gas has several interesting characteristics. First, gas is costly to transport internationally, so prices and forward curves vary regionally. Second, once a given well has begun production, gas is costly to store. Third, demand for gas in the United States is highly seasonal, with peak demand arising from heating in winter months. Thus, there is a relatively steady stream of production with variable demand, which leads to large and

6. There are costly ways to store electricity. Three examples are *pumped storage hydroelectricity* (pump water into an uphill reservoir when prices are low, and release the water to flow over turbines when electricity is expensive); *night wind storage* (refrigerated warehouses are cooled to low temperature when electricity is cheap and the temperature is allowed to rise when electricity is expensive); *compressed air energy storage* (use wind power to compress air, then use the compressed air to drive turbines when electricity is expensive). All three of these methods entail losses.

TABLE 7 Day-ahead price, by hour, for 1 megawatt-hour of electricity in New York City, March 21, 2011.

Time	Price	Time	Price	Time	Price	Time	Price
0000	\$36.77	0600	\$44.89	1200	\$53.84	1800	\$56.18
0100	\$34.43	0700	\$58.05	1300	\$51.36	1900	\$63.51
0200	\$32.22	0800	\$52.90	1400	\$50.01	2000	\$54.99
0300	\$32.23	0900	\$54.06	1500	\$49.55	2100	\$47.01
0400	\$32.82	1000	\$55.06	1600	\$49.71	2200	\$40.26
0500	\$35.84	1100	\$55.30	1700	\$51.66	2300	\$37.29

Data from Bloomberg

FIGURE 7 Specifications for the NYMEX Henry Hub natural gas contract.

Underlying	Natural gas delivered at Sabine Pipe Lines Co.'s Henry Hub, Louisiana
Where traded	New York Mercantile Exchange
Size	10,000 million British thermal units (MMBtu)
Months	72 consecutive months
Trading ends	Third-to-last business day of month prior to maturity month
Delivery	As uniformly as possible over the delivery month

predictable price swings. Whereas corn has seasonal production and relatively constant demand, gas has relatively constant supply and seasonal demand.

Figure 8 displays strips of gas futures prices for the first Wednesday in June for 4 years between 2004 and 2010. In all curves, seasonality is evident, with high winter prices and low summer prices. The 2004 and 2006 strips show seasonal cycles combined with a downward trend in prices, suggesting that the market considered prices in that year as anomalously high. For the other years, the long-term trend is upward.

Gas storage is costly and demand for gas is highest in the winter. The steady rise of the forward curve (contango) during the fall months suggests that storage occurs just before the heaviest demand. In the June 2006 forward curve, the October, November, and December 2006 prices were \$7.059, \$8.329, and \$9.599. The interest rate at that time was about 5.5%, or 0.5%/month. Interest costs would thus contribute at most a few cents to contango. Considering the October and November prices, in a carry market, storage cost would have to satisfy equation (8):

$$8.329 = 7.059e^{0.005} + \lambda$$

FIGURE 8

Forward curves for natural gas for four years. Prices are dollars per MMBtu, from CME Group/NYMEX.

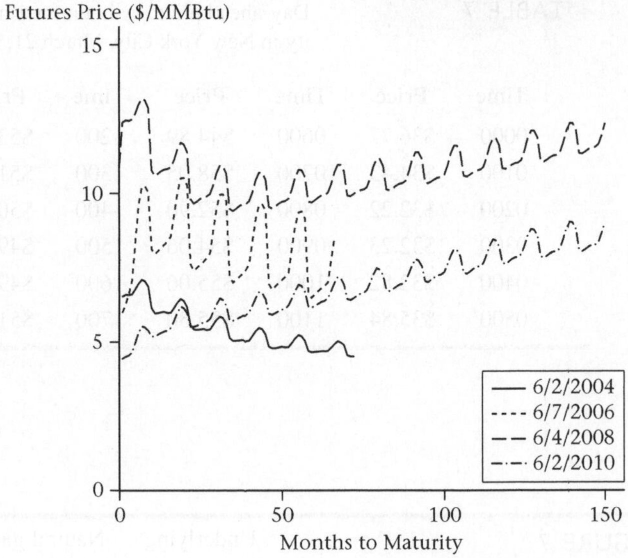

Data from Datastream.

This calculation implies an estimated expected marginal storage cost of $\lambda = \$1.235$ in November 2006. The technologies for storing gas range from pumping it into underground storage facilities to freezing it and storing it offshore in liquified natural gas tankers. By examining Figure 8 you will find different imputed storage costs in each year, but this is to be expected if marginal storage costs vary with the quantity stored.

Because of the expense in transporting gas internationally, the seasonal behavior of the forward curve can vary in different parts of the world. In tropical areas where gas is used for cooking and electricity generation, the forward curve is relatively flat because demand is relatively flat. In the Southern hemisphere, where seasons are reversed from the Northern hemisphere, the forward curve will peak in June and July rather than December and January.

Oil

Both oil and natural gas produce energy and are extracted from wells, but the different physical characteristics and uses of oil lead to a very different forward curve than that for gas. Oil is easier to transport than gas, with the result that oil trades in a global market. Oil is also easier to store than gas. Thus, seasonals in the price of crude oil are relatively unimportant. Specifications for the NYMEX light sweet crude oil contract (also known as West Texas Intermediate, or WTI) are shown in Figure 9.[7] The NYMEX forward curve on four dates is plotted in Figure 10.

7. Oil is called "sweet" if it has a relatively low sulfur content, and "sour" if the sulfur content is high.

FIGURE 9

Specifications for the NYMEX light sweet crude oil contract.

Underlying	Specific domestic crudes delivered at Cushing, Oklahoma
Where traded	New York Mercantile Exchange
Size	1000 U.S. barrels (42,000 gallons)
Months	30 consecutive months plus long-dated futures out 7 years
Trading ends	Third-to-last business day preceding the 25th calendar day of month prior to maturity month
Delivery	As uniformly as possible over the delivery month

FIGURE 10

Multi-year strips of NYMEX crude oil futures prices, $/barrel, for four different dates.

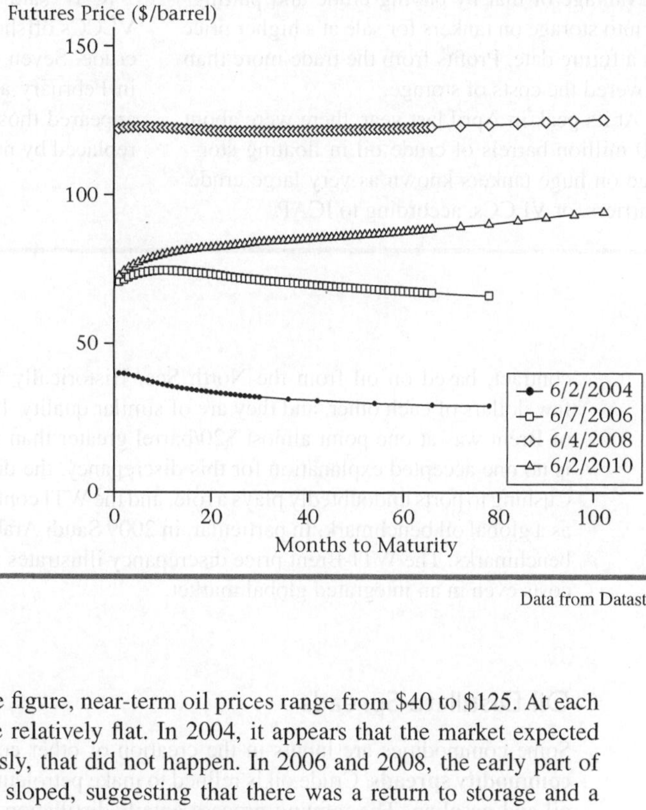

Data from Datastream.

On the four dates in the figure, near-term oil prices range from $40 to $125. At each price, the forward curves are relatively flat. In 2004, it appears that the market expected oil prices to decline. Obviously, that did not happen. In 2006 and 2008, the early part of the forward curve is steeply sloped, suggesting that there was a return to storage and a temporary surplus supply. During 2009, for example, there was substantial arbitrage activity with traders storing oil on tankers. This is discussed in Box 2.

Although oil is a global market, the delivery point for the WTI oil contract is Cushing, Oklahoma, which is landlocked. Another important oil contract is the Brent crude oil

BOX 2: Tanker-Based Arbitrage

From *The Wall Street Journal:* The huge floating stockpile of crude oil kept on tankers amid a global supply glut is showing signs of shrinking, as traders struggle to make profits from the once highly lucrative storage play.

The volume being stored at sea has nearly halved from a peak of about 90 million barrels in April last year, according to ship broker ICAP, and [is] expected to fall even further. . . .

The phenomenon of floating storage took off early last year. Oil on the spot market traded at a big discount to forward-dated contracts, in a condition known as contango. Traders took advantage of that by buying crude and putting it into storage on tankers for sale at a higher price at a future date. Profits from the trade more than covered the costs of storage.

At its peak in April last year, there were about 90 million barrels of crude oil in floating storage on huge tankers known as very large crude carriers, or VLCCs, according to ICAP.

But the spread between prompt crude-oil prices and forward prices has narrowed in recent weeks, while freight rates have increased, reducing the incentive to store oil for future delivery.

Contango has narrowed to around 40 cents a barrel, and "to cover your freight and other costs you need at least 90 cents," said Torbjorn Kjus, an oil analyst at DnB NOR Markets.

J.P. Morgan has said prices could even go into backwardation at the end of the second quarter, where spot prices are higher than those in forward contracts. This would be the first time the spread has been in positive territory since July last year.

ICAP said there were currently 21 trading VLCCs offshore with some 43 million barrels of crude. Seven of these are expected to discharge in February and one more in March. So far, it appeared those discharged cargoes wouldn't be replaced by new ones. . . .

Source: Chazan (2010)

contract, based on oil from the North Sea. Historically WTI and Brent traded within a few dollars of each other, and they are of similar quality. In early 2011, however, the price of Brent was at one point almost $20/barrel greater than the price of WTI. Though there is no one accepted explanation for this discrepancy, the difficulty of transporting oil from Cushing to ports undoubtedly plays a role, and the WTI contract in recent years has lost favor as a global oil benchmark. In particular, in 2009 Saudi Arabia dropped WTI from its export benchmarks. The WTI-Brent price discrepancy illustrates the importance of transportation costs even in an integrated global market.

Oil Distillate Spreads

Some commodities are inputs in the creation of other commodities, which gives rise to **commodity spreads**. Crude oil is refined to make petroleum products, in particular heating oil and gasoline. The refining process entails distillation, which separates crude oil into different components, including gasoline, kerosene, and heating oil. The split of oil into these different components can be complemented by a process known as "cracking"; hence, the difference in price between crude oil and equivalent amounts of heating oil and gasoline is called the **crack spread.**[8]

Oil can be processed in different ways, producing different mixes of outputs. The spread terminology identifies the number of gallons of oil as input, and the number of gallons of gasoline and heating oil as outputs. Traders will speak of "5-3-2," "3-2-1," and "2-1-1" crack spreads. The 5-3-2 spread, for example, reflects the profit from taking 5 gallons of oil as input, and producing 3 gallons of gasoline and 2 gallons of heating oil. A petroleum refiner producing gasoline and heating oil could use a futures crack spread to lock in both the cost of oil and output prices. This strategy would entail going long oil futures and short the appropriate quantities of gasoline and heating oil futures. Of course there are other inputs to production and it is possible to produce other outputs, such as jet fuel, so the crack spread is not a perfect hedge.

Example 3. A refiner in June 2010 planning for July production could have purchased July oil for \$72.86/barrel and sold August gasoline and heating oil for \$2.0279/gallon and \$2.0252/gallon. The 3-2-1 crack spread is the gross margin from buying 3 gallons of oil and selling 2 gallons of gasoline and 1 of heating oil. Using these prices, the spread is

$$2 \times \$2.0279 + \$2.0252 - 3 \times \$72.86/42 = \$0.8767$$

or $\$0.8767/3 = \$0.29221$/gallon. ■

There are crack spread swaps and options. Most commonly these are based on the difference between the price of heating oil and crude oil, and the price of gasoline and heating oil, both in a 1:1 ratio.

7. HEDGING STRATEGIES

In this section we discuss some issues when using commodity futures and forwards to hedge commodity price exposure. First, since commodities are heterogeneous and often costly to transport and store, it is common to hedge a risk with a commodity contract that is imperfectly correlated with the risk being hedged. This gives rise to *basis risk*: The price of the commodity underlying the futures contract may move differently than the price of the commodity you are hedging. For example, because of transportation cost and time, the price of natural gas in California may differ from that in Louisiana, which is the location underlying the principal natural gas futures contract (see again Figure 7). Second, in some cases one commodity may be used to hedge another. As an example of this we discuss the use of crude oil to hedge jet fuel. Finally, weather derivatives provide another example of an instrument that can be used to cross-hedge. We discuss degree-day index contracts as an example of such derivatives.

8. Spreads are also important in agriculture. Soybeans, for example, can be crushed to produce soybean meal and soybean oil (and a small amount of waste). A trader with a position in soybeans and an opposite position in equivalent quantities of soybean meal and soybean oil has a **crush spread** and is said to be "trading the crush."

Basis Risk

Exchange-traded commodity futures contracts call for delivery of the underlying commodity at specific locations and specific dates. The actual commodity to be bought or sold may reside at a different location and the desired delivery date may not match that of the futures contract. Additionally, the *grade* of the deliverable under the futures contract may not match the grade that is being delivered.

This general problem of the futures or forward contract not representing exactly what is being hedged is called *basis risk*. Basis risk is a generic problem with commodities because of storage and transportation costs and quality differences. Basis risk can also arise with financial futures, as for example when a company hedges its own borrowing cost with the Eurodollar contract.

In the same way as an individual stock could be hedged with an index futures contract, suppose we wish to hedge oil delivered on the East Coast with the NYMEX oil contract, which calls for delivery of oil in Cushing, Oklahoma. The variance-minimizing hedge ratio would be the regression coefficient obtained by regressing the East Coast price on the Cushing price. Problems with this regression are that the relationship may not be stable over time or may be estimated imprecisely.

Another example of basis risk occurs when hedgers decide to hedge distant obligations with near-term futures. For example, an oil producer might have an obligation to deliver 100,000 barrels per month at a fixed price for a year. The natural way to hedge this obligation would be to buy 100,000 barrels per month, locking in the price and supply on a month-by-month basis. This is called a **strip hedge**. We engage in a strip hedge when we hedge a stream of obligations by offsetting each individual obligation with a futures contract matching the maturity and quantity of the obligation. For the oil producer obligated to deliver every month at a fixed price, the hedge would entail buying the appropriate quantity each month, in effect taking a long position in the strip.

An alternative to a strip hedge is a **stack hedge**. With a stack hedge, we enter into futures contracts with a *single* maturity, with the number of contracts selected so that changes in the *present value* of the future obligations are offset by changes in the value of this "stack" of futures contracts. In the context of the oil producer with a monthly delivery obligation, a stack hedge would entail going long 1.2 million barrels using the near-term contract. (Actually, we would want to tail the position and go long fewer than 1.2 million barrels, but we will ignore this.) When the near-term contract matures, we reestablish the stack hedge by going long contracts in the new near month. This process of stacking futures contracts in the near-term contract and rolling over into the new near-term contract is called a **stack and roll**. If the new near-term futures price is below the expiring near-term price (i.e., there is backwardation), rolling is profitable.

There are at least two reasons for using a stack hedge. First, there is often more trading volume and liquidity in near-term contracts. With many commodities, bid-ask spreads widen with maturity. Thus, a stack hedge may have lower transaction costs than a strip hedge. Second, the manager may wish to speculate on the shape of the forward curve. You might decide that the forward curve looks unusually steep in the early months. If you undertake a stack hedge and the forward curve then flattens, you will have locked in all your oil at the relatively cheap near-term price, and implicitly made gains from not having locked in the relatively high strip prices.However, if the curve becomes steeper, it is possible to lose.

BOX 3: Metallgesellschaft A. G.

In 1992, a U.S. subsidiary of the German industrial firm Metallgesellschaft A. G. (MG) had offered customers fixed prices on over 150 million barrels of petroleum products, including gasoline, heating oil, and diesel fuel, over periods as long as 10 years. To hedge the resulting short exposure, MG entered into futures and swaps.

Much of MG's hedging was done using short-dated NYMEX crude oil and heating oil futures. Thus, MG was using stack hedging, rolling over the hedge each month.

During much of 1993, the near-term oil market was in contango (the forward curve was upward sloping). As a result of the market remaining in contango, MG systematically lost money when rolling its hedges and had to meet substantial margin calls. In December 1993, the supervisory board of MG decided to liquidate both its supply contracts and the futures positions used to hedge those contracts. In the end, MG sustained losses estimated at between \$200 million and \$1.3 billion.

The MG case was extremely complicated and has been the subject of pointed exchanges among academics—see in particular Culp and Miller (1995), Edwards and Canter (1995), and Mello and Parsons (1995). While the case is complicated, several issues stand out. First, was the stack and roll a reasonable strategy for MG to have undertaken? Second, should the position have been liquidated when and in the manner it was? (As it turned out, oil prices increased—which would have worked in MG's favor—following the liquidation.) Third, did MG encounter liquidity problems from having to finance losses on its hedging strategy? While the MG case has receded into history, hedgers still confront the issues raised by this case.

The box above recounts the story of Metallgesellschaft A. G. (MG), in which MG's large losses on a hedged position might have been caused, at least in part, by the use of a stack hedge.

Hedging Jet Fuel with Crude Oil

Jet fuel futures do not exist in the United States, but firms sometimes hedge jet fuel with crude oil futures along with futures for related petroleum products.[9] In order to perform this hedge, it is necessary to understand the relationship between crude oil and jet fuel prices. If we own a quantity of jet fuel and hedge by holding H crude oil futures contracts, our mark-to-market profit depends on the change in the jet fuel price and the change in the futures price:

$$(P_t - P_{t-1}) + H(F_t - F_{t-1}) \qquad (12)$$

where P_t is the price of jet fuel and F_t the crude oil futures price. We can estimate H by regressing the change in the jet fuel price (denominated in dollars per gallon) on the change in the crude oil futures price (denominated in dollars per gallon, which is the barrel price

9. This note has been intentionally omitted for this edition.

divided by 42). We use the nearest to maturity oil futures contract. Running this regression using daily data for January 2006–March 2011 gives[10]

$$P_t - P_{t-1} = \underset{(0.0009)}{0.0004} + \underset{(0.0192)}{0.8379}(F_t^{\text{oil}} - F_{t-1}^{\text{oil}}) \quad R^2 = 0.596 \tag{13}$$

Standard errors are below coefficients. The coefficient on the futures price change tells us that, on average, when the crude futures price increases by \$0.01, a gallon of jet fuel increases by \$0.008379.[11] The R^2 of 0.596 implies a correlation coefficient of about 0.77, so there is considerable variation in the price of jet fuel not accounted for by the price of crude. Because jet fuel is but one product produced from crude oil, it makes sense to see if adding other oil products to the regression improves the accuracy of the hedge. Adding the near term futures prices for heating oil and gasoline, we obtain

$$\begin{aligned} P_t - P_{t-1} = \underset{(0.0001)}{0.0006} + \underset{(0.0278)}{0.0897}\left(F_t^{\text{oil}} - F_{t-1}^{\text{oil}}\right) + \underset{(0.0277)}{0.8476}\left(F_t^{\text{heating oil}} - F_{t-1}^{\text{heating oil}}\right) \\ + \underset{(0.0222)}{0.0069}\left(F_t^{\text{gasoline}} - F_{t-1}^{\text{gasoline}}\right) \quad R^2 = 0.786 \end{aligned} \tag{14}$$

The explanatory power of the regression is improved, with an implied correlation of 0.886 between the actual and predicted jet fuel price. The price of heating oil is more closely related to the price of jet fuel than is the price of crude oil.

Weather Derivatives

Many businesses have revenue that is sensitive to weather: Ski resorts are harmed by warm winters, soft drink manufacturers are harmed by a cold spring, summer, or fall, and makers of lawn sprinklers are harmed by wet summers. In all of these cases, firms could hedge their risk using **weather derivatives**—contracts that make payments based upon realized characteristics of weather—to cross-hedge their specific risk.

Weather can affect both the price and consumption of energy-related products. If a winter is colder than average, homeowners and businesses will consume extra electricity, heating oil, and natural gas, and the prices of these products will tend to be high as well. Conversely, during a warm winter, energy prices and quantities will be low. While it is possible to use futures markets to hedge prices of commodities such as natural gas, hedging the quantity is more difficult. Weather derivatives can provide an additional contract with a payoff correlated with the quantity of energy used.

An example of a weather contract is the degree-day index futures contract traded at the CME Group. The contract is based on the premise that heating is used when temperatures are below 65 degrees and cooling is used when temperatures are above 65 degrees. Thus, a **heating degree-day** is the difference between 65 degrees Fahrenheit and the average daily temperature, if positive, or zero otherwise. A **cooling degree-day** is the difference between

10. This regression omits 4 days: September 11, 12, 15, and 16, 2008. The reported price of jet fuel on those days—a stressful period during the financial crisis—increased by over \$1/gallon and then on September 17 returned to its previous price.

11. In this case, crude is used to produce jet fuel, so it makes sense that dollar changes in the price of crude would be related to dollar changes in the price of jet fuel.

the average daily temperature and 65 degrees Fahrenheit, if positive, and zero otherwise. The monthly degree-day index is the sum of the daily degree-days over the month. The futures contract then settles based on the cumulative heating or cooling degree-days (the two are separate contracts) over the course of a month. The size of the contract is \$100 times the degree-day index. Degree-day index contracts are available for major cities in the United States, Europe, and Japan. There are also puts and calls on these futures.

With city-specific degree-day index contracts, it is possible to create and hedge payoffs based on average temperatures, or using options, based on ranges of average temperatures. If Minneapolis is unusually cold but the rest of the country is normal, the heating degree-day contract for Minneapolis will make a large payment that will compensate the holder for the increased consumption of energy.

8. SYNTHETIC COMMODITIES

Just as it is possible to use stock index futures to create a synthetic stock index, it is also possible to use commodity futures to create synthetic commodities. We can create a synthetic commodity by combining a commodity forward contract and a zero-coupon bond. Enter into a long commodity forward contract at the price $F_{0,T}$ and buy a zero-coupon bond that pays $F_{0,T}$ at time T. Since the forward contract is costless, the cost of this investment strategy at time 0 is just the cost of the bond, which equals the prepaid forward price: $e^{-rT}F_{0,T}$. At time T, the strategy pays

$$\underbrace{S_T - F_{0,T}}_{\text{Forward contract payoff}} + \underbrace{F_{0,T}}_{\text{Bond payoff}} = S_T$$

where S_T is the time T price of the commodity. This investment strategy creates a *synthetic commodity*, which has the same value as a unit of the commodity at time T.

During the early 2000s, indexed commodity investing became popular. Commodity funds use futures contracts and Treasury bills or other bonds to create synthetic commodities and replicate published commodity indexes. Two important indexes are the S&P GSCI index (originally created by Goldman Sachs) and the Dow Jones UBS index (originally created by AIG). Masters (2008) estimates that money invested in commodity funds grew 20-fold between 2003 and 2008, from \$13 billion to \$260 billion.[12] During this same period, commodity prices rose significantly. Figure 11 shows the performance of two commodity indexes plotted with the S&P 500. The two indexes diverge sharply in 2009 because they weight commodities differently. The S&P GSCI index, for example, is world-production

12. Index investors have to periodically exchange an expiring futures contract for a new long position. This transaction is referred to as "rolling" the position. For large index investors, the dollar amount of this futures roll can be substantial. Mou (2010) provides evidence that price effects from the roll are predictable and that front-running it can be profitable.

FIGURE 11

Value of S&P GSCI and DJ UBS indexes from 1991 to 2011, plotted against the S&P 500 index.

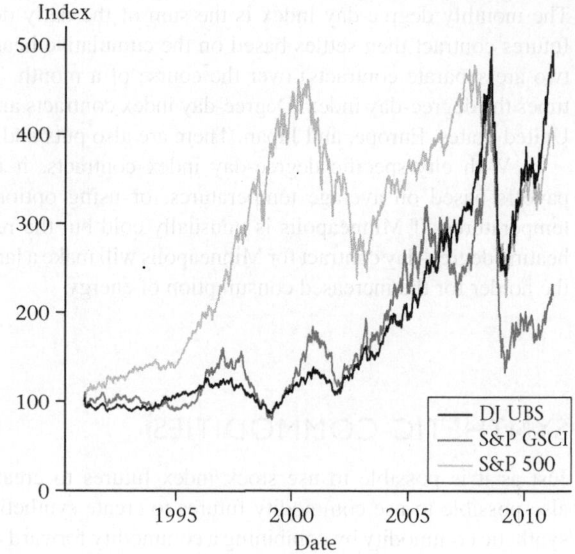

Source: Datastream

weighted and more heavily weights the petroleum sector. The DJ UBS index is designed to be more evenly weighted.[13]

You might wonder whether a commodity fund should use futures contracts to create synthetic commodities, or whether the fund should hold the physical commodity (where feasible). An important implication of the discussion in Section 3 is that it is generally preferable to invest in synthetic commodities rather than physical commodities. To see this, we can compare the returns to owning the physical commodity and owning a synthetic commodity. As before, let $\lambda(0, T)$ denote the future value of storage costs.

To invest in the physical commodity for 1 year, we can buy the commodity and prepay storage costs. This costs $S_0 + \lambda(0, 1)/(1 + R)$ initially and one period later pays $S_1 + \lambda(0, 1) - \lambda(0, 1) = S_1$.

An investment in the synthetic commodity costs the present value of the forward price, $F_{0,1}/(1 + R)$, and pays S_1. The synthetic investment will be preferable if

13. Historical commodity and futures data, necessary to estimate expected commodity returns, and thus to evaluate commodity investing as a strategy, are relatively hard to obtain. Bodie and Rosansky (1980) examine quarterly futures returns from 1950 to 1976, while Gorton and Rouwenhorst (2004) examine monthly futures returns from 1959 to 2004. Both studies construct portfolios of synthetic commodities—T-bills plus commodity futures—and find that these portfolios earn the same average return as stocks, are on average negatively correlated with stocks, and are positively correlated with inflation. These findings imply that a portfolio of stocks and synthetic commodities would have the same expected return and less risk than a diversified stock portfolio alone.

$$F_{0,1}/(1+R) < S_0 + \lambda(0, 1)/(1+R)$$

or $F_{0,1} < S_0(1+R) + \lambda(0, 1)$. Suppose, however, that $F_{0,1} > S_0(1+R) + \lambda(0, 1)$. This is an arbitrage opportunity exploitable by buying the commodity, storing it, paying storage costs, and selling it forward. Thus, if there is no arbitrage, we expect that $F_{0,1} \le S_0(1+R) + \lambda(0, 1)$ and the synthetic commodity will be the less expensive way to obtain the commodity return. Moreover, there will be equality only in a carry market. So investors will be indifferent between physical and synthetic commodities in a carry market, and will prefer synthetic commodities at all other times.

CHAPTER SUMMARY

At a general level, commodity forward prices can be described by the same formula as financial forward prices:

$$F_{0,T} = S_0 e^{(r-\delta)T} \tag{15}$$

For financial assets, δ is the dividend yield. For commodities, δ is the commodity *lease rate*—the return that makes an investor willing to buy and then lend a commodity. Thus, for the commodity owner who lends the commodity, it is like a dividend. From the commodity borrower's perspective, it is the cost of borrowing the commodity.

Different issues arise with commodity forwards than with financial forwards. For both commodities and financial assets, the forward price is the expected spot price discounted at the risk premium on the asset. (As with financial forwards, commodity forward prices are biased predictors of the future spot price when the commodity return contains a risk premium.) Storage of a commodity is an economic decision in which the investor compares the benefit from selling today with the benefit of selling in the future. When commodities are stored, the forward price must be sufficiently high so that a cash-and-carry compensates the investor for both financing and storage costs (this is called a carry market). When commodities are not stored, the forward price reflects the expected future spot price. Forward prices that are too high can be arbitraged with a cash-and-carry, while forward prices that are lower may not be arbitrageable, as the terms of a short sale should be based on the forward price. Some holders of a commodity receive a benefit from physical ownership. This benefit is called the commodity's *convenience yield*, and convenience can lower the forward price.

Forward curves provide information about individual commodities, each of which differs in the details. Forward curves for different commodities reflect different properties of storability, storage costs, production, demand, and seasonality. Electricity, gold, corn, natural gas, and oil all have distinct forward curves, reflecting the different characteristics of their physical markets. These idiosyncracies will be reflected in the individual commodity lease rates.

It is possible to create synthetic commodities by combining commodity futures and default-free bonds. In general it is financially preferable to invest in a synthetic rather than a physical commodity. Synthetic commodity indexes have been popular investments in recent years.

FURTHER READING

Geman (2005) and Siegel and Siegel (1990) provide a detailed discussion of many commodity futures. There are numerous papers on commodities. Bodie and Rosansky (1980) and Gorton and Rouwenhorst (2004) examine the risk and return of commodities as an investment. Brennan (1991), Pindyck (1993b), and Pindyck (1994) examine the behavior of commodity prices. Schwartz (1997) compares the performance of different models of commodity price behavior. Jarrow and Oldfield (1981) discuss the effect of storage costs on pricing, and Routledge et al. (2000) present a theoretical model of commodity forward curves. The websites of commodity exchanges are also useful resources, with information about particular contracts and sometimes about trading and hedging strategies.

Finally, Metallgesellschaft engendered a spirited debate. Papers written about that episode include Culp and Miller (1995), Edwards and Canter (1995), and Mello and Parsons (1995).

PROBLEMS

1. The spot price of a widget is \$70.00 per unit. Forward prices for 3, 6, 9, and 12 months are \$70.70, \$71.41, \$72.13, and \$72.86. Assuming a 5% continuously compounded annual risk-free rate, what are the annualized lease rates for each maturity? Is this an example of contango or backwardation?

2. The current price of oil is \$32.00 per barrel. Forward prices for 3, 6, 9, and 12 months are \$31.37, \$30.75, \$30.14, and \$29.54. Assuming a 2% continuously compounded annual risk-free rate, what is the annualized lease rate for each maturity? Is this an example of contango or backwardation?

3. Given a continuously compounded risk-free rate of 3% annually, at what lease rate will forward prices equal the current commodity price? (Recall the copper example in Section 3.) If the lease rate were 3.5%, would there be contango or backwardation?

4. Suppose that copper costs \$3.00 today and the continuously compounded lease rate for copper is 5%. The continuously compounded interest rate is 10%. The copper price in 1 year is uncertain and copper can be stored costlessly.

a. If you short-sell a pound of copper for 1 year, what payment do you have to make to the copper lender? Would it make sense for a financial investor to store copper in equilibrium?

b. Show that the equilibrium forward price is \$3.154.

c. In what sense is \$3.316 ($= 3 \times e^{0.10}$) a maximum possible forward price?

d. Explain the circumstances in which any price below \$3.316 could be the observed forward price, without giving rise to arbitrage. (Be sure to consider the possibility that the lease rate may not be 5%.)

5. Suppose the gold spot price is \$300/oz, the 1-year forward price is 310.686, and the continuously compounded risk-free rate is 5%.

a. What is the lease rate?

b. What is the return on a cash-and-carry in which gold is not loaned?

c. What is the return on a cash-and-carry in which gold is loaned, earning the lease rate?

For the next three problems, assume that the continuously compounded interest rate is 6% and the storage cost of widgets is $0.03 quarterly (payable at the end of the quarter). Here is the forward price curve for widgets:

Year 0	Year 1				Year 2	
Dec.	Mar.	June	Sept.	Dec.	Mar.	June
3.000	3.075	3.152	2.750	2.822	2.894	2.968

6. **a.** What are some possible explanations for the shape of this forward curve?

b. What annualized rate of return do you earn on a cash-and-carry entered into in December of Year 0 and closed in March of Year 1? Is your answer sensible?

c. What annualized rate of return do you earn on a cash-and-carry entered into in December of Year 0 and closed in September of Year 1? Is your answer sensible?

7. **a.** Suppose that you want to borrow a widget beginning in December of Year 0 and ending in March of Year 1. What payment will be required to make the transaction fair to both parties?

b. Suppose that you want to borrow a widget beginning in December of Year 0 and ending in September of Year 1. What payment will be required to make the transaction fair to both parties?

8. **a.** Suppose the March Year 1 forward price were $3.10. Describe two different transactions you could use to undertake arbitrage.

b. Suppose the September Year 1 forward price fell to $2.70 and subsequent forward prices fell in such a way that there is no arbitrage from September Year 1 and going forward. Is there an arbitrage you could undertake using forward contracts from June Year 1 and earlier? Why or why not?

9. Consider Example 1. Suppose the February forward price had been $2.80. What would the arbitrage be? Suppose it had been $2.65. What would the arbitrage be? In each case, specify the transactions and resulting cash flows in both November and February. What are you assuming about the convenience yield?

10. Using Table 6, what is your best guess about the current price of gold per ounce?

11. Consider production ratios of 2:1:1, 3:2:1, and 5:3:2 for oil, gasoline, and heating oil. Assume that other costs are the same per gallon of processed oil.

a. Which ratio maximizes the per-gallon profit if oil costs $80/barrel, gasoline is $2/gallon, and heating oil is $1.80/gallon?

b. Suppose gasoline costs $1.80/gallon and heating oil $2.10/gallon. Which ratio maximizes profit?

c. Which spread would you expect to be most profitable during the summer? Which during the winter?

12. Suppose you know nothing about widgets. You are going to approach a widget merchant to borrow one in order to short-sell it. (That is, you will take physical possession of the widget, sell it, and return a widget at time T.) Before you ring the doorbell, you want to make a judgment about what you think is a reasonable lease rate for the widget. Think about the following possible scenarios.

a. Suppose that widgets do not deteriorate over time, are costless to store, and are always produced, although production quantity can be varied. Demand is constant over time. Knowing nothing else, what lease rate might you face?

b. Suppose everything is the same as in (a) except that demand for widgets varies seasonally.

c. Suppose everything is the same as in (a) except that demand for widgets varies seasonally and the rate of production cannot be adjusted. Consider how seasonality and the horizon of your short-sale interact with the lease rate.

d. Suppose everything is the same as in (a) except that demand is constant over time and production is seasonal. Consider how production seasonality and the horizon of your short-sale interact with the lease rate.

e. Suppose that widgets cannot be stored. How does this affect your answers to the previous questions?

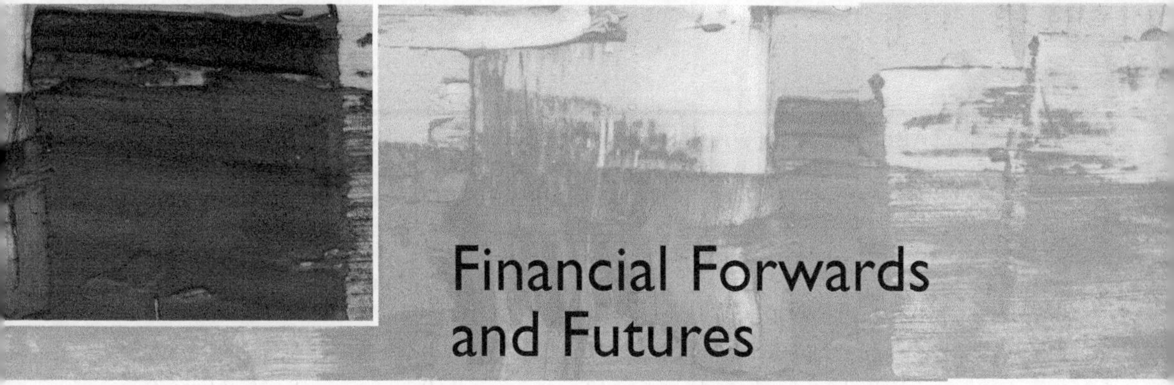

Financial Forwards and Futures

Forward contracts—which permit firms and investors to guarantee a price for a future purchase or sale—are a basic financial risk management tool. In this chapter we explore these contracts and study in detail forward and futures contracts on financial instruments, such as stocks, indexes, currencies, and interest rates. Our objectives are to understand more about the use of these contracts, how they are priced, and how market-makers hedge them.

Questions to keep in mind throughout the chapter include: Who might buy or sell specific contracts? What kinds of firms might use the contract for risk management? Why is the contract designed as it is?

1. ALTERNATIVE WAYS TO BUY A STOCK

The purchase of a share of XYZ stock has three components: (1) fixing the price, (2) the buyer making payment to the seller, and (3) the seller transferring share ownership to the buyer. If we allow for the possibility that payment and physical receipt can occur at different times—say, time 0 and time T—then once the price is fixed there are four logically possible purchasing arrangements: Payment can occur at time 0 or T, and physical receipt can occur at time 0 or T. Table 1 depicts these four possibilities, along with their customary names. Let's discuss these different arrangements.[1]

Outright purchase. The typical way to think about buying stock. You simultaneously pay the stock price in cash and receive ownership of the stock.

Fully leveraged purchase. A purchase in which you borrow the entire purchase price of the security. Suppose you borrow the share price, S_0, and agree to repay the borrowed

1. All of these arrangements can be reversed in the case of the seller. Problem 1 asks you to describe them from that perspective.

From Chapter 5 of *Derivatives Markets*, Third Edition, Robert McDonald. Copyright © 2013 by Pearson Education, Inc. Published by Pearson Prentice Hall. All rights reserved.

TABLE 1 Four different ways to buy a share of stock that has price S_0 at time 0. At time 0 you agree to a price, which is paid either today or at time T. The shares are received either at 0 or T. The interest rate is r.

Description	Pay at Time	Receive Security at Time	Payment
Outright purchase	0	0	S_0 at time 0
Fully leveraged purchase	T	0	S_0e^{rT} at time T
Prepaid forward contract	0	T	?
Forward contract	T	T	$? \times e^{rT}$

amount at time T. If the continuously compounded interest rate is r, at time T you would owe e^{rT} per dollar borrowed, or S_0e^{rT}.[2]

Prepaid forward contract. An arrangement in which you pay for the stock today and receive the stock at an agreed-upon future date.[3] The difference between a prepaid forward contract and an outright purchase is that with the former, you receive the stock at time T. We will see that the price you pay is not necessarily the stock price.

Forward contract. An arrangement in which you both pay for the stock and receive it at time T, with the time T price specified at time 0.

From Table 1 it is clear that you pay interest when you defer payment. The interesting question is how deferring the *physical receipt* of the stock affects the price; this deferral occurs with both the forward and prepaid forward contracts. What should you pay for the stock in those cases?[4]

2. PREPAID FORWARD CONTRACTS ON STOCK

A prepaid forward contract entails paying today to receive something—stocks, a foreign currency, bonds—in the future. The sale of a prepaid forward contract permits the owner to sell an asset while retaining physical possession for a period of time.

2. We use "r" to denote the interest rate. On any given date, the interest rate is typically different for different maturities, so you should always think of r as representing the rate appropriate for the maturity implied by the context. For example, the expression e^{-rT} should be interpreted as the cost today of a bond that pays \$1 at time T, and r is then implicitly the T-period interest rate. In some contexts, we will use a more precise notation to denote interest rates.

3. The term *prepaid forward contract*, or *prepay*, is used in practice to describe arrangements in which a party repays a loan with a predetermined number of shares of stock. So-called variable prepaid forwards are commonly used by large shareholders selling their stock.

4. The arrangements also differ with respect to credit risk, which arises from the possibility that the person on the other side of the transaction will not fulfill his or her end of the deal. (And of course the person on the other side of the deal may be worried about *you* fulfilling your obligation.)

We will derive the prepaid forward price using three different methods: pricing by analogy, pricing by present value, and pricing by arbitrage.

Pricing the Prepaid Forward by Analogy

Suppose you buy a prepaid forward contract on XYZ. By delaying physical possession of the stock, you do not receive dividends and have no voting or control rights. (We ignore here the value of voting and control.)

In the absence of dividends, whether you receive physical possession today or at time T is irrelevant: In either case you own the stock, and at time T it will be exactly as if you had owned the stock the whole time.[5] *Therefore, when there are no dividends, the price of the prepaid forward contract is the stock price today.* Denoting the prepaid forward price for an asset bought at time 0 and delivered at time T as $F_{0,T}^P$, the prepaid forward price for delivery at time T is

$$F_{0,T}^P = S_0 \tag{1}$$

Pricing the Prepaid Forward by Discounted Present Value

We can also derive the price of the prepaid forward using present value: We calculate the expected value of the stock at time T and then discount that value at an appropriate rate of return. The stock price at time T, S_T, is uncertain. Thus in computing the present value of the stock price, we need to use an appropriate risk-adjusted rate.

If the expected stock price at time T based on information we have at time 0 is $E_0(S_T)$, then the prepaid forward price is given by

$$F_{0,T}^P = E_0(S_T)e^{-\alpha T} \tag{2}$$

where α, the expected return on the stock, is determined using the CAPM or some other model of expected returns.

How do we compute the expected stock price? By definition of the expected return, we expect that in T years the stock will be worth

$$E_0(S_T) = S_0 e^{\alpha T}$$

Thus, equation (2) gives

$$F_{0,T}^P = E_0(S_T)e^{-\alpha T} = S_0 e^{\alpha T} e^{-\alpha T} = S_0$$

For a non-dividend-paying stock, the prepaid forward price is the stock price.

Pricing the Prepaid Forward by Arbitrage

Classical **arbitrage** describes a situation in which we can generate a positive cash flow either today or in the future by simultaneously buying and selling related assets, with no net investment of funds and with no risk. Arbitrage, in other words, is free money. An extremely

5. Suppose that someone secretly removed shares of stock from your safe and returned them 1 year later. From a purely financial point of view, you would never notice the stock to be missing.

TABLE 2 Cash flows and transactions to undertake arbitrage when the prepaid forward price, $F^P_{0,T}$, exceeds the stock price, S_0.

Transaction	Cash Flows: Time 0	Time T (expiration)
Buy stock @ S_0	$-S_0$	$+S_T$
Sell prepaid forward @ $F^P_{0,T}$	$+F^P_{0,T}$	$-S_T$
Total	$F^P_{0,T} - S_0$	0

important pricing principle, which we will use often, is that *the price of a derivative should be such that no arbitrage is possible*.

Here is an example of arbitrage. Suppose that the prepaid forward price exceeds the stock price—i.e., $F^P_{0,T} > S_0$. The arbitrageur will buy low and sell high by buying the stock for S_0 and selling the prepaid forward for $F^P_{0,T}$. This transaction makes money and it is also risk-free: Selling the prepaid forward requires that we deliver the stock at time T, and buying the stock today ensures that we have the stock to deliver. Thus, we earn $F^P_{0,T} - S_0$ today and at expiration we supply the stock to the buyer of the prepaid forward. We have earned positive profits today and offset all future risk. Table 2 summarizes this situation.

Now suppose on the other hand that $F^P_{0,T} < S_0$. Then we can engage in arbitrage by buying the prepaid forward and shorting the stock, earning $S_0 - F^P_{0,T}$. One year from now we acquire the stock via the prepaid forward and we use that stock to close the short position. The cash flows in the above table are simply reversed.

We assume that prices are at levels that preclude arbitrage. This raises a question: If prices are such that arbitrage is not profitable, who can afford to become an arbitrageur, watching out for arbitrage opportunities? We can resolve this paradox with the insight that in order for arbitrageurs to earn a living, arbitrage opportunities must occur from time to time; there must be "an equilibrium degree of disequilibrium."[6] However, you would not expect arbitrage to be obvious or easy to undertake.

The transactions in Table 2 are the same as those of a market-maker who is hedging a position. A market-maker would sell a prepaid forward if a customer wished to buy it. The market-maker then has an obligation to deliver the stock at a fixed price and, in order to offset this risk, can buy the stock. The market-maker thus engages in the same transactions as an arbitrageur, except the purpose is risk management, not arbitrage. Thus, *the transaction described in Table 2—selling the prepaid forward and buying the stock—also describes the actions of a market-maker.*

The no-arbitrage arguments we will make thus serve two functions: They tell us how to take advantage of mispricings, and they describe the behavior of market-makers managing risk.

6. The phrase is from Grossman and Stiglitz (1980), in which this idea was first proposed.

Pricing Prepaid Forwards with Dividends

When a stock pays a dividend, the prepaid forward price is less than the stock price. The owner of stock receives dividends, but the owner of a prepaid forward contract does not. It is necessary to adjust the prepaid forward price to reflect dividends that are received by the shareholder but not by the holder of the prepaid forward contract.

Discrete Dividends. To understand the effect of dividends, consider Stock A, which pays no dividend, and otherwise identical stock B, which pays a $5 dividend 364 days from today. We know that the 1-year prepaid forward price for stock A is the current stock price. What is the one-year prepaid forward price for stock B?

The $5 dividend is paid just before the prepaid forward expiration date 1 year from today. Thus, on the delivery date stock B will be priced $5 less than stock A. The prepaid forward price for stock B should therefore be lower than that for stock A by the present value of $5.

In general, the price for a prepaid forward contract will be the stock price less the present value of dividends to be paid over the life of the contract. Suppose there are multiple dividend payments made throughout the life of the forward contract: A stock is expected to make dividend payments of D_{t_i} at times t_i, $i = 1, \ldots, n$. A prepaid forward contract will entitle you to receive the stock at time T but without receiving the interim dividends. Thus, the prepaid forward price is

$$\boxed{F^P_{0,T} = S_0 - \sum_{i=1}^{n} \text{PV}_{0,t_i}(D_{t_i})} \tag{3}$$

where PV_{0,t_i} denotes the time 0 present value of a time t_i payment.

Example 1 Suppose XYZ stock costs $100 today and is expected to pay a $1.25 quarterly dividend, with the first coming 3 months from today and the last just prior to the delivery of the stock. Suppose the annual continuously compounded risk-free rate is 10%. The quarterly continuously compounded rate is therefore 2.5%. A 1-year prepaid forward contract for the stock would cost

$$F^P_{0,1} = \$100 - \sum_{i=1}^{4} \$1.25e^{-0.025i} = \$95.30 \quad \blacksquare$$

The calculation in this example implicitly assumes that the dividends are certain. Over a short horizon this might be reasonable. Over a long horizon we would expect dividend risk to be greater, and we would need to adjust the discount rate in computing the present value of expected dividends.

Continuous Dividends. For stock indexes containing many stocks, it is common to model the dividend as being paid continuously at a rate that is proportional to the level of the index; i.e., the dividend *yield* (the annualized dividend payment divided by the stock price) is constant. This is an approximation, but in a large stock index there can be dividend payments on a large proportion of days.[7] The dividend yield is not likely to be fixed in the short run: When stock prices rise, the dividend yield falls, at least temporarily. Nevertheless, we will assume a constant proportional dividend yield for purposes of this discussion.

To model a continuous dividend, suppose that the index price is S_0 and the annualized daily compounded dividend yield is δ. Then the dollar dividend over 1 day is

$$\text{Daily dividend} = \frac{\delta}{365} \times S_0$$

Now suppose that we reinvest dividends in the index. Because of reinvestment, after T years we will have more shares than we started with. Using continuous compounding to approximate daily compounding, we get

$$\text{Number of shares} = \left(1 + \frac{\delta}{365}\right)^{365 \times T} \approx e^{\delta T}$$

At the end of T years we have approximately $e^{\delta T}$ times the shares we had initially.

Now suppose we wish to invest today in order to have one share at time T. We can buy $e^{-\delta T}$ shares today. Because of dividend reinvestment, at time T, we will have $e^{\delta T}$ more shares than we started with, so we end up with exactly one share. Adjusting the initial quantity in this way in order to offset the effect of income from the asset is called **tailing** the position. Tailing enables us to offset the effect of continuous dividends. We will encounter the concept of tailing frequently.

Since an investment of $e^{-\delta T} S_0$ gives us one share at time T, this is the time 0 prepaid forward price for delivery at time T:

$$\boxed{F^P_{0,T} = S_0 e^{-\delta T}} \tag{4}$$

where δ is the dividend yield and T the time to maturity of the prepaid forward contract.

Example 2. Suppose that the index is \$125 and the annualized daily compounded dividend yield is 3%. The daily dollar dividend is

$$\text{Dividend} = (0.03 \div 365) \times \$125 = \$0.01027$$

or a little more than one penny per unit of the index. If we start by holding one unit of the index, at the end of 1 year we will have

$$e^{0.03} = 1.030455$$

shares. Thus, if we wish to end the year holding one share, we must invest in

$$e^{-0.03} = 0.970446$$

shares. The prepaid forward price is

$$\$125e^{-0.03} = \$121.306$$ ■

7. There is significant seasonality in dividend payments, which can be important in practice. A large number of U.S. firms pay quarterly dividends in February, May, August, and November. German firms, by contrast, pay annual dividends concentrated in May, June, and July.

BOX 1: Low Exercise Price Options

In some countries, including Australia and Switzerland, it is possible to buy stock options with very low strike prices—so low that it is virtually certain the option will expire in-the-money. For example, in Australia, the strike price is a penny. Such an option is called a *low exercise price option* (LEPO). These often exist in order to avoid taxes or transaction fees associated with directly trading the stock. LEPOs do not pay dividends and do not carry voting rights. As with any call option, a LEPO is purchased outright, and it entitles the option holder to acquire the stock at expiration by paying the (low) strike price. The payoff of a LEPO expiring at time T is

$$\max(0, S_T - K)$$

However, if the strike price, K, is so low that the option is certain to be exercised, this is just

$$S_T - K$$

This option has a value at time 0 of

$$F^P_{0,T} - \text{PV}(K)$$

Since the strike price of the option is close to zero, a LEPO is essentially a prepaid forward contract.

3. FORWARD CONTRACTS ON STOCK

If we know the prepaid forward price, we can compute the forward price. The difference between a prepaid forward contract and a forward contract is the timing of the payment for the stock, which is immediate with a prepaid forward but deferred with a forward. Because there is deferral of payment, the forward contract is initially costless for both the buyer and seller; the premium is zero. Also, because payment is deferred, the forward price is just the future value of the prepaid forward price:

$$F_{0,T} = \text{FV}(F^P_{0,T}) \tag{5}$$

This formula holds for any kind of dividend payment.

An important special case is that of a continuous dividend. In that case, equation (5) becomes

$$F_{0,T} = e^{rT} S_0 e^{-\delta T}$$

or

$$\boxed{F_{0,T} = S_0 e^{(r-\delta)T}} \tag{6}$$

The r in equation (6) is the yield to maturity for a default-free zero coupon bond with the same time to maturity as the forward contract. For each maturity, there is an interest rate, r, such that $e^{-r(T-t)} = P(t, T)$, where $P(t, T)$ is the time t price of a zero-coupon bond maturing at time T. We can therefore also write equation (6) as the price of the prepaid forward contract divided by the price of a zero-coupon bond:

$$F_{0,T} = S_0 e^{-\delta T} / P(0, T)$$

For forward contracts with different maturities, different values of r (and for that matter, δ) will generally be appropriate. For simplicity we will write formulas as if there is a single interest rate for all maturities, but in practice this is unlikely to be true.

As is apparent from equation (6), the forward price is generally different from the spot price. The **forward premium** is the ratio of the forward price to the spot price, defined as

$$\text{Forward premium} = \frac{F_{0,T}}{S_0} \tag{7}$$

We can annualize the forward premium and express it as a percentage, in which case we have

$$\text{Annualized forward premium} = \frac{1}{T} \ln\left(\frac{F_{0,T}}{S_0}\right)$$

For the case of continuous dividends, equation (6), the annualized forward premium is simply the difference between the risk-free rate and the dividend yield, $r - \delta$.

Occasionally it is possible to observe the forward price but not the price of the underlying stock or index. For example, the futures contract for the S&P 500 index trades at times when the NYSE is not open, so it is possible to observe the futures price but not the stock price. The asset price implied by the forward pricing formulas above is said to define **fair value** for the underlying stock or index. Equation (6) is used in this case to infer the value of the index.

Does the Forward Price Predict the Future Spot Price?

It is common to think that the forward price predicts the future spot price. Equation (9) tells us that the forward price equals the expected future spot price, but with a discount for the risk premium of the asset. Thus, the forward price *systematically* errs in predicting the future stock price. If the asset has a positive risk premium, the future spot price will on average be greater than the forward price.

The reason is straightforward. When you buy a stock, you invest money that has an opportunity cost (it could otherwise have been invested in an interest-earning asset), and you are acquiring the risk of the stock. On average you expect to earn interest as compensation for the time value of money. You also expect an additional return as compensation for the risk of the stock—this is the risk premium. Algebraically, the expected return on a stock is

$$\alpha = \underbrace{r}_{\text{Compensation for time}} + \underbrace{\alpha - r}_{\text{Compensation for risk}} \tag{8}$$

When you enter into a forward contract, there is no investment; hence, you are not compensated for the time value of money. However, the forward contract retains the risk of the stock, so you must be compensated for risk. *This means that the forward contract must earn the risk premium.* If the risk premium is positive, then on average you must expect a positive return from the forward contract. The only way this can happen is if the forward price predicts too low a stock price. In other words *the forward contract is a biased predictor of the future stock price.* This explains the discount by the risk premium in equation (9).

As an example, suppose that a stock index has an expected return of 15%, while the risk-free rate is 5%. If the current index price is 100, then on average we expect that the index will be 115 in 1 year. The forward price for delivery in 1 year will be only 105, however.

This means that a holder of the forward contract will on average earn positive profits, albeit at the cost of bearing the risk of the index.[8]

We can see the bias in another way by using equation (2). The prepaid forward price is the present value of the expected future spot price. The forward price is the future value of the prepaid forward price. Thus, we have

$$F_{0,T} = e^{rT} F^P_{0,T} = E_0(S_T)e^{-(\alpha - r)T} \tag{9}$$

The forward price is the expected future spot price, discounted at the risk premium.

This bias does not imply that a forward contract is a good investment. Rather, it tells us that *the risk premium on an asset can be created at zero cost and hence has a zero value.* Though this seems surprising, it is a result from elementary finance that if we buy any asset and borrow the full amount of its cost—a transaction that requires no investment—then we earn the risk premium on the asset. Since a forward contract has the risk of a fully leveraged investment in the asset, it earns the risk premium. This proposition is true in general, not just for the example of a forward on a non-dividend-paying stock.

Creating a Synthetic Forward Contract

A market-maker or arbitrageur must be able to offset the risk of a forward contract. It is possible to do this by creating a *synthetic* forward contract to offset a position in the actual forward contract.

In this discussion we will assume that dividends are continuous and paid at the rate δ, and hence that equation (6) is the appropriate forward price. We can then create a synthetic long forward contract by buying the stock and borrowing to fund the position. To see how the synthetic position works, recall that the payoff at expiration for a long forward position on the index is

$$\text{Payoff at expiration} = S_T - F_{0,T}$$

In order to obtain this same payoff, we buy a tailed position in the stock, investing $S_0e^{-\delta T}$. This gives us one share at time T. We borrow this amount so that we are not required to pay anything additional at time 0. At time T we must repay $S_0e^{(r-\delta)T}$ and we sell the stock for S_T. Table 3 demonstrates that borrowing to buy the stock replicates the expiration payoff to a forward contract.

Just as we can use the stock and borrowing to synthetically create a forward, we can also use the forward to create synthetic stocks and bonds. Table 4 demonstrates that we can go long a forward contract and lend the present value of the forward price to synthetically create the stock. The expiration payoff in this table assumes that equation (6) holds. Table 5 demonstrates that if we buy the stock and short the forward, we create cash flows like those of a risk-free bond. The rate of return on this synthetic bond—the construction of which is summarized in Table 5—is called the **implied repo rate**.

To summarize, we have shown that

$$\text{Forward} = \text{Stock} - \text{zero-coupon bond} \tag{10}$$

---

8. Accounting for dividends in this example would not change the magnitude of the bias, since dividends would lower the expected future price of the index and the forward price by equal amounts.

TABLE 3 Demonstration that borrowing $S_0 e^{-\delta T}$ to buy $e^{-\delta T}$ shares of the index replicates the payoff to a forward contract, $S_T - F_{0,T}$.

Transaction	Cash Flows: Time 0	Cash Flows: Time T (expiration)
Buy $e^{-\delta T}$ units of the index	$-S_0 e^{-\delta T}$	$+S_T$
Borrow $S_0 e^{-\delta T}$	$+S_0 e^{-\delta T}$	$-S_0 e^{(r-\delta)T}$
Total	0	$S_T - S_0 e^{(r-\delta)T}$

TABLE 4 Demonstration that going long a forward contract at the price $F_{0,T} = S_0 e^{(r-\delta)T}$ and lending the present value of the forward price creates a synthetic share of the index at time T.

Transaction	Cash Flows: Time 0	Cash Flows: Time T (expiration)
Long one forward	0	$S_T - F_{0,T}$
Lend $S_0 e^{-\delta T}$	$-S_0 e^{-\delta T}$	$+S_0 e^{(r-\delta)T}$
Total	$-S_0 e^{-\delta T}$	S_T

TABLE 5 Demonstration that buying $e^{-\delta T}$ shares of the index and shorting a forward creates a synthetic bond.

Transaction	Cash Flows: Time 0	Cash Flows: Time T (expiration)
Buy $e^{-\delta T}$ units of the index	$-S_0 e^{-\delta T}$	$+S_T$
Short one forward	0	$F_{0,T} - S_T$
Total	$-S_0 e^{-\delta T}$	$F_{0,T}$

We can rearrange this equation to derive other synthetic equivalents.

$$\text{Stock} = \text{Forward} + \text{zero-coupon bond}$$

$$\text{Zero-coupon bond} = \text{Stock} - \text{forward}$$

All of these synthetic positions can be reversed to create synthetic short positions.

TABLE 6 Transactions and cash flows for a cash-and-carry: A market-maker is short a forward contract and long a synthetic forward contract.

Transaction	Cash Flows: Time 0	Cash Flows: Time T (expiration)
Buy tailed position in stock, paying $S_0e^{-\delta T}$	$-S_0e^{-\delta T}$	$+S_T$
Borrow $S_0e^{-\delta T}$	$+S_0e^{-\delta T}$	$-S_0e^{(r-\delta)T}$
Short forward	0	$F_{0,T} - S_T$
Total	0	$F_{0,T} - S_0e^{(r-\delta)T}$

TABLE 7 Transactions and cash flows for a reverse cash-and-carry: A market-maker is long a forward contract and short a synthetic forward contract.

Transaction	Cash Flows: Time 0	Cash Flows: Time T (expiration)
Short tailed position in stock, receiving $S_0e^{-\delta T}$	$+S_0e^{-\delta T}$	$-S_T$
Lend $S_0e^{-\delta T}$	$-S_0e^{-\delta T}$	$+S_0e^{(r-\delta)T}$
Long forward	0	$S_T - F_{0,T}$
Total	0	$S_0e^{(r-\delta)T} - F_{0,T}$

Synthetic Forwards in Market-Making and Arbitrage

Now we will see how market-makers and arbitrageurs use these strategies. Suppose a customer wishes to enter into a long forward position. The market-maker, as the counterparty, is left holding a short forward position. He can offset this risk by creating a synthetic long forward position.

Specifically, consider the transactions and cash flows in Table 6. The market-maker is short a forward contract and long a synthetic forward contract, constructed as in Table 3. There is no risk because the total cash flow at time T is $F_{0,T} - S_0e^{(r-\delta)T}$. All of the components of this cash flow—the forward price, the stock price, the interest rate, and the dividend yield—are known at time 0. The result is a risk-free position.

Similarly, suppose the market-maker wishes to hedge a long forward position. Then it is possible to reverse the positions in Table 6. The result is in Table 7.

A transaction in which you buy the underlying asset and short the offsetting forward contract is called a **cash-and-carry**. A cash-and-carry has no risk: You have an obligation to deliver the asset but also own the asset. The market-maker offsets the short forward position with a cash-and-carry. An arbitrage that involves buying the underlying asset and selling it forward is called a **cash-and-carry arbitrage.** As you might guess, a **reverse cash-and-carry** entails short-selling the index and entering into a long forward position.

If the forward contract is priced according to equation (6), then profits on a cash-and-carry are zero. We motivated the cash-and-carry in Table 6 as risk management by a market-maker. However, an arbitrageur might also engage in a cash-and-carry. If the forward price is too high relative to the stock price—i.e., if $F_{0,T} > S_0 e^{(r-\delta)T}$—then an arbitrageur or market-maker can use the strategy in Table 6 to make a risk-free profit.

An arbitrageur would make the transactions in Table 7 if the forward were underpriced relative to the stock—i.e., if $S_0 e^{(r-\delta)T} > F_{0,T}$.

As a final point, you may be wondering about the role of borrowing and lending in Tables 6 and 7. When you explicitly account for borrowing, you account for the opportunity cost of investing funds. For example, if we omitted borrowing from Table 6, we would invest $S_0 e^{-\delta T}$ today and receive $F_{0,T}$ at time T. In order to know if there is an arbitrage opportunity, we would need to perform a present value calculation to compare the time 0 cash flow with the time T cash flow. By explicitly including borrowing in the calculations, this time-value-of-money comparison is automatic.[9]

Similarly, by comparing the implied repo rate with our borrowing rate, we have a simple measure of whether there is an arbitrage opportunity. For example, if we could borrow at 7%, then there is an arbitrage opportunity if the implied repo rate exceeds 7%. On the other hand, if our borrowing rate exceeds the implied repo rate, there is no arbitrage opportunity.

No-Arbitrage Bounds with Transaction Costs

Tables 6 and 7 demonstrate that an arbitrageur can make a costless profit if $F_{0,T} \neq S_0 e^{(r-\delta)T}$. This analysis ignores trading fees, bid-ask spreads, different interest rates for borrowing and lending, and the possibility that buying or selling in large quantities will cause prices to change. The effect of such costs will be that, rather than there being a single no-arbitrage price, there will be a no-arbitrage *bound*: a lower price F^- and an upper price F^+ such that arbitrage will not be profitable when the forward price is between these bounds.

Suppose that the stock and forward have bid and ask prices of $S^b < S^a$ and $F^b < F^a$, a trader faces a cost k of transacting in the stock or forward, and the interest rates for borrowing and lending are $r^b > r^l$. In this example we suppose that there are no transaction costs at time T, with the forward settled by delivery of the stock.

We will first derive F^+. An arbitrageur believing the observed bid forward price, F^b, is too high will undertake the transactions in Table 6: Sell the forward and borrow to buy the stock. For simplicity we will assume the stock pays no dividends. The arbitrageur will pay the transaction cost k to short the forward and pay $(S_0^a + k)$ to acquire one share of stock. The required borrowing to finance the position is therefore $S_0^a + 2k$. At time T, the payoff is

$$\underbrace{-(S_0^a + 2k)e^{r^b T}}_{\text{Repayment of borrowing}} + \underbrace{F_{0,T} - S_T}_{\text{Value of forward}} + \underbrace{S_T}_{\text{Value of stock}}$$

9. In general, arbitrageurs can borrow and lend at different rates. A pro forma arbitrage calculation needs to account for the appropriate cost of capital for any particular transaction.

Arbitrage is profitable if this expression is positive, or

$$F^b > F^+ = (S_0^a + 2k)e^{r^b T} \tag{11}$$

Thus, the upper bound reflects the fact that we pay a high price for the stock (the ask price), pay transaction costs on both the stock and forward, and borrow at a high rate.

We can derive F^- analogously. Problem 14 asks you to verify that the bound below which arbitrage is feasible is

$$F^a < F^- = (S_0^b - 2k)e^{r^l T} \tag{12}$$

This expression assumes that short-selling the stock does not entail costs other than bid-ask transaction costs when the short position is initiated.

Notice that in equations (11) and (12), the costs all enter in such a way as to make the no-arbitrage region as large as possible (for example, the low lending rate enters F^- and the high borrowing rate enters F^+). This makes economic sense: Trading costs cannot help an arbitrageur make a profit.

There are additional costs not reflected in equations (11) and (12). One is that significant amounts of trading can move prices, so that what appears to be an arbitrage may vanish if prices change when the arbitrageur enters a large order. Another challenge can be execution risk. If trades do not occur instantaneously, the arbitrage can vanish before the trades are completed.

It is likely that the no-arbitrage region will be different for different arbitrageurs at a point in time, and different across time for a given arbitrageur. For example, consider the trading transaction cost, k. A large investment bank sees stock order flow from a variety of sources and may have inventory of either long or short positions in stocks. The bank may be able to buy or sell shares at low cost by serving as market-maker for a customer order. It may be inexpensive for a bank to short if it already owns the stocks, or it may be inexpensive to buy if the bank already has a short position.

Borrowing and lending rates can also vary. For a transaction that is explicitly financed by borrowing, the relevant interest rates are the arbitrageur's marginal borrowing rate (if that is the source of funds to buy stocks) or lending rate (if stocks are to be shorted). However, at other times, it may be possible to borrow at a lower rate or lend at a higher rate. For example, it may be possible to sell T-bills being held for some other purpose as a source of short-term funds. This may effectively permit borrowing at a low rate. Finally, in order to borrow money or securities arbitrageurs must have available capital. Undertaking one arbitrage may prevent undertaking another.

The overall conclusion is not surprising: Arbitrage may be difficult, risky, and costly. Large deviations from the theoretical price may be arbitraged, but small deviations may or may not represent genuine arbitrage opportunities.

Quasi-Arbitrage

The previous section focused on explicit arbitrage. However, it can also be possible to undertake *implicit* arbitrage by substituting a low yield position for one with a higher return. We call this **quasi-arbitrage**.

Consider, for example, a corporation that can borrow at 8.5% and lend at 7.5%. Suppose there is a cash-and-carry transaction with an implied repo rate of 8%. There is no pure arbitrage opportunity for the corporation, but it would make sense to divert lending from the 7.5% assets to the 8% cash-and-carry. If we attempt explicit arbitrage by borrowing at 8.5% in order to earn 8% on the cash-and-carry, the transaction becomes unprofitable. We can arbitrage only to the extent that we are already lending; this is why it is "quasi"-arbitrage.

An Interpretation of the Forward Pricing Formula

The forward pricing formula for a stock index, equation (6), depends on $r - \delta$, the difference between the risk-free rate and the dividend yield. This difference is called the **cost of carry**.

Suppose you buy a unit of the index that costs S and fund the position by borrowing at the risk-free rate. You will pay rS on the borrowed amount, but the dividend yield will provide offsetting income of δS. You will have to pay the difference, $(r - \delta)S$, on an ongoing basis. This difference is the net cash flow if you carry a long position in the asset; hence, it is called the "cost of carry."

Now suppose you were to short the index and invest the proceeds at the risk-free rate. You would receive S for shorting the asset and earn rS on the invested proceeds, but you would have to pay δS to the index lender. We will call δ the lease rate of the index; it is what you would have to pay to a lender of the asset. The lease rate of an asset is the annualized cash payment that the borrower must make to the lender. For a non-dividend-paying stock, the lease rate is zero, while for a dividend-paying stock, the lease rate is the dividend.[10]

Here is an interpretation of the forward pricing formula:

$$\text{Forward price} = \text{Spot price} + \underbrace{\text{Interest to carry the asset} - \text{Asset lease rate}}_{\text{Cost of carry}} \tag{13}$$

The forward contract, unlike the stock, requires no investment and makes no payouts and therefore has a zero cost of carry. One way to interpret the forward pricing formula is that, to the extent the forward contract saves our having to pay the cost of carry, we are willing to pay a higher price. This is what equation (13) says.

4. FUTURES CONTRACTS

Futures contracts are essentially exchange-traded forward contracts. As with forwards, futures contracts represent a commitment to buy or sell an underlying asset at some future date. Because futures are exchange-traded, they are standardized and have specified delivery dates, locations, and procedures. Futures may be traded either electronically or in trading pits, with buyers and sellers shouting orders to one another (this is called **open outcry**). Each exchange has an associated clearinghouse.

Although forwards and futures are similar in many respects, there are differences.

- Whereas forward contracts are settled at expiration, futures contracts are settled daily. The determination of who owes what to whom is called **marking-to-market**. Frequent marking-to-market and settlement of a futures contract can lead to pricing differences between the futures and an otherwise identical forward.
- As a result of daily settlement, futures contracts are liquid—it is possible to offset an obligation on a given date by entering into the opposite position. For example, if you

10. This discussion ignores lending fees, which are generally small (several basis points).

are long the September S&P 500 futures contract, you can cancel your obligation to buy by entering into an offsetting obligation to sell the September S&P 500 contract. If you use the same broker to buy and to sell, your obligation is officially cancelled.[11]

- Over-the-counter forward contracts can be customized to suit the buyer or seller, whereas futures contracts are standardized. For example, available futures contracts may permit delivery of 250 units of a particular index in only March or June. A forward contract, by contrast, could specify April delivery of 300 units of the index.
- Because of daily settlement, the nature of credit risk is different with the futures contract. In fact, futures contracts are structured so as to minimize the effects of credit risk.
- There are typically daily price limits in futures markets (and on some stock exchanges as well). A **price limit** is a move in the futures price that triggers a temporary halt in trading. For example, there is an initial 5% limit on *down* moves in the S&P 500 futures contract. An offer to sell exceeding this limit can trigger a temporary trading halt, after which time a 10% price limit is in effect. If that is exceeded, there are subsequent 15% and 20% limits. The rules can be complicated, but it is important to be aware that such rules exist.

We will illustrate futures contracts with the S&P 500 index futures contract as a specific example.

The S&P 500 Futures Contract

The S&P 500 futures contract has the S&P 500 stock index as the underlying asset. Futures on individual stocks have recently begun trading in the United States. (See Box 2.) Figure 1 shows the specifications of a newspaper quotation for the S&P 500 index futures contract along with other stock index futures contracts. The **notional value**, or size, of the contract is the dollar value of the assets underlying one contract. In this case it is by definition $\$250 \times 1300 = \$325{,}000$.[12]

The S&P 500 is an example of a cash-settled contract: Instead of settling by actual delivery of the underlying stocks, the contract calls for a cash payment that equals the profit or loss *as if* the contract were settled by delivery of the underlying asset. On the expiration day, the S&P 500 futures contract is marked-to-market against the actual cash index. This final settlement against the cash index guarantees that the futures price equals the index value at contract expiration.

It is easy to see why the S&P 500 is cash-settled. A physical settlement process would call for delivery of 500 shares (or some large subset thereof) in the precise percentage they make up the S&P 500 index. This basket of stocks would be expensive to buy and sell. Cash settlement is an inexpensive alternative.

11. Although forward contracts may not be explicitly marketable, it is generally possible to enter into an offsetting position to cancel the obligation to buy or sell.

12. Because the S&P 500 index is a fabricated number—a value-weighted average of individual stock prices—the S&P 500 index is treated as a pure number rather than a price, and the contract is defined at maturity to have a size of $\$250 \times$ S&P 500 index.

BOX 2: Single Stock Futures

Futures contracts on individual stocks trade in various countries. In the United States, single stock futures began trading in November 2002 on OneChicago, an electronic exchange owned jointly by the Chicago Board Options Exchange, the Chicago Board of Trade, and the Chicago Mercantile Exchange. Earlier, the trading of single stock futures had been stalled by disagreements among exchanges and by a regulatory turf battle between the Securities and Exchange Commission, which regulates stocks and stock options, and the Commodity Futures Trading Commission, which regulates commodity and equity index futures.

Single stock futures were controversial even before trading began, with disagreement about how successful the product would be. What need would single stock futures serve? There was already a well-established market for buying and short-selling stocks, and investors could create synthetic stock forwards using options. Would differences in margin requirements, transaction costs, or contract characteristics make the new product successful?

Since 2002, one competitor to OneChicago (NQLX) has entered and then exited the market for single stock futures in the United States. Trading volume has proved disappointing for some advocates (see Zwick and Collins, 2004).

In 2010, OneChicago ("OCX") introduced OCX.NoDiv, a dividend-protected single-stock futures contract. The new product reduces the futures settlement price by the dividend amount on each ex-dividend day. The new contract should have a price equal to the stock price plus interest, while the standard contract will subtract the present value of dividends. The two contracts trading side-by-side permit investors to speculate on and hedge dividends.

FIGURE 1

Specifications for the S&P 500 index futures contract.

Underlying	S&P 500 index
Where traded	Chicago Mercantile Exchange
Size	$250 × S&P 500 index
Months	March, June, September, December
Trading ends	Business day prior to determination of settlement price
Settlement	Cash-settled, based upon opening price of S&P 500 on third Friday of expiration month

Margins and Marking to Market

Let's explore the logistics of holding a futures position. Suppose the futures price is 1100 and you wish to acquire a \$2.2 million position in the S&P 500 index. The notional value of one contract is $\$250 \times 1100 = \$275,000$; this represents the amount you are agreeing to pay at expiration per futures contract. To go long \$2.2 million of the index, you would enter into \$2.2 million/\$0.275 million = 8 long futures contracts. The notional value of eight contracts is $8 \times \$250 \times 1100 = \$2,000 \times 1100 = \$2.2$ million.

A broker executes your buy order. For every buyer there is a seller, which means that one or more investors must be found who simultaneously agree to sell forward the same number of units of the index. The total number of open positions (buy/sell pairs) is called the **open interest** of the contract.

Both buyers and sellers are required to post a performance bond with the broker to ensure that they can cover a specified loss on the position.[13] This deposit, which can earn interest, is called **margin** and is intended to protect the counterparty against your failure to meet your obligations. The margin is a performance bond, not a premium. Hence, futures contracts are costless (not counting, of course, commissions and the bid-ask spread).

To understand the role of margin, suppose that there is 10% margin and weekly settlement (in practice, settlement is daily). The margin on futures contracts with a notional value of \$2.2 million is \$220,000.

If the S&P 500 futures price drops by 1, to 1099, we lose \$2000 on our futures position. The reason is that eight long contracts obligate us to pay $\$2000 \times 1100$ to buy 2000 units of the index which we could now sell for only $\$2000 \times 1099$. Thus, we lose $(1099 - 1100) \times \$2000 = -\$2000$. Suppose that over the first week, the futures price drops 72.01 points to 1027.99, a decline of about 6.5%. On a mark-to-market basis, we have lost

$$\$2000 \times -72.01 = -\$144{,}020$$

We have a choice of either paying this loss directly, or allowing it to be taken out of the margin balance. It doesn't matter which we do, since we can recover the unused margin balance plus interest at any time by offsetting our position.

If the loss is subtracted from the margin balance, we have earned 1 week's interest and have lost \$144,020. Thus, if the continuously compounded interest rate is 6%, our margin balance after 1 week is

$$\$220{,}000e^{0.06\times 1/52} - \$144{,}020 = \$76{,}233.99$$

Because we have a 10% margin, a 6.5% decline in the futures price results in a 65% decline in margin. Were we to close out our position by entering into eight short index futures contracts, we would receive the remaining margin balance of \$76,233.99.

The decline in the margin balance means the broker has significantly less protection should we default. For this reason, participants are required to maintain the margin at a minimum level, called the **maintenance margin**. This is often set at 70% to 80% of the initial margin level. In this example, where the margin balance declines 65%, we would have to post additional margin. The broker would make a **margin call**, requesting additional margin. If we failed to post additional margin, the broker would close the position by selling 2000 units of the index and return to us the remaining margin. In practice, marking-to-market and settling up are performed at least daily.

Since margin you post is the broker's protection against your default, a major determinant of margin levels is the volatility of the underlying asset. The margin on the S&P 500 contract has generally been less than the 10% we assume in this example. In December

13. The exchange's clearinghouse determines a minimum margin, but individual brokers can and do demand higher margins from individual customers. The reason is that the broker is liable to the clearing corporation for customer failure to pay.

TABLE 8 Mark-to-market proceeds and margin balance over 10 weeks from long position in 8 S&P 500 futures contracts. The last column does not include additional margin payments. The final row represents expiration of the contract.

Week	Multiplier ($)	Futures Price	Price Change	Margin Balance($)
0	2000.00	1100.00	—	220,000.00
1	2000.00	1027.99	−72.01	76,233.99
2	2000.00	1037.88	9.89	96,102.01
3	2000.00	1073.23	35.35	166,912.96
4	2000.00	1048.78	−24.45	118,205.66
5	2000.00	1090.32	41.54	201,422.13
6	2000.00	1106.94	16.62	234,894.67
7	2000.00	1110.98	4.04	243,245.86
8	2000.00	1024.74	−86.24	71,046.69
9	2000.00	1007.30	−17.44	36,248.72
10	2000.00	1011.65	4.35	44,990.57

2010, for example, the initial margin on the S&P 500 futures contract was about 9% of the notional value of the contract. The maintenance margin was 80% of the initial margin.

To illustrate the effect of periodic settlement, Table 8 reports hypothetical futures price moves and tracks the margin position over a period of 10 weeks, assuming weekly marking-to-market and a continuously compounded risk-free rate of 6%. As the party agreeing to buy at a fixed price, we make money when the price goes up and lose when the price goes down. The opposite would occur for the seller.

The 10-week profit on the position is obtained by subtracting from the final margin balance the future value of the original margin investment. Week-10 profit on the position in Table 8 is therefore

$$\$44{,}990.57 - \$220{,}000e^{0.06\times 10/52} = -\$177{,}562.60$$

What if the position had been a forward rather than a futures position, but with prices the same? In that case, after 10 weeks our profit would have been

$$(1011.65 - 1100) \times \$2000 = -\$176{,}700$$

Why do the futures and forward profits differ? The reason is that with the futures contract, interest is earned on the mark-to-market proceeds. Given the prices in Table 8, the loss is larger for futures than forwards because prices on average are below the initial price and we have to fund losses as they occur. With a forward, by contrast, losses are not funded until expiration. Earning interest on the daily settlement magnifies the gain or loss compared to that on a forward contract. Had there been consistent gains on the position in this example, the futures profit would have exceeded the forward profit. Appendix B demonstrates that the ultimate payoff to a forward and futures contract can be equated in this example by adjusting the number of futures contracts so as to undo the magnifying effect of interest.

Comparing Futures and Forward Prices

An implication of Appendix B is that if the interest rate were not random, then forward and futures prices would be the same. However, what if the interest rate varies randomly? Suppose, for example, that on average the interest rate increases when the futures price increases; i.e., the two are positively correlated. Then the margin balance would grow (due to an increased futures price) just as the interest rate was higher. The margin balance would shrink as the interest rate was lower. On average in this case, a long futures position would outperform a long forward contract.

Conversely, suppose that on average the interest rate declined as the futures price rose. Then as the margin balance on a long position grew, the proceeds would be invested at a lower rate. Similarly, as the balance declined and required additional financing, this financing would occur at a higher rate. Here a long futures contract would on average perform worse than a long forward contract.

This comparison of the forward and futures payoffs suggests that when the interest rate is positively correlated with the futures price, the futures price will exceed the price on an otherwise identical forward contract: The investor who is long futures buys at a higher price to offset the advantage of marking-to-market. Similarly, when the interest rate is negatively correlated with the forward price, the futures price will be less than an otherwise identical forward price: The investor who is long futures buys at a lower price to offset the disadvantage of marking-to-market.

As an empirical matter, forward and futures prices are very similar.[14] The theoretical difference arises from uncertainty about the interest on mark-to-market proceeds. For short-lived contracts, the effect is generally small. However, for long-lived contracts, the difference can be significant, especially for long-lived interest rate futures, for which there is sure to be a correlation between the interest rate and the price of the underlying asset. For the rest of this chapter we will ignore the difference between forwards and futures.

Arbitrage in Practice: S&P 500 Index Arbitrage

We now illustrate the use of equation (6) to determine the theoretical price of an S&P 500 futures contract on a specific day. In order to compute equation (6), we need three inputs: (1) the value of the cash index (S_0), (2) the value of dividends to be paid on the index over the life of the contract (δ), and (3) the interest rate (r). The pricing exercise is summarized in Table 9.

On December 16, 2010, the closing S&P 500 index price was 1242.87. S&P 500 futures contracts expiring in March 2011 and June 2011 had closing prices of 1238.50 and 1233.60. The dividend yield on the S&P 500 in mid-December was about 1.89%. The remaining input is the risk-free interest rate. What interest rate is appropriate?

14. See French (1983) for a comparison of forward and futures prices on a variety of underlying assets.

TABLE 9 Actual and theoretical S&P 500 futures prices, December 16, 2010. The S&P 500 index closed at 1242.87 on December 16, and the dividend yield was 1.89%. Theoretical prices are computed using equation (6).

Maturity	Closing Price	T-bill Yield	Theoretical Price	LIBOR	Theoretical Price
Spot	1242.87				
March 2011	1238.50	0.13%	1237.41	0.30%	1237.94
June 2011	1233.60	0.19%	1232.35	0.46%	1234.02

Rates and dividend yield from Bloomberg.

Two interest rates that we can easily observe are the yield on U.S. Treasury bills and the London Interbank Offer Rate (LIBOR), which is a borrowing rate for large financial institutions.[15] (We will discuss LIBOR further in Section 7.) Table 9 reports 3-month and 6-month T-bill and LIBOR rates from December 16. LIBOR yields are greater than Treasury yields for two reasons. First, banks have greater default risk than the government and thus the interest rate on their deposits is greater. Second, Treasury securities are more liquid—they are easier to buy and sell—and consequently their price is greater (their yield is lower).

To think about what interest rate is appropriate, consider the economic characteristics of a futures contract. A long futures contract is like a leveraged position in the underlying asset, where the loan that provides leverage is collateralized with margin that is refreshed daily. The lender will perceive a costly default as unlikely; thus the rate can be close to risk-free. The T-bill rate includes a liquidity premium, however, while the rate implicit in a futures contract would not. The appropriate rate is therefore greater than the T-bill rate and likely lower than LIBOR.

Table 9 shows that for the 3-month contract, equation (6) yields lower prices than the observed price when using both the T-bill rate and LIBOR. For the 6-month contract, the two rates bracket the observed futures price. The percentage difference between the observed futures price and that computed using LIBOR is small for both contracts, about 0.04%.

There are a number of considerations in interpreting these differences in prices:

- Future dividends on the S&P 500 stocks are uncertain. For pricing a 3-month futures contract, one could use equation (5), with actual recent cash dividends on the underlying stocks for D_{t_i} as proxies for forthcoming dividends. There is still a risk that dividends will change over the next 3 months. The risk is greater for longer-dated futures contracts.

15. This example uses reported yields as if they were quoted as continuously compounded yields, which they are not. However, for short periods and low interest rates, there is almost no difference between effective annual and continuously compounded rates. For example, if the effective annual rate is 2%, the continuously compounded equivalent is $\ln(1.02) = 0.0198$, or 1.98%. In practice, interest rates are quoted using a variety of arcane conventions for annualizing the rate.

FIGURE 2

Specifications for the Nikkei 225 index futures contract.

Underlying	Nikkei 225 Stock Index
Where traded	Chicago Mercantile Exchange
Size	\$5 × Nikkei 225 Index
Months	March, June, September, December
Trading ends	Business day prior to determination of settlement price
Settlement	Cash-settled, based upon opening Osaka quotation of the Nikkei 225 index on the second Friday of expiration month

- There are transaction costs of arbitrage. As illustrated by equations (11) and (12), transaction costs create no-arbitrage *regions*, rather than no-arbitrage prices. In practice, a representative bid-ask spread on the index futures contract might be 20 to 30 basis points (a basis point on the S&P futures contract is 0.01—this is roughly 0.02% of the price) and 0.25% to 0.5% on the stocks in the index when traded in significant quantities. These costs are likely larger than the observed pricing difference.
- Because of transaction costs, an arbitrageur will usually not buy the entire 500-stock index, but instead either a subset of stocks or an index alternative such as Standard and Poor's Depository Receipts (SPDRs).[16] The futures contract and the offsetting position may not move exactly together. Also, when buying a large number of stocks, there is execution risk—the possibility that prices move during the time between the order being placed and the stock being actually purchased.

Arbitrageurs will need to take into account these considerations and small differences may not be worth arbitraging. Ultimately, the only way to know if arbitrage is profitable is to assess specific prices, trading costs, and borrowing and lending rates.

Quanto Index Contracts

At first glance the Chicago Mercantile Exchange's Nikkei 225 futures contract—see the details summarized in Figure 2—is a stock index contract like the S&P 500 contract. However, there is one very important difference: Settlement of the contract is in a different currency (dollars) than the currency of denomination for the index (yen).[17]

To see why this is important, consider a dollar-based investor wishing to invest in the Nikkei 225 cash index. This investor must undertake two transactions: changing dollars to yen and using yen to buy the index. When the position is sold, the investor reverses these transactions, selling the index and converting yen back to dollars. There are two sources of risk in this transaction: the risk of the index, denominated in yen, and the risk that the

16. SPDRs are unit investment trusts that are backed by a portfolio intended to mimic the S&P 500. Investors can convert units of 50,000 SPDR shares into the actual stock and can convert stock into SPDRs. This keeps SPDRs close to the S&P 500 index, but in practice SPDRs may be mispriced relative to the cash S&P 500 just as futures are.

17. There is also a yen-denominated Nikkei 225 futures contract that trades at the Osaka exchange. Since it is purely yen-denominated, this contract *is* priced according to equation (6).

yen/dollar exchange rate will change. From Figure 2, the Nikkei 225 futures contract is denominated in dollars rather than yen. Consequently, the contract insulates investors from currency risk, permitting them to speculate solely on whether the index rises or falls. This kind of contract is called a *quanto*. Quanto contracts allow investors in one country to invest in a different country without exchange rate risk.

The dollar-denominated Nikkei contract provides an interesting variation on the construction of a futures contract. Because of the quanto feature, the pricing formulas we have developed do not work for the Nikkei 225 contract.

5. USES OF INDEX FUTURES

An index futures contract resembles borrowing to buy the index. Why use an index futures contract if you can synthesize one? One answer is that index futures can permit trading the index at a lower transaction cost than actually trading a basket of the stocks that make up the index. If you are taking a temporary position in the index, either for investing or hedging, the transaction cost saving could be significant.

In this section we provide two examples of the use of index futures: asset allocation and cross-hedging a related portfolio.

Asset Allocation

Asset allocation strategies involve switching investments among asset classes, such as stocks, money market instruments, and bonds. Trading the individual securities, such as the stocks in an index, can be expensive. Our earlier discussion of arbitrage demonstrated that we can use forwards to create synthetic stocks and bonds. The practical implication is that a portfolio manager can invest in a stock index without holding stocks, commodities without holding physical commodities, and so on.

Switching from Stocks to T-bills. As an example of asset allocation, suppose that we have an investment in the S&P 500 index and we wish to temporarily invest in T-bills instead of the index. Instead of selling all 500 stocks and investing in T-bills, we can simply keep our stock portfolio and take a short forward position in the S&P 500 index. This converts our investment in the index into a cash-and-carry, creating a synthetic T-bill. When we wish to revert to investing in stocks, we simply offset the forward position, undoing the cash-and-carry.

To illustrate this, suppose that the current index price, S_0, is \$100, and the effective 1-year risk-free rate is 10%. The forward price is therefore \$110. Suppose that in 1 year, the index price could be either \$80 or \$130. If we sell the index and invest in T-bills, we will have \$110 in 1 year.

Table 10 shows that if, instead of selling, we keep the stock and short the forward contract, we earn a 10% return no matter what happens to the value of the stock. In this example 10% is the rate of return implied by the forward premium. If there is no arbitrage, this return will be equal to the risk-free rate.

General Asset Allocation. We can use forwards and futures to perform even more sophisticated asset allocation. Suppose we wish to invest our portfolio in Treasury bonds (long-term Treasury obligations) instead of stocks. We can accomplish this reallocation

TABLE 10 Effect of owning the stock and selling forward, assuming that $S_0 = \$100$ and $F_{0,1} = \$110$.

	Cash Flows		
Transaction	**Today**	**1 year, $S_1 = \$80$**	**1 year, $S_1 = \$130$**
Own stock @ \$100	−\$100	\$80	\$130
Short forward @ \$110	0	\$110 − \$80	\$110 − \$130
Total	−\$100	\$110	\$110

with two forward positions: Shorting the forward S&P 500 index and going long the forward T-bond. The first transaction converts our portfolio from an index investment to a T-bill investment. The second transaction converts the portfolio from a T-bill investment to a T-bond investment. This use of futures to convert a position from one asset category (stocks) to another (bonds) is called a **futures overlay**.

Futures overlays can have benefits beyond reducing transaction costs. Suppose an investment management company has portfolio managers who successfully invest in stocks they believe to be mispriced. The managers are judged on their performance relative to the S&P 500 stock index and consistently outperform the index by 2% per year (in the language of portfolio theory, their "alpha" is 2%). Now suppose that new clients of the company like the performance record, but want to invest in bonds rather than stocks. The investment management company could fire its stock managers and hire bond managers, but its existing investment managers are the reason for the company's success. The company can use a futures overlay to continue to invest in stocks, but to provide a bond return instead of a stock return to investors. By investing in stocks, shorting index futures, and going long bond futures, the managers continue to invest in stocks, but the client receives a bond return plus 2% rather than a stock return plus 2%. This use of futures to transform an outperforming portfolio on one asset class into an outperforming portfolio on a different asset class is called **alpha-porting**.

Cross-hedging with Index Futures

Index futures are often used to hedge portfolios that are not exactly the index. This is called *cross-hedging*.

Cross-hedging with Perfect Correlation. Suppose that we have a portfolio that is not the S&P 500, and we wish to shift the portfolio into T-bills. Can we use the S&P 500 futures contract to do this? The answer depends on the correlation of the portfolio with the S&P 500. To the extent the two are not perfectly correlated, there will be residual risk.

Suppose that we own \$100 million of stocks with a beta relative to the S&P 500 of 1.4. Assume for the moment that the two indexes are perfectly correlated. Perfect correlation means that there is a perfectly predictable relationship between the two indexes, not necessarily that they move one-for-one. Using the Capital Asset Pricing Model (CAPM), the return on our portfolio, r_p, is related to its beta, β_p, by

$$r_p = r + \beta_p(r_{\text{S\&P}} - r)$$

Assume also that the S&P 500 is 1100 with a 0 dividend yield and the effective annual risk-free rate is 6%. Hence the futures price is $1100 \times 1.06 = 1166$.

If we wish to allocate from the index into Treasury bills using futures, we need to short some quantity of the S&P 500. There are two steps to calculating the short futures quantity:

1. *Adjust for the difference in the dollar amounts of our portfolio and the S&P 500 contract.* In this case, one futures contract has a notional value of $\$250 \times 1166 = \$291{,}500$. This is denominated in future dollars; the value of one contract in current dollars is $\$291{,}500/1.06 = \$275{,}000$ (this is also the prepaid forward price). Thus, the number of contracts needed to cover \$100 million of stock is

$$\frac{\$100 \text{ million}}{\$0.275 \text{ million}} = 363.636$$

Note that both the numerator and denominator are expressed in current dollars.

2. *Adjust for the difference in beta.* Since the beta of our portfolio exceeds 1, it moves more than the S&P 500 in either direction. Thus we need to further increase our S&P 500 position to account for the greater magnitude moves in our portfolio relative to the S&P 500. This gives us

$$\text{Final hedge quantity} = 363.636 \times 1.4 = 509.09$$

Table 11 shows the performance of the hedged position. The result, as you would expect, is that the hedged position earns the risk-free rate, 6%.

Cross-Hedging with Imperfect Correlation. The preceding example assumes that the portfolio and the S&P 500 index are perfectly correlated. In practice, correlations between

TABLE 11 Results from shorting 509.09 S&P 500 index futures against a \$100m portfolio with a beta of 1.4.

S&P 500 Index	Gain on 509 Futures	Portfolio Value	Total
900	33.855	72.145	106.000
950	27.491	78.509	106.000
1000	21.127	84.873	106.000
1050	14.764	91.236	106.000
1100	8.400	97.600	106.000
1150	2.036	103.964	106.000
1200	−4.327	110.327	106.000

two portfolios can be substantially less than one. Using the S&P 500 to hedge such a portfolio would introduce basis risk, creating a hedge with residual risk.[18]

Denote the return and invested dollars on the portfolio as r_p and I_p. Assume that we short H futures contracts, each with a notional value N. The futures position earns the risk premium, $r_{\text{S\&P}} - r$. Thus, the return on the hedged position is

$$\text{Hedged return} = r_p I_p + H \times N \times (r_{\text{S\&P}} - r)$$

Repeating the analysis in the context of selecting the hedge ratio, the variance-minimizing hedge position, H^*, is

$$H^* = -\frac{I_p}{N}\frac{\text{Cov}(r_p, r_{\text{S\&P}})}{\sigma^2_{\text{S\&P}}} = -\frac{I_p}{N}\beta_p \tag{14}$$

The hedge quantity is denominated in terms of a quantity of futures contracts. The second equality follows because $\text{Cov}(r_p, r_{\text{S\&P}})/\sigma^2_{\text{S\&P}}$ is the slope coefficient when we regress the portfolio return on the S&P 500 return; i.e., it is the portfolio beta with respect to the S&P 500 index. Equation (14) is also the formula we used in concluding that, with perfect correlation, we should short 509.09 contracts.

Notice that the hedge ratio in equation (14) depends on the ratio of the market value of the portfolio, I_p, to the notional value of the S&P 500 contract, N. Thus, as the portfolio changes value relative to the S&P 500 index, it is necessary to change the hedge ratio. This rebalancing is necessary when we calculate hedge ratios using a relationship based on returns, which are percentage changes.

When we add H^* futures to the portfolio, the variance of the hedged portfolio, σ^2_{hedged}, is

$$\sigma^2_{\text{hedged}} = \sigma^2_p I^2_p \left(1 - \rho^2\right) \tag{15}$$

where ρ is the correlation coefficient between the portfolio and the S&P 500 index. This is the same as the following equation. The correlation coefficient, ρ, can be computed directly from r_p and $r_{\text{S\&P}}$, but it is also the square root of the regression r-squared (R^2) when we regress r_P on $r_{\text{S\&P}}$ in order to estimate β.

$$\sigma^2_{\text{hedged}} = N^2_w \sigma^2_w \left(1 - \rho^2\right)$$

Example 3. Suppose we are optimistic about the performance of the NASDAQ index relative to the S&P 500 index. We can go long the NASDAQ index and short the S&P 500 futures. We obtain the variance-minimizing position in the S&P 500 by using equation (14). A 5-year regression (from June 1999 to June 2004) of the daily NASDAQ return on the S&P 500 return gives

$$r_{\text{NASD}} = \underset{(0.0003)}{-\,0.0001} + \underset{(0.0262)}{1.4784} \times (r_{\text{S\&P}} - r) \qquad R^2 = 0.7188$$

18. There is additional basis risk in such a hedge because, for reasons discussed in Section 4, the S&P 500 futures contract and the cash price of the S&P 500 index may not move perfectly together.

The regression beta tells us to short a dollar value of the S&P that is 1.4784 times greater than the NASDAQ position we hold. The correlation coefficient between the two returns, ρ, is $\sqrt{0.7188} = 0.8478$.[19] The daily standard deviation of the return on the NASDAQ over this period is 2.24%. Hence, using equation (15), for a \$1 million investment the variance of the hedged position is

$$\sigma^2_{\text{NASD}} I_p^2 \left(1 - \rho^2\right) = 0.0224^2 \times (\$1m)^2 \times (1 - 0.7188) = (\$11,878)^2$$

Thus, the daily standard deviation of the hedged return is \$11,878. ■

Risk Management for Stock-Pickers. An asset manager who picks stocks is often making a bet about the relative, but not the absolute, performance of a stock. For example, XYZ might be expected to outperform a broad range of stocks on a risk-adjusted basis. If the economy suffers a recession, however, XYZ will decline in value even if it outperforms other stocks. Index futures can be used in this case to help isolate the *relative* performance of XYZ.

Suppose the return of XYZ is given by the CAPM:

$$r_{\text{XYZ}} = \alpha_{\text{XYZ}} + r + \beta_{\text{XYZ}}(r_m - r) \tag{16}$$

The term α_{XYZ} in this context represents the expected abnormal return on XYZ. If we use the S&P 500 as a proxy for the market, then we can select H according to equation (14). The result for the hedged position will be that, on average, we earn $\alpha_{\text{XYZ}} + r$. The risk of the position will be given by equation (15). Since the correlation of an individual stock and the index will not be close to 1, there will be considerable remaining risk. However, the portfolio will not have market risk.

6. CURRENCY CONTRACTS

Currency futures and forwards are widely used to hedge against changes in exchange rates. The pricing of currency contracts is a straightforward application of the principles we have already discussed. Figure 3 reports the specifications for the US dollar/euro futures contract at the CME, and Table 12 reports futures price quotes for two dates.

Many corporations use currency futures and forwards for short-term hedging. An importer of consumer electronics, for example, may have an obligation to pay the manufacturer ¥150 million 90 days in the future. The dollar revenues from selling these products are likely known in the short run, so the importer bears pure exchange risk due to the payable being fixed in yen. By buying ¥150 million forward 90 days, the importer locks in a dollar price to pay for the yen, which will then be delivered to the manufacturer.

Currency Prepaid Forward

Suppose that 1 year from today you want to have ¥1. A prepaid forward allows you to pay dollars today to acquire ¥1 in 1 year. What is the prepaid forward price? Suppose the yen-denominated interest rate is r_y and the exchange rate today (\$/¥) is x_0. We can work

19. You can, of course, also compute the correlation coefficient directly from the time series of returns.

FIGURE 3

Specifications for EUR/USD futures contract.

Underlying	Euro currency
Where traded	Chicago Mercantile Exchange
Size	125,000 euro
Months	March, June, September, December (six consecutive contracts)
Trading ends	9:16A.M. on the second business day prior to the third Wednesday of the month
Delivery	Cash-settlement

TABLE 12 Dollar cost of foreign currencies.

Date	Currency	June	Sept.	Dec.	Mar.	June	Sept.
June 6, 2007	Euro	1.351	1.355	1.358	1.361	1.363	1.365
	100 Yen	0.828	0.837	0.847	0.856	0.865	0.873
	Sterling	1.992	1.99	1.987	1.984	1.98	1.975
June 2, 2010	Euro	1.224	1.225	1.226	1.228	1.229	1.231
	100 Yen	1.085	1.087	1.089	1.092	1.095	1.098
	Sterling	1.464	1.465	1.465	1.466	1.466	1.467

Source: CMEGroup via Datastream.

backward. If we want ¥1 in 1 year, we must have e^{-r_y} in yen today. To obtain that many yen today, we must exchange $x_0 e^{-r_y}$ dollars into yen.

Thus, the prepaid forward price for a yen is

$$F_{0,T}^{P} = x_0 e^{-r_y T} \tag{17}$$

where T is time to maturity of the forward.

The economic principle governing the pricing of a prepaid forward on currency is the same as that for a prepaid forward on stock. By deferring delivery of the underlying asset, you lose income. In the case of currency, if you received the currency immediately, you could buy a bond denominated in that currency and earn interest. The prepaid forward price reflects the loss of interest from deferring delivery, just as the prepaid forward price for stock reflects the loss of dividend income. This is why equation (17) is the same as that for a stock paying a continuous dividend, equation (4).

Example 4. Suppose that the yen-denominated interest rate is 2% and that the current exchange rate is 0.009 dollars per yen. Then in order to have 1 yen in 1 year, we would invest today

$$0.009\$ /¥ \times ¥1 \times e^{-0.02} = \$.008822 \quad ■$$

Currency Forward

The prepaid forward price is the *dollar* cost of obtaining 1 yen in the future. Thus, to obtain the forward price, compute the future value using the dollar-denominated interest rate, r:

$$F_{0,T} = x_0 e^{(r-r_y)T} \tag{18}$$

The forward currency rate will exceed the current exchange rate when the domestic risk-free rate is higher than the foreign risk-free rate.[20]

Example 5. Suppose that the yen-denominated interest rate is 2% and the dollar-denominated rate is 6%. The current exchange rate is 0.009 dollars per yen. The 1-year forward rate is

$$0.009e^{0.06-0.02} = 0.009367 \quad ■$$

Notice that equation (18) is just like equation (6), for stock index futures, with the foreign interest rate equal to the dividend yield. The interest rate difference $r - r_y$ is the cost of carry for a foreign currency (we borrow at the domestic rate r and invest the proceeds in a foreign money-market instrument, earning the foreign rate r_y as an offset to our cost). If we wish to borrow foreign currency, r_y is the lease rate.

Covered Interest Arbitrage

We can synthetically create a forward contract by borrowing in one currency and lending in the other. If we want to have 1 yen in the future, with the dollar price fixed today, we can pay today for the yen, and borrow in dollars to do so. To have 1 yen in 1 year, we need to invest

$$x_0 e^{-r_y T}$$

in dollars, and we obtain this amount by borrowing. The required dollar repayment is

$$x_0 e^{(r-r_y)T}$$

which is the forward exchange rate.

Example 6. Suppose that $x_0 = 0.009$, $r_y = 2\%$, and $r = 6\%$. The dollar cost of buying 1 yen today is $0.009 \times e^{-0.02} = 0.008822$. We defer the dollar payment by borrowing at 6%, for a cost 1 year from today of $0.008822e^{0.06} = 0.009367$. This transaction is summarized in Table 13. ■

The example shows that borrowing in one currency and lending in another creates the same cash flow as a forward contract. If we offset this borrowing and lending position with an actual forward contract, the resulting transaction is called **covered interest arbitrage**.

20. Of course if you think about it, every currency transaction can be expressed in terms of either currency—for example, as yen/dollar or dollar/yen. If the forward price exceeds the current exchange rate viewed from the perspective of one currency, it must be less from the perspective of the other.

TABLE 13 Synthetically creating a yen forward contract by borrowing in dollars and lending in yen. The payoff at time 1 is ¥1 − $0.009367.

	Cash Flows			
	Year 0		Year 1	
Transaction	$	¥	$	¥
Borrow $x_0 e^{-r_y}$ dollar at 6% ($)	+0.008822	—	−0.009367	—
Convert to yen @ 0.009 $/¥	−0.008822	+0.9802	—	—
Invest in yen-denominated bill (¥)	—	−0.9802	—	1
Total	0	0	−0.009367	1

A carry trade entails borrowing in the currency with low interest rates and lending in the currency with high interest rates, without hedging. Box 3 explains carry trades.

To summarize, a forward exchange rate reflects the difference in interest rates denominated in different currencies. Imagine that you want to invest $1 for 1 year. You can do so by buying a dollar-denominated bond, or you can exchange the dollar into another currency and buy a bond denominated in that other currency. You can then use currency forwards to guarantee the exchange rate at which you will convert the foreign currency back into dollars. The principle behind the pricing of currency forwards is that a position in foreign risk-free bonds, with the currency risk hedged, pays the same return as domestic risk-free bonds.

7. EURODOLLAR FUTURES

Businesses and individuals face uncertainty about future interest rates. A manager planning to borrow money 3 months from today doesn't know today what the interest rate will be at that time. Forward and futures contracts permit hedging interest rate risk by allowing the manager to lock in now a borrowing rate for 3 months in the future.

The principles underlying interest rate contracts are exactly those we have been discussing, but interest rates seem more complicated because there are so many of them, depending upon whether you invest for 1 day, 1 month, 1 year, or 30 years. There are also implied forward interest rates between any two points in the future.[21] The Eurodollar contract is so important that we discuss it briefly here.

The Eurodollar contract, described in Figure 4, is based on a $1 million 3-month deposit earning LIBOR (the London Interbank Offer Rate), which is the average borrowing rate faced by large international London banks. The 1-month LIBOR contract is similar. Suppose that current LIBOR is 1.5% over 3 months. By convention, this is annualized by multiplying by 4, so the quoted LIBOR rate is 6%. Assuming a bank borrows $1 million for

21. In addition, there are different rates faced by different classes of borrower: government, private, and municipal. And of course there are different currencies of denomination.

BOX 3: Carry Trades

Suppose that the yen interest rate is 2% and the dollar interest rate is 6%. On the surface, it might seem to you that it would be profitable to borrow at 2% in yen, and lend at 6% in dollars. This strategy of borrowing at a low rate and lending at a high rate is often undertaken in practice and is called a **carry trade**.

If you borrow yen and invest in dollars, you face the risk that the dollars will become less valuable (the dollar will depreciate), or to say the same thing differently, that the yen will appreciate (the dollar price of a yen will increase). Thus, while a carry trade may superficially sound like a money machine, the trade has risk.

To illustrate the risk in a currency carry trade, we use the assumptions of Example 5. The yen/dollar exchange rate today is 0.009, and we suppose that in 1 year the rate can be 0.0091, 0.009367, or 0.0096. If we plan to invest ¥100,000, the trade entails borrowing \$900/0.009 = ¥100,000 at 2% and lending \$900 at 6%. Dollar profit at the three exchange rates is

- $x_1 = 0.0091$. The yen depreciates relative to the forward price, so the trade is profitable:

$$\text{Profit} = \$900 \times e^{0.06} - ¥100{,}000 \times e^{0.02} \times 0.0091 = \$27.2697$$

- $x_1 = 0.009367$. The yen equals the forward price, so the trade breaks even:

$$\text{Profit} = \$900 \times e^{0.06} - ¥100{,}000 \times e^{0.02} \times 0.009367 = 0$$

- $x_1 = 0.0096$. The yen appreciates relative to the forward price, so the trade loses money:

$$\text{Profit} = \$900 \times e^{0.06} - ¥100{,}000 \times e^{0.02} \times 0.0096 = -\$23.7404$$

This example illustrates what we already knew from studying covered interest arbitrage: The carry trade breaks even when the future exchange rate equals the forward rate. (Covered interest arbitrage adds currency futures to the carry trade, ensuring that we can buy yen at the forward price.) The behavior of the exchange rate determines the profitability of the investment.

Carry trades can be undertaken with different asset classes, e.g., by borrowing short term and lending long term in the same currency. Currency carry trades are popular because historically they have been profitable. Burnside et al. (2008) show that this profitability (relative to risk) persists even when the investor buys options to protect against large losses. The persistent profitability of currency carry trades is surprising.

3 months, a change in annualized LIBOR of 0.01% (1 basis point) would raise its borrowing cost by $0.0001/4 \times \$1$ million = \$25.

The Eurodollar futures price at expiration of the contract is

$$100 - \text{Annualized 3-month LIBOR}$$

Thus, if LIBOR is 6% at maturity of the Eurodollar futures contract, the final futures price will be $100 - 6 = 94$. It is important to understand that the Eurodollar contract settles based on current LIBOR, which is the interest rate quoted for the *next* 3 months. Thus, for example, the price of the contract that expires in June reflects the 3-month interest rate between June and September. With the futures contract, as with a \$1 million LIBOR deposit, a change of 0.01% in the rate is worth \$25.

FIGURE 4

Specifications for the Eurodollar futures contract.

Where traded	Chicago Mercantile Exchange
Size	3-month Eurodollar time deposit, \$1 million principal
Months	March, June, September, December, out 10 years, plus 2 serial months and spot month
Trading ends	5 A.M. (11 A.M. London) on the second London bank business day immediately preceding the third Wednesday of the contract month.
Delivery	Cash settlement based on 100 − British Banker's Association Futures Interest Settlement Rate for 3-Month Eurodollar Interbank Time Deposits. (This is a 3-month rate annualized by multiplying by 360/90.)

Like most money-market interest rates, LIBOR is quoted assuming a 360-day year. Thus, the annualized 91-day rate, r_{91}, can be extracted from the futures price, F, by computing the 90-day rate and multiplying by 91/90. The quarterly effective rate is then computed by dividing the result by 4:

$$r_{91} = (100 - F) \times \frac{1}{100} \times \frac{1}{4} \times \frac{91}{90} \tag{19}$$

Three-month Eurodollar contracts have maturities out to 10 years, which means that it is possible to use the contract to lock in a 3-month rate as far as 10 years in the future. If the Eurodollar futures contract maturing 60 months from today has a price of 95.25, this means that the contract can be used to lock in an annualized rate of 4.75% for a period beginning 60 months from today and terminating 63 months from today.

The Eurodollar futures strip (the set of futures prices with different maturities at one point in time) provides basic interest rate information that is commonly used to price other futures contracts and to price swaps. Figure 5 depicts the Eurodollar strip for four dates. Each point on the graph is the annualized 3-month interest rate implied by the Eurodollar futures price maturing that many months in the future.

Let's see how the Eurodollar contract can be used to hedge interest rate risk. For a borrower, for example, a short position in the contract is a hedge because it pays when the interest rate rises and requires payment when the interest rate falls. To see this, suppose that 7 months from today we plan to borrow \$1 million for 90 days, and that our borrowing rate is the same as LIBOR. The Eurodollar futures price for 7 months from today is 94; this implies a 90-day rate of $(100 - 94) \times 90/360 \times 1/100 = 1.5\%$. Now suppose that 7 months hence, 3-month LIBOR is 8%, which implies a Eurodollar futures price of 92. The implied 90-day rate is 2%. Our extra borrowing expense over 90 days on \$1 million will therefore be $(0.02 - 0.015) \times \$1\text{m} = \$5000$.

This extra borrowing expense is offset by gains on the short Eurodollar contract. The Eurodollar futures price has gone down, giving us a gain of \$25 per basis point, or

FIGURE 5

Eurodollar futures price strip for four dates.

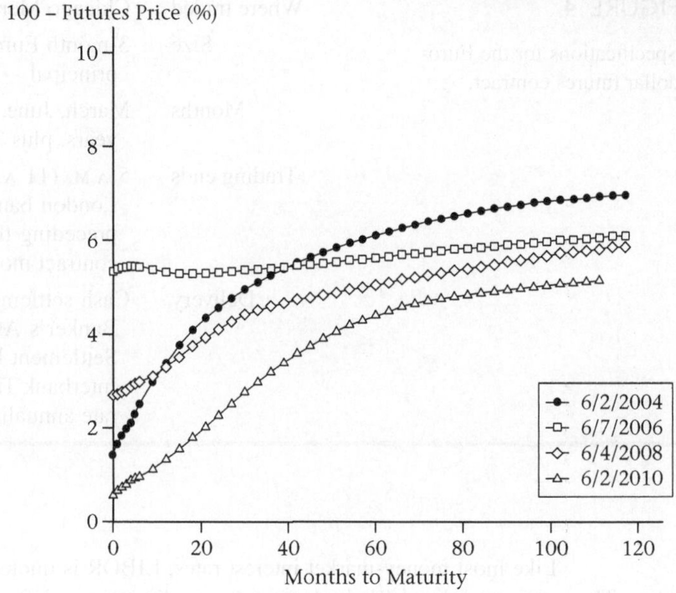

Source: Datastream.

$\$25 \times 100 \times (94 - 92) = \$5000$. The short position in the futures contract compensates us for the increase in our borrowing cost.[22] In the same way, a long position can be used to lock in a lending rate.

The Eurodollar futures price is a construct, not the price of an asset. In this sense Eurodollar futures are different from the futures contracts we have already discussed. Although Eurodollar LIBOR is closely related to a number of other interest rates, there is no one specific identifiable asset that underlies the Eurodollar futures contract.

LIBOR is quoted in currencies other than dollars, and comparable rates are quoted in different locations. In addition to LIBOR, there are PIBOR (Paris), TIBOR (Tokyo), and Euribor (the European Banking Federation).

Finally, you might be wondering why we are discussing LIBOR rather than rates on Treasury bills. Business and bank borrowing rates move more in tandem with LIBOR than with the government's borrowing rate. Thus, these borrowers use the Eurodollar futures contract to hedge. LIBOR is also a better measure of the cost of funds for a market-maker, so LIBOR is typically used to price forward contracts.

22. It might occur to you that the Eurodollar contract pays us at the time we borrow, but we do not pay interest until the loan matures, 91 days hence. Since we have time to earn interest on the change in the value of the contract, the hedge ratio should be less than 1 contract per $1 million borrowing.

CHAPTER SUMMARY

The purchase of a stock or other asset entails agreeing to a price, making payment, and taking delivery of the asset. A forward contract fixes the price today, but payment and delivery are deferred. The pricing of forward contracts reflects the costs and benefits of this deferred payment and delivery. The seller receives payment later, so the price is higher to reflect interest owed the seller, and the buyer receives possession later, so the price is lower to reflect dividends not received by the buyer. A prepaid forward contract requires payment today; hence, it separates these two effects. The price of a prepaid forward is

$$\text{Prepaid forward price} = S_0 e^{-\delta T}$$

The prepaid forward price is below the asset spot price, S_0, due to dividends forgone by deferring delivery. The forward price also reflects deferral of payment, so it is the future value of the prepaid forward price:

$$\text{Forward price} = S_0 e^{(r-\delta)T}$$

In the case of a currency forward, the dividend yield forgone by holding the forward contract instead of the underlying asset, δ, is the interest rate you could earn by investing in foreign-currency denominated assets. Thus, for currencies, $\delta = r_f$, where r_f is the foreign interest rate.

A forward contract is equivalent to a leveraged position in an asset—borrowing to buy the asset. By combining the forward contract with other assets it is possible to create synthetic stocks and bonds. These equivalents are summarized in Table 14. Since a forward contract is risky but requires no investment, it earns the risk premium. The forward price is therefore a biased predictor of the future spot price of the asset, with the bias equal to the risk premium.

The fact that it is possible to create a synthetic forward has two important implications. First, if the forward contract is mispriced, arbitrageurs can take offsetting positions in the forward contract and the synthetic forward contract—in effect buying low and selling high—and make a risk-free profit. Second, dealers who make markets in the forward or in the underlying asset can hedge the risk of their position with a synthetic offsetting position. With transaction costs there is a no-arbitrage *region* rather than a single no-arbitrage price.

Futures contracts are similar to forward contracts, except that with futures there are margin requirements and daily settlement of the gain or loss on the position. The contractual

TABLE 14 Synthetic equivalents assuming the asset pays continuous dividends at the rate δ.

Position	Synthetic Equivalent	
Long forward	$=$ Buy $e^{-\delta T}$ shares of stock	$+$ Borrow $S_0 e^{-\delta T}$
Bond paying $F_{0,T}$	$=$ Buy $e^{-\delta T}$ shares of stock	$+$ Short forward
Synthetic stock	$=$ Long forward	$+$ Lend $e^{-rT} F_{0,T}$

differences between forwards and futures can lead to pricing differences, but in most cases forward prices and futures prices are very close.

In addition to hedging, forward and futures contracts can be used to synthetically switch a portfolio invested in stocks into bonds. A portfolio invested in Asset A can remain invested in Asset A but earn the returns associated with Asset B, as long as there are forward or futures contracts on A and B. This is called a futures overlay.

The Eurodollar futures contract, based on LIBOR (London Interbank Offer Rate) is widely used for hedging interest rate risk. Because the Eurodollar futures contract does not represent the price of an asset (at settlement it is 100 − LIBOR), it cannot be priced using the formulas in this chapter.

FURTHER READING

To get a sense of the range of traded contracts, explore the websites of futures exchanges: the CME Group (www.cmegroup.com) and the London International Financial Futures Exchange (www.euronext.com), among others. These sites typically provide current prices, along with information about the contracts: the definition of the underlying asset, how the contracts are settled, and so forth. The site for One Chicago (www.onechicago.com) provides information about single stock futures in the United States.

It is well accepted that forward prices are determined by the models and considerations in this chapter. Early papers that examined futures pricing include Modest and Sundaresan (1983), Cornell and French (1983), which emphasizes tax effects in futures pricing (see Appendix A), and French (1983), which compares forwards and futures when both exist on the same underlying asset. Brennan and Schwartz (1990) explore optimal arbitrage when there are transaction costs, and Reinganum (1986) explores the arbitrage possibilities inherent in time travel. There is a more technical academic literature focusing on the difference between forward and futures contracts, including Black (1976a), Cox et al. (1981), Richard and Sundaresan (1981), and Jarrow and Oldfield (1981).

PROBLEMS

1. Construct Table 1 from the perspective of a seller, providing a descriptive name for each of the transactions.

2. A \$50 stock pays a \$1 dividend every 3 months, with the first dividend coming 3 months from today. The continuously compounded risk-free rate is 6%.

a. What is the price of a prepaid forward contract that expires 1 year from today, immediately after the fourth-quarter dividend?

b. What is the price of a forward contract that expires at the same time?

3. A \$50 stock pays an 8% continuous dividend. The continuously compounded risk-free rate is 6%.

a. What is the price of a prepaid forward contract that expires 1 year from today?

b. What is the price of a forward contract that expires at the same time?

4. Suppose the stock price is \$35 and the continuously compounded interest rate is 5%.

a. What is the 6-month forward price, assuming dividends are zero?

b. If the 6-month forward price is \$35.50, what is the annualized forward premium?

c. If the forward price is \$35.50, what is the annualized continuous dividend yield?

5. Suppose you are a market-maker in S&R index forward contracts. The S&R index spot price is 1100, the risk-free rate is 5%, and the dividend yield on the index is 0.

a. What is the no-arbitrage forward price for delivery in 9 months?

b. Suppose a customer wishes to enter a short index futures position. If you take the opposite position, demonstrate how you would hedge your resulting long position using the index and borrowing or lending.

c. Suppose a customer wishes to enter a long index futures position. If you take the opposite position, demonstrate how you would hedge your resulting short position using the index and borrowing or lending.

6. Repeat the previous problem, assuming that the dividend yield is 1.5%.

7. The S&R index spot price is 1100, the risk-free rate is 5%, and the dividend yield on the index is 0.

a. Suppose you observe a 6-month forward price of 1135. What arbitrage would you undertake?

b. Suppose you observe a 6-month forward price of 1115. What arbitrage would you undertake?

8. The S&R index spot price is 1100, the risk-free rate is 5%, and the continuous dividend yield on the index is 2%.

a. Suppose you observe a 6-month forward price of 1120. What arbitrage would you undertake?

b. Suppose you observe a 6-month forward price of 1110. What arbitrage would you undertake?

9. Suppose that 10 years from now it becomes possible for money managers to engage in time travel. In particular, suppose that a money manager could travel to January 1981, when the 1-year Treasury bill rate was 12.5%.

a. If time travel were costless, what riskless arbitrage strategy could a money manager undertake by traveling back and forth between January 1981 and January 1982?

b. If many money managers undertook this strategy, what would you expect to happen to interest rates in 1981?

c. Since interest rates *were* 12.5% in January 1981, what can you conclude about whether costless time travel will ever be possible?

10. The S&R index spot price is 1100 and the continuously compounded risk-free rate is 5%. You observe a 9-month forward price of 1129.257.

a. What dividend yield is implied by this forward price?

b. Suppose you believe the dividend yield over the next 9 months will be only 0.5%. What arbitrage would you undertake?

c. Suppose you believe the dividend yield will be 3% over the next 9 months. What arbitrage would you undertake?

11. Suppose the S&P 500 index futures price is currently 1200. You wish to purchase four futures contracts on margin.

a. What is the notional value of your position?

b. Assuming a 10% initial margin, what is the value of the initial margin?

12. Suppose the S&P 500 index is currently 950 and the initial margin is 10%. You wish to enter into 10 S&P 500 futures contracts.

a. What is the notional value of your position? What is the margin?

b. Suppose you earn a continuously compounded rate of 6% on your margin balance, your position is marked to market *weekly*, and the maintenance margin is 80% of the initial margin. What is the greatest S&P 500 index futures price 1 week from today at which you will receive a margin call?

13. Verify that going long a forward contract and lending the present value of the forward price creates a payoff of one share of stock when

a. The stock pays no dividends.

b. The stock pays discrete dividends.

c. The stock pays continuous dividends.

14. Verify that when there are transaction costs, the lower no-arbitrage bound is given by equation (12).

15. Suppose the S&R index is 800, and that the dividend yield is 0. You are an arbitrageur with a continuously compounded borrowing rate of 5.5% and a continuously compounded lending rate of 5%. Assume that there is 1 year to maturity.

a. Supposing that there are no transaction fees, show that a cash-and-carry arbitrage is not profitable if the forward price is less than 845.23, and that a reverse cash-and-carry arbitrage is not profitable if the forward price is greater than 841.02.

b. Now suppose that there is a $1 transaction fee, paid at time 0, for going either long or short the forward contract. Show that the upper and lower no-arbitrage bounds now become 846.29 and 839.97.

c. Now suppose that in addition to the fee for the forward contract, there is also a $2.40 fee for buying or selling the index. Suppose the contract is settled by delivery of the index, so that this fee is paid only at time 0. What are the new upper and lower no-arbitrage bounds?

d. Make the same assumptions as in the previous part, except assume that the contract is cash-settled. This means that it is necessary to pay the stock index transaction fee (but not the forward fee) at both times 0 and 1. What are the new no-arbitrage bounds?

e. Now suppose that transactions in the index have a fee of 0.3% of the value of the index (this is for both purchases and sales). Transactions in the forward contract still have a fixed fee of \$1 per unit of the index at time 0. Suppose the contract is cash-settled so that when you do a cash-and-carry or reverse cash-and-carry you pay the index transaction fee both at time 1 and time 0. What are the new upper and lower no-arbitrage bounds? Compare your answer to that in the previous part. (*Hint:* To handle the time 1 transaction fee, you may want to consider tailing the stock position.)

16. Suppose the S&P 500 currently has a level of 875. The continuously compounded return on a 1-year T-bill is 4.75%. You wish to hedge an \$800,000 portfolio that has a beta of 1.1 and a correlation of 1.0 with the S&P 500.

a. What is the 1-year futures price for the S&P 500 assuming no dividends?

b. How many S&P 500 futures contracts should you short to hedge your portfolio? What return do you expect on the hedged portfolio?

17. Suppose you are selecting a futures contract with which to hedge a portfolio. You have a choice of six contracts, each of which has the same variability, but with correlations of −0.95, −0.75, −0.50, 0, 0.25, and 0.85. Rank the futures contracts with respect to basis risk, from highest to lowest basis risk.

18. Suppose the current exchange rate between Germany and Japan is 0.02 €/¥. The euro-denominated annual continuously compounded risk-free rate is 4% and the yen-denominated annual continuously compounded risk-free rate is 1%. What are the 6-month euro/yen and yen/euro forward prices?

19. Suppose the spot \$/¥ exchange rate is 0.008, the 1-year continuously compounded dollar-denominated rate is 5% and the 1-year continuously compounded yen-denominated rate is 1%. Suppose the 1-year forward exchange rate is 0.0084. Explain precisely the transactions you could use (being careful about currency of denomination) to make money with zero initial investment and no risk. How much do you make per yen? Repeat for a forward exchange rate of 0.0083.

20. Suppose we wish to borrow \$10 million for 91 days beginning next June, and that the quoted Eurodollar futures price is 93.23.

a. What 3-month LIBOR rate is implied by this price?

b. How much will be needed to repay the loan?

Appendix A TAXES AND THE FORWARD RATE

Appendix available at http://www.pearsonhighered.com/mcdonald.

TABLE 15 Marking-to-market proceeds and margin balance from long position in the S&P 500 futures contract, where hedge is adjusted on a weekly basis.

Week	Multiplier ($)	Futures Price	Price Change	Margin Balance ($)
0	1979.34	1100.00	—	217,727.21
1	1981.62	1027.99	−72.01	75,446.43
2	1983.91	1037.88	9.89	95,131.79
3	1986.20	1073.23	35.35	165,372.88
4	1988.49	1048.78	−24.45	117,001.17
5	1990.79	1090.32	41.54	199,738.33
6	1993.09	1106.94	16.62	233,055.86
7	1995.39	1110.98	4.04	241,377.01
8	1997.69	1024.74	−86.24	69,573.25
9	2000.00	1007.30	−17.44	34,813.80
10	2000.00	1011.65	4.35	43,553.99

Appendix B EQUATING FORWARDS AND FUTURES

Because the futures price exceeds the prepaid forward price, marking-to-market has the effect of magnifying gains and losses. For example, the futures price on a non-dividend-paying stock is $F_{0,T} = S_0e^{rT}$. If the stock price increases by \$1 at time 0, the gain on the futures contract at time T is e^{rT}. Thus, in order to use futures to precisely hedge a position (with the hedge being settled at time T) it is necessary to hold fewer futures than forward contracts, effectively offsetting the extra volatility induced by the future value factor. In the example in Table 15, we can go long fewer than eight contracts, to make up for the effect of marking-to-market.

Table 15 shows the effect of this adjustment to the futures position and how it is adjusted over time. Initially, we go long

$$8 \times e^{-0.06\times 9/52} = 7.91735$$

contracts. This number of contracts has a multiplier of \$250 × 7.91735 = \$1979.34, the multiplier in the first row of the table. Reducing the number of contracts offsets the effect of earning interest. Each week there is less time until expiration, so we increase the number of index units we are long.

Profit on this position is

$$\$43{,}553.99 - \$217{,}727.21e^{0.06\times 10/52} = -\$176{,}700$$

which is exactly the same profit as a forward position. The example in Table 15 is unrealistic in the sense that the magnitude is too small for the adjustment to be worth the bother. However, it does demonstrate how to scale the position to offset the magnifying effect of marking-to-market, and the link between the profit on a forward and futures position.

Appendix C FORWARD AND FUTURES PRICES

Appendix available at http://www.pearsonhighered.com/mcdonald.

Interest Rate Forwards and Futures

Suppose you have the opportunity to spend \$1 one year from today to receive \$2 two years from today. What is the value of this opportunity? To answer this question, you need to know the appropriate interest rates for discounting the two cash flows. This comparison is an example of the most basic concept in finance: using interest rates to compute present values. Once we find a present value for one or more assets, we can compare the values of cash flows from those assets even if the cash inflows and cash outflows occur at different times. In order to perform these calculations, we need information about the set of interest rates prevailing between different points in time.

We begin the chapter by reviewing basic bond concepts—coupon bonds, yields to maturity, and implied forward rates. Any reader of this chapter should understand these basic concepts. We then look at interest rate forwards and forward rate agreements, which permit hedging interest rate risk. Finally, we look at bond futures and the repo market.

1. BOND BASICS

Table 1 presents information about current interest rates for bonds maturing in from 1 to 3 years. *Identical information is presented in five different ways in the table.* Although the information appears differently across columns, it is possible to take the information in any one column of Table 1 and reproduce the other four columns.[1]

In practice, a wide range of maturities exists at any point in time, but the U.S. government issues Treasury securities only at specific maturities—typically 3 months, 6 months, and 1, 2, 5, 10, and 30 years.[2] Government securities that are issued with less than 1 year to maturity and that make only a single payment, at maturity, are called Treasury *bills*. *Notes* and *bonds* pay coupons and are issued at a price close to their maturity value (i.e., they are issued at par). Notes have 10 or fewer years to maturity and bonds have more

1. Depending upon how you do the computation, you may arrive at numbers slightly different from those in Table 1. The reason is that all of the entries except those in column 1 are rounded in the last digit, and there are multiple ways to compute the number in any given column. Rounding error will therefore generate small differences among computations performed in different ways.

2. Treasury securities are issued using an auction. In the past the government also issued bonds with maturities of 3 and 7 years. Between 2002 and 2005 the government issued no 30-year bonds.

From Chapter 7 of *Derivatives Markets*, Third Edition, Robert McDonald. Copyright © 2013 by Pearson Education, Inc. Published by Pearson Prentice Hall. All rights reserved.

TABLE 1 Five ways to present equivalent information about default-free interest rates. All rates but those in the last column are effective annual rates.

Years to Maturity	(1) Zero-Coupon Bond Yield	(2) Zero-Coupon Bond Price	(3) One-Year Implied Forward Rate	(4) Par Coupon	(5) Continuously Compounded Zero Yield
1	6.00%	0.943396	6.00000%	6.00000%	5.82689%
2	6.50	0.881659	7.00236	6.48423	6.29748
3	7.00	0.816298	8.00705	6.95485	6.76586

than 10 years to maturity. The distinctions between bills, notes, and bonds are not important for our purposes; we will refer to all three as bonds. Treasury inflation protected securities are bonds for which payments are adjusted for inflation. Finally, the most recently issued government bonds are called **on-the-run**; other bonds are called **off-the-run**. These terms are used frequently in talking about government bonds since on-the-run bonds generally have lower yields and greater trading volume than off-the-run bonds. Appendix A discusses some of the conventions used in bond price and yield quotations.

In addition to government bonds there are also STRIPS. A **STRIPS**—Separate Trading of Registered Interest and Principal of Securities—is a claim to a single interest payment or the principal portion of a government bond. These claims trade separately from the bond. STRIPS are zero-coupon bonds since they make only a single payment at maturity. "STRIPS" should not be confused with the forward strip, which is the set of forward prices available at a point in time.

We need a way to represent bond prices and interest rates. Interest rate notation is, unfortunately and inevitably, cumbersome, because for any rate we must keep track of three dates: the date on which the rate is quoted, and the period of time (this has beginning and ending dates) over which the rate prevails. We will let $r_t(t_1, t_2)$ represent the interest rate from time t_1 to time t_2, prevailing on date t. If the interest rate is current—i.e., if $t = t_1$—and if there is no risk of confusion, we will drop the subscript.

Zero-Coupon Bonds

We begin by showing that the zero-coupon bond yield and zero-coupon bond price, columns (1) and (2) in Table 1, provide the same information. A **zero-coupon bond** is a bond that makes only a single payment at its maturity date. Our notation for zero-coupon bond prices will mimic that for interest rates. The price of a bond quoted at time t_0, with the bond to be purchased at t_1 and maturing at t_2, is $P_{t_0}(t_1, t_2)$. As with interest rates, we will drop the subscript when $t_0 = t_1$.

The 1-year zero-coupon bond price of $P(0, 1) = 0.943396$ means that you would pay \$0.943396 today to receive \$1 in 1 year. You could also pay $P(0, 2) = 0.881659$ today to receive \$1 in 2 years and $P(0, 3) = 0.816298$ to receive \$1 in 3 years.

The **yield to maturity** (or *internal rate of return*) on a zero-coupon bond is simply the percentage increase in dollars earned from the bond. For the 1-year bond, we end up with $1/0.943396 - 1 = 0.06$ more dollars per \$1 invested. If we are quoting interest rates as effective annual rates, this is a 6% yield.

For the zero-coupon 2-year bond, we end up with $1/0.881659 - 1 = 0.134225$ more dollars per \$1 invested. We could call this a 2-year effective interest rate of 13.4225%, but it is conventional to quote rates on an annual basis. If we want this yield to be comparable to the 6% yield on the 1-year bond, we could assume annual compounding and get $(1 + r(0, 2))^2 = 1.134225$, which implies that $r(0, 2) = 0.065$. In general,

$$P(0, n) = \frac{1}{[1 + r(0, n)]^n} \tag{1}$$

Note from equation (1) that *a zero-coupon bond price is a discount factor*: A zero-coupon bond price is what you would pay today to receive \$1 in the future. If you have a future cash flow at time t, C_t, you can multiply it by the price of a zero-coupon bond, $P(0, t)$, to obtain the present value of the cash flow. Because of equation (1), multiplying by $P(0, t)$ is the same as discounting at the rate $r(0, t)$, i.e.,

$$C_t \times P(0, t) = \frac{C_t}{[1 + r(0, t)]^t}$$

The inverse of the zero-coupon bond price, $1/P(0, t)$, provides a future value factor.

In contrast to zero-coupon bond prices, interest rates are subject to quoting conventions that can make their interpretation difficult (if you doubt this, see Appendix A). Because of their simple interpretation, we can consider zero-coupon bond prices as the building block for all of fixed income.

A graph of annualized zero-coupon yields to maturity against time to maturity is called the zero-coupon **yield curve**. A yield curve shows us how yields to maturity vary with time to maturity. In practice, it is common to present the yield curve based on coupon bonds, not zero-coupon bonds.

Implied Forward Rates

We now see how column (3) in Table 1 can be computed from either column (1) or (2). The 1-year and 2-year zero-coupon yields are the rates you can earn from year 0 to year 1 and from year 0 to year 2. There is also an *implicit* rate that can be earned from year 1 to year 2 that must be consistent with the other two rates. This rate is called the **implied forward rate**.

Suppose we could today guarantee a rate we could earn from year 1 to year 2. We know that \$1 invested for 1 year earns $[1 + r_0(0, 1)]$ and \$1 invested for 2 years earns $[1 + r_0(0, 2)]^2$. Thus, the time 0 forward rate from year 1 to year 2, $r_0(1, 2)$, should satisfy

$$[1 + r_0(0, 1)][1 + r_0(1, 2)] = [1 + r_0(0, 2)]^2$$

or

$$1 + r_0(1, 2) = \frac{[1 + r_0(0, 2)]^2}{1 + r_0(0, 1)} \tag{2}$$

Figure 1 shows graphically how the implied forward rate is related to 1- and 2-year yields. If $r_0(1, 2)$ did not satisfy equation (2), then there would be an arbitrage opportunity. Problem

FIGURE 1

An investor investing for 2 years has a choice of buying a 2-year zero-coupon bond paying $[1 + r_0(0, 2)]^2$ or buying a 1-year bond paying $1 + r_0(0, 1)$ for 1 year, and reinvesting the proceeds at the implied forward rate, $r_0(1, 2)$, between years 1 and 2. The implied forward rate makes the investor indifferent between these alternatives.

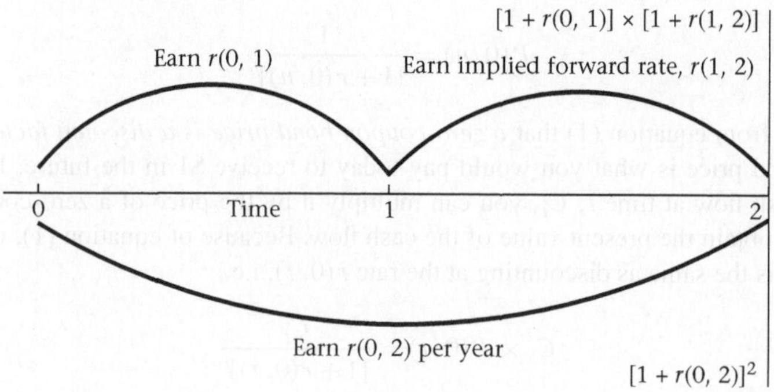

15 asks you to work through the arbitrage. In general, we have

$$[1+r_0(t_1, t_2)]^{t_2-t_1} = \frac{[1+r_0(0, t_2)]^{t_2}}{[1+r_0(0, t_1)]^{t_1}} = \frac{P(0, t_1)}{P(0, t_2)} \tag{3}$$

Corresponding to 1-year and 2-year interest rates, $r_0(0, 1)$ and $r_0(0, 2)$, we have prices of 1-year and 2-year zero-coupon bonds, $P_0(0, 1)$ and $P_0(0, 2)$. Just as the interest rates imply a forward 1-year interest rate, the bond prices imply a 1-year forward zero-coupon bond price. The implied forward zero-coupon bond price must be consistent with the implied forward interest rate. Rewriting equation (3), we have

$$P_0(t_1, t_2) = \frac{1}{[1+r_0(t_1, t_2)]^{t_2-t_1}} = \frac{[1+r_0(0, t_1)]^{t_1}}{[1+r_0(0, t_2)]^{t_2}} = \frac{P(0, t_2)}{P(0, t_1)} \tag{4}$$

The implied forward zero-coupon bond price from t_1 to t_2 is simply the ratio of the zero-coupon bond prices maturing at t_2 and t_1.

Example 1. Using information in Table 1, we want to compute the implied forward interest rate from year 2 to year 3 and the implied forward price for a 1-year zero-coupon bond purchased in year 2.

The implied forward interest rate, $r_0(2, 3)$, can be computed as

$$1 + r_0(2, 3) = \frac{[1 + r_0(0, 3)]^3}{[1 + r_0(0, 2)]^2} = \frac{(1 + 0.07)^3}{(1 + 0.065)^2} = 1.0800705$$

or equivalently as

$$1 + r_0(2, 3) = \frac{P_0(0, 2)}{P_0(0, 3)} = \frac{0.881659}{0.816298} = 1.0800705$$

The implied forward 1-year zero-coupon bond price is

$$\frac{P_0(0,3)}{P_0(0,2)} = \frac{1}{1+r_0(2,3)} = 0.925865 \quad ■$$

Coupon Bonds

Given the prices of zero-coupon bonds—column (1) in Table 1—we can price coupon bonds. We can also compute the **par coupon**—column (4) in Table 1—the coupon rate at which a bond will be priced at par. To describe a coupon bond, we need to know the date at which the bond is being priced, the start and end date of the bond payments, the number and amount of the payments, and the amount of principal. Some practical complexities associated with coupon bonds, not essential for our purposes, are discussed in Appendix A.

We will let $B_t(t_1, t_2, c, n)$ denote the time t price of a bond that is issued at t_1, matures at t_2, pays a coupon of c per dollar of maturity payment, and makes n evenly spaced payments over the life of the bond, beginning at time $t_1 + (t_2 - t_1)/n$. We will assume the maturity payment is \$1. If the maturity payment is different than \$1, we can just multiply all payments by that amount.

Since the price of a bond is the present value of its payments, at issuance time t the price of a bond maturing at T must satisfy

$$B_t(t, T, c, n) = \sum_{i=1}^{n} cP_t(t, t_i) + P_t(t, T) \tag{5}$$

where $t_i = t + i(T - t)/n$, with i being the index in the summation. Using equation (5), we can solve for the coupon as

$$c = \frac{B_t(t, T, c, n) - P_t(t, T)}{\sum_{i=1}^{n} P_t(t, t_i)}$$

A par bond has $B_t = 1$, so the coupon on a par bond is given by

$$\boxed{c = \frac{1 - P_t(t, T)}{\sum_{i=1}^{n} P_t(t, t_i)}} \tag{6}$$

Example 2. Using the information in Table 1, the coupon on a 3-year coupon bond that sells at par is

$$c = \frac{1 - 0.816298}{0.943396 + 0.881659 + 0.816298}$$
$$= 6.95485\% \quad ■$$

Equation (5) computes the bond price by discounting each bond payment at the rate appropriate for a cash flow with that particular maturity. For example, in equation (5), the coupon occuring at time t_i is discounted using the zero-coupon bond price $P_t(t, t_i)$; an alternative way to write the bond price is using the yield to maturity to discount all payments.

Suppose the bond makes m payments per year. Denoting the per-period yield to maturity as y_m, we have

$$B_t(t, T, c, n) = \sum_{i=1}^{n} \frac{c}{(1 + y_m)^i} + \frac{1}{(1 + y_m)^n} \tag{7}$$

It is common to compute the quoted annualized yield to maturity, y, as $y = m \times y_m$. Government bonds, for example, make two coupon payments per year, so the annualized yield to maturity is twice the semiannual yield to maturity.

The difference between equation (5) and equation (7) is that in equation (5), each coupon payment is discounted at the appropriate rate for a cash flow occurring at that time. In equation (7), one rate is used to discount all cash flows. By definition, the two expressions give the same price. However, equation (7) can be misleading, since the yield to maturity, y_m, is not the return an investor earns by buying and holding a bond. Moreover, equation (7) provides no insight into how the cash flows from a bond can be replicated with zero-coupon bonds.

Zeros from Coupons

We have started with zero-coupon bond prices and deduced the prices of coupon bonds. In practice, the situation is often the reverse: We observe prices of coupon bonds and must infer prices of zero-coupon bonds. This procedure in which zero coupon bond prices are deduced from a set of coupon bond prices is called **bootstrapping**.

Suppose we observe the par coupons in Table 1. We can then infer the first zero-coupon bond price from the first coupon bond as follows:

$$1 = (1 + 0.06)P(0, 1)$$

This implies that $P(0, 1) = 1/1.06 = 0.943396$. Using the second par coupon bond with a coupon rate of 6.48423% gives us

$$1 = 0.0648423P(0, 1) + 1.0648423P(0, 2)$$

Since we know $P(0, 1) = 0.943396$, we can solve for $P(0, 2)$:

$$\begin{aligned} P(0, 2) &= \frac{1 - 0.0648423 \times 0.943396}{1.0648423} \\ &= 0.881659 \end{aligned}$$

Finally, knowing $P(0, 1)$ and $P(0, 2)$, we can solve for $P(0, 3)$ using the 3-year par coupon bond with a coupon of 6.95485%:

$$1 = (0.0695485 \times P(0, 1)) + (0.0695485 \times P(0, 2)) + (1.0695485 \times P(0, 3))$$

which gives us

$$\begin{aligned} P(0, 3) &= \frac{1 - (0.0695485 \times 0.943396) - (0.0695485 \times 0.881659)}{1.0695485} \\ &= 0.816298 \end{aligned}$$

There is nothing about the procedure that requires the bonds to trade at par. In fact, we do not even need the bonds to all have different maturities. For example, if we had a 1-year bond and two different 3-year bonds, we could still solve for the three zero-coupon bond prices by solving simultaneous equations.

Interpreting the Coupon Rate

A coupon rate—for example the 6.95485% coupon on the 3-year bond—determines the cash flows the bondholder receives. However, except in special cases, it does not correspond to the rate of return that an investor actually earns by holding the bond.

Suppose for a moment that interest rates are certain; i.e., the implied forward rates in Table 1 are the rates that will actually occur in years 1 and 2. Imagine that we buy the 3-year bond and hold it to maturity, reinvesting all coupons as they are paid. What rate of return do we earn? Before going through the calculations, let's stop and discuss the intuition. We are going to invest an amount at time 0 and to reinvest all coupons by buying more bonds, and we will not withdraw any cash until time 3. *In effect, we are constructing a 3-year zero-coupon bond.* Thus, we should earn the same return as on a 3-year zero: 7%. This buy-and-hold return is different than the yield to maturity of 6.95485%. The coupon payment is set to make a par bond fairly priced, but it is not actually the return we earn on the bond except in the special case when the interest rate is constant over time.

Consider first what would happen if interest rates were certain, we bought the 3-year bond with a \$100 principal and a coupon of 6.95485%, and we held it for 1 year. The price at the end of the year would be

$$\begin{aligned} B_1 &= \frac{6.95485}{1.0700237} + \frac{106.95485}{(1.0700237)(1+0.0800705)} \\ &= 99.04515 \end{aligned}$$

The 1-period return is thus

$$\begin{aligned} \text{1-period return} &= \frac{6.95485 + 99.04515}{100} - 1 \\ &= 0.06 \end{aligned}$$

We earn 6%, since that is the 1-year interest rate. Problem 13 asks you to compute your 2-year return on this investment.

By year 3, we have received three coupons, two of which have been reinvested at the implied forward rate. The total value of reinvested bond holdings at year 3 is

$$6.95485 \times [(1.0700237)(1.0800705) + (1.0800705) + 1] + 100 = 122.5043$$

The 3-year yield on the bond is thus

$$\left(\frac{122.5043}{100}\right)^{1/3} - 1 = 0.07$$

As we expected, this is equal to the 7% yield on the 3-year zero and different from the coupon rate.

This discussion assumed that interest rates are certain. Suppose that we buy and hold the bond, reinvesting the coupons, and that interest rates are not certain. Can we still expect to earn a return of 7%? The answer is yes if we use interest rate forward contracts to guarantee the rate at which we can reinvest coupon proceeds. Otherwise, the answer in general is no.

The belief that the implied forward interest rate equals the expected future spot interest rate is a version of the **expectations hypothesis**. Forward prices are biased predictors of future spot prices when the underlying asset has a risk premium; the same is true for forward interest rates. When you own a coupon bond, the rate at which you will be able to reinvest coupons is uncertain. If interest rates carry a risk premium, then the expected return to holding the bond will not equal the 7% return calculated by assuming interest rates are certain. The expectations hypothesis will generally not hold, and you should not expect implied forward interest rates to be unbiased predictors of future interest rates.

In practice, you can guarantee the 7% return by using forward rate agreements to lock in the interest rate for each of the reinvested coupons. We discuss forward rate agreements in Section 2.

Continuously Compounded Yields

Any interest rate can be quoted as either an effective annual rate or a continuously compounded rate. (Or in a variety of other ways, such as a semiannually compounded rate, which is common with bonds. See Appendix A.) Column (5) in Table 1 presents the continuously compounded equivalents of the rates in the "zero yield" column.

In general, if we have a zero-coupon bond paying $1 at maturity, we can write its price in terms of an annualized continuously compounded yield, $r^{cc}(0, t)$, as[3]

$$P(0, t) = e^{-r^{cc}(0,t)t}$$

Thus, if we observe the price, we can solve for the yield as

$$r^{cc}(0, t) = \frac{1}{t}\ln[1/P(0, t)]$$

We can compute the continuously compounded 3-year zero yield, for example, as

$$\frac{1}{3}\ln(1/0.816298) = 0.0676586$$

Alternatively, we can obtain the same answer using the 3-year zero yield of 7%:

$$\ln(1 + 0.07) = 0.0676586$$

Any of the zero yields or implied forward yields in Table 1 can be computed as effective annual or continuously compounded. The choice hinges on convention and ease of calculation.

2. FORWARD RATE AGREEMENTS, EURODOLLAR FUTURES, AND HEDGING

We now consider the problem of a borrower who wishes to hedge against increases in the cost of borrowing. We consider a firm expecting to borrow $100m for 91 days, beginning 120 days from today, in June. This is the borrowing date. The loan will be repaid in September

3. This note has been intentionally omitted for this edition.

on the loan repayment date. In the examples we will suppose that the effective quarterly interest rate at that time can be either 1.5% or 2%, and that the implied June 91-day forward rate (the rate from June to September) is 1.8%. Here is the risk faced by the borrower, assuming no hedging:

	120 days	**211 days**	
		$r_{\text{quarterly}} = 1.5\%$	$r_{\text{quarterly}} = 2\%$
Borrow \$100m	+100m	−101.5m	−102.0m

Depending upon the interest rate, there is a variation of \$0.5m in the borrowing cost. How can we hedge this uncertainty?

Forward Rate Agreements

A **forward rate agreement** (FRA) is an over-the-counter contract that guarantees a borrowing or lending rate on a given notional principal amount. FRAs can be settled either at the initiation or maturity of the borrowing or lending transaction. If settled at maturity, we will say the FRA is settled in arrears. In the example above, the FRA could be settled on day 120, the point at which the borrowing rate becomes known and the borrowing takes place, or settled in arrears on day 211, when the loan is repaid.

FRAs are a forward contract based on the interest rate, and as such do not entail the actual lending of money. Rather, the borrower who enters an FRA is paid if a reference rate is above the FRA rate, and the borrower pays if the reference rate is below the FRA rate. The actual borrowing is conducted by the borrower independently of the FRA. We will suppose that the reference rate used in the FRA is the same as the actual borrowing cost of the borrower.

FRA Settlement in Arrears. First consider what happens if the FRA is settled in September, on day 211, the loan repayment date. In that case, the payment to the borrower should be

$$\left(r_{\text{quarterly}} - r_{\text{FRA}}\right) \times \text{notional principal}$$

Thus, if the borrowing rate is 1.5%, the payment under the FRA should be

$$(0.015 - 0.018) \times \$100\text{ m} = -\$300{,}000$$

Since the rate is lower than the FRA rate, the borrower pays the FRA counterparty.

Similarly, if the borrowing rate turns out to be 2.0%, the payment under the FRA should be

$$(0.02 - 0.018) \times \$100\text{ m} = \$200{,}000$$

Settling the FRA in arrears is simple and seems like the obvious way for the contract to work. However, settlement can also occur at the time of borrowing.

FRA Settlement at the Time of Borrowing. If the FRA is settled in June, at the time the money is borrowed, payments will be less than when settled in arrears because the borrower has time to earn interest on the FRA settlement. In practice, therefore, the FRA settlement is tailed by the reference rate prevailing on the settlement (borrowing) date. (Tailing in this context means that we reduce the payment to reflect the interest earned between June and

September.) Thus, the payment for a borrower is

$$\text{Notional principal} \times \frac{\left(r_{\text{quarterly}} - r_{\text{FRA}}\right)}{1 + r_{\text{quarterly}}} \tag{8}$$

If $r_{\text{quarterly}} = 1.5\%$, the payment in June is

$$\frac{-\$300{,}000}{1 + 0.015} = -\$295{,}566.50$$

By definition, the future value of this is $-\$300{,}000$. In order to make this payment, the borrower can borrow an extra \$295,566.50, which results in an extra \$300,000 loan payment in September. If on the other hand $r_{\text{quarterly}} = 2.0\%$, the payment is

$$\frac{\$200{,}000}{1 + 0.02} = \$196{,}078.43$$

The borrower can invest this amount, which gives \$200,000 in September, an amount that offsets the extra borrowing cost.

If the forward rate agreement covers a borrowing period other than 91 days, we simply use the appropriate rate instead of the 91-day rate in the above calculations.

Synthetic FRAs

Suppose that today is day 0. By using a forward rate agreement, we will be able to invest \$1 on day 120 and be guaranteed a 91-day return of 1.8%. We can synthetically create the same effect as with an FRA by trading zero-coupon bonds. In order to accomplish this we need to guarantee cash flows of \$0 on day 0, $-\$1$ on day 120, and $+\$1.018$ on day 211.[4]

First, let's get a general sense of the transaction. To match the FRA cash flows, we want cash going out on day 120 and coming in on day 211. To accomplish this, on day 0 we will need to borrow with a 120-day maturity (to generate a cash outflow on day 120) and lend with a 211-day maturity (to generate a cash inflow on day 211). Moreover, we want the day 0 value of the borrowing and lending to be equal so that there is no initial cash flow. This description tells us what we need to do.

In general, suppose that today is day 0, and that at time t we want to lend \$1 for the period s, earning the implied forward rate $r_0(t, t+s)$ over the interval from t to $t+s$. To simplify the notation in this section, $r_0(t, t+s)$ will denote the *nonannualized* percent return from time t to time s. Recall first that

$$1 + r_0(t, t+s) = \frac{P(0, t)}{P(0, t+s)}$$

The strategy we use is to:

1. Buy $1 + r_0(t, t+s)$ zero-coupon bonds maturing at time $t+s$.
2. Short-sell 1 zero-coupon bond maturing at time t.

4. The example in the previous section considered locking in a borrowing rate, but in this section we lock in a lending rate; the transactions can be reversed for borrowing.

TABLE 2 Investment strategy undertaken at time 0, resulting in net cash flows of $-\$1$ on day t, and receiving the implied forward rate, $1 + r_0(t, t + s)$ at $t + s$. This synthetically creates the cash flows from entering into a forward rate agreement on day 0 to lend at day t.

	Cash Flows		
Transaction	**0**	t	$t + s$
Buy $1 + r_0)t, t + s)$ zeros maturing at $t + s$	$-P(0, t + s) \times (1 + r_0(t, t + s))$	—	$1 + r_0(t, t + s)$
Short 1 zero maturing at t	$+P(0, t)$	01	—
Total	0	-1	$1 + r_0(t, t + s)$

TABLE 3 Example of synthetic FRA. The transactions in this table are exactly those in Table 2, except that all bonds are sold at time t.

	Cash Flows	
Transaction	**0**	t
Buy $1 + r_0)t, t + s)$ zeros maturing at $t + s$	$-P(0, t + s) \times [1 + r_0(t, t + s)]$	$\frac{1+r_0(t,t+s)}{1+r_1(t,t+s)}$
Short 1 zero maturing at t	$+P(0, t)$	-1
Total	0	$\frac{r_0(t,t+s)-r_1(t,t+s)}{1+r_1(t,t+s)}$

The resulting cash flows are illustrated in Table 2, which shows that transactions made on day 0 synthetically create a loan commencing on day t and paying the implied forward rate, $r_0(t, t + s)$, on day $t + s$.

This example can be modified slightly to synthetically create the cash flows from a forward rate agreement that settles on the borrowing date, day t. To make this modification, we sell at time t the bond maturing at time $t + s$. The result is presented in Table 3. Note that if we reinvested the FRA proceeds at the market rate prevailing on day t, $r_t(t, t + s)$, we would receive $r_0(t, t + s) - r_t(t, t + s)$ on day $t + s$.

Example 3. Consider the example above and suppose that $P(0, 211) = 0.95836$ and $P(0, 120) = 0.97561$, which implies a 120-day interest rate of 2.5%. In order to receive \$1.018 on day 211, we buy 1.018 211-day zero-coupon bonds. The cost of this is

$$1.018 \times P(0, 211) = \$0.97561$$

In order to have zero cash flow initially and a cash outflow on day 120, we borrow 0.97561, with a 120-day maturity. This entails borrowing one 120-day bond, since

$$\frac{0.97561}{P(0, 120)} = 1$$

The result on day 120 is that we pay \$1 to close the short position on the 120-day bond, and on day 211 we receive \$1.018 since we bought that many 211-day bonds. ■

To summarize, we have shown that an FRA is just like the stock and currency forwards we have considered, both with respect to pricing and synthesizing. If at time 0 we want to lock in a lending rate from time t to time $t + s$, we can create a rate forward synthetically by buying the underlying asset (the bond maturing at $t + s$) and borrowing (shorting) the bond maturing at day t.

In general, we have the following conclusions concerning a rate forward covering the period t_1 to t_2:

- The forward rate we can obtain is the implied forward rate—i.e., $r_{t_0}(t_1, t_2) = P_{t_0}(t_0, t_1)/P_{t_0}(t_0, t_2) - 1$.
- We can synthetically create the payoff to an FRA, $\frac{r_{t_0}(t_1,t_2)-r_{t_1}(t_1,t_2)}{1+r_{t_1}(t_1,t_2)}$, by borrowing to buy a bond maturing at t_2, i.e., by:
  1. Buying $1 + r_{t_0}(t_1, t_2)$ of the zero-coupon bond maturing on day t_2, and
  2. Shorting 1 zero-coupon bond maturing on day t_1.

Eurodollar Futures

Eurodollar futures contracts are similar to FRAs in that they can be used to guarantee a borrowing rate. There are subtle differences between FRAs and Eurodollar contracts, however, that are important to understand.

Let's consider again the example in which we wish to guarantee a borrowing rate for a \$100m loan from June to September. Suppose the June Eurodollar futures price is 92.8. Implied 3-month LIBOR is $\frac{100-92.8}{4\times 100} = 1.8\%$ over 3 months. The payoff on a single short Eurodollar contract at expiration will be[5]

$$[92.8 - (100 - r_{\text{LIBOR}})] \times 100 \times \$25$$

Thus, the payoff on the Eurodollar contract compensates us for differences between the implied rate (1.8%) and actual LIBOR at expiration.

To illustrate hedging with this contract we again consider two possible 3-month borrowing rates in June: 1.5% or 2%. If the interest rate is 1.5%, borrowing cost on \$100m will be \$1.5m, payable in September. If the interest rate is 2%, borrowing cost will be \$2m.

Suppose that we were to short 100 Eurodollar futures contracts. Ignoring marking-to-market prior to June, if the 3-month rate in June is 1.5%, the Eurodollar futures price will be 94. The payment is

$$[(92.8 - 94) \times 100 \times \$25] \times 100 = -\$300{,}000$$

5. This calculation treats the Eurodollar contract as if it were a forward contract.

We multiply by 100 twice: once to account for 100 contracts, and the second time to convert the change in the futures price to basis points. Similarly, if the borrowing rate is 2%, we have

$$[(92.8 - 92) \times 100 \times \$25] \times 100 = \$200{,}000$$

This is like the payment on an FRA paid in arrears, except that the futures contract settles in June, but our interest expense is not paid until September. Thus we have 3 months to earn or pay interest on our Eurodollar gain or loss before we actually have to make the interest payment.

Recall that when the FRA settles on the borrowing date, the payment is the *present value* of the change in borrowing cost. The FRA is thus tailed automatically as part of the agreement. With the Eurodollar contract, by contrast, we need to tail the position explicitly. We do this by shorting fewer than 100 contracts, using the implied 3-month Eurodollar rate of 1.8% as our discount factor. Thus, we enter into[6]

$$\text{Number of Eurodollar contracts} = -\frac{100}{1 + 0.018} = -98.2318$$

Now consider the gain on the Eurodollar futures position. If LIBOR = 6% ($r_{\text{quarterly}} = 1.5\%$), our total gain on the short contracts when we initiate borrowing on day 120 will be

$$98.2318 \times (92.8 - 94) \times \$2500 = -\$294{,}695$$

If LIBOR = 8% ($r_{\text{quarterly}} = 2.0\%$), our total gain on the contracts will be

$$98.2318 \times (92.8 - 92) \times \$2500 = \$196{,}464$$

Notice that the amounts are different than with the FRA: The reason is that the FRA payment is automatically tailed using the 3-month rate prevailing in June, whereas with the Eurodollar contract we tailed using 1.8%, the LIBOR rate implied by the initial futures price.

We can now invest these proceeds at the prevailing interest rate. Here are the results on day 211, when borrowing must be repaid. If LIBOR = 6% ($r_{\text{quarterly}} = 1.5\%$), we save \$300,000 in borrowing cost, and the proceeds from the Eurodollar contract are

$$-\$294{,}695 \times (1.015) = -\$299{,}115$$

If LIBOR = 8% ($r_{\text{quarterly}} = 2.0\%$), we owe an extra \$200,000 in interest and the invested proceeds from the Eurodollar contract are

$$\$196{,}464 \times (1.02) = \$200{,}393$$

Table 4 summarizes the result from this hedging position. The borrowing cost is close to 1.8%.

Convexity Bias and Tailing. In Table 4 the net borrowing cost appears to be a little less than 1.8%. You might guess that this is due to rounding error. It is not. Let's examine the numbers more closely.

6. We assume here that it is possible to short fractional contracts in order to make the example exact.

TABLE 4 Results from hedging $100m in borrowing with 98.23 short Eurodollar futures.

	Cash Flows			
	June		September	
Borrowing Rate:	1.5%	2%	1.5%	2%
Borrow $100m	+100m	+100m	−101.5m	−102.0m
Gain on 98.23 short Eurodollar contracts	−0.294695m	0.196464m		
Gain plus interest			−0.299115m	0.200393m
Net			−101.799m	−101.799m

If LIBOR = 6% ($r_{\text{quarterly}} = 1.5\%$), we pay $1.5m in borrowing cost and we lose $299,115 on the Eurodollar contract, for a net borrowing expense of $1.799115m. This is a "profit" from the Eurodollar hedge, relative to the use of an FRA, of $1.8m − $1.799115m = $884.

If LIBOR = 8% ($r_{\text{quarterly}} = 2.0\%$), we pay $2.0m in borrowing cost but make $200,393 on the Eurodollar contract, for a net borrowing expense of $1.799607m. We make a profit, relative to an FRA, of $1.8m − $1.799607m = $393.

It appears that we systematically come out ahead by hedging with Eurodollar futures instead of an FRA. You are probably thinking that something is wrong.

As it turns out, what we have just shown is that *the rate implied by the Eurodollar contract cannot equal the prevailing FRA (implied forward) rate for the same loan.* To see this, consider the borrower perspective: When the interest rate turns out to be high, the short Eurodollar contract has a positive payoff and the proceeds can be reinvested until the loan payment date at the high realized rate. When the interest rate turns out to be low, the short Eurodollar contract has a negative payoff and we can fund this loss until the loan payment date by borrowing at a low rate. Thus the settlement structure of the Eurodollar contract works *systematically* in favor of the borrower. By turning the argument around, we can verify that it systematically works against a lender.

The reason this happens with Eurodollars and not FRAs is that we have to make the tailing decision *before* we know the 3-month rate prevailing on day 120. When we tail by a fixed amount (1.8% in the above example), the actual variations in the realized rate work in favor of the borrower and against the lender. The FRA avoids this by automatically tailing—paying the present value of the change in borrowing cost—using the actual interest rate on the borrowing date.

In order for the futures price to be fair to both the borrower and lender, the rate implicit in the Eurodollar futures price must be higher than a comparable FRA rate. This difference between the FRA rate and the Eurodollar rate is called **convexity bias**. For the most part in subsequent discussions we will ignore convexity bias and treat the Eurodollar contract and FRAs as if they are interchangeable. The reason is that in many cases the effect is small. In the above example, convexity bias results in a profit of several hundred dollars out of a borrowing cost of \$1.8m. For short-term contracts, the effect can be small, but for longer-term contracts the effect can be important.[7]

In practice, convexity bias also matters before the final contract settlement. Marking-to-market a futures contract can lead to a futures price that is different from the forward price. When a futures contract is marked to market and interest rates are negatively correlated with the futures price, there is a systematic advantage to being short the futures contract. This leads to a futures price that is greater than the forward price. This is exactly what happens with the Eurodollar contract in this example. When interest rates rise, the borrower receives a payment that can be invested at the higher interest rate. When interest rates fall, the borrower makes a payment that can be funded at the lower interest rate. This works to the borrower's benefit. Marking-to-market prior to settlement is therefore another reason why the rate implied by the Eurodollar contract will exceed that on an otherwise comparable FRA.

LIBOR Versus 3-Month T-Bills. The Eurodollar futures contract is based on LIBOR, but there are other 3-month interest rates. For example, the Treasury-bill futures contract is based on the price of the 3-month Treasury bill. A borrower could use either the Eurodollar contract or the Treasury-bill futures contract to hedge their borrowing rate. Which contract is preferable?

Banks that offer LIBOR time deposits have the potential to default. Thus, LIBOR includes a default premium. (The **default premium** is an increase in the interest rate that compensates the lender for the possibility the borrower will default.) Private companies that borrow can also default, so their borrowing rates will also include a default premium.

The U.S. government, by contrast, is considered unlikely to default, so it can borrow at a lower rate than firms. In addition, in the United States and other countries, government

---

7. If future interest rates were known for certain in advance, then it would be possible to perfectly tail the position. However, with uncertainty about rates, the error is due to interest on the difference between the realized rate, $\tilde{r}$, and the forward rate, r_{forward}. Given that we tail by the forward rate, the error is measured by

$$\frac{\tilde{r}(\tilde{r} - r_{\text{forward}})}{1 + r_{\text{forward}}}$$

The expected error is

$$E\left[\frac{\tilde{r}\,(\tilde{r} - r_{\text{forward}})}{1 + r_{\text{forward}}}\right] = \frac{1}{1 + r_{\text{forward}}}\left[E\left(\tilde{r}^2\right) - E\left(\tilde{r} r_{\text{forward}}\right)\right]$$
$$= \frac{\sigma^2}{1 + r_{\text{forward}}}$$

where σ^2 is the variance of the interest rate. Rates in our example can be 2% or 1.5%, so the standard deviation is approximately 25 basis points, or 0.0025, and the variance is thus $0.0025^2 = 0.00000625$. Convexity bias is thus

$$\$100\text{m} \times \frac{0.00000625}{1.018} = \$613.95$$

The actual average convexity error in the example was (\$884 + \$393)/2, or \$638.5.

FIGURE 2

The 3-month LIBOR rate and 3-month T-bill rate (top panel) and the difference between the two (bottom panel), 1982–2011.

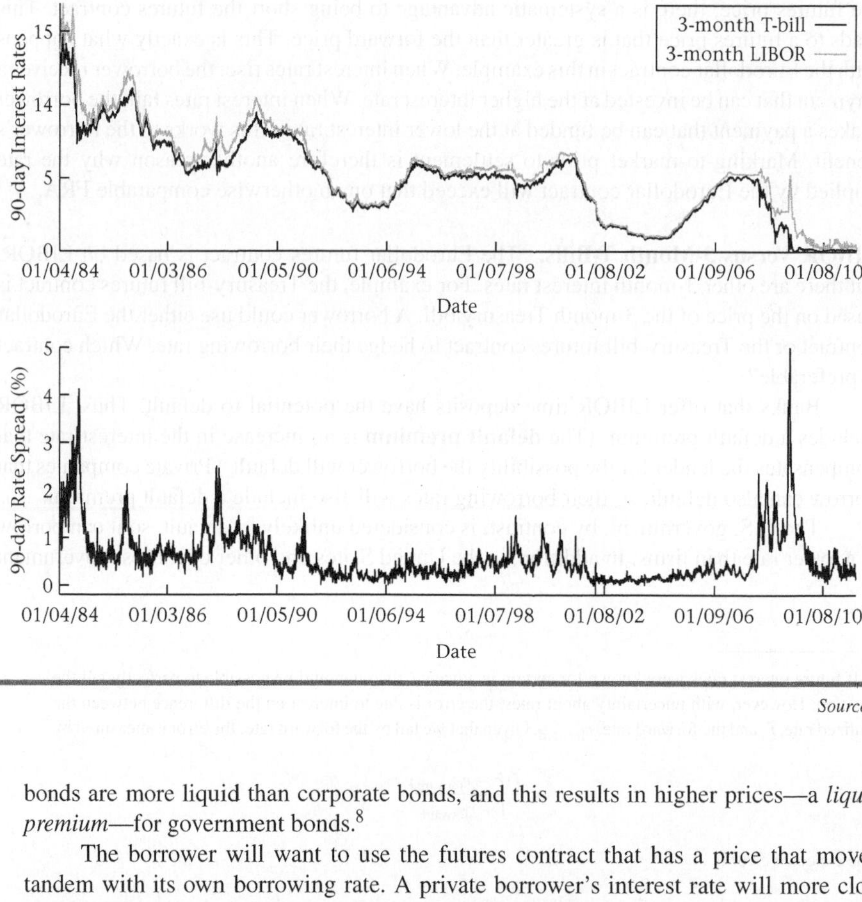

Source: Datastream.

bonds are more liquid than corporate bonds, and this results in higher prices—a *liquidity premium*—for government bonds.[8]

The borrower will want to use the futures contract that has a price that moves in tandem with its own borrowing rate. A private borrower's interest rate will more closely track LIBOR than the Treasury-bill rate. In fact, the spread between corporate borrowing rates and Treasuries moves around a great deal. A private firm's borrowing costs can increase even as the T-bill rate goes down; this can occur during times of financial distress, when investors bid up the prices of Treasury securities relative to other assets (a so-called "flight to quality"). Thus, LIBOR is commonly used in markets as a benchmark, high-quality, private interest rate.

Figure 2 shows historical 3-month LIBOR along with the difference between LIBOR and the 3-month T-bill yield, illustrating this variability.[9] It is obvious that the spread varies

8. In the United States, another reason for government bonds to have higher prices than corporate bonds is that government bond interest is exempt from state taxation.

9. The TED spread ("T-Bills over Eurodollars") is obtained by going long T-bill futures and short the Eurodollar futures contract.

considerably over time: Although the spread has been as low as a few basis points, twice in the 1990s it exceeded 100 basis points. In September of 1982, when Continental Bank failed, and during the financial crisis of 2008 (see Box 1), the spread exceeded 400 basis points. A private LIBOR-based borrower who had hedged its borrowing rate by shorting T-bill futures in August of 1982 would by September have lost money on the T-bill contract as Treasury rates declined, while the actual cost of borrowing (LIBOR) would have remained close to unchanged. This example illustrates the value of using a hedging contract that reflects the actual cost of borrowing.

The Eurodollar futures contract is far more popular than the T-bill futures contract. Trading volume and open interest on the two contracts were about equal in the early 1980s. However, in recent years, open interest on the Eurodollar contract has been millions of contracts, while the T-bill contract has had zero open interest. This is consistent with LIBOR being a better measure of private sector interest rates than the T-bill yield.

3. DURATION AND CONVEXITY

An important characteristic of a bond is the sensitivity of its price to interest rate changes, which we measure using **duration**. Duration tells us approximately how much the bond's price will change for a given change in the bond's yield. Duration is thus a summary measure of the risk of a bond, permitting a comparison of bonds with different coupons, times to maturity, and discounts or premiums relative to principal. In this section we also discuss **convexity**, which is another measure related to bond price risk.

Price Value of a Basis Point and DV01

We first compute the change in the bond price due to a change in the yield. Suppose a bond makes m coupon payments per year for T years in the amount C/m and pays M at maturity. Let y/m be the per-period yield to maturity (by convention, y is the annualized yield to maturity) and $n = m \times T$ the number of periods until maturity. The price of the bond, $B(y)$, is given by

$$B(y) = \sum_{i=1}^{n} \frac{C/m}{(1+y/m)^i} + \frac{M}{(1+y/m)^n}$$

The change in the bond price for a unit change in the yield, y, is[10]

$$\frac{\text{Change in bond price}}{\text{Unit change in yield}} = \sum_{i=1}^{n} -\frac{i}{m}\frac{C/m}{(1+y/m)^{i+1}} - \frac{n}{m}\frac{M}{(1+y/m)^{n+1}}$$

$$= -\frac{1}{1+y/m}\left[\sum_{i=1}^{n} \frac{i}{m}\frac{C/m}{(1+y/m)^i} + \frac{n}{m}\frac{M}{(1+y/m)^n}\right] \quad (9)$$

Equation (9) tells us the *dollar* change in the bond price for a change of 1.0 in y. It is natural to scale this either to reflect a change per percentage point [in which case we divide equation (9) by 100] or per basis point (divide equation (9) by 10,000). Equation (9) divided

10. This is obtained by computing the derivative of the bond price with respect to the yield, $dB(y)/dy$.

BOX 1: Was LIBOR Accurate During the Financial Crisis?

Unlike most quoted interest rates, LIBOR is not based on a transaction price. Rather, the British Bankers' Association (BBA) conducts a daily survey of 16 large banks and asks about their borrowing rate for a $1 million time deposit. A bank that is regarded as safe will be able to borrow at a lower rate than one thought to be less creditworthy.

During the financial crisis, the BBA became concerned that some of the surveyed banks were not being truthful about their borrowing rates. In April 2008, the *Wall Street Journal* reported on LIBOR:

> The world's most widely used interest rate took its largest jump since the advent of the credit crisis in a sign that banks could be responding to increasing concerns that the rate doesn't reflect their actual borrowing costs.
>
> Thursday's sudden jump in the dollar-denominated London interbank offered rate, or Libor, comes after a decision Wednesday by the British Bankers' Association to speed up an inquiry into the daily borrowing rates that banks provide to establish the Libor rate.
>
> The move by the BBA, which oversees Libor, came amid concerns among bankers that their rivals were not reporting the high rates they were paying for short-term loans for fear of appearing desperate for cash. . . .
>
> Some expect Libor to increase further. William Porter, credit strategist at Credit Suisse, said he believes the three-month dollar rate is 0.4 percentage point below where it should be. That echoes the view of Scott Peng, a Citigroup Inc. analyst who said that Libor understated banks' true borrowing costs by as much as 0.3 percentage points.
>
> *Source:* Mollenkamp 2008.

Government investigations can move slowly. Three years later, the *Financial Times* (Masters et al., 2011) reported that subpeonas were being issued to a handful of global banks as regulators investigated LIBOR manipulation between 2006 and 2008. The article noted that LIBOR is used as a benchmark for $350 trillion in financial products, explaining the concern of regulators.

by 10,000 is also known as the **price value of a basis point** (PVBP) or the dollar value of an 01 (**DV01**). To interpret PVBP for a bond, we need to know the par value of the bond.

Example 4. Consider the 3-year zero-coupon bond in Table 1 with a yield to maturity of 7%. The bond price per $100 of maturity value is $\$100/1.07^3 = \$81.62979$. At a yield of 7.01%, one basis point higher, the bond price is $\$100/1.0701^3 = \$81.60691$, a change of $-\$0.02288$ per $100 of maturity value.

As an alternative way to derive the price change, we can compute equation (9) with $C = 0$, $M = \$100$, $n = 3$, and $m = 1$ to obtain

$$-\frac{1}{1.07} \times 3 \times \frac{\$100}{1.07^3} = -\$228.87$$

In order for this to reflect a change of 1 basis point, we divide by 10,000 to obtain $-\$228.87/10{,}000 = -\$0.02289$, almost equal to the actual bond price change. This illustrates the importance of scaling equation (9) appropriately. ■

Duration

When comparing bonds with different prices and par values, it is helpful to have a measure of price sensitivity expressed *per dollar of bond price*. We obtain this by dividing equation (9) by the bond price, $B(y)$, and multiplying by -1. This gives us a measure known as **modified duration**, which is the *percentage* change in the bond price for a unit change in the yield:

$$\text{Modified duration} = -\frac{\text{Change in bond price}}{\text{Unit change in yield}} \times \frac{1}{B(y)}$$

$$\boxed{= \frac{1}{B(y)} \frac{1}{1+y/m} \left[\sum_{i=1}^{n} \frac{i}{m} \frac{C/m}{(1+y/m)^i} + \frac{n}{m} \frac{M}{(1+y/m)^n} \right]} \tag{10}$$

We obtain another measure of bond price risk—**Macaulay duration**—by multiplying equation (10) by $1 + y/m$.[11] This puts both bond price and yield changes in percentage terms and gives us an expression with a clear interpretation:

$$\text{Macaulay duration} = -\frac{\text{Change in bond price}}{\text{Unit change in yield}} \times \frac{1+y/m}{B(y)}$$

$$\boxed{= \frac{1}{B(y)} \left[\sum_{i=1}^{n} \frac{i}{m} \frac{C/m}{(1+y/m)^i} + \frac{n}{m} \frac{M}{(1+y/m)^n} \right]} \tag{11}$$

To interpret this expression, note that $(C/m)/(1+y/m)^i$ is the present value of the ith bond payment, which occurs in i/m years. The quantity $C/m/[(1+y/m)^i B(y)]$ is therefore the fraction of the bond value that is due to the ith payment. Macaulay duration is a *weighted average of the time (number of periods) until the bond payments occur*, with the weights being the percentage of the bond price accounted for by each payment. This interpretation of Macaulay duration as a time-to-payment measure explains why these measures of bond price sensitivity are called "duration."[12] For a zero-coupon bond, equation (11) implies that Macaulay duration equals time to maturity.

Macaulay duration illustrates why maturity alone is not a satisfactory risk measure for a coupon bond. A coupon bond makes a series of payments, each with a different maturity. Macaulay duration summarizes bond price risk as a weighted average of these different maturities.

Example 5. Returning to Example 4, using equation (11), Macaulay duration for the 7% bond is

$$-\frac{-\$228.87}{1} \times \frac{1.07}{\$81.62979} = 3.000 \quad ■$$

11. This measure of duration is named after Frederick Macaulay, who wrote a classic history of interest rates (Macaulay, 1938).

12. The Excel duration functions are *Duration* for Macaulay duration and *MDuration* for modified duration.

Example 6. Consider the 3-year coupon bond in Table 1. For a par bond, the yield to maturity is the coupon, 6.95485% in this case. For each payment we have

$$\%\text{Payment } 1 = \frac{0.0695485}{1.0695485} = 0.065026$$

$$\%\text{Payment } 2 = \frac{0.0695485}{(1.0695485)^2} = 0.060798$$

$$\%\text{Payment } 3 = \frac{1.0695485}{(1.0695485)^3} = 0.874176$$

Thus, with $n = 3$ and $m = 1$, Macaulay duration is

$$(1 \times 0.065026) + (2 \times 0.060798) + (3 \times 0.874176) = 2.80915$$

The interpretation of the duration of 2.81 is that the bond responds to interest rate changes as if it were a pure discount bond with 2.81 years to maturity. Modified duration is $2.80915/1.0695485 = 2.626482$. ■

Since duration tells us the sensitivity of the bond price to a change in the interest rate, it can be used to compute the approximate bond price change for a given change in interest rates. Suppose the bond price is $B(y)$ and the yield on the bond changes from y to $y + \epsilon$, where ϵ is a small change in the yield. The formula for Macaulay duration, D_{Mac}, can be written

$$D_{\text{Mac}} = -\frac{\left[B(y+\epsilon) - B(y)\right]}{\epsilon} \frac{1+y}{B(y)}$$

We can therefore rewrite this equation to obtain the new bond price in terms of the old bond price and either duration measure:

$$B(y+\epsilon) = B(y) - [D \times B(y)\epsilon] = B(y) - [D_{\text{Mac}}/(1+y) \times B(y)\epsilon] \qquad (12)$$

Example 7. Consider the 3-year zero-coupon bond with a price of \$81.63 per \$100 maturity value. The yield is 7% and the bond's Macaulay duration is 3.0. If the yield were to increase to 7.25%, the predicted price would be

$$B(7.25\%) = \$81.63 - (3/1.07) \times \$81.63 \times 0.0025 = \$81.058$$

The actual new bond price is $\$100/(1.0725)^3 = \$81.060$. The prediction error is about 0.02% of the bond price. ■

Although duration is an important concept and is frequently used in practice, it has a conceptual problem. We emphasized in the previous section that a coupon bond is a collection of zero-coupon bonds, and therefore each cash flow has its own discount rate. Yet both duration formulas are computed assuming that all cash flows are discounted by a single artificial number, the yield to maturity.

Duration Matching

Suppose we own a bond with time to maturity t_1, price B_1, and Macaulay duration D_1. We are considering a short position in a bond with maturity t_2, price B_2, and Macaulay duration

D_2. How much of the second bond should we short-sell so that the resulting portfolio—long the bond with duration D_1 and short the bond with duration D_2—is insensitive to interest rate changes?

Equation (12) gives us a formula for the change in price of each bond. Let N denote the quantity of the second bond. The value of the portfolio is

$$B_1 + NB_2$$

and, using equation (12), the change in price due to an interest rate change of ϵ is

$$\begin{aligned}&\left[B_1(y_1+\epsilon) - B_1(y_1)\right] + N\left[B_2(y_2+\epsilon) - B_2(y_2)\right] \\ &= -D_1 B_1(y_1)\epsilon/(1+y_1) - N D_2 B_2(y_2)\epsilon/(1+y_2)\end{aligned}$$

where D_1 and D_2 are Macaulay durations. If we want the net change to be zero, we choose N to set the right-hand side equal to zero. This gives

$$\boxed{N = -\frac{D_1 B_1(y_1)/(1+y_1)}{D_2 B_2(y_2)/(1+y_2)}} \tag{13}$$

When a portfolio is duration-matched in this fashion, the net investment in the portfolio will typically not be zero. That is, either the value of the short bond is less than the value of the long bond, in which case additional financing is required, or vice versa, in which case there is cash to invest. This residual can be financed or invested in very short-term bonds, with duration approximately zero, in order to leave the portfolio duration matched.

Example 8. Suppose we own a 7-year 6% coupon bond with a yield of 7% and want to find the duration-matched short position in a 10-year 8% coupon bond yielding 7.5%. Assuming annual coupon payments, the Macaulay duration and price of the two bonds is 5.882 years and \$94.611, and 7.297 years and \$103.432, respectively. Thus, if we own one of the 7-year bonds, we must hold

$$-\frac{5.882 \times 94.611/(1.07)}{7.297 \times 103.432/(1.075)} = -0.7408$$

units of the 10-year bond. The short position in the 10-year bond is not enough to pay for the 7-year bond; hence, investment in the portfolio is $1 \times 94.611 - 0.7408 \times 103.432 = 17.99$. If the yield on both bonds increases 25 basis points, the price change of the portfolio is

$$-1.289 + (-0.7408) \times -1.735 = -0.004 \;\blacksquare$$

Convexity

The hedge in Example 8 is not perfect, because duration changes as the interest rate changes.[13] *Convexity* measures the extent to which duration changes as the bond's yield

13. At the original yields, we computed a hedge ratio of 0.7408. Problem 19 asks you to compute the hedge ratio that would have exactly hedged the portfolio had both interest rates increased 25 basis points and decreased 25 basis points. The two hedge ratios are different, which means that one hedge ratio would not have worked perfectly.

changes. The formula for convexity is[14]

$$\text{Convexity} = \frac{1}{B(y)}\left[\sum_{i=1}^{n} \frac{i(i+1)}{m^2}\frac{C/m}{(1+y/m)^{i+2}} + \frac{n(n+1)}{m^2}\frac{M}{(1+y/m)^{n+2}}\right] \tag{14}$$

We can use convexity in addition to duration to obtain a more accurate prediction of the new bond price. When we include convexity, the price prediction formula, equation (12), becomes[15]

$$B(y+\epsilon) = B(y) - [D \times B(y) \times \epsilon] + 0.5 \times \text{Convexity} \times B(y) \times \epsilon^2 \tag{15}$$

where D is modified duration. Here is an example of computing a bond price at a new yield using both duration and convexity.

Example 9. Consider again Example 7. We want to predict the new price of a 3-year zero-coupon bond when the interest rate changes from 7% to 7.25%. Using equation (14) with $C = 0$, $m = 1$, and $M = \$100$, convexity of the bond is

$$\text{Convexity} = 3 \times 4 \times \frac{100}{1.07^{(3+2)}} \times \frac{1}{81.63} = 10.4812$$

Using equation (15), the price at a yield of 7.25% is

$$\begin{aligned} B(7.25\%) &= \$81.63 - (3/1.07) \times \$81.63 \times 0.0025 + 0.5 \times 10.4812 \times \$81.63 \times 0.0025^2 \\ &= \$81.060 \end{aligned}$$

The predicted price of \$81.060 is the same as the actual price at a yield of 7.25%, to an accuracy of three decimal points. In Example 7, the predicted price was slightly lower (\$81.058) than the actual new price. The difference without a convexity correction occurs because the bond's sensitivity to the interest rate changes as the interest rate changes.[16] Convexity corrects for this effect. ■

Figure 3 illustrates duration and convexity by comparing three bond positions that have identical prices at a yield of 10%. Duration is the slope of the bond price graph at a given yield, and convexity is the curvature of the graph. The 10% 10-year bond has the lowest duration and is the shallowest bond price curve. The other two bonds have almost equal durations at a yield of 10% and their slopes are equal in the figure. However, the 25-year bond exhibits greater curvature: Its price is above the 10-year bond at both lower and higher yields. This greater curvature is what it means for the 25-year bond to have greater convexity.

---

14. This is obtained by taking the second derivative of the bond price with respect to the yield to maturity, $d^2B(y)/dy^2$, and normalizing the result by dividing by the bond price.

15. If you recall calculus, you may recognize equation (12) as a Taylor series expansion of the bond price.

16. You might wonder about this statement since the bond in Example 7 is a zero-coupon bond, for which Macaulay duration is constant. Notice, however, that the bond price prediction formula, equation (12), depends on *modified* duration, which is $D_{\text{Mac}}/(1+y)$. Modified duration does change with the yield on the bond.

FIGURE 3

Comparison of the value of three bond positions as a function of the yield to maturity: 2.718 10-year zero-coupon bonds, one 10-year bond paying a 10% annual coupon, and one 25-year bond paying a 10% coupon. The duration (D) and convexity (C) of each bond at a yield of 10% are in the legend.

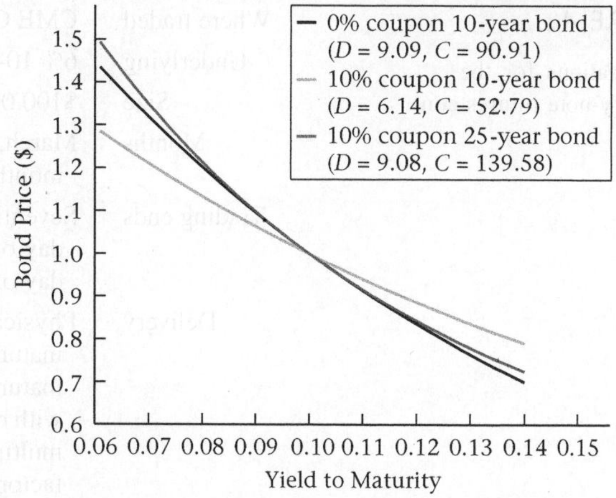

The idea that using both duration and convexity provides a more accurate model of bond price changes is not particular to bonds, but it pertains to options as well.

4. TREASURY-BOND AND TREASURY-NOTE FUTURES

The Treasury-note and Treasury-bond futures contracts are important instruments for hedging interest rate risk.[17] The specifications for the T-note contract are listed in Figure 4. The bond contract is similar except that the deliverable bond has a maturity of at least 15 years, or if the bond is callable, has 15 years to first call. The two contracts are similar; we will focus here on the T-note contract. In this discussion we will use the terms "bond" and "note" interchangeably.

The basic idea of the T-note contract is that a long position is an obligation to buy a 6% bond with between 6.5 and 10 years to maturity. To a first approximation, we can think of the underlying as being like a stock with a dividend yield of 6%. The futures price would then be computed as with a stock index: the future value of the current bond price, less the future value of coupons payable over the life of the futures contract.

This description masks a complication that may already have occurred to you. The delivery procedure permits the short to deliver any note maturing in 6.5 to 10 years. Hence, the delivered note can be one of many outstanding notes, with a range of coupons and maturities. Which bond does the futures price represent?

Of all bonds that *could* be delivered, there will generally be one that is the most advantageous for the short to deliver. This bond is called the **cheapest to deliver**. A description of the delivery procedure will demonstrate the importance of the cheapest-to-deliver bond.

17. The interest rate on the 10-year Treasury note is a commonly used benchmark interest rate; hence, the 10-year note futures are important.

FIGURE 4

Specifications for the Treasury-note futures contract.

Where traded	CME Group/CBOT
Underlying	6% 10-year Treasury note
Size	$100,000 Treasury note
Months	March, June, September, December, out 15 months
Trading ends	Seventh business day preceding last business day of month. Delivery until last business day of month.
Delivery	Physical T-note with at least 6.5 years to maturity and not more than 10 years to maturity. Price paid to the short for notes with other than 6% coupon is determined by multiplying futures price by a conversion factor. The conversion factor is the price of the delivered note ($1 par value) to yield 6%. Settlement until last business day of the month.

In fulfilling the note futures contract, the short delivers the bond in exchange for payment. The payment to the short—the *invoice price* for the delivered bond—is the futures price times the conversion factor. The conversion factor is the price of the bond if it were priced to yield 6%. Thus, the short delivering a bond is paid[18]

$$\text{Invoice price} = (\text{Futures price} \times \text{conversion factor}) + \text{accrued interest}$$

Example 10. Consider two bonds making semiannual coupon payments. Bond A is a 7% coupon bond with exactly 8 years to maturity, a price of 103.71, and a yield of 6.4%. This bond would have a price of 106.28 if its yield were 6%. Thus its conversion factor is 1.0628.

Bond B has 7 years to maturity and a 5% coupon. Its current price and yield are 92.73 and 6.3%. It would have a conversion factor of 0.9435, since that is its price at a 6% yield. ■

Now suppose that the futures contract is close to expiration, the observed futures price is 97.583, and the only two deliverable bonds are Bonds A and B. The short can decide which bond to deliver by comparing the market value of the bond to its invoice price if delivered. For Bond A we have

$$\text{Invoice price} - \text{market price} = (97.583 \times 1.0628) - 103.71 = 0.00$$

For Bond B we have

18. Appendix A contains a definition of accrued interest.

TABLE 5 Prices, yields, and the conversion factor for two bonds. The futures price is 97.583. The short would break even delivering the 8-year 7% bond, and lose money delivering the 7-year 5% bond. Both bonds make semiannual coupon payments.

Description	8-Year 7% Coupon, 6.4% Yield	7-Year 5% Coupon, 6.3% Yield
Market price	103.71	92.73
Price at 6% (conversion factor)	106.28	94.35
Invoice price (futures × conversion factor)	103.71	92.09
Invoice − market	0	−0.66

$$\text{Invoice price} - \text{market price} = (97.583 \times 0.9435) - 92.73 = -0.66$$

These calculations are summarized in Table 5.

Based on the yields for the two bonds, the short breaks even delivering the 8-year 7% bond and would lose money delivering the 7-year 5% coupon bond (the invoice price is less than the market price). In this example, the 8-year 7% bond is thus the cheapest to deliver.

In general there will be a single cheapest-to-deliver bond. You might be wondering why both bonds are not equally cheap to deliver. The reason is that the conversion factor is set by a mechanical procedure (the price at which the bond yields 6%), taking no account of the current relative market prices of bonds. Except by coincidence, two bonds will not be equally cheap to deliver.

Also, all but one of the bonds must have a negative delivery value. If two bonds had a positive delivery value, then arbitrage would be possible. The only no-arbitrage configuration in general has one bond worth zero to deliver (Bond A in Example 10) and the rest lose money if delivered. To avoid arbitrage, the futures price is

$$\text{Futures price} = \frac{\text{Price of cheapest to deliver}}{\text{Conversion factor for cheapest to deliver}} \tag{16}$$

This discussion glosses over subtleties involving transaction costs (whether you already own a bond may affect your delivery profit calculation) and uncertainty before the delivery period about which bond will be cheapest to deliver. Also the T-note is deliverable at any time during the expiration month, but trading ceases with 7 business days remaining. Consequently, if there are any remaining open contracts during the last week of the month, the short has the option to deliver any bond at a price that might be a week out of date. This provides a delivery option for the short that is also priced into the contract.

The T-bond and T-note futures contracts have been extremely successful. The contracts illustrate some important design considerations for a futures contract. Consider first how the contract is settled. If the contract designated a particular T-bond as the underlying asset, that T-bond could be in short supply, and in fact it might be possible for someone to corner the available supply. (A **market corner** occurs when someone buys most or all of the deliverable asset or commodity.) A short would then be unable to obtain the bond to deliver. In addition, the deliverable T-bond would change from year to year and the contract would become more complicated, since traders would have to price the futures differently to reflect different underlying bonds for different maturity dates.

An alternative scheme could have had the contract cash-settle against a T-bond index, much like the S&P 500. This arrangement, however, introduces basis risk, as the T-bond futures contract might then track the index but fail to track any particular bond.

In the end, settlement procedures for the T-bond and T-note contracts permitted a range of bonds and notes to be delivered. Since a high-coupon bond is worth more than an otherwise identical low-coupon bond, there had to be a conversion factor, in order that the short is paid more for delivering the high-coupon bond.

The idea that there is a cheapest to deliver is not exclusive to Treasury bonds. The same issue arises with commodities, where a futures contract may permit delivery of commodities at different locations or of different qualities.

5. REPURCHASE AGREEMENTS

A repurchase agreement, or **repo**, is the sale of a security, with the seller agreeing to buy the security back at a prespecified price at a later date. The counterparty to a repo enters into a reverse repurchase agreement, or **reverse repo**, which is the purchase of a security, with the buyer agreeing to sell it at the prespecified price at the later date. The repo is a reverse cash-and-carry—a sale coupled with a long forward position. The reverse repo is a cash-and-carry—a purchase coupled with a short forward position.

A repo is at bottom a simple idea. The borrower (the repo) owns a security and would like to temporarily obtain cash. Similarly, the lender (the reverse repo) has cash and would like to lend the cash to earn a return. The security owner is able to borrow cash using the security as collateral for the loan. While the repo is in place, however, the lender owns the bond. The party who repos, however, owns the bond both before and after the repo and therefore bears the long-run risk of owning the security. Although the mechanics of a repo can seem arcane, it is a collateralized loan. We will use the language of loans to talk about repos.

The implicit interest rate in the transaction is the repo rate: the annualized percentage difference between the sale and purchase price. Repos are common in bond markets, but a repurchase agreement can be used for any asset. Most repos are overnight. A longer-term repurchase agreement is called a **term repo**.

Example 11. Suppose you enter into a 1-week repurchase agreement for a 9-month \$1m Treasury bill. The current price of the T-bill is \$956,938, and you agree to repurchase it in 1 week for \$958,042. You have borrowed money at a 1-week rate of $958{,}042/956{,}938 - 1 = 0.115\%$, receiving cash today and promising to repay cash plus interest in a week. The security provides collateral for the loan. ■

An important feature of a repo is that the actual cash amount exchanged for the security can be less than the market value of the security serving as collateral. The amount by which the value of the collateral exceeds the amount of the loan is called a **haircut**. The haircut provides a cushion should the security fall in value and the borrower fail to repay the loan.

The size of the haircut reflects the credit risk of the borrower as well as the risk of the collateral. A 2% haircut would mean that a borrower repoing a security worth $102 would receive a loan of only $100. Collateral with a more variable price and a less liquid market is lower quality from the perspective of the lender and typically would require a greater haircut.

Repurchase agreements played an important role in the financial crisis in 2008. Box 2 discusses this.

Repurchase agreements often use government securities as collateral, and can be negotiated to require a specific security as collateral—called a *special collateral repurchase agreement*—or with any of a variety of government securities as collateral—called a *general collateral repurchase agreement*. General collateral repos have greater flexibility and hence lower transaction costs.

The repo rate on special collateral repos will generally be below that on general collateral repos. (The borrower obtains a more favorable rate because the collateral is more desirable.) With a low enough repo rate, the original bondholder can earn interest on the cash received for the bond that exceeds the repo rate. The borrower thereby profits from the specialness of the bond.

When two parties transact a repo directly with each other, the transaction is known as a bilateral repo. It is also common for the two parties to agree to a repo but then to use a tri-party agent to provide operational assistance, such as the transferring of collateral and cash between the two parties, and valuing collateral. This is called a **tri-party repo**.[19]

Repurchase agreements can be used by dealers as a form of financing. The purchase of a security requires funds. A dealer can buy a bond and then repo it overnight. The money raised with the repo, together with the haircut, provides the cash needed to pay the bond seller. The dealer then has a cost of carrying the bond equal to the repo rate plus the capital cost of the haircut. The counterparty on this transaction is a lender with cash to invest short-term, such as a money-market fund.

The same techniques can be used to finance speculative positions. A hedge fund speculating on the price difference between two Treasury bonds—a transaction known as a "convergence trade"—can finance the transaction with repos. The hedge fund will undertake the following two transactions simultaneously:

The long position. Buy bond A and repo it, using the cash received in the repo to pay for the bond. When it is time to unwind the repo, close the repo position and sell the bond, using the cash raised from the sale to repay the loan (think of the bond sale and close of the repo as happening simultaneously). Note that a low repo rate for this bond works to the arbitrageur's advantage, since it means that the interest rate on the loan is low. The arbitrageur also benefits from a price increase on the bond.

The short position. Borrow bond B by entering into a reverse repurchase agreement. Obtain the bond (collateral for the loan) via the reverse repo, sell it, and use the proceeds to lend to the counterparty. At the termination of the agreement, buy the bond back in the open market and return it, being paid the repo rate. Since we receive interest in this transaction, a high repo rate works to the arbitrageur's advantage as does a price decrease on the bond.

19. For addditional details about the workings of the repo market, with a focus on tri-party repo, see Federal Reserve Bank of New York (2010).

One well-known convergence trade involves newly issued on-the-run 30-year Treasury bonds, which typically sell at a lower yield than the almost identical off-the-run $29\frac{1}{2}$-year Treasury bond.[20] One would expect that the yields of the 30-year and $29\frac{1}{2}$-year bonds would converge as the 30-year bond aged and became off-the-run. As described above, traders making this bet would reverse repo the on-the-run bond (betting that its price will fall) and repo the off-the-run bond (betting that its price will rise). Traders profit from a convergence in price.

The arbitrageur in this situation would like a low repo rate on the purchased bond and a high repo rate on the sold bond, as well as a price increase of the purchased bond relative to the short-sold bond.[21] Even if the price gap between the two bonds closes, the arbitrage can be prohibitively costly if the difference in repo rates on the two bonds is sufficiently great. Finally, the size of the haircut will affect the desirability of the trade. Box 3 describes the use of repos by Long-Term Capital Management, a hedge fund.

CHAPTER SUMMARY

The price of a zero-coupon bond with T years to maturity tells us the value today of \$1 to be received at time T. The set of these bond prices for different maturities is the zero-coupon yield curve and is the basic input for present value calculations. There are equivalent ways to express the same information about interest rates, including the par coupon rate and implied forward rates.

Forward rate agreements (FRAs) permit borrowers and lenders to hedge the interest rate by locking in the implied forward rate. If the interest rate changes, FRAs require a payment reflecting the change in the value of the interest rate as of the loan's maturity day. Eurodollar contracts are an alternative to FRAs as a hedging mechanism. However, Eurodollar contracts make payment on the initiation date for the loan rather than the maturity date, so there is a timing mismatch between the Eurodollar payment and the interest payment date. This gives rise to convexity bias, which causes the rate implied by the Eurodollar contract to be greater than that for an otherwise equivalent FRA. Treasury bill contracts are yet another possible hedging vehicle, but suffer from basis risk since the change in the government's borrowing rate may be different from the change in the borrowing rate for a firm or individual.

PVBP and DV01 measure the dollar change in a bond's price when the yield increases by one basis point.

Modified duration is the percentage change in the bond price for a unit change in the interest rate. Macaulay duration is the percentage change in the bond price for a percentage change in the discount factor. Duration is not a perfect measure of bond price risk. A portfolio

20. An "on-the-run" Treasury bond is the most recently issued and generally the most heavily traded. Other bonds are "off-the-run." Krishnamurthy (2002) studies the behavior of the spread between the on- and off-the-run bonds.

21. Cornell and Shapiro (1989) document one well-known episode of on-the-run/off-the-run arbitrage in which the repo rate on an on-the-run (short-sold) bond went to zero, making the arbitrage position costly. Moreover, the price gap remained when the on-the-run bond became off-the-run.

BOX 2: Repo in the 2008 Financial Crisis

Repurchase agreements are not as familiar as stocks and bonds. During and after the 2008 financial crisis, however, repo transactions made headlines. Three aspects of repo were noteworthy. First, the volume of repo was enormous. Second, most repo agreements are for short time periods, often overnight. This contributed to the fragility of financial institutions that were heavily reliant on repo financing. Third, repo transactions were used to manipulate accounting reports, most notably at Lehman Brothers and Bank of America.

Surprisingly, no one knows exactly how big the repo market is. There is agreement that the outstanding amount of repo in the U.S. and Europe is in the trillions of dollars, with estimates as great as $10 trillion in each locale (Hördahl and King, 2008; Gorton and Metrick, 2010). One difficulty of measuring repo is that a given security may be repoed multiple times. For example, a money-market fund may have cash to lend and a dealer may have a bond to use as collateral. The dealer may repo the bond to another dealer who in turn repos it to the money market fund. The act of repoing a security that is itself serving as collateral is called **rehypothecation**. From an economic perspective, the same bond has been loaned twice for the same ultimate economic purpose; the multiple transactions due to rehypothecation should count as one transaction (the loan of one security for cash) rather than two.

Repurchase agreements are widely used as a way to finance the holding of a long-term asset. A bank could buy a bond (e.g., a mortgage-backed obligation) and finance the bond with a repurchase agreement. If the haircut were 5%, the bank could buy a $105 bond by investing $5 of capital and repoing the bond for $100. When the repo expires, the bank must either renew the repo or find a new repo counterparty. A risk of repo finance is that if the bank gets into trouble, or if the bond's risk increases, the counterparty might refuse to continue lending or might increase the haircut. Gorton and Metrick (2009) argue that increases in haircuts on mortgage-backed instruments caused a "run on repo." If haircuts increase significantly, a bank that is heavily repo-financed will have to sell assets, possibly realizing losses, contributing to (or revealing) price declines for the assets, and causing lenders to flee. Lenders to Bear Stears and Lehman, for example, withdrew repo financing in the days before they failed.

Finally, the bankruptcy of Lehman provided a glimpse into the use of repo to manipulate accounting statements. The Lehman bankruptcy examiner found that Lehman systematically understated its leverage on its accounting reports (Valukas, 2010). At each quarter end, Lehman engaged in a strategy known as "Repo 105," in which it would use repos to sell assets, receive cash, and use the cash to buy down debt. It would reverse the transaction at the beginning of the next quarter, borrowing to buy the assets back. The repos were reported as asset sales rather than repos. It was later disclosed that Citigroup and Bank of America did the same thing, although both banks claimed that they did not intend to create misleading financial statements (see Rapoport, 2010).

is said to be duration-matched if it consists of short and long bond positions with equal value-weighted durations. Convexity is a measure of the change in duration as the bond's yield to maturity changes.

Treasury-note and Treasury-bond futures contracts have Treasury notes and bonds as underlying assets. A complication with these contracts is that a range of bonds are

BOX 3: Long-Term Capital Management

Repurchase agreements achieved particular notoriety during the Long-Term Capital Management (LTCM) crisis in 1998. LTCM was a hedge fund with a luminous roster of partners, including star bond trader John Meriwether, former Federal Reserve Vice Chairman David Mullins, and academics Robert Merton and Myron Scholes, who won the Nobel Prize in Economics while associated with LTCM.

Many of LTCM's strategies involved convergence trades. In his book about LTCM, Lowenstein (2000, p. 45) described one trade like this: "No sooner did Long-Term buy the off-the-run bonds than it loaned them to some other Wall Street firm, which then wired cash to Long-Term as collateral. Then Long-Term turned around and used this cash as collateral on the bonds that *it* borrowed. The collateral it paid equaled the collateral it collected. In other words, Long-Term pulled off the entire \$2 billion trade *without using a dime of its own cash*." (Emphasis in original.)

When LTCM failed in the fall of 1998, it had many such transactions and thus potentially many creditors. The difficulty of unwinding all of these intertwined positions was one of the reasons the Fed brokered a buyout of LTCM by other banks, rather than have LTCM explicitly declare bankruptcy.

deliverable, and there is a cheapest to deliver. The futures price will reflect expectations about which bond is cheapest to deliver.

Repurchase agreements and reverse repurchase agreements are synthetic short-term borrowing and lending, the equivalent of reverse cash-and-carry and cash-and-carry transactions.

FURTHER READING

Basic interest rate concepts are fundamental in finance. While the bond price calculations in this chapter are useful in practice, concepts such as duration have conceptual problems.

Useful references for bond and money market calculations are Stigum (1990) and Stigum and Robinson (1996). Veronesi (2010), Sundaresan (2009) and Tuckman (1995) are fixed-income texts that go into topics in this chapter in more depth. Convexity bias is studied by Burghardt and Hoskins (1995) and Gupta and Subrahmanyam (2000). Grinblatt and Longstaff (2000) discuss the market for STRIPS and study the pricing relationships between Treasury bonds and STRIPS. The repo market is discussed in Fleming and Garbade (2002, 2003, 2004).

PROBLEMS

1. Suppose you observe the following zero-coupon bond prices per \$1 of maturity payment: 0.96154 (1-year), 0.91573 (2-year), 0.87630 (3-year), 0.82270 (4-year), 0.77611 (5-year). For each maturity year compute the zero-coupon bond yields (effective annual and continuously compounded), the par coupon rate, and the 1-year implied forward rate.

2. Using the information in the previous problem, find the price of a 5-year coupon bond that has a par payment of $1,000.00 and annual coupon payments of $60.00.

3. Suppose you observe the following effective annual zero-coupon bond yields: 0.030 (1-year), 0.035 (2-year), 0.040 (3-year), 0.045 (4-year), 0.050 (5-year). For each maturity year compute the zero-coupon bond prices, continuously compounded zero-coupon bond yields, the par coupon rate, and the 1-year implied forward rate.

4. Suppose you observe the following 1-year implied forward rates: 0.050000 (1-year), 0.034061 (2-year), 0.036012 (3-year), 0.024092 (4-year), 0.001470 (5-year). For each maturity year compute the zero-coupon bond prices, effective annual and continuously compounded zero-coupon bond yields, and the par coupon rate.

5. Suppose you observe the following continuously compounded zero-coupon bond yields: 0.06766 (1-year), 0.05827 (2-year), 0.04879 (3-year), 0.04402 (4-year), 0.03922 (5-year). For each maturity year compute the zero-coupon bond prices, effective annual zero-coupon bond yields, the par coupon rate, and the 1-year implied forward rate.

6. Suppose you observe the following par coupon bond yields: 0.03000 (1-year), 0.03491 (2-year), 0.03974 (3-year), 0.04629 (4-year), 0.05174 (5-year). For each maturity year compute the zero-coupon bond prices, effective annual and continuously compounded zero-coupon bond yields, and the 1-year implied forward rate.

7. Using the information in Table 1,

a. Compute the implied forward rate from time 1 to time 3.

b. Compute the implied forward price of a par 2-year coupon bond that will be issued at time 1.

8. Suppose that in order to hedge interest rate risk on your borrowing, you enter into an FRA that will guarantee a 6% effective annual interest rate for 1 year on $500,000.00. On the date you borrow the $500,000.00, the actual interest rate is 5%. Determine the dollar settlement of the FRA assuming

a. Settlement occurs on the date the loan is initiated.

b. Settlement occurs on the date the loan is repaid.

9. Using the same information as the previous problem, suppose the interest rate on the borrowing date is 7.5%. Determine the dollar settlement of the FRA assuming

a. Settlement occurs on the date the loan is initiated.

b. Settlement occurs on the date the loan is repaid.

Use the following zero-coupon bond prices to answer the next three questions:

Days to Maturity	Zero-Coupon Bond Price
90	0.99009
180	0.97943
270	0.96525
360	0.95238

10. What is the rate on a synthetic FRA for a 90-day loan commencing on day 90? A 180-day loan commencing on day 90? A 270-day loan commencing on day 90?

11. What is the rate on a synthetic FRA for a 180-day loan commencing on day 180? Suppose you are the counterparty for a borrower who uses the FRA to hedge the interest rate on a \$10m loan. What positions in zero-coupon bonds would you use to hedge the risk on the FRA?

12. Suppose you are the counterparty for a lender who enters into an FRA to hedge the lending rate on \$10m for a 90-day loan commencing on day 270. What positions in zero-coupon bonds would you use to hedge the risk on the FRA?

13. Using the information in Table 1, suppose you buy a 3-year par coupon bond and hold it for 2 years, after which time you sell it. Assume that interest rates are certain not to change and that you reinvest the coupon received in year 1 at the 1-year rate prevailing at the time you receive the coupon. Verify that the 2-year return on this investment is 6.5%.

14. As in the previous problem, consider holding a 3-year bond for 2 years. Now suppose that interest rates can change, but that at time 0 the rates in Table 1 prevail. What transactions could you undertake using forward rate agreements to guarantee that your 2-year return is 6.5%?

15. Consider the implied forward rate between year 1 and year 2, based on Table 1.

a. Suppose that $r_0(1, 2) = 6.8\%$. Show how buying the 2-year zero-coupon bond and borrowing at the 1-year rate and implied forward rate of 6.8% would earn you an arbitrage profit.

b. Suppose that $r_0(1, 2) = 7.2\%$. Show how borrowing the 2-year zero-coupon bond and lending at the 1-year rate and implied forward rate of 7.2% would earn you an arbitrage profit.

16. Suppose the September Eurodollar futures contract has a price of 96.4. You plan to borrow \$50m for 3 months in September at LIBOR, and you intend to use the Eurodollar contract to hedge your borrowing rate.

a. What rate can you secure?

b. Will you be long or short the Eurodollar contract?

c. How many contracts will you enter into?

d. Assuming the true 3-month LIBOR is 1% in September, what is the settlement in dollars at expiration of the futures contract? (For purposes of this question, ignore daily marking-to-market on the futures contract.)

17. A lender plans to invest \$100m for 150 days, 60 days from today. (That is, if today is day 0, the loan will be initiated on day 60 and will mature on day 210.) The implied forward rate over 150 days, and hence the rate on a 150-day FRA, is 2.5%. The actual interest rate over that period could be either 2.2% or 2.8%.

a. If the interest rate on day 60 is 2.8%, how much will the lender have to pay if the FRA is settled on day 60? How much if it is settled on day 210?

b. If the interest rate on day 60 is 2.2%, how much will the lender have to pay if the FRA is settled on day 60? How much if it is settled on day 210?

18. Consider the same facts as the previous problem, only now consider hedging with the 3-month Eurodollar futures. Suppose the Eurodollar futures contract that matures 60 days from today has a price on day 0 of 94.

a. What issues arise in using the 3-month Eurodollar contract to hedge a 150-day loan?

b. If you wish to hedge a lending position, should you go long or short the contract?

c. What 3-month LIBOR is implied by the Eurodollar futures price? Approximately what lending rate should you be able to lock in?

d. What position in Eurodollar futures would you use to lock in a lending rate? In doing this, what assumptions are you making about the relationship between 90-day LIBOR and the 150-day lending rate?

19. Consider the bonds in Example 8. What hedge ratio would have exactly hedged the portfolio if interest rates had decreased by 25 basis points? Increased by 25 basis points? Repeat assuming a 50-basis-point change.

20. Compute Macaulay and modified durations for the following bonds:

a. A 5-year bond paying annual coupons of 4.432% and selling at par.

b. An 8-year bond paying semiannual coupons with a coupon rate of 8% and a yield of 7%.

c. A 10-year bond paying annual coupons of 6% with a price of $92 and maturity value of $100.

21. Consider the following two bonds which make semiannual coupon payments: a 20-year bond with a 6% coupon and 20% yield, and a 30-year bond with a 6% coupon and a 20% yield.

a. For each bond, compute the price value of a basis point.

b. For each bond, compute Macaulay duration.

c. "For otherwise identical bonds, Macaulay duration is increasing in time to maturity." Is this statement always true? Discuss.

22. An 8-year bond with 6% annual coupons and a 5.004% yield sells for $106.44 with a Macaulay duration of 6.631864. A 9-year bond has 7% annual coupons with a 5.252% yield and sells for $112.29 with a Macaulay duration of 7.098302. You wish to duration-hedge the 8-year bond using a 9-year bond. How many 9-year bonds must we short for every 8-year bond?

23. A 6-year bond with a 4% coupon sells for $102.46 with a 3.5384% yield. The conversion factor for the bond is 0.90046. An 8-year bond with 5.5% coupons sells for $113.564 with a conversion factor of 0.9686. (All coupon payments are semiannual.) Which bond is cheaper to deliver given a T-note futures price of 113.81?

24. **a.** Compute the convexity of a 3-year bond paying annual coupons of 4.5% and selling at par.

b. Compute the convexity of a 3-year 4.5% coupon bond that makes semiannual coupon payments and that currently sells at par.

c. Is the convexity different in the two cases? Why?

25. Suppose a 10-year zero-coupon bond with a face value of \$100 trades at \$69.20205.

a. What is the yield to maturity and modified duration of the zero-coupon bond?

b. Calculate the approximate bond price change for a 50-basis-point increase in the yield, based on the modified duration you calculated in part (a). Also calculate the exact new bond price based on the new yield to maturity.

c. Calculate the convexity of the 10-year zero-coupon bond.

d. Now use the formula (equation (15)) that takes into account both duration and convexity to approximate the new bond price. Compare your result to that in part (b).

Appendix A INTEREST RATE AND BOND PRICE CONVENTIONS

This appendix will focus on conventions for computing yields to maturity for different kinds of bonds, and the conventions for quoting bond prices. When discussing yields to maturity, it is necessary to distinguish on the one hand between notes and bonds, which make coupon payments and are issued with more than 1 year to maturity, and on the other hand bills, which have no coupons and are issued with 1 year or less to maturity. The quotation conventions are different for notes and bonds than for bills. For a full treatment of bond pricing and quoting conventions, see Stigum and Robinson (1996).

Bonds

We first consider notes and bonds, which we will refer to as just "bonds." Bond coupons and yields are annualized. If a bond is described as paying a 6% semiannual coupon, this means that the bond pays $6\%/2 = 3\%$ every 6 months. Further, if the bond yield is 7%, this means that the bond's 6-month yield to maturity is $7\%/2 = 3.5\%$. Bond coupons and yields are annualized by multiplying by 2 rather than by compounding.

Suppose a bond makes semiannual coupon payments of $C/2$, and has a semiannual yield of $y/2$. The quoted coupon and yield are C and y.[22] Let d be the actual number of days until the next coupon, and d' the number of days between the previous and next coupon. We take into account a fractional period until the next coupon by discounting the cash flows for that fractional period. The price of the bond is

22. If a bond makes coupon payments m times a year, the convention is to quote the coupon rate as m times the per-period payment. The yield to maturity is computed per payment period and multiplied by m to obtain the annual quoted yield.

$$B(y) = \sum_{i=1}^{n} \frac{C/2}{(1+y/2)^{i-1+d/d'}} + \frac{M}{(1+y/2)^{n-1+d/d'}}$$

This can be rewritten as

$$B(y) = \left(\frac{1}{1+y/2}\right)^{d/d'} \left(C/2 + \frac{C/2}{y/2}\left[1 - \frac{1}{(1+y/2)^{n-1}}\right] + \frac{M}{(1+y/2)^{n-1}}\right) \tag{17}$$

In the special case when the bond has just paid a coupon, then $d = d'$, and equation (17) becomes

$$B(y) = \sum_{i=1}^{n} \frac{C/2}{(1+y/2)^{i}} + \frac{M}{(1+y/2)^{n}} \tag{18}$$

This formula assumes there is one full period until the next coupon.

Example 12. Consider a 7% \$100 maturity coupon bond that makes semiannual coupon payments on February 15 and August 15 and matures on August 15, 2012. Suppose it is August 15, 2004, and the August coupon has been paid. There are 16 remaining payments. If the semiannual yield, y, is 3.2%, then using equation (18), the price of the bond is

$$\frac{\$3.5}{0.032}\left[1 - \frac{1}{(1+0.032)^{16}}\right] + \frac{\$100}{(1+0.032)^{16}} = \$103.71$$ ■

Example 13. Consider the same bond as in Example 12. Suppose that on November 11, 2004, the semiannual yield is still 3.2%. There are 96 days until the February coupon payment and 184 days between the August and February payments. Using equation (17), the price for the bond at a 6.4% yield (3.2% semiannual) is

$$\left(\frac{1}{1.032}\right)^{96/184}\left(\$3.5 + \frac{\$3.5}{0.032}\left[1 - \frac{1}{(1.032)^{15}}\right] + \frac{\$100}{(1.032)^{15}}\right) = \$105.286$$ ■

The bond-pricing formulas in Examples 12 and 13 illustrate that even with a constant yield to maturity, the bond price will vary with the time until the next coupon payment. This occurs because equation (17) computes a bond price that fully reflects the coming coupon payment. Using this formula, the bond price rises over time as a coupon payment approaches, then falls on the coupon payment date, and so forth. The bond price quoted in this fashion is called the **dirty price**.

Intuitively, if you buy a bond three-fourths of the way from one coupon payment to the next, the price you pay should reflect three-fourths of the coming coupon payment. This prorated amount is **accrued interest**, which is included in the price in equation (17). Accrued interest is calculated as the prorated portion of the coupon since the last coupon date. With $d' - d$ days since the last coupon, accrued interest is $C \times (d' - d)/d'$.

In practice, bond prices are quoted net of accrued interest. The dirty price less accrued interest is the **clean price**, which does not exhibit the predictable rise and fall in price due to the coming coupon payment.[23]

23. Because accrued interest is amortized linearly rather than geometrically, this statement is not precisely true; see Smith (2002).

TABLE 6 Treasury bill quotations.

Maturity	Days to Maturity	Ask Discount	Ask Yield
February 13	43	3.65	3.72
December 18	351	3.87	4.04

Example 14. Consider the bond in Example 13. Accrued interest as of November 11 would be $3.5 \times (184 - 96)/184 = 1.674$. Thus, the clean price for the bond would be

$$\begin{aligned}\text{Clean price} &= \text{Dirty price} - \text{accrued interest}\\ &= \$105.286 - \$1.674 = \$103.612\end{aligned}$$ ■

Bills

Table 6 presents typical Treasury-bill quotations. Suppose today is January 1. A bond maturing February 13 has 43 days to maturity and one maturing December 18 has 351 days to maturity (assuming it is not a leap year).

The "ask yields" in this table are "bond-equivalent yields" (Stigum and Robinson, 1996), intended to make Treasury-bill yields comparable to Treasury-bond yields. To obtain the yields, we first find the market prices of the T-bills. A T-bill price is quoted on an annualized discount basis. The discount is the number subtracted from 100 to obtain the invoice price for the T-bill, P. The formula, normalizing the face value of the T-bill to be 100, is

$$P = 100 - \frac{\text{discount} \times \text{days}}{360}$$

The T-bills in Table 6 have invoice prices of

$$100 - 3.65 \times 43/360 = 99.5640$$
$$100 - 3.87 \times 351/360 = 96.2268$$

Thus, an investor pays 0.995640 per dollar of maturity value for the 43-day bill and 0.962268 for the 351-day bill. Note that these prices give us "true" 43-day and 351-day discount factors. Given the prices, what are the yields?

A 43-day bill yields $\frac{100}{99.5640} = 1.004379$ or 0.4379% over 43 days, while the 351-day bill yields 3.9212% over 351 days. The bond-equivalent yield calculations annualize these yields in a way that makes them more comparable to bond yields. This necessarily involves making arbitrary assumptions.

For bills less than 182 days from maturity, a bill is directly comparable to a maturing bond since neither makes a coupon payment over that period. In this case we need only to adjust for the fact that bonds are quoted using the actual number of days (i.e., a 365-day basis) and bills are quoted on a 360-day basis:

$$r_{be} = \frac{365 \times \text{discount}/100}{360 - \text{discount}/100 \times \text{days}}$$

where r_{be} stands for "bond-equivalent yield." Applying this formula to the 43-day T-bill, we see that

$$\frac{365 \times 0.0365}{360 - 0.0365 \times 43} = 0.0372$$

If you use this formula for the 351-day bill, however, you obtain a yield of 4.078 rather than the 4.04 listed in Table 6. The bond-equivalent yield calculation for this bill takes into account that a bond with more than 182 days to maturity would make a coupon payment. Hence, to make the bill yield comparable to that for a bond, we need to account for the imaginary coupon. The formula from Stigum and Robinson (1996) is

$$r_{be} = \frac{-\frac{2\times \text{days}}{365} + 2\sqrt{\left(\frac{\text{days}}{365}\right)^2 - \left(\frac{2\times \text{days}}{365} - 1\right)\left(1 - \frac{100}{P}\right)}}{\frac{2\times \text{days}}{365} - 1} \tag{19}$$

Applying this to the 351-day bond gives

$$\frac{-\frac{2\times 351}{365} + 2\sqrt{\left(\frac{351}{365}\right)^2 - \left(\frac{2\times 351}{365} - 1\right)\left(1 - \frac{1}{0.962268}\right)}}{\frac{2\times 351}{365} - 1} = 0.040384$$

This matches the quoted yield in Table 6. In Excel, the function TBILLEQ provides the bond-equivalent yield for a T-bill.

Swaps

A forward contract fixes a price for a transaction that will occur on a specific date in the future. However, many transactions occur repeatedly. Firms that issue bonds make periodic coupon payments. Multinational firms frequently exchange currencies. Firms that buy commodities as production inputs or that sell them make payments or receive income linked to commodity prices on an ongoing basis.

These situations raise the question: If a manager seeking to reduce risk confronts a risky payment *stream*—as opposed to a single risky payment—what is the easiest way to hedge this risk? One obvious answer is that we can enter into a separate forward contract for each payment we wish to hedge. However, it might be more convenient, and entail lower transaction costs, if we could hedge a stream of payments with a single transaction.

A **swap** is a contract calling for an exchange of payments over time. One party makes a payment to the other depending upon whether a reference price turns out to be greater or less than a fixed price that is specified in the swap contract. A swap thus provides a means to hedge a stream of risky payments. By entering into an oil swap, for example, an oil buyer confronting a stream of uncertain oil payments can lock in a fixed price for oil over a period of time. The swap payments would be based on the difference between a fixed price for oil and a market price that varies over time.

From this description, you can see that there is a relationship between swaps and forward contracts. In fact, a forward contract is a single-payment swap. It is possible to price a multi-date swap—determine the fixed price for oil in the above example—by using information from the set of forward prices with different maturities (i.e., the strip). We will see that swaps are nothing more than forward contracts coupled with borrowing and lending money.

1. AN EXAMPLE OF A COMMODITY SWAP

We begin our study of swaps by presenting an example of a simple commodity swap. Our purpose here is to understand how a swap is related to forwards, why someone might use a swap, and how market-makers hedge the risk of swaps. In later sections we present swap-price formulas and examine interest rate swaps, total return swaps, and more complicated commodity swap examples.

An industrial producer, IP Inc., is going to buy 100,000 barrels of oil 1 year from today and 2 years from today. Suppose that the forward price for delivery in 1 year is \$110/barrel

From Chapter 8 of *Derivatives Markets*, Third Edition, Robert McDonald. Copyright © 2013 by Pearson Education, Inc. Published by Pearson Prentice Hall. All rights reserved.

and in 2 years is \$111/barrel. Suppose that the 1- and 2-year annual zero-coupon bond yields are 6% and 6.5%.

IP can use forward contracts to guarantee the cost of buying oil for the next 2 years. Specifically, IP could enter into long forward contracts for 100,000 barrels in each of the next 2 years, committing to pay \$110/barrel in 1 year and \$111/barrel in 2 years. The present value of this cost is

$$\frac{\$110}{1.06} + \frac{\$111}{1.065^2} = \$201.638$$

IP could invest this amount today and ensure that it had the funds to buy oil in 1 and 2 years. Alternatively, IP could pay an oil supplier \$201.638, and the supplier would commit to delivering one barrel in each of the next 2 years. A single payment today for a single delivery of oil in the future is a prepaid forward. A single payment today to obtain *multiple* deliveries in the future is a **prepaid swap**.

Although it is possible to enter into a prepaid swap, buyers might worry about the resulting credit risk: They have fully paid for oil that will not be delivered for up to 2 years. (The prepaid forward has the same problem.) For the same reason, the swap counterparty would worry about a postpaid swap, where the oil is delivered and full payment is made after 2 years. A more attractive solution for both parties is to defer payment until the oil is delivered, while still fixing the total price.

Note that there are many feasible ways to have the buyer pay. Typically, however, a swap will call for equal payments in each year. The payment per year per barrel, x, will then have to be such that

$$\frac{x}{1.06} + \frac{x}{1.065^2} = \$201.638$$

To satisfy this equation, the payments must be \$110.483 in each year. We then say that the 2-year swap price is \$110.483. *However, any payments that have a present value of \$201.638 are acceptable.*

Physical Versus Financial Settlement

Thus far we have described the swap as if the swap counterparty supplied physical oil to the buyer. Figure 1 shows a swap that calls for physical settlement. In this case \$110.483 is the per-barrel cost of oil.

FIGURE 1

Illustration of a swap where the oil buyer pays \$110.483/year and receives one barrel of oil each year.

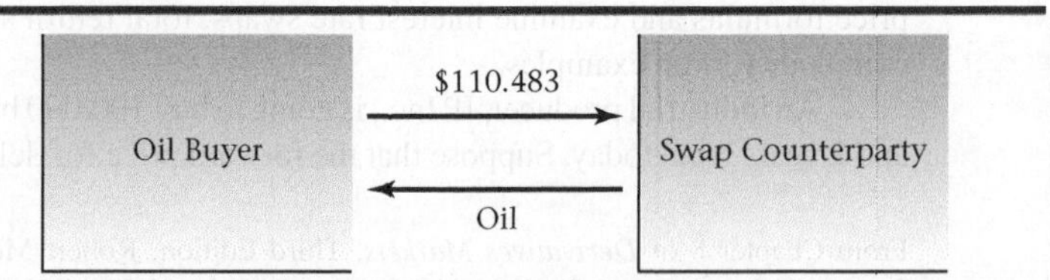

However, we could also arrange for *financial settlement* of the swap. With financial settlement, the oil buyer, IP, pays the swap counterparty the difference between \$110.483 and the spot price (if the difference is negative, the counterparty pays the buyer), and the oil buyer then buys oil at the spot price. For example, if the market price is \$115, the swap counterparty pays IP

$$\text{Spot price} - \text{swap price} = \$115 - \$110.483 = \$4.517$$

If the market price is \$108, the spot price less the swap price is

$$\text{Spot price} - \text{swap price} = \$108 - \$110.483 = -\$2.483$$

In this case, the oil buyer, IP, makes a payment to the swap counterparty. Whatever the market price of oil, the net cost to the buyer is the swap price, \$110.483:

$$\underbrace{\text{Spot price} - \text{swap price}}_{\text{Swap payment}} - \underbrace{\text{spot price}}_{\text{Spot purchase of oil}} = -\text{Swap price}$$

Figure 2 depicts cash flows and transactions when the swap is settled financially. *The results for the buyer are the same whether the swap is settled physically or financially*. In both cases, the net cost to the oil buyer is \$110.483.

We have discussed the swap on a per-barrel basis. For a swap on 100,000 barrels, we simply multiply all cash flows by 100,000. In this example, 100,000 is the **notional amount** of the swap, meaning that 100,000 barrels is used to determine the magnitude of the payments when the swap is settled financially.

To illustrate how a commodity swap would be specified in practice, Figure 3 is an abbreviated example of a **term sheet** for an oil swap. Term sheets are commonly used by broker-dealers to succinctly convey the important terms of a financial transaction. The specific example is hypothetical, but the language is from a real term sheet. This particular example is a 3-month oil swap with settlement each month based on the difference between a fixed price and the average over the month of the NYMEX near-month futures price. As you would expect, the complete documentation for such a deal is lengthy. Transaction confirmations typically make reference to standard documentation supplied by the International Swaps and Derivatives Association (ISDA). The use of standard documentation makes swaps less costly to trade and prices more comparable across dealers.

FIGURE 2

Cash flows from a transaction where the oil buyer enters into a financially settled 2-year swap. Each year the buyer pays the spot price for oil and receives spot price − \$110.483. The buyer's net cost of oil is \$110.483/barrel.

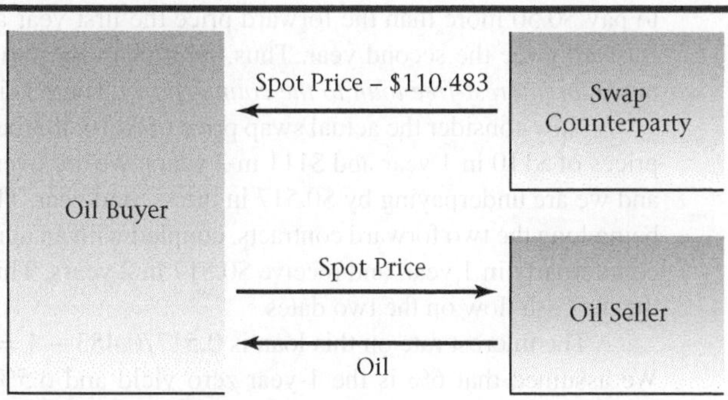

FIGURE 3

Illustrative example of the terms for an oil swap based on West Texas Intermediate (WTI) crude oil.

Fixed-Price Payer:	Broker-dealer
Floating-Price Payer:	Counterparty
Notional Amount:	100,000 barrels
Trade Date:	April 18, 2011
Effective Date:	July 1, 2011
Termination Date:	September 31, 2011
Period End Date:	Final Pricing Date of each Calculation Period as defined in the description of the Floating Price.
Fixed Price:	110.89 USD per barrel
Commodity Reference Price:	OIL-WTI-NYMEX
Floating Price:	The average of the first nearby NYMEX WTI Crude Oil Futures settlement prices for each successive day of the Calculation Period during which such prices are quoted
Calculation Period:	Each calendar month during the transaction
Method of Averaging:	Unweighted
Settlement and Payment:	If the Fixed Amount exceeds the Floating Amount for such Calculation Period, the Fixed Price Payer shall pay the Floating Price Payer an amount equal to such excess. If the Floating Amount exceeds the Fixed Amount for such Calculation Period, the Floating Price Payer shall pay the Fixed Price Payer an amount equal to such excess.
Payment Date:	5 business days following each Period End Date

Why Is the Swap Price Not \$110.50?

The swap price, \$110.483, is close to the average of the two oil forward prices, \$110.50. However, it is not exactly the same. Why?

Suppose that the swap price were \$110.50. The oil buyer would then be committing to pay \$0.50 more than the forward price the first year and would pay \$0.50 less than the forward price the second year. Thus, *relative to the forward curve, the buyer would have made an interest-free loan to the counterparty.* There is implicit lending in the swap.

Now consider the actual swap price of \$110.483/barrel. Relative to the forward curve prices of \$110 in 1 year and \$111 in 2 years, we are overpaying by \$0.483 in the first year and we are underpaying by \$0.517 in the second year. Therefore, the swap is equivalent to being long the two forward contracts, coupled with an agreement to lend \$0.483 to the swap counterparty in 1 year, and receive \$0.517 in 2 years. This loan has the effect of equalizing the net cash flow on the two dates.

The interest rate on this loan is $0.517/0.483 - 1 = 7\%$. Where does 7% come from? We assumed that 6% is the 1-year zero yield and 6.5% is the 2-year yield. Given these interest rates, 7% is the 1-year implied forward yield from year 1 to year 2. By entering into

FIGURE 4

Cash flows from a transaction where an oil buyer and seller each enters into a financially settled 2-year swap. The buyer pays the spot price for oil and receives the spot price – $110.483 each year as a swap payment. The oil seller receives the spot price for oil and receives $110.483 – spot price as a swap payment.

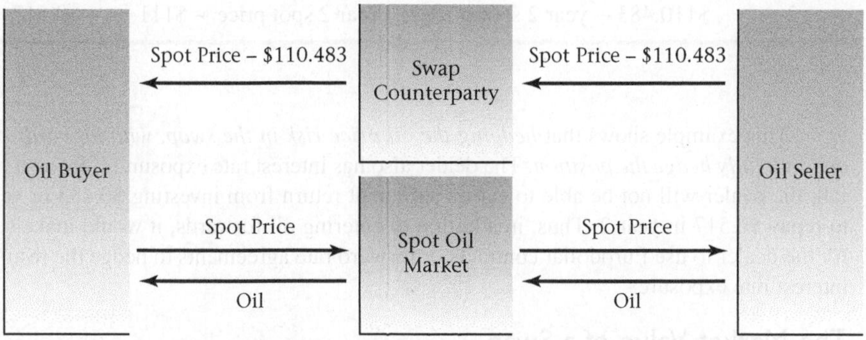

the swap, we are lending the counterparty money for 1 year beginning in 1 year. If the deal is priced fairly, the interest rate on this loan should be the implied forward interest rate.

The Swap Counterparty

The swap counterparty is a dealer who hedges the oil price risk resulting from the swap. The dealer can hedge in several ways. First, imagine that an oil seller would like to lock in a fixed selling price of oil. In this case, the dealer locates the oil buyer and seller and serves as a go-between for the swap, receiving payments from one party and passing them on to the other. In practice the fixed price paid by the buyer exceeds the fixed price received by the seller. This price difference is a bid-ask spread and is the dealer's fee.

Figure 4 illustrates how this transaction would work with financial settlement. The oil seller receives the spot price for oil and receives the swap price less the spot price, on net receiving the swap price. The oil buyer pays the spot price and receives the spot price less the swap price. The situation where the dealer matches the buyer and seller is called a **back-to-back transaction** or "matched book" transaction. The dealer bears the credit risk of both parties but is not exposed to price risk.

A more interesting situation occurs when the dealer serves as counterparty and hedges the transaction using forward markets. Let's see how this would work.

After entering the swap with the oil buyer, the dealer has the obligation to pay the spot price and receive the swap price. If the spot price rises, the dealer can lose money. The dealer has a short position in 1- and 2-year oil.

The natural hedge for the dealer is to enter into long forward or futures contracts to offset this short exposure. Table 1 illustrates how this strategy works. As we discussed earlier, there is an implicit loan in the swap and this is apparent in Table 1. The net cash flow for the hedged dealer is a loan, where the dealer receives cash in year 1 and repays it in year 2.

TABLE 1 Positions and cash flows for a dealer who has an obligation to receive the fixed price in an oil swap and who hedges the exposure by going long year 1 and year 2 oil forwards.

Year	Payment from Oil Buyer	Long Forward	Net
1	\$110.483 – year 1 spot price	Year 1 spot price – \$110	\$0.483
2	\$110.483 – year 2 spot price	Year 2 spot price – \$111	–\$0.517

This example shows that *hedging the oil price risk in the swap, with forwards only, does not fully hedge the position*. The dealer also has interest rate exposure. If interest rates fall, the dealer will not be able to earn a sufficient return from investing \$0.483 in year 1 to repay \$0.517 in year 2. Thus, in addition to entering oil forwards, it would make sense for the dealer to use Eurodollar contracts or forward rate agreements to hedge the resulting interest rate exposure.

The Market Value of a Swap

When the buyer first enters the swap, its market value is zero, meaning that either party could enter or exit the swap without having to pay anything to the other party (apart from commissions and bid-ask spreads). From the oil buyer's perspective, the swap consists of two forward contracts plus an agreement to lend money at the implied forward rate of 7%. The forward contracts and forward rate agreement have zero value, so the swap does as well.

Once the swap is struck, however, its market value will generally no longer be zero, for two reasons. First, the forward prices for oil and interest rates will change over time. New swaps would no longer have a fixed price of \$110.483; hence, one party will owe money to the other should one party wish to exit or *unwind* the swap.

Second, even if oil and interest rate forward prices do not change, the value of the swap will remain zero only *until the first swap payment is made*. Once the first swap payment is made, the buyer has overpaid by \$0.483 relative to the forward curve, and hence, in order to exit the swap, the counterparty would have to pay the oil buyer \$0.483. Thus, even if prices do not change, the market value of swaps can change over time due to the implicit borrowing and lending.

A buyer wishing to exit the swap could negotiate terms with the original counterparty to eliminate the swap obligation. An alternative is to leave the original swap in place and enter into an offsetting swap with the counterparty offering the best price. The original swap called for the oil buyer to pay the fixed price and receive the floating price; the offsetting swap has the buyer receive the fixed price and pay floating. The original obligation would be cancelled except to the extent that the fixed prices are different. However, the difference is known, so oil price risk is eliminated. (There is still credit risk when the original swap counterparty and the counterparty to the offsetting swap are different. This could be a reason for the buyer to prefer offsetting the swap with the original counterparty.)

To see how a swap can change in value, suppose that immediately after the buyer enters the swap, the forward curve for oil rises by \$2 in years 1 and 2. Thus, the year-1 forward price becomes \$112 and the year-2 forward price becomes \$113. The original swap will no longer have a zero market value.

BOX 1: Enron's Hidden Debt

When energy giant Enron collapsed in the fall of 2001, there were charges that other companies had helped Enron mislead investors. In July 2003, the Securities and Exchange Commission announced that J. P. Morgan Chase and Citigroup had each agreed to pay more than $100 million to settle allegations that they had helped Enron commit fraud. Specifically, the SEC alleged that both banks had helped Enron characterize loan proceeds as operating income.

The basic outline of the transaction with J. P. Morgan Chase is as follows. Enron entered into "prepaid forward sales contracts" (essentially a prepaid swap) with an entity called Mahonia; Enron received a lump-sum payment and agreed to deliver natural gas in the future. Mahonia in turn received a lump-sum payment from Chase and agreed to deliver natural gas in the future. Chase, which controlled Mahonia, then hedged its Mahonia transaction with Enron. With all transactions netted out, Enron had no commodity exposure, and received its lump-sum initial payment from Mahonia in exchange for making future fixed installment payments to Chase. In other words, Enron in effect had a loan with Chase. Not only did Enron not record debt from these transactions, but the company reported operating income. The transaction is illustrated in Figure 5.

The SEC complaint included a revealing excerpt from internal Chase e-mail:

> WE ARE MAKING DISGUISED LOANS, USUALLY BURIED IN COMMODITIES OR EQUITIES DERIVATIVES (AND I'M SURE IN OTHER AREAS). WITH AFEW [sic] EXCEPTIONS, THEY ARE UNDERSTOOD TO BE DISGUISED LOANS AND APPROVED AS SUCH. (Capitalization in the original.)

Assuming interest rates are unchanged, the new swap price is $112.483. (You should verify this.) The buyer could unwind the swap at this point by agreeing to sell oil at $112.483, while the original swap still calls for buying oil at $110.483. Thus, the net swap payments in each year are

$$\underbrace{(\text{Spot price} - \$110.483)}_{\text{Original swap}} + \underbrace{(\$112.483 - \text{spot price})}_{\text{New swap}} = \$2$$

The present value of this difference is

$$\frac{\$2}{1.06} + \frac{\$2}{(1.065)^2} = \$3.650$$

The buyer can receive a stream of payments worth $3.65 by offsetting the original swap with a new swap. Thus, $3.65 is the market value of the swap.

If interest rates had changed, we would have used the new interest rates in computing the new swap price.

As a practical matter, swaps and other derivatives can cause problems for regulators, accountants, and investors, all of whom would like an accurate depiction of activities within a firm. Box 1 shows an extreme example of a hedged transaction—allegedly used to hide debt and manipulate earnings—involving Enron and J. P. Morgan Chase. Figure 5, which was taken from an SEC account of the transaction, illustrates the transactions and flows.

The examples we have analyzed in this section illustrate the fundamental characteristics of swaps and their cash flows. In the rest of the chapter, we will examine swaps based

FIGURE 5

Enron's swaps with Mahonia and Chase.

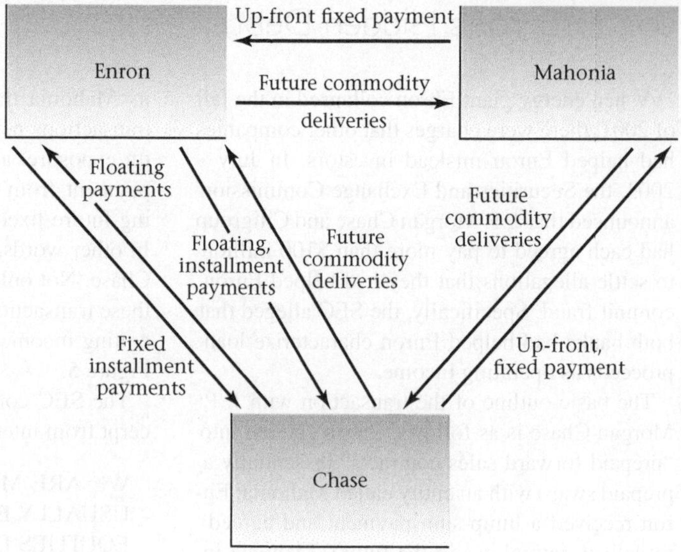

Source: Securities and Exchange Commission.

on interest rates, currencies, and commodities and see some of the ways in which we can modify the terms of a swap.

2. COMPUTING THE SWAP RATE IN GENERAL

We now present a general formula for computing the swap rate. As we saw in the previous section, the swap rate calculation equates the value of a prepaid swap with the present value of the fixed swap payments. This principle for computing the swap rate is the same for any underlying asset.

Fixed Quantity Swaps

We first consider swaps with a notional amount that is fixed over time.[1] Suppose there are n swap settlements, occurring on dates t_i, $i = 1, \ldots, n$. The forward prices on these dates are given by F_{0,t_i}. We will account for interest rates by using bond price notation. The price of a zero-coupon bond maturing on date t_i is $P(0, t_i)$. This price is the factor for discounting a fixed payment from date t_i to date 0.

If the buyer at time zero were to enter into forward contracts to purchase one unit on each of the n dates, the present value of payments would be the present value of the forward

1. A swap with payments based on 100,000 barrels of oil, as discussed before and shown in Figure 3, would be such a swap.

prices, which equals the price of the prepaid swap:

$$\text{Prepaid swap} = \sum_{i=1}^{n} F_{0,t_i} P(0, t_i) \tag{1}$$

We determine the fixed swap price, R, by requiring that the present value of the swap payments equal the value of the prepaid swap. Thus, we have

$$\sum_{i=1}^{n} RP(0, t_i) = \sum_{i=1}^{n} F_{0,t_i} P(0, t_i) \tag{2}$$

Solving for R gives

$$\boxed{R = \frac{\sum_{i=1}^{n} P(0, t_i) F_{0,t_i}}{\sum_{i=1}^{n} P(0, t_i)}} \tag{3}$$

The expression $\sum_{i=1}^{n} P(0, t_i) F_{0,t_i}$ is the present value of payments implied by the strip of forward prices. The expression $\sum_{i=1}^{n} P(0, t_i)$ is the present value of a \$1 annuity. Thus, the swap rate annuitizes the interest payments on the floating-rate bond.

A different way to motivate the swap price calculation is to note that the present value of the differences between the swap price and the forward prices must equal zero:

$$\sum_{i=1}^{n} P(0, t_i)[R - F_{0,t_i}] = 0 \tag{4}$$

This also gives rise to equation (3).

We can rewrite equation (3) to make it easier to interpret:

$$R = \sum_{i=1}^{n} \left[\frac{P(0, t_i)}{\sum_{j=1}^{n} P(0, t_j)} \right] F_{0,t_i}$$

The terms in square brackets sum to 1. This form of equation (3) emphasizes that the fixed swap rate is a weighted average of the forward prices, where zero-coupon bond prices are used to determine the weights.

Figure 6 displays a swap curve for natural gas, constructed using equation 3. The natural gas price exhibits seasonality. The swap price is a weighted average of natural gas forward prices over the life of the swap, and thus exhibits less variation. In Figure 6, the average natural gas futures price climbs so the swap curve climbs as well.

You will observe from Figure 6 that it is easier to describe the general level of the natural gas price at different horizons by referring to the swap price rather than the individual prices. The swap price is about \$5.50 at a horizon of 3 years and \$6 at a horizon of 7 years.

Swaps with Variable Quantity and Price

A commodity buyer might prefer a swap in which quantities vary over time. For example, a natural gas buyer could enter into a swap supplying a greater quantity of gas during the heating season. A buyer might also wish to fix different prices in different seasons. For example, there could be seasonal variation in the price of the output produced using natural

FIGURE 6

Natural gas swap curve, June 2, 2010. The swap curve displays the fixed price for a natural gas swap beginning June 2010 and continuing, with monthly settlement, for the number of months specified on the x-axis.

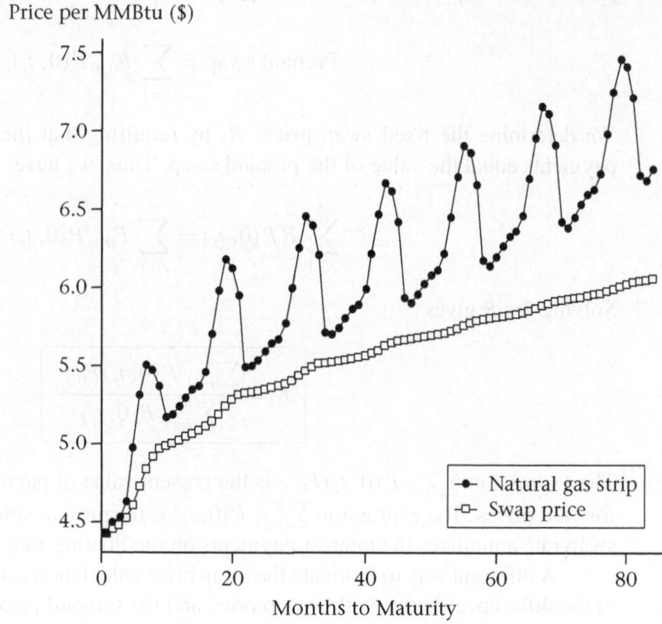

gas as an input. How do we determine the swap price with seasonally varying quantities and prices?

Let Q_{t_i} denote the quantity of the commodity to be purchased at time t_i. If a buyer pays in advance, the prepaid swap price is

$$\text{Prepaid swap} = \sum_{i=1}^{n} Q_{t_i} F_{0,t_i} P(0, t_i) \tag{5}$$

Consider a swap in which the buyer pays RQ_{t_i} for Q_{t_i} units of the commodity. The present value of these fixed payments (fixed per unit of the commodity) must equal the prepaid swap price, so that

$$\sum_{i=1}^{n} Q_{t_i} F_{0,t_i} P(0, t_i) = \sum_{i=1}^{n} Q_{t_i} R P(0, t_i)$$

Solving this equation for R gives

$$R = \frac{\sum_{i=1}^{n} Q_{t_i} P(0, t_i) F_{0,t_i}}{\sum_{i=1}^{n} Q_{t_i} P(0, t_i)} \tag{6}$$

The equation shows that if we are going to buy more gas when the forward price is high, we have to weight more heavily the forward price in those months. When $Q_t = 1$, the formula is the same as equation (3).

Once again, another way to derive this equation is to require that the present value of the quantity-weighted difference between the swap price and the forward prices is zero:

$$\sum_{i=1}^{n} P(0, t_i)Q_{t_i}\left(R - F_{0,t_i}\right) = 0$$

We can also permit prices to be time-varying. If, for example, we let the summer swap price be denoted by R_s and the winter price by R_w, then the summer and winter swap prices can be any prices for which the value of the prepaid swap equals the present value of the fixed swap payments:

$$R_s \sum_{i \in \text{summer}}^{n} P(0, t_i)Q_{t_i} + R_w \sum_{i \in \text{winter}}^{n} P(0, t_i)Q_{t_i} = \sum_{i=1}^{n} P(0, t_i)Q_{t_i}F_{0,t_i}$$

The notations $i \in$ summer and $i \in$ winter mean to sum over only the months in those seasons. This gives us one equation and two unknowns, R_s and R_w. Once we fix one of the two prices, the equation will give us the other.

3. INTEREST RATE SWAPS

Companies use interest rate swaps to modify their interest rate exposure. In this section we will begin with a simple example of an interest rate swap, similar to the preceding oil swap example. We will then present general pricing formulas and discuss ways in which the basic swap structure can be altered.

A Simple Interest Rate Swap

Suppose that XYZ Corp. has \$200m of floating-rate debt at LIBOR—meaning that every year XYZ pays that year's current LIBOR—but would prefer to have fixed-rate debt with 3 years to maturity. There are several ways XYZ could effect this change.

First, XYZ could change their interest rate exposure by retiring the floating-rate debt and issuing fixed-rate debt in its place. However, an actual purchase and sale of debt has transaction costs.

Second, they could enter into a strip of forward rate agreements (FRAs) in order to guarantee the borrowing rate for the remaining life of the debt. Since the FRA for each year will typically carry a different interest rate, the company will lock in a different rate each year and, hence, the company's borrowing cost will vary over time, even though it will be fixed in advance.

A third alternative is to obtain interest rate exposure equivalent to that of fixed rate debt by entering into a swap. XYZ is already paying a floating interest rate. They therefore want to enter a swap in which they receive a floating rate and pay the fixed rate, which we will suppose is 6.9548%. This swap is illustrated in Figure 7. Notice the similarity to the oil swap.

In a year when the fixed 6.9548% swap rate exceeds 1-year LIBOR, XYZ pays 6.9548% − LIBOR to the swap counterparty. Conversely, when the 6.9548% swap rate is less than LIBOR, the swap counterparty pays LIBOR − 6.9548% to XYZ. On net, XYZ pays 6.9548%. Algebraically, the net interest payment made by XYZ is

$$\text{XYZ net payment} = \underbrace{-\text{LIBOR}}_{\text{Floating payment}} + \underbrace{\text{LIBOR} - 6.9548\%}_{\text{Swap payment}} = -6.9548\%$$

FIGURE 7

Illustration of cash flows for a company that borrows at LIBOR and swaps to fixed-rate exposure at 6.9548%.

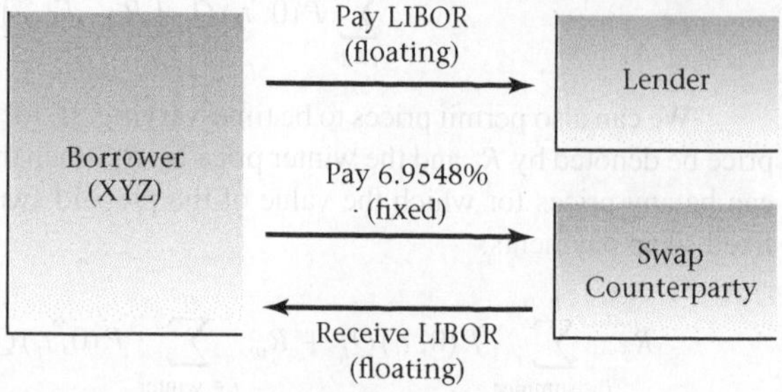

The notional principal of the swap is \$200m: It is the amount on which the interest payments—and, hence, the net swap payment—is based. The life of the swap is the **swap term** or **swap tenor**.

There are timing conventions with a swap similar to those for a forward rate agreement. At the beginning of a year, the borrowing rate for that year is known. However, the interest payment on the loan is due at the end of the year. The interest rate determination date for the floating interest payment would therefore occur at the beginning of the period. As with an FRA we can think of the swap payment being made at the end of the period (when interest is due).

With the financially settled interest rate swap, only net swap payments—in this case the difference between LIBOR and 6.9548%—are actually made between XYZ and the counterparty. If one party defaults, they owe to the other party at most the present value of net swap payments they are obligated to make at current market prices. This means that a swap generally has less credit risk than a bond: Whereas principal is at risk with a bond, only net swap payments are at risk in a swap.

The swap in this example is a construct, making payments *as if* there were an exchange of payments between a fixed-rate and floating-rate bond. In practice, a fund manager might own fixed-rate bonds and wish to have floating-rate exposure while continuing to own the bonds. A swap in which a fund manager receives a floating rate in exchange for the payments on bonds the fund continues to hold is called an **asset swap**.

Pricing and the Swap Counterparty

To understand the pricing of the swap, we will examine it from the perspective of both the counterparty and the firm. We first consider the perspective of the counterparty, who we assume is a market-maker.

The market-maker is a counterparty to the swap in order to earn fees, not to take on interest rate risk. Therefore, the market-maker will hedge the transaction. The market-maker receives the fixed rate from the company and pays the floating rate; the danger for the market-maker is that the floating rate will rise. The risk in this transaction can be hedged by entering into forward rate agreements. We express the time 0 implied forward rate between time t_i and t_j as $r_0(t_i, t_j)$ and the realized 1-year rate as $\tilde{r}_{t_i}$. The current 1-year rate, 6%, is known. With the swap rate denoted R, Table 2 depicts the risk-free (but time-varying) cash flows faced by the hedged market-maker.

TABLE 2 Cash flows faced by a market-maker who receives fixed and pays floating and hedges the resulting exposure using forward rate agreements.

Year	Payment on Forward	Net Swap Payment	Net
1	—	$R - 6\%$	$R - 6\%$
2	$\tilde{r}_2 - 7.0024\%$	$R - \tilde{r}_2$	$R - 7.0024\%$
3	$\tilde{r}_3 - 8.0071\%$	$R - \tilde{r}_3$	$R - 8.0071\%$

TABLE 3 Cash flows faced by a floating-rate borrower who enters into a 3-year swap with a fixed rate of 6.9548%.

Year	Floating-Rate Debt Payment	Net Swap Payment	Net
1	-6%	$6\% - 6.9548\%$	-6.9548%
2	$-\tilde{r}_2$	$\tilde{r}_2 - 6.9548\%$	-6.9548%
3	$-\tilde{r}_3$	$\tilde{r}_3 - 6.9548\%$	-6.9548%

How is R determined? Obviously a market-maker receiving the fixed rate would like to set a high swap rate, but the swap market is competitive. We expect R to be bid down by competing market-makers until the present value of the hedged cash flows is zero. In computing this present value, we need to use the appropriate rate for each cash flow: the 1-year rate for $R - 6\%$, the 2-year rate for $R - 7.0024\%$, and so forth. Using these rates, we compute

$$\frac{R - 6\%}{1.06} + \frac{R - 7.0024\%}{1.065^2} + \frac{R - 8.0071\%}{1.07^3} = 0$$

This formula gives us an R of 6.9548%, which is the same as the par coupon on a 3-year bond! In fact, our swap-rate calculation is a roundabout way to compute a par bond yield. On reflection, this result should be no surprise. Once the borrower has entered into the swap, the net effect is exactly like borrowing at a fixed rate. Thus the fixed swap rate should be the rate on a coupon bond.

Notice that the unhedged net cash flows in Table 2 (the "net swap payment" column) can be replicated by borrowing at a floating rate and lending at a fixed rate. In other words, *an interest rate swap is equivalent to borrowing at a floating rate to buy a fixed-rate bond*.

The borrower's calculations are just the opposite of the market-maker's. The borrower continues to pay the floating rate on its floating-rate debt, and receives floating and pays fixed in the swap. Table 3 details the cash flows.

Since the swap rate is the same as the par 3-year coupon rate, the borrower is indifferent between the swap and a coupon bond, ignoring transaction costs. Keep in mind that the borrower could also have used forward rate agreements, locking in an escalating interest rate over time: 6% the first year, 7.0024% the second, and 8.0071% the third. By using interest rate forwards the borrower would have eliminated uncertainty about future borrowing rates and created an uneven but certain stream of interest payments over time. The swap provides a way to both guarantee the borrowing rate and lock in a constant rate in a single transaction.

Swap Rate and Bond Calculations

The interest rate swap calculation we just illustrated is an application of equation (3), with the implied forward interest rate used as the forward price. There is, however, an equivalent way to express the swap rate that is helpful in the case of an interest rate swap.

The implied forward rate between times t_1 and t_2, $r_0(t_1, t_2)$, is given by the ratio of zero-coupon bond prices, i.e.,

$$r_0(t_1, t_2) = P(0, t_1)/P(0, t_2) - 1$$

Therefore equation (4) can be rewritten

$$\sum_{i=1}^{n} P(0, t_i)[R - r(t_{i-1}, t_i)] = \sum_{i=1}^{n} P(0, t_i)\left[R - \frac{P(0, t_{i-1})}{P(0, t_i)} + 1\right]$$

Setting this equation equal to zero and solving for R gives us

$$R = \frac{1 - P_0(0, t_n)}{\sum_{i=1}^{n} P_0(0, t_i)} \quad (7)$$

You may recognize this as the formula for the coupon on a par coupon bond. This in turn can be rewritten as

$$R \sum_{i=1}^{n} P(0, t_i) + P(0, t_n) = 1$$

This is the valuation equation for a bond priced at par with a coupon rate of R.

The conclusion is that *the swap rate is the coupon rate on a par coupon bond*. This result is intuitive since a firm that swaps from floating-rate to fixed-rate exposure ends up with the economic equivalent of a fixed-rate bond.

The correspondence between swap and bond calculations also extends to the change in value of the swap when interest rates change. An interest rate increase reduces the present value of the fixed payments. (The fixed-rate receiver is in the position of a bond owner and suffers a loss in value.) It is common to use the DV01 (PVBP) calculation to describe the price sensitivity of a swap.

Example 1. Consider again the swap described in Table 3. Suppose that the notional value is \$100 million. The Macaulay duration of a 6.95485% par bond is 2.80915 years. By rearranging

$$\text{Macaulay duration} = -\frac{\text{Change in bond price}}{\text{Unit change in yield}} \times \frac{1 + y/m}{B(y)}$$

$$= \frac{1}{B(y)}\left[\sum_{i=1}^{n} \frac{i}{m} \frac{C/m}{(1 + y/m)^i} + \frac{n}{m} \frac{M}{(1 + y/m)^n}\right],$$

DV01 (the change in bond price for a 1-basis-point change in yield) would therefore be

$$\begin{aligned}\text{DV01} &= \text{Duration} \times 0.0001 \times 100{,}000{,}000 \\ &= 2.80915 \times 0.0001 \times \$100{,}000{,}000 = \$28{,}091.50\end{aligned}$$

The Swap Curve

The Eurodollar futures contract provides a set of 3-month forward LIBOR rates extending out 10 years. It is possible to use this set of forward interest rates to compute the interest rate swap curve. Zero-coupon bond prices can be constructed from implied forward rates.

There is an over-the-counter market in interest rate swaps, which is widely quoted. The swap curve should be consistent with the interest rate curve implied by the Eurodollar futures contract, which is used to hedge swaps.[2]

We now use equation (3) to construct the interest rate swap curve using Eurodollar prices.[3] To compute swap rates we need forward interest rates, which we obtain from the Eurodollar futures prices, and we need zero coupon bond prices, which we build from the forward interest rates.

Column 2 of Table 4 lists near-term Eurodollar futures prices from June 2010. The third column shows the implied 91-day interest rate for a loan terminating in the month in that row. For example, the June Eurodollar futures price was 99.432. The implied quarterly (nonannualized) interest rate for June to September was

$$(100 - 99.432)\frac{91}{90}\frac{1}{400} = 0.14358\%$$

The implied June price for a \$1 cash flow in September was therefore

$$\frac{1}{1 + 0.0014358} = 0.998566$$

The implied June price for a \$1 cash flow in December is obtained by first finding the forward interest rate from September to December:

$$(100 - 99.200)\frac{91}{90}\frac{1}{400} = 0.20222\%$$

The price of a zero-coupon bond paying \$1 in December is then

$$0.998566 \times \frac{1}{1 + 0.0020222} = 0.99655$$

2. The Eurodollar contract is a futures contract, while a swap is a set of forward rate agreements. Because of convexity bias, the swap curve constructed from Eurodollar futures contracts following the procedure described in this section will be somewhat greater than the observed swap curve. This is discussed by Burghardt and Hoskins (1995) and Gupta and Subrahmanyam (2000).

3. Collin-Dufresne and Solnik (2001) point out that the credit risk implicit in the LIBOR rate underlying the Eurodollar futures contract is different than the credit risk of an interest rate swap. LIBOR is computed as an average 3-month borrowing rate for international banks with good credit. Banks that experience credit problems are dropped from the sample. Thus, by construction, the pool of banks represented in the Eurodollar contract never experience a credit downgrade. A firm with a swap, by contrast, could be downgraded.

TABLE 4 Eurodollar futures prices and implied interest rate swap rates, June 2, 2010. The second column is the Eurodollar futures price for the eurodollar contract maturing in the month in the first column. The third column is the implied quarterly interest rate for a 3-month loan maturing in that month. The fourth column is the implied June price for a zero coupon bond paying $1 in that month, and the final column is the annualized swap rate for a swap maturing in that month.

Maturity	Eurodollar Futures	Implied Rate	Zero Price	Swap Rate
Jun	99.432			
Sep	99.200	0.00144	0.99857	0.57431
Dec	99.035	0.00202	0.99655	0.69148
Mar	98.875	0.00244	0.99413	0.78601
Jun	98.665	0.00284	0.99131	0.87354

We can then use equation (3) to determine the swap rate. For the June to December swap rate, for example, we have

$$\frac{0.998566 \times 0.0014358 + 0.99655 \times 0.0020222}{0.998566 + 0.99655} = 0.17287\%$$

We multiply this rate by 4 to annualize it, giving the entry 0.69148% in Table 4.

In Figure 8 we graph the entire swap curve against quarterly forward rates implied by the Eurodollar curve. Figure 8 also displays yields on government bonds. The **swap spread** is the difference between swap rates and Treasury-bond yields for comparable maturities. As you would expect, it is positive in Figure 8.[4]

The Swap's Implicit Loan Balance

An interest rate swap behaves much like the oil swap in Section 1. At inception, the swap has zero value to both parties. If interest rates change, the present value of the fixed payments and, hence, the swap rate will change. The market value of the swap is the difference in the present value of payments between the old swap rate and the new swap rate. For example, consider the 3-year swap in Table 3. If interest rates rise after the swap is entered into, the value of the existing 6.9548% swap will fall for the party receiving the fixed payment.

Even in the absence of interest rate changes, however, the swap in Table 3 changes value over time. Once the first swap payment is made, the swap acquires negative value for

4. Beginning in late 2008, and up through the date of this writing in early 2012, 30-year swap spreads (and, less frequently, 7- and 10-year swap spreads) have been negative. That is, the yield on 30-year Treasury bonds has been *greater* than the 30-year swap rate. This is surprising because Treasury yields should be less than private yields.

FIGURE 8

Forward 3-month interest rate curve implied by the Eurodollar strip, swap rates, and constant maturity Treasury yields for June 2, 2010.

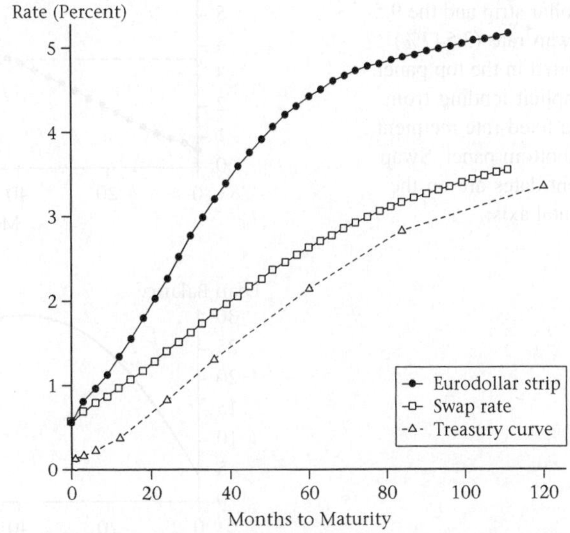

the market-maker (relative to the use of forwards) because in the second year the market-maker will make a net cash payment. Similarly, the swap will have positive value for the borrower (again relative to the use of forwards) after the first payment is made. In order to smooth payments, the borrower pays "too much" (relative to the forward curve) in the first year and receives a refund in the second year. *The swap is equivalent to entering into forward contracts and undertaking some additional borrowing and lending.*

The 9.5-year swap rate in Figure 8 is 3.547%. We can use this value to illustrate the implicit borrowing and lending in the swap. Consider an investor who pays fixed and receives floating. This investor is paying a high rate in the early years of the swap, and, hence, is lending money. About halfway through the life of the swap, the Eurodollar forward rate exceeds the swap rate and the loan balance declines, falling to zero by the end of the swap. The fixed rate recipient has a positive loan balance over the life of the swap because the Eurodollar futures rate is below the swap initially—so the fixed-rate recipient is receiving payments—and crosses the swap price once. The credit risk in this swap is therefore borne, at least initially, by the fixed-rate payer, who is lending to the fixed-rate recipient. The implicit loan balance in the swap is illustrated in Figure 9.

Deferred Swaps

We can construct a swap that begins at some date in the future, but for which the swap rate is agreed upon today. This type of swap is called a **deferred swap**. To demonstrate this type of swap, we can compute the value of a 2-period swap that begins 1 year from today. The reasoning is exactly as before: The swap rate will be set by the market-maker so that the present value of the fixed and floating payments is the same. This gives us

$$\frac{R - 0.070024}{1.065^2} + \frac{R - 0.080071}{1.07^3} = 0$$

FIGURE 9

Eurodollar strip and the 9.5-year swap rate (3.547%) are plotted in the top panel, and implicit lending from being a fixed-rate recipient in the bottom panel. Swap payment dates are on the horizontal axis.

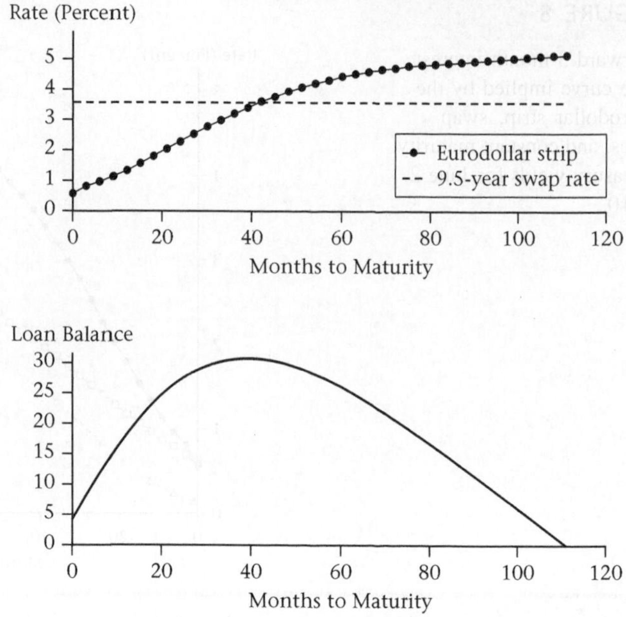

Solving for R, the deferred swap rate is 7.4854%. Using equation (3), with $F_{0,t_i} = r_0(t_{i-1}, t_i)$, the fixed rate on a deferred swap beginning in k periods (instead of 1 period) is computed as

$$R = \frac{\sum_{i=k}^{n} P_0(0, t_i) r_0(t_{i-1}, t_i)}{\sum_{i=k}^{n} P(0, t_i)} \tag{8}$$

This can also be written as

$$R = \frac{P(0, t_{k-1}) - P(0, t_n)}{\sum_{i=k}^{n} P(0, t_i)} \tag{9}$$

Equation (8) is equal to equation (3) when $k = 1$.

Related Swaps

We have so far described plain vanilla interest rate swaps in this section. Two related swaps are **overnight indexed swaps** (OIS) and **inflation swaps.**

Overnight lending is common in financial markets. One of the most important overnight markets in the U.S. is the fed funds market, in which banks lend to one another. The interest rate in this market is called the **fed funds rate**. An overnight index swap makes payments based on this rate. Rather than settle the swap each day, the swap is settled quarterly based on the geometric average of the overnight rates. The fixed rate on the swap therefore is effectively the forward price for 3 months' worth of overnight borrowing in the fed funds market.

During the financial crisis, the spread between LIBOR and OIS was an important indicator of stress in the interbank lending market. Taylor and Williams (2009) document that the LIBOR-OIS spread was approximately 10 basis points during early 2007, but spiked to almost 100 basis points in August 2007, at the onset of the crisis. The spread exceeded 400 basis points during the fall of 2008.

Inflation swaps are also of interest in fixed income markets. The vast majority of bonds are nominal bonds: they make dollar payments that do not depend on the inflation rate. (Treasury inflation-protected securities (TIPS) are a notable exception.) Lenders holding a nominal bond are harmed when the inflation rate increases and borrowers issuing a nominal bond are harmed when the inflation rate decreases. The payment on an inflation swap depends upon whether the realized inflation rate is greater or less than the fixed rate specified in the swap. Therefore, an inflation swap permits borrowers and lenders to hedge their exposure to inflation. Of course, it also permits speculation on the inflation rate.

Why Swap Interest Rates?

Managers sometimes say that they would like to borrow short-term because short-term interest rates are on average lower than long-term interest rates. Leaving aside the question of whether this view makes sense theoretically, let's take for granted the desire to borrow at short-term interest rates. The problem facing the manager is that the firm may be unable to borrow significant amounts by issuing short-term debt.

When a firm borrows by issuing long-term debt, bondholders bear both interest rate risk and the credit risk of the firm. If the firm borrows short-term (for example, by issuing commercial paper), lenders primarily bear credit risk.

In practice, short-term lenders appear unwilling to absorb large issues from a single borrower because of credit risk. For example, money-market mutual funds that hold commercial paper will not hold large amounts of any one firm's commercial paper, preferring instead to diversify across firms. This diversification minimizes the chance that a single bankruptcy will significantly reduce the fund's rate of return.

Because short-term lenders are sensitive in this way to credit risk, a firm cannot borrow a large amount of money short-term without lenders demanding a higher interest rate. By contrast, long-term lenders to corporations—for example, pension funds and insurance companies—willingly assume both interest rate and credit risk. Thus there are borrowers who wish to issue short-term debt and lenders who are unwilling to buy it. Swaps provide a way around this problem, permitting the firm to separate credit risk and interest rate risk.

Suppose, for example, that a firm borrows long-term and then swaps into short-rate exposure. The firm receives the fixed rate, pays the fixed rate to bondholders, and pays the floating rate on the swap. The net payment is the short-term rate, which is the rate the firm wanted to pay.

Credit risk does not vanish; it is still mostly held by the long-term bondholders. The swap counterparty faces credit risk since the firm could go bankrupt when the value of the swap is positive to the counterparty (this would occur if interest rates had risen). The notional principal of the loan is not at risk for the swap counterparty, however, so the credit risk in the swap is less than for a short-term loan. Thus, by swapping its interest rate exposure, the firm pays the short-term interest rate, *but the long-term bondholders continue to bear most of the credit risk.*

If it seems odd to you that the firm can use a swap to convert a high fixed rate into a low floating rate, recognize that any time there is an upward-sloping yield curve, the short-term interest rate is below the long-term interest rate. If you reduce the period for which your borrowing rate is fixed (which happens when you swap fixed for floating), you borrow at the lower short-term interest rate instead of the higher long-term interest rate.

Swaps thus permit separation of two aspects of borrowing: credit risk and interest rate risk. To the extent these risks are acquired by those most willing to hold them, swaps increase efficiency.

Amortizing and Accreting Swaps

We have assumed that the notional value of the swap remains fixed over the life of the swap. However, it is also possible to engage in a swap where the notional value is changing over time. For example, consider a floating-rate mortgage, for which every payment contains an interest and principal component. Since the outstanding principal is declining over time, a swap involving a mortgage would need to account for this. Such a swap is called an **amortizing swap** because the notional value is declining over time. It is also possible for the principal in a swap to grow over time. This is called an **accreting swap**.

Let Q_t be the relative notional amount at time t. Then the basic idea in pricing a swap with a time-varying notional amount is the same as with a fixed notional amount—the present value of the fixed payments should equal the present value of the floating payments:

$$\sum_{i=1}^{n} Q_{t_i} P(0, t_i)[R - r(t_{i-1}, t_i)] = 0 \tag{10}$$

where, as before, there are n payments on dates $t_1, t_2, \ldots, t_n$. Equation (10) can be rewritten as

$$R = \frac{\sum_{i=1}^{n} Q_{t_i} P(0, t_i) r(t_{i-1}, t_i)}{\sum_{i=1}^{n} Q_{t_i} P(0, t_i)} \tag{11}$$

The fixed swap rate is still a weighted average of implied forward rates, only now the weights also involve changing notional principal.

Many other structures are possible for swaps based on interest rates or other prices. One infamous swap structure is described in Box 2, which recounts the 1993 swap between Procter & Gamble and Bankers Trust.

4. CURRENCY SWAPS

Firms sometimes issue debt denominated in a foreign currency. A firm may do this as a hedge against revenues received in that currency, or because perceived borrowing costs in that currency are lower. Whatever the reason, if the firm later wants to change the currency to which they have exposure, there are a variety of ways to do so. The firm can use forward contracts to hedge exchange rate risk, or it can use a **currency swap**, in which payments are based on the difference in debt payments denominated in different currencies.

To understand these alternatives, let's consider the example of a dollar-based firm that has euro-denominated 3-year fixed-rate debt. The annual coupon rate is ρ. The firm is

BOX 2: The Procter & Gamble Swap

In November 1993, consumer products company Procter & Gamble (P&G) entered into a 5-year \$200m notional value swap with Bankers Trust. The contract called for P&G to receive a 5.3% fixed rate from Bankers Trust and pay the 30-day commercial paper rate less 75 basis points, plus a spread. Settlements were to be semiannual. The spread would be zero for the first settlement, and thereafter be fixed at the spread as of May 4, 1994.

The spread was determined by the difference between the 5-year constant maturity treasury (CMT) rate (the yield on a 5-year Treasury bond, but a constructed rate since there is not always a Treasury bond with exactly 5 years to expiration) and the price per \$100 of maturity value of the 6.25% 30-year Treasury bond. The formula for the spread was

$$\text{Spread} = \max\left(\frac{\frac{\text{5-year CMT \%}}{0.0578} \times 98.5 - \text{price of 30-year bond}}{100}, 0\right)$$

At inception in November 1993, the 5-year CMT rate was 5.02% and the 30-year Treasury price was 102.57811. The expression in the max function evaluated to -0.17 (-17%), so the spread was zero.

If the spread were zero on May 4, 1994, P&G would save 75 basis points per year on \$200m for 4.5 years, an interest rate reduction worth approximately \$7m. However, notice something important: If interest rates rise before the spread determination date, then the 5-year CMT goes up *and the price of the 30-year bond goes down.* Thus, the swap is really a bet on the *direction* of interest rates, not the difference in rates!

The swap is recounted in Smith (1997) and Srivastava (1998). Interest rates rose after P&G entered the swap. P&G and Bankers Trust renegotiated the swap in January 1994, and P&G liquidated the swap in March, with a loss of about \$100m. P&G sued Bankers Trust, complaining in part that the risks of the swap had not been adequately disclosed by Bankers Trust.

In the end, P&G and Bankers Trust settled, with P&G paying Bankers Trust about \$35m. (Forster (1996) and Horwitz (1996) debate the implications of the trial and settlement.) The notion that Procter & Gamble might have been uninformed about the risk of the swap, and if so, whether this should have mattered, was controversial. U.S. securities laws are often said to protect "widows and orphans." Nobel Prize–winning economist Merton Miller wryly said of the case, "Procter is the widow and Gamble is the orphan."

obligated to make a series of payments that are fixed in euro terms but variable in dollar terms.

Since the payments are known, eliminating euro exposure is a straightforward hedging problem using currency forwards. We have cash flows of $-\rho$ each year, and $-(1+\rho)$ in the maturity year. If currency forward prices are $F_{0,t}$, we can enter into long euro forward contracts to acquire at a known exchange rate the euros we need to pay to the lenders. Hedged cash flows in year t are $-\rho F_{0,t}$.

As we have seen in other examples, the forward transactions eliminate risk but leave the firm with a variable (but riskless) stream of cash flows. The variability of hedged cash flows is illustrated in the following example.

TABLE 5 Unhedged and hedged cash flows for a dollar-based firm with euro-denominated debt.

Year	Unhedged Euro Cash Flow	Forward Exchange Rate	Hedged Dollar Cash Flow
1	−€3.5	0.922	−$3.226
2	−€3.5	0.944	−$3.304
3	−€103.5	0.967	−$100.064

Example 2. Suppose the effective annual euro-denominated interest rate is 3.5% and the dollar-denominated rate is 6%. The spot exchange rate is $0.90/€. A dollar-based firm has a 3-year 3.5% euro-denominated bond with a €100 par value and price of €100. The firm wishes to guarantee the dollar value of the payments. Since the firm will make debt payments in euros, it buys the euro forward to eliminate currency exposure. Table 5 summarizes the transaction and reports the currency forward curve and the unhedged and hedged cash flows. The value of the hedged cash flows is

$$\frac{\$3.226}{1.06} + \frac{\$3.304}{1.06^2} + \frac{\$100.064}{1.06^3} = \$90 \quad \blacksquare$$

Example 2 verifies what we knew had to be true: Hedging does not change the value of the debt. The initial value of the debt in euros is €100. Since the exchange rate is $0.90/€, the debt should have a dollar value of $90, which it has.

As an alternative to hedging each euro-denominated payment with a forward contract, a firm wishing to change its currency exposure can enter into a currency swap, which entails making debt payments in one currency and receiving debt payments in a different currency. There is typically an exchange of principal at both the start and end of the swap. Compared with hedging the cash flows individually, the currency swap generates a different cash flow stream, but with equivalent value. We can examine a currency swap by supposing that the firm in Example 2 uses a swap rather than forward contracts to hedge its euro exposure.

Example 3. Make the same assumptions as in Example 2. The dollar-based firm enters into a swap where it pays dollars (6% on a $90 bond) and receives euros (3.5% on a €100 bond). The firm's euro exposure is eliminated. The market-maker receives dollars and pays euros. The position of the market-maker is summarized in Table 6. The present value of the market-maker's net cash flow is

$$\frac{\$2.174}{1.06} + \frac{\$2.096}{1.06^2} - \frac{\$4.664}{1.06^3} = 0 \quad \blacksquare$$

The market-maker's net exposure in this transaction is long a dollar-denominated bond and short a euro-denominated bond. Table 6 shows that after hedging there is a series of net cash flows with zero present value. As in all the previous examples, the effect of the swap is equivalent to entering into forward contracts, coupled with borrowing or lending. In this case, the firm is lending to the market-maker in the first 2 years, with the implicit loan repaid at maturity.

TABLE 6 Unhedged and hedged cash flows for a dollar-based firm with euro-denominated debt. The effective annual dollar-denominated interest rate is 6% and the effective annual euro-denominated interest rate is 3.5%.

Year	Forward Exchange Rate (\$/€)	Receive Dollar Interest	Pay Hedged Euro Interest	Net Cash Flow
1	0.9217	\$5.40	−€3.5 × 0.9217	\$2.174
2	0.9440	\$5.40	−€3.5 × 0.9440	\$2.096
3	0.9668	\$95.40	−€103.5 × 0.9668	−\$4.664

The fact that a currency swap is equivalent to borrowing in one currency and lending in the other is familiar from the concept of currency forwards.

Currency Swap Formulas

Currency swap calculations are the same as those for the other swaps we have discussed. To see this, consider a swap in which a dollar annuity, R, is exchanged for an annuity in another currency, R^*. Given the foreign annuity, R^*, what is R?

We start with the observation that the present value of the two annuities must be the same. There are n payments and the time-0 forward price for a unit of foreign currency delivered at time t_i is F_{0,t_i}. This gives

$$\sum_{i=1}^{n}\left[RP_{0,t_i} - R^*F_{0,t_i}P_{0,t_i}\right] = 0$$

In calculating the present value of the payment R^*, we first convert to dollars by multiplying by F_{0,t_i}. We can then compute the present value using the dollar-denominated zero-coupon bond price, P_{0,t_i}. Solving for R gives

$$R = \frac{\sum_{i=1}^{n} P_{0,t_i}R^*F_{0,t_i}}{\sum_{i=1}^{n} P_{0,t_i}} \tag{12}$$

This expression is exactly like equation (3), with the implied forward rate, $r_0(t_{i-1}, t_i)$, replaced by the foreign-currency-denominated annuity payment translated into dollars, R^*F_{0,t_i}.

When coupon bonds are swapped, we have to account for the difference in maturity value as well as the coupon payment, which is an annuity. If the dollar bond has a par value of \$1, the foreign bond will have a par value of $1/x_0$, where x_0 is the current exchange rate expressed as dollars per unit of the foreign currency. If R^* is the coupon rate on the foreign bond and R is the coupon rate on the dollar bond, the present value of the difference in payments on the two bonds is

$$\sum_{i=1}^{n}\left[RP_{0,t_i} - R^*F_{0,t_i}P_{0,t_i}/x_0\right] + P_{0,t_n}(1 - F_{0,t_n}/x_0) = 0$$

The division by x_0 accounts for the fact that a \$1 bond is equivalent to $1/x_0$ bonds with a par value of 1 unit of the foreign currency. The dollar coupon in this case is

$$R = \frac{\sum_{i=1}^{n} P_{0,t_i} R^* F_{0,t_i}/x_0 + P_{0,t_n}(F_{0,t_n}/x_0 - 1)}{\sum_{i=1}^{n} P_{0,t_i}} \tag{13}$$

The fixed payment, R, is the dollar equivalent of the foreign coupon plus the amortized value of the difference in the maturity payments of the two bonds. Problem 16 asks you to verify that equation (13) gives 6% using the assumptions in Tables 5 and 6.

Other Currency Swaps

There are other kinds of currency swaps. The preceding examples assumed that all borrowing was fixed rate. Suppose the dollar-based borrower issues a euro-denominated loan with a *floating* interest rate. In this case there are two future unknowns: the exchange rate at which interest payments are converted, and—because the bond is floating rate—the amount of the interest payment. Swapping this loan to a dollar loan is still straightforward, however; we just require one extra hedging transaction.

We first convert the floating interest rate into a fixed interest rate with a *euro* interest rate swap. The resulting fixed-rate euro-denominated exposure can then be hedged with currency forwards and converted into dollar interest rate exposure. Given the assumptions in Table 6, the euro-denominated loan would swap to a 3.5% floating-rate loan. From that point on, we are in the same position as in the previous example.

In general, we can swap fixed-to-fixed, fixed-to-floating, floating-to-fixed, and floating-to-floating. The analysis is similar in all cases.

One kind of swap that might on its face seem similar is a **diff swap**, short for differential swap. In this kind of swap, payments are made based on the difference in floating interest rates in two different currencies, with the notional amount in a single currency. For example, we might have a swap with a \$10m notional amount, but the swap would pay in dollars, based on the difference in a euro-denominated interest rate and a dollar-denominated interest rate. If the short-term euro interest rate rises from 3.5% to 3.8% with the dollar rate unchanged, the annual swap payment would be 30 basis points on \$10m, or \$30,000. This is like a standard interest rate swap, only for a diff swap, the reference interest rates are denominated in different currencies.

Standard currency forward contracts cannot be used to hedge a diff swap. The problem is that we can hedge the change in the foreign interest rate, but doing so requires a transaction denominated in the foreign currency. We can't easily hedge the exchange rate at which the value of the interest rate change is converted *because we don't know in advance how much currency will need to be converted.* In effect there is quantity uncertainty regarding the foreign currency to be converted. The diff swap is an example of a quanto swap.

5. SWAPTIONS

An option to enter into a swap is called a **swaption**. We can see how a swaption works by returning to the two-date oil swap example in Section 1. The 2-year oil swap price was \$110.483. Suppose we are willing to buy oil at \$110.483/barrel, but we would like to speculate on the swap price being even lower over the next 3 months.

Consider the following contract: If in 3 months the fixed price for a swap commencing in 9 months (1 year from today) is \$110.483 or above, we enter into the swap, agreeing to pay \$110.483 and receive the floating price for 2 years. If, on the other hand, the market swap price is below \$110.483, we have no obligation. If the swap price in 3 months is \$108, for example, we could enter into a swap at that time at the \$108 price, or we could elect not to enter any swap.

With this contract we are entering into the swap with \$110.483 as the swap price only when the market swap price is greater; hence, this contract will have a premium. In this example, we would have purchased a **payer swaption**, since we have the right, but not the obligation, to pay a fixed price of \$110.483 for 2 years of oil. The counterparty has sold this swaption.

When exercised, the swaption commits us to transact at multiple times in the future. It is possible to exercise the option and then offset the swap with another swap, converting the stream of swap payments into a certain stream with a fixed present value. Thus, the swaption is analogous to an ordinary option, with the present value of the swap obligations (the price of the prepaid swap) as the underlying asset.

The strike price in this example is \$110.483, so we have an at-the-money swaption. We could make the strike price different from \$110.483. For example, we could reduce the swaption premium by setting the strike above \$110.483.

Swaptions can be American or European, and the terms of the underlying swap—fixed price, floating index, settlement frequency, and tenor—will be precisely specified.

Example 4. Suppose we enter into a European payer oil swaption with a strike price of \$21. The underlying swap commences in 1 year and has two annual settlements. After 3 months, the fixed price on the underlying swap is \$21.50. We exercise the option, obligating us to pay \$21/barrel for 2 years. If we wish to offset the swap, we can enter into a swap to receive the \$21.50 fixed price. In year 1 and year 2 we will then receive \$21.50 and pay \$21, for a certain net cash flow each year of \$0.50. The floating payments cancel. ■

A **receiver swaption** gives you the right to pay the floating price and receive the fixed strike price. Thus, the holder of a receiver swaption would exercise when the fixed swap price is below the strike.

Although we have used a commodity swaption in this example, an interest rate or currency swaption would be analogous, with payer and receiver swaptions giving the right to pay or receive the fixed interest rate.

6. TOTAL RETURN SWAPS

A **total return swap** is a swap in which one party pays the realized total return (dividends plus capital gains) on a reference asset, and the other party pays a floating return such as LIBOR. The two parties exchange only the difference between these rates. The party paying the return on the reference asset is the *total return payer*.

As with other swaps, there are multiple settlement dates over the life of the swap. The cumulative effect for the total return payer is of being short the reference asset and long an asset paying the floating rate. The cash flows on a total return swap are illustrated in Figure 10.

FIGURE 10

Cash flows for a total return swap. The total return payer pays the per-period total return on the reference asset, receiving the floating rate from the counterparty.

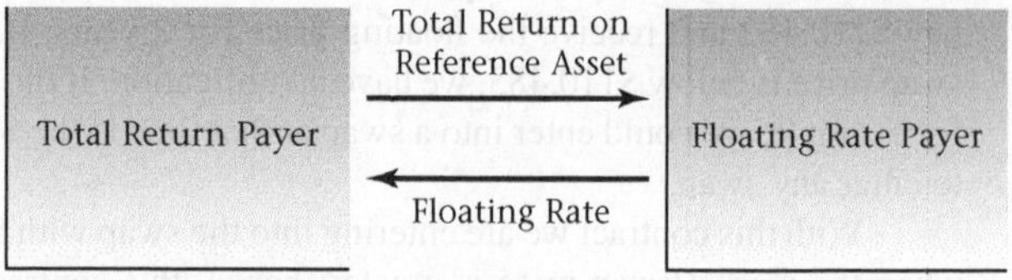

TABLE 7 Illustration of cash flows on a total return swap with annual settlement for 3 years.

Year	S&P Capital Gain	S&P Dividend	Floating Rate	Net Payment to Total Return Payer
1	5%	1.5%	7.2%	0.7%
2	−12%	1.5%	7.5%	18.0%
3	22%	1.5%	7.0%	−16.5%

Example 5. ABC Asset Management has a $2 billion investment in the S&P stock index. However, fund managers have become pessimistic about the market and would like to reduce their exposure to stocks from $2 billion to $1 billion. One way to do this is to sell $1 billion of stocks. However, the fund can retain the stock position but financially transfer the return of the stocks by engaging in a total return swap, obligating the fund to pay the total return (dividends plus capital gains) on the swapped stocks, while receiving a floating-rate return such as LIBOR on the swapped $1 billion notional amount. This avoids the transaction costs of a sale of physical stock.

Table 7 illustrates the payments on such a swap. In year 1, ABC earns 6.5% on the S&P index. However, on the portion it has swapped, it must pay the 6.5% in exchange for the 7.2% floating rate. The net payment of 0.7% leaves ABC as well off as if it had sold the index and invested in an asset paying the floating rate. In year 2, ABC receives 18%, compensating it for the difference between the 7.5% floating return and the 10.5% loss on the S&P index. Finally, in year 3 the S&P index does well, and ABC pays 16.5% to the counterparty. ■

You might wonder about the economics of a swap like this. The stock index on average earns a higher return than LIBOR. So if the fund swaps the stock index in exchange for LIBOR, it will on average make payments to the counterparty.

This observation is correct, but notice that the fund is paying the difference between the index return and a short-term interest rate—this difference is the risk premium on the index.

The average loss associated with swapping a stock index for LIBOR is the same as the average loss associated with selling the stock and buying a floating-rate note paying LIBOR. It is just that the swap makes the loss obvious since it requires a payment.

Some investors have used total return swaps to avoid taxes on foreign stocks. In many cases, countries impose withholding taxes on foreign investors, meaning that if a firm in country A pays a dividend, for example, country A withholds a fraction of that dividend from investors based in country B. A total return swap enables a country-B investor to own country-A stocks without physically holding them, and thus in many cases without having to pay withholding taxes. For example, a U.S. investor could first swap out of a U.S. stock index and then swap into a European stock index, effectively becoming the counterparty for a European investor wanting to swap out of European stock exposure. Because net swap payments are not always recognized by withholding rules, this transaction can be more tax-efficient than holding the foreign stocks directly.

Another use of total return swaps is the management of credit risk. A fund manager holding corporate debt can swap the return on a particular bond for a floating-rate return. If the company that issued the bond goes bankrupt, the debt holder receives a payment on the swap compensating for the fact that the bond is worth a fraction of its face value.

If you think about this use of total return swaps, it is a crude tool for managing credit risk specifically. The problem is that bond prices also change due to interest rate changes. A corporate bond holder might wish to retain interest rate risk but not bankruptcy risk. Thus, there are products called **default swaps**. These are essentially default options, in which the buyer pays a premium, usually amortized over a series of payments. If the reference asset experiences a "credit event" (for example, a failure to make a scheduled payment on a particular bond or class of bonds), then the seller makes a payment to the buyer. Frequently these contracts split the return on the bond into the portion due to interest rate changes (with Treasury securities used as a reference) and the portion due to credit quality changes, with the swap making payments based only on the latter.

CHAPTER SUMMARY

A swap is a contract calling for an exchange of payments, on one or more dates, determined by the difference in two prices. A single-payment swap is the same thing as a cash-settled forward contract. In the simplest swaps, a fixed payment is periodically exchanged for a floating payment. A firm can use a swap to lock in a long-term commodity price, a fixed interest rate, or a fixed exchange rate. Considering only the present value of cash flows, the same result is obtained using a strip of forward contracts and swaps. The difference is that hedging with a strip of forward contracts results in net payments that are time-varying. In contrast, hedging with a swap results in net payments that are constant over time. The value of a swap is zero at inception, though as swap payments are made over time, the value of the swap can change in a predictable way.

The fixed price in a swap is a weighted average of the corresponding forward prices. The swap formulas in different cases all take the same general form. Let $f_0(t_i)$ denote the forward price for the floating payment in the swap. Then the fixed swap payment is

$$R = \frac{\sum_{i=1}^{n} P(0, t_i) f_0(t_i)}{\sum_{i=1}^{n} P(0, t_i)} \tag{14}$$

TABLE 8 Equivalent forms of the swap-rate calculation. For the currency swap, F_{0,t_i} is the forward price for the foreign currency and R^* is an annuity in the foreign currency. For the commodity swap, F_{0,t_i} is the forward price for the commodity.

To Obtain Formula for	Substitute in Equation (14)
Interest rate swap	$f_0(t_i) = r_0(t_{i-1}, t_i)$
Currency swap (annuity)	$f_0(t_i) = R^* F_{0,t_i}$
Commodity swap	$f_0(t_i) = F_{0,t_i}$

Table 8 summarizes the substitutions to make in equation (14) to get the various swap formulas shown in the chapter. This formula can be generalized to permit time variation in the notional amount and the swap price, and the swap can start on a deferred basis.

An important characteristic of swaps is that they require only the exchange of net payments, and not the payment of principal. So if a firm enters an interest rate swap, for example, it is required only to make payments based on the difference in interest rates, not on the underlying principal. As a result, swaps have less credit risk than bonds.

Total return swaps involve exchanging the return on an asset for a floating rate such as LIBOR. The term *swap* is also used to describe agreements like the Procter & Gamble swap (Box 2), which required payments based on the difference in interest rates and bond prices, as well as default swaps.

FURTHER READING

Litzenberger (1992) provides an overview of the swap market. Turnbull (1987) discusses arguments purporting to show that the use of swaps can have a positive net present value. Default swaps are discussed by Tavakoli (1998). Because of convexity bias, the market interest rate swap curve is not exactly the same as the swap curve constructed from Eurodollar futures. This is discussed in Burghardt and Hoskins (1995) and Gupta and Subrahmanyam (2000). The SEC complaint against J. P. Morgan Chase is at http://www.sec.gov/litigation/complaints/comp18252.htm.

PROBLEMS

Some of the problems that follow use Table 9. Assume that the current exchange rate is \$0.90/€.

1. Suppose that 1- and 2-year oil forward prices are \$22/barrel and \$23/barrel. The 1- and 2-year interest rates are 6% and 6.5%. Show that the new 2-year swap price is \$22.483.

2. Suppose that oil forward prices for 1 year, 2 years, and 3 years are \$20, \$21, and \$22. The 1-year effective annual interest rate is 6.0%, the 2-year interest rate is 6.5%, and the 3-year interest rate is 7.0%.

TABLE 9

Quarter	1	2	3	4	5	6	7	8
Oil forward price	21	21.1	20.8	20.5	20.2	20	19.9	19.8
Gas swap price	2.2500	2.4236	2.3503	2.2404	2.2326	2.2753	2.2583	2.2044
Zero-coupon bond price	0.9852	0.9701	0.9546	0.9388	0.9231	0.9075	0.8919	0.8763
Euro-denominated zero-coupon bond price	0.9913	0.9825	0.9735	0.9643	0.9551	0.9459	0.9367	0.9274
Euro forward price ($/€)	0.9056	0.9115	0.9178	0.9244	0.9312	0.9381	0.9452	0.9524

a. What is the 3-year swap price?

b. What is the price of a 2-year swap beginning in one year? (That is, the first swap settlement will be in 2 years and the second in 3 years.)

3. Consider the same 3-year oil swap. Suppose a dealer is paying the fixed price and receiving floating. What position in oil forward contracts will hedge oil price risk in this position? Verify that the present value of the locked-in net cash flows is zero.

4. Consider the 3-year swap in the previous example. Suppose you are the fixed-rate payer in the swap. How much have you overpaid relative to the forward price after the first swap settlement? What is the cumulative overpayment after the second swap settlement? Verify that the cumulative overpayment is zero after the third payment. (Be sure to account for interest.)

5. Consider the same 3-year swap. Suppose you are a dealer who is paying the fixed oil price and receiving the floating price. Suppose that you enter into the swap and immediately thereafter all interest rates rise 50 basis points (oil forward prices are unchanged). What happens to the value of your swap position? What if interest rates fall 50 basis points? What hedging instrument would have protected you against interest rate risk in this position?

6. Supposing the effective quarterly interest rate is 1.5%, what are the per-barrel swap prices for 4-quarter and 8-quarter oil swaps? (Use oil forward prices in Table 9.) What is the total cost of prepaid 4- and 8-quarter swaps?

7. Using the information about zero-coupon bond prices and oil forward prices in Table 9, construct the set of swap prices for oil for 1 through 8 quarters.

8. Using the information in Table 9, what is the swap price of a 4-quarter oil swap with the first settlement occurring in the third quarter?

9. Given an 8-quarter oil swap price of $20.43, construct the implicit loan balance for each quarter over the life of the swap.

10. Using the zero-coupon bond prices and oil forward prices in Table 9, what is the price of an 8-period swap for which two barrels of oil are delivered in even-numbered quarters and one barrel of oil in odd-numbered quarters?

11. Using the zero-coupon bond prices and natural gas swap prices in Table 9, what are gas forward prices for each of the 8 quarters?

12. Using the zero-coupon bond prices and natural gas swap prices in Table 9, what is the implicit loan amount in each quarter in an 8-quarter natural gas swap?

13. What is the fixed rate in a 5-quarter interest rate swap with the first settlement in quarter 2?

14. Using the zero-coupon bond yields in Table 9, what is the fixed rate in a 4-quarter interest rate swap? What is the fixed rate in an 8-quarter interest rate swap?

15. What 8-quarter dollar annuity is equivalent to an 8-quarter annuity of €1?

16. Using the assumptions in Tables 5 and 6, verify that equation (13) equals 6%.

17. Using the information in Table 9, what are the *euro-denominated* fixed rates for 4- and 8-quarter swaps?

18. Using the information in Table 9, verify that it is possible to derive the 8-quarter dollar interest swap rate from the 8-quarter euro interest swap rate by using equation (13).

Options

Forward contracts (and futures and swaps) represent a binding commitment to buy or sell the underlying asset in the future. Because the commitment is binding, but deferred, time value of money is the main economic idea used in determining forward prices.

Options, on the other hand, need not be exercised. Intuitively, you would expect the probability distribution of the stock to affect the option price. Consequently, in discussing option pricing we use some concepts from basic probability. However, it turns out that there is much to say about options without needing to think about the probability distribution of the stock.

The binomial option pricing model assumes that the stock can move only in a very simple way, but provides the intuition underlying more complicated option

From *Derivatives Markets*, Third Edition, Robert McDonald. Copyright © 2013 by Pearson Education, Inc. Published by Pearson Prentice Hall. All rights reserved.

pricing calculations. The Black-Scholes option pricing formula is one of the most important formulas in finance.

As with forwards, futures, and swaps, option contracts are bought and sold by market-makers who hedge the risk associated with market-making.

Parity and Other Option Relationships

In this chapter we study option pricing. Contracts entailing *firm commitments*, such as forwards, futures, and swaps, do not permit either party to back away from the agreement. Optionality occurs when it is possible to avoid engaging in unprofitable transactions. The principal question in option pricing is: *How do you value the right to back away from a commitment?*

Before we delve into pricing models, we devote this chapter to refining our common sense about options. For example, Table 1 contains call and put prices for IBM for four different strikes and two different expiration dates. These are American-style options. Here are some observations and questions about these prices:

- What determines the difference between put and call prices at a given strike?
- How would the premiums change if these options were European rather than American?
- It appears that, for a given strike, the October options are more expensive than the June options. Is this necessarily true?
- Do call premiums always decrease as the strike price increases? Do put premiums always increase as the strike price increases?
- Both call and put premiums change by less than the change in the strike price. Does this always happen?

These questions, and others, will be answered in this chapter, but you should take a minute and think about the answers now. While doing so, pay attention to *how* you are trying to come up with the answers. What constitutes a persuasive argument? Along with finding the answers, we want to understand how to think about questions like these.

1. PUT-CALL PARITY

Put-call parity is perhaps the single most important relationship among option prices. Synthetic forwards (created by buying the call and selling the put) must be priced consistently with actual forwards. The basic parity relationship for European options with the same strike price and time to expiration is

$$\text{Call} - \text{put} = \text{PV}(\text{forward price} - \text{strike price})$$

From Chapter 9 of *Derivatives Markets*, Third Edition, Robert McDonald. Copyright © 2013 by Pearson Education, Inc. Published by Pearson Prentice Hall. All rights reserved.

TABLE 1 IBM option prices, dollars per share, May 6, 2011. The closing price of IBM on that day was $168.89.

		Calls		Puts	
Strike	Expiration	Bid ($)	Ask ($)	Bid ($)	Ask ($)
160	June	10.05	10.15	1.16	1.20
165	June	6.15	6.25	2.26	2.31
170	June	3.20	3.30	4.25	4.35
175	June	1.38	1.43	7.40	7.55
160	October	14.10	14.20	5.70	5.80
165	October	10.85	11.00	7.45	7.60
170	October	8.10	8.20	9.70	9.85
175	October	5.80	5.90	12.40	12.55

Source: Chicago Board Options Exchange.

The equation $\text{Call}(K, T) - \text{Put}(K, T) = \text{PV}(F_{0,T} - K)$ expresses this more precisely:

$$C(K, T) - P(K, T) = \text{PV}_{0,T}(F_{0,T} - K) \tag{1}$$
$$= e^{-rT}(F_{0,T} - K)$$

where $C(K, T)$ is the price of a European call with strike price K and time to expiration T, $P(K, T)$ is the price of a European put, $F_{0,T}$ is the forward price for the underlying asset, K is the strike price, T is the time to expiration of the options, and $\text{PV}_{0,T}$ denotes the present value over the life of the options. Note that $e^{-rT}F_{0,T}$ is the prepaid forward price for the asset and $e^{-rT}K$ is the prepaid forward price for the strike, so we can also think of parity in terms of prepaid forward prices.

The intuition for equation (1) is that buying a call and selling a put with the strike equal to the forward price ($F_{0,T} = K$) creates a synthetic forward contract and hence must have a zero price. If we create a synthetic long forward position at a price lower than the forward price, we have to pay $\text{PV}_{0,T}(F_{0,T} - K)$ since this is the benefit of buying the asset at the strike price rather than the forward price.

Parity generally fails for American-style options, which may be exercised prior to maturity. Appendix A discusses parity bounds for American options.

We now consider the parity relationship in more detail for different underlying assets.

Options on Stocks

If the underlying asset is a stock and Div is the stream of dividends paid on the stock, then $e^{-rT}F_{0,T} = S_0 - \text{PV}_{0,T}(\text{Div})$. Thus, from equation (1), the parity relationship for European options on stocks is

$$C(K, T) = P(K, T) + [S_0 - \text{PV}_{0,T}(\text{Div})] - e^{-rT}K \tag{2}$$

where S_0 is the current stock price and $\text{PV}_{0,T}(\text{Div})$ is the present value of dividends payable over the life of the option. For index options, we know that $S_0 - \text{PV}_{0,T}(\text{Div}) = S_0e^{-\delta T}$.

FIGURE 1

Cash flows for outright purchase of stock and for synthetic stock created by buying a 40-strike call and selling a 40-strike put.

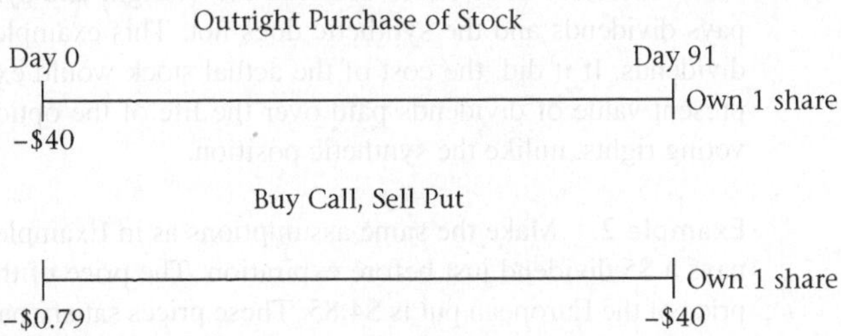

Hence, we can write

$$C(K, T) = P(K, T) + S_0 e^{-\delta T} - \text{PV}_{0,T}(K)$$

Example 1. Suppose that the price of a non-dividend-paying stock is \$40, the continuously compounded interest rate is 8%, and options have 3 months to expiration. A 40-strike European call sells for \$2.78 and a 40-strike European put sells for \$1.99. This is consistent with equation (2):

$$\$2.78 = \$1.99 + \$40 - \$40e^{-0.08 \times 0.25}$$ ■

Why does the price of an at-the-money call exceed the price of an at-the-money put by \$0.79? The answer is that buying a call and selling a put is a leveraged synthetic stock purchase, with different cash flows than an outright purchase. Figure 1 compares the synthetic purchase of the stock (buying the call and selling the put) with an outright purchase.

Notice that both positions result in the ownership of the stock 3 months from today. With the outright purchase, we pay \$40 today and own the stock for the entire 3 months. With the synthetic purchase, we pay \$0.79 today and \$40 at expiration. If the price at expiration is above \$40, we will own the stock because we exercise the call. If the stock price is below \$40, we will own the stock because we sold a put that will be exercised; as the put-writer, we have to buy the stock.

Although with the synthetic stock purchase we do not own the stock until expiration, we are still exposed to the risk of the stock. A \$1 change in the value of the stock will induce a \$1 change in the value of the synthetic stock, exactly as if we owned the stock outright.

Thus, by buying the call and selling the put we own the stock economically, but we have deferred the payment of \$40 until expiration. To obtain this deferral we must pay 3 months of interest on the \$40, the present value of which is \$0.79. *The option premiums differ by the interest on the deferral of payment for the stock*. The difference in the call and put premiums is due to interest on the strike price. This is the reason that an at-the-money European call on a non-dividend-paying stock always sells for more than an at-the-money European put with the same expiration.

Note that if we reverse the position by selling the call and buying the put, then we are synthetically short-selling the stock. In 3 months, the options will be exercised and we will receive \$40. In this case, the \$0.79 compensates us for deferring receipt of the \$40.

There are differences between the outright and synthetic positions. First, the stock pays dividends and the synthetic does not. This example assumed that the stock paid no dividends. If it did, the cost of the actual stock would exceed that of the synthetic by the present value of dividends paid over the life of the options. Second, the actual stock has voting rights, unlike the synthetic position.

Example 2. Make the same assumptions as in Example 1, except suppose that the stock pays a \$5 dividend just before expiration. The price of the European call is \$0.74 and the price of the European put is \$4.85. These prices satisfy parity with dividends, equation (2):

$$\$0.74 - \$4.85 = (\$40 - \$5e^{-0.08\times 0.25}) - \$40e^{-0.08\times 0.25}$$

The call price is higher than the put price by interest on the strike (\$0.79) and lower by the present value of the dividend (\$4.90), for a net difference of \$4.11. ■

In this example, the at-the-money call sells for less than an at-the-money put because dividends on the stock exceed the value of interest on the strike price.

It is worth mentioning a common but erroneous explanation for the higher premium of an at-the-money call compared to an at-the-money put. The profit on a call is potentially unlimited since the stock price can go to infinity, while the profit on a put can be no greater than the strike price. This explanation seems to suggest that the call should be more expensive than the put.[1] However, parity shows that the true reason for the call being more expensive (as in Example 1) is time value of money.

Synthetic stock. Parity provides a cookbook for the synthetic creation of options, stocks, and T-bills.

The example above shows that buying a call and selling a put is like buying the stock except that the timing of the payment for the stock differs in the two cases. Rewriting equation (2) gives us

$$S_0 = C(K, T) - P(K, T) + \text{PV}_{0,T}(\text{Div}) + e^{-rT}K \tag{3}$$

To match the cash flows for an outright purchase of the stock, in addition to buying the call and selling the put, we have to lend the present value of the strike and dividends to be paid over the life of the option. We then receive the stock in 91 days.

Synthetic T-bills. If we buy the stock, sell the call, and buy the put, we have purchased the stock and short-sold the synthetic stock. This transaction gives us a hedged position that has no risk but requires investment. Parity shows us that

$$S_0 + P(K, T) - C(K, T) = \text{PV}_{0,T}(K) + \text{PV}_{0,T}(\text{Div})$$

We have thus created a position that costs $\text{PV}(K) + \text{PV}_{0,T}(\text{Div})$ and that pays $K + FV_{0,T}(\text{Div})$ at expiration. This is a synthetic Treasury bill.

Since T-bills are taxed differently than stocks, the ability to create a synthetic Treasury bill with the stock and options creates problems for tax and accounting authorities. How should the return on this transaction be taxed—as a stock transaction or as interest income?

1. In fact, the argument also seems to suggest that every stock is worth more than its price!

Tax rules call for this position to be taxed as interest, but you can imagine taxpayers trying to skirt these rules.

The creation of a synthetic T-bill by buying the stock, buying a put, and selling a call is called a **conversion**. If we short the stock, buy a call, and sell a put, we have created a synthetic short T-bill position and this is called a **reverse conversion**.

Synthetic options. Parity tells us that

$$C(K,T) = S_0 - \text{PV}_{0,T}(\text{Div}) - \text{PV}_{0,T}(K) + P(K,T)$$

and that

$$P(K,T) = C(K,T) - S_0 + \text{PV}_{0,T}(K) + \text{PV}_{0,T}(\text{Div})$$

The first relation says that a call is equivalent to a leveraged position on the underlying asset $[S_0 - \text{PV}_{0,T}(\text{Div}) - \text{PV}(K)]$, which is insured by the purchase of a put. The second relation says that a put is equivalent to a short position on the stock, insured by the purchase of a call.

Options on Currencies

Suppose we have options to buy euros by paying dollars. The dollar forward price for a euro is $F_{0,T} = x_0 e^{(r-r_€)T}$, where x_0 is the current exchange rate denominated as \$/€, $r_€$ is the euro-denominated interest rate, and r is the dollar-denominated interest rate. The parity relationship for options to buy one euro by paying x_0 is then

$$C(K,T) - P(K,T) = x_0 e^{-r_€ T} - K e^{-rT} \tag{4}$$

Buying a euro call and selling a euro put is equivalent to lending euros and borrowing dollars. Equation (4) tells us that the difference in the call and put premiums simply reflects the difference in the amount borrowed and loaned, in the currency of the country in which the options are denominated.

Options on Bonds

Finally, we can construct the parity relationship for options on bonds. The prepaid forward for a bond differs from the bond price due to coupon payments (which are like dividends). Thus, if the bond price is B_0, we have

$$C(K,T) = P(K,T) + [B_0 - \text{PV}_{0,T}(\text{Coupons})] - \text{PV}_{0,T}(K) \tag{5}$$

Note that for a pure-discount bond, the parity relationship is exactly like that for a non-dividend-paying stock.

Dividend Forward Contracts

Dividends play a critical role in the parity equation. In practice, there is at least some uncertainty about future dividend payments and yields. **Dividend forward contracts** and **dividend swaps** can be used to hedge or speculate on actual dividend amounts. A dividend forward contract pays $\text{FV}_{0,T}(D) - F_{0,T}$ at time T, where $F_{0,T}$ is the dividend forward price and $\text{FV}_{0,T}(D)$ is the time T value of dividends paid between time 0 and time T. It is straightforward to determine the dividend forward price, $F_{0,T}(D)$, using put-call parity. The intuition is that prices of European options reflect expected future ex-dividend stock prices, so that comparing the stock price today with option prices, we can determine the price of a claim on dividends.[2]

Suppose a stock with price S_0 pays uncertain dividends between time 0 and time T. Consider buying the stock, borrowing Ke^{-rT}, and buying a European put and selling a European call, both with strike price K expiring at time T. The payoff to this portfolio is the future value of dividends paid between time 0 and time T:[3]

$$\underbrace{S_T + \text{FV}_{0,T}(D)}_{\text{Stock plus dividends}} - \underbrace{K}_{\text{Borrowing}} + \underbrace{K - S_T}_{\text{Options}} = \text{FV}_{0,T}(D)$$

The cost of this portfolio is therefore the time 0 price of acquiring dividends paid from 0 to T, which is the prepaid forward price for a dividend contract. Thus,[4]

$$F^P_{0,T}(D) = S_0 - Ke^{-rT} + P(K, T) - C(K, T) \tag{6}$$

This implies that the dividend forward price is

$$F_{0,T}(D) = e^{rT} F^P_{0,T}(D) = e^{rT}\left[S_0 + P(K, T) - C(K, T)\right] - K \tag{7}$$

A dividend swap can be constructed from dividend forwards using the equation

$$R = \frac{\sum_{i=1}^{n} P(0, t_i) f_0(t_i)}{\sum_{i=1}^{n} P(0, t_i)}$$

2. GENERALIZED PARITY AND EXCHANGE OPTIONS

The preceding section showed how the parity relationship works for different underlying assets. Now we will generalize parity to apply to the case where the strike asset is not necessarily cash but could be any other asset. This version of parity includes all previous versions as special cases.

Suppose we have an option to exchange one asset for another. Let the underlying asset, asset A, have price S_t, and the strike asset (the asset which, at our discretion, we surrender in exchange for the underlying asset), asset B, have the price Q_t. Let $F^P_{t,T}(S)$ denote the time t price of a prepaid forward on the underlying asset, paying S_T at time T, and let $F^P_{t,T}(Q)$ denote the time t price of a prepaid forward on asset B, paying Q_T at time T. We use the notation $C(S_t, Q_t, T - t)$ to denote the time t price of an option with $T - t$ periods to expiration, which gives us the right to give up asset B in exchange for asset A.

2. Special and extraordinary dividends are typically excluded from dividend forwards and swaps. This exclusion is consistent with the common practice of adjusting option terms to protect option holders against changes in value due to extraordinary dividends.

3. In practice, dividend forwards and swaps settle annually based on actual dividends, without taking into account the interest from reinvesting dividends.

4. van Binsbergen et al. (forthcoming) study the returns on investment strategies based on equation (6). van Binsbergen et al. (2011) show that prices on dividend futures contracts are predictors of growth for Europe, the U.S., and Japan.

$P(S_t, Q_t, T-t)$ is defined similarly as the right to give up asset A in exchange for asset B. Now suppose that the call payoff at time T is

$$C(S_T, Q_T, 0) = \max(0, S_T - Q_T)$$

and the put payoff is

$$P(S_T, Q_T, 0) = \max(0, Q_T - S_T)$$

Then for European options we have this form of the parity equation:

$$\boxed{C(S_t, Q_t, T-t) - P(S_t, Q_t, T-t) = F^P_{t,T}(S) - F^P_{t,T}(Q)} \quad (8)$$

The use of prepaid forward prices in the parity relationship completely takes into account the dividend and time value of money considerations. This version of parity tells us that there is nothing special about an option having the strike amount designated as cash. In general, options can be designed to exchange any asset for any other asset, and the relative put and call premiums are determined by prices of prepaid forwards on the underlying and strike assets.

To prove equation (8) we can use a payoff table in which we buy a call, sell a put, sell a prepaid forward on A, and buy a prepaid forward on B. This transaction is illustrated in Table 2.

If the strategy in Table 2 does not pay zero at expiration, there is an arbitrage opportunity. Thus, we expect equation (8) to hold. All European options satisfy this formula, whatever the underlying asset.

TABLE 2 Payoff table demonstrating that there is an arbitrage opportunity unless $-C(S_t, Q_t, T-t) + P(S_t, Q_t, T-t) + F^P_{t,T}(S) - F^P_{t,T}(Q) = 0$.

		Expiration	
Transaction	Time 0	$S_T \le Q_T$	$S_T > Q_T$
Buy call	$-C(S_t, Q_t, T-t)$	0	$S_T - Q_T$
Sell put	$P(S_t, Q_t, T-t)$	$S_T - Q_T$	0
Sell prepaid forward on A	$F^P_{t,T}(S)$	$-S_T$	$-S_T$
Buy prepaid forward on B	$-F^P_{t,T}(Q)$	Q_T	Q_T
Total	$-C(S_t, Q_t, T-t)$ $+P(S_t, Q_t, T-t)$ $+F^P_{t,T}(S) - F^P_{t,T}(Q)$	0	0

Example 3. Suppose that non-dividend-paying stock A has a price of \$20, and non-dividend-paying stock B has a price of \$25. Because neither stock pays dividends, their prepaid forward prices equal their prices. If A is the underlying asset and B is the strike asset, then put-call parity implies that

$$\text{Call} - \text{put} = \$20 - \$25 = -\$5$$

The put is \$5 more expensive than the call for any time to expiration of the options. ■

Options to Exchange Stock

Executive stock options are sometimes constructed so that the strike price of the option is the price of an index, rather than a fixed cash amount. The idea is to have an option that pays off only when the company outperforms competitors, rather than one that pays off simply because all stock prices have gone up. As a hypothetical example of this, suppose that Microsoft executives are given compensation options that payoff only if Microsoft outperforms Google. They will exercise these options if and only if the share price of Microsoft, S_{MSFT}, exceeds the share price of Google, S_{GOOG}, i.e., $S_{\text{MSFT}} > S_{\text{GOOG}}$. From the executives' perspective, this is a call option, with the payoff

$$\max(0, S_{\text{MSFT}} - S_{\text{GOOG}})$$

Now consider the compensation option for Google executives. They receive a compensation option that pays off only if Google outperforms Microsoft, i.e.,

$$\max(0, S_{\text{GOOG}} - S_{\text{MSFT}})$$

This is a call from the Google executives' perspective.

Here is the interesting twist: The Google call looks like a Microsoft put! And the Microsoft call looks like a Google put. Either option can be viewed as a put or call; it is simply a matter of perspective. *The distinction between a put and a call in this example depends upon what we label the underlying asset and what we label as the strike asset.*

What Are Calls and Puts?

The preceding discussion suggests that labeling an option as a call or put is always a matter of convention. It is an important convention because we use it all the time in talking about options. Nevertheless, in general we can interpret calls as being puts, and vice versa. We can see why by using an analogy.

When you go to the grocery store to obtain bananas, you typically say that you are *buying* bananas. The actual transaction involves handing cash to the grocer and receiving a banana. This is an exchange of one asset (cash) for another (a banana). We could also describe the transaction by saying that we are *selling cash* (in exchange for bananas). The point is that an exchange occurs, and we can describe it either as buying the thing we receive, or selling the thing we surrender.

Any transaction is an exchange of one thing for another. Whether we say we are buying or selling is a matter of convention. This insight may not impress your grocer, but it is important for us because it suggests that the labeling we commonly use to distinguish calls and puts is a matter of convention.

To see how an ordinary call could be considered a put, consider a call option on a stock. This is the right to exchange a given number of dollars, the strike price K, for stock worth S, if the stock is worth more than the dollars. For example, suppose that if $S > K$, we earn $S - K$. We can view this as either of two transactions:

- Buying one share of stock by paying K. In this case we exercise when $S > K$. This is a call option on stock.
- Selling K dollars in exchange for one share of stock. Again we exercise when $S > K$—i.e., when the dollars we sell are worth less than the stock. This is a put option on dollars, with a share of stock as the strike asset.

Under either interpretation, if $S < K$ we do not exercise the option. If the dollars are worth more than the stock, we would not sell them for the stock.

Now consider a put option on a stock. The put option confers the right to exchange one share of stock for a given number of dollars. Suppose $S < K$; we earn $K - S$. We can view this in either of two ways:

- Selling one share of stock at the price K.
- Buying K dollars by paying one share of stock. This is a call where we have the right to give up stock to obtain dollars.

If $S > K$ we do not exercise under either interpretation. If the dollars are worth less than the stock, we would not pay the stock to obtain the dollars.

Currency Options

The idea that calls can be relabeled as puts is commonplace in currency markets. A currency transaction involves the exchange of one kind of currency for another. In this context, it is obvious to market participants that referring to a particular currency as having been bought or sold is a matter of convention, depending upon which currency a trader regards as the home currency.

To understand how a call in one currency can be a put in the other, consider how currency options are quoted by dealers. A term sheet for a currency option might specify "EUR Call USD Put, AMT: EUR 100 million, USD 120 million." The term sheet thus says explicitly that the option can be viewed either as a call on the euro or a put on the dollar. Exercise of the option will entail an exchange of €100 million for $120 million.

If we interpret the option as a call on the euro, we have the right to pay $120 million to acquire €100 million. You can think of this as 100 million calls on the euro, each with a strike of $1.20. If we interpret the option as a put on the dollar, we have the right to sell $120 million in exchange for €100 million. Because the put is on the dollar, it is natural to think of this as 120 million options on one dollar, each with a strike of $100/120 = 0.8333$ euros.

We will say that an option is "dollar-denominated" if the strike price and premium are denominated in dollars. An option is "euro-denominated" if the strike price and premium are in euros. It is often helpful to think of a dollar-denominated option as being based on one unit of the foreign currency, and a euro- (or other currency-) denominated option as based on one dollar.

We will now use a numerical example to illustrate how to convert a call in one currency into a put in the other. Suppose the current exchange rate is $x_0 = \$1.25/€$, and consider the following two options:[5]

1. A 1-year *dollar-denominated call option* on euros with a strike price of \$1.20 and premium of \$0.06545. In 1 year, the owner of the option has the right to buy €1 for \$1.20. The payoff on this option, in dollars, is therefore

$$\max(0, x_1 - 1.20)$$

2. A 1-year *euro-denominated put option* on dollars with a strike of $\frac{1}{1.20} = €0.833$. The premium of this option is €0.04363. In 1 year the owner of this put has the right to give up \$1 and receive €0.833; the owner will exercise the put when \$1 is worth less than €0.833. The euro value of \$1 in 1 year will be $1/x_1$. Hence, the payoff of this option is

$$\max\left(0, \frac{1}{1.20} - \frac{1}{x_1}\right)$$

Because $x_1 > 1.20$ exactly when $\frac{1}{1.20} > \frac{1}{x_1}$, the euro-denominated dollar put will be exercised when, and only when, the dollar-denominated euro call is exercised.

Though the two options will be exercised under the same circumstances, they differ in two respects:

- The scale of the two options is different. The dollar-denominated euro call is based on one euro, which has a current dollar value of \$1.25, and the euro-denominated dollar put is based on one dollar, which has a current euro value of €0.8333.
- The currency of denomination is different.

We can equate the scale of the two options in one of two ways. First, we can either scale up the dollar-denominated euro calls, holding 1.20 of them, or we can scale down the euro-denominated dollar puts, holding $\frac{1}{1.20}$ of them. To see the equivalence of the euro call and the dollar put, consider the following two transactions, each of which entails exchanging \$1.20 for €1 if the exchange rate is greater than \$1.20:

1. Buy one 1-year dollar-denominated euro call option with a strike of \$1.20. If we exercise, we will give up \$1.20 for €1. The cost of the option is \$0.06545.
2. Buy 1.20 1-year euro-denominated put options on dollars with a strike of €0.833. If exercised, these options entail receiving €1 and giving up \$1.20. The cost of this in dollars is $\$1.25/€ \times 1.20 \times €0.04363 = \$0.06545$.

Table 3 compares the payoffs of these two option positions. At exercise, each position results in surrendering \$1.20 for €1 if $x_1 > 1.20$. The two positions must cost the same, or else there is an arbitrage opportunity.

We can summarize this result algebraically. The price of a dollar-denominated foreign currency call with strike K, when the current exchange rate is x_0, is $C_\$(x_0, K, T)$. The price

5. These are Black-Scholes prices with a current exchange rate of \$1.25/€, a dollar-denominated interest rate of 0.005, a euro-denominated interest rate of 0.020, and exchange rate volatility of 10%.

TABLE 3 The equivalence of buying a dollar-denominated euro call and a euro-denominated dollar put. In transaction I, we buy one dollar-denominated call option, permitting us to buy €1 for a strike price of \$1.20. In transaction II, we buy 1.20 euro-denominated puts, each with a premium of €0.04363, and permitting us to sell \$1 for a strike price of €0.833.

		Year 0		Year 1			
				$x_1 < 1.20$		$x_1 \geq 1.20$	
	Transaction	\$	€	\$	€	\$	€
I:	Buy 1 euro call	−0.06545	—	0	0	−1.20	1
II:	Convert dollars to euros,	−0.06545	0.05236				
	buy 1.20 dollar puts		−0.05236	0	0	−1.20	1

of a foreign-currency–denominated dollar put with strike $\frac{1}{K}$, when the exchange rate is $\frac{1}{x_0}$, is $P_f(\frac{1}{x_0}, \frac{1}{K}, T)$. Adjusting for currency and scale differences, the prices are related by

$$C_\$(x_0, K, T) = x_0 K P_f\left(\frac{1}{x_0}, \frac{1}{K}, T\right) \tag{9}$$

This insight—that calls in one currency are the same as puts in the other—is interesting in and of itself. Its generalization to *all* options provides a fresh perspective for thinking about the difference between calls and puts.

3. COMPARING OPTIONS WITH RESPECT TO STYLE, MATURITY, AND STRIKE

We now examine how option prices change when there are changes in option characteristics, such as exercise style (American or European), the strike price, and time to expiration. Remarkably, we can say a great deal without a pricing model and without making any assumptions about the distribution of the underlying asset.[6] Thus, *whatever* the particular option model or stock price distribution used for valuing a given option, we can still expect option prices to behave in certain ways.

Here is an example of the kind of questions we will address in this section. Suppose you have three call options, with strikes of \$40, \$45, and \$50. How do the premiums on these options differ? Common sense suggests that, with a call option on any underlying asset, the premium will go down as you raise the strike price; it is less valuable to be able

6. The so-called "theory of rational option pricing," on which this section is based, was first presented in 1973 by Robert Merton in an astonishing paper (Merton, 1973b). This material is also superbly exposited in Cox and Rubinstein (1985).

to buy at a higher price.[7] Moreover, the decline in the premium cannot be greater than \$5. (The right to buy for a \$5 cheaper price cannot be worth more than \$5.)

Following this logic, the premium will drop as we increase the strike from \$40 to \$45, and drop again when we increase the strike further from \$45 to \$50. Here is a more subtle question: In which case will the premium drop more? It turns out that the decline in the premium from \$40 to \$45 *must* be greater than the decline from \$45 to \$50, or else there is an arbitrage opportunity.

In this section we will explore the following issues for stock options (some of the properties may be different for options on other underlying assets):

- How prices of otherwise identical American and European options compare.
- How option prices change as the time to expiration changes.
- How option prices change as the strike price changes.

A word of warning before we begin this discussion: You may find option price listings reporting prices that seem to permit arbitrage. This can occur if some of the reported option prices are stale, meaning that the comparison is among option prices recorded at different times of the day. Also, an apparent arbitrage opportunity only becomes genuine when bid-ask spreads (see Table 1), commissions, costs of short-selling, and market impact are taken into account.

European Versus American Options

Since an American option can be exercised at any time, it must always be at least as valuable as an otherwise identical European option. (By "otherwise identical" we mean that the two options have the same underlying asset, strike price, and time to expiration.) Any exercise strategy appropriate to a European option can always be duplicated with an American option. Thus we have

$$C_{\text{Amer}}(S, K, T) \geq C_{\text{Eur}}(S, K, T) \tag{10a}$$

$$P_{\text{Amer}}(S, K, T) \geq P_{\text{Eur}}(S, K, T) \tag{10b}$$

We will see that there are times when the right to early-exercise is worthless, and, hence, American and European options have the same value.

Maximum and Minimum Option Prices

It is often useful to understand just how expensive or inexpensive an option can be. Here are some basic limits.

Calls. The price of a European call option:

- Cannot be negative, because the call need not be exercised.
- Cannot exceed the stock price, because the best that can happen with a call is that you end up owning the stock.

7. If you are being fastidious, you will say the option premium *cannot increase* as the strike goes up. Saying that the option premium will *decrease* as the strike increases does not account for the possibility that all the premiums are zero, and hence the premium will not go down but will remain unchanged, as the strike price increases.

- Must be at least as great as the price implied by parity with a zero put value.

Combining these statements, together with the result about American options never being worth less than European options, gives us

$$\boxed{S \geq C_{\text{Amer}}(S, K, T) \geq C_{\text{Eur}}(S, K, T) \geq \max[0, \text{PV}_{0,T}(F_{0,T}) - \text{PV}_{0,T}(K)]} \quad (11)$$

where present values are taken over the life of the option.

Puts. Similarly, a put:

- Cannot be worth more than the undiscounted strike price, since that is the most it can ever be worth (if the stock price drops to zero, the put pays K at some point).
- Must be at least as great as the price implied by parity with a zero call value.

Also, an American put is worth at least as much as a European put. This gives us

$$\boxed{K \geq P_{\text{Amer}}(S, K, T) \geq P_{\text{Eur}}(S, K, T) \geq \max[0, \text{PV}(K) - \text{PV}_{0,T}]} \quad (12)$$

Early Exercise for American Options

When might we want to exercise an option prior to expiration? An important result is that an American call option on a non-dividend-paying stock should never be exercised prior to expiration. You may, however, rationally exercise an American-style put option prior to expiration.

Calls on a non-dividend-paying stock. We can demonstrate in two ways that an American-style call option on a non-dividend-paying stock should never be exercised prior to expiration. Early exercise is not optimal if the price of an American call prior to expiration satisfies

$$C_{\text{Amer}}(S_t, K, T-t) > S_t - K$$

If this inequality holds, you would lose money by early-exercising (receiving $S_t - K$) as opposed to selling the option (receiving $C_{\text{Amer}}(S_t, K, T-t) > S_t - K$).

We will use put-call parity to demonstrate that early exercise is not rational. If the option expires at T, parity implies that

$$\begin{aligned} C_{\text{Eur}}(S_t, K, T-t) &= \underbrace{S_t - K}_{\text{Exercise value}} + \underbrace{P_{\text{Eur}}(S_t, K, T-t)}_{\text{Insurance against } S_T < K} \\ &\quad + \underbrace{K(1 - e^{-r(T-t)})}_{\text{Time value of money on } K} > S_t - K \end{aligned} \quad (13)$$

Since the put price, $P_{\text{Eur}}(S_t, K, T-t)$, and the time value of money on the strike, $K(1 - e^{-r(T-t)})$, are both positive, this equation establishes that the European call option premium on a non-dividend paying stock always is at least as great as $S_t - K$. From equation (10a), we also know that $C_{\text{Amer}} \geq C_{\text{Eur}}$. Thus we have

$$C_{\text{Amer}} \geq C_{\text{Eur}} > S_t - K$$

Since C_{Amer}, the American option premium, always exceeds $S - K$, we would lose money exercising an American call prior to expiration, as opposed to selling the option.

Equation (13) is useful because it shows us precisely *why* we would never early-exercise. Early-exercising has two effects. First, we throw away the implicit put protection should the stock later move below the strike price. Second, we accelerate the payment of the strike price.

A third effect is the possible loss from deferring receipt of the stock. However, when there are no dividends, we lose nothing by waiting to take physical possession of the stock.

We have demonstrated that if a stock pays no dividends, you should never see an option selling for less than $S_t - K$. In fact, equation (13), like equation (11), actually implies the stronger result that you should never see a call on a non-dividend-paying stock sell for less than $S_t - Ke^{-r(T-t)}$. What happens if you do observe an option selling for too low a price? If $C < S_t - K$ and the option is American, you can buy the option, exercise it, and earn $S_t - K - C_{\text{Amer}}(S_t, K, T-t) > 0$. If the option is European and cannot be exercised early, the arbitrage is: Buy the option, short the stock, and lend the present value of the strike price. Table 4 demonstrates the arbitrage in this case. The sources of profit from the arbitrage are the same as those identified in equation (13).

It is important to realize that this proposition does *not* say that you must hold the option until expiration. It says that if you no longer wish to hold the call, you should sell it rather than early-exercising it.[8]

Exercising calls just prior to a dividend. If the stock pays dividends, the parity relationship is

$$C(S_t, K, T-t) = P(S_t, K, T-t) + S_t - \text{PV}_{t,T}(\text{Div}) - \text{PV}_{t,T}(K)$$

Using this expression, we cannot always rule out early exercise as we did above. Early exercise is not optimal at any time where

$$K - \text{PV}_{t,T}(K) > \text{PV}_{t,T}(\text{Div}) \tag{14}$$

That is, if interest on the strike price (which induces us to delay exercise) exceeds the present value of dividends (which induces us to exercise), then we will for certain never early-exercise at that time. If inequality (14) is violated, this does not tell us that we *will* exercise, only that we cannot rule it out.

If dividends are sufficiently great, however, early exercise can be optimal. To take an extreme example, consider a 90-strike American call on a stock selling for \$100, which is about to pay a dividend of \$99.99. If we exercise—paying \$90 to acquire the \$100 stock—we have a net position worth \$10. If we delay past the ex-dividend date, the option is worthless.

If dividends do make early exercise rational, it will be optimal to exercise at the last moment before the ex-dividend date. By exercising earlier than that, we pay the strike price prematurely and thus at a minimum lose interest on the strike price.

Early exercise for puts. It can be optimal to early-exercise a put. To see this, suppose a company is bankrupt and the stock price falls to zero. Then a put not exercised until expiration will be worth $\text{PV}_{t,T}(K)$. If we could early-exercise, we would receive K. If the

8. Some options, such as compensation options, cannot be sold. In practice it is common to see executives exercise options prior to expiration and then sell the stock. The discussion in this section demonstrates that such exercise would be irrational if the option could be sold or if the stock could be sold short.

TABLE 4 Demonstration of arbitrage if a call option with price C sells for less than $S_t - Ke^{-r(T-t)}$ and the stock pays no dividends. Every entry in the row labeled "Total" is nonnegative.

		Expiration or Exercise, Time T	
Transaction	Time t	$S_T < K$	$S_T > K$
Buy call	$-C$	0	$S_T - K$
Short stock	S_t	$-S_T$	$-S_T$
Lend $Ke^{-r(T-t)}$	$-Ke^{-r(T-t)}$	K	K
Total	$S_t - Ke^{-r(T-t)} - C$	$K - S_T$	0

interest rate is positive, $K > \text{PV}(K)$. Therefore, early exercise would be optimal in order to receive the strike price earlier.

We can also use a parity argument to understand this. The put will never be exercised as long as $P > K - S$. Supposing that the stock pays no dividends, parity for the put is

$$P(S_t, K, T-t) = C(S_t, K, T-t) - S_t + \text{PV}_{t,T}(K)$$

The no-exercise condition, $P > K - S$, then implies

$$C(S_t, K, T-t) - S_t + \text{PV}_{t,T}(K) > K - S_t$$

or

$$C(S_t, K, T-t) > K - \text{PV}_{t,T}(K)$$

If the call is sufficiently valueless (as in the above example of a bankrupt company), parity cannot rule out early exercise. This does not mean that we *will* early-exercise; it simply means that we cannot rule it out.

Early exercise in general. We can summarize this discussion of early exercise. When we exercise an option, we receive something (the stock with a call, the strike price with a put). A necessary condition for early exercise is that we prefer to receive this something sooner rather than later. For calls, dividends on the stock are a reason to want to receive the stock earlier. For puts, interest on the strike is a reason to want to receive the strike price earlier. Thus, dividends and interest play similar roles in the two analyses of early exercise. In fact, if we view interest as the dividend on cash, then dividends (broadly defined) become the sole reason to early-exercise an option.

Similarly, dividends on the strike asset become a reason not to early-exercise. In the case of calls, interest is the dividend on the strike asset, and in the case of puts, dividends on the stock are the dividend on the strike asset.

The point of this section has been to make some general statements about when early exercise will not occur, or under what conditions it *might* occur. Early exercise is a trade-off involving time value of money on the strike price, dividends on the underlying asset, and the value of insurance on the position. In general, figuring out when to exercise requires an option pricing model.

Time to Expiration

How does an option price change as we increase time to expiration? If the options are American, the option price can never decline with an increase in time to expiration. If the options are European, the price can go either up or down as we increase time to expiration.

American options. An American call with more time to expiration is at least as valuable as an otherwise identical call with less time to expiration. An American call with 2 years to expiration, for example, can always be turned into an American option with 1 year to expiration by voluntarily exercising it after 1 year. Therefore, the 2-year call is at least as valuable as the 1-year call. For the same reason, a longer-lived American put is always worth at least as much as an otherwise equivalent European put.

European options. A European call on a non-dividend-paying stock will be at least as valuable as an otherwise identical call with a shorter time to expiration. This occurs because, with no dividends, a European call has the same price as an otherwise identical American call. With dividends, however, longer-lived European calls may be less valuable than shorter-lived European calls.

To see this, imagine a stock that will pay a liquidating dividend 2 weeks from today.[9] A European call with 1 week to expiration will have value because it is exercisable prior to the dividend. A European call with 3 weeks to expiration will have no value because the stock will have no value at expiration. This is an example of a longer-lived option being less valuable than a shorter-lived option. Note that if the options were American, we would simply exercise the 3-week option prior to the dividend.

Longer-lived European puts can also be less valuable than shorter-lived European puts. A good example of this is a bankrupt company. The put will be worth the present value of the strike price, with present value calculated until time to expiration. Longer-lived puts will be worth less than shorter-lived puts. If the options were American, they would all be exercised immediately and hence would be worth the strike price.

European options when the strike price grows over time. In discussing the effect of changing time to maturity, we have been keeping the option strike price fixed. The present value of the strike price therefore decreases with time to maturity. Suppose, however, that we keep the present value of the strike constant by setting $K_t = Ke^{rt}$. When the strike grows at the interest rate, the premiums on European calls and puts on a non-dividend-paying stock increase with time to maturity.[10] We will demonstrate this for puts; the demonstration is identical for calls.

To keep the notation simple, let $P(t)$ denote the time 0 price of a European put maturing at time t, with strike price $K_t = Ke^{rt}$. We want to show that $P(T) > P(t)$ if $T > t$. To show this, we will demonstrate an arbitrage if $P(T) \leq P(t)$.

9. A liquidating dividend occurs when a firm pays its entire value to shareholders. A firm is worthless after paying a liquidating dividend.

10. Dividends can easily be accommodated in the following way. Suppose that all dividends are reinvested in the stock. Call the resulting position a *total return portfolio* and let S_t be the price of this portfolio. Define the options so that the total return portfolio is the underlying asset. The result in this section then obtains for the total return portfolio. The reason is that the total return portfolio is a synthetic non-dividend-paying stock. If the underlying asset does pay dividends, however, then the price of a European call can decrease with time to maturity.

TABLE 5 Demonstration that there is an arbitrage if $P(T) \leq P(t)$ with $t < T$. The strike on the put with maturity t is $K_t = Ke^{rt}$, and the strike on the put with maturity T is $K_T = Ke^{rt}$. If the option expiring at time t is in-the-money, the payoff, $S_t - K_t$, is reinvested until time T. If $P(t) \geq P(T)$, all cash flows in the "total" line are nonnegative.

		Payoff at Time T			
		$S_T < K_T$		$S_T > K_T$	
		Payoff at Time t			
Transaction	Time 0	$S_t < K_t$	$S_t > K_t$	$S_t < K_t$	$S_t > K_t$
Sell $P(t)$	$P(t)$	$S_T - K_T$	0	$S_T - K_T$	0
Buy $P(T)$	$-P(T)$	$K_T - S_T$	$K_T - S_T$	0	0
Total	$P(t) - P(T)$	0	$K_T - S_T$	$S_T - K_T$	0

If the longer-lived put is not more expensive—i.e., if $P(T) \leq P(t)$—buy the put with T years to expiration and sell the put with t years to expiration. At time t the written put will expire. If $S_t > K_t$ its value is zero and we can ignore the shorter-lived option from this point on. If $S_t < K_t$, the put holder will exercise the short-lived option and our payoff is $S_t - K_t$. Suppose that we keep the stock we receive and borrow to finance the strike price, holding this position until the second option expires at time T. Here is the important step: Notice that the time-T value of this time-t payoff is $S_T - K_t e^{r(T-t)} = S_T - K_T$.

Table 5 summarizes the resulting payoffs. By buying the long-lived put and selling the short-lived put, we are guaranteed not to lose money at time T. Therefore, if $P(t) \geq P(T)$ there is an arbitrage opportunity. A practical application of this result is discussed in Box 1.

Different Strike Prices

We discussed at the beginning of this section some statements we can make about how option prices vary with the strike price. Here is a more formal statement of these propositions. Suppose we have three strike prices, $K_1 < K_2 < K_3$, with corresponding call option prices $C(K_1)$, $C(K_2)$, and $C(K_3)$ and put option prices $P(K_1)$, $P(K_2)$, and $P(K_3)$. Here are the propositions we discuss in this section:

1. A call with a low strike price is at least as valuable as an otherwise identical call with a higher strike price:

$$\boxed{C(K_1) \geq C(K_2)} \tag{15}$$

A put with a high strike price is at least as valuable as an otherwise identical put with a low strike price:

$$\boxed{P(K_2) \geq P(K_1)} \tag{16}$$

BOX 1: Portfolio Insurance for the Long Run

Historically, the rate of return from investing in stocks over a long horizon has outperformed that from investing in government bonds in the United States (see, for example, Siegel, 1998). This observation has led some to suggest that if held for a sufficiently long period of time, stocks are a safe investment relative to risk-free bonds.

Bodie (1995) suggests using put option premiums to think about the claim that stocks are safe in the long run. Specifically, what would it cost to buy a put option insuring that after T years your stock portfolio would be worth at least as much as if you had instead invested in a zero-coupon bond? If your initial investment was S_0, you could provide this insurance by setting the strike price on the put option equal to $K_T = S_0 e^{rT}$.

Bodie uses the Black-Scholes model to show that the premium on this insurance increases with T. As Bodie notes, however, this proposition must be true for any valid option pricing model. The payoffs in Table 5 demonstrate that the cost of this insurance *must* increase with T or else there is an arbitrage opportunity. Whatever the historical return statistics appear to say, the cost of portfolio insurance is increasing with the length of time for which you insure the portfolio return. Using the cost of insurance as a measure, stocks are riskier in the long run.

2. The premium difference between otherwise identical calls with different strike prices cannot be greater than the difference in strike prices:

$$\boxed{C(K_1) - C(K_2) \leq K_2 - K_1} \tag{17}$$

The premium difference for otherwise identical puts also cannot be greater than the difference in strike prices:

$$\boxed{P(K_2) - P(K_1) \leq K_2 - K_1} \tag{18}$$

3. Premiums decline at a decreasing rate as we consider calls with progressively higher strike prices. The same is true for puts as strike prices decline. This is called **convexity** of the option price with respect to the strike price:

$$\boxed{\frac{C(K_1) - C(K_2)}{K_2 - K_1} \geq \frac{C(K_2) - C(K_3)}{K_3 - K_2}} \tag{19}$$

$$\boxed{\frac{P(K_2) - P(K_1)}{K_2 - K_1} \leq \frac{P(K_3) - P(K_2)}{K_3 - K_2}} \tag{20}$$

These statements are all true for both European and American options.[11] Algebraic demonstrations are in Appendix B. It turns out, however, that these three propositions are

11. In fact, if the options are European, the second statement can be strengthened: The difference in option premiums must be less than the *present value* of the difference in strikes.

equivalent to saying that there are no free lunches: If you enter into an option spread, there must be stock prices at which you would lose money on the spread net of your original investment. Otherwise, the spread represents an arbitrage opportunity. These three propositions say that you cannot have a bull spread, a bear spread, or a butterfly spread for which you can never lose money. Specifically:

1. If inequality (15) were not true, buy the low-strike call and sell the high-strike call (this is a call bull spread). If inequality (16) were not true, buy the high-strike put and sell the low-strike put (a put bear spread).
2. If inequality (17) were not true, sell the low-strike call and buy the high-strike call (a call bear spread). If inequality (18) were not true, buy the low-strike put and sell the high-strike put (a put bull spread).
3. If either of inequalities (19) or (20) were not true, there is an asymmetric butterfly spread with positive profits at all prices.

We will illustrate these propositions with numerical examples.

Example 4. Suppose we observe the call premiums in Panel A of Table 6. These values violate the second property for calls, since the difference in strikes is 5 and the difference in the premiums is 6. If we observed these values, we could engage in arbitrage by buying the 55-strike call and selling the 50-strike call, which is a bear spread. Note that we receive \$6 initially and never have to pay more than \$5 in the future. This is an arbitrage, whatever the interest rate. ■

Now consider the third proposition, *strike price convexity*. There is a different way to write the convexity inequality, equation (19). Since K_2 is between K_1 and K_3, we can write

TABLE 6 Panel A shows call option premiums for which the change in the option premium (\$6) exceeds the change in the strike price (\$5). Panel B shows how a bear spread can be used to arbitrage these prices. By lending the bear spread proceeds, we have a zero cash flow at time 0; the cash outflow at time T is always greater than \$1.

Panel A

Strike	50	55
Premium	18	12

Panel B

		Expiration or Exercise		
Transaction	Time 0	$S_T < 50$	$50 \le S_T \le 55$	$S_T \ge 55$
Buy 55-strike call	−12	0	0	$S_T - 55$
Sell 50-strike call	18	0	$50 - S_T$	$50 - S_T$
Total	6	0	$50 - S_T$	−5

it as a weighted average of the other two strikes, i.e.,

$$K_2 = \lambda K_1 + (1-\lambda)K_3$$

where

$$\lambda = \frac{K_3 - K_2}{K_3 - K_1} \tag{21}$$

With this expression for λ, it is possible to rewrite equation (19) as

$$C(K_2) \leq \lambda C(K_1) + (1-\lambda)C(K_3) \tag{22}$$

Here is an example illustrating convexity.

Example 5. If $K_1 = 50$, $K_2 = 59$, and $K_3 = 65$, $\lambda = \frac{65-59}{65-50} = 0.4$; hence,

$$59 = 0.4 \times 50 + 0.6 \times 65$$

Call prices must then satisfy

$$C(59) \leq 0.4 \times C(50) + 0.6 \times C(65)$$

Suppose we observe the call premiums in Table 7. The change in the option premium per dollar of strike price change from 50 to 59 is $5.1/9 = 0.567$, and the change from 59 to 65 is $3.9/6 = 0.65$. Thus, prices violate the proposition that the premium decreases at a decreasing rate as the strike price increases.

To arbitrage this mispricing, we engage in an asymmetric butterfly spread: Buy four 50-strike calls, buy six 65-strike calls, and sell ten 59-strike calls.[12] By engaging in a butterfly spread, Panel B shows that a profit of at least \$3 is earned. ■

The formula for λ may look imposing, but there is an easy way to figure out what λ is in any situation. In this example, we had the prices 50, 59, and 65. It is possible to express 59 as a weighted average of 50 and 65. The total distance between 50 and 65 is 15, and the distance from 50 to 59 is 9, which is $9/15 = 0.6$ of the total distance. Thus, we can write 59 as

$$59 = (1 - 0.6) \times 50 + 0.6 \times 65$$

This is the interpretation of λ in expression (22).

Here is an example of convexity with puts.

Example 6. See the prices in Panel A of Table 8. We have $K_1 = 50$, $K_2 = 55$, and $K_3 = 70$. $\lambda = 0.75$ and $55 = 0.75 \times 50 + (1 - 0.75) \times 70$. Convexity is violated since

$$P(55) = 8 > 0.75 \times 4 + (1 - 0.75) \times 16 = 7$$

12. Note that we get exactly the same arbitrage with any number of calls as long as the ratio at the various strikes remains the same. We could also have bought 0.4 50-strike calls, sold one 59-strike call, and bought 0.6 65-strike calls.

TABLE 7 The example in Panel A violates the proposition that the rate of change of the option premium must decrease as the strike price rises. The rate of change from 50 to 59 is 5.1/9, while the rate of change from 59 to 65 is 3.9/6. We can arbitrage this convexity violation with an asymmetric butterfly spread. Panel B shows that we earn at least \$3 plus interest at time T.

Panel A

Strike	50	59	65
Call premium	14	8.9	5

Panel B

		Expiration or Exercise			
Transaction	Time 0	$S_T < 50$	$50 \le S_T \le 59$	$59 \le S_T \le 65$	$S_T > 65$
Buy four 50-strike calls	−56	0	$4(S_T - 50)$	$4(S_T - 50)$	$4(S_T - 50)$
Sell ten 59-strike calls	89	0	0	$10(59 - S_T)$	$10(59 - S_T)$
Buy six 65-strike calls	−30	0	0	0	$6(S_T - 65)$
Lend \$3	−3	$3e^{rT}$	$3e^{rT}$	$3e^{rT}$	$3e^{rT}$
Total	0	$3e^{rT}$	$3e^{rT} + 4(S_T - 50)$	$3e^{rT} + 6(65 - S_T)$	$3e^{rT}$

TABLE 8 Arbitrage of mispriced puts using asymmetric butterfly spread.

Panel A

Strike	50	55	70
Put premium	4	8	16

Panel B

		Expiration or Exercise			
Transaction	Time 0	$S_T < 50$	$50 \le S_T \le 55$	$55 \le S_T \le 70$	$S_T > 70$
Buy three 50-strike puts	−12	$3(50 - S_T)$	0	0	0
Sell four 55-strike puts	32	$4(S_T - 55)$	$4(S_T - 55)$	0	0
Buy one 70-strike put	−16	$70 - S_T$	$70 - S_T$	$(70 - S_T)$	0
Lend \$4	−4	$4e^{rT}$	$4e^{rT}$	$4e^{rT}$	$4e^{rT}$
Total	0	$4e^{rT}$	$4e^{rT} + 3(S_T - 50)$	$4e^{rT} + 70 - S_T$	$4e^{rT}$

To arbitrage this mispricing, we engage in an asymmetric butterfly spread: Buy three 50-strike puts, buy one 70-strike put, and sell four 55-strike puts. The result is in Panel B of Table 8. ■

In this case, we always make at least 4. Figure 2 illustrates the necessary shape of curves for both calls and puts relating the option premium to the strike price.

FIGURE 2

Illustration of convexity and other strike price properties for calls and puts. For calls the premium is decreasing in the strike, with a slope less than 1 in absolute value. For puts the premium is increasing in the strike, with a slope less than 1. For both, the graph is convex, i.e., shaped like the cross section of a bowl.

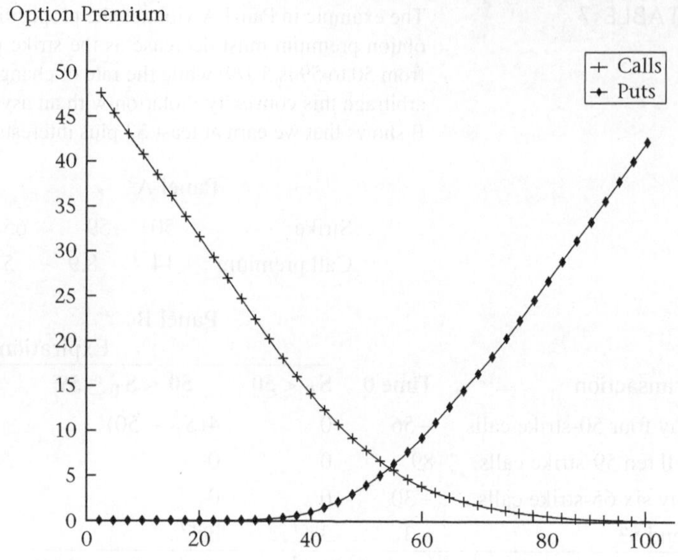

Exercise and Moneyness

If it is optimal to exercise an option, it is also optimal to exercise an otherwise identical option that is more in-the-money. Consider what would have to happen in order for this *not* to be true.

Suppose a call option on a dividend-paying stock has a strike price of \$50, and the stock price is \$70. Also suppose that it is optimal to exercise the option. This means that the option must sell for \$70 − \$50 = \$20.

Now what can we say about the premium of a 40-strike option? We know from the discussion above that the change in the premium is no more than the change in the strike price, or else there is an arbitrage opportunity. This means that

$$C\,(40) \leq \$20 + (\$50 - \$40) = \$30$$

Since the 40-strike call is worth \$30 if exercised, it must be optimal to exercise it.

Following the same logic, this is also true for puts.

CHAPTER SUMMARY

Put-call parity is one of the most important relations in option pricing. Parity is the observation that buying a European call and selling a European put with the same strike price and time to expiration is equivalent to making a leveraged investment in the underlying asset, less the value of cash payments to the underlying asset over the life of the option. Different versions of parity for different underlying assets appear in Table 9. In every case the value

TABLE 9 Versions of put-call parity. Notation in the table includes the spot currency exchange rate, x_0; the risk-free interest rate in the foreign currency, r_f; and the current bond price, B_0.

Underlying Asset	Parity Relationship
Futures contract	$e^{-rT}F_{0,T} = C(K,T) - P(K,T) + e^{-rT}K$
Stock, no-dividend	$S_0 = C(K,T) - P(K,T) + e^{-rT}K$
Stock, discrete dividend	$S_0 - \text{PV}_{0,T}(\text{Div}) = C(K,T) - P(K,T) + e^{-rT}K$
Stock, continuous dividend	$e^{-\delta T}S_0 = C(K,T) - P(K,T) + e^{-rT}K$
Currency	$e^{-r_f T}x_0 = C(K,T) - P(K,T) + e^{-rT}K$
Bond	$B_0 - \text{PV}_{0,T}(\text{Coupons}) = C(K,T) - P(K,T) + e^{-rT}K$

on the left-hand side of the parity equation is the price of the underlying asset less its cash flows over the life of the option. The parity relationship can be algebraically rearranged so that options and the underlying asset create a synthetic bond, options and a bond create a synthetic stock, and one kind of option together with the stock and bond synthetically create the other kind of option.

The idea of an option can be generalized to permit an asset other than cash to be the strike asset. This insight blurs the distinction between a put and a call. The idea that puts and calls are different ways of looking at the same contract is commonplace in currency markets.

Option prices must obey certain restrictions when we vary the strike price, time to maturity, or option exercise style. American options are at least as valuable as European options. American calls and puts become more expensive as time to expiration increases, but European options need not. European options on a non-dividend-paying stock do become more expensive with increasing time to maturity if the strike price grows at the interest rate. Dividends are the reason to exercise an American call early, while interest is the reason to exercise an American put early. A call option on a non-dividend-paying stock will always have a price greater than its value if exercised; hence, it should never be exercised early.

There are a number of pricing relationships related to changing strike prices. In particular, as the strike price increases, calls become less expensive with their price decreasing at a decreasing rate. The absolute value of the change in the call price is less than the change in the strike price. As the strike price decreases, puts become less expensive with their price decreasing at a decreasing rate. The change in the put price is less than the change in the strike price.

FURTHER READING

Much of the material in this chapter can be traced to Merton (1973b), which contains an exhaustive treatment of option properties that must hold if there is to be no arbitrage. Cox and Rubinstein (1985) also provides an excellent treatment of this material.

PROBLEMS

1. A stock currently sells for \$32.00. A 6-month call option with a strike of \$35.00 has a premium of \$2.27. Assuming a 4% continuously compounded risk-free rate and a 6% continuous dividend yield, what is the price of the associated put option?

2. A stock currently sells for \$32.00. A 6-month call option with a strike of \$30.00 has a premium of \$4.29, and a 6-month put with the same strike has a premium of \$2.64. Assume a 4% continuously compounded risk-free rate. What is the present value of dividends payable over the next 6 months?

3. Suppose the S&R index is 800, the continuously compounded risk-free rate is 5%, and the dividend yield is 0%. A 1-year 815-strike European call costs \$75 and a 1-year 815-strike European put costs \$45. Consider the strategy of buying the stock, selling the 815-strike call, and buying the 815-strike put.

   a. What is the rate of return on this position held until the expiration of the options?

   b. What is the arbitrage implied by your answer to (a)?

   c. What difference between the call and put prices would eliminate arbitrage?

   d. What difference between the call and put prices eliminates arbitrage for strike prices of \$780, \$800, \$820, and \$840?

4. Suppose the exchange rate is 0.95 \$/€, the euro-denominated continuously compounded interest rate is 4%, the dollar-denominated continuously compounded interest rate is 6%, and the price of a 1-year 0.93-strike European call on the euro is \$0.0571. What is the price of a 0.93-strike European put?

5. The premium of a 100-strike yen-denominated put on the euro is ¥8.763. The current exchange rate is 95 ¥/€. What is the strike of the corresponding euro-denominated yen call, and what is its premium?

6. The price of a 6-month dollar-denominated call option on the euro with a \$0.90 strike is \$0.0404. The price of an otherwise equivalent put option is \$0.0141. The annual continuously compounded dollar interest rate is 5%.

   a. What is the 6-month dollar-euro forward price?

   b. If the euro-denominated annual continuously compounded interest rate is 3.5%, what is the spot exchange rate?

7. Suppose the dollar-denominated interest rate is 5%, the yen-denominated interest rate is 1% (both rates are continuously compounded), the spot exchange rate is 0.009 \$/¥, and the price of a dollar-denominated European call to buy one yen with 1 year to expiration and a strike price of \$0.009 is \$0.0006.

   a. What is the dollar-denominated European yen put price such that there is no arbitrage opportunity?

   b. Suppose that a dollar-denominated European yen put with a strike of \$0.009 has a premium of \$0.0004. Demonstrate the arbitrage.

   c. Now suppose that you are in Tokyo, trading options that are denominated in yen rather than dollars. If the price of a dollar-denominated at-the-money yen call in the United States is \$0.0006, what is the price of a yen-denominated at-the-money dollar call—an option giving the right to buy one dollar, denominated in yen—in Tokyo? What is the relationship of this answer to your answer to (a)? What is the price of the at-the-money dollar put?

8. Suppose call and put prices are given by

Strike	50	55
Call premium	9	10
Put premium	7	6

What no-arbitrage property is violated? What spread position would you use to effect arbitrage? Demonstrate that the spread position is an arbitrage.

9. Suppose call and put prices are given by

Strike	50	55
Call premium	16	10
Put premium	7	14

What no-arbitrage property is violated? What spread position would you use to effect arbitrage? Demonstrate that the spread position is an arbitrage.

10. Suppose call and put prices are given by

Strike	50	55	60
Call premium	18	14	9.50
Put premium	7	10.75	14.45

Find the convexity violations. What spread would you use to effect arbitrage? Demonstrate that the spread position is an arbitrage.

11. Suppose call and put prices are given by

Strike	80	100	105
Call premium	22	9	5
Put premium	4	21	24.80

Find the convexity violations. What spread would you use to effect arbitrage? Demonstrate that the spread position is an arbitrage.

12. In each case identify the arbitrage and demonstrate how you would make money by creating a table showing your payoff.

a. Consider two European options on the same stock with the same time to expiration. The 90-strike call costs \$10 and the 95-strike call costs \$4.

b. Now suppose these options have 2 years to expiration and the continuously compounded interest rate is 10%. The 90-strike call costs \$10 and the 95-strike call costs \$5.25. Show again that there is an arbitrage opportunity. (*Hint:* It is important in this case that the options are European.)

c. Suppose that a 90-strike European call sells for \$15, a 100-strike call sells for \$10, and a 105-strike call sells for \$6. Show how you could use an asymmetric butterfly to profit from this arbitrage opportunity.

13. Suppose the interest rate is 0% and the stock of XYZ has a positive dividend yield. Is there any circumstance in which you would early-exercise an American XYZ call? Is there any circumstance in which you would early-exercise an American XYZ put? Explain.

14. In the following, suppose that neither stock pays a dividend.

a. Suppose you have a call option that permits you to receive one share of Apple by giving up one share of AOL. In what circumstance might you early-exercise this call?

b. Suppose you have a put option that permits you to give up one share of Apple, receiving one share of AOL. In what circumstance might you early-exercise this put? Would there be a loss from not early-exercising if Apple had a zero stock price?

c. Now suppose that Apple is expected to pay a dividend. Which of the above answers will change? Why?

15. The price of a non-dividend-paying stock is \$100 and the continuously compounded risk-free rate is 5%. A 1-year European call option with a strike price of $\$100 \times e^{0.05\times 1} = \$105.127$ has a premium of \$11.924. A $1\frac{1}{2}$ year European call option with a strike price of $\$100 \times e^{0.05\times 1.5} = \$107.788$ has a premium of \$11.50. Demonstrate an arbitrage.

16. Suppose that to buy either a call or a put option you pay the quoted ask price, denoted $C_a(K, T)$ and $P_a(K, T)$, and to sell an option you receive the bid, $C_b(K, T)$ and $P_b(K, T)$. Similarly, the ask and bid prices for the stock are S_a and S_b. Finally, suppose you can borrow at the rate r_H and lend at the rate r_L. The stock pays no dividend. Find the bounds between which you cannot profitably perform a parity arbitrage.

17. In this problem we consider whether parity is violated by any of the option prices in Table 1. Suppose that you buy at the ask and sell at the bid, and that your continuously compounded lending rate is 0.3% and your borrowing rate is 0.4%. Ignore transaction costs on the stock, for which the price is \$168.89. Assume that IBM is expected to pay a \$0.75 dividend on August 8, 2011. Options expire on the third Friday of the expiration month. For each strike and expiration, what is the cost if you:

a. Buy the call, sell the put, short the stock, and lend the present value of the strike price plus dividend (where appropriate)?

b. Sell the call, buy the put, buy the stock, and borrow the present value of the strike price plus dividend (where appropriate)?

18. Consider the June 165, 170, and 175 call option prices in Table 1.

a. Does convexity hold if you buy a butterfly spread, buying at the ask price and selling at the bid?

b. Does convexity hold if you sell a butterfly spread, buying at the ask price and selling at the bid?

c. Does convexity hold if you are a market-maker either buying or selling a butterfly, paying the bid and receiving the ask?

Appendix A PARITY BOUNDS FOR AMERICAN OPTIONS

The exact parity relationship discussed in the chapter only holds for European options. However, American options often come close to obeying put-call parity, especially when options have short times to expiration.

With a non-dividend-paying stock, the call will not be exercised early, but the put might be. The effect of early exercise for the put is to accelerate the receipt of the strike price. Since interest on the strike price is small for short times to maturity, parity will come close to holding for short-lived American options on non-dividend-paying stocks.

We now let P and C refer to prices of American options. The American put can be more valuable than the European put, and we have

$$P \geq C + \text{PV}(K) - S$$

However, suppose that the put were exercised early. Then it would be worth $K - S$. For example, if we think of synthetically creating the stock by buying the call and selling the put, there is a chance that we will pay K before expiration, in the event the stock price plummets and the put is early-exercised. Consequently, if we replace the present value of the strike with the undiscounted strike, we have a valid upper bound for the value of the put. It will be true (and you can verify with a no-arbitrage argument) that

$$P \leq C + K - S$$

When there are no dividends, we have $C + K - S$ as an upper bound on the put, and European parity as a lower bound (since an American put is always worth at least as much as a European put). The parity relationship can be written as a restriction on the put price or on the call price:

$$C + K - S \geq P \geq C + \text{PV}(K) - S$$
$$P + S - \text{PV}(K) \geq C \geq P + S - K$$

Thus, when there are no dividends, European parity can be violated to the extent of interest on the strike price. Since this will be small for options that are not long-lived, European parity can remain a good approximation for American options.

Dividends add the complication that the call as well as the put may be exercised early. There exists the possibility of a large parity violation because of the following "whipsaw" scenario: The call is exercised early to capture a large dividend payment, the stock price drops, and the put is then exercised early to capture interest on the strike price. The possibility that this can happen leads to a wider no-arbitrage band. With dividends, the parity relationship becomes (Cox and Rubinstein, 1985, p. 152)

$$C + K + \text{PV}(D) - S \geq P \geq C + \text{PV}(K) - S$$
$$P + S - \text{PV}(K) \geq C \geq P + S - \text{PV}(D) - K$$

The upper bound for the call is the same as in European parity, except without dividends. The intuition for the upper bound on the call option (the left-hand side) is that we can avoid the loss of dividends by early-exercising the call; hence, it is the same bound as in the European case with no dividends. The lower bound exists because it may not be optimal to exercise the call to avoid dividends, and it may be optimal to early-exercise the put.

Consider the worst case for the call. Suppose $K = \$100$ and $S = \$100$, and the stock is about to pay a liquidating dividend (i.e., $D = \$100$). We will not exercise the call, since doing so gives us nothing. The put will be exercised after the dividend is paid, once the stock is worthless. So $P = \$100$. The relationship then states

$$C \geq P + S - D - K = 100 + 100 - 100 - 100 = 0$$

And indeed, the call will be worthless in this case.

Appendix B ALGEBRAIC PROOFS OF STRIKE-PRICE RELATIONS

Appendix available at http://www.pearsonhighered.com/mcdonald.

Binomial Option Pricing: Basic Concepts

In this chapter we discuss the binomial option pricing model, with which we can compute the price of an option, given the characteristics of the stock or other underlying asset.

The binomial option pricing model assumes that, over a period of time, the price of the underlying asset can move up or down only by a specified amount—that is, the asset price follows a binomial distribution. Given this assumption, it is possible to determine a no-arbitrage price for the option. Surprisingly, this approach, which appears at first glance to be overly simplistic, can be used to price options, and it conveys much of the intuition underlying more complex (and seemingly more realistic) option pricing models. It is hard to overstate the value of thoroughly understanding the binomial approach to pricing options.

Because of its usefulness, we devote this chapter to binomial option pricing. In this chapter, we will see how the binomial model works and use it to price both European and American call and put options on stocks, currencies, and futures contracts. As part of the pricing analysis, we will also see how market-makers can create options synthetically using the underlying asset and risk-free bonds.

1. A ONE-PERIOD BINOMIAL TREE

Binomial pricing achieves its simplicity by making a very strong assumption about the stock price: At any point in time, the stock price can change to either an up value or a down value. In-between, greater or lesser values are not permitted. The restriction to two possible prices is why the method is called "binomial." The appeal of binomial pricing is that it displays the logic of option pricing in a simple setting, using only algebra to price options.

The binomial approach to pricing was first used by Sharpe (1978) as an intuitive way to explain option pricing. Binomial pricing was developed more formally by Cox et al. (1979) and Rendleman and Bartter (1979), who showed how to implement the model, demonstrated the link between the binomial model and the Black-Scholes model, and showed that the method provides a tractable way to price options for which early exercise may be optimal. The binomial model is often referred to as the "Cox-Ross-Rubinstein pricing model."

From Chapter 10 of *Derivatives Markets*, Third Edition, Robert McDonald. Copyright © 2013 by Pearson Education, Inc. Published by Pearson Prentice Hall. All rights reserved.

FIGURE 1

Binomial tree depicting the movement of XYZ stock over 1 year. The current stock price is $41.

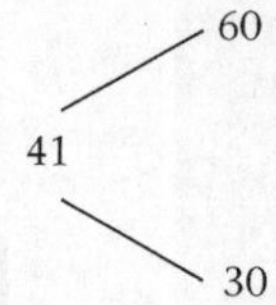

We begin with a simple example. Consider a European call option on the stock of XYZ, with a $40 strike and 1 year to expiration. XYZ does not pay dividends and its current price is $41. The continuously compounded risk-free interest rate is 8%. We wish to determine the option price.

Since the stock's return over the next year is uncertain, the option could expire either in-the-money or out-of-the-money, depending upon whether the stock price is more or less than $40. Intuitively, the valuation for the option should take into account both possibilities and assign values in each case. If the option expires out-of-the-money, its value is zero. If the option expires in-the-money, its value will depend upon how far in-the-money it is. To price the option, then, we need to characterize the uncertainty about the stock price at expiration.

Figure 1 represents the evolution of the stock price: Today the price is $41, and in 1 year the price can be either $60 or $30. This depiction of possible stock prices is called a **binomial tree**. We will see shortly how to construct a binomial tree like that in Figure 1. For now, you should take the tree as given as we work through an option pricing example. Be aware that if we had started with a different tree, the numbers that follow, including the price, would all be different.

Computing the Option Price

Now we compute the price of our 40-strike 1-year call. Consider two portfolios:

Portfolio A. Buy one call option. The cost of this is the call premium, which is what we are trying to determine.

Portfolio B. Buy 2/3 of a share of XYZ and borrow $18.462 at the risk-free rate.[1] This position costs

$$2/3 \times \$41 - \$18.462 = \$8.871$$

Now we compare the payoffs to the two portfolios 1 year from now. Since the stock can take on only two values, we can easily compute the value of each portfolio at each possible stock price.

For Portfolio A, the time 1 payoff is $\max[0, S_1 - \$40]$:

1. Of course, it is not possible in practice to buy fractional shares of stock. As an exercise, you can redo this example, multiplying all quantities by 3. You would then compare three call options (Portfolio A) to buying two shares and borrowing $18.462 × 3 = $55.386 (Portfolio B).

	Stock Price in 1 Year (S_1)	
	\$30	**\$60**
Payoff	0	\$20

In computing the payoff for Portfolio B, we assume that we sell the shares at the market price and that we repay the borrowed amount, plus interest ($\$18.462 \times e^{0.08} = \$20$). Thus we have

	Stock Price in 1 Year (S_1)	
	\$30	**\$60**
2/3 purchased shares	\$20	\$40
Repay loan of \$18.462	−\$20	−\$20
Total payoff	0	\$20

Note that Portfolios A and B have the same payoff: Zero if the stock price goes down, in which case the option is out-of-the-money, and \$20 if the stock price goes up. Therefore, both portfolios should have the same cost. Since Portfolio B costs \$8.871, then given our assumptions, *the price of one option must be \$8.871*. Portfolio B is a *synthetic* call, mimicking the payoff to a call by buying shares and borrowing.

The idea that positions that have the same payoff should have the same cost is called the **law of one price**. This example uses the law of one price to determine the option price. We will see shortly that there is an arbitrage opportunity if the law of one price is violated.

The call option in the example is replicated by holding 2/3 shares, which implies that one option has the risk of 2/3 shares. The value 2/3 is the *delta* (Δ) of the option: the number of shares that replicates the option payoff. Delta is a key concept, and we will say much more about it later.

Finally, we can say something about the expected return on the option. Suppose XYZ has a positive risk premium (i.e., the expected return on XYZ is greater than the risk-free rate). Since we create the synthetic call by borrowing to buy the stock, the call is equivalent to a leveraged position in the stock, and therefore the call will have an expected return greater than that on the stock. The option elasticity measures the amount of leverage implicit in the option.

The Binomial Solution

In the preceding example, how did we know that buying 2/3 of a share of stock and borrowing \$18.462 would replicate a call option?

We have two instruments to use in replicating a call option: shares of stock and a position in bonds (i.e., borrowing or lending). To find the replicating portfolio, we need to find a combination of stock and bonds such that the portfolio mimics the option.

To be specific, we wish to find a portfolio consisting of Δ shares of stock and a dollar amount B in lending, such that the portfolio imitates the option whether the stock rises or falls. We will suppose that the stock has a continuous dividend yield of δ, which we reinvest in the stock. Thus, if you buy one share at time t, at time $t + h$ you will have $e^{\delta h}$ shares. The up and down movements of the stock price reflect the *ex-dividend* price.

Let S be the stock price today. We can write the stock price as uS when the stock goes up and as dS when the price goes down. The stock price tree is then:

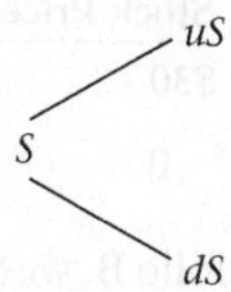

In this tree u is interpreted as one plus the rate of capital gain on the stock if it goes up, and d is one plus the rate of capital loss if it goes down. (If there are dividends, the total return is the capital gain or loss, plus the dividend.)

Let C_u and C_d represent the value of the option when the stock goes up or down, respectively. The tree for the stock implies a corresponding tree for the value of the option:

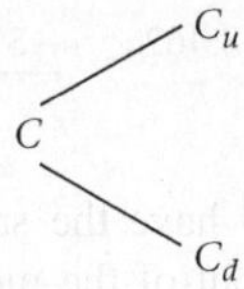

If the length of a period is h, the interest factor per period is e^{rh}. The problem is to solve for Δ and B such that our portfolio of Δ shares and B in lending duplicates the option payoff. The value of the replicating portfolio at time h, with stock price S_h, is

$$\Delta S_h e^{\delta h} + e^{rh} B$$

At the prices $S_h = dS$ and $S_h = uS$, a successful replicating portfolio will satisfy[2]

$$(\Delta \times dS \times e^{\delta h}) + (B \times e^{rh}) = C_d$$
$$(\Delta \times uS \times e^{\delta h}) + (B \times e^{rh}) = C_u$$

This is two equations in the two unknowns Δ and B. Solving for Δ and B gives

$$\boxed{\Delta = e^{-\delta h} \frac{C_u - C_d}{S(u-d)}} \tag{1}$$

$$\boxed{B = e^{-rh} \frac{uC_d - dC_u}{u-d}} \tag{2}$$

Note that when there are dividends, the formula adjusts the number of shares in the replicating portfolio, Δ, to offset the dividend income.

Given the expressions for Δ and B, we can derive a simple formula for the value of the option. The cost of creating the option is the net cash required to buy the shares and bonds. Thus, the cost of the option is $\Delta S + B$. Using equations (1) and (2), we have

$$\boxed{\Delta S + B = e^{-rh} \left(C_u \frac{e^{(r-\delta)h} - d}{u-d} + C_d \frac{u - e^{(r-\delta)h}}{u-d} \right)} \tag{3}$$

2. The term $e^{\delta h}$ arises in the following equations because the owner of the stock receives a proportional dividend that we assume is reinvested in shares.

The assumed stock price movements, u and d, should not give rise to arbitrage opportunities. In particular, we require that

$$u > e^{(r-\delta)h} > d \tag{4}$$

To see why this condition must hold, suppose $\delta = 0$. If the condition were violated, we would short the stock to hold bonds (if $e^{rh} \geq u$), or we would borrow to buy the stock (if $d \geq e^{rh}$). Either way, we would earn an arbitrage profit. Therefore the assumed process could not be consistent with any possible equilibrium. Problem 23 asks you to verify that equation (4) must hold when $\delta > 0$.

Note that because Δ is the number of shares in the replicating portfolio, it can also be interpreted as the sensitivity of the option to a change in the stock price. If the stock price changes by \$1, then the option price, $\Delta S + B$, changes by Δ. This interpretation will be quite important later.

Example 1. Here is the solution for Δ, B, and the option price using the stock price tree depicted in Figure 1. There we have $u = \$60/\$41 = 1.4634$, $d = \$30/\$41 = 0.7317$, and $\delta = 0$. In addition, the call option had a strike price of \$40 and 1 year to expiration—hence, $h = 1$. Thus $C_u = \$60 - \$40 = \$20$, and $C_d = 0$. Using equations (1) and (2), we have

$$\Delta = \frac{\$20 - 0}{\$41 \times (1.4634 - 0.7317)} = 2/3$$

$$B = e^{-0.08} \frac{1.4634 \times \$0 - 0.7317 \times \$20}{1.4634 - 0.7317} = -\$18.462$$

Hence, the option price is given by

$$\Delta S + B = 2/3 \times \$41 - \$18.462 = \$8.871 \quad \blacksquare$$

Note that *if we are interested only in the option price, it is not necessary to solve for Δ and B;* that is just an intermediate step. If we want to know only the option price, we can use equation (3) directly:

$$\begin{aligned}\Delta S + B &= e^{-0.08}\left(\$20 \times \frac{e^{0.08} - 0.7317}{1.4634 - 0.7317} + \$0 \times \frac{1.4634 - e^{0.08}}{1.4634 - 0.7317}\right)\\ &= \$8.871\end{aligned}$$

Throughout this chapter we will continue to report Δ and B, since we are interested not only in the price but also in the replicating portfolio.

Arbitraging a Mispriced Option

What if the observed option price differs from the theoretical price? Because we have a way to replicate the option using the stock, it is possible to take advantage of the mispricing and fulfill the dream of every trader—namely, to buy low and sell high.

The following examples illustrate that if the option price is anything other than the theoretical price, arbitrage is possible.

The Option is Overpriced. Suppose that the market price for the option is \$9.00, instead of \$8.871. We can sell the option, but this leaves us with the risk that the stock price at expiration will be \$60 and we will be required to deliver the stock.

We can address this risk by buying a synthetic option at the same time we sell the actual option. We have already seen how to create the synthetic option by buying 2/3 shares and borrowing \$18.462. If we simultaneously sell the actual option and buy the synthetic, the initial cash flow is

$$\underbrace{\$9.00}_{\text{Receive option premium}} - \underbrace{2/3 \times \$41}_{\text{Cost of shares}} + \underbrace{\$18.462}_{\text{Borrowing}} = \$0.129$$

We earn \$0.129, the amount by which the option is mispriced.

Now we verify that there is no risk at expiration. We have

	Stock Price in 1 Year (S_1)	
	\$30	**\$60**
Written call	\$0	−\$20
2/3 Purchased shares	\$20	\$40
Repay loan of \$18.462	−\$20	−\$20
Total payoff	\$0	\$0

By hedging the written option, we eliminate risk.

The Option is Underpriced. Now suppose that the market price of the option is \$8.25. We wish to buy the underpriced option. Of course, if we are unhedged and the stock price falls at expiration, we lose our investment. We can hedge by selling a synthetic option. We accomplish this by reversing the position for a synthetic purchased call: We short 2/3 shares and invest \$18.462 of the proceeds in Treasury bills. The cash flow is

$$\underbrace{-\$8.25}_{\text{Option premium}} + \underbrace{2/3 \times \$41}_{\text{Short-sale proceeds}} - \underbrace{\$18.462}_{\text{Invest in T-bills}} = \$0.621$$

At expiration we have

	Stock Price in 1 Year (S_1)	
	\$30	**\$60**
Purchased call	\$0	\$20
2/3 Short-sold shares	−\$20	−\$40
Sell T-bill	\$20	\$20
Total payoff	\$0	\$0

We have earned the amount by which the option was mispriced and hedged the risk associated with buying the option.

A Graphical Interpretation of the Binomial Formula

The binomial solution for Δ and B, equations (1) and (2), is obtained by solving two equations in two unknowns. Letting C_h and S_h be the option and stock value after one binomial period, and supposing $\delta = 0$, the equations for the portfolio describe a line with

FIGURE 2

The payoff to an expiring call option is the dark heavy line. The payoff to the option at the points dS and uS are C_d and C_u (at point D). The portfolio consisting of Δ shares and B bonds has intercept $e^{rh}B$ and slope Δ, and by construction goes through both points E and D. The slope of the line is calculated as $\frac{\text{Rise}}{\text{Run}}$ between points E and D, which gives the formula for Δ.

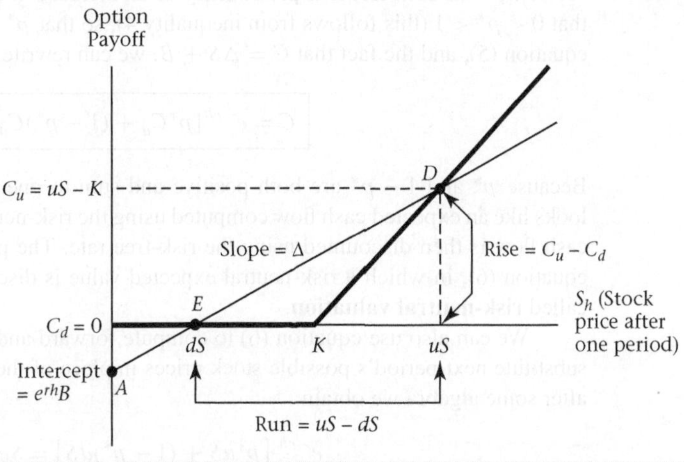

the formula

$$C_h = \Delta \times S_h + e^{rh}B$$

This is graphed as line AED in Figure 2, which shows the option payoff as a function of the stock price at expiration.

We choose Δ and B to yield a portfolio that pays C_d when $S_h = dS$ and C_u when $S_h = uS$. Hence, by construction this line runs through points E and D. We can control the slope of a payoff diagram by varying the number of shares, Δ, and its height by varying the number of bonds, B. It is apparent that a line that runs through both E and D must have slope $\Delta = (C_u - C_d)/(uS - dS)$. Also, the point A is the value of the portfolio when $S_h = 0$, which is the time-h value of the bond position, $e^{rh}B$. Hence, $e^{rh}B$ is the y-axis intercept of the line.

You can see by looking at Figure 2 that *any* line replicating a call will have a positive slope ($\Delta > 0$) and a negative intercept ($B < 0$). As an exercise, you can verify graphically that a portfolio replicating a put would have negative slope ($\Delta < 0$) and positive intercept ($B > 0$).

Risk-Neutral Pricing

In the preceding option price calculations, we did not make use of (nor did we discuss) the probability that the stock price would move up or down. The strategy of holding Δ shares and B bonds replicates the option payoff whichever way the stock moves, so the probability of an up or down movement is irrelevant for computing $\Delta S + B$, which is the option price.

Although we do not need probabilities to price the option, there is a very important probabilistic interpretation of equation (3). Define

$$\boxed{p^* = \frac{e^{(r-\delta)h} - d}{u - d}} \tag{5}$$

We call p^* the **risk-neutral probability** of an increase in the stock price. You can verify that $0 < p^* < 1$ (this follows from inequality 4), so that p^* looks like a probability. Using equation (5), and the fact that $C = \Delta S + B$, we can rewrite equation (3) as

$$\boxed{C = e^{-rh}[p^* C_u + (1 - p^*) C_d]} \tag{6}$$

Because p^* and $1 - p^*$ are both positive and sum to one, the term $p^* C_u + (1 - p^*) C_d$ looks like an expected cash flow computed using the risk-neutral probability. This expected cash flow is then discounted using the risk-free rate. The pricing procedure illustrated in equation (6), in which a risk-neutral expected value is discounted at the risk-free rate, is called **risk-neutral valuation**.

We can also use equation (6) to compute forward and prepaid forward prices. If we substitute next period's possible stock prices in place of the option prices in equation (6), after some algebra we obtain

$$e^{-rh}\left[p^* uS + (1 - p^*) dS\right] = Se^{-\delta h} \tag{7}$$

This is the prepaid forward price. If we do not discount the expected payoff, we obtain the forward price, which is a value denominated in time h dollars:[3]

$$p^* uS + (1 - p^*) dS = Se^{(r-\delta)h} = F_{t,t+h} \tag{8}$$

You can think about p^* as the probability for which the expected stock price is the forward price.

When you first encounter risk-neutral valuation, it appears peculiar. The risk-neutral probability is generally not the actual probability of the stock price going up, and the expected cash flow in equation (6) is discounted at the risk-free rate even though the option has the risk of a levered investment in the stock. Nevertheless, risk-neutral valuation is one of the most important ideas in the derivatives markets.

2. CONSTRUCTING A BINOMIAL TREE

In this section we explain the construction of the binomial tree. We will model the stock returns u and d using the equations

$$\begin{aligned} u &= e^{(r-\delta)h + \sigma\sqrt{h}} \\ d &= e^{(r-\delta)h - \sigma\sqrt{h}} \end{aligned} \tag{9}$$

where r is the continuously compounded annual interest rate, δ is the continuous dividend yield, σ is the annual volatility, and h is the length of a binomial period in years.

In all likelihood you do not find equation (9) to be immediately intuitive. Thus, in this section we explain a number of the concepts underlying equation (9). We first review some properties of continuously compounded returns and define volatility. We then explain the construction of u and d, and then discuss the estimation of historical volatility.

3. This note has been intentionally omitted for this edition.

Continuously Compounded Returns

What follows in this section relies on calculations based on continuously compounded returns. Returns can be expressed in a variety of ways. Continuously compounded returns are mathematically convenient and widely used in practice, both in pricing models and when computing volatility. Here we briefly summarize the important properties of continuously compounded returns.

- **The logarithmic function computes continuously compounded returns from prices.** Let S_t and S_{t+h} be stock prices at times t and $t+h$. The continuously compounded return between t and $t+h$, $r_{t,t+h}$ is then

$$r_{t,t+h} = \ln(S_{t+h}/S_t) \tag{10}$$

- **The exponential function computes prices from continuously compounded returns.** If we know the continuously compounded return, $r_{t,t+h}$, we can obtain S_{t+h} by exponentiating both sides of equation (10). This gives

$$S_{t+h} = S_t e^{r_{t,t+h}} \tag{11}$$

- **Continuously compounded returns are additive.** Suppose we have continuously compounded returns over consecutive periods—for example, $r_{t,t+h}$, $r_{t+h,t+2h}$, etc. The continuously compounded return over a long period is the *sum* of continuously compounded returns over the shorter periods, i.e.,

$$r_{t,t+nh} = \sum_{i=1}^{n} r_{t+(i-1)h,t+ih} \tag{12}$$

Here are some examples illustrating these statements.

Example 2. The stock price on four consecutive days is \$100, \$103, \$97, and \$98. The daily continuously compounded returns are

$$\ln(103/100) = 0.02956; \quad \ln(97/103) = -0.06002; \quad \ln(98/97) = 0.01026$$

The continuously compounded return from day 1 to day 4 is $\ln(98/100) = -0.0202$. This is also the sum of the daily continuously compounded returns:

$$r_{1,2} + r_{2,3} + r_{3,4} = 0.02956 + (-0.06002) + 0.01026 = -0.0202$$ ■

Example 3. The stock price is \$100 at time 0 and \$10 at 1 year later. The percentage return is $(10-100)/100 = -0.9 = -90\%$. The continuously compounded return is $\ln(10/100) = -2.30 = -230\%$. (A continuously compounded return can be less than 100%.) ■

Example 4. The stock price today is \$100. Over the next year the continuously compounded return is -500%. Using equation (11), the end-of-year price is $S_1 = 100e^{-5.00} =$ \$0.6738. The percentage return is $0.6738/100 - 1 = -99.326\%$. ■

Volatility

The **volatility** of an asset, defined as the standard deviation of continuously compounded returns, is a key input for any option pricing calculation. We can express volatility over different periods. For example, we could compute monthly volatility (the standard deviation of the monthly return) or annual volatility (the standard deviation of the annual return). How are these related?

Suppose that the continuously compounded return over month i is $r_{\text{monthly},i}$. From equation (12), we can sum continuously compounded returns. Thus, the annual continuously compounded return is

$$r_{\text{annual}} = \sum_{i=1}^{12} r_{\text{monthly},i}$$

The variance of the annual continuously compounded return is therefore

$$\text{Var}(r_{\text{annual}}) = \text{Var}\left(\sum_{i=1}^{12} r_{\text{monthly},i}\right) \tag{13}$$

It is common to assume that returns are uncorrelated over time; i.e., the realization of the return in one period does not affect the expected returns in subsequent periods. With this assumption, the variance of a sum is the sum of the variances. Also suppose that each month has the same variance of returns. If we let σ^2 denote the annual variance, then from equation (13) we have

$$\sigma^2 = 12 \times \sigma^2_{\text{monthly}}$$

Taking the square root of both sides and rearranging, we can express the monthly standard deviation in terms of the annual standard deviation, σ:

$$\sigma_{\text{monthly}} = \frac{\sigma}{\sqrt{12}}$$

To generalize this formula, if we split the year into n periods of length h (so that $h = 1/n$), the standard deviation over the period of length h, σ_h, is[4]

$$\boxed{\sigma_h = \sigma\sqrt{h}} \tag{14}$$

The standard deviation thus scales with the square root of time. If we know σ_h, equation (14) implies that

4. Equation (14) assumes that continuously compounded returns are independent and identically distributed. If returns are not independent, volatility estimation becomes more complicated. Commodity prices, for example, may be mean-reverting: If oil supply is temporarily reduced (e.g., due to political upheaval), the price of oil will increase in the short term but will likely revert due to decreased demand and increased supply in the future. The volatility over T years will be less than $\sigma\sqrt{T}$, reflecting the tendency of prices to revert from extreme values. Monte Carlo methods would be one way to price an option in such a case.

$$\boxed{\sigma = \frac{\sigma_h}{\sqrt{h}}} \tag{15}$$

Constructing u and d

As a starting point in constructing u and d, we can ask: What if there were no uncertainty about the future stock price? With certainty, the stock price next period must equal the forward price. The formula for the forward price is

$$F_{t,t+h} = S_t e^{(r-\delta)h} \tag{16}$$

Thus, without uncertainty we must have $S_{t+h} = F_{t,t+h}$; the rate of return on the stock must be the risk-free rate.[5]

We incorporate uncertainty into the stock return using volatility, which measures how sure we are that the stock rate of return will be close to the expected rate of return. Stocks with a larger σ will have a greater chance of a return far from the expected return. We model the stock price evolution by adding uncertainty to the forward price:

$$\begin{aligned} uS_t &= F_{t,t+h}e^{+\sigma\sqrt{h}} \\ dS_t &= F_{t,t+h}e^{-\sigma\sqrt{h}} \end{aligned} \tag{17}$$

Using equation (16), we can rewrite equation (17) to obtain equation (9). This is the formula we will use to construct binomial trees. Note that if we set volatility equal to zero (i.e., $\sigma = 0$), we will have $uS_t = dS_t = F_{t,t+h}$. Thus, with zero volatility, the price will still rise over time, just as with a Treasury bill. Zero volatility does not mean that prices are *fixed*; it means that prices are *known in advance*.

We will refer to a tree constructed using equation (9) as a "forward tree."

Estimating Historical Volatility

In selecting the parameters to use in the binomial model, the most difficult decision usually is choosing the value for σ, which we cannot observe directly. One possibility is to measure σ by computing the standard deviation of continuously compounded historical returns. Volatility computed from historical stock returns is **historical volatility**.

Table 1 lists 10 weeks of Wednesday closing prices for the S&P 500 composite index and for IBM, along with the standard deviation of the continuously compounded returns, computed using the StDev function in Excel.[6] Based on the historical returns in Table 1, the weekly standard deviation of returns was 0.02800 and 0.02486 for the S&P 500 index and IBM, respectively. These standard deviations measure the variability in weekly returns. We compute annualized standard deviations by using equation (15): Multiply the weekly

5. With the forward price given by equation (16), the total return on the stock would be the stock price increase, which is at the rate $r - \delta$, plus the dividend yield, δ.

6. We use weekly rather than daily data because computing daily statistics is complicated by weekends and holidays. In theory the standard deviation over the 3 days from Friday to Monday should be greater than over the 1 day from Monday to Tuesday. Using weekly data avoids this kind of complication. Further, using Wednesdays avoids most holidays.

TABLE 1 Weekly prices and continuously compounded returns for the S&P 500 index and IBM, from 7/7/2010 to 9/8/2010.

	S&P 500		IBM	
Date	Price	$\ln(S_t/S_{t-1})$	Price	$\ln(S_t/S_{t-1})$
7/7/2010	1060.27		127	
7/14/2010	1095.17	0.03239	130.72	0.02887
7/21/2010	1069.59	−0.02363	125.27	−0.04259
7/28/2010	1106.13	0.03359	128.43	0.02491
8/4/2010	1127.24	0.01890	131.27	0.02187
8/11/2010	1089.47	−0.03408	129.83	−0.01103
8/18/2010	1094.16	0.00430	129.39	−0.00338
8/25/2010	1055.33	−0.03613	125.27	−0.03238
9/1/2010	1080.29	0.02338	125.77	0.00398
9/8/2010	1098.87	0.01705	126.08	0.00246
Standard deviation	0.02800		0.02486	
Standard deviation × $\sqrt{52}$	0.20194		0.17926	

standard deviations by $\sqrt{52}$ (because $h = 1/\sqrt{52}$), giving annualized historical standard deviations of 20.19% for the S&P 500 index and 17.93% for IBM. We can use the estimated annualized standard deviation as σ in constructing a binomial tree.

You should not be misled by the fact that the standard deviations were estimated with weekly data. Once we annualize the estimate we can then multiply the result by $\sqrt{h}$ (as in equation (9)) to obtain the appropriate standard deviation for any size binomial step.

You might be wondering about how dividends affect the standard deviation calculation. The returns in Table 1 are based on ex-dividend prices, in particular ignoring IBM's payment of \$0.65 with an ex-dividend date of August 6, 2010. Including the dividend in the return calculation in this example changes the estimated annual standard deviation to 0.1778. Most of the time dividends are infrequent and small; the standard deviation will be similar whether you compute a standard deviation accounting for dividends or ignoring them.

The more important question is whether the standard deviation calculation *should* be based on returns that include dividends (the total return volatility). For option pricing it is generally the volatility of the price *excluding dividends* that matters. For a European option, the payoff clearly depends on the ex-dividend price, so the volatility calculation should exclude dividends. The same is true for American options: If an American call is not exercised before expiration, the payoff depends on the ex-dividend price. If it is exercised before expiration, the option holder exercises prior to a dividend. American puts are exercised ex-dividend. Thus, for standard options, the volatility that matters excludes dividends. For an option protected against dividends, it would be appropriate to base pricing upon the total return volatility, which includes dividends.

FIGURE 3

Binomial tree for pricing a European call option; assumes $S = \$41.00$, $K = \$40.00$, $\sigma = 0.30$, $r = 0.08$, $T = 1.00$ years, $\delta = 0.00$, and $h = 1.000$. At each node the stock price, option price, Δ, and B are given. Option price in ***bold italic*** signifies that exercise is optimal at that node.

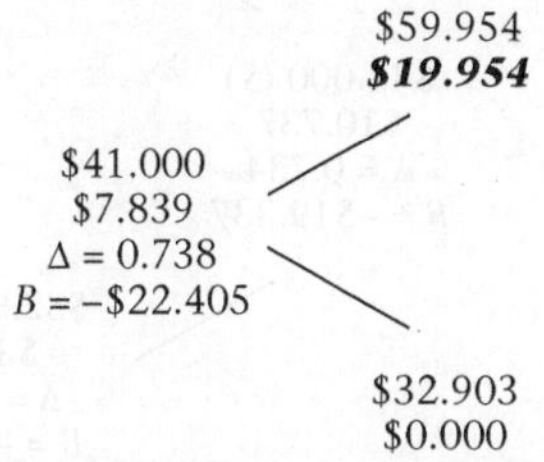

One-Period Example with a Forward Tree

We began this section by assuming that the stock price followed the binomial tree in Figure 1. The up and down stock prices of \$30 and \$60 were selected to make the example easy to follow. Now we present an example where everything is the same except that we use equation (9) to construct the up and down moves.

Suppose volatility is 30%. Since the period is 1 year, we have $h = 1$, so that $\sigma\sqrt{h} = 0.30$. We also have $S_0 = \$41$, $r = 0.08$, and $\delta = 0$. Using equation (9), we get

$$\begin{aligned} uS &= \$41e^{(0.08-0)\times 1+0.3\times\sqrt{1}} = \$59.954 \\ dS &= \$41e^{(0.08-0)\times 1-0.3\times\sqrt{1}} = \$32.903 \end{aligned} \tag{18}$$

Because the binomial tree is different than in Figure 1, the option price will be different as well.

Using the stock prices given in equation (18), we have $u = \$59.954/\$41 = 1.4623$ and $d = \$32.903/\$41 = 0.8025$. With $K = \$40$, we have $C_u = \$59.954 - \$40 = \$19.954$, and $C_d = 0$. Using equations (1) and (2), we obtain

$$\Delta = \frac{\$19.954 - 0}{\$41 \times (1.4623 - 0.8025)} = 0.7376$$

$$B = e^{-0.08}\frac{1.4623 \times \$0 - 0.8025 \times \$19.954}{1.4623 - 0.8025} = -\$22.405$$

Hence, the option price is given by

$$\Delta S + B = 0.7376 \times \$41 - \$22.405 = \$7.839$$

This example is summarized in Figure 3.

We have covered a great deal of ground in this section, but there are still many issues remaining. The simple binomial tree seems too simple to provide an accurate option price. Unanswered questions include how to handle more than one binomial period, how to price put options, and how to price American options. With the basic binomial formula in hand, we can now turn to those questions.

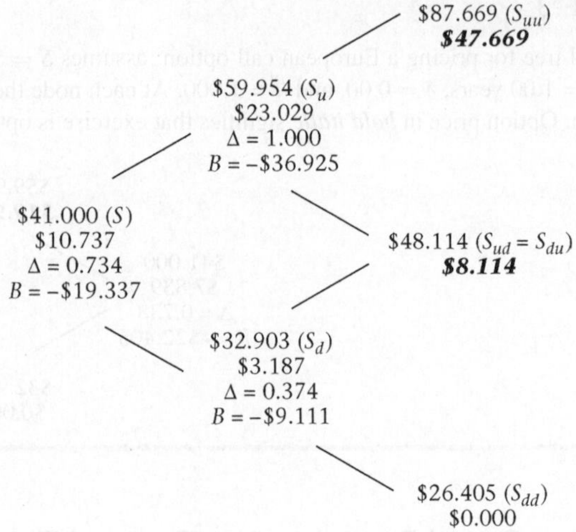

FIGURE 4

Binomial tree for pricing a European call option; assumes $S = \$41.00$, $K = \$40.00$, $\sigma = 0.30$, $r = 0.08$, $T = 2.00$ years, $\delta = 0.00$, and $h = 1.000$. At each node the stock price, option price, Δ, and B are given. Option prices in ***bold italic*** signify that exercise is optimal at that node.

3. TWO OR MORE BINOMIAL PERIODS

We now see how to extend the binomial tree to more than one period. We begin by pricing a 2-year option using a two-period binomial model. Then we will see how to accommodate many periods of arbitrary length.

A Two-Period European Call

We begin first by adding a single period to the tree in Figure 3; the result is displayed in Figure 4. We can use that tree to price a 2-year option with a \$40 strike when the current stock price is \$41, assuming all inputs are the same as before.

Since we are increasing the time to maturity for a call option on a non-dividend-paying stock, we expect the option premium to increase. In this example the two-period tree will give us a price of \$10.737, compared to \$7.839 in Figure 3.

Constructing the Tree. To see how to construct the tree, suppose that we move up in year 1, to $S_u = \$59.954$. If we reach this price, then we can move further up or down according to equation (17). We get

$$S_{uu} = \$59.954 e^{0.08+0.3} = \$87.669$$

and

$$S_{ud} = \$59.954 e^{0.08-0.3} = \$48.114$$

The subscript *uu* means that the stock has gone up twice in a row and the subscript *ud* means that the stock has gone up once and then down.

Similarly, if the price in 1 year is $S_d = \$32.903$, we have

$$S_{du} = \$32.903 e^{0.08+0.3} = \$48.114$$

and

$$S_{dd} = \$32.903e^{0.08-0.3} = \$26.405$$

Note that an up move followed by a down move (S_{ud}) generates the same stock price as a down move followed by an up move (S_{du}). This is called a **recombining tree**. If an up move followed by a down move led to a different price than a down move followed by an up move, we would have a **nonrecombining tree**.[7] A recombining tree has fewer nodes, which means less computation is required to compute an option price.

We also could have used equation (9) directly to compute the year-2 stock prices. Recall that $u = e^{0.08+0.3} = 1.462$ and $d = e^{0.08-0.3} = 0.803$. We have

$$S_{uu} = u^2 \times \$41 = e^{2\times(0.08+0.3)} \times \$41 = \$87.669$$
$$S_{ud} = S_{du} = u \times d \times \$41 = e^{(0.08+0.3)} \times e^{(0.08-0.3)} \times \$41 = \$48.114$$
$$S_{dd} = d^2 \times \$41 = e^{2\times(0.08-0.3)} \times \$41 = \$26.405$$

Pricing the Call Option. How do we price the option when we have two binomial periods? The key insight is that we work *backward* through the binomial tree. In order to use equation (3), we need to know the option prices resulting from up and down moves in the subsequent period. At the outset, the only period where we know the option price is at expiration.

Knowing the price at expiration, we can determine the price in period 1. Having determined that price, we can work back to period 0.

Figure 4 exhibits the option price at each node as well as the details of the replicating portfolio at each node. Remember, however, when we use equation (3), it is not necessary to compute Δ and B in order to derive the option price.[8] Here are details of the solution:

Year 2, Stock Price = \$87.669. Since we are at expiration, the option value is $\max(0, S - K) = \$47.669$.

Year 2, Stock Price = \$48.114. Again we are at expiration, so the option value is \$8.114.

Year 2, Stock Price = \$26.405. Since the option is out of the money, the value is 0.

Year 1, Stock Price = \$59.954. At this node we use equation (3) to compute the option value. (Note that once we are at this node, the "up" stock price, uS, is \$87.669, and the "down" stock price, dS, is \$48.114.)

$$e^{-0.08}\left(\$47.669 \times \frac{e^{0.08} - 0.803}{1.462 - 0.803} + \$8.114 \times \frac{1.462 - e^{0.08}}{1.462 - 0.803}\right) = \$23.029$$

Year 1, Stock Price = \$32.903. Again we use equation (3) to compute the option value:

$$e^{-0.08}\left(\$8.114 \times \frac{e^{0.08} - 0.803}{1.462 - 0.803} + \$0 \times \frac{1.462 - e^{0.08}}{1.462 - 0.803}\right) = \$3.187$$

7. In cases where the tree recombines, the representation of stock price movements is also (and, some argue, more properly) called a *lattice*. The term *tree* would then be reserved for nonrecombining stock movements.

8. As an exercise, you can verify the Δ and B at each node.

Year 0, Stock Price = \$41. Again using equation (3):

$$e^{-0.08}\left(\$23.029 \times \frac{e^{0.08} - 0.803}{1.462 - 0.803} + \$3.187 \times \frac{1.462 - e^{0.08}}{1.462 - 0.803}\right) = \$10.737$$

Notice the following:

- The option price is greater for the 2-year than for the 1-year option, as we would expect.
- We priced the option by working backward through the tree, starting at the end and working back to the first period.
- The option's Δ and B are different at different nodes. In particular, at a given point in time, Δ increases to 1 as we go further into the money.
- We priced a European option, so early exercise was not permitted. However, permitting early exercise would have made no difference. At every node prior to expiration, the option price is greater than $S - K$; hence we would not have exercised even if the option had been American.
- Once we understand the two-period option, it is straightforward to value an option using more than two binomial periods. The important principle is to work backward through the tree.

Many Binomial Periods

An obvious objection to the binomial calculations thus far is that the stock can only have two or three different values at expiration. It seems plausible that to increase accuracy we would want to divide the time to expiration into more periods, generating a more realistic tree. Fortunately, the generalization to many binomial periods is straightforward.

To illustrate using more binomial periods, we re-examine the 1-year European call option in Figure 3, which has a \$40 strike and initial stock price of \$41. We use equation (9) to generate the up and down moves. Suppose there are three binomial periods. With a 1-year call, the length of a period is $h = \frac{1}{3}$. We will assume that other inputs stay the same, so $r = 0.08$ and $\sigma = 0.3$. Equation (9) then automatically generates a per-period interest rate of $rh = 0.027$ and volatility of $\sigma\sqrt{h} = 0.1732$.

Figure 5 depicts the stock price and option price tree for this option. The option price is \$7.074, as opposed to \$7.839 in Figure 3. The difference occurs because the numerical approximation is different; it is quite common to see large changes in a binomial price when the number of periods, n, is changed, particularly when n is small.

Since the length of the binomial period is shorter, u and d are closer to 1 than before (1.2212 and 0.8637 as opposed to 1.462 and 0.803 with $h = 1$). Just to be clear about the procedure, here is how the second-period nodes are computed:

$$S_u = \$41e^{0.08\times 1/3+0.3\sqrt{1/3}} = \$50.071$$

$$S_d = \$41e^{0.08\times 1/3-0.3\sqrt{1/3}} = \$35.411$$

The remaining nodes are computed similarly.

The option price is computed by working backward. The risk-neutral probability of the stock price going up in a period is

FIGURE 5

Binomial tree for pricing a European call option; assumes $S = \$41.00$, $K = \$40.00$, $\sigma = 0.30$, $r = 0.08$, $T = 1.00$ years, $\delta = 0.00$, and $h = 0.333$. At each node the stock price, option price, Δ, and B are given. Option prices in ***bold italic*** signify that exercise is optimal at that node.

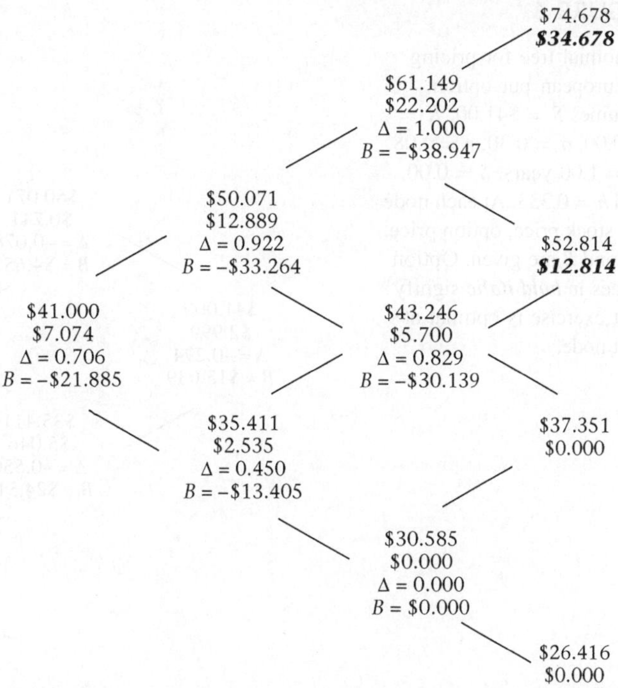

$$\frac{e^{0.08\times 1/3} - 0.8637}{1.2212 - 0.8637} = 0.4568$$

The option price at the node where $S = \$43.246$, for example, is then given by

$$e^{-0.08\times 1/3}\left([\$12.814 \times 0.4568] + [\$0 \times (1 - 0.4568)]\right) = \$5.700$$

Option prices at the remaining nodes are priced similarly.

4. PUT OPTIONS

Thus far we have priced only call options. The binomial method easily accommodates put options also, as well as other derivatives. We compute put option prices using the same stock price tree and in almost the same way as call option prices; the only difference with a European put option occurs at expiration: Instead of computing the price as $\max(0, S - K)$, we use $\max(0, K - S)$.

Figure 6 shows the binomial tree for a European put option with 1 year to expiration and a strike of \$40 when the stock price is \$41. This is the same stock price tree as in Figure 5.

FIGURE 6

Binomial tree for pricing a European put option; assumes $S = \$41.00$, $K = \$40.00$, $\sigma = 0.30$, $r = 0.08$, $T = 1.00$ years, $\delta = 0.00$, and $h = 0.333$. At each node the stock price, option price, Δ, and B are given. Option prices in ***bold italic*** signify that exercise is optimal at that node.

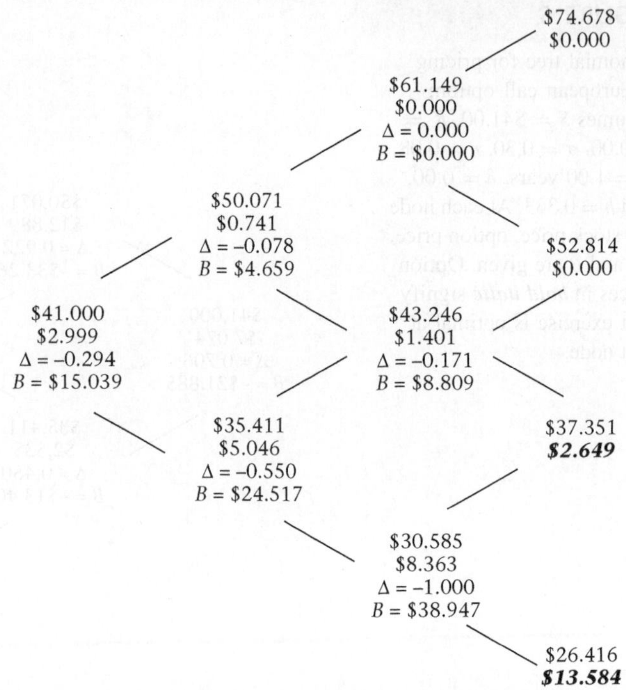

To illustrate the calculations, consider the option price at the node where the stock price is \$35.411. The option price at that node is computed as

$$e^{-0.08\times 1/3}\left(\$1.401 \times \frac{e^{0.08\times 1/3} - 0.8637}{1.2212 - 0.8637} + \$8.363 \times \frac{1.2212 - e^{0.08\times 1/3}}{1.2212 - 0.8637}\right) = \$5.046$$

Figure 6 does raise one issue that we have not previously had to consider. Notice that at the node where the stock price is \$30.585, the option price is \$8.363. If this option were American, it would make sense to exercise at that node. The option is worth \$8.363 when held until expiration, but it would be worth \$40 – \$30.585 = \$9.415 if exercised at that node. Thus, in this case the American option should be more valuable than the otherwise equivalent European option. We will now see how to use the binomial approach to value American options.

5. AMERICAN OPTIONS

Since it is easy to check at each node whether early exercise is optimal, the binomial method is well-suited to valuing American options. The value of the option if it is left "alive" (i.e., unexercised) is given by the value of holding it for another period, equation (3). The value of the option if it is exercised is given by $\max(0, S - K)$ if it is a call and $\max(0, K - S)$ if it is a put.

FIGURE 7

Binomial tree for pricing an American put option; assumes $S = \$41.00$, $K = \$40.00$, $\sigma = 0.30$, $r = 0.08$, $T = 1.00$ years, $\delta = 0.00$, and $h = 0.333$. At each node the stock price, option price, Δ, and B are given. Option prices in ***bold italic*** signify that exercise is optimal at that node.

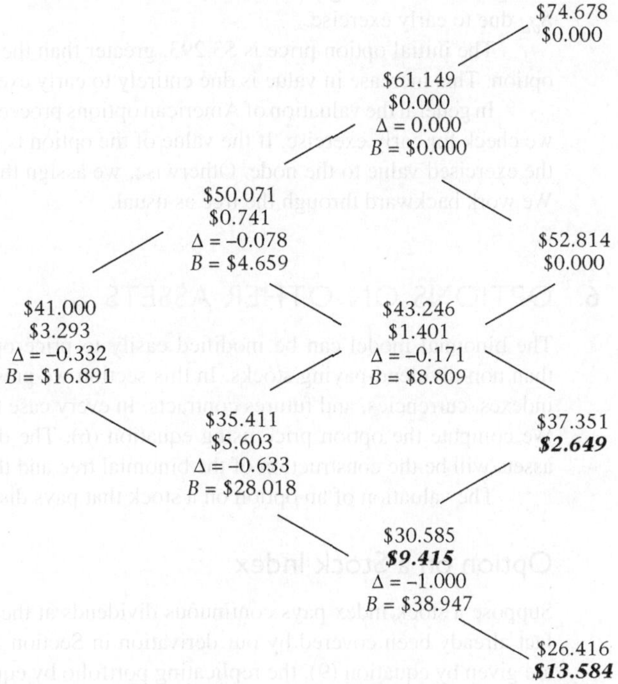

Thus, for an American put, the value of the option at a node is given by

$$P(S, K, t) = \max\left(K - S, e^{-rh}\left[P(uS, K, t+h)p^* + P(dS, K, t+h)(1-p^*)\right]\right) \tag{19}$$

where, p^* is given by equation (5),

$$p^* = \frac{e^{(r-\delta)h} - d}{u - d}$$

Figure 7 presents the binomial tree for the American version of the put option valued in Figure 6. The only difference in the trees occurs at the node where the stock price is \$30.585. The American option at that point is worth \$9.415, its early-exercise value.[9] We have just seen in the previous section that the value of the option if unexercised is \$8.363.

The greater value of the option at that node ripples back through the tree. When the option price is computed at the node where the stock price is \$35.411, the value is greater

9. In order to determine whether to exercise the option at the 30.585 node, it is necessary to compute the price of the option if it were and were not exercised, and then compare the two values. The values of Δ and B reported for the 30.585 node refer to the values for the *unexercised* option.

in Figure 7 than in Figure 6; the reason is that the price is greater at the subsequent node S_{dd} due to early exercise.

The initial option price is \$3.293, greater than the value of \$2.999 for the European option. This increase in value is due entirely to early exercise at the S_{dd} node.

In general the valuation of American options proceeds as in this example. At each node we check for early exercise. If the value of the option is greater when exercised, we assign the exercised value to the node. Otherwise, we assign the value of the option unexercised. We work backward through the tree as usual.

6. OPTIONS ON OTHER ASSETS

The binomial model can be modified easily to price options on underlying assets other than non-dividend-paying stocks. In this section we present examples of options on stock indexes, currencies, and futures contracts. In every case the general procedure is the same: We compute the option price using equation (6). The difference for different underlying assets will be the construction of the binomial tree and the risk-neutral probability.

The valuation of an option on a stock that pays discrete dividends is more complex.

Option on a Stock Index

Suppose a stock index pays continuous dividends at the rate δ. This type of option has in fact already been covered by our derivation in Section 1. The up and down index moves are given by equation (9), the replicating portfolio by equations (1) and (2), and the option price by equation (3). The risk-neutral probability is given by equation (5).[10]

Figure 8 displays a binomial tree for an American call option on a stock index. Note that because of dividends, early exercise is optimal at the node where the stock price is \$157.101. Given these parameters, we have $p^* = 0.457$; hence, when $S = \$157.101$, the value of the option unexercised is

$$e^{-0.05\times 1/3}\left[0.457 \times \$87.747 + (1 - 0.457) \times \$32.779\right] = \$56.942$$

Since $57.101 > 56.942$, we exercise the option at that node.

Options on Currencies

With a currency with spot price x_0, the forward price is $F_{0,h} = x_0 e^{(r-r_f)h}$, where r_f is the foreign interest rate. Thus, we construct the binomial tree using

$$ux = xe^{(r-r_f)h+\sigma\sqrt{h}}$$

$$dx = xe^{(r-r_f)h-\sigma\sqrt{h}}$$

There is one subtlety in creating the replicating portfolio: Investing in a "currency" means investing in a money-market fund or fixed-income obligation denominated in that currency.

10. Intuitively, dividends can be taken into account either by (1) appropriately lowering the nodes on the tree and leaving risk-neutral probabilities unchanged, or (2) by reducing the risk-neutral probability and leaving the tree unchanged. The forward tree adopts the first approach.

FIGURE 8

Binomial tree for pricing an American call option on a stock index; assumes $S = \$110.00$, $K = \$100.00$, $\sigma = 0.30$, $r = 0.05$, $T = 1.00$ years, $\delta = 0.035$, and $h = 0.333$. At each node the stock price, option price, Δ, and B are given. Option prices in ***bold italic*** signify that exercise is optimal at that node.

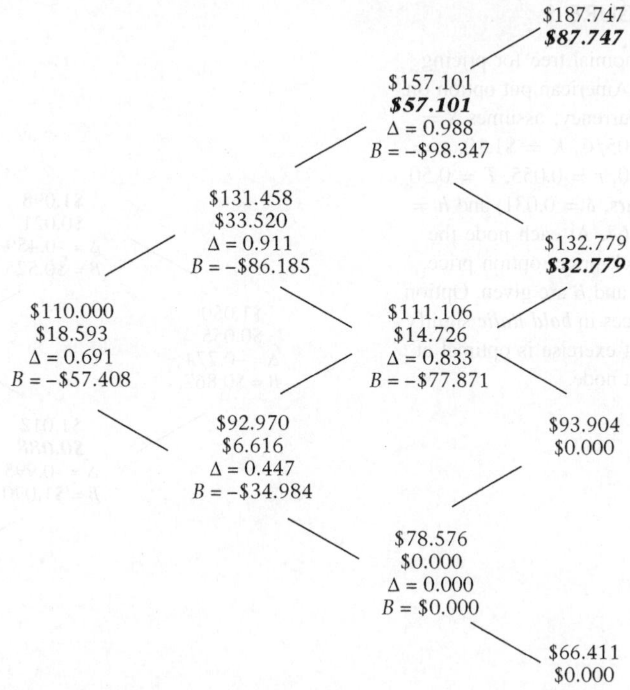

Taking into account interest on the foreign-currency-denominated obligation, the two equations are

$$\Delta \times dxe^{r_f h} + e^{rh} \times B = C_d$$

$$\Delta \times uxe^{r_f h} + e^{rh} \times B = C_u$$

The risk-neutral probability of an up move in this case is given by

$$p^* = \frac{e^{(r-r_f)h} - d}{u - d} \tag{20}$$

Notice that if we think of r_f as the dividend yield on the foreign currency, these two equations look exactly like those for an index option. In fact, the solution is the same as for an option on an index: Set the dividend yield equal to the foreign risk-free rate and the current value of the index equal to the spot exchange rate.

Figure 9 prices a dollar-denominated American put option on the euro. The current exchange rate is assumed to be \$1.05/€ and the strike is \$1.10/€. The euro-denominated interest rate is 3.1%, and the dollar-denominated rate is 5.5%.

Because volatility is low and the option is in-the-money, early exercise is optimal at three nodes prior to expiration.

FIGURE 9

Binomial tree for pricing an American put option on a currency; assumes $S =$ \$1.05/€, $K =$ \$1.10, $\sigma = 0.10$, $r = 0.055$, $T = 0.50$ years, $\delta = 0.031$, and $h = 0.167$. At each node the stock price, option price, Δ, and B are given. Option prices in ***bold italic*** signify that exercise is optimal at that node.

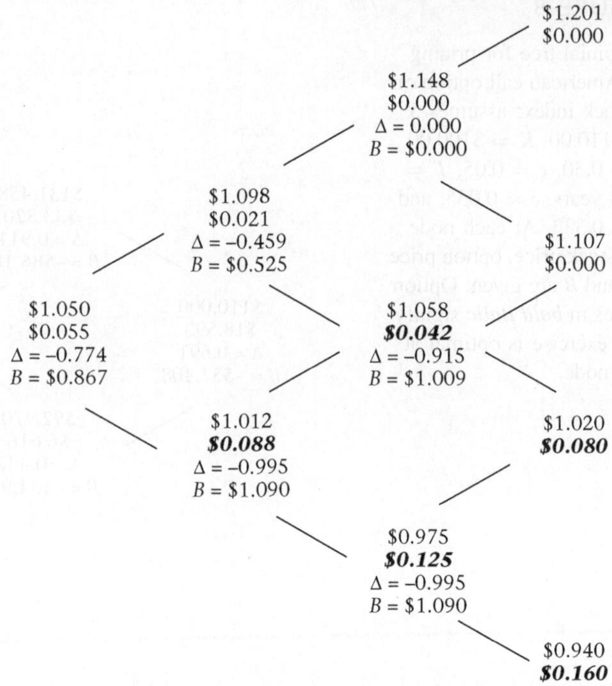

Options on Futures Contracts

We now consider options on futures contracts. We assume the forward price is the same as the futures price. Since we build the tree based on the forward price, we simply add up and down movements around the current price. Thus, the nodes are constructed as

$$u = e^{\sigma\sqrt{h}}$$
$$d = e^{-\sigma\sqrt{h}}$$

Note that this solution for u and d is exactly what we would get for an option on a stock index if δ, the dividend yield, were equal to the risk-free rate.

In constructing the replicating portfolio, recall that in each period a futures contract pays the change in the futures price, and there is no investment required to enter a futures contract. The problem is to find the number of futures contracts, Δ, and the lending, B, that replicates the option. We have

$$\Delta \times (dF - F) + e^{rh} \times B = C_d$$
$$\Delta \times (uF - F) + e^{rh} \times B = C_u$$

Solving gives[11]

$$\Delta = \frac{C_u - C_d}{F(u-d)}$$

$$B = e^{-rh}\left(C_u \frac{1-d}{u-d} + C_d \frac{u-1}{u-d}\right)$$

While Δ tells us how many futures contracts to hold to hedge the option, the value of the option in this case is simply B. The reason is that the futures contract requires no investment, so the only investment is that made in the bond. We can again price the option using equation (3).

The risk-neutral probability of an up move is given by

$$p^* = \frac{1-d}{u-d} \tag{21}$$

Figure 10 shows a tree for pricing an American call option on a gold futures contract. Early exercise is optimal when the price is \$336.720. The intuition for early exercise is that when an option on a futures contract is exercised, the option holder pays nothing, is entered into a futures contract, and receives mark-to-market proceeds of the difference between the strike price and the futures price. The motive for exercise is the ability to earn interest on the mark-to-market proceeds.

Options on Commodities

Many options exist on commodity futures contracts. However, it is also possible to have options on the physical commodity. If there is a market for lending and borrowing the commodity, then, in theory, pricing such an option is straightforward.

The *lease rate* for a commodity is conceptually similar to a dividend yield. If you borrow the commodity, you pay the lease rate. If you buy the commodity and lend it, you receive the lease rate. Thus, from the perspective of someone synthetically creating the option, the commodity is like a stock index, with the lease rate equal to the dividend yield.

11. The interpretation of Δ here is the number of futures contracts in the replicating portfolio. Another interpretation of Δ is the price sensitivity of the option when the price of the underlying asset changes. These two interpretations usually coincide, but not in the case of options on futures. The reason is that the futures price at time t reflects a price denominated in future dollars. The effect on the option price of a futures price change today is given by $e^{-rh}\Delta$. To see this, consider an option that is one binomial period from expiration and for which $uF > dF > K$. Then

$$\Delta = \frac{uF - K - (dF - K)}{F(u-d)} = 1$$

But we also have

$$\begin{aligned} B &= e^{-rh}\left[(uF - K)\frac{1-d}{u-d} + (dF - K)\frac{u-1}{u-d}\right] \\ &= e^{-rh}(F - K) \end{aligned}$$

From the second expression, you can see that if the futures price changes by \$1, the option price changes by e^{-rh}.

FIGURE 10

Binomial tree for pricing an American call option on a futures contract; assumes $S = \$300.00$, $K = \$300.00$, $\sigma = 0.10$, $r = 0.05$, $T = 1.00$ years, $\delta = 0.05$, and $h = 0.333$. At each node the stock price, option price, Δ, and B are given. Option prices in ***bold italic*** signify that exercise is optimal at that node.

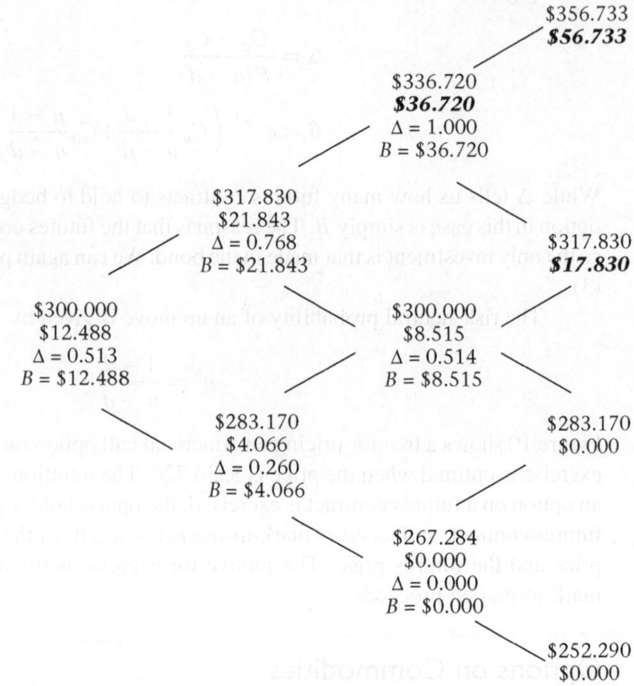

Because this is conceptually the same as the pricing exercise in Figure 8 (imagine a commodity with a price of \$110, a lease rate of 3.5%, and a volatility of 30%), we do not present a pricing example.

In practice, pricing and hedging an option based on the physical commodity can be problematic. If an appropriate futures contract exists, a market-maker could use it to hedge a commodity option. Otherwise, transactions in physical commodities often have greater transaction costs than for financial assets. Short-selling a commodity may not be possible, for many reasons. Market-making is then difficult.

Options on Bonds

Finally, we will briefly discuss options on bonds. It is useful to understand in this chapter some of the issues in pricing options on bonds. As a first approximation we could just say that bonds are like stocks that pay a discrete dividend (a coupon), and price bond options using the binomial model.

However, bonds differ from the assets we have been discussing in two important respects.

1. The volatility of a bond decreases over time as the bond approaches maturity. The prices of 30-day Treasury bills, for example, are much less volatile than the prices of 30-year Treasury bonds. The reason is that a given change in the interest rate, other things equal, changes the price of a shorter-lived bond by less.

2. We have been assuming in all our calculations that interest rates are the same for all maturities, do not change over time, and are not random. While these assumptions may be good enough for pricing options on stocks, they are logically inconsistent for pricing options on bonds: If interest rates do not change unexpectedly, neither do bond prices.

In some cases, it may be reasonable to price bond options using the simple binomial model in this chapter. For example, consider a 6-month option on a 29-year bond. The underlying asset in this case is a 29.5-year bond. As a practical matter, the volatility difference between a 29.5- and a 29-year bond is likely to be very small. Also, because it is short-lived, this option will not be particularly sensitive to the short-term interest rate, so the correlation of the bond price and the 6-month interest rate will not matter much.

On the other hand, if we have a 3-year option to buy a 5-year bond, these issues might be quite important. Another issue is that bond coupon payments are discrete, so the assumption of a continuous dividend is an approximation.

In general, the conceptual and practical issues with bonds are different enough that bonds warrant a separate treatment.

Summary

Here is the general procedure covering the other assets discussed in this section.

- Construct the binomial tree for the price of the underlying asset using

$$\begin{aligned} uS_t &= F_{t,t+h}e^{+\sigma\sqrt{h}} \quad \text{or} \quad u = \frac{F_{t,t+h}}{S_t}e^{+\sigma\sqrt{h}} \\ dS_t &= F_{t,t+h}e^{-\sigma\sqrt{h}} \quad \text{or} \quad d = \frac{F_{t,t+h}}{S_t}e^{-\sigma\sqrt{h}} \end{aligned} \tag{22}$$

  Since different underlying assets will have different forward price formulas, the tree will be different for different underlying assets.

- The option price at each node, if the option is unexercised, can then be computed as

$$\begin{aligned} p^* &= \frac{F_{t,t+h}/S_t - d}{u-d} \\ &= \frac{e^{(r-\delta)h} - d}{u-d} \end{aligned} \tag{23}$$

  and, as before,

$$C = e^{-rh}\left(p^*C_u + (1-p^*)C_d\right) \tag{24}$$

  where C_u and C_d are the up and down nodes relative to the current node. For an American option, at each node take the greater of this value and the value if exercised.

  Pricing options with different underlying assets requires adjusting the risk-neutral probability for the borrowing cost or lease rate of the underlying asset. Mechanically, this means that we can use the formula for pricing an option on a stock index with an appropriate substitution for the dividend yield. Table 2 summarizes the substitutions.

TABLE 2 Substitutions for pricing options on assets other than a stock index.

Underlying Asset	Interest Rate	Dividend Yield
Stock index	Domestic risk-free rate	Dividend yield
Currency	Domestic risk-free rate	Foreign risk-free rate
Futures contract	Domestic risk-free rate	Domestic risk-free rate
Commodity	Domestic risk-free rate	Commodity lease rate
Coupon bond	Domestic risk-free rate	Yield on bond

CHAPTER SUMMARY

In order to price options, we must make an assumption about the probability distribution of the underlying asset. The binomial distribution provides a particularly simple stock price distribution: At any point in time, the stock price can go from S up to uS or down to dS, where the movement factors u and d are given by equation (9).

Given binomial stock price movements, the option can be replicated by holding Δ shares of stock and B bonds. The option price is the cost of this replicating portfolio, $\Delta S + B$. For a call option, $\Delta > 0$ and $B < 0$, so the option is replicated by borrowing to buy shares. For a put, $\Delta < 0$ and $B > 0$. If the option price does not equal this theoretical price, arbitrage is possible. The replicating portfolio is dynamic, changing as the stock price moves up or down. Thus it is unlike the replicating portfolio for a forward contract, which is fixed.

The binomial option pricing formula has an interpretation as a discounted expected value, with the risk-neutral probability (equation (5)) used to compute the expected payoff to the option and the risk-free rate used to discount the expected payoff. This is known as risk-neutral pricing.

The up and down binomial asset price movements depend on the asset volatility, which is the annualized standard deviation of the continuously compounded return on the asset. We construct the up and down movements as the forward price multiplied by a term depending on plus or minus the per-period volatility. Historical volatility can be measured using past returns. Option prices, however, should depend on prospective volatility.

The binomial model can be used to price American and European calls and puts on a variety of underlying assets, including stocks, indexes, futures, currencies, commodities, and bonds.

FURTHER READING

This chapter has focused on the *mechanics* of binomial option pricing.

In addition to the original papers by Cox et al. (1979) and Rendleman and Bartter (1979), Cox and Rubinstein (1985) provides an excellent exposition of the binomial model.

PROBLEMS

In these problems, n refers to the number of binomial periods. Assume all rates are continuously compounded unless the problem explicitly states otherwise.

1. Let $S = \$100$, $K = \$105$, $r = 8\%$, $T = 0.5$, and $\delta = 0$. Let $u = 1.3$, $d = 0.8$, and $n = 1$.

a. What are the premium, Δ, and B for a European call?
b. What are the premium, Δ, and B for a European put?

2. Let $S = \$100$, $K = \$95$, $r = 8\%$, $T = 0.5$, and $\delta = 0$. Let $u = 1.3$, $d = 0.8$, and $n = 1$.

a. Verify that the price of a European call is \$16.196.
b. Suppose you observe a call price of \$17. What is the arbitrage?
c. Suppose you observe a call price of \$15.50. What is the arbitrage?

3. Let $S = \$100$, $K = \$95$, $r = 8\%$, $T = 0.5$, and $\delta = 0$. Let $u = 1.3$, $d = 0.8$, and $n = 1$.

a. Verify that the price of a European put is \$7.471.
b. Suppose you observe a put price of \$8. What is the arbitrage?
c. Suppose you observe a put price of \$6. What is the arbitrage?

4. Obtain at least 5 years' worth of daily or weekly stock price data for a stock of your choice.

1. Compute annual volatility using all the data.
2. Compute annual volatility for each calendar year in your data. How does volatility vary over time?
3. Compute annual volatility for the first and second half of each year in your data. How much variation is there in your estimate?

5. Obtain at least 5 years of daily data for at least three stocks and, if you can, one currency. Estimate annual volatility for each year for each asset in your data. What do you observe about the pattern of historical volatility over time? Does historical volatility move in tandem for different assets?

6. Let $S = \$100$, $K = \$95$, $\sigma = 30\%$, $r = 8\%$, $T = 1$, and $\delta = 0$. Let $u = 1.3$, $d = 0.8$, and $n = 2$. Construct the binomial tree for a call option. At each node provide the premium, Δ, and B.

7. Repeat the option price calculation in the previous question for stock prices of \$80, \$90, \$110, \$120, and \$130, keeping everything else fixed. What happens to the initial option Δ as the stock price increases?

8. Let $S = \$100$, $K = \$95$, $\sigma = 30\%$, $r = 8\%$, $T = 1$, and $\delta = 0$. Let $u = 1.3$, $d = 0.8$, and $n = 2$. Construct the binomial tree for a European put option. At each node provide the premium, Δ, and B.

9. Repeat the option price calculation in the previous question for stock prices of \$80, \$90, \$110, \$120, and \$130, keeping everything else fixed. What happens to the initial put Δ as the stock price increases?

10. Let $S = \$100$, $K = \$95$, $\sigma = 30\%$, $r = 8\%$, $T = 1$, and $\delta = 0$. Let $u = 1.3$, $d = 0.8$, and $n = 2$. Construct the binomial tree for an American put option. At each node provide the premium, Δ, and B.

11. Suppose $S_0 = \$100$, $K = \$50$, $r = 7.696\%$ (continuously compounded), $\delta = 0$, and $T = 1$.

a. Suppose that for $h = 1$, we have $u = 1.2$ and $d = 1.05$. What is the binomial option price for a call option that lives one period? Is there any problem with having $d > 1$?

b. Suppose now that $u = 1.4$ and $d = 0.6$. Before computing the option price, what is your guess about how it will change from your previous answer? Does it change? How do you account for the result? Interpret your answer using put-call parity.

c. Now let $u = 1.4$ and $d = 0.4$. How do you think the call option price will change from (a)? How does it change? How do you account for this? Use put-call parity to explain your answer.

12. Let $S = \$100$, $K = \$95$, $r = 8\%$ (continuously compounded), $\sigma = 30\%$, $\delta = 0$, $T = 1$ year, and $n = 3$.

a. Verify that the binomial option price for an American call option is \$18.283. Verify that there is never early exercise; hence, a European call would have the same price.

b. Show that the binomial option price for a European put option is \$5.979. Verify that put-call parity is satisfied.

c. Verify that the price of an American put is \$6.678.

13. Repeat the previous problem assuming that the stock pays a continuous dividend of 8% per year (continuously compounded). Calculate the prices of the American and European puts and calls. Which options are early-exercised?

14. Let $S = \$40$, $K = \$40$, $r = 8\%$ (continuously compounded), $\sigma = 30\%$, $\delta = 0$, $T = 0.5$ year, and $n = 2$.

a. Construct the binomial tree for the stock. What are u and d?

b. Show that the call price is \$4.110.

c. Compute the prices of American and European puts.

15. Use the same data as in the previous problem, only suppose that the call price is \$5 instead of \$4.110.

a. At time 0, assume you write the option and form the replicating portfolio to offset the written option. What is the replicating portfolio and what are the net cash flows from selling the overpriced call and buying the synthetic equivalent?

b. What are the cash flows in the next binomial period (3 months later) if the call at that time is fairly priced and you liquidate the position? What would you do if the option continues to be overpriced the next period?

c. What would you do if the option is underpriced the next period?

16. Suppose that the exchange rate is \$0.92/€. Let $r_\$ = 4\%$, and $r_€ = 3\%$, $u = 1.2$, $d = 0.9$, $T = 0.75$, $n = 3$, and $K = \$0.85$.

a. What is the price of a 9-month European call?

b. What is the price of a 9-month American call?

17. Use the same inputs as in the previous problem, except that $K = \$1.00$.

a. What is the price of a 9-month European put?

b. What is the price of a 9-month American put?

18. Suppose that the exchange rate is 1 dollar for 120 yen. The dollar interest rate is 5% (continuously compounded) and the yen rate is 1% (continuously compounded). Consider an at-the-money American dollar call that is yen-denominated (i.e., the call permits you to buy 1 dollar for 120 yen). The option has 1 year to expiration and the exchange rate volatility is 10%. Let $n = 3$.

a. What is the price of a European call? An American call?

b. What is the price of a European put? An American put?

c. How do you account for the pattern of early exercise across the two options?

19. An option has a gold futures contract as the underlying asset. The current 1-year gold futures price is \$300/oz, the strike price is \$290, the risk-free rate is 6%, volatility is 10%, and time to expiration is 1 year. Suppose $n = 1$. What is the price of a call option on gold? What is the replicating portfolio for the call option? Evaluate the statement: "Replicating a call option always entails borrowing to buy the underlying asset."

20. Suppose the S&P 500 futures price is 1000, $\sigma = 30\%$, $r = 5\%$, $\delta = 5\%$, $T = 1$, and $n = 3$.

a. What are the prices of European calls and puts for $K = \$1000$? Why do you find the prices to be equal?

b. What are the prices of American calls and puts for $K = \$1000$?

c. What are the time-0 replicating portfolios for the European call and put?

21. For a stock index, $S = \$100$, $\sigma = 30\%$, $r = 5\%$, $\delta = 3\%$, and $T = 3$. Let $n = 3$.

a. What is the price of a European call option with a strike of \$95?

b. What is the price of a European put option with a strike of \$95?

c. Now let $S = \$95$, $K = \$100$, $\sigma = 30\%$, $r = 3\%$, and $\delta = 5\%$. (You have exchanged values for the stock price and strike price and for the interest rate and dividend yield.) Value both options again. What do you notice?

22. Repeat the previous problem calculating prices for American options instead of European. What happens?

23. Suppose that $u < e^{(r-\delta)h}$. Show that there is an arbitrage opportunity. Now suppose that $d > e^{(r-\delta)h}$. Show again that there is an arbitrage opportunity.

Appendix A TAXES AND OPTION PRICES

Appendix available at http://www.pearsonhighered.com/mcdonald.

Binomial Option Pricing: Selected Topics

In this chapter we focus on binomial pricing, discussing selected topics and delving more deeply into the economics of the model and its underlying assumptions.

First, the binomial model can value options that may be early-exercised. We examine early exercise in detail.

Second, the binomial option pricing formula can be interpreted as the expected option payoff one period hence, discounted at the risk-free rate. This calculation is referred to as *risk-neutral pricing*. This calculation appears to be inconsistent with standard discounted cash flow valuation, in which expected cash flows are discounted at a risk-adjusted rate, not the risk-free rate. We show that, in fact, the binomial pricing formula (and, hence, risk-neutral valuation) is consistent with option valuation using standard discounted cash flow techniques.

Third, we discuss the implicit distributional assumptions in the binomial model, namely that continuously compounded returns are normally distributed in the limit, which implies that prices are lognormally distributed.

Finally, in this chapter we adapt the binomial model to price options on stocks that pay discrete dividends.

1. UNDERSTANDING EARLY EXERCISE

In deciding whether to early-exercise an option, the option holder compares the value of exercising immediately with the value of continuing to hold the option and exercises if immediate exercise is more valuable.

We obtain an economic perspective on the early-exercise decision by considering the costs and benefits of early exercise. There are three economic considerations governing the decision to exercise early. By exercising, the option holder:

From Chapter 11 of *Derivatives Markets*, Third Edition, Robert McDonald. Copyright © 2013 by Pearson Education, Inc. Published by Pearson Prentice Hall. All rights reserved.

- Receives the stock and therefore receives future dividends.
- Pays the strike price prior to expiration (this has an interest cost).
- Loses the insurance implicit in the call. By holding the call instead of exercising, the option holder is protected against the possibility that the stock price will be less than the strike price at expiration. Once the option is exercised, this protection no longer exists.

Consider an example where a call option has a strike price of \$100, the interest rate is 5%, and the stock pays continuous dividends of 5%. If the stock price is \$200, the net effect of dividends and interest encourages early exercise. Annual dividends are approximately 5% of \$200, or $0.05 \times \$200 = \$10$. The annual interest saved by deferring exercise is approximately $0.05 \times \$100 = \$5$. Thus, for a stock price of \$200 (indeed, for any stock price above \$100) dividends lost by not exercising exceed interest saved by deferring exercise.

The only reason in this case not to exercise early is the implicit insurance the option owner loses by exercising. This implicit insurance arises from the fact that the option holder could exercise and then the stock price could fall below the strike price of \$100. Leaving the option unexercised protects against this scenario. The early-exercise calculation for a call therefore implicitly weighs dividends, which encourage early exercise, against interest and insurance, which discourage early exercise.

If volatility is zero, then the value of insurance is zero, and it is simple to find the optimal exercise policy as long as r and δ are constant. For an infinitely lived call, it is optimal to defer exercise as long as interest savings on the strike exceed dividends lost, or

$$rK > \delta S$$

It is optimal to exercise when this is not true, or

$$S > \frac{rK}{\delta}$$

In the special case when $r = \delta$ and $\sigma = 0$, any in-the-money option should be exercised immediately. If $\delta = 0.5r$, then we exercise when the stock price is twice the exercise price.

The decision to exercise is more complicated when volatility is positive. In this case the implicit insurance has value that varies with time to expiration. Figure 1 displays the price above which early exercise is optimal for a 5-year option with $K = \$100$, $r = 5\%$, and $\delta = 5\%$, for three different volatilities, computed using 500 binomial steps. If it is optimal to exercise a call at a given stock price, then it is optimal to exercise at all higher stock prices. Figure 1 thus shows the *lowest* stock price at which exercise is optimal. The oscillation in this lowest price, which is evident in the figure, is due to the up and down binomial movements that approximate the behavior of the stock; with an infinite number of binomial steps, the early-exercise schedule would be smooth and continuously decreasing. Comparing the three lines, we observe a significant volatility effect. A 5-year option with a volatility of 50% should only be exercised if the stock price exceeds about \$360. If volatility is 10%, the boundary drops to \$130. This volatility effect stems from the fact that the insurance value lost by early-exercising is greater when volatility is greater.

Figure 2 performs the same experiment for put options with the same inputs. The picture is similar, as is the logic: The advantage of early exercise is receiving the strike

FIGURE 1

Early-exercise boundaries for volatilities of 10%, 30%, and 50% for a 5-year American call option. In all cases, $K = \$100$, $r = 5\%$, and $\delta = 5\%$.

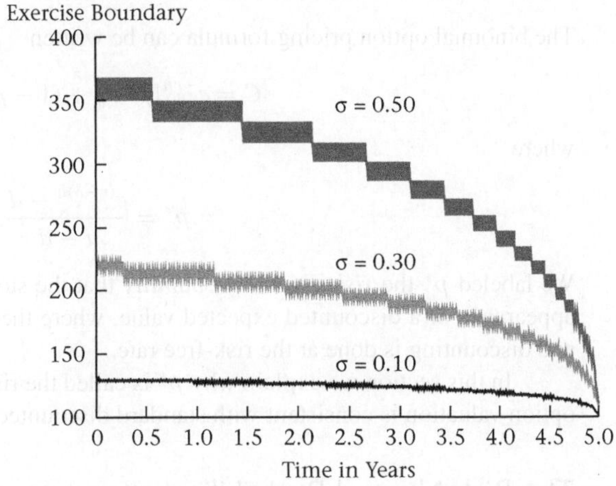

FIGURE 2

Early-exercise boundaries for volatilities of 10%, 30%, and 50% for a 5-year American put option. In all cases, $K = \$100$, $r = 5\%$, and $\delta = 5\%$.

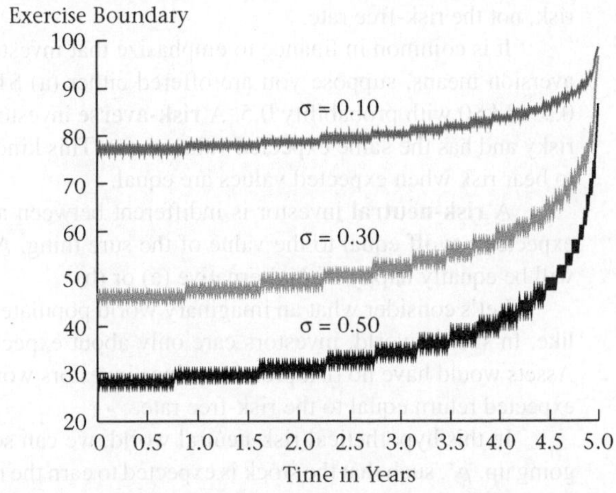

price sooner rather than later. The disadvantages are the dividends lost by giving up the stock, and the loss of insurance against the stock price exceeding the strike price.

Figures 1 and 2 also show that, other things equal, early-exercise criteria become less stringent closer to expiration. This occurs because the value of insurance diminishes as the options approach expiration.

While these pictures are constructed for the special case where $\delta = r$, the overall conclusion holds generally.

2. UNDERSTANDING RISK-NEUTRAL PRICING

The binomial option pricing formula can be written

$$C = e^{-rh}[p^* C_u + (1 - p^*)C_d] \tag{1}$$

where

$$p^* = \frac{e^{(r-\delta)h} - d}{u - d} \tag{2}$$

We labeled p^* the *risk-neutral probability* that the stock will go up. Equation (1) has the appearance of a discounted expected value, where the expected value calculation uses p^* and discounting is done at the risk-free rate.

In this section we explain why p^* is called the risk-neutral probability and show that option valuation is consistent with standard discounted cash flow calculations.

The Risk-Neutral Probability

The idea that an option price is the result of a present value calculation is reassuring, but at the same time equation (1) is puzzling. A standard discounted cash flow calculation would require computing an expected value using the true probability that the stock price would go up. Discounting would then be done using the expected return on an asset of equivalent risk, not the risk-free rate.

It is common in finance to emphasize that investors are risk averse. To see what risk aversion means, suppose you are offered either (a) \$1000, or (b) \$2000 with probability 0.5, and \$0 with probability 0.5. A **risk-averse** investor prefers (a), since alternative (b) is risky and has the same expected value as (a). This kind of investor will require a premium to bear risk when expected values are equal.

A **risk-neutral** investor is indifferent between a sure thing and a risky bet with an expected payoff equal to the value of the sure thing. A risk-neutral investor, for example, will be equally happy with alternative (a) or (b).

Let's consider what an imaginary world populated by risk-neutral investors would be like. In such a world, investors care only about expected returns and not about riskiness. Assets would have no risk premium since investors would be willing to hold assets with an expected return equal to the risk-free rate.

In this hypothetical risk-neutral world, we can solve for the probability of the stock going up, p^*, such that the stock is expected to earn the risk-free rate. In the binomial model, the probability that the stock will go up, p^*, must satisfy

$$p^* uSe^{\delta h} + (1 - p^*)dSe^{\delta h} = e^{rh}S$$

Solving for p^* gives us equation (2), which is why we refer to p^* as the *risk-neutral probability that the stock price will go up*. It is the probability that the stock price would increase in a risk-neutral world.

Not only would the risk-neutral probability, equation (2), be used in a risk-neutral world, but also all discounting would take place at the risk-free rate. Thus, the option pricing formula, equation (1), can be said to price options *as if* investors are risk-neutral. ous, It is important to note that we are not assuming that investors are actually risk-neutral, and we are not assuming that risky assets are actually expected to earn the risk-free rate of return. Rather, *risk-neutral pricing is an* interpretation *of the formulas above*. Those formulas in turn arise from finding the cost of the portfolio that replicates the option payoff.

This interpretation of the option-pricing procedure has great practical importance; risk-neutral pricing can sometimes be used where other pricing methods are too difficult. Risk-neutral pricing is the basis for Monte Carlo valuation, in which asset prices are simulated under the assumption that assets earn the risk-free rate, and these simulated prices are used to value the option.

Pricing an Option Using Real Probabilities

We are left with this question: Is option pricing consistent with standard discounted cash flow calculations? The answer is yes. We can use the true distribution for the future stock price in computing the expected payoff to the option. This expected payoff can then be discounted with a rate based on the stock's required return.

Discounted cash flow is not used in practice to price options because there is no reason to do so: However, we present two examples of valuing an option using real probabilities to see the difficulty in using real probabilities, and also to understand how to determine the risk of an option.

Suppose that the continuously compounded expected return on the stock is α and that the stock does not pay dividends. Then if p is the true probability of the stock going up, p must be consistent with u, d, and α:

$$puS + (1 - p)dS = e^{\alpha h}S \tag{3}$$

Solving for p gives us

$$p = \frac{e^{\alpha h} - d}{u - d} \tag{4}$$

For probabilities to be between 0 and 1, we must have $u > e^{\alpha h} > d$. Using p, the actual expected payoff to the option one period hence is

$$pC_u + (1 - p)C_d = \frac{e^{\alpha h} - d}{u - d}C_u + \frac{u - e^{\alpha h}}{u - d}C_d \tag{5}$$

Now we face the problem with using real as opposed to risk-neutral probabilities: At what rate do we discount this expected payoff? It is not correct to discount the option at the expected return on the stock, α, because the option is equivalent to a leveraged investment in the stock and, hence, is riskier than the stock.

Denote the appropriate per-period discount rate for the option as γ. To compute γ, we can use the fact that the required return on any portfolio is the weighted average of the returns on the assets in the portfolio.[1] An option is equivalent to holding a portfolio

1. See, for example, Brealey et al. (2011, ch. 9).

consisting of Δ shares of stock and B bonds. The expected return on this portfolio is

$$e^{\gamma h} = \frac{S\Delta}{S\Delta + B}e^{\alpha h} + \frac{B}{S\Delta + B}e^{rh} \tag{6}$$

We can now compute the option price as the expected option payoff, equation (5), discounted at the appropriate discount rate, given by equation (6). This gives

$$e^{-\gamma h}\left[\frac{e^{\alpha h} - d}{u - d}C_u + \frac{u - e^{\alpha h}}{u - d}C_d\right] \tag{7}$$

It turns out that *this gives us the same option price as performing the risk-neutral calculation.* Appendix A demonstrates algebraically that equation (7) is equivalent to the risk-neutral calculation, equation (1).

The calculations leading to equation (7) started with the assumption that the expected return on the stock is α. We then derived a consistent probability, p, and discount rate for the option, γ. You may be wondering if it matters whether we have the "correct" value of α to start with. The answer is that it does not matter: *Any* consistent pair of α and γ will give the same option price. Risk-neutral pricing is valuable because setting $\alpha = r$ results in the *simplest* pricing procedure.

A One-Period Example. To see how to value an option using true probabilities, we will compute two examples. First, consider the one-period binomial example in Figure 3. Suppose that the continuously compounded expected return on XYZ is $\alpha = 15\%$. Then the true probability of the stock going up, from equation (4), is

$$p = \frac{e^{0.15} - 0.8025}{1.4623 - 0.8025} = 0.5446$$

The expected payoff to the option in one period, from equation (5), is

$$0.5446 \times \$19.954 + (1 - 0.5446) \times \$0 = \$10.867$$

The replicating portfolio, Δ and B, does not depend on p or α. In this example, $\Delta = 0.738$ and $B = -\$22.405$. The discount rate, γ, from equation (6) is given by

$$\begin{aligned} e^{\gamma h} &= \frac{0.738 \times \$41}{0.738 \times \$41 - \$22.405}e^{0.15} + \frac{-\$22.405}{0.738 \times \$41 - \$22.405}e^{0.08} \\ &= 1.386 \end{aligned}$$

FIGURE 3

Binomial tree for pricing a European call option; assumes $S = \$41.00$, $K = \$40.00$, $\sigma = 0.30$, $r = 0.08$, $T = 1.00$ years, $\delta = 0.00$, and $h = 1.000$.

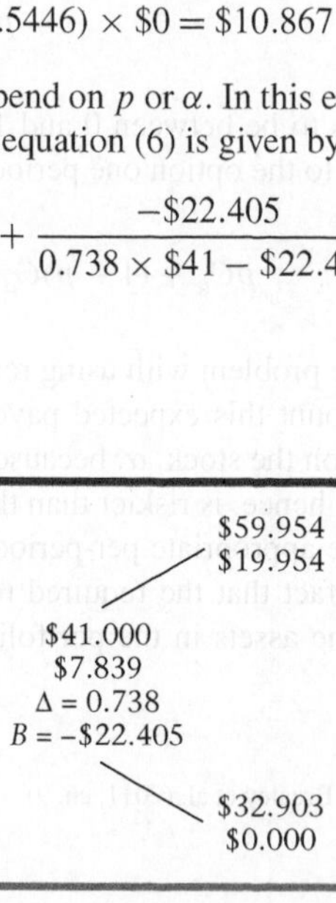

Thus, $\gamma = \ln(1.386) = 32.64\%$. The option price is then given by equation (7):

$$e^{-0.3264} \times \$10.867 = \$7.839$$

This is exactly the price we obtained before.

Notice that in order to compute the discount rate, we first had to compute Δ and B. But once we have computed Δ and B, we can simply compute the option price as $\Delta S + B$. There is no need for further computations. It can be helpful to know the actual expected return on an option, but for valuation it is pointless.

A Multi-Period Example. To demonstrate that this method of valuation works over multiple periods, Figure 4 presents a binomial tree illustrating that the true discount rate for the option, γ, is reported at each node. Given the 15% continuously compounded discount rate, the true probability of an up move in Figure 4 is

$$\frac{e^{0.15\times 1/3} - 0.8637}{1.2212 - 0.8637} = 0.5247$$

To compute the price at the node where the stock price is \$61.149, we discount the expected option price the next period at 26.9%. This gives

$$e^{-0.269\times 1/3}\left[0.5247 \times \$34.678 + (1 - 0.5247) \times \$12.814\right] = \$22.202$$

When the stock price is \$43.246, the discount rate is 49.5%, and the option price is

$$e^{-0.495\times 1/3}\left[0.5247 \times \$12.814 + (1 - 0.5247) \times \$0\right] = \$5.700$$

FIGURE 4

Binomial tree for pricing an American call option; assumes $S = \$41.00$, $K = \$40.00$, $\sigma = 0.30$, $r = 0.08$, $T = 1.00$ years, $\delta = 0.00$, and $h = 0.333$. The continuously compounded true expected return on the stock, α, is 15%. At each node the stock price, option price, and continuously compounded true discount rate for the option, γ, are given. Option price in ***bold italic*** signify that exercise is optimal at that node.

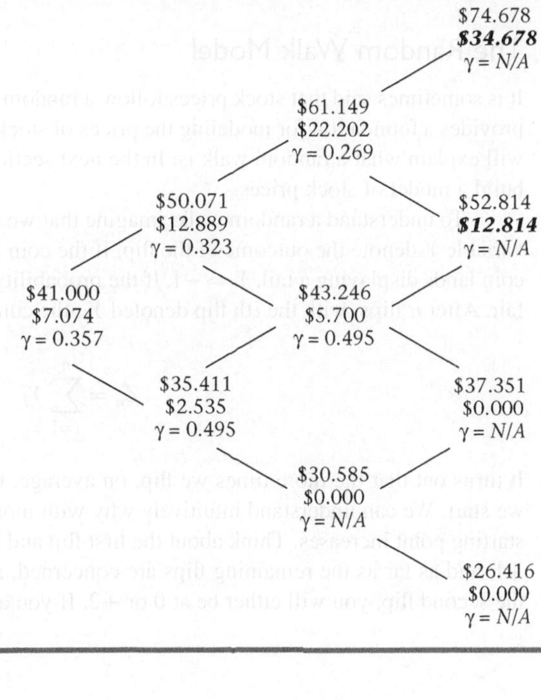

We work back through the tree. To compute the price at the node where the stock price is \$50.071, we discount the expected option price the next period at 32.3%. Thus,

$$e^{-0.323\times 1/3}\left[0.5247 \times \$22.202 + (1 - 0.5247) \times \$5.700\right] = \$12.889$$

The actual discount rate for the option changes as we move down the tree at a point in time and also over time. The required return on the option is less when the stock price is \$61.149 (26.9%) than when it is \$43.246 (49.5%). The discount rate increases as the stock price decreases because the option is equivalent to a leveraged position in the stock, and the degree of leverage increases as the option moves out of the money.

These examples illustrate that it is possible to obtain option prices using standard discounted-cash-flow techniques. Generally, however, there is no reason to do so. Moreover, the fact that risk-neutral pricing works means that it is not necessary to estimate α, the expected return on the stock, when pricing an option. Since expected returns are hard to estimate precisely, this makes option pricing a great deal easier.

Appendix B goes into more detail about risk-neutral pricing.

3. THE BINOMIAL TREE AND LOGNORMALITY

The usefulness of the binomial pricing model hinges on the binomial tree providing a reasonable representation of the stock price distribution. In this section we discuss the motivation for and plausibility of the binomial tree. We will define a lognormal distribution and see that the binomial tree approximates this distribution.

The Random Walk Model

It is sometimes said that stock prices follow a random walk. More precisely, a random walk provides a foundation for modeling the prices of stocks and other assets. In this section, we will explain what a random walk is. In the next section, we use the random walk model to build a model of stock prices.

To understand a random walk, imagine that we flip a coin repeatedly. Let the random variable Y denote the outcome of the flip. If the coin lands displaying a head, $Y = 1$. If the coin lands displaying a tail, $Y = -1$. If the probability of a head is 50%, we say the coin is fair. After n flips, with the ith flip denoted Y_i, the cumulative total, Z_n, is

$$Z_n = \sum_{i=1}^{n} Y_i \tag{8}$$

It turns out that the more times we flip, on average, the farther we will move from where we start. We can understand intuitively why with more flips the average distance from the starting point increases. Think about the first flip and imagine you get a head. You move to +1, and as far as the remaining flips are concerned, *this is your new starting point*. After the second flip, you will either be at 0 or +2. If you are at zero, it is as if you started over;

however, if you are at +2, you are starting at +2. Continuing in this way, your average distance from the starting point increases with the number of flips.[2]

Another way to represent the process followed by Z_n is in terms of the *change* in Z_n:

$$Z_n - Z_{n-1} = Y_n$$

We can rewrite this more explicitly as

$$\text{Heads:} \quad Z_n - Z_{n-1} = +1 \tag{9}$$

$$\text{Tails:} \quad Z_n - Z_{n-1} = -1 \tag{10}$$

With heads, the *change* in Z is 1, and with tails, the change in Z is -1. This random walk is illustrated in Figure 5.

The idea that asset prices should follow a random walk was articulated in Samuelson (1965). In efficient markets, an asset price should reflect all available information. By definition, new information is a surprise. In response to new information the price is equally likely to move up or down, as with the coin flip. The price after a period of time is the initial price plus the cumulative up and down movements due to informational surprises.

Modeling Stock Prices as a Random Walk

The idea that stock prices move up or down randomly makes sense; however, the description of a random walk in the previous section is not a satisfactory description of stock price movements. Suppose we take the random walk model in Figure 5 literally. Assume the beginning stock price is \$100, and the stock price will move up or down \$1 each time we flip the coin. There are at least three problems with this model:

1. If by chance we get enough cumulative down movements, the stock price will become negative. Because stockholders have limited liability (they can walk away from a bankrupt firm), a stock price will never be negative.
2. The magnitude of the move (\$1) should depend upon how quickly the coin flips occur and the level of the stock price. If we flip coins once a second, \$1 moves are excessive; in real life, a \$100 stock will not typically have 60 \$1 up or down movements in 1 minute. Also, if a \$1 move is appropriate for a \$100 stock, it likely isn't appropriate for a \$5 stock.
3. The stock on average should have a positive return. The random walk model taken literally does not permit this.

2. After n flips, the average squared distance from the starting point will be n. Conditional on the first flip being a head, your average squared distance is $0.5 \times 0 + 0.5 \times 2^2 = 2$. If your first flip had been a tail, your average squared distance after two moves would also be 2. Thus, the unconditional average squared distance is 2 after 2 flips. If D_n^2 represents your squared distance from the starting point, then

$$D_n^2 = 0.5 \times (D_{n-1} + 1)^2 + 0.5 \times (D_{n-1} - 1)^2 = D_{n-1}^2 + 1$$

Since $D_0^2 = 0$, this implies that $D_n^2 = n$. This idea that with a random walk you drift increasingly farther from the starting point is an important concept.

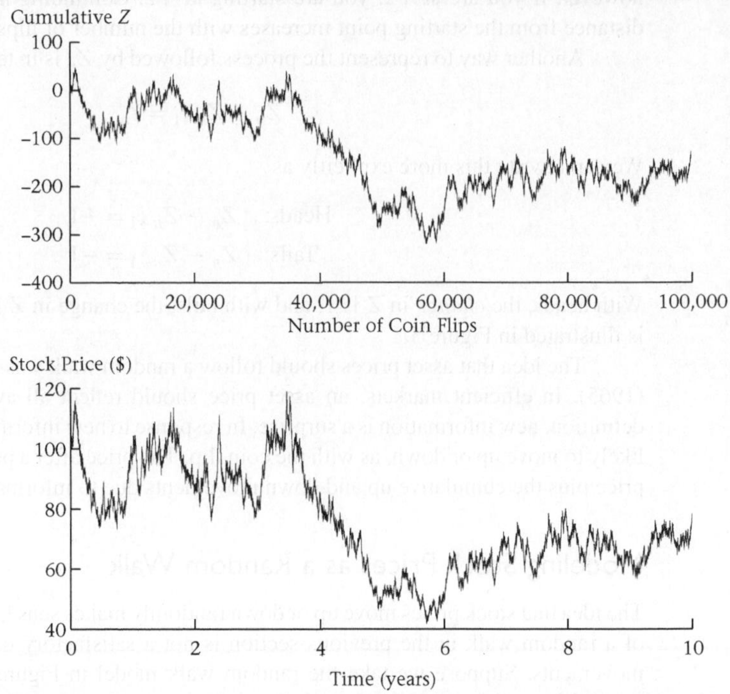

FIGURE 5

In the top panel is an illustration of a random walk, where the counter, Z, increases by 1 when a fair coin flip comes up heads, and decreases by 1 with tails. In the bottom panel is a particular path through a 10,000-step binomial tree, where the up and down moves are the same as in the top panel. Assumes $S_0 = \$100$, $r = 6\%$, $\sigma = 30\%$, $T = 10$ years, and $h = 0.0001$.

It turns out that the binomial model is a variant of the random walk model that solves all of these problems at once. The binomial model assumes that *continuously compounded returns are a random walk with drift*.

The Binomial Model

The binomial stock price is

$$S_{t+h} = S_t e^{(r-\delta)h \pm \sigma\sqrt{h}}$$

Taking logs, we obtain

$$\ln(S_{t+h}/S_t) = (r - \delta)h \pm \sigma\sqrt{h} \tag{11}$$

Since $\ln(S_{t+h}/S_t)$ is the continuously compounded return from t to $t + h$, $r_{t,t+h}$, the binomial model is simply a particular way to model the continuously compounded return. That return has two parts, one of which is certain $[(r - \delta)h]$, and the other of which is uncertain and generates the up and down stock price moves $(\pm\sigma\sqrt{h})$.

Let's see how equation (11) solves the three problems in the random walk discussed earlier:

1. The stock price cannot become negative. Even if we move down the binomial tree many times in a row, the resulting large, negative, continuously compounded return will give us a positive price.
2. As stock price moves occur more frequently, h gets smaller, therefore up and down moves get smaller. By construction, annual volatility is the same no matter how many binomial periods there are. Since returns follow a random walk, the percentage price change is the same whether the stock price is \$100 or \$5.
3. There is a $(r - \delta)h$ term, and we can choose the probability of an up move, so we can guarantee that the expected change in the stock price is positive.

The bottom panel of Figure 5 illustrates the stock price that results when the continuously compounded return follows equation (11). The figure is one particular path through a 10,000-step binomial tree, with the path generated by the same sequence of coin flips as in the top panel of Figure 5.

Lognormality and the Binomial Model

The binomial tree approximates a lognormal distribution, which is commonly used to model stock prices. The lognormal distribution is the probability distribution that arises from the assumption that *continuously compounded returns on the stock are normally distributed.* When we traverse the binomial tree, we are implicitly adding up binomial random return components of $(r - \delta)h \pm \sigma\sqrt{h}$. In the limit (as $n \to \infty$ or, the same thing, $h \to 0$), the sum of binomial random variables is normally distributed. Thus, continuously compounded returns in a binomial tree are (approximately) normally distributed, which means that the stock is lognormally distributed. We can see with an example how it works.

The binomial model implicitly assigns probabilities to the various nodes. Figure 6 depicts the construction of a tree for three binomial periods, along with the risk-neutral probability of reaching each final period node. There is only one path—sequence of up and down moves—reaching the top or bottom node (uuu or ddd), but there are three paths

FIGURE 6

Construction of a binomial tree depicting stock price paths, along with risk-neutral probabilities of reaching the various terminal prices.

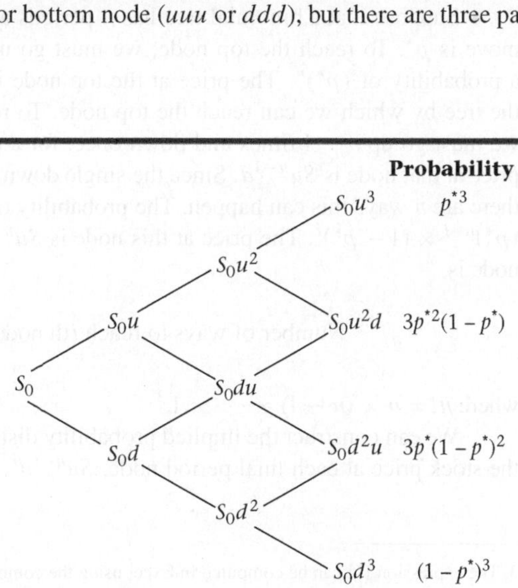

FIGURE 7

Comparison of lognormal distribution with three-period binomial approximation.

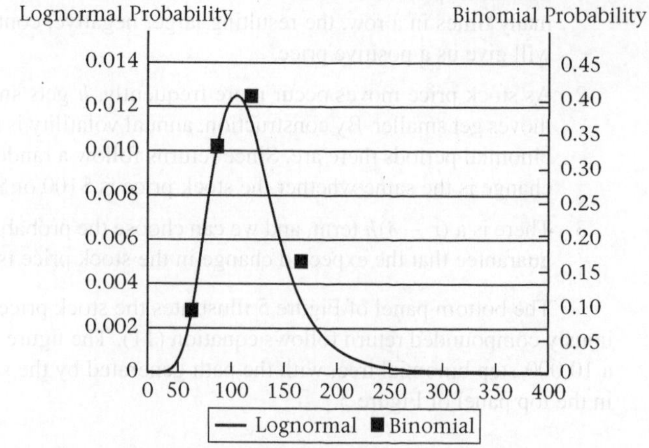

reaching each intermediate node. For example, the first node below the top (S_0u^2d) can be reached by the sequences *uud*, *udu*, or *duu*. Thus, there are more paths that reach the intermediate nodes than the extreme nodes.

We can take the probabilities and outcomes from the binomial tree and plot them against a lognormal distribution with the same parameters. Figure 7 compares a three-period binomial approximation with a lognormal distribution assuming that the initial stock price is \$100, volatility is 30%, the expected return on the stock is 10%, and the time horizon is 1 year. Because we need different scales for the discrete and continuous distributions, lognormal probabilities are graphed on the left vertical axis and binomial probabilities on the right vertical axis.

Suppose that a binomial tree has n periods and the risk-neutral probability of an up move is p^*. To reach the top node, we must go up n times in a row, which occurs with a probability of $(p^*)^n$. The price at the top node is Su^n. There is only one path through the tree by which we can reach the top node. To reach the first node below the top node, we must go up $n-1$ times and down once, for a probability of $(p^*)^{n-1} \times (1-p^*)$. The price at that node is $Su^{n-1}d$. Since the single down move can occur in any of the n periods, there are n ways this can happen. The probability of reaching the ith node below the top is $(p^*)^{n-i} \times (1-p^*)^i$. The price at this node is $Su^{n-i}d^i$. The number of ways to reach this node is

$$\text{Number of ways to reach } i\text{th node} = \frac{n!}{(n-i)!\,i!} = \binom{n}{i}$$

where $n! = n \times (n-1) \times \cdots \times 1$.[3]

We can construct the implied probability distribution in the binomial tree by plotting the stock price at each final period node, $Su^{n-i}d^i$, against the probability of reaching that

3. The expression $\binom{n}{i}$ can be computed in Excel using the combinatorial function, *Combin*(n, i).

FIGURE 8

Comparison of lognormal distribution with 25-period binomial approximation.

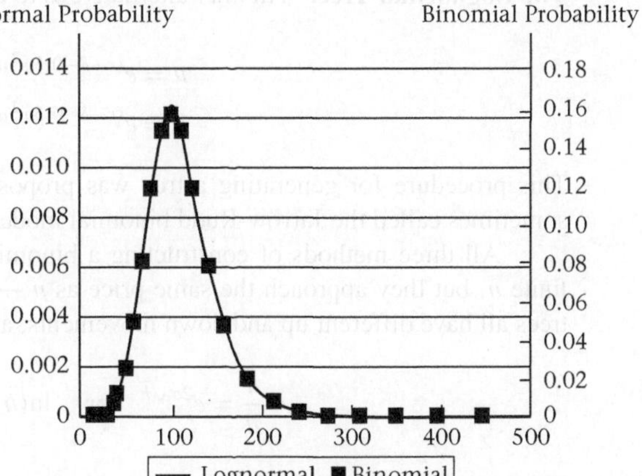

node. The probability of reaching any given node is the probability of one path reaching that node times the number of paths reaching that node:

$$\text{Probability of reaching } i\text{th node} = p^{*n-i}(1-p^*)^i \frac{n!}{(n-i)!\,i!} \tag{12}$$

Figure 8 compares the probability distribution for a 25-period binomial tree with the corresponding lognormal distribution. The two distributions appear close; as a practical matter, a 25-period approximation works fairly well for an option expiring in a few months.

Figures 7 and 8 show you what the lognormal distribution for the stock price looks like. The stock price is positive, and the distribution is skewed to the right; that is, there is a chance that extremely high stock prices will occur.

Alternative Binomial Trees

There are other ways besides equation (11) to construct a binomial tree that approximates a lognormal distribution. An acceptable tree must match the standard deviation of the continuously compounded return on the asset and must generate an appropriate distribution as the length of the binomial period, h, goes to 0. Different methods of constructing the binomial tree will result in different u and d stock movements.

The Cox-Ross-Rubinstein Binomial Tree. The best-known way to construct a binomial tree is that in Cox et al. (1979), in which the tree is constructed as

$$\begin{aligned} u &= e^{\sigma\sqrt{h}} \\ d &= e^{-\sigma\sqrt{h}} \end{aligned} \tag{13}$$

The Cox-Ross-Rubinstein approach is often used in practice. A problem with this approach, however, is that if h is large or σ is small, it is possible that $e^{rh} > e^{\sigma\sqrt{h}}$. In real applications h would be small, so this problem does not occur.

The Lognormal Tree. Another alternative is to construct the tree using

$$u = e^{(r-\delta-0.5\sigma^2)h+\sigma\sqrt{h}}$$
$$d = e^{(r-\delta-0.5\sigma^2)h-\sigma\sqrt{h}} \tag{14}$$

This procedure for generating a tree was proposed by Jarrow and Rudd (1983) and is sometimes called the Jarrow-Rudd binomial model.

All three methods of constructing a binomial tree yield different option prices for finite n, but they approach the same price as $n \to \infty$. Also, while the different binomial trees all have different up and down movements, all have the same ratio of u to d:

$$\frac{u}{d} = e^{2\sigma\sqrt{h}} \quad \text{or} \quad \ln(u/d) = 2\sigma\sqrt{h}$$

This is the sense in which, however the tree is constructed, the proportional distance between u and d measures volatility.

Is the Binomial Model Realistic?

Any option pricing model relies on an assumption about the behavior of stock prices. As we have seen in this section, the binomial model is a form of the random walk model, adapted to modeling stock prices. The lognormal random walk model in this section assumes, among other things, that volatility is constant, that "large" stock price movements do not occur, and that returns are independent over time. All of these assumptions appear to be violated in the data.

There is ample evidence that volatility changes over time (see Bollerslev et al., 1994). It also appears that on occasion stocks move by a large amount. The binomial model has the property that stock price movements become smaller as the period length, h, becomes smaller. Occasional large price movements—"jumps"—are therefore a feature of the data inconsistent with the binomial model. Finally, there is some evidence that stock returns are correlated across time, with positive correlations at the short to medium term and negative correlation at long horizons (see Campbell et al., 1997, ch. 2).

The random walk model is a useful starting point for thinking about stock price behavior, and it is widely used because of its elegant simplicity. However, it is not sacrosanct.

4. STOCKS PAYING DISCRETE DIVIDENDS

Although it may be reasonable to assume that a stock index pays dividends continuously, individual stocks pay dividends in discrete lumps, quarterly or annually. In addition, over short horizons it is frequently possible to predict the amount of the dividend. How should we price an option when the stock will pay a known dollar dividend during the life of the option? The procedure we have already developed for creating a binomial tree can accommodate this case. However, we will also discuss a preferable alternative due to Schroder (1988).

Modeling Discrete Dividends

When no dividend will be paid between time t and $t+h$, we create the binomial tree. Suppose that a dividend will be paid between times t and $t+h$ and that its future value at time $t+h$ is D. The time t forward price for delivery at $t+h$ is then

$$F_{t,t+h} = S_t e^{rh} - D$$

Since the stock price at time $t+h$ will be ex-dividend, we create the up and down moves based on the ex-dividend stock price:

$$\begin{aligned} S_t^u &= \left(S_t e^{rh} - D\right) e^{\sigma\sqrt{h}} \\ S_t^d &= \left(S_t e^{rh} - D\right) e^{-\sigma\sqrt{h}} \end{aligned} \tag{15}$$

How does option replication work when a dividend is imminent? When a dividend is paid, we have to account for the fact that the stock earns the dividend. Thus, we have

$$\left(S_t^u + D\right)\Delta + e^{rh}B = C_u$$
$$\left(S_t^d + D\right)\Delta + e^{rh}B = C_d$$

The solution is

$$\Delta = \frac{C_u - C_d}{S_t^u - S_t^d}$$

$$B = e^{-rh}\left[\frac{S_t^u C_d - S_t^d C_u}{S_t^u - S_t^d}\right] - \Delta D e^{-rh}$$

Because the dividend is known, we decrease the bond position by the present value of the certain dividend. (When the dividend is proportional to the stock price, as with a stock index, we reduce the stock position.) The expression for the option price is given by

$$C = e^{-rh}\left(p^* C_u + (1 - p^*) C_d\right)$$

Problems with the Discrete Dividend Tree

The practical problem with this procedure is that the tree does not completely recombine after a discrete dividend. In all previous cases we have examined, we reached the same price after a given number of up and down movements, regardless of the order of the movements.

Figure 9, in which a dividend with a period-2 value of \$5 is paid between periods 1 and 2, demonstrates that with a discrete dividend, the order of up and down movements affects the price. In the third binomial period there are six rather than four possible stock prices.

To see how the tree is constructed, period-1 prices are

$$\$41e^{0.08\times 1/3+0.3\times\sqrt{1/3}} = \$50.071$$
$$\$41e^{0.08\times 1/3-0.3\times\sqrt{1/3}} = \$35.411$$

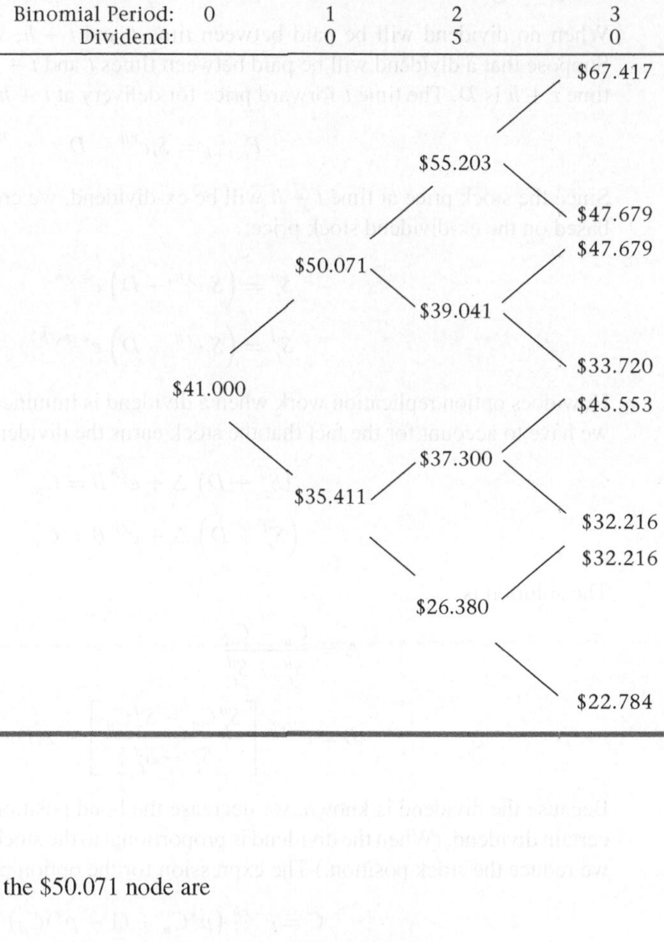

FIGURE 9

The tree depicts a discrete \$5 dividend paid between the first and second binomial periods. There are eight discrete terminal nodes (six of them distinct) rather than four. Assumes $S = \$41$, $\sigma = 0.3$, $r = 0.08$, $t = 1$ year, and $h = 0.333$.

The period-2 prices from the \$50.071 node are

$$(\$50.071e^{0.08\times 1/3} - 5) \times e^{0.3\times\sqrt{1/3}} = \$55.203$$
$$(\$50.071e^{0.08\times 1/3} - 5) \times e^{-0.3\times\sqrt{1/3}} = \$39.041$$

Repeating this procedure for the node $S = \$35.411$ gives prices of \$37.300 and \$26.380. You can see that there are now four prices instead of three after two binomial steps: The ud and du nodes do not recombine. There are six distinct prices in the final period as each set of ex-dividend prices generates a distinct tree (three prices arise from the top two prices in period 2 and three prices arise from the bottom two prices in period 2). Each discrete dividend causes the tree to bifurcate.

There is also a conceptual problem with equation (15). Since the amount of the dividend is fixed, the stock price could in principle become negative if there have been large downward moves in the stock prior to the dividend.

This example demonstrates that handling fixed dividends requires care. We now turn to a method that is computationally easier than constructing a tree using equation (15) and that will not generate negative stock prices.

A Binomial Tree Using the Prepaid Forward

Schroder (1988) presents an elegant method of constructing a tree for a dividend-paying stock that solves both problems encountered with the method in Figure 9. The key insight is that if we know for certain that a stock will pay a fixed dividend, then we can view the stock price as being the sum of two components: the dividend and the present value of the ex-dividend value of the stock—in other words, the prepaid forward price. With the dividend known, all volatility is attributed to the prepaid forward component of the stock price.

Suppose we know that a stock will pay a dividend D at time $T_D < T$, where T is the expiration date of the option. For $t < T_D$, the stock price is the sum of the prepaid forward price and the present value of the dividend:

$$S_t = F_{t,T}^P + De^{-r(T_D-t)} \tag{16}$$

where $F_{t,T}^P = S_t - De^{-r(T_D-t)}$. We construct the binomial tree by attributing all uncertainty to the prepaid forward price. As before, we have up and down movements of

$$u = e^{rh+\sigma\sqrt{h}} \qquad d = e^{rh-\sigma\sqrt{h}}$$

The observed stock price at time $t + h < T_D$ is then

$$S_{t+h} = F_t^P e^{rh\pm\sigma\sqrt{h}} + De^{-r(T_D-(t+h))}$$

We measure σ by observing movements in S_t, but σ is used in this equation to characterize movements in F_t^P. We want the total dollar volatility of the prepaid forward to equal that of the stock, so we assign a volatility to the prepaid forward using the *ad hoc* adjustment

$$\sigma_F = \sigma_s \times \frac{S}{F^P}$$

Figure 10 shows the construction of the binomial tree for a specific example, using the same initial inputs as Figure 9. Both the observed stock price and the stock price less the present value of dividends (the prepaid forward price) are included in the figure. Assuming that the dividend is paid just before the second period, the initial prepaid forward price is $F_0^P = 41 - 5e^{-0.08\times 2/3} = 36.26$. The volatility for the prepaid forward is therefore $0.3 \times \frac{\$41}{\$36.26} = 0.3392$.

To understand Figure 10, note first that $u = 1.2492$. Look at the node where the stock price is \$61.584. This is a *cum-dividend* price, just before the dividend is paid. The nodes in the last period are constructed based on the *ex-dividend* price, for example,

$$(\$61.584 - \$5) \times 1.2492 = \$70.686$$

As a final point, we obtain risk-neutral probabilities for the tree in the same way as in the absence of dividends. Because up and down movements are based on the prepaid forward, which pays no dividends, the risk-neutral probability of an up move in the prepaid forward price is given by $p^* = \frac{e^{(r-\delta)h}-d}{u-d}$, as for a non-dividend paying stock.

FIGURE 10

Binomial tree for pricing an American call option on a stock paying a discrete dividend of \$5 in 8 months; assumes $S = \$41.00$, $K = \$40.00$, $\sigma = 0.3392$, $r = 0.08$, $T = 1.00$ years, $\delta = 0.00$, and $h = 0.333$. At each node the stock price, prepaid forward price, and option price are given. Option prices in ***bold italic*** signify that exercise is optimal at that node.

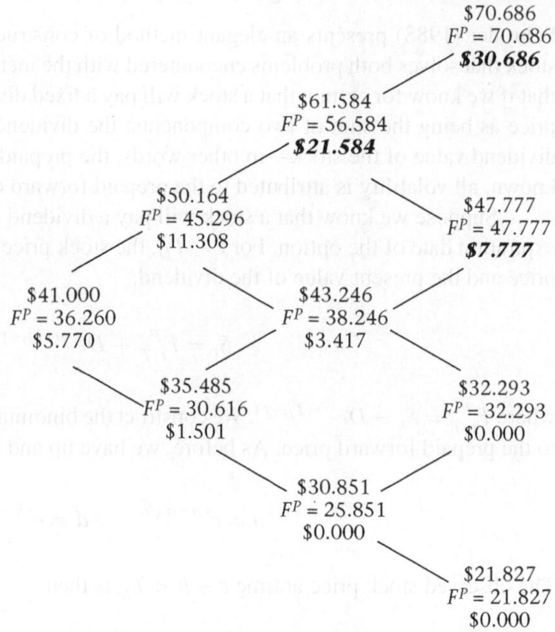

CHAPTER SUMMARY

Both call and put options may be rationally exercised prior to expiration. The early-exercise decision weighs three considerations: dividends on the underlying asset, interest on the strike price, and the insurance value of keeping the option alive. Calls will be early-exercised in order to capture dividends on the underlying stock; interest and insurance weigh against early exercise. Puts will be early-exercised in order to capture interest on the strike price; dividends and insurance weigh against early exercise. For both calls and puts, the early-exercise criterion becomes less stringent as the option has less time to maturity.

Risk-neutral option valuation is consistent with valuation using more traditional discounted cash flow methods. With risk-neutral pricing it is not necessary to estimate the expected return on the stock in order to price an option. With traditional discounted cash flow methods, the correct discount rate for the option varies along the binomial tree; thus, valuation is considerably more complicated than with risk-neutral pricing.

The binomial model, which approximates the lognormal distribution, is a random walk model adapted to modeling stock prices. The model assumes that the continuously compounded return on the stock is normally distributed, which implies that the stock price is lognormally distributed.

The binomial model can be adapted to price options on a stock that pays discrete dividends. Discrete dividends can lead to a nonrecombining binomial tree. If we assume that the prepaid forward price follows a binomial process instead of the stock price, the tree becomes recombining.

FURTHER READING

The binomial model can be used to derive the Black-Scholes model. The literature on risk-neutral pricing is fairly technical. Cox and Ross (1976) was the first paper to use risk-neutral pricing, and Harrison and Kreps (1979) studied the economic underpinnings. Two good treatments of this topic are Huang and Litzenberger (1988, ch. 8)—their treatment inspired Appendix B—and Baxter and Rennie (1996).

Campbell et al. (1997) and Cochrane (2001) summarize evidence on the distribution of stock prices. The original Samuelson work on asset prices following a random walk (Samuelson, 1965) remains a classic, modern empirical evidence notwithstanding.

Broadie and Detemple (1996) discuss the computation of American option prices, and also discuss alternative binomial approaches and their relative numerical efficiency.

PROBLEMS

Many (but not all) of these questions can be answered with the help of the BinomCall and BinomPut functions.

1. Consider a one-period binomial model with $h = 1$, where $S = \$100$, $r = 0$, $\sigma = 30\%$, and $\delta = 0.08$. Compute American call option prices for $K = \$70$, \$80, \$90, and \$100.

a. At which strike(s) does early exercise occur?

b. Use put-call parity to explain why early exercise does not occur at the higher strikes.

c. Use put-call parity to explain why early exercise is sure to occur for all lower strikes than that in your answer to (a).

2. Repeat Problem 1, only assume that $r = 0.08$. What is the greatest strike price at which early exercise will occur? What condition related to put-call parity is satisfied at this strike price?

3. Repeat Problem 1, only assume that $r = 0.08$ and $\delta = 0$. Will early exercise ever occur? Why?

4. Consider a one-period binomial model with $h = 1$, where $S = \$100$, $r = 0.08$, $\sigma = 30\%$, and $\delta = 0$. Compute American put option prices for $K = \$100$, \$110, \$120, and \$130.

a. At which strike(s) does early exercise occur?

b. Use put-call parity to explain why early exercise does not occur at the other strikes.

c. Use put-call parity to explain why early exercise is sure to occur for all strikes greater than that in your answer to (a).

5. Repeat Problem 4, only set $\delta = 0.08$. What is the lowest strike price at which early exercise will occur? What condition related to put-call parity is satisfied at this strike price?

6. Repeat Problem 4, only set $r = 0$ and $\delta = 0.08$. What is the lowest strike price (if there is one) at which early exercise will occur? If early exercise never occurs, explain why not.

For the following problems, note that the BinomCall and BinomPut functions are array functions that return the option delta (Δ) as well as the price. If you know Δ, you can compute B as $C - S\Delta$.

7. Let $S = \$100$, $K = \$100$, $\sigma = 30\%$, $r = 0.08$, $t = 1$, and $\delta = 0$. Let $n = 10$. Suppose the stock has an expected return of 15%.
   a. What is the expected return on a European call option? A European put option?
   b. What happens to the expected return if you increase the volatility to 50%?

8. Let $S = \$100$, $\sigma = 30\%$, $r = 0.08$, $t = 1$, and $\delta = 0$. Suppose the true expected return on the stock is 15%. Set $n = 10$. Compute European call prices, Δ, and B for strikes of \$70, \$80, \$90, \$100, \$110, \$120, and \$130. For each strike, compute the expected return on the option. What effect does the strike have on the option's expected return?

9. Repeat the previous problem, except that for each strike price, compute the expected return on the option for times to expiration of 3 months, 6 months, 1 year, and 2 years. What effect does time to maturity have on the option's expected return?

10. Let $S = \$100$, $\sigma = 30\%$, $r = 0.08$, $t = 1$, and $\delta = 0$. Suppose the true expected return on the stock is 15%. Set $n = 10$. Compute European put prices, Δ, and B for strikes of \$70, \$80, \$90, \$100, \$110, \$120, and \$130. For each strike, compute the expected return on the option. What effect does the strike have on the option's expected return?

11. Repeat the previous problem, except that for each strike price, compute the expected return on the option for times to expiration of 3 months, 6 months, 1 year, and 2 years. What effect does time to maturity have on the option's expected return?

12. Let $S = \$100$, $\sigma = 0.30$, $r = 0.08$, $t = 1$, and $\delta = 0$. Using equation (12) to compute the probability of reaching a terminal node and $Su^i d^{n-i}$ to compute the price at that node, plot the risk-neutral distribution of year-1 stock prices as in Figures 7 and 8 for $n = 3$ and $n = 10$.

13. Repeat the previous problem for $n = 50$. What is the risk-neutral probability that $S_1 < \$80$? $S_1 > \$120$?

14. The undiscounted risk-neutral expected stock price equals the forward price. We will verify this using the binomial tree in Figure 4.
   a. Using $S = \$100$, $r = 0.08$, and $\delta = 0$, what are the 4-month, 8-month, and 1-year forward prices?
   b. Verify your answers in (a) by computing the risk-neutral expected stock price in the first, second, and third binomial period. Use equation (12) to determine the probability of reaching each node.

15. Compute the 1-year forward price using the 50-step binomial tree in Problem 13.

16. Suppose $S = \$100, K = \$95, r = 8\%$ (continuously compounded), $t = 1, \sigma = 30\%$, and $\delta = 5\%$. Explicitly construct an eight-period binomial tree using the Cox-Ross-Rubinstein expressions for u and d:

$$u = e^{\sigma\sqrt{h}} \qquad d = e^{-\sigma\sqrt{h}}$$

Compute the prices of European and American calls and puts.

17. Suppose $S = \$100, K = \$95, r = 8\%$ (continuously compounded), $t = 1, \sigma = 30\%$, and $\delta = 5\%$. Explicitly construct an eight-period binomial tree using the lognormal expressions for u and d:

$$u = e^{(r-\delta-.5\sigma^2)h+\sigma\sqrt{h}} \qquad d = e^{(r-\delta-.5\sigma^2)h-\sigma\sqrt{h}}$$

Compute the prices of European and American calls and puts.

18. Suppose that $S = \$50$, $K = \$45$, $\sigma = 0.30$, $r = 0.08$, and $t = 1$. The stock will pay a \$4 dividend in exactly 3 months. Compute the price of European and American call options using a four-step binomial tree.

Appendix A PRICING OPTIONS WITH TRUE PROBABILITIES

In this appendix we demonstrate algebraically that computing the option price in a consistent way using α as the expected return on the stock gives the correct option price. Using the definition of γ, equation (6), we can rewrite equation (7) as

$$(\Delta S + B)\left(\frac{1}{e^{\alpha h}\Delta S + e^{rh}B}\left[\frac{e^{rh}-d}{u-d}C_u + \frac{u-e^{rh}}{u-d}C_d + \frac{e^{\alpha h}-e^{rh}}{u-d}(C_u - C_d)\right]\right) \tag{17}$$

Since $\Delta S + B$ is the call price, we need only show that the expression in large parentheses is equal to one. From the definitions of Δ and B we have

$$\frac{e^{rh}-d}{u-d}C_u + \frac{u-e^{rh}}{u-d}C_d = e^{rh}(\Delta S + B)$$

We can rewrite equation (17) as

$$(\Delta S + B)\left(\frac{1}{e^{\alpha h}\Delta S + e^{rh}B}\left[e^{rh}(\Delta S + B) + (e^{\alpha h} - e^{rh})\Delta S\right]\right) = \Delta S + B$$

This follows since the expression in large parentheses equals one.

Appendix B WHY DOES RISK-NEUTRAL PRICING WORK?

In this appendix we use the binomial model to explain the economic underpinnings of risk-neutral pricing.

Utility-Based Valuation

The starting point is that the well-being of investors is not measured in dollars, but in *utility*, which is a measure of satisfaction. Economists typically assume that investors exhibit *declining marginal utility*: Starting from a given level of wealth, the utility gained if we add \$1 to wealth is less than the utility lost if we remove \$1 from wealth. Thus, we expect that more dollars will make an investor happier, but that if we keep adding dollars, each additional dollar will make the investor less happy than the previous dollars.

Declining marginal utility implies that investors are risk-averse, which means that an investor will prefer a safer investment to a riskier investment that has the same expected return. Since losses are more costly than gains are beneficial, a risk-averse investor will avoid a fair bet, which by definition has equal expected gains and losses.[4]

To illustrate risk-neutral pricing, we imagine a world where there are two assets, a risky stock and a risk-free bond. Investors are risk-averse. Suppose the economy in one period will be in one of two states, a high state and a low state. How do we value assets in such a world? We need to know three things:

1. What utility value, expressed in terms of dollars today, does an investor attach to the marginal dollar received in each state in the future? Denote the values today of \$1 received in the high and low states as χ_H and χ_L, respectively.[5] Because the investor is risk-averse, \$1 received in the high state is worth less than \$1 received in the low state; hence, $\chi_H < \chi_L$.
2. How many dollars will an asset pay in each state? The bond pays \$1 in each state, while the risky stock pays S_H in the high state and S_L in the low state.
3. What is the probability of each state occurring? Denote the probability of the high state as p. Another name for p is the **physical probability** of an up move.

We begin by defining a state price as the price of a security that pays \$1 only when a particular state occurs. Let Q_H be the price of a security that pays \$1 when the high state occurs, and Q_L the price of a security paying \$1 when the low state occurs.[6] Since χ_H and χ_L are the value today of \$1 in each state, the price we would pay is just the value times the probability that state is reached:

$$\begin{aligned} Q_H &= p \times \chi_H \\ Q_L &= (1-p) \times \chi_L \end{aligned} \tag{18}$$

Since there are only two possible states, we can value any future cash flow using these state prices.

The price of the risky stock, S_0, is

$$S_0 = (Q_H \times S_H) + (Q_L \times S_L) \tag{19}$$

4. This is an example of *Jensen's Inequality*. A risk-averse investor has a concave utility function, which implies that

$$\mathrm{E}[U(x)] < U[\mathrm{E}(x)]$$

The expected utility associated with a gamble, $\mathrm{E}[U(x)]$, is less than the utility from receiving the expected value of the gamble for sure, $U[\mathrm{E}(x)]$.

5. Technically χ_H and χ_L are ratios of marginal utilities, discounted by the rate of time preference. However, you can think of them as simply converting future dollars in a particular state into dollars today.

6. These are often called "Arrow-Debreu" securities, named after Nobel Prize–winning economists Kenneth Arrow and Gerard Debreu.

The risk-free bond, with price B_0, pays \$1 in each state. Thus, we have

$$B_0 = (Q_H \times 1) + (Q_L \times 1) \tag{20}$$

We can calculate rates of return by dividing expected cash flows by the price. Thus, the risk-free rate is

$$\begin{aligned} 1 + r &= \frac{1}{Q_H + Q_L} \\ &= \frac{1}{B_0} \end{aligned} \tag{21}$$

The expected return on the stock is

$$\begin{aligned} 1 + \alpha &= \frac{p \times S_H + (1 - p)S_L}{Q_H \times S_H + Q_L \times S_L} \\ &= \frac{p \times S_H + (1 - p)S_L}{S_0} \end{aligned} \tag{22}$$

Standard Discounted Cash Flow

The standard discounted cash flow calculation entails computing the security price by discounting the expected cash flow at the expected rate of return. In the case of the stock, this gives us

$$\frac{pS_H + (1 - p)S_L}{1 + \alpha} = S_0$$

This is simply a rewriting of equation (22); hence, it is obviously correct. Similarly, the bond price is

$$\frac{1}{1 + r} = \text{Price of bond}$$

Risk-Neutral Pricing

The point of risk-neutral pricing is to sidestep the utility calculations above. We want probabilities we can use to compute expected cash flows *without* explicit utility adjustments, and for which discounting that expectation at the risk-free rate will provide the correct answer.

The trick is the following: Instead of utility-weighting the cash flows and computing expectations, *we utility-weight the probabilities*, creating new "risk-neutral" probabilities. Use the state prices in equation (18) to define the risk-neutral probability of the high state, p^*, as

$$p^* = \frac{p \times \chi_H}{p \times \chi_H + (1 - p) \times \chi_L} = \frac{Q_H}{Q_H + Q_L}$$

Now we compute the stock price by using the risk-neutral probabilities to compute expected cash flow, and then discounting at the risk-free rate. We have

$$\frac{p^* S_H + (1-p^*)S_L}{1+r} = \frac{\frac{Q_H}{Q_H+Q_L} S_H + \frac{Q_L}{Q_H+Q_L} S_L}{1+r}$$

$$= \frac{Q_H S_H + Q_L S_L}{(Q_H + Q_L)(1+r)}$$

$$= Q_H S_H + Q_L S_L$$

which is the price of stock, from equation (19). This shows that we can construct risk-neutral probabilities and use them to price risky assets.

Physical vs. Risk-Neutral Probabilities

The difference between the actual probability of an event and the risk-neutral probability can be expressed in terms of the risk premium on the asset. As before, we have

$$S_0 = \frac{pS_H + (1-p)S_L}{1+\alpha} \tag{23}$$

Because $1+\alpha = 1 + (\alpha - r) + r$, we can rewrite equation (23) as

$$pS_H + (1-p)S_L - S_0(\alpha - r) = (1+r)S_0$$

Notice that the right-hand side of this equation is the forward price of the stock, $F_{0,1}$. We can rewrite this equation to obtain

$$\left(p - \frac{S_0(\alpha - r)}{S_H - S_L}\right)(S_H - S_L) + S_L = (1+r)S_0$$

Rewriting and dividing by $1+r$, we have

$$\frac{\hat{p}S_H + (1-\hat{p})S_L}{1+r} = S_0 \tag{24}$$

where the new probability $\hat{p}$ is defined as

$$\hat{p} = p - \frac{S_0(\alpha - r)}{S_H - S_L} \tag{25}$$

Equation (24) is the risk-neutral valuation equation for the stock. Thus, $\hat{p}$ equals p^*, the risk-neutral probability of the high state.

Equation (25) shows that the actual probability, p, and the risk-neutral probability, $\hat{p}$, differ by a term that is proportional to the *dollar* risk premium on the stock, $S_0(\alpha - r)$. The actual probability, p, is reduced by the dollar risk premium per dollar of risk, $S_H - S_L$. Thus, the real and risk-neutral probabilities differ by an amount that is determined by investor attitudes toward risk.

Example

Table 1 contains assumptions for a numerical example.

State Prices. Using equation (18), the state prices are $Q_H = 0.52 \times \$0.87 = \$0.4524$, and $Q_L = 0.48 \times \$0.98 = \$0.4704$.

TABLE 1 Probabilities, utility weights, and equity cash flows in high and low states of the economy.

	High State	Low State
Cash flow to risk-free bond	$B_H = \$1$	$B_L = \$1$
Cash flow to stock	$S_H = \$180$	$S_L = \$30$
Probability	$p = 0.52$	$p = 0.48$
Value of \$1	$\chi_H = \$0.87$	$\chi_L = \$0.98$

Valuing the Risk-Free Bond. The risk-free bond pays \$1 in each state. Thus, using equation (20), the risk-free bond price, B_0, is

$$B_0 = Q_H + Q_L = \$0.4524 + \$0.4704 = \$0.9228 \tag{26}$$

The risk-free rate is

$$r = \frac{1}{0.9228} - 1 = 8.366\%$$

Valuing the Risky Stock Using Real Probabilities. Using equation (19), the price of the stock is

$$S_0 = 0.4524 \times \$180 + 0.4704 \times \$30 = \$95.544 \tag{27}$$

The expected cash flow on the stock in one period is

$$\text{E}(S_1) = 0.52 \times \$180 + 0.48 \times \$30 = \$108$$

The expected return on the stock is therefore

$$\alpha = \frac{\$108}{\$95.544} - 1 = 13.037\%$$

By definition, if we discount $\text{E}(S_1)$ at the rate 13.037%, we will obtain the price \$95.544.

Risk-Neutral Valuation of the Stock. The risk-neutral probability is

$$p^* = \frac{\$0.4524}{\$0.4524 + \$0.4704}$$
$$= 49.025\%$$

Now we can value the stock using p^* instead of the true probabilities and discount at the risk-free rate:

$$S_0 = \frac{0.49025 \times \$180 + (1 - 0.49025) \times \$30}{1.08366}$$
$$= \$95.544$$

We can see that risk-neutral pricing requires that investors agree about the equilibrium risk premium for assets. They will agree if each investor values and invests in both the stock and risk-free bond. In equilibrium, investors will be pleased with their investment amounts. As long as this is true, investors agree about the risk premium associated with each asset and therefore agree on the transformation that creates risk-neutral probabilities.

When would risk-neutral pricing not work? Suppose you have an asset that cannot be traded or hedged, or you have a nontradable asset with cash flows that cannot be replicated by the cash flows of traded assets. If you cannot trade or offset the risk of the asset, then there is no guarantee that the risk premium that you as an individual use to value payoffs from this asset in a given state will be the same as that used by other investors. If risk premia differ across investors, there will be disagreement about valuation and the calculations in this appendix are not possible. Valuing the nontradable stream of cash flows then requires computing the utility value of the payoffs.

The Black-Scholes Formula

In 1973 Fischer Black and Myron Scholes (Black and Scholes, 1973) published a formula—the Black-Scholes formula—for computing the theoretical price of a European call option on a stock. Their paper, coupled with closely related work by Robert Merton, revolutionized both the theory and practice of finance. The history of the Black-Scholes formula is discussed in Box 1.

In this chapter we present the Black-Scholes formula for pricing European options, explain how it is used for different underlying assets, and discuss the so-called option Greeks—delta, gamma, theta, vega, rho, and psi—which measure the behavior of the option price when inputs to the formula change. We also show how observed option prices can be used to infer the market's estimate of volatility. Finally, while there is in general no simple formula comparable to Black-Scholes for valuing options that may be exercised early, perpetual options are an exception. We present the pricing formulas for perpetual American calls and puts.

1. INTRODUCTION TO THE BLACK-SCHOLES FORMULA

To introduce the Black-Scholes formula, we first use the binomial model. When computing a binomial option price, we can vary the number of binomial steps, holding fixed the time to expiration. Table 1 computes binomial call option prices, and increases the number of steps, n. Changing the number of steps changes the option price, but once the number of steps becomes great enough we appear to approach a limiting value for the price. The last row reports the call option price if we were to use an infinite number of steps. We can't literally have an infinity of steps in a binomial tree, but it is possible to show that as the number of steps approaches infinity, the option price is given by the Black-Scholes formula. Thus, the Black-Scholes formula is a limiting case of the binomial formula for the price of a European option.

Call Options

The Black-Scholes formula for a European call option on a stock that pays dividends at the continuous rate δ is

$$\boxed{C(S, K, \sigma, r, T, \delta) = Se^{-\delta T} N(d_1) - Ke^{-rT} N(d_2)} \tag{1}$$

From Chapter 12 of *Derivatives Markets*, Third Edition, Robert McDonald. Copyright © 2013 by Pearson Education, Inc. Published by Pearson Prentice Hall. All rights reserved.

BOX 1: The History of the Black-Scholes Formula

The Black-Scholes formula was first published in the May/June 1973 issue of the *Journal of Political Economy* (*JPE*) (see Black and Scholes, 1973). By coincidence, the Chicago Board Options Exchange (CBOE) opened at almost the same time, on April 26, 1973. Initially, the exchange traded call options on just 16 stocks. Puts did not trade until 1977. In 2000, by contrast, the CBOE traded both calls and puts on over 1200 stocks.

Fischer Black told the story of the formula in Black (1989). He and Myron Scholes started working on the option-pricing problem in 1969, when Black was an independent consultant in Boston and Scholes an assistant professor at MIT. While working on the problem, they had extensive discussions with Robert Merton of MIT, who was also working on option pricing.

The first version of their paper was dated October 1970 and was rejected for publication by the *JPE* and subsequently by another prominent journal. However, in 1971, Eugene Fama and Merton Miller of the University of Chicago, recognizing the importance of their work, interceded on their behalf with the editors of the *JPE*. Later in 1973 Robert Merton published an important and wide-ranging follow-up paper (Merton, 1973b), which, among other contributions, established the standard no-arbitrage restrictions on various option prices significantly generalized the Black-Scholes formula and their derivation of the model, and provided formulas for pricing perpetual American puts and down-and-out calls.

In 1997, Robert Merton and Myron Scholes won the Nobel Prize in Economics for their work on option pricing. Fischer Black was ineligible for the prize, having died in 1995 at the age of 57.

TABLE 1 Binomial option prices for different numbers of binomial steps. All calculations assume that the stock price $S = \$41$, the strike price $K = \$40$, volatility $\sigma = 0.30$, risk-free rate $r = 0.08$, time to expiration $T = 1$, and dividend yield $\delta = 0$.

Number of Steps (n)	Binomial Call Price ($)
1	7.839
4	7.160
10	7.065
50	6.969
100	6.966
500	6.960
∞	6.961

where

$$d_1 = \frac{\ln(S/K) + (r - \delta + \frac{1}{2}\sigma^2)T}{\sigma\sqrt{T}} \tag{2a}$$

$$d_2 = d_1 - \sigma\sqrt{T} \tag{2b}$$

As with the binomial model, there are six inputs to the Black-Scholes formula: S, the current price of the stock; K, the strike price of the option; σ, the volatility of the stock; r, the continuously compounded risk-free interest rate; T, the time to expiration; and δ, the dividend yield on the stock.

The function $N(x)$ in the Black-Scholes formula is the cumulative normal distribution function, which is the probability that a number randomly drawn from a standard normal distribution (i.e., a normal distribution with mean 0 and variance 1) will be less than x. Most spreadsheets have a built-in function for computing $N(x)$. In Excel, the function is "NormSDist."

Two of the inputs (K and T) describe characteristics of the option contract. The others describe the stock (S, σ, and δ) and the discount rate for a risk-free investment (r). All of the inputs are self-explanatory with the exception of volatility. Volatility is the standard deviation of the rate of return on the stock—a measure of the uncertainty about the future return on the stock.

It is important to be clear about units in which inputs are expressed. Several of the inputs in equation (1) are expressed per unit time: The interest rate, volatility, and dividend yield are typically expressed on an annual basis. In equation (1), these inputs are all multiplied by time: The interest rate, dividend, and volatility appear as $r \times T$, $\delta \times T$, and $\sigma^2 \times T$ (or equivalently, $\sigma \times \sqrt{T}$). Thus, when we enter inputs into the formula, the specific time unit we use is arbitrary as long as we are consistent. If time is measured in years, then r, δ, and σ should be annual. If time is measured in days, then we need to use the daily equivalent of r, σ, and δ, and so forth. We will always assume inputs are per year unless we state otherwise.

Example 1. Let $S = \$41$, $K = \$40$, $\sigma = 0.3$, $r = 8\%$, $T = 0.25$ (3 months), and $\delta = 0$. Computing the Black-Scholes call price, we obtain[1]

$$\$41 \times e^{-0\times 0.25} \times N\left(\frac{\ln(\frac{41}{40}) + (0.08 - 0 + \frac{0.3^2}{2}) \times 0.25}{0.3\sqrt{0.25}}\right)$$

$$- \$40 \times e^{-0.08\times 0.25} \times N\left(\frac{\ln(\frac{41}{40}) + (0.08 - 0 - \frac{0.3^2}{2}) \times 0.25}{0.3\sqrt{0.25}}\right) = \$3.399 \blacksquare$$

There is one input that does *not* appear in the Black-Scholes formula—namely, the expected return on the stock. You might guess that stocks with a high beta would have a higher expected return; hence, options on these stocks would have a higher probability of

1. The call price here can be computed using the Black-Scholes formula call spreadsheet formula, BSCall:

$$\text{BSCall}(S, K, \sigma, r, t, \delta) = \text{BSCall}(41, 40, 0.3, 0.08, 0.25, 0) = \$3.399$$

settlement in-the-money. The higher expected return would seem to imply a higher option price. However, a high stock beta implies a high option beta, so the discount rate for the expected payoff to such an option is correspondingly greater. The net result—one of the key insights from the Black-Scholes analysis—is that beta is irrelevant: The larger average payoff to options on high beta stocks is exactly offset by the larger discount rate.

Put Options

The pricing formula for a European put follows from put-call parity:

$$P(S, K, \sigma, r, T, \delta) = C(S, K, \sigma, r, T, \delta) + Ke^{-rT} - Se^{-\delta T} \tag{3}$$

Using the Black-Scholes equation for the call, equation (1), we can also write the put formula as

$$\boxed{P(S, K, \sigma, r, T, \delta) = Ke^{-rT}N(-d_2) - Se^{-\delta T}N(-d_1)} \tag{4}$$

where d_1 and d_2 are given by equations (2a) and (2b).

Equation (4) follows from equations (1) and (3), together with the fact that for any x, $1 - N(x) = N(-x)$ (i.e., the probability that a random draw from the standard normal distribution is above x, $1 - N(x)$, equals the probability that a draw is below $-x$, $N(-x)$).

Example 2. Using the same inputs as in Example 1, the put price is \$1.607. We can compute the put price in two ways. First, computing it using equation (4), we obtain[2]

$$\$40e^{-0.08\times 0.25}N\left(-\frac{\ln(\frac{41}{40}) + (0.08 - 0 - \frac{0.3^2}{2})0.25}{0.3\sqrt{0.25}}\right)$$

$$- \$41e^{-0\times 0.25}N\left(-\frac{\ln(\frac{41}{40}) + (0.08 - 0 + \frac{0.3^2}{2})0.25}{0.3\sqrt{0.25}}\right) = \$1.607$$

Computing the price using put-call parity, equation (3), we have

$$\begin{aligned} P(41, 40, 0.3, 0.08, 0.25, 0) &= 3.339 + 40e^{-0.08\times 0.25} - 41 \\ &= \$1.607 \end{aligned}$$

When Is the Black-Scholes Formula Valid?

The derivation of the Black-Scholes formula makes a number of assumptions that can be sorted into two groups: assumptions about how the stock price is distributed, and assumptions about the economic environment. For the version of the formula we have presented, assumptions about the distribution of the stock price include the following:

- Continuously compounded returns on the stock are normally distributed and independent over time. (We assume there are no "jumps" in the stock price.)

2. The put price here can be computed using the Black-Scholes put spreadsheet formula, BSPut:

$$\text{BSPut}(S, K, \sigma, r, t, \delta) = \text{BSPut}(41, 40, 0.3, 0.08, 0.25, 0) = \$1.607$$

- The volatility of continuously compounded returns is known and constant.
- Future dividends are known, either as a dollar amount or as a fixed dividend yield.

Assumptions about the economic environment include these:

- The risk-free rate is known and constant.
- There are no transaction costs or taxes.
- It is possible to short-sell costlessly and to borrow at the risk-free rate.

Many of these assumptions can easily be relaxed. For example, with a small change in the formula, we can permit the volatility and interest rate to vary over time in a known way. Even though there are taxes, tax rates do not appear in the binomial formula; the same argument applies to the Black-Scholes formula.

As a practical matter, the first set of assumptions—those about the stock price distribution—are the most crucial. Most academic and practitioner research on option pricing concentrates on relaxing these assumptions. They will also be our focus when we discuss empirical evidence. You should keep in mind that almost *any* valuation procedure, including ordinary discounted cash flow, is based on assumptions that appear strong; the interesting question is how well the procedure works in practice.

2. APPLYING THE FORMULA TO OTHER ASSETS

The Black-Scholes formula is often thought of as a formula for pricing European options on stocks. Specifically, equations (1) and (4) provide the price of a call and put option, respectively, on a stock paying continuous dividends. In practice, we also want to be able to price European options on stocks paying discrete dividends, options on futures, and options on currencies. The binomial model can be adapted to different underlying assets by adjusting the dividend yield. The same adjustments work in the Black-Scholes formula.

We can rewrite d_1 in the Black-Scholes formula, equation (2a), as

$$d_1 = \frac{\ln(Se^{-\delta T}/Ke^{-rT}) + \frac{1}{2}\sigma^2 T}{\sigma\sqrt{T}}$$

When d_1 is rewritten in this way, it is apparent that the dividend yield enters the formula *only* to discount the stock price, as $Se^{-\delta T}$, and the interest rate enters the formula *only* to discount the strike price, as Ke^{-rT}. Notice also that volatility enters only as $\sigma^2 T$.

The prepaid forward prices for the stock and strike asset are $F^P_{0,T}(S) = Se^{-\delta T}$ and $F^P_{0,T}(K) = Ke^{-rT}$. Then we can write the Black-Scholes formula, equation (1), entirely in terms of prepaid forward prices and $\sigma\sqrt{T}$:[3]

3. We can also let $V(T) = \sigma\sqrt{T}$ represent total volatility—uncertainty about the relative time-T values of the underlying and strike assets—over the life of the option. The option price can then be written solely in terms of $F^P_{0,T}(S)$, $F^P_{0,T}(K)$, and $V(T)$. This gives us a minimalist version of the Black-Scholes formula: To price an option, you need to know the prepaid forward prices of the underlying asset and the strike asset, and the relative volatility of the two.

$$C(F^P_{0,T}(S), F^P_{0,T}(K), \sigma, T) = F^P_{0,T}(S)N(d_1) - F^P_{0,T}(K)N(d_2) \quad (5)$$

$$d_1 = \frac{\ln[F^P_{0,T}(S)/F^P_{0,T}(K)] + \frac{1}{2}\sigma^2 T}{\sigma\sqrt{T}}$$

$$d_2 = d_1 - \sigma\sqrt{T}$$

This version of the formula is interesting because the dividend yield and the interest rate do not appear explicitly; they are implicitly incorporated into the prepaid forward prices.

To price options on underlying assets other than stocks, we can use equation (5) in conjunction with the forward price formulas. For all of the examples in this chapter, we will have a strike price denominated in cash, so that $F^P_{0,T}(K) = Ke^{-rT}$.

Options on Stocks with Discrete Dividends

When a stock makes discrete dividend payments, the prepaid forward price is

$$F^P_{0,T}(S) = S_0 - \text{PV}_{0,T}(\text{Div})$$

where $\text{PV}_{0,T}(\text{Div})$ is the present value of dividends payable over the life of the option. Thus, using equation (5), we can price a European option with discrete dividends by subtracting the present value of dividends from the stock price and entering the result into the formula in place of the stock price.

Example 3. Suppose $S = \$41$, $K = \$40$, $\sigma = 0.3$, $r = 8\%$, and $T = 0.25$ (3 months). The stock will pay a \$3 dividend in 1 month, but makes no other payouts over the life of the option (hence, $\delta = 0$). The present value of the dividend is

$$\text{PV(Div)} = \$3e^{-0.08\times 1/12} = \$2.98$$

Setting the stock price in the Black-Scholes formula equal to \$41 − \$2.98 = \$38.02, the Black-Scholes call price is \$1.763. ■

Compared to the \$3.399 price computed in Example 1, the dividend reduces the option price by about \$1.64, or over half the amount of the dividend. Note that this is the price of a *European* option. An American option might be exercised just prior to the dividend, and hence would have a greater price.

Options on Currencies

We can price an option on a currency by replacing the dividend yield with the foreign interest rate. If the spot exchange rate is x (expressed as domestic currency per unit of foreign currency), and the foreign currency interest rate is r_f, the prepaid forward price for the currency is

$$F^P_{0,T}(x) = x_0 e^{-r_f T}$$

Using equation (5), the Black-Scholes formula becomes

$$C(x, K, \sigma, r, T, r_f) = xe^{-r_f T} N(d_1) - Ke^{-rT} N(d_2) \tag{6}$$

$$d_1 = \frac{\ln(x/K) + (r - r_f + \frac{1}{2}\sigma^2)T}{\sigma\sqrt{T}}$$

$$d_2 = d_1 - \sigma\sqrt{T}$$

This formula for the price of a European call on currencies is called the Garman-Kohlhagen model, after Garman and Kohlhagen (1983).

The price of a European currency put is obtained using parity:

$$P(x, K, \sigma, r, T, r_f) = C(x, K, \sigma, r, T, r_f) + Ke^{-rT} - xe^{-r_f T}$$

Example 4. Suppose the spot exchange rate is $x = \$1.25/€$, $K = \$1.20$, $\sigma = 0.10$, $r = 1\%$ (the dollar interest rate), $T = 1$, and $r_f = 3\%$ (the euro-denominated interest rate). The price of a dollar-denominated euro call is \$0.061407, and the price of a dollar-denominated euro put is \$0.03641. ■

Options on Futures

The prepaid forward price for a futures contract is just the present value of the futures price. Thus, we price a European option on a futures contract by using the futures price as the stock price and setting the dividend yield equal to the risk-free rate. The resulting formula is also known as the **Black formula**:

$$C(F, K, \sigma, r, T, r) = Fe^{-rT} N(d_1) - Ke^{-rT} N(d_2) \tag{7}$$

$$d_1 = \frac{\ln(F/K) + \frac{1}{2}\sigma^2 T}{\sigma\sqrt{T}}$$

$$d_2 = d_1 - \sigma\sqrt{T}$$

The put price is obtained using the parity relationship for options on futures:

$$P(F, K, \sigma, r, T, r) = C(F, K, \sigma, r, T, r) + Ke^{-rT} - Fe^{-rT}$$

Example 5. Suppose the 1-year futures price for natural gas is \$6.50/MMBtu and the volatility is 0.25. We have $F = \$6.50$, $K = \$6.50$, $\sigma = 0.25$, $r = 0.02$, $T = 1$, and $\delta = 0.02$ (the dividend yield is set to equal the interest rate). The Black-Scholes call price and put price are both \$0.63379. ■

3. OPTION GREEKS

Option Greeks are formulas that express the change in the option price when an input to the formula changes, taking as fixed all the other inputs.[4] One important use of Greek measures is to assess risk exposure. For example, a market-making bank with a portfolio of options would want to understand its exposure to changes in stock prices, interest rates, volatility, etc. An options investor would like to know how interest rate changes and volatility changes affect profit and loss.

Keep in mind that the Greek measures by assumption change only *one* input at a time. In real life, we would expect interest rates and stock prices, for example, to change together. The Greeks answer the question, What happens when *one and only one* input changes?

The formulas for the Greeks appear in Appendix B. Greek measures can be computed for options on any kind of underlying asset, but we will focus here on stock options.

Definition of the Greeks

The units in which changes are measured are a matter of convention. Thus, when we define a Greek measure, we will also provide the assumed unit of change.

- Delta (Δ) measures the option price change when the stock price increases by \$1.
- Gamma (Γ) measures the change in delta when the stock price increases by \$1.
- Vega measures the change in the option price when there is an increase in volatility of 1 percentage point.[5]
- Theta (θ) measures the change in the option price when there is a decrease in the time to maturity of 1 day.
- Rho (ρ) measures the change in the option price when there is an increase in the interest rate of 1 percentage point (100 basis points).
- Psi (Ψ) measures the change in the option price when there is an increase in the continuous dividend yield of 1 percentage point (100 basis points).

A useful mnemonic device for remembering some of these is that "vega" and "volatility" share the same first letter, as do "theta" and "time." Also "r" is often used to denote the interest rate and is the first letter in "rho."

We will discuss each Greek measure in turn, assuming for simplicity that we are talking about the Greek for a purchased option. The Greek for a written option is opposite in sign to that for the same purchased option.

Delta. Delta is defined as the number of shares in the portfolio that replicates the option. For a call option, delta is positive: As the stock price increases, the call price increases. Delta is also the sensitivity of the option price to a change in the stock price: If an option is replicated with 50 shares, the option should exhibit the price sensitivity of approximately 50 shares. You can think of delta as the *share-equivalent* of the option.

4. Specifically, the Greeks are mathematical derivatives of the option price formula with respect to the inputs.

5. "Vega" is not a Greek letter. "Kappa" and "lambda" are also sometimes used to mean the same thing as vega.

FIGURE 1

Call (top graph) and put (bottom graph) deltas for 40-strike options with different times to expiration. Assumes $\sigma = 30\%$, $r = 8\%$, and $\delta = 0$.

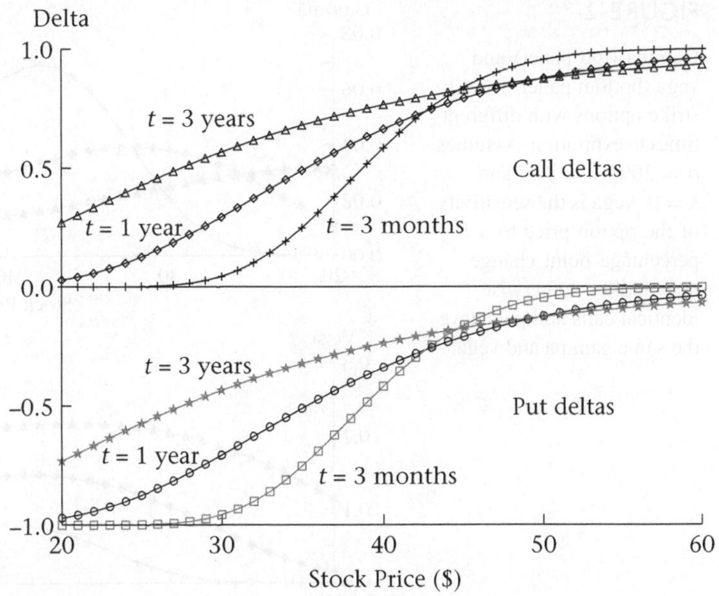

Figure 1 represents the behavior of delta for European calls and puts with differing times to expiration. The top panel in the figure illustrates that an in-the-money option will be more sensitive to the stock price than an out-of-the-money option. For example, if a call is deep in-the-money (i.e., the stock price is high relative to the strike price of \$40), it is likely to be exercised and hence the option should behave much like a leveraged position in a full share. Delta approaches 1 in this case and the share-equivalent of the option is 1. If a call is out-of-the-money, it is unlikely to be exercised and the option behaves like a position with very few shares. In this case delta is approximately 0 and the share-equivalent is 0. An at-the-money option may or may not be exercised and, hence, behaves like a position with between 0 and 1 share. Note that as time to expiration increases, the call delta is lower at high stock prices and greater at low stock prices. This behavior of delta reflects the fact that, for an option with greater time to expiration, the likelihood is greater that an out-of-the-money option will eventually become in-the-money, and the likelihood is greater that an in-the-money option will eventually become out-of-the-money.

We can use the interpretation of delta as a share-equivalent to interpret the Black-Scholes price. The formula both prices the option and also tells us what position in the stock and borrowing is equivalent to the option. The formula for the call delta is

$$\Delta = e^{-\delta T} N(d_1)$$

If we hold $e^{-\delta t} N(d_1)$ shares and borrow $Ke^{-rT} N(d_2)$ dollars, the cost of this portfolio is

$$Se^{-\delta T} N(d_1) - Ke^{-rT} N(d_2)$$

This is the Black-Scholes price. Thus, the pieces of the formula tell us what position in the stock and borrowing synthetically recreates the call. Figure 1 shows that delta changes with

FIGURE 2

Gamma (top panel) and vega (bottom panel) for 40-strike options with different times to expiration. Assumes $\sigma = 30\%$, $r = 8\%$, and $\delta = 0$. Vega is the sensitivity of the option price to a 1 percentage point change in volatility. Otherwise identical calls and puts have the same gamma and vega.

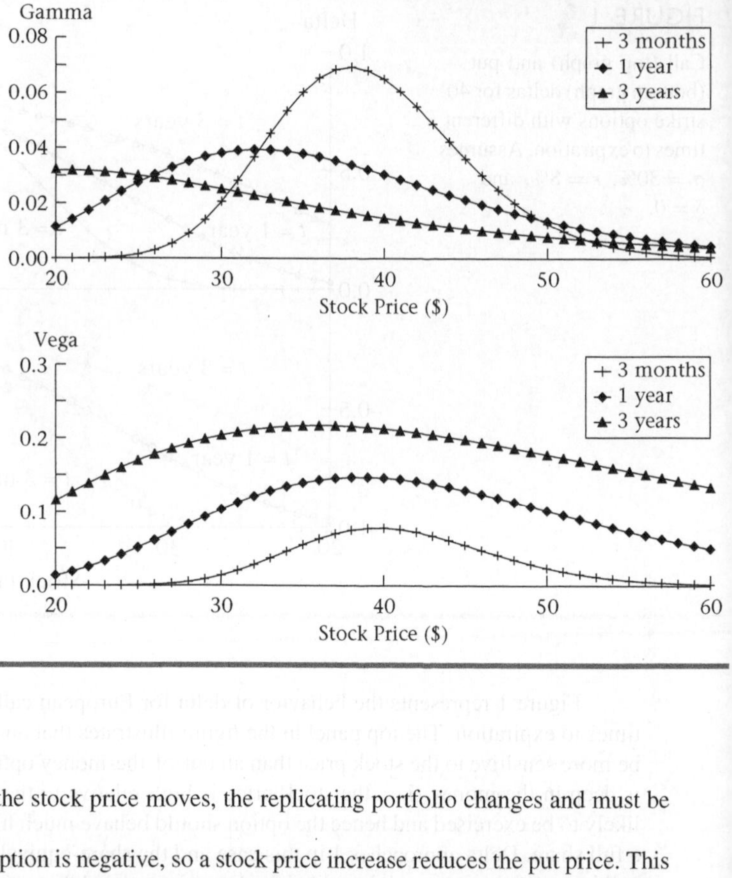

the stock price, so as the stock price moves, the replicating portfolio changes and must be adjusted dynamically.

Delta for a put option is negative, so a stock price increase reduces the put price. This relationship can be seen in the bottom panel of Figure 1. Because put-call parity implies that the put delta is the call delta minus $e^{-\delta T}$, the two panels in Figure 1 behave similarly.

Gamma. Gamma—the change in delta as the stock price changes—is always positive for a purchased call or put. As the stock price increases, delta increases. This behavior can be seen in both panels of Figure 1. For a call, delta approaches 1 as the stock price increases. For a put, delta approaches 0 as the stock price increases. Because of put-call parity, gamma is the same for a European call and put with the same strike price and time to expiration.

The top panel of Figure 2 graphs call gammas for options with three different expirations. Deep in-the-money options have a delta of about 1, and, hence, a gamma of about zero. (A delta close to 1 cannot change much as the stock price changes.) Similarly, deep out-of-the-money options have a delta of about 0 and, hence, a gamma of about 0. The large gamma for the 3-month option in Figure 2 corresponds to the steep increase in delta for the same option in Figure 1. Put-call parity implies that put gammas are the same as call gammas.

A derivative for which gamma is always positive is said to be *convex*. If gamma is positive, then delta is always increasing, and a graph of the price function will have curvature like that of the cross section of a bowl.

FIGURE 3

Call (top panel) and put (bottom panel) prices for options with different strikes at different times to expiration. Assumes $S = \$40$, $\sigma = 30\%$, $r = 8\%$, and $\delta = 0$.

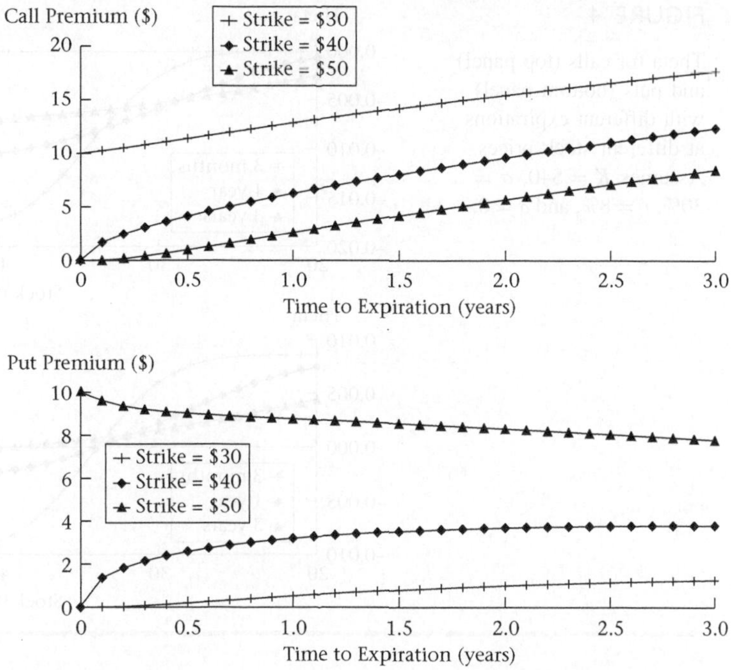

Vega. Vega measures the change in the option price due to a specified change in volatility. It is common to express vega as the change in option price for a *1 percentage point* (0.01) change in volatility.[6] The bottom panel of Figure 2 shows that vega tends to be greater for at-the-money options, and greater for options with moderate than with short times to expiration.[7] Because of put-call parity, vega, like gamma, is the same for calls and puts with the same strike price and time to expiration.

Theta. Options generally—but not always—become less valuable as time to expiration decreases. Figure 3 depicts call and put premiums for out-of-the-money, at-the-money, and in-the-money options as a function of the time to expiration. For the at-the-money (strike = \$40) call and put, time decay is rapid at expiration.

Time decay can be positive for European options in some special cases. Deep in-the-money call options on an asset with a high dividend yield and deep in-the-money puts are two examples. In both cases we would want to exercise the options early if possible. Since we cannot, the option effectively becomes a T-bill, appreciating as it gets close to expiration.

6. Vega is the derivative of the option price with respect to σ. It is expressed as the result of a percentage point change in volatility by dividing the derivative by 100.

7. The behavior of vega can be different for very long-lived options. With a 20-year option and pricing inputs otherwise identical to those in Figure 2, vega is greatest for out-of-the-money calls and, for the range of prices in the figure, lower than that for a 3-year call.

FIGURE 4

Theta for calls (top panel) and puts (bottom panel) with different expirations at different stock prices. Assumes $K = \$40$, $\sigma = 30\%$, $r = 8\%$, and $\delta = 0$.

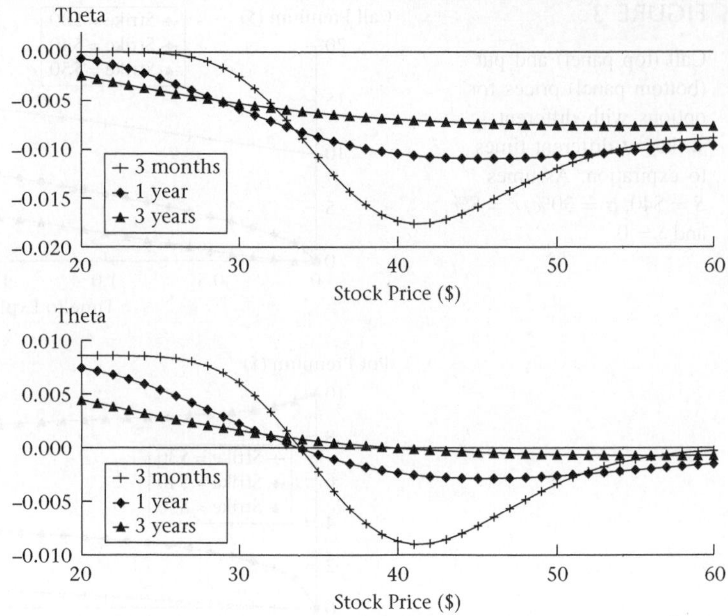

This effect is evident in the bottom panel of Figure 3, in which the in-the-money (50-strike) put becomes more valuable, other things equal, as expiration approaches.

Graphs of call and put thetas are in Figure 4. The top panel of the Figure 4 graphs theta explicitly for calls with three different times to expiration, showing that time decay is greatest (theta is most negative) for the at-the-money short-term option. In the bottom panel, theta for in-the-money puts is positive, showing that these options behave like T-bills, appreciating as they approach maturity.

Theta in Figure 4 assumes a 1-day change in the time to expiration. It is also common in practice to compute theta over longer periods, such as 10 days.

Rho. Rho, the change in premium due to a change in the interest rate, is positive for an ordinary stock call option. Exercising a call entails paying the fixed strike price to receive the stock; a higher interest rate reduces the present value of the strike. Similarly, for a put, rho is negative, since the put entitles the owner to receive cash, and the present value of this is lower with a higher interest rate. The top panel of Figure 5 shows that as the time to expiration increases and as a call option becomes more in-the-money, rho is greater. Figure 5 assumes a 1 percentage point (100 basis point) change in the interest rate.

Psi. Psi, the change in the option premium due to a change in the dividend yield, is negative for an ordinary stock call option and positive for a put. A call entitles the holder to receive the stock, but without receiving the dividends paid on the stock prior to exercising the option. Thus, the present value of the stock to be received is lower, the greater the dividend yield. Owning a put entails an obligation to deliver the stock in the future in exchange for cash. The present value of the stock to be delivered goes down when the dividend yield goes

FIGURE 5

Rho (top panel) and psi (bottom panel) at different stock prices for call options with different maturities. Assumes $K = \$40$, $\sigma = 30\%$, $r = 8\%$, and $\delta = 0$.

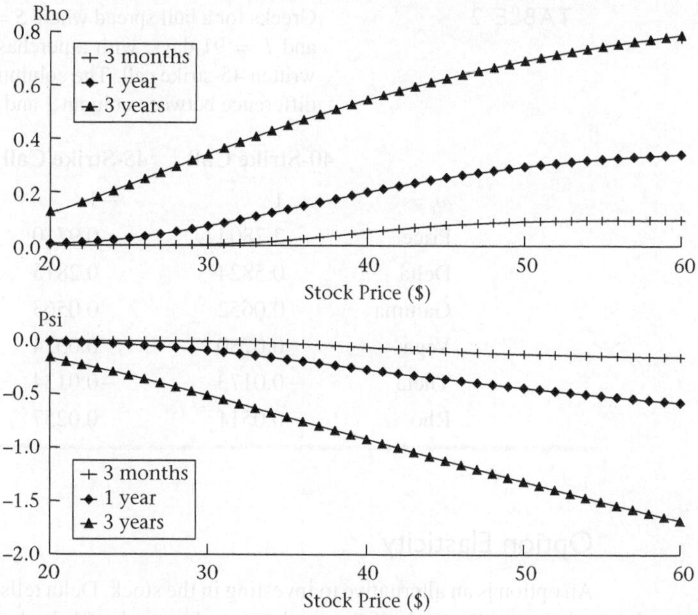

up, so the put is more valuable when the dividend yield is greater. Hence, psi for a put is positive.

The bottom panel of Figure 5 shows that the absolute value of psi increases with time to expiration. An increase in the dividend yield has little effect with a short time to maturity, but dividends lost by not owning the stock increase with time to maturity. Note that in Figure 5 the bottom panel (psi) is almost a mirror image of the top panel (rho).

Greek Measures for Portfolios

The Greek measure of a portfolio is the sum of the Greeks of the individual portfolio components. This relationship is important because it means that the risk of complicated option positions is easy to evaluate. For a portfolio containing N options with a single underlying stock, where the quantity of each option is given by n_i, we have

$$\Delta_{\text{portfolio}} = \sum_{i=1}^{N} n_i \Delta_i$$

The same relation holds true for the other Greeks as well.

Example 6. Table 2 lists Greek measures for a 40–45 bull spread. Greeks for the spread are Greeks for the 40-strike call less those for the 45-strike call. ■

TABLE 2 Greeks for a bull spread where $S = \$40$, $\sigma = 0.3$, $r = 0.08$, and $T = 91$ days, with a purchased 40-strike call and a written 45-strike call. The column titled "combined" is the difference between column 1 and column 2.

	40-Strike Call	45-Strike Call	Combined
ω_i	1	−1	—
Price	2.7804	0.9710	1.8094
Delta	0.5824	0.2815	0.3009
Gamma	0.0652	0.0563	0.0088
Vega	0.0780	0.0674	0.0106
Theta	−0.0173	−0.0134	−0.0040
Rho	0.0511	0.0257	0.0255

Option Elasticity

An option is an alternative to investing in the stock. Delta tells us the dollar risk of the option relative to the stock: If the stock price changes by \$1, by how much does the option price change? The option elasticity, by comparison, tells us the risk of the option relative to the stock in percentage terms: If the stock price changes by 1%, what is the percentage change in the value of the option?

Dollar Risk of the Option. If the stock price changes by ϵ, the change in the option price is

$$\begin{aligned}\text{Change in option price} &= \text{Change in stock price} \times \text{option delta}\\ &= \epsilon \times \Delta\end{aligned}$$

Example 7. Suppose that the stock price is $S = \$41$, the strike price is $K = \$40$, volatility is $\sigma = 0.30$, the risk-free rate is $r = 0.08$, the time to expiration is $T = 1$, and the dividend yield is $\delta = 0$. The call price is \$6.961. Delta is 0.6911. If we own options to buy 1000 shares of stock, the delta of the position is

$$1000 \times \Delta = 691.1 \text{ shares of stock}$$

Thus, the option position at this stock price has a "share-equivalent" of 691 shares. If the stock price changes by \$0.50, we expect an option price change of approximately[8]

$$1000 \times \Delta \times \$0.50 = \$345.55$$ ■

Percentage Risk of the Option. The **option elasticity** computes the percentage change in the option price relative to the percentage change in the stock price. The percentage change

8. A more accurate measure of the option price change is obtained by using both delta and gamma.

in the stock price is simply ϵ/S. The percentage change in the option price is the dollar change in the option price, $\epsilon\Delta$, divided by the option price, C:

$$\frac{\epsilon\Delta}{C}$$

The option elasticity, denoted by Ω, is the ratio of these two:

$$\Omega \equiv \frac{\%\text{ change in option price}}{\%\text{ change in stock price}} = \frac{\frac{\epsilon\Delta}{C}}{\frac{\epsilon}{S}} = \frac{S\Delta}{C} \tag{8}$$

The elasticity tells us the percentage change in the option for a 1% change in the stock. It is effectively a measure of the leverage implicit in the option.

For a call, $\Omega \geq 1$. A call option is replicated by a levered investment in the stock. A levered position in an asset is always riskier than the underlying asset.[9] Also, the implicit leverage in the option becomes greater as the option is more out-of-the-money. Thus, Ω decreases as the strike price decreases.

For a put, $\Omega \leq 0$. This occurs because the replicating position for a put option involves shorting the stock.

Example 8. Suppose $S = \$41$, $K = \$40$, $\sigma = 0.30$, $r = 0.08$, $T = 1$, and $\delta = 0$. The option price is \$6.961 and $\Delta = 0.6911$. Hence, the call elasticity is

$$\Omega = \frac{\$41 \times 0.6911}{\$6.961} = 4.071$$

The put has a price of \$2.886 and Δ of -0.3089; hence, the elasticity is

$$\Omega = \frac{\$41 \times -0.3089}{\$2.886} = -4.389 \quad ■$$

Figure 6 shows the behavior of elasticity for a call, varying both the stock price and time to expiration. The 3-month out-of-the-money calls have elasticities exceeding 8. For longer time-to-expiration options, elasticity is much less sensitive to the moneyness of the option.

The Volatility of an Option. The volatility of an option is the elasticity times the volatility of the stock:

$$\sigma_{\text{option}} = \sigma_{\text{stock}} \times |\Omega| \tag{9}$$

where $|\Omega|$ is the absolute value of Ω. Since elasticity is a measure of leverage, this calculation is analogous to the computation of the standard deviation of levered equity by multiplying the unlevered beta by the ratio of firm value to equity. Based on Figure 6, for a stock with a 30% volatility, an at-the-money option could easily have a volatility of 120% or more.

The Risk Premium and Beta of an Option. Elasticity measures the percentage sensitivity of the option relative to the stock; therefore, it tells us how the risk premium of the option compares to that of the stock.

9. This follows because $S\Delta = Se^{-\delta t}N(d_1) > C(S)$.

FIGURE 6

Elasticity for a call option for different stock prices and times to expiration. Assumes $K = \$40$, $\sigma = 0.3$, $r = 0.08$, and $\delta = 0$.

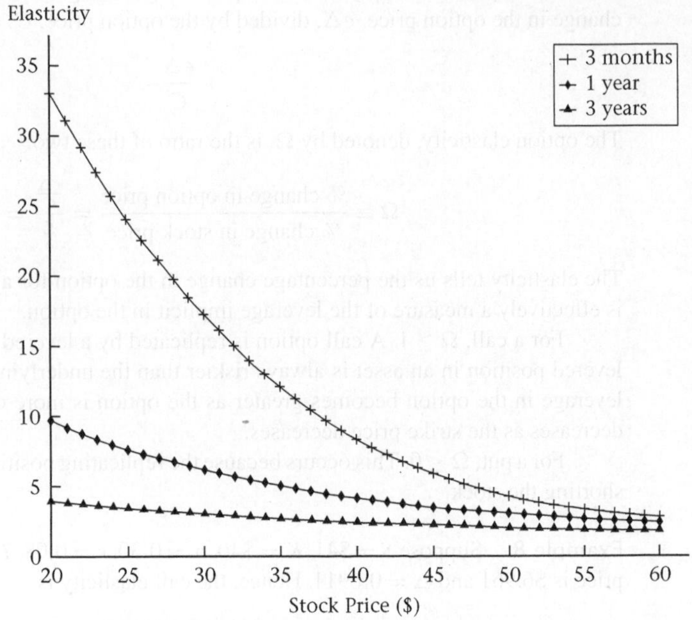

At a point in time, the option is equivalent to a position in the stock and in bonds; hence, the return on the option is a weighted average of the return on the stock and the risk-free rate. Let α denote the expected rate of return on the stock, γ the expected return on the option, and r the risk-free rate. We have

$$\gamma = \frac{\Delta S}{C(S)}\alpha + \left(1 - \frac{\Delta S}{C(S)}\right) r$$

Because $\Delta S / C(S)$ is the elasticity, this can also be written

$$\gamma = \Omega\alpha + (1 - \Omega)r$$

or

$$\gamma - r = (\alpha - r) \times \Omega \tag{10}$$

Thus, the risk premium on the option equals the risk premium on the stock times Ω.

In the capital asset pricing model, the beta of an asset is proportional to the risk premium. Thus, since the risk premium scales with elasticity, so does beta:

$$\beta_{\text{option}} = \beta_{\text{asset}} \times \Omega \tag{11}$$

Using our earlier facts about elasticity, we conclude that if the stock has a positive risk premium, then a call always has an expected return at least as great as the stock and that, other things equal, the expected return on an option goes down as the stock price goes up. In terms of the capital asset pricing model, we would say that the option beta goes down as the option becomes more in-the-money. For puts, we conclude that if the stock risk premium is positive, the put has an expected return less than that of the stock.

The Sharpe Ratio of an Option. The Sharpe ratio for any asset is the ratio of the risk premium to volatility:

$$\text{Sharpe ratio} = \frac{\alpha - r}{\sigma} \tag{12}$$

Using equations (9) and (10), the Sharpe ratio for a call is

$$\text{Sharpe ratio for call} = \frac{\Omega(\alpha - r)}{\Omega\sigma} = \frac{\alpha - r}{\sigma} \tag{13}$$

Thus, the Sharpe ratio for a call equals the Sharpe ratio for the underlying stock. This equivalence of the Sharpe ratios is obvious once we realize that the option is always equivalent to a levered position in the stock, and that leverage *per se* does not change the Sharpe ratio.[10]

The Elasticity and Risk Premium of a Portfolio. The elasticity of a portfolio is the *weighted average* of the elasticities of the portfolio components. This is in contrast to the Greeks expressed in dollar terms (delta, gamma, etc.), for which the portfolio Greek is the *sum* of the component Greeks.

To understand this, suppose there is a portfolio of N calls with the same underlying stock, where the ith call has value C_i and delta Δ_i, and where n_i is the quantity of the ith call. The portfolio value is then $\sum_{i=1}^{N} n_i C_i$. For a \$1 change in the stock price, the change in the portfolio value is

$$\sum_{i=1}^{N} n_i \Delta_i \tag{14}$$

The elasticity of the portfolio is the percentage change in the portfolio divided by the percentage change in the stock, or

$$\Omega_{\text{portfolio}} = \frac{\frac{\sum_{i=1}^{N} n_i \Delta_i}{\sum_{j=1}^{N} n_j C_j}}{\frac{1}{S}} = \sum_{i=1}^{N} \left(\frac{n_i C_i}{\sum_{j=1}^{N} n_j C_j} \right) \frac{S\Delta_i}{C_i} = \sum_{i=1}^{N} \omega_i \Omega_i \tag{15}$$

where ω_i is the fraction of the portfolio invested in option i. Using equation (10), the risk premium of the portfolio, $\gamma - r$, is just the portfolio elasticity times the risk premium on the stock, $\alpha - r$:

$$\gamma - r = \Omega_{\text{portfolio}}(\alpha - r) \tag{16}$$

10. There is one subtlety: While the Sharpe ratio for the stock and option is the same at every point in time, it is not necessarily the same when measured using realized returns. For example, suppose you perform the experiment of buying a call and holding it for a year and then evaluate the after-the-fact risk premium and standard deviation using historical returns. A standard way to do this would be to compute the average risk premium on the option and the average volatility and then divide them to create the Sharpe ratio. You would find that the call will have a lower Sharpe ratio than the stock. This is purely a result of dividing one *estimated* statistic by another.

TABLE 3 Value of 40-strike call option at different stock prices and times to expiration. Assumes $r = 8\%$, $\sigma = 30\%$, $\delta = 0$.

	Time to Expiration			
Stock Price ($)	12 Months	6 Months	3 Months	0 (Expiration)
36	3.90	2.08	1.00	0
38	5.02	3.02	1.75	0
40	6.28	4.16	2.78	0
42	7.67	5.47	4.07	2
44	9.15	6.95	5.58	4

4. PROFIT DIAGRAMS BEFORE MATURITY

Now we will see how to draw payoff and profit diagrams for options prior to expiration. We will illustrate the calculations with two strategies: buying a call option, and entering a calendar spread (buying and selling options with different times to expiration).

Purchased Call Option

If we buy a call option and sell it prior to expiration, profit will depend upon the changes in the stock price and time to expiration. Table 3 shows the Black-Scholes value of a call option for five different stock prices at four different times to expiration. By varying the stock price for a given time to expiration, keeping everything else the same, we are able to graph the value of the call.

Figure 7 plots Black-Scholes call prices for stock prices ranging from \$20 to \$60, including the values in Table 3. Notice that the value of the option prior to expiration is a smoothed version of the value of the option at expiration.

The payoff diagram depicted in Figure 7 does not take into account the original cost of the option. We compute profit by subtracting from the value of the option at each stock price the original cost of the position, plus interest.[11] For example, if we buy a 1-year option and hold it for 9 months, the resulting profit diagram is the payoff for a 3-month option less the original cost plus interest of the 1-year option. The "held 9 months" line in the bottom panel of Figure 7 is thus the "3 months" line from the top panel less $\$6.674 = \$6.285e^{0.08\times 0.75}$.

Example 9. The 1-year option in Table 3 costs \$6.285 at a stock price of \$40. If after 1 day the stock price is still \$40, the value of the option will have fallen to \$6.274, and the 1-day holding period profit is $\$6.274 - \$6.285 \times e^{0.08/365} = -\$0.012$. This loss reflects the theta of the option. If the stock price were to increase to \$42, the option premium would increase to \$7.655, and the 1-day holding period profit would be $\$7.655 - \$6.285 \times e^{0.08/365} = \$1.369$.

11. This is like assuming the option is financed by borrowing.

FIGURE 7

Payoff and profit diagram for a purchased call option. Top panel shows payoff diagrams for options with different remaining times to expiration. Bottom panel shows profit diagrams for a one-year call bought when the stock price was \$40 and then held for different lengths of time. Assumes $K = \$40$, $r = 8\%$, $\delta = 0$, and $\sigma = 30\%$.

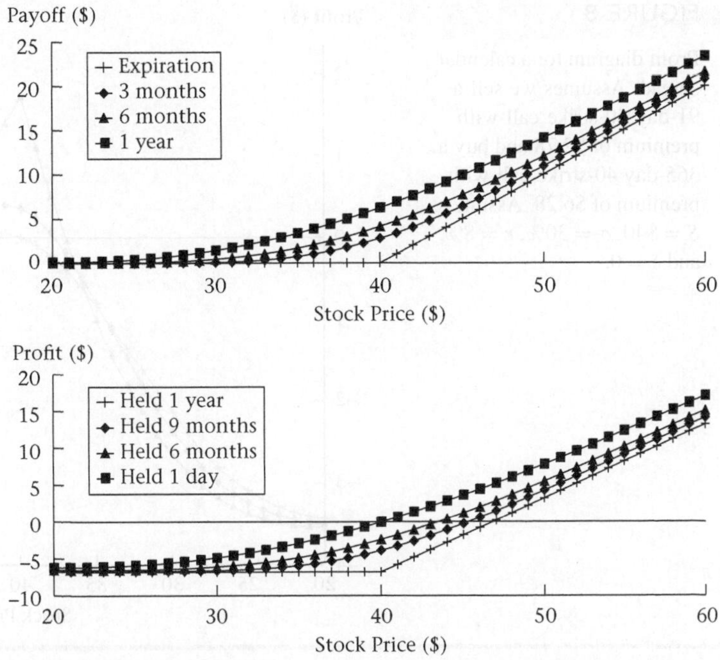

After 6 months, the holding period profit at a price of \$40 would be $\$4.155 - \$6.285 \times e^{0.08\times 0.5} = -\$2.386$. Even if the stock price had risen to \$42, the holding period return would still be $-\$1.068$. These profit calculations are illustrated in the bottom panel of Figure 7. ■

The option premium graphs in Figure 7 illustrate the behavior of delta and gamma discussed in Section 3. In all cases the slope of the call option graph is positive. This corresponds to a positive delta. In addition, the slope becomes greater as the stock price increases. Delta increasing with the stock price corresponds to a positive gamma. The fact that gamma is always positive implies that the graphs will be curved like the cross section of a bowl, i.e., the option price is *convex*. A positive gamma implies convex curvature. A negative gamma implies the opposite (concave) curvature.

Calendar Spreads

There are a number of option spreads that permit you to speculate on the volatility of a stock, including straddle, strangle, and butterfly spreads. These spreads all contain options with the same time to expiration and different strikes. To speculate on volatility you could also enter into a **calendar spread**, in which the options you buy and sell have different expiration dates.

Suppose you want to speculate that XYZ's stock price will be unchanged over the next 3 months. An alternative to a written straddle or a written butterfly spread is simply to

FIGURE 8

Profit diagram for a calendar spread. Assumes we sell a 91-day 40-strike call with premium of \$2.78 and buy a 365-day 40-strike call with premium of \$6.28. Assumes $S = \$40$, $\sigma = 30\%$, $r = 8\%$, and $\delta = 0$.

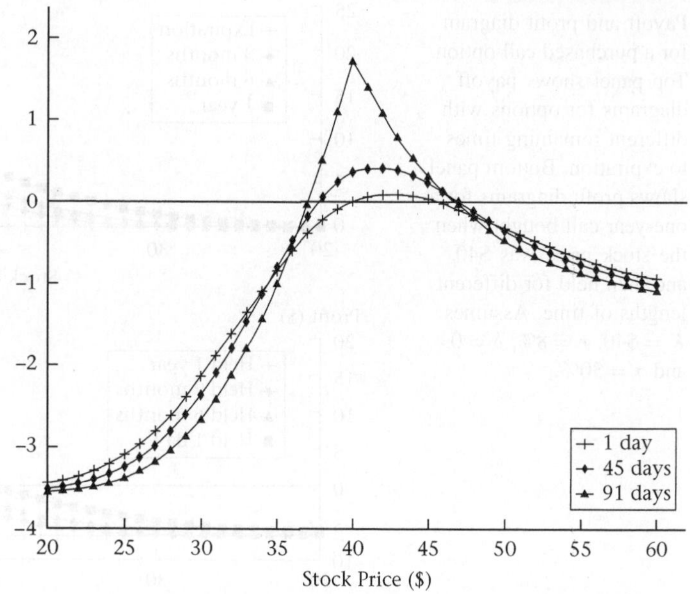

sell a call or put, in the hope that the stock price will remain unchanged and you will earn the premium. The potential cost is that if the option does move into the money, you can have a large loss.

To protect against a stock price increase when selling a call, you can simultaneously buy a call option with the same strike and greater time to expiration. For example, suppose you sell a 40-strike call with 91 days to expiration and buy a 40-strike call with 1 year to expiration. At a stock price of \$40, the premiums are \$2.78 for the 91-day call and \$6.28 for the 1-year call. The profit diagram for this position for holding periods of 1 day, 45 days, and 91 days is displayed in Figure 8. You can see that you earn maximum profit over 91 days if the stock price does not change.

We can understand the behavior of profit for this position by considering the theta of the two options. The top panel of Figure 4 shows that theta is more negative for the 91-day call (−0.0173) than for the 1-year call (−0.0104). Thus, if the stock price does not change over the course of 1 day, the position will make money because the written option loses more value than the purchased option. Over 91 days, the written 91-day option will lose its full value (its price declines from \$2.78 to 0), while the 1-year option will lose only about \$1 (its price declines from \$6.28 to \$5.28) if the stock price does not change. The difference in the rates of time decay generates profit of approximately \$1.78.

Figure 8 shows that at the initial stock price of \$40, delta is positive: The delta of the written 91-day call is 0.5825 and that of the purchased 1-year call is 0.6615, for a net positive delta of 0.0790. Thus, over 1 day, the maximum profit occurs if the stock price rises by a small amount.

5. IMPLIED VOLATILITY

To price an option we need volatility as an input. Specifically, we require an estimate of *prospective* volatility: What is the future uncertainty about the return on the underlying asset? The vega diagram in Figure 2 shows that option prices, particularly for near-the-money options, can be quite sensitive to volatility. Moreover, volatility is unobservable, which raises the question of how options are priced in practice.[12]

One approach is to compute historical volatility using the history of returns. A problem with historical volatility is that expected future volatility can be different from historical volatility. For example, political turbulence, or predictable events such as earnings announcements and government information releases, can create periods in which investors expect uncertainty to be unusually high. Sophisticated statistical models can improve upon simple historical volatility estimates, but ultimately you cannot count on history to always provide you with a reliable estimate of future volatility.

We obtain a different perspective by thinking of an option market as the venue where volatility is traded and *revealed*. Options are claims that investors use to hedge and speculate on future values of the stock price. Therefore the option price should reveal the market's expectations about the future stock price distribution. (The price of a deep out-of-the-money put, for example, depends upon the market's assessment that the stock will decline enough for the put to be valuable.) One way to extract information from an option price is by computing the option's **implied volatility**, which is the volatility that, when put into a pricing formula, yields the observed option price.[13]

Computing Implied Volatility

To compute a Black-Scholes implied volatility, assume that we observe the stock price S, strike price K, interest rate r, dividend yield δ, and time to expiration T. The implied call volatility is the $\hat{\sigma}$ that solves

$$\text{Market option price} = C(S, K, \hat{\sigma}, r, T, \delta) \tag{17}$$

By definition, if we use implied volatility to price an option, we obtain the market price of the option. Thus, we cannot use implied volatility to assess whether an option price is correct, but implied volatility does tell us the market's assessment of volatility.

Equation (17) cannot be solved directly for the implied volatility, $\hat{\sigma}$, so it is necessary to use an iterative procedure to solve the equation. Any pricing model can be used to calculate an implied volatility, but Black-Scholes implied volatilities are frequently used as benchmarks.

12. Of the five other inputs to the Black-Scholes formula, we also cannot observe future dividends. Over short horizons, however, dividends are typically stable, so usually past dividends can be used to forecast future dividends.

13. You might wonder: If options are priced by market participants based on assessments of future uncertainty, what is the role of an option pricing formula? An answer is that any financial formula is just a guide, a way to organize and categorize information and understanding. The Black-Scholes analysis provides an economic framework for thinking about options, and it has proven hugely influential even though it is not just a mechanical means of obtaining the "correct" answer.

Example 10. A 45-strike 6-month European call has a premium of \$8.07. The stock price is \$50, the interest rate is 8%, and the dividend yield is zero. The option price as a function of volatility is

$$\$8.07 = \text{BSCall}(50, 45, \sigma, 0.08, 0.5, 0)$$

By trial and error (or by using a tool such as Excel's Goalseek), we find that setting $\sigma = 28.7\%$ gives us a call price of \$8.07.[14] ■

Implied volatility computed using a pricing model is a characteristic of an individual option, so it is interesting to compare implied volatilities for options across strike prices and times to expiration. The top panel of Figure 9 displays implied volatilities for Apple, and the bottom panel displays implied volatilities for the S&P 500 index.

Figure 9 exhibits patterns commonly found for equity and index options. Frequently, implied volatility is greatest for out-of-the-money puts (in-the-money calls) and lowest for near-the-money options. As the expiration date changes, implied volatility for a given strike can go either up or down. Implied volatility differences across strikes can be substantial.

The volatility plots in Figure 9 exhibit different patterns. A **volatility smile** is symmetric, with volatility lowest for at-the-money options, and high for in-the-money and out-of-the-money options. A lopsided smile is a "smirk" and an upside-down smile would be a "frown." A difference in volatilities between in-the-money and out-of-the-money options, evident in Figure 9, is referred to as **volatility skew**. Explaining such patterns and modifying pricing models to account for them is a challenge for option pricing theory.

Figure 9 graphs put implied volatilities. Implied volatilities for calls will exhibit similar patterns. For European options (such as the S&P 500 index options), call and put volatilities should be the same because of put-call parity. For American options, the possibility of early exercise can introduce differences. Even for European options, implied volatilities in practice differ for puts and calls because of transaction costs, bid-ask spreads, and so forth. It is common to report separate implied volatilities for option bid and ask prices.

In addition to computing implied volatility using the Black-Scholes, there is also a so-called model-free calculation that is the basis of the S&P 500 VIX volatility index, known as the VIX. The VIX calculation uses option prices for all available strike prices to compute a single implied volatility.

Figure 10 graphs the VIX index since 1990. You can see on the graph that during the financial crisis, the VIX exceeded 80% for a brief period. Overall, it is apparent that volatility is volatile. The VIX is widely watched and reported upon. It is often described as the "fear index" because it generally rises during times of financial stress. There are also both futures and options based on the VIX.

Using Implied Volatility

Implied volatility is a standard descriptive measure with important practical uses.

14. This note has been intentionally omitted for this edition.

FIGURE 9

Implied put volatilities for Apple and the S&P 500 on October 27, 2010. The top panel shows implied volatility curves for Apple and the bottom panel shows the same for the S&P 500 index, each for three different maturities. Closing prices for Apple and the S&P 500 were 307.83 and 1182.45.

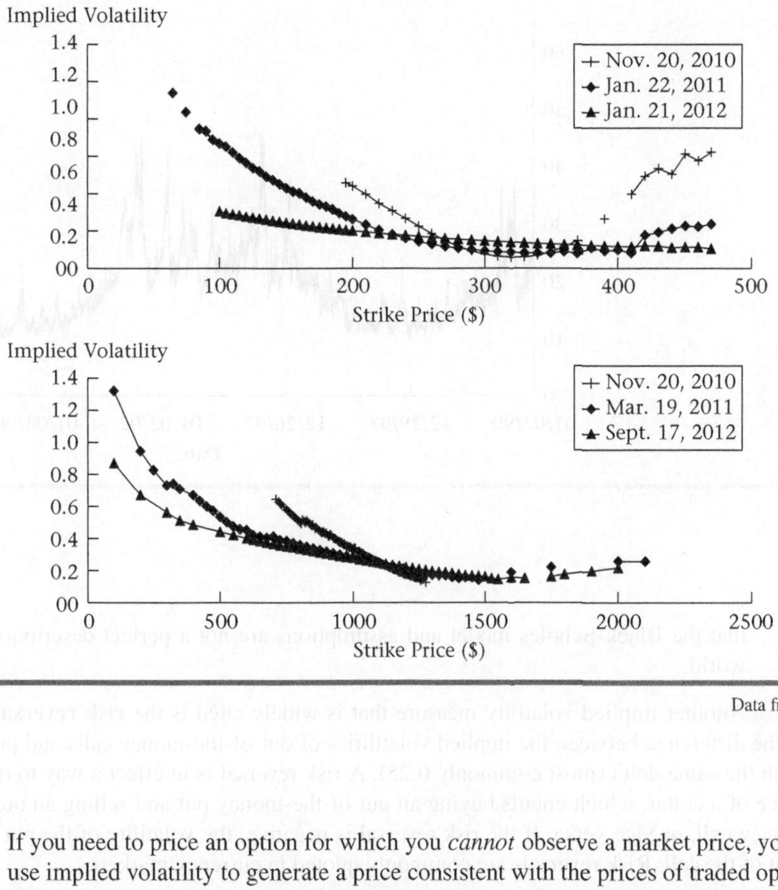

Data from OptionMetrics.

- If you need to price an option for which you *cannot* observe a market price, you can use implied volatility to generate a price consistent with the prices of traded options. Market-makers, for example, will price options consistently with prices of similar options.
- Implied volatility is often used as a quick way to describe the level of option prices on a given underlying asset: you could quote option prices in terms of volatility, rather than as a dollar price. There are typically numerous options on a given asset; implied volatility can be used to succinctly describe the general level of option prices for a given underlying asset.
- Volatility skew provides a measure of the extent to which pricing deviates from the assumptions underlying the Black-Scholes model. If the Black-Scholes model were literally true, implied volatilities for a given underlying asset would be the same at all strike prices and maturities. One common test of the Black-Scholes model is to check the empirical validity of this assumption. The existence of volatility skew suggests

FIGURE 10

S&P 500 implied volatility (VIX) from January 1990 to May 2011.

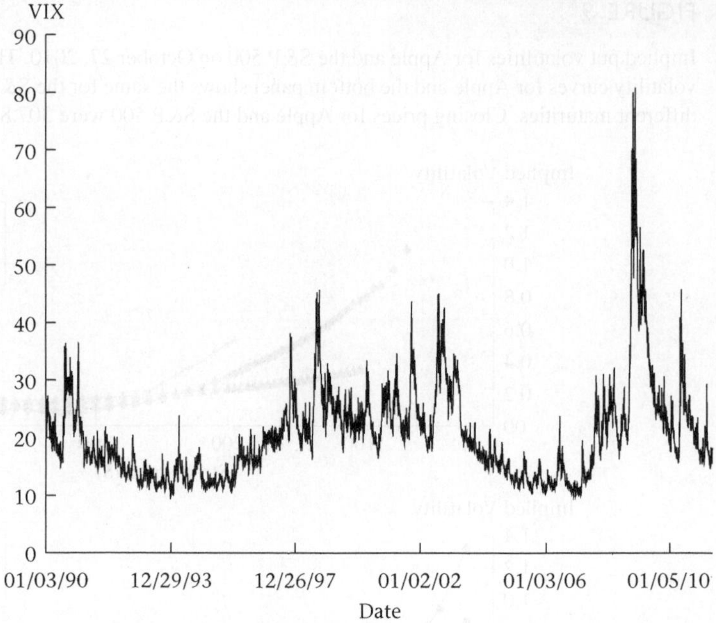

Data from Yahoo.

that the Black-Scholes model and assumptions are not a perfect description of the world.

Another implied volatility measure that is widely cited is the **risk reversal**, which is the difference between the implied volatilities of out-of-the-money calls and puts, each with the same delta (most commonly 0.25). A risk reversal is in effect a way to quote the price of a collar, which entails buying an out-of-the-money put and selling an out-of-the-money call, or vice versa. If the risk reversal is negative, the volatility of the put exceeds that of the call. Risk reversals are commonly quoted in currency markets.

6. PERPETUAL AMERICAN OPTIONS

The Black-Scholes formula prices options that can only be exercised at expiration. In this section we present formulas, based on Merton (1973b), for the prices of calls and puts that never expire, which are known as **perpetual options** or "expirationless options."

American options are harder to price than European options because it is difficult to characterize the optimal exercise strategy.

Perpetual American options are different because such an option always has the same time to expiration, namely infinity. Because time to expiration is constant, the option exercise problem will look the same today, tomorrow, and forever. Thus, the price at which it is optimal to exercise the option is constant. The optimal exercise strategy entails picking the exercise barrier that maximizes the value of the option and then exercising the option the first time the stock price reaches that barrier.

Valuing Perpetual Options

In this section we present the formulas for perpetual calls and puts. The formulas provide the option price and also the price of the underlying asset at which exercise is optimal.

First, define h_1 and h_2:

$$h_1 = \frac{1}{2} - \frac{r-\delta}{\sigma^2} + \sqrt{\left(\frac{r-\delta}{\sigma^2} - \frac{1}{2}\right)^2 + \frac{2r}{\sigma^2}}$$

$$h_2 = \frac{1}{2} - \frac{r-\delta}{\sigma^2} - \sqrt{\left(\frac{r-\delta}{\sigma^2} - \frac{1}{2}\right)^2 + \frac{2r}{\sigma^2}}$$

The value of a perpetual American call with strike price K that is exercised when $S \geq H_c$ is

$$\boxed{(H_c - K)\left(\frac{S}{H_c}\right)^{h_1}} \tag{18}$$

where H_c is given by

$$H_c = K\left(\frac{h_1}{h_1 - 1}\right) \tag{19}$$

You can verify that if $\delta = 0$, then $H_c = \infty$: It is never optimal to exercise a call option on a non-dividend-paying stock.

Notice that equation (18), the value of the call, is a function of H_c, the price at which it is exercised. It is straightforward to show (using calculus) that the H_c given by equation (19) maximizes the value of the call. The option holder chooses an exercise strategy that makes the call as valuable as possible.

The value of a perpetual American put with strike price K that is exercised when $S \leq H_p$ is

$$\boxed{(K - H_p)\left(\frac{S}{H_p}\right)^{h_2}} \tag{20}$$

where H_p is given by

$$H_p = K\frac{h_2}{h_2 - 1} \tag{21}$$

You can verify that if $r = 0$, then $H_p = 0$: It is never optimal to exercise a put option when the interest rate is non-positive. As with the call, H_p in equation (21) maximizes the value of the put.

Example 11. Let $S = \$45$, $K = \$40$, $\sigma = 0.30$, $r = 0.05$, and $\delta = 0.02$. Using equation (18), a perpetual American call has a premium of \$25.41 and will be exercised when $S = \$211.05$. A perpetual American put has a premium of \$9.66 and will be exercised when $S = \$18.95$.[15] ■

Barrier Present Values

If you look at equation (18), you will see that the formula for the value of a perpetual call is the number of dollars received at exercise $(H_c - K)$ times the factor $(S/H_c)^{h_1}$. The value at time 0, of \$1 received when the stock price reaches H, assuming $H > S_0$, is

$$\text{Value of \$1 received when } S \text{ first reaches } H \text{ from below} = \left(\frac{S_0}{H}\right)^{h_1} \tag{22}$$

Similarly, the value at time 0 of \$1 received when the stock price reaches H, assuming $H < S_0$, is

$$\text{Value of \$1 received when } S \text{ first reaches } H \text{ from above} = \left(\frac{S_0}{H}\right)^{h_2} \tag{23}$$

We will refer to the expressions in equations (22) and (23) as "barrier present values."

CHAPTER SUMMARY

Under certain assumptions, the Black-Scholes formula provides an exact formula—approximated by the binomial formula—for pricing European options. The inputs to the Black-Scholes formula are the same as for the binomial formula: the stock price, strike price, volatility, interest rate, time to expiration, and dividend yield. As with the binomial formula, the Black-Scholes formula accommodates different underlying assets by changing the dividend yield.

Option Greeks measure the change in the option price (or other option characteristic) for a change in an option input. Delta, gamma, vega, theta, rho, and psi are widely used in practice to assess the risk of an option position. The option elasticity is the percentage change in the option's price for a 1% change in the stock price. The volatility and beta of an option are the volatility and beta of the stock times the option elasticity. Thus, an option and the underlying stock have the same Sharpe ratio.

Of the inputs to the Black-Scholes formula, volatility is hardest to estimate. In practice it is common to use the formula in backward fashion to infer the market's estimate of volatility from the option price. This implied volatility is computed by finding the volatility for which the formula matches observed market prices for options. In theory, all options of a given maturity should have the same implied volatility. In practice they do not.

Although there is no simple formula for valuing a finitely lived American option, there are simple formulas in the special case of perpetual puts and calls.

15. This note has been intentionally omitted for this edition.

FURTHER READING

The classic early papers on option pricing are Black and Scholes (1973) and Merton (1973b). The details of how the binomial model converges to the Black-Scholes model are in Cox et al. (1979). The perpetual put formula is derived in Merton (1973b). The link between the perpetual call and put formulas is discussed by McDonald and Siegel (1986).

PROBLEMS

In answering many of these problems you can use the functions BSCall, BSPut, CallPerpetual, and PutPerpetual and the accompanying functions for the Greeks.

1. Use a spreadsheet to verify the option prices in Examples 1 and 2.

2. Using the BinomCall and BinomPut functions, compute the binomial approximations for the options in Examples 1 and 2. Be sure to compute prices for $n = 8, 9, 10, 11$, and 12. What do you observe about the behavior of the binomial approximation?

3. Let $S = \$100$, $K = \$120$, $\sigma = 30\%$, $r = 0.08$, and $\delta = 0$.

  a. Compute the Black-Scholes call price for 1 year to maturity and for a variety of very long times to maturity. What happens to the option price as $T \rightarrow \infty$?

  b. Set $\delta = 0.001$. Repeat (a). Now what happens to the option price? What accounts for the difference?

4. Let $S = \$120$, $K = \$100$, $\sigma = 30\%$, $r = 0$, and $\delta = 0.08$.

  a. Compute the Black-Scholes call price for 1 year to maturity and for a variety of very long times to maturity. What happens to the price as $T \rightarrow \infty$?

  b. Set $r = 0.001$. Repeat (a). Now what happens? What accounts for the difference?

5. The exchange rate is ¥95/€, the yen-denominated interest rate is 1.5%, the euro-denominated interest rate is 3.5%, and the exchange rate volatility is 10%.

  a. What is the price of a 90-strike yen-denominated euro put with 6 months to expiration?

  b. What is the price of a 1/90-strike euro-denominated yen call with 6 months to expiration?

  c. What is the link between your answer to (a) and your answer to (b), converted to yen?

6. Suppose XYZ is a non-dividend-paying stock. Suppose $S = \$100$, $\sigma = 40\%$, $\delta = 0$, and $r = 0.06$.

  a. What is the price of a 105-strike call option with 1 year to expiration?

  b. What is the 1-year forward price for the stock?

  c. What is the price of a 1-year 105-strike option, where the underlying asset is a futures contract maturing at the same time as the option?

7. Suppose $S = \$100$, $K = \$95$, $\sigma = 30\%$, $r = 0.08$, $\delta = 0.03$, and $T = 0.75$.

a. Compute the Black-Scholes price of a call.

b. Compute the Black-Scholes price of a call for which $S = \$100 \times e^{-0.03 \times 0.75}$, $K = \$95 \times e^{-0.08 \times 0.75}$, $\sigma = 0.3$, $T = 0.75$, $\delta = 0$, $r = 0$. How does your answer compare to that for (a)?

8. Make the same assumptions as in the previous problem.

a. What is the 9-month forward price for the stock?

b. Compute the price of a 95-strike 9-month call option on a futures contract.

c. What is the relationship between your answer to (b) and the price you computed in the previous question? Why?

9. Assume $K = \$40$, $\sigma = 30\%$, $r = 0.08$, $T = 0.5$, and the stock is to pay a single dividend of \$2 tomorrow, with no dividends thereafter.

a. Suppose $S = \$50$. What is the price of a European call option? Consider an otherwise identical American call. What is its price?

b. Repeat, only suppose $S = \$60$.

c. Under what circumstance would you not exercise the option today?

10. "Time decay is greatest for an option close to expiration." Use the spreadsheet functions to evaluate this statement. Consider both the dollar change in the option value and the percentage change in the option value, and examine both in-the-money and out-of-the-money options.

11. In the absence of an explicit formula, we can estimate the change in the option price due to a change in an input—such as σ—by computing the following for a small value of ϵ:

$$\text{Vega} = \frac{\text{BSCall}(S, K, \sigma + \epsilon, r, t, \delta) - \text{BSCall}(S, K, \sigma - \epsilon, r, t, \delta)}{2\epsilon}.$$

a. What is the logic behind this calculation? Why does ϵ need to be small?

b. Compare the results of this calculation with results obtained from BSCallVega.

12. Suppose $S = \$100$, $K = \$95$, $\sigma = 30\%$, $r = 0.08$, $\delta = 0.03$, and $T = 0.75$. Using the technique in the previous problem, compute the Greek measure corresponding to a change in the dividend yield. What is the predicted effect of a change of 1 percentage point in the dividend yield?

13. Consider a bull spread where you buy a 40-strike call and sell a 45-strike call. Suppose $S = \$40$, $\sigma = 0.30$, $r = 0.08$, $\delta = 0$, and $T = 0.5$. Draw a graph with stock prices ranging from \$20 to \$60 depicting the profit on the bull spread after 1 day, 3 months, and 6 months.

14. Consider a bull spread where you buy a 40-strike call and sell a 45-strike call. Suppose $\sigma = 0.30$, $r = 0.08$, $\delta = 0$, and $T = 0.5$.

a. Suppose $S = \$40$. What are delta, gamma, vega, theta, and rho?

b. Suppose $S = \$45$. What are delta, gamma, vega, theta, and rho?

c. Are any of your answers to (a) and (b) different? If so, why?

15. Consider a bull spread where you buy a 40-strike put and sell a 45-strike put. Suppose $\sigma = 0.30$, $r = 0.08$, $\delta = 0$, and $T = 0.5$.

a. Suppose $S = \$40$. What are delta, gamma, vega, theta, and rho?

b. Suppose $S = \$45$. What are delta, gamma, vega, theta, and rho?

c. Are any of your answers to (a) and (b) different? If so, why?

d. Are any of your answers different in this problem from those in Problem 14? If so, why?

16. Assume $r = 8\%$, $\sigma = 30\%$, $\delta = 0$. In doing the following calculations, use a stock price range of \$60–\$140, stock price increments of \$5, and two different times to expiration: 1 year and 1 day. Consider purchasing a 100-strike straddle, i.e., buying one 100-strike put and one 100-strike call.

a. Compute delta, vega, theta, and rho of the call and put separately, for the different stock prices and times to expiration.

b. Compute delta, vega, theta, and rho of the purchased straddle (do this by adding the Greeks of the individual options). As best you can, explain intuitively the signs of the straddle Greeks.

c. Graph delta, vega, theta, and rho of the straddle with 1 year to expiration as a function of the stock price. In each case explain why the graph looks as it does.

17. Assume $r = 8\%$, $\sigma = 30\%$, $\delta = 0$. Using 1-year-to-expiration European options, construct a position where you sell two 80-strike puts, buy one 95-strike put, buy one 105-strike call, and sell two 120-strike calls. For a range of stock prices from \$60 to \$140, compute delta, vega, theta, and rho of this position. As best you can, explain intuitively the signs of the Greeks.

18. Consider a perpetual call option with $S = \$50$, $K = \$60$, $r = 0.06$, $\sigma = 0.40$, and $\delta = 0.03$.

a. What is the price of the option and at what stock price should it be exercised?

b. Suppose $\delta = 0.04$ with all other inputs the same. What happens to the price and exercise barrier? Why?

c. Suppose $r = 0.07$ with all other inputs the same. What happens to the price and exercise barrier? Why?

d. Suppose $\sigma = 50\%$ with all other inputs the same. What happens to the price and exercise barrier? Why?

19. Consider a perpetual put option with $S = \$50$, $K = \$60$, $r = 0.06$, $\sigma = 0.40$, and $\delta = 0.03$.

a. What is the price of the option and at what stock price should it be exercised?

b. Suppose $\delta = 0.04$ with all other inputs the same. What happens to the price and exercise barrier? Why?

c. Suppose $r = 0.07$ with all other inputs the same. What happens to the price and exercise barrier? Why?

d. Suppose $\sigma = 50\%$ with all other inputs the same. What happens to the price and exercise barrier? Why?

20. Let $S = \$100$, $K = \$90$, $\sigma = 30\%$, $r = 8\%$, $\delta = 5\%$, and $T = 1$.

a. What is the Black-Scholes call price?

b. Now price a put where $S = \$90$, $K = \$100$, $\sigma = 30\%$, $r = 5\%$, $\delta = 8\%$, and $T = 1$.

c. What is the link between your answers to (a) and (b)? Why?

21. Repeat the previous problem, but this time for perpetual options. What do you notice about the prices? What do you notice about the exercise barriers?

Appendix A THE STANDARD NORMAL DISTRIBUTION

The *standard normal probability density function* is given by

$$\phi(x) \equiv \frac{1}{\sqrt{2\pi}} e^{-\frac{1}{2}x^2} \tag{24}$$

The *cumulative standard normal distribution function*, evaluated at a point x, for example, tells us the probability that a number randomly drawn from the standard normal distribution will fall below x, or

$$N(x) \equiv \int_{-\infty}^{x} \phi(x)dx \equiv \int_{-\infty}^{x} \frac{1}{\sqrt{2\pi}} e^{-\frac{1}{2}x^2} dx \tag{25}$$

Excel computes the cumulative distribution using the built-in function NORMSDIST. Note that $N'(x_1) = \phi(x_1)$.

Appendix B FORMULAS FOR OPTION GREEKS

In this section we present formulas for the Greeks for an option on a stock paying continuous dividends.[16]

Delta (Δ)

Delta measures the change in the option price for a \$1 change in the stock price:

16. If you wish to derive any of these formulas for yourself, or if you find that different authors use formulas that appear different, here are two useful things to know. The first is a result of the normal distribution being symmetric around 0:

$$N(x) = 1 - N(-x)$$

With some effort, the second can be verified algebraically:

$$Se^{-\delta T} N'(d_1) = Ke^{-rT} N'(d_2)$$

$$\text{Call delta} = \frac{\partial C(S, K, \sigma, r, T-t, \delta)}{\partial S} = e^{-\delta(T-t)}N(d_1)$$

$$\text{Put delta} = \frac{\partial P(S, K, \sigma, r, T-t, \delta)}{\partial S} = -e^{-\delta(T-t)}N(-d_1)$$

Gamma (Γ)

Gamma measures the change in delta when the stock price changes:

$$\text{Call gamma} = \frac{\partial^2 C(S, K, \sigma, r, T-t, \delta)}{\partial S^2} = \frac{e^{-\delta(T-t)}N'(d_1)}{S\sigma\sqrt{T-t}}$$

$$\text{Put gamma} = \frac{\partial^2 P(S, K, \sigma, r, T-t, \delta)}{\partial S^2} = \text{Call gamma}$$

The second equation follows from put-call parity.

Theta (θ)

Theta measures the change in the option price with respect to calendar time (t), holding fixed time to expiration (T):

$$\begin{aligned}\text{Call theta} &= \frac{\partial C(S, K, \sigma, r, T-t, \delta)}{\partial t} \\ &= \delta S e^{-\delta(T-t)}N(d_1) - rKe^{-r(T-t)}N(d_2) - \frac{Ke^{-r(T-t)}N'(d_2)\sigma}{2\sqrt{T-t}}\end{aligned}$$

$$\begin{aligned}\text{Put theta} &= \frac{\partial P(S, K, \sigma, r, T-t, \delta)}{\partial t} \\ &= \text{Call theta} + rKe^{-r(T-t)} - \delta S e^{-\delta(T-t)}\end{aligned}$$

If time to expiration is measured in years, theta will be the *annualized* change in the option value. To obtain a per-day theta, divide by 365.

Vega

Vega measures the change in the option price when volatility changes. Some writers also use the terms *lambda* or *kappa* to refer to this measure:

$$\text{Call vega} = \frac{\partial C(S, K, \sigma, r, T-t, \delta)}{\partial \sigma} = Se^{-\delta(T-t)}N'(d_1)\sqrt{T-t}$$

$$\text{Put vega} = \frac{\partial P(S, K, \sigma, r, T-t, \delta)}{\partial \sigma} = \text{Call vega}$$

It is common to report vega as the change in the option price *per percentage point* change in the volatility. This requires dividing the vega formula above by 100.

Rho (ρ)

Rho is the partial derivative of the option price with respect to the interest rate:

$$\text{Call rho} = \frac{\partial C(S, K, \sigma, r, T - t, \delta)}{\partial r} = (T - t)Ke^{-r(T-t)}N(d_2)$$

$$\text{Put rho} = \frac{\partial P(S, K, \sigma, r, T - t, \delta)}{\partial r} = -(T - t)Ke^{-r(T-t)}N(-d_2)$$

These expressions for rho assume a change in r of 1.0. We are typically interested in evaluating the effect of a change of 0.01 (100 basis points) or 0.0001 (1 basis point). To report rho as a change per percentage point in the interest rate, divide this measure by 100. To interpret it as a change per basis point, divide by 10,000.

Psi (ψ)

Psi is the partial derivative of the option price with respect to the continuous dividend yield:

$$\text{Call psi} = \frac{\partial C(S, K, \sigma, r, T - t, \delta)}{\partial \delta} = -(T - t)Se^{-\delta(T-t)}N(d_1)$$

$$\text{Put psi} = \frac{\partial P(S, K, \sigma, r, T - t, \delta)}{\partial \delta} = (T - t)Se^{-\delta(T-t)}N(-d_1)$$

To interpret psi as a price change per percentage point change in the dividend yield, divide by 100.

Market-Making and Delta-Hedging

At least as important as the Black-Scholes *formula* is the Black-Scholes *technique* for deriving the formula. In this chapter we explore the Black-Scholes technique by considering the market-maker perspective on options. What issues confront the market professionals who supply the options that customers want to buy? The insights we gain from studying this question apply not only to pricing call and put options but also to derivatives pricing and risk management in general.

The Black-Scholes approach to deriving the option pricing formula assumes that market-makers are profit-maximizers in a competitive market who want to hedge the risk of their option positions. Market-makers can hedge by taking a stock position that offsets the option's delta. Because option deltas change as the stock price changes, market-makers must continually review and modify their hedging decisions.

We will see that the costs of carrying a hedged option position can be expressed in terms of delta, gamma, and theta. On average, competitive market-makers should expect to break even by hedging. Under certain assumptions about the behavior of the stock price, the market-maker's break-even price is the Black-Scholes option price. Thus, as with any other good in a competitive market, the price of an option should equal the market-maker's cost of producing it.

1. WHAT DO MARKET-MAKERS DO?

A **market-maker** stands ready to sell to buyers and to buy from sellers. The owner of an appliance store, for example, is a market-maker. The store owner buys televisions at a low price (the wholesale price) and sells them at cost plus a markup (the retail price), earning the difference. The markup must at a minimum cover the cost of doing business—rent, salaries, utilities, and advertising—so that the retail price covers the cost of acquiring televisions plus all other costs of doing business. The appliance dealer has both a bid price and an ask price. The bid price is the price at which the dealer buys the television, also known as the wholesale price. The ask price is the price at which the dealer will sell the television, also known as the retail price.

An appliance seller does not select which models to sell based on personal preference and does not expect to profit by speculating on the price of a television. Rather, the appliance dealer selects inventory based on expected customer demand and earns profit based on the markup. The store maintains an inventory, and the owner is able to satisfy customers

From Chapter 13 of *Derivatives Markets*, Third Edition, Robert McDonald. Copyright © 2013 by Pearson Education, Inc. Published by Pearson Prentice Hall. All rights reserved.

who walk in and want to buy a television immediately. Market-makers supply *immediacy*, permitting customers to trade whenever they wish.

Proprietary trading, which is conceptually distinct from market-making, is trading to express an investment strategy. Customers and proprietary traders typically expect their positions to be profitable depending upon whether the market goes up or down. In contrast, market-makers profit by buying at the bid and selling at the ask. The position of a market-maker is the result of whatever order flow arrives from customers.

A difference between appliance sellers and financial market-makers is that an appliance store must possess a physical television in order to sell one. A financial market-maker, by contrast, can supply an asset by short-selling (borrowing shares and selling those shares), thereby generating inventory as needed.

In some cases market-makers may trade as customers, but then the market-maker is paying the bid-ask spread and therefore not serving as a market-maker.

2. MARKET-MAKER RISK

Without hedging, an active market-maker will have an arbitrary position generated by fulfilling customer orders. An arbitrary portfolio has uncontrolled risk. An adverse price move has the potential to bankrupt the market-maker. Consequently, market-makers attempt to hedge the risk of their positions.

Market-makers can control risk by **delta-hedging**. The market-maker computes the option delta and takes an offsetting position in shares. We say that such a position is *delta-hedged*. In general a delta-hedged position is not a zero-value position: The cost of the shares required to hedge is not the same as the cost of the options. Because of the cost difference, the market-maker must invest capital to maintain a delta-hedged position.

A key idea in derivatives is that such a hedged position should earn the risk-free rate: You have money tied up so you should earn a return on it, and you have no risk so you should earn the risk-free rate. The notion that a hedged position earns the risk-free rate is a linchpin of almost all derivative pricing models. It was the fundamental idea exploited by Black and Scholes in their derivation of the option pricing model.

With the help of a simple numerical example, we can understand not only the intuition of the Black-Scholes model, but the mathematics as well. Delta-hedging is key to pricing because it is the technique for offsetting the risk of an option position. If we think of option producers as selling options at cost, then delta-hedging provides us with an understanding of what the cost of the option is when it is replicated. Delta-hedging is thus both a technique widely used in practice and a key to understanding option pricing.

Option Risk in the Absence of Hedging

If a customer wishes to buy a 91-day call option, the market-maker fills this order by selling a call option. To be specific, suppose that $S = \$40$, $K = \$40$, $\sigma = 0.30$, $r = 0.08$ (continuously compounded), and $\delta = 0$. We will let T denote the expiration time of the option and t the present, so time to expiration is $T - t$. Let $T - t = 91/365$. The price, delta, gamma, and theta for this call are listed in Table 1.

Because the market-maker has written the option, the sign of the Greek measures for the position is opposite those of a purchased option. In particular, the written option is like shorting shares of stock (negative delta) and the option gains in value over time (positive

TABLE 1 Price and Greek information for a call option with $S = \$40$, $K = \$40$, $\sigma = 0.30$, $r = 0.08$ (continuously compounded), $T - t = 91/365$, and $\delta = 0$.

	Purchased	Written
Call price	2.7804	−2.7804
Delta	0.5824	−0.5824
Gamma	0.0652	−0.0652
Theta	−0.0173	0.0173

theta). Because delta is negative, the risk for the market-maker who has written a call is that the stock price will rise.

Suppose that the market-maker does not hedge the written option and the stock price rises to \$40.75. We can measure the profit of the market-maker by **marking-to-market** the position. Marking-to-market answers the question: If we liquidated the position today, what would be the gain or loss? In the case of an option price increase, the market-maker would need to buy the option back at a higher price than that at which it was sold, and therefore would lose money. At a stock price of \$40.75, the call price would increase to \$3.2352, so the market-maker profit on a per-share basis would be \$2.7804 − \$3.2352 = −\$0.4548.[1]

Figure 1 graphs the overnight profit of the unhedged written call option as a function of the stock price, against the profit of the option at expiration. In computing overnight profit, we are varying the stock price holding fixed all other inputs to the Black-Scholes formula except for time to expiration, which decreases by 1 day. It is apparent from the graph that the risk for the market-maker is a rise in the stock price. Although it is not obvious from the graph, if the stock price does not change, the market-maker will profit because of time decay: It would be possible to liquidate the option position by buying options at a lower price the next day than the price at which they were sold originally.

Delta and Gamma as Measures of Exposure

Since delta tells us the price sensitivity of the option, it also measures the market-maker's exposure. The delta of the call at a stock price of \$40 is 0.5824, which suggests that a \$1 increase in the stock price should increase the value of the option by approximately \$0.5824. A \$0.75 increase in the stock price would therefore increase the option price by $\$0.75 \times 0.5824 = \$0.4368$. However, the actual increase in the option's value is \$0.4548, greater by \$0.0180.

This discrepancy occurs because delta varies with the stock price: As the stock price increases and the option moves more into the money, delta also increases. At a stock price of \$40.75, delta is 0.6301. Thus, using the delta at \$40 will *understate* the actual change in the value of the option due to a price increase.

1. For simplicity, this calculation ignores the overnight interest that the market-maker can earn on the proceeds from selling the option. In this case, interest per share is $(\exp(.08/365) - 1) \times \$2.7804 = \$0.0006$. Later examples will account for interest.

FIGURE 1

Depiction of overnight and expiration profit from writing a call option on one share of stock, if the market-maker is unhedged.

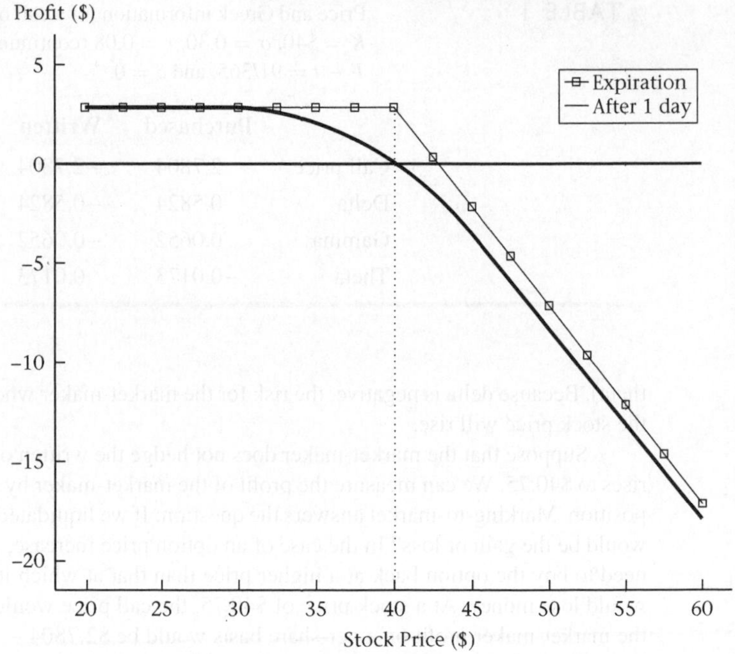

Similarly, the delta at $40 will *overstate* the decline in the value of the option due to a stock price decrease. If the stock price had fallen $0.75 to $39.25, the option price would have declined to $2.3622, which would result in a gain of $0.4182 to the market-maker. Using delta, we would have predicted a price decline of $-\$0.75 \times 0.5824 = -\$0.4368$, which is greater than the actual decline. This occurs because the option delta decreases as the stock price declines. The delta at this new price is 0.5326.

Gamma measures the change in delta when the stock price changes. In the example above, the gamma of 0.0652 means that delta will change by approximately 0.0652 if the stock price moves $1. This is why delta did not accurately predict the change in the option price: The delta itself was changing as the stock price changed. The ultimate change in the option price is a result of the *average* delta during the stock price change, not just the delta at the initial stock price. As you might guess, we can use gamma in addition to delta to better approximate the effect on the value of the option of a change in the stock price. We will discuss this adjustment later.

3. DELTA-HEDGING

Suppose a market-maker sells one call option and hedges the position with shares. With the sale of a call, the market-maker is short delta shares. To hedge this position, the market-maker can buy delta shares to delta-hedge the position.

We now will consider the risk of a delta-hedged position by assuming that the market-maker delta-hedges and marks-to-market daily. We first look at numerical examples and then in Section 4 explain the results algebraically.

An Example of Delta-Hedging for 2 Days

Day 0. Consider the 40-strike call option described above, written on 100 shares of stock. The market-maker sells the option and receives \$278.04. Since $\Delta = 0.5824$, the market-maker also buys 58.24 shares. (We will permit fractional share purchases in this example.) The net investment is

$$(58.24 \times \$40) - \$278.04 = \$2051.56$$

At an 8% interest rate, the market-maker has an overnight financing charge of $\$2051.56 \times (e^{0.08/365} - 1) = \$0.45$.

Day 1: Marking-to-Market. Without at first worrying about rebalancing the portfolio to maintain delta-neutrality, we can ask whether the market-maker made money or lost money overnight. Suppose the new stock price is \$40.50. The new call option price with 1 day less to expiration and at the new stock price is \$3.0621. Overnight mark-to-market profit is a gain of \$0.50, computed as follows:

Gain on 58.24 shares	$58.24 \times (\$40.50 - \$40) = \$29.12$
Gain on written call option	$\$278.04 - \$306.21 = -\$28.17$
Interest	$-(e^{0.08/365} - 1) \times \$2051.56 = -\$0.45$
Overnight profit	**\$0.50**

Day 1: Rebalancing the Portfolio. The new delta is 0.6142. Since delta has increased, we must buy $61.42 - 58.24 = 3.18$ additional shares. This transaction requires an investment of $\$40.50 \times 3.18 = \$128.79$. Since the readjustment in the number of shares entails buying at the current market price, it does not affect the mark-to-market profits for that day.

Day 2: Marking-to-Market. The stock price now falls to \$39.25. The market-maker makes money on the written option and loses money on the 61.42 shares. Interest expense has increased over the previous day because additional investment was required for the extra shares. The net result from marking-to-market is a loss of $-\$3.87$:

Gain on 61.42 shares	$61.42 \times (\$39.25 - \$40.50) = -\$76.78$
Gain on written call option	$\$306.21 - \$232.82 = \$73.39$
Interest	$-(e^{0.08/365} - 1) \times \$2181.30 = -\$0.48$
Overnight profit	**−\$3.87**

Interpreting the Profit Calculation

At the end of day 1, we show a \$0.50 profit from the mark-to-market calculation. Conceptually, we can think of the profit or loss as measuring the extent to which the portfolio requires cash infusions in order to maintain a delta-neutral hedge. When we show a positive profit, as in this case, we can take cash out of the portfolio.

To see that mark-to-market profit measures the net cash infusions required to maintain the delta-neutral position, suppose that a lender is willing at all times to lend us the value of securities in the portfolio. Initially, we buy 58.24 shares of stock, which costs \$2329.60, but this amount is offset by the \$278.04 option premium, so the net cash we require is \$2051.56. This is also the net value of our portfolio (stock less the option), so we can borrow this amount.[2]

As time passes, there are three sources of cash flow into and out of the portfolio:

1. **Borrowing:** Our borrowing capacity equals the market value of securities in the portfolio; hence, borrowing capacity changes as the net value of the position changes. On day 0, the net value of our securities was \$2051.56. On day 1, the share price rose and we bought additional shares; the market value of the position was 61.42 × \$40.50 − \$306.21 = \$2181.30. Thus our borrowing capacity increased by \$129.74. The change in the option value changes borrowing capacity, but there is no cash flow since we are not changing the number of options.
2. **Purchase or sale of shares:** We buy or sell shares as necessary to maintain delta-neutrality. In the above example, we increased shares in our portfolio from 58.24 to 61.42. The price at the time was \$40.50, so we spent 3.18 × \$40.50 = \$128.79.
3. **Interest:** We pay interest on the borrowed amount. On day 1 we owed \$0.45.

Thus, we need \$128.79 to buy more shares and \$0.45 to pay interest expense. The change in our borrowing capacity—the extra amount the bank will lend us—is \$129.74. The difference between what the bank will lend us on the one hand and the cost of additional shares plus interest on the other is

$$\$129.74 - \$128.79 - \$0.45 = \$0.50$$

Since the bank is willing to lend us the value of our securities, we are free to pocket the \$0.50 that is left over.

This example demonstrates that the mark-to-market profit equals the net cash flow generated by always borrowing to fully fund the position. Another way to see the equality of mark-to-market profit and net cash flow is by examining the sources and uses of funds, and the extent to which it is necessary to inject additional cash into the position in order to maintain the delta-neutral hedge. We can calculate the net cash flow from the portfolio as

$$\begin{aligned}\text{Net cash flow} = {} & \text{Change in borrowing capacity} \\ & - \text{cash used to purchase additional shares} \\ & - \text{interest}\end{aligned}$$

Let Δ_i denote the option delta on day i, S_i the stock price, C_i the option price, and MV_i the market value of the portfolio. Borrowing capacity on day i is $MV_i = \Delta_i S_i - C_i$; hence, the change in borrowing capacity is

$$MV_i - MV_{i-1} = \Delta_i S_i - C_i - (\Delta_{i-1} S_{i-1} - C_{i-1})$$

The cost of purchasing additional shares is $S_i(\Delta_i - \Delta_{i-1})$, and interest owed on day i depends on the previous day's borrowing, rMV_{i-1}. Thus, on day i we have

2. In practice the market-maker would be able to borrow only part of the funds required to buy securities, with market-maker capital making up the difference.

$$\begin{aligned}\text{Net cash flow} &= \text{MV}_i - \text{MV}_{i-1} - S_i(\Delta_i - \Delta_{i-1}) - r\text{MV}_{i-1} \\ &= \Delta_i S_i - C_i - (\Delta_{i-1} S_{i-1} - C_{i-1}) - S_i(\Delta_i - \Delta_{i-1}) - r\text{MV}_{i-1} \\ &= \Delta_{i-1}(S_i - S_{i-1}) - (C_i - C_{i-1}) - r\text{MV}_{i-1}\end{aligned}$$

The last expression is the overnight gain on shares, less the overnight gain on the option, less interest; this result is identical to the profit calculation we performed above. In the numerical example, we have

$$\begin{aligned}\text{MV}_1 - \text{MV}_0 - S_1(\Delta_1 - \Delta_0) - r\text{MV}_0 &= \$2181.30 - \$2051.56 - \$128.79 - \$0.45 \\ &= \$0.50\end{aligned}$$

This value is equal to the overnight profit we calculated between day 0 and day 1.

Thus, we can interpret the daily mark-to-market profit or loss as the amount of cash that we can pocket (if there is a profit) or that we must pay (if there is a loss) in order to fund required purchases of new shares and to continue borrowing exactly the amount of our securities. When we have a positive profit, as on day 1, we can take money out of the portfolio, and when we have a negative profit, as on day 2, we must put money into the portfolio.

A hedged portfolio that never requires additional cash investments to remain hedged is **self-financing**. One of the questions we will answer is under what conditions a delta-hedged portfolio is self-financing.

Delta-Hedging for Several Days

We can continue the example by letting the market-maker rebalance the portfolio each day. Table 2 summarizes delta, the net investment, and profit each day for 5 days. The profit line in the table is *daily* profit, not cumulative profit.

What determines the pattern of gain and loss in the table? There are three effects, attributable to gamma, theta, and the carrying cost of the position.

1. **Gamma:** For the largest moves in the stock, the market-maker loses money. For small moves in the stock price, the market-maker makes money. The loss for large moves

TABLE 2 Daily profit calculation over 5 days for a market-maker who delta-hedges a written option on 100 shares.

	Day					
	0	1	2	3	4	5
Stock ($)	40.00	40.50	39.25	38.75	40.00	40.00
Call ($)	278.04	306.21	232.82	205.46	271.04	269.27
100 × delta	58.24	61.42	53.11	49.56	58.06	58.01
Investment ($)	2051.58	2181.30	1851.65	1715.12	2051.35	2051.29
Interest ($)		−0.45	−0.48	−0.41	−0.38	−0.45
Capital gain ($)		0.95	−3.39	0.81	−3.62	1.77
Daily profit ($)		0.50	−3.87	0.40	−4.00	1.32

results from gamma: If the stock price changes, the position becomes unhedged. In this case, since the market-maker is short the option, a large move generates a loss. As the stock price rises, the delta of the call increases and the call loses money faster than the stock makes money. As the stock price falls, the delta of the call decreases and the call makes money more slowly than the fixed stock position loses money. In effect, the market-maker becomes unhedged net long as the stock price falls and unhedged net short as the stock price rises. The losses on days 2 and 4 are attributable to gamma. For all of the entries in Table 2, the gamma of the written call is about −0.06 per share.

2. **Theta:** If a day passes with no change in the stock price, the option becomes cheaper. This time decay works to the benefit of the market-maker who could unwind the position more cheaply. Time decay is especially evident in the profit on day 5, but is also responsible for the profit on days 1 and 3.
3. **Interest cost:** In order to hedge, the market-maker must purchase stock. The net carrying cost is a component of the overall cost.

FIGURE 2

Overnight profit as a function of the stock price for a delta-hedged market-maker who has written a call.

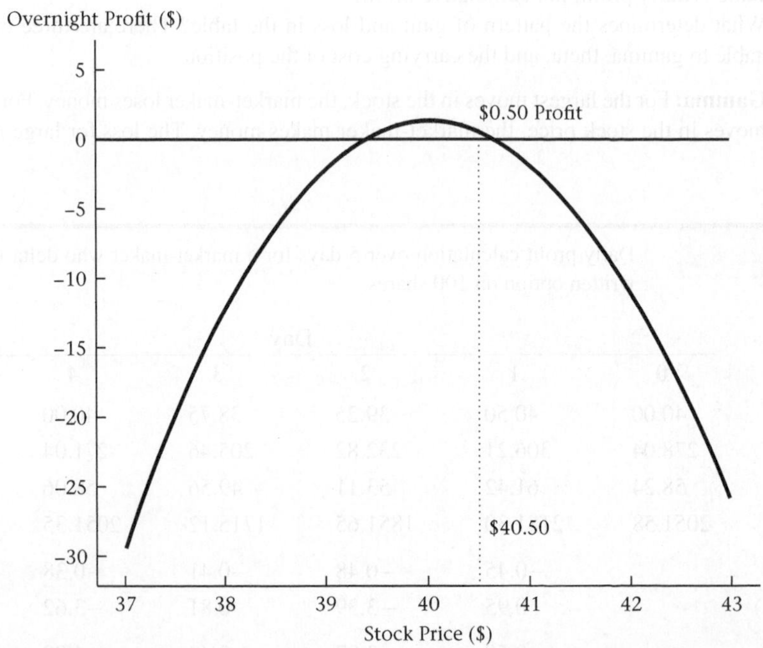

TABLE 3 Daily profit calculation over 5 days for a market-maker who delta-hedges a written option on 100 shares, assuming the stock price moves up or down 1 σ each day.

	Day					
	0	1	2	3	4	5
Stock ($)	40.000	40.642	40.018	39.403	38.797	39.420
Call ($)	278.04	315.00	275.57	239.29	206.14	236.76
100 × delta	58.24	62.32	58.27	54.08	49.80	54.06
Investment ($)	2051.58	2217.66	2056.08	1891.60	1725.95	1894.27
Interest ($)		−0.45	−0.49	−0.45	−0.41	−0.38
Capital gain ($)		0.43	0.51	0.46	0.42	0.38
Daily profit ($)		−0.02	0.02	0.01	0.01	0.00

Figure 2 graphs overnight market-maker profit on day 1 as a function of the stock price on day 1. At a stock price of $40.50, for example, the profit is $0.50, just as in the table. The graph is generated by recomputing the first day's profit per share for a variety of stock prices between $37 and $43. The graph verifies what is evident in the table: The delta-hedging market-maker who has written a call wants small stock price moves and can suffer a substantial loss with a big move. In fact, should the stock price move to $37.50, for example, the market-maker would lose $20.

If the market-maker had purchased a call and shorted delta shares, the profit calculation would be reversed. The market-maker would lose money for small stock price moves and make money with large moves. The profit diagram for such a position would be a mirror image of Figure 2.

A Self-Financing Portfolio: The Stock Moves One σ

In the previous example, the stock price changes by varying amounts and our daily profit varies substantially. However, in Figure 2, there is an up move and a down move for the stock such that the market-maker exactly breaks even in our profit calculations. If the stock always moved by this amount, the portfolio would be self-financing: No cash inflows are required to maintain delta-neutrality. It turns out that the portfolio is self-financing if the stock moves by one standard deviation.

Table 3 shows the results of the stock moving up, down three times, and then up. You can see that the market-maker comes close to breaking even each day. If the stock moves according to the binomial model, therefore, the portfolio is approximately self-financing.

4. THE MATHEMATICS OF DELTA-HEDGING

Clearly, delta, gamma, and theta all play a role in determining the profit on a delta-hedged position. In this section we examine these relationships more closely in order to better understand the numerical example above. What we do here is a kind of financial forensics: Once we learn how the stock price changed, we seek to discover why we earned the profit we did.

Using Gamma to Better Approximate the Change in the Option Price

Delta alone is an inaccurate predictor of the change in the option price because delta changes with the stock price. When delta is very sensitive to the stock price (gamma is large), the inaccuracy will be relatively great. When delta is not sensitive to the stock price (gamma is small), the inaccuracy will be relatively small. Since gamma measures the change in delta, we can use gamma to develop a better approximation for the change in the option price.

If the stock price were \$40.75 instead of \$40, the option price would be \$3.2352 instead of \$2.7804. For the purpose of computing the change in the option price, we want to know the average rate of price increase between \$40 and \$40.75, which we can approximate by averaging the deltas at \$40 and \$40.75:

$$\Delta_{\text{average}} = \frac{\Delta_{40} + \Delta_{40.75}}{2}$$

We could then approximate the option price at \$40.75 by computing

$$C(\$40.75) = C(\$40) + 0.75 \times \Delta_{\text{average}} \tag{1}$$

When we average the deltas at \$40 and \$40.75, we have to compute deltas at two different stock prices. A different approach is to approximate the average delta by using only the delta evaluated at \$40 together with gamma. Since gamma measures the change in delta, we can approximate the delta at \$40.75 by adding $0.75 \times \Gamma$ to Δ_{40}:

$$\Delta_{40.75} = \Delta_{40} + 0.75 \times \Gamma$$

Using this relationship, the average delta is

$$\begin{aligned}\Delta_{\text{average}} &= \frac{\Delta_{40} + (\Delta_{40} + 0.75 \times \Gamma)}{2} \\ &= \Delta_{40} + \frac{1}{2} \times 0.75 \times \Gamma\end{aligned}$$

Using equation (1), we can then approximate the call price as

$$\begin{aligned}C(\$40.75) &= C(\$40) + 0.75 \times \Delta_{\text{average}} \\ &= C(\$40) + 0.75 \times \left(\Delta_{40} + \frac{1}{2} \times 0.75 \times \Gamma\right) \\ &= C(\$40) + 0.75 \times \Delta_{40} + \frac{1}{2} \times 0.75^2 \times \Gamma \qquad (2)\end{aligned}$$

The use of delta and gamma to approximate the new option price is called a **delta-gamma approximation**.[3]

3. This note has been intentionally omitted for this edition.

Example 1. If the stock price rises from \$40 to \$40.75, the option price increases from \$2.7804 to \$3.2352. Using a delta approximation alone, we would estimate $C(\$40.75)$ as

$$C(\$40.75) = C(\$40) + 0.75 \times 0.5824 = \$3.2172$$

Using a delta-gamma approximation, we obtain

$$C(\$40.75) = C(\$40) + 0.75 \times 0.5824 + \frac{1}{2} \times 0.75^2 \times 0.0652 = \$3.2355$$

The delta-gamma approximation is significantly closer to the true option price at \$40.75 than is the delta approximation.

Similarly, for a stock price decline to \$39.25, the true option price is \$2.3622. The delta approximation gives

$$C(\$39.25) = C(\$40) - 0.75 \times 0.5824 = \$2.3436$$

The delta-gamma approximation gives

$$C(\$39.25) = C(\$40) - 0.75 \times 0.5824 + \frac{1}{2} \times 0.75^2 \times 0.0652 = \$2.3619$$

Again, the delta-gamma approximation is more accurate. ■

Delta-Gamma Approximations

We now repeat the previous arguments using algebra. For a "small" move in the stock price, we know that the rate at which delta changes is given by gamma. Thus, if over a time interval of length h the stock price change is

$$\epsilon = S_{t+h} - S_t$$

then gamma is the change in delta per dollar of stock price change, or

$$\Gamma(S_t) = \frac{\Delta(S_{t+h}) - \Delta(S_t)}{\epsilon}$$

Rewriting this expression, delta will change by approximately the magnitude of the price change, ϵ, times gamma, $\epsilon\Gamma$:

$$\Delta(S_{t+h}) = \Delta(S_t) + \epsilon\Gamma(S_t) \tag{3}$$

If the rate at which delta changes is constant (meaning that gamma is constant), this calculation is exact.

How does equation (3) help us compute the option price change? If the stock price changes by ϵ, we can compute the option price change if we know the *average* delta over the range S_{t+h} to S_t. If Γ is approximately constant, the average delta is simply the average of $\Delta(S_t)$ and $\Delta(S_{t+h})$, or (using equation (3))

$$\frac{\Delta(S_t) + \Delta(S_{t+h})}{2} = \Delta(S_t) + \frac{1}{2}\epsilon\Gamma(S_t) \tag{4}$$

The option price at the new stock price is the initial option price, $C(S_t)$, plus the average delta times the change in the stock price, or

$$C(S_{t+h}) = C(S_t) + \epsilon \left[\frac{\Delta(S_t) + \Delta(S_{t+h})}{2} \right]$$

Using equation (4), we can rewrite this to express $\Delta(S_{t+h})$ in terms of $\Gamma(S_t)$:

$$C(S_{t+h}) = C(S_t) + \epsilon\Delta(S_t) + \frac{1}{2}\epsilon^2\Gamma(S_t) \tag{5}$$

The gamma correction is independent of the direction of the change in the stock price because gamma is multiplied by ϵ^2, which is always positive. When the stock price goes up, delta alone predicts too little a change in the call price, and we have to add something to correct the prediction. When the stock price goes down, delta alone predicts too much of a decrease in the option price, and we again have to add something to correct the prediction.

The new predicted call price is not perfect because gamma changes as the stock price changes. We could add a term correcting for the change in gamma, and a term correcting for the change in the change in gamma, and so forth, but the gamma correction alone dramatically improves the accuracy of the approximation. You might recognize equation (5) as a second-order (because it uses the first and second derivatives, delta and gamma) *Taylor series approximation* for the change in the call price. Taylor series approximations are discussed in Appendix A.

Figure 3 shows the result of approximating the option price using the delta and delta-gamma approximations. The delta approximation is a straight line tangent to the option price curve and is always below the option price curve. Because of this, the delta approximation understates the option price, whether the stock price rises or falls. The delta-gamma approximation uses the squared stock price change, which generates a curve more closely approximating the option price curve.

Theta: Accounting for Time

The preceding calculations measured the option risk that arises from price changes alone. Of course, as the price changes, time is passing and the option is approaching maturity.

The option's theta (θ) measures the option's change in price due to time passing, holding the stock price fixed. For a period of length h, the change in the option price will be θh. For example, consider the 91-day option in Section 3 and consider the effect of a day passing, with no change in the stock price. Since the variables in the option pricing formula are expressed as annual values, a one-unit change in $T - t$ implies a θ of -6.33251. Since h is 1/365, the implied daily option price change is $-6.33251/365 = -0.01735$.

Adding theta to our previous option price prediction equation, we have

$$\begin{aligned} C(S_{t+h}, T - t - h) = {} & C(S_t, T - t) \\ & + \epsilon\Delta(S_t, T - t) + \tfrac{1}{2}\epsilon^2\Gamma(S_t, T - t) + h\theta(S_t, T - t) \end{aligned} \tag{6}$$

The experiment reflected in this equation is this: Starting with an option with $T - t$ periods until expiration and a stock price of S_t, we want to express the new option price as a function of the old price and the delta, gamma, and theta evaluated at the original price and time to

FIGURE 3

Delta- and delta-gamma approximations of option price. The true option price is represented by the bold line, and approximations by dashed lines.

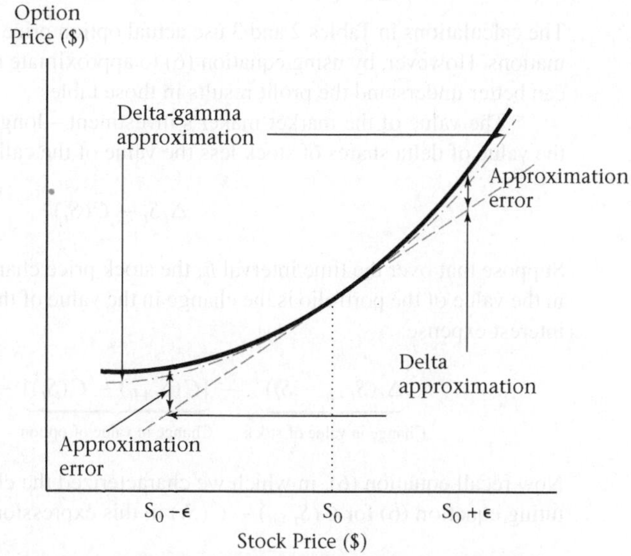

TABLE 4

Predicted option price over a period of 1 day, assuming stock price move of \$0.75, using equation (6). Assumes that $\sigma = 0.3$, $r = 0.08$, $T - t = 91$ days, and $\delta = 0$, and the initial stock price is \$40.

					Option Price 1 Day Later ($h = 1$ day)	
	Starting Price	$\epsilon\Delta$	$\frac{1}{2}\epsilon^2\Gamma$	θh	Predicted	Actual
$S_{t+h} = \$40.75$	\$2.7804	0.4368	0.0183	−0.0173	\$3.2182	\$3.2176
$S_{t+h} = \$39.25$	\$2.7804	−0.4368	0.0183	−0.0173	\$2.3446	\$2.3452

expiration. This formula is quite accurate for relatively small changes in time and in the stock price.

Example 2. Table 4 shows the results from using equation (6) to predict the option price change when prices move by \$0.75 ($\epsilon = \pm 0.75$). In this example, $\Delta = 0.5824$, $\Gamma = 0.0652$, and $h\theta = -0.0173$. Note that in each case the formula slightly overstates the change, but the predicted price is close to the actual price. ■

Understanding the Market-Maker's Profit

The calculations in Tables 2 and 3 use actual option price changes over 1 day, not approximations. However, by using equation (6) to approximate the change in the option price we can better understand the profit results in those tables.

The value of the market-maker's investment—long delta shares and short a call—is the value of delta shares of stock less the value of the call, or

$$\Delta_t S_t - C(S_t)$$

Suppose that over the time interval h, the stock price changes from S_t to S_{t+h}. The change in the value of the portfolio is the change in the value of the stock and option positions, less interest expense:

$$\underbrace{\Delta_t(S_{t+h} - S_t)}_{\text{Change in value of stock}} - \underbrace{[C(S_{t+h}) - C(S_t)]}_{\text{Change in value of option}} - \underbrace{rh[\Delta_t S_t - C(S_t)]}_{\text{Interest expense}}$$

Now recall equation (6), in which we characterized the change in the option price. Substituting equation (6) for $C(S_{t+h}) - C(S_t)$ in this expression tells us

$$\begin{aligned}\Delta_t(S_{t+h} - S_t) - [\Delta_t(S_{t+h} - S_t) + \frac{1}{2}(S_{t+h} - S_t)^2\Gamma_t + \theta_t h] - rh[\Delta_t S_t - C(S_t)] \\ = -\left(\frac{1}{2}\epsilon^2\Gamma_t + \theta_t h + rh\left[\Delta_t S_t - C(S_t)\right]\right)\end{aligned} \tag{7}$$

This expression gives us the profit of the market-maker when the stock price changes by ϵ over an interval of length h.

On the right-hand side of equation (7) we see the effects of gamma, theta, and interest:

1. **Gamma:** The effect of gamma is measured by $-\frac{1}{2}\epsilon^2\Gamma_t$. Since the gamma of the call is positive, by writing the call the market-maker will lose money in proportion to the square of the stock price change. The larger the stock move, the greater is the loss.
2. **Theta:** The effect of theta is measured by $-\theta_t h$. Since theta for the call is negative, the option writer benefits from theta.
3. **Interest cost:** Interest is measured by $-rh[\Delta_t S_t - C(S_t)]$. The option writer has a net investment because Δ_t shares are more expensive than one option. Hence, interest is a net cost.

Since θ is negative, time decay benefits the market-maker, whereas interest and gamma work against the market-maker.

Let's examine how ϵ, the change in the stock price, enters equation (7). Note first that because we have delta-hedged, ϵ itself does not affect market-maker profit. However, profit *does* depend on the *squared* change in the stock price, ϵ^2. Consequently, as we saw in Table 2, it is the magnitude—not the direction of the stock price move—that determines profit.

Table 5 calculates equation (7) for various moves in the stock price. Because equation (7) depends only on the *squared* stock price move, the calculation is the same for moves up and down.

TABLE 5 Predicted effect, using equation (7), of different-sized stock price moves on the profit of a delta-hedged market-maker.

Absolute Value of Price Move, $\|\epsilon\|$	$-\frac{1}{2}\epsilon^2\Gamma - \theta h - rh[\Delta S_t - C(S_t)]$
0.0000	1.283
0.2500	1.080
0.5000	0.470
0.6281	0.000
0.7500	−0.546
1.0000	−1.970
1.5000	−6.036

If the stock price moves \$0.6281, equation (7) is exactly zero. We have already seen in Table 3 that the market-maker approximately breaks even for a one-standard-deviation move in the stock. Here we arrive at the same result. Let's explore this idea further.

If σ is measured annually, then a one-standard-deviation move over a period of length h is $\sigma S_t \sqrt{h}$. Therefore a squared one-standard-deviation move is

$$\epsilon^2 = \sigma^2 S_t^2 h \tag{8}$$

Substituting this expression for ϵ^2, we can rewrite equation (7) as

$$\text{Market-maker profit} = -\left(\frac{1}{2}\sigma^2 S_t^2 \Gamma_t + \theta_t + r\left[\Delta_t S_t - C(S_t)\right]\right) h \tag{9}$$

This expression gives us market-maker profit when the stock moves one standard deviation. As an example, let $h = 1/365$ and $\sigma = 0.3$. Then $\sigma S \sqrt{h} = \$0.6281$. From Table 5, with this stock price move equation (9) is *exactly* zero! (Problem 13 asks you to verify this.) It is not an accident that equation (9) is zero for this price move. We explain this result in Section 5.

In Table 5, the loss from a \$1 move is substantially larger in absolute value than the gain from no move. However, small moves are more probable than big moves. If we think of returns as being approximately normally distributed, then stock price moves greater than one standard deviation occur about one-third of the time. The market-maker thus expects to make small profits about two-thirds of the time and larger losses about one-third of the time. On average, the market-maker will break even.

5. THE BLACK-SCHOLES ANALYSIS

We have discussed how a market-maker can measure and manage the risk of a portfolio containing options. What is the link to pricing an option?

The Black-Scholes Argument

If a stock moves one standard deviation, then a delta-hedged position will exactly break even, taking into account the cost of funding the position. This finding is not a coincidence; it reflects the arguments Black and Scholes used to derive the option pricing formula.

Imagine, for example, that the stock always moves exactly one standard deviation every minute.[4] A market-maker hedging every minute will be hedged over an hour or over any period of time. Black and Scholes argued that the money invested in this hedged position should earn the risk-free rate since the resulting income stream is risk-free.

Equation (9) gives us an expression for market-maker profit when the stock moves one standard deviation. Setting this expression to zero gives

$$-\left(\frac{1}{2}\sigma^2 S_t^2 \Gamma_t + \theta_t + r\left[\Delta_t S_t - C(S_t)\right]\right) h = 0$$

If we divide by h and rearrange terms, we get

$$\boxed{\frac{1}{2}\sigma^2 S_t^2 \Gamma_t + r S_t \Delta_t + \theta_t = rC(S_t)} \qquad (10)$$

This is the equation Black and Scholes used to characterize the behavior of an option. The Greeks Γ, Δ, and θ are partial derivatives of the option price. Equation (10) is the well-known Black-Scholes partial differential equation, or just Black-Scholes equation (as opposed to the Black-Scholes *formula* for the price of a European call). This relationship among the Greeks is as fundamental in valuing risky cash flows as is e^{-rT} when valuing risk-free cash flows.

Equation (10) embodies numerous assumptions, among them that the underlying asset does not pay a dividend, the option itself does not pay a dividend, the interest rate and volatility are constant, and the stock does not make large discrete moves. With these assumptions, equation (10) holds for calls, puts, American options, European options, and most of the exotic variants. With simple modifications, an equation like (10) will also hold for options on dividend-paying stocks, currencies, futures, bonds, etc. The link between delta-hedging and pricing is one of the most important ideas in finance.

Delta-Hedging of American Options

Equation (10) holds for American options as well as for European options, but it does not hold at times when it is optimal to early-exercise the option. Consider a deep in-the-money American put option and suppose the option should be exercised early. Since early exercise is optimal, the option price is $K - S$; hence, $\Delta = -1$, $\Gamma = 0$, and $\theta = 0$. In this case, equation (10) becomes

$$\left[r \times (-1) \times S_t\right] + \left(\frac{1}{2} \times 0\right) + 0 = r \times (K - S_t)$$

Note that $-rS_t$ appears on both sides of the equation. Thus, we can rewrite the equation as

4. There are $365 \times 24 \times 60 = 525{,}600$ minutes in a year. Thus, if the stock's annual standard deviation is 30%, the per-minute standard deviation is $0.3/\sqrt{525{,}600} = 0.04\%$, or \$0.016 for a \$40 stock.

$$0 = rK$$

Since this equation is false, something is wrong. We began by assuming that the put was so far in-the-money that it should be early-exercised. This means that interest received on the strike exceeds the loss of the implicit call option. Thus, if the option should be exercised but you own it, delta-hedge it, and *do not exercise it*, then you lose interest on the strike you are not receiving. Similarly, if you have written the option and delta-hedged, and the owner does not exercise, then you are earning arbitrage profit of rK.

Thus, equation (10) is only valid in a region where early exercise is not optimal. If an option should be exercised but is not exercised, then behavior is irrational and there is no reason why a delta-hedged position should earn the risk-free rate and thus no reason that equation (10) should hold.

What Is the Advantage to Frequent Re-Hedging?

In practice, because of transaction costs, it is expensive for a market-maker to trade shares for every change in an option delta. Instead, a delta-hedger will wait for the position to become somewhat unhedged before trading to reestablish delta-neutrality. We assume that market-makers maintain their hedged position at all times. What does the market-maker lose by hedging less frequently?

Boyle and Emanuel (1980) considered a market-maker who delta-hedges at set intervals, rather than every time the stock price changes. Let x_i denote the number of standard deviations the stock price moves—we can think of x_i as being drawn randomly from the standard normal distribution. Also let $R_{h,i}$ denote the period-i return to a delta-hedged market-maker who has purchased a call. Boyle and Emanuel show that this return can be written as[5]

$$R_{h,i} = \frac{1}{2}S^2\sigma^2\Gamma(x_i^2 - 1)h \tag{11}$$

where Γ is the option's gamma and h is the time interval between hedge readjustments. For a delta-hedging call writer, the return has the opposite sign. From Boyle and Emanuel, the variance of $x_i^2 - 1$ is 2; hence,

$$\text{Var}(R_{h,i}) = \frac{1}{2}\left(S^2\sigma^2\Gamma h\right)^2 \tag{12}$$

We assume—as in the binomial model—that the stock return is uncorrelated across time, so that x_i is uncorrelated across time.

Now let's compare hedging once a day against hedging hourly (suppose trading occurs around the clock). The daily variance of the return earned by the market-maker who hedges once a day is given by

$$\text{Var}(R_{1/365,1}) = \frac{1}{2}\left(S^2\sigma^2\Gamma/365\right)^2$$

The daily return of the market-maker who hedges hourly is the sum of the hourly returns. Assuming for the sake of simplicity that S and Γ do not change much, that variance is

5. This expression can be derived by assuming that the stock price move, ϵ, is normally distributed with standard deviation $S\sigma\sqrt{h}$, and subtracting equation (9) from (7).

$$\text{Var}\left(\sum_{i=1}^{24} R_{h,i}\right) = \sum_{i=1}^{24} \frac{1}{2}\left[S^2\sigma^2\Gamma/(24 \times 365)\right]^2$$
$$= \frac{1}{24} \times \text{Var}(R_{1/365,1})$$

Thus, by hedging hourly instead of daily the market-maker's total return variance is reduced by a factor of 24.

Here is the intuition for this result. Whatever the hedging interval, about two-thirds of the price moves will be less than a single standard deviation, whereas one-third will be greater. Frequent re-hedging does not avoid these large or small moves, since they can occur over any interval. However, frequent hedging does permit better *averaging* of the effects of these moves. Whether you hedge once a day or once an hour, the typical stock price move you encounter will likely not be close to one standard deviation. However, if you hedge every hour, over the course of a day you will have 24 moves and 24 opportunities to re-hedge. The *average* move over this period is likelier to be close to one standard deviation. The gains from small moves and losses from large moves will tend to average over the course of a day. In effect, the more frequent hedger benefits from diversification over time.[6]

Example 3. Using Boyle and Emanuel's formulas to study the market-maker problem in Section 3, the standard deviation of profit is about \$0.075 for a market-maker who hedges hourly. Since hedging errors are independent from hour to hour, the daily standard deviation for an hourly hedger would be $\$0.075 \times \sqrt{24} = \$0.37$. If the market-maker were to hedge only daily as in our example, the daily standard deviation would be about \$1.82. ■

As you would expect, the *mean* return on a delta-hedged position is the risk-free rate, even if the hedge is not frequently readjusted.

Delta-Hedging in Practice

The Black-Scholes analysis outlined here is the linchpin of modern option pricing theory *and* practice. Market-makers use equation (10) to price options, subject to qualifications mentioned above.

We have seen, however, that delta-hedging does not eliminate risk. One problem, which we emphasized above, is that a delta-hedged portfolio with negative gamma can sustain losses due to large moves in the price of the underlying asset. Consequently, a delta-hedging market-maker needs to worry about gamma. Another problem, discussed in Box 1, is that firms can unexpectedly change their dividend payments.

There are at least four ways a market-maker can try to reduce the risk of extreme price moves. Note that some of these strategies require the market-maker to acquire specific option positions, which means that the market-maker may have to pay the bid-ask spread. Since the bid-ask spread is revenue for the market-maker, paying the spread is undesirable.

---

6. This resembles the problem faced by an insurance company. If the company insures one large asset, the standard deviation of the loss is $\sqrt{n}$ greater than if it insures n small assets, with the same total insured value in each case. Similarly, we can view the return over each hedging interval as being an independent draw from a probability distribution.

First, just as market-makers can adopt a delta-neutral position, they can also adopt a gamma-neutral position. This position cannot be achieved with the stock alone, since the gamma of the stock is zero. Thus, to be gamma-neutral the market-maker must buy or sell options so as to offset the gamma of the existing position.[7] We provide an example of gamma-neutrality below.

Second, in a related strategy, market-makers can use **static option replication**, a strategy in which options are used to hedge options. In our delta-hedging example, the market-maker might not be able to buy an exactly offsetting call option to hedge the written call, but by selectively setting the bid and ask prices for related options, might be able to acquire an option position requiring only infrequent rebalancing. To take a simple example, if the market-maker were able to buy a put with the same strike price and maturity as the written call (e.g., by setting the bid price to attract any seller of that option), then by buying 100 shares to offset the risk of the position, the market-maker would have used put-call parity to create a hedge that is both gamma- and delta-neutral for the life of the options.

Third, a market-maker can buy out-of-the-money options as insurance. In our example of delta-neutral hedging of a written option, the market-maker could buy a deep out-of-the-money put and a deep out-of-the-money call. The two options would be relatively inexpensive and would protect against large moves in the stock. One problem with this solution is that, since option positions in the aggregate sum to zero, the market-making community as a whole can buy protective options only if investors in the aggregate are willing to sell them. Investors, however, are usually thought to be insurance buyers rather than insurance sellers.

Fourth, a market-maker can create a financial product by selling the hedging error, as discussed by Carr and Madan (1998). For example, to hedge a negative-gamma, delta-neutral position, the market-maker would make a payment to a counterparty if the stock makes a small move in either direction, and receive payment from the counterparty if the stock makes a large move in either direction. This is effectively a variance swap. The point is that the market-maker can potentially solve the delta-hedging problem by creating a new product.

Gamma-Neutrality

Let's explore gamma-hedging in more depth. Suppose we wish to both delta-hedge and gamma-hedge the written option described in Table 1. We cannot do this using just the stock, because the gamma of stock is zero. Hence, we must acquire another option in an amount that offsets the gamma of the written call. Table 6 presents information for the 3-month 40-strike call, and also for a 4-month 45-strike call. We will use the latter to gamma-hedge the former.

7. Market-makers sometimes buy and hold over-the-counter options issued by a firm. For example, in the late 1990s some firms sold put options on their own stock. These options were reportedly held by dealers and delta-hedged. One possible motivation for dealers to undertake such a transaction would be to acquire positive gamma. See McDonald (2004) for a discussion.

BOX 1: Dividend Risk

Market-makers price options taking into account the dividends they expect a stock to pay. If a firm announces a significant change in dividend policy, delta-hedgers can make or lose money depending on their position and depending on whether the derivatives they hold are protected against dividend changes.

In 1998, Daimler-Benz surprised option market-makers by announcing a special one-time dividend, creating a dividend payout of about 14%, or 10 times the usual dividend yield. The Deutsche Terminbörse (DTB), the exchange where Daimler options were traded, decided not to adust the terms of exchange-traded options to account for the dividend. The DTB was criticized for this, and some dealers were said to have sustained significant losses.

The stated policy of the Options Clearing Corporation (1994, 2003 supplement) in the United States is that typically there is adjustment only for "extraordinary" cash dividends or distributions, i.e., those exceeding "10% of the market value of the underlying security outstanding. Determinations . . . are made on a case-by-case basis."

In July 2004 Microsoft announced that it would make a special one-time payment of \$3/share, a dividend yield in excess of 10% based on Microsoft's price at the time of the announcement. The Options Clearing Corporation in the United States responded by declaring that it would reduce strike prices on Microsoft options by \$3 when the dividend was paid.

The ratio of the gamma of the two options is[8]

$$\frac{\Gamma_{K=40,t=0.25}}{\Gamma_{K=45,t=0.33}} = \frac{0.0651}{0.0524} = 1.2408 \tag{13}$$

Thus, we need to buy 1.2408 of the 45-strike 4-month options for every 40-strike 3-month option we have sold. The Greeks resulting from the position are in the last column of Table 6. Since delta is −0.1749, we need to buy 17.49 shares of stock to be both delta- and gamma-hedged.

Figure 4 compares this delta- and gamma-hedged position to the delta-hedged position, discussed earlier, in which the same call was written. The delta-hedged position has the problem that large moves always cause losses. The gamma-hedged position loses less if there is a large move down, and can make money if the stock price increases. Moreover, as Table 6 shows, the gamma-hedged position has a positive vega. Why would anyone *not* gamma-hedge?

There are two reasons. First, as noted already, gamma-hedging requires the use of additional options. The market-maker will have to obtain the required option position from another market-maker, paying the bid-ask spread. In this example, all profits earned from writing the 40-strike call will go to pay the market-maker who sells the 45-strike call used in gamma-hedging. In a large portfolio, however, with many options bought and sold, naturally

8. The gammas in equation (13) are rounded. The actual gammas are 0.065063 and 0.052438, the ratio of which is 1.2408.

TABLE 6 Prices and Greeks for 40-strike call, 45-strike call, and the (gamma-neutral) portfolio resulting from selling the 40-strike call for which $T - t = 0.25$ and buying 1.2408 45-strike calls for which $T - t = 0.33$. By buying 17.49 shares, the market-maker can be both delta- and gamma-neutral. Assumes $S = \$40$, $\sigma = 0.3$, $r = 0.08$, and $\delta = 0$.

	40-Strike Call	45-Strike Call	Sell 40-Strike Call, Buy 1.2408 45-Strike Calls
Price ($)	2.7847	1.3584	−1.0993
Delta	0.5825	0.3285	−0.1749
Gamma	0.0651	0.0524	0.0000
Vega	0.0781	0.0831	0.0250
Theta	−0.0173	−0.0129	0.0013
Rho	0.0513	0.0389	−0.0031

FIGURE 4

Comparison of 1-day holding period profit for delta-hedged position described in Table 2 and delta- and gamma-hedged position described in Table 6.

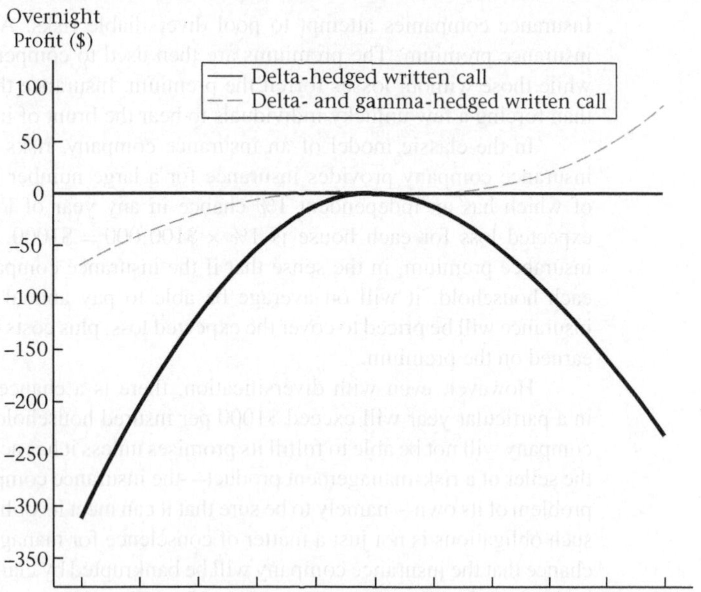

offsetting one another, gamma-hedging the net exposure would not require many option transactions.

Second, if end-users on average buy puts and calls, then in the aggregate they have positive gamma (the end-users "buy gamma," to use market-making parlance). By definition, market-makers in the aggregate must then have negative gamma. Thus, while in principle any one market-maker could gamma-hedge, not all market-makers could be gamma-neutral. If investors want to buy insurance, they will not be gamma-neutral, and, hence, market-makers cannot in the aggregate be gamma-neutral.

In addition to gamma, other risks, such as vega and rho, can be hedged in the same fashion as delta.

6. MARKET-MAKING AS INSURANCE

The preceding discussion suggests that market-makers who write options can sustain large losses, even if they delta-hedge. This conclusion suggests that option market-making (and derivatives market-making more generally) has more in common with insurance than you might at first think.

Insurance

Insurance companies attempt to pool diversifiable risks. All insured individuals pay an insurance premium. The premiums are then used to compensate those who suffer losses, while those without losses forfeit the premium. Insurance thereby spreads the pain rather than forcing a few unlucky individuals to bear the brunt of inevitable losses.

In the classic model of an insurance company, risks are independent. Suppose an insurance company provides insurance for a large number of identical households, each of which has an independent 1% chance in any year of losing \$100,000 in a fire. The expected loss for each house is $1\% \times \$100{,}000 = \$1000$. This is the "actuarially fair" insurance premium, in the sense that if the insurance company collects this amount from each household, it will on average be able to pay annual insurance claims. In general insurance will be priced to cover the expected loss, plus costs of doing business, less interest earned on the premium.

However, even with diversification, there is a chance that actual insurance claims in a particular year will exceed \$1000 per insured household, in which case the insurance company will not be able to fulfill its promises unless it has access to additional funds. Thus, the seller of a risk-management product—the insurance company—has a risk-management problem of its own—namely to be sure that it can meet its obligations to customers. Meeting such obligations is not just a matter of conscience for management; if there is a significant chance that the insurance company will be bankrupted by claims, there will be no customers in the first place!

Insurance companies have two primary ways to ensure that they meet claims:

1. **Capital:** Insurance companies hold capital, i.e., a buffer fund in case there is an unusually large number of claims. Because of diversification, for any given bankruptcy probability insurers can use a smaller reserve fund per insured house as the number of insured houses grows. Capital in the form of reserves has traditionally been an important buffer for insurance companies against unexpectedly large claims.

2. **Reinsurance:** There is always the possibility of a loss that can exceed any *fixed* amount of capital. An insurance company can in turn buy insurance against large losses, in order to be able to make large payouts if necessary. Insurance for insurance companies is called reinsurance. Insurance companies buy insurance from reinsurance firms to cover the event that claims exceed a certain amount. Reinsurance is a put option: The reinsurance claim gives the insurance company the right to sell to the reinsurers claims that have lost money. Reinsurance does not change the aggregate need for capital, but it does permit further diversification.

Market-Makers

Now consider again the role of market-makers. Suppose that investors, fearful of a market crash, wish to buy out-of-the-money puts. Out-of-the-money put writers are selling insurance against large market moves. It is precisely when large market moves occur that delta-hedging breaks down. Just like an insurance company, a market-maker requires capital as a cushion against losses. Since capital has a cost, market-makers may also raise the cost of written options that require a disproportionately large commitment of capital per dollar of premium.

Reinsurance for a market-maker would entail buying out-of-the-money put options to move some risk to another market-maker, but ultimately if the financial industry is a net writer of insurance, there must be capital in the event of losses.

The importance of capital and the analogy to insurance becomes more obvious when we consider new derivatives markets. For example, think about weather derivatives. Financial institutions have hedged ski-resort operators against warm winters, soft-drink manufacturers against cold summers, and lawn sprinkler manufacturers against wet summers. Ultimately, there must be a counterparty willing to absorb the risk. If you think about the risks in weather insurance, on a *global* basis they are like traditional insurance. Weather contracts in the United States can be diversified with weather contracts in Asia, and ultimately the global capital committed to insurance absorbs the reinsurance risk. Global capital markets broadly defined are thus the natural party to absorb these risks.

Some risk, however, is not globally diversifiable. Consider writing puts on the S&P 500. If the U.S. stock market suffers a large decline, other markets around the world are likely to follow. The risk of writing out-of-the-money index puts is one possible explanation for the behavior of implied volatility. Ultimately, it is capital—usually in the form of shareholders willing to absorb risk—that safeguards the financial industry. Delta-hedging plays a key role, but in the end there is always risk that must be absorbed by capital.

CHAPTER SUMMARY

Market-makers buy and sell to satisfy customer demand. A derivatives market-maker can use the underlying stock to delta-hedge the resulting position. By definition, the return on a delta-hedged position does not depend on the *direction* in which the stock price moves, but it does depend on the *magnitude* of the stock price move. A position with zero delta and negative gamma makes money for small stock price moves and loses money for large stock price moves. If the gamma of the position is positive, it makes money for large moves and loses money for small moves. Either way, the delta-hedged position breaks even if the stock moves one standard deviation.

Using a delta-gamma-theta approximation to characterize the change in the value of the delta-hedged portfolio, we can demonstrate that there are three factors that explain the profitability of the portfolio. First, gamma measures the tendency of the portfolio to become unhedged as the stock price moves. Second, theta measures the gain or loss on the portfolio due to the passage of time alone. Third, the market-maker will have interest income or expense on the portfolio.

If we assume that the stock price moves one standard deviation and impose the condition that the market-maker earns zero profit, then a fair option price satisfies a particular relationship among delta, gamma, and theta. This relationship, equation (10), is the foundation of the Black-Scholes option pricing analysis and applies to derivatives in general, not just to calls and puts.

Ultimately, market-making is risky and requires capital. If customers on average buy puts and calls, and if we think of options as insurance, then market-makers are in the same business as insurance companies. This requires capital, since if an extreme event occurs, delta-hedging will fail.

FURTHER READING

The main example in this chapter assumed that the Black-Scholes formula provided the correct option price and illustrated the behavior of the formula, viewed from the perspective of a delta-hedging market-maker.

PROBLEMS

In the following problems assume, unless otherwise stated, that $S = \$40$, $\sigma = 30\%$, $r = 8\%$, and $\delta = 0$.

1. Suppose you sell a 45-strike call with 91 days to expiration. What is delta? If the option is on 100 shares, what investment is required for a delta-hedged portfolio? What is your overnight profit if the stock tomorrow is \$39? What if the stock price is \$40.50?

2. Suppose you sell a 40-strike put with 91 days to expiration. What is delta? If the option is on 100 shares, what investment is required for a delta-hedged portfolio? What is your overnight profit if the stock price tomorrow is \$39? What if it is \$40.50?

3. Suppose you buy a 40–45 bull spread with 91 days to expiration. If you delta-hedge this position, what investment is required? What is your overnight profit if the stock tomorrow is \$39? What if the stock is \$40.50?

4. Suppose you enter into a put ratio spread where you buy a 45-strike put and sell two 40-strike puts. If you delta-hedge this position, what investment is required? What is your overnight profit if the stock tomorrow is \$39? What if the stock is \$40.50?

5. Reproduce the analysis in Table 2, assuming that instead of selling a call you sell a 40-strike put.

6. Reproduce the analysis in Table 3, assuming that instead of selling a call you sell a 40-strike put.

7. Consider a 40-strike 180-day call with $S = \$40$. Compute a delta-gamma-theta approximation for the value of the call after 1, 5, and 25 days. For each day, consider stock prices of \$36 to \$44.00 in \$0.25 increments and compare the actual option premium at each stock price with the predicted premium. Where are the two the same?

8. Repeat the previous problem for a 40-strike 180-day put.

9. Consider a 40-strike call with 91 days to expiration. Graph the results from the following calculations.

   a. Compute the actual price with 90 days to expiration at \$1 intervals from \$30 to \$50.

   b. Compute the estimated price with 90 days to expiration using a delta approximation.

   c. Compute the estimated price with 90 days to expiration using a delta-gamma approximation.

   d. Compute the estimated price with 90 days to expiration using a delta-gamma-theta approximation.

10. Consider a 40-strike call with 365 days to expiration. Graph the results from the following calculations.

    a. Compute the actual price with 360 days to expiration at \$1 intervals from \$30 to \$50.

    b. Compute the estimated price with 360 days to expiration using a delta approximation.

    c. Compute the estimated price with 360 days to expiration using a delta-gamma approximation.

    d. Compute the estimated price with 360 days to expiration using a delta-gamma-theta approximation.

11. Repeat Problem 9 for a 91-day 40-strike put.

12. Repeat Problem 10 for a 365-day 40-strike put.

13. Using the parameters in Table 1, verify that equation (9) is zero.

14. Consider a put for which $T = 0.5$ and $K = \$45$. Compute the Greeks and verify that equation (9) is zero.

15. You own one 45-strike call with 180 days to expiration. Compute and graph the 1-day holding period profit if you delta- and gamma-hedge this position using a 40-strike call with 180 days to expiration.

16. You have sold one 45-strike put with 180 days to expiration. Compute and graph the 1-day holding period profit if you delta- and gamma-hedge this position using the stock and a 40-strike call with 180 days to expiration.

17. You have written a 35–40–45 butterfly spread with 91 days to expiration. Compute and graph the 1-day holding period profit if you delta- and gamma-hedge this position using the stock and a 40-strike call with 180 days to expiration.

18. Suppose you enter into a put ratio spread where you buy a 45-strike put and sell two 40-strike puts, both with 91 days to expiration. Compute and graph the 1-day holding period profit if you delta- and gamma-hedge this position using the stock and a 40-strike call with 180 days to expiration.

19. You have purchased a 40-strike call with 91 days to expiration. You wish to delta-hedge, but you are also concerned about changes in volatility; thus, you want to *vega-hedge* your position as well.

a. Compute and graph the 1-day holding period profit if you delta- and vega-hedge this position using the stock and a 40-strike call with 180 days to expiration.

b. Compute and graph the 1-day holding period profit if you delta-, gamma-, and vega-hedge this position using the stock, a 40-strike call with 180 days to expiration, and a 45-strike put with 365 days to expiration.

20. Repeat the previous problem, except that instead of hedging volatility risk, you wish to hedge interest rate risk, i.e., to *rho-hedge*. In addition to delta-, gamma-, and rho-hedging, can you delta-gamma-rho-vega hedge?

Appendix A TAYLOR SERIES APPROXIMATIONS

We have seen that the change in the option price can be expressed in terms of delta, gamma, and theta. The resulting expression is really just a particular approximation to the option price, called a Taylor series approximation.

Let $G(x, y)$ be a function of two variables. Taylor's theorem says that the value of the function at the point $G(x + \epsilon_x, y + \epsilon_y)$ may be approximated using derivatives of the function, as follows:

$$
\begin{aligned}
&G(x + \epsilon_x, y + \epsilon_y) = \\
&G(x, y) + \epsilon_x G_x(x, y) + \epsilon_y G_y(x, y) \\
&+ \frac{1}{2}\left[\epsilon_x^2 G_{xx}(x, y) + \epsilon_y^2 G_{yy}(x, y) + 2\epsilon_x\epsilon_y G_{x,y}(x, y)\right] \\
&+ \frac{1}{6}\left[\epsilon_x^3 G_{xxx}(x, y) + 3\epsilon_x^2\epsilon_y G_{xxy}(x, y) + 3\epsilon_x\epsilon_y^2 G_{xyy}(x, y) + \epsilon_y^3 G_{yyy}G(x, y)\right] \\
&+ \cdots \qquad (14)
\end{aligned}
$$

The approximation may be extended indefinitely, using successively higher-order derivatives. The nth term in the expansion is

$$\frac{1}{n!}\sum_{i=0}^{n}\binom{n}{i}\epsilon_x^i\epsilon_y^{n-i}G_{x^i,y^{n-i}}(x, y)$$

where the notation $G_{x^i, y^{n-i}}(x, y)$ means take the ith derivative with respect to x and the $(n-i)$th derivative with respect to y. The Taylor series is useful when the approximation is reasonably accurate with few terms.

For our purposes, it is enough to note that the delta-gamma approximation, equation (6), looks like a Taylor series approximation that stops with the second derivative. You may wonder, however, why there is no second derivative with respect to time. You may also wonder why the approximation stops with the second derivative.

Appendix B GREEKS IN THE BINOMIAL MODEL

The Black-Scholes Greeks are obtained by differentiating the option price. However, the general binomial option price calculation is not a formula but an algorithm. How can option Greeks be computed using the binomial tree? We can use some of the relations between delta, gamma, and theta discussed in this chapter to compute the binomial Greeks.

The option price and stock price for the first two time steps in the binomial model can be represented as in Figure 5. Delta at the initial node is computed using the formula

$$\Delta(S, 0) = e^{-\delta h} \frac{C_u - C_d}{uS - dS} \tag{15}$$

Gamma is the change in delta. We cannot compute the change in delta for the time-0 delta, since only one delta at a single stock price is defined at that point. But we can compute the change in delta at time h using the two deltas that are defined there. Thus, we have

$$\Gamma(S_h, h) = \frac{\Delta(uS, h) - \Delta(dS, h)}{uS - dS} \tag{16}$$

This is an approximation since we wish to know gamma at time 0, not at time h, and at the price S_0. However, even with a small number of binomial steps, the approximation works reasonably well.

With theta we are interested in the pure effect on the option price of changing time. We can calculate this using delta and gamma. Define

$$\epsilon = udS - S$$

FIGURE 5

Option price and stock price trees, assuming that the stock can move up or down u or d each period.

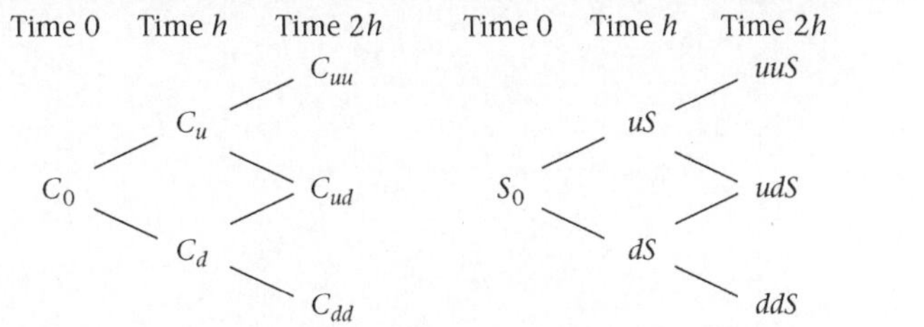

Using the delta-gamma-theta approximation, equation (6), we can write the option price at time $2h$ and node udS as

$$C(udS, 2h) = C(S, 0) + \epsilon\Delta(S, 0) + \frac{1}{2}\epsilon^2\Gamma(S, 0) + 2h\theta(S, 0)$$

Solving for $\theta(S, 0)$ gives

$$\theta(S, 0) = \frac{C(udS, 2h) - \epsilon\Delta(S, 0) - \frac{1}{2}\epsilon^2\Gamma(S, 0) - C(S, 0)}{2h} \tag{17}$$

Exotic Options I

By altering the terms of standard contracts like standard options, futures, and swaps, you obtain a "nonstandard" or "exotic" option. Exotic options can provide precise tailoring of risk exposures, and they permit investment strategies difficult or costly to realize with standard options and securities. In this chapter we discuss some basic kinds of exotic options, including Asian, barrier, compound, gap, and exchange options.

1. INTRODUCTION

Suppose that XYZ Corp., a dollar-based multinational corporation with sizable European operations, has a large monthly inflow of euros that are eventually converted to dollars. XYZ is considering the purchase of 1-year put options as insurance against a fall in the euro but is also interested in exploring alternatives. In thinking about how to hedge this position, you might reason as follows: "A standard 1-year put option would hedge the firm against the level of the euro *on the one day the option expires*. This hedge would have significant basis risk since the price at expiration could be quite different from the average price over the year. Buying a strip of put options in which one option expires every month would have little basis risk but might be expensive. Over the course of the year what really matters is the *average* exchange rate over this period; the ups and downs around the average rate cancel out by definition."

This train of thought leads you to construct a new kind of option—based on the average price, rather than the price at a point in time—with a payoff that addresses a particular business concern: It provides a more precise hedge against the risk that matters, namely the average exchange rate. This example demonstrates that exotic options can solve a particular business problem in a way that standard options do not. Generally, an **exotic option** (or **nonstandard option**) is simply an option with some contractual difference from standard options. Although we will focus on hedging examples, these products can also be used to speculate.

It is not hard to invent new kinds of options. The challenge is to invent new options that are potentially attractive to buyers and that can be priced and hedged without too much difficulty. A market-maker can delta-hedge an option position. Thus the price of an option is equivalent to the cost of synthetically manufacturing the option. In particular, an option is fairly priced when there is a certain relationship among the Greeks of the option.

From Chapter 14 of *Derivatives Markets*, Third Edition, Robert McDonald. Copyright © 2013 by Pearson Education, Inc. Published by Pearson Prentice Hall. All rights reserved.

Options with exotic features can generally be priced and delta-hedged in the same way as ordinary options.[1] As a consequence, exotic derivative products are quite common in practice and the technology for pricing and hedging them is well understood. In fact, since many such options are in common use, the term "exotic" is an anachronism. We will continue to use it, however.

The goal in this chapter is *not* to master the mathematical details of particular products, but rather to gain an intuitive understanding of the trade-offs in design and pricing. Consequently, most of the formulas appear in the chapter appendix.

Since exotic options are often constructed by tweaking ordinary options in minor ways, ordinary options are useful as benchmarks for exotics. To understand exotic options you should ask questions like these:

- How does the payoff of the exotic compare to that of a standard option?
- Can the exotic option be approximated by some portfolio of other options?
- Is the exotic option cheap or expensive relative to standard options? Understanding the economics of the option is a critical step in understanding its pricing and use.
- What is the rationale for the use of the exotic option?
- How easily can the exotic option be hedged? An option may be desirable to a customer, but it will not be sold unless the risk arising from market-making can be controlled.

2. ASIAN OPTIONS

An **Asian option** has a payoff that is based on the average price over some period of time. An Asian option is an example of a **path-dependent option**, which means that the value of the option at expiration depends upon the path by which the stock arrived at its final price.[2] Such an option has the potential to solve XYZ's hedging problem.

There are many practical applications in which we average prices. In addition to cases where the firm cares about the average exchange rate (as with XYZ), averaging is also used when a single price at a point in time might be subject to manipulation or price swings induced by thin markets. Bonds convertible into stock, for example, often base the terms of conversion on the average stock price over a 20-day period at the end of the bond's life. Settlement based on the average is called an **Asian tail**, since the averaging occurs only at the termination of the contract.

As we will see, Asian options are worth less at issuance than otherwise equivalent ordinary options. The reason is that the averaged price of the underlying asset is less volatile than the asset price itself, and an option on a lower volatility asset is worth less.

1. However, there are options that are quite difficult to hedge even though they are easy to price.

2. You can think of path dependence in the context of a binomial pricing model. In the binomial model, *udu* and *duu* are a series of up and down stock price moves—paths—occurring in a different order but which lead to the same final stock price. Thus, both yield the same payoff for a European option. However, with a path-dependent option, these two paths would yield different final option payoffs because the intermediate stock prices were different.

XYZ's Hedging Problem

Let's think more about XYZ's currency hedging problem. Suppose that XYZ has a monthly euro inflow of €100m, reflecting revenue from selling products in Europe. Its costs, however, are primarily fixed in dollars. Let x_i denote the dollar price of a euro in month i. At the end of the year, the converted amount in dollars is

$$€\,100\text{m} \times \sum_{i=1}^{12} x_i e^{r(12-i)/12} \tag{1}$$

We have numerous strategies available for hedging the end-of-year cash flow. Here are a few obvious ones:

- **Strip of forward contracts:** Sell euro forward contracts maturing each month over the year. The premium of this strategy is zero.
- **Euro swap:** Swap euros for dollars. Except for the timing of cash flows, a swap produces the same result as hedging with the strip of forwards. A swap also has a zero premium.
- **Strip of puts:** Buy 12 put options on €100m, each maturing at the end of a different month. The cost is the 12 option premiums.

The difference between the forward and option strategies is the ability to profit from a euro appreciation, but we pay a premium for the possibility of earning that profit. You can probably think of other strategies as well.

The idea of an Asian option stems from expression (1): What we really care about is the future value of the *sum* of the converted cash flows. This in turn depends on the sum of the month-end exchange rates. If for simplicity we ignore interest, what we are trying to hedge is

$$\sum_{i=1}^{12} x_i = 12 \times \left(\frac{\sum_{i=1}^{12} x_i}{12} \right) \tag{2}$$

The expression in parentheses is the month-end arithmetic average exchange rate, which motivates the idea of an option on the average.

Options on the Average

As a logical matter there are eight basic kinds of Asian options, depending upon whether the option is a put or a call, whether the average is computed as a geometric or arithmetic average, and whether the average asset price is used in place of the price of the underlying asset or the strike price. Here are details about some of these alternatives.

The Definition of the Average. It is most common in practice to define the average as an *arithmetic average*. Suppose we record the stock price every h periods from time 0 to T; there are then $N = T/h$ periods. The arithmetic average is defined as

$$A(T) = \frac{1}{N} \sum_{i=1}^{N} S_{ih} \tag{3}$$

While arithmetic averages are typically used, they are mathematically inconvenient.[3] It is computationally easier, but less common in practice, to use the *geometric average* stock price, which is defined as

$$G(T) = \left(S_h \times S_{2h} \times \cdots \times S_{Nh}\right)^{\frac{1}{N}} \tag{4}$$

The following example illustrates the difference between an arithmetic and geometric average.

Example 1. Suppose that we compute the average based on quarterly stock prices over 1 year. We observe stock prices of \$55, \$72, \$61, and \$85. The arithmetic average is

$$\frac{\$55 + \$72 + \$61 + \$85}{4} = \$68.250$$

The geometric average is

$$(\$55 \times \$72 \times \$61 \times \$85)^{0.25} = \$67.315 \quad \blacksquare$$

The chapter appendix has (relatively simple) formulas for pricing European options based on the geometric average.

Whether the Average Is Used as the Asset Price or the Strike. The payoff at maturity can be computed using the average stock price either as the price of the underlying asset or as the strike price. When the average is used as the asset price, the option is called an *average price option.* When the average is used as the strike price, the option is called an *average strike option.* Here are the four variants of options based on the geometric average:

$$\text{Geometric average price call} = \max[0, G(T) - K] \tag{5}$$

$$\text{Geometric average price put} = \max[0, K - G(T)] \tag{6}$$

$$\text{Geometric average strike call} = \max[0, S_T - G(T)] \tag{7}$$

$$\text{Geometric average strike put} = \max[0, G(T) - S_T] \tag{8}$$

The terms "average price" and "average strike" refer to whether the average is used in place of the asset price or the strike price. In each case the average could also be computed as an arithmetic average, giving us our eight basic kinds of Asian options.

Comparing Asian Options

Table 1 shows values of geometric average price calls and puts. If the number of averages, N, is 1, then the average is the final stock price. In that case the average price call is an ordinary call.

Intuitively, averaging reduces the volatility of $G(T)$ relative to the volatility of the stock price at expiration, S_T, and thus we should expect the value of an average price option to decrease with the number of stock prices used to compute the average. This is evident in Table 1, which shows the decline in value of the average price option as the frequency of averaging increases.

3. Because the sum of lognormal variables is not lognormally distributed, there are no simple pricing formulas for options based on the arithmetic average.

TABLE 1 Premiums of at-the-money geometric average price and geometric average strike calls and puts, for different numbers of prices averaged, N. The case $N = 1$ for the average price options is equivalent to Black-Scholes values. Assumes $S = \$40$, $K = \$40$, $r = 0.08$, $\sigma = 0.3$, $\delta = 0$, and $t = 1$.

	Average Price ($)		Average Strike ($)	
N	Call	Put	Call	Put
1	6.285	3.209	0.000	0.000
2	4.708	2.645	2.225	1.213
3	4.209	2.445	2.748	1.436
5	3.819	2.281	3.148	1.610
10	3.530	2.155	3.440	1.740
50	3.302	2.052	3.668	1.843
1000	3.248	2.027	3.722	1.868
∞	3.246	2.026	3.725	1.869

Table 1 also shows that, in contrast to average price calls, the price of an average strike call increases with the number of averaging periods. The average of stock prices between times 0 and T is positively correlated with the stock price at time T, S_T. If $G(T)$ is high, S_T is likely to be high as well. More frequent averaging makes the average strike option more valuable because it reduces the correlation between S_T and $G(T)$. To see this pattern, consider what happens if the average is computed only using the final stock price. The value of the call is

$$\max[0, S_T - G(T)]$$

If only one stock price observation is used, $G(T) = S_T$, and the value of the option is zero for sure. With more frequent averaging the correlation is reduced and the value of the average strike option increases.

When would an average strike option make sense? Such an option pays off when there is a difference between the average asset price over the life of the option and the asset price at expiration. Such an option could be used for insurance in a situation where we accumulated an asset over a period of time and then sold the entire accumulated position at one price.

An Asian Solution for XYZ

If XYZ receives euros and its costs are fixed in dollars, profits are reduced if the euro depreciates—that is, if the number of dollars received for a euro is lower. We could construct an Asian put option that puts a floor, K, on the average exchange rate received. The per euro payoff of this option would be

$$\max\left(0, K - \frac{1}{12}\sum_{i=1}^{12} x_i\right) \tag{9}$$

TABLE 2 Comparison of costs for alternative hedging strategies for XYZ. The price in the second row is the sum of premiums for puts expiring after 1 month, 2 months, and so forth, out to 12 months. The first, third, and fourth row premiums are calculated assuming 1 year to maturity, and then multiplied by 12. Assumes the current exchange rate is \$0.9/€, option strikes are 0.9, $r_\$ = 6\%$, $r_€ = 3\%$, and dollar/euro volatility is 10%.

Hedge Instrument	Premium (\$)
Put option expiring in 1 year	0.2753
Strip of monthly put options	0.2178
Geometric average price put	0.1796
Arithmetic average price put	0.1764

For example, if we wanted to guarantee an average exchange rate of \$0.90 per euro, we would set $K = \$0.9$. If the average exchange rate was less than that, we would be paid the difference between \$0.9 and the average. Since we repatriate €1.2b over the course of a year, we would buy contracts covering €1.2b.

Do you recognize the kind of option described by equation (9)? The average is arithmetic, the average is used in place of the asset price, and it is a put. Hence, it is an *arithmetic average price Asian put*.

There are other hedging strategies XYZ could use. Table 2 lists premiums for several alternatives. The single put expiring at year-end is the most expensive option. As discussed earlier, it has basis risk because the year-end exchange rate could be quite different from the average. Two other strategies have signficantly less basis risk: the strip of European puts expiring monthly and the arithmetic Asian put. The strip of puts protects against low exchange rates month-by-month, whereas the Asian option protects the 12-month average. The Asian put is cheaper since there will be situations in which some of the individual puts are valuable (for example, if the exchange rate takes a big swing in one month that is reversed subsequently), but the Asian put does not pay off. The geometric option hedges less well than the arithmetic option since the quantity being hedged (equation (1)) is an arithmetic, not a geometric, average.

Finally, be aware that this example ignores several subtleties. The option strikes, for example, might be made to vary with the forward curve for the exchange rate. The effect of interest in equation (1) could also be taken into account.

3. BARRIER OPTIONS

A **barrier option** has a payoff depending upon whether, over the life of the option, the price of the underlying asset reaches a specified level, called the *barrier*. Barrier puts and calls either come into existence or go out of existence the first time the asset price reaches the barrier. If they are in existence at expiration, they are equivalent to ordinary puts and calls.

Box 1: Are All Barrier Options Created Equal?

One difficulty in designing a barrier option is defining the barrier. What does it mean for the S&P 500 index, for example, to "hit" the level 1500? Does it mean that the closing price exceeds 1500? Does it mean that, at some point during the day, the reported index exceeds that level? If so, whose report of the price is to be used?

What about manipulation of the index? Suppose the index reaches 1499.99 and then there is a large trade in a single stock, pushing the index to 1500.01. Is it possible that someone entered a buy order with the intention of manipulating the index? Since either the buyer or seller could try to manipulate the price, it is common to define a barrier using a price average computed over some period of time. An average of this type is less easily manipulated. (Concern about manipulation is one reason for the use of Asian tails, often used in securities convertible into stock.)

Barrier options sold by different firms may use different definitions of the barrier. Thus, a company might find that the barrier option it bought from Bank A to offset the option it sold to Bank B is not really an offset, because the definition of the barrier for the two options is slightly different. Hsu (1997) discusses many of the practical problems that arise with barrier options.

It can be tricky to define what it means for the stock price to reach a barrier. See the box above for a discussion.

Since barrier puts and calls never pay more than standard puts and calls, they are no more expensive than standard puts and calls. Barrier options are another example of a path-dependent option.

Barrier options are widely used in practice. One appeal of barrier options may be their lower premiums, although the lower premium of course reflects a lower average payoff.

Types of Barrier Options

There are three basic kinds of barrier options:

1. **Knock-out options:** These go out of existence (are "knocked-out") if the asset price reaches the barrier. If the price of the underlying asset has to fall to reach the barrier, the option is a **down-and-out**. If the price of the underlying asset has to rise to reach the barrier, the option is an **up-and-out**.
2. **Knock-in options:** These come into existence (are "knocked-in") if the barrier is touched. If the price of the underlying asset has to fall to reach the barrier, the option is a **down-and-in**. If the asset price has to rise to reach the barrier, it is an **up-and-in**.
3. **Rebate options:** These make a fixed payment if the asset price reaches the barrier. The payment can occur either at the time the barrier is reached, or at the time the option expires, in which case it is a deferred rebate. Rebate options can be either "up rebates" or "down rebates," depending on whether the barrier is above or below the current price.

FIGURE 1

Illustration of a price path where the initial stock price is \$100 and the barrier is \$75. At $t = 0.5$, the stock hits the barrier.

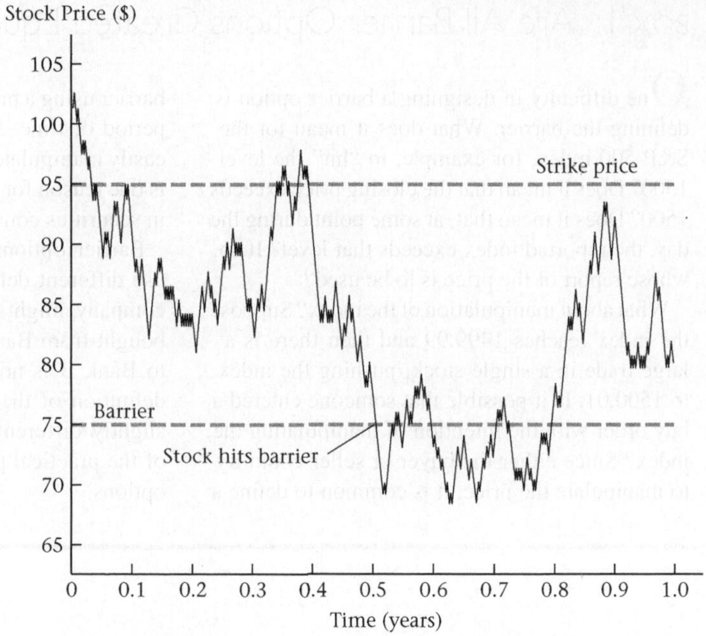

Figure 1 illustrates how a barrier option works. The stock price starts at around \$100, ends at \$80, and hits the barrier of \$75 about halfway through the year. If the option were a 95-strike down-and-in put, the option would knock in and pay \$15 (\$95 − \$80) at expiration. If the option were a down-and-out put, it would be worthless at expiration. If the option were a down-and-in call, it would knock in at \$75 but still be worthless at expiration because the stock price is below the strike price.

The important parity relation for barrier options is

$$\boxed{\text{“Knock-in” option} + \text{“Knock-out” option} = \text{Ordinary option}} \tag{10}$$

For example, for otherwise equivalent options, we have

$$\text{Down-and-in call} + \text{Down-and-out call} = \text{Standard call}$$

Since these option premiums cannot be negative, this equation demonstrates directly that barrier options have lower premiums than standard options.

Currency Hedging

Consider once again XYZ. Here we will focus on hedging only the cash flow occurring in 6 months to see how barrier puts compare to standard puts.

What kinds of barrier puts make sense in the context of XYZ's hedging problem? We are hedging against a decline in the exchange rate, which makes certain possibilities

TABLE 3 Premiums of standard, down-and-in, and up-and-out currency put options with strikes K. The column headed "standard" contains prices of ordinary put options. Assumes $x_0 = 0.9$, $\sigma = 0.1$, $r_\$ = 0.06$, $r_€ = 0.03$, and $t = 0.5$.

	Standard	Down-and-In Barrier ($)		Up-and-Out Barrier ($)		
Strike ($)	($)	0.8000	0.8500	0.9500	1.0000	1.0500
$K = 0.8$	0.0007	0.0007	0.0007	0.0007	0.0007	0.0007
$K = 0.9$	0.0188	0.0066	0.0167	0.0174	0.0188	0.0188
$K = 1.0$	0.0870	0.0134	0.0501	0.0633	0.0847	0.0869

less attractive. A down-and-out put would be worthless when we needed it. Similarly, an up-and-in put would provide insurance only if, prior to the exchange rate falling below the strike, the exchange rate had risen so the option could knock in.

This leaves down-and-ins and up-and-outs to consider. Table 3 presents prices of standard, down-and-in, and up-and-out puts with different strikes and different barriers. Consider first the row where $K = 0.8$. Notice that all options appear to have the same price. It is a useful exercise in the logic of barrier options to understand why they appear equally priced. In fact, here is an exercise to solve before reading further: Can you deduce which of the six premiums with $K = 0.8$ are exactly equal and which are merely close?

The option prices in Table 3 tell us something about the relative likelihood of different scenarios for the exchange rate. The ordinary put premium when the strike is 0.8 reflects the (risk-neutral) probability that the exchange rate will be below 0.8 at maturity. Both of the down-and-ins, having strikes below the starting exchange rate of 0.9 and at least 0.8, will necessarily have knocked in should the exchange rate fall below 0.8. Described differently, a down-and-in put with a barrier above the strike is equivalent to an ordinary put. Therefore, the first three option premiums in the $K = 0.8$ row are identical.

Now consider the knock-out puts with $K = 0.8$. The difference between the ordinary put and the up-and-out put with a 0.95 barrier is that sometimes the exchange rate will drift from 0.9 to above 0.95, and then below 0.8. In this case, the ordinary put will have a payoff but the knock-out put will not.

How likely is this scenario? The low premium of 0.0007 for the ordinary put tells us that it is relatively unlikely the exchange rate will drift from 0.9 to 0.8 over 6 months. It is even less likely that the exchange rate will hit 0.95 *in those cases* when it does fall below 0.8. A knock-out may be likely, but it is rare to have a knock-out occur *in those cases when an ordinary put with a strike of 0.8 would pay off*. Thus, the knock-out feature is not subtracting much from the value of the option. This argument is even stronger for the knock-out barriers of 1.0 and 1.05. Nevertheless, since there is a chance these options will knock out and then end up in-the-money, the premiums are less than for the knock-in puts and are increasing with the barrier. Thus, the up-and-out prices in the $K = 0.8$ row are slightly less than the price of an ordinary put.

When the strike price is 1.0, the up-and-outs with barriers of 1.0 and 1.05 have substantially all the value of the ordinary put with the same strike. The interpretation is that most of the value of the puts comes from scenarios in which the option remains in-the-money; in those scenarios in which the option knocks out, the exchange rate on average does not fall enough for the option to be valuable.

4. COMPOUND OPTIONS

A **compound option** is an option to buy an option. If you think of an ordinary option as an asset—analogous to a stock—then a compound option is similar to an ordinary option.

Compound options are a little more complicated than ordinary options because there are two strikes and two expirations, one each for the underlying option and for the compound option. Suppose that the current time is t_0 and that we have a compound option which at time t_1 will give us the right to pay x to buy a European call option with strike K. This underlying call will expire at time $T > t_1$. Figure 2 compares the timing of the exercise decisions for this compound option with the exercise decision for an ordinary call expiring at time T.

If we exercise the compound call at time t_1, then the price of the option we receive is $C(S, K, T - t_1)$. At time T, this option will have the value $\max(0, S_T - K)$, the same as an ordinary call with strike K. At time t_1, when the compound option expires, the value of the compound option is

$$\max[C(S_{t_1}, K, T - t_1) - x, 0]$$

We only exercise the compound option if the stock price at time t_1 is sufficiently great that the value of the call exceeds the compound option strike price, x. Let S^* be the critical stock price above which the compound option is exercised. By definition, S^* satisfies

$$C(S^*, K, T - t_1) = x \tag{11}$$

FIGURE 2

The timing of exercise decisions for a compound call option on a call compared with an ordinary call option.

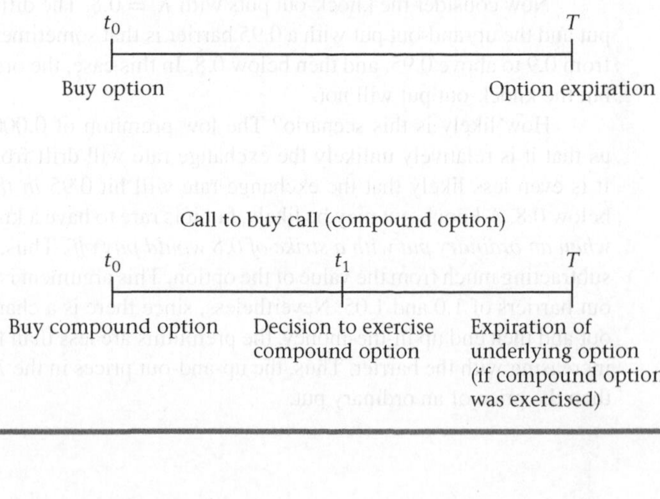

The compound option is exercised for $S_{t_1} > S^*$.

Thus, in order for the compound call to ultimately be valuable, there are two events that must take place. First, at time t_1 we must have $S_{t_1} > S^*$; that is, it must be worthwhile to exercise the compound call. Second, at time T we must have $S_T > K$; that is, it must be profitable to exercise the underlying call. Because two events must occur, the formula for a compound call contains a bivariate cumulative normal distribution, as opposed to the univariate distribution in the Black-Scholes formula.

Formulas for the four compound options—an option to buy a call (CallOnCall), an option to sell a call (PutOnCall), an option to buy a put (CallOnPut), and an option to sell a put (PutOnPut)—are in the chapter appendix. Valuing a compound option is different from valuing an ordinary option in part for mathematical rather than for conceptual reasons. The Black-Scholes formula assumes that the stock price is lognormally distributed. However, the price of an option—because there is a significant probability that it will be worthless—cannot be lognormally distributed. Thus, while an option on an option is conceptually similar to an option on a stock, it is mathematically different.[4] The trick in deriving a formula for the price of a compound option is to value the option based on the value of the stock, which *is* lognormally distributed, rather than the price of the underlying option, which is not lognormally distributed.

Compound Option Parity

As you might guess, there are parity relationships among the compound option prices. Suppose we buy a call on a call, and sell a put on a call, where both have the same strike, underlying option, and time to maturity. When the compound options expire, we will acquire the underlying option by paying the strike price x. If the stock price is high, we will exercise the compound call, and if the stock price is low, the compound put will be exercised and we will be forced to buy the call. Thus, the difference between the call on call and put on call premiums, plus the present value of x, must equal the premium to acquire the underlying option outright. That is,

$$\begin{aligned} &\text{CallOnCall}(S, K, x, \sigma, r, t_1, t_2, \delta) - \text{PutOnCall}(S, K, x, \sigma, r, t_1, t_2, \delta) + xe^{-rt_1} \\ &\qquad = \text{BSCall}(S, K, \sigma, r, t_2, \delta) \end{aligned} \tag{12}$$

An analogous relationship holds for puts.

Options on Dividend-Paying Stocks

It is possible to price American options on dividend-paying stocks using the binomial model. It turns out that the compound option model also permits us to price an option on a stock that will pay a single discrete dividend prior to expiration.

Suppose that at time t_1 the stock will pay a dividend, D. We have a choice of exercising the option at the cum-dividend price,[5] $S_{t_1} + D$, or holding the call, which will have a value reflecting the ex-dividend price, S_{t_1}. Thus, at t_1, the value of the call option is the greater of its

4. Geske (1979) was the first to derive the formula for a compound option.

5. The stock is *cum-dividend* if a purchaser of the stock will receive the dividend. Once the stock goes *ex-dividend*, the purchaser will not receive the dividend.

exercise value, $S_{t_1} + D - K$, and the option valued at the ex-dividend price, $C(S_{t_1}, T - t_1)$:

$$\max\left[C(S_{t_1}, T - t_1), S_{t_1} + D - K\right] \tag{13}$$

By put-call parity, at time t_1 we can write the value of the ex-dividend unexercised call as

$$C(S_{t_1}, T - t_1) = P(S_{t_1}, T - t_1) + S_{t_1} - Ke^{-r(T-t_1)}$$

Making this substitution in equation (13) and rewriting the result, we obtain

$$S_{t_1} + D - K + \max\left(P[S_{t_1}, T - t_1] - \left[D - K(1 - e^{-r(T-t_1)})\right], 0\right) \tag{14}$$

The value of the option is the present value of this expression.

Equation (14) tells us that we can value a call option on a dividend-paying stock as the sum of the following:

1. The stock, with present value S_0. (S_0 is the present value of $S_{t_1} + D$.)
2. Less the present value of the strike price, Ke^{-rt_1}.
3. Plus the value of a compound option—a call option on a put option—with strike price $D - K(1 - e^{-r(T-t_1)})$ and maturity date t_1, permitting the owner to buy a put option with strike price K and maturity date T.

In this interpretation, exercising the compound option corresponds to keeping the option on the stock unexercised. To see this, notice that if we exercise the compound option in equation (14), we give up the dividend and gain interest on the strike in order to acquire the put. The total is

$$S_{t_1} + P(S_{t_1}, T - t_1) - Ke^{-r(T-t_1)}$$

If we do not exercise the compound option, we receive the stock plus dividend, less the strike:

$$S_{t_1} + D - K$$

This valuation exercise provides a way to understand early exercise. We can view exercising an American call as *not* exercising the compound option to buy a put in equation (14). The cost of not exercising is that we lose the dividend, less interest on the strike. This is exactly the intuition governing early exercise.

Example 2. Suppose a stock with a price of \$100 will pay a \$5 dividend in 91 days ($t_1 = 0.2493$). The prepaid forward price for the stock, assuming receipt of the share *after* the dividend (at the time denoted 0.2493^+) is

$$F^P_{0,0.2493^+}(S_0) = \$100 - \$5 \times e^{-0.08\times 0.2493} = \$95.0987$$

An option with a strike price of \$90 will expire in 152 days ($T = 0.4164$). Assume $\sigma = 0.3$ and $r = 0.08$. The value of a European call on the stock is

$$\text{BSCall}(95.0987, \$90, 0.3, 0.08, 0.4164, 0) = \$11.764$$

The value of an American call is computed as the present value of equation 14, with the exercise price for the compound option equal to $5 - 90(1 - e^{-0.08\times(0.4164-0.2493)}) =$

3.8047, and time to maturity 0.2493 for the compound option and 0.4164 for the underlying option. The price of the compound option is

$$\begin{aligned}&\text{CallOnPut}\,(S, K, x, \sigma, r, t_1, T, \delta)\\&\quad= \text{CallOnPut}(95.0987, 90, 3.8047, 0.30, 0.08, 0.2493, 0.4164, 0) = \$1.7552\end{aligned}$$

Thus, the value of the American option is,[6] from equation (14), the cum-dividend stock price, less the present value of the strike, plus the value of the option to buy a put by paying the dividend less interest on the strike:

$$\$100 - \$90e^{-0.2493\times0.08} + \$1.7552 = \$13.5325$$

The compound option should be exercised if the ex-dividend stock price is below \$89.988.[7] Since exercise of the compound option is equivalent to leaving the original call *unexercised*, the original call should be exercised at time $t_1 = 0.2493$ if the stock price *exceeds* \$89.988.

Currency Hedging with Compound Options

Compound options provide yet another variation on possible currency-hedging strategies. Instead of buying a 6-month put option on the euro, we could buy a call option on a put option. In effect, this compound option is giving us the opportunity to wait and see what happens.

Suppose that after 3 months we will decide whether to buy the put option. Here is one way to structure such a transaction. We could figure out what premium a 3-month put with a strike of \$0.9 would have, if the exchange rate were still at 0.9. The Black-Scholes formula tells us that a 3-month at-the-money option with a strike of \$0.9 would have a premium of \$0.0146. (This value compares with the premium of \$0.0188 for the 6-month option from Table 3.)

Now we can use the compound pricing formula to price a call on a put, setting the strike to equal \$0.0146. The price of this compound call is \$0.0093. So by paying less than two-thirds the premium of the 6-month at-the-money option, we can buy an option that permits us to pay \$0.0146 for a 3-month option. By selecting this strike, we have constructed the option so that we will exercise it if the exchange rate is below 0.9. If the exchange rate goes up, we will not exercise the option and save the premium. If the exchange rate goes down, we will acquire an in-the-money option for the price of an at-the-money option. Many other structures are possible.

5. GAP OPTIONS

A call option pays $S - K$ when $S > K$. The strike price, K, here serves to determine both the range of stock prices where the option makes a payoff (when $S > K$) and also the size of the payoff ($S - K$). However, we could imagine separating these two functions of the strike

6. It is possible to obtain the same result for the American option price by using the binomial calculation in the "Fixed Dividends" tab of *OptAll2.xls*. With 500 iterations, the call price is 13.5294.

7. The VBA function CallOnPut is an array function. The second value returned is the stock price below which the compound option is exercised.

FIGURE 3

A gap call, paying $S - \$90$ when $S > \$100$.

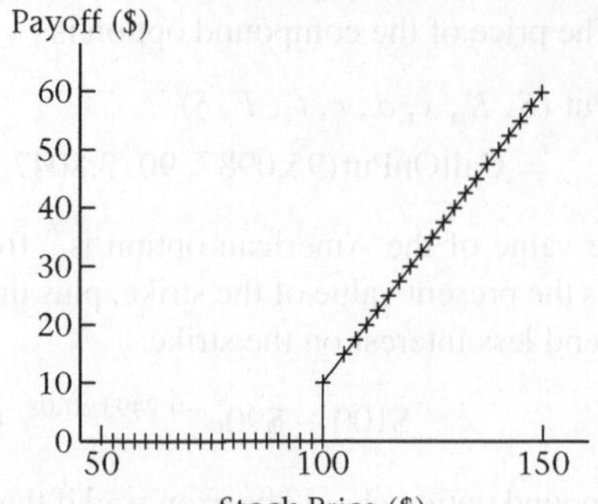

price. Consider an option that pays $S - 90$ when $S > 100$. Note that there is a difference between the prices that govern when there is a payoff ($100) and the price used to determine the size of the payoff ($90). This difference creates a discontinuity—or gap—in the payoff diagram, which is why the option is called a **gap option**.

Figure 3 shows a gap call option with payoff $S - 90$ when $S > 100$. The gap in the payoff occurs when the option payoff jumps from $0 to $10 as a result of the stock price changing from $99.99 to $100.01.

Figure 4 depicts a gap put that pays $90 - S$ when $S < 100$. This option demonstrates that a gap option can be structured to require, for some stock prices, a payout from the option holder at expiration. You should compare Figure 4 with Figure 12—the gap put looks very much like a paylater strategy.[8] Note that the owner of the put in Figure 4 is *required* to exercise the option when $S < 100$.[9]

The pricing formula for a gap call, which pays $S - K_1$ when $S > K_2$, is obtained by a simple modification of the Black-Scholes formula. Let K_1 be the strike price (the price the option holder pays at expiration to acquire the stock) and K_2 the payment trigger (the price at which payment on the option is triggered). The formula is then

$$C(S, K_1, K_2, \sigma, r, T, \delta) = Se^{-\delta T}N(d_1) - K_1 e^{-rT}N(d_2) \tag{15}$$

$$d_1 = \frac{\ln(Se^{-\delta T}/K_2 e^{-rT}) + \frac{1}{2}\sigma^2 T}{\sigma\sqrt{T}}$$

$$d_2 = d_1 - \sigma\sqrt{T}$$

The modification to the put formula is similar.[10]

8. A gap option *must* be exercised when $S > K_1$ for a call or $S < K_1$ for a put. Since the owner can lose money at exercise, the term "option" is a bit of a misnomer.

9. The paylater strategy for hedging a share of stock entails selling n puts at strike K_2 and buying $n + 1$ puts at strike $K_1 < K_2$, with n selected so that the net option premium is zero. It is possible to show that as $K_2 \to K_1$, there is a gap call that has the same profit diagram as the paylater strategy. In the limit, the paylater strategy is the same as a gap option.

10. This note has been intentionally omitted for this edition.

FIGURE 4

A gap put, paying \$90 − S when S < \$100.

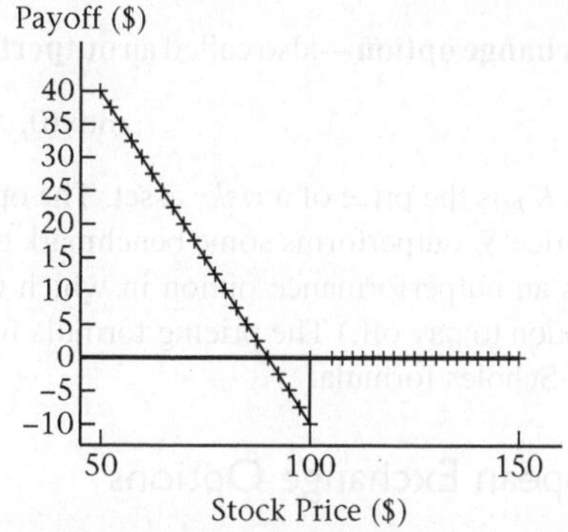

TABLE 4

Premiums of ordinary and gap put options with strikes K_1 and payment triggers K_2. Assumes $x_0 = 0.9$, $\sigma = 0.1$, $r_\$ = 0.06$, $r_€ = 0.03$, and $t = 0.5$.

		Payment Trigger (K_2) (\$)		
Strike (K_1) (\$)	Put (\$)	0.8	0.9	1.0
0.8000	0.0007	0.0007	−0.0229	−0.0888
0.9000	0.0188	0.0039	0.0188	−0.0009
1.0000	0.0870	0.0070	0.0605	0.0870

Returning to the XYZ currency hedging example, let's examine the use of gap options as a hedging instrument. The intuitive appeal of a gap option is that we can purchase insurance with which we are fully protected if the loss exceeds a certain amount.

Table 4 lists gap put premiums for different strikes and payment triggers. When the strike equals the payment trigger, the premium is the same as for an ordinary put. For a given strike, increasing the payment trigger reduces the premium. The reason is that when the payment trigger is above the strike, the option holder will have to make a payment to the option writer in some cases. For example, consider the case when the strike is \$0.8 and the payment trigger is \$1. If the exchange rate is 0.95, the gap put holder is obligated to sell euros worth \$0.95 for only \$0.8, a loss of \$0.15. The option premium in this case is −\$0.0888, reflecting the possibility that the option buyer will end up making a payment at maturity to the option seller. A hedger believing it highly likely that the exchange rate would be below 0.8 might be willing to receive a premium in exchange for the risk that the exchange rate would end up between 0.8 and 1.0.

Note that for a given trigger, K_2, you can always find a strike, K_1, that will make the option premium zero. Thus, gap options permit us to accomplish something similar to the paylater strategy.

6. EXCHANGE OPTIONS

An **exchange option**—also called an **outperformance option**—is an option with the payoff

$$\max(0, S_T - K_T)$$

where K_T is the price of a *risky* asset. The option thus pays off only if the underlying asset with price S_t outperforms some benchmark asset with price K_t. (You can view an ordinary call as an outperformance option in which the stock has to outperform cash in order for the option to pay off.) The pricing formula for this kind of option is a simple variant of the Black-Scholes formula.

European Exchange Options

Suppose an exchange call maturing T periods from today provides the right to obtain 1 unit of risky asset 1 in exchange for 1 unit of risky asset 2. (We could think of this as, for example, the right to obtain the Nikkei index by giving up the S&P 500.) Let S_t be the price of risky asset 1 and K_t the price of risky asset 2 at time t, with dividend yields δ_S and δ_K, and volatilities σ_S and σ_K. Let ρ denote the correlation between the continuously compounded returns on the two assets. The payoff to this option is

$$\max(0, S_T - K_T)$$

The formula for the price of an exchange option (see Margrabe, 1978) is

$$\boxed{C(S, K, \sigma, \delta_K, T, \delta_S) = Se^{-\delta_S T}N(d_1) - Ke^{-\delta_K T}N(d_2)} \tag{16}$$

where

$$d_1 = \frac{\ln(Se^{-\delta_S T}/Ke^{-\delta_K T}) + \frac{1}{2}\sigma^2 T}{\sigma\sqrt{T}}$$

$$d_2 = d_1 - \sigma\sqrt{T}$$

$$\sigma = \sqrt{\sigma_S^2 + \sigma_K^2 - 2\rho\sigma_S\sigma_K} \tag{17}$$

The volatility, σ, is the volatility of the *difference* in the continuously compounded returns of S and K over the life of the option. This is sometimes called the "blended volatility." The pricing formula for the exchange option therefore turns out to be a simple variant of the Black-Scholes formula: The strike price is replaced by the price of the benchmark asset, the risk-free rate is replaced by the dividend yield on the benchmark asset, and the appropriate volatility is the volatility of the difference in continuously compounded returns on the two assets.

We can also interpret the pricing formula for an exchange option by considering the version of the Black-Scholes formula written in terms of prepaid forward prices. The expression $Ke^{-\delta_K T}$ is the prepaid forward price for the strike asset. The formula for an infinitely lived American exchange option is in the chapter appendix.

By setting the dividend yields and volatility appropriately, equation (16) yields the formulas for ordinary calls and puts:

- With a call, we give up cash to acquire stock. The dividend yield on cash is the interest rate. Thus, if we set $\delta_S = \delta$ (the dividend yield on stock), $\delta_K = r$ (the risk-free rate), and $\sigma_K = 0$ (asset 2 is risk-free), the formula reduces to the standard Black-Scholes formula for a call.

- With a put, we give up stock to acquire cash. Thus, if we set $\delta_S = r$, $\delta_K = \delta$ (the dividend yield on stock), and $\sigma_S = 0$, the formula reduces to the Black-Scholes formula for a put on stock. (Try this to verify that it works.)

Example 3. Consider an option for which the owner receives a share of Microsoft only if Microsoft outperforms the S&P 500 index. This is a Microsoft call with the appropriately scaled S&P index as the strike asset. On January 5, 2011, the price of Microsoft was \$28 and the S&P Index was at 1276.56. Thus, one share of Microsoft had the same value as $28/1276.56 = 1/45.591$ units of the S&P index. Microsoft's previous quarterly dividend had been \$0.16/share, for an annual dividend yield of about 2.286%. The dividend yield on the S&P index was about 1.85%. Their historical volatilities during 2010 had been 26.51% (Microsoft) and 17.52% (the S&P index) with a return correlation of 0.8361. The volatility of the relative prices, σ, is therefore

$$\begin{aligned}\sigma &= \sqrt{0.2651^2 + 0.1752^2 - 2 \times .8361 \times 0.2651 \times 0.1752}\\ &= 0.1526\end{aligned}$$

Suppose the option is issued at-the-money, so it permits exchanging one share of Microsoft for 1/45.591 units of the S&P index. The price of a 1-year at-the-money outperformance call would be

$$\text{BSCall}(\$28.00, 1275.56/45.591, 0.1526, 0.0185, 1, 0.02286) = \$1.6095$$

Because the S&P index is the strike asset, we replace the risk-free rate with the dividend yield on the index. By contrast, assuming a risk-free rate of 0.5%, a plain 1-year at-the-money call on Microsoft would be worth

$$\text{BSCall}(\$28.00, \$28.00, 0.2651, 0.005, 1, 0.02286) = \$2.6194$$

The outperformance option is less expensive because the blended volatility is substantially less than Microsoft's volatility. ■

Problem 19 asks you to think about the circumstances under which XYZ might hedge currency risk using exchange options.

CHAPTER SUMMARY

An exotic option is created by altering the contractual terms of a standard option. Exotic options permit hedging solutions tailored to specific problems and speculation tailored to particular views. Examples of exotic options include the following:

- *Asian options* have payoffs that are based on the average price of the underlying asset over the life of the option. The average price can be used in place of either the underlying asset (an *average price option*) or in place of the strike price (an *average strike option*). Averages can be arithmetic or geometric.

- *Barrier options* have payoffs that depend upon whether the price of the underlying asset has reached a barrier over the life of the option. These options can come into existence (*knock-in options*) or go out of existence (*knock-out options*) when the barrier is reached.
- *Compound options* are options on options: Put or call options with put or call options as the underlying asset.
- *Gap options* are options where the option payoff jumps at the price where the option comes into the money.
- *Exchange options* are options that have risky assets as both the underlying asset and the strike asset.

It is helpful in analyzing exotic options to compare them to standard options: In what ways does an exotic option resemble a standard option? How will its price compare to that of an ordinary option? When might someone use the exotic option instead of a standard option?

FURTHER READING

General books covering exotic options include Briys and Bellala (1998), Haug (1998), Wilmott (1998), and Zhang (1998). Rubinstein (1991b) discusses exchange options, Rubinstein (1991a) discusses compound options, and Rubinstein and Reiner (1991a) discuss barrier options.

PROBLEMS

To answer many of these questions you can use the exotic option functions.

1. Obtain monthly stock prices for 5 years for three stocks. Compute the arithmetic and geometric average month-end price for each stock. Which is greater?
2. Suppose you observe the prices {5, 4, 5, 6, 5}. What are the arithmetic and geometric averages? Now you observe {3, 4, 5, 6, 7}. What are the two averages? What happens to the difference between the two measures of the average as the standard deviation of the observations increases?
3. Suppose that $S = \$100$, $K = \$100$, $r = 0.08$, $\sigma = 0.30$, $\delta = 0$, and $T = 1$. Construct a standard two-period binomial stock price tree.
   - **a.** Consider stock price averages computed by averaging the 6-month and 1-year prices. What are the possible arithmetic and geometric averages after 1 year?
   - **b.** Construct a binomial tree for the *average*. How many nodes does it have after 1 year? (*Hint*: While the moves *ud* and *du* give the same year-1 price, they do *not* give the same average in year 1.)
   - **c.** What is the price of an Asian arithmetic average price call?
   - **d.** What is the price of an Asian geometric average price call?

4. Using the information in the previous problem, compute the prices of

a. An Asian arithmetic average strike call.

b. An Asian geometric average strike call.

5. Repeat Problem 3, except construct a *three*-period binomial tree. Assume that Asian options are based on averaging the prices every 4 months.

a. What are the possible geometric and arithmetic averages after 1 year?

b. What is the price of an Asian arithmetic average price call?

c. What is the price of an Asian geometric average price call?

6. Let $S = \$40$, $K = \$45$, $\sigma = 0.30$, $r = 0.08$, $T = 1$, and $\delta = 0$.

a. What is the price of a standard call?

b. What is the price of a knock-in call with a barrier of \$44? Why?

c. What is the price of a knock-out call with a barrier of \$44? Why?

7. Let $S = \$40$, $K = \$45$, $\sigma = 0.30$, $r = 0.08$, $\delta = 0$, and $T = \{0.25, 0.5, 1, 2, 3, 4, 5, 100\}$.

a. Compute the prices of knock-out calls with a barrier of \$38.

b. Compute the ratio of the knock-out call prices to the prices of standard calls. Explain the pattern you see.

8. Repeat the previous problem for up-and-out puts assuming a barrier of \$44.

9. Let $S = \$40$, $K = \$45$, $\sigma = 0.30$, $r = 0.08$, and $\delta = 0$. Compute the value of knock-out calls with a barrier of \$60 and times to expiration of 1 month, 2 months, and so on, up to 1 year. As you increase time to expiration, what happens to the price of the knock-out call? What happens to the price of the knock-out call *relative to* the price of an otherwise identical standard call?

10. Examine the prices of up-and-out puts with strikes of \$0.9 and \$1.0 in Table 3. With barriers of \$1 and \$1.05, the 0.90-strike up-and-outs appear to have the same premium as the ordinary put. However, with a strike of 1.0 and the same barriers, the up-and-outs have lower premiums than the ordinary put. Explain why. What would happen to this pattern if we increased the time to expiration?

11. Suppose $S = \$40$, $K = \$40$, $\sigma = 0.30$, $r = 0.08$, and $\delta = 0$.

a. What is the price of a standard European call with 2 years to expiration?

b. Suppose you have a compound call giving you the right to pay \$2 1 year from today to buy the option in part (a). For what stock prices in 1 year will you exercise this option?

c. What is the price of this compound call?

d. What is the price of a compound option giving you the right to *sell* the option in part (a) in 1 year for \$2?

12. Make the same assumptions as in the previous problem.

a. What is the price of a standard European put with 2 years to expiration?

b. Suppose you have a compound call giving you the right to pay \$2 1 year from today to buy the option in (a). For what stock prices in 1 year will you exercise this option?

c. What is the price of this compound call?

d. What is the price of a compound option giving you the right to *sell* the option in part (a) in 1 year for \$2?

13. Consider the hedging example using gap options, in particular the assumptions and prices in Table 4.

a. Implement the gap pricing formula. Reproduce the numbers in Table 4.

b. Consider the option with $K_1 = \$0.8$ and $K_2 = \$1$. If volatility were zero, what would the price of this option be? What do you think will happen to this premium if the volatility increases? Verify your answer using your pricing model and explain why it happens.

14. Use the technique of computing approximate Greek measures for an option to compute delta for the gap option in Figure 3, for stock prices ranging from \$90 to \$110 and for times to expiration of 1 week, 3 months, and 1 year. How easy do you think it would be to hedge a gap call?

15. This problem has been intentionally omitted for this edition.

16. Let $S = \$40$, $\sigma = 0.30$, $r = 0.08$, $T = 1$, and $\delta = 0$. Also let $Q = \$60$, $\sigma_Q = 0.50$, $\delta_Q = 0.04$, and $\rho = 0.5$. What is the price of a standard 40-strike call with S as the underlying asset? What is the price of an exchange option with S as the underlying asset and $0.667 \times Q$ as the strike price?

17. Let $S = \$40$, $\sigma = 0.30$, $r = 0.08$, $T = 1$, and $\delta = 0$. Also let $Q = \$60$, $\sigma_Q = 0.50$, $\delta_Q = 0$, and $\rho = 0.5$. In this problem we will compute prices of exchange calls with S as the price of the underlying asset and Q as the price of the strike asset.

a. Vary δ from 0 to 0.1. What happens to the price of the call?

b. Vary δ_Q from 0 to 0.1. What happens to the price of the call?

c. Vary ρ from -0.5 to 0.5. What happens to the price of the call?

d. Explain your answers by drawing analogies to the effects of changing inputs in the Black-Scholes call pricing formula.

18. Let $S = \$40$, $\sigma = 0.30$, $r = 0.08$, $T = 1$, and $\delta = 0$. Also let $Q = \$40$, $\sigma_Q = 0.30$, $\delta_Q = 0$, and $\rho = 1$. Consider an exchange call with S as the price of the underlying asset and Q as the price of the strike asset.

a. What is the price of an exchange call with S as the underlying asset and Q as the strike price?

b. Now suppose $\sigma_Q = 0.40$. What is the price of the exchange call?

c. Explain your answers to (a) and (b).

19. XYZ wants to hedge against depreciations of the euro and is also concerned about the price of oil, which is a significant component of XYZ's costs. However, there is a positive correlation between the euro and the price of oil: The euro appreciates when the price of oil rises. Explain how an exchange option based on oil and the euro might be used to hedge in this case.

20. A **chooser option** (also known as an **as-you-like-it option**) becomes a put or call at the discretion of the owner. For example, consider a chooser on the S&R index for which both the call, with value $C(S_t, K, T-t)$, and the put, with value $P(S_t, K, T-t)$, have a strike price of K. The index pays no dividends. At the choice date, t_1, the payoff of the chooser is

$$\max[C(S_{t_1}, K, T-t_1), P(S_{t_1}, K, T-t_1)]$$

a. If the chooser option and the underlying options expire simultaneously, what ordinary option position is this equivalent to?

b. Suppose that the chooser must be exercised at t_1 and that the underlying options expire at T. Show that the chooser is equivalent to a call option with strike price K and maturity T plus $e^{-\delta(T-t_1)}$ put options with strike price $Ke^{-(r-\delta)(T-t_1)}$ and expiration t_1.

21. Suppose that $S = \$100$, $\sigma = 30\%$, $r = 8\%$, and $\delta = 0$. Today you buy a contract which, 6 months from today, will give you one 3-month to expiration *at-the-money* call option. (This is called a **forward start** option.) Assume that r, σ, and δ are certain not to change in the next 6 months.

a. Six months from today, what will be the value of the option if the stock price is \$100? \$50? \$200? (Use the Black-Scholes formula to compute the answer.) In each case, what fraction of the stock price does the option cost?

b. What investment *today* would guarantee that you had the money in 6 months to buy an at-the-money option?

c. What would you pay today for the forward start option in this example?

d. How would your answer change if the option were to have a strike price that was 105% of the stock price?

22. You wish to insure a portfolio for 1 year. Suppose that $S = \$100$, $\sigma = 30\%$, $r = 8\%$, and $\delta = 0$. You are considering two strategies. The *simple insurance strategy* entails buying one put option with a 1-year maturity at a strike price that is 95% of the stock price. The *rolling insurance strategy* entails buying one 1-month put option each month, with the strike in each case being 95% of the then-current stock price.

a. What is the cost of the simple insurance strategy?

b. What is the cost of the rolling insurance strategy? (*Hint*: See the previous problem.)

c. Intuitively, what accounts for the cost difference?

Appendix A PRICING FORMULAS FOR EXOTIC OPTIONS

In this appendix we present formulas for some of the options discussed in this chapter.

Asian Options Based on the Geometric Average

The average can be used in place of either the asset price (an average price option) or the strike price (an average strike option).

Average Price Options. Suppose the risk-free rate is r and the stock has a dividend yield δ and volatility σ. We compute the average using N equally spaced prices from 0 to T, with the first observation at time T/N. A European geometric average price option can then be valued using the Black-Scholes formula for a call by setting the dividend yield and volatility equal to

$$\delta^* = \frac{1}{2}\left[r\frac{N-1}{N} + (\delta + 0.5\sigma^2)\frac{N+1}{N} - \frac{\sigma^2}{N^2}\frac{(N+1)(2N+1)}{6}\right] \tag{18}$$

and

$$\sigma^* = \frac{\sigma}{N}\sqrt{\frac{(N+1)(2N+1)}{6}} \tag{19}$$

With continuous sampling, i.e., $N = \infty$, the formulas reduce to

$$\delta^* = \frac{1}{2}\left(r + \delta + \frac{1}{6}\sigma^2\right)$$

and

$$\sigma^* = \sigma\sqrt{\frac{1}{3}}$$

Average Strike Options. In order to value the geometric average strike option, we need to know the correlation between the average, $G(T)$, and the terminal stock price, S_T. We also need to recognize that the strike asset is the average; hence, we value the option like an exchange option (see Section 6), in which we exchange the time-T stock price for its average.

The average strike option can be valued using the Black-Scholes formula, with the following substitutions:

- Replace the risk-free rate with the "dividend yield," equation (18).
- Replace the volatility with

$$\sigma^{**} = \sigma\sqrt{1 + \frac{(N+1)(2N+1)}{6N^2} - 2\rho\sqrt{\frac{(N+1)(2N+1)}{6N^2}}}$$

where the correlation between $\ln(S_T)$ and $G(T)$ is given by

$$\rho = \frac{1}{2}\sqrt{\frac{6(N+1)}{2N+1}}$$

- Use the current stock price as the strike price.
- The dividend yield remains the same.

Compound Options

Letting ρ denote the correlation coefficient between normally distributed z_1 and z_2, we denote the cumulative bivariate standard normal distribution as

$$\Pr(z_1 < a, z_2 < b; \rho) = \text{NN}(a, b; \rho)$$

This function is implemented in the spreadsheets as BINORMSDIST.

Suppose we have a compound call option to buy a call option. Let t_1 be the time to maturity of the compound option, and t_2 the time to maturity of the underlying option (obviously, we require that $t_2 > t_1$). Also let K be the strike price on the underlying option and x the strike price on the compound option; i.e., we have the right on date t_1 to pay x to acquire a call option with time to expiration $t_2 - t_1$. Define S^* as in equation (11); that is, S^* is the stock price at which the option is worth the strike that must be paid to get it.[11]

The formula for the price of a call option on a call option is

$$\begin{aligned} &\text{CallOnCall}(S, K, x, \sigma, r, t_1, t_2, \delta) \\ &= Se^{-\delta t_2}\text{NN}\left(a_1, d_1; \sqrt{\frac{t_1}{t_2}}\right) - Ke^{-rt_2}\text{NN}\left(a_2, d_2; \sqrt{\frac{t_1}{t_2}}\right) - xe^{-rt_1}N\left(a_2\right) \end{aligned} \tag{20}$$

where

$$a_1 = \frac{\ln(S/S^*) + (r - \delta + 0.5\sigma^2)t_1}{\sigma\sqrt{t_1}}$$

$$a_2 = a_1 - \sigma\sqrt{t_1}$$

$$d_1 = \frac{\ln(S/K) + (r - \delta + 0.5\sigma^2)t_2}{\sigma\sqrt{t_2}}$$

$$d_2 = d_1 - \sigma\sqrt{t_2}$$

Notice that d_1 and d_2 are identical to the Black-Scholes d_1 and d_2, and relate to ultimate exercise of the underlying option, while a_1 and a_2 differ only in the strike price and time to expiration and relate to exercise of the compound option. The last term in equation (20) reflects payment of the compound option strike price and the condition under which it is paid. The sign on the correlation term, $\sqrt{t_1/t_2}$, reflects whether exercise of the compound option is associated with an increase or decrease in the likelihood of exercising the underlying option. (The correlation is positive for a call on a call. For a call on a put, an increase in the stock price reduces the value of the put and also reduces the value of the option to buy the put; hence, the correlation is again positive.)

This discussion suggests that we can guess how the remaining compound option formulas will look. We would like to value puts on calls, calls on puts, and puts on puts.

The put on the call requires a positive sign on Ke^{-rt} and a negative sign on $Se^{-\delta t}$, since the option if ultimately exercised will require the owner to be a call writer. The underlying option is in-the-money if $S > K$; hence, we want positive d_1 and d_2. The compound option will be exercised and the strike x received if $S < S^*$, which requires negative a_1 and a_2 and a positive sign on x. Finally, if the stock price goes up, this increases the value of the call

11. The spreadsheet function to compute S^* is called BSCallImpS, which is similar to the implied volatility function BSCallImpVol, except that it computes the stock price consistent with an option price, rather than the volatility.

and decreases the value of the put on the call; hence, the correlation must be negatively signed. Thus, the formula is

$$\text{PutOnCall}(S, K, x, \sigma, r, t_1, t_2, \delta) = -Se^{-\delta t_2}\text{NN}\left(-a_1, d_1; -\sqrt{\frac{t_1}{t_2}}\right)$$
$$+ Ke^{-rt_2}\text{NN}\left(-a_2, d_2; -\sqrt{\frac{t_1}{t_2}}\right) + xe^{-rt_1}N(-a_2) \tag{21}$$

Similar arguments give us the following formulas:

$$\text{CallOnPut}(S, K, x, \sigma, r, t_1, t_2, \delta) = -Se^{-\delta t_2}\text{NN}\left(-a_1, -d_1; \sqrt{\frac{t_1}{t_2}}\right)$$
$$+ Ke^{-rt_2}\text{NN}\left(-a_2, -d_2; \sqrt{\frac{t_1}{t_2}}\right) - xe^{-rt_1}N(-a_2) \tag{22}$$

$$\text{PutOnPut}(S, K, x, \sigma, r, t_1, t_2, \delta)$$
$$= Se^{-\delta t_2}\text{NN}\left(a_1, -d_1; -\sqrt{\frac{t_1}{t_2}}\right)$$
$$- Ke^{-rt_2}\text{NN}\left(a_2, -d_2; -\sqrt{\frac{t_1}{t_2}}\right) + xe^{-rt_1}N(a_2) \tag{23}$$

As an exercise, we can check that as t_1 approaches 0, the compound option formula simplifies to the greater of the value of the underlying option or zero.

Infinitely Lived Exchange Option

The logic of exchange options extends directly to the case of an infinitely lived American option. A key insight is that the optimal exercise level H really depends on the *ratio* of the values of the asset being received to the asset being given up; the absolute level is unimportant. Thus, if it is optimal to exchange stock A for stock B when the price of A is 100 and the price of B is 200, then it will be optimal to exchange A for B when their prices are 1 and 2. We therefore just need to find the *ratio* of prices at which exercise is optimal.

The formula for the infinitely lived option to exchange stock 1 for stock 2 is

$$C^{\infty}(S_1, S_2, \sigma_1, \sigma_2, \rho, \delta_1, \delta_2) = (s-1)S_2\left(\frac{S_1/S_2}{s}\right)^h$$

where δ_i is the dividend yield on asset i, σ_i is the volatility of asset i, ρ is the correlation between stock 1 and stock 2, and

$$s = \frac{h}{1-h}$$

is the ratio of S_1 to S_2 at which it is optimal to exercise the option. Let $\sigma^2 = \sigma_1^2 + \sigma_2^2 - 2\rho\sigma_1\sigma_2$ and

$$h = \frac{1}{2} - \frac{\delta_2 - \delta_1}{\sigma^2} + \sqrt{\left(\frac{\delta_2 - \delta_1}{\sigma^2} - \frac{1}{2}\right)^2 + \frac{2\delta_2}{\sigma^2}}$$

It is possible to show that if we set $\delta_2 = r$ and $\sigma_2 = 0$, we get the formula for an infinite call, while if we set $\delta_1 = r$ and $\sigma_1 = 0$, we get the put formula.

Financial Engineering and Applications

Forwards, swaps, and options (including exotic options) are used as stand-alone financial claims. These claims can be used as financial building blocks to create new claims, and derivatives pricing theory can help us understand corporate financial policy and the valuation of investment projects.

It is possible to construct and price bonds that make payments that, instead of being denominated in cash, are denominated in stocks, commodities, and different currencies. Such bonds can be structured to contain embedded options. Such claims can be used for risk management and their issuance can be motivated by tax and regulatory considerations.

From *Derivatives Markets*, Third Edition, Robert McDonald. Copyright © 2013 by Pearson Education, Inc. Published by Pearson Prentice Hall. All rights reserved.

Financial Engineering and Security Design

Forwards, calls, puts, and common exotic options can be added to bonds or otherwise combined to create new securities. For example, many traded securities are effectively bonds with embedded options. Individual derivatives thus become building blocks—ingredients used to construct new kinds of financial products. In this chapter we will see how to assemble the ingredients to create new products. The process of constructing new instruments from these building blocks is called **financial engineering**.

1. THE MODIGLIANI-MILLER THEOREM

The starting point for any discussion of modern financial engineering is the analysis of Franco Modigliani and Merton Miller (Modigliani and Miller, 1958). Before their work, financial analysts would puzzle over how to compare the values of firms with similar *operating* characteristics but different *financial* characteristics. Modigliani and Miller realized that different financing decisions (for example, the choice of the firm's debt-to-equity ratio) may carve up the firm's cash flows in different ways, but if the *total* cash flows paid to all claimants is unchanged, the total value of all claims would remain the same. They showed that if firms differing only in financial policy differed in market value, profitable arbitrage would exist. Using their famous analogy, the price of whole milk should equal the total prices of the skim milk and butterfat that can be derived from that milk.[1]

The Modigliani-Miller analysis requires numerous assumptions: For example, there are no taxes, no transaction costs, no bankruptcy costs, and no private information. Nevertheless, the basic Modigliani-Miller result provided clarity for a confusing issue, and it created a starting point for thinking about the effects of taxes, transaction costs, and the like, revolutionizing finance.

All of the no-arbitrage pricing arguments we have been using embody the Modigliani-Miller spirit. For example, we could synthetically create a forward contract using options, a call option using a forward contract, bonds, and a put, and so forth. An option could also be synthetically created from a position in the stock and borrowing or lending. If prices of actual claims differ from their synthetic equivalents, arbitrage is possible.

1. Standard corporate finance texts offer a more detailed discussion of the Modigliani-Miller results. The original paper (Modigliani and Miller, 1958) is a classic.

From Chapter 15 of *Derivatives Markets*, Third Edition, Robert McDonald. Copyright © 2013 by Pearson Education, Inc. Published by Pearson Prentice Hall. All rights reserved.

Financial engineering is an application of the Modigliani-Miller idea. We can combine claims such as stocks, bonds, forwards, and options and assemble them to create new claims. The price for this new security is the sum of the pieces combined to create it. When we create a new instrument in this fashion, as in the Modigliani-Miller analysis, value is neither created nor destroyed. Thus, financial engineering has no value in a pure Modigliani-Miller world. However, in real life, the new instrument may have different tax, regulatory, or accounting characteristics, or may provide a way for the issuer or buyer to obtain a particular payoff at lower transaction costs than the alternatives. Financial engineering thus provides a way to create instruments that meet specific needs of investors and issuers. To illustrate this, Box 1 discusses the application of financial engineering to satisfy religious restrictions.

As a starting point, you can ask the following questions when you confront new financial instruments:

- What is the payoff of the instrument?
- Is it possible to synthetically create the same payoffs using some combination of assets, bonds, and options?
- Who might issue or buy such an instrument?
- What problem does the instrument solve?

We begin by discussing structured notes without and with options. We then turn to examples of engineered products.

2. STRUCTURED NOTES WITHOUT OPTIONS

An ordinary note or bond has interest and maturity payments that are fixed at the time of issue.[2] A **structured note** has interest or maturity payments that are not fixed in dollars but are contingent in some way. Structured notes can make payments based on stock prices, interest rates, commodities, or currencies, and the payoffs may or may not contain options.

We first discuss bonds that make a single payment and then bonds that make multiple payments (such as coupon bonds), all without options. In the next section we will introduce structures with options.

Single Payment Bonds

A single payment bond is a financial instrument for which you pay today and that makes a single payment at time T.[3] The payment could be \$1, a share of stock, an ounce of gold, or a bushel of corn. A single payment bond is equivalent to a prepaid forward contract on the asset or commodity.

Because the price of a single payment bond is the value today of a future payment, it also is equivalent to a discount factor—a value that translates future payments into a value today. This interpretation will play an important role in our discussion.

---

2. We will use the terms "bond" and "note" interchangeably, though in common usage a note has a medium time to maturity (2–10 years) and a bond has a longer maturity.

3. In this chapter, "zero-coupon bond" will mean a single payment bond that pays in cash.

BOX 1: Islamic Finance*

Shariah, the religious law of Islam, places restrictions on financial transactions. Four verses in the Qur'an, the holy book of Islam, prohibit the payment of interest. By scholarly interpretation, the Qur'an also requires that business transactions must both pertain to real assets and have an ethical purpose. These restrictions and requirements have given rise to a practice known as *Islamic Finance*. The primary elements of Islamic Finance are

- No interest or usury
- No gambling
- No speculation
- Strive for fair and just business practices
- Avoid prohibited goods and services (alcohol, weapons, hedonism)

Obviously, standard financial practices in major financial markets may run afoul of one or more of these elements. There is no religious objection to making a profit on a real asset, but interest as profit on money is prohibited. Practitioners in Islamic Finance face the challenge of constructing transactions that serve a genuine business purpose and adhere to the tenets above. The process of constructing such transactions is a form of financial engineering.

As an example, consider a residential mortgage. There are at least three ways an owner can borrow money to finance a purchase:

Murabaha The bank purchases the home and resells it to the client at a markup, which can include financing cost.

Musharaka The buyer and bank enter into a joint venture where the bank owns a percentage of the house, and as the client makes payments the bank's ownership percentage declines.

Ijara The buyer can lease to own.

In all of these transactions, the bank owns the property for some period of time and can thus attribute gains to profit from ownership rather than as a return to the lending of money.

Islamic Finance also maintains a general objection to speculative uses of derivatives, stemming both from concerns about speculation and also from the idea that derivatives are removed from the primary underlying transaction, not directly furthering its real economic purpose. Derivatives are acceptable, however, as a way to manage risk. Calls are effected by the buyer making a down payment with the right to walk away, and puts with a third party guarantee against loss. Derivatives on gold, silver, and currency are prohibited. See Jobst and Solé (2012) for a comprehensive discussion of derivatives in Islamic Finance.

*I am grateful to Karen Hunt-Ahmed for her assistance with this box.

The most basic financial instrument is a zero-coupon bond that pays \$1 at maturity. Let $r_s(t, T)$ represent the annual continuously compounded interest rate prevailing at time $s \leq t$, for a loan from time t to time T. Similarly, the price of a zero-coupon bond purchased at time t, maturing at time T, and quoted at time s is $P_s(t, T)$. Thus, we have

$$P_s(t, T) = e^{-r_s(t,T)(T-t)}$$

When there is no risk of misunderstanding, we will assume that the interest rate is quoted at time $t_0 = 0$, and the bond is also purchased then. We will denote the rate $r_0(0, T) = r(T)$, or just r, and the corresponding bond price P_T. So we will write

$$P_T = e^{-r(T)T}$$

P_T is the time 0 price of a T-period zero-coupon bond.

We can describe P_T as a bond price, as a discount factor and as the prepaid forward price for \$1 delivered at time T:

Zero-coupon bond price = Discount factor for \$1 = Prepaid forward price for \$1

A single payment bond that pays a unit of an asset or commodity is equivalent to a prepaid forward contract for that asset or commodity. Thus, the time 0 price of the bond is $F^P_{0,T}$. It is helpful to keep in mind the link between the prepaid forward price, the forward price, and the spot price of the asset or commodity.

Because the only difference between a forward contract and a prepaid forward is the timing of the payment for the underlying asset, the prepaid forward price is the present value of the forward price, discounted at the risk-free rate:

$$F^P_{0,T} = e^{-rT} F_{0,T} \tag{1}$$

The difference between the current spot price, S_0, and the prepaid forward price can be expressed as a yield:

$$F^P_{0,T} = S_0 e^{-\delta T} \tag{2}$$

If S_0 is the price of a financial asset, then δ represents a payment such as dividends or interest. If S_0 is the price of a commodity, δ is the commodity lease rate.

Zero-coupon equity-linked bond. From equation (2), the value of a single-payment bond that pays a share of stock at time T is $F^P_{0,T} = S_0 e^{-\delta T}$.

Example 1. Suppose that XYZ stock has a price of \$100 and pays no dividends, and that the annual continuously compounded interest rate is 6%. In the absence of dividends, the prepaid forward price equals the stock price. Thus, we would pay \$100 to receive the stock in 5 years. ■

We define an equity-linked bond as selling for par value if the bond price equals the maturity payment of the bond. The bond in Example 1 is at par because the bond pays one share of stock at maturity and the price of the bond equals the price of one share of stock today.

If the stock pays dividends and the bond makes no coupon payments, the bond will sell at less than par because you are not entitled to receive dividends.

Example 2. Suppose the price of XYZ stock is \$100, the quarterly dividend is \$1.20, and the annual continuously compounded interest rate is 6% (the quarterly interest rate is therefore 1.5%). Using the equation $F^P_{0,T} = S_0 - \sum_{i=1}^{n} \text{PV}_{0,t_i}(D_{t_i})$, the price of an equity-linked bond that pays one share in 5 years is

$$\$100 - \sum_{i=1}^{20} \$1.20e^{-0.015\times i} = \$79.42 \quad ■$$

Zero-coupon commodity-linked bond. If a bond pays a unit of a commodity for which there are traded futures contracts, it is possible to value the bond by using the futures price.

Example 3. Suppose the spot price of gold is $S_0 = \$400$/oz, the 3-year forward price is $F_{0,3} = \$455$/oz, and the 3-year continuously compounded interest rate is 6.25%. Then using equation (1), a zero-coupon note paying 1 ounce of gold in 3 years would sell for

$$F_{0,T}^P = \$455e^{-0.0625\times 3} = \$377.208$$

The lease rate in this case is

$$\delta_l = r - \frac{1}{T}\ln(F_{0,T}/S_0) = 0.0625 - \frac{1}{3}\ln(455/400) = 0.019556$$

An alternative way to compute the present value uses equation (2):

$$F_{0,3}^P = S_0 e^{-\delta_l 3} = 400e^{-.019556\times 3} = 377.208$$

This amount is less than the spot price of \$400 because the lease rate is positive. ■

Zero-Coupon Currency-Linked Bond. From the equation $F_{0,T}^P = x_0 e^{-r_y T}$, a bond that pays one unit of foreign currency at time T has a time zero value of

$$F_{0,T}^P = x_0 e^{-r_f T}$$

where x_0 is the time 0 exchange rate denominated in units of the home currency per unit of the foreign currency, and r_f is the foreign interest rate. With a currency-linked bond, the foreign interest rate plays the same role as the dividend yield for stocks and the lease rate for commodities.

Multiple Payment Bonds

You can easily construct and value multiple payment bonds as a portfolio of single payment bonds. A common design question with multiple payment bonds (and structured products in general) is how to construct them so that they sell at par.

First we examine bonds that pay in cash. Consider a bond that pays the coupon, c, n times over the life of the bond, makes the maturity payment M, and matures at time T. We will denote the price of this bond as $B(0, T, c, n, M)$. The time between coupon payments is T/n, and the ith coupon payment occurs at time $t_i = i \times T/n$.

We can value this bond by discounting its payments at the interest rate appropriate for each payment. This bond has the price

$$\begin{aligned} B(0, T, c, n, M) &= \sum_{i=1}^{n} ce^{-r(t_i)t_i} + Me^{-r(T)T} \\ &= \sum_{i=1}^{n} cP_{t_i} + MP_T \end{aligned} \tag{3}$$

This valuation equation shows us how to price the bond and also how to replicate the bond using zero-coupon bonds. Suppose we buy c zero-coupon bonds maturing in 1 year, c maturing in 2 years, and so on, and $c + M$ zero-coupon bonds maturing in T years. This set of zero-coupon bonds will pay c in 1 year, c in 2 years, and $c + M$ in T years. We can say that the coupon bond is *engineered* from a set of zero-coupon bonds with the same maturities as the cash flows from the bond.

In practice, bonds are usually issued at par, meaning that the bond sells today for its maturity value, M. The bond will sell at par if we set the coupon so that the price of the bond is M. Using equation (3), $B(0, T, c, n, M) = M$ if the coupon is set so that

$$c = M\frac{(1 - P_T)}{\sum_{i=1}^{n} P_{t_i}} \tag{4}$$

In the special case of a constant interest rate, equation (4) becomes

$$c = M\frac{1 - e^{-rT}}{\sum_{i=1}^{n} e^{-rt_i}} \tag{5}$$

If a bond has payments denominated in stock, commodities, or a foreign currency instead of cash, simply replace the discount factor for cash, P_{t_i}, with the prepaid forward price, F_{0,t_i}^P, which is the discount factor for a noncash payment. If a bond makes some payments in cash and some in stock (for example), simply discount each payment using the appropriate discount factor.

For example, suppose a bond pays one share of stock at maturity, and that coupon payments are fractions of a share rather than a fixed number of dollars. To price such a bond, we represent the number of fractional shares received at each coupon payment as c^*. The value at time 0 of a share received at time t is $F_{0,t}^P$. Thus, the formula for V_0 the value of the note at time t_0, is

$$V_0 = c^* \sum_{i=1}^{n} F_{0,t_i}^P + F_{0,T}^P$$

The number of fractional shares that must be paid each year for the note to be initially priced at par, i.e., for $V_0 = S_0$, is

$$c^* = \frac{S_0 - F_{0,T}^P}{\sum_{i=1}^{n} F_{0,t_i}^P} \tag{6}$$

When we pay coupons as shares rather than cash, the coupons have variable value. Thus, it is appropriate to use the prepaid forward for the stock as a discount factor rather than the prepaid forward for cash. The interpretation of equation (6) is the same as that of equation (4). The numerator is the difference between the current price of one unit of the underlying asset today and in the future. The difference is amortized using the annuity factor for the underlying asset.

In the special case of a constant expected continuous dividend yield, δ, this equation becomes

$$c^* = \frac{1 - e^{-\delta T}}{\sum_{i=1}^{n} e^{-\delta t_i}} \tag{7}$$

This expression resembles equation (4).

Comparing the equations (5) and (7), we can see that the par coupon is determined from the lease rate on the underlying asset. In the case of a bond denominated in cash, the lease rate is the interest rate, while in the case of a bond completely denominated in shares, the lease rate is the dividend yield.

Equity-linked bonds. Example 2 illustrated a single payment equity-linked bond that sold for less than the stock price because the stock paid dividends. It is possible for the bond to sell at par (the current stock price) if it makes coupon payments, compensating the holder for dividends not received. To see this, if the bond pays cash coupons and also pays a share at maturity, the present value of the payments is

$$\begin{aligned} B(0, T, c, n, S_T) &= c \sum_{i=1}^{n} P_{t_i} + F_{0,t_i}^P \\ &= c \sum_{i=1}^{n} P_{t_i} + S_0 - \sum_{i=1}^{n} P_{t_i} D_{t_i} \end{aligned}$$

We can see that the price of the bond, B, will equal the stock price, S_0, as long as the present value of the bond's coupons (the first term on the right-hand side) equals the present value of the stock dividends (the third term on the right-hand side).

Example 4. Consider XYZ stock as in Example 2. If the note promised to pay \$1.20 quarterly—a coupon equal to the stock dividend—the note would sell for \$100. ■

A note that pays in shares of stock can be designed in different ways. Coupon payments can be paid in cash or in shares of XYZ. The instrument might be labelled either a stock or a bond, depending on regulatory or tax considerations. Dividends may change unexpectedly over the life of the note, so the note issuer must decide whether the buyer or seller bears the dividend risk. The coupon on the note could change to match the dividend paid by the stock, or the coupon could be fixed at the outset as in Example 4.

Commodity-linked bonds. Suppose a note pays one unit of a *commodity* at maturity. In order for such a note to sell at par (which we take to be the current price of the commodity), the present value of coupon payments on the note must equal the present value of the lease payments on the commodity.[4] The commodity lease rate plays the same role in a commodity-linked note as does the dividend yield when pricing an equity-linked note; both the lease rate and dividend yield create a difference between the prepaid forward price and the current spot price.

Example 5. Suppose the spot price of gold is \$400/oz, the 3-year forward price is \$455/oz, the 1-year continuously compounded interest rate is 5.5%, the 2-year rate is 6%, and the 3-year rate is 6.25%. The annual coupon denominated in cash is

$$c = \frac{\$400 - \$455e^{-0.0625\times 3}}{e^{-0.055} + e^{-0.06\times 2} + e^{-0.0625\times 3}} = \$8.561$$

The annual coupon on a 3-year gold-linked note is therefore about 2% of the spot price. ■

4. A lease rate can be negative if there are storage costs. In this case, the holder of a commodity-linked note benefits by not having to pay storage costs associated with the physical commodity and will therefore pay a price above maturity value (in the case of a zero-coupon note) or else the note must carry a negative dividend, meaning that the holder must make coupon payments to the issuer.

A 2% yield in this example might seem inexpensive compared to the 5.5% risk-free rate, but this is only because the lease rate on gold is less than the lease rate on cash (the interest rate).

Perpetuities. A perpetuity is an infinitely lived coupon bond. To illustrate, we can use equations (7) and (5) to consider two types: one that makes annual payments in dollars and another that makes payments in units of a commodity. Suppose we want the dollar perpetuity to have a price of M and the commodity perpetuity to have a price of S_0. Using standard perpetuity calculations, if we let $T \to \infty$ in equation (5) (this also means that $n \to \infty$), the coupon rate on the dollar bond is

$$c = M \frac{1}{\frac{e^{-r}}{1-e^{-r}}} = M(e^r - 1) = \hat{r} M$$

where $\hat{r}$ is the effective annual interest rate, $e^r - 1$. Similarly, for a perpetuity paying a unit of a commodity, equation (7) becomes

$$c^* = S_0 \frac{1}{\frac{e^{-\delta}}{1-e^{-\delta}}} = S_0(e^{\delta} - 1) = \hat{\delta} S_0$$

where $\hat{\delta}$ is the effective annual lease rate, $e^{\delta} - 1$. Thus, in order for a commodity perpetuity to be worth one unit of the commodity, it must pay the lease rate in units of the commodity. For example, if the effective annual lease rate is 2%, the bond pays 0.02 units of the commodity per year.

What if a bond pays one unit of the commodity per year, forever? We know that if it pays $\hat{\delta} S_t$ in perpetuity it is worth S_0. Thus, if it pays S_t it is worth

$$\frac{S_0}{\hat{\delta}} \tag{8}$$

This is the commodity equivalent of a perpetuity, with the lease rate taking the place of the interest rate.

Currency-linked bonds. A bond completely denominated in a foreign currency will have a coupon given by equation (4), only using foreign zero-coupon bonds (and hence foreign interest rates):

$$c^F = M \frac{1 - P_T^F}{\sum_{i=1}^{n} P_{t_i}^F}$$

The superscript F indicates that the price is denominated in the foreign currency.

If the bond has principal denominated in the home currency and coupons denominated in the foreign currency, we can discount the foreign currency coupon payments using the foreign interest rate, and then translate their value into dollars using the current exchange rate, x_0 (denominated as \$/unit of foreign currency). The value of the ith coupon is $x_0 P_i^F c$, and the value of the bond is

$$B(0, T, c^F, n, M) = x_0 c^F \sum_{i=1}^{n} P_{t_i}^F + M P_T$$

You could also translate the future coupon payment into dollars using the forward currency rate, $F_{0,t}$, and then discount back at the dollar-denominated interest rate, P_t. The value of the bond in this case is

$$B(0, T, c^F, n, M) = c^F \sum_{i=1}^{n} F_{0,t_i} P_{t_i} + M P_T$$

The two calculations give the same result since the currency forward rate, from equation (18) is given by

$$F_{0,t} = x_0 e^{r(t)t} e^{-r_F(t)t} = x_0 \frac{P_t^F}{P_t}$$

The forward price for foreign exchange is set so that it makes no difference whether we convert the currency and then discount, or discount and then convert the currency.

3. STRUCTURED NOTES WITH OPTIONS

We now consider the pricing of bonds with embedded options. Any option or combination of options can be added to a bond. A purchased option raises the price of the bond and a written option lowers it. Because options change the price, they also change the par coupon.

Figure 1 displays the payoff diagrams for four common structures with options:[5]

- **Convertible bond**, which is created by combining an ordinary bond with calls
- **Reverse convertible bond**, which is created by combining an ordinary bond with a written put
- **Tranched payoff**, which makes payments based on a limited range of returns of the underlying asset
- **Variable prepaid forward** (VPF, also called a **prepaid variable forward**), which resembles a combination of the convertible and reverse convertible

The structures in Figure 1 are merely illustrative; they can be customized in an infinity of ways. By adding a purchased low-strike put to the reverse convertible, for example, one could create a reverse convertible with a minimum payoff. In general, one could add or subtract options so as to change the basic payoff structure. Also, for all of these structures, put-call parity tells us that there are other ways to create the same structure.

In this section, we use examples to illustrate structures that contain options, specifically panels (a)–(d) in Figure 1. In the next section, we will discuss additional structures with payoffs resembling that in panel (d).

We consider default-free structures where the underlying asset is that of a third party (for example, a bank might issue an insured deposit linked to the S&P 500 index).

5. In addition to convertible bonds offered by firms, there are bonds offered under many names for different kinds of equity-linked notes—for example, DECS (Debt Exchangeable for Common Stock), PEPS (Premium Equity Participating Shares), and PERCS (Preferred Equity Redeemable for Common Stock), all of which are effectively bonds coupled with options.

FIGURE 1

Four basic payoffs: Panel (a) is a convertible bond, where the bond converts to the asset if its price is above \$100. Panel (b) is a reverse convertible, where the bond pays \$100 if the asset price is above \$100, and converts into the asset below. Panel (c) is a tranche, in which the instrument pays 0 if the asset price is below \$60, \$40 if the asset price is above \$100, and the asset price less \$60 otherwise. Panel (d) is a variable prepaid forward, where the bond pays the asset value for prices below \$100, \$100 between \$100 and \$125, and $\$100 + 0.80(S - \$125)$ for asset prices above \$125.

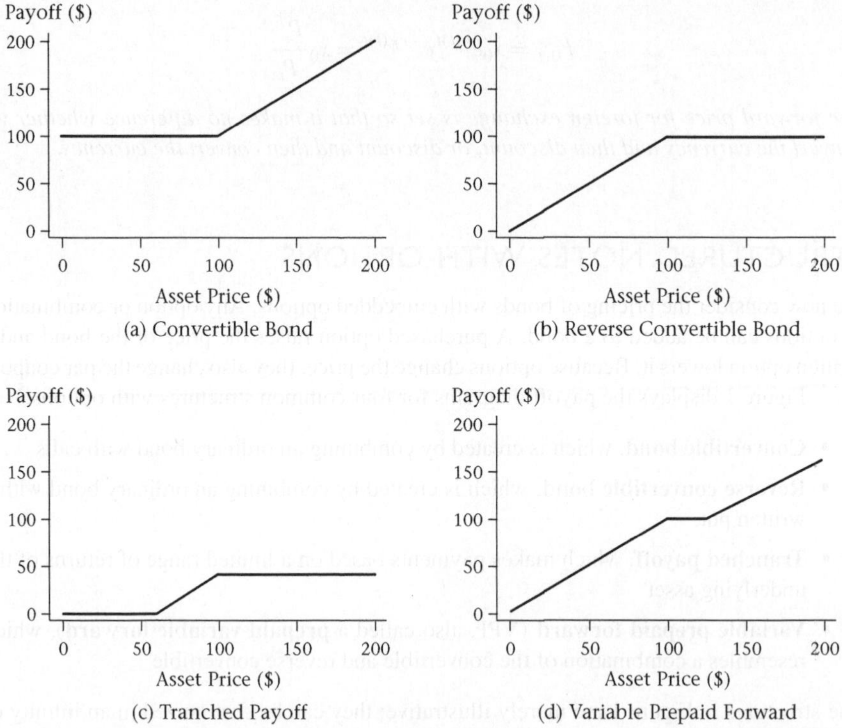

Convertible Bonds

Standard convertible bonds, also sometimes called equity-linked notes, have a minimum payoff and convert into units of the underlying asset when the underlying asset performs well. This payoff is depicted in panel (a) of Figure 1. We obtain this structure by embedding call options in the bond. We will use the terms "bond" and "note" interchangeably, though in common usage a note has a medium time to maturity (2–10 years) and a bond has a longer maturity.

Consider a note convertible into stock. Let γ denote the extent to which the note participates in the appreciation of the underlying stock; we will call γ the **price participation** of the note. In general, the value V_0 of a note with fixed maturity payment M, coupon c, maturity T, strike price K, and price participation γ can be written

$$V_0 = MP_T + c\sum_{i=1}^{n} P_{t_i} + \gamma \text{BSCall}(S_0, K, \sigma, r, T, \delta) \tag{9}$$

Equation (9) assumes that the principal payment is cash. It could just as well be shares. Equation (9) also assumes that the note has a single embedded call option.

Given equation (9), we could arbitrarily select M, T, c, K, and γ and then value the note, but it is common to structure notes in particular ways. To take one example, suppose that the initial design goals are as follows:

1. The note's initial price should equal the price of a share, i.e., $V_0 = S_0$.
2. The note should guarantee a return of at least zero, i.e., $M = V_0$.
3. The note should pay some fraction of stock appreciation above the initial price, i.e., $K = V_0$.

These conditions imply that $V_0 = S_0 = M = K$, and thus the price of the note satisfies the equation

$$S_0 = c\sum_{i=1}^{n} P_{t_i} + S_0 P_T + \gamma \ \text{BSCall}(S_0, S_0, \sigma, r, T, \delta) \tag{10}$$

Given these constraints, equation (10) implies a relationship between the coupon, c, and price participation, γ. Given a coupon, c, we can solve for γ, and vice versa.

Valuing and Structuring an Equity-Linked CD

Valuing the CD. Suppose the S&P index at issue is S_0 and is $S_{5.5}$ at maturity. The CD pays no coupons ($c = 0$), and it gives the investor 0.7 at-the-money calls ($\gamma = 0.7$ and $K = S_0$). After 5.5 years the CD pays

$$S_0 + 0.7 \times \max\left(S_{5.5} - S_0, 0\right) \tag{11}$$

Using equation (9), the value of this payoff at time 0 is

$$S_0 \times P_{5.5} + 0.7 \times \text{BSCall}(S_0, S_0, \sigma, r, 5.5, \delta) \tag{12}$$

where $P_{5.5} = e^{-r \times 5.5}$.

To compute equation (12), we need to make assumptions about the interest rate, the volatility, and the dividend yield on the S&P 500 index. Suppose the 5.5-year interest rate is 6%, the 5-year index volatility is 30%, the S&P index is 1300, and the dividend yield is 1.5%. We have two pieces to value. The zero-coupon bond paying \$1300 is worth

$$\$1300e^{-0.06\times 5.5} = \$934.60$$

One call option has a value of

$$\text{BSCall}(\$1300, \$1300, 0.3, 0.06, 5.5, 0.015) = \$441.44$$

The two pieces together, assuming they could be purchased without fees or spreads in the open market, would therefore cost

$$\$934.60 + 0.7 \times \$441.44 = \$1243.61$$

This is \$56.39 less than the \$1300 initial investment. This difference suggests that the sellers earn a 4.3% commission (56.39/1300) for selling the CD. If the bank had offered 100% of market appreciation, it would have lost money, selling the CD for less than it was worth.

You can think of equation (12) as describing the *wholesale* cost of the CD—it is the theoretical cost to the bank of this payoff. As a retailer, an issuing bank typically does not accept the market risk of issuing the CD. Banks offering products like this often hedge the option exposure by buying call options from an investment bank or dealer. The bank itself need not have option expertise in order to offer this kind of product. The bank is a retailer, expecting to make a profit by selling the CD.

The originating bank will hedge the CD, and must either bear the cost and risks of delta-hedging, or else buy the underlying option from another source. Retail customers may have trouble comparing subtly different products offered by different banks. Customers who have not studied derivatives might not understand option pricing, and hence will be unable to calculate the theoretical value of the CD. On balance, it is not surprising that we find the value of the CD to be several percent less than its retail cost. Here are some other considerations:

- It would have been costly for retail customers to duplicate this payoff, particularly since 5-year options were not readily available to public investors at the time of issue.
- Investors buying this product are spared the need to learn as much about options and, for example, taxes on options, as they would were they to replicate this payoff for themselves.[6]
- The price we have just computed is a ballpark approximation: It is not obvious what the appropriate volatility and dividend inputs are for a 5.5-year horizon.

Any specific valuation conclusion obviously depends entirely on the interest rate, volatility, and dividend assumptions. However, Baubonis et al. (1993) suggest that fees of several percent are common for equity-linked CD products.

Structuring the Product. Many issues arise when designing an equity-linked CD. For example:

- What index should we link the note to? Possibilities besides the S&P include the Dow Jones Industrials, the NYSE, the NASDAQ, sector indexes such as high-tech, and foreign indexes, with or without currency exposure.
- How much participation in the market should the note provide? The CD we have been discussing provides 70% of the return (if positive) over the life of the CD.
- Should the note make interest payments? (The example CD does not.)
- How much of the original investment should be insured? (The example CD fully insures the investment.)

Alternative Structures. Numerous other variations in the structure of the CD are possible. Some examples follow:

6. It turns out that the tax treatment in the United States of an equity-linked CD such as this one is fairly complicated. A bond with a payment linked to a stock index is considered to be "contingent interest debt." The bondholder must pay tax annually on imputed interest, and there is a settling-up procedure at maturity. Issuers of such bonds frequently recommend that they be held in tax-exempt accounts.

- Use Asian options instead of ordinary options.
- Cap the market participation rate, turning the product into a collar.
- Incorporate a put instead of a call.
- Make the promised payment different from the price.

We will consider the first two alternatives in this section. Problems 9 and 11 cover the other two.

Asian options. The payoff discussed above depends on the simple return over a period of 5.5 years. We could instead compute the return based on the average of year-end prices. An Asian option is worth less than an otherwise equivalent ordinary option. Therefore, when an Asian option is used, the participation rate will be greater than with an ordinary call.

Suppose we base the option on the geometric average price recorded five times over the 5.5-year life of the option, and set the strike price equal to the current index level. The value of this Asian call is \$240.97 as opposed to \$441.44 for an ordinary call. Assuming the equity-linked note pays no coupon and keeping the present value the same, the participation rate with this geometric-average Asian option is

$$0.7 \times \frac{441.44}{240.97} = 1.28$$

If instead we base the option on the arithmetic average, the option price is \$273.12, giving us a participation rate of

$$0.7 \times \frac{441.44}{273.12} = 1.13$$

The arithmetic Asian option has a higher price than one based on the geometric average, and hence we get a lower participation rate.

Increasing the number of prices averaged would lower the price of either option, raising the participation rate.

Capped participation. Another way to raise the participation rate is to cap the level of participation. For example, suppose we set a cap of k times the initial price. Then the investor writes to the issuer a call with a strike of kS_0, and the valuation equation for the CD becomes

$$S_0(1-\alpha) = S_0 e^{-r\times t} + \gamma \times [\text{BSCall}(S_0, S_0, \sigma, r, t, \delta) - \text{BSCall}(S_0, kS_0, \sigma, r, t, \delta)]$$

Example 6. Suppose we set a cap of a 100% return. Then the investor writes a call with a strike of \$2600 to the issuer, and the valuation equation for the CD becomes

$$1300(1-0.043) = 1300e^{-0.06\times 5.5} + \gamma \times [\text{BSCall}(1300, 1300, 0.3, 0.06, 5.5, 0.015) - \text{BSCall}(1300, 2600, 0.3, 0.06, 5.5, 0.015)]$$

The value of the written 2600-strike call is \$162.48. The participation rate implied by this equation is 1.11. ■

Reverse Convertible Bonds

Standard reverse convertible bonds have a maximum payoff and convert into the asset when it performs poorly, as in Panel B of Figure 1. The reverse convertible structure is implicit in corporate bonds, which pay investors in full when the firm performs well and not when the firm declares bankruptcy. Financial institutions have also issued hundreds of explicit reverse convertibles in recent years.

To take one example, in February 2009, Barclay's issued a reverse convertible based on the U.S. Oil exchange traded fund. The issue had 6 months to maturity and paid an 11% coupon (5.5% for 6 months). The note was issued at par, which we assume is \$100. If the price of U.S. Oil had risen over the 6-month period, the note would pay \$100. If U.S. Oil fell, the payoff on the reverse convertible was contingent on the amount by which U.S. Oil declined:

- If the U.S. Oil price fell by 50% (the "protection price") during the 6-month period, the bond would pay \$100 or the value of the U.S. Oil ETF, whichever was less.
- If the ETF price did not fall by 50% during the 6-month period, the bond would pay \$100.

The maturity payoff of the reverse convertible therefore looks like a flat line at \$100 if the ETF does not decline by 50%, and like panel B otherwise.

You may recognize that this structure embeds a written down-and-in put, which is a barrier option. The value of the bond is

$$e^{-rT}(M + C) - \text{PutDownIn}(S_0, M, \sigma, r, T, \delta, P)$$

where M is the maturity payment, C is the coupon, σ is the volatility, r the interest rate, P the protection price, T the time to expiration, δ the dividend yield, and PutDownIn is the down-and-in put pricing function.

If we assume that $\sigma = 60\%$ and $r = 3\%$, we have

$$\begin{aligned} e^{-rT}105.5 - \text{PutDownIn}(100, 100, \sigma, r, 0.5, 0, 50) &= \$103.929 - \$6.629 \\ &= \$97.300 \end{aligned}$$

Given these assumptions, the bond is worth 2.7% less than its \$100 price.

If there had been no barrier, the option would be an ordinary put and the price would have been

$$\begin{aligned} e^{-rT}105.5 - \text{BSPut}(100, 100, \sigma, r, 0.5, 0) &= \$103.929 - \$15.940 \\ &= \$87.989 \end{aligned}$$

In order for a bond with a nonbarrier option to sell at par, the coupon would need to have been much larger. To achieve a value of 97.30, the coupon would have needed to be \$13.48, or about 27%.[7] The barrier structure thus puts the coupon in a typical range.

It is probably obvious to you that many similar structures could be created and that it is not easy for a typical investor to analyze such structures.[8] Box 2 illustrates that regulators

7. You can verify this by solving for C:

$$e^{-rT}(100 + C) - \text{BSPut}(100, 100, 0.60, 0.03, 0.5, 0) = 97.30$$

8. Henderson and Pearson (2011) study the pricing of SPARQS (Stock Participation Accreting Redemption Quarterly-Pay Securities) and conclude that the market price of the instruments is on average 8% greater than the cost of dynamically creating the same payoff.

BOX 2: Do Investors Understand Structured Notes?

The U.S. Securities and Exchange Commission (SEC) and the Financial Industry Regulatory Authority (FINRA) issued a press release in June 2011 to warn investors about risks of investing in structured notes. Here are excerpts from the release:

> The SEC's Office of Investor Education and Advocacy and FINRA have issued an investor alert called *Structured Notes with Principal Protection: Note the Terms of Your Investment* to educate investors about the risks of structured notes with principal protection, and to help them understand how these complex financial products work. The retail market for these notes has grown in recent years, and while these structured products have reassuring names, they are not risk-free.
>
> Structured notes with principal protection typically combine a zero-coupon bond—which pays no interest until the bond matures with an option or other derivative product whose payoff is linked to an underlying asset, index or benchmark. The underlying asset, index or benchmark can vary widely, from commonly cited market benchmarks to currencies, commodities and spreads between interest rates. The investor is entitled to participate in a return that is linked to a specified change in the value of the underlying asset. However, investors should know that these notes might be structured in a way such that their upside exposure to the underlying asset, index or benchmark is limited or capped.
>
> Investors who hold these notes until maturity will typically get back at least some of their investment, even if the underlying asset, index or benchmark declines. But protection levels vary, with some of these products guaranteeing as little as 10 percent—and any guarantee is only as good as the financial strength of the company that makes that promise. . . .
>
> FINRA and the SEC's Office of Investor Education and Advocacy are advising investors that structured notes with principal protection can have complicated pay-out structures that can make it hard to accurately assess their risk and potential for growth. Additionally, investors considering these notes should be aware that they could tie up their principal for upwards of a decade with the possibility of no profit on their initial investment.

Source: SEC/FINRA

in the U.S. share this concern, particularly with respect to products advertising "principal protection." The U.S. Oil reverse convertible described above has no principal protection (if the U.S. Oil price were to fall to zero, the note would pay only the coupon), but it would be possible to add protection by including a purchased barrier put in the structure.

Tranched Payoffs

Tranching refers to splitting up cash flows to create new derivative instruments that make payments dependent on the return on an underlying asset being in a specific range.[9] Tranched securities were prominent in discussions of the financial crisis. A mortgage originator (such as a bank) would lend to a homebuyer. The bank would combine (or *pool*) thousands of

9. If this definition sounds to you as if it should apply to option spreads such as bull and bear spreads, you are correct.

TABLE 1 Payment at maturity on a variable prepaid forward contract, showing the dependence of the maturity payment on the future price of the underlying stock. In Panel D of Figure 1, $K_1 = \$100$, $K_2 = \$125$, and $\lambda = 0.80$.

Time T Share Price	Payment to VPF Holder
$S_T < K_1$	S_T
$K_1 \le S_T \le K_2$	K_1
$K_2 < S_T$	$K_1 + \lambda(S_T - K_2)$

similar mortgages. The resulting mortgage pool would then be converted into financial securities (called collateralized mortgage obligations, or CMOs) that were sold to investors. The products sold to investors often were typically tranched: the mortgage payments were split into different groups depending on performance (i.e., whether the homeowner paid the mortgage early or not at all), and the returns on the groups went to different tranched securities.

Consider a bull spread constructed using options. Suppose that an investor buys a 60-strike call and sells a 100-strike call, as in panel (c) of Figure 1. At expiration of the options, the investor will pay \$60 to acquire the stock if the stock price is between \$60 and \$100. Below \$60 the position is worthless, and above \$100 the position is worth its maximum value of \$40. We could say that the return on the stock has been tranched, with the investor receiving a variable return when the price is between \$60 and \$100, and no incremental exposure for other stock prices. This is effectively how mortgage tranching worked, with some investors buying tranches that paid with a high probability (analogous to a low-strike tranche, which is deep in-the-money and likely to pay in full even if the stock performs poorly), and others being paid with low probability (analogous to a high-strike tranche, which is out-of-the-money and pays in full only if the stock performs unusually well).

Mortgage tranches were effectively bull spreads on the underlying mortgage pool. The tranches likely to pay in full were priced like low-risk bonds and carried low yields. The tranches unlikely to pay in full were priced like high-risk bonds and carried high yields. To make things more complicated, dealers would sometimes pool intermediate tranches and sell new tranched securities created out of old tranched securities. This process resulted in products with risk that was extremely difficult to analyze.

Variable Prepaid Forwards

The payment at maturity on a typical VPF is in Table 1. A VPF has two special prices, K_1 and K_2, also called the "floor" and the "cap." The VPF holder receives the value of the stock at prices below K_1, K_1 for intermediate stock prices, and $K_1 + \lambda(S_T - K_2)$ for prices above K_2. Typically, $\lambda = k_1/k_2$. Versions of this structure have other names, such as PEPS and Upper DECs, but the general idea is the same. You should verify that if you set $K_1 = \$100$, $K_2 = \$125$, and $\lambda = 0.80$, you obtain the payoff in Panel D of Figure 1.

A common use of a VPF would be for a large shareholder to hedge a stock position.[10] VPFs are generally over-the-counter instruments, so the shareholder would sell a VPF to a dealer, receiving the VPF price at time 0, V_0. At time T, the VPF settles, and the shareholder is obligated to make the payments in Table 1. The profit for a shareholder selling a VPF would then be

$$\underbrace{S_T - S_0e^{rT}}_{\text{Stock profit}} - \underbrace{[S_T - \max(0, S_T - K_1) + \lambda \max(0, S_T - K_2) - V_0e^{rT}]}_{\text{VPF profit}}$$
$$= \max(0, S_T - K_1) - \lambda \max(0, S_T - K_2) + V_0e^{rT} - S_0e^{rT} \quad (13)$$

Note that in computing profit on the position it is necessary to take into account the opportunity cost of holding the stock, which the shareholder could have sold at time 0 for S_0.

This example illustrates the net result from owning shares and selling a VPF.

Example 7. Consider a VPF with $K_1 = \$100$, $K_2 = \$125$. Suppose that $S_0 = \$100$, $r = 0.06$, $\sigma = 0.30$, $\delta = 0$, and $T = 5$. We have

$$C(K_1) = \text{BSCall}(100, 100, 0.30, 0.06, 5, 0) = \$37.969$$
$$C(K_2) = \text{BSCall}(100, 125, 0.30, 0.06, 5, 0) = \$29.155$$

With $\lambda = k_1/k_2 = 0.8$ the value at time 0 of the VPF is

$$V_0 = \$100 - \$37.969 + 0.8 \times \$29.155 = \$85.355$$

The profit from owning a share and hedging with the VPF is in Figure 2. The profit below \$100 is $-\$19.769$. ■

The net profit line in Figure 2 has a positive slope above \$125. This is because $\lambda = 0.80$; for every dollar by which the stock price increases, the VPF pays \$0.80 and the VPF seller keeps \$0.20. The slope will vary with λ; in particular, if $\lambda = 1$, the line would be flat above \$125.

4. STRATEGIES MOTIVATED BY TAX AND REGULATORY CONSIDERATIONS

A common use of financial engineering is to create financial structures with particular tax and regulatory characteristics. Many such structures resemble the variable prepaid forward structure (panel (d) in Figure 1). This section focuses on two functional examples using instruments with a payoff like the variable prepaid forward: the deferral of capital gains taxes and an instrument that provides tax-deductible equity capital for a bank holding company.

---

10. VPFs can more generally be used to monetize a stock position. For example, in 2001, Howard Schultz, CEO of Starbucks, sold a VPF for 1.7 million Starbucks shares in order to raise funds to become a part owner of the Seattle Supersonics. By selling a VPF he retained the votes on the underlying shares.

FIGURE 2

Profit from owning one share and selling a variable prepaid forward contract.

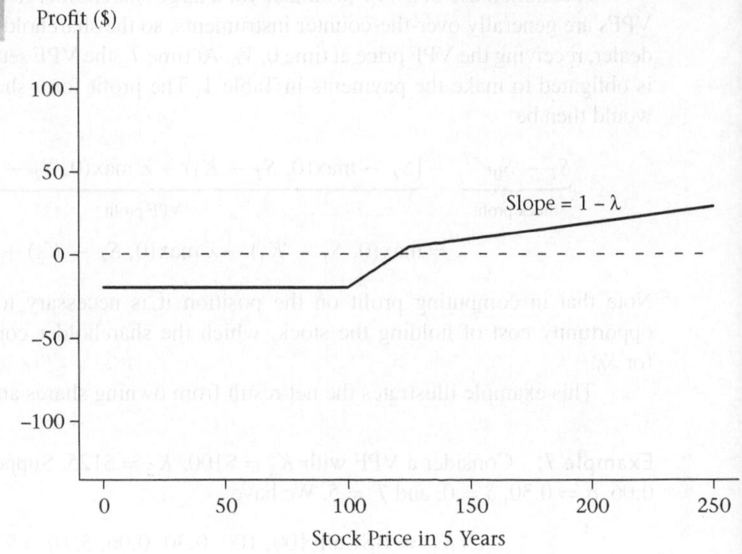

Capital Gains Deferral

If you sell a financial asset at a price greater than your cost, the difference is a capital gain, which is taxed as income in many countries.[11] The United States and many other countries tax capital gains only when an asset is sold. This brings up a practical question: How do you determine when an asset is sold?

You might think that it is obvious how to define the sale of an asset. However, suppose you own shares of a stock and you sell those shares forward for delivery in 5 years. The cash flows from this transaction resemble those of a risk-free bond. You still hold the asset but you bear none of its risk. Have you sold the asset? In some respects you have performed the economic equivalent of a sale. Should you therefore pay capital gains taxes as if you had sold the asset?

Since 1997, holding an asset and selling it forward has constituted a *constructive sale* of the asset for tax purposes in the United States. Box 3 discusses some history related to this provision. The concept of a constructive sale is inherently ambiguous, however. For example, suppose that the investor hedges an asset by buying a collar instead of selling the asset forward. As long as the collar has sufficient distance between the strikes, this transaction is not considered a constructive sale.

Hedging a stock position without selling it is a way to defer capital gains on the hedged portion. This deferral can be valuable. Suppose you have stock worth \$10 million with capital gains of \$7 million. If taxed at the 15% long-term capital gains tax rate, the tax on a sale of this position would be 15% × \$7 million = \$1.05 million. If the after-tax

11. A sale at a loss is a capital loss. Capital losses typically can be subtracted from capital gains when figuring tax, but they cannot be used to a significant extent to reduce taxes on other forms of income.

BOX 3: Constructive Sales

In late 1995, Estee Lauder and Ronald Lauder sold 13.8 million shares of Revlon (see Henriques, 1997). The capital gains *tax* owed on a direct sale of these shares was estimated at $95 million. The Lauders did not directly sell the shares they owned, however. Instead they borrowed 13.8 million shares from family members, and sold those borrowed shares. Technically they still owned their original shares and owed shares to relatives, but they had received money from selling the borrowed shares. This maneuver is known as "shorting-against-the-box." Clearly shorting-against-the-box has the earmarks of a sale, in that the shareholder has no remaining risk of ownership and has received cash for the stock.

Astounding as it may seem, shorting-against-the-box was for years a well-known and legal strategy for deferring the payment of capital gains taxes. Taxes on the position were not owed until the short position was closed by returning the borrowed shares. Unfortunately for the Lauders, their transaction received publicity and was widely criticized.

Congress in 1997 passed a tax bill that made a short-against-the-box equivalent to a sale of the stock. The Lauder transaction was believed to be one reason for this tax rule. The idea was that a transaction that was the economic equivalent of a sale would be deemed a constructive sale and taxed like a sale. Facing IRS action, the Lauders in 1997 sold their shares and paid a large tax bill.

A short-against-the-box is a constructive sale because the shareholder has no remaining risk from the shares. What if a hedging transaction leaves some risk? When does a hedge become a constructive sale? The 1997 bill permits shareholders to defer realization if they entered into hedges with sufficient residual risk, such as collars with a large enough difference between the call and put strikes. The bill left it to the Treasury Department to specify the regulations that would codify permissible tax deferral strategies, but as of 2011, the Treasury had not clarified the exact rules for collars.

interest rate is 4% and the capital gains tax can be deferred for 5 years, the gain to the investor would be

$$\$1{,}050{,}000 - \frac{\$1{,}050{,}000}{1.04^5} = \$186{,}977$$

Deferring the tax payment is like receiving an interest-free loan from the government for the amount of the tax.

Hedging by Corporate Insiders. Corporate insiders can enter into collars and variable prepaid forward contracts as a way to hedge their shareholdings. In one widely reported example, Paul Allen, a cofounder of Microsoft, entered into collars on 76 million Microsoft shares during October and November of 2000 (McMurray, 2001). Once a stock position has been collared or hedged, and the risk of the stock position reduced, the hedged stock can serve as collateral for a loan. For example, suppose an executive enters into a zero-cost collar with a put strike of $90. The executive is guaranteed to receive at least $90 at maturity, so a bank can lend the present value of $90 using the stock plus put as collateral.

Bettis et al. (2010) examined SEC filings between 1996 and 2006 and found over 2000 instances of insiders entering into hedging contracts, including zero-cost collars, exchange funds, and VPFs.[12] In the early part of this period, insiders predominantly used zero-cost collars and exchange funds, which are trusts funded by the contributions of insider shareholdings from different companies.[13] Later in the period, after 2001, insiders most commonly sold VPFs, which combine hedging and lending.[14]

Both Bettis et al. (2010) and Jagolinzer et al. (2007) (who also examined prepaid forwards) find that the sale of a VPF tends to precede poor performance by the company, suggesting that shareholders might have been hedging their shares in anticipation of adverse information about the company.

To consider one prominent example of a VPF transaction, in August 2003 Walt Disney Co vice-chairman Roy Disney sold a 5-year VPF covering a large percentage of his Disney stock holdings. The contract called for Disney to deliver to Credit Suisse First Boston a variable number of shares in 5 years. To quote from the Form 4 filed with the SEC:

> The VPF Agreement provides that on August 18, 2008 ("Settlement Date"), [Roy Disney] will deliver a number of shares of Common Stock to CSFB LLC (or . . . the cash equivalent of such shares) as follows: (a) if the average VWAP ["Value Weighted Average Price"] of the Common Stock for the 20 trading days preceding and including the Settlement Date ("Settlement Price") is less than $21.751, a delivery of 7,500,000 shares; (b) if the Settlement Price is equal to or greater than $21.751 per share ("Downside Threshold") but less than or equal to $32.6265 per share ("Upside Threshold"), a delivery of shares equal to the Downside Threshold/Settlement Price × 7,500,000; and (c) if the Settlement Price is greater than the Upside Threshold, a delivery of shares equal to (1 − (10.8755/Settlement Price)) × 7,500,000.

The profit picture for Disney resembled Figure 2 with $K_1 = 21.751$, $K_2 = 32.6265$, and $\lambda = 1$. This transaction permitted Disney to retain the voting rights in the shares, receive substantial cash, and presumably defer any capital gains he had on the position. The data in Jagolinzer et al. (2007) and Bettis et al. (2010) shows that shareholders had undertaken over a hundred similar transactions prior to the Disney deal, and hundreds more afterwards.

Tax Deferral for Corporations. Corporations may also wish to sell an asset without creating a constructive sale. A corporation has an alternative not open to most investors—namely, the issuance of a note with a payoff linked to the price of the appreciated stock. A well-known example of this is the 1996 issuance by Times-Mirror Co of an equity-linked note, where the note was linked to the stock price of Netscape.

In April 1995, Times Mirror had purchased 1.8 million shares of Netscape in a private placement. The price (adjusted for subsequent share splits) was $2/share. The stock was restricted and could not be resold publicly for 2 years even if Netscape were to go public. In order to sell the stock, Times Mirror would have had to find a qualified buyer (a wealthy or

12. For purposes of SEC reporting, an insider is an officer, director, or beneficial owner of more than 10% of a company's shares. Insider trades and holdings are generally reported on SEC Forms 3, 4, and 5. The SEC's website (www.sec.gov) is an excellent resource for understanding reporting requirements.

13. Bettis et al. (2001) studied the use by executives of zero-cost collars from 1996 to 1998. They found that those who used zero-cost collars on average collared one-third of their stock. Almost no executive used equity swaps, which would likely have resulted in a constructive sale.

14. The collars and VPFs in the Bettis et al. (2010) sample both had an average life of about 3 years. Collars had a median ceiling-to-floor ratio of 1.59 and a price to floor ratio of 1.11, while VPFs had a median ceiling-to-floor ratio of 1.34 and a price to floor ratio of 1.01.

BOX 4: Constructive Sales, Part II

A dealer is typically the buyer of a VPF. In order to hedge this exposure to the stock, the dealer will short shares, and therefore must borrow them. In some cases, dealers have borrowed shares from the VPF seller. The IRS announced in 2006 that if a shareholder both sells a VPF *and* lends shares to the dealer, the two transactions together constitute a sale for tax purposes—the transaction is a constructive sale.

In July 2010, the U.S. Tax Court, in *Anschutz Company v. Commissioner* (135 T.C. No. 5 (July 22, 2010)), agreed with the IRS that the combination of a VPF sale coupled with a share lending agreement did constitute a sale. The tax issues were quite complex (see Humphreys, 2010, for a detailed discussion), but two important facts in the case are that the lender had the ability to recall the shares, and the dealer had the right to accelerate the settlement of the VPF were it unable to hedge the transaction. Thus, the share lending and sale of the VPF appeared to be linked.

This may strike you as splitting hairs. The fact is that the tax code has numerous interlocking provisions that have accumulated over decades. Tax lawyers and financial engineers create structures that they hope will yield favorable results for the client. At the same time, the IRS tries to draw lines to avoid unreasonable results. In the end, the tax courts have to adjudicate the resulting disputes.

The fundamental issue is that the tax law draws sharp distinctions between positions that are economically similar. Given this, it is difficult to write rules that lawyers and financial engineers cannot exploit.

professional investor) and sell the shares in a private placement.[15] In August 1995, Netscape issued shares publicly. In March 1996, Times Mirror had approximately \$85 million in capital gains on the stock. If the shares had been sold on the open market, the tax liability would have been approximately $0.35 \times \$85\text{ m} = \$29.75$ million. Although tax law did not at that time define a constructive sale, a sufficiently wide collar seemed likely to avoid challenge by the tax authorities. Times Mirror's Netscape stake was too large to collar with exchange-traded options. An over-the-counter deal would have left an investment bank with a difficult hedging problem.

Times Mirror elected to hedge its position in Netscape by issuing a five-year equity-linked note that was essentially a VPF. The structure was called a PEPS (Premium Equity Participating Shares) security with $K_1 = \$39.25$, $K_2 = \$45.14$, and $\lambda = 0.8696$. The security was issued for \$39.25 and differed from a typical VPF in paying 4.25% interest (paid quarterly based on the issue price of \$39.25). The shares were ultimately redeemable in cash or stock, at the discretion of Times Mirror.

The effect of issuing the PEPS was like that of Roy Disney selling the variable prepaid forward. Times Mirror received cash at issuance and could deliver shares at maturity. In order to avoid challenge as a constructive sale, the issuance left Times Mirror imperfectly hedged. If at maturity the Netscape stock price was less than \$39.25, Times Mirror

15. Stock with these restrictions is called "144A" stock, after the Securities Act section that defined it.

would lose the interest payments. Above \$45.14, Times Mirror had the risk of holding approximately 13% of the shares.[16]

Marshall & Ilsley SPACES

Banks are required to have capital to cover potential losses on loans and investments. The specific rules are in flux, but generally speaking, "tier 1" capital is equity, retained earnings, and preferred stock, while "tier 2" capital is subordinated debt. Prior to the 2010 Dodd-Frank financial regulation bill, banks were permitted to count limited amounts of so-called trust preferred securities as tier 1 capital.[17] Trust preferred securities are complicated, but their basic design resembles a variable prepaid forward.

The goal of trust preferred securities is to have a financing instrument that has a significant equity component and can serve as tier 1 capital, yet for which the payments are at least partially tax-deductible. Under U.S. tax law, interest payments on corporate debt are tax-deductible for the issuing firm, while dividend payments on equity are not. The distinction between debt and equity may at first seem clear-cut, but with financial engineering it is possible to blur the distinction. For example, suppose a firm issues equity-linked notes that promise coupon payments (like debt) but have a payment at maturity contingent on the firm's stock price (like equity). Is such a financial claim debt or equity for tax purposes?

Here we describe a trust preferred security issued by the bank holding company Marshall & Ilsley Corp. (M&I), and discuss some of the considerations that entered into the design. With a security like the M&I convertible, myriad details hinge on complex tax, accounting, and regulatory considerations. Our purpose in discussing the bond is to understand at a general level the kinds of issues that financial engineering can address. We ignore specific details that aren't needed in conveying a sense of the transaction.

The M&I Issue. In July 2004, M&I raised \$400 million issuing convertible securities with a payoff that resembled that of a variable prepaid forward contract. The M&I offering actually consisted of two components: an ownership stake in a trust containing M&I bonds, and a stock purchase contract requiring that the convertible bondholder make a future payment in exchange for shares. These two components are in theory separable: An investor could hold one without the other. Here are some of the details on these two pieces:

- *Interest in the trust:* M&I issued \$400 million of subordinated debt (debt with very low priority in the event of bankruptcy) maturing in 2038, paying a 3.9% coupon. These bonds were placed into a trust.[18] Each unit of the convertible bond contains an interest in the trust for \$25 par value worth of these subordinated bonds. After 3 years, the bond coupon will be reset so that the bond trades at par. The bonds are subordinated so they can count as regulatory capital.
- *Stock purchase contract:* Each stock purchase contract pays a 2.6% coupon and requires the investor, after 3 years, to pay \$25 for between 0.5402 and 0.6699 shares.

16. Note that \$39.25 × 1.15 = \$45.14, and for the slope, 0.8696 = 1/1.15. Thus the collar width and slope above \$45.14 are both determined using 15%.

17. The Dodd-Frank bill calls for a study of trust preferred securities as tier 1 capital.

18. A trust is an entity holding an asset for the benefit of another party. A trust is controlled by a trustee.

(At the time of the offering, the M&I share price was \$37.32. The value of 0.6699 shares was \$25.) The number of shares that the investor receives after 3 years depends on the M&I stock price at that time, S_{MI}:

$$\begin{array}{ll} 0.6699 \text{ shares} & \text{if } S_{MI} \leq \$37.32 \\ \$25/S_{MI} \text{ shares} & \text{if } \$37.32 < S_{MI} < \$46.28 \\ 0.5402 \text{ shares} & \text{if } S_{MI} \geq \$46.28 \end{array}$$

The bonds held in trust serve as collateral to ensure that the investor can pay the \$25 to buy shares in 3 years, eliminating credit risk for M&I.

The total coupon paid by the trust security was 6.5%: 3.9% for the bond and 2.6% for the stock purchase contract. At maturity the investor would exercise the stock purchase contract, paying for the stock with the bonds. Because the instrument effectively settled in shares of Marshall & Ilsley's own stock, it was a mandatorily convertible bond.

You can verify that the payoff for holding $1/0.6699 = 1.4928$ of the securities resembled panel (d) in Figure 1, with $K_1 = 37.32$, $K_2 = 46.28$, and $\lambda = 0.80639$. Buying 1.4928 bonds is therefore equivalent to owning 1 prepaid forward on the stock, selling 1 call with a strike price of \$37.32, and buying 0.80639 calls with a strike price of \$46.28. Holders of the bond forgo both approximately 20% of the appreciation on the stock above \$46.28 as well as the 2% dividend on the stock.

Although the bond payoff resembles a stock coupled with written and purchased calls, the payments on the bond attributable to the subordinated bonds are nevertheless partially tax-deductible for the issuer. For this reason, trust preferred securities are sometimes called "tax-deductible equity."

Design Considerations. How can we understand the pricing of the convertible? Think of the investor as having paid \$25 for the 3.9% bonds and nothing for the stock purchase contract. If you compare the stock purchase contract with 0.6699 shares of M&I, there are both costs and benefits of the stock purchase contract relative to the stock: The investor is obligated in 3 years to pay the offering day price for 0.6699 shares (\$25) but could in 3 years receive as few as 0.5402 shares. The investor also does not receive the 2% dividend on the underlying M&I shares. However, the investor can acquire future shares for the offering day price. Taking all three considerations into account, the investor receives a 2.6% dividend in return for entering into the stock purchase contract at a zero initial cost.[19]

At this point, it may be helpful to answer some questions that may occur to you:

- *Why didn't M&I simply issue a single instrument, convertible into stock, with the same payoff?* A single instrument with the structure of the M&I convertible—with no minimum promised payment—would probably have been deemed too equity-like and the payment would not have been tax-deductible. The inclusion of an actual bond among the components of the structure created the possibility of tax-deductibility.
- *The bondholder bought the trust unit (containing subordinated bonds) plus a stock purchase contract. If you have to hold these as a unit, isn't this the same thing as holding a single instrument?* The key to allowing tax-deductibility of the interest is that the bonds and stock purchase contract do not have to be held as a unit. The

19. Problem 23 asks you to analyze the pricing of the contract.

subordinated bonds expire 30 years after the stock purchase contract matures. They are documented as distinct entities. Moreover, the convertible-holder has the right to hold the stock purchase contract but to substitute Treasury securities as collateral in place of the stake in the trust.

- *What if interest rates in 3 years have risen and the value of the subordinated bond has fallen below $25?* The bonds are issued subject to a *remarketing agreement*. This means that in 3 years the interest rate on the bonds will be reset so that the bonds sell at par ($25). Thus, the bonds will be worth $25 at exactly the time when the shareholders need to pay $25 for the variable number of shares.[20]
- *Why did the stock purchase contract have a kink, instead of just being a simple forward contract?* The dividend on the forward purchase contract compensates the investor for the possibility of receiving fewer than 0.6699 shares at maturity and the loss of the dividend on the underlying shares, less the gain from deferring the $25 share cost. In exchange for giving up more appreciation, the investor receives a greater dividend. The kink is determined by the willingness of seller and buyers to trade appreciation for current income.

Many financial institutions have used a trust structure like that in the M&I transaction. For example, in November 2007 Citigroup issued a $7.5 billion trust preferred security to Abu Dhabi's state investment fund.[21] Related structures under different names (for example, "Upper DECS") are used by companies wishing to obtain partially tax-deductible equity-like financing.

5. ENGINEERED SOLUTIONS FOR GOLDDIGGERS

Gold-Linked Notes

Any hedger using a forward (or futures) contract to hedge faces the risk that the forward contract will suffer a loss prior to expiration of the hedge. That loss generally must be funded when it occurs.[22] This need to fund interim losses arises from the structure of the hedging instrument, in particular the fact that it is a zero-investment contract linked to the price of gold, meant to serve as a hedging instrument and not as a financing instrument.

20. We have not discussed the possibility that remarketing would fail or what would happen if M&I enters bankruptcy. The publicly available prospectus for the bond discusses these details.

21. See Eric Dash and Andrew Ross Sorkin, "Citigroup Sells Abu Dhabi Fund $7.5 Billion Stake," *New York Times*, November 27, 2007.

22. As discussed earlier, forward contracts and swaps typically have collateralization requirements. In practice, a company must have capital to cover a large loss on a financial contract, even when there is an offsetting gain. For example, in a well-known incident in 1999, Ashanti Goldfields had sold forward eight times annual production. The company suffered a $500 million loss on its forward gold sales when the gold price rose significantly. Although Ashanti had gold in the ground, it did not have cash to cover this loss. Ultimately, Ashanti was able to keep operating by giving warrants on 15% of its stock to its counterparties on the forward sale. For details, see Cooper (2000) and the *Wall Street Journal* (October 7, 1999, p. C1).

Instead of shorting a forward contract, Golddiggers could issue a note promising to pay an ounce of gold 1 year from now. Such a note is effectively debt collateralized by future sales of gold. Ordinarily we would think a risky commodity like gold to be poor collateral for a debt issue. But if a *gold-mining firm* issues gold-linked debt, the risk of the bond and the risk of the collateral are the same. Bondholders provide financing as well as absorbing gold price risk.

We begin with the following information: The current price of gold is \$405/oz, the forward price is \$420, and the effective annual interest rate is 5%. The effective annual lease rate is therefore $0.05 - (420/405 - 1) = 1.296\%$. We wish to construct a debt contract that raises \$405 today (the cost of 1 ounce of gold), pays 1 ounce of gold 1 year from today, and if necessary, pays a coupon, c.

We have already seen that the lease rate plays the role of a dividend. Thus, if the bond has a coupon equal to the lease payment on an ounce of gold, it should be priced fairly. A bond with these characteristics should pay a coupon of $1.296\% \times \$405 = \$5.25$.

We can verify that such a bond is fairly priced. The payoff to the bond in 1 year is \$5.25 plus 1 ounce of gold. We know we can sell the gold in 1 year for \$420 since that is the forward price. The present value of the payoff is therefore the value of the coupon plus the prepaid forward price for gold:

$$\$5.25 \times P_1 + F_{0,1}^P = \frac{\$5.25}{1.05} + \frac{\$420}{1.05} = \$405$$

Because the lease rate is paid as interest, the bond sells at par.

We should verify that the bond serves as an appropriate hedge for Golddiggers. Table 2 summarizes the payoffs to Golddiggers and the bondholders at different gold prices in 1 year. The table assumes that Golddiggers invests the \$405 at 5%—this yields the \$425.25 that is labeled "FV(gross bond proceeds)." The net cash flow is determined by adding profits without consideration of bond payments (column 2) to the difference between the invested bond proceeds (column 3) and the payment to bondholders (column 4). In this case, issuing the bond achieves the same result as selling a forward contract, so Golddiggers is completely hedged.

TABLE 2 Dollar bond payments and net cash flow to Golddiggers with gold-linked bond paying 1 ounce of gold plus \$5.25. The cost of producing 1 ounce of gold is \$380.

Price of Gold (\$)	Profit Before Bond Flows (\$)	FV(Gross Bond Proceeds) (\$)	Payment to Bondholders (\$)	Net Cash Flow (\$)
350	−30	425.25	−355.25	40
400	20	425.25	−405.25	40
450	70	425.25	−455.25	40
500	120	425.25	−505.25	40

The chief difference between the gold-linked note and the forward contract is that the former provides financing, the latter doesn't. If Golddiggers seeks financing (in order to construct the mine, for example), the issuance of a gold-linked note might be preferable to borrowing and hedging separately.

Notes with Embedded Options

A gold-linked bond leaves bondholders with the risk of a loss should the gold price drop. Golddiggers could instead offer a bond that promises bondholders that they will receive interest plus appreciation of gold above \$420.

Such a bond implicitly gives holders a call option on gold with a strike price of \$420. From one calculation, the cost of this option today is \$8.77, with a future value of $\$8.77 \times 1.05 = \$9.21$. Let the promised payment on the bond be the \$405 issue price plus the coupon, c. In 1 year, the bond is worth

$$\$405 + c + \max(0, S_1 - \$420)$$

The valuation equation for the bond is

$$\frac{\$405 + c}{1.05} + \$8.77 = \$405$$

Solving for c gives $c = \$11.04$, which is a yield of 2.726%. Golddiggers thus issues a bond for \$405, with a 2.726% coupon, with additional payments to bondholders if the price of gold exceeds \$420. The difference between the 2.726% coupon and 5% is due to the value of the embedded call option.

What is the result for Golddiggers from having issued this bond? If Golddiggers invests at 5% the \$405 bond proceeds, then it will have \$425.25 cash in 1 year. Recall that costs are \$380/oz. If the gold price in 1 year exceeds \$420, Golddiggers will show profits of

$$\$420 + \$9.21 - \$380 = \$49.21$$

whereas if gold is less than \$420, Golddiggers will make

$$S_1 + \$9.21 - \$380$$

Table 3 summarizes the cash flows to bondholders and to Golddiggers from the issuance of this bond. You can verify that this is exactly the same payoff as obtained when Golddiggers hedges by writing a call. The commodity-linked bond achieves the same effect.

Instead of having a low coupon and protection against low gold prices, bondholders might be willing to bear the risk of a decline in the price of gold in exchange for a higher coupon. For example, Golddiggers could issue a bond in which bondholders sell a 420-strike put to Golddiggers. Golddiggers in turn would have to pay greater interest to compensate bondholders for selling the put. The bond would be structured as follows:

- The initial bond price is \$405.
- The promised payment on the bond is \$434.46, a 7.274% rate of interest.
- If gold sells for less than \$420, the payment is reduced by $\$420 - S_1$.

The bondholders have written a put option to Golddiggers and hence in 1 year receive the future value of the premium. If the price of gold is above \$420, Golddiggers makes

TABLE 3 Dollar bond payments and net cash flow to Golddiggers with gold-linked bond providing gold appreciation to bondholders.

Price of Gold ($)	Profit Before Bond Flows ($)	FV(Gross Bond Proceeds) ($)	Payment to Bondholders ($)	Net Cash Flow ($)
350	−30	425.25	−416.04	−20.79
400	20	425.25	−416.04	29.21
450	70	425.25	−446.04	49.21
500	120	425.25	−496.04	49.21

TABLE 4 Dollar bond payments and net cash flow to Golddiggers with gold-linked bond in which bondholders sell put option to Golddiggers.

Price of Gold ($)	Profit Before Bond Flows ($)	FV(Gross Bond Proceeds) ($)	Payment to Bondholders ($)	Net Cash Flow ($)
350	−30	425.25	−364.46	30.79
400	20	425.25	−414.46	30.79
450	70	425.25	−434.46	60.79
500	120	425.25	−434.46	110.79

$$\$425.25 - \$434.46 + (S_1 - \$380) = S_1 - \$380 - \$9.21$$

If gold is below \$420, Golddiggers makes

$$\$425.25 - \$434.46 + (\$420 - S_1) + (S_1 - \$380) = \$30.79$$

With this bond, Golddiggers in effect buys a 420-strike put. Table 4 depicts the net cash flow to Golddiggers from issuing this bond.

CHAPTER SUMMARY

Zero-coupon bonds, forwards, calls, and puts serve as building blocks that can be used to engineer new financial products. Fair pricing of a product will depend upon volatility, the dividend or lease rate, and the currency of denomination. Ordinary bonds that are simply denominated in something other than cash follow a simple pricing principle: The lease rate of the underlying asset becomes the coupon rate on the bond.

The specific characteristics of a financial product can be varied, though when one characteristic is changed, another must be changed to keep the value the same. The dials that we can turn include the participation in the underlying asset (via embedded calls and puts), the guaranteed minimum, and the coupon. Pricing theory tells us how to make these tradeoffs.

Instruments can be designed specifically to take advantage of tax rules and regulations. The Disney prepaid forward, Netscape PEPS, and M&I convertible bond are examples of this.

FURTHER READING

In this chapter we focused on the creation of engineered instruments using basic building blocks such as assets, bonds, forward contracts, and options. However, using the Black-Scholes technology based on delta-hedging, it is possible to engineer more complicated instruments.

The SEC's press release about structured notes is at http://www.sec.gov/news/press/2011/2011-118.htm. Readings about structured products (including some not discussed in this chapter) include Baubonis et al. (1993), McConnell and Schwartz (1992), Arzac (1997), and Crabbe and Argilagos (1994). For more information about Western-Southern, a deal similar to Times-Mirror Netscape PEPS, see http://www.kellogg.northwestern.edu/faculty/petersen/html.

PROBLEMS

Some of the problems that follow use Table 5 and the following assumptions: The spot price of oil is \$20.90. Let S_t denote the time price of the S&P 500 index and assume that the price of the S&P 500 index is $S_0 = \$1200$ and the continuous annual dividend yield on the S&P 500 index is 1.5%.

1. Consider a 5-year equity-linked note that pays one share of XYZ at maturity. The price of XYZ today is \$100, and XYZ is expected to pay its annual dividend of \$1 at the end of this year, increasing by \$0.50 each year. The fifth dividend will be paid the day before the note matures. The appropriate discount rate for dividends is a continuously compounded risk-free rate of 6%.

Suppose that the day after the note is issued, XYZ announces a permanent dividend increase of \$0.25. What happens to the price of the equity-linked note?

2. Suppose the effective semiannual interest rate is 3%.

TABLE 5 Table for problems.

	Quarter							
	1	2	3	4	5	6	7	8
Oil forward price (\$)	21.0	21.1	20.8	20.5	20.2	20.0	19.9	19.8
Zero-coupon bond price (\$)	0.9852	0.9701	0.9546	0.9388	0.9231	0.9075	0.8919	0.8763

a. What is the price of a bond that pays one unit of the S&P index in 3 years?

b. What semiannual dollar coupon is required if the bond is to sell at par?

c. What semiannual payment of fractional units of the S&P index is required if the bond is to sell at par?

3. Use information from Table 5.

a. What is the price of a bond that pays one unit of the S&P index in 2 years?

b. What quarterly dollar coupon is required if the bond is to sell at par?

c. What quarterly payment of fractional units of the S&P index is required if the bond is to sell at par?

4. Assume that the volatility of the S&P index is 30%.

a. What is the price of a bond that after 2 years pays $S_2 + \max(0, S_2 - S_0)$?

b. Suppose the bond pays $S_2 + [\lambda \times \max(0, S_2 - S_0)]$. For what λ will the bond sell at par?

5. Assume that the volatility of the S&P index is 30%.

a. What is the price of a bond that after 2 years pays $S_0 + \max(0, S_2 - S_0)$?

b. Suppose the bond pays $S_0 + [\lambda \times \max(0, S_2 - S_0)]$ in year 2. For what λ will the bond sell at par?

6. Assume that the volatility of the S&P index is 30% and consider a bond with the payoff $S_2 + \lambda \times [\max(0, S_2 - S_0) - \max(0, S_2 - K)]$.

a. If $\lambda = 1$ and $K = \$1500$, what is the price of the bond?

b. Suppose $K = \$1500$. For what λ will the bond sell at par?

c. If $\lambda = 1$, for what K will the bond sell at par?

The next six problems will deal with the equity-linked CD in Section 3. If necessary, use the assumptions in that section.

7. Explain how to synthetically create the equity-linked CD in Section 3 by using a forward contract on the S&P index and a put option instead of a call option. (*Hint:* Use put-call parity. Remember that the S&P index pays dividends.)

8. Consider the equity-linked CD in Section 3. Assuming that profit for the issuing bank is zero, draw a graph showing how the participation rate, γ, varies with the coupon, c. Repeat assuming the issuing bank earns profit of 5%.

9. Compute the required semiannual cash dividend if the expiration payoff to the CD is $\$1300 - \max(0, 1300 - S_{5.5})$ and the initial price is to be \$1300.

10. Compute λ if the dividend on the CD is 0 and the payoff is $\$1300 - \max(0, 1300 - S_{5.5}) + \lambda \times \max(0, S_{5.5} - 2600)$ and the initial price is to be \$1300.

11. Compute λ if the dividend on the CD is 0, the initial price is \$1300, and the payoff is $\$1200 + \lambda \times \max(0, S_{5.5} - 1300)$.

12. Consider the equity-linked CD example in Section 3.

a. What happens to the value of the CD as the interest rate, volatility, and dividend yield change? In particular, consider alternative volatilities of 20% and 40%, interest rates of 0.5% and 7%, and dividend yields of 0.5% and 2.5%.

b. For each parameter change above, suppose that we want the product to continue to earn a 4.3% commission. What price participation, γ, would the CD need to have in each case to keep the same market value?

13. Use the information in Table 5.

a. What is the price of a bond that pays one barrel of oil 2 years from now?

b. What annual cash payment would the bond have to make in order to sell for $20.90?

14. Using the information in Table 5, suppose we have a bond that pays one barrel of oil in 2 years.

a. Suppose the bond pays a fractional barrel of oil as an interest payment after 1 year and after 2 years, in addition to the one barrel after 2 years. What payment would the bond have to make in order to sell for par ($20.90)?

b. Suppose that the oil payments are quarterly instead of annual. How large would they need to be for the bond to sell at par?

15. Using the information in Table 5, suppose we have a bond that after 2 years pays one barrel of oil plus $\lambda \times \max(0, S_2 - 20.90)$, where S_2 is the year-2 spot price of oil. If the bond is to sell for $20.90 and oil volatility is 15%, what is λ?

16. Using the information in Table 5, assume that the volatility of oil is 15%.

a. Show that a bond that pays one barrel of oil in 1 year sells today for $19.2454.

b. Consider a bond that in 1 year has the payoff $S_1 + \max(0, K_1 - S_1) - \max(0, S_1 - K_2)$. Find the strike prices K_1 and K_2 such that $K_2 - K_1 = \$2$, and the price of the bond is $19.2454. How would you describe this payoff?

c. Now consider a claim that in 1 year pays $S_1 - \$20.50 + \max(0, K_1 - S_1) - \max(0, S_1 - K_2)$, where K_1 and K_2 are from the previous answer. What is the value of this claim? What have you constructed?

17. Swaps often contain caps or floors. In this problem, you are to construct an oil contract that has the following characteristics: The initial cost is zero. Then in each period, the buyer pays the market price of oil if it is between K_1 and K_2; otherwise, if $S < K_1$, the buyer pays K_1, and if $S > K_2$, the buyer pays K_2 (there is a floor and a cap). Assume that $K_2 - K_1 = \$2$ and that oil volatility is 15%.

a. If there is a single settlement date in 1 year, what are K_1 and K_2?

b. If the swap settles quarterly for eight quarters, what are K_1 and K_2?

18. You have been asked to construct an oil contract that has the following characteristics: The initial cost is zero. Then in each period, the buyer pays $S - \overline{F}$, with a cap of $\$21.90 - \overline{F}$ and a floor of $\$19.90 - \overline{F}$. Assume oil volatility is 15%. What is $\overline{F}$?

19. This problem has been intentionally omitted for this edition.

20. Consider again the Netscape PEPS discussed in this chapter and assume the following: the price of Netscape is \$39.25, Netscape is not expected to pay dividends, the interest rate is 7%, and the 5-year volatility of Netscape is 40%. What is the theoretical value of the PEPS?

21. A DECS contract pays two shares if $S_T < 27.875$, 1.667 shares if the price is above $S_T > 33.45$, and \$27.875 and \$55.75 otherwise. The quarterly dividend is \$0.87. Value this DECS assuming that $S = \$26.70$, $\sigma = 35\%$, $r = 9\%$, and $T = 3.3$ and that the underlying stock pays a quarterly dividend of \$0.10.

The next two problems are based on the M&I stock purchase contract.

22. A stock purchase contract with a zero initial premium calls for you to pay for one share of stock in 3 years. The stock price is \$100 and the 3-year interest rate is 3%.

- **a.** If you expect the stock to have a zero dividend yield, what price in 3 years would you agree to pay for the stock?
- **b.** If the stock has a 2% dividend yield, what price in 3 years would you agree to pay for the stock?
- **c.** Now suppose that the stock purchase contract calls for you to pay \$100 in 3 years for one share of stock. What annual payment on the stock purchase contract would be fair if the dividend yield on the stock is zero? What if it is 4%?

23. Value the M&I stock purchase contract assuming that the 3-year interest rate is 3% and the M&I volatility is 15%. How does your answer change if volatility is 35%?

Corporate Applications

In this chapter we look at some contexts in which firms issue derivatives, either explicitly or implicitly. First, Black and Scholes (1973) observed that common debt and equity can be viewed as options, with the firm's assets as the underlying asset. We show how this insight can be used to price debt subject to default, as well as the implications for determining how leverage affects the expected return on equity. We also examine warrants, convertible debt, and callable debt as examples of securities that explicitly contain options.

Second, many firms grant options as compensation to employees. These options typically cannot be exercised for some period of time and cannot be sold, so they raise interesting valuation issues. In addition, compensation options often have nonstandard features.

Third, merger deals in which firm A offers their own stock to buy firm B sometimes offer price protection to firm B shareholders. This protection can take the form of a collar. We examine one merger—Northrop Grumman–TRW—that used a collar for this purpose.

1. EQUITY, DEBT, AND WARRANTS

Firms issue explicit derivatives, such as warrants. However, firms also issue implicit derivatives, such as ordinary debt and equity, which have values determined by the asset value of the firm. In this section we see how option theory helps us understand corporate finance. You will see that it is natural to think of stocks, bonds, and other instruments as options.

Debt and Equity as Options

Consider a firm with the following very simple capital structure. The firm has non-dividend-paying equity outstanding, along with a single zero-coupon debt issue. Represent the time t values of the assets of the firm, the debt, and the equity as A_t, B_t, and E_t. The debt matures at time T and has maturity value $\bar{B}$.

We assume throughout this section that there are no taxes, bankruptcy costs, transaction costs, or other market imperfections.

The value of the debt and equity at time T will depend upon the value of the firm's assets. Equity-holders are the legal owners of the firm; in order for them to have unambiguous possession of the firm's assets, they must pay the debt-holders $\bar{B}$ at time T. If $A_T > \bar{B}$, equity-holders will pay $\bar{B}$ to the bondholders since equity will then be worth the

From Chapter 16 of *Derivatives Markets*, Third Edition, Robert McDonald. Copyright © 2013 by Pearson Education, Inc. Published by Pearson Prentice Hall. All rights reserved.

value of the assets less the payment to bondholders, or $A_T - \overline{B} > 0$. However, if $A_T < \overline{B}$, equity-holders would have to inject additional funds in order to pay off the debt. In this case equity-holders would declare bankruptcy, permitting the bondholders to take possession of the assets. Therefore, the value of the equity at time T, E_T, is

$$E_T = \max(0, A_T - \overline{B}) \tag{1}$$

This expression is the payoff to a call option with the assets of the firm as the underlying asset and $\overline{B}$ as the strike price.

Because equity-holders control the firm, bondholders receive the *smallest* payment to which they are legally entitled. If the firm is bankrupt—i.e., if $A_T < \overline{B}$—the bondholders receive A_T. If the firm is solvent—i.e., if $A_T \geq \overline{B}$—the bondholders receive $\overline{B}$. Thus the value of the debt is

$$B_T = \min(A_T, \overline{B}) \tag{2}$$

This expression can be written[1]

$$\begin{aligned} B_T &= A_T + \min(0, \overline{B} - A_T) \\ &= A_T - \max(0, A_T - \overline{B}) \end{aligned} \tag{3}$$

Equation (3) says that the bondholders own the firm but have written a call option to the equity-holders. This way of expressing the debt value explains where the call option in equation (1) comes from. Summing equations (1) and (2) gives the total value of the firm—equity plus debt—as A_T.

A different way to write equation (2) is the following:

$$\begin{aligned} B_T &= \overline{B} + \min(0, A_T - \overline{B}) \\ &= \overline{B} - \max(0, \overline{B} - A_T) \end{aligned} \tag{4}$$

The interpretation of equation (4) is that the bondholders own risk-free debt with a payoff equal to $\overline{B}$ but have written a put option on the assets with strike price $\overline{B}$.[2]

Example 1. Suppose a firm has issued zero-coupon debt with a face value of $\overline{B} = \$6000$. The maturity value of the equity is given by equation (1) and the maturity value of the debt is given by equation (4). The two payoffs are graphed in Figure 1 as a function of corporate assets at maturity. ■

If we assume that the assets of the firm are lognormally distributed, then we can use the Black-Scholes model to value the payoffs to the firm's equity and debt, equations (1)

1. To follow these derivations, note that $\min(0, x - y) = -\max(0, y - x)$.

2. A bond with a payoff specified as in equation (2) is a **debenture**—a bond for which payments are secured only by the general creditworthiness of the company. Such a bond is said to be *unsecured*. It is also possible for bonds to be secured by specific collateral. For example, lenders to airlines may have an airplane as collateral for their bond.

FIGURE 1

Value of debt and equity at maturity of the debt, as a function of assets, for a firm that has a single issue of zero-coupon debt with a maturity value of $6000.

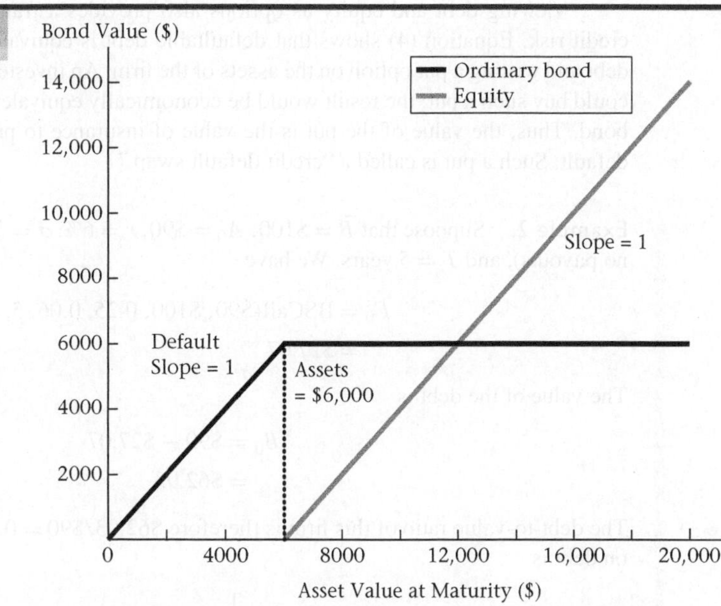

and (4). For purposes of option pricing, the firm's assets are the underlying asset, the strike price is the promised payment on debt, $\overline{B}$, the volatility of the firm's assets, σ, is volatility, and the payout rate from the firm becomes the dividend yield. If the risk-free rate is r and the debt matures at time T, we have

$$E_t = \text{BSCall}(A_t, \overline{B}, \sigma, r, T - t, \delta) \tag{5}$$

$$B_t = A_t - E_t \tag{6}$$

Assuming that the debt is zero-coupon, we can compute the yield to maturity on debt, ρ. By definition of the yield to maturity, we have $B_t = \overline{B}e^{-\rho(T-t)}$; hence, we can solve for ρ to obtain

$$\rho = \frac{1}{T - t}\ln(\overline{B}/B_t) \tag{7}$$

Equity and debt are options, so they have the familiar characteristics of options. For example, if the value of the underlying assets increases by \$1, then from equation (5) the value of the equity will increase by the call delta, Δ_E, and from equation (6), the value of the debt will increase by $1 - \Delta_E$. If the volatility of assets goes up by one percentage point, the value of equity will increase by the call vega and the value of the debt will decrease by vega, and so forth.

This model of the firm is very simple, in that we have not incorporated coupons or dividends, refinancings or subsequent debt issues, etc. It is possible to create more complicated models of a firm's capital structure; nevertheless, this model provides a starting point for understanding how leverage affects returns on debt and equity and determines the yield on risky debt.

Viewing debt and equity as options also provides a framework for thinking about credit risk. Equation (4) shows that defaultable debt is equivalent to owning default-free debt and writing a put option on the assets of the firm. An investor owning a corporate bond could buy such a put; the result would be economically equivalent to owning a default-free bond. Thus, the value of the put is the value of insurance to protect bondholders against default. Such a put is called a "credit default swap."

Example 2. Suppose that $\overline{B} = \$100$, $A_0 = \$90$, $r = 6\%$, $\sigma = 25\%$, $\delta = 0$ (the firm makes no payouts), and $T = 5$ years. We have

$$E_0 = \text{BSCall}(\$90, \$100, 0.25, 0.06, 5, 0) = \$27.07$$

The value of the debt is

$$B_0 = \$90 - \$27.07 = \$62.93$$

The debt-to-value ratio of this firm is therefore $\$62.93/\$90 = 0.699$. The yield to maturity on debt is

$$\rho = \frac{1}{5}\ln(100/62.93) = 0.0926$$

The debt yield of 9.26% is 326 basis points greater than the risk-free rate.

By put-call parity, the value of the debt can be written as the value of a \$100 risk-free bond less a put with a \$100 strike price:

$$B_0 = \$100e^{-0.06\times 5} - \text{BSPut}(\$90, \$100, 0.25, 0.06, 5, 0) = \$74.08 - \$11.15 = \$62.93$$

The cost of an insurance contract on the bond is the cost of the put, \$11.15. Stated differently, buying a bond for \$62.93 plus an insurance contract on the bond for \$11.15 creates a risk-free position costing \$74.08. ■

Leverage and the Expected Return on Debt and Equity

Example 2 shows that, because of the possibility of bankruptcy, the yield to maturity on debt exceeds the risk-free rate. However, a bondholder earns the yield to maturity only if the firm does not go bankrupt. Accounting for the possibility of bankruptcy, the investor on average will earn a return less than the yield to maturity and greater than the risk-free rate. In effect, debt that can default bears some of the risk of the assets, sharing this risk with the equity-holders.

We can compute the expected return on both debt and equity using the concept of *option elasticity*. The elasticity of an option tells us the relationship between the expected return on the underlying asset and that on the option. Using the equation $\gamma - r = (\alpha - r) \times \Omega$, we can compute the expected return on equity as

$$r_E = r + (r_A - r) \times \Omega_E \tag{8}$$

where r_A is the expected return on assets, r is the risk-free rate, and Ω_E is the elasticity of the equity. Using equation (5), elasticity is

$$\Omega_E = \frac{A_t \Delta_E}{E_t} \tag{9}$$

where Δ_E is the option delta.

We can compute the expected return on debt using the debt elasticty, Ω_B:

$$r_B = r + (r_A - r) \times \Omega_B \tag{10}$$

The elasticity calculation is slightly more involved for debt than for equity. Since we compute debt value as $B_t = A_t - E_t$, the elasticity of debt is a weighted average of the asset and equity elasticities:

$$\Omega_B = \frac{A_t}{A_t - E_t}\Omega_A - \frac{E_t}{A_t - E_t}\Omega_E \tag{11}$$

The elasticity of any asset with respect to itself is 1, so we have $\Omega_A = 1$.

Using equations (8)–(11), you can verify that if you owned a proportional interest in the debt and equity of the firm, the expected return on your portfolio would be the expected return on the assets of the firm:

$$(\%\text{Equity} \times r_E) + (\%\text{Debt} \times r_B) = r_A \tag{12}$$

It bears emphasizing that this relationship requires that r_B represent the *expected return* on debt, not the yield to maturity.

It is instructive to compare the expected return calculation for equity in equation (8) with a common alternative calculation. If we assume the debt is risk-free, the expected return on equity is[3]

$$\hat{r}_E = r + (r_A - r)\frac{1}{\%\text{Equity}} \tag{13}$$

This is the familiar Modigliani-Miller expression for the expected return on levered equity. Equation (13) can be obtained from equation (8) by assuming that the delta of the equity is one, which implies that the delta of the debt is zero. Viewing debt and equity as options, by contrast, allows us take into the account the effects of possible bankruptcy. Equation (8) assumes that debt- and equity-holders share the risk of the assets, so equation (13) will give a higher r_E than equation (8).

Example 3. Use the same assumptions as in Example 2, and suppose that the expected return on assets, r_A, is 10%. The equity delta is

$$\text{BSCallDelta}(90, 100, 0.25, 0.06, 5, 0) = 0.735$$

The debt delta is $1 - 0.735 = 0.265$. Thus, if the asset value increases by \$1, the value of the equity increases by \$0.735 and the value of the debt increases by \$0.265.

3. This expression is also sometimes written as $r_E = r_A + (r_A - r) \times D/E$.

Using equation (9), the equity elasticity is

$$\frac{90 \times 0.735}{27.07} = 2.443$$

The expected return on equity is therefore

$$\begin{aligned} r_E &= 0.06 + (0.1 - 0.06) \times 2.443 \\ &= 0.1577 \end{aligned}$$

Using equation (11), the debt elasticity is

$$\frac{90}{90 - 27.07} \times 1 - \frac{27.07}{90 - 27.07} \times 2.443 = 0.3793$$

The expected return on debt is therefore

$$\begin{aligned} r_B &= 0.06 + (0.1 - 0.06) \times 0.3793 \\ &= 0.0752 \end{aligned}$$

Note that the 7.52% expected return on debt is greater than the risk-free rate (6%) and less than the yield to maturity on debt (9.26%).

If we owned equity and debt in the same proportion in which they were issued by the firm, we would have a return of

$$\frac{27.07}{90} \times 0.1577 + \frac{90 - 27.07}{90} \times 0.0752 = 0.1000$$

Since 10% is the expected return on assets, this illustrates equation (12).

Finally, if we were to (erroneously) assume that debt is risk-free and use equation (13) to compute the expected return on equity, we would obtain

$$\begin{aligned} \hat{r}_E &= 0.06 + \frac{1}{27.07/90}(0.1 - 0.06) \\ &= 0.1929 \end{aligned}$$

This calculation gives an expected return on equity substantially greater than 15.77%. ■

This example computes expected returns for a particular leverage ratio. As the firm becomes more levered, equity-holders bear more asset risk per dollar of equity. If assets have a positive beta, the expected return on equity will increase with leverage. At the same time, debt also becomes riskier as leverage increases and there is increased chance of default on the debt.

Figure 2 graphs the debt-to-asset ratio (computed using equation 5) and the expected return on equity (computed using equation 8) as a function of the asset value of the firm, using the assumptions in Example 3. For very low asset values, the debt-to-asset ratio is almost 1 and the expected return on equity is almost 40%.

You can also see that as the debt-to-asset ratio declines, so does the expected return on equity. For very low asset values (where there is high leverage), the expected return on equity is about 40%, dropping to 12% for high asset values (where there is low leverage). The decline in the expected return on equity evident in Figure 2 was the focus of controversy during the debate on financial reform in 2010 and afterwards. See Box 1.

For purposes of comparison, Figure 2 also graphs the expected return on equity, computed assuming that the debt is risk-free. For asset values close to \$200, the difference

FIGURE 2

The top panel graphs the debt-to-asset ratio as a function of the asset value of the firm, using the Black-Scholes formula to compute the value of the debt. The bottom panel graphs the expected return on equity as a function of the asset value of the firm, using equations (13) (dashed line) and (8) (solid line). Both graphs assume that there is a single zero-coupon debt issue with maturity value \$100 and 5 years to maturity, and also assume that $r = 6\%$, $\sigma = 25\%$ (for the assets), and $\delta = 0$.

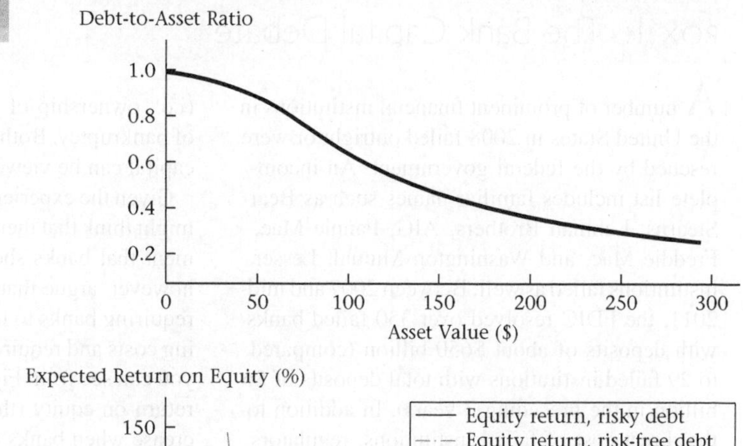

is less than 20 basis points. For a very highly levered (low asset value) firm, however, the difference in Figure 2 is dramatic.

Conflicts Between Debt and Equity. The idea that equity is a call option on the firm and that corporate bonds are risky provides insights into relations between debt- and equity-holders. Since equity-holders control the firm, bondholders may be concerned that equity-holders will take actions that would harm them, or may fail to take actions that would help them.

There are two decisions equity-holders make that affect the relative value of debt and equity. First, equity-holders can affect the volatility of assets. Equity-holders can increase asset volatility in numerous ways—for example, by increasing the operating risk of existing assets, by "asset substitution," (replacing existing assets with riskier assets) or by engaging in financial speculation. An increase in volatility, other things equal, increases the value of the equity-holder's call option and therefore reduces the value of debt. In Example 2, the vega of the equity is 0.66, so an increase in asset volatility of 0.01 leads to an increase in the market value of equity of \$0.66, which is $0.66/27.07 = 2.4\%$ of equity value. Debt value would decline by \$0.66.

A second decision that equity-holders can make is the size of payouts to shareholders, such as dividends and share repurchases. To see why payouts are a potential problem for bondholders, suppose that the firm makes an unexpected one-time \$1 payout to shareholders. This payout reduces assets by \$1. The delta of the equity with respect to assets is less than one, so the value of equity declines by less than \$1. Since the value of debt plus

BOX 1: The Bank Capital Debate

A number of prominent financial institutions in the United States in 2008 failed outright or were rescued by the federal government. An incomplete list includes familiar names such as Bear Stearns, Lehman Brothers, AIG, Fannie Mae, Freddie Mac, and Washington Mutual. Lesser institutions failed as well: Between 2007 and mid-2011, the FDIC resolved over 350 failed banks with deposits of about \$650 billion (compared to 29 failed institutions with total deposits of \$6 billion in the preceding 7 years). In addition to the direct cost of failed institutions, regulators worry about spillover effects: Banks have deep financial ties to one another, so that a large failed bank could lead to a cascade of failures among connected banks.

Can bank failures be avoided? Like other firms, a bank fails when its assets are insufficient to meet its debt obligations. The probability of a bank failing can be reduced by requiring banks to have a higher ratio of equity to assets. It can also be reduced if banks issue debt that converts to stock before the bank fails. Such securities, originally proposed by Flannery (2005) (see also McDonald (2012)), are called *contingent capital*. Ordinary debt, by contrast, converts to stock (i.e., ownership of the assets) only at the time of bankruptcy. Both ordinary debt and contingent capital can be viewed as reverse convertibles.

Given the experience of the financial crisis, you might think that there would be widespread agreement that banks should use less debt. Bankers, however, argue that equity is expensive and that requiring banks to use less debt will raise financing costs and require them to reduce lending.* As you can see from Figure 2, however, the expected return on equity (the cost of equity) should decrease when banks use less debt, so the bankers' argument is at the very least incomplete (see Admati et al. (2010)).

Banks are complicated and play a central role in the economy. Banks are also regulated and protected by government policy (especially the largest banks), so banks' debt cost may be artifically low, which would lead banks to prefer debt finance. In the wake of the financial crisis, regulators will require banks to increase the amount of equity they issue for details (see www.bis.org), but arguments persist over whether the required increase is sufficient to protect the financial system.

*See http://tinyurl.com/4yu86d7 (Reuters.com).

equity equals assets, *the value of the debt must decline by one less the delta of the equity.* Unanticipated payouts to equity-holders therefore can hurt bondholders.

Bondholders are well aware of the potentially harmful effects of asset substitution and dividends. Bond covenants (legal restrictions on the firm) often limit the ability of the firm to change assets or pay dividends. Viewing debt and equity as options makes it clear why such restrictions exist.

Bondholders also encounter problems from actions that shareholders fail to take. Suppose the firm has a project worth \$2 that requires shareholders to make a \$1 investment. If shareholders make the investment, they pay \$1, the value of the assets increases by \$2 and the value of the shares rises by $2 \times \Delta_E$. The gain to shareholders is less than the increase in the value of assets. The difference of $2 - 2 \times \Delta_E$ goes to the bondholders. In making a positive NPV investment, shareholders help bondholders.

The shareholders in this example only will make the investment if the value of shares goes up by more than the \$1 they invest, which will only occur if $\Delta_E > 0.5$. In order for shareholders to be willing to invest, the NPV must be great enough that shareholders gain after allowing for the value increase that is lost to debt-holders.[4] Thus, because of debt, the shareholders may fail to make positive NPV investments. A related problem is asset substitution: Shareholders might make negative NPV investments that increase asset risk, thereby transferring value from bondholders to stockholders.

Multiple Debt Issues

The option-based model of debt accommodates multiple issues of zero-coupon debt with different seniorities. By definition, more senior debt has priority in the event of bankruptcy. Suppose that there are three debt issues, with maturity values of \$30, \$30, and \$40, ranked in seniority from highest to lowest. We will refer to each distinct level of seniority as a *tranche*. The value of equity will be the same as in Example 2, since it is still necessary for equity-holders to pay \$100 to receive ownership of the assets. However, the option pricing approach permits us to assign appropriate yields to each level of debt.

Senior debt-holders are the first in line to be paid. They own the firm and have written a call option permitting the next set of bondholders to buy the firm from them by paying the maturity value of the senior debt, \$30. Intermediate debt-holders own a call option permitting them to buy the firm for \$30, and have sold a call option permitting the junior bondholders to buy the firm for \$60. Junior bondholders in turn own the call option to buy the firm for \$60, and have written a call option permitting the equity-holders to buy the firm for \$100. The values of these options are

$$\text{BSCall}(\$90, \$30, 0.25, 0.06, 5, 0) = \$67.82 \tag{14}$$

$$\text{BSCall}(\$90, \$60, 0.25, 0.06, 5, 0) = \$47.25 \tag{15}$$

$$\text{BSCall}(\$90, \$100, 0.25, 0.06, 5, 0) = \$27.07 \tag{16}$$

Table 1 summarizes the value, yield to maturity, and expected return of each tranche of debt. The junior tranche has a yield to maturity of 13.69%, very close to the required return on equity. The senior tranche, according to the model, is almost risk-free.

The expected returns in Table 1 are computed using option elasticities. To illustrate the calculation, consider the junior bond, which is created by buying a 60-strike call on the assets of the firm and selling a 100-strike call.[5] The two option elasticities are 1.7875 (60-strike) and 2.4432 (100-strike). Using the fact that the elasticity of a portfolio is a weighted average of the elasticities of the portfolio components, the elasticity of the junior bond is

$$\frac{47.25}{47.25 - 27.07} \times 1.7875 - \frac{27.07}{47.25 - 27.07} \times 2.4432 = 0.9077$$

The expected return on the junior debt is therefore

$$r_{\text{junior}} = 0.06 + (0.10 - 0.06) \times 0.9077 = 0.0963$$

4. The idea that the debt may harm investment incentives is developed in Myers (1977).

5. The junior bond is a bull spread on the assets of the firm.

TABLE 1 Market values, yields, and expected returns on three debt tranches.

Claim	Owns	Writes	Value ($)	Yield (%)	Expected Return (%)
Senior bonds	Assets	C(30)	22.18	6.04	6.04
Intermediate bonds	C(30)	C(60)	20.57	7.54	7.03
Junior bonds	C(60)	C(100)	20.18	13.69	9.63
Equity	C(100)		27.07		15.77

Table 1 makes it clear why debt cannot be treated as a single homogeneous class when firms with complex capital structures enter bankruptcy. The interests of the most junior debt-holders may well resemble the interests of equity-holders more than those of senior debt-holders.

Warrants

Firms sometimes issue options explicitly. If a firm issues a call option on its own stock, it is known as a **warrant**. (The term "warrant" is used here to denote options on a firm issued by the firm itself, though in practice the term includes traded options issued in fixed supply.) When a warrant is exercised, the warrant-holder pays the firm the strike price, K, and receives a share worth more than K (or else the holder would not have exercised the warrant). Thus, the act of exercise is dilutive to other shareholders in the sense that the firm has sold a share for less than it is worth. Of course, existing shareholders are aware of warrants outstanding and anticipate this potential exercise. The problem is how to value the warrant, and how to value the equity given the existence of warrants. This valuation problem does not arise with ordinary options, because they are traded by third parties and their exercise has no effect on the firm.

To see how to value a warrant, suppose the firm has n shares outstanding, and that the outstanding warrants are European, on m shares, with strike price K. The asset value is A.

At expiration, if warrant-holders exercise the warrants, they pay K per share and receive m shares. After the warrants are exercised, the firm has assets worth $A + mK$; hence, exercised warrants are worth

$$\frac{A + mK}{n + m} - K = \frac{n}{n + m}\left(\frac{A}{n} - K\right) \tag{17}$$

The expression A/n is the value of a share of equity in the absence of warrants. Thus, equation (17) suggests that we can value a warrant in two steps. First, we compute an option price with A/n as the underlying asset and K as the strike price, ignoring dilution. Second, we multiply the result by a dilution correction factor, $n/(n + m)$. This second step accounts for the fact that warrant exercise changes the number of shares outstanding, with the new shares issued at a "below-market" price of K. The warrant can be valued by using the Black-Scholes formula:

$$\frac{n}{n+m} \text{BSCall}\left(\frac{A}{n}, K, \sigma, r, t, \delta\right) \tag{18}$$

Convertible Bonds

In addition to issuing warrants directly, firms can issue warrants embedded in bonds, i.e., convertible bonds. A simple convertible bond resembles the equity-linked notes, except that the bond is convertible into the company's own shares rather than the shares of a third party. The call option in the bond gives the bondholder the right to surrender the bond's maturity payment, M, in exchange for q shares. The valuation of a convertible bond entails valuing both debt subject to default and a warrant.

Suppose there are m bonds with maturity payment M, each of which is convertible into q shares. The value of the firm at time T is A_T. If there are n original shares outstanding, then there will be $n + mq$ shares if the bond is converted. At expiration, the bondholders will convert if the value per share of the assets after conversion, $A_T/(n + mq)$, exceeds the value per share of the maturity payment that bondholders would forgo:

$$\frac{A_T}{n+mq} > \frac{M}{q}$$

or

$$\frac{n}{n+mq}\left(\frac{A_T}{n} - \frac{M}{q}\frac{n+mq}{n}\right) > 0 \tag{19}$$

This expression is different from equation (12) for warrants, because rather than injecting new cash into the firm when they convert, the bondholders instead avoid taking cash out of the firm.

Conversion occurs if the assets increase sufficiently in value. If the assets decrease, the firm could default on the promised maturity payment. Assuming the convertible is the only debt issue, bankruptcy occurs if assets are worth less than the promised payment to all convertible holders, or $A_T < mM$. The payoff of the convertible at maturity, time T, is

$$\underbrace{mM}_{\text{Bond}} - \underbrace{\max\left(0, mM - A_T\right)}_{\text{Written put}} + \underbrace{mq \times \frac{n}{n+mq} \times \max\left(0, \frac{A_T}{n} - \frac{M}{q}\frac{n+mq}{n}\right)}_{mq\,\text{Purchased warrants}} \tag{20}$$

Thus, owning m convertibles can be valued as owning a risk-free bond with maturity payment mM, selling a put on the firm's assets, and buying mq warrants with strike $M/q \times (n + mq)/n$.

Equation (20) can be rewritten as

$$\max\left[\min\left(mM, A_T\right), \frac{mq}{n+mq} A_T\right] \tag{21}$$

This version of the convertible payoff can be interpreted as follows: Shareholders give bondholders the least they can ($\min[M, A_T/m]$); if it is optimal to do so, convertible holders can then exchange this amount for the conversion value, which is their proportionate share of the assets ($mq/[n + mq] \times A_T$).

FIGURE 3

Maturity payoffs for the aggregate value of an ordinary bond and a convertible bond, using the parameters in Example 4.

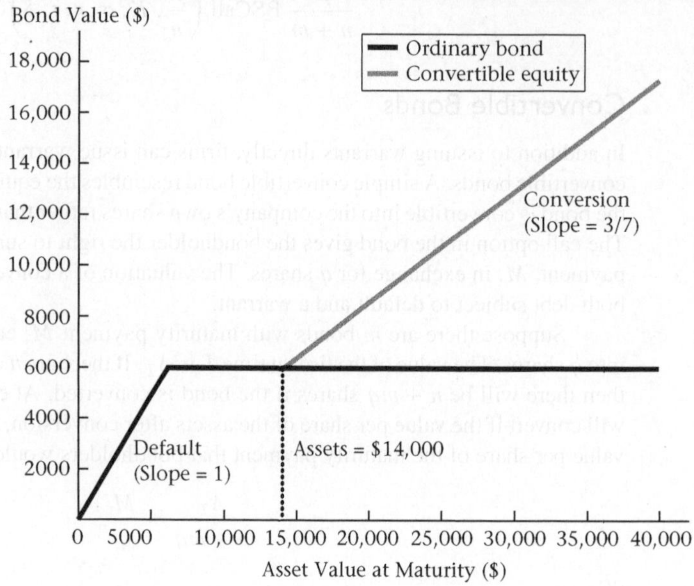

Example 4. Suppose a firm has issued $m = 6$ convertible bonds, each with maturity value $M = \$1000$ and convertible into $q = 50$ shares. The firm has $n = 400$ common shares outstanding. Figure 3 shows the maturity payoff for the aggregate value of the convertible bonds, comparing it with the maturity payoff of otherwise identical nonconvertible bonds issued by the same firm. The six bonds have a total promised maturity value of \$6000, so default occurs when assets are below that level. Equation (19) implies that conversion occurs when assets exceed $\$1000 \times 700/50 = \$14{,}000$. The slope of the convertible payoff above \$14,000 is $mq/(n + mq) = 3/7$, less than the slope in default, because convertible investors share gains with existing shareholders, but once in default, convertible bondholders bear additional losses alone (in default, shares are already worthless). ■

Just as we valued ordinary zero-coupon bonds with the Black-Scholes formula, we can also use the Black-Scholes formula to value a bond convertible at maturity.

Example 5. Suppose a firm has assets of \$10,000 with a single debt issue consisting of six zero-coupon bonds, each with a maturity value of \$1000 and with $T = 5$ years to maturity. The asset volatility is $\sigma = 30\%$ and the risk-free rate is $r = 6\%$. The firm makes no payouts.

If the single debt issue is not convertible, the price is

$$\$1000 \times e^{-0.06\times 5} - \text{BSPut}\left(\frac{\$10,000}{6}, \$1000, 0.30, 0.06, 5, 0\right) = \$701.27$$

The yield on the nonconvertible bond is $\ln(1000/701.27)/5 = 0.0710$, greater than the risk-free rate because of the risk of bankruptcy.

Suppose the debt issue is instead the convertible bond described in Example 4. Using equation (20), the value of all convertible bonds is

$$6 \times \$1000 \times e^{-0.06\times 5} - \text{BSPut}\,(\$10{,}000, 6 \times \$1000, 0.30, 0.06, 5, 0)$$
$$+ 6 \times 50 \times \frac{400}{400 + 6 \times 50} \times \text{BSCall}\left(\frac{\$10{,}000}{400}, \frac{\$1000}{50}\frac{400 + 6 \times 50}{400}, 0.30, 0.06, 5, 0\right)$$
$$= \$5276.35$$

Each bond has a price of \$879.39. The yield on a bond is ln(\$1000/\$879.39)/5 = 0.0257. This is below the yield on an otherwise equivalent nonconvertible bond because of the conversion option: The bondholders have a call option for which they pay by accepting a lower yield on the debt. The value of a share is (\$10,000 − \$5276.35)/400 = \$11.809. Bondholders will convert if at maturity the assets are worth more than

$$M \times (n + mq)/q = \$1000 \times (400 + 6 \times 50)/50 = \$14{,}000$$ ■

Convertible bonds are typically issued at terms such that a significant increase in the stock price is required for conversion to be worthwhile. In Example 5, each bond gives the holder the right to convert into 50 shares, so the strike price is \$1000/50 = \$20. Since the stock price is \$11.809, the ratio of the strike price to the stock price, which is called the **conversion premium**, is \$20/\$11.809 − 1 = 69.4%. In practice, conversion premiums are most commonly between 20% and 40%.

Why do firms issue convertible bonds? One explanation is that convertible bonds resolve one of the conflicts between equity- and debt-holders. Shareholders can take value from holders of ordinary bonds by increasing volatility, even if this action has no beneficial effect from the perspective of the firm as a whole. However, convertibles are harmed less than ordinary debt by an increase in volatility, and may even be helped. Financing with convertibles instead of ordinary debt thus reduces the incentive of shareholders to raise volatility.

In practice, valuation of convertible bonds is more complicated than in this example. First, convertible bonds are typically American options, convertible for much of the life of the bond. Second, convertible bonds typically are not zero-coupon. The payment of coupons complicates the analysis because bankruptcy becomes possible at times other than expiration and the reduction in assets stemming from the payment of the coupon (or any other cash payment to the firm's security-holders). This coupon reduces assets but is also paid to the bondholders. Third, many companies pay dividends. If the dividends that can be earned by converting the bond into stock exceed the bond coupon, there can be a reason for bondholders to convert before maturity. Finally, interest rates and volatility can change, and the circumstances of default may be more complicated than we have assumed (for example, when there are other debt issues, default could occur prior to maturity). The value of the bond can then change for reasons other than stock price changes.

It is possible to value convertible bonds incorporating early exercise, dividends, and callability.[6] It is also possible to incorporate interest rate risk using various techniques.

6. Ingersoll (1977) and Brennan and Schwartz (1977) discuss the valuation of convertible bonds.

Callable Bonds

Many bonds are *callable*, meaning that, prior to maturity, the company has the right to give bondholders a predetermined payment in exchange for the bonds. The idea underlying a callable bond is that the bond issuer can buy the bond back at a relatively cheap price if it becomes expensive. A bond can become expensive because interest rates have fallen, in which case the issuer would like to exchange the existing bonds for new bonds carrying a lower coupon rate. A bond can also become expensive if the market perceives that the company is less likely to default. Again, in this case the company would like to exchange the existing bond for a newly issued bond with a lower default premium. A firm can always buy bonds back at a market price, but there is generally no advantage to doing so. Callability permits the company to buy bonds back at a relatively low price. Of course the company pays for this right by receiving a lower price when it issues the bond.

The predetermined price at which a company can call a bond is specified by a **call schedule**. Bonds are typically noncallable for several years after issuance, a period during which the bond is said to have **call protection**. Callability is, in effect, an option that investors sell to the bond issuer. In return, the company issuing the bonds pays a higher yield on the bonds.

Convertible bonds are typically callable. When the issuer calls a convertible bond, the holder of the bond has the choice of surrendering the bond in exchange for the call price or converting. Callability is a way for issuers to shorten the life of the bond, potentially forcing holders to convert prior to maturity. The issuer—acting in the interests of shareholders—follows a call strategy that *minimizes* the value of the bond. Bondholders, by contrast, follow a conversion strategy that *maximizes* the value of the bond.

Since bonds can be called prior to expiration, we cannot value the call provision using Black-Scholes. However, we can value a callable bond binomially. The call strategy for an issuer is like the exercise of an American option: The issuer calls if it is more valuable to do so than to leave the bond outstanding for another period.

Figure 4 presents binomial valuation examples for four bonds: an ordinary bond, a convertible bond, a callable bond, and a callable convertible bond. We examine noncallable bonds as benchmarks in order to better understand the effect of callability. We value these bonds using the binomial pricing model. In each case, the assets of the firm are the underlying asset, and the value of the bonds is determined by the value of the assets. To perform the valuation, we move backward through the tree. The assumptions in Figure 4 are the same as those in Example 5, so the results in the example and figure are comparable for the ordinary and convertible bonds.

Callable Nonconvertible Bonds. We first consider the binomial valuation of an ordinary, noncallable bond (panel (b) in Figure 4) and its callable counterpart (panel (d) in Figure 4). The yield on the callable bond (7.57%) exceeds that on the noncallable bond (7.29%) because of the option that bondholders have written to the firm.

How are bond prices in Figure 4 computed? For the ordinary bond, the value in year 5 is

$$B_5 = \min(mM, A_5) = \min(\$6000, A_5)$$

There are six \$1000 bonds outstanding, and shareholders will pay to these bondholders the value of the firm or \$6000, whichever is less. Note that default occurs at the bottom node in year 5 since the value of assets is less than the required bond payment, \$6000. Prior to maturity, the value at each node is calculated as in a typical binomial valuation, with

$$B_t = e^{-rh}[pB^+_{t+h} + (1-p)B^-_{t+h}]$$

For a given node at time t, B^+_{t+h} is the bond value if assets move up from that node, and B^-_{t+h} is the bond value if assets move down from that node.

The binomial valuation of the callable bond is straightforward. Let K^{call}_t denote the call schedule. The call price in this example is set to equal the price of a bond yielding 6.75%. At time 1.67, for example, the company could call by paying the bondholders \$4791.10, which, for a bond maturing in 3.33 years, is a yield of 6.75%. We assume that the risk-free rate is fixed; thus the only reason for the company to call the bond is if the company could issue replacement bonds at a lower coupon due to a decrease in default risk.

Shareholders wish to minimize the value of the bonds; hence, their value is

$$\begin{aligned} B_t &= \min\left[\text{ Leave the bond outstanding, call }\right] \\ &= \min\left[e^{-rh}(pB^+_{t+h} + (1-p)B^-_{t+h}),\ K^{\text{call}}_t\right] \end{aligned} \tag{22}$$

If you compare the binomial trees in panels (b) and (d), it is apparent why the callable bond has a lower price at issue than the ordinary bond. At the top node in year 1.67, the noncallable bonds are worth \$4912.38, for a yield of 6%. (If assets reach that node, default will not occur.) The firm calls the callable bond at that node since it is now possible to issue default-free debt. The prospect of this call prevents the bondholders from receiving a capital gain. This in turn lowers the initial price of the bond. Problem 15 asks you to compute share prices at each node so that you can see the effect on shareholders of the different bonds.

Callable Convertible Bonds. We now consider noncallable and callable convertible bonds, panels (e) and (f) in Figure 4. Note first that, as in Example 5, the yield on the convertible noncallable bond (2.39%) is lower than that on the ordinary bond (7.29%) because convertible bondholders receive a call option and pay for this with a lower yield.

Using equation (21), the year 5 value for the convertible bond is

$$\max\left[\min(mM, A_5),\ \frac{mq}{n+mq}A_5\right]$$

In panel (e) in Figure 4, bondholders convert at the top two nodes in year 5, receive the maturity payment in cash at the next node, and the firm defaults at the bottom node.

Prior to maturity, the convertible investor values the bond as the greater of its conversion value and the value of letting the bond live one more period:

$$\begin{aligned} B_t &= \max\left[\text{ Continue to hold, convert }\right] \\ &= \max\left[e^{-rh}(pB^+_{t+h} + (1-p)B^-_{t+h}),\ \frac{mq}{n+mq}A_t\right] \end{aligned} \tag{23}$$

B_t is the total value of the bonds.

When the bond is both convertible and callable, there is a tug-of-war between the firm and the bond investors. We can imagine the bond value being determined as follows: The bondholders decide whether to hold or convert (maximizing the bond value). Given this decision, the firm decides whether to call (minimizing the bond value). If the firm calls, bondholders revisit their decision about whether or not to convert (again maximizing the bond value, conditional upon the behavior of the firm). This chain of reasoning implies the

FIGURE 4

Binomial valuation of a callable nonconvertible and a callable convertible bond. The assumptions are the same as those in Example 5. The binomial tree for assets in panel (a) is generated using a forward tree with $u = 1.6279$, $d = 0.7503$, $p^* = 0.40444$, $T = 5$, and three binomial time steps (hence the time between binomial periods is $h = 5/3 = 1.67$). In each case there are six bonds outstanding with a total maturity value of \$6000. Convertible bonds convert into 50 shares. The yield for each bond is computed as $\ln(6000/B_0)/5$, where B_0 is the time 0 value of the six bonds. The price is $B_0/6$. The call schedule in panel (c) is the price of a zero-coupon bond maturing in year 5 and yielding 6.75%. Callable bonds are call-protected until year 1.67. Prices in *italics* denote calls of the bond; prices in **bold** denote conversions, and prices in ***bold italics*** denote conversions in response to a call.

	Year			
Panel	**0**	**1.67**	**3.33**	**5**
(a) Firm assets	10,000.00	16,279.12	26,500.98	43,141.27
		7502.88	12,214.03	19,883.36
			5629.32	9164.04
				4223.61
(b) Ordinary bond	4166.82	4912.38	5429.02	6000.00
Price = \$694.47		4396.40	5429.02	6000.00
Yield = 7.29%			4471.64	6000.00
				4223.61
(c) Call schedule	N/A	4791.10	5361.58	6000.00
(d) Callable bond	4109.14	*4791.10*	*5361.58*	6000.00
Price = \$684.86		4371.73	*5361.58*	6000.00
Yield = 7.57%			4471.64	6000.00
				4223.61
(e) Convertible bond	5324.34	7578.78	11,357.56	**18,489.12**
Price = \$887.39		4733.96	6351.59	**8521.44**
Yield = 2.39%			4471.64	6000.00
				4223.61
(f) Callable convertible bond	4908.85	***6976.77***	***11,357.56***	**18,489.12**
Price = \$818.14		4371.73	*5361.58*	**8521.44**
Yield = 4.01%			4471.64	6000.00
				4223.61

following valuation equation:

$$B_t = \max\{\min[\max(\text{Continue to Hold, Convert}), \text{Call}], \text{Convert}\}$$

$$= \max\left\{\min\left[\max\left(\underbrace{e^{-rh}[pB^+_{t+h} + (1-p)B^-_{t+h}]}_{\text{Hold}}, \underbrace{\frac{mq}{n+mq}A_t}_{\text{Convert}}\right), \underbrace{K_t^{\text{call}}}_{\text{Call}}\right],\right.$$

$$\left.\underbrace{\frac{mq}{n+mq}A_t}_{\text{Convert}}\right\} \tag{24}$$

As you would expect, the ability to call a convertible bond lowers its price, raising its yield from 2.39% to 4.01%. By comparing panels (e) and (f) in Figure 4, you can see why this happens. In year 1.67 at the top node, it is optimal to wait to convert if the bond is noncallable. This gives a bond value in panel (e) of \$7578.78. However, if the bond is callable using the call schedule in panel (c), the firm will call at the top node in year 1.67. In response, the bondholders convert, giving them 50 shares worth \$6976.66. The bond is worth less because shareholders cannot delay the conversion. The firm does not call at the lower node in year 1.67 because the credit quality of the bond deteriorates at that node.

Bond Valuation Based on the Stock Price

The binomial examples in Figure 4 assume that the assets of the firm follow a binomial process and use the resulting tree to value a convertible bond. This approach becomes complicated when the firm's capital structure contains multiple bonds and convertible securities.

An alternative approach, often used in practice, is to base valuation of a convertible bond on a binomial tree for the stock, rather than on assets. A standard binomial tree for the stock, however, will never reach a zero stock price, and thus a convertible bond valued on this tree will be priced as if it were default-free. This raises the question: How can we incorporate bond default risk into the pricing procedure?

Tsiveriotis and Fernandes (1998) suggest valuing separately the bond income and the stock income from an optimally managed convertible bond. Their procedure accounts for default by discounting bond income at a rate greater than the risk-free rate, while the component of the bond income related to conversion into stock is discounted at the risk-free rate.

Other Bond Features

It is possible to issue bonds that are considerably more complex than those we have considered. Conversion and call schedules can vary with time in complicated ways. Bonds can be *puttable*, meaning that the investor can sell them back to the firm at a predetermined price. Bonds can pay *contingent interest*, meaning that if a particular event occurs, the interest rate on the bond changes.

Particular structures are often a response to tax and accounting considerations. Another example is the use of *contingent convertible* bonds, also known as "co-co's."

Firms report earnings on a *per share* basis. For a firm that has issued only shares and ordinary debt, computing earnings per share (EPS) is straightforward since there is no ambiguity about the number of shares outstanding. However, if a firm has issued convertible debt or warrants, how many shares should the firm use in computing EPS? Under financial accounting rules in the United States, the firm must compute the worst-case fully diluted earnings per share. When the firm has issued a convertible security, this generally means adding back to earnings after-tax interest on the convertible, and adding the number of convertible shares to shares outstanding.

In recent years firms have issued **contingent convertible bonds**, which are securities that for a time received different accounting treatment than ordinary convertibles. Holders of such bonds can convert only when a contingency—such as the stock price being sufficiently high—has occurred. Prior to 2005, firms were permitted to ignore such bonds in computing fully diluted EPS. However, the FASB ruled that such bonds had to be treated as convertibles, and a number of firms that had issued such bonds were forced to change the way they accounted for them.

General Motors in 2004 would have had to reduce earnings by 15% if it altered its accounting for the $8 billion in contingent convertibles that it had issued. In the end, GM altered the bonds to permit settlement in cash rather than stock, and avoided the earnings reduction.[7]

Put Warrants

Many companies that had share repurchase programs during the 1990s also sold put options on their own stock.[8] A commonly stated rationale for issuing such put warrants (see, for example, Thatcher et al., 1994) is that the put sales are a hedge against the cost of repurchasing shares. Intel, Microsoft, and Dell, for example, all sold significant numbers of puts, with Microsoft alone earning well over $1 billion in put premiums during the 1990s. Here is a quote from Microsoft's 1999 10-K describing the put program:

> Microsoft enhances its repurchase program by selling put warrants. . . . On June 30, 1999, 163 million warrants were outstanding with strike prices ranging from $59 to $65 per share. The put warrants expire between September 1999 and March 2002. The outstanding put warrants permit a net-share settlement at the Company's option and do not result in a put warrant liability on the balance sheet.

The sale of a put allows the firms to implicitly buy and sell their own shares in response to price changes. Dealers purchased the puts written by firms such as Microsoft, Intel, and Dell. The dealers reportedly held the puts and delta-hedged the position, thus reducing their risk. Moreover, the transactions, including the dealer's hedging trades, occurred without

7. See "New Bond Rules to Dent GM Earnings," by James Mackintosh and Jenny Wiggins, *Financial Times*, London ed., July 22, 2004, p. 26. and "GM Acts on New Co-Co Bond Rules," by Jeremy Grant, *Financial Times*, London ed., August 6, 2004, p. 24.

8. Generally these companies had large stock option programs and repurchased shares in order to prevent their compensation programs from causing an increase in the number of shares outstanding. (Corporate finance theory offers no justification for this practice, but firms seem to believe that it is important.)

any public announcement. In effect, put-selling firms transacted with shareholders using the dealer as a conduit. When the share price rose, the delta of the dealer's purchased put, which was negative, increased toward zero and the dealer would sell the shares it had purchased to hedge the put. When the share price fell, delta would have decreased to negative one and the dealer would then have bought additional shares to hedge its position. Thus, the dealer, acting on behalf of the firm, bought as the share price fell and sold as the share price rose.

Problem 19 asks you to examine a binomial example of this transaction, showing first that the firm could accomplish the same end as put writing by transacting directly in its shares. Second, the problem asks you to show how the counterparty dealer delta-hedges the transaction.

2. COMPENSATION OPTIONS

Many firms pay executives and other employees with call options on the company's own stock. The use of such *compensation options* is common and significant in many companies, but has declined since the early 2000s.

The Use of Compensation Options

Microsoft provides an illustration of the evolution in the use of option grants. The firm estimated in its 1999 annual report (10-K) that its 78 million option grants that year were worth about $1.6 billion. This was approximately $52,000 per employee (Microsoft had 31,000 employees). Microsoft also reported that the June 30, 1999, market value of total outstanding options (on 766 million shares, with 5 billion shares outstanding) was $69 billion, or $2 *million* per employee. In 2004, Microsoft largely switched from the use of stock options to share grants; see Box 2.

Many companies besides Microsoft made significant use of compensation options. Eberhart (2005) found in a sample of 1800 firms using compensation options in 1999 that options were on average 12% of shares outstanding. Moreover, the use of options was not restricted to executives: Core and Guay (2001) found in a sample of 750 companies that two-thirds of option grants were to nonexecutive employees.

As at Microsoft, however, the use of compensation options declined more generally. Murphy (forthcoming) finds that between 2001 and 2009, option grants declined from over half to less than one-quarter of compensation for S&P 500 CEOs, with the percentage of CEOs receiving options falling from 85% in 2000 to 65% in 2009.

What caused the decline in the use of compensation options? One likely factor is the decline in stock prices during the early 2000s, particularly for high-tech stocks. This decline left many employees with deep out-of-the-money options and created morale problems for companies heavily dependent upon options. Boxes 2 and 4 discuss Microsoft's and Google's responses to their overhang of out-of-the-money options in 2003 and 2009.

A second important factor is that both the Financial Accounting Standards Board (FASB) in the United States and the International Accounting Standards Board (IASB) announced that they would require companies to recognize employee option grants as a compensation expense. Throughout the 1990s most companies had treated grants of

BOX 2: Compensation Options at Microsoft

In July 2003, the *Wall Street Journal* proclaimed: "The golden age of stock options is over." (See "Microsoft Ushers Out the Era of Options," by Robert A. Guth and Joann S. Lublin, *Wall Street Journal*, July 14, 2003.) Microsoft stock had fallen and many employees had out-of-the-money options. CEO Steve Ballmer said employees had "angst" about the low stock price, and Microsoft's CFO said that employees could no longer expect to become wealthy from stock options:

> "If you think what happened in the nineties is going to happen again—it's not," said Microsoft Chief Financial Officer John Connors. In a recent interview he described the PC market boom as a "phenomenon" that "nobody will ever likely repeat."

Microsoft announced that in the future it would issue restricted stock instead of options. (Restricted stock cannot be sold for a period of time.)

In addition, Microsoft engaged JP Morgan Chase on a one-time basis to buy options from employees. The bank bought the options at modified terms: In particular, maturities were reduced to a maximum of three years. As a result employees sold their options for a price that in some cases was significantly less than the unrestricted price for an otherwise equivalent traded option. JP Morgan Chase, which would hold the options it acquired, informed Microsoft employees that it would be short-selling shares in order to delta-hedge the option position. Slightly more than half of employee options were sold in this fashion.

Microsoft's avoidance of options appeared to be part of a general trend. One survey found a 50% reduction in the value of option grants between 2001 and 2003. (See "Stock Option Awards Sharply Cut," by Ruth Simon, *Wall Street Journal*, December 14, 2004, p. D3.)

In 2005, Microsoft chairman Bill Gates told a group of business writers, "I regret that we ever used stock options." (Reuters, "Gates Regrets Paying with Stock Options," www.cnn.com, May 3, 2005). Between 2008 and 2010, the company granted options on 12 million shares, but those grants were in conjunction with acquisitions.

---

compensation options as worthless when computing earnings.[9] An attempt by the FASB to require option expensing in the early 1990s was defeated by companies opposed to expensing. Many of these companies were concerned about the decline in reported earnings that would result from expensing.

The logic behind requiring companies to expense option grants is straightforward. If a company pays cash to an employee, the company deducts the payment as an expense. If an otherwise identical company replaces some of the cash with an option grant, that company will report systematically higher earnings than the first *unless* the value of the option grant is also deducted as an expense.[10]

9. SFAS 123 did require companies to report the value of options in a footnote. This value—frequently computed using the Black-Scholes formula—did not affect reported earnings.

10. You can also perform the following thought experiment: Suppose that an option-issuing firm hedges its obligations by buying an insurance contract from a third party. This third party would pay the firm the value of the option when the employee exercises it. A firm granting an option and buying the hedging contract would bear the cost of the hedge. If a firm does not buy such a contract, it self-insures. The shareholders

In December 2004, the FASB issued Statement of Financial Accounting Standards (SFAS) 123R, which contained the final rules, effective in June 2005, for companies to follow in expensing options:

> [A] public entity [is required] to measure the cost of employee services received in exchange for an award of equity instruments based on the grant-date fair value of the award (with limited exceptions). That cost will be recognized over the period during which an employee is required to provide service in exchange for the award—the requisite service period (usually the vesting period).[11]

A company might grant options that vest after 3 years and expire after 7 years. Under SFAS 123R, the company could value these options using the Black-Scholes or the binomial formula, and then expense 1/3 of their value over each year of the vesting period.

Compensation options are generally granted at-the-money, so both the reported value and the value to the recipient depend on the share price at the grant date. An academic researcher discovered in the early 2000s that numerous companies had retrospectively chosen grant dates to make valuable options appear less valuable at grant. Box 3 discusses the resulting uproar.

Valuation of Compensation Options

The valuation of compensation options is complicated by the fact that there are many special considerations in valuing them:

- Compensation options cannot be sold and typically are not fully vested (i.e., the employee does not own them) for several years.
- The executive may resign, be fired, die, or become disabled, or the company may be acquired. Any of these may affect the value of the option grant, either by forcing early exercise (as may happen with a death) or requiring that the options be forfeited (in the event the executive is fired).
- The term of the options can be 10 years or more, which makes volatility and dividend estimates difficult.
- The company may not have a publicly traded stock, in which case the stock price must be estimated.
- There may be unusual contractual features of the compensation option contract. For example, the strike price may be an industry stock price index.

Such considerations make it harder to value compensation options than short-lived exchange-traded options, but they do not imply that the option has zero value. We will now discuss some of the issues that arise in option expensing.

Whose Valuation. Compensation options cannot be traded. An employee who cannot sell options will typically discount their value. As a result, you can expect that firms and

---

then bear the present value of the option exercise cost, which should equal the cost of the insurance. Either way, the shareholders bear the cost of the compensation option.

11. Statement of Financial Accounting Standards No. 123R, p. ii.

BOX 3: Option Backdating

Executives receive stock option awards on a specific date. The options are typically granted at-the-money, so the stock price on this date determines the strike price of the options. Lie (2005) (following an earlier study by Yermack, 1997) documented a remarkable fact: Between 1992 and 2002, abnormal company stock returns were on average negative before the date of option grants and positive thereafter. This finding catalyzed both news coverage and regulatory investigations. Ultimately, investigators found convincing evidence that over 100 companies had systematically selected the low stock price of the quarter when granting options at the end of the quarter. This practice was called **option backdating**.

In addition to backdating, companies also engaged in "spring-loading" (granting options prior to a release of good news), "bullet-dodging" (delaying an option grant until after the release of bad news), and possible outright lying to the IRS about the date on which an executive had exercised options (Cicero, 2009). (For ordinary nonqualified compensation options, the gain at exercise is taxed as ordinary income. Claiming that the option was exercised when prices were low would reduce taxes.)

Ultimately, abnormal return patterns around option grant dates were sharply reduced (see Heron and Lie, 2007) when, beginning in August 2002, the Sarbanes-Oxley Act required firms to report option grants no later than two days following the grant.

The *New York Times* in 2010 summarized the status of backdating prosecutions:*

> On the civil side, the S.E.C. filed about 50 cases. The largest one involved Dr. William W. McGuire, the former chief executive of the UnitedHealth Group, who paid $468 million in civil fines and restitution to the company.
>
> Irrespective of whether stock-options backdating resulted in penalties, the practice turned out to be relatively common. About 150 companies issued restatements because of allegations of backdating stock options, a list that included Apple and Cablevision.

*See http://tinyurl.com/3wghxyx.

employees will value compensation options differently. Such a difference in valuation can occur for any compensation other than immediate cash.

Accounting standards require that companies deduct the *cost to the company*. The goal is to measure cost to nonemployee shareholders, not value to employees. For example, suppose a company grants employees nontradable membership in a golf club costing $15,000 per year. An employee who does not play golf might value the membership at zero. Nevertheless, shareholders bear the $15,000 cost. *The fact that the employee discounts the membership's value does not reduce the cost to the firm.* For shareholders, the issue is how much options cost the company, given the behavior of employees.

Valuation Inputs. SFAS 123R calls for the valuation to measure fair market value of the option. This requires that companies estimate the likely behavior of employees with respect to exercise and forfeiture of options, and also that the company estimate prospective volatility and dividends.[12] To illustrate several practical issues in measuring cost to the

12. Since dividends reduce the value of an option, it is possible that widespread use of compensation options has resulted in a reduction in corporate dividends.

company, we again consider Microsoft as an example. In accord with SFAS 123, Microsoft in 1999 valued its options using the Black-Scholes formula and disclosed this value in a footnote. The options vested in $4\frac{1}{2}$ years and expired after 7 years. Here is the discussion from Microsoft's 1999 10-K:

> [Option] value was estimated using an expected life of 5 years, no dividends, volatility of 0.32 in 1999 and 1998 and 0.30 in 1997, and risk-free interest rates of 6.5%, 5.7%, and 4.9% in 1997, 1998, and 1999.

Microsoft does not document how it chose volatilities, but these are close to historical volatilities in each year.[13]

Why did Microsoft use a 5-year expiration to value options expiring in 7 years? It is never optimal to early-exercise a publicly traded call option on a non-dividend-paying stock since it can be sold for more than its intrinsic value. However, compensation options cannot be sold. Thus, the value of the options *to the holder* may be less than intrinsic value. In this case, employees may exercise the options before expiration.[14] In addition to exercise by continuing employees, options are often canceled due to death, termination, or retirement of the employee. Taxes can also potentially affect the exercise decision, although a common tax-motivated argument for early exercise is incorrect.[15] Finally, compensation options cannot be exercised until they vest. A realistic valuation would account for the likelihood of these various factors. The assumed 5-year life is intended to account for the *expected* life of an option.[16]

It is possible to modify both the Black-Scholes and binomial models to account for complications due to early exercise. For example, suppose that 4-year options vest after 3 years and the company estimates that 5% of outstanding options will be forfeited each year during the vesting period. Furthermore, the company believes that half of the remaining options will be exercised at vesting, with the other half exercised at expiration. One could then value the option grant as being partially a 3-year option and partially a 4-year option:

$$(1 - 0.05)^3 \left[0.5 \times \text{3-year option} + (1 - 0.05) \times 0.5 \times \text{4-year option}\right] \quad (25)$$

In this expression, each option price is weighted by the fraction of employees who historically exercised at that time. A problem with this approach is that it does not recognize that employee behavior depends on the stock price. If the option is deeply in-the-money in the

13. Using weekly data, historical volatilities for Microsoft for July to June were 32% for 1996–1997, 30% for 1997–1998, and 39% for 1998–1999.

14. See Kulatilaka and Marcus (1994) for a discussion of the employee's valuation of options. In practice, executives frequently exercise a large fraction of their in-the-money options as soon as they vest. Huddart (1998) shows that options are disproportionately exercised on the first through fourth anniversaries of the grant, in blocks of 25% of the grant. Since it is common for grants to vest 25% annually, this finding suggests that many options are being exercised as soon as possible.

15. An employee is taxed at ordinary income rates on the exercise of a nonqualified option, with subsequent gains on the stock being taxed at capital gains rate. Some have argued that employees optimistic about the share price should exercise compensation options early in order to maximize the percentage of income taxed at the favorable capital gains rate. This argument is incorrect. However, if the ordinary income rate is expected to increase, early exercise can be optimal. For a discussion, see McDonald (2003).

16. If a company alters its assumption about the exercise behavior of employees, the estimated value of newly issued options will change. Cisco, for example, changed its assumed option life from 5.6 to 3.3 years, reducing the estimated value of its option grants by 23%, from \$1.3 to \$1.0 billion. See "Cisco May Profit on New Option Assumptions," by Scott Thurm, *Wall Street Journal*, December 7, 2004, p. C1.

early years, fewer employees are likely to resign before the options vest. If the option is out-of-the-money in year 3, all employees who do not resign will wait before deciding whether to exercise, which lengthens option maturity. Thus, the assumptions about exercise behavior will generally be incorrect. Bodie et al. (2003) point out that for these reasons, equation (25) will undervalue the option. A binomial model or Monte Carlo valuation permits a more flexible and realistic treatment of early exercise.

An alternative approach to expensing options was suggested by Bulow and Shoven (2005). A discussion of their approach is in Appendix A.

Repricing of Compensation Options

If a company is heavily dependent on compensation options, a decline in the stock price can cause morale problems for employees who are hoping their options will be valuable. The delta of a deep out-of-the-money option is low, so that subsequent stock price changes will not have much effect on the value of employee options. As a result, companies will sometimes substitute at-the-money options for already-granted options that have become out-of-the-money. Reducing the exercise price of compensation options in response to a decline in the stock price is called option **repricing.** Many companies have repriced, including Oracle, Netscape Communications, Apple Computer, Bay Networks, Best Buy, and Oxford Health Plans during the 1990s, and Google, Intel, and Starbucks in 2009.[17] If the repricing increases the value of the options, the company is required to record an expense for the increase in value. To avoid recording an expense, Starbucks granted employees fewer at-the-money options than the number of retired out-of-the-money options. Google, on the other hand, exchanged options one-for-one and recognized an expense. See Box 4 for a discussion of Google's approach to compensation options.

If you expect that options will be repriced if the price falls, how valuable is the option grant in the first place? We can answer this question using barrier options. An option that is going to be repriced if the stock price reaches a certain level can be modeled as a knock-out option (the originally granted option vanishes), plus a knock-in option (a new option replaces it) with the same barrier. Specifically, suppose that the option strike is K, and that at the barrier, H, a new at-the-money option will be issued in place of the original option. A repriceable option is then worth

$$\text{CallDownOut}(S, K, \sigma, r, T, \delta, H) + \text{CallDownIn}(S, H, \sigma, r, T, \delta, H) \qquad (26)$$

The second term reflects the knock-in call being at-the-money when it knocks-in.

Example 6. Suppose $S = \$100$, $\sigma = 0.4$, $r = 0.06$, $t = 10$, $\delta = 0.01$, and that options will be repriced if the stock price hits \$60. The value of an option that will *not* be repriced is

$$\text{BSCall}(\$100, \$100, 0.4, 0.06, 10, 0.01) = \$54.43$$

The value of an otherwise equivalent option that will be repriced at \$60 is

$$\text{CallDownOut}(\$100, \$100, 0.4, 0.06, 10, 0.01, 60)$$
$$+ \text{CallDownIn}(\$100, \$60, 0.4, 0.06, 10, 0.01, 60) = \$41.11 + \$20.30 = \$61.41$$

Thus, the possibility of repricing increases the value of the option by 13%. ■

17. See Morgenson (1998) for a discussion of the debate about accounting for repricing.

Box 4: Google and Compensation Options

Microsoft renounced compensation options in 2003, but Google and other companies continue to use them. In late 2008, Google employees lost considerable value on their compensation options when Google's stock tumbled almost 50%. Google responded in early 2009 by repricing those options, permitting employees to exchange existing high-strike price options for new at-the-money options with additional vesting time. Google anticipated a $460 million expense as a result of employees exchanging less valuable for more valuable options.

Another issue with options is that when they vest, employees typically have to choose whether to hold the options or exercise them prior to expiration, which reduces their value. In 2007, Google introduced transferable stock options (TSOs) to partially address this problem, as well as to provide prices for options. Google typically grants options with 10 years to expiration, and the options vest after 4 years. Once an option vests, employees using the TSO program can offer to sell their options to investment banks, which bid for the options in an internal market. Any options sold in this way have a maximum maturity of 2 years. As a consequence, an employee whose options have just vested, and which therefore have 6 years to expiration, faces a substantial loss in theoretical value by selling the options, shortening the maturity by 4 years. However, the options will be more valuable than if the employee were to exercise them at that point. Moreover, employees can observe the internal market price for options and can thereby place a lower bound on the value of their vested, unexercised options.

Google's TSO program is similar to the one-time option purchase program Microsoft offered when it eliminated options (see Box 2). One ramification of the TSO program for Google is that tradable options will have a longer life than nontradable options—employees who would have exercised options upon vesting will sell them instead, extending the life by 2 years. This increase in the expected life of the options increases their theoretical value when they are granted. Google's reported option compensation expense will therefore be greater as a result of the TSO program.

Reload Options

A **reload option** gives the option-holder new call options when existing call options are exercised. The idea is that the option-holder uses shares to pay for exercise, and new at-the-money options are granted for each share given up in this fashion. This type of option is best explained with an example. Assume that a 10-year option grant for 1000 shares with a strike price of $100 permits a single reload. Suppose the employee exercises the option when the stock price is $250, with 4 years of option life remaining. The exercise price requires a payment of $\$100 \times 1000 = \$100{,}000$. This amount can be paid in cash or by surrendering $\$100{,}000/\$250 = 400$ shares. An executive paying the strike price by surrendering shares receives 400 new at-the-money options with 4 years to expiration.

Arnason and Jagannathan (1994) pointed out that there are two important characteristics of reload options. First, the reload feature is valuable: A reload option can be worth 30% more than an otherwise equivalent option without the reload feature. Second, reload options cannot be valued using the Black-Scholes formula because reload options may be early-exercised. However, they can be valued using the binomial option pricing model.

Reload options might seem esoteric, but Saly et al. (1999) show that 1135 reload options were granted, in 1997, out of a total of 9673 grants reported in the S&P Execucomp

FIGURE 5

Binomial valuation of ordinary option (binomial tree on the left) and reload option (binomial tree on the right). The calculations assume that $S = \$100$, $K = \$100$, $\sigma = 0.3$, $r = 0.08$, $\delta = 0$, $T = 4$, $h = 2$, and that there is a single reload. Stock prices and option prices are shown at each node, with the reload value in italics. A reload occurs at the boxed stock price. In this example, we have $u = 1.794$, $d = 0.768$, and $p = 0.395$.

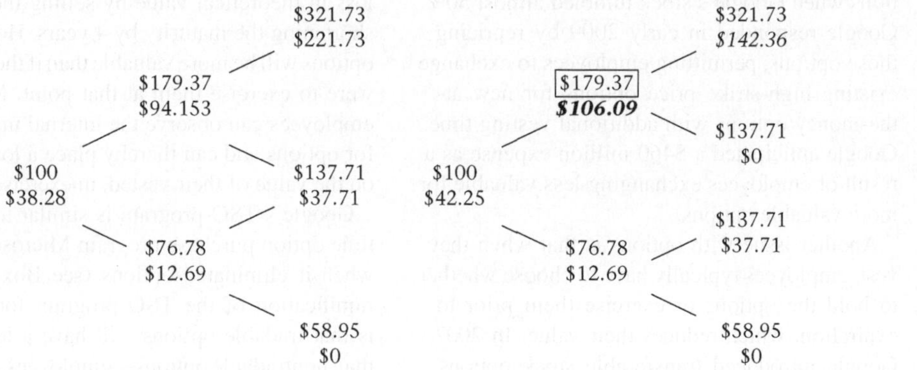

database. SFAS 123R accounts for reloads by ignoring the extra value of the reload feature when the option is granted, and accounting for the additional expense when the option is exercised and reloaded.[18] This treatment is in the spirit of the Bulow-Shoven expensing proposal, discussed in Appendix A.

Reload options can be valued binomially. This is accomplished by replacing the exercise amount at the time of exercise, $S - K$, with the value of a new reload option. We will illustrate this in the simplest possible fashion, with a two-period binomial example.

Figure 5 shows the binomial valuation of an ordinary option and a reload option with a single reload. The binomial price for an option without a reload provision is \$38.28. (The Black-Scholes price for this option is \$36.76.) The reload price, by contrast, is \$42.25, and a reload optimally occurs in the second binomial period. Let's examine how this works.

First, consider the valuation without a reload. When $S = \$179.37$ in period 1, the value of the option left alive is \$94.153, while the value exercised is \$79.37. As we would expect since there are no dividends, the option is not exercised early; the value in period 0 is \$38.28.

When a reload is permitted, the one candidate node for a reload is when $S = \$179.37$. (A reload would have no value at $S = \$100$ or in the final period.) If a reload occurs, the option-holder receives \$79.37 for exercising the option, and 100/179.37 options are issued with a strike price of \$179.37 and 2 years to maturity. Thus, we calculate the value of the

18. Saly et al. (1999) suggest that reload options may be a way to give management undisclosed compensation.

option at this node as

$$\$79.37 + \frac{100}{179.37}e^{-0.08\times 2}\left(0.395 \times \$142.36 + 0.605 \times \$0\right) = \$106.09 \quad (27)$$

From Figure 5, the value of the reload option is \$42.25, 10.5% greater than in the absence of the reload.

In general, we can compute the value of the reload at every node by solving another binomial pricing problem valuing the appropriate number of newly issued options. The option-holder reloads if doing so is more valuable than not doing so, just like the exercise decision for an American option.[19]

Level 3 Communications

Level 3 Communications was one of the first companies to deduct the cost of compensation options in computing earnings. However, Level 3 also granted unusually complex and valuable options and did not take this complexity and extra value into account when expensing. In a June 1998 proxy statement, Level 3 described its outperform stock options (OSO), granted to employees. This is how they are described in the proxy:

> Participants in the OSO Program do not realize any value from awards unless the Level 3 Common Stock outperforms the Standard & Poor's 500 Index. When the stock price gain is greater than the corresponding gain on the Standard & Poor's 500 Index, the value received for awards under the OSO Program is based on a formula involving a Multiplier related to how much the Common Stock outperforms the Standard & Poor's 500 Index.

The multiplier is then described as follows:

> The Multiplier shall be based on the "Outperform Percentage" . . . for the Period, determined on the date of exercise. The Outperform Percentage shall be the excess of the annualized percentage change . . . in the Fair Market Value of the Common Stock over the Period . . . over the annualized percentage increase or decrease . . . in the Standard & Poor's 500 Index over the Period. . . .

The multiplier is computed based on the outperform percentage as follows:

Outperform Percentage	Multiplier
$x \le 0$	0
$0 < x \le 11\%$	$x \times \frac{8}{11} \times 100$
$x > 11\%$	8.0

Because of the multiplier, if Level 3 outperforms the S&P 500 index by at least an annual average of 11%, the option recipient will have the payoff of eight options. The options have a 4-year maturity and are exercisable and fully vested after 2 years.

19. When n reloads are permitted, the problem can be solved by having the binomial pricing function call itself, along with the information that one less reload remains. This is simple to program but computationally very slow because of the large number of binomial valuations. See Saly et al. (1999) for a discussion.

Example 7. Suppose that at the grant of an option, the price of Level 3 is \$100, and the S&P 500 index is at 1300. After 4 years, the price of Level 3 is \$185, and the S&P 500 index is at 1950. A "nonmultiplied" outperformance option would have had a payoff of

$$\$185 - \$100 \times \frac{1950}{1300} = \$35$$

The (nonannualized) returns on Level 3 and the S&P 500 index are 85% and 50%. The outperform percentage is

$$1.85^{0.25} - 1.50^{0.25} = 5.957\%$$

The multiplier is therefore

$$0.05957 \times \frac{8}{11} \times 100 = 4.332$$

The payment on the option is

$$\left(\$185 - \$100 \times \frac{1950}{1300}\right) \times 4.332 = \$151.64 \quad ■$$

This option is worth between 0 and 8 times as much as an ordinary option. How can we get an intuitive sense for the value of the difference? We will first examine the effect of the outperformance feature and then consider the effect of the multiplier.

Valuing the Outperformance Feature. First, what would be the value of an ordinary 4-year-to-maturity at-the-money call? Using a volatility of 25% (which Level 3 says in its 1998 Annual Report is the "expected volatility" of its common stock), and a risk-free rate of 6%, we obtain an option price of

$$\text{BSCall}(\$100, \$100, 0.25, 0.06, 4, 0) = \$30.24$$

The Level 3 1998 Annual Report discusses the valuation of the outperformance option as follows:

> The fair value of the options granted was calculated by applying the Black-Scholes method with an S&P 500 expected dividend yield rate of 1.8% and an expected life of 2.5 years. The Company used a blended volatility rate of 24% between the S&P 500 expected volatility rate of 16% and the Level 3 Common Stock expected volatility rate of 25%. The expected correlation factor of 0.4 was used to measure the movement of Level 3 stock relative to the S&P 500.

To value an outperformance option, we use the Black-Scholes formula but make the following substitutions:

$$\sigma_{\text{Level 3}} \rightarrow \hat{\sigma} = \sqrt{\sigma^2_{\text{Level 3}} + \sigma^2_{\text{S\&P}} - 2\rho\sigma_{\text{Level 3}}\sigma_{\text{S\&P}}}$$

$$r \rightarrow \delta_{\text{S\&P}}$$

where ρ is the correlation between Level 3 and S&P 500 returns and r is the risk-free rate. The net effect on value of granting an outperformance call depends upon the effect of these substitutions. The "blended" volatility, $\hat{\sigma}$, can be greater or less than $\sigma_{\text{Level 3}}$. In recent years, $\delta_{S\&P}$ has been less than r. The calculation Level 3 makes for the blended volatility is

$$\hat{\sigma} = \sqrt{0.25^2 + 0.16^2 - 2 \times 0.4 \times 0.25 \times 0.16}$$
$$= 0.2368$$

which is rounded to 24%. The price of the outperformance option is therefore

$$\text{BSCall}(\$100, \$100, 0.2368, 0.018, 4, 0) = \$21.75$$

This is about $\frac{2}{3}$ of the value of the ordinary option. This reduction in value is primarily due to replacing the 6% interest rate with a 1.8% dividend yield. The volatility reduction by itself lowers the option price only to \$29.44.

Accounting for the Multiplier. Now consider the effect of the multiplier. We can approximate the value of the multiplied option using gap options. The multiplier in effect provides additional options as outperformance increases. For every $\frac{11}{8} = 1\frac{3}{8}\%$ per year by which Level 3 outperforms the S&P 500, the multiplier increases by 1. Thus, we can approximate the effect of the multiplier by valuing a strip of gap outperformance options.

For example, the multiplier is 2 if over 4 years Level 3 outperforms the S&P 500 by a factor of $1.0275^4 = 1.1146$, nonannualized. We can use a set of gap options to approximate the value of the option. If outperformance is between 0 and 1.375% per year, the option-holder receives nothing. Between 1.375% and 2.75%, the option-holder receives one option, etc. Above 11% per year, the option-holder receives eight options. For example, the option received if performance is between 2.75% and 4.125% per year would pay $S_{\text{Level 3}} - S_{\text{S\&P}}$ if $S_{\text{Level 3}} > 1.0275^4 \times S_{\text{S\&P}}$.

Figure 6 shows the payoff of a single nonmultiplied option, plotted against the exact payoff and the payoff approximated by gap options. Note that the exact and gap approximation are not identical, but they are quite close.

Table 2 shows that, using the gap option approximation, the value of the compensation option is about seven times the value of a single option. A more precise binomial valuation using 100 binomial steps gives a value for the option of \$156.25, so the gap approximation of \$153 is quite close. Monte Carlo valuation provides an alternative way to value the Level 3 option.

Finally, it is interesting to note that it may be rational to exercise the Level 3 option early even in the absence of dividends. Suppose the option is close to expiration and the outperformance percentage is slightly above 11%. If the holder exercises, the multiplier is 8. If the share price rises further, the multiplier remains 8. However, if the share price falls, the multiplier may fall to 7; by waiting to exercise, the option-holder can lose options. This extra loss from a share price decline can provide an incentive to exercise early. For very high prices, there is no incentive to exercise early since the multiplier remains constant. For low prices, the potential increase in the multiplier offsets the potential reduction in the multiplier. Thus, early exercise is potentially optimal only for intermediate prices and close to expiration.

FIGURE 6

Payoff to Level 3 compensation option with multiplier, as a function of relative return on Level 3 stock and the S&P 500 index. "Approximate payoff" is the result of buying a strip of eight gap options, designed to approximate the exact payoff.

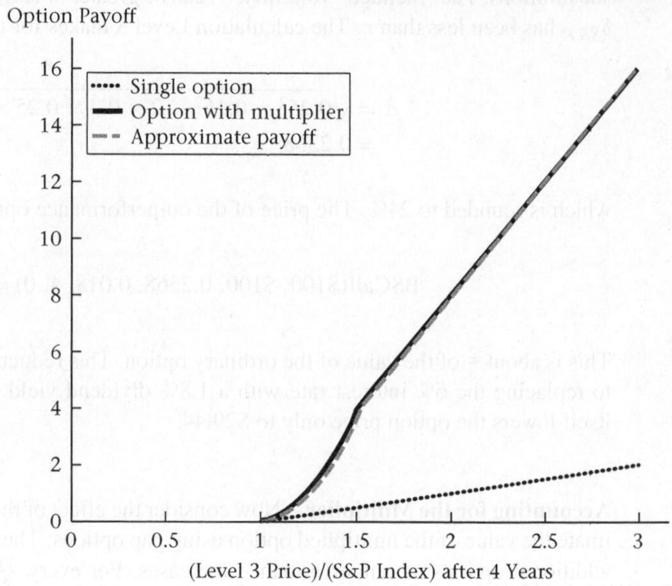

TABLE 2

Valuation of Level 3 option approximated as sum of gap options. For each row, the option value is computed as a gap call option ($C(S, K_1, K_2, \sigma, r, T, \delta) = Se^{-\delta T}N(d_1) - K_1 e^{-rT}N(d_2)$), where $S = \$100$, $K_1 = \$100$, $K_2 = \$100\alpha$, $r = 0.018$, $\sigma = 0.2368$, $T = 4$, and $\delta = 0$.

Multiplier	Outperformance (α)	Gap Option Value ($)
1	1.056	21.63
2	1.115	21.28
3	1.175	20.72
4	1.239	19.96
5	1.305	19.04
6	1.373	17.98
7	1.444	16.81
8	1.518	15.58
Total		153.00

3. THE USE OF COLLARS IN ACQUISITIONS

A common financial transaction is for one firm (the *acquirer*) to buy another (the *target*) by buying its common stock. The acquirer can pay for these shares with cash or by exchanging its own shares for target firm shares. Collarlike structures are frequently used in these transactions.

Suppose that under the purchase agreement, each target share will be exchanged for x shares of the acquirer (x is the *exchange ratio*). Once the target agrees to the purchase, the acquisition will generally take time to complete, often 6 months or more.[20] Target shareholders will be concerned that the acquirer's stock will drop before the merger is completed, in which case the dollar value of x acquirer shares will be lower. To protect against a price drop, it is possible to exchange whatever number of shares have a fixed dollar value. (For example, if the acquirer price is \$100, exchange one share for each target share. If the acquirer price is \$50, exchange two shares for each target share.) However, target shareholders may also wish to participate in share price gains that the acquirer experiences; this suggests fixing the exchange ratio rather than the dollar value. There are four common offer structures that address considerations such as these:[21]

- **Fixed stock offer:** A offers to pay B a fixed number of A shares per B share.
- **Floating stock offer:** A offers to pay B however many shares have a given dollar value, based on A's share price just before the merger is completed.
- **Fixed collar offer:** There is a range for A's share price within which the offer is a fixed stock offer. Outside this range the deal can become a floating stock offer or may be subject to cancellation.
- **Floating collar offer:** There is a range for A's share price within which the offer is a floating stock offer. Outside this range the deal can become a fixed stock offer or may be subject to cancellation.

Figure 7 illustrates these four types of acquisition offers. As this list shows, it is possible to modify the extent to which the target bears the risk of a change in the stock price of the acquirer. More complicated structures are also possible.

The Northrop Grumman—TRW merger

Northrop Grumman's 2002 bid for TRW is an example of a merger offer with a collar. In July 2002, Northrop Grumman and TRW agreed that Northrop would pay \$7.8 billion for TRW. News headlines stated that Northrop offered "\$60 per share," but the offer actually resembled a collar. The number of Northrop Grumman shares to be exchanged for each TRW share would be determined by dividing \$60 by the average Northrop Grumman price over the 5 days preceding the close of the merger, with the exchange ratio to be no less than 0.4348 (\$60/\$138) and no more than 0.5357 (\$60/\$112). Thus, if the price of Northrop Grumman at the merger closing was below \$112, TRW shareholders would receive 0.5357 shares. If the price was above \$138, TRW shareholders would receive 0.4348 shares. If the price, S, was in between \$112 and \$138, TRW shareholders would receive $\$60/S$, which

20. In many cases, for example, regulatory agencies examine the acquisition to see if it is anticompetitive.

21. Fuller (2003) discusses the kinds of offers and the motives for using alternative kinds of collars.

FIGURE 7

Four acquisition offer types: (a) a fixed stock offer of one share for one share; (b) a floating stock offer for \$50 worth of acquirer shares; (c) and (d) fixed and floating collar offers with strike prices of \$40 and \$60.

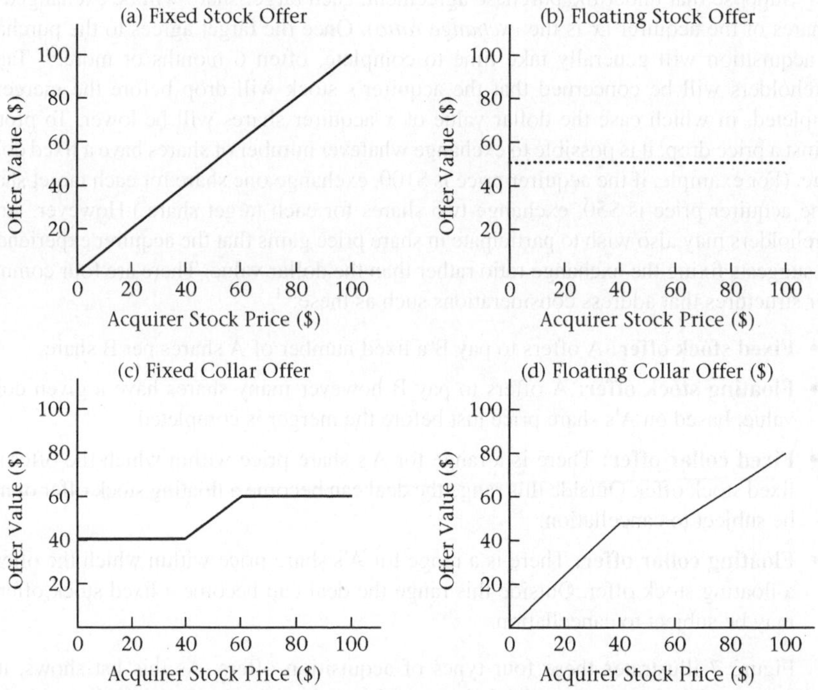

is \$60 worth of shares.[22] The deal closed on December 11, 2002, when the closing price of Northrop Grumman was \$96.50; TRW shareholders therefore received shares worth

$$0.5357 \times \$96.50 = \$51.69$$

How would TRW shareholders value the Northrop offer? Suppose that TRW shareholders were certain the merger would occur at time T, but uncertain about the future Northrop Grumman stock price, S. TRW shareholders could then value the offer by noting that the offer is equivalent to buying 0.5357 shares of Northrop Grumman, selling 0.5357 112-strike calls, and buying 0.4348 138-strike calls. In addition, the TRW shareholders would not receive Northrop dividends paid prior to closing and would continue to receive

22. The acquisition terms changed between February and July. Initially, Northrop offered to exchange \$47 worth of Northrop Grumman stock for each TRW share: The number of shares to be exchanged was to be no more than 0.4563 (\$47/\$103) or less than 0.4159 (\$47/\$113). In May, the value of the bid was increased to \$53 (no more than 0.4690 shares (\$53/\$113) or less than 0.4309 (\$53/\$123) shares).

FIGURE 8

Value of Northrop Grumman offer for TRW at closing of the merger and with $4\frac{1}{2}$ months until closing.

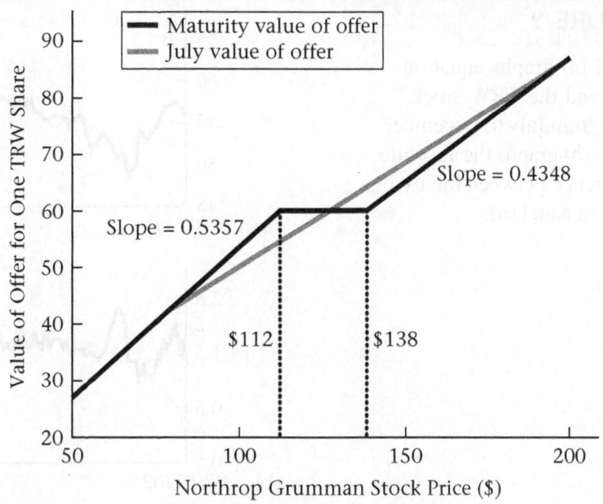

TRW dividends. The time t value of TRW shares would then be

$$0.5357 \times \left[Se^{-\delta(T-t)} - \text{BSCall}(S, 112, \sigma, r, T-t, \delta) \right] + 0.4348 \times \text{BSCall}(S, 138, \sigma, r, T-t, \delta) + \text{PV}_{t,T}(\text{TRW Dividends}) \tag{28}$$

If the exchange ratio had been fixed, then the TRW share would simply be a fractional prepaid forward for Northrop, plus expected TRW dividends over the life of the offer.

Figure 8 graphs the value of the Northrop Grumman offer for one TRW share, as a function of the Northrop Grumman share price. The figure depicts the value of the offer both at closing and assuming there are 5 months to expiration.[23] Because of the structure of the offer, the value of a TRW share could either exceed or be less than the expiration value.

Figure 9 depicts equation (28) using the historical Northrop Grumman stock price from July to December 2002, assuming that the offer would close on December 11.[24] The theoretical value of a TRW share under the terms of the offer is consistently greater than the market price of a TRW share. This is what we would expect to see, since in order to induce the target company to accept an offer, the acquirer generally has to offer a price greater than the perceived value of the target as a stand-alone company. Since there is some chance the merger might not occur, the target share price is below the value of the offer. The difference between the value of a TRW share and the theoretical value of the offer declined toward zero as December approached. Had the merger been cancelled for some reason, the value of a TRW share would have diverged from the value under the terms of the offer.

23. The calculation also assumes a risk-free rate of 1.5%, dividend yield of 1.25%, and volatility of 36%.

24. It was necessary for Northrop Grumman and TRW to receive regulatory approval from European authorities, the U. S. Department of Defense, and the U. S. Department of Justice. Final approval from the Department of Justice was on December 10 and the merger was completed on December 11.

FIGURE 9

Panel (a) graphs equation (27) and the TRW stock price from July to December. Panel (b) graphs the absolute difference between the two lines in panel (a).

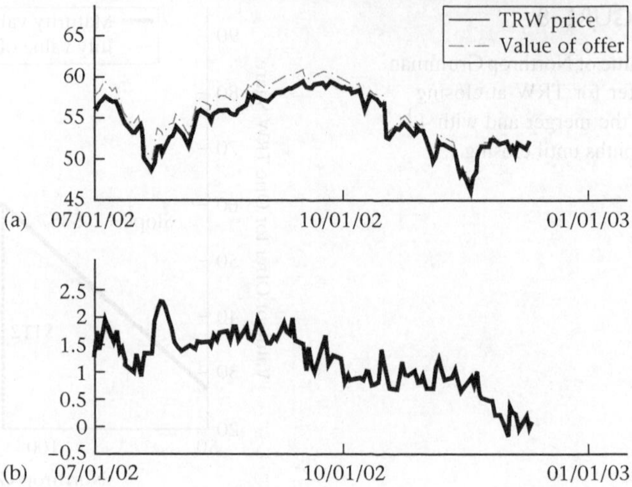

Risk arbitrageurs take positions in the two stocks in order to speculate on the success or failure of the merger.[25] Equation (27) tells us that the offer is equivalent to a portfolio of Northrop shares and options. Thus, using the option replication technique, we can hold Northrop shares and borrowing or lending to synthetically create a position equivalent to the offer. Because the price of TRW is less than the offer value, an arbitrageur speculating that the merger would succeed could then take a long position in TRW shares and a short position in the offer, short-selling delta shares of Northrop. If the offer succeeds, the position earns the difference in price depicted in Figure 9; if the offer fails, the difference should diverge and the arbitrageur would lose money.

CHAPTER SUMMARY

Three corporate contexts in which options appear, either explicitly or implicitly, are capital structure (debt, equity, and warrants), compensation, and acquisitions.

If we view the assets of the firm as being like a stock, then debt and equity can be valued as options with the assets of the firm as the underlying asset. Viewing corporate securities as options provides a natural way to measure bankruptcy risk, and illuminates conflicts between bondholders and stockholders.

Compensation options are an explicit use of options by corporations. They exhibit a variety of complications, some naturally occurring (early exercise decisions by risk-averse employees) and some created by the issuer (repricing, reloads, outperformance, and multipliers). For this reason they provide an interesting context in which to use the exotic pricing formulas.

25. Mitchell and Pulvino (2001) examine the historical returns earned by risk arbitrageurs.

Offers by one firm to purchase another sometimes have embedded collars. The Grumman offer to buy TRW was an example of this.

FURTHER READING

The idea that debt and equity are options was first pointed out by Black and Scholes (1973). Merton (1974, 1977) analyzed the pricing of perpetual debt and demonstrated that the Modigliani-Miller theorem holds even with (costless) bankruptcy. Two principal applications of this idea are the determination of the fair yield on risky debt and the assessment of bankruptcy probabilities. Galai and Masulis (1976) derived the link between the return on assets and the return on the firm's stock.

The Bank of International Settlements in Basel (http://bis.org) is the international body promulgating official recommendations and rules for bank capital and liquidity requirements, and so forth. Papers that discuss issues related to bank capital are Flannery (2005), Admati et al. (2010), and McDonald (2012).

The discussion of warrants and convertible bonds in this chapter assumes that the options are European. With American warrants the optimal exercise strategy can be more complicated than with European options. The reason is that exercise alters the assets of the firm. The problem of optimal American warrant exercise is studied by Emanuel (1983), Constantinides (1984), and Spatt and Sterbenz (1988). McDonald (2004) examines the tax implications of warrant issues, including put warrants. Complications also arise with convertible bonds, which in practice are almost always callable. Thus, valuing a convertible bond requires understanding the call strategy. Classic papers studying the pricing of convertibles include Brennan and Schwartz (1977) and Ingersoll (1977). Harris and Raviv (1985) discuss how asymmetric information affects the decision to call the bond, and Stein (1992) discusses the decision to issue convertibles in the first place. Finally, there is a large empirical literature on the convertible call decision; for example, see Asquith (1995). Güntay et al. (2004) examine the decision to issue callable bonds.

Papers on compensation options include Saly et al. (1999), Johnson and Tian (2000a), and Johnson and Tian (2000b). Repricing is studied by Chance et al. (2000) and Acharya et al. (2000). Petrie (2000) examines the use of collars in acquisitions.

PROBLEMS

For all problems, unless otherwise stated assume that the firm has assets worth $A = \$100$, and that $\sigma = 30\%$, $r = 8\%$, and the firm makes no payouts prior to the maturity date of the debt.

1. There is a single debt issue with a maturity value of \$120. Compute the yield on this debt assuming that it matures in 1 year, 2 years, 5 years, or 10 years. What debt-to-equity ratio do you observe in each case?

2. There is a single debt issue. Compute the yield on this debt assuming that it matures in 1 year and has a maturity value of \$127.42, 2 years with a maturity value of \$135.30, 5 years with a maturity value of \$161.98, or 10 years with a maturity value of \$218.65. (The maturity value increases with maturity at a 6% rate.) What debt-to-equity ratio do you observe in each case?

3. There are four debt issues with different priorities, each promising $30 at maturity.

   a. Compute the yield on each debt issue assuming that all four mature in 1 year, 2 years, 5 years, or 10 years.

   b. Assuming that each debt issue matures in 5 years, what happens to the yield on each when you vary σ? When you vary r?

4. Suppose there is a single 5-year zero-coupon debt issue with a maturity value of $120. The expected return on assets is 12%. What is the expected return on equity? The volatility of equity? What happens to the expected return on equity as you vary A, σ, and r?

5. Repeat the previous problem for debt instead of equity.

6. In this problem we examine the effect of changing the assumptions in Example 1.

   a. Compute the yield on debt for asset values of $50, $100, $150, $200, and $500. How does the yield on debt change with the value of assets?

   b. Compute the yield on debt for asset volatilities of 10% through 100%, in increments of 5%.

For the next three problems, assume that a firm has assets of $100 and 5-year-to-maturity zero-coupon debt with a face value of $150. Assume that investment projects have the same volatility as existing assets.

7. The firm is considering an investment project costing $1. What is the amount by which the project's value must exceed its cost in order for shareholders to be willing to pay for it? Repeat for project values of $10 and $25.

8. Now suppose the firm finances the project by issuing debt that has *lower* priority than existing debt. How much must a $1, $10, or $25 project be worth if the shareholders are willing to fund it?

9. Now suppose the firm finances the project by issuing debt that has *higher* priority than existing debt. How much must a $10 or $25 project be worth if the shareholders are willing to fund it?

10. Assume there are 20 shares outstanding. Compute the value of the warrant and the share price for each of the following situations.

   a. Warrants for 2 shares expire in 5 years and have a strike price of $15.

   b. Warrants for 15 shares expire in 10 years and have a strike of $20.

11. A firm has outstanding a bond with a 5-year maturity and maturity value of $50, convertible into 10 shares. There are also 20 shares outstanding. What is the price of the warrant? The share price? Suppose you were to compute the value of the convertible as a risk-free bond plus an option, valued using the Black-Scholes formula and the share price you computed. How accurate is this?

12. Suppose a firm has 20 shares of equity, a 10-year zero-coupon debt with a maturity value of $200, and warrants for 8 shares with a strike price of $25. What is the value of the debt, the share price, and the price of the warrant?

13. Suppose a firm has 20 shares of equity and a 10-year zero-coupon convertible bond with a maturity value of \$200, convertible into 8 shares. What is the value of the debt, the share price, and the price of the warrant?

14. Using the assumptions of Example 4, and the stock price derived in Example 5 suppose you were to perform a "naive" valuation of the convertible as a risk-free bond plus 50 call options on the stock. How does the price you compute compare with that computed in Example 5?

15. Consider Panels B and D in Figure 4. Using the information in each panel, compute the share price at each node for each bond issue.

16. As discussed in the text, compensation options are prematurely exercised or canceled for a variety of reasons. Suppose that compensation options both vest and expire in 3 years and that the probability is 10% that the executive will die in year 1 and 10% in year 2. Thus, the probability that the executive lives to expiration is 80%. Suppose that the stock price is \$100, the interest rate is 8%, the volatility is 30%, and the dividend yield is 0.

a. Value the option by computing the expected time to exercise and plugging this into the Black-Scholes formula as time to maturity.

b. Compute the expected value of the option given the different possible times until exercise.

c. Why are the answers for the two calculations different?

17. XYZ Corp. compensates executives with 10-year European call options, granted at the money. If there is a significant drop in the share price, the company's board will reset the strike price of the options to equal the new share price. The maturity of the repriced option will equal the remaining maturity of the original option. Suppose that $\sigma = 30\%$, $r = 6\%$, $\delta = 0$, and that the original share price is \$100.

a. What is the value at grant of an option that will not be repriced?

b. What is the value at grant of an option that is repriced when the share price reaches \$60?

c. What repricing trigger maximizes the initial value of the option?

18. Suppose that top executives of XYZ are told they will receive at-the-money call options on 10,000 shares each year for the next 3 years. When granted, the options have 5 years to maturity. XYZ's stock price is \$100, volatility is 30%, and $r = 8\%$. Estimate the value of this promise.

19. Suppose that $S = \$100$, $\sigma = 30\%$, $r = 6\%$, $t = 1$, and $\delta = 0$. XYZ writes a European put option on one share with strike price $K = \$90$.

a. Construct a two-period binomial tree for the stock and price the put. Compute the replicating portfolio at each node.

b. If the firm were synthetically creating the put (i.e., trading to obtain the same cash flows as if it issued the put), what transactions would it undertake?

c. Consider the bank that buys the put. What transactions does it undertake to hedge the transaction?

d. Why might a firm prefer to issue the put warrant instead of borrowing and repurchasing shares?

20. Firm A has a stock price of \$40 and has made an offer for firm B where A promises to pay \$60/share for B, as long as A's stock price remains between \$35 and \$45. If the price of A is below \$35, A will pay 1.714 shares, and if the price of A is above \$45, A will pay 1.333 shares. The deal is expected to close in 9 months. Assume $\sigma = 40\%$, $r = 6\%$, and $\delta = 0$.

a. How are the values 1.714 and 1.333 arrived at?

b. What is the value of the offer?

c. How sensitive is the value of the offer to the volatility of A's stock?

21. Firm A has a stock price of \$40, and has made an offer for firm B where A promises to pay 1.5 shares for each share of B, as long as A's stock price remains between \$35 and \$45. If the price of A is below \$35, A will pay \$52.50/share, and if the price of A is above \$45, A will pay \$67.50/share. The deal is expected to close in 9 months. Assume $\sigma = 40\%$, $r = 6\%$, and $\delta = 0$.

a. How are the values \$52.50 and \$67.50 arrived at?

b. What is the value of the offer?

c. How does the value of this offer compare with that in Problem 20?

22. The strike price of a compensation option is generally set on the day the option is issued. On November 10, 2000, the CEO of Analog Devices, Jerald Fishman, received 600,000 options. The stock price was \$44.50. Four days later, the price rose to \$63.25 after an earnings release:

> Maria Tagliaferro of Analog said the timing of the two events [option grant and earnings release] is irrelevant because company policy is that no option vests until at least three years from its granting date. "What happens to the stock price in the day, the hour, the year the option is granted is not relevant to that option," she said. "The stock price only becomes relevant after that option has vested."[26]

In its annual report for 2000, Analog Devices reported that the expected life of its options granted that year was 4.9 years, with a 56.6% volatility and 6% risk-free rate. The company paid no dividends until 2003.

a. Using the inputs from the annual report, and assuming no dividends, estimate the value to the CEO of an at-the-money option grant at a stock price of \$44.50.

b. Estimate the value of an at-the-money grant at a price of \$63.25.

c. Estimate the value of a newly granted option at a strike of \$44.50 when the stock price is \$63.25.

d. Do you agree with Maria Tagliaferro? Why or why not?

---

26. See "SEC Probes Analog Devices' Options," *Wall Street Journal*, December 2, 2004, p. B6.

23. Four years after the option grant, the stock price for Analog Devices was about \$40. Using the same input as in the previous problem, compute the market value of the options granted in 2000, assuming that they were issued at strikes of \$44.50 and \$63.25.

24. Suppose that a firm offers a 3-year compensation option that vests immediately. An employee who resigns has two years to decide whether to exercise the option. Compute annual compensation option expense using the stock price tree in the example in Appendix A. Verify that the present value of the option deductions is \$28.15.

Appendix A AN ALTERNATIVE APPROACH TO EXPENSING OPTION GRANTS

Appendix available at http://www.pearsonhighered.com/mcdonald.

Real Options

Although financial assets are important, many of the most important decisions that firms make concern *real assets*, a term that broadly encompasses factories, mines, office buildings, research and development, and other nonfinancial firm assets. In this chapter we will see that it is possible to analyze investment and operating decisions for real assets using various pricing models for financial options.

To illustrate how it can be possible to evaluate an investment decision as an option, consider a firm that is deciding whether or not to build a factory. Compare the following two descriptions:

- A *call option* is the right to pay a *strike price* to receive the present value of a stream of future cash flows (represented by the *price of the underlying asset*).
- An *investment project* is the right to pay an *investment cost* to receive the present value of a stream of future cash flows (represented by the *present value of the project*).

Do you notice the similarities in these two statements? We have

Investment Project		Call Option
Investment cost	=	Strike price
Present value of project	=	Price of underlying asset

This comparison suggests that we can view any investment project as a call option, with the investment cost equal to the strike price and the present value of cash flows equal to the asset price. The exploitation of this and other analogies between real investment projects and financial options has come to be called **real options**, which we define as the application of derivatives theory to the operation and valuation of real investment projects. Note the phrase "operation *and* valuation." We will see in this chapter that you cannot value a real asset without also understanding how you will operate it. You cannot value any option without understanding when you will exercise it.

1. INVESTMENT AND THE NPV RULE

We first consider a simple investment decision of the sort you would encounter in a basic finance course when studying net present value (NPV). Despite its simplicity, the example illustrates the issues that will arise again later in this chapter.

From Chapter 17 of *Derivatives Markets*, Third Edition, Robert McDonald. Copyright © 2013 by Pearson Education, Inc. Published by Pearson Prentice Hall. All rights reserved.

Suppose we can invest in a machine, costing \$10, that will produce one widget a year forever. In addition, each widget costs \$0.90 to produce. The price of widgets will be \$0.55 next year and will increase at 4% per year. The effective annual risk-free rate is 5% per year. We can invest, at any time, in one such machine. There is no uncertainty.

Before reading further, you should try to answer this question: What is the most you would pay to acquire the rights to this project?

Static NPV

A natural first step is to compute the NPV if we invested in the project today. We obtain

$$\begin{aligned} \text{NPV}_{\text{Invest today}} &= \$0.55 \times \left(\frac{1}{1.05} + \frac{1.04}{1.05^2} + \frac{1.04^2}{1.05^3} + \cdots \right) \\ &\quad - \$0.9 \times \left(\frac{1}{1.05} + \frac{1}{1.05^2} + \frac{1}{1.05^3} + \cdots \right) - \$10 \\ &= \frac{\$0.55}{1.04} \times \left(\frac{1}{\frac{1.05}{1.04} - 1} \right) - \frac{\$0.9}{0.05} - \$10 = \frac{\$0.55}{0.01} - \$28 = \$27 \end{aligned} \tag{1}$$

This calculation tells us that if widget production were to start next year, we would pay \$27 for the project. For reasons that will become obvious, we call this the project's **static NPV**.

Notice that in the early years, the project has an operating loss. If we activate the project today, then next year we will have negative operating cash flows, spending \$0.90 to produce a \$0.55 widget. In addition, at a 5% rate of interest, the opportunity cost of the \$10 investment is \$0.50/year.

Why is NPV positive if we will be producing at a loss? Although the initial cash flows are negative, the widget price is growing. The project *will become* profitable in the future. This eventual profitability is why NPV is positive. This analysis suggests that we might consider waiting until later to invest.

Suppose we wait 5 years to invest instead of investing immediately. NPV is then

$$\begin{aligned} \text{NPV}_{\text{Wait 5 years}} &= \frac{1}{1.05^5} \left[(1.04)^5 \frac{\$0.55}{0.01} - \$28 \right] \\ &= \$30.49 \end{aligned}$$

Thus, it is better to wait 5 years than to invest today. What is the maximum NPV we can attain?

Common sense points to an approximate answer: We should not invest until annual widget revenue covers marginal production cost (\$0.90) plus the opportunity cost of the project (\$0.50); i.e., cost is at least \$1.40. The widget price will be \$1.40 when n satisfies

$$(1 + .04)^n 0.55 = 1.40$$

Solving for n gives us $n = 23.82$.[1] After 23.82 years, the widget price will have reached a break-even level. The value today of waiting that long to invest in the project is

---

1. The price must increase by a factor of 1.40/0.55 to reach \$1.40, so we have $\ln(1.40/0.55) / \ln(1.04) = 23.82$.

$$\left[\frac{(1.04)^{23.82}\$0.55}{0.01} - \frac{\$0.90}{0.05} - \$10\right]\frac{1}{(1+0.05)^{23.82}} = \$35.03$$

Problem 4 asks you to verify this result. You will discover that 23.82 years is not exactly optimal. Rather, waiting approximately 24.32 years—not 23.82 years—maximizes NPV. At this point the widget price will be about $1.43.

We will see the reason for this slight difference in Section 4. It occurs because the effective annual interest and growth rates of 5% and 4% are not the relevant rates since the decision to put off the investment is made on a day-to-day basis. It is instead the equivalent *continuously compounded* rates that matter.

This example demonstrates the important point that making an investment decision requires thinking carefully about alternatives, even under certainty.

We are left with (at least) two questions:

- How do we approach this kind of problem in general?
- Why didn't the NPV rule work? Or did it?

The Correct Use of NPV

The NPV rule worked correctly in the above example. The NPV rule for making investment decisions entails two steps:

1. Compute NPV by discounting expected cash flows at the opportunity cost of capital.
2. Accept a project if and only if its NPV is positive *and it exceeds the NPV of all mutually exclusive alternative projects.*[2]

When we computed the widget machine's NPV in equation (1), we neglected to take into account the NPV of alternative mutually exclusive projects, namely investing in the project tomorrow or at some other future date. Static NPV—NPV if we accept the project today—ignores project delay. Because static NPV measures the value of an action we could take, namely investing today, it at least provides a lower bound on the value of the project.

In this example it would be correct to invest in the project today *if not activating the project today meant that we would lose it forever.* Under this assumption, the mutually exclusive alternative (never taking the project) has a value of 0, so taking it today would be correct.

To decide whether and when to invest in an arbitrary project, we need to be able to compute the value of delaying that investment. As suggested at the start of the chapter, option pricing theory can help us to value delay.

The Project as an Option

The decision to invest in the project involves a comparison of net present values. In what sense is this an option?

We can interpret equation (1) so as to make the option analogy more apparent. When we take the project, we pay $10 and we commit to paying $0.90/year forever. The present

2. Introductory finance textbooks state the NPV rule correctly, but in casual discussions it is sometimes stated incorrectly.

value of this stream of costs is

$$\text{Present value of costs} = \$10 + \frac{\$0.90}{0.05} = \$28$$

As we discussed earlier, we can view this present value as analogous to the exercise price in an option valuation. In return for paying \$28, we receive a cash flow with a present value of

$$\text{Present value of widget revenue} = \frac{S_{+1}}{0.01}$$

where S_{+1} is the widget price the year after we make the investment. When $S_{+1} = \$0.55$, the present value of cash flow is \$55. This present value of widget revenue is the price the revenue stream would have if it were traded separately. It is analogous to the stock price in an option valuation, and therefore it is sometimes called the **twin security** or the **traded present value** of the project.

The dividends forgone by not acquiring the asset today, the interest saved by deferring the payment of the strike price, and the value of the insurance that is lost by exercising the option. It turns out that the same three considerations govern the decision to invest in the widget project.

First, by delaying investment, we lose the cash flow from selling widgets. The cash flow we do not receive is analogous to stock dividends we do not receive by holding an option rather than the underlying stock. The first period cash flow is \$0.55. The present value of future cash flows is \$0.55/0.01 = \$55. Thus, the dividend yield is approximately 1%. (We can also think of the dividend yield as the difference between the discount rate [5%] and the growth rate of the cash flows [4%].)

Second, once we begin widget production, we are committed to spending the present value of the marginal widget cost, \$18, along with the \$10 initial investment. The annual value of delaying investment is interest on the total investment cost, or $0.05 \times \$28 = \$1.40$ per year.

Third and finally, in the widget project, there is no uncertainty and therefore no insurance value to delaying investment.

We can compute the value of the widget project option using the perpetual call calculation. The formula assumes continuously compounded rates, so for the interest rate we use $\ln(1.05) = 4.879\%$, and for the dividend yield we use the difference between the continuously compounded interest rate and growth rate, or $\ln(1.05) - \ln(1.04) = 0.9569\%$.

With $S = \$55$ (the present value of revenue), $K = \$28$ (the present value of costs), $r = 0.04879$, $\sigma = 0$,[3] and $\delta = 0.009569$, the equation $(H_c - K)\left(\frac{S}{H_c}\right)^{h_1}$ gives an option price of \$35.03 and investment when the widget price equals \$1.4276. We will call this price the **investment trigger price**. We reach this price after about 24.32 years, which verifies the answer we discussed earlier.

The example in this section illustrates the importance of thinking dynamically about a project and shows how this specific problem can be modeled as an option.

3. It is necessary to set σ to a small positive number such as 0.00001 to avoid a zero-divide error.

2. INVESTMENT UNDER UNCERTAINTY

In this section we discuss the valuation of real investment projects when cash flows are uncertain. With the widget project in the previous section, waiting to invest was optimal because project dividends were initially less than the interest gained from deferring the project. If we add uncertainty about project cash flows, the value of insurance (the implicit put option) also influences the decision to delay the project. In such a case, waiting to invest provides information about the value of the project. In this section we will use a binomial tree to value a project with uncertain cash flows.

As before, the decision to invest in such a project is like exercising an American option: We pay the investment cost (strike price) to receive the asset (present value of future cash flows).

A Simple DCF Problem

We first examine a particularly simple valuation problem in order to better understand the link between discounted cash flow (DCF), real options, and financial options.

Suppose an analyst is evaluating a project that will generate a single cash flow, X, occurring at time T. As with many investment projects, it is not possible to observe market characteristics of the project. There is no way to directly estimate project returns, project volatility, or the covariances of the project with the stock market. Instead, suppose the analyst considers the economic fundamentals of the project and makes educated inferences about these characteristics. The analyst might also look for public firms with a business resembling the project. The analyst could then use information about these public firms to infer characteristics (such as beta) of the project.

After examining all available data, the analyst estimates that the cash flow will be X_u if the economy is doing well—an event with the probability p—and X_d if the economy is doing poorly. The project requires expenditures of I_0 at time 0 and I_T at time T. The analyst determines that projects with comparable risk have an effective annual expected rate of return of α.

We can use this description to compute the value of the project, V. The standard discounted cash flow methodology calls for computing the expected cash flow, and using as a discount rate the expected return on a project of comparable risk:

$$V = \frac{pX_u + (1-p)X_d}{(1+\alpha)^T} \tag{2}$$

Assuming that we either take the project now or never, we invest in the project if $V \geq I_0 + I_T/(1+r)^T$.

Example 1. Suppose that the risk-free rate is $r = 6\%$, the expected return on the market is $r_M = 10\%$, the project beta is $\beta = 1.25$, $p = 0.60$, $T = 1$, $X_u = \$120$, and $X_d = \$80$. The expected return on an asset with the same risk as the project is

$$\alpha = 0.06 + 1.25 \times (0.10 - 0.06) = 0.11$$

The expected cash flow is

$$E(X) = 0.60 \times \$120 + 0.40 \times \$80 = \$104$$

Using (2), the present value of the project cash flows is

$$V = \frac{\$104}{1+0.11} = \$93.694$$

Suppose that $I_0 = \$10$ and $I_1 = \$95$ and that the manager commits at time 0 to paying the \$95 at time 1. Then net present value is

$$\begin{aligned} V - I_0 - I_1/(1+r) &= 93.694 - \$10 - \$95/1.06 \\ &= -\$5.929 \quad \blacksquare \end{aligned}$$

Valuing Derivatives on the Cash Flow

The calculation in Example 1 is standard but it is nevertheless based on strong assumptions: We have specified the future cash flows in different states, the probabilities of those states, and the comparability of the project to a traded asset.[4] It turns out that in valuing the project *we have already made all the assumptions we need to make in order to value derivatives related to the project*.

To see how to perform capital budgeting calculations involving options, suppose that if we invest I_0 to start the project, the subsequent investment of I_1 is optional: We make this further investment only if the project at time 1 has sufficient value. Since the project has a good and bad outcome, it is natural to think about using binomial option valuation. In order to do so, we need to know the risk-neutral probability of the high outcome.[5]

Fortunately, we can easily compute risk-neutral probabilities for this project. The expected risk-neutral price is the forward price. We have computed V, which is the price of an asset paying a single cash flow at time T. The forward price is

$$F_{0,T} = V(1+r)^T$$

The risk-neutral probability must therefore satisfy

$$p^* X_u + (1-p^*) X_d = F_{0,T}$$

Thus, we have

$$p^* = \frac{F_{0,T} - X_d}{X_u - X_d}$$

This gives us the binomial tree (X_u and X_d) and the risk-neutral probability of a high outcome (p^*). Notice that if we value the project using the risk-neutral distribution, then *by construction* we will obtain the original project value, V.

4. The last assumption in particular deserves some additional comment. We are assuming that the returns of the project are *spanned* by existing traded assets; in other words, the addition of the project to the universe of assets does not materially change the opportunities available to investors. If this were not true, we would have to know more about the preferences of investors in order to evaluate the project.

5. In general we also need to know volatility to value an option. Volatility determines the vertical *distance* between binomial nodes. Thus, in specifying the tree, we implicitly specified volatility.

Example 2. Consider the same parameters as in Example 1. The forward price for the project is

$$F_{0,1} = \$93.694 \times (1.06) = \$99.315$$

The risk-neutral probability of the good outcome is

$$p^* = \frac{99.315 - 80}{120 - 80} = 0.4829$$

If we value the project using the risk-neutral probability, we obtain

$$\frac{0.4829 \times \$120 + (1 - 0.4829) \times \$80}{1.06} = \$93.694$$

Now make the same assumptions as in Example 1, except that we decide at time 1 whether to incur the \$95 cost. We will choose to produce output in time 1 only when the cash flow is \$120, since we would lose \$15 by paying \$95 to produce when the output sells for \$80. The value of the project is

$$\frac{p^* \max[0, X_u - I_1] + (1 - p^*) \max[0, X_L - I_1]}{1 + r} - I_0$$

$$= \frac{0.4829 \times \$25 + (1 - 0.4829) \times 0}{1.06} - \$10 = \$1.389 \blacksquare$$

Given the risk-neutral probability and the cash flow distribution, we can value projects with options or other nonlinear cash flows.[6]

You may be thinking that there appears to be little difference between standard discounted cash flow valuation and real options valuation. Recognize that *any* financial valuation entails assigning a dollar value today to a (possibly uncertain) cash flow that occurs in the future. This description applies to the valuation of a project, as well as to valuing a bond, a stock, or an option.

When we value an option on a stock, we rely on the market to have already performed part of the valuation—namely, valuing the stock. When we value an option on a project, we have to estimate the value of the project since we cannot observe it. *This is true whether or not the project contains options.*

This discussion illustrates the point that risk-neutral pricing and discounted cash flow are alternative means of valuing a future cash flow. If done using the same assumptions, the two methods give the same answer. In practice, of course, it is common to make simplifying assumptions for tractability. Answers may differ because the simplifying assumptions for different valuation methods are inconsistent.

Evaluating a Project with a 2-Year Investment Horizon

We now consider the problem of when to invest in a risky project. As before, the decision to invest in such a project is like exercising an American option: We pay the investment cost

6. Problem 9 asks you to value a project paying the squared cash flow.

(strike price) to receive the asset (present value of future cash flows). The widget project in the previous section had cash flows that were certain.

Suppose a project costs \$100 and begins producing an infinite stream of cash flows 1 year after investment. Expected annual cash flows for the first year are \$18, and are expected to grow annually at a rate of 3%. Suppose further that the risk-free rate is 7%, the risk premium on the market is 6%, and the beta of the project is 1.33. Using the Capital Asset Pricing Model (CAPM), we compute the discount rate for the project in the usual way:

$$\begin{aligned} r_{\text{project}} &= r_{\text{risk-free}} + \beta(r_{\text{market}} - r_{\text{risk-free}}) \\ &= 0.07 + 1.33(0.06) \\ &= 0.15 \end{aligned}$$

To value the project, we perform a standard discounted cash flow calculation. Since the project lives forever, we treat it as a perpetual growing annuity. The present value is

$$\begin{aligned} \text{PV} &= \frac{\text{E}(\text{CF}_1)}{r_{\text{project}} - \text{growth rate}} \\ &= \frac{\$18}{0.15 - 0.03} \\ &= \$150 \end{aligned}$$

Static NPV is therefore \$150 − \$100 = \$50.

Suppose we have 2 years in which to decide whether to accept the project; at the end of that time, we either invest in the project or lose it. (Imagine, for example, that the licensing rights for a technology will revert at that time to the original owner.) The static NPV rule will apply after 2 years because further deferral is not possible. However, at time 0, we must evaluate the option to wait.

The forgone initial cash flow (the dividend on the project) is \$18 and the interest saving is \$7 (7% × 100). Thus, considering only dividends and interest, it makes sense to start the project immediately. However, the project also has implicit insurance that we lose by investing in the project. To value the insurance we need to know the project volatility.

A Tree for Project Value. Suppose that cash flows are lognormally distributed with a 50% volatility. Figure 1 uses the Cox-Ross-Rubinstein approach to construct a binomial tree for the evolution of cash flows with a binomial period of 1 year. If we wait to take the project, initial cash flows in 1 year will be either $\$18e^{0.5} = \$29.677$ or $\$18e^{-0.5} = \$10.918$. Since the project value is proportional to cash flows, the value of the project is also lognormally distributed with a 50% volatility.

In 1 year, project value will be either \$29.677/(0.15 − 0.03) = \$247.31 or \$10.918/(0.15 − 0.03) = \$91. If we will continue to learn about the project at the same rate over time, we can build a binomial tree with constant volatility that shows the evolution of project value. This tree, constructed by discounting at each node the cash flows in Figure 1, is in Figure 2.

Figure 2 describes the evolution of the project's present value. The project does not exist prior to investment, but the tree provides the information we need in order to decide whether to invest. The tree in Figure 2 is exactly the same tree we would construct for the stock price of a company that had the project as its only asset and that paid dividends equal to the cash flow of the project. Such a stock would have an initial price of \$150 and a 50% volatility.

FIGURE 1

Binomial tree for project cash flows, assuming binomial distribution with 50% volatility.

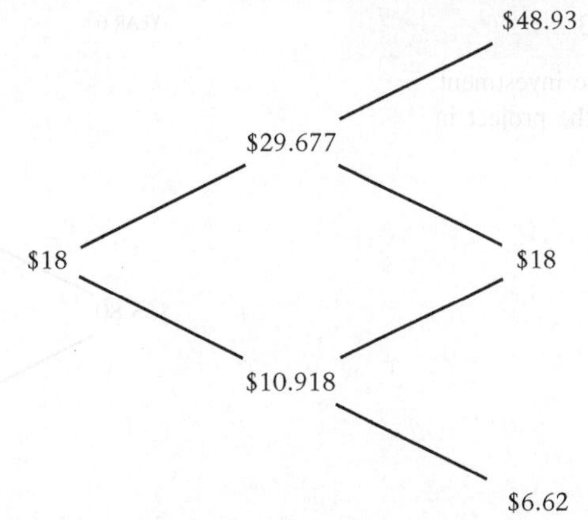

FIGURE 2

Binomial tree for project value, assuming 50% volatility. The value at each node is the project value if investment occurs at that node.

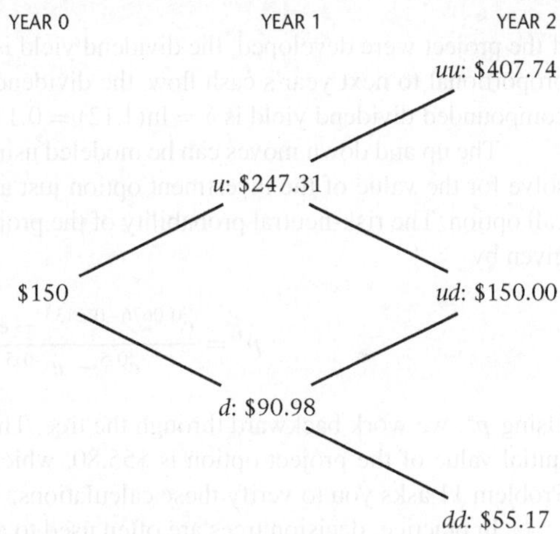

It may trouble you that in valuing this project, option pricing formulas are being used in a context where literal replication of the option is not possible because the twin security does not exist. *The binomial procedure also works in a setting where we perform valuation using the CAPM or other pricing model.* Thus, we are using option pricing formulas to create *fair prices*, not *arbitrage-free* prices.

Solving for the Optimal Investment Decision. We can use Figure 2 to solve the investment problem exactly as we would use it in a binomial option pricing problem. The inputs are initial project value, $S = \$150$; investment cost, $K = \$100$; continuously compounded risk-free rate, $r = \ln(1.07) = 6.766\%$; volatility, $\sigma = 0.50$; and time to expiration, $t = 2$ years. Since the market value of the project today is $150 and the cash flow in a year would be $18

FIGURE 3

Value of the investment option for the project in Figure 2.

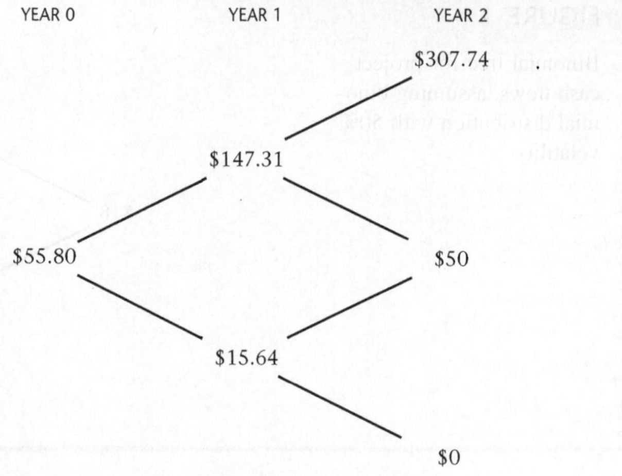

if the project were developed, the dividend yield is 12% (\$18/\$150). Since project value is proportional to next year's cash flow, the dividend yield never changes. The continuously compounded dividend yield is $\delta = \ln(1.12) = 0.1133$.

The up and down moves can be modeled using any of the binomial trees. We can then solve for the value of the investment option just as we solve for the price of an American call option. The risk-neutral probability of the project value increasing in any period, p^*, is given by

$$p^* = \frac{e^{0.0676-0.1133} - e^{-0.5}}{e^{0.5} - e^{-0.5}} = 0.335$$

Using p^*, we work backward through the tree. The results are in Figure 3. Notice that the initial value of the project option is \$55.80, which is greater than the static NPV of \$50. Problem 11 asks you to verify these calculations.

In practice, decision trees are often used to analyze this kind of problem. Figure 2—like any binomial option problem—*is* a decision tree, albeit with probabilities and nodes constructed in a very particular way. If the discount rate applicable to the underlying asset is constant, then when valuing an option using true probabilities, the correct discount rate varies across the nodes of the tree. Analysts using a decision tree often use true (not risk-neutral) probabilities and a constant discount rate along the tree.[7] Binomial pricing per se does not imply that any particular true expected return is constant; instead, it tells us how to perform valuation so that the assumptions about the project and the assumptions about the tree are consistent with each other.

7. This is not necessarily incorrect; as a logical matter, a constant discount rate for the option could be correct *if* the tree for the underlying asset had discount rates that varied across the nodes. However, in decision tree analysis in practice, the issue of discount rate determination is often glossed over.

Evaluating the Project with an Infinite Investment Horizon

The above example assumes that we must start the project by year 2 and that we evaluate it annually. Suppose instead that the project can be started at any time and then will live forever. The project is then a perpetual call option that we can evaluate using the perpetual option pricing formula. Using continuously compounded inputs, we compute

$$\text{CallPerpetual}(\$150, \$100, 0.50, 0.0676, 0.1133) = \{\$63.396, \$245.71\}$$

When the project value is \$150, the option value is \$63.396 and the optimal investment trigger is \$245.71. In other words, we invest when the project is worth \$245.71, more than twice the investment cost. If we invest immediately, the project is worth \$50. The ability to wait increases that value by \$13.396.

3. REAL OPTIONS IN PRACTICE

Real investment decisions often have optionlike features. Consider the following:

1. The decision about whether and when to invest in investment projects.
2. The ability to shut down, restart, and permanently abandon projects.
3. The ability to invest in projects that may give rise to future options.
4. The ability to be flexible in the future about the choice of inputs, outputs, or production technologies.

We have already discussed the first—an investment project is a call option. We can view the ability to shut down a money-losing project (item 2 in the list above) as having the project plus a put option—an insurance policy to protect against even greater losses. The ability to invest in a way that gives rise to future investment options (item 3, sometimes called "strategic options") should remind you of a compound option (an option to buy an option). So-called flexibility options (item 4) are analogous to a type of exotic option called a rainbow option.

Despite the many similarities between real options and financial options, there is usually no simple and straightforward way to make real-life investment problems fit an option pricing formula. As with any valuation problem, it is necessary to analyze the specific problem. In this section, we look at two examples that use option analysis to value assets: peak-load electricity generation and pharmaceutical research and development. Box 1 describes an investment problem at Intel that was similar to a peak-load problem.

Peak-Load Electricity Generation[8]

Electricity forward prices can vary over the course of a day. They also vary seasonally: In the United States, electricity forward prices are high in the summer and low in the winter. In addition to this predictable variation, electricity prices can be volatile. On extremely hot days, for example, prices can spike to 100 times their average price.

8. I thank David Moore of El Paso Corporation for helpful discussions and for providing representative data.

BOX 1: Peak-Load Manufacturing at Intel

Manufacturers investing in production capacity and facing uncertain demand experience the same peak-load production problem as electricity producers. Consider a manufacturer investing in production capacity and facing uncertain demand. How should the manufacturer choose plant capacity? Consider choosing the plant's capacity to meet expected demand. If demand turns out to be less than forecast, the firm will either produce at a loss or have an idle plant. If demand is greater, the firm will forgo revenue. If it is necessary to produce whether demand is high or low, then extra capacity has no option value. However, if it is possible to idle an unused plant when demand is low, then *extra production capacity is like a peak-load facility*. The extra capacity gives the firm a call option.

Intel in 1997 had to decide upon the capacity of a new plant. Semiconductor fabrication facilities ("fabs") cost about \$2 billion and take 2 years to construct, 1 year for the shell—the building—and 1 year for the equipment. The shell cost was about \$350 million, with the rest reflecting equipment cost.

Intel analysts proposed building a shell 1 year ahead of schedule. If demand were high, the firm would be able to install equipment a year early and earn an extra year of revenue. If demand were low, the firm would maintain the building until needed, which was relatively inexpensive.

The planners sought to persuade senior management that early construction of a shell provided benefits. Intel analysts developed a simple binomial model that illustrated the costs and benefits of early construction. They verified that the Black-Scholes formula gave approximately the same option value. Intel then built the shell 1 year early.

A peak-load plant, as the name suggests, produces only when it is profitable to do so, exploiting spikes in the price of electricity. Such plants are designed so that they can be idled when the price of electricity is less than the cost of fuel, but they can be quickly brought online to produce power when the price of electricity is high or when the price of fuel declines. Because it is turned on only when profitable, owning a peak-load plant is like owning a strip of call options, with options maturing daily.[9] The underlying asset is electricity. The strike price is the cost of inputs required to produce a unit of electricity, including the cost of the fuel—typically natural gas—and other variable costs associated with operating the plant.[10] The **heat rate**, H, of a plant is the efficiency with which it turns gas into electricity (the number of MMBtus required to produce a megawatt hour (MWh)).[11]

For the moment, let's consider only electricity and gas prices, and assume that we can ignore distribution costs and marginal operating, maintenance, and other costs. Then

9. Operators will think not only about day-to-day operations, but hour-to-hour as well, since a plant may be operated during the day and not at night.

10. In practice, the term "strike price" is sometimes used to refer only to nongas variable costs.

11. The definition of heat rate is the number of BTUs required to produce 1 kilowatt/hour of electricity. The heat rate times 1000 is the number of British Thermal Units (BTUs) to produce 1 MWh. For example, if the heat rate is 9000, then $9000 \times 1000 = 9$ m BTUs is required to produce 1 megawatt/hour of electricity. If the price of natural gas is \$3/MMBtu, then the gas cost of producing 1 MWh of electricity is \$27.

FIGURE 4

Forward price (top panel) and volatility (middle panel) curves for electricity and natural gas. The bottom panel depicts the spark spread implied by the forward price curves, assuming a heat rate of 9000.

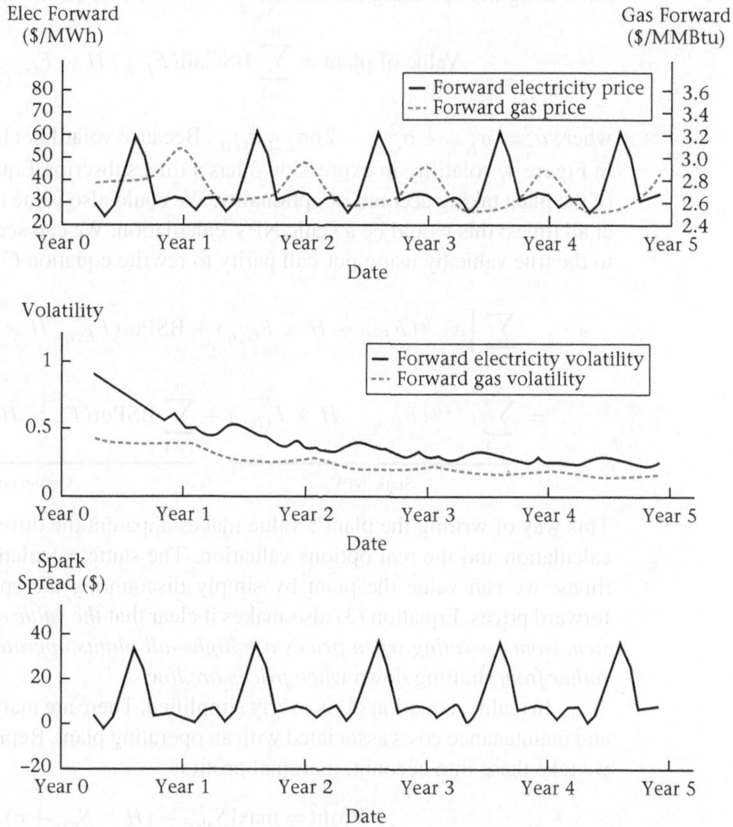

the profit of the plant is

$$\text{Profit} = \max(S_{\text{elec}} - H \times S_{\text{gas}}, 0)$$

This is the payoff to a European exchange option. The difference between the price of electricity and the cost of generation, $S_{\text{elec}} - H \times S_{\text{gas}}$, is called the **spark spread**. There are operating costs besides gas, but the spark spread is the variable component of marginal profit.

In order to value the option we need forward prices and volatilities for electricity and gas and the correlation between the two. The top panel in Figure 4 shows representative forward curves for electricity and gas. The price curve for gas has a shape that exhibits seasonal winter peaks. The electricity curve, by contrast, exhibits summer peaks. The bottom panel shows the spark spread implied by the prices in the first panel.

The value of a plant is the sum of the operating options it provides. Let F_{E,t_i} and F_{G,t_i} represent the time 0 forward prices for electricity and gas delivered at time t_i. If we ignore other marginal operating costs, then the value of the operating plant is[12]

$$\text{Value of plant} = \sum_{i=1}^{n} \text{BSCall}(F_{E,t_i}, H \times F_{G,t_i}, \hat{\sigma}_{t_i}, r, t_i, r) \tag{3}$$

where $\hat{\sigma}_{t_i}^2 = \sigma_{E,t_i}^2 + \sigma_{G,t_i}^2 - 2\rho\sigma_{E,t_i}\sigma_{G,t_i}$. Because volatility changes with the time horizon in Figure 4, volatility in expression 3 has a time subscript. Equation (3) provides the value of the plant taking account of optionality. We could also value the plant assuming operation at all times; this would be a static NPV calculation. We can see how the static value relates to the true value by using put-call parity to rewrite equation (3):

$$\sum_{i=1}^{n} \left[e^{-rt_i}(F_{E,t_i} - H \times F_{G,t_i}) + \text{BSPut}(F_{E,t_i}, H \times F_{G,t_i}, \hat{\sigma}_{t_i}, r, t_i, r) \right] \tag{4}$$

$$= \underbrace{\sum_{i=1}^{n} e^{-rt_i}(F_{E,t_i} - H \times F_{G,t_i})}_{\text{Static NPV}} + \underbrace{\sum_{i=1}^{n} \text{BSPut}(F_{E,t_i}, H \times F_{G,t_i}, \hat{\sigma}_{t_i}, r, t_i, r)}_{\text{Option not to operate}}$$

This way of writing the plant's value makes apparent the difference between a static NPV calculation and the real options valuation. The static calculation assumes operation at all times; we can value the plant by simply discounting the spark spread computed using forward prices. Equation (3) also makes it clear that *the value of a peak-load plant does not stem from operating when prices are high—all plants operate when prices are high—but rather from* shutting down *when prices are low*.

In reality, equation (4) is overly simplified. There are marginal distribution, operation, and maintenance costs associated with an operating plant. Represent these costs as c. When we take these into account, marginal profit is

$$\text{Profit} = \max[S_{\text{elec}} - (H \times S_{\text{gas}} + c), 0]$$

This payoff is that of a **spread option**, since the payoff is positive if the spread $S_{\text{elec}} - H \times S_{\text{gas}}$ exceeds c. An option with this payoff cannot be valued using the Black-Scholes formula because neither $S_{\text{elec}} - H \times S_{\text{gas}}$ nor $H \times S_{\text{gas}} + c$ is lognormally distributed. Equation (3) is therefore an approximation once nonfuel costs are added to the strike price.[13]

When we include other costs, the static NPV of a peak-load plant is typically negative. Adding the shutdown option, however, makes NPV positive. One implication is that, in equilibrium, after the optimal number of peak-load plants have been constructed, electricity prices will continue to be variable. Otherwise, the marginal peak-load plant would have negative NPV. Thus, *the existence of peak-load technology will not eliminate equilibrium variability in electricity prices.*

As a final point, note that the volatility curves in Figure 4 are declining over time. From the standpoint of year 0, a 2-year volatility is less than a 1-year volatility. This is in contrast with stocks, for which we typically assume volatility is constant over time.

The assumption that a stock price follows a random walk implies that volatility increases with the square root of time. Thus, volatility enters the Black-Scholes model as

12. Because the underlying asset is a forward price, the risk-free rate, r, is used as the dividend yield. This is the Black formula.

13. Haug (1998, p. 59) discusses approximations that can be used to value spread options.

$\sigma\sqrt{T-t}$; this expression measures the volatility of the stock price over the horizon from t to T. By contrast, we do not expect electricity prices to follow a random walk. When the electricity price is high, users consume less electricity and producers increase production. When prices are low, users consume more and producers produce less. Thus, the price of electricity reverts to a level reflecting the cost of production. When prices revert in this fashion, *volatility grows with T at a rate less than* $\sqrt{T-t}$.

To consider a specific example, suppose it is January. From this perspective, the July price this year and the July price next year have similar distributions; we won't learn much about the July price this year or next until we approach July. (This is not strictly true because economic activity and even weather can follow long-term cycles, but suppose that it is a good approximation.) To compute an option price, we require *annualized* volatility, σ, which the option pricing formula transforms into volatility over the life of the option, $\sigma\sqrt{T-t}$. If you believe the uncertainty this July and next July is the same, the annualized volatility will be lower for next July since a given amount of uncertainty, when annualized, is spread across a greater period of time. If $\sigma\sqrt{T_i - t}$ is the same for two different T_is, the σs will be different and the volatility curve will decline with horizon.

Research and Development

Research and development is a capital expenditure like any other, in that it involves paying R&D costs today to receive cash flows later. If R&D is successful, a project using the new technology can be undertaken if its NPV is positive. This final option is a call option, just like the other projects we have analyzed. The R&D leading up to this project is therefore like an option premium: We pay R&D costs to acquire the project. R&D can be thought of as acquiring future investment options.

Drug development by pharmaceutical firms provides a particularly clear example of the options in R&D, since the drug development process has clearly delineated points at which there is a decision to abandon or continue development. Figure 5, based on a description in Schwartz and Moon (2000), summarizes the process, along with the probabilities of progressing from one stage to the next. In practice, stages sometimes run together, but Figure 5 reflects a standard description of the process.

As R&D costs are paid over time, pharmaceutical firms are able to resolve uncertainties about their technical ability to produce and market the product. Specifically, they answer the questions: Will the project work, and, if it works, will anyone want it? At all

FIGURE 5

The development process for a new drug. Probabilities are the percentage of pharmaceutical drugs proceeding from one stage to the next. For example, 74% of drugs submitted for FDA approval receive it.

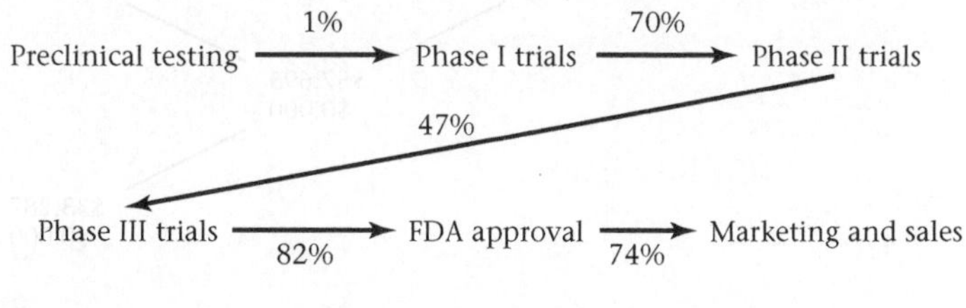

Schwartz and Moon (2000).

times, project managers have the option to continue or stop the research. In effect, each ongoing investment purchases an option to continue development.

Figure 5 shows that most potential drugs are abandoned before Phase I trials. As with peak-load electricity generation, value arises from what is not done. A pharmaceutical company that pursued all potential drugs, no matter how unpromising, would reap full rewards from successful drugs but would be bankrupted by the unsuccessful drugs. The put option to abandon a drug is what creates value for the firm.

How do we evaluate pharmaceutical investments? The underlying asset is the value of the drug if brought to market. How do we find the value of this asset? With the peak-load electricity plant, we have forward prices for both the input (natural gas) and the output (electricity). We can estimate volatilities from market prices. However, in pharmaceuticals, we must estimate development costs, potential revenues, volatilities, and correlations without the benefit of observing market prices. Project payoffs will vary with the state of the economy and, hence, have systematic risk, which must also be estimated.

Assuming that all of these inputs are known, we can evaluate the sequential investment as in Figure 6. The figure presents an example in which, in each period, it is necessary to

FIGURE 6

An example of staged investment. The value of the project, if developed, is in the top line at each node. The value of the option to develop the project is shown below the value of the project. In each year, it is necessary to pay the amount in the Investment row to keep the project alive in the next period. The tree is generated as a forward tree assuming $S_0 = \$100$, $\sigma = 0.50$, $r = 0.10$, and $\delta = 0.15$.

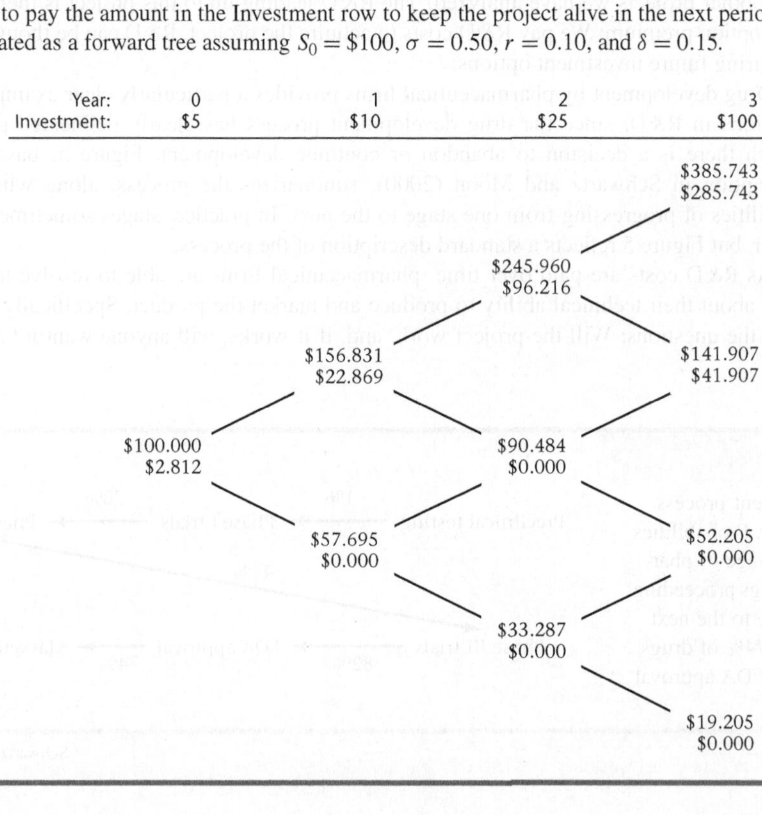

pay an investment cost (shown in the "investment" row) to keep the project alive for another period. The static NPV of the project is negative, since the initial value of the developed investment is \$100, but the present value of the investment costs at a 10% rate of interest is \$108.60. This static calculation ignores the staging of the investment, which permits making later-year investment costs only if the project shows promise. With staging, the value of the development option is \$2.812. Schwartz and Moon (2000), building on work by Pindyck (1993a), developed a general valuation model, with staging, which is applicable to pharmaceutical R&D.

Peak-load pricing and research and development are examples of how option techniques are used in making investment decisions. In the next two sections we develop an extended example of commodity extraction, which is yet another area in which real option considerations are essential.

4. COMMODITY EXTRACTION AS AN OPTION

Natural resources investments are an important application of option techniques to investment decisions.[14] The extraction of a resource from the ground exhibits many similarities to the exercise of a financial option. The resource has a value that can be realized by paying an extraction cost. The market for the resource is typically competitive so that the behavior of one producer does not affect the price.

In this section we will consider the problem of extracting oil from the ground. There is an initial cost to sink a well to commence production, after which we assume we keep producing forever.

Our goal in studying the oil extraction problem will be to understand the *economics* of this problem. The analysis is an example illustrating the costs and benefits of deferring investment and stopping and starting production. The specific formulas do not apply in every situation.

Single-Barrel Extraction under Certainty

Suppose there is a plot of land that contains one barrel of oil. The current price of a barrel of oil is \$15, the oil forward curve is such that the effective annual lease rate, δ, is 4% (constant over time and across maturities at a point in time), and the effective annual risk-free rate, r, is 5% (also constant over time). There is no uncertainty about the future price of oil. The barrel can be extracted at any time by paying \$13.60, which we denote X. Finally, to make matters simple, suppose that the land is completely worthless once the oil is extracted.

If the price of oil at time 0 is S_t, the time 0 forward price for delivery at time T is given by

$$F_{0,T} = S_0 \left(\frac{1+r}{1+\delta}\right)^T \tag{5}$$

Since prices are certain, the future spot price will equal the forward price; hence, the spot price of oil will grow forever at the rate $(1+r)/(1+\delta) - 1 = 1.05/1.04 - 1 = 0.9615\%$ per year.

---

14. See in particular Brennan and Schwartz (1985), McDonald and Siegel (1986), and Paddock et al. (1988).

How much would you pay for this plot of land? The obvious answer—a bid of \$1.40 (= \$15 − \$13.60)—ignores the possibility of delaying investment. As with the widget project, *you cannot value the land without first deciding under what circumstances you will extract oil from the ground*. A bid of \$1.40 is too low. The correct answer is to select T to maximize the present value of net extraction revenue,

$$\frac{S_T - X}{(1+r)^T} \tag{6}$$

Using equation (3) to model the change in the oil price over time, we can mechanically find the T that maximizes expression (6). However, we want to discuss the reasons for delaying investment.

Optimal Extraction. The costs and benefits of extraction are probably familiar by now. If we delay extraction, the barrel of oil in the ground appreciates at 0.9615% per year, less than the risk-free rate. We lose 4% per year—the lease rate—on the value of the barrel. However, extracting the barrel costs \$13.60. By delaying extraction 1 year we earn another year's interest on this amount.

Thinking about costs and benefits in this way suggests a simple decision rule, familiar from the widget project: Delay extraction as long as the cost exceeds the benefit. The benefit in this case is constant from year to year since the extraction cost is constant, but the cost of delaying extraction—the forgone dollar lease payment—grows with the oil price.

This line of thinking leads to a back-of-the-envelope extraction rule. Since the interest rate (5%) is 25% greater than the dividend yield (4%), the dividend yield lost by not investing will equal the interest saved when $S = 1.25 \times \$13.60 = \$17$. Thus, we should expect it to be optimal to extract the oil when $S \approx \$17$.

A more precise calculation is to compare the NPV of investing today with that of investing tomorrow. At a minimum, if we are to invest, we must decide that the NPV of investing today exceeds that of waiting until tomorrow to invest. If we let r_d and δ_d represent the daily interest rate and lease rate, then we defer investing as long as the present value of producing tomorrow exceeds the value of producing today. Since tomorrow's oil price is today's oil price times $(1+r_d)/(1+\delta_d)$, we delay investing as long as

$$\frac{1}{1+r_d}\left(S\frac{1+r_d}{1+\delta_d} - X\right) > S - X$$

This expression shows that we defer investment as long as

$$\frac{S}{X} < \frac{\frac{r_d}{1+r_d}}{\frac{\delta_d}{1+\delta_d}} \tag{7}$$

In this case we have $r_d = 1.05^{1/365} - 1 = 0.013368\%$, with the daily lease rate $\delta_d = 0.010746\%$. The trigger price, at which $S = X\frac{r_d}{\delta_d}\left(\frac{1+\delta_d}{1+r_d}\right)$, is \$16.918.

Note that, since daily rates are essentially the same as continuously compounded rates, we get the same answer by using continuous compounding. We invest when

$$S_t = \frac{\ln(1.05)}{\ln(1.04)} \times \$13.60 = \$16.918$$

This shows why our back-of-the-envelope answer of \$17 is not exactly right. Instead of computing the ratio of effective annual rates (5%/4%), we want to compute the ratio of continuously compounded rates (ln(1.05)/ ln(1.04)).

Value and Appreciation of the Land. We know that we will extract when oil reaches a price of \$16.918/barrel. How long will this take? The annual growth rate of the price of oil is $1.05/1.04 - 1 = 0.9615\%$. We have to find the t such that $\$15 \times (1.009615)^t = \$16.918$. Solving gives us $t = 12.575$ years. At that point the value of extraction will be \$16.918 – \$13.60. Hence, NPV today is

$$\frac{\$16.918 - \$13.60}{1.05^{12.575}} = \$1.796$$

This is what we would pay for the land today. This substantially exceeds the value of \$1.40 were we to extract the oil immediately.

At what rate does the land appreciate? The oil in the land is appreciating at 0.9615% per year; nevertheless, *the land itself appreciates at 5%.* If the land appreciated at less than 5%, no one would be willing to own it since bonds would earn a higher return. In fact, our valuation procedure ensures that the land earns 5% since that is the rate at which we discount the future payoff. *The properly operated oil reserve, whether producing or not, must at all times pay the owner a fair return* (in this case, 5%).

Using the Option Pricing Formula. This problem is equivalent to deciding when to exercise a call option. By paying the extraction cost (the strike price), we can receive oil (the stock). As with a financial call, early exercise is a trade-off between interest saved by delaying exercise and dividends forgone. Once we have possession of the oil, we can lease it; hence, oil's lease rate is the dividend yield. We can verify our answers by using the formula for a perpetual call option, CallPerpetual. Set $S = \$15$, $K = \$13.60$, $\sigma = 0.0001$, $r = \ln(1.05)$, and $\delta = \ln(1.04)$.[15] We get

$$\text{CallPerpetual}(\$15, \$13.60, 0.0001, \ln(1.05), \ln(1.04)) = \{\$1.796, \$16.918\}$$

The option price is \$1.796 and the optimal decision is to exercise when the oil price reaches \$16.918, exactly the answer we just obtained. The option formula implicitly makes the same calculations.

Like the widget example, this situation illustrates the similarity between the exercise of a financial and a real option.

Changing Extraction Costs. What if the cost of extraction, X, changes over time? Inflation might cause X to grow, while technological progress might cause X to decline. Intuitively, real growth in the extraction cost will accelerate investment. The reason is that the benefit from delaying investment is less: We earn interest on money set aside to fund extraction, but some of that money has to be reinvested to fund the growth in extraction cost. Thus, if g is the growth rate of the extraction cost, our benefit from delay is $r - g$ instead of r.

If we view the option to extract oil as a general option to exchange one asset (cash) for another (oil), our willingness to make the exchange depends on the relative dividend

15. This note has been intentionally omitted for this edition.

yields of the two assets. The option is equivalent to being long the underlying asset without receiving its dividend, and short the strike asset without having to pay its dividend. A high dividend yield on the asset we are giving up (the strike asset) makes us less willing to make the exchange, other things equal. Positive growth in the extraction cost reduces the dividend yield on the asset we are giving up, making us more anxious to give it up; hence, there is a lower trigger price.

In the example, if the growth rate of the extraction cost is 0.5% per annum (effective annual), then we would invest when, using continuously compounded rates,

$$S = \frac{r - g}{\delta}X = \frac{0.04879 - 0.00498}{0.03922}\$13.60 = \$15.19$$

It will take 1.32 years to reach this price, and the land would therefore be worth

$$(\$15.19 - \$13.60 \times (1.005)^{1.32})/1.05^{1.32} = \$1.407$$

Growth in the extraction cost hastens extraction and lowers the value of the property.

Gold Extraction. We can see that if the lease rate of gold were zero, it would never be optimal to mine gold.[16] If a commodity has a zero lease rate, then the cost of delaying extraction is zero: It is always preferable to wait to extract.

To see why a zero lease rate implies that we would never extract gold, think about the comparison we just made between extracting oil today or tomorrow. If oil had a zero lease rate, then by definition the forward curve would be growing at the risk-free rate. The present value of oil tomorrow would be the value of oil today; nothing is lost by leaving it in the ground. The gain to deferral, however, would be interest saved on the extraction cost. Thus there would have been no reason ever to extract the oil. In effect, oil in the ground is worth as much as oil out of the ground, so why pay the extraction cost? Equation (7) and the option pricing formula give the same answer, with the extraction barrier approaching infinity as the lease rate approaches zero. Thus, *gold, or any extractive resource, will never be extracted if the lease rate is zero.*

This discussion provides an answer to the question of why gold has a positive lease rate. Investors hold a large stock of gold above ground *despite* the positive lease rate. The lease rate must therefore reflect a convenience yield earned by gold investors. This convenience yield is reflected in the forward curve as a positive lease rate. The positive lease rate in turn makes producers willing to extract new gold.

Single-Barrel Extraction under Uncertainty

Now we consider the effects of uncertainty on the oil extraction decision. Before proceeding, try to answer this question: If we keep all variables unchanged (the lease rate, extraction cost, and so forth), except that the oil price is uncertain, how do the extraction trigger price and the value of the undeveloped land change?

Option reasoning gives unambiguous answers to this question: The extraction trigger price goes up and the land becomes more valuable. The comparison of dividends (the lease rate) to interest savings in the previous example captures two of the three reasons for early exercise. The third is insurance that results from the ability to delay taking the project. With uncertainty the insurance has value, which increases the value of delay. The forgone

16. This also assumes that extraction cost grows less than the risk-free rate.

dividend has to be greater before it is worth giving up the implicit insurance. Another way to think about the investment decision is that by deferring extraction of the oil, we have more time to see if the oil price will decline or rise further. This effect induces additional delay, in the sense that we will optimally invest at a higher price.

If we decide to extract the oil when the price is $\overline{S}$, we will receive $\overline{S} - X$ when S reaches $\overline{S}$. Using the equation

$$\text{Value of \$1 received when } S \text{ first reaches } H \text{ from below} = \left(\frac{S_0}{H}\right)^{h_1},$$

the value of the extraction option is

$$(\overline{S} - \$13.60)\left(\frac{S}{\overline{S}}\right)^{h_1}$$

where

$$h_1 = \frac{1}{2} - \frac{r-\delta}{\sigma^2} + \sqrt{\left(\frac{r-\delta}{\sigma^2} - \frac{1}{2}\right)^2 + \frac{2r}{\sigma^2}}$$

This is the present value of our investment strategy.

By varying $\overline{S}$, we can see how the present value of the project is affected by different extraction trigger prices. Figure 7 compares the value of the land under different rules about when to pay \$13.60 and extract the oil. When oil price volatility is 15%, the trigger price is higher and the land is more valuable. The trigger price that maximizes the value of the land is $\overline{S} = 25.3388$. At this price, we have a project value of

$$(\$25.3388 - \$13.60)\left(\frac{\$15}{25.3388}\right)^{h_1} = \$3.7856$$

FIGURE 7

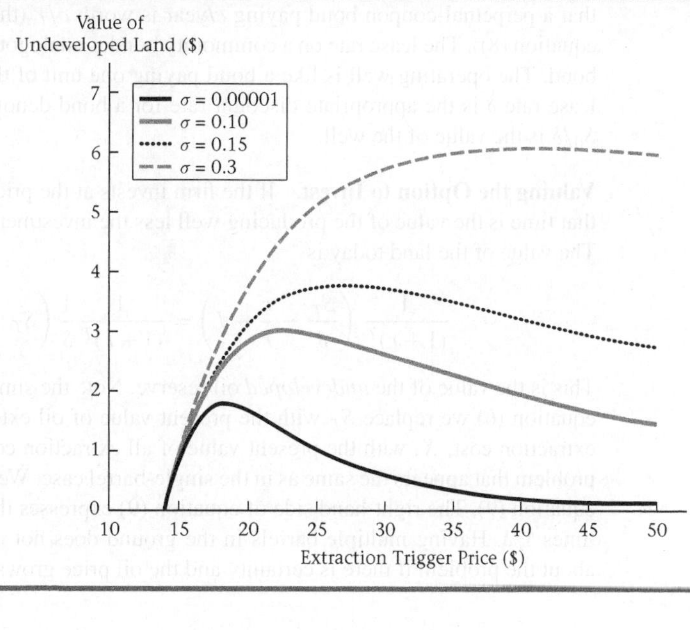

Value of land containing one barrel of oil as a function of the trigger extraction price, $\overline{S}$, for four different oil volatilities. For the curve where $\sigma = 0.00001$, the maximum is attained at $\overline{S} = \$16.918$ with a corresponding value of \$1.796. For the curve where $\sigma = 0.15$, the maximum is attained at $\overline{S} = \$25.3388$ with a corresponding value of \$3.786.

We can verify this calculation by exploiting the insight that for option pricing purposes the lease rate is the dividend yield, and use the perpetual call formula:

$$\text{CallPerpetual}[\$15, \$13.60, 0.15, \ln(1.05), \ln(1.04)] = \{\$3.7856, \$25.3388\}$$

The perpetual call calculation also gives $\bar{S} = \$25.3388$ as the price at which exercise should occur.

Valuing an Infinite Oil Reserve

Now suppose that the land contains an infinite number of barrels of oil that can be extracted at the rate of one barrel per year. We will assume that the firm can at any time invest I in order to turn the undeveloped reserve into a developed reserve. Exactly 1 year after that, the reserve will begin to produce one barrel of oil a year forever at a cost c per barrel. We solve this problem by working backward. We first compute the value of the firm supposing that it is already producing, and we then study the decision about when to invest.

Valuing the Producing Firm. Once the firm has invested, it will continue producing forever since the price of oil is always rising. The lease rate is the discount rate linking the future commodity price with the current commodity price. Thus, the time t value of a barrel received at time T is $\text{PV}_t(F_{t,T}) = F_{t,T}/(1+r)^{T-t} = S_t/(1+\delta)^{T-t}$. The value of the producing firm at time 0 is therefore

$$\begin{aligned} \sum_{i=1}^{\infty} \frac{F_{0,i} - c}{(1+r)^i} &= \sum_{i=1}^{\infty} \left(\frac{S_0}{(1+\delta)^i} - \frac{c}{(1+r)^i} \right) \\ &= \frac{S_0}{\delta} - \frac{c}{r} \end{aligned} \tag{8}$$

You might wonder why the present value of a barrel of oil a year forever is S_0/δ. We know that a perpetual-coupon bond paying c/year is worth c/r (the second term on the right in equation (8)). The lease rate on a commodity bond is analogous to the interest rate on a cash bond. The operating well is like a bond paying one unit of the commodity forever, so the lease rate δ is the appropriate discount rate for a bond denominated in a commodity, and S_0/δ is the value of the well.

Valuing the Option to Invest. If the firm invests at the price S_T, the value of the land at that time is the value of the producing well less the investment cost, I, or $S_T/\delta - c/r - I$. The value of the land today is

$$\frac{1}{(1+r)^T}\left(\frac{S_T}{\delta} - \frac{c}{r} - I\right) = \frac{1}{(1+r)^T}\frac{1}{\delta}\left(S_T - \delta\left[\frac{c}{r} + I\right]\right) \tag{9}$$

This is the value of the *undeveloped* oil reserve. Note the similarity with equation (6). If in equation (6) we replace S_T with the present value of oil extracted, S_T/δ, and replace the extraction cost, X, with the present value of all extraction costs, $c/r + I$, then we have a problem that appears the same as in the single-barrel case. We want to select T to maximize equation (9). The right-hand side of equation (9) expresses the value on a per-barrel basis, times $1/\delta$. Having multiple barrels in the ground does not change anything fundamental about the problem if there is certainty and the oil price grows indefinitely.

Example 3. Suppose $S_0 = \$15$, $r = 5\%$, $\delta = 4\%$, $c = \$8$, and the value of the producing well is $\$15/0.04 - \$8/0.05 = \$215$. If the investment cost, I, is \$180, then the *per-barrel* extraction cost is $\delta(c/r + I) = 0.04 \times (\$8/0.05 + \$180) = \$13.60$. The problem is the same as having $1/\delta$ options to extract at a cost of \$13.60; hence, the solution is exactly the same as in the single-barrel case. To appreciate the similarity, use the option pricing formula:

$$\text{CallPerpetual}\left[\frac{\$15}{0.04}, \frac{\$8}{0.05} + 180, 0.000001, \ln(1.05), \ln(1.04)\right] = \{\$44.914, \$422.956\}$$

The value of the well at which extraction occurs is \$422.956. Thus, extraction occurs when $S = 0.04 \times \$422.956 = \$16.918$. ■

With uncertainty, we could have the ability to shut a producing well. We will assume for the moment that production continues forever. In that case, the problem is the same as in the single-barrel case.

Example 4. Make the same assumptions as in Example 3, except suppose that the price of oil is lognormally distributed with a constant lease rate and volatility is $\sigma = 0.15$. The land value and optimal extraction decision is given by

$$\text{CallPerpetual}\left[\frac{\$15}{0.04}, \frac{\$8}{0.05} + \$180, 0.15, \ln(1.05), \ln(1.04)\right] = \{\$94.639, \$633.469\}$$

The well is worth \$94.639 and we invest when it is worth $S/0.04 = \$633.469$, or when $S = \$25.3388$. On a per-barrel basis, the well is worth $0.04 \times \$94.639 = \$3.7856$. With these assumptions, the solution is the same as in the single-barrel case. ■

In the absence of any shutdown options, the single- and infinite-barrel cases differ only in scale. The interesting difference arises when it is possible to avoid operating losses by shutting down, which matters only in the multiple-barrel case.

5. COMMODITY EXTRACTION WITH SHUTDOWN AND RESTART OPTIONS

With production occurring over time and uncertainty about the price of oil, we face two new operating decisions: whether to keep the well operating, or, if it has been shut down, whether to reopen it. There are thus three stages of production:

Initial investment in the well. We begin with an empty field containing oil. This is an undeveloped well. At what point do we drill the well and begin extraction? We answered this question in Section 4, assuming that the well operates until the resource is exhausted.

Continuing to produce. Once we have made the investment in an oil well, we say that the property is *developed*. However, a developed well may or may not be producing. If we are extracting oil from the ground, we have a *developed and producing* well. However, if the oil price drops below extraction cost, it may make sense to pay a cost in order to shut down the well and avoid future operating losses. Then it is a *shutdown* well.

FIGURE 8

Investment and operating decisions for an oil well. Initial investment occurs when the oil price crosses the investment trigger price, $\overline{S}$, at point A. Shutdown of production occurs when the price falls to the shutdown trigger, S_* (point B). Production is restarted at the restart trigger, S^*, at point C.

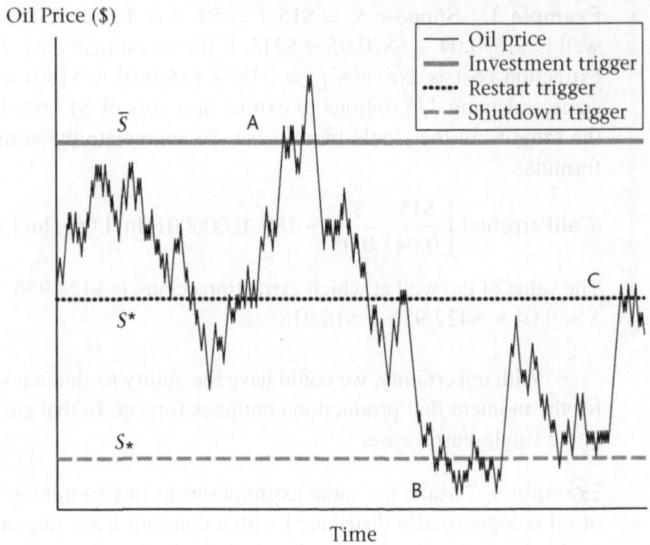

Restarting an operating well. Having shut down the well, if the oil price rises again, it may be possible to pay a cost and *restart* the well, turning it back into a producing well.

Thus, the well can be in one of three states: undeveloped, producing, and shutdown (developed but not producing). Figure 8 shows a hypothetical price path of oil over time and possible operating rules. Investment occurs the first time the oil price reaches the investment trigger price, $\overline{S}$. Production is shut down at the shutdown trigger price, S_*, and restarted at the restart trigger price, S^*. Thus, before point A the well is undeveloped. Between points A and B, and after C, the well is producing. Between B and C the well is shutdown. Key questions are: How do we determine the investment, shutdown, and restart triggers, $\overline{S}$, S_*, and S^*, and what is the value of the land on which the oil is located?

Once again, we have to work backward, as in the binomial valuation of a stock option. Before we can decide the rule for investing (determining $\overline{S}$), we have to determine the value of a producing well (this is the present value of future cash flows at the point we invest). In order to value a producing well, we need to understand operating decisions, specifically how S_* and S^* are determined.

It is helpful to analyze shutting down and restarting by considering three separate cases:

1. Production can be shut down once permanently. After the well has been shut, the land has no additional value.

2. Production can be shut down once, then restarted once, this time permanently.
3. Production can be shut down and restarted an infinite number of times.[17]

Each case layers a new option on the previous case. In addition to allowing additional shutting down and restarting, we can impose costs of doing so. We focus in this section on the case where the well can be shut down never or once after the initial investment. Appendix B adds restarting to the analysis.

Permanent Shutting Down

Suppose that we are operating the well. If the current price is S and we ignore shutting down, the value of the operating well is simply

$$V_{\text{operating, no shutdown}} = \frac{S}{\delta} - \frac{c}{r} \tag{10}$$

Suppose that we can at any time pay a cost of k_s, abandon the well, and never produce again. S_* is the price at which we shut down.

What is the value of shutting down? There are three considerations:

1. Once we shut down, we no longer sell oil. Thus, we give up the revenue stream with present value S/δ.
2. We no longer pay the extraction cost, so we gain the present value c/r.
3. We give up k_s, the shutdown cost.

Thus, the value of shutting down at price S_* at a cost of k_s is

$$-\frac{S_*}{\delta} + \frac{c}{r} - k_s = \left(\frac{c}{r} - k_s\right) - \frac{S_*}{\delta} \tag{11}$$

This is the payoff to a put option with strike price $c/r - k_s$ and asset price S_*/δ. If we are operating and the price is S, we can value this put to determine the value of the option to shut down, as well as the trigger price, S_*, for shutting down.

Example 5. Suppose the oil well is operating and the oil price is $S = \$10$. We also have $c = \$8$, $\sigma = 0.15$, and effective annual r and δ are 5% and 4%, respectively. If $k_s = \$0$, the value of the option to shut down is

$$\text{PutPerpetual}[\$10/0.04, \$8/0.05, 0.15, \ln(1.05), \ln(1.04)] = \{\$9.633, \$106.830\}$$

Thus, we shut down production when $S/\delta = \$106.83$ or when $S = 0.04 \times \$106.83 = \$4.273$. At this point, the present value of continuing to produce is

$$\frac{\$4.273}{0.04} - \frac{\$8.00}{0.05} = -\$53.17$$

By shutting down production, we avoid losses of \$53.17.

17. The model with infinite shutdown and restart was first analyzed in Brennan and Schwartz (1985) and subsequently by Dixit (1989).

When $k_s = \$25$, the shutdown solution is

$$\text{PutPerpetual}(\$10/0.04, \$8/0.05 - 25, 0.15, 0.04879, 0.03922) = \{\$5.778, \$90.137\}$$

The shutdown trigger is then $S = 0.04 \times \$90.137 = \$3.605$. We pay \$25 to avoid losses with a present value of $-\$69.863$. ■

To interpret the shutdown results, there are two natural benchmark prices to consider. The first is the price at which the NPV of the operating will become zero, which occurs when $S = \delta \times c/r = \$6.40$. The second is the price equal to the marginal cost of production, $c = \$8$. If $S > \$8$, then we are making money by operating and we will not shut down. If $\$8 > S > \$6.40$, then we are losing money on an operating basis but the NPV of operating the well is positive. In this case we would consider shutting down if we could later restart production, but, because the NPV of operation is positive, we would not shut the well if the shutdown were permanent. Finally, if $S < \$6.40$, it may make sense to shut the well even if the shutdown were permanent. Note that in all cases, the initial investment is sunk and therefore irrelevant.

In Example 5, shutdown is permanent so the zero NPV price ($S = \$6.40$) is the natural benchmark. The usual option exercise logic applies: We won't shut down as soon as present value is negative, because the decision is irreversible. In fact, we wait until the price is below \$5. The price *might* subsequently increase; by shutting down we are unable to benefit from this reversal. This is the counterpart to not investing as soon as NPV is positive.

The value of the producing well. Given that shutdown is possible, what is the value of a producing well? The answer is that the value of the well is the value of the perpetually producing well plus the value of the shutdown option:

$$\begin{aligned} V_{\text{operating}}(S) &= V_{\text{no shutdown}}(S) + V_{\text{shutdown option}}(S) \\ &= \frac{S}{\delta} - \frac{c}{r} + \text{PutPerpetual}\left[\frac{S}{\delta}, \frac{c}{r} - k_s, \sigma, \ln(1+r), \ln(1+\delta)\right] \end{aligned} \tag{12}$$

Figure 9 graphs equation (12) for a range of oil prices and four different volatilities, along with the value of the well without a shutdown option. Without the shutdown option, the value of the well is like a stock and declines to $-c/r = -\$160$ when $S = 0$. With the option, the well is worth zero once it is shut. (Recall that once the well has been shut, the land has no additional value.)

When the oil price is significantly above the shutdown price, the shutdown option is worth little and the value of the well changes by $1/\delta$ for each \$1 change in the oil price. (The Δ of the well is $1/\delta$.) Close to the shutdown price, however, the value of the well becomes less sensitive to the oil price, because the shutdown option is increasing in value to absorb the effect of declines in the oil price. In each case, the value of the well smoothly approaches zero as we approach the shutdown price.

This example illustrates how the shutdown option affects valuation of an operating well. The next question is how the shutdown option affects the decision to invest in the well in the first place.

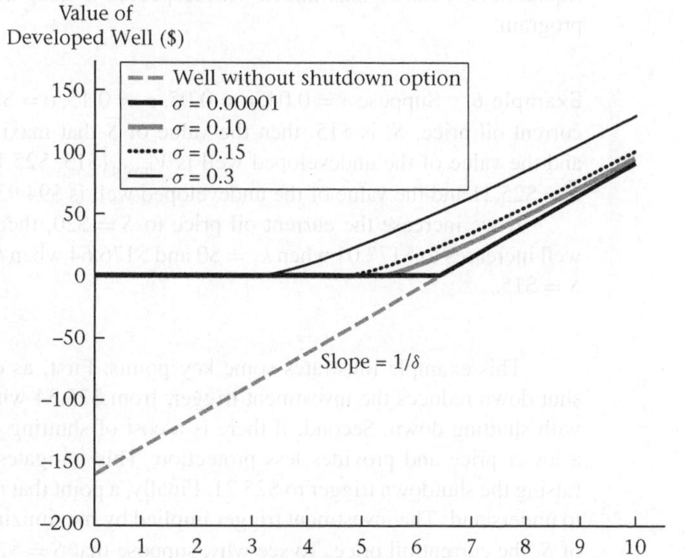

FIGURE 9

Value of a producing well that can never be shut down (equation (8)), and that can be shut once with no shutdown cost (equation (12)). The shutdown triggers for the different volatilities are \$6.40 ($\sigma = 0.00001$), \$5.01 ($\sigma = 0.10$), \$4.27 ($\sigma = 0.15$), and \$2.68 ($\sigma = 0.30$).

Investing When Shutdown Is Possible

How does the ability to shut the well affect the initial investment decision? Once we drill the well, the maximum potential loss is less because of the shutdown option. The ability to shut down makes us willing to invest sooner.

To account for the value of the shutdown option we work backward. Equation (12) gives the value of a producing well. Call this $V_p(S)$. If we invest at the price $\overline{S}$, paying an investment cost of I, then the value *at the time we invest* is

$$\begin{aligned} &\text{Value of well at time of investment} = V_p(\overline{S}) - I \\ &= \frac{\overline{S}}{\delta} - \frac{c}{r} + \text{PutPerpetual}\left[\frac{\overline{S}}{\delta}, \frac{c}{r} - k_s, \sigma, \ln(1+r), \ln(1+\delta)\right] - I \end{aligned} \tag{13}$$

To solve for $\overline{S}$, we need to find the *present value* of equation (13), and then choose $\overline{S}$ to maximize this present value. For a given $\overline{S}$, equation (13) tells us the value of investing when $S = \overline{S}$. If the oil price today is $S < \overline{S}$, we can compute the present value of equation (13) using equation (14). The value will depend upon the current oil price (the lower the price, the longer it will take to hit $\overline{S}$), so we denote it as $V_{\text{Invest}}(S; \overline{S})$. This present value is

$$\begin{aligned} &V_{\text{invest}}(S; \overline{S}) = \left(\frac{S}{\overline{S}}\right)^{h_1} \\ &\times \left(\frac{\overline{S}}{\delta} - \frac{c}{r} + \text{PutPerpetual}\left[\frac{\overline{S}}{\delta}, \frac{c}{r} - k_s, \sigma, \ln(1+r), \ln(1+\delta)\right] - I\right) \end{aligned} \tag{14}$$

Equation (14) can be maximized with respect to $\overline{S}$ using a spreadsheet or other numerical program.

Example 6. Suppose $\delta = 0.04, r = 0.05, \sigma = 0.15, c = \$8, k_s = \$0$, and $I = \$180$. If the current oil price, S, is \$15, then the value of $\overline{S}$ that maximizes equation (14) is \$25.12, and the value of the undeveloped well is $V_{\text{invest}}(\$15, \$25.12) = \$95.13$. If $k_s = \$25$, then $\overline{S} = \$25.21$ and the value of the undeveloped well is \$94.93.

If we increase the current oil price to $S = \$20$, then the value of the undeveloped well increases to \$177.01 when $k_s = \$0$ and \$176.64 when $k_s = \$25$. $\overline{S}$ is the same as when $S = \$15$. ■

This example illustrates some key points. First, as discussed earlier, the ability to shut down reduces the investment trigger, from \$25.34 with no shutting down, to \$25.12 with shutting down. Second, if there is a cost of shutting down, shutting down occurs at a lower price and provides less protection. This mitigates the benefit of shutting down, raising the shutdown trigger to \$25.21. Finally, a point that may be obvious but is important to understand: The investment trigger implied by maximizing equation (14) is independent of S, the current oil price. To see why, suppose that $\overline{S} = \$25$. If $S = \$15$, it must pass \$20 before reaching \$25. Thus, if we evaluate the option when $S = \$20$, we must obtain the same $\overline{S}$ as when $S = \$15$. Thus, $\overline{S}$ is independent of S.

Restarting Production

The preceding example assumed that the firm could never restart once it had shut down. In this section we examine the restart strategy if the firm could restart after it permanently had shut down.

Suppose the firm can pay k_r to restart production. The ability to restart is a call option in which the firm receives S/δ by paying $c/r + k_r$, future production costs plus the restart cost.

Example 7. The value of a shutdown well is

$$\text{CallPerpetual}\left[\frac{S}{\delta}, \frac{c}{r} + k_r, \sigma, log(1+r), log(1+\delta)\right]$$

Assuming that $S = \$10$, $\delta = 0.04$, $r = 0.05$, $\sigma = 0.15$, $c = \$8$, and $k_r = \$0$, the option pricing formula gives us the value of the well as \$94.46, and \$11.92 as the price at which to restart. ■

The ability to restart affects the decision to shut down. When we shut down, we not only cut off future losses but *we also acquire a call option to restart*. In equation (14) we acquired a put option when we invested, so in this case we acquire a call option when we exercise the put option! And when we invest in the first place, we acquire the put option to shut down, but the value of that put now implicitly contains the call option to restart. The solution for this problem appears in Appendix B.

TABLE 1 Comparison of investment ($\overline{S}$), shutdown (S_*), and restart (S^*) triggers under different assumptions. k_s is the cost of shutting down the well and k_r is the cost of restarting once it is shut. In all cases, $r = 5\%$ and the lease rate is $\delta = 4\%$.

Parameters			Number of Times		Triggers		
σ	k_s	k_r	Shutdown	Restart	$\overline{S}$	S_*	S^*
0.0	—	—	0	0	16.92	—	—
0.15	—	—	0	0	25.34	—	—
0.15	0	—	1	0	25.12	4.27	—
0.15	25	—	1	0	25.14	3.60	—
0.15	0	0	1	1	25.00	6.03	11.92
0.15	25	25	1	1	25.17	4.33	13.79
0.15	25	25	∞	∞	25.17	4.37	13.18

Additional Options

The firm might be able to restart and shut down production many times. We can determine triggers and solve for the value of the well by following the strategy in the previous sections. Details of the solution are in Appendix B.

Table 1 summarizes the price triggers for several different cases. The qualitative results are intuitive. As with any American option, we require that the oil well have positive NPV before we invest—we are reluctant to kill the put option implicit in the option to take the project. If shutting down in the future is possible, there is an additional put option available besides that from deferring investment, and we are willing to invest at a lower price. The addition of an option to restart once we have shut down makes us more willing to shut down, and, hence, more willing to invest. Adding costs to restarting and shutting down makes us more reluctant to restart, to shut down, and, hence, to invest initially. More options generally mean more value and investment at a lower price; greater costs mean lower value and investment at a higher price.

The results in Table 1 illustrate a phenomenon called **hysteresis**, which Dixit (1989, p. 622) defines as "the failure of an effect to reverse itself as the underlying cause is reversed." Suppose that all oil producers have a marginal extraction cost of \$8. The current oil price is \$7, following a period in which it was \$30, and there is a shutdown cost. Oil production is currently unprofitable, and we would not invest in new capacity at this price, but production from existing wells is not unprofitable enough to shut down production. We are in a situation where the cause (the oil price) reversed itself, but the effect (the creation of an oil well) did not. Oil producers lose money on an operating basis, but are not losing enough to shut down production.

Real-life investment decisions exhibit hysteresis. To illustrate hysteresis in a different context, Dixit (1989) considers investment decisions of a manufacturer with operations in a foreign country. Exchange rate fluctuations will change the profitability of the foreign investment. However, since investing and disinvesting are costly, it will be optimal to wait until the investment is sufficiently profitable before investing, and sufficiently unprofitable before disinvesting. What appear to be sluggish investment decisions may simply result from costs of undoing what has been done.

CHAPTER SUMMARY

Real options is the analysis of investment decisions taking into account the ability to revise future operating decisions. Examples of real options include timing options (the ability to choose when to make an investment), shutdown options (the ability to stop production in order to avoid losses), sequential investments where the decision to make later investments depends on the outcome of earlier investments (common in R&D), and natural resource extraction. Investment decisions in which such options are present can be analyzed using pricing tools, such as the Black-Scholes model, perpetual options, binomial trees, and barrier present value calculations. In some cases the optimal decision is equivalent to the problem of when to exercise an American option. In general, however, as illustrated by the oil extraction problem, a simple option formulation is just a starting point for analysis.

Even when standard option pricing models are not directly applicable, understanding the economics of derivatives is helpful in understanding the economics of investment and operation decisions.

FURTHER READING

Early papers that used techniques from financial options to analyze real assets include Brennan and Schwartz (1985) and McDonald and Siegel (1985, 1986). These papers study investment timing and the option to shut down and restart. Brennan (2000) insightfully summarizes the literature since then. There are several valuable books on real options, including Dixit and Pindyck (1994) and Trigeorgis (1996).

A number of papers have applied real options to understanding the real estate market. These include Titman (1985), Grenadier (1996), and Grenadier (1999).

Many firms use capital budgeting techniques more sophisticated than simple discounted cash flow. Triantis and Borison (2001) survey managers on their use of real options, identifying three categories of real options usage: as an analytical tool, as a language and framing device for investment problems, and as an organizational process. McDonald (2000) argues that the use of high hurdle rates in capital budgeting could be an approximate way to account for real options.

PROBLEMS

1. Suppose you have a project that will produce a single widget. Widgets today cost \$1 and the project costs \$0.90. The risk-free rate is 5%. Under what circumstances would you invest immediately in the project? What conditions would lead you to delay the project?

2. You have a project costing \$1.50 that will produce *two* widgets, one each the first and second years after project completion. Widgets today cost \$0.80 each, with the price growing at 2% per year. The effective annual interest rate is 5%. When will you invest? What is the value today of the project?

3. Consider again the project in Problem 2, only suppose that the widget price is unchanging and the cost of investment is declining at 2% per year. When will you invest? What is the value today of the project?

4. Consider the widget investment problem outlined in Section 1. Show the following in a spreadsheet.

   a. Compute annual widget prices for the next 50 years.

   b. For each year, compute the net present value of investing in that year.

   c. Discount the net present value for each year back to the present. Verify that investing when the widget price reaches \$1.43 is optimal.

5. Again consider the widget investment problem in Section 1. Verify that with $S = \$50$, $K = \$30$, $r = 0.04879$, $\sigma = 0$, and $\delta = 0.009569$, the perpetual call price is \$30.597 and exercise optimally occurs when the present value of cash flows is \$152.957. What happens to the value of the project and the investment trigger when you change S? Why? What happens to the value of the project and the investment trigger when you increase volatility? Why?

6. The stock price of XYZ is \$100. One million shares of XYZ (a negligible fraction of the shares outstanding) are buried on a tiny, otherwise worthless plot of land in a vault that would cost \$50 million to excavate. If XYZ pays a dividend, you will have to dig up the shares to collect the dividend.

   a. If you believe that XYZ will never pay a dividend, what would you pay for the land?

   b. If you believe that XYZ will pay a liquidating dividend in 10 years, and the continuously compounded risk-free rate is 5%, what would you pay for the land?

   c. Suppose that XYZ has a 1% dividend yield and a volatility of 0.3. At what price would you excavate and what would you pay for the land?

7. Repeat Problem 6, only assume that after the stock is excavated, the land has an alternative use and can be sold for \$30m.

8. Consider the widget investment problem of Section 1 with the following modification. The expected growth rate of the widget price is zero. (This means there is no reason to consider project delay.) Each period, the widget price will be \$0.25 with probability 0.5 or \$2.25 with probability 0.5. Each widget costs \$1 to produce.

   a. What is the expected widget price?

   b. If the firm produces a widget each period, regardless of the price, what is the NPV of the widget project?

   c. If the firm can choose to produce widgets only when the widget price is greater than \$1, what is the NPV?

d. What happens to the NPV if the widget price can be \$0.10 or \$2.40 with equal probability?

9. To answer this question, use the assumptions of Example 1 and the risk-neutral valuation method (and risk-neutral probability) described in Example 2.

a. Compute the value of a claim that pays the square root of the cash flow in period 1.

b. Compute the value of a claim that pays the square of the cash flow in period 1.

c. Given your answers above computed using risk-neutral valuation, back out the *true* discount rate that would give you the same value for each claim. In each case is this rate bigger or smaller than the 11% discount rate for the cash flow itself? Why?

10. Consider a project that in one year pays \$50 if the economy performs well (the stock market goes up) and that pays \$100 if the economy performs badly (the stock market goes down). The probability of the economy performing well is 60%, the effective annual risk-free rate is 6%, the expected return on the market is 10%, and the beta of the project is −0.50.

a. Compute the present value of the project's cash flows using the true probabilities and expected return on the project.

b. Compute the risk-neutral probability of the economy performing well, then repeat the valuation of the project using risk-neutral valuation.

11. Verify the binomial calculations in Figure 3.

12. A project costing \$100 will produce perpetual net cash flows that have an annual volatility of 35% with no expected growth. If the project existed, net cash flows today would be \$8. The project beta is 0.5, the effective annual risk-free rate is 5%, and the effective annual risk premium on the market is 8%. What is the static NPV of the project? What would you pay to acquire the rights to this project if investment rights lasted only 3 years? What would you pay to acquire perpetual investment rights?

13. A project has certain cash flows today of \$1, growing at 5% per year for 10 years, after which the cash flow is constant. The risk-free rate is 5%. The project costs \$20 and cash flows begin 1 year after the project is started. When should you invest and what is the value of the option to invest?

14. Consider the oil project with a single barrel, in which $S = \$15$, $r = 5\%$, $\delta = 4\%$, and $X = \$13.60$. Suppose that, in addition, the land can be sold for the residual value of $R = \$1$ after the barrel of oil is extracted. What is the value of the land?

15. Verify in Figure 2 that if volatility were 30% instead of 50%, immediate exercise would be optimal.

16. Consider the last row of Table 1. What is the solution for S_* and S^* when $k_s = k_r = 0$? (This answer does not require calculation.)

In the following five problems, assume that the spot price of gold is $300/oz, the effective annual lease rate is 3%, and the effective annual risk-free rate is 5%.

17. A mine costing $275 will produce 1 ounce of gold on the day the cost is paid. Gold volatility is zero. What is the value of the mine?

18. A mine costing $1000 will produce 1 ounce of gold per year forever at a marginal extraction cost of $250, with production commencing 1 year after the mine opens. Gold volatility is zero. What is the value of the mine?

19. Repeat Problems 17 and 18 assuming that the annual volatility of gold is 20%.

20. Repeat Problem 18 assuming that the volatility of gold is 20% and that once opened, the mine can be costlessly shut down forever. What is the value of the mine? What is the price at which the mine will be shut down?

21. Repeat Problem 18 assuming that the volatility of gold is 20% and that once opened, the mine can be costlessly shut down once, and then costlessly reopened once. What is the value of the mine? What are the prices at which the mine will be shut down and reopened?

Appendix A CALCULATION OF OPTIMAL TIME TO DRILL AN OIL WELL

Appendix available at http://www.pearsonhighered.com/mcdonald.

Appendix B THE SOLUTION WITH SHUTTING DOWN AND RESTARTING

Appendix available at http://www.pearsonhighered.com/mcdonald.

Advanced Pricing Theory and Applications

The standard derivation of the Black-Scholes model of pricing derivatives has two components: an assumption about how the stock price behaves, and the idea that prices are determined by competitive delta-hedging market-makers.

The form of the Black-Scholes model arises from straightforward lognormal probability calculations. The Monte Carlo pricing method is a powerful and flexible technique widely used to price derivatives.

Black and Scholes assumed that stocks follow geometric Brownian motion and used a mathematical tool called Itô's Lemma to solve the problem they posed.

From *Derivatives Markets*, Third Edition, Robert McDonald. Copyright © 2013 by Pearson Education, Inc. Published by Pearson Prentice Hall. All rights reserved.

The Lognormal Distribution

It is common in option pricing to assume the lognormality of asset prices. The purpose of this chapter is to explain the meaning of this assumption. We first review the normal distribution, which gives rise to the lognormal distribution. We then define lognormality and illustrate some common calculations based on lognormality. These calculations result in terms that look much like the parts of the Black-Scholes formula. Finally, we examine stock returns to see whether stock price data seem consistent with lognormality.

We will find that stock prices are not exactly lognormal. Nevertheless, the lognormal assumption is the basis for many frequently used pricing formulas. Moreover, it is difficult to understand more realistic models used in practice without first understanding models based on the lognormal distribution.

1. THE NORMAL DISTRIBUTION

A random variable, $\tilde{x}$, obeys the **normal distribution**—or is *normally distributed*—if the probability that $\tilde{x}$ takes on a particular value is described by the normal density function, which we represent by ϕ. The formula for the normal density function is[1]

$$\boxed{\phi(x;\mu,\sigma) \equiv \frac{1}{\sigma\sqrt{2\pi}} e^{-\frac{1}{2}\left(\frac{x-\mu}{\sigma}\right)^2}} \tag{1}$$

Notice in equation (1) that in order to calculate a value for ϕ, in addition to x, you need to supply two numbers: a mean, μ, and a standard deviation, σ. For this reason, the normal distribution is said to be a *two-parameter distribution*; it is completely described by the mean and the standard deviation.

Figure 1 graphs equation (1) for two different standard deviations (1 and 1.5), and for the same mean (0). The normal density with $\mu = 0$ and $\sigma = 1$ is called the *standard normal density*. When working with the standard normal density, we will write $\phi(x)$, without a mean and standard deviation.

1. You can calculate the normal density in Excel using NormDist(x, μ, σ,*False*).

From Chapter 18 of *Derivatives Markets*, Third Edition, Robert McDonald. Copyright © 2013 by Pearson Education, Inc. Published by Pearson Prentice Hall. All rights reserved.

FIGURE 1

Two normal densities with mean 0, one with $\sigma = 1$ (the standard normal), the other with $\sigma = 1.5$.

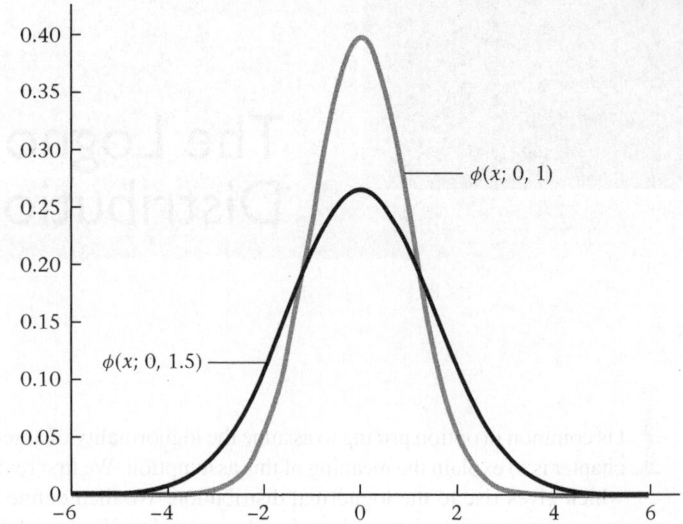

Compared to the standard normal density, the normal density with $\sigma = 1.5$ assigns lower probabilities to values of x close to 0, and greater probabilities for x farther from 0. Increasing the variance spreads out the distribution. The mean locates the center of the distribution, and the standard deviation tells you how spread out it is. The normal density is symmetric about the mean, μ, meaning that

$$\phi(\mu + a; \mu, \sigma) = \phi(\mu - a; \mu, \sigma)$$

If a random variable x is normally distributed with mean μ and standard deviation σ, we write this as

$$x \sim \mathcal{N}(\mu, \sigma^2)$$

We will use z to represent a random variable that has the standard normal distribution:

$$z \sim \mathcal{N}(0, 1)$$

We can use the normal distribution to compute the probability of different events, but we have to be careful about what we mean by an event. Since the distribution is continuous, there are an infinite number of events that can occur when we randomly draw a number from the distribution. (This is unlike the binomial distribution, in which an event can have only one of two values.) The probability of any *particular* number being drawn from the normal distribution is zero. Thus, we use the normal distribution to describe the probability that a number randomly selected from the normal distribution will be in a particular *range*.

We could ask, for example, what is the probability that if we draw a number from the standard normal distribution, it will be less than some number a? The area under the curve to the left of a, denoted $N(a)$, equals this probability, $\Pr(z < a)$. We call $N(a)$ the **cumulative normal distribution function**. The integral from $-\infty$ to a is the area under the density over that range; it is cumulative in that it sums the probabilities from $-\infty$ to a.

FIGURE 2

Top panel: Area under the normal curve to the left of 0.3. *Bottom panel:* Cumulative normal distribution. The height at $x = 0.3$, given by $N(0.3)$, is 0.6179.

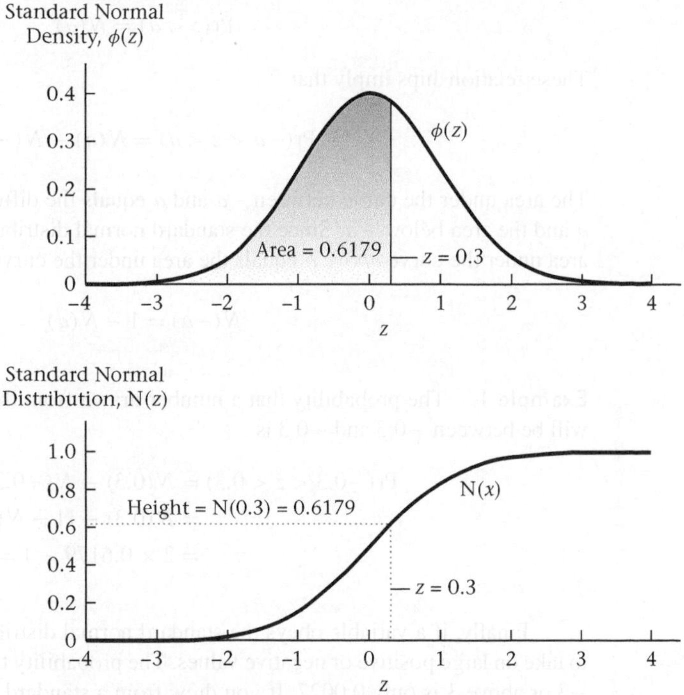

Mathematically, this is accomplished by integrating the standard normal density, equation (1) with $\mu = 0$ and $\sigma = 1$, from $-\infty$ to a:

$$N(a) \equiv \int_{-\infty}^{a} \frac{1}{\sqrt{2\pi}} e^{-\frac{1}{2}x^2} dx \tag{2}$$

As an example, $N(0.3)$ is shown in Figure 2. In the top panel, $N(0.3)$ is the area under the normal density curve between $-\infty$ and 0.3. In the bottom panel, $N(0.3)$ is a point on the cumulative distribution. The range $-\infty$ to $+\infty$ covers all possible outcomes for a single draw from a normal distribution. The probability that a randomly drawn number will be less than ∞ is 1; hence, $N(\infty) = 1$. As you may already have surmised, the $N(a)$ defined above is the same $N(\,)$ used in computing the Black-Scholes formula.

There is no simple formula for the cumulative normal distribution function, equation (2), but it is a frequent-enough calculation that modern spreadsheets have it as a built-in function. (In Excel the function is called NormSDist.) The area under the normal density from $-\infty$ to 0.3 is 0.6179. Thus, if you draw a number from the standard normal distribution, 61.79% of the time the number you draw will be less than 0.3.

Suppose that we wish to know the probability that a number drawn from the standard normal distribution will be between a and $-a$. We have

$$\Pr(z < -a) = N(-a)$$
$$\Pr(z < a) = N(a)$$

These relationships imply that

$$\Pr(-a < z < a) = N(a) - N(-a)$$

The area under the curve between $-a$ and a equals the difference between the area below a and the area below $-a$. Since the standard normal distribution is symmetric about 0, the area under the curve *above a* equals the area under the curve *below* $-a$. Thus,

$$N(-a) = 1 - N(a) \tag{3}$$

Example 1. The probability that a number drawn from the standard normal distribution will be between −0.3 and +0.3 is

$$\begin{aligned}\Pr(-0.3 < z < 0.3) &= N(0.3) - N(-0.3)\\ &= N(0.3) - [1 - N(0.3)]\\ &= 2 \times 0.6179 - 1 = 0.2358 \quad ■\end{aligned}$$

Finally, if a variable obeys the standard normal distribution, it is extremely unlikely to take on large positive or negative values. The probability that a single draw will be below −3 or above 3 is only 0.0027. If you drew from a standard normal distribution every day, you would draw above 3 or below −3 only about once a year. The probability of being below −4 or above 4 is 0.000063, which, with daily draws, would occur on average about once every 43.25 years.

Converting a Normal Random Variable to Standard Normal

If we have an arbitrary normal random variable, it is easy to convert it to standard normal. Suppose

$$x \sim \mathcal{N}(\mu, \sigma^2)$$

Then we can create a standard normal random variable, z, by subtracting the mean and dividing by the standard deviation:

$$z = \frac{x - \mu}{\sigma} \tag{4}$$

Using this fact, we can compute the probability that x is less than some number b:

$$\begin{aligned}\Pr(x < b) &= \Pr\left(\frac{x - \mu}{\sigma} < \frac{b - \mu}{\sigma}\right)\\ &= N\left(\frac{b - \mu}{\sigma}\right)\end{aligned} \tag{5}$$

Using equation (3), the complementary probability is

$$\begin{aligned}\Pr(x > b) &= 1 - \Pr(x < b) \\ &= 1 - N\left(\frac{b-\mu}{\sigma}\right) \\ &= N\left(\frac{\mu - b}{\sigma}\right)\end{aligned} \tag{6}$$

This result will be helpful in interpreting the Black-Scholes formula.

If we have a standard normal random variable z, we can generate a variable $x \sim \mathcal{N}(\mu, \sigma^2)$, using the following:

$$x = \mu + \sigma z \tag{7}$$

Example 2. Suppose that $x \sim \mathcal{N}(3, 25)$ and $z \sim \mathcal{N}(0, 1)$. Then

$$\frac{x-3}{5} \sim \mathcal{N}(0, 1)$$

and

$$3 + 5 \times z \sim \mathcal{N}(3, 25) \quad ■$$

Sums of Normal Random Variables

Suppose we have n jointly distributed random variables x_i, $i = 1, \ldots, n$, with mean and variance $\mathrm{E}(x_i) = \mu_i$, $\mathrm{Var}(x_i) = \sigma_i^2$, and covariance $\mathrm{Cov}(x_i, x_j) = \sigma_{ij}$. (The covariance between two random variables measures their tendency to move together. We can also write the covariance in terms of ρ_{ij}, the correlation between x_i and x_j: $\sigma_{ij} = \rho_{ij}\sigma_i\sigma_j$.) Then the weighted sum of the n random variables has mean

$$\mathrm{E}\left(\sum_{i=1}^{n} \omega_i x_i\right) = \sum_{i=1}^{n} \omega_i \mu_i \tag{8}$$

and variance

$$\mathrm{Var}\left(\sum_{i=1}^{n} \omega_i x_i\right) = \sum_{i=1}^{n}\sum_{j=1}^{n} \omega_i \omega_j \sigma_{ij} \tag{9}$$

where ω_i and ω_j represent arbitrary weights. These formulas for the mean and variance are true for any distribution of the x_i.

In general, the distribution of a sum of random variables is different from the distribution of the individual random variables. However, the normal distribution is an example of a **stable distribution**. A distribution is stable if sums of random variables have the same distribution as the original random variables. In this case, the sum of jointly-normally distributed random variables is normal. Thus, if x_i are jointly-normally distributed,

$$\sum_{i=1}^{n} \omega_i x_i \sim \mathcal{N}\left(\sum_{i=1}^{n} \omega_i \mu_i, \sum_{i=1}^{n}\sum_{j=1}^{n} \omega_i \omega_j \sigma_{ij}\right) \tag{10}$$

A familiar special case of this occurs with the sum of two random variables:

$$ax_1 + bx_2 \sim \mathcal{N}\left(a\mu_1 + b\mu_2, a^2\sigma_1^2 + b^2\sigma_2^2 + 2ab\rho\sigma_1\sigma_2\right)$$

The Central Limit Theorem. Why does the normal distribution appear in option pricing (and frequently in other contexts)? The normal distribution is important because it arises naturally when random variables are added. The normal distribution was originally discovered by mathematicians studying series of random events, such as gambling outcomes and observational errors.[2] Suppose, for example, that a surveyor is making observations to draft a map. The measurements will always have some error, and the error will differ from measurement to measurement. Errors can arise from observational error, imprecise use of the instruments, or simply from recording the wrong number. Whatever the reason, the errors will in general be accidental and, hence, *uncorrelated*. If you were using such error-prone data, you would like to know the statistical distribution of these errors in order to assess the reliability of your conclusions for a given number of observations, and also to decide how many observations to make to achieve a given degree of reliability. It would seem that the nature of the errors would differ depending on who made them, the kind of equipment used, and so forth. The remarkable result is that sums of such errors are approximately normal.

The normal distribution is therefore not just a convenient, aesthetically pleasing distribution, but it arises in nature when outcomes can be characterized as sums of independent random variables with a finite variance. The distribution of such a sum approaches normality. This result is known as the **central limit theorem**.[3]

In the context of asset returns, the continuously compounded stock return over a year is the sum of the daily continuously compounded returns. If news and other factors are the shocks that cause asset prices to change, and if these changes are independent, then it is natural to think that longer-period continuously compounded returns are normally distributed. Since the central limit theorem is a theorem about what happens in the limit, sums of just a few random variables may not appear normal. But the normality of continuously compounded returns is a reasonable starting point for thinking about stock returns.

2. THE LOGNORMAL DISTRIBUTION

A random variable, y, is said to be **lognormally distributed** if $\ln(y)$ is normally distributed. Put another way, if x is normally distributed, y is lognormal if it can be written in either of two equivalent ways:

$$\ln(y) = x$$

or

$$y = e^x$$

This last equation is the link between normally distributed continuously compounded returns and lognormality of the stock price.

2. The history of statistics—including the story of the normal distribution—is entertainingly related in Bernstein (1996).

3. Most statistics books discuss one or more versions of the central limit theorem. See, for example, Casella and Berger (2002, pp. 236–239), DeGroot (1975, pp. 227–231), or Mood et al. (1974, pp. 233–236).

By definition, the continuously compounded return from 0 to t is

$$R(0, t) = \ln(S_t/S_0) \tag{11}$$

Suppose $R(0, t)$ is normally distributed. By exponentiating both sides, we obtain

$$S_t = S_0 e^{R(0,t)} \tag{12}$$

Equation (12) shows that if continuously compounded returns are normally distributed, then the stock price is lognormally distributed. Exponentiation converts the continuously compounded return, $R(0, t)$, into one plus the effective total return from 0 to t, $e^{R(0,t)}$. Notice that because S_t is created by exponentiation of $R(0, t)$, *a lognormal stock price cannot be negative.*

We saw that the sum of normal variables is normal. For this reason, the *product* of lognormal random variables is lognormal. If x_1 and x_2 are normal, then $y_1 = e^{x_1}$ and $y_2 = e^{x_2}$ are lognormal. The product of y_1 and y_2 is

$$y_1 \times y_2 = e^{x_1} \times e^{x_2} = e^{x_1+x_2}$$

Since $x_1 + x_2$ is normal, $e^{x_1+x_2}$ is lognormal. Thus, because normality is preserved by addition, lognormality is preserved by multiplication. However, just as the product of normal random variables is not normal, the sum of lognormal random variables is not lognormal.

The binomial model generates a stock price distribution that appears lognormal; this was an example of the central limit theorem. In the binomial model, the continuously compounded stock return is binomially distributed. Sums of binomial random variables approach normality. Thus, in the binomial model, the continuously compounded return approaches normality and the stock price distribution approaches lognormality.

If $\ln(y) \sim \mathcal{N}(m, v^2)$, the lognormal density function is given by

$$g(y; m, v) \equiv \frac{1}{yv\sqrt{2\pi}} e^{-\frac{1}{2}\left(\frac{\ln(y)-m}{v}\right)^2}$$

Figure 3 displays three different lognormal densities for various values of m and v. Notice that the lognormal distribution is nonnegative and skewed to the right. The distribution for which the underlying normal distribution has a high mean (1.5) and low standard deviation (0.2) most resembles the normal distribution. It is still bounded below by zero and skewed to the right. Two of the distributions in Figure 3 are based upon exponentiating the distributions in Figure 1.

We can compute the mean and variance of a lognormally distributed random variable. If $x \sim \mathcal{N}(m, v^2)$, then the expected value of e^x is given by

$$\boxed{\mathrm{E}(e^x) = e^{m+\frac{1}{2}v^2}} \tag{13}$$

We prove this in Appendix A, but it is intuitive that the mean of the exponentiated variable will be greater than the exponentiated mean of the underlying normal variable. Exponentiation is asymmetric: A positive random draw generates a bigger increase than an identical negative random draw does a decrease. To see this, consider a mean zero binomial random variable that is 0.5 with probability 0.5 and −0.5 with probability 0.5. You can verify that $e^{0.5} = 1.6487$. Thus, $\frac{e^{0.5}+e^{-0.5}}{2} = \frac{1.6487+0.6065}{2} = 1.128$, which is obviously greater than $e^0 = 1$.

FIGURE 3

Graph of the lognormal density for y, where $\ln(y) \sim \mathcal{N}(0, 1)$, $\ln(y) \sim \mathcal{N}(0, 1.5)$, and $\ln(y) \sim \mathcal{N}(1.5, 0.2)$.

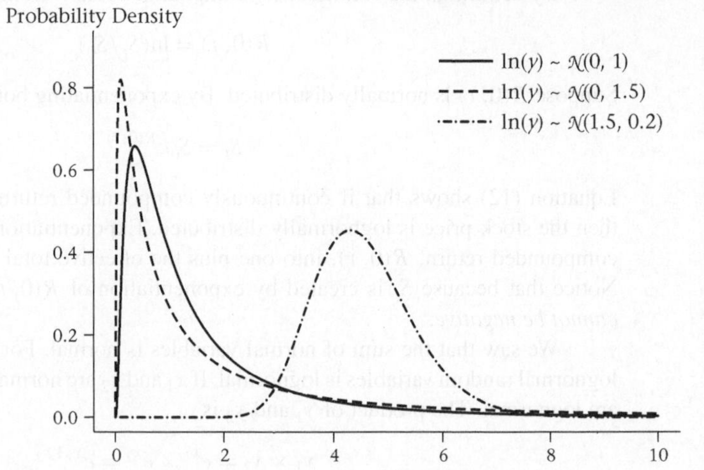

This is a specific example of **Jensen's inequality**: The expectation of a function of a random variable is not generally equal to the function evaluated at the expectation of the random variable. In the context of this example, $\mathrm{E}(e^x) \neq e^{\mathrm{E}(x)}$. Since the exponential function is convex, Jensen's inequality implies that $\mathrm{E}(e^x) > e^{\mathrm{E}(x)}$. Derivatives theory is replete with examples of Jensen's inequality.

The variance of a lognormal random variable is

$$\mathrm{Var}(e^x) = e^{2m+v^2}\left(e^{v^2} - 1\right) \tag{14}$$

While we can compute the variance of a lognormal variable, it is much more convenient to use only the variance of $\ln(y)$, which is normal.

3. A LOGNORMAL MODEL OF STOCK PRICES

How do we implement lognormality as a model for the stock price? If the stock price S_t is lognormal, we can write

$$\frac{S_t}{S_0} = e^x$$

where x, the continuously compounded return from 0 to t, is normally distributed. We want to find a specification for x that provides a *useful* way to think about stock prices.

Let the continuously compounded return from time t to some later time s be $R(t, s)$. Suppose we have times $t_0 < t_1 < t_2$. By the definition of the continuously compounded return, we have

$$S_{t_1} = S_{t_0} e^{R(t_0, t_1)}$$
$$S_{t_2} = S_{t_1} e^{R(t_1, t_2)}$$

The stock price at t_2 can therefore be expressed as

$$\begin{aligned} S_{t_2} &= S_{t_1} e^{R(t_1, t_2)} \\ &= S_{t_0} e^{R(t_0, t_1)} e^{R(t_1, t_2)} \\ &= S_{t_0} e^{R(t_0, t_1) + R(t_1, t_2)} \end{aligned}$$

Thus, the continuously compounded return from t_0 to t_2, $R(t_0, t_2)$, is the sum of the continuously compounded returns over the shorter periods:

$$R(t_0, t_2) = R(t_0, t_1) + R(t_1, t_2) \tag{15}$$

Example 3. Suppose the stock price is initially \$100 and the continuously compounded return on a stock is 15% one year and 3% the next year. The price after 1 year is $\$100e^{0.15} = \$116.1834$, and after 2 years is $\$116.1834e^{0.03} = \$119.722$. This equals $100e^{0.15+0.03} = 100e^{0.18}$. ■

Equation (15), together with the assumption that returns are independent and identically distributed over time, implies that the mean and variance of returns over different horizons are proportional to the length of the horizon. Take the period of time from 0 to T and carve it up into n intervals of length h, where $h = T/n$. We can then write the continuously compounded return from 0 to T as the sum of the n returns over the shorter periods:

$$\begin{aligned} R(0, T) &= R(0, h) + R(h, 2h) + \cdots + R[(n-1)h, T] \\ &= \sum_{i=1}^{n} R[(i-1)h, ih] \end{aligned}$$

Let $\mathrm{E}(R[(i-1)h, ih]) = \alpha_h$ and $\mathrm{Var}(R[(i-1)h, ih]) = \sigma_h^2$. Then over the entire period, the mean and variance are

$$\mathrm{E}[R(0, T)] = n\alpha_h \tag{16}$$

$$\mathrm{Var}[R(0, T)] = n\sigma_h^2 \tag{17}$$

Thus, if returns are independent and identically distributed, *the mean and variance of the continuously compounded returns are proportional to time*. This result corresponds with the intuition that both the mean and variance of the return should be greater over long horizons than over short horizons.

Now we have enough background to present an explicit lognormal model of the stock price. Generally we will let t be denominated in years and α and σ be the annual mean and standard deviation, with δ the annual dividend yield on the stock. We will assume that the continuously compounded capital gain from 0 to t, $\ln(S_t/S_0)$, is normally distributed with mean $(\alpha - \delta - 0.5\sigma^2)t$ and variance $\sigma^2 t$:

$$\boxed{\ln(S_t/S_0) \sim \mathcal{N}[(\alpha - \delta - 0.5\sigma^2)t, \sigma^2 t]} \tag{18}$$

This gives us two equivalent ways to write an expression for the stock price.

First, recall from equation (7) that we can convert a standard normal random variable, Z, into one with an arbitrary mean or variance by multiplying by the standard deviation and adding the mean. We can write

$$\ln(S_t/S_0) = (\alpha - \delta - \frac{1}{2}\sigma^2)t + \sigma\sqrt{t}Z \tag{19}$$

Second, we can exponentiate equation (19) to obtain an expression for the stock price:

$$\boxed{S_t = S_0 e^{(\alpha-\delta-\frac{1}{2}\sigma^2)t+\sigma\sqrt{t}Z}} \tag{20}$$

We will use equation (20) often in what follows.

You may be wondering how to interpret equations (18), (19), and (20). The subtraction of the dividend yield, δ, is necessary since, other things equal, a higher dividend yield means a lower future stock price. But why do we subtract $\frac{1}{2}\sigma^2$ in the mean?

To understand equation (20) it helps to compute the expected stock price. We can do this by breaking up the right-hand side of equation (20) into two terms, one of which contains the random variable Z and the other of which does not:

$$S_t = S_0 e^{(\alpha-\delta-\frac{1}{2}\sigma^2)t} e^{\sigma\sqrt{t}Z}$$

Next, evaluate the expectation of $e^{\sigma\sqrt{t}Z}$ using equation (13). Since $z \sim \mathcal{N}(0, 1)$, we have

$$\mathrm{E}\left(e^{\sigma\sqrt{t}Z}\right) = e^{\frac{1}{2}\sigma^2 t}$$

This gives us

$$\mathrm{E}(S_t) = S_0 e^{(\alpha-\delta-\frac{1}{2}\sigma^2)t} e^{\frac{1}{2}\sigma^2 t} = S_0 e^{(\alpha-\delta)t} \tag{21}$$

We therefore have

$$\boxed{\ln \mathrm{E}\left(\frac{S_t}{S_0}\right) = (\alpha - \delta)t} \tag{22}$$

The expression $\alpha - \delta$ is the continuously compounded expected rate of appreciation on the stock. If we did not subtract $\frac{1}{2}\sigma^2$ in equation (20), then the expected rate of appreciation would be $\alpha - \delta + \frac{1}{2}\sigma^2$. This is fine (we can define things as we like), except that it renders α difficult to interpret.

Thus, the issue is purely one of creating an expression where it is easy to interpret the parameters. If we want $\alpha - \delta$ to have an interpretation as the continuously compounded expected capital gain on the stock, then because of equation (13), we need to subtract $\frac{1}{2}\sigma^2$.

The median stock price—the value such that 50% of the time prices will be above or below that value—is obtained by setting $Z = 0$ in equation (20). The median is thus

$$S_0 e^{(\alpha-\delta-\frac{1}{2}\sigma^2)t} = \mathrm{E}(S_t) e^{-\frac{1}{2}\sigma^2 t}$$

This equation demonstrates that the median is below the mean. *More than 50% of the time, a lognormally distributed stock will earn below its expected return.* Perhaps more surprisingly, if σ is large, a lognormally distributed stock will lose money ($S_t < S_0$) more than half the time!

Example 4. Suppose that the stock price today is \$100, the expected rate of return on the stock is $\alpha = 10\%/\text{year}$, and the standard deviation (volatility) is $\sigma = 30\%/\text{year}$. If the stock is lognormally distributed, the continuously compounded 2-year return is 20% and the 2-year volatility is $0.30 \times \sqrt{2} = 0.4243$. Thus, we have

$$S_2 = \$100e^{(0.1-\frac{1}{2}0.3^2)\times 2+\sigma\sqrt{2}Z}$$

The expected value of S_2 is

$$\text{E}(S_2) = \$100e^{(0.1\times 2)} = \$122.14$$

The median stock price is

$$\$100e^{(0.1-0.5\times 0.3^2)\times 2} = \$111.63$$

If the volatility were 60%, the expected value would still be \$122.14, but the median would be

$$\$100e^{(0.1-0.5\times 0.6^2)\times 2} = \$85.21$$

Half the time, after 2 years the stock price would be below this value. ■

We can also define a "one standard deviation move" in the stock price. Since z has the standard normal distribution, then if $Z = 1$, the continuously compounded stock return is the mean plus one standard deviation, and if $Z = -1$, the continuously compounded stock return is the mean minus one standard deviation.

Example 5. Using the same assumptions as in Example 4, a one standard deviation move up over 2 years is given by

$$S_2 = \$100e^{(0.1-\frac{1}{2}0.3^2)\times 2+\sigma\sqrt{2}\times 1} = \$170.62$$

A one standard deviation move down is given by

$$S_2 = \$100e^{(0.1-\frac{1}{2}0.3^2)\times 2-\sigma\sqrt{2}\times 1} = \$73.03$$

We can think of these prices as logarithmically centered around the mean price of \$122.14. ■

In the three different ways to construct a binomial model, all had up and down stock price moves of the form

$$S_u = Se^{\alpha h+\sigma\sqrt{h}}; \qquad S_d = Se^{\alpha h-\sigma\sqrt{h}}$$

where α differed for the three models. In all cases, we generated up and down moves by setting $Z = \pm 1$. As $h \to 0$ the three models converge; the effects of the different α's in each case are offset by the different risk-neutral probabilities.

4. LOGNORMAL PROBABILITY CALCULATIONS

If S_t is lognormally distributed, we can use this fact to compute a number of probabilities and expectations. For example, we can compute the probability that an option will expire in the money, and, given that it expires in the money, the expected stock price. In this section we will present formulas for these calculations.

Probabilities

If the stock price today is S_0, what is the probability that $S_t < K$, where K is some arbitrary number? Note that $S_t < K$ exactly when $\ln(S_t) < \ln(K)$. Since $\ln(S_t)$ is normally distributed, we can just use the normal calculations we developed above. We have

$$\ln(S_t/S_0) \sim \mathcal{N}[(\alpha - \delta - 0.5\sigma^2)t, \sigma^2 t]$$

or, equivalently,

$$\ln(S_t) \sim \mathcal{N}\left[\ln(S_0) + (\alpha - \delta - 0.5\sigma^2)t, \sigma^2 t\right]$$

We can create a standard normal number random variable, Z, by subtracting the mean and dividing by the standard deviation:

$$Z = \frac{\ln(S_t) - \ln(S_0) - (\alpha - \delta - 0.5\sigma^2)t}{\sigma\sqrt{t}}$$

We have $\Pr(S_t < K) = \Pr[\ln(S_t) < \ln(K)]$. Subtracting the mean from both $\ln(S_t)$ and $\ln(K)$ and dividing by the standard deviation, we obtain

$$\Pr(S_t < K) =$$
$$\Pr\left[\frac{\ln(S_t) - \ln(S_0) - (\alpha - \delta - 0.5\sigma^2)t}{\sigma\sqrt{t}} < \frac{\ln(K) - \ln(S_0) - (\alpha - \delta - 0.5\sigma^2)t}{\sigma\sqrt{t}}\right]$$

Since the left-hand side is a standard normal random variable, the probability that $S_t < K$ is

$$\Pr(S_t < K) = \Pr\left[Z < \frac{\ln(K) - \ln(S_0) - (\alpha - \delta - 0.5\sigma^2)t}{\sigma\sqrt{t}}\right]$$

Since $Z \sim \mathcal{N}(0, 1)$, $\Pr(S_t < K)$ is

$$\Pr(S_t < K) = N\left[\frac{\ln(K) - \ln(S_0) - (\alpha - \delta - 0.5\sigma^2)t}{\sigma\sqrt{t}}\right]$$

This can also be written

$$\boxed{\Pr(S_t < K) = N(-\hat{d}_2)} \quad (23)$$

where $\hat{d}_2$ is the standard Black-Scholes argument with the risk-free rate, r, replaced with the actual expected return on the stock, α. We can also perform the complementary calculation.

We have $\Pr(S_t > K) = 1 - \Pr(S_t < K)$, so

$$\boxed{\Pr(S_t > K) = N(\hat{d}_2)} \tag{24}$$

The expression $N(\hat{d}_2)$ contains the true expected return on the stock, α. If we replace α with r, the risk-free rate in equations (23) and (24), we obtain the risk-neutral probabilities that S_t is above or below K. It is exactly these risk-neutral versions of equations (23) and (24) that appear in the Black-Scholes call and put option pricing formulas.

Lognormal Prediction Intervals

We can now answer questions about future prices, such as "What is the range of prices such that there is a 95% probability that the stock price will be in that range 1 year from today?" To answer this question, we compute the 95% prediction intervals for a number of different time horizons.

Suppose we would like to know the prices S_t^L and S_t^U such that $\Pr(S_t < S_t^L) = p/2$ and $\Pr(S_t > S_t^U) = p/2$. If the stock price is S_0, we can generate S_t^L and S_t^U as follows. We know from equation (23) that

$$\Pr(S < S_t^L) = N(-\hat{d}_2)$$

where

$$\hat{d}_2 = [\ln(S_0/S_t^L) + (\alpha - \delta - 0.5\sigma^2)t]/\sigma\sqrt{t}$$

Thus, we want to find the S_t^L such that the probability that S_t is less than S_t^L is $p/2$, or

$$p/2 = N(-\hat{d}_2)$$

In order to do this, we need to invert the cumulative standard normal distribution function—i.e., ask what number $\hat{d}_2$ corresponds to a given probability. We can write this inverse cumulative normal probability function as $N^{-1}(p)$. Then by definition, $N^{-1}[N(x)] = x$. Fortunately, this is a standard calculation, and Excel and other spreadsheets contain a built-in function that does this. (In Excel it is NormSInv().) We have

$$N^{-1}(p/2) = -\hat{d}_2$$

Solving explicitly for S_t^L gives us

$$S_t^L = S_0 e^{(\alpha-\delta-\frac{1}{2}\sigma^2)t+\sigma\sqrt{t}N^{-1}(p/2)}$$

Similarly, we can solve for the upper bound S_t^U such that

$$N^{-1}(1 - p/2) = -[\ln(S_0/S_t^U) + (\alpha - \delta - 0.5\sigma^2)t]/\sigma\sqrt{t}$$

This gives us

$$S_t^U = S_0 e^{(\alpha-\delta-\frac{1}{2}\sigma^2)t+\sigma\sqrt{t}N^{-1}(1-p/2)}$$

Thus, to generate a prediction interval for a lognormal price, we need only find the values of z corresponding to the same prediction interval for a $\mathcal{N}(0, 1)$ variable, and then substitute those values into the expression for the lognormal price.

Example 6. If $p = 5\%$, $N^{-1}(0.025) = -1.96$ and $N^{-1}(0.975) = 1.96$. That is, there is a 5% probability that a standard normal random variable will be outside the range $(-1.96, 1.96)$. Thus, if $S_0 = \$100$, $t = 2$, $\alpha = 0.10$, $\delta = 0$, and $\sigma = 0.30$, we have

$$\begin{aligned} S_t^L &= S_0 e^{(\alpha-\delta-\frac{1}{2}\sigma^2)t-\sigma\sqrt{t}1.96} \\ &= S_0 e^{(0.10-\frac{1}{2}0.3^2)\times 2-0.3\times\sqrt{2}\times 1.96} \\ &= \$48.599 \end{aligned}$$

Similarly, for S_t^U we have

$$\begin{aligned} S_t^U &= S_0 e^{(\alpha-\delta-\frac{1}{2}\sigma^2)t+\sigma\sqrt{t}1.96} \\ &= \$256.40 \quad \blacksquare \end{aligned}$$

Example 7. Suppose we have a lognormally distributed \$50 stock with a 15% continuously compounded expected rate of return, a zero dividend yield, and a 30% volatility. Consider a horizon of 1 month ($t = \frac{1}{12}$). The monthly continuously compounded mean return is

$$\begin{aligned} (\alpha - \delta - \frac{1}{2}\sigma^2)t &= \left(0.15 - 0 - \frac{1}{2}0.3^2\right)\frac{1}{12} \\ &= 0.00875 \end{aligned}$$

and the monthly standard deviation is

$$\begin{aligned} \sigma\sqrt{t} &= 0.3\sqrt{\frac{1}{12}} \\ &= 0.0866 \end{aligned}$$

For the standard normal distribution, there is a 68.27% probability of drawing a number in the interval $(-1, +1)$, and a 95.45% probability of drawing a number in the interval $(-2, +2)$. Thus, over a 1-month horizon, there is a 68.27% chance that the continuously compounded return on the stock will be 0.00875 ± 0.0866 (i.e., the return is between -7.88% and 9.54%), and a 95.45% chance that the return will be $0.00875 \pm 2 \times 0.0866$ (the return will be between -16.44% and 18.19%):

$$-0.0788 \le \ln\left(\frac{S_{\text{one month}}}{50}\right) \le 0.0954 \quad \text{prob} = 68.27\%$$

$$-0.1644 \le \ln\left(\frac{S_{\text{one month}}}{50}\right) \le 0.1819 \quad \text{prob} = 95.45\%$$

Equivalently, by exponentiating all of these terms (for example, $\$50e^{-0.0788} = \$46.22$, $e^{\ln\left(\frac{S_{\text{one month}}}{50}\right)} = S_{\text{one month}}/50$, etc.), we can express the prediction interval in terms of prices

$$\$46.22 \le S_{\text{one month}} \le \$55.06 \quad \text{prob} = 68.27\%$$

$$\$42.35 \le S_{\text{one month}} \le \$62.09 \quad \text{prob} = 95.45\%$$

Using this same logic, we can compute one standard deviation and two standard deviation intervals over different horizons. This will give us 68.27% and 95.45% prediction intervals

TABLE 1 Stock prices ($) corresponding to −2, −1, 1, and 2 standard deviations from the initial stock price of 50.

Horizon	Fraction of a Year	-2σ	-1σ	$+1\sigma$	$+2\sigma$
1 Day	0.0027	48.47	49.24	50.81	51.61
1 Month	0.0849	42.35	46.22	55.06	60.09
1 Year	1	30.48	41.14	74.97	101.19
2 Years	2	26.40	40.36	94.28	144.11
5 Years	5	22.10	43.22	165.31	323.33

over those horizons, which are displayed in Table 1. For example, there is a 95.45% chance over a 1-day horizon that a $50 stock will be between $48.47 and $51.61. Over a 5-year horizon, there is a 95.45% chance that the stock price will be between $22.10 and $323.33. ■

The calculation in Example 7 is often used to compute loss probabilities and risk exposure. This is how value at risk (VaR) is calculated. The idea behind VaR is to assess the magnitude of a possible loss on a position that can occur with a given probability over a given horizon. So, for example, if we examine the 1-day horizon in Table 1, there is a 2.275% probability that over a 1-day horizon the stock price will drop below $48.47.[4] In practice, it is common to evaluate the magnitude of moves of 1.96σ since this corresponds to a 5% ("once in 20 days") probability of occurrence.

Box 1 illustrates how the probability calculations in this section can be used to analyze the cost of portfolio insurance over time.

The Conditional Expected Price

Given that an option expires in-the-money, what is the expected stock price? The answer to this question is the expected stock price *conditional* upon the option expiring in-the-money. For a put with strike price K, we want to calculate $\mathrm{E}(S_t|S_t < K)$, the expected stock price conditional on $S_t < K$. To compute this expectation, we need to take into account only the portion of the probability density representing stock prices below K.

To understand the calculations we are going to perform in this section, consider a binomial model in which the strike price is $50, and the stock price at expiration can be $20, $40, $60, or $80, with probabilities 1/8, 3/8, 3/8, and 1/8. If a put is in the money at expiration, the stock price is either $20 or $40. Suppose that for these two values we sum the stock price times the probability. We obtain

$$\sum_{S_t<50} \Pr(S_t) \times S_t = \left(\frac{1}{8} \times \$20\right) + \left(\frac{3}{8} \times \$40\right) = \$17.50 \tag{25}$$

4. You can verify the 2.275% probability by computing $N(-2)$.

BOX 1: Portfolio Insurance for the Long Run

The cost of insuring a stock portfolio so that it performs at least as well as a zero-coupon bond is increasing with the time to maturity of the insurance. The demonstration of this relies on the absence of arbitrage, which is incontrovertible but does not always provide intuition about the result. Using the results in this section, we can reconcile the historical low probability of stocks underperforming bonds with the increasing cost of insurance as we insure over a longer horizon.

The probability that $S_T < K$ is given by equation (23). By setting the strike price to equal the forward price, i.e., $K_T = S_0 e^{rT}$, we can use equation (23) to calculate the probability that stocks bought at time 0 will have underperformed bonds at time T. After simplification, equation (23) can be written

$$\Pr(S_T < K_T) = N\left(\frac{\frac{1}{2}\sigma^2 - (\alpha - r)}{\sigma}\sqrt{T}\right)$$

Thus, if the stock is lognormally distributed, the probability of the stock underperforming a zero-coupon bond depends on the size of the risk premium on stocks, $\alpha - r$, relative to one-half the variance, $\frac{1}{2}\sigma^2$. If the risk premium is high, puts will be increasingly less likely to pay off in the long run, even though the put price is increasing with horizon.

The put price depends in part on the *risk-neutral* probability that the stock will underperform bonds, $\Pr^*(S_T < K)$. This is obtained by setting $\alpha = r$, and we then have

$$\Pr^*(S_T < K_T) = N\left(\frac{1}{2}\sigma\sqrt{T}\right)$$

The *risk-neutral* probability that the put will pay off is increasing with time. This fact does not by itself explain the price of the put increasing with time, since the put price also depends on the conditional expectation of the stock price when the put is in the money. However, this example does illustrate how historical *true* probabilities can mislead about the price of insurance.

The value \$17.50 is clearly not an expected stock price since it is below the lowest possible price (\$20). We call \$17.50 the **partial expectation** of the stock price conditional upon $S_t <$ \$50. When we compute a conditional expectation, we are conditioning upon the event $S_t <$ \$50, which occurs with probability 0.5. We can convert a partial expectation into a conditional expectation by dividing by the probability of the conditioning event ($S_t <$ \$50). Thus, the conditional expectation is

$$\frac{1}{\Pr(S_t < 50)} \sum_{S_t < 50} \Pr(S_t) \times S_t = \frac{1}{0.5}\left[\left(\frac{1}{8} \times \$20\right) + \left(\frac{3}{8} \times \$40\right)\right]$$
$$= \$35 \qquad (26)$$

The calculations for a lognormally distributed price are analogous, using integrals rather than summations.

The partial expectation of S_t, conditional on $S_t < K$, is

$$\int_0^K S_t g(S_t; S_0) dS_t = S_0 e^{(\alpha-\delta)t} N\left(\frac{\ln(K) - [\ln(S_0) + (\alpha - \delta + 0.5\sigma^2)t]}{\sigma\sqrt{t}}\right) \tag{27}$$

$$= S_0 e^{(\alpha-\delta)t} N(-\hat{d}_1)$$

where $g(S_t; S_0)$ is the probability density of S_t conditional on S_0, and $\hat{d}_1$ is the Black-Scholes d_1 with α replacing r.

The probability that $S_t < K$ is $N(-\hat{d}_2)$. Thus, the expectation of S_t conditional on $S_t < K$ is

$$\boxed{\mathrm{E}(S_t | S_t < K) = S_0 e^{(\alpha-\delta)t} \frac{N(-\hat{d}_1)}{N(-\hat{d}_2)}} \tag{28}$$

For a call, we are interested in the expected price conditional on $S_t > K$. The partial expectation of S_t conditional on $S_t > K$ is

$$\int_K^\infty S_t g(S_t; S_0) dS_t = S_0 e^{(\alpha-\delta)t} N\left(\frac{\ln(S_0) - \ln(K) + (\alpha - \delta + 0.5\sigma^2)t}{\sigma\sqrt{t}}\right) \tag{29}$$

$$= S_0 e^{(\alpha-\delta)t} N(\hat{d}_1)$$

As before, except for the fact that it contains the expected rate of return on the stock, α, instead of the risk-free rate, the second term is just the Black-Scholes expression, $N(d_1)$. The conditional expectation is

$$\boxed{\mathrm{E}(S_t | S_t > K) = S_0 e^{(\alpha-\delta)t} \frac{N(\hat{d}_1)}{N(\hat{d}_2)}} \tag{30}$$

The Black-Scholes Formula

Using equations (23), (24), (28), and (30), we can now heuristically derive the Black-Scholes formula. The Black-Scholes formula can be derived by assuming risk-neutrality. In this case, the expected return on stocks, α, will equal r, the risk-free rate. If we let g^* denote the risk-neutral lognormal probability density, E^* denote the expectation taken with respect to risk-neutral probabilities, and $\Pr^*$ denote those probabilities, the price of a European call option on a stock will be

$$C(S, K, \sigma, r, t, \delta) = e^{-rt} \int_K^\infty (S_t - K) g^*(S_t, S_0) dS_t$$

$$= e^{-rt} \mathrm{E}^*(S - K | S > K) \times \Pr^*(S > K)$$

We can rewrite this as

$$C(S, K, \sigma, r, t, \delta) = e^{-rt} \mathrm{E}^*(S | S > K) \times \Pr^*(S > K)$$

$$- e^{-rt} \mathrm{E}^*(K | S > K) \times \Pr^*(S > K)$$

Using (23) and (30), with $\alpha = r$, this becomes

$$C(S, K, \sigma, r, t, \delta) = e^{-\delta t} S N(d_1) - K e^{-rt} N(d_2)$$

which is the Black-Scholes formula.

Similarly, the formula for a European put option on a stock is derived by computing

$$P(S, K, \sigma, r, t, \delta) = e^{-rt}\mathrm{E}^*(K - S|K > S) \times \Pr^*(K > S)$$

We can rewrite this as

$$\begin{aligned} P(S, K, \sigma, r, t, \delta) &= e^{-rt}\mathrm{E}^*(K|K > S) \times \Pr^*(K > S) \\ &\quad - e^{-rt}\mathrm{E}^*(S|K > S) \times \Pr^*(K > S) \end{aligned}$$

and using (24) and (28), with $\alpha = r$, this becomes

$$P(S, K, \sigma, r, t, \delta) = Ke^{-rt}N(-d_2) - e^{-\delta t}SN(-d_1)$$

5. ESTIMATING THE PARAMETERS OF A LOGNORMAL DISTRIBUTION

In this section we will see how to estimate the mean and variance of lognormally distributed price data.

When stocks are lognormally distributed, a price S_t evolves from the previous price observed at time $t - h$, according to

$$S_t = S_{t-h}e^{(\alpha-\delta-\sigma^2/2)h+\sigma\sqrt{h}z}$$

Suppose we have daily observations. How would we estimate the mean and standard deviation? We have

$$\ln(S_t) = \ln(S_{t-h}) + (\alpha - \delta - \sigma^2/2)h + \sigma\sqrt{h}z$$

Thus

$$\begin{aligned} \mathrm{E}\left[\ln\left(S_t/S_{t-h}\right)\right] &= (\alpha - \delta - \sigma^2/2)h \\ \mathrm{Var}\left[\ln\left(S_t/S_{t-h}\right)\right] &= \sigma^2 h \end{aligned}$$

By using the log ratio of prices at adjacent points in time, we can compute the continuously compounded mean and variance. Note that to estimate α, we have to add one-half the estimate of the variance to the estimate of the mean.

Example 8. Table 2 contains seven weekly stock price observations along with continuously compounded returns computed from those observations. You can compute the mean and standard deviation of the values in the third column (for example, using the Average and Stdev functions in Excel). Since these are weekly observations, we are estimating the *weekly* mean of the log price ratio and the *weekly* standard deviation.

The mean of the second column in Table 2 is 0.006745 and the standard deviation is 0.038208. The annualized standard deviation is

$$\text{Annualized standard deviation} = 0.038208 \times \sqrt{52} = 0.2755$$

Two adjustments are needed to interpret the mean. First, we have to annualize it. Second, since we computed the mean of the log returns, we have to add back one-half the variance.

TABLE 2 Hypothetical weekly stock price observations and corresponding weekly continuously compounded returns, $\ln(S_t/S_{t-1})$

Week	Price ($)	$\ln(S_t/S_{t-1})$
1	100	—
2	105.04	0.0492
3	105.76	0.0068
4	108.93	0.0295
5	102.50	−0.0608
6	104.80	0.0222
7	104.13	−0.0064

Thus, we obtain

$$\text{Annualized expected return} = 0.006745 \times 52 + 0.5 \times 0.2755^2 = 0.3887$$

The prices were generated randomly assuming using a standard deviation of 30% and a mean of 10%. Despite having only six observations, the standard deviation estimate is quite close to the true value of 30%. The estimated mean, however, is quite far off. ■

We used hypothetical data in this example in order to compare the estimates to the true underlying parameters, something we cannot do with real data. As this example illustrates, mean returns are hard to estimate precisely because the mean is determined by the difference between where you start and where you end. If you start at a price of $100 and end at a price of $104, the in-between prices are irrelevant: If you had a big negative weekly return (say −20%), it must have been offset by a big positive return (on the order of +20%), or you would not have ended up at 104! Having many frequent observations is not helpful in estimating mean returns. What is helpful is having a long time interval, and seven weeks is not long.

Statistical theory tells us the precision of our estimate of the mean. With a normally distributed random variable, the standard deviation of the estimated mean is the standard deviation of the variable divided by the square root of the number of observations. The data in this example were generated using an actual weekly σ of $0.3/\sqrt{52} = 0.0416$. Divide this by $\sqrt{6}$ (since there are six return observations) to get 0.017. Thus, one standard deviation for our estimate of the mean is 1.7% on a weekly basis, or 12.25% annualized. There is a 68% probability that the annualized continuously compounded mean falls in the range 38% ± 12.25%! A 95% confidence interval is 38% ± 24.5%. This is a wide range. Even with 10 years of weekly data, one standard deviation for our estimated annualized mean would be $30\%/\sqrt{520} = 1.3\%$.

When we estimate a standard deviation, we are interested in the movement of the price. The more observations we have, the more precisely we can estimate movement. With six observations, an approximate 95% confidence interval for the standard deviation is approximately ±18 percentage points.[5] With only 26 weekly observations, the 95% confidence interval shrinks to ±8 percentage points. Moreover, unlike the mean, we can increase the precision of our estimate of the standard deviation by making more frequent observations. In general, standard deviations are easier to estimate than means.

In this discussion we have assumed that the variance is not changing over time. There is good evidence, however, that the variance does change over time, and sophisticated statistical methods can be used to estimate changing variances.

You should also be aware that, in practice, using data from very tiny intervals (e.g., hourly prices) may not increase precision. Over short time periods, factors such as bid-ask bounce—the movement of the price between the bid and ask spreads due to some orders being sells and others being buys—can introduce into prices noise that is not related to the values we are trying to measure.

6. HOW ARE ASSET PRICES DISTRIBUTED?

The lognormal model assumes that stock returns are independent over time (today's return does not affect future returns), that mean and volatility are constant over time, and that the distribution of continuously compounded returns is normal. However, implied volatilities differ for options with different strikes. One possible explanation is that stock prices are not lognormally distributed. How can we tell whether lognormality (or some other particular distribution) is a reasonable approximation for actual stock prices?

Histograms

One way to assess lognormality is simply to plot the continuously compounded returns as a histogram and see whether the resulting distribution appears normal. The top row of Figure 4 presents histograms for daily returns over a 10-year period for the S&P 500 index and for IBM. The bottom row is histograms for weekly returns. Also plotted on each graph is a normal distribution, computed using the historical mean and standard deviation for each return series.[6] Several observations are pertinent.

None of the histograms appears exactly normal. All of the histograms exhibit a peak around zero; the presence or absence of this peakedness is referred to as *kurtosis* (a measure of how "sharp" the peak of the distribution is), and the graph displays *leptokurtosis* (*lepto*

5. The variability of the variance estimate is described by the chi-squared distribution. (The chi-squared distribution is the distribution of sums of squared independent standard normal variables; hence, it describes the distribution of the estimated variance when observations are independent.) Suppose we wish to test the null hypothesis that our variance estimate $s^2 = \sigma_0^2$ and that we have n observations. The variable $(n-1)s^2/\sigma_0^2$ has the chi-squared distribution with $n-1$ degrees of freedom. If we wish to perform a two-tailed test when we have six observations, the critical values for 0.975 and 0.025 confidence are 0.831 and 12.832. If our null hypothesis is that $\sigma_0^2 = 0.09$, then the 95% confidence interval is 0.01496 – 0.23097. This corresponds to a range of standard deviations of 12.23% – 48.06%, or approximately 30% ± 18%. The calculation for 26 observations is similar.

6. An equivalent approach would be to normalize returns by subtracting the estimated mean and dividing by the estimated standard deviation. The resulting series should then be standard normal if returns are truly lognormal.

FIGURE 4

Histograms for daily and weekly returns on the S&P 500 index and IBM, from July 1, 2001 to July 1, 2011.

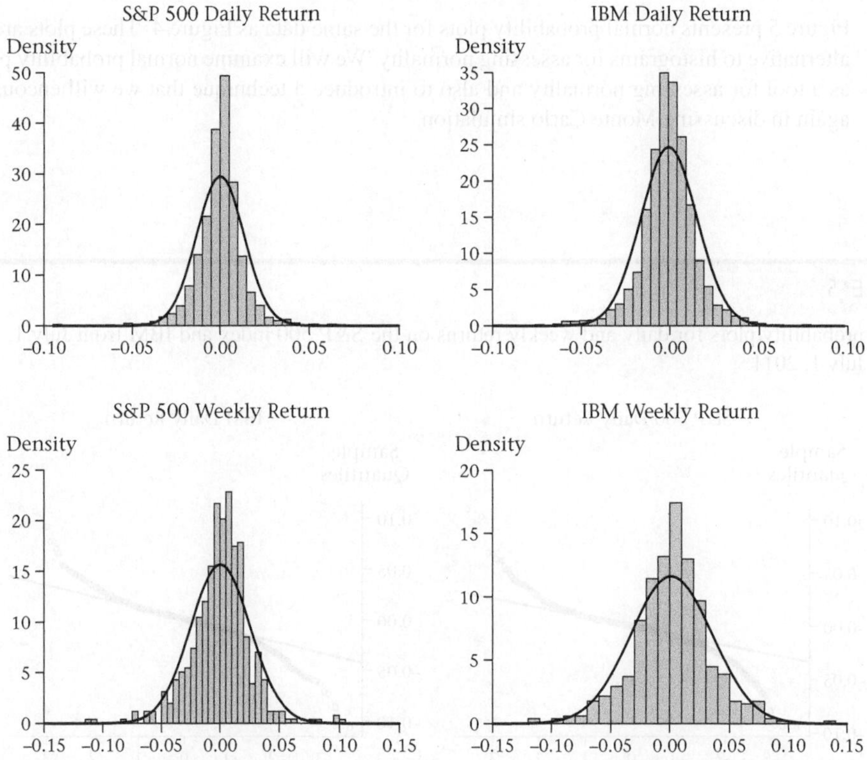

meaning "small, thin, delicate").[7] For a normally distributed random variable, kurtosis is 3. For the data plotted in Figure 4, kurtosis for the S&P and IBM are 8.03 and 9.54 for daily returns, and 4.68 and 5.21 for weekly returns. Accompanying the peaks are *fat tails*, large returns that occur more often than would be predicted by the lognormal model. These shapes are typical for stock returns.

There are several possible explanations for returns appearing nonnormal. One is that stock prices can jump discretely from time to time. Another explanation is that returns are normally distributed, but with a variance that changes over time. If actual daily returns are drawn from a distribution that has a 1% volatility half the time and a 2% volatility half the time, the stock price histogram will appear fat-tailed. This blend of two distributions is

7. The kurtosis of a distribution is the fourth central moment (i.e., $E[(x-\mu)^4]$, where μ is the mean) divided by σ^4.

commonly referred to as a **mixture of normals** model. Long-horizon returns, which result from summing short-horizon returns, will still appear normal.

Normal Probability Plots

Figure 5 presents normal probability plots for the same data as Figure 4. These plots are an alternative to histograms for assessing normality. We will examine normal probability plots as a tool for assessing normality and also to introduce a technique that we will encounter again in discussing Monte Carlo simulation.

FIGURE 5

Normal probability plots for daily and weekly returns on the S&P 500 index and IBM from July 1, 2001 to July 1, 2011.

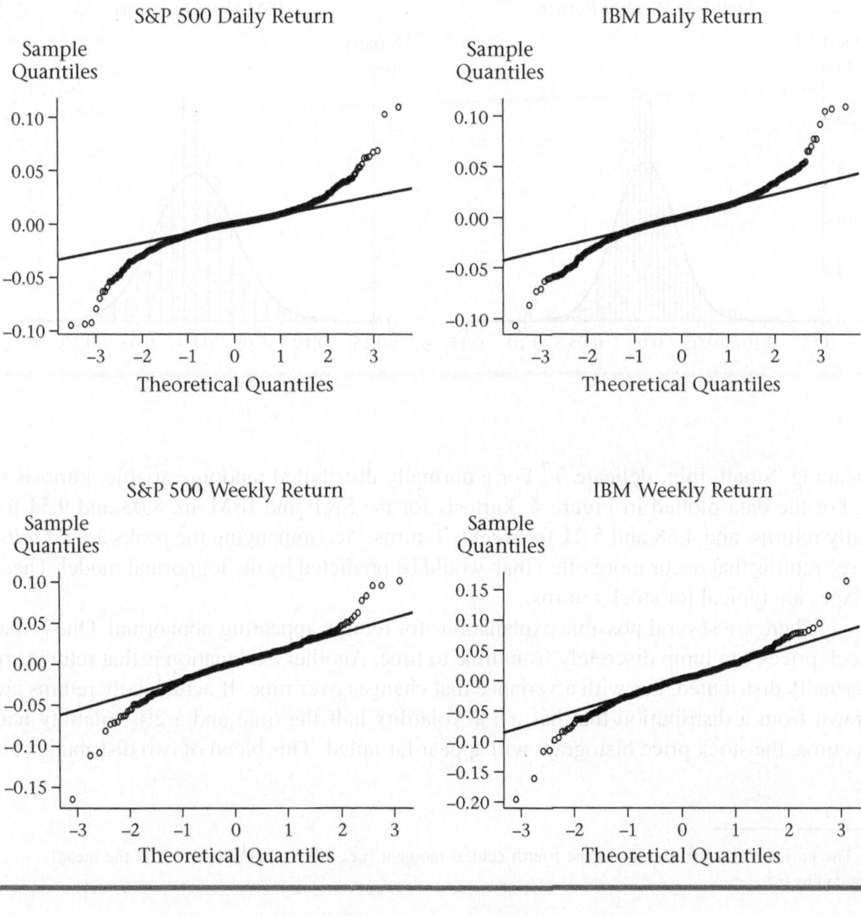

The interpretation of these plots is straightforward: If the data points (plotted with a "+") lie along the straight line in the graph, the data are consistent with a normal distribution. If the data plot is curved, the data are less likely to have come from a normal distribution. In both cases it appears the data are not normal. There are too many points to the left of the line for low values and to the right of the line for high values. The interpretation of the plots is that extreme low and high returns occur more often than with a normal distribution.

For both the S&P index and IBM, the weekly returns appear more normal than daily returns, in that the observations more closely resemble the straight line. This is the relationship we would expect from the central limit theorem. Weekly returns are the sum of daily returns. If daily returns are independent and identically distributed, the summed daily returns will tend toward normality.

We will consider a simple example to see how a normal plot is constructed. First we have to define two concepts, *order statistics* and *quantiles*. Suppose that we randomly draw n random variables x_i, $i = 1, \ldots, n$, from some distribution with the cumulative distribution function $F(x)$. (For the normal distribution, $F(x) = N(x)$). If we sort the data in ascending order, the sorted data are called **order statistics**.

Example 9. Suppose we draw from a distribution five times and obtain the values {7, 3, 11, 5, 4}. The order statistics are {3, 4, 5, 7, 11}. ■

The qth **quantile** of the distribution F is the smallest value x such that $F(x) \geq q$. In words, the qth quantile is the x such that there is at least probability q of drawing a value from the distribution less than or equal to x.

Example 10. Suppose z is standard normal. The 10% quantile is the value such that there is a 10% chance that a draw from the standard normal distribution is less than that number. Using the inverse cumulative distribution, $N^{-1}(0.10) = -1.282$. Thus, the 10% quantile is -1.281. The 30% quantile is $N^{-1}(0.3) = -0.524$. ■

The idea of the normal probability plot (which can be done for any distribution, not just normal) is to compare the distance between the quantiles of the data with the distance between the quantiles of the normal distribution. If they are the same, the normal probability plot is a straight line.

To see how this works, suppose we have the five values in Example 9. We want to assign quantiles to the data points, so with five data points we need five quantiles. Divide the range 0–100% into 0–20%, 20%–40%, and so forth. Assign the order statistics (the ordered data points) to the midpoints of these ranges, so that 3 is assigned a quantile value of 10%, 4 a quantile value of 30%, 5 to 50%, 7 to 70%, and 11 to 90%.[8] The normal probability plot then graphs these points against the points from the corresponding quantiles of the standard normal distribution.

The top left panel of Figure 6 presents the normal plot for the data in Example 9 with the data points plotted against the corresponding z-values of the standard normal distribution. Appendix B explains the construction of this plot. The top right panel is exactly the same, except that the y-axis is labeled with probabilities corresponding to the z-values.

8. With six data points, we would have assigned quantile ranges of 0–16.67, 16.67–33.33, etc., and the order statistics would then be assigned to the quantiles 8.333, 25, 41.67, etc.

The data do not appear normal, though with only five points there is a large possibility for error.

The bottom row of Figure 6 presents normal probability plots with two different y-axes for 1000 randomly generated points from a $\mathcal{N}(0, 1)$ distribution. In this case the data lie along the line and, hence, appear normal. In all of the normal probability plots, the straight

FIGURE 6

Normal probability plots for the five data points in Example 9: 3, 4, 5, 7, and 11 (top) and 1000 points randomly generated from a $\mathcal{N}(0, 1)$ distribution (bottom).

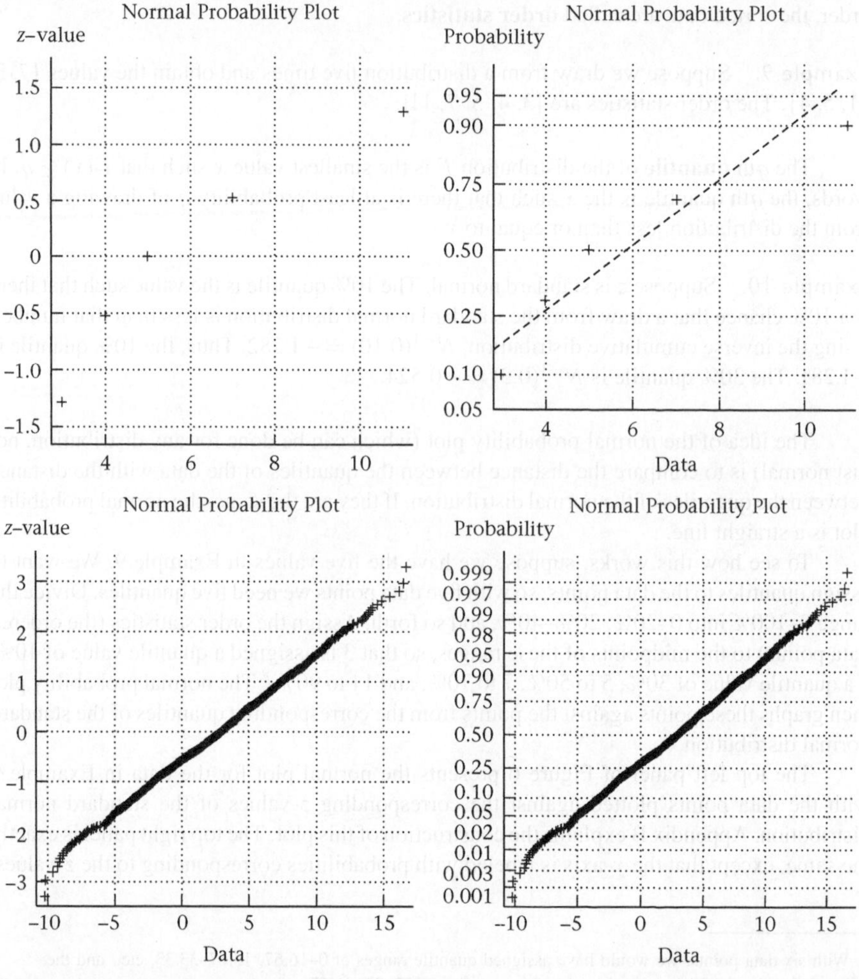

line is drawn connecting the 25% and 75% quantiles of the data.[9] In essence, the normal probability plot *changes the scale on the y-axis so the cumulative normal distribution is a straight line rather than an S-shaped curve.*

CHAPTER SUMMARY

The normal distribution has these characteristics:

- It is symmetric; i.e., the right and left sides are mirror images of each other.
- It runs to plus and minus infinity, which means it is possible (albeit perhaps unlikely) that *any* number could occur when you draw from the distribution.
- It is unimodal; i.e., it has a single hump, which occurs at the mean.
- Sums of normal random variables are normal.

The lognormal distribution arises from assuming that continuously compounded returns are normally distributed. The lognormal distribution has these characteristics:

- It is skewed to the right.
- It runs from zero to plus infinity, which means that negative outcomes are impossible.
- It is unimodal (i.e., it has a single hump), which occurs to the left of the mean.
- Products of lognormal random variables are lognormal.

The Black-Scholes formula arises from a straightforward lognormal probability calculation using risk-neutral probabilities. The contribution of Black and Scholes was not the particular formula but rather the appearance of the risk-free rate in the formula.

From examining histograms and normal probability plots for daily and weekly continuously compounded returns, we can see that there are too many large returns relative to normally distributed returns. Although continuously compounded returns do not appear to be exactly normal, the Black-Scholes model and the accompanying assumption of lognormality is used frequently. We will explore extensions that are consistent with departures from normality we have seen in this chapter.

FURTHER READING

Both the histogram and normal probability plot verify that continuously compounded returns in practice are not normally distributed. The question is whether this matters for pricing, and if so, how to modify the assumed price distributions and pricing formulas to obtain more accurate derivative prices. Two modifications allow the stock to jump discretely and to permit volatility to be stochastic.

---

9. The straight line can be fitted in numerous ways. Matlab and R by default connect the quantiles. In the case of the sample data, the 10% and 30% quantiles are 3 and 4, so by interpolation the 25% quantile is 3.75. Similarly, the 70% and 90% quantiles are 7 and 11, so by interpolation the 75% quantile is 8.

An excellent discussion of the basic characteristics of stock returns is Campbell et al. (1997, chs. 1 and 2). The history of the normal distribution is entertainingly recounted in Bernstein (1996). (See in particular the accounts of DeMoivre, Gauss, and Galton.)

PROBLEMS

1. You draw these five numbers randomly from a normal distribution with mean −8 and variance 15: {−7, −11, −3, 2, −15}. What are the equivalent draws from a standard normal distribution?

2. You draw these five numbers from a standard normal distribution: {−1.7, 0.55, −0.3, −0.02, .85}. What are the equivalent draws from a normal distribution with mean 0.8 and variance 25?

3. Suppose $x_1 \sim \mathcal{N}(1, 5)$ and $x_2 \sim \mathcal{N}(-2, 2)$. The covariance between x_1 and x_2 is 1.3. What is the distribution of $x_1 + x_2$? What is the distribution of $x_1 - x_2$?

4. Suppose $x_1 \sim \mathcal{N}(2, 0.5)$ and $x_2 \sim \mathcal{N}(8, 14)$. The correlation between x_1 and x_2 is −0.3. What is the distribution of $x_1 + x_2$? What is the distribution of $x_1 - x_2$?

5. Suppose $x_1 \sim \mathcal{N}(1, 5)$, $x_2 \sim \mathcal{N}(2, 3)$, and $x_3 \sim \mathcal{N}(2.5, 7)$, with correlations $\rho_{1,2} = 0.3$, $\rho_{1,3} = 0.1$, and $\rho_{2,3} = 0.4$. What is the distribution of $x_1 + x_2 + x_3$? $x_1 + (3 \times x_2) + x_3$? $x_1 + x_2 + (0.5 \times x_3)$?

6. If $x \sim \mathcal{N}(2, 5)$, what is $\mathrm{E}(e^x)$? What is the median of e^x?

7. Suppose you observe the following month-end stock prices for stocks A and B:

	Day				
	0	**1**	**2**	**3**	**4**
Stock A	100	105	102	97	100
Stock B	100	105	150	97	100

For each stock:

a. Compute the mean monthly continuously compounded return. What is the annual return?

b. Compute the mean monthly standard deviation. What is the annual standard deviation?

c. Evaluate the statement: "The estimate of the mean depends only on the beginning and ending stock prices; the estimate of the standard deviation depends on all prices."

For the following five problems, unless otherwise stated, assume that $S_0 = \$100$, $\alpha = 0.08$, $\sigma = 0.30$, and $\delta = 0$.

8. What is $\Pr(S_t > \$105)$ for $t = 1$? How does this probability change when you change t? How does it change when you change σ?

9. What is $\mathrm{E}(S_t | S_t > \$105)$ for $t = 1$? How does this expectation change when you change t, σ, and r?

10. What is $\Pr(S_t < \$98)$ for $t = 1$? How does this probability change when you change t?

11. Let $t = 1$. What is $\mathrm{E}(S_t | S_t < \$98)$? What is $\mathrm{E}(S_t | S_t < \$120)$? How do both expectations change when you vary t from 0.05 to 5? Let $\sigma = 0.1$. Does either answer change? How?

12. Let $K_T = S_0 e^{rT}$. Compute $\Pr(S_T < K_T)$ and $\Pr(S_T > K_T)$ for a variety of Ts from 0.25 to 25 years. How do the probabilities behave? How do you reconcile your answer with the fact that *both* call and put prices increase with time?

13. Consider $\Pr(S_t < K)$, equation (23), and $\mathrm{E}(S_t | S_t < K)$, equation (28). Verify that it is possible to pick parameters such that changes in t can have ambiguous effects on $\Pr(S_t < K)$ (experiment with very short and long times to maturity, and set $\alpha > 0.5\sigma^2$). Is the effect of t on $\mathrm{E}(S_t | S_t < K)$ ambiguous?

14. Select a stock or index and obtain at least 5 years of daily or weekly data. Estimate the annualized mean and volatility, using all data and 1 year at a time. Compare the behavior of your estimates of the mean with those of the standard deviation.

15. Select a stock that has at least 5 years of daily data. Create data sets consisting of daily data and weekly data, Wednesday to Wednesday. (The weekday function in Excel will tell you the day of the week corresponding to a date. Wednesday is 4.) For both data sets, create a histogram of returns and a normal plot. Are the stock prices lognormal?

Appendix A THE EXPECTATION OF A LOGNORMAL VARIABLE

In this appendix we verify equation (13). Suppose that $y \sim \mathcal{N}(\mu, \sigma^2)$; hence, e^y is lognormally distributed. The normal distribution is given by

$$\phi(x; \mu, \sigma^2) \equiv \frac{1}{\sigma\sqrt{2\pi}} e^{-\frac{1}{2}\left(\frac{x-\mu}{\sigma}\right)^2}$$

Hence, we can directly compute the expectation:

$$\mathrm{E}(e^y) = \int_{-\infty}^{\infty} e^x \frac{1}{\sigma\sqrt{2\pi}} e^{-\frac{1}{2}\left(\frac{x-\mu}{\sigma}\right)^2} dx$$

Collect the exponentiated terms under the integral. This gives us

$$\mathrm{E}(e^y) = \int_{-\infty}^{\infty} \frac{1}{\sigma\sqrt{2\pi}} e^{-\frac{1}{2\sigma^2}[(x-\mu)^2 - 2\sigma^2 x]} dx \tag{31}$$

Now focus on the exponentiated term in the square brackets. We have

$$\begin{aligned}(x-\mu)^2 - 2\sigma^2 x &= x^2 + \mu^2 - 2x(\mu+\sigma^2)\\ &= x^2 + (\mu+\sigma^2)^2 - 2x(\mu+\sigma^2) + \mu^2 - (\mu+\sigma^2)^2\\ &= [x-(\mu+\sigma^2)]^2 - \sigma^4 - 2\mu\sigma^2\end{aligned}$$

We can now substitute this expression into (31), obtaining

$$\begin{aligned}\mathrm{E}(e^y) &= \int_{-\infty}^{\infty} \frac{1}{\sigma\sqrt{2\pi}}\, e^{-\frac{1}{2\sigma^2}([x-(\mu+\sigma^2)]^2-\sigma^4-2\mu\sigma^2)}\,dx\\ &= e^{\mu+\frac{1}{2}\sigma^2}\int_{-\infty}^{\infty} \frac{1}{\sigma\sqrt{2\pi}}\, e^{-\frac{1}{2\sigma^2}([x-(\mu+\sigma^2)]^2)}\,dx\\ &= e^{\mu+\frac{1}{2}\sigma^2}\end{aligned}$$

The last equality follows because the integral expression is one: It is the total area under a normal density with mean $\mu+\sigma^2$ and variance σ^2. Thus we obtain equation (13).

Appendix B CONSTRUCTING A NORMAL PROBABILITY PLOT

Appendix available at http://www.pearsonhighered.com/mcdonald.

Monte Carlo Valuation

Derivatives have a (relatively simple) valuation formula, or can be valued binomially. For many common derivatives, however, a different approach is necessary. For example, consider arithmetic Asian options. There is no simple valuation formula for such options, and the binomial pricing approach is difficult because the final payoff depends on the specific path the stock price takes through the tree—i.e., the payoff is path-dependent. A pricing method that can be used in such cases is **Monte Carlo valuation**. In Monte Carlo valuation we simulate future stock prices and then use these simulated prices to compute the discounted expected payoff of the option.

Monte Carlo valuation is performed using the risk-neutral distribution, where we assume that assets earn the risk-free rate on average, and we then discount the expected payoff using the risk-free rate. We will see in this chapter that risk-neutral pricing is a cornerstone of Monte Carlo valuation; using the actual distribution instead would create a complicated discounting problem.

With Monte Carlo you simulate the possible future values of the security; therefore, as a byproduct you generate the *distribution* of payoffs. The distribution can be extremely useful when you want to compare two investment strategies that have different distributions of outcomes. Computing value-at-risk for complicated portfolios is a common use of Monte Carlo.

In this chapter we will see why risk-neutral valuation is important for Monte Carlo, see how to produce normal random numbers, discuss the efficiency of Monte Carlo, introduce the Poisson distribution to help account for nonlognormal patterns in the data, and see how to create correlated random stock prices.

1. COMPUTING THE OPTION PRICE AS A DISCOUNTED EXPECTED VALUE

Option valuation can be performed *as if* all assets earned the risk-free rate of return and investors performed all discounting at this rate. Specifically, we compute the time price of

From Chapter 19 of *Derivatives Markets*, Third Edition, Robert McDonald. Copyright © 2013 by Pearson Education, Inc. Published by Pearson Prentice Hall. All rights reserved.

a claim, $V[S(0), 0]$, as

$$V[S(0), 0] = e^{-rT} \mathrm{E}_0^*[V(S(T), T)] \tag{1}$$

where E_0^* is the expectation computed at time 0 using the risk-neutral distribution. Monte Carlo valuation exploits this procedure. We *assume* that assets earn the risk-free rate of return and simulate their returns. For example, for any given stock price 3 months from now, we can compute the payoff on a call. We perform the simulation many times and average the outcomes. This provides an estimate of $\mathrm{E}_0^*[V(S_T), S_T]$. Since we use risk-neutral valuation, we then discount the average payoff at the risk-free rate in order to arrive at the price.

As a practical matter, Monte Carlo valuation depends critically on risk-neutral valuation. In order to see why this is so, we will compute an option price as an expected value with both risk-neutral and true probabilities.

Valuation with Risk-Neutral Probabilities

We can interpret the one-period binomial option pricing calculation as an expected value, in which the expectation is computed using the risk-neutral probability p^* and discounting is at the risk-free rate.

In a multiperiod tree, we repeat this process at each node. For a European option, the result obtained by working backward through the tree is equivalent to computing the expected option price in the final period, and discounting at the risk-free rate.

If there are n binomial periods, the equation

$$\text{Probability of reaching } i\text{th node} = p^{*n-i}(1-p^*)^i \frac{n!}{(n-i)!\,i!}$$

gives the probability of reaching any given stock price at expiration. Let n represent the number of binomial steps and i the number of stock price down moves. We can value a European call option by computing the expected option payoff at the final node of the binomial tree and then discounting at the risk-free rate. For example, for a European call,

$$\text{European call price} \\ = e^{-rT} \sum_{i=0}^{n} \max[0, Su^{n-i}d^i - K](p^*)^{n-i}(1-p^*)^i \frac{n!}{(n-i)!\,i!} \tag{2}$$

To illustrate this calculation, Figure 1 shows the stock price tree with the total risk-neutral probabilities of reaching each of the terminal nodes. Figure 1 demonstrates that the option can be priced by computing the expected payoff at expiration using the probability of reaching each final node, and then discounting at the risk-free rate.

We can also use the tree in Figure 1 to illustrate Monte Carlo valuation. Imagine a gambling wheel divided into four unequal sections, where each section has a probability corresponding to one of the option payoffs in Figure 1: 9.5% (\$34.678), 34% (\$12.814), 40.4% (0), and 16% (0). Each spin of the wheel therefore selects one of the final stock price nodes and option payoffs in Figure 1. If we spin the wheel numerous times and then average the resulting option values, we will have an estimate of the expected payoff. Discounting this expected payoff at the risk-free rate provides an estimate of the option value.

FIGURE 1

Binomial tree showing stock price paths, along with risk-neutral probabilities of reaching the various terminal prices. Assumes $S = \$41.00$, $K = \$40.00$, $\sigma = 0.30$, $r = 0.08$, $t = 1.00$ years, $\delta = 0.00$, and $h = 0.333$. The risk-neutral probability of going up is $p^* = 0.4568$. At the final node the stock price and terminal option payoff (beneath the price) are given.

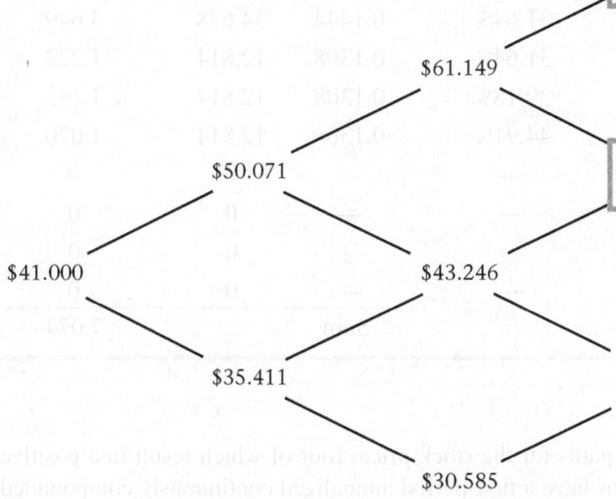

Price and Payoff	Probability	$e^{-0.08}$ × Prob. × Payoff
\$74.678 ***\$34.678***	p^{*3} = 0.095	\$3.052
\$52.814 ***\$12.814***	$3p^{*2}(1-p^*)$ = 0.340	\$4.022
\$37.351 \$0.000	$3p^*(1-p^*)^2$ = 0.404	\$0.000
\$26.416 \$0.000	$(1-p^*)^3$ = 0.160	\$0.000
Total	1.000	\$7.074

It is easy to compute the actual expected payoff for the option in Figure 1 without using a gambling wheel. However, the example illustrates how random trials can be used to perform valuation.

Valuation with True Probabilities

The simple procedure we used to discount payoffs for the risk-neutral tree in Figure 1 *does not work* when we use actual probabilities. In fact, if we are to compute an option price as an expected value using true probabilities, we need to compute the discount rate *for each*

TABLE 1 Computation of option price using expected value calculation and true probabilities. The column entitled "Discount Rates Along Path" reports the node-specific true annualized continuously compounded discount rates from that figure. "Discount Rate for Path" is the compound annualized discount rate for the entire path. "Prob. of Path" is the probability that the particular path will occur, computed using the true probability of an up move (52.46%). The last column is the probability times the payoff, discounted at the continuously compounded rate for the path.

Path	Discount Rates Along Path			Discount Rate for Path	Prob. of Path	Payoff ($)	Discounted ($) (Prob. × Payoff)
uuu	35.7%	32.3%	26.9%	31.64%	0.1444	34.678	3.649
uud	35.7%	32.3%	26.9%	31.64%	0.1308	12.814	1.222
udu	35.7%	32.3%	49.5%	39.18%	0.1308	12.814	1.133
duu	35.7%	49.5%	49.5%	44.91%	0.1308	12.814	1.070
udd	—	—	—	—	—	0	0
dud	—	—	—	—	—	0	0
ddu	—	—	—	—	—	0	0
ddd	—	—	—	—	—	0	0
					Sum		7.074

path. There are eight possible paths for the stock price, four of which result in a positive option payoff. All of these paths have a first-period annualized continuously compounded discount rate of 35.7%. The subsequent discount rates depend on the path the stock takes. Table 1 verifies that discounting payoffs at path-dependent discount rates gives the correct option price. To take just the first row, the discounted expected option payoff for that row is computed as follows:

$$e^{-(0.357\times\frac{1}{3}+0.323\times\frac{1}{3}+0.269\times\frac{1}{3})} \times (0.5246)^3 \times (\$74.678 - \$40) = \$3.649$$

This calculation uses the fact that the actual probability that the stock price will move up in any period is 52.46%.

As Table 1 illustrates, it is necessary to have a different cumulative discount rate along each *path* the stock can take. A call option is a high-beta security when it is out-of-the-money and it has a lower beta (but still higher than the stock) when it is in-the-money. This variation in the discount rate complicates discounting if we are using the true distribution of stock prices.[1]

1. Here is why a single discount rate does not work. Suppose we represent the terminal option price associated with a particular pattern of stock price up and down movements by $C_i(T)$ and the compound discount factor for that path by β_i. Since both the payoff and the discount rates are uncertain, we need to compute $\mathrm{E}[C_i(T)/(1+\beta_i)]$. However, if we average the payoff and then separately average the discount

Risk-neutral valuation neatly sidesteps the hardest problem about using discounted cash flow valuation techniques with an option. While it is easy to compute the expected payoff of an option if the stock is lognormally distributed, it is hard to compute the discount rate. If we value options *as if* the world were risk-neutral, this complication is avoided.

2. COMPUTING RANDOM NUMBERS

In this section we discuss how to compute the normally distributed random numbers required for Monte Carlo valuation. The uniform distribution is defined on a specified range, over which the probability is 1, and assigns equal probabilities to every interval of equal length on that range. A random variable, u, that is uniformly distributed on the interval (a, b), has the distribution $\mathcal{U}(a, b)$. The uniform probability density, $f(x; a, b)$, is defined as

$$f(x; a, b) = \frac{1}{b-a}; a \leq x \leq b \tag{3}$$

and is 0 otherwise. When $a = 0$ and $b = 1$, the uniform distribution is a flat line at a height of 1 over the range 0 to 1.

Drawing uniformly distributed random variables is very common; virtually all programming languages and spreadsheets have a way to do this.[2] The Rand built-in function in Excel does this, for example. It turns out that once we have a way to compute uniformly distributed random variables, it is possible compute random numbers drawn from *any* distribution.

Suppose that $u \sim \mathcal{U}(0, 1)$ and $z \sim \mathcal{N}(0, 1)$. The *cumulative distribution function*, denoted $U(w)$ for the uniform and $N(y)$ for the normal, is the probability that $u < w$ or $z < y$, i.e.,

$$U(w) = \Pr(u \leq w)$$
$$N(y) = \Pr(z \leq y)$$

where w is the $U(w)$ quantile and y is the $N(y)$ quantile of the two distributions. If we randomly draw a uniform number u, how can we use u to construct a corresponding normal random number, z?

We can generate a normal random number from a uniform random number. Instead of interpreting a random draw from the uniform distribution as a *number*, we interpret it as a *quantile*. So, for example, if we draw 0.7 from a $\mathcal{U}(0, 1)$ distribution, we interpret this as a draw corresponding to the 70% quantile. We then use the inverse distribution function, $N^{-1}(u)$, to find the value from the normal distribution corresponding to that quantile.[3] This

---

factors, we are computing the ratio of the averages, $E[C_i(T)]/E[(1 + \beta_i)]$, rather than the average of the ratios. Jensen's inequality tells us that these are not the same calculation.

2. Since computers are ultimately deterministic devices, it is virtually impossible to compute "true" random numbers. See Judd (1998, pp. 285–287) for a discussion and additional references.

3. The Excel function NormSInv computes the inverse cumulative normal distribution. Unfortunately, there is a serious bug in this function in Office 97 and Office 2000. In both versions of Excel, NormSInv (0.9999996) = 5.066, and NormSInv(0.9999997) = 5,000,000. Because of this, Excel will on occasion

technique works because, for any distribution, quantiles are uniformly distributed: If you draw from a distribution, by definition any quantile is equally likely to be drawn.

The algorithm is therefore as follows:

1. Generate a uniformly distributed random number between 0 and 1. Suppose this is 0.7.
2. Ask: What is the value of z such that $N(z) = 0.7$? The answer to this question is computed using the *inverse cumulative distribution function*. In this case we have $N^{-1}(0.7) = 0.5244$. This value is a single draw of a standard normal random variable (0.5244).
3. Repeat.

This procedure simulates draws from a normal distribution. To simulate a log-normal random variable, simulate a normal random variable and exponentiate the draws.

This procedure of using the inverse cumulative probability distribution is valuable because it works for any distribution for which you can compute the inverse cumulative distribution.[4]

3. SIMULATING LOGNORMAL STOCK PRICES

If $Z \sim \mathcal{N}(0, 1)$, a lognormal stock price can be written

$$S_T = S_0 e^{(\alpha - \delta - \frac{1}{2}\sigma^2)T + \sigma\sqrt{T}Z} \tag{4}$$

Suppose we wish to draw random stock prices for 2 years from today. From equation (4), the stock price is driven by the normally distributed random variable Z. Set $T = 2$, $\alpha = 0.10$, $\delta = 0$, and $\sigma = 0.30$. If we then randomly draw a set of standard normal Z's and substitute the results into equation (4), the result is a random set of lognormally distributed S_2's. The continuously compounded mean return will be 20% (10% per year) and the continuously compounded standard deviation of $\ln(S_2)$ will be $0.3 \times \sqrt{2} = 42.43\%$.

Simulating a Sequence of Stock Prices

There is another way to create a random set of prices 2 years from now. We can also generate *annual* random prices and compound these to get a 2-year price. This will give us exactly the same distribution for 2-year prices. Here is how to do it:

- Compute the 1-year price, S_1, as

$$S_1 = S_0 e^{(0.1 - \frac{1}{2}0.3^2)\times 1 + \sigma\sqrt{1}Z(1)}$$

produce a randomly drawn normal value of 5,000,000, which ruins a Monte Carlo valuation. I thank Mark Broadie for pointing out this problem with using Excel to produce random normal numbers.

4. Problem 2 asks you to construct the histogram of $\sum_i^{12} u_i - 6$, where the u_i are independent and uniformly distributed. This illustrates a different way to simulate a normally distributed random variable, relying on the central limit theorem.

- Using this S_1 as the starting price, compute S_2:

$$S_2 = S_1 e^{(0.1-\frac{1}{2}0.3^2)\times 1+0.3\sqrt{1}Z(2)}$$

In these expressions, $Z(1)$ and $Z(2)$ are two draws from the standard normal distribution.

If we substitute the expression for S_1 into S_2, we get

$$S_2 = S_0 e^{(0.1-\frac{1}{2}0.3^2)\times 2+0.3\sqrt{1}[Z(1)+Z(2)]} \tag{5}$$

The difference between this expression and equation (4) is that instead of the term $\sqrt{2}Z$, we have $[Z(1) + Z(2)]$. Note that

$$\text{Var}(\sqrt{2}Z) = 2$$

and

$$\text{Var}[Z(1) + Z(2)] = 2$$

Therefore, equations (4) and (5) generate S_2's with the same distribution.

If we really want to simulate a random stock price after 2 years, there is no reason to draw two random variables instead of one. But if we want to simulate the *path* of the stock price over 2 years (for example, to price a path-dependent option), then we can do so by splitting up the 2 years into multiple periods.

In general, if we wish to split up a period of length T into intervals of length h, the number of such intervals will be $n = T/h$. We have

$$S_h = S_0 e^{(\alpha-\delta-\frac{1}{2}\sigma^2)h+\sigma\sqrt{h}Z(1)}$$

$$S_{2h} = S_h e^{(\alpha-\delta-\frac{1}{2}\sigma^2)h+\sigma\sqrt{h}Z(2)}$$

and so on, up to

$$S_{nh} = S_{(n-1)h} e^{(\alpha-\delta-\frac{1}{2}\sigma^2)h+\sigma\sqrt{h}Z(n)}$$

These n stock prices can be interpreted as equally spaced points on the stock price path between times 0 and T. Note that if we substitute S_h into the expression for S_{2h}, the expression for S_{2h} into that for S_{3h}, and so on, we get

$$\begin{aligned} S_T &= S_0 e^{(\alpha-\delta-\frac{1}{2}\sigma^2)T+\sigma\sqrt{h}\left[\sum_{i=1}^{n} Z(i)\right]} \\ &= S_0 e^{(\alpha-\delta-\frac{1}{2}\sigma^2)T+\sigma\sqrt{T}\left[\frac{1}{\sqrt{n}}\sum_{i=1}^{n} Z(i)\right]} \end{aligned} \tag{6}$$

Since $\frac{1}{\sqrt{n}}\sum_{i=1}^{n} Z(i) \sim \mathcal{N}(0, 1)$, we get the same distribution at time T with equation (6) as if we had drawn a single $\mathcal{N}(0, 1)$ random variable, as in equation (4). By splitting up the problem into n draws, however, we simulate the path taken by S. The simulation of a path is useful in computing the value of path-dependent derivatives, such as Asian and barrier options.

4. MONTE CARLO VALUATION

In Monte Carlo valuation, we perform a calculation similar to that in equation (2). The option payoff at time T is a function of the stock price, S_T. Represent this payoff as $V(S_T, T)$. The time-0 Monte Carlo price, $V(S_0, 0)$, is then

$$V(S_0, 0) = \frac{1}{n} e^{-rT} \sum_{i=1}^{n} V(S_T^i, T) \tag{7}$$

where $S_T^1, \ldots, S_T^n$ are n randomly drawn time-T stock prices. For the case of a call option, for example, $V(S_T^i, T) = \max(0, S_T^i - K)$.

Both equations (2) and (7) use approximations to the time-T stock price distribution to compute an option price. Equation (2) uses the binomial distribution to approximate the lognormal stock price distribution, while equation (7) uses simulated lognormal prices to approximate the lognormal stock price distribution.

As an illustration of Monte Carlo techniques, we will first work with a problem for which we already know the answer. Suppose we have a European option that expires in T periods. The underlying asset has volatility σ and the risk-free rate is r. We can use the Black-Scholes option pricing formula to price the option, but we will price the option using *both* Black-Scholes and Monte Carlo so that we can assess the performance of Monte Carlo valuation.

Monte Carlo Valuation of a European Call

We assume that the stock price follows the risk-neutral version of equation (4), obtained by setting $\alpha = r$. We generate random standard normal variables, Z, substitute them into equation (4), and generate many random future stock prices. Each Z creates one trial. Suppose we compute N trials. For each trial, i, we compute the value of a call as

$$\max(0, S_T^i - K) = \max\left(0, S_0 e^{(r-\delta-0.5\sigma^2)T + \sigma\sqrt{T} Z_i} - K\right); \quad i = 1, \ldots, N$$

Average the resulting values:

$$\frac{1}{N} \sum_{i=1}^{N} \max(0, S_T^i - K)$$

This expression gives us an estimate of the expected option payoff at time T. We discount the average payoff back at the risk-free rate in order to get an estimate of the option value:

$$\overline{C} = e^{-rT} \frac{1}{N} \sum_{i=1}^{N} \max(0, S_T^i - K)$$

Example 1. Suppose we wish to value a 3-month European call option where the stock price is \$40, the strike price is \$40, the risk-free rate is 8%, the dividend yield is zero, and the volatility is 30%. We draw random 3-month stock prices by using the expression

$$S_{3\,\text{months}} = S_0 e^{(0.08 - 0.3^2/2) \times 0.25 + 0.3\sqrt{0.25} Z}$$

TABLE 2 Results of Monte Carlo valuation of European call with $S = \$40$, $K = \$40$, $\sigma = 30\%$, $r = 8\%$, $t = 91$ days, and $\delta = 0$. The Black-Scholes price is \$2.78. Each trial uses 500 random draws.

Trial	Computed Price (\$)
1	2.98
2	2.75
3	2.63
4	2.75
5	2.91
Average	2.804

For each stock price, we compute

$$\text{Option payoff} = \max(0, S_{3\text{ months}} - \$40)$$

We repeat this procedure many times, average the resulting option payoffs, and discount the average back 3 months at the risk-free rate. With a single estimate using 2500 draws, we get an answer of \$2.804 (see Table 2), close to the true value of \$2.78. ■

In this example we priced a European-style option. We will discuss in Section 6 the use of Monte Carlo simulation to value American-style options.

Accuracy of Monte Carlo

There is no need to value a European call using Monte Carlo methods, but doing so allows us to assess the accuracy of Monte Carlo valuation for a given number of simulated stock price paths. The key question is how many simulated stock prices suffice to value an option to a desired degree of accuracy. Monte Carlo valuation is simple but relatively inefficient. There are methods that improve the efficiency of Monte Carlo; we discuss several of these in Section 5.

To assess the accuracy of a Monte Carlo estimate, we can run the simulation different times and see how much variability there is in the results. Of course in this case, we also know that the Black-Scholes solution is \$2.78.

Table 2 shows the results from running five Monte Carlo valuations, each containing 500 random stock price draws. The result of 2500 simulations is close to the correct answer (\$2.804 is close to \$2.78). However, there is considerable variation among the individual trials of 500 simulations.

To assess accuracy, we need to know the standard deviation of the estimate. Let $C(\tilde{S}_i)$ be the call price generated from the randomly drawn $\tilde{S}_i$. If there are n trials, the Monte Carlo estimate is

$$\overline{C}_n = \frac{1}{n} \sum_{i=1}^{n} C(\tilde{S}_i)$$

Let σ_C denote the standard deviation of one draw and σ_n the standard deviation of n draws. The variance of a mean, given independent and identically distributed $\tilde{S}_i$'s, is

$$\sigma_n^2 = \frac{1}{n}\sigma_C^2$$

or

$$\sigma_n = \frac{1}{\sqrt{n}}\sigma_C$$

Thus, the standard deviation of the Monte Carlo estimate is inversely proportional to the square root of the number of draws.

In the Monte Carlo results reported in Table 2, the standard deviation of a draw is about \$4.05. (This value is computed by taking the standard deviation of the 2500 price estimates used to compute the average.) For 500 draws, the standard deviation is

$$\frac{\$4.05}{\sqrt{500}} = \$0.18$$

Given that the correct price is \$2.78, a \$0.18 standard deviation is a substantial percentage of the option price (6.5%). With 2500 observations, the standard deviation is cut to \$0.08, suggesting that the \$2.80 estimate from averaging the five answers was only accidentally close to the correct answer. In order to have a 1% (\$0.028) standard deviation, we would need to have 21,000 trials.

Arithmetic Asian Option

In the previous example of Monte Carlo valuation, we valued an option that we already could value with the Black-Scholes formula. In practice, Monte Carlo valuation is useful under these conditions:

- Where the number of random elements in the option valuation problem is too great to permit direct numerical solution.
- Where underlying variables are distributed in such a way that direct solutions are difficult.
- Where options are path-dependent, i.e., the payoff at expiration depends upon the path of the underlying asset price.

For the case of a path-dependent option, the use of Monte Carlo estimation is straightforward. As discussed above, we can simulate the path of the stock as well as its terminal value. For example, consider the valuation of a security that at the end of 3 months makes a payment based on the arithmetic average of the stock price at the end of months 1, 2, and 3. This is an arithmetic average price Asian option: "Asian" because the payoff is based on an average, and "arithmetic average price" because the arithmetic average stock price replaces the actual stock price at expiration.

How will the value of an option on the average compare with an option that settles based on the actual expiration-day stock price? Intuitively, averaging should reduce the likelihood of large gains and losses. Any time the stock ends up high (in which case the call will have a high value at expiration), it will have traversed intermediate stock prices in

FIGURE 2

Histograms for risk-neutral stock price distribution after 3 months (top panel) and risk-neutral distribution for the average stock price created by averaging the three month-end stock prices during the same period (bottom panel). Assumes $S_0 = \$40$, $r = 8\%$, $\sigma = 30\%$, and $\delta = 0$. These histograms were generated using 100,000 trials.

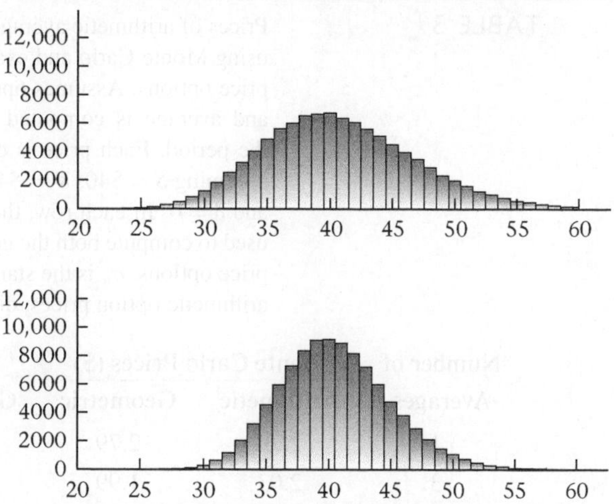

the process of reaching a high value. The payoff to the Asian option will reflect these lower intermediate prices, and, hence, large payoffs will be much less likely.

We compute the 1-month, 2-month, and 3-month stock prices as follows:

$$S_1 = 40e^{(r-\delta-\sigma^2/2)T/3+\sigma\sqrt{T/3}Z(1)}$$

$$S_2 = S_1e^{(r-\delta-\sigma^2/2)T/3+\sigma\sqrt{T/3}Z(2)}$$

$$S_3 = S_2e^{(r-\delta-\sigma^2/2)T/3+\sigma\sqrt{T/3}Z(3)}$$

where $Z(1)$, $Z(2)$, and $Z(3)$ are independent draws from a standard normal distribution. We repeat the trial many times and draw many Z_i's. The value of the security is then computed as

$$C_{\text{Asian}} = e^{-rT} E\left(\max[(S_1 + S_2 + S_3)/3 - K, 0]\right) \tag{8}$$

Example 2. Let r = 8%, $\sigma = 0.3$, and suppose that the initial stock price is \$40. Figure 2 compares histograms for the actual risk-neutral stock price distri- bution after 3 months and that for the average stock price created by averaging the three month-end prices. As expected, the nonaveraged distribution has significantly higher tail probabilities and a lower probability of being close to the initial stock price of \$40. ■

Table 3 lists prices of Asian options computed using 10,000 Monte Carlo trials each.[5] The first row (where a single terminal price is averaged) represents the price of an ordinary call option with 3 months to expiration. The others represent more frequent averaging. The

5. A trial in this case means the computation of a single option price at expiration. When 40 prices are averaged over 3 months, each trial consists of drawing 40 random numbers; hence, 400,000 random numbers are drawn in order to compute the price.

TABLE 3 Prices of arithmetic average-price Asian options estimated using Monte Carlo and exact prices of geometric average price options. Assumes option has 3 months to expiration and average is computed using equal intervals over the period. Each price is computed using 10,000 trials, assuming $S = \$40$, $K = \$40$, $\sigma = 30\%$, $r = 8\%$, $T = 0.25$, and $\delta = 0$. In each row, the same random numbers were used to compute both the geometric and arithmetic average price options. σ_n is the standard deviation of the estimated arithmetic option prices, divided by $\sqrt{10{,}000}$.

Number of	Monte Carlo Prices ($)		Exact	
Averages	Arithmetic	Geometric	Geometric Price ($)	σ_n
1	2.79	2.79	2.78	0.0408
3	2.03	1.99	1.94	0.0291
5	1.78	1.74	1.77	0.0259
10	1.70	1.66	1.65	0.0241
20	1.66	1.61	1.59	0.0231
40	1.63	1.58	1.56	0.0226

Asian price declines as the averaging frequency increases, with the largest price decline obtained by moving from no averaging (the first row in Table 3) to monthly averaging (the second row of Table 3).

Note also in Table 3 that, in any row, the arithmetic average price is always above the geometric average price. This is Jensen's inequality at work: Geometric averaging produces a lower average stock price than arithmetic averaging, and hence a lower option price.

5. EFFICIENT MONTE CARLO VALUATION

We have been describing what might be called "naive" or simple Monte Carlo, making no attempt to reduce the variance of the simulated answer for a given number of trials. There are a number of methods to achieve faster Monte Carlo valuations.[6]

Control Variate Method

We have seen that naive Monte Carlo estimation of an arithmetic Asian option requires many simulations. In Table 3, even with 10,000 simulations, there is still a standard deviation of several percent in the option price.

6. Excellent overviews are Boyle et al. (1997) and Glasserman (2004). See also Judd (1998, ch. 8), which in turn contains other references, and Campbell et al. (1997, ch. 9).

In each row of Table 3, the same random numbers are used to estimate the option price. As a result, the errors in the estimated arithmetic and geometric prices are correlated: When the estimated price for the geometric option is high, this occurs because we have had high returns in the stock price simulation. This should result in a high arithmetic price as well.

This observation suggests the **control variate method** to increase Monte Carlo accuracy. The idea underlying this method is to estimate the error on each trial by using the price of a related option that does have a pricing formula. The error estimate obtained from this control price can be used to improve the accuracy of the Monte Carlo price on each trial.

Asian options illustrate this idea.[7] Because we have a formula for the price of a geometric Asian option, we know whether the geometric price from a Monte Carlo valuation is too high or too low. For a given set of random stock prices, the arithmetic and geometric prices will typically be too high or too low in tandem, so we can use information on the error in the geometric price to adjust our estimate of the arithmetic price, for which there is no formula.

To be specific, we use the same simulation to estimate both the arithmetic price, $\overline{A}$, and the geometric price, $\overline{G}$. Let G and A represent the true geometric and arithmetic prices. The error for the Monte Carlo estimate of the geometric price is $(G - \overline{G})$. We want to use this error to improve our estimate of the arithmetic price. Consider calculating

$$A^* = \overline{A} + \beta\left(G - \overline{G}\right) \tag{9}$$

This is a control variate estimate. Monte Carlo provides an unbiased estimate of G: $E(\overline{G}) = G$. Therefore, the estimate of A is also unbiased: $E(A^*) = E(\overline{A}) = A$. The variance of A^* is

$$\text{Var}(A^*) = \text{Var}(\overline{A}) + \beta^2\,\text{Var}(\overline{G}) - 2\beta\,\text{Cov}(\overline{A}, \overline{G}) \tag{10}$$

The variance $\text{Var}(A^*)$ is minimized by setting $\beta = \hat{\beta}$, where $\hat{\beta} = \text{Cov}(\overline{A}, \overline{G})/\text{Var}(\overline{G})$. You might recognize $\hat{\beta}$ as the slope coefficient from regressing $\overline{A}$ on $\overline{G}$. With β selected to minimize $\text{Var}(A^*)$, the control variate Monte Carlo variance is

$$\text{Var}(A^*) = \text{Var}(\overline{A})(1 - \rho^2) \tag{11}$$

where ρ is the correlation between $\overline{A}$ and $\overline{G}$. In general, the variance of the control variate estimate will be less than that of naive Monte Carlo. If β is optimally chosen, it is never worse.[8] One can estimate $\hat{\beta}$ by performing a small number of Monte Carlo trials and running a regression of equation (10) to obtain $\hat{\beta}$. The optimal value of β will vary depending on the application.

If the simulated claim and the control are highly correlated, the variance reduction from the control variate method can be dramatic. Figure 3 compares the results from a

7. This example follows Kemna and Vorst (1990), who used the control variate method to price arithmetic Asian options.

8. Boyle et al. (1997) first suggested using equation (9) for control variate estimates. They pointed out that if β is not optimally chosen (for example, if one always sets $\beta = 1$), the variance of the control variate estimate can be greater than that of the Monte Carlo estimate.

FIGURE 3

Histograms comparing simple and efficient Monte Carlo estimates. All panels depict the distribution of 100 valuations using 200 estimates per valuation. The top two panels show the distribution of estimates for a 1-year arithmetic Asian option with monthly averaging. The top left panel shows the distribution obtained with simple Monte Carlo ($\sigma_n = \$0.399$), and the top right for the control variate estimate ($\sigma_n = \$0.042$). The estimated value using all control variate trials is \$3.42. The bottom panel shows 100 valuations using 200 estimates per valuation for a European call. The left panel is simple Monte Carlo ($\sigma_n = \$0.606$) and the right panel uses stratified sampling ($\sigma_n = \$0.042$). The Black-Scholes price is \$6.28, which is also the average of the stratified sampling estimates. In all cases $S = \$40, K = \$40, \sigma = 0.3, r = 0.08, T = 1.00$, and $\delta = 0$.

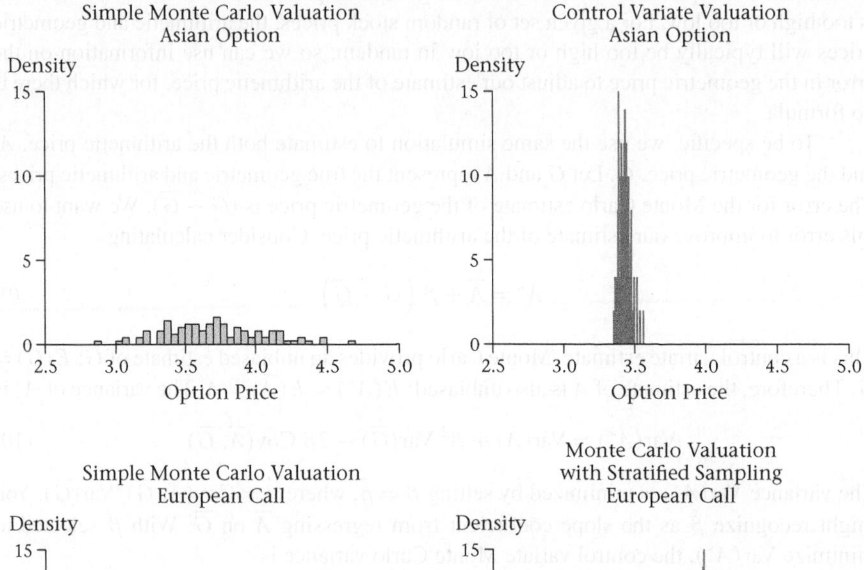

simple Monte Carlo calculation with those from a control variate calculation. The standard deviation of the control variate estimate is 10% that of the simple Monte Carlo calculation.

Other Monte Carlo Methods

The control variate example is but one method for improving the efficiency of Monte Carlo valuation. There are a variety of other methods discussed in more depth in Boyle et al. (1997) and Glasserman (2004). The **antithetic variate method** uses the idea that for every simulated realization, there is an opposite and equally likely realization. For example, if we draw a random normal number of 0.5, we could just as well have drawn −0.5. By using the opposite of each normal draw we can get two simulated outcomes for each random path we draw. There can be an efficiency gain because the two estimates are negatively correlated; adding them reduces the variance of the estimate. Notably, if you draw an extreme estimate from one tail of the distribution, you will also draw an extreme estimate from the other tail, balancing the effect of the first draw. Boyle et al. (1997) find modest benefits from using the antithetic variate method.

Another important class of methods controls the region in which random numbers are generated. Such methods are generally called **stratified sampling**. Suppose you have 100 uniform random numbers, u_i, $i = 1, \ldots, 100$. With simple Monte Carlo you would compute $z_i = N^{-1}(u_i)$. This calculation treats each random number as representing a random draw from the cumulative distribution. However, because of random variation, 100 uniform random numbers can create a distribution for the z_i's that does not look normal. Certain areas can be under- or over-represented. We can improve the distribution of the u_i, and therefore of the z_i, if we treat each number *as a random draw from each percentile of the uniform distribution*. Thus, take the first draw, u_1, and divide it by 100. The resulting $\hat{u}_1$ is now uniformly distributed over [0, 0.01]. Take the second draw, divide it by 100, and add 0.01. The resulting $\hat{u}_2$ is uniformly distributed over (0.01, 0.02). For the ith draw, compute $\hat{u}_i = (i - 1 + u_i)/100$. This value is uniformly distributed over the ith percentile. Proceeding in this way we are guaranteed to generate a random number for each percentile of the normal distribution. You can select a number of intervals different from 100, and you can repeat the simulation multiple times. A generalization of this technique when the payoff depends on more than one random variable is *Latin hypercube sampling*.

The bottom panels of Figure 3 compare simple Monte Carlo valuation with estimates using stratified sampling. The figure on the bottom left is the histogram of European call prices computed using 200 random draws. The figure on the bottom right uses stratified sampling, where a random number is drawn for one-half percentile of the distribution. The standard deviation of the estimate is less than one tenth that obtained with simple Monte Carlo.

A refinement of stratified sampling is *importance sampling*, in which the generation of random numbers is concentrated in the region where they have the most value for pricing a particular claim. Finally, it is possible to construct carefully selected deterministic points, called *low discrepancy sequences*, to create more uniform coverage of the distribution. These methods are particularly helpful for high-dimensional problems.[9]

If you are performing a one-time calculation, simple Monte Carlo is appealing. However, if you are performing a Monte Carlo valuation repeatedly, you may achieve

9. Tan and Boyle (2000) discuss low discrepancy sequences in the context of derivatives valuation.

FIGURE 4

Assumes $S_0 = 1.0$, $K = 1.1$, and $r = 6\%$. Prices in **bold** are nodes where early exercise might be optimal.

	Stock Price Paths			
Path	$t = 0$	$t = 1$	$t = 2$	$t = 3$
1	1.00	**1.09**	**1.08**	1.34
2	1.00	1.16	1.26	1.54
3	1.00	1.22	**1.07**	**1.03**
4	1.00	**0.93**	**0.97**	**0.92**
5	1.00	1.11	1.56	1.52
6	1.00	**0.76**	**0.77**	**0.90**
7	1.00	**0.92**	**0.84**	**1.01**
8	1.00	**0.88**	1.22	1.34

Data from Longstaff and Schwartz (2001).

large efficiency gains by analyzing the problem and using one or more variance reduction techniques to increase efficiency.

6. VALUATION OF AMERICAN OPTIONS

It is generally more difficult to value American-style options than to value European-style options, and this remains true when using Monte Carlo valuation. Standard Monte Carlo entails simulating stock price paths *forward*, then averaging and discounting the maturity payoffs. In American option valuation, the difficulty is knowing when to exercise the option; this requires working *backward* to determine the times at which the option should be exercised. Recently, Broadie and Glasserman (1997) and Longstaff and Schwartz (2001) have demonstrated feasible methods for using Monte Carlo to value American options.

We will discuss pricing a 3-year put option with a strike of \$1.10, the example used in Longstaff and Schwartz (2001). In order to analyze early exercise we need to consider times before maturity, so we must simulate stock price *paths*. Figure 4, taken from Longstaff and Schwartz (2001), illustrates eight hypothetical simulation paths, with intermediate stock prices generated annually. The in-the-money nodes (those for which $S < \$1.10$) are candidate nodes for exercise of the option; in Figure 4 they are in bold (this ignores exercise at time 0). How do we determine at which of these nodes early exercise is optimal?

The idea underlying any method of American option valuation is to compare the value of immediate exercise to the **continuation value** of the option—i.e., the value of keeping the option alive.[10] The problem is therefore to estimate the continuation value at each point in time.

It is worth noting one potential problem in estimating continuation value, which stems from the use of future stock prices on a given path to decide whether to exercise on that path. Consider path 1 in Figure 4. The option is out-of-the-money, and therefore worthless, at $t = 3$. Therefore, on this path we would be better off at $t = 2$ exercising rather than waiting.

10. This note has been intentionally omitted for this edition.

However, in deciding to exercise by looking ahead on the path, we are using knowledge of the future stock price, which is information we will not have in real life. Valuing the option assuming we know the future price will give us too high a value. The way to mitigate such "lookahead bias" is to base an exercise decision on *average* outcomes from a given point forward. There are at least two ways to characterize the average outcome from a given point. One is to use a regression to characterize the continuation value based on analysis of multiple paths. This is the method proposed by Longstaff and Schwartz (2001). Another is to create additional branches from each node, providing multiple outcomes that we can average to characterize continuation value at that node. This is the basis for the Broadie and Glasserman (1997) procedure.

To price the option using regression analysis, we work backward through the columns of Figure 4, running a regression at each time to estimate continuation value as a function of the stock price. We work backward because the continuation value at $t = 1$ will depend upon whether exercise is optimal on a given path at $t = 2$. At $t = 2$, there are five paths (1, 3, 4, 6, and 7) where the option is in-the-money and exercise could be optimal. For each of these paths, we know the value of exercising immediately and the value of waiting. Longstaff and Schwartz run a regression of the present value of waiting to exercise (i.e., the continuation value) against the stock price and stock price squared. At time 2, we obtain the following result:

$$\text{Continuation value at time } 2 = -1.07 + 2.98 \times S - 1.81 \times S^2$$

where S is the time 2 stock price. Now for each node where exercise could be optimal, we insert the stock price at that node into the regression equation and obtain an estimate of continuation value. By comparing this to intrinsic value, we decide whether to exercise at that node. For example, when $S = 1.08$ in row 1, the estimated value of waiting to exercise is

$$-1.07 + 2.98 \times 1.08 - 1.81 \times 1.166 = 0.037 \qquad (12)$$

Since the immediate exercise value is $1.10 - 1.08 = 0.02$, which is less than 0.037, we wait at that node. Table 4 summarizes the results.

We then repeat the analysis at $t = 1$, using the results at $t = 2$. The final decision about where to exercise the option is summarized in Figure 5. We can value the option by computing the present value of cash flows based on exercising at the nodes where doing so is optimal. The final American put value is \$0.1144, compared with \$0.0564 for a European value computed using the same simulated paths.

A problem with the regression approach is that it is not obvious how to select an appropriate functional form for the continuation regression. Longstaff and Schwartz (2001) report obtaining similar results for a variety of functional forms, but for each new problem it will be desirable to experiment with different functions.

Broadie and Glasserman (1997) adopt a different approach, pointing out that American option valuations are subject to different kinds of biases. As we discussed above, an estimator will give too high a valuation to the extent it uses information about the future to decide whether to exercise at a given time. Estimators will be biased low to the extent that early exercise is suboptimal (because optimal exercise maximizes the value of the option). To address the two errors, Broadie and Glasserman use two estimators, one with high bias and one with low bias. In constructing these estimators, they create sample paths in which there are multiple branches from each node. The resulting set of paths resembles a nonrecombining binomial tree with more than two branches from each node.

TABLE 4 Exercise analysis at $t = 2$ for those nodes in Figure 4 where $S < \$1.10$ at $t = 2$.

Path	PV(Wait)	S	S^2	Exercise	Continuation	Result
1	0.000	1.08	1.166	0.02	0.037	Wait
3	0.066	1.07	1.145	0.03	0.046	Wait
4	0.170	0.97	0.941	0.13	0.118	Exercise
6	0.188	0.77	0.593	0.33	0.152	Exercise
7	0.085	0.84	0.706	0.26	0.156	Exercise

FIGURE 5

Summary of results showing the nodes at which exercise is optimal (in **bold**) for the paths in Figure 4.

	Stock Price Paths			
Path	$t = 0$	$t = 1$	$t = 2$	$t = 3$
1	1.00	1.09	1.08	1.34
2	1.00	1.16	1.26	1.54
3	1.00	1.22	1.07	**1.03**
4	1.00	**0.93**	0.97	0.92
5	1.00	1.11	1.56	1.52
6	1.00	**0.76**	0.77	0.90
7	1.00	**0.92**	0.84	1.01
8	1.00	**0.88**	1.22	1.34

The high bias estimator assesses the continuation value by averaging the discounted values on branches emanating from a point and exercising if the value of doing so is greater than the value of continuing. Because the subsequent branches are constructed by simulation, there will be sampling error. To see the effects of such error, suppose exercise is optimal at a node. If the subsequent branches are too high due to sampling error, we will not exercise and assign an even higher value to the node than would be obtained by (optimally) exercising. Now suppose that exercise is not optimal at a node but subsequent branches are too low due to sampling error. We will then exercise and again assign a higher value to the node than we should, given the subsequent branch values.[11]

The low bias estimator is obtained by splitting the branches from each node into two sets. Using the first set, we estimate the value of continuation and decide whether to exercise. If it is optimal to continue, we use the second set of nodes to estimate the continuation value.

11. Note that the other two kinds of sampling errors do not matter for assessing the value of early exercise. If it is not optimal to exercise and subsequent branches are too high, we will not exercise and therefore not erroneously attribute value to exercising. Similarly, if it is optimal to exercise and subsequent values are too low, we will exercise, giving the correct value to early exercise.

By using separate sets of nodes to make the exercise decision and to estimate continuation value, this estimator avoids the "high bias" discussed above. But to the extent the exercise decision is suboptimal, the inferred option value will be too low. Both estimators are biased, but both also converge to the true option value as the number of paths increases.

The Broadie and Glasserman approach is computationally involved, but it provides a general method for accommodating early exercise in a simulation model.

7. THE POISSON DISTRIBUTION

We have seen that the lognormal distribution assigns a low probability to large stock price moves. One approach to generating a more realistic stock price distribution is to permit large stock price moves to occur randomly. Occasional large price moves can generate the fat tails.

The **Poisson distribution** is a discrete probability distribution that counts the number of events—such as large stock price moves—that occur over a period of time. The Poisson distribution is summarized by the parameter λ, where λh is the probability that one event occurs over the short interval h. A Poisson-distributed event is very unlikely to occur more than once over a sufficiently short interval. Thus, λ is like an annualized probability of the event occurring over a short interval.[12]

Over a longer period of time, t, the probability that the event occurs exactly m times is given by

$$p(m, \lambda t) = \frac{e^{-\lambda t}(\lambda t)^m}{m!}$$

The cumulative Poisson distribution is then the probability that there are m or fewer events from 0 to t.[13]

$$\mathcal{P}(m, \lambda t) = \Pr(x \leq m; \lambda t) = \sum_{i=0}^{m} \frac{e^{-\lambda t}(\lambda t)^i}{i!}$$

Given an expected number of events, the Poisson distribution tells us the probability that we will see a particular number of the events over a given period of time.[14] The mean of the Poisson distribution is λt.

---

12. By definition, the number of occurrences of an event is Poisson-distributed if four assumptions are satisfied:

1. The probability that one event will occur in a small interval h is proportional to the length of the interval.
2. The probability that more than one event will occur in a small interval h is substantially smaller than the probability that a single event will occur.
3. The number of events in nonoverlapping time intervals is independent.
4. The expected number of events between time t and time $t + s$ is independent of t.

The Poisson distribution can be derived from these four assumptions. See Casella and Berger (2002).

13. In Excel, you can compute $p(m, \lambda t)$ as Poisson(m, λt, *false*), and the cumulative distribution, $\mathcal{P}(m, \lambda t)$, as Poisson($m$, λt, *true*).

14. The probability that no event occurs between time 0 and time t is $p(0, \lambda t) = e^{-\lambda t}$. The probability that one or more events occurs between 0 and t is therefore $1 - e^{-\lambda t}$. This expression is also the cumulative

FIGURE 6

Graph of Poisson distribution for λt of 0.010, 0.025, and 0.050. This graph may be interpreted as the distribution of the number of events observed over a 10-year period, given annual event probabilities of 1%, 2.5%, and 5%. In any of the cases, there is a tiny probability of seeing more than five events over the 10-year period.

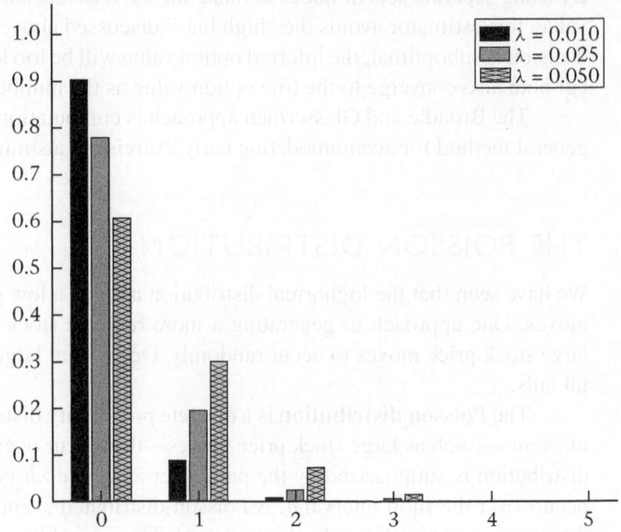

Example 3. Suppose the probability of a market crash over a short period of length h is λh, where $\lambda = 0.02$. Then the probability of seeing no market crashes in any given year can be computed as $p(0, 0.02 \times 1) = 0.9802$. The probability of seeing no crashes over a 10-year period would be $p(0, 0.02 \times 10) = 0.8187$. The probability of seeing exactly two crashes over a 10-year period would be $p(2, 0.02 \times 10) = 0.0164$. ■

Figure 6 graphs the Poisson distribution for three values of the Poisson parameter, λt. Suppose we are interested in the number of times an event will occur over a 10-year period. Figure 6 shows us the distribution for $t = 10$ and $\lambda = 0.01$ (1% per year), $\lambda = 0.025$ (2.5% per year), and $\lambda = 0.05$ (5% per year). The likeliest occurrence in all three scenarios is that no events occur. It is also extremely unlikely that four or more events occur.

The Poisson distribution only counts the number of events. If an event occurs, we need to determine the magnitude of the jump as an independent draw from some other density; the lognormal is frequently used. Thus, in those periods when a Poisson event occurs, we would draw a separate random variable to determine the magnitude of the jump.

Using the inverse cumulative distribution function for a Poisson random variable, it is easy to generate a Poisson-distributed random variable. Even without the inverse cumulative distribution function (which Excel does not provide), we can construct the inverse distribution function from the cumulative distribution function.

Table 5 calculates the Poisson distribution for a mean of 0.8. Using this table we can easily see how to randomly draw a Poisson event. First we draw a uniform (0,1) random

---

distribution of the **exponential distribution**, which models the time until the first event. The density function of the exponential distribution is $f(t, \lambda) = \lambda e^{-\lambda t}$.

TABLE 5 Values of Poisson distribution and cumulative Poisson distribution with mean $(\lambda t) = 0.8$.

Number of Events	Probability	Cumulative Probability
0	0.4493	0.4493
1	0.3595	0.8088
2	0.1438	0.9526
3	0.0383	0.9909

variable. Then we use the values in the table to decide how many events occur. If the uniform random variable is less than 0.4493, we say that no events occur. If the value is between 0.4493 and 0.8088, we say that one event occurs, and so forth.

8. SIMULATING JUMPS WITH THE POISSON DISTRIBUTION

As we discussed, stock prices sometimes move more than would be expected from a lognormal distribution. If market volatility is 20% and the expected return is 15%, a 1-day 5% drop in the market occurs about once every 2.5 million days. (See Problem 8.) A 20% 1-day drop (as in October 1987) is virtually impossible if prices are lognormally distributed with a reasonable volatility.

Merton (1976) introduced the use of the Poisson distribution in an option pricing context. The Poisson distribution counts the number of events that occur in a given period of time. If each event is a jump in the price, we can then use the lognormal (or other) distribution to compute the size of the jump. This Poisson-lognormal model assumes that jumps are independent. In addition to independence, we will assume that jumps are idiosyncratic, meaning that jumps can be diversified. In this case, the possibility of a jump does not affect the risk premium of the asset. (This is a common assumption made for tractability, but it is not always appropriate. While some jumps are idiosyncratic, a large market move is by definition systematic.)

Let the lognormally distributed jump magnitude Y be given by

$$Y = e^{\alpha_J - 0.5\sigma_J^2 + \sigma_J W}$$

where W is a standard normal variable. If S is the pre-jump price, YS is the post-jump price. e^{α_J} is the expected jump and σ_J is the standard deviation of the log of the jump. The expected percentage jump is

$$E\left(\frac{YS - S}{S}\right) = e^{\alpha_J} - 1 = k \tag{13}$$

Simulating the Stock Price with Jumps

To simulate the stock price over a period of time h, we first pick two uniform random variables to determine the number of jumps and the ordinary (nonjump) lognormal return.

If there are m jumps, we must then pick m additional random variables to determine the magnitudes of the jumps. Each jump has a multiplicative effect on the stock price.

Specifically, suppose the stock price is S_t. If a stock cannot jump, its price at time $t+h$ is

$$S_{t+h} = S_t e^{(\alpha-\delta-0.5\sigma^2)h+\sigma\sqrt{h}Z}$$

where α is the expected return.

Now consider an otherwise identical stock that can jump, with price $\hat{S}_t$. The stock price will have two components, one with and one without jumps. The no-jump lognormal component is

$$S_t e^{(\hat{\alpha}-\delta-0.5\sigma^2)h+\sigma\sqrt{h}Z}$$

where the expected stock return, conditional on no jump, is $\hat{\alpha}$. We will see in a moment why we use a different notation for the expected return in this expression. If the stock jumps m times between t and $t+h$, each jump changes the price by a factor of

$$Y_i = e^{\alpha_J - 0.5\sigma_J^2 + \sigma_J W(i)}$$

Where Z and $W(i)$, $i = 1, \ldots, m$ are standard normal random variables. The cumulative jump is the product of the Y_i's, or

$$\prod_{i=1}^{m} Y_i = e^{m(\alpha_J - 0.5\sigma_J^2) + \sigma_J \Sigma_{i=1}^{m} W(i)}$$

Notice that the cumulative jump is lognormal, since it is the product of lognormal random variables. The stock price at time $t+h$, taking account of both the normal lognormal return and jumps, is then

$$\hat{S}_{t+h} = \hat{S}_t e^{(\hat{\alpha}-\delta-0.5\sigma^2)h+\sigma\sqrt{h}Z} \times e^{m(\alpha_J-0.5\sigma_J^2)+\sigma_J \Sigma_{i=1}^{m} W(i)} \tag{14}$$

It is possible to simulate $\hat{S}_{t+h}$ using this expression. There are three steps:

1. Select a standard normal Z.
2. Select m from the Poisson distribution.
3. Select m draws, $W(i)$, $i = 1, \ldots, m$, from the standard normal distribution.

By inserting these values into equation (14), we generate $\hat{S}_{t+h}$, which is lognormal since it is a product of lognormal expressions.

We have not answered the question: What is $\hat{\alpha}$? There is a subtlety associated with modeling jumps. When a jump occurs, the expected percentage change in the stock price is $e^{\alpha_J} - 1$. If $\alpha_J \neq 0$, jumps will induce average up or down movement in the stock, depending upon whether $\alpha_J > 0$ or $\alpha_J < 0$. Recall, however, that we assumed jumps are idiosyncratic. When jumps have no systematic risk, the jump does not affect the stock's expected return. Therefore, *the unconditional (meaning that we do not know whether jumps will occur) expected return for a stock that does not jump should be the same as the unconditional expected return for an otherwise identical stock that does jump*. We have to adjust the nonjump expected return, $\hat{\alpha}$, in order for jumps not to affect the expected return. For example, if the average jump return is -10%, then over time the stock price will drift down on average due to jumps. In equilibrium, the stock must appreciate when not jumping in order to give the owner a fair return unconditionally. If $\alpha_J = -10\%$, we would need to raise the average expected return on the stock in order for it to earn a fair rate of return on average.

We adjust for α_J by subtracting λk from the no-jump expected return, where λ is the Poisson parameter and k is given by equation (13). Thus,

$$\hat{\alpha} = \alpha - \lambda k \tag{15}$$

With this correction, if the expected jump is positive, we lower the expected return on the stock when it is not jumping, and vice versa for a negative expected jump.

The final expression for the stock price is thus

$$\begin{aligned} \hat{S}_{t+h} &= \hat{S}_t e^{(\alpha-\delta-\lambda k-0.5\sigma^2)h+\sigma\sqrt{h}Z} \prod_{i=0}^{m} e^{\alpha_J-0.5\sigma_J^2+\sigma_J W_i} \\ &= \hat{S}_t e^{(\alpha-\delta-\lambda k-0.5\sigma^2)h+\sigma\sqrt{h}Z} e^{m(\alpha_J-0.5\sigma_J^2)+\sigma_J \Sigma_{i=0}^{m} W_i} \end{aligned} \tag{16}$$

where α_J and σ_J are the mean and standard deviation of the jump magnitude, Z and W_i are random standard normal variables, and m is a Poisson-distributed random variable. A similar expression appears in Merton (1976).

Figure 7 displays two simulated stock price series, one for which jumps do not occur, and one generated using equation (16). In the absence of jumps, the stock price is assumed to follow a lognormal process with $\alpha = 8\%$ and $\sigma = 30\%$. For the jump component, we assume $\lambda = 3$ (an average of three jumps per year), $\alpha_J = -2\%$, and $\sigma_J = 5\%$. In the figure, we can detect jumps because the no-jump series is drawn using the same random Z's. Some

FIGURE 7

Simulated stock price paths over 10 years (3650 days). One stock cannot jump; the other is the same except that jumps can occur. The simulation assumes that $\alpha = 9\%$, $\delta = 0$, $\sigma = 30\%$, $\lambda = 3$, $\alpha_j = -2\%$, and $\sigma_j = 5\%$.

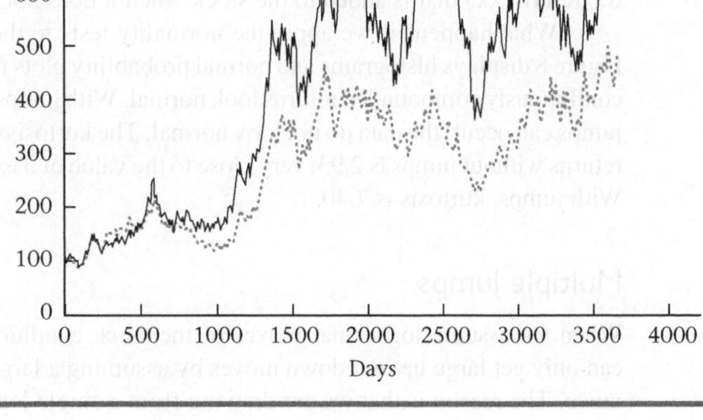

FIGURE 8

Histograms and normal probability plots for the daily returns generated from the two series in Figure 7. Graphs on the left are for the no-jump series.

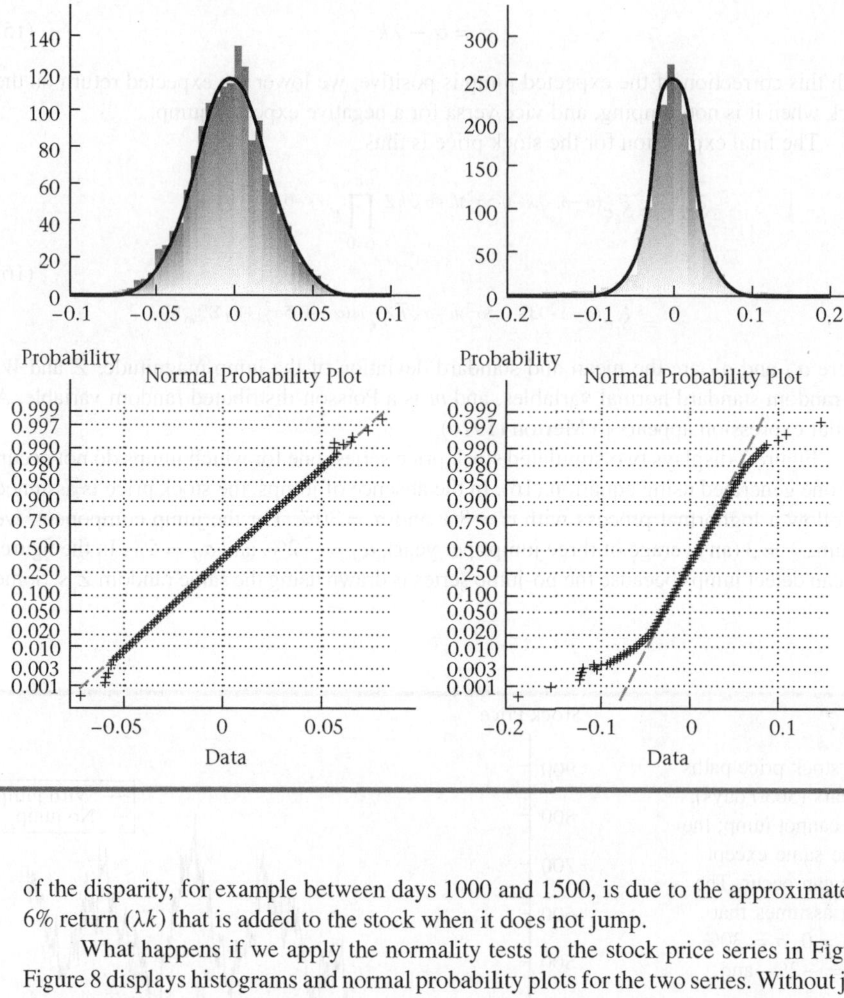

of the disparity, for example between days 1000 and 1500, is due to the approximate extra 6% return (λk) that is added to the stock when it does not jump.

What happens if we apply the normality tests to the stock price series in Figure 7? Figure 8 displays histograms and normal probability plots for the two series. Without jumps, continuously compounded returns look normal. With jumps, the data look nonnormal. When jumps can occur, the data do not look normal. The kurtosis of the continuously compounded returns without jumps is 2.93, very close to the value of 3 expected for a normal distribution. With jumps, kurtosis is 7.40.

Multiple Jumps

When we assume lognormal moves of the stock conditional on a single jump event, we can only get large up *and* down moves by assuming a large standard deviation of the jump move. The reason is that we are drawing from a single lognormal distribution, conditional on the Poisson event. An alternative is to assume there are *two* (or more) Poisson variables, one controlling up jumps and one controlling down jumps. The lognormal moves associated with each can have different means and standard deviations. This obviously provides for a richer and potentially more realistic set of outcomes.

9. SIMULATING CORRELATED STOCK PRICES

Suppose that S and Q are both lognormally distributed stock prices such that

$$\ln(S_t) = \ln(S_0) + (\alpha_S - 0.5\sigma_S^2)t + \sigma_S\sqrt{t}W$$

$$\ln(Q_t) = \ln(Q_0) + (\alpha_Q - 0.5\sigma_Q^2)t + \sigma_Q\sqrt{t}Z$$

If S and Q are uncorrelated, then we can simulate both prices by drawing independent W and Z. However, suppose that the correlation between S and Q is ρ. Here is how to simulate these two random variables taking account of their correlation.

Let ϵ_1 and ϵ_2 be independent and distributed as $\mathcal{N}(0, 1)$. Let

$$W = \epsilon_1$$

$$Z = \rho\epsilon_1 + \epsilon_2\sqrt{1-\rho^2} \tag{17}$$

Then $\text{Corr}(Z, W) = \rho$, and Z is distributed $\mathcal{N}(0, 1)$.

To see this, note first that Z and W both have zero mean. Compute the covariance between Z and W and the variance of Z:

$$\text{E}(WZ) = \text{E}[\epsilon_1(\rho\epsilon_1 + \epsilon_2\sqrt{1-\rho^2})] = \rho E(\epsilon_1^2) = \rho$$

$$\text{E}(Z^2) = \text{E}[(\rho\epsilon_1 + \epsilon_2\sqrt{1-\rho^2})^2] = \rho^2 + 1 - \rho^2 = 1$$

Thus, W and Z are both $\mathcal{N}(0, 1)$ and have a correlation coefficient of ρ.

Now we will check that the continuously compounded returns of S and Q have correlation ρ. The covariance between $\ln(S_t)$ and $\ln(Q_t)$ is

$$\begin{aligned}\text{E}\left[(\ln(S_t) - \text{E}[\ln(S_t)])(\ln(Q_t) - \text{E}[\ln(Q_t)])\right] &= \text{E}\left(\sigma_S W\sqrt{t}\sigma_Q Z\sqrt{t}\right)\\ &= \sigma_S\sigma_Q\rho t\end{aligned}$$

The correlation coefficient is

$$\text{Correlation} = \frac{\sigma_S\sigma_Q\rho t}{\sigma_S\sqrt{t}\sigma_Q\sqrt{t}} = \rho$$

Thus, if W and Z have correlation ρ, so will the continuously compounded returns of S and Q.

Generating n Correlated Lognormal Random Variables

Suppose we have n correlated lognormal variables. The question we address here is how to generalize the previous analysis. The first of the n random variables will have $n - 1$ pairwise correlations with the others. The second will have $n-2$ (not counting its correlation with the first, which we have already counted). Continuing in this way, we will have

$$n-1+n-2+\cdots+1=\frac{1}{2}n(n-1)$$

pairwise correlations we have to take into account. We will denote the correlation between variables i and j as $\rho_{i,j}$.

We denote the original uncorrelated random $\mathcal{N}(0,1)$ variables as $\epsilon_1, \epsilon_2, \ldots, \epsilon_n$. The correlated random variables are $Z(1), Z(2), \ldots, Z(n)$, with

$$\mathrm{E}[Z(i)Z(j)]=\rho_{i,j}$$

We can generate the $Z(i)$ as

$$Z(i)=\sum_{j=1}^{i} a_{i,j}\epsilon_j$$

where the $a_{i,j}$ are coefficients selected to make sure the pairwise correlations are correct.

Creating the coefficients $a_{i,j}$ has a recursive solution. That is, we construct $Z(1)$, then $Z(2)$ using the solution to $Z(1)$, and so on. The formula for the $a_{i,j}$ is

$$\begin{aligned} a_{i,j} &= \frac{1}{a_{j,j}}\left[\rho_{i,j}-\sum_{k=1}^{j-1} a_{j,k}a_{i,k}\right] \qquad i>j \\ a_{i,i} &= \sqrt{1-\sum_{k=1}^{i-1} a_{i,k}^2} \end{aligned} \tag{18}$$

For the case of two random variables, this reduces to equation (17).

The matrix of $a_{i,j}$'s is called the **Cholesky decomposition** of the original correlation matrix.[15] In order for equation (18) to give correct coefficients, the set of correlations must be **positive-definite**, which means that the correlations must be such that there is no way to sum random variables and compute a negative variance. This is *not* an arbitrary condition: If this condition is not satisfied, the set of correlations is not valid.[16]

15. Formally, if Ω is a correlation matrix, the Cholesky decomposition is the triangular matrix L such that $\Omega = L'L$. The procedure outlined in equation (18) generates L.

16. Suppose there are three random variables, a, b, and c, each with a variance of 1. Suppose that a is perfectly correlated with b ($\rho_{a,b}=1$) and b is perfectly correlated with c ($\rho_{b,c}=1$). It must then be the case that c is perfectly correlated with a. If $\rho_{a,c}\neq 1$, the matrix of correlations is not positive-definite. To see this, suppose that $\rho_{a,c}=0$, then compute Var$(a-b+c)$. You will find that the variance is -1, which is impossible. To take a different example, suppose $\rho_{a,c}=0.9$. You will then find that Var$(a-2b+c)=-0.2$, which is again impossible. If a matrix of correlations is not positive-definite, it means that there is some combination of the random variables for which you will compute a negative variance. (For many combinations the variance will still be positive.) The interpretation of a negative variance is that you had an invalid correlation matrix to start with.

The point—and the reason for mentioning this—is that correlations and covariances cannot be arbitrary. In practice, depending upon how a covariance matrix is estimated, this can be an important concern. The *true* covariances among hundreds of bonds, stocks, currencies, and commodities *must* create a positive-definite covariance matrix. However, *estimated* covariances might not be positive-definite. If there are m assets and $n > m$ observations, the covariance matrix estimated from these data will be positive-definite. However, if different covariances are estimated from different data sets, positive-definiteness is not assured. The results of a simulation based on such covariances may produce nonsensical results.

CHAPTER SUMMARY

Monte Carlo methods entail simulating asset returns in order to obtain a future distribution for prices. This distribution can then be used to price claims on the asset (for example, Asian options) or to assess the risk of the asset. Performing simulations requires that we draw random numbers from an appropriate distribution (for example, the normal) in order to generate future asset prices. There are adjustments, such as the control variate method, which can dramatically increase the speed with which Monte Carlo estimates converge to the correct price.

It is possible to incorporate jumps in the price by mixing Poisson and log-normal random variables. Simulated correlated random variables can be created using the Cholesky decomposition.

FURTHER READING

The first use of Monte Carlo methods to price options was Boyle (1977), and the technique is now quite widespread. Two excellent discussions of the use of Monte Carlo to value derivatives are Boyle et al. (1997) and Glasserman (2004). Bodie and Crane (1999) use Monte Carlo to analyze retirement investment products. Schwartz and Moon (2000) use Monte Carlo to value a firm by simulating future cash flows.

The papers by Broadie and Glasserman (1997) and Longstaff and Schwartz (2001), which present techniques for using Monte Carlo to value American-style options, have clear discussions of their respective methodologies.

Merton (1976) derived an option pricing formula in the presence of idiosyncratic jumps. Naik and Lee (1990) illustrate option pricing in the presence of systematic jumps. Risk aversion affects the option price in such cases.

PROBLEMS

1. Let $u_i \sim \mathcal{U}(0, 1)$. Draw 1000 random u_i and construct a histogram of the results. What are the mean and standard deviation?

2. Let $u_i \sim \mathcal{U}(0, 1)$. Compute $\sum_{i=1}^{12} u_i - 6$, 1000 times. (This will use 12,000 random numbers.) Construct a histogram and compare it to a theoretical standard normal density. What are the mean and standard deviation? (This is a way to compute a random approximately normally distributed variable.)

3. Suppose that $x_1 \sim \mathcal{N}(0, 1)$ and $x_2 \sim \mathcal{N}(0.7, 3)$. Compute 2000 random draws of e^{x_1} and e^{x_2}.

a. What are the means of e^{x_1} and e^{x_2}? Why?

b. Create a graph that displays a frequency distribution in each case.

4. The Black-Scholes price for a European put option with $S = \$40$, $K = \$40$, $\sigma = 0.30$, $r = 0.08$, $\delta = 0$, and $t = 0.25$ is \$1.99. Use Monte Carlo to compute this price. Compute the standard deviation of your estimates. How many trials do you need to achieve a standard deviation of \$0.01 for your estimates?

5. Let $r = 0.08$, $S = \$100$, $\delta = 0$, and $\sigma = 0.30$. Using the risk-neutral distribution, simulate $1/S_1$. What is $E(1/S_1)$? What is the forward price for a contract paying $1/S_1$?

6. Suppose $S_0 = 100$, $r = 0.06$, $\sigma_S = 0.4$ and $\delta = 0$. Use Monte Carlo to compute prices for claims that pay the following:

a. S_1^2

b. $\sqrt{S_1}$

c. S_1^{-2}

7. Suppose that $\ln(S)$ and $\ln(Q)$ have correlation $\rho = -0.3$ and that $S_0 = \$100$, $Q_0 = \$100$, $r = 0.06$, $\sigma_S = 0.4$, and $\sigma_Q = 0.2$. Neither stock pays dividends. Use Monte Carlo to find the price today of claims that pay the following:

a. $S_1 Q_1$

b. S_1/Q_1

c. $\sqrt{S_1 Q_1}$

d. $1/(S_1 Q_1)$

e. $S_1^2 Q_1$

8. Assume that the market index is 100. Show that if the expected return on the market is 15%, the dividend yield is zero, and volatility is 20%, then the probability of the index falling below 95 over a 1-day horizon is approximately 0.0000004.

9. Suppose that on any given day the annualized continuously compounded stock return has a volatility of either 15%, with a probability of 80%, or 30%, with a probability of 20%. This is a mixture of normals model. Simulate the daily stock return and construct a histogram and normal plot. What happens to the normal plot as you vary the probability of the high volatility distribution?

10. For stocks 1 and 2, $S_1 = \$40$, $S_2 = \$100$, and the return correlation is 0.45. Let $r = 0.08$, $\sigma_1 = 0.30$, $\sigma_2 = 0.50$, and $\delta_1 = \delta_2 = 0$. Generate 1000 1-month prices for the two stocks. For each stock, compute the mean and standard deviation of the continuously compounded return. Also compute the return correlation.

11. Assume $S_0 = \$100$, $r = 0.05$, $\sigma = 0.25$, $\delta = 0$, and $T = 1$. Use Monte Carlo valuation to compute the price of a claim that pays \$1 if $S_T > \$100$, and 0 otherwise. (This is called a *cash-or-nothing call*. The actual price of this claim is \$0.5040.)

a. Running 1000 simulations, what is the estimated price of the contract? How close is it to \$0.5040?

b. What is the standard deviation of your Monte Carlo estimate? What is the 95% confidence interval for your estimate?

c. Use a 1-year at-the-money call as a control variate and compute a price using equation (9), setting $\beta = 1$.

d. Again use a 1-year at-the-money call as a control variate, only this time use equation (9) and set β optimally. What is the standard deviation of your estimate?

For the following three problems, assume that $S_0 = \$100$, $r = 0.08$, $\alpha = 0.20$, $\sigma = 0.30$, and $\delta = 0$. Perform 2000 simulations. Note that most spreadsheets have built-in functions to compute skewness and kurtosis. (In Excel, the functions are Skew and Kurt.) For the normal distribution, skewness, which measures asymmetry, is zero. Kurtosis equals 3.

12. Let $h = 1/52$. Simulate both the continuously compounded actual return and the actual stock price, S_{t+h}. What are the mean, standard deviation, skewness, and kurtosis of both the continuously compounded return on the stock and the stock price? Use the same random normal numbers and repeat for $h = 1$. Do any of your answers change? Why?

13. An options trader purchases 1000 1-year at-the-money calls on a non-dividend-paying stock with $S_0 = \$100$, $\alpha = 0.20$, and $\sigma = 0.25$. Assume the options are priced according to the Black-Scholes formula and $r = 0.05$.

a. Use Monte Carlo (with 1000 simulations) to estimate the expected return, standard deviation, skewness, and kurtosis of the return on the call when it is held until expiration. Interpret your answers.

b. Repeat for an at-the-money put.

14. Repeat the previous problem, only assume that the options trader purchases 1000 1-year at-the-money *straddles*.

15. Refer to Table 1.

a. Verify the regression coefficients in equation (12).

b. Perform the analysis for $t = 1$, verifying that exercise is optimal on paths 4, 6, 7, and 8, and not on path 1.

16. Refer to Figure 2.

a. Verify that the price of a European put option is \$0.0564.

b. Verify that the price of an American put option is \$0.1144. Be sure to allow for the possibility of exercise at time 0.

17. Assume $S_0 = \$50$, $r = 0.05$, $\sigma = 0.50$, and $\delta = 0$. The Black-Scholes price for a 2-year at-the-money put is \$10.906. Suppose that the stock price is lognormal but can also jump, with the number of jumps Poisson-distributed. Assume $\alpha = 0.05$

(the expected return to the stock is equal to the risk-free rate), $\sigma = 0.50$, $\lambda = 2$, $\alpha_J = -0.04$, $\sigma_J = 0.08$.

a. Using 2000 simulations incorporating jumps, simulate the 2-year price and draw a histogram of continuously compounded returns.

b. Using Monte Carlo incorporating jumps, value a 2-year at-the-money put. Is this value significantly different from the Black-Scholes value?

Appendix A FORMULAS FOR GEOMETRIC AVERAGE OPTIONS

Appendix available at http://www.pearsonhighered.com/mcdonald.

Brownian Motion and Itô's Lemma

This chapter addresses three important topics. First, stock and other asset prices are commonly assumed to follow a stochastic process called geometric Brownian motion. This chapter explains what this means and develops the notation and assumptions underlying the Black-Scholes model.

Second, given that an asset price follows geometric Brownian motion, we want to characterize the behavior of a claim—such as an option—that has a payoff dependent upon the asset price. For this purpose we need Itô's Lemma, which tells us the process followed by a claim that is a function of the stock price.

Third, it is typical when pricing derivatives to use the risk-neutral process for an asset rather than the actual process. We illustrate risk-neutral pricing when the stock follows an Itô process.

Practitioners and academic derivatives researchers alike rely on the concepts and techniques we discuss here.

1. THE BLACK-SCHOLES ASSUMPTION ABOUT STOCK PRICES

The vast majority of technical option pricing discussions, including the original paper by Black and Scholes, begin by assuming that the price of the underlying asset follows a process like the following:

$$\frac{dS(t)}{S(t)} = (\alpha - \delta)dt + \sigma dZ(t) \tag{1}$$

In this expression, $S(t)$ is the stock price, $dS(t)$ is the instantaneous change in the stock price, α is the continuously compounded expected return on the stock, σ is the standard deviation of the instantaneous return (volatility), and $Z(t)$ is a normally distributed random variable that follows a process called Brownian motion. The variable $dZ(t)$ represents the change in $Z(t)$ over a short period of time. A stock obeying equation (1) is said to follow a process called *geometric Brownian motion*. Expressions like equation (1) are called *stochastic differential equations*.

From Chapter 20 of *Derivatives Markets*, Third Edition, Robert McDonald. Copyright © 2013 by Pearson Education, Inc. Published by Pearson Prentice Hall. All rights reserved.

One goal of this chapter is to understand the meaning of equations like (1). For our purposes, there are two important implications of this equation:

1. If the stock price follows equation (1), the distribution of $S(T)$, conditional upon the current price $S(0)$, is lognormal, i.e.,

$$\ln[S(T)] \sim \mathcal{N}(\ln[S(0)] + [\alpha - \delta - 0.5\sigma^2]T, \sigma^2 T)$$

   The assumption that the stock follows geometric Brownian motion thus provides a foundation for our assumption that the stock price is lognormally distributed.

2. Lognormality tells us about the distribution of the stock price at a point in time. For many purposes, however, we are interested not just in the distribution at a terminal point but also the *path* the stock price takes in getting to that terminal point. With barrier options, for example, the price of the option depends upon the probability that the asset price reaches the barrier. Geometric Brownian motion allows us to describe this path.

Our goal is to provide a heuristic, rather than technical, understanding of equations like (1).

2. BROWNIAN MOTION

A **stochastic process** is a random process that is a function of time. **Brownian motion**, which is a basic building block for standard derivatives pricing models, is a stochastic process that evolves in continuous time, with movements that are continuous. A careful mathematical formulation of Brownian motion requires mathematics beyond the scope and purpose of this chapter.[1] Our goal here is to provide an intuitive understanding.

Definition of Brownian Motion

Brownian motion is a continuous stochastic process, $Z(t)$, with the following characteristics:

- $Z(0) = 0$.
- $Z(t + s) - Z(t)$ is normally distributed with mean 0 and variance s.
- $Z(t + s_1) - Z(t)$ is independent of $Z(t) - Z(t - s_2)$, where $s_1, s_2 > 0$. In other words, nonoverlapping increments are independently distributed.
- $Z(t)$ is continuous (you can draw a picture of Brownian motion without lifting your pencil).

These properties imply that $Z(t)$ is a **martingale**: a stochastic process for which $\mathrm{E}[Z(t + s)|Z(t)] = Z(t)$. The process $Z(t)$ is also called a **diffusion process**. Brownian motion is an example of a **random walk**, which is a stochastic process with independent increments.

1. The developments in this section draw heavily on Cox and Miller (1965, ch. 5) and Merton (1990). For a more rigorous approach to this material, see Duffie (2001) and Karatzas and Shreve (1991).

We can obtain a heuristic understanding of Brownian motion by modeling the change in $Z(t)$ as binomial, times a scale factor that makes the change in $Z(t)$ small over a small period of time. Brownian motion is then the limit of a sum of infinitesimal increments over a period of time. Denote the short period of time as h, and let $Y(t)$ be a random draw from a binomial distribution, where $Y(t)$ is ± 1 with probability 0.5. Note that $\mathrm{E}[Y(t)] = 0$ and $\mathrm{Var}[Y(t)] = 1$. We can write

$$Z(t+h) - Z(t) = Y(t+h)\sqrt{h} \tag{2}$$

Over any period of time longer than h, Z will be the sum of the binomial increments specified in equation (2). Let $n = T/h$ be the number of intervals of length h between 0 and T. We have

$$Z(T) - Z(0) = \sum_{i=1}^{n} (Z[ih] - Z[(i-1)h]) = \sum_{i=1}^{n} Y(ih)\sqrt{h}$$

Since $h = T/n$, we can also write this as

$$Z(T) - Z(0) = \sqrt{T}\left[\frac{1}{\sqrt{n}}\sum_{i=1}^{n} Y(ih)\right] \tag{3}$$

To understand the properties of $Z(T)$, we must first understand the properties of the term in square brackets in equation (3). Since $\mathrm{E}[Y(ih)] = 0$, we have

$$\mathrm{E}\left[\frac{1}{\sqrt{n}}\sum_{i=1}^{n} Y(ih)\right] = 0$$

Also, since $\mathrm{Var}[Y(ih)] = 1$, and the Y's are independent, we have

$$\mathrm{Var}\left[\frac{1}{\sqrt{n}}\sum_{i=1}^{n} Y(ih)\right] = \frac{1}{n}\sum_{i=1}^{n} 1 = 1$$

Thus, the term in square brackets has mean 0 and variance 1, since it is the sum of n independent random variables with mean 0 and variance 1, divided by $\sqrt{n}$.

By the central limit theorem, the distribution of the sum of independent binomial random variables approaches normality. We have

$$\lim_{n\to\infty} \frac{1}{\sqrt{n}}\sum_{i=1}^{n} Y(ih) \sim \mathcal{N}(0, 1)$$

The division by $\sqrt{n}$ in this expression prevents the variance from going to infinity as n goes to infinity.

Returning to equation (3), the multiplication by $\sqrt{T}$ on the right-hand side multiplies the variance by T. Thus, in the limit we have

$$Z(T) - Z(0) \to \mathcal{N}(0, T)$$

To summarize, we have verified that the $Z(T)$ we have constructed has some of the characteristics of Brownian motion: It is normally distributed with mean zero and variance T, and increments to $Z(T)$ are independent.

We have not verified that the $Z(T)$ defined in equation (3) is a continuous process; hence, we have not demonstrated that it is true Brownian motion. However, it is plausible that $Z(T)$ is continuous because the magnitude of the increments is $\sqrt{h} = \sqrt{T/n}$, and $h \to 0$ as $n \to \infty$.

We can write an expression denoting the Brownian increment. As h becomes small, rename h as dt and the change in Z as $dZ(t)$. We then have

$$dZ(t) = Y(t)\sqrt{dt} \tag{4}$$

This representation of the Brownian process is mathematically informal but surprisingly useful nevertheless. Equation (4) is just like equation (2), except that $Z(t+h) - Z(t)$ is now called $dZ(t)$, and $\sqrt{h}$ is now $\sqrt{dt}$.[2] Equation (4) is a mathematical way to say, "Over small periods of time, changes in the value of the process are normally distributed with a variance that is proportional to the length of the time period."

Although expressions like equation (4) appear in the derivatives literature, it is mathematically appropriate to deal with sums of increments rather than increments. These sums are written as integrals, for example:

$$Z(T) = Z(0) + \lim_{n\to\infty} \sqrt{T}\left[\frac{1}{\sqrt{n}}\sum_{i=1}^{n} Y(ih)\right] \to Z(0) + \int_0^T dZ(t) \tag{5}$$

The integral in expression (5) is called a stochastic integral.[3]

Properties of Brownian Motion

We now use equation (3) to understand some additional properties of Brownian motion. The following derivations will be informal, intended to provide intuition rather than actual proofs. In particular, we continue to use the binomial approximation to the Brownian process.

The **quadratic variation** of a process is defined as the sum of the squared increments to the process. Thus, the quadratic variation of the Brownian process $Z(t)$ is

$$\lim_{n\to\infty}\sum_{i=1}^{n}(Z[ih] - Z[(i-1)h])^2 = \lim_{n\to\infty}\sum_{i=1}^{n}\left(\sqrt{h}Y_{ih}\right)^2 = \lim_{n\to\infty}\sum_{i=1}^{n} hY_{ih}^2$$

Since we are treating Y_i as binomial, taking on the values ± 1, we have $Y_{ih}^2 = 1$ and hence

$$\lim_{n\to\infty}\sum_{i=1}^{n} hY_{ih}^2 = \lim_{n\to\infty}\sum_{i=1}^{n}\frac{T}{n} = T$$

2. Should we think of $Y(t)$ as being binomially or normally distributed? For any t and ϵ, $Z(t+\epsilon) - Z(t)$ is the sum of infinitely many $dZ(t)$'s. Therefore, we can think of $Y(t)$ as binomial or normal; either way, $Z(t)$ is normal for any finite interval.

3. Because $dZ(t)$ is a random variable, considerable care is required in defining equation (5). See Neftci (2000, ch. 9) for a discussion of stochastic integration. Karatzas and Shreve (1991) provide a more advanced treatment.

In other words,

$$\lim_{n\to\infty}\sum_{i=1}^{n}(Z[ih]-Z[(i-1)h])^2=T \tag{6}$$

Surprisingly, the quadratic variation of a Brownian process from time 0 to time T is not a random variable, but it is finite and equal to T. The fact that quadratic variation is finite implies that higher-order variations are zero. Thus, for example, the sum of the cubed increments is zero. The finite quadratic variation of a Brownian process turns out to be an extremely important result that we will encounter again.

The **total variation** of the Brownian process is

$$\lim_{n\to\infty}\sum_{i=1}^{n}|\sqrt{h}Y_{ih}|=\lim_{n\to\infty}\sum_{i=1}^{n}\sqrt{h}|Y_{ih}|$$

Again, treating Y_{ih} as binomial, we have $|Y_{ih}|=1$, and hence

$$\lim_{n\to\infty}\sum_{i=1}^{n}\sqrt{h}|Y_{ih}|=\lim_{n\to\infty}\sqrt{T}\sum_{i=1}^{n}\frac{1}{\sqrt{n}}=\sqrt{T}\lim_{n\to\infty}\sqrt{n}=\infty$$

In words, the absolute length of a Brownian path is infinite over any finite interval. In order for a path to have infinite length over a finite interval of time, it must move up and down rapidly. This behavior implies the *infinite crossing* property, which states that a Brownian path will cross its starting point an infinite number of times in an interval of any finite length.

Arithmetic Brownian Motion

The Brownian motion process described above is a building block for more elaborate and realistic processes. With pure Brownian motion, the expected change in Z is 0, and the variance per unit time is 1. We can generalize this to allow an arbitrary variance and a nonzero mean. To make this generalization, we can write

$$X(t+h)-X(t)=\alpha h+\sigma Y(t+h)\sqrt{h}$$

This equation implies that $X(T)$ is normally distributed. Since $h=T/n$, we have

$$\begin{aligned}X(T)-X(0)&=\sum_{i=1}^{n}\left(\alpha\frac{T}{n}+\sigma Y(ih)\sqrt{\frac{T}{n}}\right)\\&=\alpha T+\sigma\left(\sqrt{T}\sum_{i=1}^{n}\frac{Y(ih)}{\sqrt{n}}\right)\end{aligned}$$

We have seen that as $n\to\infty$, the term in parentheses on the right-hand side has the distribution $\mathcal{N}(0,T)$. We can write

$$X(T)-X(0)=\alpha T+\sigma Z(T) \tag{7}$$

The differential form of this expression is

$$dX(t)=\alpha dt+\sigma dZ(t) \tag{8}$$

This process is called **arithmetic Brownian motion**. We say that α is the instantaneous mean per unit time and σ^2 is the instantaneous variance per unit time. The variable $X(t)$ is the sum of the individual changes dX. An implication of equation (8) is that $X(T)$ is normally distributed, or

$$X(T) - X(0) \sim \mathcal{N}(\alpha T, \sigma^2 T)$$

As before, there is an integral representation of equation (8):

$$X(T) = X(0) + \int_0^T \alpha dt + \int_0^T \sigma dZ(t)$$

This expression is equivalent to equation (7).

Here are some of the properties of the process in equation (8):

- $X(t)$ is normally distributed because it is a scaled Brownian process.
- The random term has been multiplied by a scale factor that enables us to specify the variance of the process. Since $dZ(t)$ has a variance of 1 per unit time, $\sigma dZ(t)$ will have a variance of σ^2 per unit time.
- The αdt term introduces a nonrandom *drift* into the process. Adding αdt has the effect of adding α per unit time to $X(t)$.

Being able to adjust the drift and variance is a big step toward a more useful model, but arithmetic Brownian motion has several drawbacks:

- There is nothing to prevent X from becoming negative, so it is a poor model for stock prices.
- The mean and variance of changes in dollar terms are independent of the level of the stock price. In practice, if the price of a stock doubles, we would expect both the dollar expected return and the dollar standard deviation of returns to approximately double.

The Ornstein-Uhlenbeck Process

Another modification of the arithmetic Brownian process permits mean reversion. It is natural to consider mean reversion when modeling commodity prices or interest rates. For example, if the interest rate becomes sufficiently high, it is likely to fall, and if the value is sufficiently low, it is likely to rise. Commodity prices may also exhibit this tendency to revert to the mean. We can incorporate mean reversion by modifying the drift term:

$$dX(t) = \lambda[\alpha - X(t)]\, dt + \sigma dZ(t) \tag{9}$$

Equation (9) is called an **Ornstein-Uhlenbeck process**.

Equation (9) has the implication that if X rises above α, the drift, $\lambda[\alpha - X(t)]$, will become negative. If X falls below α, the drift becomes positive. The parameter λ measures the speed of the reversion: If λ is large, reversion happens more quickly. In the long run, we expect X to revert toward α. As with arithmetic Brownian motion, X can still become negative.

3. GEOMETRIC BROWNIAN MOTION

In general, we can write both the drift and volatility as functions of X (or other variables):

$$dX(t) = \alpha[X(t)]\,dt + \sigma[X(t)]\,dZ(t) \tag{10}$$

This equation, in which the drift, α, and volatility, σ, depend on $X(t)$, is called an **Itô process**.

Suppose we modify arithmetic Brownian motion to make the instantaneous mean and standard deviation proportional to $X(t)$:

$$dX(t) = \alpha X(t)\,dt + \sigma X(t)\,dZ(t)$$

This is an Itô process that can also be written

$$\frac{dX(t)}{X(t)} = \alpha dt + \sigma dZ(t) \tag{11}$$

This equation says that the dollar mean and standard deviation of $X(t)$ are $\alpha X(t)$ and $\sigma X(t)$, proportional to the level of $X(t)$. Thus, *the percentage change in $X(t)$ is normally distributed with instantaneous mean α and instantaneous variance σ^2*. The process in equation (11) is known as **geometric Brownian motion**. For the rest of the chapter, we will frequently assume that prices of stocks and other assets follow equation (11).

The integral representation for equation (11) is

$$X(T) - X(0) = \int_0^T \alpha X(t)\,dt + \int_0^T \sigma X(t)\,dZ(t)$$

Lognormality

We now circle back to our discussion of lognormality because of this fact: A variable that follows geometric Brownian motion is lognormally distributed. Suppose we start a process at $X(0)$ and it follows geometric Brownian motion. Because the mean and variance at time t are proportional to $X(t)$, the evolution of X implied by equation (11) generates compounding (the change in X is proportional to X) and, hence, nonnormality.

While X is not normal, $\ln[X(t)]$ is normally distributed:

$$\ln[X(t)] \sim \mathcal{N}(\ln[X(0)] + (\alpha - 0.5\sigma^2)t, \sigma^2 t) \tag{12}$$

As a result, we can write

$$X(t) = X(0)e^{\left(\alpha - 0.5\sigma^2\right)t + \sigma\sqrt{t}Z} \tag{13}$$

where $Z \sim \mathcal{N}(0, 1)$. This is the link between Brownian motion and lognormality. If a variable is distributed in such a way that instantaneous percentage changes follow geometric Brownian motion, then over discrete periods of time, the variable is lognormally distributed.

Given that X follows (11), we can compute the expected value of X at a point in the future. It follows from the equation that

$$\begin{aligned} \mathrm{E}[X(t)] &= X(0)e^{(\alpha-0.5\sigma^2)t}\mathrm{E}_0(e^{\sigma\sqrt{t}Z}) \\ &= X(0)e^{\left(\alpha-0.5\sigma^2\right)t}e^{0.5\sigma^2 t} \\ &= X(0)e^{\alpha t} \end{aligned} \tag{14}$$

Thus, α in equation (11) is the continuously compounded expected return on X.

Relative Importance of the Drift and Noise Terms

Consider the discrete counterpart for arithmetic Brownian motion:

$$X(t+h) - X(t) = \alpha h + \sigma Y(t)\sqrt{h}$$

Over a short interval of time, there are two components to the change in X: a deterministic component, αh, and a random component, $\sigma Y(t)\sqrt{h}$. An important fact is that *over short periods of time, the character of the Brownian process is determined almost entirely by the random component*. The drift can be undetectable amid all the up and down movement generated by the random term.

To understand why the random term is important over short horizons, consider the ratio of the standard deviation to the drift:

$$\frac{\sigma\sqrt{h}}{\alpha h} = \frac{\sigma}{\alpha\sqrt{h}}$$

This ratio becomes infinite as h approaches dt.

A numerical example shows this concretely. Suppose $\alpha = 10\%$ and $\sigma = 10\%$. Over a year, the mean and standard deviations are the same. Table 1 shows that the ratio increases as the time interval becomes smaller. Over a period of 1 day, the standard deviation is 19 times larger than the mean. This is important in practice since it means that when you look at daily returns, you are primarily seeing the movement of a random variable following pure Brownian motion.[4] The deterministic drift (the expected return) is virtually undetectable.

As the time interval becomes longer than a year, the reverse happens: The mean becomes more important than the standard deviation. Since the mean is proportional to h while the standard deviation is proportional to $\sqrt{h}$, the mean comes to dominate over longer horizons.[5]

Multiplication Rules

The dominance of the noise term over short intervals has another implication. Since the behavior of dX is dominated by the noise term, the squared return, $(dX)^2$, reflects primarily

4. There are other considerations when you look at prices over short periods of time, including the bouncing of prices between the bid and the ask, and the effects of trades such as large blocks that may temporarily depress prices. Brownian motion implies that even in the absence of these effects, prices would still bounce around significantly.

5. Table 1 also holds for geometric Brownian motion in the following sense. If $X(t)$ is lognormally distributed, we can perform the same analysis using the coefficients of the process for $\ln[X(t)]$, which follows arithmetic Brownian motion.

TABLE 1 The last column computes the ratio of the per-period standard deviation to the per-period mean for different time intervals. The ratio becomes infinite as the time interval goes to zero.

Period Length	h	αh	$\sigma\sqrt{h}$	$\frac{\sigma\sqrt{h}}{\alpha h}$
5 years	5	0.5	0.2236	0.447
1 year	1	0.100	0.100	1.000
1 month	0.0833	0.0083	0.0289	3.464
1 day	0.0027	0.00027	0.0052	19.105
1 minute	0.000002	0.0000002	0.00014	724.983

the noise term. We have

$$[X(t+h) - X(t)]^2 = \left[\alpha X(t)h + \sigma X(t)Y(t)\sqrt{h}\right]^2$$

Expanding this expression and simplifying, we have

$$[X(t+h) - X(t)]^2 = \alpha^2 X(t)^2 h^2 + 2\alpha\sigma X(t)^2 Y(t) h^{1.5} + \sigma^2 X(t)^2 Y(t)^2 h$$

Suppose that h is 1 day. Then $h = 0.00274$, $h^{1.5} = 0.000143$, and $h^2 = 0.0000075$. If h is 1 hour, then $h = 0.000114$, $h^{1.5} = 0.0000012$, and $h^2 = 0.00000001$. Clearly, the relative magnitude of the term multiplied by h is much greater than the other terms as h becomes very small. In addition, if we think of Y as binomial, then $Y(t)^2 = 1$. This leads us to write

$$[X(t+h) - X(t)]^2 \approx \sigma^2 X(t)^2 h$$

or

$$[dX(t)]^2 = \sigma^2 X(t)^2 dt$$

essentially ignoring all terms that are higher powers of h. This equation tells us that if we look at the squared stock price change over a small interval, all we are seeing is the effect of the variance.

We can also consider terms like

$$[X(t+h) - X(t)]h$$

Rewriting this expression gives us

$$\left[\alpha X(t)h + \sigma X(t)Y(t)\sqrt{h}\right] h = \alpha X(t)h^2 + \sigma X(t)Y(t)h^{1.5}$$

Since the smallest power of h is 1.5, this entire term vanishes relative to h as h goes to zero.

One way to make these calculations mechanical is to use the following so-called multiplication rules for terms containing dt and dZ:

$$dt \times dZ = 0 \tag{15a}$$
$$(dt)^2 = 0 \tag{15b}$$
$$(dZ)^2 = dt \tag{15c}$$

The reasoning behind these multiplication rules is that the multiplications resulting in powers of dt greater than 1 vanish in the limit.

Modeling Correlated Asset Prices

Some derivatives have a payoff depending on more than one asset price. In order to price such a derivative it is necessary to specify the pairwise correlations among the various assets. To be concrete, suppose that we have m asset processes

$$dX_i/X_i = (\alpha_i - \delta_i)dt + \sigma_i dZ_i \quad i = 1, \ldots, m \tag{16}$$

The correlation between X_i and X_j will be generated by correlation between the uncertain part of the returns, the Brownian processes $Z_i(t)$ and $Z_j(t)$. We can create correlated diffusion processes by expressing dZ_i and dZ_j as sums of independent diffusions.

An example will illustrate how to construct correlated $dZ_i(t)$'s. Suppose that we want the returns on stocks 1 and 2 to have correlation ρdt. This means that $dZ_1(t)$ and $dZ_2(t)$—which are the source of randomness—must exhibit a correlation of ρdt. Let $W_1(t)$ and $W_2(t)$ be independent Brownian motions and define

$$dZ_1(t) = dW_1(t); \qquad dZ_2(t) = \rho dW_1(t) + \sqrt{1-\rho^2}\, dW_2(t)$$

This is known as the Cholesky decomposition. In order to evaluate the product $dZ_1(t)dZ_2(t)$, we need to evaluate both $dW_1(t)^2$ and $dW_1(t)dW_2(t)$. We know from our previous discussion of multiplication rules that $dW_1(t)^2 = dt$. But how do we evaluate the product $dW_1(t)dW_2(t)$?

The independence of $W_1(t)$ and $W_2(t)$ implies that

$$\mathrm{E}_t\{[W_1(t+s) - W_1(t)][W_2(t+s) - W_2(t)]\} = 0$$

(You can think of the increments to each process as generated by independent binomial random variables.) Using the differential notation, we can write $dW_i(t) \times dW_j(t) = 0$.

We therefore have

$$\begin{aligned} dZ_1(t)dZ_2(t) &= dW_1(t)[\rho dW_1(t) + \sqrt{1-\rho^2} dW_2(t)] \\ &= \rho dW_1(t)^2 + \sqrt{1-\rho^2}\, dW_1(t)dW_2(t) \\ &= \rho\, dt \end{aligned}$$

We can generalize this example to n processes as follows. We construct the dZ_i in equation (16) as

$$dZ_i(t) = \sum_{k=1}^{n} \lambda_{i,k} dW_k(t) \tag{17}$$

where we scale the coefficients so that $\sum_{k=1}^{n} \lambda_{i,k}^2 = 1$. (In the previous example, the squared coefficients also summed to 1.) Because the Brownian increments are jointly-normally distributed, their sum is normal. We also have

$$\text{Var}\left[dZ_i(t)\right] = \text{Var}\left(\sum_{k=1}^{n} \lambda_{i,k} dW_k(t)\right) = \sum_{k=1}^{n} \lambda_{i,k}^2 dW_k(t)^2 = dt$$

The correlation depends on the sum of the product of the weights:[6]

$$dZ_i(t)dZ_j(t) = \sum_{k=1}^{n} \lambda_{i,k} dW_k(t) \sum_{k=1}^{n} \lambda_{j,k} dW_k(t) = \sum_{k=1}^{n} \lambda_{i,k}\lambda_{j,k} dt \equiv \rho_{i,j} dt$$

where $\rho_{i,j} \equiv \sum_{k=1}^{n} \lambda_{i,k}\lambda_{j,k}$. This calculation uses the fact that $dW_i(t)$ and $dW_j(t)$ are independent if $i \neq j$, so that $dW_i(t)dW_j(t) = 0, i \neq j$.

Example 1. Let $X_i(t)$ be given by equation (16), with $dZ_i(t)$ given by equation (17). Using the multiplication rules, we can compute $dX_i(t)^2$ and $dX_i(t)dX_j(t)$:

$$\begin{aligned} dX_i(t)^2 &= X_i(t)^2\left[(\alpha_i - \delta_i)dt^2 + (\alpha_i - \delta_i)\sigma_i dt dZ_i + \sigma_i^2 dZ_i^2\right] \\ &= X_i(t)^2\sigma_i^2 dt \end{aligned} \tag{18}$$

$$\begin{aligned} dX_i(t)dX_j(t) &= X_i(t)X_j(t)\Big[(\alpha_i - \delta_i)(\alpha_j - \delta_j)dt^2 + (\alpha_i - \delta_i)\sigma_j dt dZ_j \\ &\quad + (\alpha_j - \delta_j)\sigma_i dt dZ_i + \sigma_i\sigma_j dZ_i dZ_j\Big] \\ &= X_i(t)X_j(t)\sigma_i\sigma_j\rho_{i,j} dt \end{aligned} \tag{19}$$

where $\rho_{i,j} = \sum_{k=1}^{n} \lambda_{i,k}\lambda_{j,k} dt$. ■

4. ITÔ'S LEMMA

The price of a call option depends on the stock price. If the stock price follows an Itô process (e.g., geometric Brownian motion), the price of the call option will also follow an Itô process. Itô's Lemma, which we discuss in this section, is a tool for deriving the process followed by a call (or any other derivative with a payoff depending on the stock price) when the underlying stock follows an Itô process.

We will assume that the stock price, S(t), follows the Itô process given by

$$dS(t) = \left\{\hat{\alpha}[S(t), t] - \hat{\delta}[S(t), t]\right\} dt + \hat{\sigma}[S(t), t]\, dZ(t) \tag{20}$$

In this equation, the expected return, α, the dividend yield, δ, and the volatility, σ, can be functions of the stock price and time. When we specify that $S(t)$ follows geometric Brownian motion, then we are assuming specifically that $\hat{\alpha}[S(t), t] = \alpha S(t)$, $\hat{\delta}[S(t), t] = \delta S(t)$, and $\hat{\sigma}[S(t), t] = \sigma S(t)$.

6. The Cauchy inequality states that $\left(\sum_{k=1}^{n} \lambda_{i,k}\lambda_{j,k}\right)^2 \equiv \rho_{i,j}^2 \leq \sum_{k=1}^{n} \lambda_{i,k}^2 \sum_{k=1}^{n} \lambda_{j,k}^2$. Because we assumed that $\sum_{k=1}^{n} \lambda_{i,k}^2 = 1$, we have $-1 \leq \rho_{i,j} \leq 1$.

FIGURE 1

Illustration of Jensen's inequality. The function $V[S(t)]$ is convex. Equally spaced changes in $S(t)$ give rise to unequally spaced changes in $V(S(t))$. In particular, $V[S(t)+\epsilon] - V[S(t)] > V[S(t)-\epsilon]$ because V is an increasing convex function of S.

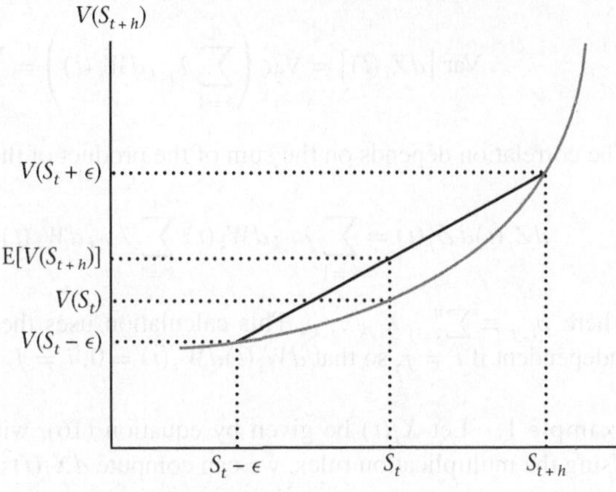

Functions of an Itô Process

Consider an option with price $V(S_t, t)$, where S_t is the time t stock price. To understand how the option will behave, consider a stock price process in which S obeys a geometric random walk with equal probabilities of up and down moves. Figure 1 illustrates this situation. Notice that equal changes up and down in S do not give rise to equal changes in $V(S, t)$. Since V is an increasing convex function of S, a change to $S+\epsilon$ increases V by more than a change to $S-\epsilon$ decreases V. Thus, if the expected change in S is zero, the expected change in V will not be zero. Intuitively, the actual expected change in V will depend on the curvature of V and the probability distribution of S, which tells us the expected size of the up and down moves.

In Figure 1, the second derivative is positive; that is, the slope of V becomes greater as S increases. As is evident in the figure, the expected change in V will then be positive. The figure illustrates Jensen's inequality: $V[E(S)] \leq E[V(S)]$ if V is convex.

Using a Taylor series expansion, we can see how V depends on S. We have

$$\begin{aligned} V(S+dS, t+dt) = {} & V(S,t) + V_S dS + V_t dt \\ & + \frac{1}{2}V_{SS}(dS)^2 + \frac{1}{2}V_{tt}(dt)^2 + V_{St}dSdt \\ & + \text{terms in } (dt)^{3/2} \text{ and higher} \end{aligned}$$

The multiplication rules already discussed in Section 3 tell us that since S is an Itô process, the terms $(dt)^2$ and $dS \times dt$ vanish, along with all higher-order terms. Intuitively, since the interval of time is short, the noise term dominates, and the squared noise term is the same order of magnitude as the drift.[7] This result stems from the property of quadratic variation that we discussed in Section 2. If we integrate the Taylor expansion with respect to time,

7. See Karatzas and Shreve (1998) or Merton (1990) for more details.

then the term containing squared changes will be proportional to time. Higher-order terms will sum to zero. This calculation is the basis for Itô's Lemma.

Proposition 1 (Itô's Lemma) Let the change in the stock price be given by equation (20). If $C[S(t), t]$ is a twice-differentiable function of $S(t)$, then the change in C, $dC[S(t), t]$, is

$$dC(S, t) = C_S dS + \frac{1}{2}C_{SS}(dS)^2 + C_t dt \tag{21}$$

$$= \left\{[\hat{\alpha}(S, t) - \hat{\delta}(S, t)]C_S + \tfrac{1}{2}\hat{\sigma}(S, t)^2 C_{SS} + C_t\right\} dt + \hat{\sigma}(S, t)C_S dZ$$

(We use the notation $C_S = \partial C/\partial S$, $C_{SS} = \partial^2 C/\partial S^2$, and $C_t = \partial C/\partial t$.) The terms in braces are the expected change in the option price.

In the case where $S(t)$ follows geometric Brownian motion, we have $\hat{\alpha}[S(t), t] = \alpha S(t)$, $\hat{\delta}[S(t), t] = \delta S(t)$, and $\hat{\sigma}[S(t), t] = \sigma S(t)$; hence,

$$dC(S, t) = \left[(\alpha - \delta)SC_S + \tfrac{1}{2}\sigma^2 S^2 C_{SS} + C_t\right] dt + \sigma SC_S dZ \quad \blacksquare$$

If there is no uncertainty ($\sigma = 0$) or if $C(S, t)$ is linear ($C_{SS} = 0$), then Itô's Lemma reduces to the calculation of a total derivative familiar from ordinary calculus:

$$dC(S, t) = C_S dS + C_t dt$$

The extra term involving the variance arises from $(dS)^2$ and is the Jensen's inequality correction stemming from the uncertainty of the stochastic process coupled with the curvature of $C(S, t)$.

Consider the following equation:

$$C[S(t+h), t+h] - C[S(t), t] \approx [S(t+h) - S(t)]\Delta[S(t), t] + \tfrac{1}{2}[S(t+h) - S(t)]^2\Gamma[S(t), t] + \theta[S(t), t]h$$

Make the substitutions $h \to dt$ and $S(t+h) - S(t) \to dS$, and Γ, Δ, and θ are just partial derivatives of the option price:

$$\Delta \equiv C_S; \qquad \Gamma \equiv C_{SS}; \qquad \theta = C_t$$

The delta-gamma approximation over a very short period of time is just Itô's Lemma.

We can use Itô's Lemma to verify that the expression for a lognormal stock price satisfies the equation for geometric Brownian motion, equation (20).

Example 2. The expression for a lognormal stock price is

$$S(t) = S(0)e^{(\alpha - \delta - \frac{1}{2}\sigma^2)t + \sigma Z(t)} \tag{22}$$

The stock price is a function of the Brownian process $Z(t)$. We can use Itô's Lemma to characterize the behavior of the stock as a function of $Z(t)$. We have

$$\frac{\partial S(t)}{\partial t} = \left(\alpha - \delta - \frac{1}{2}\sigma^2\right) S(t); \qquad \frac{\partial S(t)}{\partial Z(t)} = \sigma S(t); \qquad \frac{\partial^2 S(t)}{\partial Z(t)^2} = \sigma^2 S(t)$$

Itô's Lemma states that $dS(t)$ is given as

$$\begin{aligned} dS(t) &= \frac{\partial S(t)}{\partial t}\,dt + \frac{\partial S(t)}{\partial Z(t)}\,dZ(t) + \frac{1}{2}\frac{\partial^2 S(t)}{\partial Z(t)^2}[dZ(t)]^2 \\ &= \left(\alpha - \delta - \frac{1}{2}\sigma^2\right) S(t)dt + \sigma S(t)dZ(t) + \frac{1}{2}\sigma^2 S(t)\,dt \\ &= (\alpha - \delta)S(t)\,dt + \sigma S(t)\,dZ(t) \end{aligned}$$

In going from the second line to the third we have used the fact that $dZ(t)^2 = dt$. This calculation demonstrates that by using Itô's Lemma to differentiate equation (22), we recover equation (20). ■

Example 3. Let $Y(t) = \ln[S(t)]$. Then

$$d\ln[S(t)] = \frac{dS(t)}{S(t)} - \frac{1}{2}\frac{dS(t)^2}{S(t)^2} = \frac{dS(t)}{S(t)} - \frac{1}{2}\sigma^2 dt \quad ■ \tag{23}$$

Thus, $d\ln[S(t)]$ follows the same process as $dS(t)/S(t)$, except with a drift term arising from the concavity of the logarithmic function. This is due to Jensen's inequality.

Note that equation (23) implies that continuously compounded returns—measured as $\ln(S(T)/S(0))$—are lower than the instantaneous return, $\alpha - \delta$, by the factor $0.5\sigma^2$.

Multivariate Itô's Lemma

So far we have considered the case where the value of an option depends on a single Itô process. A derivative may have a value depending on more than one price, in which case we can use a multivariate generalization of Itô's Lemma.

Proposition 2 (Multivariate Itô's Lemma) Suppose we have n correlated Itô processes:

$$\frac{dS_i(t)}{S_i(t)} = \alpha_i\,dt + \sigma_i\,dZ_i, \quad i = 1, \ldots, n$$

Denote the pairwise correlations as $\mathrm{E}(dZ_i \times dZ_j) = \rho_{i,j}\,dt$. If $C(S_1, \ldots, S_n, t)$ is a twice-differentiable function of the S_i's, we have

$$dC(S_1, \ldots, S_n, t) = \sum_{i=1}^{n} C_{S_i}\,dS_i + \tfrac{1}{2}\sum_{i=1}^{n}\sum_{j=1}^{n} dS_i dS_j C_{S_i S_j} + C_t\,dt$$

The expected change in C per unit time is

$$\frac{1}{dt}\mathrm{E}\left[dC(S_1, \ldots, S_n, t)\right] = \sum_{i=1}^{n} \alpha_i S_i C_{S_i} + \tfrac{1}{2}\sum_{i=1}^{n}\sum_{j=1}^{n} \sigma_i\sigma_j\rho_{ij}S_i S_j C_{S_i S_j} + C_t \quad ■$$

Example 4. Suppose $C(S_1, S_2) = S_1S_2$. Then by Itô's Lemma we have

$$d(S_1S_2) = S_2dS_1 + S_1dS_2 + dS_1dS_2$$

This implies that

$$\mathrm{E}(dC) = (\alpha_1 + \alpha_2 + \rho\sigma_1\sigma_2)S_1S_2dt$$

Note that since $C(S_1, S_2)$ does not depend explicitly on time, $C_t = 0$. ■

Example 4 is interesting because we know that the product of lognormal variables is lognormal. Hence, we might expect that the drift for the product of two lognormal variables would just be the sum of the drifts. However, the drift has an extra term, due to the covariation between the two variables.

Example 5. Suppose $C(S_1, S_2) = S_1/S_2$. Then by Itô's Lemma we have

$$d\left(\frac{S_1}{S_2}\right) = dS_1\frac{1}{S_2} - dS_2\frac{S_1}{S_2^2} + 0.5\left[2(dS_2)^2\frac{S_1}{S_2^3} - 2dS_1dS_2\frac{1}{S_2^2}\right]$$

This implies that

$$d\left(\frac{S_1}{S_2}\right)\frac{S_2}{S_1} = (\alpha_1 - \alpha_2 + \sigma_2^2 - \rho\sigma_1\sigma_2)dt + \sigma_1 dZ_1 - \sigma_2 dZ_2 \tag{24}$$

From the earlier discussion of correlated Itô processes, we can also write (24) as

$$d\left(\frac{S_1}{S_2}\right)\frac{S_2}{S_1} = (\alpha_1 - \alpha_2 + \sigma_2^2 - \rho\sigma_1\sigma_2)dt + \hat{\sigma}dZ$$

where $\hat{\sigma} = \sigma_1^2 + \sigma_2^2 - 2\rho\sigma_1\sigma_2$ and $dZ = (\sigma_1 dZ_1 - \sigma_2 dZ_2)/\hat{\sigma}$. ■

Even if S_1 and S_2 have equal drifts (i.e., $\alpha_1 = \alpha_2$), the ratio of the two prices will not generally have zero drift because of Jensen's inequality.

5. THE SHARPE RATIO

If asset i has expected return α_i, the risk premium is defined as

$$\text{Risk premium}_i = \alpha_i - r$$

where r is the risk-free rate. The **Sharpe ratio** for asset i is the risk premium, $\alpha_i - r$, per unit of volatility, σ_i:

$$\text{Sharpe ratio}_i = \frac{\alpha_i - r}{\sigma_i} \tag{25}$$

The main point of this section is to present and discuss the result that two assets with prices driven by the same dZ, and hence with returns that are perfectly correlated, will have the same Sharpe ratio.

At the outset, we should note that the Sharpe ratio is commonly used to compare well-diversified portfolios and is not intended to compare individual assets. In particular, if diversifiable risk is different, two assets with the same σ can have different risk premiums (and hence different Sharpe ratios) if they have different covariances with the market. However, we *can* use the Sharpe ratio to compare two perfectly correlated claims, such as a derivative and its underlying asset.

To see that two perfectly correlated assets must have the same Sharpe ratio, consider the processes for two non-dividend-paying stocks:

$$dS_1 = \alpha_1 S_1 dt + \sigma_1 S_1 dZ \tag{26}$$

$$dS_2 = \alpha_2 S_2 dt + \sigma_2 S_2 dZ \tag{27}$$

Because the two stock prices are driven by the same dZ, it must be the case that $(\alpha_1 - r)/\sigma_1 = (\alpha_2 - r)/\sigma_2$, or else there will be an arbitrage opportunity.

The arbitrage is straightforward. Suppose that the Sharpe ratio for asset 1 is greater than that for asset 2. We then buy $1/(\sigma_1 S_1)$ shares of asset 1 and short $1/(\sigma_2 S_2)$ shares of asset 2. These two positions will generally have different costs, so we invest (or borrow) the cost difference, $1/\sigma_1 - 1/\sigma_2$, by buying (or borrowing) the risk-free bond, which has the rate of return rdt. The return on the two assets and the risk-free bond is

$$\frac{1}{\sigma_1 S_1} dS_1 - \frac{1}{\sigma_2 S_2} dS_2 + \left(\frac{1}{\sigma_2} - \frac{1}{\sigma_1}\right) rdt = \left(\frac{\alpha_1 - r}{\sigma_1} - \frac{\alpha_2 - r}{\sigma_2}\right) dt \tag{28}$$

This demonstrates that if the Sharpe ratio of asset 1 is greater than that of asset 2, we can construct a zero-investment portfolio with a positive risk-free return. Therefore, to preclude arbitrage, assets 1 and 2 must have the same Sharpe ratio.[8]

The Sharpe ratio for a stock and an option on the stock are the same. The reason is that the stock and option have the same underlying source of risk—the same dZ. They do not have the same volatility—the volatility of a call option is greater than that of the stock—and, hence, they do not have the same risk premium. However, they do have the same Sharpe ratio.

6. RISK-NEUTRAL VALUATION

In this section we provide some examples of risk-neutral valuation of some simple claims when an asset price, $S(t)$, follows geometric Brownian motion:

$$\frac{dS(t)}{S(t)} = (\alpha - \delta)dt + \sigma d\tilde{Z}(t) \tag{29}$$

Equation (29) describes the evolution of the stock price in the real world: the physical distribution. The corresponding risk-neutral distribution for the stock is

$$\frac{dS(t)}{S(t)} = (r - \delta)dt + \sigma dZ(t) \tag{30}$$

We have previously used the fact that if a claim has the time T payoff $V(S(T), T)$, we can compute its price, $V(S(0), 0)$, by computing the expected payoff under the risk-neutral

8. Problem 12 asks you to show that if $dS_2 = \alpha_2 S_2 dt - \sigma_2 S_2 dZ$, the Sharpe ratios sum to zero.

distribution and discounting that expectation at the risk-free rate:

$$V(S(0), 0) = e^{-rT}\mathrm{E}_0^*\left[V(S(T), T)\right] \tag{31}$$

where E_0^* represents an expectation under the risk-neutral distribution. In this section we will illustrate valuation for some simple claims using equation (31).

A Claim That Pays $S(T)^a$

Consider a claim that pays $V(S(T), T) = S(T)^a$. Because S follows geometric Brownian motion, the terminal price, $S(T)$, is lognormally distributed. The expected payoff to the claim is

$$S(T)^a = S(0)^a e^{a(r-\delta-0.5\sigma^2)T + a\sigma Z(T)}$$

Computing the expectation of a lognormal variable, and discounting at the risk-free rate, we have

$$\begin{aligned} e^{-rT}\mathrm{E}[S(T)^a] &= e^{-rT}S(0)^a e^{a(r-\delta-0.5\sigma^2)T + 0.5a^2\sigma^2 T} \\ &= e^{-rT}S(0)^a e^{[a(r-\delta)+0.5a(a-1)\sigma^2]T} \end{aligned}$$

This is the present value—or alternatively, the prepaid forward price—for a claim that pays $S(T)^a$. The forward price is the expectation without discounting.[9]

Proposition 3 Suppose that $S(t)$ follows the process given by equation (30) and that the risk-free rate is constant. The value at time 0 of a claim paying $S(T)^a$—the prepaid forward price—is

$$F_{0,T}^P[S(T)^a] = e^{-rT}S(0)^a e^{\left[a(r-\delta)+\frac{1}{2}a(a-1)\sigma^2\right]T} \tag{32}$$

The forward price for $S(T)^a$ is

$$F_{0,T}[S(T)^a] = S(0)^a e^{\left[a(r-\delta)+\frac{1}{2}a(a-1)\sigma^2\right]T} \tag{33}$$

An alternative way to compute $\mathrm{E}[S(T)^a]$ is to use Itô's Lemma to derive the process followed by $S(t)^a$. We have

$$\begin{aligned} dS^a &= aS^{a-1}dS + 0.5a(a-1)S^{a-2}dS^2 \\ &= aS^a\frac{dS}{S} + 0.5a(a-1)S^a\sigma^2 dt \end{aligned}$$

Using equation (30), this implies that

$$\frac{dS(t)^a}{S^a} = [a(r-\delta) + 0.5a(a-1)\sigma^2]\,dt + a\sigma\, dZ \tag{34}$$

The solution to equation (34) is

$$S(T)^a = S(0)^a e^{a(r-\delta+0.5a(a-1)\sigma^2)T - 0.5a^2\sigma^2 T + a\sigma Z(T)}$$

---

9. Appendix A shows how this claim can be valued using discounted cash flow.

You can see this by analogy with the solution for dS/S, in which the deterministic term in the exponent is the drift minus one-half the variance. Computing $E_0^*[S(0)^a]$ using this equation yields equation (33).

Finally, it is important to note that, whereas the present value of a non-dividend-paying stock is today's stock price, the present value of a claim paying $S(T)^a$ is *not* $S(0)^a$. The reason is Jensen's inequality. When $a > 1$, the payoff is convex and investors will pay extra in order to obtain the boost to returns afforded by that convexity (gains on the stock benefit from an increase in the delta of the claim, while losses are damped by a decrease in delta). When $a < 1$, the payoff is concave and investors value the claim at less than $S(0)^a$ because positive returns are damped (gains on the stock are reduced on the claim due to the reduction in delta, while losses are enhanced by the increase in delta). You can see these effects in equation (32), where the price of the claim depends upon $a - 1$. One simple way to summarize this is that $S(0)$ and $S(0)^a$ cannot simultaneously be the fair prices for claims paying $S(T)$ and $S(T)^a$. If the stock is a traded asset, then the price of a claim paying S^a requires a Jensen's inequality adjustment.

Specific Examples

We now examine four special cases of equations (32) and (33): $a = -1, 0, 1$, and 2.

Claims on S. First, suppose $a = 1$. Equation (32) then gives us

$$V(0) = S(0)e^{-\delta T}$$

This is the prepaid forward price on a stock.

Claims on S^0. If $a = 0$, the claim does not depend on the stock price; rather, since $S^0 = 1$, it is a bond. Setting $a = 0$ gives us

$$V(0) = e^{-rT}$$

This is the price of a T-period pure discount bond.

Claims on S^2. When $a = 2$, the claim pays $S(T)^2$. From equation (33), the forward price is

$$\begin{aligned} F_{0,T}(S^2) &= e^{rT}\, S(0)^2 e^{-[-r+2\delta-\sigma^2]T} \\ &= S(0)^2 e^{2(r-\delta)T} e^{\sigma^2 T} \\ &= \left[F_{0,T}(S)\right]^2 e^{\sigma^2 T} \end{aligned} \qquad (35)$$

Thus, the forward price on the squared stock price is the squared forward price times a variance term. The squared forward price is intuitive, but the variance term requires some discussion.

One way to think about equation (35) is to perform the following thought experiment. Suppose that we have an ordinary stock with a price denominated in dollars. Now imagine that we have a second stock that is identical to the first *except* that instead of receiving dollars when we sell the stock, we receive one share of ordinary stock for each dollar in the quoted price of the second stock. This conversion from dollars to shares is what it means to have a squared security.

With the squared stock, when the stock price goes up, we not only receive the extra dollars a share of stock is worth, but we also receive the appreciated value of each share that we receive in lieu of dollars. We therefore receive an extra gain when the stock price goes up.

The effect works in reverse when the price goes down. In that case, we receive fewer dollars per share, and each share received in lieu of dollars is worth less as well. However, the lower price per share hurts us less because we receive fewer shares! Thus, on average, the extra we receive when the price goes up exceeds the loss when the price goes down. This effect becomes more important as the variance is greater, since large losses and large gains become more likely.

The result is that we will pay extra for the security, and the extra amount is positively related to the variance.

Claims on 1/S. Finally, let $a = -1$, so the claim pays $1/S$. Using equation (33) with $a = -1$, we get

$$F_{0,T}(1/S) = \left[1/S(0)\right] e^{(\delta - r)T} e^{\sigma^2 T}$$

$$= F_{0,T}^{-1} e^{\sigma^2 T}$$

As with the squared security, the forward price is increasing in volatility.

The payoffs for both the S^2 and $1/S$ securities are convex; hence, Jensen's inequality tells us that the price is higher when the asset price is risky than when it is certain. In both cases the forward price contains a volatility term, and in both cases the price is increasing in volatility. If we considered a concave claim—for example, $\sqrt{S}$—the effect of increased volatility would be to lower the value of the claim. Problems 5–8 provide examples.

Valuing a Claim on $S^a Q^b$

We now consider a claim based on the product of two asset prices. Consider a claim paying $S(T)^a Q(T)^b$ where S and Q follow the risk-neutral processes

$$\frac{dS}{S} = (r - \delta_S)dt + \sigma_S dZ_S \tag{36}$$

and Q follows

$$\frac{dQ}{Q} = (r - \delta_Q)dt + \sigma_Q dZ_Q \tag{37}$$

where

$$dZ_S dZ_Q = \rho dt$$

Proposition 4 Suppose that S and Q follow the processes given by equations (36) and (37). The forward prices for S^a and Q^b are given by Proposition 3. The forward price for $S^a Q^b$ is the product of those two forward prices times a covariance correction factor:

$$F_{t,T}(S^a Q^b) = F_{t,T}(S^a) F_{t,T}(Q^b) e^{ab\rho\sigma_S\sigma_Q(T-t)}$$

The variance of $S^a Q^b$ is given by

$$a^2\sigma_S^2 + b^2\sigma_Q^2 + 2ab\rho\sigma_S\sigma_Q \quad \blacksquare$$

The squared security, S^2, is a special case of Proposition 4. When $S = Q, a = b = 1$, and $\rho = 1$ (since a variable is perfectly correlated with itself), the covariance term becomes

$$ab\rho\sigma_S\sigma_Q = \sigma_S^2$$

This gives us the same result as equation (35) for the forward price for a squared stock.

We obtain the price for the claim by computing $e^{-r(T-t)}\mathrm{E}_t^*\left[S(T)^a Q(T)^b\right]$. We can compute the expectation by using the fact that $S(T)^a$ and $Q(T)^b$ are both lognormal. We have

$$\begin{aligned} S(T)^a Q(T)^b &= S(0)^a e^{a(r-\delta_S-0.5\sigma_S^2)T + a\sigma_S Z_S(T)} Q(0)^b e^{b(r-\delta_Q-0.5\sigma_Q^2)T + b\sigma_Q Z_Q(T)} \\ &= S(0)^a Q(0)^b e^{a(r-\delta_S-0.5\sigma_S^2)T + b(r-\delta_Q-0.5\sigma_Q^2)T} e^{a\sigma_S Z_S(T) + b\sigma_Q Z_Q(T)} \end{aligned}$$

Note that the expectation of the second exponential term is

$$e^{0.5\left[a^2\sigma_S^2 + b^2\sigma_Q^2 + 2ab\sigma_S\sigma_Q\rho\right]T}$$

The expected time-T value of $S^a Q^b$ under the risk-neutral measure is therefore

$$\mathrm{E}_0^B[S(T)^a Q(T)^b] = S(0)^a Q(0)^b e^{[a(r-\delta_S)+b(r-\delta_Q)+\frac{1}{2}a(a-1)\sigma_S^2+\frac{1}{2}b(b-1)\sigma_Q^2+ab\rho\sigma_S\sigma_Q]T}$$

Using Proposition 3—in particular, equation (33)—this expression can be rewritten as

$$F_{0,T}(S^a Q^b) = F_{0,T}(S^a)F_{0,T}(Q^b)e^{ab\rho\sigma_S\sigma_Q T} \tag{38}$$

The expression on the right is the product of the forward prices times a factor that accounts for the covariance between the two assets.

This is an important result: The price that results when we multiply two prices together requires a correction for the covariance.

Proposition 4 can be generalized. Suppose there are n stocks, each of which follows the process

$$\frac{dS_i}{S_i} = (\alpha_i - \delta_i)dt + \sigma_i dz_i \tag{39}$$

where $dz_i dz_j = \rho_{ij}dt$. Let

$$V(t) = \prod_{i=1}^{n} S_i^{a_i} \tag{40}$$

The forward price for V is then

$$F_{0,T}(V) = \prod_{i=1}^{n}[F_{0,T}(S_i)]^{a_i} e^{\sum_{i=1}^{n-1}\sum_{j=i+1}^{n}\rho_{ij}\sigma_i\sigma_j a_i a_j T} \tag{41}$$

7. JUMPS IN THE STOCK PRICE

A practical objection to the Brownian process as a model of the stock price is that Brownian paths are continuous—there are no discrete jumps in the stock price. In practice, asset prices occasionally do seem to jump; a famous example is October 19, 1987, when the Dow Jones index fell 22% in a single day. A move of this size is exceedingly unlikely in the lognormal model. On a smaller scale, consider the stock price of a company that reports unexpectedly favorable earnings. To account for such nonlognormal behavior, Merton (1976) proposed modeling the stock price as lognormal with an occasional discrete jump.

We can use the Poisson to count the number of jumps that occur in any interval. Conditional on a jump occurring, we assign some distribution to the change in the stock price. The lognormal is a convenient choice for computing the price change if the jump occurs.

We can write a stock price process with jumps as follows. With the Poisson process, the probability of a jump event is proportional to the length of time. Furthermore, for an infinitesimal interval dt, the probability of more than a single jump is zero (this is part of the definition of the Poisson process). Let $q(t)$ represent the cumulative jump and dq the change in the cumulative jump. Most of the time, there is no jump and $dq = 0$. When there is a jump, the random variable Y denotes the magnitude of the jump, and $k = E(Y) - 1$ is then the expected percentage change in the stock price. If λ is the expected number of jumps per unit time over an interval dt, then

$$\Pr(\text{jump}) = \lambda dt$$

$$\Pr(\text{no jump}) = 1 - \lambda dt$$

We can then write the stock price process as

$$dS(t)/S(t) = (\alpha - \lambda k)dt + \sigma dZ + dq \tag{42}$$

where

$$dq = \begin{cases} 0 & \text{if there is no jump} \\ Y - 1 & \text{if there is a jump} \end{cases}$$

and $\mathrm{E}(dq) = \lambda k dt$. The drift term contains $-\lambda k dt$ for the following reason: The dq term has a nonzero expectation, so we subtract $\lambda k dt$ in order to preserve the interpretation of α as the expected return on the stock. We have

$$\mathrm{E}(dS/S) = (\alpha - \lambda k)dt + \mathrm{E}(\sigma dZ) + \mathrm{E}(dq) = \alpha dt$$

Thus, for example, if there is on average a downward jump, then $k < 0$, and, when no jump is occurring, we need extra drift of $-\lambda k dt > 0$ to compensate for the occasional bad times due to the jump.

The upshot of this model is that when no jump is occurring, the stock price S evolves as geometric Brownian motion. When the jump occurs, the new stock price is YS.

Proposition 5 Suppose an asset follows equation (42). If $C(S, t)$ is a twice continuously differentiable function of the stock price, the process followed by C is

$$dC(S, t) = C_S dS + \tfrac{1}{2} C_{SS}\sigma^2 S^2 dt + C_t dt + \lambda E_Y[C(SY, t) - C(S, t)] \tag{43}$$

The last term in equation (43) is the expected change in the option price conditional on the jump times the probability of the jump.

The last term in equation (43) accounts for the jump. That term is not present in the version of Itô's Lemma for a stock that cannot jump, equation (21).

CHAPTER SUMMARY

A stochastic process $Z(t)$ is a Brownian motion if it is normally distributed, changes independently over time, has variance proportional to time, and is continuous. The change in Brownian motion is denoted $dZ(t)$. The process $Z(t)$ and its change $dZ(t)$ provide the foundation for modern derivatives pricing models. The Brownian process $Z(t)$ by itself would be a poor model of an asset price, but its change, $dZ(t)$, provides a model for asset risk. By multiplying $dZ(t)$ by a scale factor and adding a drift term, we can control the variance and mean, and thereby construct more realistic processes. Such processes are called Itô processes or diffusion processes. Black and Scholes used just such a process in their original derivation of the option pricing model.

Given that a stock follows a particular Itô process, Itô's Lemma permits us to compute the process followed by an option or other claim on the stock. The pricing of claims with payoffs S^a and $S^a Q^b$, where S and Q follow geometric Brownian motion, illustrates the use of Itô's Lemma.

An important objection to Brownian motion as a driving process for a stock is the continuity of its path. It is possible to add jumps to a Brownian process, and there is a version of Itô's Lemma for such cases.

FURTHER READING

Many books cover the material in this chapter at a more advanced level. Merton (1990) in particular is an outstanding introduction. Other good sources include Neftci (2000), Duffie (2001), Wilmott (1998), Karatzas and Shreve (1991), and Baxter and Rennie (1996).

PROBLEMS

For the following four problems, use Itô's Lemma to determine the process followed by the specified equation, assuming that $S(t)$ follows (a) arithmetic Brownian motion, equation (8); (b) a mean reverting process, equation (9); and (c) geometric Brownian motion, equation (11).

1. Use Itô's Lemma to evaluate $d[\ln(S)]$.

2. Use Itô's Lemma to evaluate dS^2.

3. Use Itô's Lemma to evaluate dS^{-1}.

4. Use Itô's Lemma to evaluate $d(\sqrt{S})$.

5. Suppose that S follows equation (36) and Q follows equation (37). Use Itô's Lemma to find the process followed by $S^2 Q^{0.5}$.

6. Suppose that S follows equation (36) and Q follows equation (37). Use Itô's Lemma to find the process followed by $\ln(SQ)$.

7. Suppose $S(0) = \$100$, $r = 0.06$, $\sigma_S = 0.4$, and $\delta = 0$. Use equation (32) to compute prices for claims that pay the following:

a. S^2

b. $\sqrt{S}$

c. S^{-2}

Compare your answers to the answers you obtained to Problem 6.

8. Suppose that $\ln(S)$ and $\ln(Q)$ have correlation $\rho = -0.3$ and that $S(0) = \$100$, $Q(0) = \$100$, $r = 0.06$, $\sigma_S = 0.4$, and $\sigma_Q = 0.2$. Neither stock pays dividends. Use equation (38) to find the price today of claims that pay

a. SQ

b. S/Q

c. $\sqrt{SQ}$

d. $1/(SQ)$

e. S^2Q

Compare your answers to the answers you obtained to Problem 7.

9. Suppose that $X(t)$ follows equation (9). Use Itô's Lemma to verify that a solution to this differential equation is

$$X_t = X(0)e^{-\lambda t} + \alpha\left(1 - e^{-\lambda t}\right) + \sigma \int_0^t e^{\lambda(s-t)} dZ_s$$

(*Hint:* Note that when t increases by a small amount, the integral term changes by $dZ(t)$.)

10. Suppose that S follows equation (20), with α replaced by r, and that $\mathrm{E}^*(dV) = rV dt$. Use Itô's Lemma to verify that the value of the call, $V(S)$, satisfies this equation:

$$\frac{1}{2}\sigma^2 S^2 V_{SS} + (r - \delta)SV_S - rV = 0$$

11. Suppose that the processes for S_1 and S_2 are given by these two equations:

$$dS_1 = \alpha_1 S_1 dt + \sigma_1 S_1 dZ_1$$
$$dS_2 = \alpha_2 S_2 dt + \sigma_2 S_2 dZ_2$$

Note that the diffusions dZ_1 and dZ_2 are different. In this problem we want to find the expected return on Q, α_Q, where Q follows the process

$$dQ = \alpha_Q Q dt + Q\left(\eta_1 dZ_1 + \eta_2 dZ_2\right)$$

Show that, to avoid arbitrage,

$$\alpha_Q - r = \frac{\eta_1}{\sigma_1}(\alpha_1 - r) + \frac{\eta_2}{\sigma_2}(\alpha_2 - r)$$

(*Hint:* Consider the strategy of buying one unit of Q and shorting $Q\eta_1/S_1\sigma_1$ units of S_1 and $Q\eta_2/S_2\sigma_2$ units of S_2. Finance any net cost using risk-free bonds.)

12. Suppose that S_1 follows equation (26) with $\delta = 0$. Consider an asset that follows the process

$$dS_2 = \alpha_2 S_2\, dt - \sigma_2 S_2\, dZ$$

Show that $(\alpha_1 - r)/\sigma_1 = -(\alpha_2 - r)/\sigma_2$. (*Hint*: Find a zero-investment position in S_1 and S_2 that eliminates risk.)

13. Suppose that S and Q follow equations (36) and (37). Derive the value of a claim paying $S(T)^a Q(T)^b$ by each of the following methods:

a. Compute the expected value of the claim and discounting at an appropriate rate. (*Hint:* The expected return on the claim can be derived using the result of Problem 11.)

b. Compute the lease rate and substituting this into the formula for the forward price.

14. Assume that one stock follows the process

$$dS/S = \alpha dt + \sigma dZ \tag{44}$$

Another stock follows the process

$$dQ/Q = \alpha_Q dt + \sigma dZ + dq_1 + dq_2 \tag{45}$$

(Note that the σdZ terms for S and Q are identical.) Neither stock pays dividends. dq_1 and dq_2 are both Poisson jump processes with Poisson parameters λ_1 and λ_2. Conditional on either jump occurring, the percentage change in the stock price is $Y_1 - 1$ or $Y_2 - 1$. Consider the two stock price processes, equations (44) and (45).

a. If there were no jump terms (i.e., $\lambda_1 = \lambda_2 = 0$), what would be the relation between α and α_Q?

b. Suppose there is just one jump term ($\lambda_2 = 0$) and that $Y_1 > 1$. In words, what does it mean to have $Y_1 > 1$? What can you say about the relation between α and α_Q?

c. Write an expression for α_Q when both jump terms are nonzero. Explain intuitively why α_Q might be greater or less than α.

Appendix A VALUATION USING DISCOUNTED CASH FLOW

Appendix available at http://www.pearsonhighered.com/mcdonald.

The Black-Scholes-Merton Equation

In deriving the option pricing formula, Black and Scholes studied the problem faced by a delta-hedging market-maker. The market-maker who sells a call option buys shares to offset the risk of the written call. To analyze this situation it is necessary to characterize the risk of the position as a function of the share price. Itô's Lemma provides a tool that permits us to see how the option price changes in response to the stock price.

Black and Scholes assumed that the stock follows geometric Brownian motion and used Itô's Lemma to describe the behavior of the option price. Their analysis yields a partial differential equation, which the correct option pricing formula must satisfy.

In this chapter we study the Black-Scholes approach to pricing options.[1] This methodology is important not only for pricing European call options; it provides the intellectual foundation for pricing virtually all derivatives, and also underpins the risk-management practices of modern financial institutions.

1. DIFFERENTIAL EQUATIONS AND VALUATION UNDER CERTAINTY

The end result of the Black-Scholes derivation is a partial differential equation that describes the price of an option. At first glance the idea of using a differential equation to perform valuation may seem perplexing and special to options. However, differential equations can also be used to motivate even very simple calculations that appear in an elementary finance course. The valuation of stocks and bonds when payouts are known provides simple examples. We will demonstrate this in order to provide some context for the discussion of the Black-Scholes model.

1. Robert Merton also contributed fundamentally to understanding the option pricing problem, In practice, the equation and approach may be named either "Black-Scholes" or, increasingly, "Black-Scholes-Merton." The chapter title is the latter, but for brevity we will predominantly use the former in the text.

From Chapter 21 of *Derivatives Markets*, Third Edition, Robert McDonald. Copyright © 2013 by Pearson Education, Inc. Published by Pearson Prentice Hall. All rights reserved.

The Valuation Equation

A familiar equation from introductory finance is the following:

$$S(t) = \frac{D(t+h)h + S(t+h)}{(1+r_h)} \tag{1}$$

This equation says that the stock price today, $S(t)$, is the discounted value of the future stock price, $S(t+h)$, plus dividends paid over the period of length h, $D(t+h)h$. The discount rate over a period of length h is r_h. We can also interpret $S(t)$ as the price of a bond and $D(t)$ as the coupon payment.

Whatever the interpretation, we can write

$$\underbrace{S(t+h) - S(t)}_{\text{Change in stock price}} + \underbrace{D(t+h)h}_{\text{Cash payout}} = \underbrace{r_h S(t)}_{\text{Return on stock}} \tag{2}$$

Written in this form, the equation says that the change in the stock price plus cash payouts (such as dividends) equals the return on the stock. Equation (2) is written to emphasize how the stock price should *evolve* over time, rather than the value of the stock at a point in time.

Dividing by h and letting $h \to 0$ in equation (2), we obtain

$$\frac{dS(t)}{dt} + D(t) = rS(t) \tag{3}$$

Equation (3) is a differential equation stating the condition that the stock must appreciate to earn an appropriate rate of return. The transformation from equation (1) to equation (3) illustrates the sense in which an equation describing the evolution of the price is linked to valuation.

Bonds

Let $S(t)$ represent the price of a zero-coupon bond that pays \$1 at time T. Since the bond makes no payouts, the evolution of the bond price satisfies equation (3) with $D = 0$. The interpretation is that at every time, t, the percentage change in the price of the bond $[\frac{dS(t)}{dt}/S(t)]$ equals the interest rate. This is a familiar condition that the bond should satisfy if it is fairly priced. The general solution to this equation is[2]

$$S(t) = Ae^{-r(T-t)} \tag{4}$$

where A can be any number. You can check that this is in fact a solution by differentiating it to be sure that it satisfies the differential equation.

The differential equation describes the bond's behavior over time but does not tell us what A is. In order to price the bond we also need to know the bond price at some particular point in time. This price is called a **boundary condition**. If the bond is worth \$1 at maturity, we have the boundary condition $S(T) = \$1$. Examining equation (4) shows that $S(T)$ can equal \$1 only if $A = \$1$. Thus, the bond price is

$$S(t) = \$1 \times e^{-r(T-t)}$$

2. You might wish to verify that $S(t) = Ae^{-r(T-t)} + a$ satisfies the differential equation only if $a = 0$.

The condition $S(T) = \$1$ is called a terminal boundary condition because it sets the bond price at its maturity date. If instead we knew the bond price today, $S(0)$, we could set A so that the equation gave the correct value for $S(0)$. That value would be an initial boundary condition.

The solution confirms what you already know: The price of the bond is the present value of \$1.

Dividend-Paying Stocks

We can interpret $S(t)$ as the price of a risk-free stock that pays a continuous fixed dividend of D and has a price of $\bar{S}$ at time T. Equation (3) then says that at every time, t, dividends plus capital gains on the stock provide the risk-free rate of return.

Since we know the value at time T will be $\bar{S}$, we also have the boundary condition

$$S(T) = \bar{S}$$

Equation (3) with this boundary condition has the solution

$$S(t) = \int_t^T De^{-r(s-t)}ds + \bar{S}e^{-r(T-t)}$$

The stock price today is the discounted value of dividends to be paid between now and time T, plus the present value of the stock at time T. Again, the discrete time version of this equation is the standard present value formula taught in every introductory finance class.

The General Structure

Under certainty, a bond or stock will be priced so that the owner receives a risk-free return. The differential equation in these examples describes how the security *changes* from a given point. The boundary condition describes the price at some point in the security's life (such as at a bond's maturity date). By combining the differential equation and the boundary condition, we can determine the price of the bond at any point in time.

By analogy, if at every point you know an automobile's speed and direction, and if you know where it stops, you can work backward to figure out where it started. Essentially the same idea is used to price options: We know the price of the option at maturity (for a call it is $\max[0, S - K]$), and we then need to know how the option price changes over time.

2. THE BLACK-SCHOLES EQUATION

Consider the problem of owning an option and buying or selling enough shares to create a riskless position. Assume that the stock price follows geometric Brownian motion:

$$\frac{dS}{S} = (\alpha - \delta)dt + \sigma dZ \tag{5}$$

where α is the expected return on the stock, σ is the stock's volatility, and δ is the continuous dividend yield on the stock. The option value depends on the stock price, $S(t)$, and time, t, so we write it as $V[S(t), t]$. Also suppose there are risk-free bonds that pay the return r. If we invest W in these bonds, the change in the value of the bond position is

$$dW = rWdt \tag{6}$$

Let I denote the total investment in the option, stocks, and the risk-free bond. Suppose that we buy N shares of stock to hedge the option and invest W in risk-free bonds so that our total investment is zero. Then we have

$$I = V(S, t) + NS + W = 0 \tag{7}$$

The zero-investment condition ensures that we keep track of financing costs. It imposes the requirement that in order to buy more of one asset we have to sell something else. To buy stock, for example, we can short-sell bonds.

Applying Itô's Lemma to equation (7), we have

$$\begin{aligned} dI &= dV + N(dS + \delta S dt) + dW \\ &= V_t dt + V_S dS + \tfrac{1}{2}\sigma^2 S^2 V_{SS} dt + N(dS + \delta S dt) + rW dt \end{aligned} \tag{8}$$

If we own the physical stock, we receive dividends; this accounts for the $N\delta S dt$ term.[3]

We delta-hedge the position to eliminate risk. The option's delta (Δ) is V_S. We delta-hedge by setting

$$N = -V_S$$

Holding this number of shares has two results. First, the dS and, hence, dZ terms in equation (8) vanish, so the portfolio is no longer affected by changes in the stock price—the portfolio is risk-free. Second, because we are also maintaining zero investment (equation (7)) our holding of bonds is whatever is necessary to finance the net purchase or sale of the option and the hedging position in stock:

$$W = V_S S - V \tag{9}$$

Substituting $N = -V_S$ and this expression for W into equation (8) gives

$$dI = V_t dt + \tfrac{1}{2}\sigma^2 S^2 V_{SS} dt - V_S \delta S dt + r(V_S S - V)dt \tag{10}$$

With a zero-investment, zero-risk portfolio, we should expect to earn a zero return or else there is arbitrage, so that $dI = 0$. Imposing this condition in equation (10) and dividing by dt gives

$$\boxed{V_t + \tfrac{1}{2}\sigma^2 S^2 V_{SS} + (r - \delta)S V_S - rV = 0} \tag{11}$$

This is the famous Black-Scholes partial differential equation (PDE), which we will call the Black-Scholes *equation*.[4] (We will refer to the formula giving us the price of a European call as the Black-Scholes *formula*.) Appendix A derives the generalization of equation (11) when the value of V depends on more than one underlying asset.

The significance of equation (11) is that the price of an option must satisfy this equation, or else there is an arbitrage opportunity. The delta, gamma, and theta of a fairly priced option has to be related in a certain way. Since V_{SS} is the option's gamma, V_S the

---

3. Similarly, if we short the stock, we have to pay the dividends.

4. When the derivative claim makes a payout, $D(t)dt$, then equation (11) becomes

$$V_t + \tfrac{1}{2}\sigma^2 S^2 V_{SS} + (r - \delta)S V_S + D(t) - rV = 0$$

option's delta, and V_t the option's theta, equation (11) describes the same relationship among the Greeks.

We started this discussion by supposing that we owned an option that we wished to delta-hedge. Nothing in the derivation uses the fact that V is the price of a call option or indeed any particular kind of option at all. Thus, equation (11) *describes the change in value of any contingent claim for which the underlying assumptions are met*.[5] To be sure, we have assumed a great deal: That (a) the underlying asset follows geometric Brownian motion with constant volatility, (b) the underlying asset pays a continuous proportional dividend at the rate δ (this can be zero), (c) the contingent claim itself pays no dividend and has a payoff depending on S, (d) the interest rate is fixed, with equal borrowing and lending rates, and (e) there are no transaction costs.

These assumptions are unquestionably violated in practice. There are transaction costs, volatility and interest rates change over time, asset prices can jump, etc. However, our goal is to have a thorough understanding of how derivatives pricing and hedging works in this basic setting. This is a starting point for developing more realistic models.

Verifying the Formula for a Derivative

We can now answer the main question of option pricing: Given that asset prices follow geometric Brownian motion (equation (5)), what is the correct formula for the price of an option? As discussed in Section 1, there are two conditions. The pricing formula must satisfy the Black-Scholes equation, (11), and it must also satisfy the appropriate boundary conditions for the option. If we satisfy both conditions, we have the correct option price.

Several nonstandard option formulas solve the Black-Scholes equation.[6] The pricing formulas seem different, but they differ only in the boundary conditions. Here, we discuss several particular solutions in order to convey the basic idea of how the Black-Scholes equation works.

Simple Present Value Calculations. Let's begin by considering two familiar calculations: the price of a zero-coupon bond and the prepaid forward contract for a stock.

Suppose the bond matures at time T and pays \$1. The boundary condition is that it must be worth \$1 at time T. In addition it must satisfy the Black-Scholes equation, equation (11). Consider this formula for the price of the bond:

$$V^1(t, T) = e^{-r(T-t)} \tag{12}$$

First, this satisfies the boundary condition since $V^1(T, T) = \$1$. Second, the price of the bond does not depend on the price of a stock. Thus, $V_S = 0$ and $V_{SS} = 0$. Equation (11) then becomes

$$V_t^1 = rV^1$$

Equation (12) satisfies this equation, with the boundary condition $V^1(T, T) = \$1$.

5. Equation (11) holds for unexercised American options as well as for European options.

6. The exception is Asian options. Since the Asian option payoff is based on the average stock price, prices of those options solve a different partial differential equation in which there is a term reflecting the evolution of the average.

Now consider the prepaid forward contract for a share of stock. We know the value is

$$V^2[S(t), t] = S(t)e^{-\delta(T-t)} \tag{13}$$

Since this contract pays a share at maturity, the boundary condition is that it is worth a share at maturity:

$$V^2[S(T), T] = S(T)$$

We will verify that equation (13) solves the Black-Scholes equation. We have

$$V_S^2 = e^{-\delta(T-t)}$$
$$V_{SS}^2 = 0$$
$$V_t^2 = \delta S(t)e^{-\delta(T-t)}$$

Substituting these into the Black-Scholes equation gives

$$\tfrac{1}{2}\sigma^2 S(t)^2 \times 0 + (r - \delta)S(t) \times e^{-\delta(T-t)} + \delta S(t)e^{-\delta(T-t)} - rS(t)e^{-\delta(T-t)} = 0$$

Equation (13) thus satisfies the Black-Scholes equation and the boundary condition.

Notice that for both claims, $V_{SS} = 0$; their gamma is zero. We can replicate a prepaid forward by buying a tailed position in the stock. No further trading is necessary. This static hedging strategy works because gamma is zero.

Call Option. A European call option has the boundary condition

$$V[S(T), T] = \max[0, S(T) - K] \tag{14}$$

Let's verify that the Black-Scholes formula does satisfy the boundary condition. We can examine the behavior of the formula as t approaches T, the option expiration date. The value of the call is

$$Se^{-\delta(T-t)}N(d_1) - Ke^{-r(T-t)}N(d_2)$$

For an option at expiration, since $t = T$, the terms $e^{-\delta(T-t)}$ and $e^{-r(T-t)}$ are both equal to 1. What happens to $N(d_1)$ and $N(d_2)$?

We will rewrite slightly the definitions of d_1 and d_2:

$$d_1 = \frac{\ln(S/K)}{\sigma\sqrt{T-t}} + \left(r - \delta + \tfrac{1}{2}\sigma^2\right)\frac{\sqrt{T-t}}{\sigma}$$

$$d_2 = d_1 - \sigma\sqrt{T-t}$$

As t approaches T, the difference between d_1 and d_2 goes to zero, since the term $-\sigma\sqrt{T-t}$ goes to zero. Moreover, the term $(r - \delta + \frac{1}{2}\sigma^2)\sqrt{T-t}$ also goes to zero. Thus, both d_1 and d_2 are governed by the term $\ln(S/K)/\sigma\sqrt{T-t}$.

If $S > K$, then the option is in-the-money and $\ln(S/K) > 0$. If $S < K$, the option is out-of-the-money and $\ln(S/K) < 0$. Thus, as $t \to T$, we have

$$S > K \Rightarrow \ln(S/K) > 0 \Rightarrow \frac{\ln(S/K)}{\sigma\sqrt{T-t}} \rightarrow +\infty \Rightarrow N(d_1) = N(d_2) = 1$$

$$S < K \Rightarrow \ln(S/K) < 0 \Rightarrow \frac{\ln(S/K)}{\sigma\sqrt{T-t}} \rightarrow -\infty \Rightarrow N(d_1) = N(d_2) = 0$$

Thus, at expiration the Black-Scholes formula for a call equals $S - K$ if $S > K$, and 0 if $S < K$, so it satisfies the boundary condition, equation (14). The call formula also satisfies equation (11), but we will not verify that here.

Puts can be analyzed just like calls. European puts have the boundary condition

$$V[S(T), T] = \max[0, K - S(T)]$$

The put formula contains $N(-d_1)$ and $N(-d_2)$; as a result, the $N()$ expressions at maturity equal 1 when $S < K$, and 0 when $S > K$.

All-Or-Nothing Options. Both terms in the Black-Scholes formula *individually* satisfy the Black-Scholes equation. Consequently, each of the two expressions

$$V^3[S(t), t] = e^{-\delta(T-t)} S \times N\left(\frac{\ln[S(t)/K] + [r - \delta + 0.5\sigma^2][T-t]}{\sigma\sqrt{T-t}}\right) \tag{15}$$

$$V^4[S(t), t] = e^{-r(T-t)} \times N\left(\frac{\ln[S(t)/K] + [r - \delta - 0.5\sigma^2][T-t]}{\sigma\sqrt{T-t}}\right) \tag{16}$$

on its own is a legitimate price of a derivative. What are they the prices of?

An **asset-or-nothing option** pays one share of stock if $S(T) > K$, and nothing otherwise.[7] Examine V^3 closely. We have $V^3[S(T), T] = 0$ if $S(T) < K$, and $V^3[S(T), T] = S(T)$ if $S(T) > K$. Thus, at time T, V^3 has the same value as an asset-or-nothing option. Moreover, because V^3 satisfies the Black-Scholes equation, it gives the correct value at time t for this payoff. Thus, V^3 is the value of an asset-or-nothing option.

A **cash-or-nothing** option pays \$1 at time T if $S(T) > K$, and nothing otherwise.[8] Equation (16) has the same value at maturity as a cash-or-nothing option and satisfies the Black-Scholes equation. Thus, equation (16) gives us the time-t value of a cash-or-nothing option. Both asset-or-nothing and cash-or-nothing options are examples of all-or-nothing options, which pay a discrete amount or nothing.

A European call option is equivalent to buying one asset-or-nothing option and selling K cash-or-nothing options, both maturing at time T. The price of a European call is the cost of this strategy:

$$V^3[S(t), t] - K \times V^4[S(t), t]$$

You should verify that this is in fact the Black-Scholes formula. (See Problem 7.)

The fact that V^3 and V^4 solve the Black-Scholes equation gives us pricing formulas for two new derivatives, asset-or-nothing and cash-or-nothing options. Also, however, because V^4 by itself solves the Black-Scholes equation, we could have sold any number of cash-or-nothing options and still had a valid price for a derivative claim. In order to create a standard

7. This claim is also called a **digital share**.

8. This claim is also called **digital cash**.

call, we buy one asset-or-nothing option and sell K cash-or-nothing options. However, suppose we had instead sold $0.5K$ cash-or-nothing options. The resulting claim would have paid $S(T) - 0.5K$ if $S(T) > K$ and 0 otherwise. This is a *gap option*.[9]

The boundary conditions we have considered thus far are all *terminal* boundary conditions, meaning that they are satisfied by an option at expiration. American options and some nonstandard options have a boundary condition that must be satisfied prior to expiration. For example, barrier options have boundary conditions prior to expiration related to knocking in or out. Nevertheless, their price still solves equation (11).

The Black-Scholes Equation and Equilibrium Returns

In the foregoing derivation of the option pricing formula we required that a delta-hedged position earn the risk-free rate of return. A different approach to pricing an option is to impose the condition that the actual expected return on the option must equal the equilibrium expected return.[10] In the context of the binomial model, the expected return on the option changes as the option moves into or out of the money.

We can decompose the return on the option into expected and unexpected components. Using Itô's Lemma, we have

$$dV = \underbrace{\left[\frac{1}{2}\sigma^2 S^2 V_{SS} + (\alpha - \delta) S V_S + V_t\right] dt}_{\text{Expected return}} + \underbrace{S V_S \sigma dZ}_{\text{Unexpected return}}$$

Thus, the instantaneous expected return on the option is

$$\begin{aligned}\frac{1}{dt}\frac{E(dV)}{V} &= \frac{1}{dt}\frac{\left[\frac{1}{2}\sigma^2 S^2 V_{SS} + (\alpha - \delta) S V_S + V_t\right] dt}{V} \\ &\equiv \alpha_{\text{option}}\end{aligned} \tag{17}$$

The unexpected portion of the return is

$$\frac{E(dV)}{V} - \frac{dV}{V} = \frac{S V_S}{V}\sigma dZ \tag{18}$$

$$\equiv \sigma_{\text{option}} dZ \tag{19}$$

In interpreting this expression, recall that $S V_S / V$ is the option's elasticity, Ω. Thus, we have

$$\sigma_{\text{option}} = |\Omega| \sigma \tag{20}$$

Two assets with returns generated by the same dZ must have the same Sharpe ratio. Thus, we have

$$\frac{\alpha - r}{\sigma} = \frac{\alpha_{\text{option}} - r}{\sigma_{\text{option}}} \tag{21}$$

9. In practice, all-or-nothing and gap options are difficult to delta-hedge.

10. Black and Scholes also used this method to solve for the option price in their original paper.

Using equation (20), we can rewrite equation (21) to give

$$\alpha_{\text{option}} - r = \frac{SV_S}{V}(\alpha - r) \tag{22}$$

In words, the risk premium on the option is the risk premium on the stock times the option elasticity. We can interpret equation (22) as stating an *equilibrium* condition that the option must obey. In other words, if we view the option as just another asset, it must be priced so that its expected return is related to the expected return on the stock in a particular way.

Using equation (17), substitute for α_{option} in equation (22). This gives

$$\frac{1}{dt}\frac{\left[\frac{1}{2}\sigma^2 S^2 V_{SS} + (\alpha - \delta)SV_S + V_t\right]dt}{V} - r = \frac{SV_S}{V}(\alpha - r) \tag{23}$$

When we multiply both sides by V and rearrange terms, the expected return on the stock, α, vanishes: We once again obtain the Black-Scholes PDE, equation (11). Thus, an interpretation of the Black-Scholes equation is that the option is priced so as to earn its equilibrium expected return.

When we equate expected and actual returns, we can interpret the result as giving us a *fair* price for the option, as opposed to a no-arbitrage price. This is *equilibrium* pricing. The no-arbitrage and equilibrium prices are the same. The equilibrium approach makes clear that determining a fair price for the option using the Black-Scholes equation does not depend upon the assumption that hedging is actually possible.

What If the Underlying Asset Is Not an Investment Asset?

So far we have been discussing option pricing when the underlying asset is an investment asset, meaning that the asset is priced so as to be held by investors. Stocks and bonds are investment assets, but many commodities are not. Suppose that widgets generate no dividends, and that the price of widgets, S, follows the process

$$\frac{dS}{S} = \mu dt + \sigma dZ \tag{24}$$

From this equation, widget price risk is generated by the term dZ. Let ϕ represent the Sharpe ratio associated with dZ and let $\hat{\alpha}$ represent the expected return for an asset with σdZ risk. Since the Sharpe ratio is $\phi = (\hat{\alpha} - r)/\sigma$, we have

$$\hat{\alpha} = r + \sigma\phi$$

The important characteristic of an investment asset is that $\mu = \hat{\alpha}$. What happens if an asset is not an investment asset and $\mu < \hat{\alpha}$?

Consider again equation (20), which says that the expected return on the option equals the actual return on the option. When we derive this equation again using $\hat{\alpha}$ as the equilibrium expected return for an asset with risk dZ and μ as the actual expected return for widgets, we obtain

$$\frac{V_t + \frac{1}{2}\sigma^2 S^2 V_{SS} + \mu SV_S}{V} - r = \frac{SV_S}{V}(\hat{\alpha} - r) \tag{25}$$

Rearranging this equation, we obtain

$$\boxed{V_t + \tfrac{1}{2}\sigma^2 S^2 V_{SS} + [r - (\hat{\alpha} - \mu)]SV_S - rV = 0} \tag{26}$$

If you compare equation (26) with (11), the dividend yield, δ, has been replaced with $\hat{\alpha} - \mu$, the difference between the equilibrium expected return and the actual expected return on noninvestment widgets.[11]

Let $\hat{\delta} = \hat{\alpha} - \mu$. We can interpret $\hat{\delta}$ as follows: μ is the return you get from holding a widget and $\hat{\alpha}$ is the return you must expect if you are to voluntarily hold a widget. Thus, in order for you to hold a widget you would need an additional return of $\hat{\delta} = \hat{\alpha} - \mu$. Given the expected widget price change, μ, the only way to receive the extra return is through a dividend. This is the reason that $\hat{\alpha} - \mu$ replaces the dividend yield in the Black-Scholes equation.

We have encountered this concept before: $\hat{\delta}$ is the *lease rate* for the widget, or more generally the lease rate for an asset with expected capital gain μ and risk σdZ. When you lend a commodity, you receive its capital gains. The lease rate is the extra income you need to make you willing to buy and lend the asset. In the same way, $\hat{\delta}$ is the extra income you need to make you willing to hold a widget as an investment asset.

In practice, a widget-linked bond could be used to hedge the risk of a widget option. If the widget bond were constructed so that its price equalled the widget price today and at maturity, the bond would pay the widget lease rate as a coupon. This coupon, being a cash payment on the underlying asset, would play the role in the option pricing formula of a dividend on the underlying asset. This idea of a hypothetical lease-rate-paying, widget-linked security is also like a *twin security*. It provides an investment vehicle for owning the risk dZ. If such a twin security existed, we could use it to hedge the risk of the option, and its dividend yield, $\hat{\delta}$, would appear in the option price.

An equivalent way to write equation (26) is to replace $\hat{\alpha}$ with $r + \phi\sigma$. We then obtain

$$\boxed{V_t + \tfrac{1}{2}\sigma^2 S^2 V_{SS} + (\mu - \phi\sigma)SV_S - rV = 0} \tag{27}$$

In this version, the coefficient on the SV_S term is the drift on the widget less the risk premium appropriate for widgets.

Note that when the asset is an investment asset, $\hat{\alpha} = \alpha$ and $\mu = \alpha - \delta = r + \phi\sigma - \delta$. Both equations (26) and (27) reduce to equation (11).

To summarize, the Black-Scholes PDE, equation (11), also characterizes derivative prices for assets that are not investment assets. In the case of an asset that is not an investment asset, the dividend yield, δ, is replaced with the lease rate of the asset, $\hat{\delta}$.

Example 1. To see how to use equation (26), suppose we have an option for which the maturity payoff is based upon the stock price raised to a power, S^a. This type of option is called a **power option**. For example, we could have a call option with a payoff of

$$\max(S^a - K^a, 0)$$

11. This modification to the Black-Scholes equation is discussed in Constantinides (1978) and McDonald and Siegel (1984).

The lease rate on an asset paying S^a is $\delta^* = r - a(r - \delta) - \frac{1}{2}a(a - 1)\sigma^2$. From Itô's Lemma, the volatility is $a\sigma$. Thus, using equation (26), we can price the option by using S^a as the stock price, K^a as the strike price, δ^* as the dividend yield, and $a\sigma$ as the volatility. ■

3. RISK-NEUTRAL PRICING

The expected return on the stock, α, does not appear in the Black-Scholes equation, equation (11). Thus, when pricing derivatives on investment assets, only the risk-free rate matters; the actual expected return on a stock is irrelevant for pricing an option on the stock. The binomial pricing formula also depends only on the risk-free rate.

This observation led Cox and Ross (1976) to the following important observation: Because only the risk-free rate appears in the Black-Scholes PDE, it must be consistent with any possible world in which there is no arbitrage. If we are trying to value an option, we can assume that we are in the world in which it is easiest to value the option. Valuation will be easiest in a risk-neutral world, in which (if it actually existed) all assets would earn the risk-free rate of return and we would discount expected future cash flows at the risk-free rate. Thus, we can value options and other derivative claims by *assuming* that the stock earns the risk-free rate of return and calculate values based on that premise. We assume that the stock in this world follows the process

$$\frac{dS}{S} = (r - \delta)dt + \sigma d\tilde{Z} \tag{28}$$

As we keep emphasizing, the risk-neutral distribution is *not* an assumption about investor risk preferences. It is a device that can be used when pricing by arbitrage is possible (see Appendix B for a discussion).

Interpreting the Black-Scholes Equation

The actual expected change in the option price is given by

$$\frac{1}{dt}\mathrm{E}_t(dV) = V_t + \tfrac{1}{2}\sigma^2 S^2 V_{SS} + (\alpha - \delta)SV_S \tag{29}$$

Let E^* represent the expectation with respect to the risk-neutral distribution. Under the risk-neutral distribution, the expected change in the stock price is $\mathrm{E}^*(dS) = (r - \delta)dt$. The drift in the option price can thus be written

$$\frac{1}{dt}\mathrm{E}_t^*(dV) = V_t + \tfrac{1}{2}\sigma^2 S^2 V_{SS} + (r - \delta)SV_S \tag{30}$$

The Black-Scholes equation, (11), can therefore be rewritten as

$$\frac{1}{dt}\mathrm{E}_t^*(dV) = rV \tag{31}$$

Under the risk-neutral process, the option appreciates on average at the risk-free rate.

The Backward Equation

Closely related to equation (31) are the following equations, which characterize both the actual and risk-neutral probability distributions:

$$\frac{1}{dt}\mathrm{E}_t(dV) = 0 \tag{32}$$

$$\frac{1}{dt}\mathrm{E}_t^*(dV) = 0 \tag{33}$$

For the risk-neutral process, equation (33) is

$$\boxed{V_t + \tfrac{1}{2}\sigma^2 S^2 V_{SS} + (r - \delta)SV_S = 0} \tag{34}$$

Equation (34) is called the **Kolmogorov backward equation** for the geometric Brownian motion process given by equation (28). Whereas the Black-Scholes PDE characterizes prices, the backward equation characterizes probabilities. The backward equation is just like the Black-Scholes PDE except that there is no rV term.[12]

The Black-Scholes equation can be interpreted as saying that the expected return on the option must equal the risk-free rate. The backward equation pertains to probabilities of events, such as the probability that an option will expire in-the-money. To understand how such probabilities should behave, suppose we decide that the probability is 0.65 that the stock price 1 year from today will be greater than \$100. We know today that if the stock price goes up tomorrow, we will then assign a greater probability to this event. If the stock price goes down tomorrow, our estimate of the probability will go down. However, we should not expect our estimate of the probability to change on average: Our expectation *today*, of *tomorrow's* probability, must also be 0.65. If today's estimate of tomorrow's probability were not 0.65, then 0.65 could not have been the correct probability today.

Thus, whereas the price of a financial asset is expected to change over time, the expected change in the probability of an event is zero. This is why the backward equation does not have the rV term.

If $f(S_T; S_t)$ is the probability density for S_T given that the price today is S_t, both of these expressions would satisfy the backward equation:

$$\int_K^\infty f(S_T; S_t)dS_T$$

$$\int_K^\infty S_T f(S_T; S_t)dS_T$$

The first is the *probability* a call is in-the-money at time T. The second is the *partial expectation* of the stock price, conditional on $S_T > K$. Both are undiscounted. The backward equation holds for both the true and risk-neutral distributions generated by Itô processes.

Derivative Prices as Discounted Expected Cash Flows

The solution to equation (31) is equivalent to computing an expected value of the derivative payoff under the risk-neutral probability distribution and discounting at the risk-free rate. The specific form of the integral depends upon boundary conditions and payouts. We can see how this works with our assumptions (in particular a constant risk-free interest rate) by considering a simple European call option on a stock that pays continuous dividends at

12. The backward equation is covered in detail in standard texts; see, for example, Cox and Miller (1965) and Karlin and Taylor (1981). Wilmott (1998, ch. 10) contains a particularly clear heuristic derivation of equation (34).

the rate δ. In that case, equation (11), along with the boundary condition that the option at expiration is worth max$[0, S(T) - K]$, is equivalent to the discounted expectation

$$C[S(t), K, \sigma, r, T-t, \delta] = e^{-r(T-t)} \int_K^\infty [S(T) - K] f^*[S(T), \sigma, r, \delta; S(t)] dS(T)$$

where $f^*[S(T), \sigma, r, \delta; S(t)]$ is the *risk-neutral* probability density for $S(T)$, conditional on the time-t price being $S(t)$. In general, it is possible to write the solution to equation (11), with appropriate boundary conditions, as an explicit integral.[13]

If a probability $W(S, t)$ satisfies the backward equation under the risk-neutral distribution, expression (33), then $V(S, t) = e^{-r(T-t)} W(S, t)$, the present value of $W(S, t)$, will satisfy the Black-Scholes equation, equation (31). To see this, suppose that $W(S, t)$ satisfies the backward equation, i.e.,

$$\frac{1}{dt} \mathrm{E}_t^* [dW(S, t)] = 0$$

Since $V = e^{-r(T-t)} W$, we have

$$\begin{aligned} \frac{1}{dt} \mathrm{E}_t^* [dV(S, t)] &= \frac{1}{dt} \mathrm{E}_t^* \left\{ d \left[e^{-r(T-t)} W(S, t) \right] \right\} \\ &= rV + e^{-r(T-t)} \frac{1}{dt} \mathrm{E}_t^* [dW(S, t)] \\ &= rV \end{aligned}$$

This is the Black-Scholes PDE, equation (11).

This result means that *discounted risk-neutral probabilities and partial expectations* are prices of derivatives. Thus, any risk-neutral probability or partial expectation also has a corresponding derivative price. As an example of this, the Black-Scholes term $N(d_2)$ is the risk-neutral probability that an option is in-the-money at expiration. The discounted probability, $e^{-r(T-t)} N(d_2)$, is therefore the price of a derivative that pays \$1 if the option is in-the-money at expiration.

4. CHANGING THE NUMERAIRE

Now we consider what happens when the number of options (or other derivative contracts) that we receive at expiration is random, determined by some asset price. This odd-sounding payoff is common. Consider the following example.

Example 2. The price today of a nondividend-paying stock is \$100, and the forward price is \$106.184. Joe bets Sarah that in 1 year the stock price will be greater than \$106.184. Joe wants the loser to pay one share to the winner. Sarah wants the loser to pay \$106.184 to the winner.

The share received by Joe would be worth more than \$106.184 if he wins. Similarly, Sarah's desired payoff of \$106.184 is worth more than one share if she wins. Are either of these fair bets? If not, who has the more valuable side of the bet if it is denominated in shares? Who has the more valuable side of the bet if it is denominated in cash? ■

13. See, for example, Cox et al. (1985a, Lemma 4). The integral form of the Black-Scholes equation is also called the Feynman-Kac solution. See Karlin and Taylor (1981, pp. 222–224) and Duffie (1996, ch. 5).

If Sarah wins (i.e., the share price is below \$106.184), a payment of \$106.184 will exceed the value of one share. If Joe wins (i.e., the share price is greater than \$106.184), a payment of one share will be worth more than \$106.184. However, it is not obvious which bet has a greater fair value given a current stock price of \$100. Assuming no inside information about the stock, would an investor pay a greater price for Joe's desired bet or Sarah's desired bet?

We can describe the two forms of the bet as each having a different **numeraire**, or *unit of denomination*. Joe's desired bet is denominated in shares, whereas Sarah's desired bet is denominated in dollars. You can interpret the share-denominated bet as paying either a fixed number of shares (one) or a variable number of dollars (the dollar price of one share). The dollar-denominated bet pays a fixed number of dollars (\$106.184) or a variable number of shares (the number of shares with the value \$106.184). The general question we want to answer is how a change in the numeraire (unit of denomination) for a derivative changes the price of the derivative.

Here are some other examples where a change of denomination is relevant:

- **Currency translation:** A cash flow originating in yen (for example) can be valued in yen, or in some other currency.
- **Quantity uncertainty:** An agricultural producer who wants to insure production of an entire field must hedge total revenue—the product of price and quantity—rather than quantity alone.
- **All-or-nothing options:** All-or-nothing options, which we briefly discussed earlier, can be structured either to pay cash if a certain event occurs (such as the stock price exceeding the strike) or shares. The payoffs to the stock price bets above are in fact all-or-nothing payoffs; thus, the bets can be valued as all-or-nothing options.

To see what happens when we change the denomination of an option, suppose Q is the price of an asset that follows

$$\frac{dQ}{Q} = (\alpha_Q - \delta_Q)dt + \sigma_Q dZ_Q \tag{35}$$

Let $V(S, t)$ represent the price of an option denominated in cash, where S follows the process in equation (5). The correlation between dZ_Q and dZ is ρ. Suppose we receive the time-T payoff

$$Y[Q(T), S(T), T] = Q(T)^b V[S(T), K, \sigma, r, T, \delta] \tag{36}$$

Equation (36) represents a random number, Q^b, of claims, V. The value of this payoff is given in the following proposition.

Proposition 1 Suppose the process for S is given by equation (5) and the process for Q by equation (35), with ρ the correlation between dS and dQ. Let $V(S, K, \sigma_S, r, T-t, \delta_S)$ represent the price of a European derivative claim on S expiring at time T. The price of a claim paying $Q^b V$ is given by

$$Q(t)^b e^{(r-\delta^*)(T-t)} V[S(t), K, \sigma_S, r, T-t, \eta] \tag{37}$$

where $\eta = \delta - b\rho\sigma\sigma_Q$ and $\delta^* = r - b(r - \delta_Q) - \frac{1}{2}b(b-1)\sigma_Q^2$. In other words, to value Q^b claims, each with value V, we replace the dividend yield on S, δ, by η and multiply the resulting price by $Q(t)^b e^{(r-\delta^*)(T-t)}$.

The proof is in Appendix B. Equation (37) is quite important and deserves further comment. The term δ^* is the lease rate for Q^b. Thus $Q(t)^b e^{(r-\delta^*)(T-t)}$ is the forward price for a claim paying Q^b. The value of a claim paying $Q^b V$ is thus the forward price for Q^b times V evaluated at a modified dividend yield. If Q and S are correlated (in which case Q and V are correlated), there must also be a covariance term. The term η replaces the dividend yield δ to account for this covariance.

Example 3. We will now value the share-price bets described in Example 2. Let V^+ denote the value of a bet that pays \$1 at time T if $S(T) > K$, and V^- the value of a bet that pays \$1 at time T when $S(T) < K$. Both bets are cash-or-nothing options; therefore, from equation (16) we have that

$$V^+[S(0), K, \sigma, r, T, \delta] = e^{-rT} N\left(\frac{\ln[S(0)/K] + [r - \delta - 0.5\sigma^2]T}{\sigma\sqrt{T}}\right)$$
$$= e^{-rT} N(d_2)$$

This expression is the discounted risk-neutral probability that the bet pays off; it is also the second term in the Black-Scholes formula. If you hold both a bet that pays \$1 when $S(T) > K$ and a bet that pays \$1 when $S(T) < K$ then for certain you will receive \$1 at time T. Therefore, $V^+ + V^- = e^{-rT}$, and we have

$$V^-[S(0), K, \sigma, r, T, \delta] = e^{-rT} - V^+[S(0), K, \sigma, r, T, \delta]$$
$$= e^{-rT}[1 - N(d_2)]$$

Now consider the bets denominated in shares. Let Y^+ denote the value of a bet that pays one share when $S(T) > K$ and Y^- the value of a bet paying one share when $S(T) < K$. Holding a share-denominated bet is like having a random number, $S(T)$, of cash bets. By Proposition 1, the value of the share bet is obtained by multiplying V by the forward price for S, and replacing δ with $\delta - \sigma^2$ (we have $b = 1$ and $\rho = 1$ since S multiplies a claim based on S). Making these substitutions, the value of the share bet is $S(0)e^{(r-\delta)T} V[S(0), K, \sigma, r, T, \delta - \sigma^2]$, or

$$Y^+[S(0), K, \sigma, r, T, \delta] = S(0)e^{-\delta T} N\left(\frac{\ln[S(0)/K] + [r - \delta + 0.5\sigma^2]T}{\sigma\sqrt{T}}\right)$$
$$= S(0)e^{-\delta T} N(d_1)$$

This is the value of an asset-or-nothing option, equation (15), and it is the first term in the Black-Scholes formula.[14] Thus, we can view the first Black-Scholes term as a discounted risk-neutral probability with a change of numeraire.

If you hold both a share-denominated bet paying one share when $S(T) > K$, and also a bet that pays one share when $S(T) < K$, then you will for certain receive a share at time T. Thus, $Y^+ + Y^- = e^{-\delta T} S_0$, and we therefore have

$$Y^-[S(0), K, \sigma, r, T, \delta] = S(0)e^{-\delta T} - Y^+[S(0), K, \sigma, r, T, \delta]$$
$$= S(0)e^{-\delta T} - S(0)e^{-\delta T} N(d_1)$$

14. This argument linking the two terms in the Black-Scholes equation by changing the units of denomination is due to Geman et al. (1995).

In the case of Joe and Sarah's bet, suppose that the share-price volatility is 30%, the continuously compounded risk-free rate is 6%, the time to expiration is 1 year, and the share pays no dividends. Joe bets that the share price will be above \$106.184. The value of this bet is

$$\text{Value of Joe's bet} = Y^{+}[100, 106.184, 0.30, 0.08, 1, 0] = \$55.962$$

The opposite side of Joe's bet—receiving one share when $S(T) < \$106.184$—has the value $\$100 - \$55.962 = \$44.038$.

Sarah's bet pays \$106.184 if the price is below \$106.184; this bet has the value

$$\text{Value of Sarah's bet} = e^{-0.08\times 1} - V^{+}[100, 106.184, 0.30, 0.08, 1, 0] = \$55.962$$

The opposite side of Sarah's bet pays $e^{-0.08} \times \$106.184 - \$55.962 = \$44.038$. Thus, both Sarah and Joe wish to denominate the bet in their favor. Moreover, Sarah and Joe's desired bets have the same value. ■

Problem 8 asks you to find the strike prices such that the cash and share-denominated bets have equal value.

5. OPTION PRICING WHEN THE STOCK PRICE CAN JUMP

Jumps pose a problem for the Black-Scholes option pricing methodology. When the stock price can jump discretely as well as move continuously, a position that hedges against small moves will not also hedge against big moves.

The fact that jumps cannot be hedged does not mean that option pricing is impossible; rather, it means that *risk-neutral* option pricing may be impossible. When moves in the option price cannot be hedged, we can still price the option by computing discounted expected payoffs using the actual probability density rather than the risk-neutral probability density. The problem is that the option has the risk of a leveraged position in the stock, and we do not know what discount rate is appropriate. Some assumption about appropriate discount rates (which is really an assumption about investor preferences) will then be necessary to price an option.[15]

Merton (1976) derived an option pricing formula when the stock price can jump by assuming that the jump risk is diversifiable. This assumption neatly sidesteps the discounting issue since diversifiable risk does not affect expected returns. While jump risk for a broad index is not diversifiable, arguably many of the discrete moves for individual stocks are. In that case, by holding a portfolio of delta-hedged positions, the market-maker can diversify the effects of jump risk.

Ultimately, the importance of jumps and their systematic component is an empirical issue. Nevertheless, Merton's formulas provide useful insights into the effects of jumps.

Merton's Solution for Diversifiable Jumps

Suppose that the stock follows the process

15. See Naik and Lee (1990) for an example of equilibrium option pricing when there are jumps that cannot be hedged.

$$dS(t)/S(t) = (\alpha - \lambda k)dt + \sigma dZ + dq \tag{38}$$

where, over an interval dt, a jump occurs with probability λdt, and $dq = 0$ if there is no jump and $Y - 1$ if there is a jump. The jump magnitude, Y, is lognormally distributed such that

$$\ln(Y) \sim \mathcal{N}(\alpha_J, \sigma_J^2) \tag{39}$$

Thus, if the stock price is S before a jump, it is YS following the jump, where $Y - 1$ is the percentage change in the stock price due to the jump and $k = \mathrm{E}(Y - 1)$ is the expected percentage jump. Assume that the occurrence and magnitude of the jump are uncorrelated with the stock return.

Merton (1976) shows that with the stock following equation (38), and with jumps diversifiable, the Black-Scholes PDE becomes

$$V_t + \tfrac{1}{2}V_{SS}\sigma^2 S^2 + V_S(r - \delta - \lambda k)S + \lambda \mathrm{E}_Y[V(SY, t) - V(S, t)] = rV \tag{40}$$

When jumps are lognormal, as in equation (39), Merton shows that the price of a European call is[16]

$$\sum_{i=0}^{\infty} \frac{e^{-\lambda' T}(\lambda' T)^i}{i!} \text{BSCall}\left(S, K, \sqrt{\sigma^2 + i\sigma_J^2/T}, r - \lambda k + i\alpha_J/T, T, \delta\right) \tag{41}$$

where $\lambda' = \lambda e^{\alpha_J}$. The price of a call is obtained by put-call parity.

Equation (41) provides the option value as an expectation of European option prices with respect to the probability of a given number of jumps occurring. Conditional on i jumps, we replace the variance, $\sigma^2 T$, with $\sigma^2 T + i\sigma_J^2$, a quantity that reflects the added variance from having i discrete lognormal price moves. We also replace the risk-free rate, r, with $(r - \lambda k)T + i\alpha_J$. The instantaneous drift, $r - \lambda k$, is increased by the cumulative mean of i jumps, $i\alpha_J$.[17]

An interesting special case occurs when the only possible jump that can occur is a jump of the stock price to zero. If the stock jumps to zero, a call option becomes worthless: $V(SY, t) = 0$, and $\lambda k = -\lambda$. Hence, with a jump to zero, the PDE for a call becomes

$$V_t + \tfrac{1}{2}V_{SS}\sigma^2 S^2 + V_S(r + \lambda - \delta)S = (r + \lambda)V$$

Every occurrence of r is replaced by $r + \lambda$; hence, when the stock can jump to zero with instantaneous probability λdt, the value of a European call, BSCall_λ, is

$$\text{BSCall}_\lambda(S, K, \sigma, r, T - t, \delta) = \text{BSCall}(S, K, \sigma, r + \lambda, T - t, \delta) \tag{42}$$

16. Jumps need not be lognormal. Merton (1976) shows that the general solution for calls is obtained as an expected value of the Black-Scholes formula:

$$\sum_{i=0}^{\infty} \frac{e^{-\lambda T}(\lambda T)^i}{i!} \mathrm{E}_i\left[\text{BSCall}\left(SY_n e^{-\lambda k T}, K, \sigma, r, T, \delta\right)\right]$$

where E_i denotes the expectation conditional on i jumps.

17. This footnote has been intentionally omitted for this edition.

The formula for a put, BSPut_λ, is then obtained by put-call parity:[18]

$$\begin{aligned}&\text{BSPut}_\lambda(S, K, \sigma, r, T-t, \delta)\\&\quad= \text{BSCall}(S, K, \sigma, r+\lambda, T-t, \delta, \lambda) - Se^{-\delta(T-t)} + Ke^{-r(T-t)}\end{aligned}$$

CHAPTER SUMMARY

The Black-Scholes equation, equation (11), characterizes the behavior of a derivative as a function of the price of one or more underlying assets. We can interpret the Black-Scholes equation as requiring that a derivative earn an appropriate rate of return, which occurs when the delta, gamma, and theta of an asset satisfy a particular relationship. The Black-Scholes equation is thus a generalization of the idea, familiar from introductory finance, that zero-coupon bonds appreciate at the risk-free rate. Probabilities and partial expectations satisfy a related condition known as the backward equation. Along with the Black-Scholes equation, a derivative must satisfy an appropriate boundary condition.

A change of the units of an option payoff is called a change of numeraire. Proposition 1 shows that the price effect of a change of numeraire is accounted for with a simple transformation of the pricing formula.

FURTHER READING

Two classic papers on option pricing are Black and Scholes (1973) and Merton (1973b). Merton (1976) extends the Black-Scholes model to allow diversifiable jumps in the stock price, and Naik and Lee (1990) develop a model to price options when jumps are systematic. The Heston model is described in Heston (1993). In addition to Bakshi et al. (1997) and Bates (2000), recent empirical studies of volatility skew include Benzoni (2001), Andersen et al. (2002), Eraker (2001), and Pan (2002).

Cox and Miller (1965) and Wilmott (1998, ch. 10) discuss the backward equation and its counterpart, the forward equation, which characterizes the probability density for S_t, conditional on S_T. Geman et al. (1995) studied the role of changing the numeraire as a pricing technique. Schroder (1999) extends their results, including examples with stochastic volatility and jump-diffusion models. Ingersoll (2000) provides some additional examples of the use of this technique. Marcus and Modest (1984, 1986) examine quantity uncertainty in agricultural production.

---

18. For a put option, the solution does *not* entail replacing every occurrence of r with $r+\lambda$. The reason is that the PDE for the put option is different from the PDE for the call option in the case of a jump. There is a different boundary condition when the stock jumps to zero,

$$P(0, t) = Ke^{-rT}$$

rather than 0 in the case of a call.

PROBLEMS

1. Verify that equation (12) satisfies the Black-Scholes equation. What is the boundary condition for which this is a solution?

2. Verify that $AS^a e^{\gamma t}$ satisfies the Black-Scholes PDE for

$$a = \left(\frac{1}{2} - \frac{r-\delta}{\sigma^2}\right) \pm \sqrt{\left(\frac{r-\delta}{\sigma^2} - \frac{1}{2}\right)^2 + \frac{2(r-\gamma)}{\sigma^2}}$$

3. This problem has been intentionally omitted for this edition.

4. This problem has been intentionally omitted for this edition.

5. Verify that $S(t)e^{-\delta(T-t)}N(d_1)$ satisfies the Black-Scholes equation.

6. Verify that $e^{-r(T-t)}N(d_2)$ satisfies the Black-Scholes equation.

7. Use the answers to the previous two problems to verify that the Black-Scholes formula satisfies the Black-Scholes equation. Verify that the boundary condition $V[S(T), T] = \max[0, S(T) - K]$ is satisfied.

8. Consider Joe and Sarah's bet in Examples 2 and 3.

   a. In this bet, note that \$106.184 is the forward price. A bet paying \$1 if the share price is above the forward price is worth less than a bet paying \$1 if the share price is below the forward price. Why?

   b. Suppose the bet were to be denominated in cash. If we want the bet to pay x if $S > x$, what would x have to be in order to make the bet fair?

   c. Now suppose that we pay one share if $S > x$. What would x have to be in this case to make the bet fair?

9. Consider again the bet in Example 3. Suppose the bet is $S -$ \$106.184 if the price is above \$106.184, and \$106.184 $- S$ if the price is below \$106.184. What is the value of this bet to each party? Why?

10. Suppose that a derivative claim makes continuous payments at the rate Γ. Show that the Black-Scholes equation becomes

$$V_t + \frac{1}{2}\sigma^2 S^2 V_{SS} + (r-\delta)SV_S + \Gamma - rV = 0$$

For the following four problems, assume that S follows equation (5) and Q follows equation (35). Suppose $S_0 = \$50$, $Q_0 = \$90$, $T = 2$, $r = 0.06$, $\delta = 0.02$, $\delta_Q = 0.01$, $\sigma = 0.3$, $\sigma_Q = 0.5$, and $\rho = -0.2$. Use Proposition 1 to find solutions to the problems. *Optional:* For each problem, verify the solution using Monte Carlo.

11. What is the value of a claim paying $Q(T)^2 S(T)$?

12. What is the value of a claim paying $Q(T)^{-1} S(T)$?

13. You are offered the opportunity to receive for free the payoff

$$[Q(T) - F_{0,T}(Q)] \times \max[0, S(T) - K]$$

(Note that this payoff can be negative.) Should you accept the offer?

14. An agricultural producer wishes to insure the value of a crop. Let Q represent the quantity of production in bushels and S the price of a bushel. The insurance payoff is therefore $Q(T) \times V[S(T), T]$, where V is the price of a put with $K = \$50$. What is the cost of insurance?

Appendix A MULTIVARIATE BLACK-SCHOLES ANALYSIS

Consider a claim for which the payoff depends on the n asset prices, $S_1, S_2, \ldots, S_n$, where

$$\frac{dS_i}{S_i} = (\alpha_i - \delta_i)dt + \sigma_i dZ_i \tag{43}$$

The pairwise correlation between S_i and S_j is ρ_{ij}. Let $V(S_1, S_2, \ldots, S_n, t, T)$ be the value of this claim. Consider a portfolio consisting of the claim, the n assets, and bonds, W, such that

$$I = V + \sum_{i=1}^{n} N_i S_i + W$$

Using the multivariate version of Itô's Lemma, the change in the value of the portfolio is

$$dI = V_t dt + \sum_{i=1}^{n} V_{S_i} dS_i + \frac{1}{2}\sum_{i=1}^{n}\sum_{j=1}^{n} dS_i dS_j V_{S_i S_j} dt + \sum_{i=1}^{n} N_i dS_i + dW$$

In order to delta-hedge V, set $N_i = -V_{S_i}$. Hold bonds to finance the residual such that $I = 0$. The same analysis used to derive equation (11) leads to the following PDE for V:

$$V_t + \sum_{i=1}^{n}(r - \delta_i)S_i V_{S_i} + \frac{1}{2}\sum_{i=1}^{n}\sum_{j=1}^{n} \sigma_i \sigma_j \rho_{i,j} S_i S_j V_{S_i S_j} = rV \tag{44}$$

Appendix B PROOF OF PROPOSITION 1

In this section we will verify the solution in Proposition 1. We begin by assuming that we have a derivative price $V(S, \sigma, r, T - t, \delta)$ that satisfies

$$V_t + (r - \delta)SV_S + \tfrac{1}{2}\sigma^2 S^2 V_{SS} = rV \tag{45}$$

By the multivariate Black-Scholes equation described in Appendix A, the claim $Y(S, Q, t)$ must satisfy

$$Y_t + (r - \delta)SY_S + (r - \delta_Q)QY_Q + \tfrac{1}{2}\left(\sigma^2 S^2 Y_{SS} + \sigma_Q^2 Q^2 Y_{QQ} + 2\rho\sigma\sigma_Q SQY_{SQ}\right) = rY$$

Guess the solution $Y = Ae^{-(r-\delta^*)t}Q^b W$, where A is determined by boundary conditions, δ^* is to be determined, and W satisfies the same boundary condition as V. Compute the derivatives of this guess and substitute them into equation (44). After simplification (in particular, the Y multiplying every term divides out), this yields

$$\begin{aligned} &\delta^* - r + b(r - \delta_Q) + \tfrac{1}{2}\sigma_Q^2 b(b-1) \\ &\quad + \frac{1}{W}\left\{W_t + [r - (\delta - b\rho\sigma\sigma_Q)]SW_S + \tfrac{1}{2}\sigma^2 S^2 W_{SS}\right\} = r \end{aligned} \tag{46}$$

The term in braces is the same as equation (45), except that δ is replaced with $\eta = \delta - b\rho\sigma\sigma_Q$. Thus, W is the same as V except that δ is replaced by η. With this replacement, from equation (45), the term in parentheses equals rW. Equation (46) becomes

$$\delta^* - r + b(r - \delta_Q) + \tfrac{1}{2}\sigma_Q^2 b(b-1) + \frac{rW}{W} = r$$

This equation is satisfied if $\delta^* = r - b(r - \delta_Q) - \frac{1}{2}\sigma_Q^2 b(b-1)$. Thus, with the η and δ^* in Proposition 1, the candidate solution solves equation (44). The parameter A is set so, at the point the option is exercised, $A = e^{(r-\delta^*)t}$. For a European option, set $A = e^{(r-\delta^*)T}$ to solve the terminal boundary condition.

Appendix C SOLUTIONS FOR PRICES AND PROBABILITIES

Appendix available at http://www.pearsonhighered.com/mcdonald.

Risk-Neutral and Martingale Pricing

In this chapter we discuss the economic justification for risk-neutral pricing. In the process, we will learn about a different approach to pricing derivatives—namely, martingale pricing.[1]

It is common to assume that the observed price of stock i follows the process

$$\frac{dS_i}{S_i} = (\alpha_i - \delta_i)dt + \sigma_i d\tilde{Z}_i \tag{1}$$

where α_i is the expected return on the stock and δ_i the dividend yield. For most stocks, $\alpha_i > r$: The risk premium is positive. When pricing derivatives, by contrast, we use the risk-neutral stock return process:

$$\frac{dS_i}{S_i} = (r - \delta_i)dt + \sigma_i dZ_i \tag{2}$$

We assume that the stock follows this process and then value derivative claims by computing the expected derivative payoff using equation (2) and discounting this expected payoff at the risk-free rate.

The transformation from equation (1) to equation (2) is the main subject of this chapter. To obtain equation (2), we replace α_i in equation (1) with the risk-free rate r, and the diffusion $d\tilde{Z}_i$ with dZ_i. The justification for using equation (2) is far from obvious, but the effect is powerful. In many applications we simply assume that the asset follows (2) and we then proceed with pricing.

Given its importance, it is helpful to understand how equation (2) arises. The transformation from equation (1) to equation (2) has an economic interpretation, and there are related transformations that are useful in pricing particular derivatives, particularly in fixed income.

1. The purpose of the chapter is to explain the economic foundation for risk-neutral pricing, and derivative pricing in general. The interested reader can delve more deeply into the topic with an asset pricing book such as Duffie (2001). Even if you do not read the entire chapter, Sections 1 and 2 will provide an overview of the framework and a sense of why this material is important, albeit optional.

From Chapter 22 of *Derivatives Markets*, Third Edition, Robert McDonald. Copyright © 2013 by Pearson Education, Inc. Published by Pearson Prentice Hall. All rights reserved.

In order to understand the economic underpinnings of equation (2), we need first to understand how investors make portfolio decisions. All investors must decide how much to hold of each asset; this is called the portfolio selection problem. An investor selecting a portfolio must value each of the assets, assessing and discounting their future payoffs. This valuation provides the link between portfolio selection and risk-neutral valuation: *The solution to the portfolio problem implies a valuation procedure that is central in financial economics, and that gives rise to risk-neutral valuation.*

Prior to this point you might have wondered how to tell whether a derivative pricing model is legitimate. Can we write down equation (2) for *any* asset or financial quantity? The answer is that a pricing procedure is legitimate if it is consistent with the solution to the portfolio problem. This consistency takes a surprisingly simple form: An acceptable pricing model is one in which *ratios* of asset prices follow a martingale:

$$\mathrm{E}_t^*\left(\frac{S_{1,T}}{S_{2,T}}\right) = \frac{S_{1,t}}{S_{2,t}} \qquad t < T \tag{3}$$

Here $S_{1,t}$ and $S_{2,t}$ are the prices of two non-dividend-paying assets that investors can own and E_t^* is computed with respect to a probability distribution under which the martingale condition, equation (3), is true. We will see that risk-neutral pricing arises when the denominator asset in equation (3) is an account that pays the short-term risk-free rate. Different assumptions about the numeraire are convenient in other contexts, such as pricing interest rate derivatives. You may find equation (3) puzzling at this point, but we will discuss it at greater length below.

The rest of the chapter provides an economic explanation of the martingale approach and examples of its use. A key part of the martingale approach to derivatives pricing is the concept of a change of measure, which means transforming the probability distribution for assets into a new probability distribution. In continuous time, this change of measure is achieved using Girsanov's theorem, which we briefly summarize. We then present specific examples of changes of measure, including the risk-neutral measure. Finally, we discuss Warren Buffett's critique of using the Black-Scholes formula to price long-term put options.

As you read the chapter, it is important to keep in mind that pricing a derivative, or *any* financial claim, amounts to asking how investors would value a particular risky cash flow. This chapter is meant to illuminate the link between investor portfolio decisions and derivatives pricing.

1. RISK AVERSION AND MARGINAL UTILITY

All investors face two fundamental problems: first, whether to consume today or in the future (the savings/consumption decision) and second, which assets to hold in the savings portfolio (the portfolio selection problem). The two decisions are linked because the savings portfolio is a source of funds for future consumption.[2] Portfolio selection is also tied to valuation because an investment decision requires assessing and discounting future payoffs.

2. There is a large literature studying consumption and portfolio selection. Two books that provide an introduction are Cochrane (2001) and Duffie (2001).

The solution to the portfolio selection problem determines demand for an asset. At a point in time there is a given supply of assets, which are priced so that they are held willingly by investors. For each asset the risk premium (the difference between the expected return and the risk free rate) is at the level necessary to equate asset demand and supply. In equilibrium, assets have a positive risk premium only for risks that cannot be eliminated by diversification. We assume in what follows that markets are complete, i.e., that all risks are tradeable, and that all investors are unconstrained in selecting their portfolios.

It is helpful to think of each possible economic outcome as a distinct event, which is called a **state**. Strictly speaking, every set of different outcomes is a distinct state. For example, the state in which the level of the S&P index is 1300 is different from the state in which it is 1301. We will use the term more generally to refer to economically distinct conditions, for example referring to "good states" (in which investors are well off) and "bad states" (in which investors are not well off). The price of stock i in state j at time t is $S_i(t, j)$.

The basic structure of the portfolio selection problem is as follows. At time t in state j investors must select an amount to consume, $C(t, j)$. Investors do not care about consumption *per se*; rather, they care about the *utility* of consumption: their perceived level of well-being due to consumption. Investors consume part of their wealth and invest the remainder. At a future time T, they consume again, saving what they do not consume, and so on. This can continue indefinitely. Each period, investors choose the level of consumption and the portfolio that maximizes their utility, taking into account the implications of their choice for future consumption.

Consumption of $C(t)$ at time t produces utility of $U[C(t), t]$. Since utility is received at different times, it is necessary to express utility in terms of a common unit. We will implicitly assume that all utility is expressed in terms of time 0 utility.[3] Looking forward from any time t, wealth at a future time T is a random variable, with the investor assigning probabilities to the different states that are possible. Because the future state is unknown, consumption at a future date is a random variable that we will denote $\tilde{C}(T)$. Thus, the present value of time T utility is $\mathrm{E}_t[U[\tilde{C}(T), T]]$. If consumption in state j is $C(T, j)$, this means that the investor has decided to consume $C(T, j)$, taking into account the amount of wealth they have at that time and the investment and consumption opportunities they face going forward.

We assume that investors have a utility function resembling that in Figure 1. The two important features of this utility function are that first, it is increasing (the investor prefers consuming more to less), and second, it is concave (utility increases at a decreasing rate). An investor with a utility function like that in Figure 1 is *risk-averse*. Such an investor will not accept a fair bet.[4]

---

3. You can think of there being a discount factor for utility, which we implicitly take into account via the time argument in the utility function. As an alternative, it is common to write utility as $e^{-\beta t}U[C(t)]$. This notation makes explicit the discounting of utility at the rate β.

4. This is a consequence of *Jensen's Inequality*. A risk-averse investor has a concave utility function, which implies that

$$\mathrm{E}[U(x)] < U(\mathrm{E}[x])$$

In words, the expected utility associated with a gamble, $\mathrm{E}[U(x)]$, is less than the utility from receiving the expected value of the gamble for sure, $U(\mathrm{E}[x])$.

FIGURE 1

A utility function that exhibits decreasing marginal utility. Marginal utility is high when consumption and utility are low; marginal utility is low when consumption and utility are high.

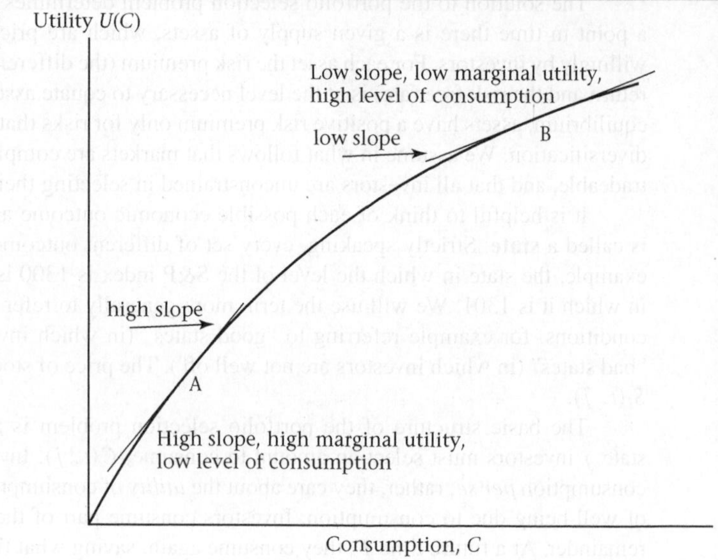

A critical concept in the following discussion is that of **marginal utility**, which is the additional utility that an investor receives from a one-unit increase in $C(t)$. Mathematically, the marginal utility in state j is

$$\frac{\partial U[C(t, j), t]}{\partial C(t, j)} \equiv U'[C(t, j), t]$$

Where it does not cause confusion, we will abbreviate $U'[C(t, j), t]$ as $U'(t)$.

The important idea in Figure 1 is that *marginal utility is a measure of whether consumption is high or low*, and thus whether investors are in a good state or a bad state. You can see in Figure 1 that the slope of the utility function decreases as the level of consumption is greater: Marginal utility is decreasing with the level of consumption. Risk-averse investors with high consumption (those at point B in Figure 1) assign less value to an *additional* dollar than when consumption is low (those at point A in Figure 1). Thus, investors at point A have low consumption and high marginal utility (this is the bad state), while investors at point B have high consumption and low marginal utility (this is the good state). The more you are able to consume, the less you value \$1 of additional consumption.

2. THE FIRST-ORDER CONDITION FOR PORTFOLIO SELECTION

Suppose that the investor allocates savings across n assets: $n - 1$ non-dividend-paying risky assets with prices $S_i(t)$ $(i = 1, \ldots, n - 1)$ and a default-free *money-market account*, which always earns the currently prevailing short-term risk-free rate, $r(t)$. An investment of $B(t)$

in the money-market account at time t will accumulate to $B(t)\exp[\int_t^T r(s)ds]$ at time T. If the interest rate is stochastic, $B(T)$ will be a random variable.

The statement of the investor's problem along with the solution is presented in Appendix A. The main result is given by equation (42). This equation must be satisfied by a utility-maximizing investor who can freely invest (either long or short) in all assets. We say that such an investor is "unconstrained" with respect to portfolio choices.[5] The result is that for each asset i, we have

$$E_t\left[U'(T)\frac{S_i(T)}{S_i(t)}\right] = U'(t) \tag{4}$$

We have simplified the notation to let $U'(T)$ denote the random variable $U'[C(T, j), T]$, when the state j is not known. The marginal utility $U'(T)$ is a random variable from the perspective of time t. Equation (4) states that the expected product of the future marginal utility of consumption times one plus the *realized* return on asset i equals the marginal utility of consumption today. Note that at time t, $U'(T)$ and $S_i(T)$ are both random variables, whereas $U'(t)$ and $S_i(t)$ are both known. The interpretation of equation (4) is that the investor is indifferent between consuming one unit less today ($U'(t)$) and consuming an uncertain extra amount in the future. The expected marginal benefit from consuming in the future—the left-hand side of equation (4)—is the same for all assets, and is equal to $U'(t)$.

Equation (4) holds for an individual investor who has made an optimal portfolio decision. Without additional assumptions, the equation does not tell you what that optimum is and it does not tell you how much of each asset the investor holds. In addition, equation (4) has buried in it information about the investor's optimism concerning different assets (in the expectation) and about the investor-specific level of risk aversion (in the utility functions).

In equilibrium, asset prices will be such that the aggregate demand by investors for assets equals their supply. This equilibrium does not imply or require that investors agree about the prospects for all assets, and in general investors will not all hold the same portfolios. Instead, equilibrium means that, given their chosen portfolios and the market prices for assets, investors have no desire to change their position. An implication is that all investors will agree on asset prices; if they did not, investors with a high valuation would buy from investors with a low valuation.[6]

By moving $S_i(t)$ to the right-hand side of equation (4), we can also write the equation as

$$E_t\left[\frac{U'(T)}{U'(t)}S_i(T)\right] = S_i(t) \tag{5}$$

The marginal value in utility terms of an extra unit of asset i in state j is $U'[C(T, j), T]$ $S_i(T, j)$. In equation (5), future cash flows are weighted by both marginal utility and probability. The ratio of the future uncertain marginal utility to the present known marginal utility, $U'(T)/U'(t)$, is called the **stochastic discount factor**. Equation (5) makes clear the

5. This discussion assumes an idealized market in which we ignore transaction costs, short-sale restrictions, liquidity impacts of trading, etc.

6. The idea that investors agree might seem puzzling: What if investor A is more optimistic about the stock than investor B? In such a case, investor A will hold relatively more of the stock. Specifically, investor A will hold enough additional stock so that the expected gain implied by optimistic beliefs is offset by the additional risk from lack of diversification due to holding a large quantity of the stock.

reason for this terminology: The future stock price is discounted by the ratio of marginal utilities in order to determine the current stock price.

To interpret equation (5), recall that marginal utility, $U'(T)$, is low in good times. Equation (5) will assign a low weight (low marginal utility) to stock prices that occur in good times and a high weight to stock prices that occur in bad times. Thus, if there are two stocks with the same expected future price, the stock that has higher prices in bad times will be worth today more than the stock that has high prices occurring in good times.

It is instructive to compare equation (5) with traditional discounted cash flow (DCF). With standard DCF, we compute an expected cash flow and discount it at a rate that appropriately adjusts for the risk of the asset. Thus, for a stock, we would write

$$\frac{\mathrm{E}_t[S_i(T)]}{1+\mu_i} = S_i(t) \tag{6}$$

where μ_i is the specific discount factor for stock i. From examining equation (5), it is clear that μ_i implicitly incorporates marginal utilities. (See equation (47) in Appendix A for an explicit expression for μ_i.)

By contrast, if we let $1/(1+\tilde{\mu}_j) = U'(C(T, j), T)/U'(t)$, equation (5) can be written

$$\mathrm{E}_t\left[\frac{S_i(T, j)}{1+\tilde{\mu}_j}\right] = S_i(t) \tag{7}$$

Here, $\tilde{\mu}_j$ is a random variable, which is a rewritten version of the stochastic discount factor. The discount factor $1+\tilde{\mu}_j$ differs across states, changing with the level of consumption, but for a given state it is the same for every asset.

Thus, we can have either a set of asset-specific state-independent discount rates (traditional DCF, equation (6)), or we can have an asset-independent, state-dependent discount rate that correctly discounts all cash flows (the stochastic discount factor, equation (7)). In practice it is common to use DCF. However, understanding the stochastic discount factor approach is helpful in understanding both derivative pricing and DCF. *When implemented correctly, the two approaches give the same present value.*

3. CHANGE OF MEASURE AND CHANGE OF NUMERAIRE

In the preceding section we showed that there is a direct link between discounting and the solution to the portfolio selection problem, summarized by equation (4). Another way to write equation (4) is

$$\mathrm{E}_t\left[\frac{U'(T)}{U'(t)}\frac{S_i(T)}{S_i(t)}\right] = 1 \tag{8}$$

In this section we show that equation (8) implies that marginal utilities can be used to redefine the probability distribution of future returns: We will create new probabilities by using marginal utility to reweight the original probabilities. The process of moving from one probability distribution to another is called a *change of measure*. When defining a change of measure, it is also typical to redefine the units in which a payoff is measured; this is called a *change of numeraire*. We begin by reviewing some results from probability theory and we then show the link to the portfolio selection problem.

Change of Measure

Suppose there is a discrete random variable with m possible outcomes. Denote the probability of the ith outcome as p_i. Probabilities are nonnegative and the sum over all possible outcomes is one. Thus, we have

$$p_i \geq 0 \quad i \in \{1 \ldots m\} \quad \text{and} \quad \sum_{i=1}^{m} p_i = 1$$

If E[·] is the expectation operator for the process, and if $\tilde{x}$ is a random variable that takes a defined value, x_i, over each of the m outcomes, we can write

$$\mathrm{E}(\tilde{x}) = \sum_{i=1}^{m} p_i x_i$$

Now suppose that $\tilde{x}$ is a nonnegative random variable defined over the m events, such that

$$\sum_{i=1}^{m} p_i x_i = 1 \tag{9}$$

Thus, x has a mean of 1. The key step is to define the new probability p_i^x:

$$p_i^x = x_i p_i \tag{10}$$

We are using the random variable x to reweight the probabilities p_i to obtain new probabilities p_i^x. This is a change of measure: We are assigning new probabilities to states. The p_i^x are probabilities because $p_i^x \geq 0$ (p_i and x_i are both nonnegative) and $\sum_{i=1}^{m} p_i^x = 1$ (from equation (9)). Whether this new probability distribution is interesting or useful depends upon x_i, which determines how the probabilities are transformed. Whenever $x_i > 1$, we will have $p_i^x > p_i$. We can see this by rewriting (10)

$$p_i^x = p_i + p_i \times [x_i - 1] \tag{11}$$

To summarize this discussion, a nonnegative random variable with a mean of 1 can be used to perform a change of measure. If you look back at equation (8), you can see why we are discussing this. The expectation operator in equation (8), E_t, is taken with respect to the actual or *physical* probabilities of different returns on the stock. However, marginal utilities and asset prices are nonnegative, and the ratio in equation (8) has an expectation of 1. Thus, we can use the ratio $U'(T)S_i(T)/U'(t)S_i(t)$ to construct a new probability distribution, i.e., a change of measure.

The Martingale Property

From equation (5), the valuation equation for asset k is

$$S_k(t) = \mathrm{E}_t\left[\frac{U'(T)S_k(T)}{U'(t)}\right]$$

If there are m possible states and we explicitly write out the probabilities, we can rewrite the valuation equation for $S_k(t)$ as

$$S_k(t) = \sum_{j=1}^{m} p_j \frac{U'[C(T,j),T]}{U'(t)} S_k(T,j) \tag{12}$$

We are now going to construct a new probability distribution using an arbitrary asset, which we will call asset number 1. We can multiply and divide the marginal utilities by $S_1(T)$ and $S_1(t)$. (It's important to keep a careful watch on subscripts because we are valuing asset k using a probability distribution constructed using asset 1.) We obtain

$$\frac{S_k(t)}{S_1(t)} = \sum_{j=1}^{m} p_j \frac{U'[C(T,j),T]S_1(T,j)}{U'(t)S_1(t)} \frac{S_k(T,j)}{S_1(T,j)} \tag{13}$$

Note that we are measuring the payoff $S_k(T, j)$ in terms of units of asset 1. This is a change of numeraire.[7] We can also say that we use the price $S_1(t)$ as a **deflator**. Now we perform a change of measure, where we define a new probability, $p_j^{S_1}$, obtained by weighting the physical probabilities by marginal utilities:

$$p_j^{S_1} = p_j \frac{U'[C(T,j),t]S_1(T;j)}{U'(t)S_1(t)} \tag{14}$$

We can then write equation (13) as

$$\frac{S_k(t)}{S_1(t)} = \sum_{j=1}^{m} p_j^{S_1} \frac{S_k(T,j)}{S_1(T,j)} \tag{15}$$

Equation (15) is equivalent to the original valuation problem but embodies two changes. First, we measure the value and payoff in terms of units of asset 1; this is the change in numeraire. Second, the probabilities $p_j^{S_1}$ define a new probability distribution; this is a change of measure.

How do probabilities change with a change of measure? From equation (11), the new measure has the effect of increasing the probability in those states where the product of marginal utility and the asset price is greater than average. If the numeraire asset is risk-free (for example, a default-free zero-coupon bond maturing at time T), then probabilities are increased (relative to physical probabilities) when the state of the economy is bad, i.e., when marginal utilities are high, and reduced when the state of the economy is good.

We have been writing $\mathrm{E}_t[\cdot]$ to denote an expectation with respect to the original, physical measure. We can similarly write $\mathrm{E}_t^{S_1}[\cdot]$ to denote an expectation computed using the $p_j^{S_1}$ defined in equation (14). We can then write the valuation equation for $S_k(t)$ as

7. A *numeraire* is a unit of account; it is how we measure prices. We commonly denominate assets in dollars or some other currency: A stock is worth \$100 or €80. However, we can adopt different numeraires. In particular, we can express the value of an asset in terms of the price of another asset. For example, we could value a position in Microsoft using IBM as numeraire. Suppose $S_{\mathrm{MSFT}} = \$30$ and $S_{\mathrm{IBM}} = \$95$. One share of Microsoft is then $30/95 = 0.3158$ IBMs. With a change in numeraire we simply count the value of our position in terms of something other than dollars.

$$\boxed{\frac{S_k(t)}{S_1(t)} = \mathrm{E}_t^{S_1}\left[\frac{\tilde{S}_k(T)}{S_1(T)}\right]} \tag{16}$$

Equation (16) shows that, when using the probability measure induced by the numeraire—S_1 in this case—the asset price ratio $S_k(t)/S_1(t)$ is a martingale. We could have selected any asset as numeraire.[8] The fact that price ratios are martingales is an important observation, and we will see that it places strong restrictions on acceptable pricing models.

A change of measure can be used in performing a valuation. Suppose there is a random future cash flow $\tilde{x}(T)$ with present value $x(t)$. We wish to compute $x(t)$. From equation (4) we have[9]

$$x(t) = \mathrm{E}_t\left[\frac{\tilde{U}'(T)}{U'(t)}\tilde{x}(T)\right]$$

With a change of numeraire and a change of measure, we can rewrite this valuation as

$$\frac{x(t)}{S_1(t)} = \mathrm{E}_t^{S_1}\left[\frac{\tilde{x}(T)}{S_1(T)}\right]$$

We will see examples where such a transformation is extremely helpful.

Girsanov's Theorem

Thus far, nothing we have discussed in this section presumes that the asset follows any particular stochastic process. However, in many applications it is natural to assume that the price of an asset follows an Itô process. In that case, Girsanov's theorem provides a way to construct a change of measure. Girsanov's theorem is often summarized as showing the equivalence of a change of drift and a change of measure.

A Brownian motion is a martingale: $\mathrm{E}_t[Z(t+s)] = Z(t)$. A process is a martingale only for a specific probability distribution (a weighting of future outcomes). If $Z(t)$ is a martingale under the original measure, it will not generally be a martingale if we alter the measure (create a new probability distribution). Similarly, if we construct a new process

8. You should convince yourself (look carefully at equation (14)) that it is possible to change from one measure to another as follows:

$$p_j^{S_k} = p_j^{S_1}\frac{S_k(T,j)}{S_k(t)}\frac{S_1(t)}{S_1(T,j)}$$

9. Because we are using the portfolio first-order condition to value $x(T)$, we are implicitly assuming either that the cash flow is traded or else that its risk is spanned by the m traded assets, which means that the payoff can be replicated with a portfolio of traded assets. For example, we could have $x(T) = \sum_{i=1}^{n}\omega_i S_i(T)$ for some weights ω_i. Spanning can also exist when we have multiple periods between t and T, and $x(T)$ can be replicated by following some dynamic trading strategy (see Duffie and Huang, 1985). In either case, the investor has already evaluated the risks of the n assets, so the valuation of cash flows that are functions of those assets can effectively piggyback on the portfolio selection work the investor has already done. If instead $x(T)$ is a completely new and untradeable risk, then equation (4) generally does not hold for that risk. It is common to make assumptions that nevertheless permit the use of equation (4), effectively assuming that the risk of $x(T)$ is approximately spanned.

$\hat{Z}(t) = Z(t) + \eta t$, this new process will not be a martingale under the original measure, but it will be a martingale if we can construct an appropriate new measure. Girsanov's theorem shows how to transform the original probability distribution so that $Z(t) + \eta t$ *is* a martingale under the new, transformed distribution. (Of course, $Z(t)$ will not be a martingale under this new distribution.) Specifically, the following is possible:

1. Start with a Brownian process dZ and add a drift to it, to obtain the process $d\hat{Z} = dZ + \eta dt$.
2. Multiply the original probability distribution for $Z(t)$ by $\zeta(t) = \exp[-\eta Z(t) - 0.5\eta^2 t]$; this process is a positive martingale with a mean of 1. The original distribution multiplied by $\zeta(t)$ defines a new probability distribution.
3. Under this new probability distribution, $\hat{Z}(t)$ is a martingale.

Girsanov's theorem tells us that if we add a drift to a Brownian motion, we can then alter the probability distribution so as to convert the Brownian motion plus drift into a Brownian motion which has zero drift under the new distribution.

The importance of Girsanov's theorem is that it assures us that it is possible to create the risk-neutral and other distributions that arise when we change numeraire and wish to use the associated measure. Girsanov's theorem also tells us how to construct this transformation should that be necessary. We will not make active use of Girsanov's theorem, but we will refer to it. Appendix B discusses Girsanov's theorem in greater detail.

4. EXAMPLES OF NUMERAIRE AND MEASURE CHANGE

We now have most of the background to understand how changes of numeraire and measure are used in pricing derivatives. We select a convenient asset price ratio to be a martingale. We then adhere to this martingale restriction in modeling asset prices.[10]

The requirements for a pricing model that is consistent with investor utility maximization are embodied in equation (15) and its counterparts: Under the measure associated with asset i, the value of any other asset is a martingale when asset i is used as numeraire. This requirement imposes tight restrictions on the form of an acceptable pricing model. There are two issues worth emphasizing:

- *The choice of a particular numeraire provides an internally consistent framework for valuation.* Once you select a numeraire/measure combination, you are restricted by that choice. For example, we will see that standard risk-neutral pricing arises when we choose as numeraire a default-free money-market account. Under this framework, you can assume that investors expect all assets to appreciate at the current short-term risk-free rate. However, this statement is not true when using other assets as numeraire, and it is not true for objects that are not asset prices.

- *The martingale restriction does not provide any additional guidance about selecting the particular statistical process to use in modeling asset returns.* It is common to assume that a stock follows geometric Brownian motion. This is a specific, often-reasonable assumption that gives rise to analytically convenient and widely used

10. Many of the results in this section are due to Geman et al. (1995).

pricing formulas. However, *the theory we have outlined does not imply that geometric Brownian motion is correct or necessary.* Other assumptions are possible and in practice the selection should be based on empirical plausibility and practicality. Theory simply tells us that whatever process we assume must satisfy the martingale restriction associated with a particular numeraire and measure.

Throughout this section we will assume that assets do not pay dividends. You can think of this as an assumption that investors own prepaid forward contracts instead of the underlying asset. Suppose the stock follows the process

$$\frac{dS}{S} = (\alpha - \delta)dt + \sigma d\tilde{Z}$$

The prepaid forward contract price is $F^P_{t,T}(S) = S_t e^{-\delta(T-t)}$. By Itô's Lemma, the prepaid forward price follows the process

$$\frac{dF^P}{F^P} = \alpha dt + \sigma d\tilde{Z}$$

By assuming that we invest in prepaid forward contracts it is often possible to ignore dividends. Once we obtain a solution, we can express the answer in terms of the stock price by replacing $F^P_{t,T}$ with $S_t e^{-\delta(T-t)}$. Thus, in this section, we assume that all risky assets follow the process

$$\frac{dS_i(t)}{S_i(t)} = \alpha_i dt + \sigma_i d\tilde{Z}_i \tag{17}$$

We now present three commonly used numeraires and measures.

The Money-Market Account as Numeraire (Risk-Neutral Measure)

The risk-neutral measure arises when we select the money-market account as numeraire. With this numeraire choice, we measure prices of other assets in terms of money-market units.[11] We act as if asset returns follow equation (2).

The Money-Market Account. Between time t and time $t + dt$, the money-market account earns the current instantaneous risk-free rate, $r(t)$, which can be random but is known at a moment in time. An instant later, the account will appreciate at whatever rate prevails at that time, and so forth. The money-market account thus follows the process

$$\frac{dB(t)}{B(t)} = r(t)dt \tag{18}$$

If we start with an initial investment of $B(0)$ in the account, then after t periods, the value of the account is

11. You might be wondering: Why not simply use the currency (for example, dollars) as numeraire? After all, in real life we denominate prices of assets and goods in currency units. The issue is that currency does not pay interest and therefore is dominated by money-market accounts, which do pay interest. (It is of course common to hold small amounts of currency for transaction purposes, but generally not as an asset.) The use of a money-market account as numeraire effectively measures the return on one asset against another.

$$B(t) = B(0)e^{\int_0^t r(s)ds} \tag{19}$$

The value $B(t)$ is the *realized* value of the account. If $r(s)$ in equation (19) is a random variable, then $B(t)$ is also a random variable, with a value depending on the realizations of $r(s)$. At this point you can view $r(t)$ as a general stochastic process.

The Money-Market Account as Numeraire. With the money-market account as numeraire, equation (15) implies that for each of the n assets,

$$\frac{S_i(t)}{B(t)} = \mathrm{E}_t^B\left[\frac{S_i(T)}{B(T)}\right] \tag{20}$$

This states that under the measure generated by the money-market account, the ratio of the asset price to the money-market account is a martingale. Multiplying both sides by $B(t)$ and using equation (19), this can be rewritten as

$$\boxed{S_i(t) = \mathrm{E}_t^B\left[S_i(T)e^{-\int_t^T r(s)ds}\right]} \tag{21}$$

The asset price today is the expectation under the risk-neutral measure of the future asset price discounted at the *realized* money-market return. It is important to understand that the discount factor in equation (21), $\exp[-\int_t^T r(s)ds]$, is random. In general, the realizations of the stock price and the realizations of the discount factor can be correlated. This is the proper definition of risk-neutral pricing: The expected payoff is evaluated using the probability measure induced by the money-market account and discounted for each particular outcome using the realized return on the money-market account for that outcome.

In the special case when r is nonstochastic, we have

$$S_i(t) = e^{-\int_t^T r(s)ds}\mathrm{E}_t^B\left[S_i(T)\right] \tag{22}$$

This will likely seem more familiar than equation (21) because we have previously assumed that interest rates were nonstochastic.

Constructing a Process for $S_i(t)$. Assuming that $S_i(t)$ follows an Itô process, as in equation (1), Itô's Lemma implies that under the physical measure we have

$$d\left[\frac{S_i(t)}{B(t)}\right]\left[\frac{B(t)}{S_i(t)}\right] = (\alpha_i - r)dt + \sigma_i d\tilde{Z}_i \tag{23}$$

The ratio $S_i(t)/B(t)$ will not be a martingale when $\alpha \neq r$. However, we know from equation (20) that we can construct a measure such that $S_i(t)/B(t)$ is a martingale.

Let $dZ_i^B = d\tilde{Z}_i + \frac{\alpha_i - r}{\sigma_i}dt$. We can then rewrite the physical process for the stock to obtain the risk-neutral process:

$$\begin{aligned}\frac{dS_i(t)}{S_i(t)} &= \alpha_i dt + \sigma_i d\tilde{Z}_i(t)\\ &= rdt + \sigma_i\left(d\tilde{Z}_i(t) + \frac{\alpha_i - r}{\sigma_i}dt\right)\\ &= rdt + \sigma_i dZ_i^B(t) \qquad (24)\end{aligned}$$

In equilibrium, the risk premium, $\alpha - r$, is determined by investor demands resulting from utility maximization. Generally speaking, if investors are more risk-averse, $\alpha - r$ will be greater. Therefore, when we use the Sharpe ratio to construct the new measure, we implicitly account for marginal utility.

Girsanov's theorem tells us that there is a probability distribution such that $dZ_i^B(t)$ is a martingale. (Of course, $d\tilde{Z}_i(t)$ is not a martingale under this alternative distribution.) Treating $dZ_i^B(t)$ as a martingale, we can once again evaluate $d\left[S_i(t)/B(t)\right]$, obtaining

$$d\left[\frac{S_i(t)}{B(t)}\right] \times \left[\frac{B(t)}{S_i(t)}\right] = (r - r)dt + \sigma dZ_i^B = \sigma dZ_i^B \qquad (25)$$

Under the measure for which dZ^B is a martingale, $S_i(t)/B(t)$ is a martingale.

In practice, we can use the risk-neutral measure by simply replacing α_i with r for every asset.

Interpretation. It is possible for $d\tilde{Z}_i$ and dZ_i^B to both be martingales, albeit under different measures, because they represent different perspectives.

A statistician examining historical asset returns is looking at the physical measure. From this perspective, the Brownian increment $d\tilde{Z}_i$ is a martingale. The ratio $S_i(t)/B(t)$ is not a martingale when the drift on stock i and on the money-market fund are different. Someone who states that "stocks on average outperform bonds" is asserting that $\alpha_i > r$, which is a statement about the physical measure.

For a risk-averse investor, the *utility* earned from $d\tilde{Z}_i$ is *not* a martingale. It is apparent from Figure 1 that the utility gain from a unit increase in $\tilde{Z}$ will be less than the magnitude of the utility loss from a unit decrease in $\tilde{Z}$. The risk-averse investor who will not take a fair bet also will not invest in an asset with a return that is a martingale because the expected utility value is negative. This is the reason the average asset has a positive risk premium: The risk premium offsets the loss from bearing risk that is a martingale. The portfolio first-order condition, equation (5), tells us that in equilibrium, the net effect is such that returns weighted by marginal utility are a martingale.

In equation (24), we add the Sharpe ratio to $d\tilde{Z}_i$ to obtain dZ_i^B. By adding a positive Sharpe ratio to $d\tilde{Z}$, we increase the probability of outcomes when marginal utility is low (good outcomes) and decrease the probability when marginal utility is high (bad outcomes). This makes dZ^B a martingale when evaluated in terms of marginal utility. The risk-neutral process thus implicitly incorporates marginal utility into the change of measure, using the risk premium to construct the new probabilities. The economic intuition behind the change of measure is that investors in equilibrium are indifferent to a small change in the allocation of their portfolio between risky and risk-free assets. The Sharpe ratio appears in the transformation because it measures the equilibrium risk premium that investors require in order to absorb additional risk.

Although we invoked Girsanov's theorem in obtaining equation (25), in practice it is sufficient to replace α with $r(t)$ in equation (1) and discount expected payoffs at the risk-free rate. No special work is required to use the risk-neutral process; we simply proceed as if the stock had an expected return equal to the risk-free rate. The discussion in this section explains the logic behind the risk-neutral measure, but it is not necessary to duplicate these steps in practical applications.

Risky Asset as Numeraire

An arbitrary risky asset can also be numeraire. If we select asset 1, then under the associated measure, $S_i(t)/S_1(t)$ must be a martingale for each asset. To see how this works, start by assuming that all assets follow equation (2), with $\delta_i = 0$, under the risk-neutral measure. Using Itô's Lemma, we have

$$d\left[\frac{S_i(t)}{S_1(t)}\right]\frac{S_1(t)}{S_i(t)} = \frac{dS_i(t)}{S_i(t)} - \frac{dS_1(t)}{S_1(t)} + \sigma_1^2 dt - \sigma_1\sigma_i\rho_{1,i}dt$$
$$= \sigma_i dZ_i^B - \sigma_1 dZ_1^B + \sigma_1^2 dt - \sigma_1\sigma_i\rho_{1,i}dt \tag{26}$$

In general, $\sigma_1^2 \neq \sigma_1\sigma_i\rho_{1,i}$, so this expression is not a martingale. To understand the necessary change of measure when S_1 is numeraire, suppose that asset i in equation (26) is the money-market account, for which $\sigma_B^2 = 0$. Equation (26) then becomes

$$d\left[\frac{B(t)}{S_1(t)}\right]\frac{S_1(t)}{B(t)} = -\sigma_1 dZ_1^B + \sigma_1^2 dt \tag{27}$$

From equation (26), the change of measure that makes the numeraire asset a martingale is

$$dZ_1^{S_1} = dZ_1^B - \sigma_1 dt$$

Given this process for $dZ_1^{S_1}$, $S_i(t)/S_1(t)$ is a martingale provided that $dZ_i^{S_1} = dZ_i^B - \rho_{1,i}\sigma_1\sigma_i dt$. Thus, we can write

$$\frac{dS_i}{S_i} = rdt + \sigma_i dZ_i^B$$
$$= (r + \sigma_1\sigma_i\rho_{1,i})dt + \sigma_i dZ_i^{S_1} \tag{28}$$

The drift for asset i under the S_1 measure is greater by the covariance of asset i and asset 1 $(\rho_{1,i}\sigma_1\sigma_i)$, divided by the standard deviation of asset i (σ_i).

Zero Coupon Bond as Numeraire (Forward Measure)

An important special case of a risky asset as numeraire occurs when we select a zero-coupon bond maturing at time T as numeraire. The resulting measure is called the **forward measure**. Mathematically this case is identical to the preceding, but the interpretation is important enough to discuss it separately.

To understand the "forward measure" terminology, we should remember that the no-arbitrage forward price is $F_{t,T} = S_i(t)/P_t(t, T)$, where $P_t(t, T)$ is the time t price of a zero-coupon bond maturing at time T. Any time-T forward price is a martingale when the zero-coupon bond maturing at time T is used as numeraire. Thus, under the forward measure we can write

$$dF_{t,T} = \sigma dZ^F$$

The forward measure and the risk-neutral measure are different, although both use fixed income assets as numeraire. The forward measure tells us that prices deflated by zero-coupon bonds are martingales, while the risk-neutral measure tells us that prices deflated by the money-market account are martingales. Under the risk-neutral measure, asset expected returns over the next instant are equal to the instantaneous risk-free rate, $r(t)$. Under the forward measure, asset expected returns over the next instant are equal to $r(t) + \rho_{P,i}\sigma_P\sigma_i$, where $\rho_{P,i}$ is the correlation between the returns on the bond and asset i, and σ_P is the standard deviation of the bond return.

The forward measure plays an important role in interest rate models.

5. EXAMPLES OF MARTINGALE PRICING

In this section we illustrate how one can use the martingale property of asset price ratios to derive various option pricing formulas in a relatively simple fashion. We will price both an ordinary and an outperformance call option. In the first example, we will go slowly through the derivation to be clear about the logic.

We first derive the prices of two binary options: a cash-or-nothing call, which pays \$1 when $S_T > K$, and an asset-or-nothing call, which pays one share (worth S_T) when $S_T > K$. As a by-product, we will obtain the Black-Scholes formula. However, we will also obtain the pricing formula for an outperformance option and for an option where a zero-coupon bond is the underlying asset (the Black formula).

Cash-or-Nothing Call

A cash-or-nothing call pays \$1 if $S_T > K$ and 0 otherwise. We can rewrite the condition for a payoff as $S_T > KP_T(T,T)$, where $P_t(s,T)$ is the time t value of a default-free \$1 zero-coupon bond bought at s and expiring at T. By definition, we have $P_T(T,T) = 1$. Writing the strike price in this way emphasizes that the strike asset can be viewed as K zero-coupon bonds. We can also view the claim, if it is in-the-money, as paying a zero-coupon bond. The payoff can therefore be written

$$V(S_T, T) = P_T(T,T)\mathbf{1}[S_T > KP_T(T,T)] \tag{29}$$

where $\mathbf{1}(x)$ is an indicator function that takes the value one if the event x occurs and zero otherwise.

Using the stochastic discount factor to compute the value of the payoff at time 0, we have

$$\begin{aligned} V(S_0, 0) &= \mathrm{E}_0\left[\frac{U'(T)}{U'(0)}P_T(T,T) \quad \mathbf{1}[S(T) \geq KP_T(T,T)]\right] \\ &= P_0(0,T)\mathrm{E}_0\left[\frac{U'(T)P_T(T,T)}{U'(0)P_0(0,T)} \quad \mathbf{1}\left(\frac{S(T)}{P_T(T,T)} \geq K\right)\right] \\ &= P_0(0,T)\mathrm{E}_0^{P(T)}\left[\mathbf{1}\left(\frac{S(T)}{P_T(T,T)} \geq K\right)\right] \end{aligned} \tag{30}$$

In going from the second to the third line, we have implicitly multiplied the physical probabilities in the expectation by $U'(T)P_T(T,T)/U'(0)P_0(0,T)$, effecting a change of measure. The expectation $\mathrm{E}^{P(T)}$ is computed with respect to the measure that uses the zero-coupon bond as numeraire—namely, the forward measure. Under this measure, the price of any asset divided by the bond price is a martingale. The valuation problem entails computing

$$\mathrm{E}_0^{P(T)}\left[\mathbf{1}\left(\frac{S(T)}{P_T(T,T)}\geq K\right)\right]=\Pr{}^{P(T)}\left(\frac{S(T)}{P_T(T,T)}\geq K\right) \tag{31}$$

where $\mathrm{E}^{P(T)}$ and $\Pr^{P(T)}$ denote calculations with respect to the forward measure.

In order to compute equation (31), we must specify a stochastic process for the price ratio $S(t)/P_t(t,T)$; theory requires only that this process be a martingale. We will use the familiar assumption that the price ratio follows a Brownian motion with constant volatility; a different specification will lead to a different pricing model. Note that $S(t)/P_t$ is the forward price of the stock, so we are assuming that the forward price has a constant volatility.

With the constant volatility assumption, we can write

$$d\left[\frac{S(t)}{P_t(t,T)}\right]\times\frac{P_t(t,T)}{S(t)}=\sigma dZ$$

Taking the natural log of the price ratio, we have

$$d\ln\left[\frac{S(t)}{P_t(t,T)}\right]=-0.5\sigma^2 dt+\sigma dZ$$

This implies that

$$\ln\left[\frac{S(T)}{P_T(T,T)}\right]=\ln\left[\frac{S(t)}{P_t(t,T)}\right]-0.5\sigma^2(T-t)+z\sigma\sqrt{T-t}$$

where z is a standard normal random variable. The probability the option expires in-the-money is therefore

$$\begin{aligned}&\Pr{}^{P(T)}\left[\ln\left(S(T)/P_T(T,T)\right)\geq\ln(K)\right]\\&=\Pr\left[\ln(S(t)/P_t(t,T))-0.5\sigma^2(T-t)+z\sigma\sqrt{T-t}\geq\ln(K)\right]\\&=\Pr\left[-z\leq\frac{\ln[S(t)/KP_t(t,T)]-0.5\sigma^2(T-t)}{\sigma\sqrt{T-t}}\right]\end{aligned}$$

Referring back to equation (30), we have

$$V(S_t,t)=P_t(t,T)N\left(\frac{\ln[S(t)/KP_t(t,T)]-0.5\sigma^2(T-t)}{\sigma\sqrt{T-t}}\right) \tag{32}$$

Note that we can write $\ln(P_t(t,T))=-r(T-t)$, where r is the continuously compounded yield to maturity on the zero-coupon bond. Equation (32) is therefore the second term in the Black-Scholes formula:

$$V(S_t,t)=e^{-r(T-t)}N\left(\frac{\ln(S_t/K)+(r-0.5\sigma^2)(T-t)}{\sigma\sqrt{T-t}}\right)$$

Interpretation of Volatility. The derivation permitted both the stock and bond returns to be stochastic. In this case, the instantaneous σ will be the blended volatility of S_t and $P_t(t, T)$:

$$\sigma^2 = \sigma_S^2 + \sigma_P^2 - 2\rho\sigma_S\sigma_P$$

where $\rho dt = dZ_S \times dZ_P$. In practice, σ is often treated as if it were the stock volatility. For short-term options, the volatility of the stock will be substantially greater than the volatility of the bond, so that $\sigma \approx \sigma_S$. For long-term options, it is more important to account for bond price uncertainty.

An additional issue is that the volatility of the bond will change over time, generally diminishing as the bond approaches maturity. The appropriate volatility will then be the integral of the blended volatility over the life of the option.[12]

Dividends. The foregoing derivation assumed that the underlying asset did not pay a dividend. When the asset does pay a dividend, we can view the price as a prepaid forward price. It is then simple to express the derivative price in terms of the stock price, rather than the prepaid forward, by replacing the price S_t with $S_t e^{-\delta(T-t)}$. Doing so, we obtain the formula when the stock pays a continuous dividend.

Asset-or-Nothing Call

An asset-or-nothing call pays one share worth S_T if $S_T > K$ and 0 otherwise. As with the cash-or-nothing call, we compute the time 0 value of the payoff:

$$\begin{aligned} W(S_0, 0) &= \mathrm{E}_0\left[\frac{U'(T)}{U'(0)}S(T) \quad \mathbf{1}[S(T) \geq KP_T(T,T)]\right] \\ &= S(0)\mathrm{E}_0\left[\frac{U'(T)S(T)}{U'(0)S(0)} \quad \mathbf{1}[S(T) \geq KP_T(T,T)]\right] \\ &= S(0)\mathrm{E}_0^S\left\{[\mathbf{1}[S(T) \geq KP_T(T,T)]\right\} \end{aligned} \tag{33}$$

This resembles the derivation of the cash-or-nothing call. Because the payoff is a share, however, it is natural to use the stock measure rather than the forward measure. Equation (33) can be rewritten

$$\mathrm{E}_0^S\left[\mathbf{1}\left(\frac{1}{K} \geq \frac{P_T(T,T)}{S(T)}\right)\right] = \Pr{}^S\left[\frac{1}{K} \geq \frac{P_T(T,T)}{S(T)}\right] \tag{34}$$

We evaluate this probability by using the fact that, under the $S(t)$ measure, the ratio $P_t(t, T)/S(t)$ is a martingale.

Before proceeding, it is instructive to compare equation (34) with equation (31). In equation (31), $S(t)/P_t(t, T)$ is a martingale; in equation (34), the other case, the inverse is a martingale. Itô's Lemma tells us that the drifts of x and $1/x$ differ by $\sigma^2 dt$. This is the reason that the d_1 and d_2 terms in the Black-Scholes formula differ by $\sigma^2 T$.

---

12. Merton (1973b, pp. 162–169) was the first to derive a formula for a European option when interest rates are stochastic. He shows that the correct measure of total variance in the pricing formula is $\int_0^T V^2(t)dt$, where $V(t)$ is the blended volatility of the return difference between the stock and bond. This formulation assumes that the stock and bond volatility are possibly time-varying, but non-stochastic.

As in the case of the cash-or-nothing call, we will assume that the ratio is a martingale with a constant standard deviation:

$$d\left[\frac{P_t(t,T)}{S(t)}\right] \times \frac{S(t)}{P_t(t,T)} = \sigma dZ$$

Taking the natural log of the price ratio and using Itô's Lemma, we have

$$d \ln\left[\frac{P_t(t,T)}{S(t)}\right] = -0.5\sigma^2 dt + \sigma dZ$$

With this process, we have

$$\ln\left[\frac{P_T(T,T)}{S(T)}\right] = \ln\left[\frac{P_t(t,T)}{S(t)}\right] - 0.5\sigma^2(T-t) + \sigma z\sqrt{T-t}$$

where $z \sim \mathcal{N}(0, 1)$. The probability at time t is therefore

$$\Pr\left[\ln\left(P_T(T,T)/S(T)\right) \leq \ln\left(1/K\right)\right]$$

$$= \Pr\left[\ln(P_t(t,T)/S(t)) - 0.5\sigma^2(T-t) + z\sigma\sqrt{T-t} \leq \ln(1/K)\right]$$

Rearranging terms and referring back to equation (33), we have

$$W(S_0, 0) = S_0 N\left(\frac{\ln[S(t)/P_t(t,T)K] + 0.5\sigma^2(T-t)}{\sigma\sqrt{T-t}}\right) \tag{35}$$

Again, by substituting $\ln[P_t(t,T)] = -r(T-t)$, this becomes $SN(d_1)$, the first term in the Black-Scholes formula.

As with the cash-or-nothing option, the volatility is the blended volatility of the bond and stock. For the same reason as before, it is common in many applications to assume that $\sigma \approx \sigma_S$.

You may be surprised by the relative simplicity of this derivation. The first term in the Black-Scholes equation requires evaluating the conditional expectation $\mathrm{E}[S_T | S_T \geq K]$, yet we only compute a probability. The simplicity is due to the change of numeraire: When we denominate the payoff in terms of the stock, we no longer receive S_T *dollars*—instead, we receive *one share*. The payoff is then either 0 (shares) or 1 (share). The expectation of a quantity that is either 0 or 1 is equivalent to a probability calculation. The change of numeraire simplifies the derivation by converting the calculation of a conditional expectation into the calculation of a probability. These remarkable derivations are due to Geman et al. (1995).

The Black-Scholes Formula

The payoff to a call is replicated by buying one asset-or-nothing option, with value given by equation (35), and subtracting K cash-or-nothing calls, with a value given by K times equation (32):

$$S_0 N\left(\frac{\ln[S(t)/P_t(t,T)K]+0.5\sigma^2(T-t)}{\sigma\sqrt{T-t}}\right)$$
$$-KP_t(t,T)N\left(\frac{\ln[S(t)/KP_t(t,T)]-0.5\sigma^2(T-t)}{\sigma\sqrt{T-t}}\right) \tag{36}$$

The interest rate appropriate for valuing the option is the yield on a default-free bond with the same maturity as the option, and that the volatility is that of the difference between the returns on the stock and on the zero-coupon default-free bond.

European Outperformance Option

An outperformance option has the payoff $\max[S_1(T) - KS_2(T), 0]$. To value this option we can take the difference of two asset-or-nothing options, one that pays S_1 if $S_1(T) > KS_2(T)$, and the other that pays $KS_2(T)$ under the same condition. This is exactly the problem we just solved. The solution for the cash-or-nothing outperformance option is equation (32) with $P_t(t, T)$ replaced by $S_2(t)$, and the solution for the first is equation (35) with the same substitution. As before the volatility is the blended volatility.

Although outperformance options are typically discussed as if they were different than ordinary options, they are really the same. For an ordinary option, the strike asset is a zero coupon bond, while for an outperformance option, the strike asset is a stock or index.

Option on a Zero-Coupon Bond

Consider a call option expiring at time T that permits the holder to pay K to buy a zero-coupon bond with s periods to maturity. We can write the payoff as

$$\max\left[0, P_T(T, T+s) - KP_T(T, T)\right] \tag{37}$$

This is an option where the underlying asset is a zero-coupon bond maturing at time $T + s$ and the strike asset is K zero-coupon bonds maturing at time T. The structure of this option is the same as an ordinary call on a stock, with the stock price replaced by the price of the bond maturing at $T + s$. Equation (36) with S_t replaced by $P_t(t, T + s)$ is called the Black formula.

6. EXAMPLE: LONG-MATURITY PUT OPTIONS

In this section we discuss the pricing of long-dated put options. In his 2009 *Letter to Shareholders*, Berkshire-Hathaway CEO Warren Buffett offered a critique of the Black-Scholes formula for pricing puts (Buffett, 2009, pp. 18–21). See the excerpt on the next page. In this passage, Buffett explains why he thinks the Black-Scholes price for an at-the-money put option with 100 years to expiration is too high.[13]

Buffett implicitly asks how we know whether an option price is correct. We will address this question in the context of Buffett's example. Our answer will hinge on an

13. Berkshire-Hathaway had sold long-term, at-the-money put options on both domestic and foreign indices, with total strikes of \$37.1 billion. In the *Letter*, Buffett explained his rationale for this transaction.

BOX 1: Warren Buffett's Written Put Option

The following is an excerpt from Buffett (2009):

> We use [the Black-Scholes formula] when valuing our equity put options for financial statement purposes. . . . If the formula is applied to extended time periods, however, it can produce absurd results. . . .
>
> It's often useful in testing a theory to push it to extremes. So let's postulate that we sell a 100-year \$1 billion put option on the S&P 500 at a strike price of 903 (the index's level on 12/31/08). Using the implied volatility assumption for long-dated contracts that we do, and combining that with appropriate interest and dividend assumptions, we would find the "proper" Black-Scholes premium for this contract to be \$2.5 million.
>
> To judge the rationality of that premium, we need to assess whether the S&P will be valued a century from now at less than today. Certainly the dollar will then be worth a small fraction of its present value (at only 2% inflation it will be worth roughly 14¢). So that will be a factor pushing the stated value of the index higher. . . . Far more important, however, is that one hundred years of retained earnings will hugely increase the value of most of the companies in the index. Considering everything, I believe the probability of a decline in the index over a one-hundred-year period to be far less than 1%. But let's use that figure and also assume that the most likely decline—should one occur—is 50%. Under these assumptions, the mathematical expectation of loss on our contract would be \$5 million (\$1 billion × 1% × 50%). But if we had received our theoretical premium of \$2.5 million up front, we would have only had to invest it at 0.7% compounded annually to cover this loss expectancy. Everything earned above that would have been profit. Would you like to borrow money for 100 years at a 0.7% rate?
>
> Let's look at my example from a worst-case standpoint. Remember that 99% of the time we would pay nothing if my assumptions are correct. But even in the worst case among the remaining 1% of possibilities—that is, one assuming a total loss of \$1 billion—our borrowing cost would come to only 6.2%. Clearly, either my assumptions are crazy or the formula is inappropriate.

understanding of the difference between the physical and risk-neutral measures, and in particular the role of marginal utility in pricing.

The Black-Scholes Put Price Calculation

In the excerpt, Buffett does not state his assumptions. It turns out that it is easy to reproduce his price and probability calculations using the Black-Scholes formula with reasonable inputs.[14] In Buffett's example, the written options are at-the-money, so both S and K are \$1 billion, and $T = 100$. We assume that $\sigma = 0.20$, $r = 0.044$, and $\delta = 0.015$. The 4.4% interest rate is slightly greater than the 30-year rate in early 2009. The strike price is denominated in dollars and the interest rate is nominal; no adjustment is necessary for inflation. There

14. Because Buffett is discussing the Black-Scholes formula, we assume that the options are not protected against dividends. In practice, it would be possible and perhaps desirable to incorporate dividend protection into a long-term option.

are no observable 100-year option prices, and therefore we cannot obtain implied volatility or implied dividend estimates.

With these inputs, the Black-Scholes put price is $2,412,997, close to Buffett's $2.5 million. To place this price in perspective, at a 4.4% rate of interest, the $1 billion strike price has a 100-year present value of $12.277 million. The put premium of $2.4 million therefore is equal to 20% of the present value of the option's *maximum* payoff.

Is the Put Price Reasonable?

We now want to discuss Buffett's argument that the $2.4 million put price is unreasonably high. As a starting point, we should remember that the Black-Scholes formula provides the correct option price within a specific, internally consistent economic model that implicitly incorporates the investor portfolio selection problem we discussed earlier in this chapter. Given this setting, the Black-Scholes put price is a mathematical result. Any complaint about the model price must therefore be a complaint about the underlying assumptions or the posited economic model. To assess the plausibility of the assumptions, it is helpful to think about the *economics* of the option.

The Likelihood of Exercise and Expected Payoff. The option price is determined by the risk-neutral probability that the option will expire in-the-money, and the conditional expected payoff of the option. Buffett states that the probability of the put ending up in-the-money is below 1%. This is a statement about the *physical* probability that the value of the index will have increased over a 100-year horizon. If stock prices are lognormally distributed, we can compute this probability as $N(-d_2^*)$, where d_2^* uses the actual expected return on the market in place of the risk-free rate. For example, if we assume that the equity index risk premium is 4%, we would substitute 8.4% for the 4.4% risk-free rate, obtaining $N(-d_2^*) = 0.0071$, a probability less than 1%.

Buffett assumes that the expected loss on the index, conditional on the index underperforming bonds, will be 50%. This is again a statement about the physical distribution. With an 8.4% expected return on the market, the expectation of $1 billion of the index conditional on $S_{100} < S_0$ is $596,452,294, or 59.6% of the current index value. Again, this is close to Buffett's assumption.

The probability and value of the index conditional on the put being in-the- money are presented in Table 1, for a variety of assumed risk premiums. Calculations under the risk-neutral measure are in the first row, where the risk premium is zero. Calculations in the other rows are under the physical measure and depend upon the assumed risk premium. Given the other assumed Black-Scholes inputs, Buffett's statements about the likely future behavior of the index correspond to assuming that the risk premium is about 4%.

It is worth noting that Buffett's calculations ignore the different marginal utilities associated with good and bad performance of the index. If the S&P index were to sustain a 50% loss over the next 100 years, the economy would have performed poorly and we would expect marginal utility at that time to be high. This is why the Black-Scholes price may seem high.

Understanding the Option Price. Following Buffett, we can view put writing as borrowing and compute the expected borrowing cost. The expected payout on the option is the expected payoff conditional upon the option expiring in-the-money, times the probability that it expires in-the-money. We can divide this expected cost by the option price and convert it to a rate of return. Buffett's calculation assumes that the option seller receives $2.5 million

TABLE 1 Risk premium, physical probability of put exercise, and expected index value conditional on exercise. Assumes the underlying asset is \$1 billion of the index, the strike equals \$1 billion, and $\sigma = 0.20$, $T = 100$ years, $\delta = 0.015$, and $r = 0.044$. The expected index return is the risk-free rate plus the risk premium. The Black-Scholes put price for these inputs is \$2.413 million.

Risk Premium	Expected Index Return	Physical Probability that $S_T \leq K$	$E_0(S_T \mid S_T < K)$ (Millions of \$)
0.00	0.044	0.3264	\$397.77
0.01	0.054	0.1711	\$458.88
0.02	0.064	0.0735	\$511.91
0.03	0.074	0.0256	\$557.45
0.04	0.084	0.0071	\$596.45
0.05	0.094	0.0016	\$629.93

today and in 100 years will pay \$500 million with a 1% probability:

$$\frac{1}{T}\ln\left[\frac{E_0(K - S_T \mid S_T < K) \times \Pr(S_T < K)}{\text{Put price}}\right] = \frac{1}{100}\ln\left[\frac{(1000 - 500) \times 0.01}{2.500}\right] = 0.007 \tag{38}$$

This is an expected borrowing cost of 0.7%. Using the numbers we computed above for a 4% risk premium, the written option looks like an even better deal:

$$\frac{1}{100}\ln\left[\frac{(1000 - 596.45) \times 0.0071}{2.412}\right] = 0.002$$

The expected annual borrowing cost here is 0.2%.

In contrast to calculations under the physical measure, the risk-neutral calculation implicitly weights the physical probabilities by marginal utilities, and therefore takes into account the high marginal utility associated with a market decline. Examine the first row of Table 1. The risk-neutral probability that the put will be in-the-money is $N(-d_2) = 0.326$. The expected value of the index conditional on the put being in-the-money is \$397.77 million, giving a conditional average payoff equal to 60% of the maximum possible payoff.

Repeating the expected borrowing cost calculation in equation (38), but using risk-neutral quantities, there is a 32.6% probability that the option will be exercised. When the put is exercised, the average payoff will be 60% of the maximum possible payoff. The implicit borrowing cost in this case is

$$\frac{1}{T}\ln\left[\frac{E_0(K - S_T \mid S_T < K) \times \Pr(S_T < K)}{\text{Put price}}\right] = \frac{1}{100}\ln\left[\frac{(1000 - 397.77) \times 0.3264}{2.412}\right] = 0.044$$

In other words, under the risk-neutral measure the expected cost of borrowing by selling a 100-year put is 4.4%. This is the risk-free rate used to price the put. The Black-Scholes put price formula is internally consistent, as it must be.

You can repeat Buffett's analysis for different rows in Table 1. The greater the risk premium you assume, the lower will be the expected borrowing cost under the physical measure.

Discussion

As we discussed earlier in the chapter, an investor who is optimally selecting a portfolio, and who is unconstrained, would invest in different risky assets to the point where the risk premium for an asset just compensates for the additional risk due to the additional investment. This is the investor described by the portfolio first-order condition, equation (5). Such an investor would be indifferent to small portfolio reallocations and would have no incentive to take an additional large leveraged bet on the market.

An investor who, by contrast, is constrained—who for some reason is not able to take as long or short a position as desired—would look for opportunities to invest in a fashion that makes the constraint less binding. To take one example, consider an investor who is fully invested in stocks but nevertheless finds the risk premium for stocks attractively high. Some ways to exploit this perception would include borrowing to buy more of the index, entering into an index swap or forward contract, buying an index call, or selling an index put. All of these are simply leveraged equity bets that make money if the index outperforms bonds. Buffett's sale of index put options is thus consistent with an optimistic view about the stock index that has not been completely offset by investing in the index.[15] An end-of-chapter problem asks you to speculate about why Buffett selected put writing as opposed to some of these other strategies.

A more general version of Buffett's argument is that stocks are a good investment for the "long run" because stocks on average are expected to outperform bonds. Such discussions typically do not take into account the difference in marginal utilities associated with gains and losses. One example of a decision based on the positive risk premium is presented in Box 2, which discusses the Pension Benefit Guaranty Corporation's trust fund, in what assets it should be invested, how it should be hedged, and the role that the risk premium plays in its risk-management decisions.

CHAPTER SUMMARY

Investors at all times must decide how to invest their savings. This portfolio decision by investors determines the equilibrium demand for different assets and thus the pricing of assets. Investors selecting optimal portfolios give up utility today for expected utility in the future. The portfolio selection first-order condition (the mathematical condition that holds when an investor holds an optimal portfolio) states that the utility investors give up

15. There are also explanations for option-selling that rely on investors having different utility functions. Leland (1980) and Brennan and Solanki (1981) show that investors will demand concave payoffs (e.g., selling a call or put) if their absolute risk aversion increases less rapidly than that of the aggregate investor.

BOX 2: Hedging the PBGC's Liabilities

The Pension Benefit Guaranty Corporation (PBGC) is a quasi-public corporation that was created in 1974 by the U.S. Congress as part of the Employee Retirement Income Security Act (ERISA). The PBGC insures defined-benefit corporate pension plans, in which the corporation promises retirees a fixed sum for the rest of their lives. (In the other leading form of retirement plan, "defined contribution," employees fund their own retirement with their accumulated savings.) Prior to ERISA, if the corporation failed, its retirees most likely lost their pensions. Corporations pay for PBGC insurance by making annual insurance payments into the PBGC's trust fund, which is used to rescue failed pension plans.

How should the PBGC invest its trust fund? To answer this, we first need to understand the risk the PBGC faces. The PBGC must make pension payments if two things occur. First, a company must fail, and second, the pension must have insufficient assets to meet its obligations. The PBGC on average will make insurance payments when the stock market falls—some companies will fail, and their pension funds will also likely have declined in value. The delta of the PBGC insurance liability is therefore positive: When the stock market falls, the PBGC expects to make greater payments. The logic of delta-hedging suggests that in order to hedge its exposure, the PBGC trust fund should *short* the shares of companies it insures.

To restate this from an economic perspective, PBGC insurance will be called upon at times when marginal utility is high. Logically, the insurer should invest in positions that increase in value, or at least do not decrease, when marginal utility increases. Government bonds and short-equity positions both satisfy this requirement.

You can probably imagine the corporate and congressional reaction if a government entity were to short-sell corporate stock. With shorting politically infeasible, the PBGC could instead invest the trust fund in government bonds. In practice, what does the PBGC do?

Prior to 2008, the trust fund had largely been invested in bonds. In 2008, at the urging of PBGC director Charles E. F. Millard, the PBGC board adopted an Investment Policy Statement calling for it to invest more in stocks. The rationale was that the fund would earn the higher average return on stocks. Of course, from a risk-management perspective, investing the PBGC's trust fund in stocks is a "Texas Hedge": a strategy that increases risk rather than reducing it. Boston University Finance Professor Zvi Bodie "likened the agency's strategy to a company that insures against hurricane damage and then invests the premiums in beachfront property" ("Pension Insurer Shifted to Stocks," *Boston Globe*, March 30, 2009).

Ultimately, 18 months after announcing it would invest more in stocks, and in the wake of much criticism, the PBGC board decided to reduce investment in public equities.

today to buy an asset must equal the additional utility expected in the future. This first-order condition also implies that the ratio of any two asset prices is a martingale under an appropriately constructed probability distribution.

Price ratios arise naturally when we choose a numeraire—i.e., denominate the value of an asset in terms of another asset. Given a numeraire, the construction of a new probability distribution is called a change of measure. Each choice of numeraire implies a change of measure under which asset price ratios are a martingale. The requirement that asset price ratios be a numeraire imposes a restriction on the behavior of asset price ratios and thus on asset prices.

Selecting different assets as numeraire gives rise to different standard asset pricing models. When a risk-free money-market account is the numeraire, the distribution that makes price ratios a martingale is the risk-neutral distribution. When a zero-coupon bond price is selected as numeraire, bond and interest rate forward prices are martingales.

The idea that asset price ratios are martingales can be used to simplify derivations of pricing formulas. The two components of the Black-Scholes formula, for example, can be separately derived, each using a different numeraire.

The fact that derivative pricing formulas are intimately connected with portfolio decisions by investors provides insight into the economics underlying derivative pricing models. For example, Warren Buffett's argument that the Black-Scholes put price gives unreasonable prices for very long-term puts must ultimately be interpretable in terms of the pricing of stocks and bonds.

FURTHER READING

Risk-neutral pricing is implicit in the original option pricing derivation in Black and Scholes (1973). However, Cox and Ross (1976) were the first to systematically exploit the idea that one could price options as if investors were risk-neutral. The link between risk-neutral pricing and the consumption and portfolio choice problems was first articulated in Harrison and Kreps (1979). Finally, the systematic development of the martingale approach to pricing is presented in Geman et al. (1995). Warren Buffett's discussion of his option writing strategy is in Buffett (2009; see especially pp. 19–21).

PROBLEMS

1. Let c be consumption. Under what conditions on the parameters λ_0 and λ_1 could the following functions serve as utility functions for a risk-averse investor? (Remember that marginal utility must be positive and the function must be concave.)

a. $U(c) = \lambda_0 \exp(\lambda_1 c)$

b. $U(c) = \lambda_0 c^{\lambda_1}$

c. $U(c) = \lambda_0 c + \lambda_1 c^2$

2. Use a change of numeraire and measure to verify that the value of a claim paying K if $S_T < K$ is $Ke^{-rT}N(-d_2)$. (Note that this is the first term in the Black-Scholes put price. You can mimic the derivation in the text for a cash-or-nothing call.)

3. Use a change of numeraire and measure to verify that the value of a claim paying S_T if $S_T < K$ is $SN(-d_1)$. (Note that this is the second term in the Black-Scholes put price. You can mimic the derivation in the text for an asset-or-nothing call.)

4. Suppose that S_1 and S_2 follow geometric Brownian motion and pay continuous proportional dividends at the rates δ_1 and δ_2. Use the martingale argument to show that the value of a claim paying $S_1(T)$ if $S_1(T) > KS_2(T)$ is

$$S_1(t)e^{-\delta_1(T-t)}N\left(\frac{\ln(S_1(t)/KS_2(t)) + (\delta_2 - \delta_1 + 0.5\sigma^2)(T-t)}{\sigma\sqrt{T-t}}\right)$$

where $\sigma^2 = \sigma_1^2 + \sigma_2^2 - 2\rho_{1,2}\sigma_1\sigma_2$ and δ_1 and δ_2 are the dividend yields on the two stocks.

5. Under the same assumptions as the previous problem, show that the value of a claim paying $S_2(T)$ if $S_1(T) > KS_2(T)$ is

$$S_2(t)e^{-\delta_2(T-t)}N\left(\frac{\ln(S_1(t)/KS_2(t)) + (\delta_2 - \delta_1 - 0.5\sigma^2)(T-t)}{\sigma\sqrt{T-t}}\right)$$

where σ^2, δ_1, and δ_2 are defined as in the previous problem.

In the next set of problems you will use Monte Carlo valuation. Assume that $S_0 = \$41$, $K = \$40$, $P_0 = 0.9802$, $\sigma = 0.30$, $T = 0.25$, and $\delta = 0$.

6. In this problem we will use Monte Carlo to simulate the behavior of the martingale S_t/P_t, with P_t as numeraire. Let $x_0 = S_0/P_0(0, T)$. Simulate the process

$$x_{t+h} = (1 + \sigma\sqrt{h}Z_{t+h})x_t$$

Let h be approximately 1 day.

a. Evaluate $P_0\text{E}\left[S_T/P_T(T, T) > K\right]$.

b. Compute the mean and standard deviation of the difference $x_T - x_0$. Did you simulate a martingale?

c. Verify that the result is approximately the same as the price of a cash-or-nothing call computed as $e^{-rT}N(d_2)$ ($0.5766 for the above parameters).

7. We now use Monte Carlo to simulate the behavior of the martingale P_t/S_t, with S_t as numeraire. Let $x_0 = P_0(0, T)/S_0$. Simulate the process

$$x_{t+h} = (1 + \sigma\sqrt{h}Z_{t+h})x_t$$

Let h be approximately 1 day.

a. Evaluate $S_0\text{E}\left[P_T(T, T)/S_T < 1/K\right]$.

b. Compute the mean and standard deviation of the difference $x_T - x_0$. Verify that you have simulated a martingale.

c. Verify that the result is approximately the same as the price of an asset-or-nothing call computed as $S_0N(d_1)$ ($26.4617 for the above parameters).

8. Suppose that the stock price follows a jump-diffusion process. Let the jump intensity be $\lambda = 0.75$, the expected jump $\exp(\alpha_J)$, with $\alpha_J = -0.15$, and let the jump volatility be $\sigma_J = 0.25$. You can simulate the behavior of the martingale S_t/P_t as

$$x_{t+h} = [1 - \lambda kh + \sigma\sqrt{h}Z_{t+h} + J(Y-1)]x_t$$

where $k = \exp(\alpha_J) - 1$, $J = 1$ indicates a jump and $J = 0$ otherwise, and $Y = e^{\alpha_J - 0.5\sigma_J^2 + \sigma_J W_t}$, with W_t standard normal. Let h be approximately 1 day.

a. Evaluate $P_0\text{E}\left[S_T/P_T(T, T) > K\right]$.

b. Compute the mean and standard deviation of the difference $x_T - x_0$. Verify that you have simulated a martingale.

c. Verify that the result is approximately the same as the price of a cash-or-nothing call ($0.5865 for the above parameters).

9. Suppose that S_1 and S_2 are correlated, non-dividend-paying assets that follow geometric Brownian motion. Specifically, let $S_1(0) = S_2(0) = \$100$, $r = 0.06$, $\sigma_1 = 0.35$, $\sigma_2 = 0.25$, $\rho = 0.40$ and $T = 1$. Verify that the following two procedures for valuing an outperformance option give a price of approximately \$13.464.

a. Use Monte Carlo simulation to simulate both $S_1(T)$ and $S_2(T)$ to value the payoff

$$\max(0, S_1(T) - S_2(T))$$

(*Hint:* Make sure that you account for the correlation between S_1 and S_2.)

b. Use Monte Carlo simulation to simulate only $S_1(T)/S_2(T)$, and value the payoff

$$S_2(0)\max(0, S_1(T)/S_2(T) - 1)$$

10. Repeat the previous problem assuming that $\delta_1 = 0.05$ and $\delta_2 = 0.12$. Verify that both procedures give a price of approximately \$15.850.

11. Suppose there are 1-, 2-, and 3-year zero-coupon bonds, with prices given by P_1, P_2, and P_3. The implied forward interest rate from year 1 to 2 is $r_0(1, 2) = P_1/P_2 - 1$, and from year 2 to 3 is $r_0(2, 3) = P_2/P_3 - 1$. Denote the rates as $r(1)$ and $r(2)$. Suppose that you select the 3-year bond as numeraire.

a. Explain why $r(2)$ is a martingale, but $r(1)$ is not.

b. The price ratio P_1/P_3 is a martingale. What is the interpretation of this ratio?

c. Suppose that P_1/P_3 and P_2/P_3 both follow geometric Brownian motion with zero drift, volatilies σ_{13} and σ_{23}, and correlation $\rho\, dt$. What is the process followed by $r(1)$?

12. Assume the same bonds and numeraire as in the previous question. Suppose that P_1/P_3 is a martingale following a geometric Brownian process with annual standard deviation $\sigma_1 = 0.10$, and that P_2/P_3 is a martingale following a geometric Brownian process with annual standard deviation $\sigma_2 = 0.05$. The correlation between the two processes is 0.9.

a. Verify by simulation that the drift per unit time for $(P_1/P_3)/(P_2/P_3)$ is $\sigma_2^2 - \rho\sigma_1\sigma_2$.

b. Discuss the implications of the answer to (a) if you are pricing a claim, such as a swaption, for which the payoff depends upon both $r(1)$ and $r(2)$.

13. A box in the chapter discusses the following result: If the strike price of a European put is set to equal the forward price for the stock, the put premium increases with maturity.

a. How is this result related to Warren Buffett's critique of put-pricing, discussed in Section 6?

b. This problem is intentionally omitted for this edition.

14. Under the social security system in the United States, workers pay taxes and receive a monthly annuity after retirement. Some have argued that the United States should invest the social security tax proceeds in stocks. The rationale is that, over time, there is a decreasing probability that stocks will underperform bonds. The social security system would thus benefit from the higher expected return on stocks.

Making use of the put-pricing discussion in Section 6, comment on this proposal.

15. Warren Buffett stated in the 2009 *Letter to Shareholders*: "Our derivatives dealings require our counterparties to make payments to us when contracts are initiated. Berkshire therefore always holds the money, which leaves us assuming no meaningful counterparty risk." Buffett also was not required to make collateral payments to counterparties on these contracts. With these considerations in mind, explain how you think Buffett might have evaluated the costs and benefits of the following long investment strategies: purchased call, written put, long index swap, long index futures, written collar.

Appendix A THE PORTFOLIO SELECTION PROBLEM

An investor at time t has wealth $W(t)$, consumes $C(t)$, and invests the difference, $W(t) - C(t)$. As a result of consuming $C(t)$, the investor receives utility $U[C(t), t]$, which is denominated in terms of time 0 utility units. The investor can select from among n different assets. We will analyze the portfolio selection problem without specifying the assets, but among them are ordinary stocks, a money-market account, and a zero-coupon bond.

In the examples in this appendix, investors make portfolio selections in discrete time. The theory generalizes to continuous time, but our goal is to provide intuition and context rather than to present the general theory.

The One-Period Portfolio Selection Problem

In the simplest version of the problem, the investor consumes at times t and $t + h$, selecting a portfolio at time t. This version of the problem considers the first two entries on the timeline in Figure 2, ignoring the rest. Let $S_i(t)$ denote the time t price of asset i and $N_i(t)$ the number of units invested in asset i. The total investment must equal wealth remaining after consumption, so we have

$$W(t) - C(t) = \sum_{i=1}^{n} N_i(t)S_i(t) \tag{39}$$

At $t + h$, there are new prices for the n securities, and wealth is

FIGURE 2

Timeline illustrating the consumption and portfolio investment decisions.

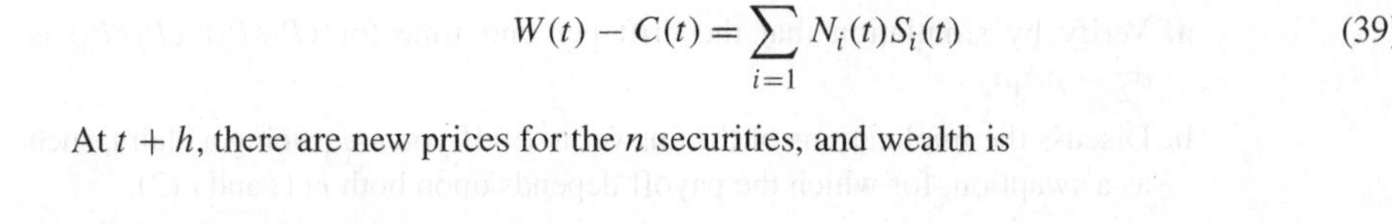

$$W(t+h) = \sum_{i=1}^{n} N_i(t)S_i(t+h) \tag{40}$$

This expression evaluates wealth given the quantities selected at time t. The investor's problem is to choose $C(t)$ and $N_i(t)$, $i = \{1, 2, \ldots, n\}$, so as to maximize

$$U[C(t), t] + \mathrm{E}_t\{U[C(t+h), t+h]\} \tag{41}$$

If there are only two periods, the investor consumes everything at time $t+h$, so $C(t+h) = W(t+h)$.

We can solve for the investor's optimal portfolio by replacing $C(t)$ in equation (41) with equation (39) and $C(t+h)$ with $W(t+h)$ from (40). The sole-choice variables are then the n portfolio weights, $N_i(t)$.

The first-order conditions for maximizing equation (41) are

$$U'(t)S_i(t) = \mathrm{E}_t[U'(t+h)S_i(t+h)] \quad i = 1, \ldots, n \tag{42}$$

where $U'(t) \equiv \partial U[C(t)]/\partial C(t)$ with $U'(t+h)$ defined analogously. We refer to $U'(t)$ and $U'(t+h)$ as the marginal utility of consumption at time t and $t+h$. Define the ratio of marginal utilities as

$$\chi_{t,t+h} \equiv \frac{U'(t+h)}{U'(t)} \tag{43}$$

The expression $\chi_{t,t+h}$ is the stochastic discount factor or **pricing kernel**. The factor $\chi_{t,t+h}$ is a random variable because $U'(t+h)$ depends on the investment portfolio's rate of return; $U'(t+h)$ is large when the return is low and low when the return is large. Because marginal utilities are nonnegative, $\chi_{t,t+h}$ is nonnegative.

Equation (42) is the key equation that we will use to discuss risk-neutral pricing. It is helpful to rewrite the first-order conditions using the stochastic discount factor. Dividing both sides of equation (42) by $U'(t)S_i(t)$, we obtain

$$1 = \mathrm{E}_t\left[\chi_{t,t+h}\frac{S_i(t+h)}{S_i(t)}\right] \tag{44}$$

Equation (44) states that the present value of the gross return on the stock is \$1.[16] In equation (44), the stochastic discount factor serves as a present value factor. Equation (44) states that the present value of \$1 invested in any asset is \$1. A different way to say the same thing is that the expectation of the product of the stochastic discount factor and 1 plus an asset return is 1.

The stochastic discount factor is closely related to the interest rate. In the special case where asset i is a \$1 default-free zero-coupon bond maturing at time $t+h$, we have

$$1 = \mathrm{E}_t\left[\chi_{t,t+h}\frac{1}{P_t(t, t+h)}\right]$$

We therefore have

$$P_t(t, t+h) = \mathrm{E}_t\left[\chi_{t,t+h}\right]$$

16. Put differently, an investment of \$1 in the stock will purchase $1/S_i(t)$ shares, yielding $S_i(t+h)/S_i(t)$. Thus, the condition states that the present value of \$1 invested in a stock is \$1.

Thus, the price of a zero-coupon bond is the expected stochastic discount factor. Rewriting this expression, we see that the return on the zero-coupon bond is the inverse of the expectation of the stochastic discount factor:

$$\frac{1}{P_t(t, t+h)} = \frac{1}{\mathrm{E}_t[\chi_{t,t+h}]} \tag{45}$$

The Risk Premium of an Asset

The solution to the portfolio problem tells us whether assets have a positive or negative risk premium. First, recall that by the definition of covariance, if x and y are random variables, we have

$$\mathrm{Cov}(x, y) = \mathrm{E}(xy) - \mathrm{E}(x)\mathrm{E}(y)$$

Using this expression, we can rewrite equation (44) (which tells us that $\mathrm{E}(xy) = 1$) as

$$1 = \mathrm{E}_t\left[\chi_{t,t+h}\right]\mathrm{E}_t\left[\frac{S_i(t+h)}{S_i(t)}\right] + \mathrm{Cov}\left[\chi_{t,t+h}, \frac{S_i(t+h)}{S_i(t)}\right]$$

Dividing by the expected stochastic discount factor and using equation (45), we obtain

$$\mathrm{E}_t\left[\frac{S_i(t+h)}{S_i(t)}\right] - \frac{1}{P_t(t, t+h)} = -\,\mathrm{Cov}\left[\chi_{t,t+h}, \frac{S_i(t+h)}{S_i(t)}\right]\frac{1}{P_t(t, t+h)} \tag{46}$$

The left-hand side of this expression is the difference between the expected return on the asset and the return on the h-period zero-coupon bond. The right-hand side is the negative of the covariance between the asset and the stochastic discount factor.

The key to understanding equation (46) is to think about the relationship between consumption and asset returns, keeping in mind that the stochastic discount factor is high (marginal utility is high) when consumption is low and vice versa. Thus, an asset that has a low return when the stochastic discount factor is high (a negative covariance) is one that has a low return when consumption is low. Investors will require a positive risk premium to hold such an asset, and this is confirmed by equation (46).

By contrast, an asset that has a high return when the stochastic discount factor is high (consumption is low) provides insurance. Such an asset will have a negative risk premium, again as confirmed by equation (46).

Equation (46) implies a discount factor for the stock. We can write

$$S_i(t) = \frac{\mathrm{E}_t[S_i(t+h)]}{1+\alpha}$$

where

$$1+\alpha = \frac{1}{P_t(t, t+h)}\left(1 - \mathrm{Cov}\left[\chi_{t,t+h}, S_i(t+h)\right]\right) \tag{47}$$

The discount factor over a period of length h is the zero-coupon bond yield adjusted by the covariance between the stock price and the marginal utility of consumption.

Multiple Consumption and Investment Periods

What if the investor makes saving and investment decisions for more than two periods? The first-order conditions will look the same. The maximization problem is harder because a decision at time t has ramifications for all periods after t, rather than just one period. The two-period problem is special, but it shares important features with the more general problem. See Cochrane (2001) and Duffie (2001) as references.

The relationship in equation (42) holds for any two dates in the future. Suppose there were a time $T+s$, and that we solved the consumption and portfolio problem for times t and T, and for T and $T+s$. The conditions for optimality look the same each period, so the solution for portfolio holdings at time T would look like the solution at time t. For stocks, we would have

$$\begin{aligned} S_t U'(C_t) &= \mathrm{E}_t\left[U'(C_T)S_T\right] \\ &= \mathrm{E}_t\left[\mathrm{E}_T\{U'(C_{T+s})S_{T+s}\}\right] \\ &= \mathrm{E}_t\left[U'(C_{T+s})S_{T+s}\right] \end{aligned}$$

The second line computes the time t expectation of the time T expectation. The expectation $\mathrm{E}_t\mathrm{E}_T$ becomes E_t: We don't expect a change in the expectation as time progresses. This is called the *law of iterated expectations*. It is possible to generalize this problem with additional assets and time periods, but equation (42) remains the cornerstone of modern asset pricing.

Appendix B GIRSANOV'S THEOREM

Girsanov's theorem shows how a Brownian process, $Z(t)$, can be transformed into a new process, $d\tilde{Z}(t) = dZ(t) + \eta dt$, that is a martingale under a transformed probability distribution.[17]

The Theorem

Theorem 1 (Girsanov's theorem) Let $Z(t)$ be a Brownian motion under the probability density $f(t)$. Then $\tilde{Z}(t) = Z(t) + \eta t$ is a Brownian motion under the probability density $\zeta(t) f(t)$, where $\zeta(t) = \exp(-\eta Z(t) - 0.5\eta^2 t)$.

Note that under the original probability distribution, $\zeta(t) > 0$ and $\mathrm{E}_t\zeta(t+h) = 1$, so $\zeta(t)$ is positive and a martingale. Adding a drift to $dZ(t)$ makes some outcomes more likely and others less likely. The Girsanov transformation effectively increases the probability density for those outcomes rendered less likely, and decreases it for those rendered more likely.

To understand this result, the probability density function for a normal variable with variance t is

$$f(t) = \exp\left[-\frac{1}{2t}Z(t)^2\right]\frac{1}{\sqrt{2\pi t}}$$

17. An early appearance of Girsanov's theorem in the context of asset pricing is in Harrison and Kreps (1979). The result is discussed in depth in Duffie (2001), Karatzas and Shreve (1991, sect. 3.5), Baxter and Rennie (1996), and Neftci (2000, chap. 14).

You can see how the Girsanov transformation works by examining $\zeta(t)f(t)$. Writing out $\zeta(t)$ and combining terms, we obtain

$$\zeta(t)\exp\left[-\frac{1}{2t}Z(t)^2\right]\frac{1}{\sqrt{2\pi t}}=\exp\left[-\frac{1}{2t}(Z(t)+\eta t)^2\right]\frac{1}{\sqrt{2\pi t}}$$

The last expression is the probability density for a normally distributed variable with mean $-\eta t$ and variance t. The process $\tilde{Z}(t)$ is a martingale with respect to this distribution, which changes the distribution so as to subtract the drift that has been added.

Constructing Multi-Asset Processes from Independent Brownian Motions

To facilitate understanding of multi-asset processes and change of measure, it is helpful to write the processes for a set of risky assets based on m independent Brownian motions, $dW_k(t)$. Specifically, consider two equivalent ways to write a process for S_i. First, we write

$$\frac{dS_i(t)}{S_i(t)}=\alpha_i dt+\hat{\sigma}_i dZ_i$$

Then, we write dZ_i as the weighted sum of independent Brownian motions by letting $\hat{\sigma}_i dZ_i=\sum_{k=1}^m \sigma_{ik}dW_k$, where $\sum_{k=1}^m \sigma_{ik}^2=\hat{\sigma}_i^2$. We therefore have

$$\frac{dS_i(t)}{S_i(t)}=\alpha_i dt+\sum_{k=1}^m \sigma_{ik}dW_k \tag{48}$$

The covariance between stock i and stock j will be

$$\sigma_{i,j}=\sum_{k=1}^m \sigma_{ik}\sigma_{jk}$$

If we have n correlated assets, then using the set of $\hat{\sigma}_i$, and pairwise covariance among the n stocks, it is straightforward to construct the equivalent processes in terms of m independent Brownian motions by using the Cholesky decomposition.

Risk-Neutral Measure. Each source of risk, dW_k, has its own Sharpe ratio, ϕ_k.[18] In general, a stock will be driven by multiple sources of risk, so its total expected return will depend on the weighting of these risks. For stock i, we have

$$\alpha_i-r=\sum_{k=1}^m \sigma_{ik}\phi_k$$

With these substitutions, we can write the process for dS_i, equation (48), as

18. If a stock followed the process $dS_i/S_i=\alpha_i dt+\sigma_{i1}dW_1$, with $\sigma_{ik}=0$ for $k>1$, it would have the drift $\alpha_i=r+\sigma_{i1}\phi_1$.

$$
\begin{aligned}
\frac{dS_i(t)}{S_i(t)} &= \left(r + \sum_{k=1}^{m} \sigma_{ik}\phi_k \right) dt + \sum_{k=1}^{m} \sigma_{ik} dW_k \\
&= r dt + \sum_{k=1}^{m} \sigma_{ik}(dW_k + \phi_k dt) \\
&= r dt + \sum_{k=1}^{m} \sigma_{ik} dW_k^B
\end{aligned} \tag{49}
$$

We obtain the second equality by invoking Girsanov's theorem, which allows us to construct a new measure under which the new diffusions, $dW_k^B = dW_k + \phi_k$, are martingales.

Risky Asset as Numeraire. Each asset follows the risk-neutral process in equation (49). From equation (26), the n diffusion terms of the numeraire risky asset (asset 1) must follow the process

$$
dW_k^{S_1} = dW_k - \sigma_{1,k} dt
$$

Note that diffusions with $\sigma_{1,k} = 0$ are unadjusted. Writing the diffusion as a sum of independent diffusions makes clear that there is a unique way to adjust the processes that drive all assets.

Now consider the ratio S_i/S_1. Under the risk-neutral measure, this follows the process

$$
d\left[\frac{S_i(t)}{S_1(t)}\right]\frac{S_1(t)}{S_i(t)} = \sum_{k=1}^{m} \sigma_{ik} dW_k - \sum_{k=1}^{m} \sigma_{1k} dW_k + \sum_{k=1}^{m} \sigma_{1k}^2 dt - \sum_{i=1}^{m} \sigma_{1k}\sigma_{ik} dt
$$

We can simplify this as follows:

$$
\begin{aligned}
d\left[\frac{S_i(t)}{S_1(t)}\right]\frac{S_1(t)}{S_i(t)} &= \sum_{k=1}^{m} \sigma_{ik}(dW_k - \sigma_{1k} dt) - \sum_{k=1}^{m} \sigma_{1k}(dW_k - \sigma_{1k} dt) \\
&= \sum_{k=1}^{m} \sigma_{ik} dW_k^{S_1} - \sum_{k=1}^{m} \sigma_{1k} dW_k^{S_1}
\end{aligned}
$$

Thus, the ratio is a martingale under the S_1 measure.

Appendix C RISK-NEUTRAL PRICING AND MARGINAL UTILITY IN THE BINOMIAL MODEL

Appendix available at http://www.pearsonhighered.com/mcdonald.

Exotic Options II

There are two main themes in this chapter. First, we introduce a variety of simple options such as all-or-nothing options that can be used as components for building more complex options. Second, we will examine options that depend on prices of more than one asset, such as quantos and rainbow options.

Throughout this chapter, we will assume that there are two assets that follow the processes

$$\frac{dS}{S} = (\alpha - \delta)dt + \sigma dZ \tag{1}$$

$$\frac{dQ}{Q} = (\alpha_Q - \delta_Q)dt + \sigma_Q dZ_Q \tag{2}$$

The correlation between dZ and dZ_Q is ρdt.

1. ALL-OR-NOTHING OPTIONS

We begin with a discussion of simple all-or-nothing options, which pay the holder a discrete amount of cash or a share if some particular event occurs. These are described as all-or-nothing (also called *binary* or *digital* options) because the payoff can be thought of as 0 or 1: Either you receive the cash or share, or you do not.

Terminology

There are many different kinds of all-or-nothing options; payoffs can be contingent on the stock price at expiration, as well as on whether the stock price has hit a barrier over the life of the option. We are interested in these options in and of themselves, and also because they are building blocks, useful for constructing variants of ordinary puts and calls as well as barrier options.

Naming all of these options can be a complex task. Table 1 describes the naming scheme we will use. The terminology will make sense as we introduce the various claims.

To see how the naming scheme works, consider the cash-or-nothing option. One kind of cash-or-nothing option pays the holder \$1 at time T if the stock price is greater than K.

From Chapter 23 of *Derivatives Markets*, Third Edition, Robert McDonald. Copyright © 2013 by Pearson Education, Inc. Published by Pearson Prentice Hall. All rights reserved.

TABLE 1 Option nomenclature used in this chapter.

Notation	Meaning
Asset	Payment at expiration is one unit of the asset
Cash	Payment at expiration is \$1
Call	Payment received if $S_T > K$
Put	Payment received if $S_T < K$
UI	Up and in: Payment received only if barrier $H > S_0$ is hit
DI	Down and in: Payment received only if barrier $H < S_0$ is hit
UO	Up and out: Payment received only if barrier $H > S_0$ is not hit
DO	Down and out: Payment received only if barrier $H < S_0$ is not hit
UR	Up rebate: Rebate received at the time the barrier, $H > S_0$, is hit
DR	Down rebate: Rebate received at the time the barrier, $H < S_0$, is hit
URDeferred	Same as UR, except \$1 paid at expiration
DRDeferred	Same as DR, except \$1 paid at expiration

The condition under which it pays off, $S_T > K$, is like that for an ordinary call option, but it is not an ordinary call, because it pays \$1 instead of $S_T - K$. We will identify an option like this as a "cash call" (*CashCall*), i.e., a contract that pays cash under the same condition as a call—when $S_T > K$.

Some options make payments only if multiple events occur. For example, consider a cash-or-nothing call that pays \$1 only if $S_T > K$ and the barrier $H > S_0$ has not been hit. We will refer to this as a "cash up and out call" (CashUOCall): "Cash" because it pays \$1, "up and out" because payment does not occur if the stock price rises to the barrier, and "call" because payment requires $S_T > K$. Similarly, we will use the terms "asset" to refer to options that pay off in shares and "put" to refer to options that pay off only when $S_T < K$. To simplify the formulas in this chapter, we will use the notation in Table 2.

Cash-or-Nothing Options

The risk-neutral probability that $S_T > K$ is given by $N(d_2)$ from the Black-Scholes formula. Discounted risk-neutral probabilities are prices of derivatives. Thus, the price for a cash-or-nothing call—which pays \$1 if $S_T > K$ and zero otherwise—is

$$\text{CashCall}(S, K, \sigma, r, T-t, \delta) = e^{-r(T-t)}N(d_2) \tag{3}$$

Equation (3), multiplied by the strike price, K, is the second term in the Black-Scholes formula for a call option. If you were to be paid x if $S > K$, you could value this as x cash-or-nothing options:

$$xe^{-r(T-t)}N(d_2)$$

TABLE 2 Definitions of expressions used in pricing formulas in this chapter.

$$d_1 = [\ln(S_t/K) + (r - \delta + 0.5\sigma^2)(T - t)]/\sigma\sqrt{T - t}$$
$$d_2 = d_1 - \sigma\sqrt{T - t}$$
$$d_3 = [\ln(H^2/S_t K) + (r - \delta + 0.5\sigma^2)(T - t)]/\sigma\sqrt{T - t}$$
$$d_4 = d_3 - \sigma\sqrt{T - t}$$
$$d_5 = [\ln(S_t/H) + (r - \delta + 0.5\sigma^2)(T - t)]/\sigma\sqrt{T - t}$$
$$d_6 = d_5 - \sigma\sqrt{T - t}$$
$$d_7 = [\ln(H/S_t) + (r - \delta + 0.5\sigma^2)(T - t)]/\sigma\sqrt{T - t}$$
$$d_8 = d_7 - \sigma\sqrt{T - t}$$

You could also have a security that pays \$1 if S is *less than* K. This is equivalent to a security that pays \$1, less a security that pays \$1 if S_T is greater than K. Such an option is called a **cash-or-nothing put**. The value is

$$\begin{aligned}\text{CashPut}(S, K, \sigma, r, T - t, \delta) &= e^{-r(T-t)} - e^{-r(T-t)}N(d_2) \\ &= e^{-r(T-t)}N(-d_2)\end{aligned} \tag{4}$$

Example 1. Suppose $S = \$40$, $K = \$40$, $\sigma = 0.3$, $r = 0.08$, $T - t = 0.25$, and $\delta = 0$. The value of a claim that pays \$1 if $S > K$ in 3 months is \$0.5129, computed using equation (3). The value of a claim that pays \$1 if $S < K$ is \$0.4673, using equation (4). The combined value of the two claims is $e^{-0.08\times0.25} = \$0.9802$. ■

We know that equations (3) and (4) are correct since both formulas satisfy the Black-Scholes equation (equation (11)) and the appropriate boundary conditions.

Asset-or-Nothing Options

An asset-or-nothing call is an option that gives the owner a unit of the underlying asset if the asset price exceeds a certain level and zero otherwise. The price of an asset-or-nothing call is obtained from the price of a cash-or-nothing by replacing the dividend yield, δ, in the cash-or-nothing formula with $\delta - \sigma^2$, and multiplying the result by the forward price for the stock. The result is

$$Se^{(r-\delta)(T-t)}e^{-r(T-t)}N\left(\frac{\ln[S_t/K] + [r - (\delta - \sigma^2) - 0.5\sigma^2][T - t]}{\sigma\sqrt{T - t}}\right)$$

$$= Se^{-\delta(T-t)}N(d_1)$$

This is the first term in the Black-Scholes formula.

Thus, the formula for an asset-or-nothing call that pays one unit of stock is

$$\text{AssetCall}(S, K, \sigma, r, T-t, \delta) = e^{-\delta(T-t)} S N(d_1) \tag{5}$$

We could also have an option in which we receive the stock if $S_T < K$, in which case the value is

$$Se^{-\delta(T-t)} - Se^{-\delta(T-t)} N(d_1) = Se^{-\delta(T-t)} N(-d_1)$$

Thus, the value of the asset-or-nothing put is

$$\text{AssetPut}(S, K, \sigma, r, T-t, \delta) = e^{-\delta(T-t)} S N(-d_1)$$

Example 2. Suppose $S = \$40$, $K = \$40$, $\sigma = 0.3$, $r = 0.08$, $T - t = 0.25$, and $\delta = 0$. The value of a claim that pays one share if $S > K$ in 3 months is \$23.30, computed using equation (5). The value of a claim that pays one share if $S < K$ is \$16.70. The combined value of the two claims is \$40. ■

Figure 1 graphs the maturity payoffs of cash and asset calls.

Ordinary Options and Gap Options

We can construct an ordinary call by buying a European asset-or-nothing call with strike price K and selling K European cash-or-nothing calls with strike price K. That is,

FIGURE 1

Payoff at maturity to one asset call and 40 cash calls. Assumes $K = \$40$, $\sigma = 0.30$, $r = 0.08$, and $\delta = 0$. The payoff to both is zero for $S < \$40$.

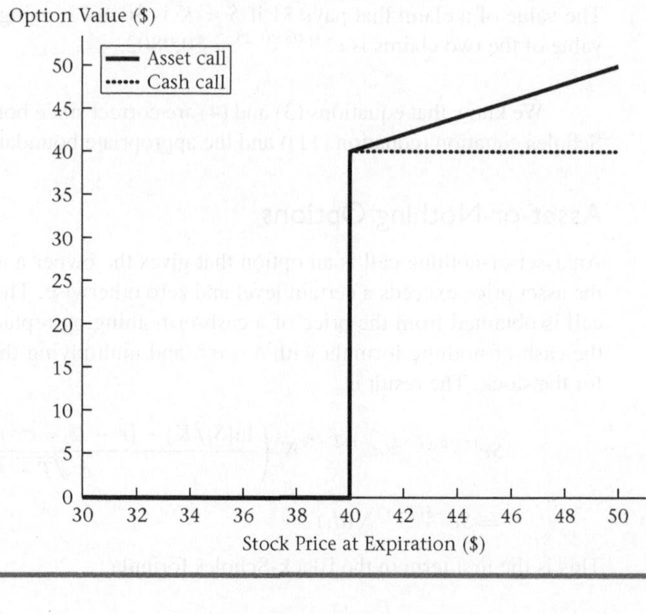

$$\begin{aligned}&\text{BSCall}(S, K, \sigma, r, T - t, \delta)\\&= \text{AssetCall}(S, K, \sigma, r, T - t, \delta) - K \times \text{CashCall}(S, K, \sigma, r, T - t, \delta)\\&= Se^{-\delta(T-t)}N(d_1) - Ke^{-r(T-t)}N(d_2)\end{aligned}$$

This is the Black-Scholes formula.

Similarly, we can construct a put:

$$\begin{aligned}&\text{BSPut}\ (S, K, \sigma, r, T - t, \delta)\\&= K \times \text{CashPut}(S, K, \sigma, r, T - t, \delta) - \text{AssetPut}(S, K, \sigma, r, T - t, \delta)\end{aligned}$$

Finally, we can construct a gap option using asset-or-nothing options. Consider a call option that pays $S - K_1$ if $S > K_2$. The value of this is

$$\text{AssetCall}(S, K_2, \sigma, T - t, r, \delta) - K_1 \times \text{CashCall}(S, K_2, \sigma, T - t, r, \delta)$$

We buy an asset call and sell K_1 cash calls, both with the strike price K_2.

Example 3. Suppose $S = \$40$, $K = \$40$, $\sigma = 0.3$, $r = 0.08$, $T - t = 0.25$, and $\delta = 0$. The price of an ordinary call is an asset call less 40 cash calls. Using results in Examples 1 and 2, the price of the ordinary call is $23.30 – 40 × $0.5129 = $2.7848.

The price of a gap call in which the owner pays $20 ($K_1$) if the stock is greater than $40 ($K_2$) at expiration is $23.20 – 20 × $0.5129 = $13.0427. ■

Delta-Hedging All-or-Nothing Options

All-or-nothing options appear frequently in writings about options, but they are relatively rare in practice. The reason is that they are easy to price but hard to hedge. To understand why, think about the position of a market-maker when such an option is close to expiration. The nightmare scenario for a market-maker is that the option is close to expiration *and* close to the strike price. In this case a small swing in the stock price can determine whether the option is in- or out-of-the-money, with the payoff changing discretely. This potential for a small price change to have a large effect on the option value is evident in Figure 1.

To assess hedging difficulty, Figure 2 graphs the price and delta of cash calls paying $1 with 3 months to expiration and 2 minutes to expiration. With 3 months to go, hedging is straightforward and delta is well-behaved. However, with 2 minutes to go until expiration, the cash call delta at $40 is 15. For the at-the-money option, delta and gamma approach infinity at expiration because an arbitrarily small change in the price can result in a $1 change in the option's value.

An ordinary call or put is easier to hedge because the payoff is continuous—there is no discrete jump at the strike price as the option approaches expiration. Supershares provide an alternative technology for creating complex payoffs.

FIGURE 2

Price and delta of a cash call at two different times to expiration: 3 months (top panel) and 2 minutes (bottom panel). Assumes $K = \$40$, $\sigma = 0.30$, $r = 0.08$, and $\delta = 0$.

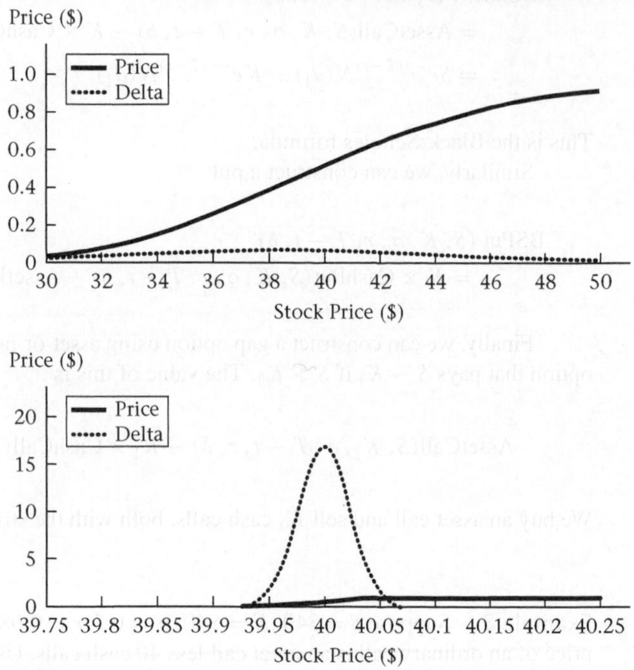

2. ALL-OR-NOTHING BARRIER OPTIONS

Barrier options are options in which the option comes into or goes out of existence if the price of the underlying asset hits a barrier.[1] There are down-and-out options, which become worthless if the stock price hits a barrier price below the initial stock price, as well as up-and-out, down-and-in, and up-and-in options. We can construct options such as these using *all-or-nothing barrier options*.

Suppose we take a cash-or-nothing call paying \$1 if $S_T > K$, but modify it by adding the additional requirement that it will only pay \$1 at expiration if the stock has also hit the barrier H sometime during the life of the option. If $H < S(0)$, this is a down-and-in cash call. Using the notation in Table 1, this would be a CashDICall. Just as we were able to construct ordinary options from digital options, we will also be able to construct barrier options from digital barrier options.

We will examine three different kinds of barrier options:

- A contract that pays \$1 contingent on either a barrier having or not having been reached (*cash-or-nothing barrier options*).

1. Three comprehensive discussions of barrier options are Rubinstein and Reiner (1991a), Rubinstein and Reiner (1991b), and Derman and Kani (1993).

BOX 1: Supershares

Hakannson (1976) proposed a concept known as **supershares**, which could be used to create exotic option-like payoffs without the need for delta-hedging by a dealer. The idea of a supershare is to create shares that pay \$1 in particular circumstances, and to use these as building blocks for more complicated instruments. Supershares can be illustrated with a simple example.

Suppose that the risk-free rate is 10%, the market index is 100, and over the next year there are three possible values of the market index: \$60, \$110, and \$160. (The use of three possible prices is just for simplicity.) Define three supershares that pay \$1 if the market in 1 year is \$60, \$1 if the market is \$110, and \$1 if the market is \$160. Call these shares "down," "middle," and "up."

We can create a fund with a \$100 million investment in the index, and finance it by selling 60 million down shares, 110 million middle shares, and 160 million up shares.* If the market is \$60 in 1 year, the entire \$60 million is paid to the holders of the down shares. If the market is \$160, the entire amount is paid to the holders of the up shares. Note that if you were to buy all of these shares, you would earn a return equivalent to a \$100 million investment in the index. (You could also buy 6 down shares, 11 middle shares, and 16 up shares for a small position in the index.) If you bought 100 each of the down, middle, and up shares, you would have a risk-free zero-coupon bond paying \$100. By buying just the down shares, you could replicate the payoff to a cash-or-nothing put, and so forth.

Although the supershare payoffs resemble the payoffs of cash-or-nothing options, the elegant simplicity of the supershare idea is that the shares are created as fully collateralized contingent claims on a fund. No delta-hedging is required. Relative pricing of the components is determined by the willingness of investors to hold them, but the portfolios replicating a bond and the index must be priced correctly or else there would be arbitrage.

Supershares were actually brought to market in November 1992 by Leland, O'Brien, and Rubinstein (the first and third named principals are finance professors). The product consisted of exchange-traded money-market and index funds, which could be decomposed into four supershares that could be traded individually at the Chicago Board Options Exchange. There were significant regulatory hurdles to introducing supershares, described in Lux (1992). Trading volume was weak and after several years the product was abandoned. The exchange-traded index fund, however, was the precursor to current popular products such as exchange-traded funds and SPDRs.

*In the examples in Hakannson (1976), shares are created paying returns every percentage point between −50% and +60%.

- A contract that pays a share of stock worth S contingent on either a barrier having or not having been reached (*asset-or-nothing barrier options*).
- A contract that pays \$1 at the time a barrier is reached (*rebate options*) or that pays \$1 at expiration as long as the barrier has been reached during the life of the option (*deferred rebate options*).

By valuing these pieces and adding them together we can price any standard barrier option. The assumption that the stock follows geometric Brownian motion makes it possible to derive relatively simple formulas for these options.

There are 16 basic kinds of all-or-nothing barrier options. First, consider cash-or-nothing barrier options that pay \$1 at expiration. Such options can knock in or knock out; they can be calls (pay cash if $S_T > K$) or puts (pay cash if $S_T < K$); and the barrier event can occur if the barrier is above the price (up-and-ins or up-and-outs) or below the price (down-and-ins or down-and-outs). This gives us $2^3 = 8$ basic cash-or-nothing barrier options to value. By the same reasoning there are also 8 basic asset-or-nothing barrier options, for a total of 16 all-or-nothing barrier options.

Cash-or-Nothing Barrier Options

We first consider the valuation of barrier cash-or-nothing options. To anticipate the results in this section, we will first see how to value one particular barrier cash-or-nothing option, a down-and-in cash call. From this one formula we will be able to value the remaining seven cash-or-nothing options and deferred rebate options.

Assume that the option is issued at time 0 and expires at time T. Let $\overline{S}_t$ denote the greatest stock price between times 0 and t (where $t \le T$) and let $\underline{S}_t$ denote the lowest stock price between times 0 and t. Suppose the barrier is below the initial stock price, i.e., $H < S_0$. A cash down-and-in call (CashDICall) is an option that pays \$1 if two conditions are satisfied. First, at some point prior to maturity, the stock price drops to reach H, i.e., $\underline{S}_T \le H$. Second, at expiration, the stock price is greater than the strike price, K.

We can analyze this option by first examining the risk-neutral probability that this joint event ($\underline{S}_T \le H$ and $S_T \ge K$) occurs. This probability should satisfy three conditions:

1. Once the barrier has been hit ($\underline{S}_t \le H$) the probability equals the probability that $S_T \ge K$ (the barrier at this point is irrelevant).
2. If at time T, $\underline{S}_T \le H$ and $S_T \ge K$, the probability equals 1.
3. If at time T, $\underline{S}_T > H$ or $S_T < K$, the probability equals 0.

Assume that $H \le K$, and consider this expression:

$$\Pr(\underline{S}_T \le H \quad \text{and} \quad S_T > K) = \left(\frac{H}{S}\right)^{2\frac{r-\delta}{\sigma^2}-1} N(d_4) \tag{6}$$

The terms d_1 through d_8 are defined in Table 2. An expression of this form solves the backward equation. We also want to verify that it satisfies the three boundary conditions described above.

First, at the point where $S_t = H$, equation (6) collapses to $N(d_2)$, which is the risk-neutral probability that $S_T > K$. (This occurs because when $H = S_t$, $d_1 = d_3$. You should examine equation (6) to verify that this happens.) Thus, once we hit the barrier, the barrier value H drops out of the expression because it is irrelevant. Second, if at expiration $\underline{S}_T \le H$ and $S_T > K$, then equation (6) equals 1. The reason is that the probability equals $N(d_2)$ once the barrier is hit, and if $S_T > K$, $N(d_2) = 1$. Finally, if $\underline{S}_T > H$, i.e., S_t never reaches H, then at expiration $H^2 < S_T K$ (recall that $H \le K$) and equation (6) collapses to 0. Thus, equation (6) both satisfies the backward equation and obeys the appropriate boundary conditions.

Equation (6) assumes that $H \le K$. Why is this important? The answer is that if $H > K$, the boundary conditions may be violated. Consider the case where at expiration $S_T = \$55$, $K = \$45$, and $H = \$54$ (thus violating the condition $H \le K$) and the boundary has not been hit. In this case a correct expression for the probability will evaluate to zero at expiration. However, $\ln(H^2/S_T K) = \ln(54^2/45 \times 55) = 0.164$, so equation (6) at maturity will equal 1 when the event has not occurred.

As a final comment on equation (6), you might ask why it is necessary to multiply $N(d_4)$ by the term $(H/S)^{2(r-\delta)/\sigma^2-1}$. The answer is simply that $N(d_4)$ by itself does not solve the backward equation, whereas equation (6) *does* solve the backward equation.

To handle the case where $H > K$ we need a more complicated version of equation (6). When $H > K$, we have

$$\Pr(S_T \leq H \quad \text{and} \quad S_T > K) = N(d_2) - N(d_6) + \left(\frac{H}{S}\right)^{2\frac{r-\delta}{\sigma^2}-1} N(d_8) \tag{7}$$

Problem 3 asks you to verify that this equation satisfies the boundary conditions. Note that when $S = H$, $N(d_6) = N(d_8)$; the formula again reduces to $N(d_2)$.

Down-And-In Cash Call. Equations (6) and (7) give us expressions for the probability that the barrier is hit and $S_T > K$. What is the value of a claim that pays \$1 when this event occurs? To answer this question we can use the fact that discounted risk-neutral probabilities are prices of derivative claims. Discounting equations (6) and (7), we have

$$\text{CashDICall}(S, K, \sigma, r, T-t, \delta, H) = \begin{cases} e^{-r(T-t)} \left(\frac{H}{S}\right)^{2\frac{r-\delta}{\sigma^2}-1} N(d_4) & H \leq K \\ e^{-r(T-t)} \left[N(d_2) - N(d_6) + \left(\frac{H}{S}\right)^{2\frac{r-\delta}{\sigma^2}-1} N(d_8) \right] & H > K \end{cases} \tag{8}$$

Equation (8) gives us the value for a cash down-and-in call when $S_0 > H$. There are three closely related options we can now price: cash down-and-out calls (CashDOCall), cash down-and-in puts (CashDIPut), and cash down-and-out puts (CashDOPut). We can value each of these using only the formula for the cash down-and-in call, equation (8). In addition, we can value a deferred down rebate option.

Deferred Down Rebate Option. We first value a deferred down rebate, which is a claim that pays \$1 at time T as long as the barrier has been hit over the life of the option. The payoff to this claim does not depend on a strike price: It pays \$1 as long as the barrier has been hit. We will call this claim a **deferred down rebate**. It is a "down rebate" because it pays \$1 if we reach the barrier, and it is "deferred" because the payment is at expiration rather than at the time we reach the barrier. We obtain the value of this claim by setting $K = \$0$ in equation (8). Since we always have $S_T > 0$, the result is a claim that pays \$1 at T as long as $S_T \leq H$. Thus, we have[2]

$$\text{DRDeferred}(S, \sigma, r, T-t, \delta, H) = \text{CashDICall}(S, 0, \sigma, r, T-t, \delta, H) \tag{9}$$

Note that since we set $K = 0$, the value of the deferred down rebate does not depend on the strike price.

Now we can compute the value of the remaining three options.

2. In peforming this calculation, to avoid a zero-divide error it is necessary to set K to be small, such as $K = \$0.000001$, rather than exactly \$0.

Down-And-Out Cash Call. We can create a synthetic cash call by buying down-and-in and down-and-out cash calls with the same barrier; this combination is guaranteed to pay \$1 if $S_T > K$. Thus, the value of a down-and-out cash call is

$$\begin{aligned}\text{CashDOCall}(S, K, \sigma, r, T-t, \delta, H) = &\ \text{CashCall}(S, K, \sigma, r, T-t, \delta) \\ &- \text{CashDICall}(S, K, \sigma, r, T-t, \delta, H)\end{aligned} \tag{10}$$

Down-And-In Cash Put. If you buy a down-and-in cash put with strike price K, you receive \$1 if the barrier is reached and $S_T < K$. If you buy a down-and-in cash call, you receive \$1 if the barrier is reached and $S_T \geq K$. Thus, if you buy *both* a down-and-in call and put, you receive \$1 as long as the barrier is hit. This is the same payoff as a deferred rebate; thus, we have

$$\begin{aligned}\text{CashDIPut}(S, K, \sigma, r, T-t, \delta, H) = &\ \text{DRDeferred}(S, \sigma, r, T-t, \delta, H) \\ &- \text{CashDICall}(S, K, \sigma, r, T-t, \delta, H)\end{aligned} \tag{11}$$

Down-And-Out Cash Put. Buying down-and-in and down-and-out cash puts creates an ordinary cash put. Thus, the value of the down-and-out put is

$$\begin{aligned}\text{CashDOPut}(S, K, \sigma, r, T-t, \delta, H) = &\ \text{CashPut}(S, K, \sigma, r, T-t, \delta) \\ &- \text{CashDIPut}(S, K, \sigma, r, T-t, \delta, H)\end{aligned} \tag{12}$$

As a final point, we can compute the risk-neutral probability that we reach the barrier. The deferred down rebate option pays \$1 at expiration as long as the barrier is hit. Thus the price of this option is the present value of the risk-neutral probability that the barrier is reached. Therefore,

$$e^{r(T-t)}\text{DRDeferred}(S, 0, \sigma, r, T-t, \delta) \tag{13}$$

is the risk-neutral probability that the barrier is reached during the life of the option.

Example 4. Suppose $S = \$40$, $\sigma = 0.3$, $r = 0.08$, $\delta = 0$, and $T - t = 1$. The value of a claim that pays \$1 if the stock hits the barrier $H = \$35$ over the next year is computed by setting $K = \$0$ in equation (8):

$$\text{CashDICall}(\$40, \$0.0000001, 0.3, 0.08, 1, 0, \$35) =$$

$$e^{-r(T-t)}\left[1 - N(d_6) + \left(\frac{H}{S}\right)^{2(r-\delta)/\sigma^2-1} N(d_8)\right] = \$0.574$$

The risk-neutral probability that the stock will hit the barrier is the undiscounted value of this claim, or $0.574 \times e^{0.08} = 0.622$.

The value of a claim that pays \$1 if the stock hits the barrier, \$35, and then is also greater than $K = \$35$ at the end of the year is

$$e^{-r(T-t)}\left(\frac{H}{S}\right)^{2(r-\delta)/\sigma^2-1} N(d_4) = \$0.309$$

This is the value of CashDICall(\$40, \$35, 0.3, 0.08, 1, 0, \$35). The risk-neutral probability of hitting the barrier and being above \$35 is $0.309 \times e^{0.08} = 0.335$. ■

This example illustrates an interesting point. The value of the claim that pays \$1 at expiration when the stock at expiration is greater than \$35 and has hit the \$35 barrier

(\$0.309) is approximately one-half the value of the claim that pays \$1 at expiration as long as the stock has hit the \$35 barrier (\$0.574). The reason is that once the stock has hit \$35, it subsequently has about a 50% chance of being above or below that value. This observation suggests that the probability of being above \$35 conditional upon having hit \$35 is $0.5 \times 0.622 = 0.311$. The actual probability is greater than that, however. The reason is that the lognormal drift is $r - 0.5\sigma^2 = 0.035$, which is positive. Thus, after having hit \$35, the stock on average drifts higher.

To verify this intuition, suppose we set the lognormal drift equal to zero. We can do this by setting the risk-free rate to 0.045, which gives us $r - 0.5\sigma^2 = 0.045 - 0.5 \times 0.3^2 = 0$. We might expect that the value of a claim paying \$1 at T if the barrier is hit is one-half the value of a claim paying \$1 at T if the barrier is hit and the stock price at expiration is greater than the barrier. Put differently, when $r = 0.5\sigma^2$, the probability of hitting and ending up above \$35 is half the unconditional probability of hitting \$35. The next example shows that this intuition works.

Example 5. Suppose $S = \$40$, $\sigma = 0.3$, $r = 0.045$, $\delta = 0$, and $T - t = 1$. The value of a claim paying \$1 if the stock hits the barrier $H = \$35$ over the next year is

$$e^{-r(T-t)}\left[1 - N(d_6) + \left(\frac{H}{S}\right)^{2(r-\delta)/\sigma^2 - 1} N(d_8)\right] = \$0.6274$$

The corresponding risk-neutral probability is $e^{0.045} \times 0.6274 = 0.6562$.

The value of a claim paying \$1 if the stock hits the barrier and is then greater than $K = \$35$ at the end of the year is

$$e^{-r(T-t)}\left(\frac{H}{S}\right)^{2(r-\delta)/\sigma^2 - 1} N(d_4) = \$0.3137$$

This is one-half of \$0.6274. The corresponding risk-neutral probability is $e^{0.045} \times 0.3137 = 0.3281$. ■

Up-And-In Cash Put. Now we consider cash-or-nothing options when the barrier is *above* the current stock price. First, consider the following formula for an up-and-in cash put, which pays \$1 when $\overline{S}_T > H$ and $S_T < K$:

$$\text{CashUIPut}(S, K, \sigma, r, T - t, \delta, H) =$$
$$\begin{cases} e^{-r(T-t)}\left(\frac{H}{S}\right)^{2\frac{r-\delta}{\sigma^2}-1} N(-d_4) & H \geq K \\ e^{-r(T-t)}\left[N(-d_2) - N(-d_6) + \left(\frac{H}{S}\right)^{2\frac{r-\delta}{\sigma^2}-1} N(-d_8)\right] & H < K \end{cases} \tag{14}$$

If you compare this formula to equation (8), you will see that $N(d_2)$ is replaced with $N(-d_2)$, $N(d_4)$ with $N(-d_4)$, and so forth. These terms also solve the Black-Scholes equation. The effect of these changes is to reverse the effect of the d_i terms. As a consequence, equation (8), which prices a down-and-in cash call, is transformed into an equation pricing an up-and-in cash put. Problem 4 asks you to verify that equation (14) solves the appropriate boundary conditions for an up-and-in cash put.

Deferred Up Rebate. Given equation (14), the procedure for obtaining the prices of the other three cash-or-nothing options when $H > S_0$ is analogous to that before. First, by setting $K = \infty$ in equation (14), we obtain the price of a claim paying \$1 at expiration as long as the barrier is reached:[3]

$$\text{URDeferred}(S, \sigma, r, T - t, \delta, H) = \text{CashUIPut}(S, \infty, \sigma, r, T - t, \delta, H) \quad (15)$$

With this equation, we can solve for the price of the other cash-or-nothing options.

Up-And-Out Cash Put. Buying up-and-in and up-and-out cash puts gives an ordinary cash put; hence,

$$\begin{aligned} \text{CashUOPut}(S, K, \sigma, r, T - t, \delta, H) &= \text{CashPut}(S, K, \sigma, r, T - t, \delta) \\ &\quad - \text{CashUIPut}(S, K, \sigma, r, T - t, \delta, H) \end{aligned} \quad (16)$$

Up-And-In Cash Call. Buying an up-and-in cash call and an up-and-in cash put yields the same payoff as a deferred up rebate. Thus, we have

$$\begin{aligned} \text{CashUICall}(S, K, \sigma, r, T - t, \delta, H) &= \text{URDeferred}(S, \sigma, r, T - t, \delta, H) \\ &\quad - \text{CashUIPut}(S, K, \sigma, r, T - t, \delta, H) \end{aligned} \quad (17)$$

Up-And-Out Cash Call. Buying up-and-in and up-and-out cash calls gives an ordinary cash call; hence,

$$\begin{aligned} \text{CashUOCall}(S, K, \sigma, r, T - t, \delta, H) &= \text{CashCall}(S, K, \sigma, r, T - t, \delta) \\ &\quad - \text{CashUICall}(S, K, \sigma, r, T - t, \delta, H) \end{aligned} \quad (18)$$

Asset-or-Nothing Barrier Options

We now wish to find the eight pricing formulas for asset-or-nothing options corresponding to those for the eight cash-or-nothing options. Fortunately, there is a simple way to do this. If we view asset-or-nothing options as cash-or-nothing options denominated in shares rather than cash, we can use a proposition dealing with a change of numeraire, to transform the pricing formulas for cash-or-nothing options into formulas for asset-or-nothing options. In each case, we replace δ by $\delta - \sigma^2$, and we multiply the cash-or-nothing formula by $S_0 e^{(r-\delta)(T-t)}$, the forward price for the stock. For example, we have

$$\begin{aligned} &\text{AssetDICall}(S, K, \sigma, r, T - t, \delta, H) \\ &\quad = S e^{(r-\delta)(T-t)} \text{CashDICall}(S, K, \sigma, r, T - t, \delta - \sigma^2, H) \end{aligned} \quad (19)$$

The other seven asset-or-nothing pricing formulas—AssetDOCall, AssetDIPut, AssetDOPut, AssetUICall, AssetUOCall, AssetUIPut, and AssetUOP—can be created in exactly the same way.

Rebate Options

Rebate options pay \$1 if the barrier is hit. We have already seen how to price deferred rebate options, which pay the \$1 at expiration. If the option pays at the time the barrier is hit, we will call the claim a **rebate option** or *immediate rebate option*.

We have already seen in equations (9) and (15) how to price deferred rebates. The formulas for rebates paid when the barrier is hit are more complicated because the discount

3. To evaluate equation (14) at $K = \infty$, we simply set $N(-d_2) = 1$.

factor for the $1 payment depends on the time at which the barrier is hit. In effect there is a random discount factor.

The formula for the price of a down rebate when $S > H$ is

$$\text{DR}(S, \sigma, r, T-t, \delta, H) = \left(\frac{S}{H}\right)^{h_1} N(Z_1) + \left(\frac{S}{H}\right)^{h_2} N(Z_2) \tag{20}$$

where

$$Z_1 = [\ln(H/S) - g\sigma^2(T-t)]/\sigma\sqrt{T-t}$$
$$Z_2 = [\ln(H/S) + g\sigma^2(T-t)]/\sigma\sqrt{T-t}$$
$$g = \sqrt{\left(\frac{r-\delta}{\sigma^2} - \frac{1}{2}\right)^2 + \frac{2r}{\sigma^2}}$$
$$h_1 = \left(\frac{1}{2} - \frac{r-\delta}{\sigma^2}\right) + g; \qquad h_2 = \left(\frac{1}{2} - \frac{r-\delta}{\sigma^2}\right) - g$$

This formula satisfies (as it must) both the Black-Scholes equation and the boundary conditions for a rebate option. Suppose that the barrier is not hit over the life of the option. Then $H < S$ and both terms go to 0 as $t \to T$. At the point when the barrier is hit, $H = S$ and $\ln(H/S) = 0$. Because the normal distribution is symmetric around 0,

$$N\left[\frac{-g\sigma^2(T-t)}{\sigma\sqrt{T-t}}\right] + N\left[\frac{g\sigma^2(T-t)}{\sigma\sqrt{T-t}}\right] = 1$$

Thus, the formula evaluates to 1 when the barrier is hit.

The up rebate formula is symmetric:

$$\text{UR}(S, \sigma, r, T-t, \delta, H) = \left(\frac{S}{H}\right)^{h_1} N(-Z_1) + \left(\frac{S}{H}\right)^{h_2} N(-Z_2) \tag{21}$$

where all variables are defined as above for the down rebate.

Perpetual American Options

If we set $T = \infty$ in (21), we obtain the price of a perpetual claim that pays $1 the first time S reaches H from below. Note that $g > 0$. Therefore, when $T \to \infty$, equation (21) becomes

$$\text{UR}(S, \sigma, r, \infty, \delta, H) = \left(\frac{S}{H}\right)^{h_1} \qquad S < H \tag{22}$$

H_c maximizes the value of the call. Similarly, using the down rebate formula, we have

$$\text{DR}(S, \sigma, r, \infty, \delta, H) = \left(\frac{S}{H}\right)^{h_2} \qquad S > H \tag{23}$$

3. BARRIER OPTIONS

At this point it is easy to construct barrier option formulas using the preceding formulas. A down-and-out call, for example, can be valued as

$$\begin{aligned}\text{CallDownOut}(S, K, \sigma, r, T-t, \delta, H) &= \text{AssetDOCall}(S, K, \sigma, r, T-t, \delta, H)\\ &\quad - K \times \text{CashDOCall}(S, K, \sigma, r, T-t, \delta, H)\end{aligned}$$

Up-and-outs, down-and-ins, and so forth are all constructed analogously. See Table 3 for a listing of formulas for barrier calls and puts.

As another example of the use of all-or-nothing options as building blocks, **capped options** are single options that have the payoff of bull spreads, except that the option is exercised the first time the stock price reaches the upper strike price. An example of an American capped option is an option with a strike price of \$100 and a cap of \$120. When the stock hits \$120, the option pays \$20. If the option expires without the stock having hit \$120, then the payoff is $\max(S_T - 100, 0)$. This option can be priced as the sum of the following two options:

- A rebate call, which pays the \$20 when the stock hits \$120 prior to expiration.
- A knock-out call with a strike of \$100, which knocks out at \$120.

If the stock reaches \$120 prior to expiration, the rebate is triggered and the call knocks out. If the stock has not hit \$120 prior to expiration but is above \$100, the knock-out call pays $S - \$100$. The table below illustrates the payoffs, assuming that the option strike is K, the cap is H, and the option expires at T:

	H **Hit**	H **Not Hit**
Purchased Knock-Out	0	$\max(0, S_T - K)$
Rebate	$H - K$ at Hit	0
Total	$H - K$ at Hit	$\max(0, S_T - K)$

Note that a European capped option is simpler to price. Since the payoff does not occur until expiration, this option is just an ordinary vertical spread (buy a 100-strike call and sell a 120-strike European call with the same times to expiration).

TABLE 3 Formulas for barrier puts and calls. In each case, the arguments for the functions are $(S, K, \sigma, r, T-t, \delta, H)$.

	Call	Put
Up-and-In	AssetUICall − K × CashUICall	K × CashUIPut − AssetUIPut
Up-and-Out	AssetUOCall − K × CashUOCall	K × CashUOPut − AssetUOPut
Down-and-In	AssetDICall − K × CashDICall	K × CashDIPut − AssetDIPut
Down-and-Out	AssetDOCall − K × CashDOCall	K × CashDOPut − AssetDOPut

Example 6. Consider the capped call discussed in the text above and suppose that $S = \$100$, $\sigma = 0.3$, $r = 0.08$, $T - t = 1$, and $\delta = 0$. We can compute the price of an up-and-out call as

$$\begin{aligned}\text{CallUpOut}(S, K, \sigma, r, T - t, \delta, H) &= \text{AssetUOCall}(S, K, \sigma, r, T - t, \delta, H) \\ &\quad - K \times \text{CashUOCall}(S, K, \sigma, r, T - t, \delta, H)\end{aligned}$$

The price of the capped call is

$$\begin{aligned}&20 \times \text{UR}(\$100, 0.3, 0.08, 1, 0, \$120) + \text{CallUpOut}(\$100, \$100, 0.3, 0.08, 1, 0, \$120) \\ &= 20 \times \$0.5649 + \$0.4298 = \$11.73\end{aligned}$$

The price of a European bull spread for the same parameters would be

$$\begin{aligned}\text{BSCall}(\$100, \$100, 0.3, 0.08, 1, 0) - \text{BSCall}(\$100, \$120, 0.3, 0.08, 1, 0) \\ = \$15.7113 - \$7.8966 = \$7.8147\end{aligned}$$

The capped call is more expensive because all of the stock price paths that cross \$120 and end up lower result in the maximum payout on the capped call but a lower payout on the bull spread. ■

4. QUANTOS

A U.S. investor wishing to invest in a foreign stock index can purchase the foreign index directly or hold futures based on that index. However, the investor then bears two risks: the risk of the foreign index, and currency (exchange rate) risk.

For example, suppose that a U.S. investor wishes to invest in the Nikkei 225 index, expecting that it will increase over the next month. The investor can take a position in the Nikkei by directly investing in the cash Nikkei index or by investing in yen-denominated futures, such as a Nikkei futures contract trading in Japan. Both strategies have a payoff denominated in yen. If the Nikkei appreciates but the yen depreciates, *the investor can lose money despite being correct about the movement of the Nikkei.*

You could try to reduce the problem of exchange rate risk by hedging the Nikkei investment using currency futures. However, the quantity of yen to be exchanged is high when the index has a high return and low when the index has a low return. Thus, *there is no way to know in advance how many yen to short*. This price uncertainty creates quantity uncertainty with respect to the yen exposure.

We could imagine a synthetic Nikkei investment in which the quantity of currency forwards depended upon the Nikkei's yen return. Such a contract would permit an investor in one currency to hold an asset denominated in another currency, without exchange rate risk. This contract is called an **equity-linked forward**, or **quanto**. For reasons that will become clear below, a quanto is also sometimes defined as a derivative having a payoff that depends on the product or ratio of two prices.

The Nikkei 225 index futures contract, traded at the CME, is an example of a quanto contract. This futures contract is marked-to-market daily in *dollars,* even though it settles

TABLE 4 Parameters used in the Nikkei/yen quanto example.

Dollar-denominated interest rate	r	0.08
Yen-denominated interest rate	r_f	0.04
Current Nikkei index	Q_0	¥20,000
Nikkei dividend yield	δ_Q	0.02
Nikkei volatility (¥)	σ_Q	0.15
Current exchange rate ($/ ¥)	x_0	0.0100
Exchange rate volatility	s	0.1
Nikkei-exchange rate ($/¥) correlation	ρ	0.2
Time to expiration	T	1 year

based on a yen-denominated price.[4] There is also a yen-denominated Nikkei futures contract that trades in Osaka. Both futures are based on the Nikkei 225 contract, but they differ in currency of denomination. We will see in this section how their pricing differs. A box on a later page discusses Nikkei put warrants, which were another example of a quanto contract. Table 4 lists the symbols and specific numbers used throughout the examples in this section.

The Yen Perspective

The yen-based investor is interested in the yen price of $1 and, hence, faces an exchange rate of $1/x_0 = 100$ ¥/$. Because the Nikkei index and the yen price of a dollar are both denominated in yen, we use the usual formulas to find forward prices for the yen and Nikkei. For the Nikkei, we have

$$\text{Nikkei forward (¥): } F_{0,T}(Q) = Q_0 e^{(r_f - \delta_Q)T} \tag{24}$$

For the exchange rate, the dollar-denominated interest rate is the yield on dollars, so the forward price is

$$\text{Exchange rate forward (¥/\$): } F_{0,T}(1/x) = \frac{1}{x_0} e^{(r_f - r)T} \tag{25}$$

These will be the forward prices observed in Japan.

A yen-based investor would construct binomial trees for the yen and Nikkei in the usual fashion. Figure 3 depicts trees for the dollar and Nikkei. The nodes on the dollar tree are constructed as

$$(1/x_T) = (1/x_0)e^{(r_f - r)T \pm s\sqrt{T}}$$

and on the Nikkei tree as

4. To illustrate dollar settlement, suppose the Nikkei 225 is at 22,000. Under the terms of the CME contract, a one-point move corresponds to $5, so the notional value of one contract is 22,000 × $5 = $110,000. If instead the Nikkei had been 22,100, the notional value of the contract would be $110,500, a difference of $500.

FIGURE 3

Binomial trees for the dollar and the Nikkei index from the perspective of a yen-based investor. Both are forward trees constructed using the parameters in Table 4. The risk-neutral probabilities of up moves are 0.4750 in the dollar tree and 0.4626 in the Nikkei tree.

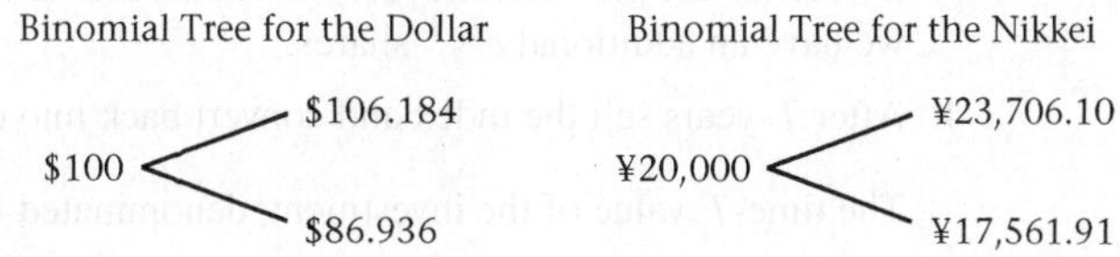

$$Q_T = Q_0 e^{(r_f - \delta_Q)T \pm \sigma_Q \sqrt{T}}$$

Example 7. Given the parameters in Table 4, the 1-year yen-denominated forward price for the Nikkei index is

$$F_{0,1}(Q) = ¥20{,}000e^{(0.04-0.02)\times 1} = ¥20{,}404.03$$

and that for the exchange rate is

$$F_{0,1}(1/x) = ¥100e^{(0.04-0.08)\times 1} = ¥96.079$$

We can also compute the forward prices on both trees as expected values. For the dollar tree we have

$$F_{0,1}(1/x) = 0.4750 \times \$106.184 + (1 - 0.4750) \times \$86.936 = \$96.079$$

For the Nikkei tree we have[5]

$$F_{0,1}(Q) = ¥0.4626 \times ¥23{,}706.10 + (1 - 0.4626) \times ¥17{,}561.91 = ¥20{,}404.03$$ ■

The Dollar Perspective

Now we consider yen and Nikkei investments from the perspective of a dollar-based investor. The yen forward price is given by

$$\text{Exchange rate forward (\$/¥): } F_{0,T}(x) = x_0 e^{(r - r_f)T} \tag{26}$$

However, from the dollar perspective, the forward price of the Nikkei is not so straightforward.

As discussed above, any Nikkei investment entails a combination of currency and index risk. To see why, suppose a dollar-based investor buys $e^{-\delta_Q T}$ units of the Nikkei and holds it for T years. The actual steps in this transaction are as follows:

---

5. The calculation shown here uses rounded numbers and therefore does not exactly equal ¥20,404.03.

1. Exchange $Q_0 x_0 e^{-\delta_Q T}$ dollars into yen (this is enough dollars to buy $e^{-\delta_Q T}$ units of the index).
2. Buy $e^{-\delta_Q T}$ units of the Nikkei index and hold for T periods.
3. Dividends are paid continuously over time and reinvested in the index; after T years we have an additional $e^{\delta_Q T}$ shares.
4. After T years sell the index and convert back into dollars.

The time-T value of the investment, denominated in dollars, is

$$Y(T) = x_T Q_T$$

The payoff is a *combination* of yen and Nikkei risk; we will call this investment the **currency-translated index**. Here is a point that is crucial for understanding what follows: *From the perspective of a dollar-based investor, the dollar-translated price of a yen-denominated asset, Y_T, is just like any other dollar-denominated asset.* However, Q_T is *not* the price of an asset for a dollar-based investor, because there is no simple way to obtain the risk of Q without also bearing currency risk.[6]

The price Y_t is that of a dollar-denominated asset. Hence, the forward price for Y_T for a dollar-based investor is[7]

$$F_{0,T}(Y) = Y_0 e^{(r-\delta_Q)T} \tag{27}$$

Because we can trade shares of the currency-translated index, we can undertake arbitrage if the forward price is anything other than equation (27).

We know that

$$F_{0,T}(Y) = F_{0,T}(x) F_{0,T}(Q) e^{\rho\sigma_Q s T} \tag{28}$$

You should be sure you understand that all three forward prices in equation (28) are those for a dollar-denominated investor. Assume that both S and Q were traded assets; the point is to find the price of a traded asset that paid the product of two traded assets. In this context, both Y and x are dollar assets, so we can simply solve for the dollar-denominated forward price for Q.

6. To convince yourself that Y_T really is like any other dollar-denominated asset, ask how you know whether you are investing in a "real" U.S. stock or in a currency-translated investment. For example, suppose you invest in an American Depositary Receipt (ADR) for the Nikkei index. (An ADR is a claim to a trust containing a foreign stock.) The ADR holds in trust shares of the Nikkei. The value at any time is $Y_t = x_t Q_t$ and it has dividend yield of $\delta_Q dt$. This ADR is indistinguishable from other dollar-denominated investments, and in fact most firms have some foreign investments among their assets. Without investigating, you would not know whether or not you were investing in assets denominated in a foreign currency.

7. If S and Q are asset prices, then the forward price for SQ contained a covariance term. You may be wondering why there is no such covariance term in equation (27). In general, if an asset with price S_0 is traded and can be held by investors, then its forward price is $S_0 e^{(r-\delta)T}$. This is a no-arbitrage result. We assume that S and Q are both prices of assets that can be held directly by investors. In that case, SQ does not represent the price of an asset. By contrast, in the discussion here, xQ and x are the prices of assets that can be held directly by investors, but Q cannot be held directly. Jensen's inequality implies that S, Q, and SQ cannot all simultaneously be the prices of traded assets.

Substituting for $F_{0,T}(Y)$ and $F_{0,T}(x)$ in equation (28), we have

$$x_0 Q_0 e^{(r-\delta_Q)T} = x_0 e^{(r-r_f)T} F_{0,T}(Q) e^{\rho\sigma_Q s T} \tag{29}$$

Solving for $F_{0,T}(Q)$, we have

$$F_{0,T}(Q) = Q_0 e^{(r_f-\delta_Q-\rho\sigma_Q s)T} \tag{30}$$

The dollar-denominated forward price for the Nikkei index is the same as the yen-denominated forward price, with a covariance correction. The prepaid quanto index forward price is

$$F^P_{0,T}(Q) = Q_0 e^{(r_f-\delta_Q-\rho\sigma_Q s-r)T} \tag{31}$$

The role of the covariance term in equation (30) is intuitive. Consider a dollar-denominated investor who buys the cash Nikkei index and ultimately converts yen back to dollars. Suppose the index and the exchange rate (measured in dollars/yen) are positively correlated. When the index does well, there are many yen to exchange. If ρ is positive, on average the exchange rate is favorable when there are many yen to exchange. When the index does poorly, there are fewer yen to exchange so the decline in the exchange rate does not matter as much. Thus, other things equal, the positive correlation systematically benefits the unhedged investment in the Nikkei relative to a contract with a fixed exchange rate. Consequently, if the exchange rate is fixed, as in a quanto contract, the price for the index settling in dollars will be lower in order to compensate the buyer for the loss of beneficial correlation between the index and exchange rate.

Example 8. Using equation (30) and the information in Table 4, the yen forward price is

$$F_{0,1} = x_0 e^{(r-r_f)t} = 0.01\$/¥ e^{(0.08-0.04)} = 0.010408\$/¥$$

The forward price for the currency-translated Nikkei is

$$F_{0,1} = x_0 Q_0 e^{(r-\delta_Q)t} = 0.01\$/¥ \times ¥20{,}000 e^{(0.08-0.02)} = \$212.367$$

Finally, using equation (30), the quanto forward price is

$$V_{0,1}(\$200, 0.01\$/¥) = ¥20{,}000 e^{(0.04-0.02-0.2\times0.1\times0.15)}$$
$$= ¥20{,}342.91$$

This is lower than the yen-denominated Nikkei forward price of ¥20,404 in Example 7. ■

A Binomial Model for the Dollar-Denominated Investor

As another way to understand quanto pricing, we can construct a binomial tree that simultaneously models the currency-translated index and the exchange rate. In addition to this particular application of two-variable binomial trees, some options have prices that depend on two state variables.

In Figure 3 we constructed separate binomial trees for the yen-based investor. For the dollar-based investor we need to construct a tree that takes account of the correlation between the Nikkei and the yen. We can do so by first modeling the behavior of the yen in the usual way, and then, *conditional upon the yen*, model the movement in the Nikkei.[8] Since for each yen move there are two Nikkei moves, the tree will have four binomial nodes. We will denote these as $\{uu, ud, du, dd\}$, with the first letter denoting the yen move and the second the Nikkei move. We have a choice of constructing a joint tree for the yen and Nikkei or the yen and dollar-translated Nikkei, but we obtain the same answer either way. Here we will model the yen and Nikkei. Problem 17 asks you to jointly model the yen and dollar-translated Nikkei.

The basic idea underlying the joint binomial model for x and Q is as follows. If x and Q are lognormal, they evolve like this:

$$x_h = x_0 e^{(r-r_f)h+s\sqrt{h}Z_1} \tag{32a}$$

$$Q_h = Q_0 e^{(r-\delta_Q)h+\sigma_Q\sqrt{h}Z_2} \tag{32b}$$

In the standard binomial model, we simply approximate Z_1 and Z_2 binomially, so that $Z_i = \pm 1$. However, we want to induce correlation between Z_1 and Z_2. We can create correlation by using Cholesky decomposition. Begin by rewriting equation (32a):

$$x_h = x_0 e^{(r-r_f)h+s\sqrt{h}\epsilon_1} \tag{33a}$$

$$Q_h = Q_0 e^{(r_f-\delta_Q)h+\sigma_Q\sqrt{h}\left(\epsilon_1\rho+\epsilon_2\sqrt{1-\rho^2}\right)} \tag{33b}$$

Thus, $Z_1 = \epsilon_1$ and $Z_2 = \rho\epsilon_1 + \sqrt{1-\rho^2}\epsilon_2$. By construction, this Z_1 and Z_2 have correlation ρ. Now we construct the binomial tree by setting $\epsilon_1 = \pm 1$ (the exchange rate moves up or down) and $\epsilon_2 = \pm 1$ (the index moves up or down). There are four possible outcomes, which we will label A ($\epsilon_1 = 1; \epsilon_2 = 1$), B ($\epsilon_1 = 1; \epsilon_2 = -1$), C ($\epsilon_1 = -1; \epsilon_2 = 1$), and D ($\epsilon_1 = -1; \epsilon_2 = -1$).

For a dollar-based investor, the possible yen moves are

$$x_A = x_B = x_0 e^{(r-r_f)h+s\sqrt{h}} = x_0 u \tag{34a}$$

$$x_C = x_D = x_0 e^{(r-r_f)h-s\sqrt{h}} = x_0 d \tag{34b}$$

For each yen move, there are two Nikkei moves:

$$Q_A = Q_0 e^{(r_f-\delta_Q)h+\sigma_Q\sqrt{h}\left(\rho+\sqrt{1-\rho^2}\right)} = Q_0 A \tag{35a}$$

$$Q_B = Q_0 e^{(r_f-\delta_Q)h+\sigma_Q\sqrt{h}\left(\rho-\sqrt{1-\rho^2}\right)} = Q_0 B \tag{35b}$$

$$Q_C = Q_0 e^{(r_f-\delta_Q)h+\sigma_Q\sqrt{h}\left(-\rho+\sqrt{1-\rho^2}\right)} = Q_0 C \tag{35c}$$

$$Q_D = Q_0 e^{(r_f-\delta_Q)h+\sigma_Q\sqrt{h}\left(-\rho-\sqrt{1-\rho^2}\right)} = Q_0 D \tag{35d}$$

Finally, we have to determine the risk-neutral probabilities associated with the nodes. The risk-neutral probability for an up move of the currency is

8. This is similar to the two-variable binomial model in Rubinstein (1994). See also Boyle et al. (1989) for a procedure to generate n-asset binomial trees.

$$p = \frac{e^{(r-r_f)h} - d}{u - d} \tag{36}$$

where u and d are implied by equation (34a) and (34b). The risk-neutral probability for an up move in the currency is 0.4750.

Recall that the risk-neutral probability arises from the requirement that an investment in the asset earn the risk-free rate. Specifically, for the currency, we consider an investment in the yen-denominated risk-free asset, hedged to remove currency risk when the investment is turned back into dollars. This investment earns the dollar-denominated risk-free return if the probability of an up move is given by equation (36).

We need a similar argument for the Nikkei. Since we cannot own the Nikkei index without bearing currency risk, we model an investment in the dollar-translated Nikkei. Let p^* denote the probability of an up move in the Nikkei, conditional on the move in the yen. We require that the dollar-translated Nikkei investment earn the dollar-denominated risk-free rate. This gives us

$$\begin{aligned} x_u Q_A p p^* + x_u Q_B p(1-p^*) + x_d Q_C (1-p) p^* + x_d Q_D (1-p)(1-p^*) \\ = x_0 Q_0 e^{(r-\delta_Q)h} \end{aligned} \tag{37}$$

Solving for p^* gives

$$\begin{aligned} p^* &= \frac{x_0 Q_0 e^{(r-\delta_Q)h} - x_u Q_B p - x_d Q_D (1-p)}{p x_u (Q_A - Q_B) + (1-p) x_d (Q_C - Q_D)} \\ &= \frac{e^{(r-\delta_Q)h} - uBp - dD(1-p)}{pu(A-B) + (1-p)d(C-D)} \end{aligned} \tag{38}$$

This expression is a generalization of the one-variable formula for a risk-neutral probability, taking account of the two up and two down states for Q.

Figure 4 depicts the binomial tree constructed using equations (34a) and (35a), and probabilities of each node constructed using equations (36) and (38). The quanto forward price can be constructed as the expectation $E(Y_1/x_1)$.

FIGURE 4

The binomial process for the dollar/yen exchange rate (x) and the Nikkei (Q). The last two columns contain the value of the currency-translated Nikkei and the risk-neutral probability of each node, computed using equations (36) and (38).

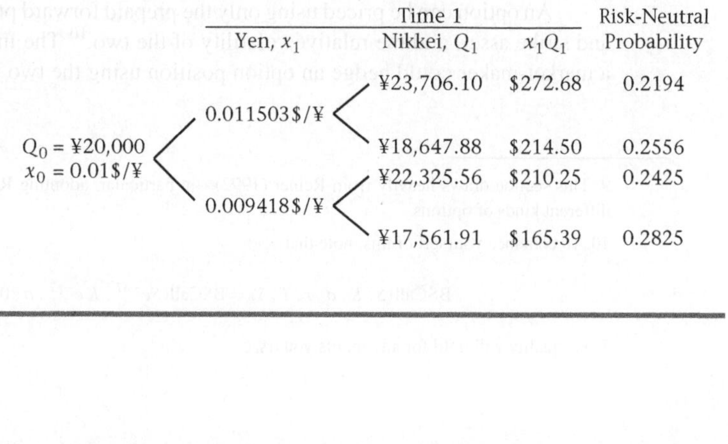

Example 9. Using Figure 4, we can compute forward prices for the yen, the dollar-translated Nikkei, and the quanto Nikkei. The risk-neutral probability of an up move in the yen is 0.4750. The yen forward price is

$$F_{0,1}(x) = 0.4750 \times 0.011503\$/¥ + (1 - 0.4750) \times 0.009418\$/¥ = 0.010408\$/¥$$

The forward price for the currency-translated Nikkei is

$$\begin{aligned} F_{0,1}(xQ) = {} & 0.2194 \times \$272.68 + 0.2556 \times \$214.50 \\ & + 0.2425 \times \$210.25 + 0.2825 \times \$165.39 = \$212.367 \end{aligned}$$

Finally, the quanto forward price is

$$\begin{aligned} F_{0,1}(Q) = {} & 0.2194 \times \frac{\$272.68}{0.011503\$/¥} + 0.2556 \times \frac{\$214.50}{0.011503\$/¥} \\ & + 0.2425 \times \frac{\$210.25}{0.009418\$/¥} + 0.2825 \times \frac{\$165.39}{0.009418\$/¥} = ¥20{,}342.91 \end{aligned}$$

All of the prices computed from the tree match those in Example 8. ■

The tree in Figure 4 can be extended to multiple periods. Rubinstein (1994) shows that in general, with n steps, there are $(n+1)^2$ nodes; for example, with two steps there are nine nodes. To see why, if we add another binomial period to the tree, there are $4^2 = 16$ combinations of the up-down moves ($AA, AB, \ldots, DD$). The order of the moves is irrelevant, so, for example, $AB = BA$. This equivalence eliminates $n \times (n-1) = 6$ nodes, leaving 10. Further, from equation (35a), $AB = CD$. Because $n = 2$, this leaves $(n+1)^2 = 9$ unique nodes.

5. CURRENCY-LINKED OPTIONS

There are several common ways to construct options on foreign assets, for which the return has an exchange rate component.[9] The different variants permit investors to assume different amounts of currency and equity risk. In this section we examine four variants and their pricing formulas. We will continue to use the notation and numbers from Table 4.

An option can be priced using only the prepaid forward prices for the underlying asset and strike asset, and the relative volatility of the two.[10] The intuition for this result is that a market-maker could hedge an option position using the two prepaid forwards, neither of

9. This section draws heavily from Reiner (1992)—in particular, adopting Reiner's terminology for the different kinds of options.

10. To convince yourself of this, note that

$$\text{BSCall}(S, K, \sigma, r, T, \delta) = \text{BSCall}(Se^{-\delta T}, Ke^{-rT}, \sigma, 0, T, 0)$$

This equality will hold for any inputs you try.

BOX 2: Nikkei Put Warrants

An example of quanto options is the Nikkei 225 put warrants that traded on the American Stock Exchange beginning in 1990. Ryan and Granovsky (2000) provide an interesting account of the history of these options, in which Nikkei risk was repackaged and transformed several times by various global financial players.

Japanese institutional investors in the late 1980s bought Nikkei bull notes. These were bonds that carried a high coupon and contained an embedded written put spread: The note principal was not paid in full if the Nikkei fell below ¥32,000. The issuer of the notes was a European bank that sold the embedded put spread to an investment bank and entered into a currency swap to achieve dollar-denominated financing without any Nikkei risk. Japanese buyers were willing to pay a price that made it profitable for the European bank to issue the notes and hedge the resulting exposure. The investment bank, having bought the put spread, had short exposure to the Nikkei. It sold dollar-denominated Nikkei puts to a European sovereign, which in turn sold dollar-denominated Nikkei puts to investors who wanted dollar-denominated Nikkei exposure in the form of SEC-registered securities without investment bank credit risk. (The sovereign issuer bore the investment bank credit risk and the notes carried sovereign risk.)

The net result of this chain of transactions was that Japanese institutional investors were betting—via the bull notes—that the Nikkei would rise. Buyers of the dollar-denominated Nikkei put warrants were betting that the Nikkei would fall. In the end, the Nikkei index suffered a long decline and the put warrant buyers won the bet.

which, by definition, makes any payouts. In the discussions to follow, we will use this result to simplify the valuation of seemingly complex options.

Foreign Equity Call Struck in Foreign Currency

If we want to speculate on a foreign index, one possibility is to buy an option completely denominated in a foreign currency. The value of this option at expiration is

$$V(Q_T, T) = \max(0, Q_T - K_f)$$

where K_f denotes the strike denominated in the foreign currency.

As an example, we might have a 1-year call option to buy the Nikkei index by paying ¥19,500. An investor based in the foreign currency would use this kind of option; thus, it can be priced using the Black-Scholes formula from the perspective of the foreign currency. Only yen inputs—the yen-denominated interest rate and the Nikkei volatility and dividend yield—enter the pricing formula. The dollar price can be obtained by converting the option price at the current exchange rate.

$$C_{¥} = Q_0 e^{-\delta_Q t} N(d_1) - K_f e^{-r_f t} N(d_2)$$

$$d_1 = \frac{\ln(Q_0 e^{-\delta_Q t}/K_f e^{-r_f t}) + \frac{1}{2}\sigma_Q^2 t}{\sigma_Q \sqrt{t}} \tag{39}$$

$$d_2 = d_1 - \sigma_Q \sqrt{t}$$

Thus, we price this option by using the Black-Scholes formula with inputs appropriate for the asset being denominated in a different currency.

Example 10. Using the parameters in Table 4 and assuming a strike price of ¥19,500, we price the call by setting $S = ¥20{,}000e^{-0.02}$ (the current Nikkei prepaid forward price), $K = ¥19{,}500e^{-0.04}$ (the prepaid forward price for the strike), $\sigma_Q = 0.15$ (the Nikkei volatility in yen), $T = 1$, and with zeros for the interest rate and dividend yield (they are already accounted for in the prepaid forward prices). We obtain BSCall(¥20,000$e^{-0.02}$; ¥19,500$e^{-0.04}$; 0.15; 0; 1; 0) = ¥1632.16.

We can also price the option by using the Black-Scholes formula in the conventional way: BSCall(¥20,000, ¥19,500; 0.15; 0.04; 1; 0.02) = ¥1632.16. The dollar price is \$16.32. ■

Foreign Equity Call Struck in Domestic Currency

Suppose we have a call option to buy the Nikkei but we denominate the strike, K, in *dollars*. If we exercise the option, we pay K dollars to acquire the Nikkei, which is worth $x_T Q_T$. Thus, at expiration, the option is worth

$$V(x_T Q_T, T) = \max(0, x_T Q_T - K)$$

In order to price this option, recognize that $Y(T) = x_T Q_T$, the currency-translated index, is priced like any domestic asset. Equation 27 gives the forward price for the currency-translated index, so the prepaid forward price is $x_0 Q_0 e^{-\delta_Q T}$. The prepaid forward price for the strike is Ke^{-rT}. The value of the option will depend upon the distribution of $x_T Q_T$; thus, the volatility that enters the option pricing formula is that of the currency-translated index. The volatility of $x_t Q_t$ is

$$\nu = \sqrt{\sigma_Q^2 + s^2 + 2\rho\sigma_Q s} \tag{40}$$

Using this volatility and the prepaid forward prices, we have

$$C = x_0 Q_0 e^{-\delta T} N(d_1) - e^{-rt} K N(d_2) \tag{41}$$

$$d_1 = \frac{\ln(x_0 Q_0 e^{-\delta T}/e^{-rt} K) + \frac{1}{2}\nu^2 t}{\nu\sqrt{t}}$$

$$d_2 = d_1 - \nu\sqrt{t}$$

You can interpret this formula in terms of prepaid forward prices or as the Black-Scholes formula with $x_0 Q_0$ as the stock price, δ_Q as the dividend yield, ν as the volatility, the domestic interest rate r as the risk-free rate, and K as the strike price.

Example 11. Using the parameters in Table 4, the volatility is

$$\nu = \sqrt{0.15^2 + 0.1^2 + (2 \times 0.2 \times 0.15 \times 0.1)} = 0.1962$$

and assuming a strike price of \$195, we price the call using prepaid forwards as

$$\text{BSCall}(x_0 Q_0 e^{-\delta T}, Ke^{-rT}, \nu, 0, T, 0)$$

$$= \text{BSCall}(0.01\$/¥ \times ¥20{,}000e^{-0.02}, \$195 \times e^{-0.08}, 0.1962, 0, 1, 0) = \$24.0719$$ ■

Fixed Exchange Rate Foreign Equity Call

Suppose we have a foreign equity call denominated in the foreign currency, but with the option proceeds to be repatriated at a predetermined exchange rate. This is a quanto option, analogous to the quanto forward, with the value of the option translated into dollars at a fixed exchange rate. Let $\bar{x}$ represent this rate. The payoff to this option with strike price K_f (denominated in the foreign currency) is

$$V(Q_T, T) = \bar{x} \times \max(0, Q_T - K_f)$$
$$= \max(0, \bar{x}Q_T - \bar{x}K_f)$$

Once again we can construct the pricing formula by thinking in terms of forward prices for the underlying and strike assets. From a dollar perspective, the underlying asset, $\bar{x}Q_T$, is a quanto index investment. The strike asset is simply a fixed number of dollars, with K_f converted at the rate $\bar{x}$. Since $\bar{x}$ is just a scale factor, we can set $\bar{x} = 1$.

Because the exchange rate is fixed, the volatility that affects the value of the option is that of the foreign-currency–denominated foreign index, σ_Q. We can obtain the pricing formula by using the prepaid forwards for the underlying and strike asset:

$$C = F_{0,T}^P(Q)N(d_1) - e^{-rT}K_f N(d_2) \tag{42}$$
$$d_1 = \frac{\ln[F_{0,t}^P(Q)/e^{-rT}K_f] + \frac{1}{2}\sigma_Q^2 T}{\sigma_Q\sqrt{T}}$$
$$d_2 = d_1 - \sigma_Q\sqrt{t}$$

The formula for $F_{0,T}^P(Q)$ is given in equation (31). Note that all values are dollar-denominated since $\bar{x}$ implicitly multiplies all prices. By substituting for $F_{0,t}^P$, equation (42) is the Black-Scholes formula with Q_0 as the stock price, $\delta_Q + \rho s \sigma_Q + r - r_f$ as the dividend yield, the domestic interest rate r as the risk-free rate, K_f as the strike, and σ_Q as the volatility.

Example 12. Using the parameters in Table 4 and assuming a strike price of ¥19,500 with a fixed exchange rate of $\bar{x} = 0.01\$/¥$, we price the call by using the Black-Scholes formula. We obtain

$$\text{BSCall}(F_{0,T}^P(Q), K_f e^{-rT}, \sigma_Q, 0, T, 0) =$$
$$\text{BSCall}(0.01\$/¥ \times ¥20,000 \times e^{-(0.02+0.2\times0.1\times0.15+0.08-0.04)}, 0.01\$/¥ \times ¥19,500e^{-0.08},$$
$$0.15, 0, 1, 0) = \$15.3187$$

Problem 6 asks you to verify that you obtain the same answer with $x_0 Q_0$ as the underlying asset and an appropriate choice of the dividend yield. ■

Equity-Linked Foreign Exchange Call

If we invest in a foreign asset, we might like to insure against low exchange rates when we convert back to the domestic currency, while still having the ability to profit from favorable exchange rates. Buying an exchange rate put is insufficient because the quantity of currency to be exchanged is uncertain. What we want is an option that guarantees a minimum exchange rate *when we convert the asset value back to the domestic currency.*

Such an option must therefore protect a variable quantity of currency. This is an *equity-linked foreign exchange option*, which is another example of a quanto option.

Let K be the minimum exchange rate. Then the payoff to such an insured position would be

$$\begin{aligned} Q_T x_T + Q_T \max(0, K - x_T) &= Q_T K + Q_T \max(0, x_T - K) \\ &= Q_T K + \max(0, x_T Q_T - Q_T K) \end{aligned} \tag{43}$$

The expression to the left of the equals sign in equation (43) is the unprotected currency-translated Nikkei investment plus Q_T exchange rate puts with strike K. The equivalent expression on the right is a quanto investment with the fixed exchange rate equal to K, plus Q_T exchange rate calls. Either way, the protection entails receiving the payoff to a random number of options. All cash flows are denominated in the home currency.

We can value the option in equation (43) as follows. $x_T Q_T$ is the currency translated index and $Q_T K$ is a quanto. The prepaid forward price for $Q_T x_T$ is $Q_0 x_0 e^{-\delta_Q T}$, with volatility given by equation 40. The prepaid forward price for the strike asset is $K F^P_{0,T}(Q)$ (see equation (31)). The relevant variance is that of $\ln(x_T Q_T / Q_T)$, which is just the variance of x_T, the exchange rate. (If you look at equation (43), you can see that exercise depends on whether $x_T > K$; thus only the variance of x_T matters.)

The price of the call is therefore

$$C = x_0 Q_0 e^{-\delta_Q T} N(d_1) - K Q_0 e^{(r_f - \delta_Q - \rho\sigma_Q s - r)T} N(d_2) \tag{44}$$

$$d_1 = \frac{\ln\left(x_0 Q_0 e^{-\delta_Q T} / K Q_0 e^{(r_f - \delta_Q - \rho\sigma_Q s - r)T}\right) + 0.5 s^2 T}{s\sqrt{T}}$$

$$d_2 = d_1 - s\sqrt{T}$$

This is the price of a call option with $x_0 Q_0$ as the stock price, $K Q_0$ as the strike price, $r + \delta_Q + \rho\sigma_Q s - r_f$ as the risk-free rate, δ_Q as the dividend yield, and s as the volatility. It is perhaps surprising that only the volatility of the exchange rate matters. This occurs because the underlying option is a currency option and the change of numeraire does not affect the volatility.

Example 13. Using the parameters in Table 4 and assuming a strike price of ¥19,500 with a fixed exchange rate of $\bar{x} = 0.01\$/¥$, we price the call as

$$\begin{aligned} &\text{BSCall}\,(F^P_{0,T}(Q), K_f e^{-rT}, \sigma_Q, 0, T, 0) = \\ &\quad \text{BSCall}(0.01\$/¥ \times ¥20{,}000 \times e^{-(0.02+0.2\times0.1\times0.15+0.08-0.04)}, \\ &\quad 0.01\$/¥ \times ¥19{,}500 e^{-0.08}, 0.15, 0, 1, 0) = \$15.3187 \end{aligned}$$

6. OTHER MULTIVARIATE OPTIONS

There are many options that have a payoff depending on the prices of two or more assets. In this section we examine two kinds of options that can be priced either by modifying the Black-Scholes formula or by using the bivariate normal distribution. Throughout this section, we assume that the assets S and Q follow the processes given by equations (1) and (2).

Options on the Best of Two Assets

Suppose an investor allocates a portfolio to both the S&P index and the currency-translated Nikkei. Allocating the portfolio to the index that the investor believes will obtain the highest return is called **market-timing**. A perfect market-timer would invest in the S&P when it outperformed the Nikkei and the Nikkei when it outperformed the S&P. What is the value of being able to infallibly select the portfolio with the superior performance?

We can answer this question by valuing an option giving us the greater of the two returns. This option would have the payoff $\max(S_T, Q_T)$, where S is the S&P index and the Q the Nikkei index. Note that

$$\max(S_T, Q_T) = Q_T + \max(S_T - Q_T, 0)$$

Thus, an option on the best of two assets is the same as owning one asset plus an option to exchange that asset for the other asset. The function $\max(S_T - Q_T, 0)$ can be viewed either as a call on S with strike asset Q, or as a put on Q with strike asset S.

An investor allocating funds between the S&P index and the Nikkei index might also want to include cash in the comparison, so that there is a guaranteed minimum return. If K represents this minimum return, the payoff for a perfect market-timer is then

$$\max(K, S_T, Q_T)$$

This option, called a **rainbow option**, has no simple one-variable solution. Instead, valuing this option requires the use of the bivariate normal distribution.[11] The bivariate normal distribution is defined as

$$\Pr(z_1 < a, z_2 < b; \rho) = \mathrm{NN}(a, b; \rho) \tag{45}$$

where z_1 and z_2 are standard normal random variables with correlation coefficient ρ.

The formula for a rainbow option is

$$\begin{aligned}
&\text{RainbowCall}(S, Q, K, \sigma, \sigma_Q, \rho, \delta, \delta_Q, T-t) \\
&\quad = Se^{-\delta(T-t)}\{N(d_{SQ}) - \mathrm{NN}[-d_1(S), d_{SQ}, (\rho\sigma_Q - \sigma)/\hat{\sigma}]\} \\
&\qquad + Qe^{-\delta_Q(T-t)}\{N(d_{QS}) - \mathrm{NN}[-d_1(Q), d_{QS}, (\rho\sigma - \sigma_Q)/\hat{\sigma}]\} \\
&\qquad + Ke^{-r(T-t)}\mathrm{NN}[-d_2(S), -d_2(Q), \rho]
\end{aligned} \tag{46}$$

where

$$d_1(S) = \frac{\ln(S/K) + (r - \delta + 0.5\sigma^2)(T-t)}{\sigma\sqrt{T-t}}$$

$$d_1(Q) = \frac{\ln(Q/K) + (r - \delta_Q + 0.5\sigma_Q^2)(T-t)}{\sigma_Q\sqrt{T-t}}$$

$$d_2(S) = d_1(S) - \sigma\sqrt{T-t}$$

11. Stulz (1982) first valued a rainbow option. See also Rubinstein (1991c) for a discussion.

$$d_2(Q) = d_1(Q) - \sigma_Q\sqrt{T-t}$$

$$d_{SQ} = \frac{\ln(S/Q) + (\delta_Q - \delta + 0.5\hat{\sigma}^2)(T-t)}{\hat{\sigma}\sqrt{T-t}}$$

$$d_{QS} = \frac{\ln(Q/S) + (\delta - \delta_Q + 0.5\hat{\sigma}^2)(T-t)}{\hat{\sigma}\sqrt{T-t}}$$

$$\hat{\sigma} = \sqrt{\sigma^2 + \sigma_Q^2 - 2\rho\sigma\sigma_Q}$$

You can understand this daunting formula by recognizing that, at maturity, the option must be worth either S, Q, or K. By setting $t = T$, you can verify that the formula satisfies this boundary condition. The formula for an option that pays $\min(S, Q, K)$—a rainbow put—is obtained by putting a minus sign in front of each "d" argument in the normal and bivariate normal functions.

Certain related options can be valued using the rainbow option formula.[12] For example, consider an option on the maximum of two assets with the payoff

$$\max[0, \max(S, Q) - K]$$

This is equal to $\max(S, Q, K) - K$, which has the value

$$\text{RainbowCall}(S, Q, K, \sigma, \sigma_Q, \rho, \delta, \delta_Q, r, T-t) - Ke^{-r(T-t)}$$

Some options that seem as if they might be valued using the rainbow option formula, however, cannot be. For example, consider the valuation of peak-load electricity plants and encountered spread options, which have the payoff

$$\max(0, S - Q - K)$$

While there are approximations for valuing such an option (see Haug, 1998, pp. 59–61), more exact solutions require Monte Carlo or two-state binomial trees.

Basket Options

Basket options have payoffs that depend upon the average of two or more asset prices. Basket options are frequently used in currency hedging. A multinational firm dealing in multiple currencies, for example, might care only about hedging the average exchange rate, rather than each exchange rate individually. As another example, an option on the S&P index might pay off only if the S&P outperforms an average of the currency-translated Nikkei and Dax (German stock) indices. With equal weights on the Nikkei and Dax, the payoff to such an option would be

$$\max[0, S_{\text{S\&P}} - 0.5 \times (S_{\text{Nikkei}} + S_{\text{Dax}})]$$

You may be able to guess the problem with deriving a simple formula to value such a payoff. The arithmetic average of two indices does not follow geometric Brownian motion. (In fact,

12. Rubinstein (1991c) provides a thorough discussion of these related options, as well as discussing which options *cannot* be valued as rainbow options.

if an index is an arithmetic average of stocks, the index itself does not follow geometric Brownian motion. We have been making the common, yet inconsistent, assumption that both stocks and indices containing those stocks follow geometric Brownian motion.)

Because the payoff can depend on many random variables and there is no easy formula, Monte Carlo is a natural technique for valuing basket options. Moreover, basket options provide a natural application for the control variate method to speed up Monte Carlo. A basket option based on the geometric average can be valued using Black-Scholes with appropriate adjustments to the volatility and dividend yield. This price can then serve as a control variate for the more conventional basket option based on an arithmetic average.

CHAPTER SUMMARY

It is possible to build new derivative claims by using simpler claims as building blocks. Important building blocks include all-or-nothing options, which pay either cash or an asset under certain conditions. Assuming that prices are lognormal with constant volatility, it is straightforward to value cash-or-nothing and asset-or-nothing options both with and without barriers. Cash-or-nothing claims can be priced as discounted risk-neutral probabilities, and a change of numeraire can then be used to price asset-or-nothing options. These claims can be used to create, among other things, ordinary options, gap options, and barrier options. While these options are straightforward to price, they may be quite difficult to hedge because of discontinuities in the payoff created by the all-or-nothing characteristic.

Quantos are claims for which the payoff depends on the product or quotient of two prices. Quantos can be used to remove the currency risk from an investment in a foreign stock index and thus are used in international investing. It is possible to construct bivariate binomial trees to price quantos. International investors can also use currency-linked options to tailor their exposure to currency. The standard currency options can be priced using prepaid forwards and change of numeraire.

Other options, such as rainbow and basket options, have payoffs depending on two or more asset prices. Some of these options have simple pricing formulas; others must be valued binomially, using Monte Carlo, or in some other way.

FURTHER READING

Mark Rubinstein and Eric Reiner published a series of papers on exotic options in *Risk* magazine in the early 1990s. These provide a comprehensive discussion of pricing formulas on a wide variety of options. Some of the material in this chapter is based directly on those papers, which can be hard to obtain. Ingersoll (2000) also provides examples of the use of all-or-nothing options as building blocks. An alternative approach to two-state binomial pricing is detailed in Boyle et al. (1989).

If you are interested in more pricing formulas, Haug (1998) presents numerous formulas and discusses approximations when those simple formulas are not available. Wilmott (1998) also has a comprehensive discussion emphasizing the use of partial differential equations (which, as we have seen, underlie all derivatives pricing). Zhang (1998) and Briys and

Bellala (1998) discuss exotic options, including many not discussed in this chapter. In practice, the hitting of a barrier is often determined on a daily or other periodic basis. Broadie et al. (1997) provide a simple correction term that makes the barrier pricing formulas more accurate when monitoring of the barrier is not continuous. One class of options we have not discussed is lookback options, which pay out based on the highest (or lowest) price over the life of the option. These are discussed in Goldman et al. (1979a) and Goldman et al. (1979b) and are covered in Problems 13 and 14.

PROBLEMS

1. A **collect-on-delivery call** (COD) costs zero initially, with the payoff at expiration being 0 if $S < K$, and $S - K - P$ if $S \geq K$. The problem in valuing the option is to determine P, the amount the option-holder pays if the option is in-the-money at expiration. The premium P is determined once and for all when the option is created. Let $S = \$100$, $K = \$100$, $r = 5\%$, $\sigma = 20\%$, $T - t = 1$ year, and $\delta = 0$.
   a. Value a European COD call option with the above inputs. (*Hint:* Recognize that you can construct the COD payoff by combining an ordinary call option and a cash-or-nothing call.)
   b. Compute delta and gamma for a COD option. (You may do this by computing the value of the option at slightly different prices and calculating delta and gamma directly, rather than by using a formula.) Consider different stock prices and times to expiration, in particular setting t close to T.
   c. How hard is it to hedge a COD option?
2. A **barrier COD** option is like a COD except that payment for the option occurs whenever a barrier is struck. Price a barrier COD put for the same values as in the previous problem, with a barrier of \$95 and a strike of \$90. Compute the delta and gamma for the paylater put. Compare the behavior of delta and gamma with that for a COD. Explain the differences, if any.
3. Verify that equation (7) satisfies the appropriate boundary conditions for $\Pr(\underline{S}_T \leq H \text{ and } S_T > K)$.
4. Verify that equation (14) (for both cases $K > H$ and $K < H$) solves the boundary conditions for an up-and-in cash put.
5. Assume that $S = \$45$, $K = \$40$, $r = 0.05$, $\delta = 0.02$, and $\sigma = 0.30$. Using the up rebate formula (equation (21)), find the value of H that maximizes $(H - K) \times \text{UR}(S, \sigma, r, T, \delta)$, for $T = 1$, 10, 100, 1000, and 10,000. Compare both H and $(H - K) \times \text{UR}$ to the perpetual option solution. Explain the differences.
6. Verify in Example 12 that you obtain the same answer if you use $x_0 Q_0$ as the stock price, $\delta_Q + \rho s \sigma_Q + r - r_f$ as the dividend yield, r as the interest rate, and σ_Q as the volatility.
7. In this problem you will price various options with payoffs based on the Eurostoxx index and the dollar/euro exchange rate. Assume that $Q = 2750$ (the index), $x = 1.25$ (\$/€), $s = 0.08$ (the exchange rate volatility), $\sigma = 0.2$ (index volatility), $r = 0.01$ (the U.S. risk-free rate), $r_f = 0.03$ (the euro-denominated risk-free rate), $\delta_Q = 0.02$ (the

dividend yield on the index), $\rho = 0.25$ (the index exchange rate correlation), and $T = 1$. Verify the following prices (all are in dollars):

a. Equity index call denominated in euros: $\max(Q_T - K, 0)$, $K = 2500$ ($457.775)

b. Foreign equity call struck in domestic currency: $\max(x_T Q_T - K_d, 0)$, $K_d =$ $3200 ($414.574)

c. Fixed exchange rate foreign equity call: $\bar{x}\max(Q_T - K, 0)$; $\bar{x} = 1.25$, $K =$ 2500 ($456.988)

d. Equity-linked foreign exchange call: $\max(x_T Q_T - K Q_T, 0)$, $K = \$1.20$ ($152.561)

8. This problem has been intentionally omitted for this edition.

9. In this problem we use the lognormal approximation to draw one-step binomial trees from the perspective of a yen-based investor. Use the information in Table 4.

a. Construct a one-step tree for the Nikkei index.

b. Construct a one-step tree for the exchange rate (yen/dollars).

c. Use the trees to price Nikkei and dollar forwards. Compare your answers with those in Example 7.

10. Suppose an option knocks in at $H_1 > S$, and knocks out at $H_2 > H_1$. Suppose that $K < H_2$ and the option expires at T. Call this a "knock-in, knock-out" option. Here is an equation summarizing the payoff to this option (note that because $H_2 > H_1$, it is not possible to hit H_2 without hitting H_1):

$$\textit{Payoff} = \begin{cases} 0 & \text{if } H_1 \text{ not hit} \\ \max(0, S_T - K) & \text{if } H_1 \text{ hit and } H_2 \text{ not hit} \\ 0 & \text{if } H_1 \text{ hit and } H_2 \text{ hit} \end{cases}$$

What is the value of this option?

11. Suppose the stock price is $50, but that we plan to buy 100 shares if and when the stock reaches $45. Suppose further that $\sigma = 0.3$, $r = 0.08$, $T - t = 1$, and $\delta = 0$. This is a noncancellable limit order.

a. What transaction could you undertake to offset the risk of this obligation?

b. You can view this limit order as a liability. What is its value?

12. Covered call writers often plan to buy back the written call if the stock price drops sufficiently. The logic is that the written call at that point has little "upside," and, if the stock recovers, the position could sustain a loss from the written call.

a. Explain in general how this buy-back strategy could be implemented using barrier options.

b. Suppose $S = \$50$, $\sigma = 0.3$, $r = 0.08$, $t = 1$, and $\delta = 0$. The premium of a written call with a $50 strike is $7.856. We intend to buy the option back if the stock hits $45. What is the net premium of this strategy?

A European **lookback call** at maturity pays $S_T - \underline{S}_T$. A European **lookback put** at maturity pays $\overline{S}_T - S_T$. (Recall that $\overline{S}_T$ and $\underline{S}_T$ are the maximum and minimum prices over the life of the option.) Here is a formula that can be used to value both options:

$$
\begin{aligned}
W(S_t, \tilde{S}_t, \sigma, r, T-t, \delta, \omega) &= \omega S_t e^{-\delta(T-t)} \left[N(\omega d_5') - \frac{\sigma^2}{2(r-\delta)} N(-\omega d_5') \right] \\
&- \omega \tilde{S}_t e^{-r(T-t)} \left[N(\omega d_6') - \frac{\sigma^2}{2(r-\delta)} \left(\frac{S_t}{\tilde{S}_t} \right)^{1-2\frac{r-\delta}{\sigma^2}} N(\omega d_8') \right]
\end{aligned}
\tag{47}
$$

where

$$
\begin{aligned}
d_5' &= [\ln(S_t/\tilde{S}_t) + (r - \delta + 0.5\sigma^2)(T-t)]/\sigma\sqrt{T-t} \\
d_6' &= d_5' - \sigma\sqrt{T-t} \\
d_7' &= [\ln(\tilde{S}_t/S_t) + (r - \delta + 0.5\sigma^2)(T-t)]/\sigma\sqrt{T-t} \\
d_8' &= d_7' - \sigma\sqrt{T-t}
\end{aligned}
$$

The value of a lookback call is obtained by setting $\tilde{S}_t = \underline{S}_t$ and $\omega = 1$. The value of a lookback put is obtained by setting $\tilde{S}_t = \overline{S}_t$ and $\omega = -1$.

13. For the lookback call:

a. What is the value of a lookback call as S_t approaches zero? Verify that the formula gives you the same answer.

b. Verify that at maturity the value of the call is $S_T - \underline{S}_T$.

14. For the lookback put:

a. What is the value of a lookback put if $S_t = 0$? Verify that the formula gives you the same answer.

b. Verify that at maturity the value of the put is $\overline{S}_T - S_T$.

15. A European **shout option** is an option for which the payoff at expiration is $\max(0, S - K, G - K)$, where G is the price at which you shouted. (Suppose you have an XYZ shout call with a strike price of \$100. Today XYZ is \$130. If you shout at \$130, you are guaranteed a payoff of $\max(\$30, S_T - \$130)$ at expiration.) You can only shout once, irrevocably.

a. Demonstrate that shouting at some arbitrary price $G > K$ is better than never shouting.

b. Compare qualitatively the value of a shout option to (i) a lookback option (which pays $\max[0, \overline{S}_T - K]$, where $\overline{S}_T$ is the greatest stock price over the life of the option) and (ii) a **ladder option** (which pays $\max(0, S - K, L - K)$ if the underlying hits the value L at some point over the life of the option).

c. Explain how to value this option binomially. (*Hint:* Think about how you would compute the value of the option at the moment you shout.)

16. Consider the Level 3 outperformance option with a multiplier. This can be valued binomially using the single state variable $S_{\text{Level 3}}/S_{\text{S\&P}}$, and multiplying the resulting value by $S_{\text{S\&P}}$.

a. Compute the value of this option if it were European, assuming the Level 3 stock price is \$100, the S&P index is 1300, and the volatilities and dividend yields are 25% and 0 for the Level 3 and 16% and 1.8% for the S&P. The Level 3–S&P correlation is 0.4 and the option has 4 years to expiration.

b. Repeat the valuation assuming the option is American.

c. In the absence of a multiplier, would you expect the option ever to be early-exercised? Under what circumstances does early exercise occur with the multiplier?

17. Consider AAAPI, the Nikkei ADR in disguise. To answer this question, use the information in Table 4.

a. What is the volatility of Y, the price of AAAPI?

b. What is the covariance between Y and x, the dollar-yen exchange rate?

c. What is the correlation between Y and x, the dollar-yen exchange rate?

d. Using this information on the volatility of Y and the correlation between Y and x, construct a joint binomial tree for x and Y. Use this tree to price a Nikkei quanto forward.

Appendix A THE REFLECTION PRINCIPLE

Appendix available at http://www.pearsonhighered.com/mcdonald.

Volatility

Volatility is a critical input necessary for pricing options, but it is not directly observable and it is not constant over time.[1] Consequently, both theorists and practitioners are concerned with the behavior of volatility and the construction of option pricing models in which volatility can change. Hedging volatility risk is also an important issue for market-makers.

In this chapter we will discuss specific techniques for measuring stock price volatility and also demonstrate how volatility models can be incorporated into the Black-Scholes pricing framework.

The chapter is divided into four general topics:

- Implied volatility: What information do option prices provide about volatility, both at a point in time and over time?
- Volatility estimation: Given the past history of stock returns, what can you say about volatility?
- Volatility hedging: What instruments are available to hedge volatility risk?
- Option pricing: How can we price options when volatility is stochastic?

You should keep in mind when reading this chapter that the distribution of asset prices remains an area in which there is significant ongoing research. Statistical techniques for measuring volatility continue to evolve, and there is a search for pricing models that best explain observed option prices.

1. Throughout the chapter we will discuss volatility as an input into pricing models. The implicit assumption is that volatility is a parameter of the (known) distribution of the underlying asset. However, we can also think of option markets as determining prices for claims on the future value of the underlying asset, for which we may not know the return distribution. An option pricing model then provides an *interpretation* of these prices, with volatility simply a parameter of the model. The point is that you can learn something from studying volatility even if you do not take the models literally.

From Chapter 24 of *Derivatives Markets*, Third Edition, Robert McDonald. Copyright © 2013 by Pearson Education, Inc. Published by Pearson Prentice Hall. All rights reserved.

1. IMPLIED VOLATILITY

To provide a context for the discussion in this chapter, we begin by reviewing implied volatility. Figure 1 depicts implied volatilities for exchange-traded IBM and S&P 500 index options on January 18, 2012, an arbitrarily chosen date. The patterns are typical, with in-the-money (low strike) calls having higher implied volatilities than at-the-money and out-of-the-money calls. In addition, the implied volatility curve is flatter for options with longer time to maturity. You may see volatilities such as those in Figure 1 plotted in a three-dimensional graph, with time to maturity on one axis and strike prices on a different axis. Such a plot is called a **volatility surface**.

The pattern of implied volatilities generally is referred to as the *volatility skew*. However, specific patterns are frequently observed. If you use your imagination, the implied volatility plot in Figure 1 resembles a lopsided grin or a smirk. The pattern in the figure is sometimes called a *volatility smirk*. When the plot of implied volatility against strike prices looks like a smile, it is called a **volatility smile**. *Volatility frowns* may also be observed.

Implied volatility may seem like a natural way to measure the volatility that is expected to prevail over a future period of time. However, the fact that implied volatilities are not constant across strike prices and over time raises at least two issues. First, it is common to measure implied volatility using the Black-Scholes model, which assumes that volatility is constant. The volatility skew may reflect pricing or specification error in the Black-Scholes

FIGURE 1

Implied volatilities for options on IBM (top panel) and on the S&P 500 index (bottom panel), January 18, 2012. Closing prices for IBM and the S&P 500 index on this day were 181.07 and 1308.04.

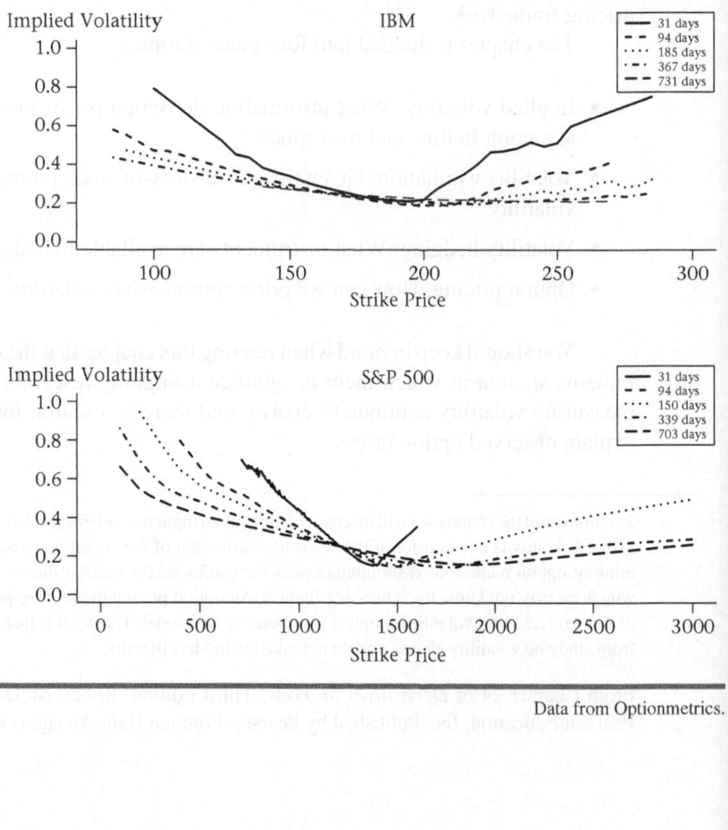

Data from Optionmetrics.

FIGURE 2

VIX (top panel) and VIX minus VXO (bottom panel), January 1990–March 2012.

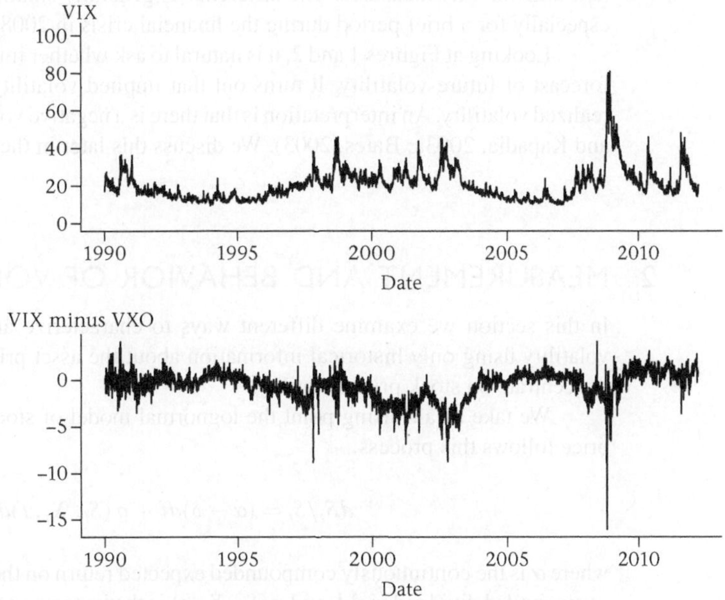

Source: Yahoo.

model, which raises the question of what implied volatility actually measures. Second, since there is no single measure of implied volatility (for the same asset, implied volatilities differ across strikes and across option maturities), how should we interpret the implied volatility numbers? Should we look at volatility at a particular "moneyness"? Is there some way to average the different volatilities? We will see later in this chapter that some theoretical pricing models are able to account for implied volatility patterns such as those in Figure 1.

In addition to examining the pattern of implied volatilities at a point in time, we can track implied volatilities over time. Since 1993 the Chicago Board Options Exchange (CBOE) has reported an index of implied volatility called the "VIX" (its ticker symbol). Originally, the CBOE reported implied volatility for the S&P 100 index, computed from near-the-money options. This original index is now called the "Old VIX," with ticker symbol VXO. Beginning in 2003, the CBOE began reporting implied volatility for the S&P 500 index, based on a new methodology that we will describe later in this chapter. Both volatility measures have been computed for previous dates.

The top panel of Figure 2 plots the new VIX index from 1990 to 2012. The spike in the VIX during Fall 2008 is evident. On November 20, 2008, the VIX reached its post-1990 maximum of 80.86.[2] The bottom panel of Figure 2 shows the difference between the

2. During October 1987—not shown in Figure 1—the VIX exceeded 100% on October 19, 20, 22, and 26. This period corresponds to the October 19, 1987, market crash, in which the Dow Jones index declined over 20% on 1 day.

new and old VIX measures. The difference is generally small, but has been large at times, especially for a brief period during the financial crisis in 2008.

Looking at Figures 1 and 2, it is natural to ask whether implied volatility is an accurate forecast of future volatility. It turns out that implied volatility on average *exceeds* future realized volatility. An interpretation is that there is a negative volatility risk premium (Bakshi and Kapadia, 2003a; Bates, 2003). We discuss this later in the chapter.

2. MEASUREMENT AND BEHAVIOR OF VOLATILITY

In this section we examine different ways to characterize and measure the behavior of volatility using only historical information about the asset price. In our examples we will concentrate on stock price volatility.

We take as a starting point the lognormal model of stock prices. Suppose the stock price follows this process:

$$dS_t/S_t = (\alpha - \delta)dt + \sigma(S_t, X_t, t)dZ \tag{1}$$

where α is the continuously compounded expected return on the stock, δ is the continuously compounded dividend yield, and $\sigma(S_t, X_t, t)$ is the instantaneous volatility. In equation (1), volatility at a point in time can depend on the level of the stock price S, other variables, X, and time. By comparison, the standard Black-Scholes assumption is that $\sigma(S_t, X_t, t) = \sigma_0$, a constant. Equation (1) is an example of a stock price process with **stochastic volatility**, in which instantaneous volatility can change randomly.[3]

Given a series of stock prices that we observe every h periods, we can compute continuously compounded returns, ϵ:

$$\epsilon_{t+h} = \ln(S_{t+h}/S_t)$$

We will assume throughout this section that h is small, and therefore that we can ignore the mean return.

Historical Volatility

The natural starting point for examining volatility is historical volatility, which we compute using past stock returns. Suppose that we observe n continuously compounded stock returns over a period of length T, so that $h = T/n$. Under the assumption that volatility is constant, we can estimate the historical annual variance of returns, σ^2, as

$$\hat{\sigma}_{\mathrm{H}}^2 = \frac{1}{h}\left[\frac{1}{(n-1)}\sum_{i=1}^{n}\epsilon_i^2\right] \tag{2}$$

3. Note that there are no jumps in equation (1), and we will assume that the volatility, $\sigma(S, X, t)$, also does not jump. It is possible to permit jumps for both; for example, see Duffie et al. (2000).

The multiplication by $1/h$ annualizes the variance estimate in square brackets.[4] This calculation differs from the usual formula for variance since it assumes the per-period mean is zero. This assumption makes little difference if h is small.

It is natural to estimate volatility using daily returns for all trading days. It is important to recognize, however, that not all calendar days, and not even all trading days, exhibit the same volatility. For example, if all days were the same, return volatility over a weekend (from Friday's close of trading to Monday's close of trading) should be $\sqrt{3}$ times the weekday volatility. However, French and Roll (1986) showed that returns from Friday to Monday were significantly less volatile than returns over three consecutive weekdays. Individual stock price volatilities are also greater on the days when firms make earnings announcements, and this greater volatility affects option prices (Patell and Wolfson, 1979, 1981; Dubinsky and Johannes, 2004). Thus, while equation (2) provides an estimate of annualized volatility, the volatilities on individual days can vary.

Exponentially Weighted Moving Average

Because volatility in appears to be changing over time, it is natural to try to take this variation into account when estimating volatility. We might reason that if volatility is changing, we want to emphasize more recent observations at the expense of more distant observations. One way to do this is to compute an *exponentially weighted moving average* (EWMA) of the squared stock returns.

The EWMA formula computes volatility at time t as a weighted average of the time $t-1$ EWMA estimate, $\hat{\sigma}^2_{\text{EWMA},t-1}$, and the time $t-1$ squared stock price change, ϵ^2_{t-1}. Thus, we have

$$\hat{\sigma}^2_{\text{EWMA},t} = (1-b)\epsilon^2_{t-1} + b\hat{\sigma}^2_{\text{EWMA},t-1} \tag{3}$$

where b is the weight applied to the previous EWMA estimate. We can lag equation (3) and substitute the resulting expression for $\hat{\sigma}^2_{\text{EWMA},t-1}$ into the right-hand side of equation (3). Continuing in this way, we obtain the EWMA estimator as a weighted average of past squared returns:

$$\hat{\sigma}^2_{\text{EWMA},t} = \sum_{i=1}^{\infty}\left[(1-b)b^{i-1}\right]\epsilon^2_{t-i} \tag{4}$$

4. Suppose r_i is computed daily. It is important to annualize *after* computing the standard deviation of the daily returns, as opposed to annualizing the daily returns and then computing the standard deviation. To see why, let $\{r_i\}$ be the set of nonannualized daily returns. The annualized standard deviation is

$$\sqrt{252} \times \sqrt{\text{Var}(\{r_i\})}$$

If instead we first annualize the returns by multiplying them by 252 and then compute the standard deviation, we obtain

$$\sqrt{\text{Var}(252 \times \{r_i\})} = 252 \times \sqrt{\text{Var}(\{r_i\})}$$

Annualizing returns before computing the standard deviation creates a return series that has too much volatility.

The term in square brackets in equation (4) is the weight applied to historical returns. The weights decline at the rate b, with the most recent return receiving the greatest weight. Because $\sum_{i=1}^{\infty}(1-b)b^{i-1}=1$, the weights on past squared returns sum to 1.

It is also possible to use a moving window when estimating EWMA volatility. For example, we might use only the previous n days of data. In this case, equation (4) becomes

$$\begin{aligned}\hat{\sigma}^2_{\text{EWMA},t} &= \sum_{i=1}^{n}\left[\frac{(1-b)b^{i-1}}{\sum_{j=1}^{n}(1-b)b^{j-1}}\right]\epsilon^2_{t-i}\\ &= \sum_{i=1}^{n}\left[\frac{(1-b)b^{i-1}}{1-b^n}\right]\epsilon^2_{t-i}\end{aligned} \tag{5}$$

Because $\sum_{i=1}^{n}(1-b)b^{i-1}=1-b^n$, the weights again sum to 1.

There is also a simple updating formula, analogous to equation (3), in the case of a moving window estimate. Each period we add the latest observation and drop the oldest observation. Equation (5) is equivalent to

$$\hat{\sigma}^2_{\text{EWMA},t} = b\hat{\sigma}^2_{\text{EWMA},t-1} + \frac{1-b}{1-b^n}\left[\epsilon^2_{t-1} - b^n\epsilon^2_{t-1-n}\right] \tag{6}$$

Example 1. Suppose $b=0.94$ and $n=60$. We have $1-b^n=0.9756$. The first term in equation (6) is then

$$\frac{(1-0.94)}{0.9756}=0.0615$$

This compares with a weight of $1/60=0.0167$ for each observation in the equal-weighted estimator in equation (2). Subsequent (earlier) observations have weights of 0.0578, 0.0543, 0.0511, etc. ■

Figure 3 illustrates two different historical volatility calculations. The top panel displays the historical 60-day volatility for IBM and the S&P 500 index from 1990 to 2012. Each day, the preceding 60 trading days are used to compute the standard deviation of the continuously compounded daily return. The resulting standard deviation is multiplied by $\sqrt{252}$ to produce an annualized standard deviation. The use of overlapping 60-day intervals induces smoothness in the series, since each day's return affects the next 60 days of volatility calculations. Even so, there is a great deal of variability in the standard deviation.

The bottom panel in Figure 3 displays the EWMA estimate for $b=0.94$ and $n=60$ days. Note that the EWMA estimator exhibits more variability than the standard historical volatility estimate. This additional variability occurs because the most recent observation has four times the weight in the EWMA estimator as in the standard estimator. Thus a particularly large return will create a large effect on the estimate. This effect will then decay at the rate b.

There are two problems with the EWMA estimator, one practical and one conceptual. First, if we use the EWMA estimator in equation (3) to forecast future volatility, we obtain a constant expected volatility at any horizon. The reason is that the forecast of ϵ_t^2 is $\hat{\sigma}^2_{t-1}$, so that all forecasts of future volatility would equal $\hat{\sigma}^2_{t-1}$. Thus, the EWMA estimator does not forecast patterns in future volatility. Second, the EWMA estimator is not derived from a

FIGURE 3

Sixty-day volatility estimates for IBM and the S&P 500 index from January 1990 to March 2012. The top panel shows volatility estimates using equation (2), whereas the bottom panel uses equation (5), with $b = 0.94$.

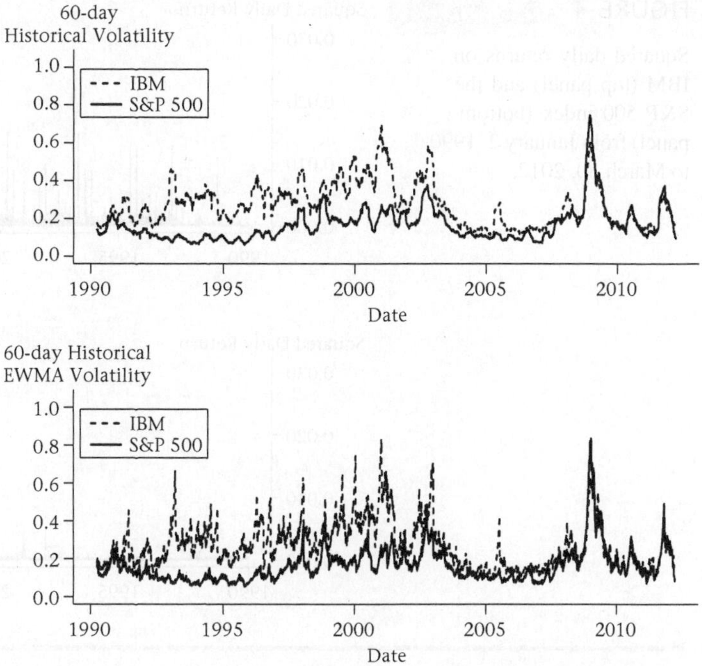

Source: Stock price data from Yahoo.

formal statistical model in which volatility can vary over time. ARCH and GARCH, which we discuss next, address both problems.

Time-Varying Volatility: ARCH

A casual examination of data, such as looking at historical volatilities (Figure 3), or looking at the behavior over time of implied volatilities (Figure 2), suggests that volatilities are not constant.[5] What do we do once we formally accept that volatilities change over time? Ideally we would have a statistical model that permits volatility changes to occur. Such a model could serve both to provide better estimates of volatility and also to provide a building block for better pricing models.

Research on the behavior of volatility shows that for many assets, there are periods of turbulence and periods of calm: high volatility tends to be followed by high volatility and

5. We can perform a back-of-the-envelope calculation by assuming that continuously compounded returns are normally distributed. In that case, the ratio of variances drawn from independent time periods has the F distribution. If we estimate two annual volatilities using 252 observations, the ratio of the two estimated variances is distributed $F(\alpha, 251, 251)$. The 99.5% and 0.005% confidence levels are obtained from $F^{-1}(p, 251, 251)$, where $p = 0.995$ or $p = 0.005$. At a 1% significance level, the two bounds for the ratio of estimated variances are 1.386 and 0.722, corresponding to volatility ratios of 1.177 and 0.849. Thus, if volatility in one year is 15%, a subsequent measured volatility outside the range 12.74%–17.66% rejects the hypothesis of constant variance at a 1% significance level.

FIGURE 4

Squared daily returns on IBM (top panel) and the S&P 500 index (bottom panel) from January 2, 1990, to March 30, 2012.

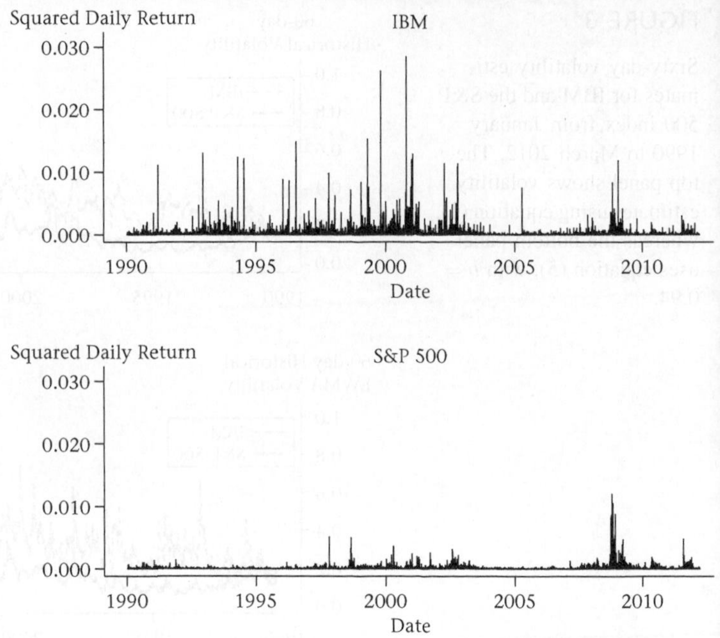

Source: Stock price data from Yahoo.

low volatility by low volatility. Put differently, during a period when measured volatility is high, the typical day tends to exhibit high volatility. (High volatility could in principle also arise from an increased chance of large but infrequent price moves.) Figure 4 displays squared daily returns for the S&P 500 index and IBM. At a casual level, this figure exhibits this effect, with periods in which many of the daily squared returns are large, and periods when many are small. This is called **volatility clustering**.

If volatility is persistent, a volatility measure should weight recent returns more heavily than more distant returns. This difference in weighting is exactly how an EWMA volatility estimate differs from the ordinary equally weighted volatility measure. ARCH and GARCH models also give more weight to recent returns.

The ARCH Model. The autoregressive conditional heteroskedasticity (ARCH) model of Engle (1982) and the subsequent GARCH (Generalized ARCH) model of Bollerslev (1986) are important and widely used volatility models that attempt to capture statistically the ebb and flow of volatility.[6] Engle in fact won the 2003 Nobel Prize in economics for his work in this area (see the box on the next page). The basic idea motivating ARCH is that if volatility is high today it is likelier than average to be high tomorrow. Engle (1982) provided a statistical framework for modeling this effect.

6. Bollerslev et al. (1994) surveys the literature on ARCH and its variants. Two accessible introductions were written as a result of the 2003 Nobel Prize: Diebold (2004) and Royal Swedish Academy of Sciences (2003). Nelson (1991) proposed exponential GARCH, which models the behavior of $\ln(\sigma^2)$.

BOX 1: A Nobel Prize for Volatility

The 2003 Nobel Prize in economics was awarded to Robert F. Engle and Clive Granger for their work in statistical methods in economics. Engle was cited for his work in studying the behavior of volatility. This quote, from the Royal Swedish Academy of Science press release announcing the award of the 2003 economics prize, describes Engle's contribution:

> Random fluctuations over time—volatility—are particularly significant because the value of shares, options and other financial instruments depends on their risk. Fluctuations can vary considerably over time; turbulent periods with large fluctuations are followed by calmer periods with small fluctuations. Despite such time-varying volatility, in want of a better alternative, researchers used to work with statistical methods that presuppose constant volatility. Robert Engle's discovery was therefore a major breakthrough. He found that the concept of autoregressive conditional heteroskedasticity (ARCH) accurately captures the properties of many time series and developed methods for statistical modeling of time-varying volatility. His ARCH models have become indispensable tools not only for researchers, but also for analysts on financial markets, who use them in asset pricing and in evaluating portfolio risk.
>
> *Source:* Royal Swedish Academy of Science, Press Release, October 2003.

Granger was cited for his work in cointegration, a statistical method important for studying the long-run behavior of economic time series.

A statistical model for asset prices could take the form

$$\ln(S_t/S_{t-h}) = (\alpha - \delta - 0.5\sigma^2)h + \epsilon_t \tag{7}$$

In this specification, the error term would have variance

$$\text{Var}(\epsilon_t) = \sigma^2 h \tag{8}$$

If σ^2 is constant over time, we say the error term, ϵ_t, is **homoskedastic**. Based on Figure 4, however, a more reasonable specification would be to assume that the variance of ϵ_t varies over time, in which case it is **heteroskedastic**.

If the time interval in equation (7) is short, then, the mean, $(\alpha - \delta - 0.5\sigma^2)h$, is small, and ϵ_t^2 is essentially the squared return. We will continue to assume that h is short enough so that we can ignore the drift in equation (7).

Let Ψ_t denote the information that is available up to and including time t, and therefore information that we have available at time t. The idea behind Engle's ARCH model is that squared returns have a variance that changes over time according to a statistical model. Specifically, let q_t be the conditional (upon information available at time $t-1$) value of the return variance, i.e.,

$$q_t \equiv E(\epsilon_t^2|\Psi_{t-1})$$

The ARCH model supposes that we can write

$$q_t = a_0 + \sum_{i=1}^{m} a_i\epsilon_{t-i}^2 \tag{9}$$

where $a_0 > 0$, $a_i \geq 0$, $i = 1, \ldots, m$. Equation (9) is an ARCH(m) model, signifying that there are m lagged terms. In order for volatility to be well-behaved, we must have $\sum_{i=1}^{n} a_i < 1$. This model states that volatility at a point in time depends upon recent observed volatility.

At this point we can understand the meaning of "autoregressive conditional heteroskedasticity." *Autoregressive* means that the value at a point in time depends on past values. *Heteroskedasticity* means that variances are not equal. The unconditional variance is the variance estimated over a long period of time. The *conditional* variance is the variance estimated at a point in time, taking into account ("conditional upon") recent volatility. Thus, *autoregressive conditional heteroskedasticity* essentially means that the level of variance depends on recent past levels of variance. This is the behavior captured by equation (9).

ARCH Volatility Forecasts. An important practical question is how many lags we need in order to estimate equation (9). To better understand the behavior of an ARCH model, let's consider a single lag, where we set $a_1 > 0$ and $a_i = 0$, $i > 1$. The volatility equation is then

$$E(\epsilon_t^2 | \Psi_{t-1}) = a_0 + a_1 \epsilon_{t-1}^2 \tag{10}$$

where $a_0 > 0$ and $a_1 < 1$. Equation (10) is an ARCH(1) model.

Suppose we forecast volatility at time $t+1$, $t+2$, etc., using only the information we have at time t. Equation (10) implies that for a one-period-ahead forecast of q_t we have

$$\begin{aligned} E(\epsilon_{t+1}^2 | \Psi_{t-1}) &= a_0 + a_1 E(\epsilon_t^2 | \Psi_{t-1}) \\ &= a_0 + a_1 \left(a_0 + a_1 \epsilon_{t-1}^2 \right) \end{aligned}$$

Similarly, for a two-period-ahead forecast,

$$\begin{aligned} E(\epsilon_{t+2}^2 | \Psi_{t-1}) &= a_0 + a_1 E(\epsilon_{t+1}^2 | \Psi_{t-1}) \\ &= a_0 + a_1 \left[a_0 + a_1 \left(a_0 + a_1 \epsilon_{t-1}^2 \right) \right] \end{aligned}$$

Continuing in this way, for an n-period-ahead forecast, we have

$$E(\epsilon_{t+n}^2 | \Psi_{t-1}) = a_0 \left(1 + \sum_{i=1}^{n} a_1^i \right) + a_1^n \epsilon_{t-1}^2 \tag{11}$$

This predicted pattern of volatility persistence is very specific and inflexible. A large squared return today implies larger squared returns at all future dates, but the effect decays per period by the factor a_1. Shocks to volatility are expected to die off at a constant rate.

Equation (11) implies that unconditional volatility (the value we would estimate as a long-run average) is

$$\bar{\sigma}^2 = a_0(1 + a_1 + a_1^2 + \ldots) = \frac{a_0}{1 - a_1} \tag{12}$$

Thus, with estimates of a_0 and a_1 we can compute the unconditional volatility.

In practice, if markets become more turbulent, they may remain more turbulent for a period of time. Equation (9) with a single lag cannot account for a period of *sustained* high volatility. As you might guess, more than one lag—generally many lags—are necessary for ARCH to fit the data.

The GARCH Model

The GARCH model, due to Bollerslev (1986), is a variant of ARCH that allows for infinite lags yet can be estimated with a small number of parameters. The GARCH model has the form

$$q_t = a_0 + \sum_{i=1}^{m} a_i \epsilon_{t-i}^2 + \sum_{j=1}^{n} b_i q_{t-i} \tag{13}$$

where $a_0 > 0$, $a_i \geq 0$, $i = 1, \ldots, m$, $b_i \geq 0$, $i = 1, \ldots, n$, and $\sum_{i=1}^{m} a_i + \sum_{i=1}^{n} b_i < 1$. This model states that volatility at a point in time depends upon recent volatility as well as recent squared returns. Equation (13) is a GARCH(m, n) model.

GARCH(1,1) is frequently used in practice. The GARCH(1,1) model is

$$q_t = a_0 + a_1 \epsilon_{t-1}^2 + b_1 q_{t-1} \tag{14}$$

It is instructive to compare the GARCH(1,1) model to the ARCH(1) model, equation (10). To do this, we can rewrite equation (14) to eliminate q_{t-1} on the right-hand side. Lagging equation (14) and substituting the result for q_{t-1} on the right-hand side of equation (14), we obtain

$$q_t = a_0 + a_1 \epsilon_{t-1}^2 + b_1 \left(a_0 + a_1 \epsilon_{t-2}^2 + b_1 q_{t-2} \right)$$

Continuing in this way, we obtain

$$\begin{aligned} q_t &= a_0 \sum_{i=0}^{\infty} b_1^i + a_1 \sum_{i=0}^{\infty} b_1^i \epsilon_{t-1-i}^2 \\ &= \frac{a_0}{1 - b_1} + \frac{a_1}{1 - b_1} \sum_{i=0}^{\infty} (1 - b_1) b_1^i \epsilon_{t-1-i}^2 \end{aligned} \tag{15}$$

A GARCH(1,1) model is therefore equivalent to an ARCH(∞) model in which the lag coefficients decline at the rate b_1. Notice that the last term in equation (15) can be rewritten in terms of an EWMA volatility estimator (5):

$$q_t = \frac{a_0}{1 - b_1} + \frac{a_1}{1 - b_1} \hat{\sigma}_{\text{EWMA}}^2 \tag{16}$$

It is important to note that the parameter b_1 in the EWMA expression in equation (16) is not arbitrarily chosen, as in equation (3), but is estimated as part of the GARCH estimation procedure.

Maximum Likelihood Estimation of a GARCH Model. Given the assumption that continuously compounded returns have a distribution that is conditionally normal, with variance q_t and mean zero, we can estimate a GARCH model using maximum likelihood.[7]

7. Alexander (2001) discusses the estimation of GARCH models and is replete with examples.

The probability density for ϵ_t, conditional on q_t, is

$$f(\epsilon_t; q_t) = \frac{1}{\sqrt{2\pi q_t}} e^{-0.5\epsilon_t^2/q_t} \tag{17}$$

Since the ϵ_t are conditionally independent, the probability of observing the particular set of n returns is the product of the probabilities, which gives us the likelihood function:

$$\prod_{i=1}^{n} f(\epsilon_i|q_i) = \prod_{i=1}^{n} \frac{1}{\sqrt{2\pi q_i}} e^{-0.5\epsilon_i^2/q_i}$$

For a GARCH(1,1), q_i is a function of a_0, a_1, and b_1. The maximum likelihood estimate is the set of parameters—a_0, a_1, and b_1—that maximizes the probability of observing the returns we actually observed. Typically, it is easiest to maximize the log of the likelihood function, in which case maximizing the likelihood is the same as maximizing

$$\sum_{i=1}^{n} \left[-0.5 \ln(q_i) - 0.5\epsilon_i^2/q_i \right] \tag{18}$$

We omit the term $-0.5\ln(2\pi)$ since it does not affect the solution. The maximization of equation (18) can be performed in statistical packages or even using Solver in Excel.

Volatility Forecasts. We can forecast volatility in the GARCH(1,1) model as we did in the ARCH(1) model. To understand the calculation, recognize that since $q_t = E(\epsilon_t^2|\Psi_{t-1})$, we then have $E(q_t|\Psi_{t-j}) = E(\epsilon_t^2|\Psi_{t-j})$ for $j \geq 1$. Thus, using equation (14), we have

$$\begin{aligned} E(q_{t+1}|\Psi_{t-1}) &= a_0 + a_1 E(\epsilon_t^2|\Psi_{t-1}) + b_1 E(q_t|\Psi_{t-1}) \\ &= a_0 + (a_1 + b_1) E(q_t|\Psi_{t-1}) \\ &= a_0 + (a_1 + b_1)(a_0 + a_1\epsilon_{t-1}^2 + b_1 q_{t-1}) \end{aligned}$$

The goal in this calculation is to express the forecasted value of q_{t+1} in terms of what we can observe at time t—namely, ϵ_{t-1} and q_{t-1}. Following the same procedure, we obtain

$$E(q_{t+2}|\Psi_{t-1}) = a_0 + a_0(a_1 + b_1) + (a_1 + b_1)^2(a_0 + a_1\epsilon_{t-1}^2 + b_1 q_{t-1})$$

For a k step-ahead forecast, we have

$$E(q_{t+k}|\Psi_{t-1}) = a_0 + a_0 \sum_{i=1}^{k} (a_1 + b_1)^i + (a_1 + b_1)^k (a_1\epsilon_{t-1}^2 + b_1 q_{t-1})$$

As we let k go to infinity, we obtain an estimate of unconditional volatility in the GARCH(1,1) model:

$$\bar{\sigma}^2 = a_0 \sum_{i=0}^{\infty} (a_1 + b_1)^i = \frac{a_0}{1 - a_1 - b_1} \tag{19}$$

Using equations (16) and (19), we can express the GARCH(1,1) equation in terms of the EWMA estimate of volatility:

$$q_t = \alpha\bar{\sigma}^2 + (1 - \alpha)\hat{\sigma}_{\text{EWMA}}^2 \tag{20}$$

where $\alpha = (1 - a_1 - b_1)/(1 - b_1)$. Thus, the GARCH(1,1) expected volatility at a point in time is a weighted average of the unconditional variance, $\bar{\sigma}^2$, and the current estimated EWMA volatility, $\hat{\sigma}^2_{\text{EWMA}}$.

Example 2. Estimating a GARCH(1,1) model for IBM using daily return data from January 1999 to December 2003 yields the GARCH volatility estimate

$$q_t = 0.000001305 + 0.0446\epsilon^2_{t-1} + 0.9552q_{t-1}$$

The implied estimate of the unconditional annualized volatility is

$$\sqrt{\frac{0.000001305}{1 - 0.0446 - 0.9552} \times 252} = 1.5318$$

The historical volatility during this period was 39.85%. An estimated unconditional volatility of 153% suggests that the GARCH(1,1) model has trouble fitting the data. In this case, it turns out that the problem is caused by large returns on days during which IBM announced earnings.

During the 1999–2003 period there were 4 days on which the absolute 1-day return exceeded 12%. On each of these days (April 21, 1999; October 20, 1999; July 19, 2000; and October 17, 2000), IBM announced earnings. The 153% volatility illustrates the GARCH model's difficulty in explaining these large magnitude returns under the assumption that returns are normally distributed. If we omit these 4 days from the sample, the estimated GARCH model is[8]

$$q_t = 0.000002203 + 0.0507\epsilon^2_{t-1} + 0.9462q_{t-1}$$

These parameters imply an unconditional volatility of

$$\sqrt{\frac{0.000002203}{1 - 0.0507 - 0.9462} \times 252} = 0.4229$$

The other parameters do not change much, and this unconditional volatility estimate of 42.29% is more reasonable. This example illustrates that a GARCH model estimated using normally distributed returns can be sensitive to extreme data points. In addition to eliminating earnings announcement days, one could permit a fatter-tailed return distribution (e.g., see Bollerslev, 1987). ■

Realized Quadratic Variation

The quadratic variation (the sum of squared increments) of a Brownian motion from t to T is $T - t$. That is, suppose we frequently sample a diffusion process, $\sigma Z(t)$. Letting $n = (T - t)/h$ and $Z(i) = Z(t + ih)$, we have

$$\sum_{i=1}^{n} [\sigma Z(i+1) - \sigma Z(i)]^2 \approx \sigma^2 (T - t)$$

8. In order to obtain an unbiased estimate for nonearnings announcement days, the correct procedure would be to eliminate *all* earnings announcement days, not just those which, after the fact, exhibited high squared returns.

Quadratic variation therefore provides an estimate of the total variance of the process over time.

Suppose stock returns are generated by equation (1), in which volatility varies over time. Consider what happens if we compute the quadratic variation of the log stock price. In order to do this, we would need to observe the stock price at a high frequency—for example, using multiple prices over the course of the trading day. Suppose we observe continuously compounded returns from time t to T every h periods. To simplify notation, let $S(t+ih) = S(i)$, and $\sigma(i) = \sigma(S_{t+ih}, X_{t+ih}, t+ih)$. The **realized quadratic variation** of the stock price from time t to time T is then the sum of squared, continuously compounded returns:[9]

$$\sum_{i=1}^{n} \ln[S(i)/S(i-1)]^2$$

$$= \sum_{i=1}^{n} \left\{[\alpha - \delta - 0.5\sigma(i-1)^2]h + \sigma(i-1)[Z(i) - Z(i-1)]\right\}^2 \tag{21}$$

$$\approx \sum_{i=1}^{n} \sigma(i-1)^2 h$$

When h is small, the drift term in the summation is small relative to the diffusion term, so that the squared change in $Z(t)$ dominates the summation.[10] The right-hand side is an estimate of the total stock price variance from time t to T.

One well-known difficulty with using high-frequency data is that some observed price movements occur simply because transactions alternate between customer purchases (made at the dealer's offer price) and customer sales (made at the dealer's bid price). The resulting up and down movement in the price is called "bid-ask bounce." Andersen et al. (2003) demonstrate a way to deal with intraday data when they use currency data to compare realized quadratic variation with other variance estimates, such as GARCH(1,1). They calculate realized quadratic variation as follows. At 30-minute intervals, they observe the bid and ask prices immediately preceding and following the 30-minute mark. They interpolate

9. Unfortunately, there does not appear to be a standard terminology for the realized quadratic variation of an asset price. It is common to call σ the "volatility." It would seem consistent to refer to the sum of squared returns as the "realized variance," and the "realized volatility" would then be the square root of the realized variance. In practice, however, the sum of squared returns is sometimes called the "realized volatility." See, for example, Andersen et al. (2003). Moreover, the realized quadratic variation only measures the variance of the stock price diffusion, σ^2, under certain regularity conditions. Thus, for clarity, we will use the term "realized quadratic variation," which is unambiguous, albeit clumsy.

10. You may wonder about the difference between estimating historical volatility and realized quadratic variation. Recall the historical variance estimate, equation (2). Multiplying by $1/h$ in equation (2) is the same as multiplying by n/T. Thus, the historical variance estimate can be rewritten as

$$\hat{\sigma}_{\mathrm{H}}^2 = \frac{1}{T}\left[\frac{n}{(n-1)}\sum_{i=1}^{n}\epsilon_i^2\right]$$

Apart from the $n/(n-1)$ term, this appears to be the same as annualized realized quadratic variation. In practice, the term "historical volatility" usually implies the use of daily or less frequent data over medium to long horizons, while "quadratic variation" implies the use of intraday data over short horizons.

the averaged bid and ask prices to impute a price at 30-minute intervals. They then use this imputed price to measure the 30-minute continuously compounded return, from which they construct realized quadratic variation. In comparing forecasts based on realized quadratic variation with other methods of forecasting volatility, both in- and out-of-sample over one- and ten-day horizons, they find that realized quadratic variation is generally at least as good as other estimates.

3. HEDGING AND PRICING VOLATILITY

In this section we discuss derivative claims that have volatility as an underlying asset. We begin by discussing volatility and variance swaps (including one contract based on the VIX). We then look at an example of pricing a variance swap. Finally, we discuss the construction of the history of the VIX volatility index reported by the Chicago Board Options Exchange (CBOE). In this section we will let V denote measured volatility and V^2 measured variance.

Variance and Volatility Swaps

A **variance swap** is a forward contract that pays the difference between a forward price, $F_{0,T}(V^2)$, and some measure of the realized stock price variance, $\hat{V}^2$, over a period of time multiplied by a notional amount. The payoff to a variance swap is

$$[\hat{V}^2 - F_{0,T}(V^2)] \times N$$

where N is the notional amount of the contract. There are numerous measurement details that we have to specify in order to write the contract for a variance swap:

- How frequently the return is measured.
- Whether returns are continuously compounded or arithmetic.
- Whether the variance is measured by subtracting the mean or by simply squaring the returns.
- The period of time over which variance is measured.
- How to handle days on which, unexpectedly, trading does not occur.

Most of these design issues are straightforward, but the last deserves some comment. Most futures contracts settle based upon a final observable price. A variance contract, by contrast, settles based upon a *series* of prices. Therefore, failing to observe a price (for example, because the market is unexpectedly closed) creates a problem for measuring the realized variance. If the market is unexpectedly closed on day t, then the next measured return will be a *2-day* return, which will have a greater expected variance than a 1-day return. The following example shows how one contract deals with this issue.

Example 3. Three-month S&P 500 variance futures traded on the Chicago Futures Exchange are an example of a variance swap. The payoff is based on the annualized sum of squared, continuously compounded daily returns over a 3-month period, $\hat{V}^2$. The measured price is quoted as $\hat{V}^2 \times 10{,}000$, and by definition a one-unit change in this number (called a *variance point*) is worth \$50.

For simplicity, we treat the payoff as if it were a forward contract, settling on one day. Let ϵ_i be the continuously compounded return on day i. The payoff at expiration is

$$\$50 \times \left[10{,}000 \times 252 \times \sum_{i=1}^{n_a - 1} \frac{\epsilon_i^2}{n_e - 1} - F_{0,T}(V^2) \right]$$

In this formula, n_a is the actual number of S&P prices used in constructing V^2 (hence there are $n_a - 1$ returns), and n_e is the number of expected trading days at the outset of the contract. Thus, in the event of an unexpected trading halt, the sum of squared returns will be divided by a number larger than the number of squared returns. The reason for this is that the trading halt will not necessarily change the total variance over the period (if the trading halt is on a Tuesday, for example, the Monday to Wednesday return will typically reflect 2 days of volatility). Dividing the sum of squared returns by n_a would mechanically increase the measured variance when there is a trading halt. Dividing by n_e prevents this. ■

A **volatility swap** is like a variance swap except that it pays based on volatility rather than variance. The payoff is

$$(\hat{V} - F_{0,T}(V)) \times N$$

where $F_{0,T}(V)$ is the forward price for volatility.

Example 4. The Chicago Board Options Exchange volatility index, the VIX, is the basis for a volatility futures contract that trades on the Chicago Futures Exchange. Unlike the variance futures contract, the volatility futures contract settles based upon the VIX index. The payoff is

$$1000 \times [\text{VIX}_T - F_{0,T}(V)]$$ ■

In comparing the volatility futures contract (Example 4) with the variance futures contract (Example 3), note that the two contracts are based on volatility measured over different periods of time. The variance contract settles based on realized quadratic variation over the period from 0 to T, and thus the futures price reflects volatility expectations from time 0 to time T. The VIX contract, since it is based on the VIX index, measures volatility expectations from time T to time $T + 30$ days. Thus, the volatility contract measures volatility going forward from the settlement date, while the variance contract looks backward from the settlement date.

There are at least two reasons that the variance contract is in some sense more "natural" than a volatility contract. First, we will see below that it is possible to price and hedge a variance forward contract (given some assumptions) using option prices. The pricing of a volatility forward contract is more complicated due to Jensen's inequality. Because the volatility is the square root of the variance, Jensen's inequality implies that the volatility forward price will be less than the square root of the variance forward price of the variance.

Second, variance swaps arise naturally from dealers hedging their option positions. The profit of a delta-hedging dealer depends on the squared stock price change. Dealers can hedge this risk in realized variance by using variance swaps. For example, a dealer with a negative gamma position could enter a swap that pays the dealer when the stock has a large price change.

Pricing Volatility

We will see in this section one way to determine the fair price for a forward contract on variance.

Consider a variance contract that pays the sum of squared price changes from time 0 to time T. If price changes are measured over an interval of length $h = T/n$, the contract would have the payoff

$$\text{Payoff} = \sum_{i=1}^{n} \left(\frac{S_{(i+1)h} - S_{ih}}{S_{ih}} \right)^2 \tag{22}$$

Note that, since arithmetic and continuously compounded returns are close over small intervals, this is the same as the realized quadratic variation measure discussed in the previous section. As h gets small, this equation (22) becomes

$$\text{Payoff} = \int_0^T \sigma(S_t, X_t, t)^2 dt \tag{23}$$

where $\sigma(S, X, t)$ is the diffusion coefficient in equation (1). We want to answer two closely related questions. First, how is it possible to replicate the payoff to such a contract? Second, how should the contract be priced? As you might suspect, replicating the contract yields a way to price it.

In principle, the price of a forward contract on variance will be the expectation of equation (23) under the risk-neutral measure. In practice, how do we compute such an expectation? The following section will provide one answer.

The Log Contract. Neuberger (1994) pointed out that a forward contract that pays

$$\ln(S_T/S_0) \tag{24}$$

could be used to hedge and speculate on variance. A claim with the payoff in equation (24) is a **log contract**. As of 2012, there is no exchange-traded log contract in existence, but for the moment, suppose such a contract does exist.

Assuming the stock price follows equation (1), we can use Itô's Lemma to characterize the process followed by the log of the stock price. (Note that we assume that the stock price does not jump.) Equation (1) permits a wide range of processes for the volatility, but the prospective volatility over the next instant is known. Applying Itô's Lemma, we have

$$d[\ln(S_t)] = \frac{1}{S} dS - 0.5 \frac{1}{S^2} dS^2$$

Thus,

$$0.5\sigma(t)^2 dt = \frac{1}{S} dS - d[\ln(S_t)]$$

Integrating this equation, we have

$$0.5 \int_0^T \sigma^2(t) dt = \int_0^T \frac{1}{S} dS - \int_0^T d[\ln(S_t)] dt$$

The integral on the left-hand side is quadratic variation over 0 to T. Let $\hat{\sigma}^2$ denote annualized realized volatility from time 0 to time T. We can then rewrite this as

$$0.5T\hat{\sigma}^2 = \int_0^T \frac{1}{S} dS - \ln(S_T/S_0) \tag{25}$$

The right-hand side of equation (25) is the cumulative return to an investment in $1/S$ shares, less the return on a contract paying the realized continuously compounded return on the stock price from time 0 to time T. The left-hand side is annualized realized quadratic variation, which from equation (23) is also the payoff on a variance contract. Equation (25) demonstrates the connection between the payoff to the log contract and volatility.

Take expectations of both sides of equation (25) with respect to the risk-neutral stock price distribution. The expectation of dS/S under the risk-neutral distribution is rdt. Hence we obtain

$$\begin{aligned} 0.5T\mathrm{E}_0^*\left[\hat{\sigma}^2\right] &= \mathrm{E}^*\left[\int_0^T \frac{1}{S} dS - \ln(S_T/S_0)\right] \\ &= rT - \mathrm{E}_0^*\left[\ln(S_T/S_0)\right] \end{aligned} \tag{26}$$

This expression seems to be of little help in pricing volatility. There is a trick, however, for pricing the log contract using other instruments.

Valuing the Log Contract. Demeterfi et al. (1999) and Carr and Madan (1998) independently showed that it is possible to use a portfolio of options to replicate the payoff on the log contract. Note first that

$$\int_a^b \frac{1}{K^2}(K - S_T)dK = \left[\ln(K) + \frac{S_T}{K}\right]_a^b = \ln(b) - \ln(a) + \frac{S_T}{b} - \frac{S_T}{a}$$

Use this to obtain the following identity, for any S_T (see Demeterfi et al., 1999):[11]

$$-\ln\left(\frac{S_T}{S_*}\right) = -\frac{S_T - S_*}{S_*} + \int_0^{S_*} \frac{1}{K^2} \max(K - S_T, 0)dK + \int_{S_*}^{\infty} \frac{1}{K^2} \max(S_T - K, 0)dK$$

Notice that if we take expectations of both sides with respect to the risk-neutral distribution for S_T, the integrals on the right-hand side become undiscounted option prices, and the expected stock price is the forward price. We can add and subtract $\ln(S_0)$ to the left-hand side and then take expectations, to obtain

11. To interpret the expression on the right-hand side, notice that for any given S_T, the value of the first integral is zero for K below S_T, and the value of the second integral is zero for K above S_T. Thus, the effective integration bounds are not 0 and ∞, but they instead depend upon S_T. For example, if $S_T = \bar{S} < K, S_*$, the equation becomes

$$-\ln\left(\frac{\bar{S}}{S_*}\right) = -\frac{\bar{S} - S_*}{S_*} + \int_{\bar{S}}^{S_*} \frac{1}{K^2} \max(K - \bar{S}, 0)dK + 0$$

$$-\mathrm{E}^*\ln\left(\frac{S_T}{S_0}\right)+\ln\left(\frac{S^*}{S_0}\right)$$
$$=-\left[\frac{F_{0,T}(S)-S_*}{S_*}\right]+e^{rT}\left[\int_0^{S_*}\frac{1}{K^2}P(K)dK+\int_{S_*}^{\infty}\frac{1}{K^2}C(K)dK\right]$$

Use this expression to substitute for $\mathrm{E}^*[\ln(S_T/S_0)]$ in equation (26). The result is

$$\hat{\sigma}^2=\frac{2}{T}\left[rT-\ln\left(\frac{S_*}{S_0}\right)-\frac{F_{0,T}(S)-S_*}{S_*}+e^{rT}\left(\int_0^{S_*}\frac{1}{K^2}P(K)dK+\int_{S_*}^{\infty}\frac{1}{K^2}C(K)dK\right)\right]\quad(27)$$

Finally, note that if we set $S_*=F_{0,T}(S)$, the first three terms on the right-hand side of equation (27) vanish, and we have

$$\hat{\sigma}^2=\frac{2e^{rT}}{T}\left[\int_0^{F_{0,T}}\frac{1}{K^2}P(K)dK+\int_{F_{0,T}}^{\infty}\frac{1}{K^2}C(K)dK\right]\quad(28)$$

Remarkably, this formula gives us an estimate of expected realized variance that we compute using the observed prices of out-of-the-money puts and calls! ("Out-of-the-money" here is with respect to the forward price rather than the current stock price.) It is important to note that we have *not* assumed that options are priced using the Black-Scholes formula or any other specific model.

One important characteristic of equation (28) is that the variance estimate can be replicated by trading options. It is possible to buy the strip of out-of-the-money puts and calls, weighted by the inverse squared strike price, to create a portfolio that has the value of $\hat{\sigma}^2$.

To get a sense of why equation (28) works, we can examine the vega of a portfolio of options held in proportion to $1/K^2$. Figure 5 graphs vegas for a set of options and also displays the vega of a portfolio where the option holdings are weighted by the inverse squared strike price. The resulting portfolio has a vega that is not zero and is constant over a wide range of stock prices. If you hold such a portfolio, you make or lose money depending on volatility changes.

Computing the VIX. We can now explain the formula used to compute the CBOE's new volatility index. The calculation is based on equation (28). In practice, option strike prices are discrete and there may be no option for which the strike price equals the index forward price. The actual formula used by the CBOE is a discrete approximation to equation (28):

$$\hat{\sigma}^2=\frac{2}{T}\sum_{K_i\le K_0}\frac{\Delta K_i}{K_i^2}e^{rT}\,\mathrm{Put}(K_i)+\frac{2}{T}\sum_{K_i>K_0}\frac{\Delta K_i}{K_i^2}e^{rT}\,\mathrm{Call}(K_i)-\frac{1}{T}\left[\frac{F_{0,T}}{K_0}-1\right]^2\quad(29)$$

FIGURE 5

Solid lines depict vegas of options with (from left to right) strikes of 25, 30, 35, 40, 45, 50, and 55. The dashed line is the weighted sum of the vegas, with each divided by the squared strike price, times 600. The calculations assume $\sigma = 0.30$, $r = 0.08$, $T = 0.25$, and $\delta = 0$.

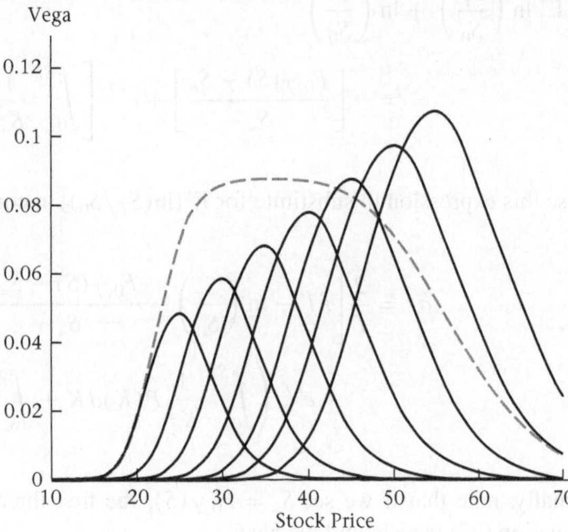

where K_0 is the first strike below the forward price for the index and $\Delta K_i = (K_{i+1} - K_{i-1})/2$.[12] The last term is a correction for the fact that there may be no option with a strike equal to the forward price.

4. EXTENDING THE BLACK-SCHOLES MODEL

In this section we examine three pricing models that are capable of generating volatility skew patterns resembling those observed in option markets. The goal is both to understand how the Black-Scholes model can be extended and also to gain a sense of how these extensions help us to better understand the data. We consider three models: (1) the Merton jump diffusion model, which relaxes the assumption that stock price moves are continuous; (2) the constant elasticity of variance model, primarily due to Cox, which relaxes the assumption that volatility is constant; and (3) the Heston stochastic volatility model, which allows volatility to follow an Itô process that is correlated with the stock price process. These models have all been significantly generalized, but we can use them as touchstones for better understanding the economics of departures from the Black-Scholes lognormality assumption.

At the outset, note that the Black-Scholes model easily accommodates time-varying volatility if the volatility pattern is deterministic. Specifically, Merton (1973b) showed that if volatility is a deterministic function of time, then it is possible to price a European option with $T - t$ periods to maturity by substituting $\int_t^T \sigma^2(s)ds$ for $\sigma^2(T - t)$ in the Black-Scholes formula. We can think about this result in the context of a delta-hedging market-maker. As long as the market-maker knows the volatility at each point in time, the

12. For the highest strike, ΔK_i is the difference between the high strike and the next highest strike. ΔK_i for the lowest strike is defined as the difference between the low strike and the next highest strike.

delta-hedge will work the same as if volatility were constant. What creates a problem is a *random* change in volatility.

Jump Risk and Implied Volatility

In this section we see how the jump model can account for the implied volatility patterns like those in Figure 1.

The Merton jump model assumes that stock prices have a different distribution than that assumed by the Black-Scholes model. If prices in the real world were generated by the Merton jump model, and if we then used the Merton jump model to compute implied volatilities, we would find that all options had the same implied volatility.[13] In real life, however, we don't know exactly what distribution generated the observed option prices. Black-Scholes implied volatilities are a way to interpret observed prices, telling us how the distribution implied by option prices differs from the lognormal model in the Black-Scholes formula.

Figure 6 shows Black-Scholes implied volatilities for option prices computed using Merton's jump formula. All of the plots assume that the diffusive standard deviation is $\sigma = 20\%$ and the mean jump is $\alpha_J = -10\%$. The jump intensity, λ, and jump volatility, σ_J, vary across the panels.

As in Figure 1, the short-term options in Figure 6 have a more pronounced smile than long-term options. In general, smiles are more pronounced when the jump volatility is greater because the chance is greater of a large stock price change that will move an out-of-the-money option into the money. A larger volatility increase is required for out-of-the-money options to account for the resulting option price increase.

In addition to affecting the amount of the smile, jumps also increase the level of implied volatilities. As λ and σ_J increase, the total effective stock price volatility increases, which results in a higher implied volatility (for example, the curves in the bottom right panel are higher than curves in other panels). For options with 1 year to maturity, there is more a smirk than a smile. Jumps raise overall volatility, but induce less of a smile for longer-term options.

The calculations here illustrate how a nonlognormally distributed underlying asset can give rise to implied volatility patterns similar to those observed in markets. It is important to keep in mind that the Merton model assumes that jumps are diversifiable, hence there is no risk premium associated with jumps. Also, nonjump volatility is constant. We have seen that volatility changes over time, and the empirical evidence (which we discuss below) is that there are risk premia associated with both volatility and jumps.

Constant Elasticity of Variance

Cox (1975) proposed the constant elasticity of variance (CEV) model, in which volatility varies with the level of the stock price. Specifically, Cox assumed that the stock follows the process

$$dS = (\alpha - \delta)S dt + \bar{\sigma} S^{\beta/2} dZ \tag{30}$$

13. In order to compute implied volatilities for the Merton model, we would also need to compute implied λ, α_J, and σ_J. We would therefore need at least four option prices to fit the pricing model to the data.

FIGURE 6

Implied volatilities computed using the Black-Scholes formula when option prices are computed using the Merton jump formula. Each panel has an implied volatility plot for three different times to expiration. The individual panels show plots for an expected number of jumps per year, λ, of 0.5 and 4, and jump volatilities of 0.1 and 0.3. In all cases $S_0 = \$100$, $\sigma = 30\%$, $r = 8\%$, $\delta = 0$, and $\alpha_J = -0.10$.

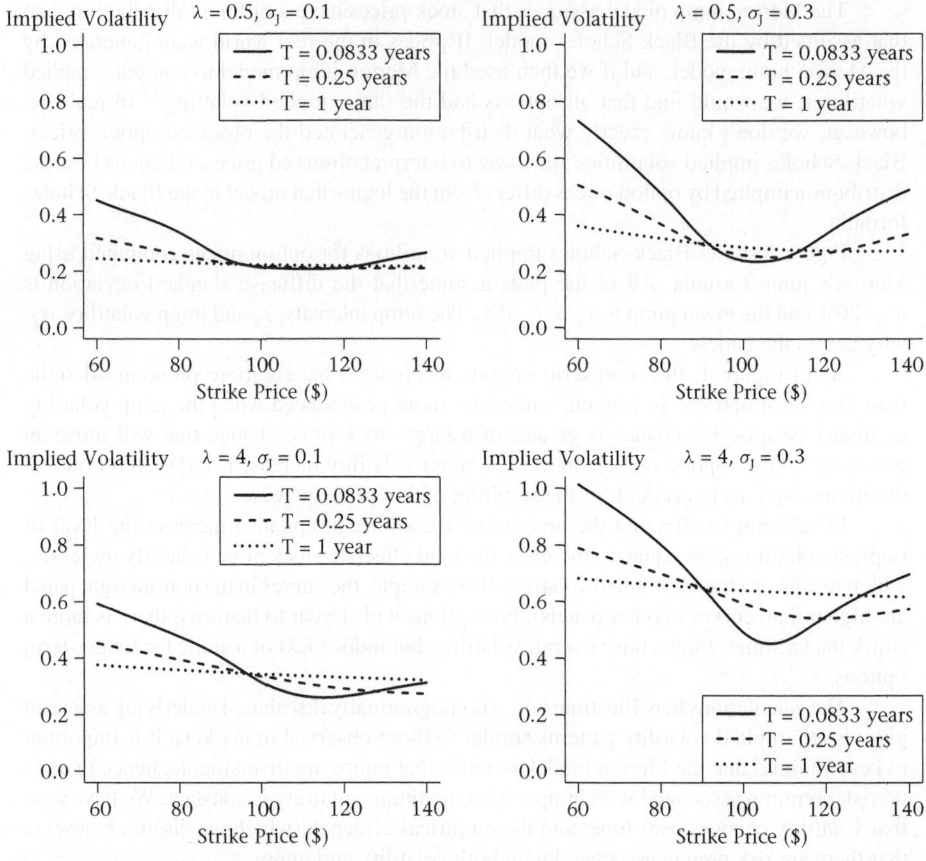

Equation (30) describes the instantaneous dollar return on the stock. The instantaneous rate of return on the stock is

$$\frac{dS}{S} = (\alpha - \delta)dt + \bar{\sigma} S^{(\beta-2)/2} dZ \tag{31}$$

The instantaneous standard deviation of the stock return is therefore

$$\sigma(S) = \bar{\sigma} S^{(\beta-2)/2} \tag{32}$$

When $\beta < 2$, the CEV model implies that volatility is decreasing with the stock price. Volatility increases with the stock price when $\beta > 2$. When $\beta = 2$, the CEV model yields the standard lognormal process.

It is important to be clear that $\bar{\sigma}$ is a parameter that determines volatility, but the instantaneous rate of return volatility is $\bar{\sigma} S^{(\beta-2)/2}$. Thus, if we want the stock to have a volatility of σ_0 at the current stock price, S_0, we must then set $\bar{\sigma}$ so that $\sigma_0 = \bar{\sigma} S^{(\beta-2)/2}$, or

$$\bar{\sigma} = \sigma_0 S^{(2-\beta)/2}$$

From equation (30), the elasticity of the instantaneous stock price variance with respect to the stock price is a constant, β:

$$\frac{\partial(\bar{\sigma}^2 S^\beta)}{\partial S} \times \frac{S}{\bar{\sigma}^2 S^\beta} = \beta$$

This is where the name "constant elasticity of variance" comes from.

One motivation for the CEV model was the finding in Black (1976b) (see also Christie, 1982) that volatility increases when stock prices fall. One potential explanation for this stems from thinking about the effect on equity risk from a fall in leverage. As the stock price decreases, the debt-to-equity ratio rises, and the equity volatility should therefore increase. Thus, the negative correlation between stock prices and volatility is called the **leverage effect**.

A drawback of the CEV model may already have occurred to you. If the stock price declines and $\beta < 2$, the CEV model implies that volatility will increase *permanently*. In practice and in theory, such a deterministic relationship between volatility and the stock price level seems implausible. However, such a relationship seems more reasonable when modeling interest rates. The interest rate in the CIR model, for example, follows a CEV process.

The CEV Pricing Formula. There is a relatively simple pricing formula for a European call when the stock price follows the CEV process.[14] Following Schroder (1989), define

$$\kappa = \frac{2(r-\delta)}{\bar{\sigma}^2(2-\beta)\left(e^{(r-\delta)(2-\beta)T}-1\right)}$$

$$x = \kappa S^{2-\beta} e^{(r-\delta)(2-\beta)T}$$

$$y = \kappa K^{2-\beta}$$

The CEV pricing formula for a European call is different for the cases $\beta < 2$ and $\beta > 2$. Let $Q(a, b, c)$ denote the noncentral chi-squared distribution function with b degrees of freedom and noncentrality parameter c, evaluated at a.[15] The CEV call price is given by

14. Cox (1996) originally derived a pricing formula in terms of infinite series for the case $\beta < 2$. Emanuel and MacBeth (1982) generalized Cox's analysis to the case where $\beta > 2$. Schroder (1989) showed that both cases could be expressed more compactly in terms of the noncentral chi-squared cumulative distribution function. Davydov and Linetsky (2001) derive pricing formulas barrier and lookback options under a CEV process.

15. The pricing formula is sometimes written in terms of the *complementary* noncentral chi-squared distribution, which is $1 - Q(a, b, c)$. The noncentral chi-squared distribution, unlike the chi-squared distribution, is not typically a standard function built into spreadsheets. However, it is available in software programs such as Matlab and Mathematica.

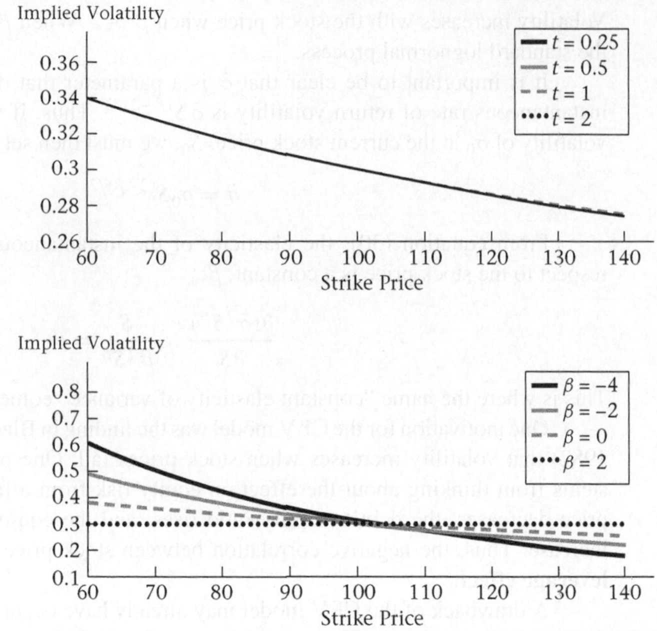

FIGURE 7

Implied volatility in the CEV model. Both panels assume that $S = \$100$, $\sigma_0 = 0.30$, $r = 0.08$, and $T = 1$. In the top panel, $\beta = 1$, while in the bottom panel, $T = 0.5$.

$$
\begin{array}{ll}
Se^{-\delta T}\left[1 - Q(2y, 2 + 2/(2-\beta), 2x)\right] - Ke^{-rT}Q(2x, 2/(2-\beta), 2y) & \beta < 2 \\
Se^{-\delta T}\left[1 - Q(2x, 2/(\beta-2), 2y)\right] - Ke^{-rT}Q(2y, 2 + 2/(\beta-2), 2x) & \beta > 2
\end{array} \qquad (33)
$$

Implied Volatility in the CEV Model. When $\beta < 2$, the CEV model generates a Black-Scholes implied volatility skew curve resembling that in Figure 1: Implied volatility decreases with the option strike price. To understand why the CEV model generates this volatility skew, note from equation (31) that when $\beta < 2$ and the stock price falls, volatility increases. Thus compared with the case of a constant volatility, an out-of-the-money put option has a greater chance of exercise and is likely to be deeper in-the-money when it is exercised. The only way for the Black-Scholes model to account for this higher price is with a higher volatility. As the strike price increases, less of the option value is due to the stock price behavior at low prices, and volatility therefore need not increase as much.

Figure 7 plots implied volatility curves generated by using the Black-Scholes formula to compute implied volatility for prices generated by the CEV model. The top panel shows that, for the given parameters, the implied volatility curve is unaffected by changing time to maturity.

The Heston Model

In the CEV model, the instantaneous volatility of the stock evolves stochastically with the stock price, but volatility is a nonstochastic function of the stock price. A more general approach is to permit volatility to follow a stochastic process. The **Heston model** (Heston,

1993) allows volatility to vary stochastically but still to be correlated with the stock.[16] This generates a different option pricing model than the CEV process and also implies that market-makers must hedge both stock price and volatility risk. In the CEV model, market-makers need only hedge with the stock since volatility depends on the stock price.

Let $v(t)$ be the instantaneous stock return variance; hence, $\sqrt{v(t)}$ is the volatility. Suppose that the stock follows the process

$$\frac{dS}{S} = (\alpha - \delta)dt + \sqrt{v(t)}dZ_1 \tag{34}$$

Assume that the variance, $v(t)$, follows the mean-reverting process

$$dv(t) = \kappa[\bar{v} - v(t)]dt + \sigma_v\sqrt{v(t)}dZ_2 \tag{35}$$

We assume that $\mathrm{E}(dZ_1dZ_2) = \rho dt$.

The equation for volatility, equation (35), has two noteworthy characteristics. First, the instantaneous variance, $v(t)$, is mean-reverting, tending toward the value $\bar{v}$, with a speed of adjustment given by κ. Second, the volatility of variance, $\sigma_v\sqrt{v(t)}$, depends on the square root of $v(t)$, and variance is therefore said to follow a *square root process*.

Suppose that the risk premium for the risk $\sigma_v\sqrt{v(t)}dZ_2$ can be written as $v(t)\beta_v$, where we assume β_v is constant. This assumption that the risk premium is proportional to the level of the variance is analytically convenient. Given this assumption about the risk premium, the risk-neutral variance process is

$$\begin{aligned} dv(t) &= \left\{\kappa[\bar{v} - v(t)] - v(t)\beta_v\right\} dt + \sigma_v\sqrt{v(t)}dZ_2^* \\ &= \kappa^*\left[\bar{v}^* - v(t)\right] dt + \sigma_v\sqrt{v(t)}dZ_2^* \end{aligned} \tag{36}$$

where $\kappa^* = \kappa + \beta_v$ and $\bar{v}^* = \bar{v}\kappa/(\kappa + \beta_v)$. This model of stochastic variance is the Heston model.

Let $V[S(t), v(t), t]$ represent the price of a derivative on the stock when the stock price and volatility are given by equations (34) and (35). Suppose we proceed with the Black-Scholes derivation, in which we hold the option and try to hedge the resulting risk. We immediately encounter the problem that there are *two* sources of risk, dZ_1 and dZ_2. A position in the stock will hedge dZ_1, but what can we use to hedge risk resulting from stochastic volatility? Apart from other options, there will typically be no asset that is a perfect hedge for volatility.[17] In that case, we rely on the equilibrium approach to pricing the option. The PDE for the derivative $V[S(t), v(t), t]$ is then

$$\begin{aligned} &\tfrac{1}{2}v(t)S^2V_{SS} + \tfrac{1}{2}\sigma_v^2v(t)V_{vv} + \rho v(t)\sigma_v SV_{Sv} \\ &\quad + (r - \delta)SV_S + \left\{\kappa[\bar{v} - v(t)] - v(t)\beta_v\right\} V_v + V_t = rV \end{aligned} \tag{37}$$

16. Earlier papers that modeled volatility as following a stochastic process included Hull and White (1987), Scott (1987), and Wiggins (1987). The Heston model has been generalized significantly by Duffie et al. (2000), who allow both jumps in the asset price and jumps in volatility.

17. It might be possible to use other options on the same stock to hedge volatility, but the option would then be priced *relative* to the price of the option used as a hedge.

The third term is due to the covariance between the stock return and variance. Since there is no asset to hedge variance, the coefficient on the V_v term has a correction for the risk premium associated with variance.

Heston (1993) shows that equation (37) has an integral solution that can be evaluated numerically. Given this solution, we can see how implied volatility behaves when volatility is stochastic. We price options for different strikes and expirations under the stochastic volatility model and then use Black-Scholes to compute implied volatilities. We assume that the stock price is \$100 and compute implied volatilities for options with strike prices ranging from \$6 to \$140 and with maturities from 1 month to 1 year.

Figure 8 shows the result of this experiment for two different values of σ_v and ρ. In the figure the long-run volatility, $\sqrt{\bar{v}^*}$, is 25%, less than the current volatility, $\sqrt{v(t)}$, of 32%. Because volatility reverts to the mean, implied volatility decreases with time to maturity in every case. In the panel where $\sigma_v = 0.25$ and $\rho = 0$, there is almost no skew, although the mean reversion in volatility is apparent. When $\sigma_v = 75\%$ and $\rho = 0$, the figure exhibits both symmetric skew and mean reversion. The asymmetric skew in both right-hand panels of Figure 8 arises from assuming a negative correlation between volatility and the stock price. In comparing Figures 6 and 8, it is clear that jumps and stochastic volatility affect the implied volatility curve in different ways, with jumps having a greater effect on short-term options and stochastic volatility a similar smile for both long and short maturities.

Evidence

The main challenge for an option pricing model is to match the observed volatility skew.[18] The literature investigating ways to do this is too large to adequately summarize here. Instead, we will sketch the nature of findings in the literature and highlight issues that arise when trying to match models to data.

The pricing models in this section illustrate ways in which modifying the Black-Scholes assumptions can enable a pricing model to better fit observed option prices. For example, all the pricing models we have discussed are capable of generating higher implied volatilities for out-of-the-money (low-strike) puts. The Merton jump model and the CEV model in the examples above both generate implied volatility curves that are flatter as time to maturity increases.[19] Combinations of the models, such as a Heston model that also allows jumps, seem able to reproduce *qualitative* features of Figure 1. However, matching models to data is a more involved exercise than just a visual comparison of implied volatility curves.

18. The true model should give equal implied volatilities for options at different strikes and maturities. For example, if the Heston stochastic volatility model were true and option prices were consistent with equation (37), then Black-Scholes implied volatilities would exhibit skew, but if the Heston model were used to compute implied volatility, then the options in Figure 8 would all have implied volatilities of 32%.

19. It is not obvious how to interpret the change with respect to maturity in implied volatility curves such as those in Figures 1, 6, 7, and 8. The issue is that the economic distinction between a \$50 strike and a \$55 strike is greater with one week to expiration than with one year to expiration; therefore, other things equal, we might expect to see flatter volatility curves as time to expiration increases. Bates (2000) corrects for this effect by scaling strike prices by $\sigma\sqrt{T}$, effectively measuring distance between strikes in "standard deviation units."

FIGURE 8

Implied volatilities computed using the Black-Scholes formula when option prices are computed using the Heston formula. Each panel has an implied volatility plot for three different times to expiration. The individual panels show plots for a volatility of volatility, σ_v, of 0.25 and 0.75, and a correlation between the stock return and volatility of 0 and −0.3. In all cases $S_0 = \$100$, $v_0 = 0.32^2$, $\bar{v} = 0.25^2$, $r = 8\%$, and $\delta = 0$.

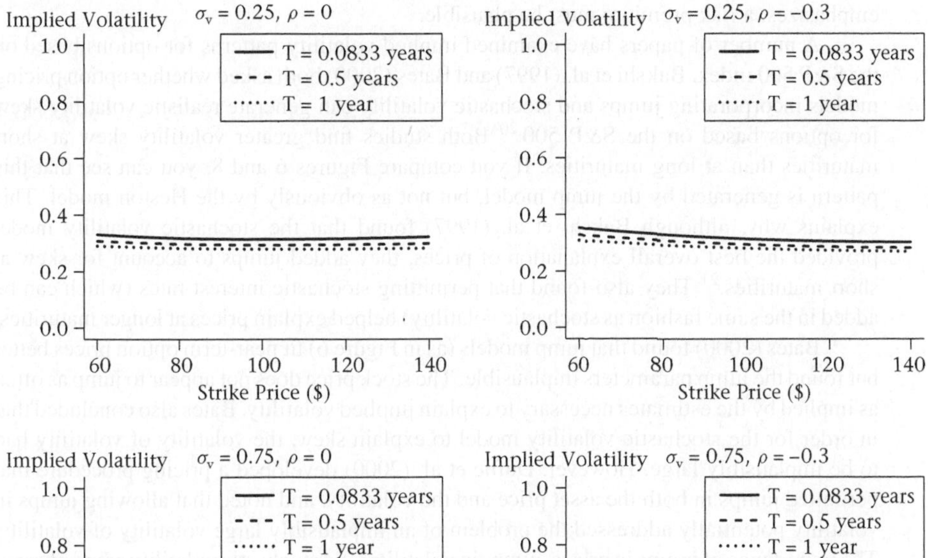

To illustrate the issues, suppose you want to match the Heston stochastic volatility model to data. There are a number of ways you might proceed. First, on a given day, you could find a set of model inputs that best matches the volatility curves for that day. This entails finding a return variance ($v(t)$), a volatility of volatility (σ_v), a mean reversion rate (κ^*), a long-run risk-neutral variance ($\bar{v}^*$), and a correlation between volatility and the stock return (ρ), that match the data for a particular day.

Matching implied volatilities across a set of options on a given day is a *cross-sectional* test of the model. Once you admit multiple days of data, the model has *time-series* implications as well. Equations (35) and (36) imply that volatility evolves over time in a specific way. If you look at the evolution of volatility over time, does it match equation (35)? Are the parameters that enable the model to fit the cross-section consistent with those implied by the volatility time series? When there is a risk premium in the equilibrium pricing model (as in the Heston model), it is potentially easier to reconcile the behavior of the stock with option prices because there is an additional parameter. However, as Bates (2003) emphasizes, a risk premium must be plausible.

A number of papers have examined implied volatility patterns for options based on the S&P 500 index. Bakshi et al. (1997) and Bates (2000) both asked whether option pricing models incorporating jumps and stochastic volatility can generate realistic volatility skew for options based on the S&P 500.[20] Both studies find greater volatility skew at short maturities than at long maturities. If you compare Figures 6 and 8, you can see that this pattern is generated by the jump model, but not as obviously by the Heston model. This explains why, although Bakshi et al. (1997) found that the stochastic volatility model provided the best overall explanation of prices, they added jumps to account for skew at short maturities.[21] They also found that permitting stochastic interest rates (which can be added in the same fashion as stochastic volatility) helped explain prices at longer maturities.

Bates (2000) found that jump models (as in Figure 6) fit near-term option prices better but found the jump parameters implausible: The stock price does not appear to jump as often as implied by the estimates necessary to explain implied volatility. Bates also concluded that in order for the stochastic volatility model to explain skew, the volatility of volatility had to be implausibly large. However, Duffie et al. (2000) developed a pricing procedure that permitted jumps in both the asset price and the volatility, and noted that allowing jumps in volatility potentially addressed the problem of an implausibly large volatility of volatility. The importance of jumps in prices, jumps in volatility, and stochastic volatility are confirmed by Broadie et al. (2007), who also find a role for volatility jump risk premia. Todorov (2010) also confirms the importance of variance and jump risk premia, and finds that these risk premia rise after big market moves.

It is also possible to measure volatility risk premia directly by looking at the returns on portfolios that are hedged against stock price risk and exposed to volatility. For example, Coval and Shumway (2001) find large negative returns on zero-delta written straddles on the S&P 100 and S&P 500 indexes, a finding confirmed by Bakshi and Kapadia (2003a), who examine delta-hedged portfolios. Because a delta-hedged position loses money when volatility increases, this result is consistent with a negative volatility risk premium. (A negative premium means that investors will pay extra to have a position that hedges against volatility increases.) Bakshi and Kapadia (2003b) find smaller risk premia associated with delta-hedged individual stocks than with index options.

To add one more layer of complication, casual observation suggests that in some cases volatility changes deterministically over time. When a firm announces earnings, for example, volatility will be higher than on ordinary days (Patell and Wolfson, 1979,

20. Bakshi et al. (1997) examined European options on the S&P 500 index, while Bates (2000) examined options on the S&P 500 futures contract.

21. Carr and Wu (2003) formalize the intuition that jumps matter more if there is a short time to expiration.

1981; Dubinsky and Johannes, 2004). This finding suggests that in addition to the use of increasingly sophisticated mathematical pricing models, careful option pricing requires data sets that identify *anticipated* days of unusual volatility.[22]

CHAPTER SUMMARY

For options on a given underlying asset on a given day, implied volatility generally varies across option strikes and maturities. Implied volatility also varies over time. As a result there is great interest in measuring volatilities and in pricing options when volatility can vary.

Methods of measuring volatility using past data include historical volatility, exponentially weighted moving average volatility, ARCH, GARCH, and realized quadratic variation. ARCH and GARCH estimates are based upon a formal statistical model in which volatility is random. Realized quadratic variation exploits high frequency data to obtain a reliable volatility estimate using data from a short time horizon.

Both variance and volatility swaps permit hedging and speculation on volatility. The variance forward price can be obtained as a weighted sum of the prices of traded European options, a calculation that is the basis for the VIX measure of implied volatility.

The Black-Scholes model does not perfectly explain observed option prices; there is volatility skew, which means that implied volatility varies with the strike price and time to expiration. Two modifications to the model are to permit jumps in the stock price and to allow volatility to be stochastic. Both changes generate option prices that exhibit volatility skew and that better fit the data than the unmodified Black-Scholes model.

Attempts to explain prices of traded options suggest that it is important to account for jumps in both the asset price and volatility, and that risk premiums on one or both jumps may be important.

FURTHER READING

Early studies of stock returns (e.g., Fama, 1965) found that continuously compounded returns exhibit too many large returns to be consistent with normality. In recent years, research has focused on specifying stock price processes that give theoretical option prices consistent with observed prices. Introductions to GARCH models include Royal Swedish Academy of Sciences (2003) and Bollerslev et al. (1994). Alexander (2001) is a readable text for less technical readers. Realized quadratic variation as a measure of volatility is presented and applied in Andersen et al. (2003).

Demeterfi et al. (1999) present a clear and well-written discussion of volatility hedging, and the paper also develops the volatility measure used now to construct the VIX. See also Chicago Board Options Exchange (2003).

22. This is not just an issue for individual firms. Governments make economic announcements on prespecified days at set times, and these announcements sometimes generate large moves in prices. For example, Hanweck (1994) shows that implied volatility in Eurodollar futures options is greater on days when the government announces aggregate employment.

The first papers to suggest alternative assumptions about the stock price for option pricing were Cox and Ross (1976), Cox (1996), and Merton (1976). Merton noted in his paper that the jump model had the potential to explain volatility skew patterns noted by practitioners at the time. The first stochastic volatility models were proposed by Hull and White (1987), Scott (1987), and Wiggins (1987). The Heston (1993) model has been generalized by Duffie et al. (2000), who develop a pricing framework that can accommodate jumps in volatility as well as in the stock price.

The empirical literature examining the ability of option pricing models to fit observed prices is rapidly evolving. Well-known papers include Bakshi et al. (1997), Bates (2000), and Pan (2002). Current research (which include citations to numerous other papers) include Andersen et al. (2005) and Broadie et al. (2004). Patell and Wolfson (1979, 1981) and Dubinsky and Johannes (2004) examine deterministic volatility changes, such as those due to earnings announcements.

PROBLEMS

1. Using weekly price data (constructed Wednesday to Wednesday), compute historical *annual* volatilities for IBM, Xerox, and the S&P 500 index for 1991 through 2004. Annualize your answer by multiplying by $\sqrt{52}$. Also compute volatility for each for the entire period.

2. Compute daily volatilities for 1991 through 2004 for IBM, Xerox, and the S&P 500 index. Annualize by multiplying by $\sqrt{252}$. How do your answers compare to those in Problem 1?

3. For the period 1999–2004, using daily data, compute the following:

a. An EWMA estimate, with $b = 0.95$, of IBM's volatility using all data.

b. An EWMA estimate, with $b = 0.95$, of IBM's volatility, at each date using only the previous 60 days of data.

Plot both estimates. How different are they?

4. Estimate a GARCH(1,1) for the S&P 500 index, using data from January 1999 to December 2003.

5. Replicate the GARCH(1,1) estimation in Example 2, using daily returns from on IBM from January 1999 to December 2003. Compare your estimates with and without the four largest returns.

6. Use the following inputs to compute the price of a European call option: $S = \$100$, $K = \$50$, $r = 0.06$, $\sigma = 0.30$, $T = 0.01$, $\delta = 0$.

a. Verify that the Black-Scholes price is \$50.0299.

b. Verify that the vega for this option is almost zero. Why is this so?

c. Verify that if you compute the option price with volatilities ranging from 0.05 to 1.00, you get essentially the same option price and vega remains about zero. Why is this so? What happens if you set $\sigma = 5.00$ (i.e., 500%)?

d. What can you conclude about difficulties in computing implied volatility for very short-term, deep in-the-money options?

7. Use the same inputs as in the previous problem. Suppose that you observe a bid option price of \$50 and an ask price of \$50.10.

a. Explain why you cannot compute an implied volatility for the bid price.

b. Compute an implied volatility for the ask price, but be sure to set the initial volatility at 200% or greater. Explain why the implied volatility for the ask price is extremely large.

c. (Optional) Examine the code for the *BSCallImpVol* function. Explain why changing the starting volatility can affect whether or not you obtain an answer.

d. What can you conclude about difficulties in computing and interpreting implied volatilities for deep in-the-money options?

8. Use the following inputs to compute the price of a European call option: $S = \$50$, $K = \$100$, $r = 0.06$, $\sigma = 0.30$, $T = 0.01$, $\delta = 0$.

a. Verify that the Black-Scholes price is zero.

b. Verify that the vega for this option is zero. Why is this so?

c. Suppose you observe a bid price of zero and an ask price of \$0.05. What answers do you obtain when you compute implied volatility for these prices. Why?

d. Why would market-makers set such prices?

e. What can you conclude about difficulties in computing and interpreting implied volatility for very short-term, deep out-of-the-money options?

9. Compute January 12 2004 bid and ask volatilities (using the Black-Scholes implied volatility function) for IBM options expiring January 17. For which options are you unable to compute a plausible implied volatility? Why?

10. Compute January 12 2004 bid and ask volatilities (using the Black-Scholes implied volatility function) for IBM options expiring February 21.

a. Do you observe a volatility smile?

b. For which options are you unable to compute a plausible implied volatility? Why?

11. Compute January 12 2004 implied volatilities using the *average* of the bid and ask prices for IBM options expiring February 21 (use the Black-Scholes implied volatility function). Compare your answers to those in the previous problem. Why might someone prefer to use implied volatilities based on the average of the bid and ask prices, rather than the bid and ask volatilities individually?

12. In this problem you will compute January 12 2004 bid and ask volatilities (using the Black-Scholes implied volatility function) for 1-year IBM options expiring the following January. Note that IBM pays a dividend in March, June, September, and December.

a. Compute implied volatilities ignoring the dividend.

b. Take dividends into account using the discrete dividend correction to the Black-Scholes formula. For simplicity, discount all observed future dividends at a 2% continuously compounded rate. How much difference does this correction make in implied volatility?

c. Take dividends into account by computing a dividend yield for IBM based on its annualized dividend rate as of January 12. Use this dividend yield in the Black-Scholes model. How different are the implied volatilities from those you obtain in the previous part?

d. Do you observe a volatility smile?

13. For this problem, use the implied volatilities for the options expiring in January 2005, computed in the preceding problem. Compare the implied volatilities for calls and puts. Where is the difference largest? Why does this occur?

14. Suppose $S = \$100$, $r = 8\%$, $\sigma = 30\%$, $T = 1$, and $\delta = 0$. Use the Black-Scholes formula to generate call and put prices with the strikes ranging from \$40 to \$250, with increments of \$5. Compute the implied volatility from these prices by using the formula for the VIX (equation (29)). What happens to your estimate if you use strikes that differ by \$1 or \$10, or strikes that range only from \$60 to \$200?

15. Explain why the VIX formula in equation (29) overestimates implied volatility if options are American.

The following three problems use the Merton jump formula. As a base case, assume $S = \$100$, $r = 8\%$, $\sigma = 30\%$, $T = 1$, and $\delta = 0$. Also assume that $\lambda = 0.02$, $\alpha_J = -0.20$, and $\sigma_J = 0.30$.

16. Using the Merton jump formula, generate an implied volatility plot for $K = 50, 55, \ldots 150$.

a. How is the implied volatility plot affected by changing α_J to -0.40 or -0.10?

b. How is the implied volatility plot affected by changing λ to 0.01 or 0.05?

c. How is the implied volatility plot affected by changing σ_J to 0.10 or 0.50?

17. Using the base case parameters, plot the implied volatility curve you obtain for the base case against that for the case where there is a jump to zero, with the same λ.

18. Repeat Problem 16, except let $\alpha_J = 0.20$, and in part (b) consider expected alternate jump magnitudes of 0.10 and 0.50.

The following two problems both use the CEV option pricing formula. Assume in both that $S = \$100$, $r = 8\%$, $\sigma_0 = 30\%$, $T = 1$, and $\delta = 0$.

19. Using the CEV option pricing model, set $\beta = 1$ and generate option prices for strikes from 60 to 140, in increments of 5, for times to maturity of 0.25, 0.5, 1.0, and 2.0. Plot the resulting implied volatilities. (This should reproduce Figure 7.)

20. Using the CEV option pricing model, set $\beta = 3$ and generate option prices for strikes from 60 to 140, in increments of 5, for times to maturity of 0.25, 0.5, 1.0, and 2.0. Plot the resulting implied volatilities.

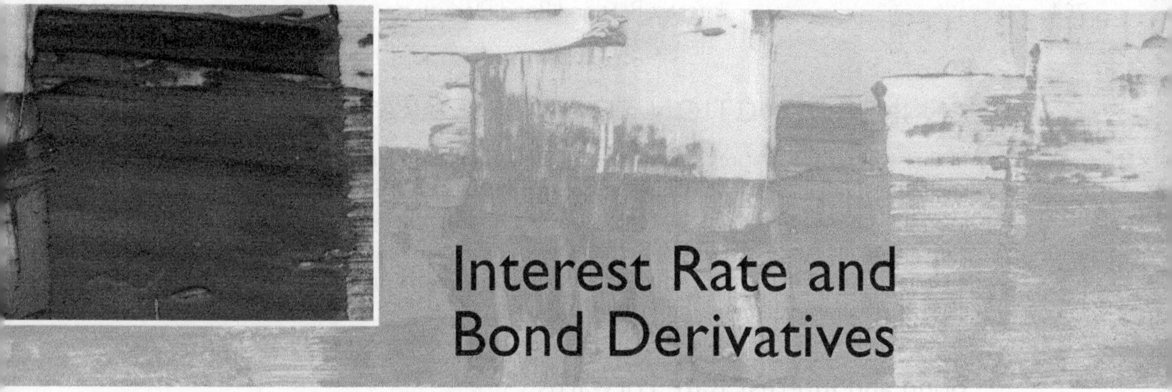

Interest Rate and Bond Derivatives

In this chapter we discuss fixed income pricing models, i.e., derivatives with payoffs depending on bond prices and interest rates. The primary goals are to introduce a number of standard fixed income pricing models, and to explore the economic underpinnings of these models.[1] Interest rate derivatives are a large topic, so this chapter can only present an overview.

We begin in Section 1 with a brief review of bond and interest rate notation and a discussion of forward pricing. We then discuss bond and interest rate options, and show that contracts with payments based on an interest rate can typically be transformed into contracts with payments based on a bond price. Thus, if you understand options on bonds, you understand options on rates. We also explain how the large number of pricing models in the chapter can be put into two buckets—short-rate models and market models—according to the economic idea underlying the calculation. This grouping of the models should help to organize your understanding of the many models in this chapter.

The following three sections discuss short-rate models. Section 2 shows how the Black-Scholes-Merton approach to pricing options applies to bonds. We discuss the role of the interest rate risk premium. Section 3 describes continuous-time short-rate models, including the Vasicek and Cox-Ingersoll-Ross models. Section 4 discusses binomial and trinomial interest rate trees as a way to implement short-rate models for cases where there is no closed-form pricing formula. Specifically, the Black-Derman-Toy model provides an example of a binomial interest rate tree, and the Hull-White model is an example of a trinomial tree. Finally, Section 5 discusses market models, including the Black model and LIBOR market model.

Some of the models we discuss have explicit formulas for bond prices and others are numerical solutions, using either a tree (binomial or trinomial) or simulation. You should keep in mind the distinction between the underlying economic model and the solution method. The choice of an economic model for a particular problem is governed by the characteristics of cash flows and interest rates. The solution method can then be a pragmatic choice.

---

1. This note has been intentionally omitted for this edition.

From Chapter 25 of *Derivatives Markets*, Third Edition, Robert McDonald. Copyright © 2013 by Pearson Education, Inc. Published by Pearson Prentice Hall. All rights reserved.

1. AN INTRODUCTION TO INTEREST RATE DERIVATIVES

In this section we first review the basic notation and forward pricing formulas for bonds and interest rates. Next, we define options on interest rates and bonds and show that the two kinds of options—products that may seem quite different—are in fact the same: Options with payments based on interest rates can be transformed into options with payments based on bond prices. Finally, we explain that the pricing models in this chapter fit into two broad categories: short-rate models and market models.

Bond and Interest Rate Forwards

We let $P_t(t_1, t_2)$ denote the time t price of a bond bought at $t_1 \geq t$ and maturing at $t_2 \geq t_1$. If $t < t_1$, the price is a bond forward price. When we buy a bond at the current market price, then by definition $t = t_1$. If there is no ambiguity, we will write the time t price of a bond maturing at time T as $P(t, T)$.

The forward price quoted at time t, to purchase a bond at time T that matures at time $T + s$, is

$$F_{t,T,T+s} \equiv P_t(T, T+s) = \frac{P_t(t, T+s)}{P_t(t, T)} \tag{1}$$

The time T payoff to a long bond forward, with the forward bought at t, is

$$\text{Payoff to bond forward} = P_T(T, T+s) - P_t(T, T+s)$$

Similarly, $R_t(T, T+s)$ is the nonannualized interest rate that can be obtained at time t for a loan commencing at T that is repaid in a lump sum at time $T + s$.[2] If $T > t$, the interest rate is a forward rate agreement (FRA).

The forward rate quoted at time t for a loan commencing at time T with repayment at time $T + s$ is

$$R_t(T, T+s) = \frac{P_t(t, T)}{P_t(t, T+s)} - 1 \tag{2}$$

Note that $R_t(T, T+s) = 1/F_{t,T,T+s} - 1$.

The time $T + s$ payoff to a long position on a forward rate agreement created at time t is the difference between the spot s-period rate, $R_T(T, T+s)$, and the forward rate, $R_t(T, T+s)$:

$$\text{Payoff to FRA at time } T+s = R_T(T, T+s) - R_t(T, T+s)$$

We could also settle the FRA at time T in an economically equivalent way by paying the present value of the time $T + s$ payoff:

$$\text{Payoff to FRA at time } T = \frac{R_T(T, T+s) - R_t(T, T+s)}{1 + R_T(T, T+s)}$$

---

2. "Nonannualized" means that if you invest \$1 at time T at the forward rate, after s periods you will have $1 + R_t(T, T+s)$.

Finally, it is possible to write a bond price in terms of a series of forward interest rates. Suppose we have a series of nonoverlapping forward interest rates spanning the time from T to $T+s$. Let h be the length of a single forward rate agreement and let $n = s/h$. We have

$$P_t(T, T+s) = \prod_{i=1}^{n} \frac{1}{1 + R_t(T + (i-1)h, T + ih)} \tag{3}$$

To see why the equation holds with forward rates, rewrite equation (3) using equation (2) to replace forward interest rates with bond price ratios:

$$P_t(T, T+s) = \prod_{i=1}^{n} \frac{P_t(t, T+ih)}{P_t(t, T+(i-1)h)} = \frac{P_t(t, T+s)}{P_t(t, T)}$$

This gives us equation (1).

Example 1. Let the prices of zero-coupon bonds be $P_0(0, 1) = 0.9625$, $P_0(0, 2) = 0.9137$, $P_0(0, 3) = 0.8585$, and $P_0(0, 4) = 0.8004$. The forward price for a 1-year bond purchased in year 2 is

$$P_0(2, 3) = P_0(0, 3)/P_0(0, 2) = 0.9396$$

The implied 1-year forward rates for years 0 through 3 are 0.03896, 0.05341, 0.06430, and 0.07259. For example, the implied forward interest rate from year 2 to 3 is

$$R_0(2, 3) = P_0(0, 2)/P_0(0, 3) - 1 = 0.06430$$

The price of a 3-year bond can be written in terms of forward rates:

$$P_0(0, 3) = \frac{1}{1.03896} \times \frac{1}{1.05341} \times \frac{1}{1.06430} = 0.8585 \quad \blacksquare$$

Options on Bonds and Rates

We now define the payoffs on bond and interest rate options, and demonstrate the equivalence between a put option on a bond and a call option on an interest rate.

Bond Options. First, consider call and put options on an s-period zero-coupon bond, where the options expire at time T. If the strike price is K, the maturity payment is

$$\text{Call}(P_T(T, T+s), K, T) = \max[0, P_T(T, T+s) - K P_T(T, T)] \tag{4}$$

$$\text{Put}(P_T(T, T+s), K, T) = \max[0, K P_T(T, T) - P_T(T, T+s)] \tag{5}$$

We write the strike price as $K P_T(T, T)$ (where $P_T(T, T) \equiv \$1$) in order to emphasize that a claim paying K at time T is a zero-coupon bond.

Interest Rate Options. We can also have options on interest rates. An interest rate **caplet** makes a payment if the interest rate is above the strike rate, K_r. A caplet would be a hedge for a borrower, paying if rates are high. Similarly, an interest rate **floorlet** makes a payment if the interest rate is below the strike rate. A floorlet is a hedge for a lender, paying if rates are low. A **cap** is a series of caplets and a **floor** is a series of floorlets.

With payment made at time $T+s$, the caplet and floorlet have payoffs with a time T value of

$$\text{Caplet}(P_T(T,T+s),T)=\frac{1}{1+R_T(T,T+s)}\max[0,R_T(T,T+s)-K_R P_T(T,T)] \tag{6}$$

$$\text{Floorlet}(P_T(T,T+s),T)=\frac{1}{1+R_T(T,T+s)}\max[0,K_R P_T(T,T)-xR_T(T,T+s)] \tag{7}$$

Note that we are using the market rate at time T to discount the payment.

Equivalence of a Bond Put and an Interest Rate Call

Options on bonds can be converted into options on interest rates. A borrower who is hedging wants a contract that makes a payment when interest rates rise. Intuitively, either a call option on the interest rate or a put option on a bond will accomplish this. In fact, we can transform one into the other.

Using the fact that $P_T(T,T)=1$, we can rewrite the caplet payoff, equation (6), as

$$\begin{aligned}&(1+K_R)\max\left[0,\frac{R_T(T,T+s)-K_R}{(1+R_T(T,T+s))(1+K_R)}\right]\\&=(1+K_R)\max\left[0,\frac{1}{1+K_R}-\frac{1}{1+R_T(T,T+s)}\right]\end{aligned} \tag{8}$$

The right-hand side of equation (8) is the payoff of $1+K_R$ put options on an s-period bond with strike price $1/(1+K_R)$. A model that can price bond options can therefore be used to price interest rate options, and vice versa.

Example 2. Consider a caplet with a strike of 6%, paying $\max(0,R_T-0.06)/(1+R_T(T,T+s))$. This is equivalent to 1.06 bond put options with a strike of $K=1/1.06$, paying $1.06\times\max[0,1/1.06-P_T(T,T+s)]$, where $P_T(T,T+s)\equiv 1/(1+R_T(T,T+s))$. ■

Taxonomy of Interest Rate Models

All of the pricing models in this chapter fall into one of two categories: short-rate models and market models. Here we will briefly explain each pricing model.

Short-Rate Models. In a short-rate model, we assume that the short-term interest rate, $r(t)$, follows some process. We can then value a claim with the payoff $X(T)$ by computing[3]

$$\boxed{X(t)=\mathrm{E}_t^B\left[X(T)e^{-\int_t^T r(s)ds}\right]} \tag{9}$$

3. This note has been intentionally omitted for this edition.

where $r(s)$ follows the assumed process and E^B is the expectation with respect to the risk-neutral distribution. For example, in order to value a zero-coupon bond paying \$1 at time T, we compute

$$P_t(t, T) = E_t^B \left[e^{-\int_t^T r(s)ds} \right] \tag{10}$$

All of the short-rate models in this chapter use equation (9), or approximate it, in order to compute the prices of bonds and derivatives.

To evaluate equation (9), we must specify a risk-neutral process for $r(t)$. Different specifications give rise to different pricing models. Models in this class include Vasicek (1977), Cox et al. (1985b), Ho and Lee (1986), Hull and White (1990), Black et al. (1990), and Black and Karasinski (1991). In some cases it is possible to compute a closed-form solution to equation (9), typically by assuming that the short-term interest rate follows an Itô process and then solving an appropriate form of the Black-Scholes-Merton partial differential equation. Alternatively, it is possible to approximate the behavior of the interest rate binomially or trinomially, and calculate an approximation to equation (9). In other cases, simulation may be best. There is great leeway in modeling $r(t)$. The goal is to pick a model that generates bond and option prices matching those observed in markets, and that is not too difficult to compute.

Short-rate models and equation (9) arise from choosing as numeraire a default-free account that earns the short-term rate of interest. If we invest $B(t)$ in this account, we earn the instantaneous return $r(t)B(t)dt$, where $r(t)$ can be random.[4] With reinvestment, at time T the account will be worth $B(T) = B(t)e^{\int_t^T r(s)ds}$. The risk-neutral measure is then defined as the probability distribution under which the price ratio $S(t)/B(t)$ is a martingale for all non-dividend-paying assets $S(t)$. Under this distribution, the instantaneous expected return on all stocks and assets equals $r(t)$.

Market Models. Models assuming that forward prices are martingales are sometimes called *market models*. If we also assume that the forward price is lognormally distributed with volatility σ, we can write the process for the forward price in a market model as

$$dF_{t,T} = \sigma F_{t,T} dZ(t) \tag{11}$$

Given a process like equation (11), how do we value payoffs that depend on a forward price?

One example arises when computing the price of an option on a zero-coupon bond. We can write the payoff to a call, for example, in terms of the forward price of the bond:

$$\max(0, P_T(T, T+s) - P_T(T, T)K) = P_T(T, T) \max\left(0, \frac{P_T(T, T+s)}{P_T(T, T)} - K\right)$$

We saw in Section 5 that the time t value of this payoff is computed using the distribution under which the forward price is a martingale:

4. An account like this is often referred to as a "money-market account" because it resembles real-world accounts of that name. Real-world money-market accounts are similar, but they may not pay the short-term interest rate and may not be default-free.

$$\text{Time } t \text{ value} = P_t(t, T)\mathrm{E}_t^F\left[\max\left(0, \frac{P_T(T, T+s)}{P_T(T, T)} - K\right)\right] \tag{12}$$

The result is the Black formula for an option on a forward contract.

As another example, suppose that a specific forward interest rate satisfies equation (11). From equation (3), we can value a zero-coupon bond using forward rates. However, Jensen's inequality restricts the set of rates that can simultaneously be martingales. We discuss in Section 5 which rates are martingales, as well as the processes followed by the other rates.

The theoretical justification for equation (11) arises from the choice of a zero-coupon bond, $P_t(t, T)$, as numeraire. An asset price divided by $P_t(t, T)$ is a forward price, so the result that all such price ratios are martingales means that all forward prices with maturity T are martingales. Such a price ratio can represent the forward price for bonds (when the numerator is $P_t(t, T+s)$) or for nonannualized interest rates (when the numerator is $P_t(t, T-s)$).

2. INTEREST RATE DERIVATIVES AND THE BLACK-SCHOLES-MERTON APPROACH

In this section we see how the Black-Scholes-Merton approach can be applied to price bonds and interest rate derivatives. The Black-Scholes-Merton derivation characterizes the fair option price for a delta-hedging market-maker. Vasicek (1977) used the same approach for pricing bonds, assuming that the short-term interest rate followed an Itô process.

We assume in this section that the short-term interest rate follows the Itô process

$$dr(t) = a(r, t)dt + \sigma(r, t)dZ \tag{13}$$

This is the physical process, as opposed to the risk-neutral process. In equation (13), the drift and standard deviation are functions of r. A special case of equation (13) is

$$dr = [\theta(t) + a(t)(b - r)]\, dt + \sigma(t)r^{\beta}dZ \tag{14}$$

with either $\beta = 0$ or $\beta = 1/2$.[5] This interest rate process was studied by Hull and White (1990). Many well-known models of the short-term interest rate are special cases of equation (14), including those of Vasicek (1977), Ho and Lee (1986), and Cox et al. (1985b).

We should consider the reason to start with equation (13) rather than with a similar equation for bonds. We could, for example, model a zero-coupon bond the same way we model a stock, by assuming that the bond price, $P_t(t, T)$, follows an Itô process:[6]

$$\frac{dP}{P} = \alpha(r, t)dt - q(r, t)dZ \tag{15}$$

5. A process of this form with $\beta = 0$ or $\beta = 1/2$ is said to be **affine**. A function $L(x)$ is **linear** if $L(x_1 + x_2) = L(x_1) + L(x_2)$ and $L(\lambda x) = \lambda L(x)$. A function $f(x)$ is affine if $f(x) = a + bL(x)$, where $L(x)$ is linear. An Itô process dr is affine if $\mathrm{E}(dr) \times (1/dt)$ and $(dr)^2 \times (1/dt)$ are both affine. You can verify that equation 14 is affine in r if $\beta = 0$ or $\beta = 1/2$.

6. The sign of dZ differs in equations (15) and (13) because interest rates and bond prices move inversely.

This is the physical process for the bond. For this equation to be reasonable, $\alpha(r, t)$ and $q(r, t)$ must be carefully specified functions of the interest rate and time. A zero-coupon bond must be worth \$1 at maturity; this boundary condition is not automatically satisfied by the price in equation (15). Also, the volatility of the bond should decrease as the bond approaches maturity. The finite life of a bond constrains the coefficients. As a result, it is typically more convenient to start with the interest rate process in equation (13) and to then compute the price of the bond, taking into account the necessary boundary condition that $P_T(T, T) = \$1$. The implied $\alpha(r, t)$ and $q(r, t)$ are then correctly specified.

The logic of the Vasicek approach to pricing bonds is identical to the Black-Scholes approach to analyzing options: We think about the problem faced by a market-maker and see what it tells us about bond price behavior. We will focus on pricing zero-coupon bonds since they are a building block for all fixed-income products.

An Equilibrium Equation for Bonds

We now consider how to price a bond given that the interest rate follows equation (13). One approach would be to start with a risk-neutral version of equation (13) and then compute equation (10). Instead, however, we will treat equation (13) as the *physical* interest rate process and work through the hedging argument. We will end up with the same pricing formula and we will have a better appreciation for the role of the risk premium in bond pricing.

Vasicek (1977) showed how to adapt the Black-Scholes-Merton pricing approach to bonds by considering the hedging problem faced by a delta-hedging market-maker. To begin, it helps to characterize the bond price process (which we do not know) in terms of the interest rate process in equation (13). From Itô's Lemma, the bond, which is a function of the interest rate and time, follows the process

$$\begin{aligned} dP(r, t, T) &= \frac{\partial P}{\partial r}dr + \frac{1}{2}\frac{\partial^2 P}{\partial r^2}(dr)^2 + \frac{\partial P}{\partial t}dt \\ &= \left[a(r)\frac{\partial P}{\partial r} + \frac{1}{2}\frac{\partial^2 P}{\partial r^2}\sigma(r)^2 + \frac{\partial P}{\partial t}\right]dt + \frac{\partial P}{\partial r}\sigma(r)dZ \end{aligned} \tag{16}$$

This equation does not look like equation (15), but we can define terms so that it does. Let

$$\alpha(r, t, T) = \frac{1}{P(r, t, T)}\left[a(r)\frac{\partial P}{\partial r} + \frac{1}{2}\frac{\partial^2 P}{\partial r^2}\sigma(r)^2 + \frac{\partial P}{\partial t}\right] \tag{17}$$

$$q(r, t, T) = -\frac{1}{P(r, t, T)}\frac{\partial P}{\partial r}\sigma(r) \tag{18}$$

Equation (16) is then

$$\frac{dP(r, t, T)}{P(r, t, T)} = \alpha(r, t, T)dt - q(r, t, T)dZ \tag{19}$$

By using equations (17) and (18) to define α and q, equations (15) and (19) are the same. Note that α and q depend on both the interest rate and on the time to maturity of the bond.

We now analyze the delta-hedging problem. We buy one bond maturing at time T_2, hedge by buying N bonds maturing at time T_1 (N can be negative), and finance the difference by buying or selling a money-market fund, which earns the short-term interest rate, $r(t)$.

The resulting portfolio has the value

$$I = NP(t, T_1) + P(t, T_2) + W = 0 \tag{20}$$

Since the money-market fund is invested in short-term bonds, we have

$$dW = r(t)W dt \tag{21}$$

We then apply Itô's Lemma to the delta-hedged bond portfolio, the value of which is given by equation (20). Substituting into the result equations (17) and (18), we have

$$\begin{aligned} dI = N\left[\alpha(r, t, T_1)dt - q(r, t, T_1)dZ\right] P(r, t, T_1) \\ + \left[\alpha(r, t, T_2)dt - q(r, t, T_2)dZ\right] P(r, t, T_2) + rW dt \end{aligned} \tag{22}$$

In order to eliminate interest rate risk, we set

$$N = -\frac{P(r, t, T_2)}{P(r, t, T_1)}\frac{q(r, t, T_2)}{q(r, t, T_1)}$$

By using the definition of q, equation (18), this can be rewritten

$$N = -\frac{P_r(r, t, T_2)}{P_r(r, t, T_1)} \tag{23}$$

The delta-hedged portfolio has no risk and no investment; it should therefore earn a zero return:

$$dI = 0$$

Substituting equation (23) into equation (22) and setting $dI = 0$, we obtain

$$\frac{\alpha(r, t, T_1) - r}{q(r, t, T_1)} = \frac{\alpha(r, t, T_2) - r}{q(r, t, T_2)} \tag{24}$$

This equation says that *the Sharpe ratio for the two bonds is equal*. Since both bond prices are driven by the same random term, dZ, they must have the same Sharpe ratio if they are fairly priced.

Equation (24) seems to leave us at an impasse. We can treat the Sharpe ratio as a parameter, however, and solve for the bond price as a function of the Sharpe ratio. Denote the Sharpe ratio for dZ as $\phi(r, t)$. For any bond we then have

$$\frac{\alpha(r, t, T) - r}{q(r, t, T)} = \phi(r, t)$$

Substituting equations (17) and (18) for α and q then gives us

$$\boxed{\frac{1}{2}\sigma(r)^2\frac{\partial^2 P}{\partial r^2} + [a(r) + \sigma(r)\phi(r, t)]\frac{\partial P}{\partial r} + \frac{\partial P}{\partial t} - rP = 0} \tag{25}$$

When the short-term interest rate is the only source of uncertainty, *this partial differential equation must be satisfied by any zero-coupon bond*. Different bonds will have different maturity dates and therefore different boundary conditions. All bonds solve the same PDE, however. The Black-Scholes equation characterizes claims that are a function of the stock price. Equation (25) is the analogous equation for derivative claims that are a function of the interest rate.

A difference between equation (25) and the Black-Scholes equation is the explicit appearance of the risk premium, $\sigma(r, t)\phi(r, t)$, in the bond equation. It is important to understand the reason.

In the context of stock options, we hedge an option with a stock, which is an investment asset. The stock is expected to earn its risk premium, $\phi^S\sigma$. Thus, for the stock, the drift term, which is analogous to $a(r)$, equals $r + \phi^S\sigma$. The delta-hedging procedure eliminates the risk premium on the stock, so we are left with the risk-free rate, r, as the coefficient on the $\partial V/\partial S$ term in the Black-Scholes equation.

The interest rate, by contrast, is not the price of an investment asset. The interest rate risk premium does not disappear when we delta-hedge the bond. The interest rate is a *characteristic* of an asset, not an asset by itself. The risk-neutral process for the interest rate is obtained by subtracting the risk premium from the drift.[7] The risk-neutral process for the interest rate is therefore

$$\boxed{dr = [a(r) + \sigma(r)\phi(r, t)]dt + \sigma(r)d\tilde{Z}} \tag{26}$$

The drift in this equation is what appears in equation (25).

Given a zero-coupon bond (which has a terminal boundary condition that the bond is worth \$1 at maturity), Cox et al. (1985b) show that equation (10) is a solution to equation (25). Thus, the bond price solution using the Black-Scholes-Merton approach is the same as that in equation (10).[8]

Finally, the expected change in the bond price under the risk-neutral distribution of the interest rate, equation (26), is

$$\frac{1}{dt}\mathrm{E}^*(dP) = \frac{1}{2}\sigma(r)^2\frac{\partial^2 P}{\partial r^2} + [a(r) + \sigma(r)\phi(r, t)]\frac{\partial P}{\partial r} + \frac{\partial P}{\partial t}$$

Equation (25) therefore says that

$$\frac{1}{dt}\mathrm{E}^*(dP) = rP \tag{27}$$

Under the risk-neutral distribution, bonds on average earn the instantaneous risk-free rate.

The fact that bonds satisfy equation (27) means that the delta-gamma-theta approximation for the change in a bond price holds exactly if the interest rate moves one standard deviation.

To summarize, we can compute the price of a bond by assuming a model for the interest rate and then using equation (25) to obtain a partial differential equation that describes

7. The risk premium for the bond is $q(r, t, T)\phi$; the risk premium for the interest rate will have the opposite sign of that for the bond, so we subtract $-\sigma(r)\phi$, which results in a positive sign on the risk premium in equation (25).

8. This equivalence also follows from the Feynman-Kac representation theorem. See Steele (2010, Chapter 15).

the bond price. Using the PDE together with boundary conditions, we can determine the price of the bond. This is the same procedure we used to price options on stock.

The derivation of equation (25) assumes that bond prices are a function of a single-state variable, the short-term interest rate $r(t)$. It is possible to allow bond prices to depend on additional state variables, and there is empirical support for having bond prices depend on more than one state variable. Litterman and Scheinkman (1991) estimate a factor model for Treasury bond returns and find that a three-factor model typically explains more than 95% of the variability in a bond's return. They identify the three factors as level, steepness, and curvature of the yield curve. The single most important factor, the level of interest rates, accounts for almost 90% of the movement in bond returns. The overwhelming importance of the level of interest rates explains why duration-based hedging, despite its conceptual problems, is widely used. We will focus in this chapter on models with a single state variable.

3. CONTINUOUS-TIME SHORT-RATE MODELS

In this section we discuss several bond pricing models in which the instantaneous short-term interest rate, $r(t)$, follows a form of equation (13) and bond prices are determined by equation (25). The three pricing models we discuss—Rendleman-Bartter, Vasiçek, and Cox-Ingersoll-Ross—differ in their specification of $\alpha(r)$, $\sigma(r)$, and $\phi(r)$. These differences can result in very different pricing implications.

The Rendelman-Bartter Model

The simplest models of the short-term interest rate are those in which the interest rate follows arithmetic or geometric Brownian motion. For example, we could write

$$dr = a dt + \sigma dZ \tag{28}$$

In this specification, the short-rate is normally distributed with mean $r_0 + at$ and variance $\sigma^2 t$. There are several objections to this model:

- The short-rate can be negative. It is not reasonable to think the *nominal* short-rate can be negative, since if it were, investors would prefer holding cash under a mattress to holding bonds.
- The drift in the short-rate is constant. If $a > 0$, for example, the short-rate will drift up over time forever. In practice if the short-rate rises, we expect it to fall; i.e., it is *mean-reverting*.
- The volatility of the short-rate is the same whether the rate is high or low. In practice, we expect the short-rate to be more volatile if rates are high.

The Rendleman and Bartter (1980) model, by contrast, assumes that the short-rate follows geometric Brownian motion:

$$dr = ar dt + \sigma r dZ \tag{29}$$

While interest rates can never be negative in this model, they can be arbitrarily high. In practice we would expect rates to exhibit mean reversion; if rates are high, we expect them on average to decrease. The Rendleman-Bartter model, on the other hand, says that the probability of rates going up or down is the same whether rates are 100% or 1%.

The Vasicek Model

The Vasicek model incorporates mean reversion:

$$\boxed{dr = a(b - r)dt + \sigma dZ} \tag{30}$$

This is an Ornstein-Uhlenbeck process. The drift term induces mean reversion. Suppose we set $a = 20\%$ and $b = 10\%$. The parameter b is the level to which short-term interest rates revert. If $r < b$, the short-rate is expected to rise. For example, if $r(t) = 5\%$, the instantaneous expected change in the interest rate is 0.01. If $r > b$, the short-rate is expected to decrease: If $r(t) = 20\%$, the instantaneous expected change in the interest rate is -0.02.

Note also that the standard deviation of interest rates, σ, is independent of the level of the interest rate. This formulation implies that it is possible for interest rates to become negative and that the variability of interest rates is independent of the level of rates. For example, if $\sigma = 1\%$, a one-standard-deviation move for the short-rate is 100 basis points, whatever the level of the rate.

In the Rendleman-Bartter model, the interest rate is lognormal, so it cannot be negative. In the Vasicek model, by contrast, rates can become negative because the variance is constant.

Vasicek used equation (30) simply to illustrate the pricing methodology outlined in Section 2, without claiming that it was a plausible empirical description of interest rates. The Vasicek model can have unreasonable pricing implications, including negative yields for long-term bonds.

Let the Sharpe ratio for interest rate risk be a constant, ϕ. With the Vasicek interest rate dynamics, equation (30), equation (25) becomes

$$\frac{1}{2}\sigma^2 \frac{\partial^2 P}{\partial r^2} + [a(b - r) + \sigma\phi]\frac{\partial P}{\partial r} + \frac{\partial P}{\partial t} - rP = 0$$

The bond price formula that solves this equation subject to the boundary condition $P(T, T, r) = 1$, and assuming $a \neq 0$, is[9]

$$P[t, T, r(t)] = A(t, T)e^{-B(t,T)r(t)} \tag{31}$$

9. When $a = 0$, the solution is equation (31), with

$$A = e^{-0.5\sigma\phi(T-t)^2+\sigma^2(T-t)^3/6}$$
$$B = T - t$$

When $a = 0$, the interest rate follows a random walk; therefore, $\bar{r}$ is undefined.

where

$$A(t,T) = e^{\bar{r}(B(t,T)+t-T)-B(t,T)^2\sigma^2/4a}$$

$$B(t,T) = (1-e^{-a(T-t)})/a$$

$$\bar{r} = b + \sigma\phi/a - 0.5\sigma^2/a^2$$

with $\bar{r}$ being the yield to maturity on an infinitely lived bond.[10]

The Cox-Ingersoll-Ross Model

The Cox-Ingersoll-Ross (CIR) model (Cox et al., 1985b) assumes a short-term interest rate model of the form

$$\boxed{dr = a(b-r)dt + \sigma\sqrt{r}dZ} \tag{32}$$

The standard deviation of the interest rate is proportional to the square root of the interest rate, instead of being constant as in the Vasicek model. Because of this subtle difference, the CIR model satisfies the objections to the earlier models:

- It is impossible for interest rates to be negative. If $r = 0$ (and assuming that $b > 0$ and $a > 0$), the drift in the rate is positive and the variance is zero, so the rate will become positive. If $2ab > \sigma^2$, the interest rate will never reach zero.
- The volatility of the short-rate increases with the level of the short-rate.
- The short-rate exhibits mean reversion.

The assumption that the variance is proportional to $\sqrt{r}$ also turns out to be convenient analytically—Cox, Ingersoll, and Ross (CIR) derive bond and option pricing formulas using this model. The Sharpe ratio in the CIR model takes the form

$$\phi(r,t) = \bar{\phi}\sqrt{r}/\sigma \tag{33}$$

With this specification for the risk premium and equation (32), the CIR interest rate dynamics, the partial differential equation for the bond price is

$$\frac{1}{2}\sigma^2 r\frac{\partial^2 P}{\partial r^2} + [a(b-r) + r\bar{\phi}]\frac{\partial P}{\partial r} + \frac{\partial P}{\partial t} - rP = 0$$

10. Jamshidian (1989) shows that in the Vasicek model, a call option with T periods to maturity on an s-period bond can be priced using the following variant of the Black-Scholes formula:

$$C(r,K,T,T+s) = P_t(t,T+s)N(d_1) - KP_t(t,T)N(d_2)$$

where

$$d_1 = (\ln[P_t(t,T+s)/KP_t(t,T)] + 0.5\sigma_p^2)/\sigma_p, \qquad d_2 = d_1 - \sigma_p$$

and $\sigma_p = \sigma\sqrt{(1-e^{-2a(T-t)}/2a}(1-e^{-as})/a$. In the same paper, Jamshidian shows that it is possible to price an option on a coupon bond, which is a portfolio of zero-coupon bonds. In the Vasicek model, the bonds in the portfolio replicating the coupon bond are perfectly correlated, so pricing a coupon bond is feasible.

The CIR bond price looks similar to that for the Vasicek dynamics, equation (31), but with $A(t, T)$ and $B(t, T)$ defined differently:[11]

$$P[t, T, r(t)] = A(t, T)e^{-B(t,T)r(t)} \tag{34}$$

where

$$A(t, T) = \left[\frac{2\gamma e^{(a-\bar{\phi}+\gamma)(T-t)/2}}{(a-\bar{\phi}+\gamma)(e^{\gamma(T-t)}-1)+2\gamma} \right]^{2ab/\sigma^2}$$

$$B(t, T) = \frac{2(e^{\gamma(T-t)}-1)}{(a-\bar{\phi}+\gamma)(e^{\gamma(T-t)}-1)+2\gamma}$$

$$\gamma = \sqrt{(a-\bar{\phi})^2 + 2\sigma^2}$$

With the CIR process, the yield on a long-term bond approaches the value $\bar{r} = 2ab/(a - \bar{\phi} + \gamma)$ as time to maturity goes to infinity.

Comparing Vasicek and CIR

How different are the prices generated by the CIR and Vasicek models? What is the role of the different variance specifications in the two models?

Figure 1 illustrates the yield curves generated by the Vasicek and by the CIR models, assuming that the current short-term rate, r, is 5%, $a = 0.2$, and $b = 10\%$. Volatility in the Vasicek model is 2% in the top panel and 10% in the bottom panel. The volatility, σ, has a different interpretation in each model. In the Vasicek model, volatility is absolute, whereas in the CIR model, volatility is scaled by the square root of the current interest rate. To make the CIR volatility comparable at the initial interest rate, it is set so that $\sigma_{\text{CIR}}\sqrt{r} = \sigma_{\text{Vasicek}}$, or 0.0894 in the top panel and 0.447 in the bottom panel. The interest rate risk premium is assumed to be zero.

The two models can exhibit very different behavior. The bottom panel has a relatively high volatility. For short-term bonds—with a maturity extending to about 2.5 years—the yield curves look similar. This is a result of setting the CIR volatility to match the Vasicek volatility. Beyond that point the two diverge, with Vasicek yields below CIR yields. The long-run interest rate in the Vasicek model is −0.025, whereas that in the CIR model is 0.0463. This difference is evident in Figure 1 as the Vasicek yields approach zero (in the long run approaching −0.025).

What accounts for the difference in medium to long-term bonds? As discussed earlier, the pricing formulas are based on averages of interest rate paths, as in equation (9). Some of the interest rate paths in the Vasicek model will be negative. Although the *typical* path will be positive because of mean reversion—rates will be pulled toward 10%—there will be paths on which rates are negative. Because of Jensen's inequality, these paths will be disproportionately important. Over sufficiently long horizons, large negative interest rates become more likely and this leads to negative yields. In the CIR model, this effect results

11. Both the Vasicek and CIR models are examples of affine short-rate models. See Dai and Singleton (2000) for a comprehensive discussion of affine term structure models.

FIGURE 1

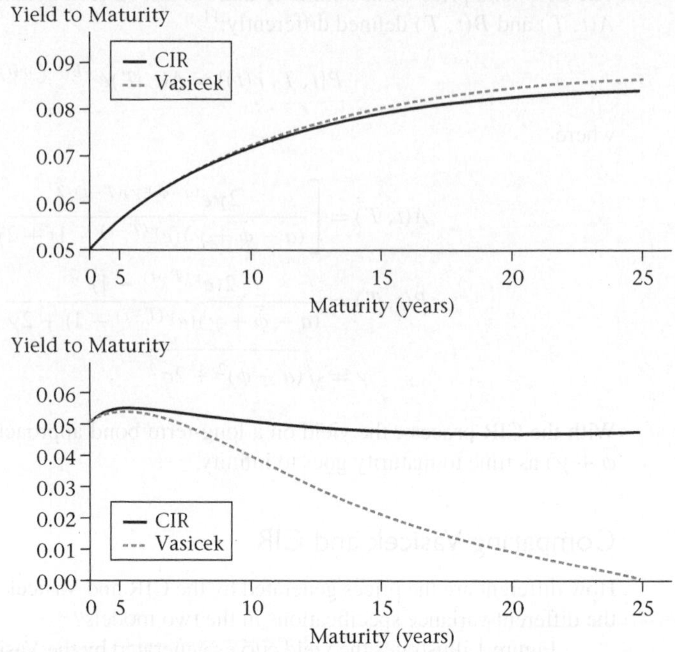

Yield curves implied by the Vasicek and CIR models, assuming that $r = 0.05$, $a = 0.2$, $b = 0.1$. In the top panel, $\sigma = 0.02$ in the Vasicek model and $\sigma = 0.02/\sqrt{0.05} = 0.0894$ in the CIR model. In the bottom panel, $\sigma = 0.10$ in the Vasicek model and $\sigma = 0.10/\sqrt{0.05} = 0.447$ in the CIR model. In all cases, $\phi = 0$.

in the long-run yield decreasing with volatility. Negative yields are impossible in the CIR model, however, since the short-term interest rate can never become negative.

In the top panel, with relatively low volatility, both yield curves are upward sloping. The effect of mean reversion outweighs that of volatility. In the long run, the Vasicek yield exceeds the CIR yield because volatility increases with the level of the interest rate in the CIR model. Consequently, the Jensen's inequality effect is more pronounced in the CIR model than in the Vasicek model.

Duration and Convexity Revisited

Duration and convexity are measures of a bond's sensitivity to interest rates. In a short-rate model, we can compute this sensitivity by computing the analogues of delta and gamma, namely, P_r and P_{rr}. There are two reasons for expecting delta and gamma to differ from duration and convexity.

First, duration and convexity are defined with respect to a change in the bond's yield to maturity, whereas in a short-rate model delta and gamma are defined with respect to a change in the current short rate. These are two different calculations. Second, duration and convexity are defined assuming that the yield curve is flat (all zero-coupon bonds at all maturities have the same yield to maturity) and that when the yield curve changes, yields for all bonds change uniformly so that the yield curve remains flat. It turns out that this simple and intuitive behavior of the yield curve does not satisfy equation (25).

Suppose that the interest rate follows equation (13) and that all zero-coupon bonds have the price

$$P(t, T) = e^{-r(t)(T-t)} \tag{35}$$

In this specification, every bond has yield to maturity $r(t)$. We can compute the derivatives of $P(t, T)$:

$$\frac{\partial P}{\partial r} = -(T-t)P; \qquad \frac{\partial^2 P}{\partial r^2} = (T-t)^2 P; \qquad \frac{\partial P}{\partial t} = rPdt$$

Substituting these expressions into equation (25), we obtain

$$\frac{1}{2}\sigma^2(r)(T-t) = a(r) + \sigma(r)\phi$$

This equation can hold for at most a single value of $T - t$, and thus it can hold for at most one bond. We conclude that equation (35) is not an acceptable bond pricing model.

Delta and gamma are thus fundamentally different calculations than duration and convexity, and the assumed yield curve shift in computing duration and convexity is inconsistent with the bond pricing equation. By how much do duration and convexity differ from delta and gamma? The following example illustrates that in the CIR model, delta and gamma can differ substantially from the traditional measures of duration and convexity. The conclusion to draw from this example is that if one is using a bond pricing model, it makes sense to use the sensitivities implied by the model, which can be very different from duration and convexity.

Example 3. Consider a 5-year zero-coupon bond priced using the CIR model, and suppose that $a = 0.2$, $b = 0.1$, $r = 0.08$, $\bar{\phi} = 0$, and $\sigma = 0.2$. The bond price is \$0.667. Because it is a 5-year zero-coupon bond, Macaulay duration is 5 and convexity is 25. However, in the CIR model with these parameters, $P_r = -1.918$ and $P_{rr} = 5.518$. The scale-free sensitivities to the short-term rate are $-P_r/P = 2.876$ (instead of 5) and $P_{rr}/P = 8.273$ (instead of 25). ■

4. SHORT-RATE MODELS AND INTEREST RATE TREES

In this section we discuss the use of binomial and trinomial interest rate trees to compute bond and option prices.[12] Just as with stock price trees, interest rate trees permit valuing American options, and also allow more flexibility in selecting an appropriate interest rate process.

With any numerical pricing procedure two issues arise: First, how should the tree be constructed and second, how can the procedure be calibrated, i.e., how can the parameters of the procedure be selected to match existing price data? We will discuss both questions in the context of short-rate models proposed by Black et al. (1990) and Hull and White (1994).

An Illustrative Tree

We begin this section with a simple illustrative interest rate tree. As before, the goal is to value cash flows using equation (9), using cumulative discount rates on a path-by-path basis. The tree models the evolution of the continuously compounded short-term interest rate, which we define as the rate prevailing from time t to time $t + h$, where h is the length

12. Early binomial bond pricing models include Rendleman and Bartter (1980) and Ho and Lee (1986).

FIGURE 2

Three-period interest rate tree showing the evolution of the continuously compounded 1-year rate. The state at each node (represented by time index i and level index j) are in braces at each node. The risk-neutral probability of an up move is p.

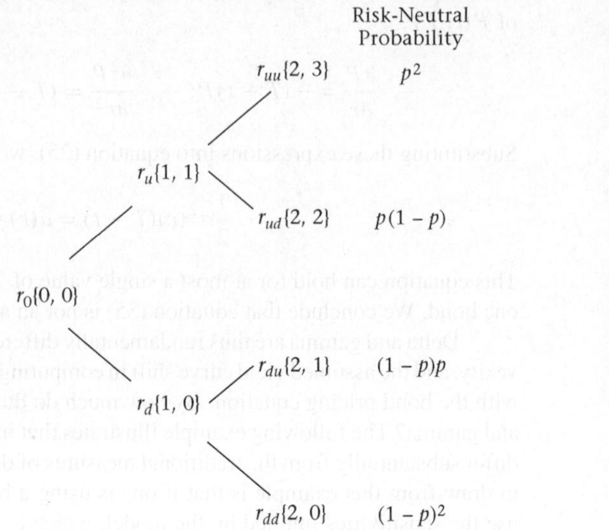

between nodes on the tree.[13] For this example we set $h = 1$; we are thus using movements in the one-year rate to approximate changes in the instantaneous short-rate.

We construct the 1-year rate tree by starting with today's 1-year rate, which we can observe. We assume the 1-year rate moves up or down the second year, and again the third year. This behavior gives us the tree in Figure 2, which is drawn so that it need not recombine. Figure 2 uses two different systems to identify interest rates. First, rates are identified by the sequence of up and down moves by which they are reached, e.g., r_0, r_u, r_{ud}, etc. Second, the rates can be identified by the binomial period and the state within that period: $r(0, 0)$, $r(1, 1)$, $r(2, 2)$, etc. The timing in the tree is such that the final nodes represent one-period rates observed 2 periods from today. Thus, the tree in Figure 2 can price bonds up to 3 years in maturity. Let p denote the risk-neutral probability of an up move. We will assume that rates are continuously compounded in this example.

Zero-Coupon Bond Prices. We calculated the one-period bond price at each node by discounting at the one-period rate prevailing at that node:

$$P(i, j, h) = e^{-r(i,j)h} \tag{36}$$

$P(i, j, h)$ in this equation represents the price of an h-period zero-coupon bond when the one-period rate at time i is $r(i, j)$. We can value a two-period bond by discounting the expected one-period bond price, one period hence. At any node we can value an n-period zero-coupon bond by proceeding in this way recursively. Beginning in period $i + n$, we value one-period bonds, then in period $i + n - 1$ we have two-period bond values, and so forth. The tree can thus be used at any node to value zero-coupon bonds (and therefore

13. A discrete tree necessarily is based on rates covering discrete periods of time, which only approximates a continuous series of short-rates.

implied forward rates) of any maturity, constrained only by the size of the tree. The tree also implies *volatilities* of bond prices and interest rates.

With the tree in Figure 2, we obtain the following valuation equations. For the one-period bond we have

$$P(0, 0, 1) = e^{-r_0 h} \tag{37}$$

The 2-year bond is priced by working backward along the tree. In the second period, the price of the bond is \$1. One year from today, the bond will have the price e^{-r_u} with probability p or e^{-r_d} with probability $1 - p$. The price of the bond is therefore

$$\begin{aligned} P(0, 0, 2) &= e^{-r_0 h}\left[pe^{-r_u h} + (1-p)e^{-r_d h}\right] \\ &= e^{-r_0 h}\left[pP_1(1, 2, 1) + (1-p)P_1(1, 1, 1)\right] \end{aligned} \tag{38}$$

Thus, we can price the 2-year bond using either the interest rate tree or the implied bond prices.

Finally, the 3-year bond is again priced by traversing the entire tree. The price is \$1 after 3 years. After 2 years, the price will be \$1 discounted at r_{uu}, r_{ud}, r_{du}, or r_{dd}. Continuing in this way, the price is

$$\begin{aligned} P(0, 0, 3) = e^{-r_0}[pe^{-r_u}(pe^{-r_{uu}} + (1-p)e^{-r_{ud}}) \\ + (1-p)e^{-r_d}\left(pe^{-r_{du}} + (1-p)e^{-r_{dd}}\right)] \end{aligned} \tag{39}$$

By collecting terms in equation (39), we can rewrite the 3-year bond calculation in terms of cumulative discount rates:

$$\begin{aligned} P(0, 0, 3) = p^2 e^{-(r_0+r_u+r_{uu})} + p(1-p)e^{-(r_0+r_u+r_{ud})} \\ + (1-p)pe^{-(r_0+r_d+r_{du})} + (1-p)^2 e^{-(r_0+r_d+r_{dd})} \end{aligned} \tag{40}$$

This way of writing the valuation equation makes it clear that we are valuing the bond with a discrete approximation to equation (9): We discount the \$1 payoff separately for each *path* the interest rate can take, and take an expectation over those paths using risk-neutral probabilities. In general, letting r_i represent the realized time-i rate, we have

$$\boxed{P(0, 0, nh) = \mathrm{E}^*\left(e^{-\sum_{i=0}^{n} r_i h}\right)} \tag{41}$$

Example 4. Figure 3 constructs an interest rate tree assuming that the current 1-year rate is 10% and that each year the 1-year rate moves up or down 4%, with probability $p = 0.5$. We can use this tree to price 1-, 2-, and 3-year zero-coupon default-free bonds.

1-year bond. From equation (37), the price of the 1-year bond is

$$P(0, h) = e^{-0.10} = \$0.9048 \tag{42}$$

2-year bond. From equation (38), the two-period bond price is

$$\begin{aligned} P(0, 2) &= e^{-0.10}\left(0.5e^{-0.14} + 0.5e^{-0.06}\right) \\ &= \$0.8194 \end{aligned}$$

FIGURE 3

Three-period interest rate tree assuming that the interest rate moves up or down 0.04 each year. The risk-neutral probability of an up move is 0.5.

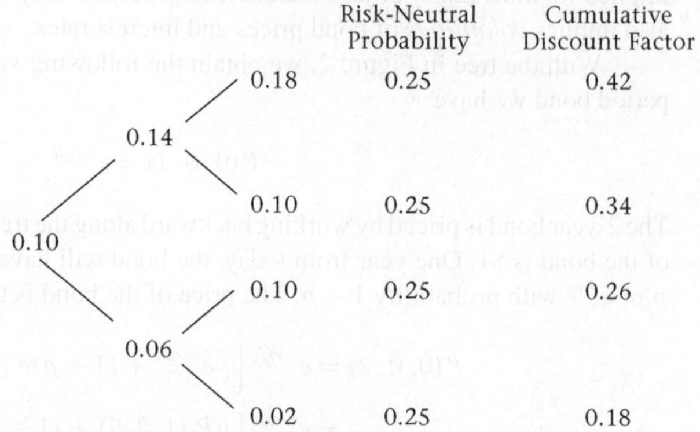

3-year bond. Finally, from equation (39), the price of the 3-year bond is

$$P(0, 3) = e^{-0.10}[0.5e^{-0.14}(0.5e^{-0.18} + 0.5e^{-0.10}) + 0.5e^{-0.06}(0.5e^{-0.10} + 0.5e^{-0.02})] = \$0.7438$$

Equation (41) also gives \$0.7438 as the price of the three-period zero-coupon bond.

Yields and Expected Interest Rates. In Figure 3, we assume that $p = 0.5$ and the up and down moves are symmetric—the interest rate follows a random walk. Consequently, the expected interest rate at each node is 10%. The yields on the two- and three-period bonds, however, are *not* 10%. The yield on the two-period bond is

$$-\ln[P(0, 2)]/2 = -\ln(0.8194)/2 = 0.0996$$

The yield on the three-period bond is

$$-\ln[P(0, 3)]/3 = -\ln(0.7438)/3 = 0.0987$$

Yields are less than 10% on the two- and three-period bonds because of Jensen's inequality: *Uncertainty causes bond yields to be lower than the expected average interest rate.* We cannot discount a cash flow by using the expected interest rate. Rather, we use the expected discount factor. The discrepancy between yields and average interest rates increases with volatility. (Problem 7 asks you to verify this relationship by constructing a different interest rate tree and repeating the bond valuation.)

Option Pricing. Suppose we have a call option with strike price K on a T-year zero-coupon bond. The expiration value of the option at node $\{i, j\}$ is

$$V(i, j) = \max[0, P(i, j, T) - K] \tag{43}$$

To price the option, we can work recursively backward through the tree using risk-neutral pricing, as with an option on a stock. The value one period earlier at the node j' is[14]

$$V(i-1, j') = P(i-1, j', h) \times \left[p \times V(i, j+1) + (1-p) \times V(i, j)\right] \quad (44)$$

We continue in this way to obtain the option value in period 0. In the same way, we can value an option on a yield, or an option on any instrument that is a function of the interest rate.

Delta-hedging works for the bond option just as for a stock option. If the option has t periods until expiration, the underlying asset is a zero-coupon bond maturing at $t + T$, since that will be a T-period bond at expiration. Each period, the delta-hedged portfolio of the option and underlying asset is financed by the short-term bond, paying whatever one-period interest rate prevails at that node.

Example 5. Suppose we have a 2-year put on a 1-year zero-coupon bond and the strike price is \$0.88. The payoff in year 2 at node j is

$$\max[0, \$0.88 - P(2, j, 1)]$$

The option price is computed based on the 1-year bond price in year 2.

From Figure 3, there is only one node at which the put will be exercised, namely, that where the interest rate is 0.18 and, hence, the bond price is $e^{-0.18} = \$0.8353$. Using the interest rates along the tree, and multiplying by the 0.25 risk-neutral probability of reaching that one node, we obtain an option price of

$$(\$0.88 - \$0.8353)e^{-(0.14+0.10)} \times 0.25 = \$0.0088 \quad ■$$

The Black-Derman-Toy Model

The preceding example illustrated the use of a binomial interest rate tree to price bonds and options, but we did not discuss how to construct the tree. In practice we want a tree that correctly prices zero-coupon bonds (in which case it will correctly price forwards and swaps) and options. Selecting parameters for a model so that it fits the data is called *calibration*. In this section and the next, we illustrate this process.

Yield curves can have various shapes depending on the interest rate process and the parameters that can be chosen. For example, a binomial random walk model has two parameters: the starting interest rate and the volatility generating up and down moves. The CIR and Vasicek models have four parameters (a, b, r, and σ) and generate yield curves with particular stylized shapes that may or may not match the data.

The Black-Derman-Toy model is a binomial tree of short-term interest rates with a flexible structure.[15] We assume in this discussion that the length of a binomial period is 1 year, although that is arbitrary.

---

14. If you look at Figure 2, you can see that from node $\{i-1, j\}$, we move "up" to $\{i, j+1\}$, or "down" to $\{i, j\}$.

15. Following Rebonato (1996, Chapter 12), the Black-Derman-Toy model can be written as $r(t) = R(t)e^{\sigma(t)Z(t)}$. Taking the log of both sides and computing $d\ln(r(t))$, we obtain:

TABLE 1 Hypothetical bond-market data. Bond prices and yields are the observed prices and effective annual yields for zero-coupon bonds with the indicated maturity. Volatility refers to the volatility of the bond yield 1 year from today.

Maturity (years)	Yield to Maturity	Bond Price ($)	Volatility in Year 1
1	10%	0.9091	N/A
2	11%	0.8116	10%
3	12%	0.7118	15%
4	12.5%	0.6243	14%

Table 1 lists market information about bonds that we would like to construct a tree to match. We follow the example in Black et al. (1990), using effective annual yields rather than continuously compounded yields. Since the table contains prices of zero-coupon bonds, we can infer the term structure of implied forward interest rates. There is also information about the volatility of interest rates. The column headed "Volatility in Year 1" is the standard deviation of the natural log of the *yield* for that bond 1 year hence. (We could, if we wished, convert this into a standard deviation of the bond price in a year.) The volatility for the n-year bond tells us the uncertainty about the year-1 yield on an $(n-1)$-year bond. The volatility in year 1 of the 2-year bond is 10%; this tells us that the 1-year yield in year 1 will have a 10% volatility. Similarly, the volatility in year 1 of the 4-year bond (which will be a 3-year bond in year 1) is 14%. While the tree matches observed yields and volatilities, it makes no attempt to capture the evolution of the yield curve over time. The yield curve evolution is of course implicit in the tree, but the tree is not calibrated with this in mind.

The BDT approach provides enough flexibility to match this data. Black, Derman, and Toy describe their tree as driven by the short-term rate, which they assume is lognormally distributed. The general structure of the resulting tree is illustrated in Figure 4. We assume that the risk-neutral probability of an up move in the interest rate is 50%.

For each period in the tree there are two parameters. R_{ih} can be thought of as a rate level parameter at a given time and σ_i as a volatility parameter. These parameters can be used to match the tree with the data. In an ordinary lognormal stock-price tree, the ratio of the up node to the down node is $Ae^{\sigma\sqrt{h}}/Ae^{-\sigma\sqrt{h}} = e^{2\sigma\sqrt{h}}$. The ratio between adjacent nodes is the same in Figure 4.

The volatilities in Table 1 are measured in the tree as follows. Let the time-h price of a zero-coupon bond maturing at T when the time-h short-term rate is $r(h)$ be $P[h, T, r(h)]$. The annualized yield of the bond is

$$y[h, T, r(h)] = P[h, T, r(h)]^{-1/(T-h)} - 1$$

$$d\ln(r) = \left[d\ln(R) - \frac{\sigma'(t)}{\sigma(t)}(\ln(R) - \ln(r))\right] dt + \sigma(t)dZ(t)$$

Thus, the BDT model resembles the Vasicek model, only applied to $\ln(r)$ rather than r. If volatility is decaying over time ($\sigma'(t) < 0$), the interest rate is mean-reverting. In any event, the Black-Derman-Toy model is affine in $\ln(r)$. (See footnote 5.)

FIGURE 4

General form of a Black-Derman-Toy interest rate tree. The probability of going up or down from each node is 50%.

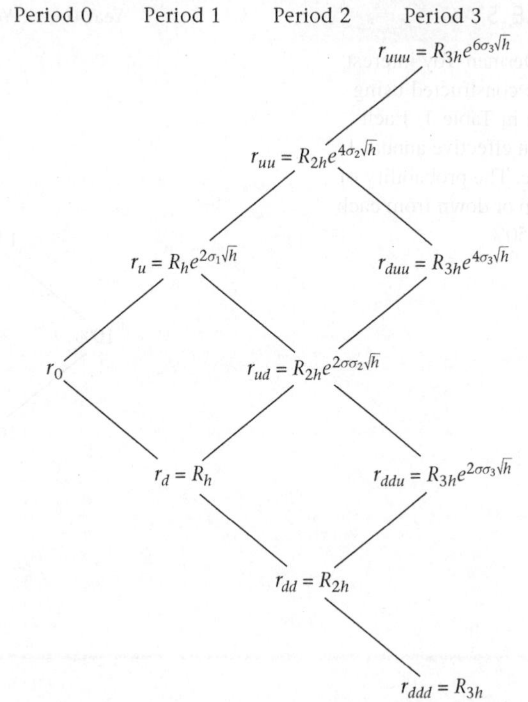

At time h the short-term rate can take on the two values r_u or r_d. The annualized lognormal yield volatility is then

$$\text{Yield volatility} = 0.5 \times \ln\left[\frac{y(h, T, r_u)}{y(h, T, r_d)}\right] \times \frac{1}{\sqrt{h}} \tag{45}$$

We multiply by 0.5 since the distance between nodes is twice the exponentiated volatility.

The tree in Figure 5, which depicts 1-year effective annual rates, was constructed using the data in Table 1. The tree behaves differently from binomial trees we have seen thus far. Unlike a stock-price tree, the nodes are not necessarily centered on the previous period's nodes. For example, in year 1, the lowest interest rate node is above the year-0 interest rate. If we track the minimum interest rate along the bottom of the tree, it increases, then decreases, then increases again. The maximum interest rate in year 3 is below the maximum rate in year 2.

These oddities arise because we constructed the tree to match the data in Table 1. Although bond yields steadily increase with maturity, volatilities do not. In order to match the pattern of volatilities given the structure of the BDT tree, rates must behave in what seems like an unusual fashion.

It is straightforward to verify that the tree in Figure 5 matches the data in Table 1. We can compute the prices of zero-coupon bonds to verify that the tree matches the yield curve. To verify the volatilities, we need to compute the prices of 1-, 2-, and 3-year zero-coupon bonds at year 1 and then compute the yield volatilities of those bonds using equation (45).

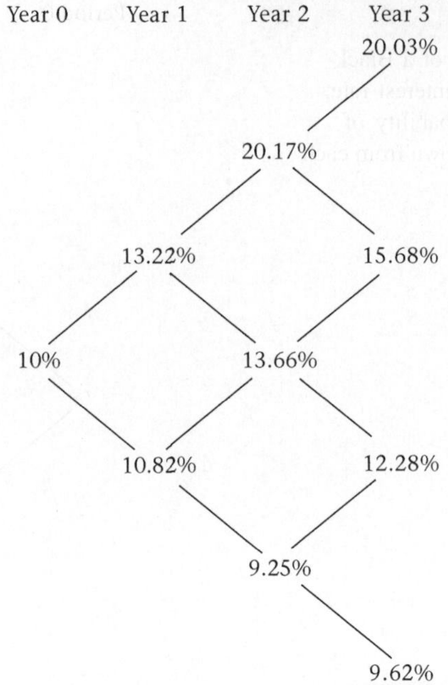

FIGURE 5

Black-Derman-Toy interest rate tree constructed using the data in Table 1. Each rate is an effective annual 1-year rate. The probability of going up or down from each node is 50%.

Constructing the tree in the first place is a matter of running verification in reverse. We build the tree out, starting from period 1. If we have a tree with $n - 1$ periods, we can construct the nth period by simultaneously matching the yield of the n-period bond and the volatility of the $n - 1$ period bond in period 1. Appendix A shows how to construct Figure 5.

Example 6. Figure 6 computes the cap payments on a \$100 4-year loan with annual interest payments, assuming a 12% cap settled annually. The payments in the figure are the *present value* of the cap payments for the interest rate at that node. For example, consider the topmost node in year 2. The realized interest rate is 20.173%. The caplet payment made at the node, 2 years from today, is therefore

$$\text{Caplet payment} = \frac{\$100 \times (0.2017 - 0.12)}{1 + 0.2017} = \$6.799$$

Since 20.17% is the observed 1-year rate 2 years from today, 3 years from today the borrower will owe an interest payment of \$20.17. The \$6.799 payment can be invested at the rate of 20.17%, so the net interest payment will be

$$\$20.17 - (\$6.799 \times 1.2017) = \$12.00$$

In the same way, we can compute the caplet payment at the middle node in year 2, \$1.463. The payment at the bottom node is zero since 9.254% is below the 12% cap.

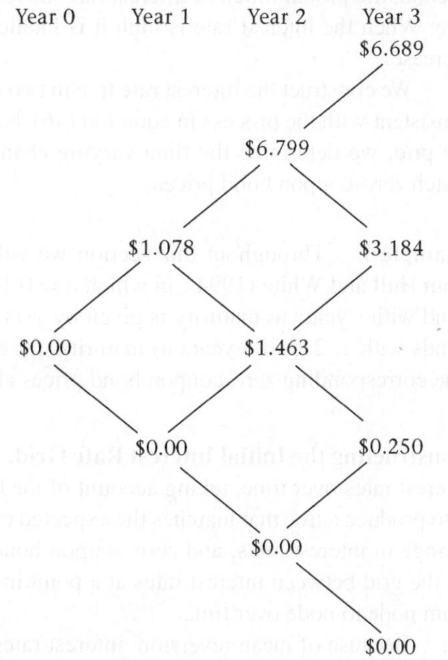

FIGURE 6

Tree showing the payoff to a 12% interest rate cap on a \$100 3-year loan, assuming that interest rates evolve according to Figure 5. Each amount is the present value of the cap payment made at the interest payment date.

We can value the year-3 caplet binomially by working back through the tree in the usual way. The calculation is

$$\text{Value of year-3 cap payment} = \$0.9091 \times [0.5 \times \$0.8832 \times (0.5 \times \$6.799 + 0.5 \times \$1.463) + 0.5 \times \$0.9023 \times (0.5 \times 1.463 + 0.5 \times 0)] = \$1.958$$

The value of the cap is the value of the sum of the caplets. Problem 10 asks you to verify that the value of the cap is \$3.909. ■

Hull-White Model

Following Hull and White (1994), we will illustrate in detail a numerical procedure for fitting a trinomial tree to the interest rate process

$$dr(t) = [\theta(t) - ar(t)]\,dt + \sigma dZ(t) \tag{46}$$

This is a mean-reverting process where the instantaneous volatility, σ, is a constant. However, the interest rate volatility over a discrete period depends upon both σ and a. The Hull-White model provides a different parameterization of the interest rate process than does the Black-Derman-Toy model, which focuses on matching the term structure of volatilities.

Mean reversion in the Hull-White model will have two important consequences. First, the drift term in equation (46) becomes more important as the difference between r and $\theta(t)/a$ becomes larger. A consequence is that extreme high and low interest rates become increasingly unlikely. Therefore, at each point in time we will be able to specify maximum and minimum values of the interest rate, an approximation that simplifies calculations.

Second, the probabilities of interest rate movements will vary with the level of the interest rate: When the interest rate is high it is likelier to decrease, and when low it is likelier to increase.

We construct the interest rate tree in two steps. First, we construct an interest rate grid consistent with the process in equation (46), but assuming that $\theta(t) = 0$. After constructing the grid, we determine the time-varying change in the interest rate, $\theta(t)$, so that we can match zero-coupon bond prices.

Example 7. Throughout this section we will work with a specific numerical example, from Hull and White (1994), in which $a = 0.10$ and $\sigma = 0.01$. The yield on a zero-coupon bond with t years to maturity is given by $y(t) = 0.08 - 0.05e^{-0.18t}$. The annual yields on bonds with 1, 2, and 3 years to maturity, for example, are 3.824%, 4.512%, and 5.086%. The corresponding zero-coupon bond prices are 0.962, 0.914, and 0.858. ■

Constructing the Initial Interest Rate Grid. We begin by constructing a grid of possible interest rates over time, taking account of the behavior implied by equation (46). The goal is to produce a tree that matches the expected change in the interest rate, the volatility of the change in interest rates, and zero-coupon bond yields. We need to determine the distance on the grid between interest rates at a point in time, as well as the probabilities of moving from node to node over time.

Because of mean reversion, interest rates on the grid will attain a minimum value of $\underline{r}$ and a maximum value $\overline{r}$. There are n_r steps, which implies a step size of $\epsilon = (\overline{r} - \underline{r})/n_r$. Possible interest rates are then $\underline{r}, \underline{r} + \epsilon, \underline{r} + 2\epsilon, \ldots, \underline{r} + (n_r - 1)\epsilon, \overline{r}$. Hull and White (1994) suggest setting $\epsilon = \sigma\sqrt{3h}$ and the number of grid points equal to $n_r = 2k + 1$, where k is the smallest integer greater than $0.184/ah$.[16] Along the time axis, if we have n_t time steps, the distance between times is $h = T/n_t$.

The resulting grid appears in Figure 7. This grid approximates the process in equation (46), assuming that $\theta(t) = 0$. The one-period discount factors implied by the rates in Figure 7 are $e^{0.0346}$, $e^{0.0173}$, e^{0}, $e^{-0.0173}$, and, $e^{-0.0346}$.

Probabilities. We now compute the probabilities associated with the various interest rate movements in Figure 7. There will be three possible patterns of interest rate movements on the grid, illustrated in Figure 8. Pattern (a) occurs for the maximum interest rate, pattern (b) for the minimum interest rate, and pattern (c) for other interest rates. We will derive the probabilities for scenario (a); the derivations for (b) and (c) will be analogous.

The central node in Figure 7—the tree before calibration—corresponds to an interest rate of 0. If there are J nodes, the index runs from $j_{\min} \equiv -(J-1)/2$ to $j_{\max} \equiv (J-1)/2$ (by virtue of symmetry and being centered at zero, J is odd). At node j, the interest rate is then $\hat{r}_j = j\epsilon$. The expected change in the interest rate is $-a\hat{r}_j h$. The interest rate can transition to one of three rates the following period: $\hat{r} - \epsilon, \hat{r}$, or $\hat{r} + \epsilon$. Denoting probabilities of up, middle, and down rates as q_u, q_m, and q_d, the equation matching the expected change in the process is

16. It is also necessary that $k < 0.816/M$. Hull and White's suggestions about step sizes and grid points address numerical issues. Do not expect them to be intuitive.

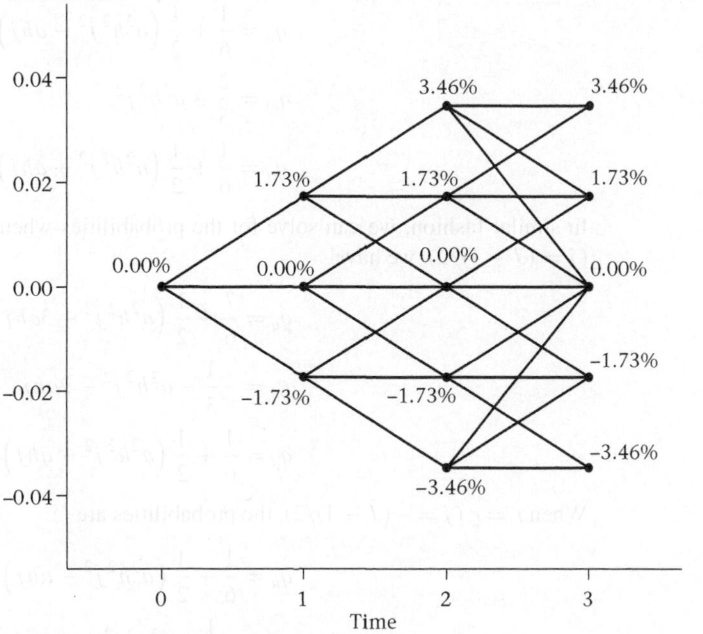

FIGURE 7

Hull-White interest rate grid prior to matching zero coupon bond prices. The time step is $h = 1$ and the interest rate difference between nodes is $\epsilon = 0.0173$. Assumes $a = 0.10$ and $\sigma = 0.01$.

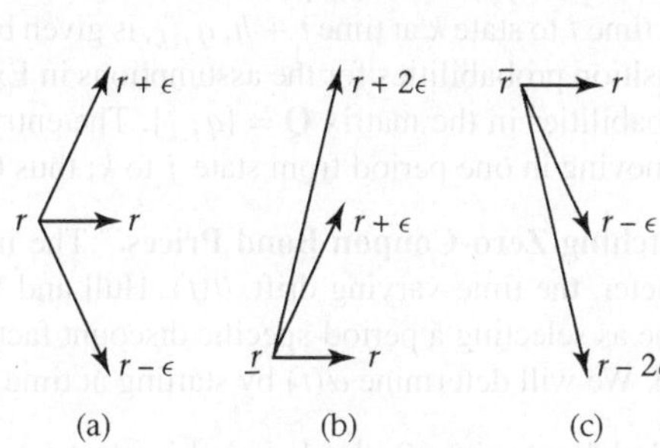

FIGURE 8

Possible movements of interest rates in the Hull-White interest rate grid. Pattern (b) occurs when the interest rate is at its minimum level, (c) when the interest rate is at its maximum level, and (a) otherwise.

$$
\begin{aligned}
-a\hat{r}h &= q_u[\hat{r} + \epsilon - \hat{r}] + q_m[\hat{r} - \hat{r}] + q_d[\hat{r} - \epsilon - \hat{r}] \\
&= (q_u - q_d)\epsilon
\end{aligned}
$$

The variance of the change in the interest rate is

$$
\sigma^2 h = q_u[\epsilon - (-a\hat{r}h)]^2 + q_m[a\hat{r}h]^2 + q_d[-\epsilon - (-a\hat{r}h)]^2
$$

Imposing $q_u + q_m + q_d = 1$ and solving for the probabilities, we have[17]

$$
\begin{aligned}
q_u &= \frac{1}{6} + \frac{1}{2}\left(a^2h^2j^2 - ahj\right) \\
q_m &= \frac{2}{3} - a^2h^2j^2 \\
q_d &= \frac{1}{6} + \frac{1}{2}\left(a^2h^2j^2 + ahj\right)
\end{aligned} \tag{47}
$$

In similar fashion, we can solve for the probabilities when $r = \bar{r}$ and $r = \underline{r}$. When $r = \bar{r}$ ($j = (J - 1)/2$), we have

$$
\begin{aligned}
q_u &= \frac{7}{6} + \frac{1}{2}\left(a^2h^2j^2 + 3ahj\right) \\
q_m &= -\frac{1}{3} - a^2h^2j^2 - 2ahj \\
q_d &= \frac{1}{6} + \frac{1}{2}\left(a^2h^2j^2 + ahj\right)
\end{aligned} \tag{48}
$$

When $r = \underline{r}$ ($j = -(J - 1)/2$), the probabilities are

$$
\begin{aligned}
q_u &= \frac{1}{6} + \frac{1}{2}\left(a^2h^2j^2 - ahj\right) \\
q_m &= -\frac{1}{3} - a^2h^2j^2 + 2ahj \\
q_d &= \frac{7}{6} + \frac{1}{2}\left(a^2h^2j^2 - 3ahj\right)
\end{aligned} \tag{49}
$$

To recap, there are J possible interest rate nodes. The probability of a move from state j at time t to state k at time $t + h$, $q_{j,k}$, is given by equations (47)–(49). Table 2 contains the transition probabilities for the assumptions in Example 7. We can summarize the transition probabilities in the matrix $\mathbf{Q} = \{q_{j,k}\}$. The entry in row j and column k is the probability of moving in one period from state j to k; thus $\mathbf{Q}$ is the same as Table 2.

Matching Zero-Coupon Bond Prices. The interest rate process has one additional parameter, the time-varying drift, $\theta(t)$. Hull and White (1994) show that setting $\theta(t)$ is the same as selecting a period-specific discount factor $e^{-\alpha(t)}$ by which to shift the interest rate grid. We will determine $\alpha(t)$ by starting at time 0 and working forward through the tree.

Period 1. At time 0, the 1-period interest rate, 3.824%, is known. Thus, we set $\alpha(1) = 0.03824$. You can see this is the rate at the first node in Figure 9.

Period 2. There are three possible interest rates in period 2. If we number the nodes so that the center node is node 0, we can determine the price of a two-period zero-coupon bond as follows:

$$
P_0(0, 2) = \left[q_{0,1}e^{0.0173} + q_{0,0}e^{0} + q_{0,-1}e^{-0.0173}\right] e^{-(0.03824+\alpha(2))}
$$

Solving for $\alpha(2)$, we obtain $\alpha(2) = 0.052046$.

17. In Hull and White (1994), $ah \equiv M$.

TABLE 2 Probabilities of transitioning from state j (row) to state k (column), constructed using equations (47)–(49) and the assumptions in Example 7.

	To State:				
From State:	2	1	0	−1	−2
2	0.887	0.0267	0.0867	0.0000	0.000
1	0.122	0.6567	0.2217	0.0000	0.000
0	0.000	0.1667	0.6667	0.1667	0.000
−1	0.000	0.0000	0.2217	0.6567	0.122
−2	0.000	0.0000	0.0867	0.0267	0.887

FIGURE 9

Hull-White interest rate grid after matching zero-coupon bond prices. The time step is $h = 1$ and the interest rate difference between nodes is $\epsilon = 0.0173$.

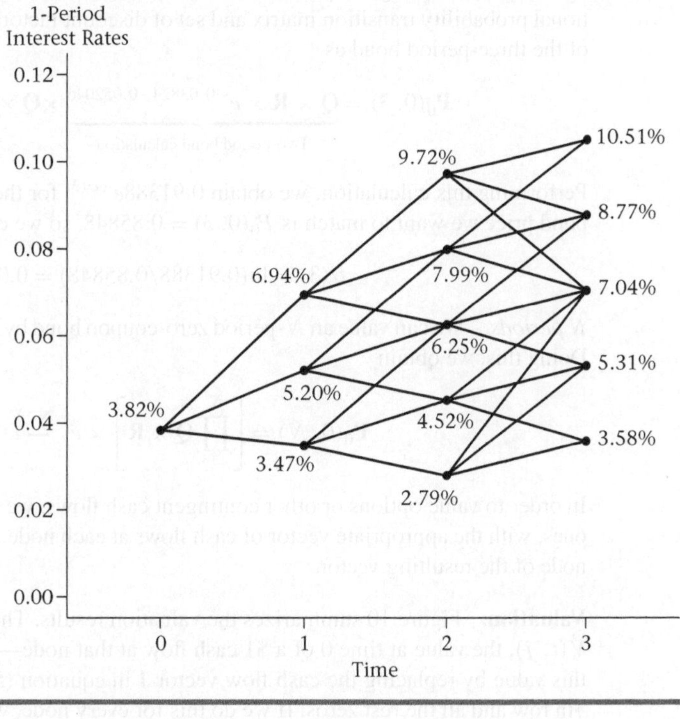

Before moving on to 3-period valuation, we will solve for $\alpha(2)$ using a different notation that will be useful in subsequent periods. We can write the calculation for $P_0(0, 2)$ using the probability transition matrix **Q**. At any point in Figure 7, there are five possible interest rates, although in period 2 we have a positive probability of reaching only three of them. Let **R** denote the matrix with $e^{(j_{\max}-(j-1))\epsilon}$ on the jth element of the diagonal ($j_{max} = 2$ in this example):

$$\mathbf{R} = \begin{pmatrix} e^{0.0346} & 0 & 0 & 0 & 0 \\ 0 & e^{0.0173} & 0 & 0 & 0 \\ 0 & 0 & e^{0} & 0 & 0 \\ 0 & 0 & 0 & e^{-0.0173} & 0 \\ 0 & 0 & 0 & 0 & e^{-0.0346} \end{pmatrix}$$

With $\mathbf{Q}$ as the matrix describing the probability of transiting from row i at time t to column j at time $t+h$, the probability of transiting to a node times the (uncalibrated) discount rate at that node is $\mathbf{Q} \times \mathbf{R}$. Let $\mathbf{1}$ be a column vector of ones of length 5: $\mathbf{1} = (1\ 1\ 1\ 1\ 1)'$. We can write the value of the two-period bond as

$$\mathbf{P}_0(0, 2) = \mathbf{Q} \times \mathbf{R} \times e^{-0.03824-0.052046} \times \mathbf{1}$$

This calculation actually computes *five* bond prices, with each price corresponding to one of five possible initial one-period interest rates. We are calibrating the tree based on the center node, however (see Figure 7), so we use only the bond price at that node.

Period 3. Following the procedure used to value the two-period bond, we have an additional probability transition matrix and set of discount factors. Thus, we can write the value of the three-period bond as

$$\mathbf{P}_0(0, 3) = \underbrace{\mathbf{Q} \times \mathbf{R} \times e^{-0.03824-0.052046}}_{\text{Two-period bond calculation}} \times \mathbf{Q} \times \mathbf{R} \times e^{-\alpha(3)} \times \mathbf{1}$$

Performing this calculation, we obtain $0.91388e^{-\alpha(3)}$ for the uncalibrated bond price. The bond price we want to match is $P_0(0, 3) = 0.85848$, so we compute $\alpha(3)$ as

$$\alpha(3) = \ln(0.91388/0.85848) = 0.06254$$

N periods. We can value an N-period zero-coupon bond by repeating the procedure above. Doing this, we obtain

$$\mathbf{P}_0(0, N) = \left[\prod_{i=2}^{N} \mathbf{Q} \times \mathbf{R} \right] \times e^{-\sum_{i=1}^{N} \alpha(i)} \times \mathbf{1} \tag{50}$$

In order to value options or other contingent cash flows, we simply replace $\mathbf{1}$, the vector of ones, with the appropriate vector of cash flows at each node. The value is that at the middle node of the resulting vector.

Valuation. Figure 10 summarizes the valuation results. The number at node j at time t is $V(t, j)$, the value at time 0 of a \$1 cash flow at that node—a state price. We can compute this value by replacing the cash flow vector $\mathbf{1}$ in equation (50) with a vector with 1 in the jth row and all the rest zeros. If we do this for every node, we obtain an $n_r \times n_T$ matrix V that we can use for valuation.[18]

18. We can also compute $V(t, j)$ recursively by multiplying the time t value vector by the probabilities of reaching node j at time $t+h$ and discounting at the appropriate rate. The time 0 value of this cash flow is thus

$$\mathbf{V}(t+h, \cdot)' = \mathbf{V}(t, \cdot)'\, \mathbf{Q}\, \mathbf{R}\, e^{-\alpha(t+h)} \tag{51}$$

FIGURE 10

State prices in the Hull-White interest rate grid. Each square represents an interest rate, and the amount below the square is the time 0 value of \$1 paid in that state. The time step is $h = 1$ and the interest rate difference between nodes is $\epsilon = 0.0173$. The assumptions are given in Example 7.

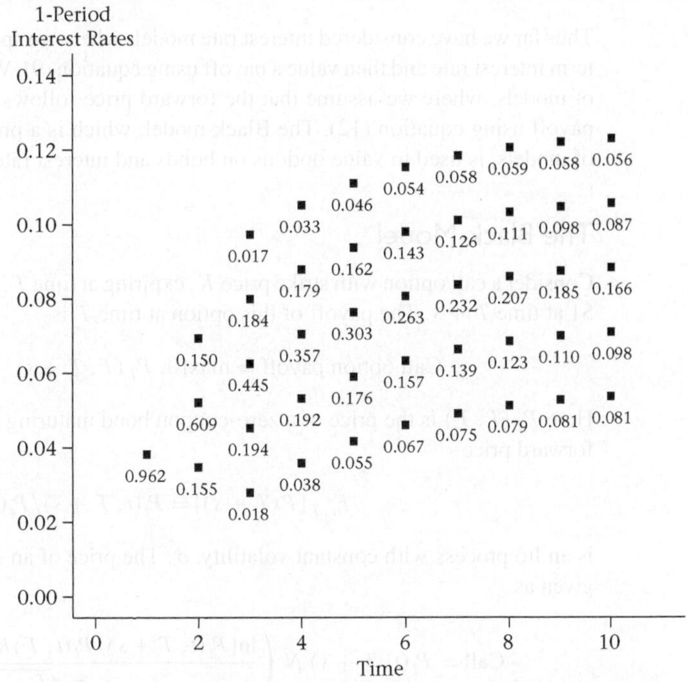

Looking at Figure 10, the value of \$1 paid at time 1 is $e^{-0.0382} = 0.962$. The time 0 value of \$1 paid at time 3 at the top node in Figure 10 is \$0.017. These are the time 0 state prices corresponding to each interest rate node. We can compute the price of a 3-year zero-coupon bond by summing the time 3 entries in Figure 10.

Example 8. Consider a 4-year 8% annual interest rate cap. From Figure 9, over 4 years there are three nodes at which the interest rate exceeds 8%: 9.72%, 10.51%, and 8.77%. The value of the cap per dollar of notional amount is

$$0.017 \times (0.0972 - 0.08) + 0.033 \times (0.1051 - 0.08) + 0.179 \times (0.0877 - 0.08) = 0.00251$$

Example 9. Consider a 3-year call option on a 1-year bond with a strike price of $K = 0.94$. The applicable rates are 1-year rates for a bond bought in period 3 and paying \$1 in period 4. The two in-the-money nodes are those in period 3 where rates are 5.31% and 3.58%. The value of the option is

$$0.194 \times \max\left[0, e^{-0.0531} - 0.94\right] + 0.018 \times \max\left[0, e^{-.0358} - 0.94\right] = 0.00366$$

5. MARKET MODELS

Thus far we have considered interest rate models where we specify the behavior of the short-term interest rate and then value a payoff using equation (9). We now consider a second class of models, where we assume that the forward price follows equation (11) and we value a payoff using equation (12). The Black model, which is a prominent example of this class of models, is used to value options on bonds and interest rates.

The Black Model

Consider a call option with strike price K, expiring at time T, on a zero-coupon bond paying \$1 at time $T+s$. The payoff of this option at time T is

$$\text{Call option payoff} = \max[0,\ P_T(T, T+s) - K\,P_T(T, T)] \tag{52}$$

Here $P_T(T, T)$ is the price of a zero-coupon bond maturing at time T. We assume that the forward price

$$F_{t,T}[P(T+s)] = P_t(t, T+s)/P_t(t, T) \tag{53}$$

is an Itô process with constant volatility, σ. The price of an option with this payoff is then given as

$$\begin{aligned}\text{Call} = {} & P_t(t, T+s)\, N\left(\frac{\ln[P_t(t, T+s)/P_t(t, T)K] + 0.5\sigma^2(T-t)}{\sigma\sqrt{T-t}}\right) \\ & - K\,P_t(t, T)\, N\left(\frac{\ln[P_t(t, T+s)/K\,P_t(t, T)] - 0.5\sigma^2(T-t)}{\sigma\sqrt{T-t}}\right)\end{aligned} \tag{54}$$

The volatility in equation (54) is the volatility of the forward price for the bond, where the forward contract calls for time-T delivery of the bond maturing at $T+s$. Equation (54) can also be written in terms of the forward price:

$$P_t(t, T)\left[F_{t,T}[P(T+s)]\,N(d_1) - K\,N(d_2)\right] \tag{55}$$

where

$$d_1 = \frac{\ln(F_{t,T}[P(T+s)]/K) + 0.5\sigma^2(T-t)}{\sigma\sqrt{T-t}}$$

$$d_2 = d_1 - \sigma\sqrt{T}$$

This is the Black formula for a call option on a bond. The formula for a put can be obtained by put-call parity. As we saw in Section 1, the formula can also be used to price caplets and floorlets.

The Black formula assumes that the volatility of the forward price is constant. The volatility of any particular bond varies over time, typically decreasing as it approaches maturity. The volatility of a forward price, however, is the volatility of the *ratio* in the prices of bonds with different maturities. A variation in the interest rate affects the discounting of *both* the underlying asset (the bond maturing at time $T+s$) and the bond maturing at time T, so this volatility plausibly could be constant.

In practice, the implied volatility from the Black formula is often used for quoting prices of caplets and floorlets. For example, the statement that a particular caplet is priced at a volatility of 90 basis points (using the Black formula) tells us the volatility of a specific forward interest rate and provides a general sense of prices. The difference in implied volatilities across maturities provides information about the relative volatilities along different portions of the forward curve.

For an example using the Black formula to price caplets and caps, suppose a borrower has a floating rate loan with interest payments at times t_i, $i = 1, \ldots, n$. A cap would make the series of payments

$$\text{Cap payment at time } t_{i+1} = \max[0, R_{t_i}(t_i, t_{i+1}) - K_R] \tag{56}$$

The value of the cap is the summed value of the individual caplets.

Example 10. One-year and 2-year zero-coupon bonds with a \$1 maturity value have prices of \$0.9091 and \$0.8116. The 1-year implied forward 1-year bond price is therefore \$0.8116/\$0.9091 = \$0.8928, with an implied forward rate of 12.01%. Suppose the volatility of the forward bond price is 2%. The price of a 1-year put option to sell the 1-year bond for a price of \$0.88 is

$$\text{BSPut}(0.8116, 0.9091 \times 0.88, 0.02, 0, 1, 0) = 0.002228$$

We can also price the option using the Black formula:

$$0.9091 \times \text{BSPut}(0.8116/0.9091, 0.88, 0.02, 0, 1, 0) = 0.002228 \quad ■$$

LIBOR Market Model

The Black model values a cash flow based on a single interest rate or bond price. In some circumstances a valuation may depend on several interest rates or bond prices (e.g., coupon bonds and swaps). The LIBOR market model, due to Brace et al. (1997), extends the framework of the Black model to value such claims.[19]

To understand the LIBOR market model, suppose we select time T as the date for which all forward contracts are martingales. Figure 11 illustrates the set of forward interest rates that are martingales. For example, consider the ratio $P_t(t, T - 4h)/P_t(t, T)$. This is the nonannualized forward interest rate for a loan beginning at time $T - 4h$ and ending at time T, which we denote $R_t(T - 4h, T)$. If we invest \$1 at time $T - 4h$ earning the rate we locked in at time t, then at time T we will have $1 + R_t(T - 4h, T)$.

The forward interest rates in Figure 11 that are martingales all represent *overlapping* periods of time, and all have different maturities, but all mature at date T and are therefore computed with $P_t(t, T)$ as the denominator. The rate $R_t(T - 2h, T - h)$, which is an h-period rate prevailing from $T - 2h$ to $T - h$, is *not* a martingale. Jensen's inequality is the reason. We can represent $R_t(T - 2h, T - h)$ as the ratio of forward rates that *are* martingales:

$$1 + R_t(T - 2h, T - h) = \frac{1 + R_t(T - 2h, T)}{1 + R_t(T - h, T)}$$

19. Heath et al. (1992) was the first paper to model stochastic forward rates and to demonstrate the necessary restrictions on the forward rate processes.

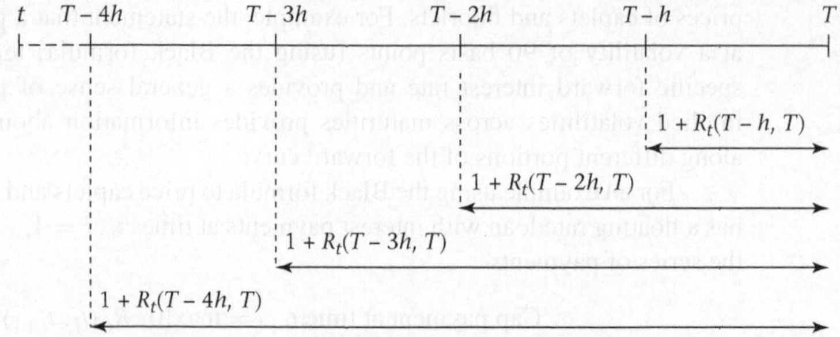

FIGURE 11

Forward interest rates that are martingales when the zero-coupon bond maturing at time T is numeraire.

Jensen's inequality tells us that if both $1 + R_t(T - 2h, T)$ and $1 + R_t(T - h, T)$ are martingales, their ratio cannot be a martingale.[20]

The insight of the LIBOR market model is that we can use the processes for rates that are martingales to compute the process for forward rates that are not martingales under the same measure, such as $R_t(T - ih, T - (i - 1)h)$. We will call these one-period rates *LIBOR* rates, denoted $L_i(t)$.

To simplify the notation, for a given T and h define $R_i(t) = R_t(T - ih, T)$. With $P_t(t, T)$ as numeraire, $R_i(t)$ is a martingale:

$$\frac{dR_i(t)}{R_i(t)} = \nu_i(t)dZ$$

We assume that the annualized LIBOR rate follows the process

$$\frac{dL_i(t)}{L_i(t)} = \mu_i(t)dt + \sigma_i(t)dZ(t) \tag{57}$$

Because $L_i(t)$ is annualized (unlike the R_i), the actual interest paid over a period h_i is $h_i L_i$. We wish to find the appropriate μ_i and σ_i given that the $R_i(t)$ are martingales.

We begin by noting that for the first period, $h_1 L_1(t) = R_1(t)$. Thus, $L_1(t)$ is a martingale:

$$h_1 dL_1(t) = dR_1(t)$$

Moving back one period, the forward rate formula implies that $1 + h_2 L_2(t) = (1 + R_2(t))/(1 + h_1 L_1(t))$. Take logs of both sides:

$$\ln[1 + R_2(t)] = \ln[1 + h_2 L_2(t)] + \ln[1 + h_1 L_1(t)] \tag{58}$$

Let $h_i L_i(t)/(1 + h_i L_i(t)) = \phi_i(t)$ denote the present value of interest on a loan at rate $L_i(t)$. From Itô's Lemma, we have

20. A different way to see this is that the forward rate from $T - 2h$ to $T - h$ has in the denominator the bond maturing at time $T - h$ rather than the bond maturing at T. If the measure is determined by the bond maturing at T, the only martingales under this measure are ratios in which the bond maturing at T is the denominator.

$$d \ln[1 + R_2(t)] = -0.5\nu_2^2 dt + \nu_2 dZ$$
$$d \ln[1 + h_1 L_1(t)] = -0.5\phi_1(t)^2\sigma_1^2 dt + \phi_1(t)\sigma_1 dZ$$
$$d \ln[1 + h_2 L_2(t)] = \phi_2(t)\mu_2 dt - 0.5\phi_2(t)^2\sigma_2^2 dt + \phi_2(t)\sigma_2 dZ$$

Using equation (58), we can equate coefficients on the dZ and dt terms to obtain

$$\nu_2(t) = \phi_2(t)\sigma_2(t) + \phi_1(t)\sigma_1(t)$$

and

$$\mu_2\phi_2(t) = 0.5\phi_1(t)^2\sigma_1^2 + 0.5\phi_2(t)^2\sigma_2^2 - 0.5\nu_2^2$$

Substituting the expression for $\nu_2(t)$ into that for $\mu_2\phi_2(t)$, we obtain the process for $L_2(t)$:

$$\frac{dL_2(t)}{L_2(t)} = -\frac{h_1 L_1(t)}{1 + h_1 L_1(t)}\sigma_1\sigma_2 + \sigma_2 dZ$$

Continuing in this way in general, we obtain

$$\frac{dL_n(t)}{L_n(t)} = -\sum_{j=1}^{n-1} \frac{h_j L_j(t)\sigma_j(t)}{1 + h_j L_j(t)}\sigma_n(t)dt + \sigma_n(t)dZ \tag{59}$$

This solution uses $P_t(t, T)$ as numeraire.

Equation (59) defines processes for the complete set of LIBOR rates in an internally consistent manner. These rates can be used to construct bond prices and to determine the values of caps and swaptions. It is possible to select the individual LIBOR volatilities to match implied volatilities for different maturities.

You may encounter variants of equation (59) constructed using a different zero-coupon bond as numeraire. These solutions will look different, but this occurs because a different maturity is the starting point.

CHAPTER SUMMARY

Two important classes of interest rate and bond derivatives are those based on the evolution of the short-rate and those based on forward prices. Short-rate models generally value a zero-coupon bond by specifying a process for the short-term interest rate, $r(t)$, and then computing

$$\mathrm{E}_t^B\left[e^{-\int_t^T r(s)ds}\right]$$

The Vasicek and Cox-Ingersoll-Ross short-rate models assume different mean-reverting processes for the short-rate and result in closed-form bond pricing models.

For many short-rate processes there is not a closed-form solution. In these cases a binomial or trinomial tree can be used to approximate the calculation. The Black-Derman-Toy tree is a binomial interest rate tree calibrated to match zero-coupon yields and a particular set of volatilities. The Hull-White model illustrates a trinomial calculation approximating a mean-reverting short-rate process.

Under the assumption that the forward price for a bond is lognormally distributed, the Black model provides a simple closed-form pricing model (essentially the Black-Scholes formula) that can be used to price bond and interest rate options. The LIBOR market model is a generalization of the Black model that specifies the process for an entire set of forward interest rates.

FURTHER READING

Fixed income texts at roughly the level of this chapter include Sundaresan (2009), Tuckman and Serrat (2012), and Veronesi (2010). Classic treatments of bond pricing with interest rate uncertainty are Vasicek (1977) and Cox et al. (1985b). These are examples of affine term structure models, discussed more generally in Duffie and Kan (1996) and Dai and Singleton (2000).

Binomial treatments include Rendleman and Bartter (1980), Ho and Lee (1986), and Black et al. (1990). Heath et al. (1992) have been extremely influential insofar as they provide an equilibrium characterization of the evolution of forward rates. See also Brace et al. (1997) and Miltersen et al. (1997). More in-depth treatments of interest rate derivatives can be found in Hull (2000, chs. 20–22), Rebonato (1996), Jarrow (1996), and James and Webber (2001).

Litterman and Scheinkman (1991) is a classic study of factors affecting bond returns. Bliss (1997) surveys this literature.

PROBLEMS

For the first three problems, use the following information:

Bond maturity (years)	1	2	3	4
Bond price	0.9259	0.8495	0.7722	0.7020
1-year forward price volatility		0.1000	0.1050	0.1100

1. **a.** What is the 1-year bond forward price in year 1?

b. What is the price of a call option that expires in 1 year, giving you the right to pay \$0.9009 to buy a bond expiring in 1 year?

c. What is the price of an otherwise identical put?

d. What is the price of an interest rate caplet that provides an 11% (effective annual rate) cap on 1-year borrowing 1 year from now?

2. **a.** What is the 2-year forward price for a 1-year bond?

b. What is the price of a call option that expires in 2 years, giving you the right to pay \$0.90 to buy a bond expiring in 1 year?

c. What is the price of an otherwise identical put?

d. What is the price of an interest rate caplet that provides an 11% (effective annual rate) cap on 1-year borrowing 2 years from now?

3. What is the price of a 3-year interest rate cap with an 11.5% (effective annual) cap rate?

4. Suppose the yield curve is flat at 8%. Consider 3- and 6-year zero-coupon bonds. You buy one 3-year bond and sell an appropriate quantity of the 6-year bond to duration-hedge the position. Any additional investment is in short-term (zero-duration) bonds. Suppose the yield curve can move up to 8.25% or down to 7.75% over the course of 1 day. Do you make or lose money on the hedge? What does the result tell you about the (impossible) flat yield curve model discussed in Section 2?

5. Suppose the yield curve is flat at 6%. Consider a 4-year 5%-coupon bond and an 8-year 7%-coupon bond. All coupons are annual.

a. What are the prices and durations of both bonds?

b. Consider buying one 4-year bond and duration-hedging by selling an appropriate quantity of the 8-year bond. Any residual is financed with short-term (zero-duration) bonds. Suppose the yield curve can move up to 6.25% or down to 5.75% over the course of 1 day. What are the results from the hedge?

6. Consider two zero-coupon bonds with 2 years and 10 years to maturity. Let $a = 0.2$, $b = 0.1$, $r = 0.05$, $\sigma_{\text{Vasicek}} = 10\%$, and $\sigma_{\text{CIR}} = 44.721\%$. The interest rate risk premium is zero in each case. We will consider a position consisting of one \$100 par value 2-year bond, which we will hedge with a position in the 10-year bond.

a. Compute the prices, deltas, and gammas of the bonds using the CIR and Vasicek models. How do delta and gamma compare to duration and convexity?

b. Suppose the Vasicek model is true. You wish to hedge the 2-year bond using the 10-year bond. Consider a 1-day holding period and suppose the interest rate moves one standard deviation up or down. What is the return on the duration-hedged position? What is the return on the Vasicek delta-hedged position?

c. Repeat the previous part, only use the CIR model in place of the Vasicek model.

7. Construct a four-period, three-step (eight terminal node) binomial interest rate tree where the initial interest rate is 10% and rates can move up or down by 2%; model your tree after that in Figure 3. Compute prices and yields for 1-, 2-, 3-, and 4-year bonds. Do yields decline with maturity? Why?

For the next eight problems, you may find it helpful to read online Appendix A.

8. Verify that the 4-year zero-coupon bond price generated by the tree in Figure 5 is \$0.6243.

9. Verify that the 1-year yield volatility of the 4-year zero-coupon bond price generated by the tree in Figure 5 is 0.14.

10. Verify that the price of the 12% interest rate cap in Figure 6 is \$3.909.

11. Verify that the 1-year forward rate 3 years hence in Figure 5 is 14.0134%.

For the next four problems, here are two BDT interest rate trees with effective annual interest rates at each node.

Tree #1

0.08000	0.07676	0.08170	0.07943	0.07552
	0.10362	0.10635	0.09953	0.09084
		0.13843	0.12473	0.10927
			0.15630	0.13143
				0.15809

Tree #2

0.08000	0.08112	0.08749	0.08261	0.07284
	0.09908	0.10689	0.10096	0.08907
		0.13060	0.12338	0.10891
			0.15078	0.13317
				0.16283

12. What are the 1-, 2-, 3-, 4-, and 5-year zero-coupon bond prices implied by the two trees?

13. What volatilities were used to construct each tree? (You computed zero-coupon bond prices in the previous problem; now you have to compute the year-1 yield volatility for 1-, 2-, 3-, and 4-year bonds.) Can you unambiguously say that rates in one tree are more volatile than the other?

14. For years 2–5, compute the following:

a. The forward interest rate, r_f, for a forward rate agreement that settles at the time borrowing is repaid. That is, if you borrow at $t - 1$ at the 1-year rate $\tilde{r}$, and repay the loan at t, the contract payoff in year t is

$$(\tilde{r} - r_f)$$

b. The forward interest rate, r_e, for a Eurodollar-style forward rate agreement that settles at the time borrowing is *initiated*. That is, if you borrow at $t - 1$ at the 1-year rate $\tilde{r}$, and repay the loan at t, the contract payoff in year $t - 1$ is

$$(\tilde{r} - r_e)$$

c. How is the difference between r_f and r_e affected by volatility (you can compare the two trees) and time to maturity?

15. You are going to borrow \$250m at a floating rate for 5 years. You wish to protect yourself against borrowing rates greater than 10.5%. Using each tree, what is the price of a 5-year interest rate cap? (Assume that the cap settles each year at the time you repay the borrowing.)

16. Suppose that the yield curve is given by $y(t) = 0.10 - 0.07e^{-0.12t}$, and that the short-term interest rate process is $dr(t) = (\theta(t) - 0.15r(t)) + 0.01dZ$. Compute the calibrated Hull-White tree for 5 years, with time steps of $h = 1$.

a. What is the probability transition matrix Q?

b. What is the price of a 5-year 7.5% interest rate cap on a \$1 million notional amount?

17. Using Monte Carlo, simulate the process $dr = a(b - r)dt + \sigma dZ$, assuming that $r = 6\%$, $a = 0.2$, $b = 0.08$, $\phi = 0$, and $\sigma = 0.02$. Compute the prices of 1-, 2-, and 3-year zero-coupon bonds, and verify that your answers match those of the Vasicek formula.

18. Repeat the previous problem, but set $\phi = 0.05$. Be sure that you simulate the risk-neutral process, obtained by including the risk premium in the interest rate process.

19. This problem builds on the previous problem using the same parameters, only valuing a call option instead of a bond. Using Monte Carlo, simulate the Vasicek process for 3 years. For each simulation trial, at the end of 3 years, use the Vasicek formula to compute the price of a 1-year zero-coupon bond, $P_3(3, 4)$. (Note that this price will depend upon the short-term interest rate in your simulation trial after 3 years.) For each trial compute $\max(0, P_3(3, 4) - 0.95)$, and discount this at $e^{-\sum_{i=1}^{N} r(i)h}$, where h is the time step. Take the mean of these calculations and compare your answer to that obtained using the formula in footnote 10. If you have several thousand iterations, it should be close.

20. Using Monte Carlo, simulate the process $dr = a(b - r)dt + \sigma\sqrt{r}dZ$, assuming that $r = 6\%$, $a = 0.2$, $b = 0.08$, $\phi = 0$ and $\sigma = 0.02$. Compute the prices of 1-, 2-, and 3-year zero coupon bonds, and verify that your answers match those of the Cox-Ingersoll-Ross formula. What numerical problem can arise in this simulation? How did you address it?

Appendix A CONSTRUCTING THE BDT TREE

Appendix available at http://www.pearsonhighered.com/mcdonald.

Value at Risk

Financial and nonfinancial firms routinely assess risks and engage in both financial and operational risk management. Risk assessment entails evaluating the distribution of possible outcomes, with a focus on the worst that might happen. Insurance companies, for example, assess the likelihood of insured events, and the resulting possible losses for the insurer. Financial institutions must understand their portfolio risks in order to determine the capital buffer needed to support their business.

In this chapter, we discuss *value at risk*, which is commonly used to measure the possible losses on a portfolio of financial assets.

The implicit tension in risk management is the tradeoff between safety on the one hand and the possibility of great success and profitability on the other. There is a risk-return tradeoff in portfolio theory. This tension is evident in extraordinarily productive but specialized firms that are vulnerable to physical disruption. The 2011 earthquake in Japan and flood in Thailand, for example, wreaked havoc with supply chains.[1] This chapter will focus on financial models, but as you read the chapter, you should keep in mind that this tradeoff is pervasive.

1. VALUE AT RISK

A financial institution might have a complex portfolio containing stocks, bonds with different maturities and with various embedded options, and instruments denominated in different currencies. The form of these instruments could be simple notes or complex options. **Value at risk** (VaR) is one way to perform risk assessment for such a portfolio. The idea of value at risk is to estimate the losses on a portfolio that occur with a given probability.

With an estimate of the distribution of outcomes we can either ask about the probability of losing a given sum (e.g., what is the chance our loss exceeds $5m?) or ask, for a given

1. "The disaster in Japan [the 2011 earthquake and tsunami] was only one of several during a year that became, in absolute terms, the costliest ever for natural catastrophes—highlighting the vulnerabilities of a complex global supply chain system that has developed over decades" (Gray, 2012).

From Chapter 26 of *Derivatives Markets*, Third Edition, Robert McDonald. Copyright © 2013 by Pearson Education, Inc. Published by Pearson Prentice Hall. All rights reserved.

probability, how much we might lose (what level of loss do we exceed with a 1% probability?). For example, a derivatives market-maker could estimate that for a given portfolio, over one day there is a 1% chance of losses in excess of \$500,000. The amount \$500,000 is then the 1-day value at risk with a 99% level of confidence.[2] In general, computing value at risk means finding the value of a portfolio such that there is a specified probability that the portfolio will be worth at least this much over a given horizon. The choice of horizon and probability will depend on how VaR is to be used. A related and often preferable measure that we discuss below in Section 2 is tail VaR, which is the expected loss should the VaR level be exceeded.

The standard version of VaR was developed in the 1990s and presented in J.P. Morgan/Reuters (1996). The obvious challenge with a risk model is calibration: determining return distributions for assets and correlations across assets. There is also the question of *which* risks are being measured and controlled.

Risk assessment can be important in contexts other than the measurement of portfolio risk—for example, project selection.[3] Suppose a firm has \$10 million in capital and can select one of two investment opportunities, each costing \$10 million. There will be additional investment opportunities the following year. Investment A returns \$12 million in 1 year for certain, while investment B returns \$24 million with probability one-half and \$0 with probability one-half. Suppose further that the risk-free rate is 10% and the risk of investment B is idiosyncratic. Portfolio theory implies that we should assess both projects as having the same positive NPV. With investment B, however, half of the time the firm will earn a zero return, depleting capital. The firm would have to raise additional capital in order to make additional investments. If capital raising is costly, A and B may no longer seem equally attractive. This illustrates the general point that managers may want to know how much of a firm's capital is at risk with a given project.

Distributions of outcomes matter at the personal level as well. If you are planning for retirement, you must decide both how much to save and how to allocate your savings among stocks, bonds, and other assets. For any strategy, a key question is this: What is the probability that by following this strategy you will fail to achieve a desired minimum level of retirement savings by the time you retire?[4] This is not the only question to ask, but a strategy with a high probability of leaving you penniless—no matter how desirable on other grounds—should call for careful consideration. We will not discuss personal financial planning in this chapter, but the ideas underlying risk assessment can be used in making personal decisions as well as corporate decisions.

There are at least three common uses of value at risk. First, regulators can use VaR to access capital requirements for financial institutions. See the box on the next page for an example. Second, managers can use VaR as an input in making risk-taking and risk-management decisions. Third, managers can also use VaR to assess the quality of the bank's models. For example, if the models say that there is a 5% chance that a particular trading operation will lose \$1m over a 1-day horizon, then on average once every 20 days (5%

2. In this example, the market-maker loses \$500,000 with a 1% probability and performs better 99% of the time. It is common to speak of 99% as the "confidence level." Since VaR is always based upon tail probabilities, in practice it will be obvious that a "99% VaR" and a "1% VaR" refer to the same quantity.

3. See Stulz (1996) for a detailed discussion of the link between investment decisions and risk assessment.

4. Bodie and Crane (1999), for example, use Monte Carlo simulation to examine return distributions to assess the suitability of financial products for retirement savings.

BOX 1: Value-at-Risk and Bank Regulation

The Basel Committee on Banking Supervision (BCBS) is an international organization housed in the Bank of International Settlements (BIS), that promulgates banking rules which are then adopted (possibly in modified form) by national banking regulators. Some of these rules rely on VaR calculations.

One important feature of the Basel rules is the requirement that banks maintain a capital buffer in order to protect the bank's bondholders, depositors, and the government (in case of bail-outs) against losses. The rules impose capital charges for various positions and risks. The "banking book" consists of assets typically held until maturity, such as loans. The "trading book" includes positions subject to market risks, such as positions acquired as part of a trading strategy, and thus likely to be resold or to realize gains or losses in the near future, as well as positions with exposure to stocks, commodities, interest rates, and foreign exchange. (Other categories of risk are *credit risk* and *operational risk*.) The BCBS rules treat these positions differently.

Capital rules for the banking book require a greater capital buffer for specific asset classes, with more capital for classes deemed riskier. Capital rules for the trading book, however, recognize the difficulty of characterizing the risk of complicated positions. The Basel II rules (BIS, 1996) created regulations basing capital requirements for the trading book on value-at-risk calculations. Basel rules since 2009, called Basel 2.5 (BIS, 2009), have called for banks to compute **stressed value-at-risk** for the trading book BIS (2009, p. 14):

> . . . a bank must calculate a "stressed value-at-risk" measure . . . based on the 10-day, 99th percentile, one-tailed confidence interval value-at-risk measure of the current portfolio, with model inputs calibrated to historical data from a continuous 12-month period of significant financial stress relevant to the bank's portfolio. . . . As an example, for many portfolios, a 12-month period relating to significant losses in 2007/2008 would adequately reflect a period of such stress . . .

Stressed VaR is intended to address the problem of using historical data at the onset of a crisis. During the 2008 crisis, volatilities increased and asset movements became more correlated. Of course, different scenarios could occur during the next crisis, but stressing in this fashion should help alleviate the obvious problem of using the previous year's data at the onset of a crisis. An additional problem is that the stressed scenario could lead banks to take risks not adequately reflected in the stress scenario.

of the time) the trading operation *should* lose \$1 million. If losses of this size occur more frequently, the models are assigning too little risk to the bank's activities. If such losses occur less frequently, the models are assigning too much risk.

Most of the examples in this section use lognormally distributed stocks and linear normal approximations to illustrate VaR calculations. Currencies and commodities can be modeled in this way as well. Although for long horizons it might not be reasonable to treat commodities as lognormally distributed, for short horizons this is generally a reasonable assumption. We ignore the possibility of jumps. We discuss bonds separately.

The question of how best to perform risk assessment is unsettled in the wake of the economics events from 2006 to 2009. Variants such as stressed value at risk may address shortcomings. One well-known critique is discussed in the box on the next page.

BOX 2: Black Swans

The most significant events are among the most surprising. Few predicted the destruction of the World Trade Center in 2001 (although there had been a prior attempt by different means) or the depth of the financial crisis in 2008 (although some warned of high real estate prices). Taleb (2010) has argued that history is shaped by such unpredictable events, and that because of their low probability and extreme nature they generally lie beyond the scope of standard risk evaluation models. He terms these events "black swans," alluding to the idea that a single unexpected event (the sighting of a black swan) can fundamentally change understanding (a belief that all swans are white).

Taleb specifically criticizes reliance on financial risk models based on normally distributed returns. The examples in this chapter, for example, mostly rely on normality and lognormality. This assumption is not essential, but it is common.

To evaluate Taleb's critique, it can be helpful to think about risk assessment for ordinary and extraordinary events as two separate activities. Extraordinary events can be transformative, but most times are ordinary, and poorly managed firms can fail for foreseeable reasons. The monitoring of routine risks can increase the chance that identifiable risks are controlled, and large losses avoided. There are a number of famous episodes in which firms lost significant sums in a way that suggested failure of routine risk controls:

- Sumitomo Corporation lost over $2 billion as a result of unauthorized copper trading (WuDunn, 1996).
- Amaranth Trading lost over $6 billion in natural gas trading (Anderson, 2006).
- Société Générale lost almost €5 billion from hidden derivatives trades (Bennhold and Clark, 2008).
- J.P. Morgan Chase lost over $5 billion on a credit default swap trade (Eavis and Craig, 2012).

These losses are small compared to some in the 2008 financial crisis, but large for the firms involved. They demonstrate the potential value of risk management; there is no way to know how many such incidents were prevented by conventional risk management.

What about managing the risk of extraordinary events? Taleb in effect warns against relying narrowly on models to justify actions which would be disastrous if the models failed. This is a straw man: Thoughtful managers and regulators have always been concerned about the validity of risk calculations under extreme conditions. The extreme events discussed by Taleb are in the background, but difficult to prepare for. The financial crisis of 2008 illustrates that it is easy with hindsight to see what failed, but difficult if not impossible to anticipate the next major failing. Models should of course be stress-tested, but major failures are almost by definition outside the bounds of modeling and stress testing. Anticipated failures are addressed in advance and thus less likely to occur. Perrow (1999), in describing "normal accidents," provides a framework for thinking about system failures, and the challenges in anticipating and controlling risks. Ultimately, whatever the business, investment, or activity, some risks will not be anticipated and cannot be controlled. Unmodeled extreme events should be considered, but they cannot be avoided.

Value at Risk for One Stock

Suppose $\tilde{x}_h$ is the dollar return on a portfolio over the horizon h, and $f(x, h)$ is the distribution of returns. Define the value at risk of the portfolio as the return, $x_h(c)$, such that $\Pr(\tilde{x}_h \le x_h(c)) = c$. In other words, $x_h(c)$ is the c quantile of the return distribution over the horizon h.

Value at risk measures the loss that will occur with a given probability over a specified period of time. Notice that the definition of value at risk requires that we specify both a horizon, h, and a probability, c.

Suppose a portfolio consists of a single stock and we wish to compute value at risk over the horizon h. If the distribution of the stock price after h periods, S_h, is lognormal, we have

$$\ln(S_h/S_0) \sim \mathcal{N}[(\alpha - \delta - 0.5\sigma^2)h, \sigma^2 h] \tag{1}$$

If we pick a stock price $\bar{S}_h$, then the probability that the stock price will be below $\bar{S}_h$ is

$$\Pr(S_h < \bar{S}_h) = N\left(\frac{\ln(\bar{S}_h) - \ln(S_0) - (\alpha - \delta - 0.5\sigma^2)h}{\sigma\sqrt{h}}\right) \tag{2}$$

The complementary calculation is to compute the $\bar{S}_h(c)$ corresponding to the probability c. By the definition of $\bar{S}_h(c)$, we have

$$c = N\left(\frac{\ln(\bar{S}_h(c)) - \ln(S_0) - (\alpha - \delta - 0.5\sigma^2)h}{\sigma\sqrt{h}}\right) \tag{3}$$

We can solve for $\bar{S}_h(c)$ by using the inverse cumulative probability distribution, N^{-1}. Applying this function to both sides of equation (3), we have

$$N^{-1}(c) = \frac{\ln(\bar{S}_h(c)) - \ln(S_0) - (\alpha - \delta - 0.5\sigma^2)h}{\sigma\sqrt{h}} \tag{4}$$

Solving for $\bar{S}_h(c)$ gives

$$\bar{S}_h(c) = S_0 e^{(\alpha-\delta-0.5\sigma^2)h+\sigma\sqrt{h}N^{-1}(c)} \tag{5}$$

In equation (5), $N^{-1}(c)$ takes the place of a standard normal random variable.

Example 1. Suppose we own \$3m worth of stock A, which has an expected return of 15% and a 30% volatility, and pays no dividend. Moreover, assume A is lognormally distributed. The value of the position in 1 week, V, is

$$V = \$3\text{m} \times e^{(0.15-0.5\times0.3^2)\frac{1}{52}+0.3\sqrt{\frac{1}{52}}Z} \tag{6}$$

where $Z \sim \mathcal{N}(0, 1)$.

Given this assumed stock price distribution, a 5% loss will occur if Z satisfies

$$\$3\text{m} \times e^{(0.15-0.5\times0.3^2)\frac{1}{52}+0.3\sqrt{\frac{1}{52}}Z} = 0.95 \times \$3\text{m}$$

or

$$Z = \frac{\ln(0.95) - (0.15 - 0.5 \times 0.3^2)\frac{1}{52}}{0.3 \times \sqrt{\frac{1}{52}}} = -1.2815$$

We have

$$\text{NormSDist}(-1.2815) = 0.1000$$

Thus, we expect that 10% of the time there will be a weekly loss in excess of 5%. With 95% probability, the value of the portfolio over a 1-week horizon will exceed

$$\$3\text{m} \times e^{(0.15-0.5\times0.3^2)\frac{1}{52}+0.3\sqrt{\frac{1}{52}}\times(-1.645)} = \$2.8072\text{m}$$

where $N^{-1}(0.05) = -1.645$. In this case, we would say the 95% value at risk is \$2.8072m − \$3m = −\$0.1928m. ■

If the assumption of lognormality is valid and if the inputs are correct, a 1-week loss of this magnitude occurs on average once every 20 weeks.

In practice it is common to simplify the VaR calculation by assuming a normal return rather than a lognormal return. The standard lognormal model is generated by assuming normal returns over very short horizons. We can therefore approximate the exact lognormal result with a normal approximation:

$$S_h = S_0\left(1 + \alpha h + z\sigma\sqrt{h}\right) \tag{7}$$

We could also further simplify by ignoring the mean:

$$S_h = S_0\left(1 + z\sigma\sqrt{h}\right) \tag{8}$$

Both equations (7) and (8) become less reasonable as h grows.

Example 2. Using the same assumptions as in Example 1, equation (7) gives

$$\$3\text{m} \times \left[1 + \frac{0.15}{52} + \left(\frac{0.3}{\sqrt{52}} \times (-1.645)\right)\right] = \$2.8033\text{m}$$

VaR is therefore \$2.8033m − \$3m = −\$0.1966m. Ignoring the mean, equation (8) gives

$$\$3\text{m} \times \left(1 + \frac{0.3}{\sqrt{52}} \times (-1.645)\right) = \$2.7947\text{m}$$

VaR is \$2.7947m − \$3m = −\$0.2053m. ■

Figure 1 compares the three models—lognormal, normal with mean, and normal without mean—over horizons of 1 day to 1 year. As you would expect, the approximation ignoring the mean (equation (8)) is less accurate over longer horizons. In practice the mean is often ignored for two reasons. First, means are hard to estimate precisely. Second, for short horizons the mean is less important than the diffusion term in an Itô process.

FIGURE 1

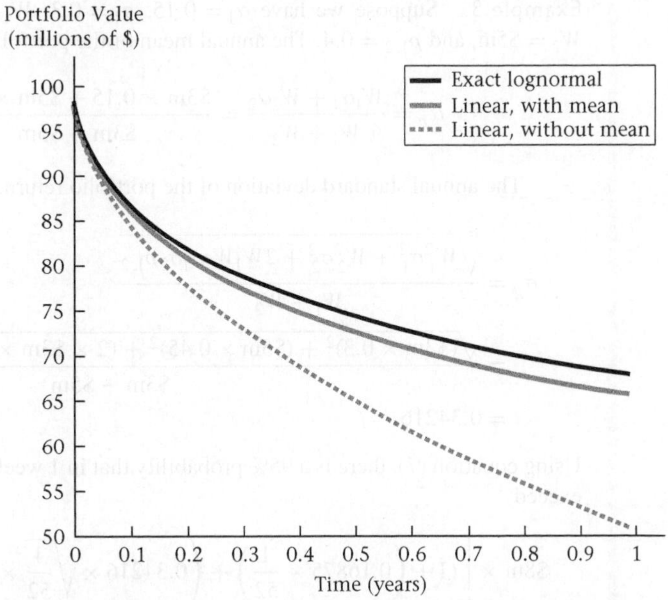

Comparison of VaR for a single stock over different horizons using the lognormal solution (equation (4)), normality with a positive mean (equation (7)), and normality assuming a zero mean (equation (8)). Assumes the same parameters as in Example 2.

VaR for Two or More Stocks

When we consider a portfolio having two or more stocks, the distribution of the future portfolio value is the sum of lognormally distributed random variables and is therefore not lognormal. Since the lognormal distribution is no longer exact, we can use the normal approximation or we can use Monte Carlo simulation to obtain the exact distribution.

Let the annual mean and standard deviation of the realized return on stock i, $\tilde{\alpha}_i$, be α_i and σ_i, with the correlation between stocks i and j being ρ_{ij}. The dollar investment in stock i is W_i. The value of a portfolio containing n stocks is

$$W = \sum_{i=1}^{n} W_i$$

The return on the portfolio over the horizon h, R_h, is

$$\text{Portfolio return} = R_h = \frac{1}{W} \sum_{i=1}^{n} \tilde{\alpha}_{i,h} W_i$$

Assuming that returns are joint-normally distributed, the annualized distribution of the portfolio return is

$$R_h \sim \mathcal{N}\left(\frac{1}{W} \sum_{i=1}^{n} \alpha_i h W_i, \; \frac{1}{W^2} \sum_{i=1}^{n} \sum_{j=1}^{n} \sigma_i \sigma_j \rho_{ij} h W_i W_j \right) \tag{9}$$

Example 3. Suppose we have $\alpha_1 = 0.15$, $\sigma_1 = 0.3$, $W_1 = \$3\text{m}$, $\alpha_2 = 0.18$, $\sigma_2 = 0.45$, $W_2 = \$5\text{m}$, and $\rho_{1,2} = 0.4$. The annual mean of the portfolio return is

$$\alpha_p = \frac{W_1\alpha_1 + W_2\alpha_2}{W_1 + W_2} = \frac{\$3\text{m} \times 0.15 + \$5\text{m} \times 0.18}{\$3\text{m} + \$5\text{m}} = 0.16875$$

The annual standard deviation of the portfolio return, σ_p, is

$$\begin{aligned}\sigma_p &= \frac{\sqrt{W_1^2\sigma_1^2 + W_2^2\sigma_2^2 + 2W_1W_2\sigma_1\sigma_2\rho_{1,2}}}{W_1 + W_2} \\ &= \frac{\sqrt{(\$3\text{m} \times 0.3)^2 + (\$5\text{m} \times 0.45)^2 + (2 \times \$3\text{m} \times \$5\text{m} \times 0.3 \times 0.45 \times 0.4)}}{\$3\text{m} + \$5\text{m}} \\ &= 0.34216\end{aligned}$$

Using equation (7), there is a 95% probability that in 1 week, the value of the portfolio will exceed

$$\$8\text{m} \times \left[(1 + \left(0.16875 \times \frac{1}{52}\right) + \left(0.34216 \times \sqrt{\frac{1}{52}} \times (-1.645)\right)\right] = \$7.40154\text{m}$$

The 1-week 95% VaR is therefore \$7.40154m − \$8m = −\$0.5985m. Using equation (8), which ignores the mean, we have a 95% chance that the value of the portfolio will exceed

$$\$8\text{m} \times \left(1 + 0.34216 \times \sqrt{\frac{1}{52}} \times (-1.645)\right) = \$7.3756\text{m}$$

The 1-week VaR ignoring the mean is therefore \$7.3756m − \$8m = −\$0.6244m. ■

This example illustrates the effects of diversification. Although stock 2, which constitutes more than half of the portfolio, has a standard deviation of 45%, the portfolio standard deviation is only about 34%. Problem 5 asks you to consider the effects of different correlations.

If there are n assets, the VaR calculation requires that we specify at least the standard deviation (and possibly the mean) for each stock, along with all pairwise correlations.

VaR for Nonlinear Portfolios

If a portfolio contains options as well as stocks, it is more complicated to compute the distribution of returns. Specifically, suppose the portfolio consists of n different stocks with ω_i shares of stock i worth $\omega_i S_i = W_i$. There are also N_i options worth $C(S_i)$ for each stock i. The portfolio value is therefore $W = \sum_{i=1}^{n}[\omega_i S_i + N_i C_i(S_i)]$. We cannot easily compute the exact distribution of this portfolio; not only is the sum of the lognormally distributed stock prices not lognormal, but the option price distribution is complicated.

We will explore two different approaches to handling nonlinearity. First, we can create a linear approximation to the option price by using the option delta. Second, we can value the option using an appropriate option pricing formula and then perform Monte Carlo simulation to obtain the return distribution.[5]

Delta Approximation. If the return on stock i is $\tilde{\alpha}_i$, we can approximate the return on the option as $\Delta_i \tilde{\alpha}_i$, where Δ_i is the option delta. The expected annual return on the stock and option portfolio is then

$$R_p = \frac{1}{W} \sum_{i=1}^{n} \alpha_i S_i (\omega_i + N_i \Delta_i) \tag{10}$$

The term $\omega_i + N_i \Delta_i$ measures the exposure to stock i. The variance of the return is

$$\sigma_p^2 = \frac{1}{W^2} \sum_{i=1}^{n} \sum_{j=1}^{n} S_i S_j (\omega_i + N_i \Delta_i)(\omega_j + N_j \Delta_j) \sigma_i \sigma_j \rho_{ij} \tag{11}$$

With this mean and variance, we can mimic the n-stock analysis. First, however, we will compute an example with a single stock for which we know the exact solution.

Example 4. Suppose we own 30,000 shares of a non-dividend-paying stock and have sold 105-strike call options, with 1 year to expiration, on 25,000 shares. The stock price is \$100, the stock volatility is 30%, the expected return on the stock is 15%, and the risk-free rate is 8%. The Black-Scholes option price is \$13.3397 and the value of the portfolio is

$$W = 30{,}000 \times \$100 - 25{,}000 \times \$13.3397 = \$2{,}666{,}507$$

(Since the written options are a liability, we subtract their value in computing the value of the portfolio.) The delta of the option is 0.6003. Using equations (10) and (11), we obtain $R_p = 0.084343$ and $\sigma_p = 0.16869$. The written options reduce the mean and volatility of the portfolio. Therefore, there is a 95% chance that the value of the portfolio in 1 week will exceed

$$\begin{aligned} &\$2{,}666{,}507 \times \left(1 + 0.084343 \times \frac{1}{52} + 0.16869 \times \sqrt{\frac{1}{52}} \times (-1.645)\right) \\ &= \$2{,}568{,}220 \end{aligned} \tag{12}$$

Value at risk using the delta approximation is therefore \$2,568,220 − \$2,666,507 = −\$98,287.

We can compute the exact value at risk by first determining the stock price that we will exceed with a 95% chance, and then computing the exact portfolio value at that price. With 95% probability, we will exceed the stock price

$$\$100 \times e^{(0.15 - 0.5 \times 0.3^2)\frac{1}{52} + 0.3\sqrt{\frac{1}{52}} \times (-1.645)} = \$93.574$$

5. A third alternative is to use a delta-gamma approximation, which is more accurate than a delta approximation. However, because the gamma term depends on the squared change in the stock price, the approximation is harder to implement than the delta approximation. The *Riskmetrics Technical Document* (Morgan/Reuters 1996, pp. 129–133) discusses an approach for implementing the delta-gamma approximation.

FIGURE 2

Comparison of exact portfolio value after 1 week with a delta approximation. Assumes the position is long 30,000 shares of stock at \$100 and short 25,000 call options with a strike price of \$105. Value at risk is the difference between the original portfolio value and that at the 5% stock price.

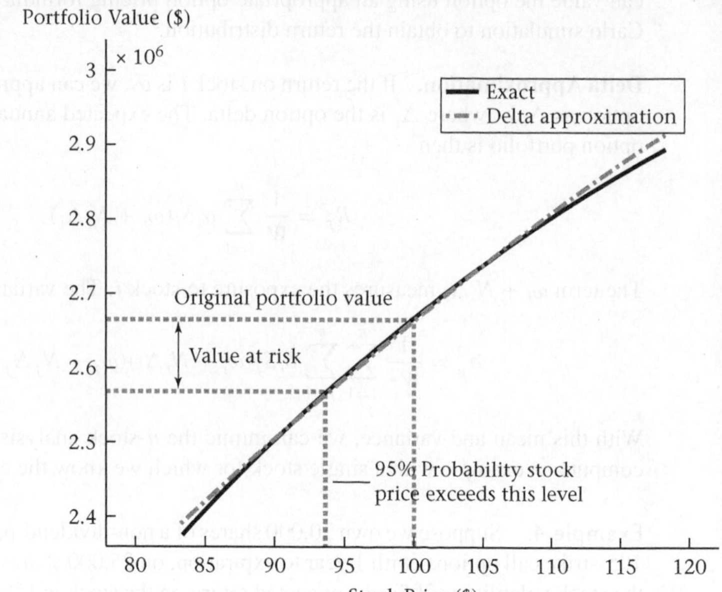

If this is the stock price 1 week later, the option price will be \$9.5913, and the value of the portfolio will be

$$(\$93.574 \times 30{,}000) - (\$9.5913 \times 25{,}000) = \$2{,}576{,}438$$

The exact 95% value at risk is therefore \$2,576,438 − \$2,666,507 = −\$99,069. ■

Figure 2 graphs the exact value of the portfolio as a function of the stock price 7 days later, compared to the value implied by the delta approximation. The delta approximation is close, but the VaR derived using delta is slightly low. The delta approximation also fails to account for theta—the time decay in the option position. Because the option is written, time decay over the 1-week horizon increases the return of the portfolio. This increased return is barely perceptible in Figure 2 as the exact portfolio value exceeds the delta approximation when the stock price is close to \$100.

Example 5. Suppose we have two stocks along with written call options on those stocks. Information for the stocks and options is in Table 1. Using this information, we obtain a portfolio value of

$$\begin{aligned} W &= (30{,}000 \times \$100) - (25{,}000 \times \$13.3397) \\ &\quad + (50{,}000 \times \$100) - (60{,}000 \times 10.3511) = \$7{,}045{,}440 \end{aligned}$$

Using equations (10) and (11), the annual mean and standard deviation are 8.392% and 16.617%. There is a 95% chance that the portfolio value will exceed

TABLE 1 Information about two stocks and call options on those stocks. Assumes the risk-free rate is 8% and that neither stock pays a dividend. The correlation between the stocks is 0.4.

	Stock Information				Option Information				
Stock	S	# Shares	α	σ	$C(S)$	Strike	Δ	Expiration	# Shares
# 1	\$100	30,000	0.15	0.30	\$13.3397	\$105	0.6003	1.0	−25,000
# 2	\$100	50,000	0.18	0.45	\$10.3511	\$110	0.4941	0.5	−60,000

$$W \times \left[1 + (R_p \times h) + (\sigma_p \times \sqrt{h} \times z)\right]$$

$$= \$7{,}045{,}440 \times \left[1 + 0.08392 \times \frac{1}{52} + 0.16617 \times \sqrt{\frac{1}{52}} \times (-1.645)\right] = \$6{,}789{,}740$$

The 95% value at risk over a 1-week horizon is therefore

$$\text{VaR} = \$6{,}789{,}740 - \$7{,}045{,}440 = -\$255{,}700$$ ■

Monte Carlo Simulation. The delta approximation can work poorly for nonlinear portfolios. For example, consider an at-the-money written straddle (a written call and written put, both with the same strike price). The straddle suffers a loss if the stock price increases or decreases, which is not a situation suited to a linear approximation. Because of losses from stock moves in either direction, we need to consider both tails when computing VaR. Monte Carlo simulation works well in this situation since the simulation produces the distribution of portfolio values.

To use Monte Carlo simulation in the case of a single stock, we randomly draw a set of stock prices. For multiple stocks, we can use the appropriate parameters for each stock and use the Cholesky decomposition to ensure the appropriate correlation among stock prices. Once we have the portfolio values corresponding to each draw of random prices, we sort the resulting portfolio values in ascending order. The 5% lower tail of portfolio values, for example, is used to compute the 95% value at risk.

We will look at two examples in which we compute VaR for a position using Monte Carlo simulation. First we will examine a straddle on a single stock, and then a straddle-like position that contains a written call on one stock and a written put on the other.

Example 6. Consider the 1-week 95% value at risk of an at-the-money written straddle on 100,000 shares of a single stock. Assuming that $S = \$100$, $K = \$100$, $\sigma = 30\%$, $r = 8\%$, $T = 30$ days, and $\delta = 0$, the initial value of the straddle is −\$685,776. Because the underlying asset is a single stock, we can compute the VaR of the position directly without Monte Carlo simulation. Figure 3 graphs the exact value of the straddle after 1 week, compared with its initial value.[6] The expected return on the stock is 15% in this calculation.

6. The increase in value of the straddle if the stock price does not change is due to theta.

FIGURE 3

The value of a portfolio, as a function of the stock price, containing 100,000 written call options with a \$100 strike and 100,000 written put options with a \$100 strike. Assumes $\sigma = 30\%$, $r = 8\%$, $t = 23$ days, and $\delta = 0$.

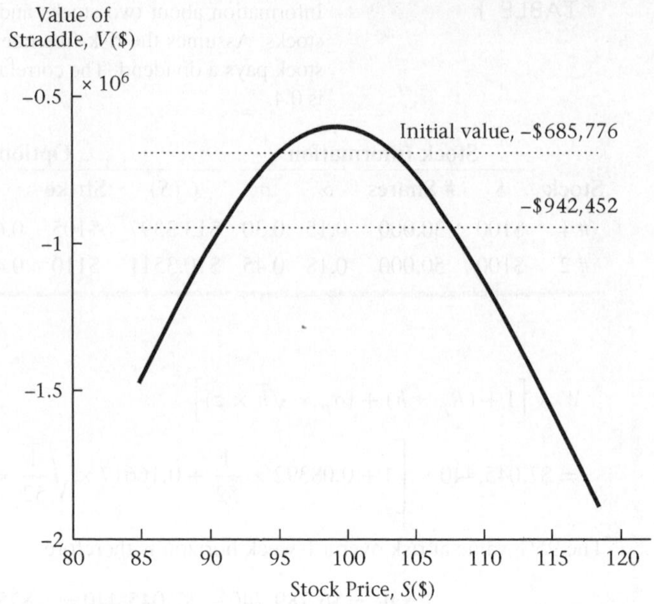

Table 2 shows a subset of the values plotted in Figure 3. Examine the boxed entries in Table 2. If the stock price declines, there is a 0.9% probability that the value of the position will be less than −\$942,266. If the stock price rises, there is a 4% chance that the position value will be less than −\$942,639. Thus, in total, there is a 4.9% probability of a loss in excess of about \$942,452, which is the average of the boxed numbers. The 1-week 95% VaR is therefore approximately −\$942,452 − (−\$685,776) = −\$256,676. Even in this one-stock example, calculating the VaR for this two-tailed position is not as simple as computing the stock prices that are exceeded with 2.5% probability.

Monte Carlo simulation simplifies the analysis. To use Monte Carlo, we randomly draw a set of $z \sim \mathcal{N}(0, 1)$ and construct the stock price as

$$S_h = S_0 e^{(\alpha - \delta - 0.5\sigma^2)h + \sigma\sqrt{h}z} \tag{13}$$

We compute the Black-Scholes call and put prices using each stock price, which gives us a distribution of straddle values. We then sort the resulting straddle values in ascending order. The 5% value is used to compute the 95% value at risk.

Figure 4 plots the histogram of values resulting from 100,000 random simulations of the value of the straddle. There is a 95% chance the straddle value will exceed −\$943,028; hence, value at risk is −\$943,028 − (−\$685,776) = −\$257,252. This result is very close to the value we inferred from Table 2. ■

As a second example we suppose that instead of the written put and call having the same underlying stock, they have different, correlated underlying stocks.

TABLE 2 Value of written straddle, V, for different stock prices, S. Values in the z column are standard normal values with the corresponding cumulative probabilities in the $N(z)$ column. Over 1 week there is approximately a 5% probability that the stock price will be outside the range \$90.87 – \$107.77. The option values are computed using the Black-Scholes formula with $\sigma = 30\%$, $r = 8\%$, $t = 23$ days, and $\delta = 0$. The stock price movement assumes $\alpha = 15\%$.

z	S(\$)	V (\$)	$N(z)$	z	S (\$)	V (\$)	$N(z)$
−2.50	90.30	−985,970	0.006	1.70	107.55	−926,472	0.955
−2.45	90.49	−971,234	0.007	1.75	107.77	−942,639	0.960
−2.40	90.68	−956,663	0.008	1.80	107.99	−959,111	0.964
−2.35	90.87	−942,266	0.009	1.85	108.22	−975,880	0.968
−2.30	91.06	−928,050	0.011	1.90	108.44	−992,939	0.971

Example 7. Suppose that there are two stocks. Stock 1 is the same as the stock in Example 6. Stock 2 has the same parameters and a correlation of 0.40 with stock 1. Because the stocks have the same volatility and dividend yield, the initial option values are the same and the written straddle has an initial value of −\$685,776. Based on 100,000 simulated prices for both stocks, the portfolio has a 95% chance of having a value greater than \$1,135,421. Hence, the 95% value at risk is −\$1,135,421 − (−\$685,776) = −\$449,645. The histogram for this calculation is in Figure 5. ■

A comparison of the results in Examples 6 and 7 shows that writing the straddle on two different stocks increases value at risk. If we examine the distributions in Figures 4 and 5, we can see why this happens.

Notice first that in Figure 4, the value of the portfolio never exceeds about −\$597,000. The reason is that, since the call and put are written on the same stock, *stock price moves can never induce the two options to appreciate together*. They can appreciate due to theta, but a change in the stock price will induce a gain in one option and a loss in the other. The same effect limits a loss, since the two options can never lose money together.

When the options are written on different stocks, as in Figure 5, it is possible for both to gain or lose simultaneously. As a result, the distribution of prices has a greater variance and increased value at risk.

As a final comment, all the value at risk calculations in this section assumed an expected return for the stocks that was positive and different from the risk-free rate. Because the horizon was only 7 days, the results are not too different from those obtained assuming the drift is zero or equal to the risk-free rate. For longer horizons the particular assumption about expected return would make more of a difference.

VaR for Bonds

In this section we see how to compute VaR for bonds, using information about the volatilities and correlations of yields for bonds at different maturities.

FIGURE 4

Histogram from a Monte Carlo simulation of the value of a written straddle after 7 days. Both the call and the put are written on the same stock. Assumes at-the-money calls and puts are written on 100,000 shares, with $S = \$100$, $\sigma = 30\%$, $r = 8\%$, $T = 23$ days, and $\delta = 0$.

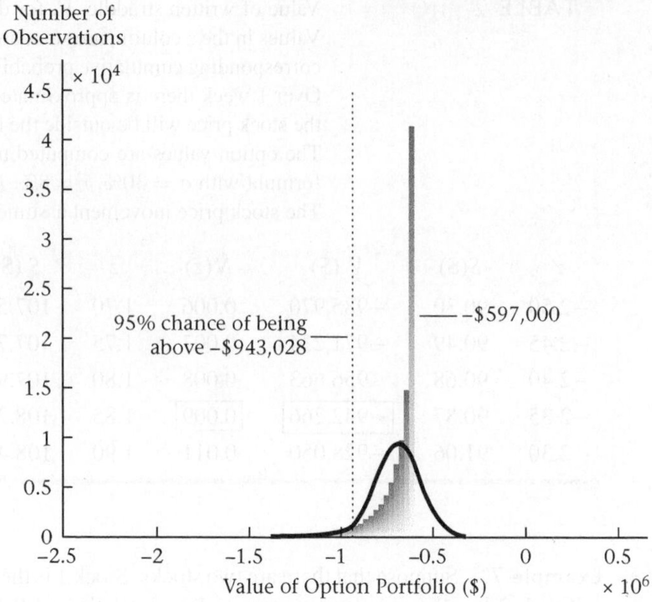

At any point in time there are numerous interest-rate sensitive claims, including bonds, FRAs, and swaps, all of which can have different maturities and be denominated in different currencies. We can simplify the problem of risk modeling for interest-rate sensitive claims by considering that all of these claims can be decomposed into zero-coupon bonds. Thus, the problem of assessing the risk of a bond, FRA, or swap reduces to one of decomposing the claim into its constitutent zero-coupon bonds and assessing the risk of these. The risk of the bond or other claim can then be measured as the risk of a portfolio of zero-coupon bonds.

It is natural to characterize risk in terms of the bond yield rather than the bond price. Yield uncertainty implies price uncertainty.

Here is an example of how to measure VaR for a zero-coupon bond. Suppose that a zero-coupon bond matures at time T and has price $P(T)$, and that the annualized yield volatility of the bond is σ_T. For a zero-coupon bond, duration equals maturity. Thus, if the yield changes by ϵ, the percentage change in the bond price will be approximately ϵT. Using this linear approximation based on duration, and ignoring the mean return on the bond, over the horizon h the bond has a 95% chance of being worth more than

$$P(T)[1 + \sigma_T T\sqrt{h} \times (-1.645)]$$

Example 8. Suppose a bond has $T = 10$ years to maturity. Its yield to maturity is 5.5% and the annualized yield volatility is 1%. The 1-week VaR on a \$10m position in these bonds is

$$\$10\text{m} \times \left[1 + 0.01 \times 10 \times \sqrt{\frac{1}{52}} \times (-1.645)\right] - \$10\text{m} = -\$228,120 \quad \blacksquare$$

FIGURE 5

Histogram from a Monte Carlo simulation over 7 days of a portfolio containing 100,000 written call options on one stock with a \$100 strike and 100,000 written put options on a different stock with a \$100 strike. For both stocks, and options, assume $\sigma = 30\%$, $r = 8\%$, $T = 23$ days, and $\delta = 0$. The correlation between the two stocks is 40%.

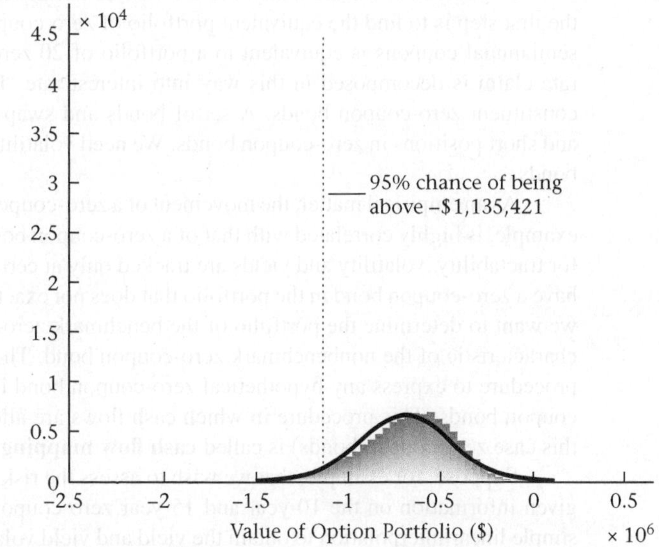

Now suppose that instead of a single bond we have a portfolio of zero-coupon bonds. In particular, suppose we own W_1 of a bond maturing at T_1 with annualized yield volatility σ_{T_1} and W_2 of a bond maturing at T_2 with annualized yield volatility σ_{T_2}. Let ρ represent the correlation between the yields on the two bonds. (This yield volatility information could be estimated using historical data or using implied volatilities.) As with a portfolio of stocks, we can use the delta approximation, only here instead of two correlated stock returns we have two correlated bond yields.

Example 9. Let $T_1 = 10$, $T_2 = 15$, $\sigma_{T_1} = 0.01$, $\sigma_{T_2} = 0.012$, $\rho = 0.985$, $W_1 = \$6\text{m}$, and $W_2 = \$4\text{m}$. Since the portfolio is 60% invested in the 10-year bond and 40% invested in the 15-year bond, the variance of the bond portfolio is

$$(0.6 \times 0.01 \times 10)^2 + (0.4 \times 0.012 \times 15)^2$$
$$+ (2 \times 0.985 \times 0.6 \times 0.4 \times 0.01 \times 10 \times 0.012 \times 15) = 0.01729$$

The volatility is $\sqrt{0.01729} = 0.1315$. The 95% 1-week VaR for this portfolio is therefore

$$\$10\text{m} \times [1 + 0.1315\sqrt{1/52} \times (-1.645)] - \$10\text{m} = -\$301{,}638 \quad \blacksquare$$

Duration here is used mechanically to compute the price change for a bond for a given change in the bond's own yield. This is a delta approximation to the actual bond price change. The conceptual problem with duration becomes problematic when we use duration to compute a hedge ratio for *two* bonds. The hedge ratio calculation assumes that the yield to maturity for the two bonds changes by the same amount. By contrast, in Example 9 each bond has a different yield volatility and there is an imperfect correlation between the two yields; thus, we do *not* assume that all yields to maturity change by the same amount—i.e., that there is a parallel yield curve shift. (For a parallel yield curve shift, we would need each bond to have the same annualized yield volatility and $\rho = 1$.)

In general, if we are analyzing the risk of an instrument with multiple cash flows, the first step is to find the equivalent portfolio of zero-coupon bonds. A 10-year bond with semiannual coupons is equivalent to a portfolio of 20 zero-coupon bonds. Every interest rate claim is decomposed in this way into interest rate "buckets" containing the claim's constituent zero-coupon bonds. A set of bonds and swaps reduces to a portfolio of long and short positions in zero-coupon bonds. We need volatilities and correlations for all these bonds.

As an empirical matter, the movement of a zero-coupon bond at an 8-year maturity, for example, is highly correlated with that of a zero-coupon bond at an $8\frac{1}{2}$-year maturity. Thus, for tractability, volatility and yields are tracked only at certain benchmark maturities. If we have a zero-coupon bond in the portfolio that does not exactly match a benchmark maturity, we want to determine the portfolio of the benchmark zero-coupon bonds that matches the characteristic of the nonbenchmark zero-coupon bond. The goal is to find an interpolation procedure to express any hypothetical zero-coupon bond in terms of the benchmark zero-coupon bonds. This procedure in which cash flows are allocated to benchmark claims (in this case zero-coupon bonds) is called **cash flow mapping**.

Suppose, for example, that we wish to assess the risk of a 12-year zero-coupon bond, given information on the 10-year and 15-year zero-coupon bonds. It is reasonable to use simple linear interpolation to obtain the yield and yield volatility for the 12-year bond from those of the 10-year and 15-year bonds. For example, if the yield and volatility of the t-year bond are y_t and σ_t, linear interpolation gives us

$$y_{12} = (0.6 \times y_{10}) + (0.4 \times y_{15}) \tag{14}$$

$$\sigma_{12} = (0.6 \times \sigma_{10}) + (0.4 \times \sigma_{15}) \tag{15}$$

These interpolations enable us to determine the price and volatility of \$1 paid in year 12. In particular, the price is $e^{-y_{12}\times 12}$. However, we are not finished, because these interpolations do *not* provide correlations between the 12-year zero and the adjacent benchmark bonds. We need these correlations because we could have a portfolio containing 10-, 12-, and 15-year bonds.

The next step is to ask what combination of the 10- and 15-year zero-coupon bonds would have the same volatility as the hypothetical 12-year bond. If we let ω equal the fraction allocated to the 10-year bond, we must solve

$$\sigma_{12}^2 = (\omega^2\sigma_{10}^2) + [(1-\omega)^2\sigma_{10}^2] + [2\rho_{10,15}\omega(1-\omega)\sigma_{10}\sigma_{15}] \tag{16}$$

Since this is a quadratic equation, there are two solutions for ω. Typically, as in the following example, one of the two solutions will be economically appealing and the other will seem unreasonable.

Example 10. Suppose we have a \$1 cash flow occurring in year 12 and that we wish to map to the 10- and 15-year zero-coupon bonds. Suppose that $y_{10} = 5.5\%$, $y_{15} = 5.75\%$, $\sigma_{10} = 1\%$, $\sigma_{15} = 1.2\%$, and $\rho = 0.985$. The yield and volatility of the hypothetical 12-year zero-coupon bond are

$$y_{12} = (0.6 \times 0.055) + (0.4 \times 0.0575) = 0.056$$
$$\sigma_{12} = (0.6 \times 0.01) + (0.4 \times 0.012) = 0.0108$$

We next need to find the cash flow mapping that matches the volatility. Solving equation (16) gives the two solutions $\omega = 6.2097$ and $\omega = 0.5797$. The first solution maps the cash flow by going long 621% of the 10-year bond and short 520% of the 15-year bond. The second, more economically reasonable solution entails going long 57.97% of the 10-year bond and 42.03% of the 15-year bond. ■

Notice that the solution $\omega = 0.5797$ is close to the 60%–40% split you might have guessed at the outset. Given these weights, value at risk for the 12-year bond can be computed in the same way as VaR for the bond portfolio in Example 9.

If you find this procedure confusing, recognize that if we had mapped the 12-year bond by assigning 60% of it to the 10-year bond and 40% to the 15-year bond, then *we would not have matched the yield and volatility given by equations (14) and (15).* Because of the nonlinear relationship between prices and yields, an interpolation based on the yield will give a different cash flow map than an interpolation based on prices.

Although we have discussed cash flow mapping in the context of bonds, mapping can be applied to any claim with multiple cash flows.

Estimating Volatility

Volatility is the key input in any VaR calculation. In most of the examples in this chapter, return volatility over the horizon h is $\sigma\sqrt{h}$, with σ constant. This calculation assumes both that the volatility, σ, does not change, and that returns are independent over time. In practice, both assumptions may be violated. One response is to use stressed VaR.

When using ordinary VaR, it is straightforward to estimate historical volatilities given a time series of returns. However, volatility is typically not constant over time. As a consequence, it is necessary to update volatility estimates when VaR is computed. There are a number of ways to estimate volatility: simple historical volatility, exponentially weighted moving average, GARCH, realized volatility, and implied volatility. Keep in mind, however, that when volatility is stochastic, there can be a risk premium for volatility that will affect the option price. Inferring the volatility from option prices when volatility is stochastic requires careful modeling, since it is necessary to disentangle the true implied volatility and the risk premium. This is an area of ongoing research.

Depending on the asset, returns may be correlated over time. To a first approximation, stock returns are independent over time. However, over horizons as short as a day, returns may be negatively correlated due to factors such as bid-ask bounce. There is some evidence of negative correlation at longer horizons, though the effect is more subtle.

When returns are correlated, volatility does not scale with $\sqrt{h}$. If returns are negatively correlated over time, then high returns are followed by low returns. Thus, negative return correlation dampens volatility relative to the independent returns case. If returns are positively correlated, high returns follow high returns, which results in a higher volatility than in the independent returns case.

With commodities, return independence may depend on the horizon. For example, high copper prices lead to increased supply and reduced demand, which eventually induces the price to fall. So return independence is not reasonable for long horizons. However, independence may be reasonable over horizons short enough that supply and demand responses do not have time to occur.

Finally, we also require correlation estimates in order to compute volatilities of portfolios. Correlations can be estimated using historical data the same way as volatilities. However, it is important to be aware that, just as volatilities will change in times of financial stress, correlations will change as well. When there is a stock market crash, for example, by definition all stocks move together, exhibiting a temporarily high positive correlation. One of the surprises during 2006–2008 was that housing prices in markets across the country simultaneously fell. It is important, therefore, to test correlation assumptions. One way to do this is by evaluating scenarios in which asset prices undergo large moves and asset correlations become extreme.

Bootstrapping Return Distributions

It is possible to use observed past returns to create an empirical probability distribution of returns that can then be used for simulation. This procedure is called **bootstrapping**. The idea of bootstrapping is to sample, with replacement, from observed historical returns under the assumption that future returns will be drawn from the same distribution. For example, if the stock price over a 5-day period has returns of $\{-0.02, 0.015, -0.01, 0.10, 0.03\}$, then this distribution can be bootstrapped by randomly selecting one of these returns each time a new 1-day return is needed. In effect, bootstrapping randomly shuffles past returns to create hypothetical future returns.

We have seen how the lognormal model has trouble accounting for events like the 1987 market crash. The advantage of bootstrapping is that, since it is not based on a particular assumed distribution, it is consistent with any distribution of returns. For example, if an event like a significant market crash occurs once every 10 years historically, it will occur on average once every 10 years in the bootstrapped distribution.

A disadvantage of simple bootstrapping is that key features of the data might be lost when the data are reshuffled. For example, if historical returns exhibit persistence in volatility, randomly reshuffled historical returns will not exhibit such persistence. It is possible to bootstrap a distribution while preserving correlation; this is called a *dependent bootstrap*.[7] First, it is possible to bootstrap by randomly selecting blocks of data at a time. The use of blocks preserves correlation across time within the blocks. Second, given a specification for the correlated series, we can estimate the correlated process and use this to bootstrap. For example, suppose we believe that a commodity price is generated by the process

$$S_{t+h} = a + \rho S_t + \epsilon_{t+h} \tag{17}$$

If we fit this process to the data, we obtain an estimate of ρ and a time series of errors, ϵ_{t+h}. These errors should be uncorrelated if equation (17) is correctly specified. We can then simulate the process in equation (17) by randomly drawing from the estimated errors. This will generate a series with the observed correlation and with errors drawn from the data.

7. Two general discussions of bootstrapping that also discuss bootstrapping of dependent data are Shao and Tu (1995, Chap. 9) and Horowitz (2001).

2. ISSUES WITH VaR

VaR provides a single number that is easy to interpret and communicate. However, VaR is not the only way to assess risk, and it has conceptual shortcomings. In this section we discuss some alternatives to simple VaR and introduce the concept of *subadditive* risk measures. In the course of comparing risk measures, we will also discuss the use of the true price distribution in computing VaR as compared to the risk-neutral distribution, which we use in pricing derivatives.

Alternative Risk Measures

Consider again the VaR for a single stock. Suppose the current stock price is S_0 and we wish to assess the risk of this investment at time T. As before, if the confidence level is c, define $\bar{S}(c)$ as the stock price such that there is a c probability that the stock price at time T will be worth less than $\bar{S}(c)$. In addition to VaR, we can compute two additional risk measures based on the VaR: the tail VaR, which we define below, and the cost of insurance against outcomes below the VaR level.

Tail VaR. A shortcoming of VaR is that it specifies the *minimum* loss that will occur with a given probability. In practice we would like to know the expected magnitude of the loss should a loss occur. This is called the **tail VaR, conditional VaR (CVaR)**, or the **expected tail loss**. For the simple case where the portfolio consists of one stock, we can assess the severity of the loss by computing the average loss conditional upon the stock price being less than $\bar{S}(c)$. Whereas VaR specifies the level, $\bar{S}(c)$, that will be breached with probability c, tail VaR measures the average severity of the breach. For the single stock case, tail VaR is defined as

$$\mathrm{E}[S_0 - S_T | S_T < \bar{S}(c)] = S_0 - \mathrm{E}[S_T | S_T < \bar{S}(c)] \tag{18}$$

Example 11. Assume that we own stock with a current price of \$100, a volatility of 30%, an expected return of 15%, and a dividend yield of 0. Also assume that the risk-free rate is 8%. Let $T = 0.5$.

Figure 6 depicts the probability density for S_T, the stock price at the 5% quantile, and the conditional expected stock price. To compute the VaR, we first need to compute $\bar{S}(0.05)$:

$$\begin{aligned}\bar{S}(0.05) &= \$100e^{(0.15-0.5\times0.3^2)\times0.5-1.645\times0.30\times\sqrt{0.5}}\\ &= \$74.347\end{aligned}$$

Thus, VaR is

$$\mathrm{VaR} = \$100 - \$74.347 = \$25.653$$

The calculation of tail VaR is based on the expected stock price conditional upon $S_T < \$74.347$. We obtain

$$\begin{aligned}\mathrm{E}(S_T | S_T < \$74.347) &= \frac{100 \times e^{0.15\times0.5} N(-\hat{d}_1)}{N(-\hat{d}_2)}\\ &= \$68.244\end{aligned}$$

FIGURE 6

The probability distribution for S_T, the VaR price level ($\bar{S}(0.05)$), and the tail VaR price level ($E[S_T|S_T < \bar{S}(0.05)]$).

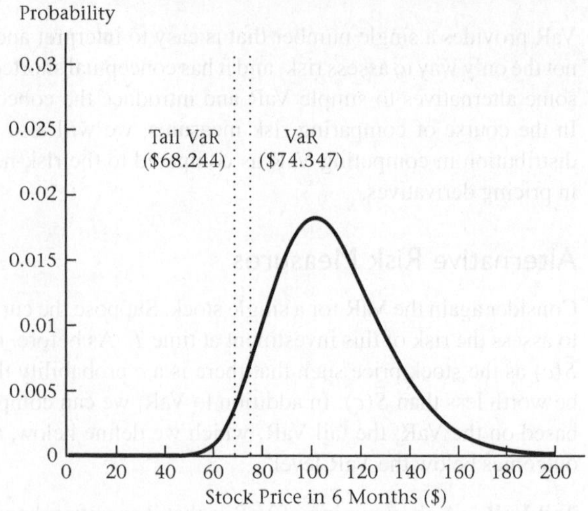

where

$$\hat{d}_1 = -\frac{\ln(100/74.347) + (0.15 + 0.5 \times 0.30^2) \times 0.5}{0.30\sqrt{0.5}}$$

$$\hat{d}_2 = \hat{d}_1 - 0.30\sqrt{0.5}$$

Tail VaR is therefore

$$\text{Tail VaR} = \$100 - \$68.244 = \$31.756$$

Figure 6 depicts the probability density for the stock price in 6 months, the VaR price level, and the tail VaR price level. ■

It is possible to interpret tail VaR as an average of VaRs with different confidence levels. We can approximate the conditional expectation of the stock price below $\bar{S}(c)$ by averaging the stock prices associated with VaRs at levels lower than c. For example, suppose we were to compute VaR at a series of different confidence levels: 0.005, 0.01, 0.015, etc. We would first compute a series of stock prices: $\bar{S}(0.005)$, $\bar{S}(0.01)$, $\bar{S}(0.015)$, etc. By definition, each of these stock prices is a quantile. While the probability that S_T is *below* each of these stock prices is different, there is an equal probability that S_T is approximately equal to any of these stock prices. More precisely, the probability of the stock price being between $\bar{S}(0.005)$ and $\bar{S}(0.01)$ is equal to the probability of S_T being between $\bar{S}(0.01)$ and $\bar{S}(0.015)$, etc. By averaging the stock prices $\bar{S}(0.005)$, $\bar{S}(0.01)$, $\bar{S}(0.015)$, . . . , $\bar{S}(0.05)$, we approximate the conditional expectation of the stock price below $\bar{S}(0.05)$, which is \$68.244.

Figure 7 illustrates this calculation. The two panels show quantiles below 5%. The average of these quantiles is approximately equal to the conditional expectation of \$68.244. As we average more quantiles, we approximate the conditional expectation more closely. In most applications there will be no simple formula for the conditional expectation. It is then possible to approximate tail VaR by averaging quantiles.

FIGURE 7

The top panel depicts quantiles from 0.0025 to 0.05 at intervals of 0.0025. The average of these quantiles is \$68.809. The bottom panel depicts quantiles from 0.001 to 0.05 at intervals of 0.001. The average of these quantiles is \$68.496. Assumes the same parameters as in Example 11.

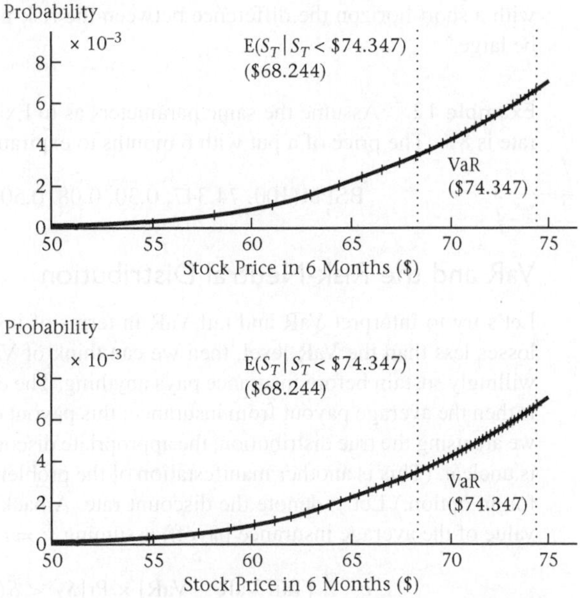

The Cost of Insurance. One application of VaR and VaR-like calculations is to compute the capital required to support a risky business. Capital is a resource that permits the firm to sustain losses and still meet its business obligations. As an alternative to capital, we could imagine a firm purchasing insurance against a loss. The capital required to undertake the business would then be the price of this insurance. The market price of this insurance provides another way to measure risk.

Returning to our example of a single stock portfolio, if we insure against losses due to a stock price below $\bar{S}(c)$, then the time-T payoff on such an insurance policy will be

$$\max[0, \bar{S}(c) - S_T]$$

Thus, the insurance premium is the value of a put option with strike price $\bar{S}(c)$ and time to expiration T. We can obtain the value of the put by computing

$$\begin{aligned} &e^{-rT}\mathrm{E}^*[\bar{S}(c) - S_T | S_T < \bar{S}(c)] \times \mathrm{Pr}^*[S_T < \bar{S}(c)] \\ &= e^{-rT}\left\{\bar{S}(c) \times -\mathrm{E}^*[S_T | S_T < \bar{S}(c)]\right\} \times \mathrm{Pr}^*[S_T < \bar{S}(c)] \end{aligned} \tag{19}$$

where E* and Pr* represent the expectation and probability computed with respect to the risk-neutral distribution. The put price calculation appears similar to the conditional price calculation used in computing tail VaR, but the two calculations are not identical. One obvious difference is that tail VaR is computed using the conditional expectation of the stock price under the true distribution, while the option price uses the risk-neutral distribution. Note that while $\mathrm{Pr}[S_T < \bar{S}(c)] = c$, $\mathrm{Pr}^*[S_T < \bar{S}(c)] \neq c$ unless the risk premium on the asset is zero ($\alpha = r$). Also, the put price is discounted, while the tail VaR is not.

VaR horizons are often short, so that discounting may not be an important issue. Also, with a short horizon the difference between the risk-neutral and true distribution may not be large.[8]

Example 12. Assume the same parameters as in Example 11, and also that the risk-free rate is 8%. The price of a put with 6 months to expiration and a strike of \$74.347 is

$$\text{BSPut}(100, 74.347, 0.30, 0.08, 0.50, 0) = \$0.4289 \quad \blacksquare$$

VaR and the Risk-Neutral Distribution

Let's try to interpret VaR and tail VaR in terms of insurance. If we are willing to accept losses less than the VaR level, then we can think of VaR as a deductible: It is the loss we willingly sustain before insurance pays anything. The difference between tail VaR and VaR is then the average payout from insurance; this payout occurs with true probability c. Since we are using the true distribution, the appropriate discount rate for a conditional expectation is unclear. (This is another manifestation of the problem of obtaining a "true" discount rate for an option.) Let γ denote the discount rate. A back-of-the-envelope calculation for the value of the average insurance payoff, assuming $\gamma = r$, is[9]

$$\begin{aligned} e^{-\gamma T} & [\text{Tail VaR} - \text{VaR}] \times \Pr[S_T < \bar{S}(c)] \\ &= e^{-\gamma T}\{S_0 - \text{E}[S_T | S_T < \bar{S}(c)] - [S_0 - \bar{S}(c)]\} \times c \\ &= e^{-0.08\times 0.50} \times (74.347 - \$68.244) \times 0.05 \\ &= 0.2932 \end{aligned} \tag{20}$$

The value of insurance inferred from the VaR calculation is substantially less than that computed using the Black-Scholes formula. There are two reasons why this calculation gives the wrong answer.

First, 5% is the VaR probability under the true distribution, not under the risk-neutral distribution. The risk-neutral probability that $S_T < 74.347$ is 6.945%. The risk-neutral probability is greater than the true probability because the 8% risk-free rate is less than the 15% expected return on the stock (i.e., $\alpha > r$).

Second, the conditional expected stock price under the risk-neutral distribution is less than that under the true distribution:

$$\text{E}^*\left(S_T | S_T < \$74.347\right) = \$67.919$$

Again, the true conditional expectation exceeds the risk-neutral conditional expectation because $\alpha > r$.

8. When prices move continuously and the hedging of risks is possible, the difference between the true and risk-neutral distributions depends upon the risk premium, $(\alpha - r)h$. When h is small, the risk premium will be small. When jumps are possible, the risk premium associated with the jump could create a significant difference between the risk-neutral and true distributions even over short horizons.

9. If there is no risk premium on the stock—i.e., $\alpha = r$—this calculation produces the Black-Scholes put price.

We can change the probability and conditional expectation to their risk-neutral values and repeat the calculation in equation 20. We then obtain

$$e^{-0.08\times 0.50} \times (\$74.347 - \$67.919) \times 0.06945 = \$0.4289$$

This is the same as the put premium in Example 12.

As a final comment, note that the 5% VaR will also be different depending upon whether we use the true or risk-neutral distribution. In this discussion we continued to use \$74.347—computed under the true distribution—as the VaR stock price.

The conclusion of this discussion is that we need to be cautious when interpreting VaR and tail VaR calculations. Economically, when $\alpha > r$, VaR-style calculations computed using the true stock-price distribution understate the insurance cost because they fail to properly account for the risk premium as a component of the drift on the asset. The risk premium is compensation for the fact that when the stock earns a low return, investors generally have suffered losses on their investments (their marginal utility of consumption is high). Insurance hedges against this outcome and is therefore valuable to investors. The Black-Scholes calculation properly accounts for the role of the risk premium, while the back-of-the-envelope calculation using VaR does not.

Subadditive Risk Measures

Artzner et al. (1999) point out a conceptual problem with VaR. As we have discussed, a common use of a risk measure is to decide how much capital is required to support an activity. Artzner et al. argue that a reasonable risk measure (or measure of required capital) should have certain properties, among them **subadditivity**.[10] If $\rho(X)$ is the risk measure associated with activity X (the capital required to support activity X), then ρ is subadditive if for two activities X and Y,

$$\rho(X+Y) \le \rho(X) + \rho(Y) \tag{21}$$

This simply says that the risk measure for the two activities combined should be less than that for the two activities separately. Because combining activities creates diversification, the capital required to support two activities together should be no greater than that required to support the two separately. If capital requirements are imposed using a rule that is not subadditive, then firms can reduce required capital by splitting up activities.

VaR is not subadditive. To show this, Artzner et al. provide an example using European out-of-the-money cash-or-nothing options having the same time to expiration and written on a single stock. Option A, a cash-or-nothing call, pays \$1 if $S_T > H$, while option B, a cash-or-nothing put, pays \$1 if $S_T < L$. Represent the premiums of the two options as P_A and P_B and suppose that either option has a 0.8% probability of paying off. The probability that either option expires out-of-the-money is 99.2%, and the probability that *both* options expire out-of-the-money is 98.4%.

---

10. Artzner et al. (1999) define *coherent* risk measures as those satisfying four properties: (1) *subadditivity*; (2) *monotonicity*: if $X \le Y$, $\rho(X) \ge \rho(Y)$ (if the loss is greater, the risk measure is greater); (3) *translation invariance*: $\rho(X+a) = \rho(X) - a$ (if you add \$1 to the cash flow, the risk measure is reduced by \$1); and (4) *positive homogeneity*: $\rho(\lambda X) = \lambda\rho(X)$ for $\lambda > 0$ (if you multiply the risk by 10, the risk measure increases by 10).

Consider a financial institution that *writes* such options. For either option considered alone, the bank is confident at a 99% level that the option will not be exercised, in which case the bank keeps the premium. Thus, VaR at a 99% confidence level is $-P_A$ (for option A) or $-P_B$ (for option B). VaR is *negative* because with 99% confidence, the option writer will keep the premium without the option being exercised.

Now suppose the institution sells both options. Because the two written options have the same underlying stock, they are perfectly negatively correlated. Therefore, the probability that one of the two options will be exercised is $0.8\% + 0.8\% = 1.6\%$. In the lowest 1% of the return distribution, one of the two options will be exercised. The VaR at the 99% level for the writer of the two options is therefore $\$1 - P_A - P_B$. We have

$$\text{VaR}(-A - B) = \$1 - P_A - P_B > -P_A - P_B = \text{VaR}(-A) + \text{VaR}(-B)$$

This expression has the opposite inequality as equation (21), so VaR is not subadditive in this example. In words, the institution can eliminate risk, as measured by 99% VaR, by undertaking the two activities in separate entities.

As a different example that illustrates this point, suppose you are comparing activity C, which generates a \$1 loss with a 1.1% probability, with activity D, which generates a \$1m loss with a 0.9% probability. Any reasonable rule should assign greater risk (and require more capital) for activity D, but a 1% VaR would be greater for C than for D.

These examples highlight an intuitively undesirable property of VaR as a risk measure: A small change in the VaR probability can cause VaR to change by a large amount. For the written cash-or-nothing call in this example, a 0.81% VaR is $-P_A$, while the 0.79% VaR is $\$1 - P_A$.

In contrast with VaR, tail VaR and the cost of insurance are both subadditive. Intuitively, tail VaR takes into account the distribution of losses beyond the VaR level, so it does not change abruptly when we change the VaR probability. To see that it is subadditive in our examples, the tail VaRs at the 99% level for A and B are

$$\rho(A) = 0.8 \times (1 - P_A) + 0.2 \times (-P_A) = 0.8 - P_A$$
$$\rho(b) = 0.8 \times (1 - P_B) + 0.2 \times (-P_B) = 0.8 - P_B$$

With the same confidence level, tail VaR at the 99% level for A and B together is

$$\rho(A + B) = 1 - P_A - P_B$$

We then have

$$\rho(A + B) = 1 - P_A - P_B < \rho(A) + \rho(B) = 1.6 - P_A - P_B$$

Thus, tail VaR in this example is subadditive.

As for the subadditivity of insurance premiums, Merton (1973b) demonstrated that options on portfolios are no more expensive than a portfolio of options on the portfolio constituents. Insurance premiums are therefore subadditive.

CHAPTER SUMMARY

Value at risk (VaR) is used to measure and manage risk—for example, in computing capital requirements. VaR deals primarily with so-called "market risks": price changes of stocks, currencies, interest rates, and commodities. The value at risk of a portfolio is the level of loss that will be exceeded a given percentage of the time over a specified horizon. Computing value at risk requires approximating the return distribution of the portfolio, which in turn requires information on the variance and covariance of assets in the portfolio. When portfolios are simple—for example, containing only stocks—standard portfolio risk calculations can be used to compute VaR. When portfolios contain options and other nonlinear assets, Monte Carlo simulation is commonly used to assess the return distribution of the portfolio. It is possible to construct examples in which VaR is an ill-behaved risk measure. Tail VaR, which takes into account the distribution of losses beyond the VaR level and the cost of insurance against losses exceeding the VaR level, may provide better alternatives.

FURTHER READING

Pearson (2002) provides an excellent overview of VaR, with very clear discussions of relevant mathematical techniques. Jorion (2001) provides a broad overview of the regulatory, practical, and analytical issues in computing VaR. Hendricks (1996) compares the results from computing VaR in a variety of different ways. Artzner et al. (1999) is an influential paper offering some important warnings about the use of VaR as a decision-making tool. Further explorations along these lines include Acerbi (2002), Acerbi and Tasche (2002), and other papers in the July 2002 special issue of the *Journal of Banking and Finance*.

Taleb (2010) is a combative, alternative take on risk management.

PROBLEMS

In the following problems, assume that the risk-free rate is 0.08 and that there are three stocks with a price of $100 and the following characteristics:

	α	σ	δ	**Correlation with B**	**Correlation with C**
Stock A	0.15	0.30	0.00	0.25	0.20
Stock B	0.18	0.45	0.02	1.00	0.30
Stock C	0.16	0.50	0.00	0.30	1.00

1. Consider the expression in equation (6). What is the exact probability that, over a 1-day horizon, stock A will have a loss?

2. Assuming a $10m investment in one stock, compute the 95% and 99% VaR for stocks A and B over 1-day, 10-day, and 20-day horizons.

3. Assuming a $10m investment that is 40% stock A and 60% stock B, compute the 95% and 99% VaR for the position over 1-day, 10-day, and 20-day horizons.

4. What are 95% and 99% 1-, 10-, and 20-day VaRs for a portfolio that has $4m invested in stock A, $3.5m in stock B, and $2.5m in stock C?

5. Using the same assumptions as in Example 3, compute VaR with and without the mean, assuming correlations of −1, −0.5, 0, 0.5, and 1. Is risk eliminated with a correlation of −1? If not, why not?

6. Using the delta-approximation method and assuming a \$10m investment in stock A, compute the 95% and 99% 1-, 10-, and 20-day VaRs for a position consisting of stock A plus one 105-strike put option for each share. Use the same assumptions as in Example 4.
7. Repeat the previous problem, only use Monte Carlo simulation.
8. Compute the 95% 10-day VaR for a written strangle (sell an out-of-the-money call and an out-of-the-money put) on 100,000 shares of stock A. Assume the options have strikes of \$90 and \$110 and have 1 year to expiration. Use the delta-approximation method and Monte Carlo simulation. What accounts for the difference in your answers?
9. Using Monte Carlo, compute the 95% and 99% 1-, 10-, and 20-day tail VaRs for the position in Problem 2.
10. Compute the 95% 10-day tail VaR for the position in Problem 8.
11. Suppose you write a 1-year cash-or-nothing put with a strike of \$50 and a 1-year cash-or-nothing call with a strike of \$215, both on stock A.
    a. What is the 1-year 99% VaR for each option separately?
    b. What is the 1-year 99% VaR for the two written options together?
    c. What is the 1-year 99% tail VaR for each option separately and the two together?
12. Suppose the 7-year zero-coupon bond has a yield of 6% and yield volatility of 10% and the 10-year zero-coupon bond has a yield of 6.5% and yield volatility of 9.5%. The correlation between the 7-year and 10-year yields is 0.96. What are 95% and 99% 10-day VaRs for an 8-year zero-coupon bond that pays \$10m at maturity?
13. Using the same assumptions as in Problem 12, compute the 10-day 95% VaR for a claim that pays \$3m each year in years 7–10.

Credit Risk

The risk that a counterparty will fail to meet a contractual payment obligation is called **credit risk**. Such risk exists anytime one party promises to make a future payment to another. Credit risk arises with loans, corporate bonds, and derivative contracts, and is therefore a risk that permeates the financial system. The failure to make a promised payment is a **default**. More generally, the term **credit event** is often used in contracts to refer to specific occurrences that suggest that a default is likely or has occurred. Examples of credit events are declaration of bankruptcy, failure to make a bond payment, repudiation of an obligation, or a credit downgrade.[1]

In this chapter we discuss theory and practice relating to credit risk. We first present a framework for analyzing credit risk and discuss the Merton model, which essentially uses the Black-Scholes model to study credit risk. We then discuss credit ratings, which are widely used by market participants to judge the credit-worthiness of instruments and firms. Finally, we consider the instruments used to modify, hedge, and trade credit risk, including credit default swaps and collateralized debt obligations.

Defaults and fear of defaults played a central role in the financial crisis of 2008, so you may recognize many of the terms and concepts in this chapter. Credit risk is important because routine financial dealings presume the credit-worthiness of a counterparty. Also, many investors seek assets that have a low risk of default. Thus, assessing and managing credit risk are of critical importance in modern financial markets.

1. DEFAULT CONCEPTS AND TERMINOLOGY

In this section we introduce basic concepts and terminology related to default in the context of pricing a zero-coupon bond. Suppose that a firm with asset value A_0 issues a zero-coupon bond maturing at time T, with a promised payment of $\bar{B}$. Let B_T denote the market value of the bond at time T. At time T, there are two possible outcomes:

1. A company that fails to make a promised payment may seek court protection—or a quick resolution of its dilemma—by declaring bankruptcy. Bankruptcy is a legal concept, with specific bankruptcy rules varying by country. In practice, default generally leads to bankruptcy, so we will use those terms interchangeably, without regard to their precise legal meaning.

From Chapter 27 of *Derivatives Markets*, Third Edition, Robert McDonald. Copyright © 2013 by Pearson Education, Inc. Published by Pearson Prentice Hall. All rights reserved.

- $A_T > \bar{B}$. Since assets are worth more than the repayment owed bondholders, shareholders will repay bondholders in full, so $B_T = \bar{B}$.
- $A_T < \bar{B}$. Shareholders will walk away from the firm, surrendering it to bondholders. The value of the bonds at time T is then $B_T = A_T$.

Let $g^*(A_T; A_0)$ denote the risk-neutral probability density for the time T asset value, conditional upon the time 0 asset value, A_0. Then we can write the initial debt value, B_0, as

$$B_0 = e^{-rT}\left[\int_0^{\bar{B}} A_T g^*(A_T; A_0) dA_T + \bar{B}\int_{\bar{B}}^{\infty} g^*(A_T; A_0) dA_T\right] \quad (1)$$

The first integral on the right-hand side is the risk-neutral partial expectation of the asset value, conditional on bankruptcy. The second integral is the risk-neutral probability that the firm is not bankrupt. Thus, we can rewrite the value of the bonds as

$$B_0 = e^{-rT}\{\mathrm{E}^*(A_T|\text{Default}) \times \Pr{}^*(\text{Default}) + \bar{B} \times [1 - \Pr{}^*(\text{Default})]\}$$

where E^* and $\Pr^*$ are computed with respect to the risk-neutral measure. Since $B_T = A_T$ in default, we can also write this as

$$B_0 = e^{-rT}\{\mathrm{E}^*\left(B_T|\text{Default}\right) \times \Pr{}^*(\text{Default}) + \bar{B} \times [1 - \Pr{}^*(\text{Default})]\} \quad (2)$$

If we set the probability of default equal to zero, equation (2) yields the standard formula for the value of a default-free bond, $B_0 = e^{-rT}\bar{B}$. Equation (2) also illustrates that default introduces two new elements: the default probability ($\Pr^*$[Default]), and the payoff conditional on default ($\mathrm{E}^*\left[B_T|\text{Default}\right]$).

The payoff conditional on default can be expressed in different ways. The **recovery rate** is the amount the debt-holders receive as a fraction of what they are owed. Thus, in the case where a firm issues a single zero-coupon bond, the risk-neutral expected recovery rate is

$$\mathrm{E}^*(\text{Recovery rate}) = \frac{\mathrm{E}^*\left(B_T|\text{Default}\right)}{\bar{B}} \quad (3)$$

The **loss given default** is the difference between what the bondholders are owed and what they receive, as a fraction of the promised payment:

$$\mathrm{E}^*(\text{Loss given default}) = 1 - \mathrm{E}^*(\text{Recovery rate}) \quad (4)$$

Conventionally any such measure is expressed as a percentage.

Finally, we can express the **credit spread**—the difference between the yield to maturity on a defaultable bond and an otherwise equivalent default-free bond—in terms of the risk-neutral default probability and expected loss given default. In equation (2), divide both sides by $\bar{B}$ and take the natural logarithm of both sides. Recall that the annual yield to maturity on the bond, ρ, is

$$\rho = \frac{1}{T}\ln\left(\frac{\bar{B}}{B_0}\right)$$

After some rearrangement, we obtain the following expression from equation (2):

$$\rho - r = \frac{1}{T}\ln\left[\frac{1}{1 - \text{Pr}^*(\text{Default}) \times \text{E}^*(\text{Loss given default})}\right] \tag{5}$$

The left-hand side of equation (5) is the credit spread. Both the probability of default and the expected loss given default are less than 1, so, as we would expect, the credit spread is greater than or equal to zero. If either the probability of default or the expected loss given default is zero, the bond yield equals the risk-free rate.

By taking a Taylor series expansion of the right-hand side of equation (5), we obtain

$$\rho - r \approx \frac{1}{T}\,\text{Pr}^*(\text{Default}) \times \text{E}^*(\text{Loss given default})$$

Thus, the credit spread approximately equals the annualized product of the risk-neutral default probability and the expected loss given default.

2. THE MERTON DEFAULT MODEL

Owning zero-coupon debt subject to default is the same thing as owning a default-free bond and writing a put option on the assets of the firm. This is an example of a *structural* approach to modeling bankruptcy: We create an explicit model for the evolution of the firm's assets, coupled with a rule governing default.

If we assume that the assets of the firm are lognormally distributed, then we can use lognormal probability calculations to compute either the risk-neutral or actual probability that the firm will go bankrupt. This approach to bankruptcy modeling has come to be called the *Merton model* since Merton (1974) used continuous-time methods to provide a model of the credit spread. The Merton default model has in recent years been the basis for credit risk analyses provided by Moody's KMV.

Default at Maturity

Assume that the assets of the firm, A, follow the process

$$\frac{dA}{A} = (\alpha - \delta)dt + \sigma dZ \tag{6}$$

where α is the expected return on the firm assets and δ is the cash payout made to claim holders on the firm. Suppose the firm has issued a single zero-coupon bond with promised payment $\bar{B}$, that matures at time T and makes no payouts. Default occurs at time T if $A_T < \bar{B}$. The probability of bankruptcy at time T, conditional on the value of assets at time t, is

$$\begin{aligned}\Pr(A_T < \bar{B}|A_t) &= N\left[-\frac{\ln(A_t/\bar{B}) + (\alpha - \delta - \frac{1}{2}\sigma^2)(T-t)}{\sigma\sqrt{T-t}}\right] \\ &= N(-\hat{d}_2)\end{aligned} \tag{7}$$

In this equation, $\hat{d}_2$ is the Black-Scholes d_2 term with r replaced by α.

The expression $\hat{d}_2$ is called the **distance to default** and measures the size (in standard deviations) of the random shock required to induce bankruptcy. To understand this interpretation, recall that when assets are lognormally distributed, the expected log asset value at time T is

$$E[\ln(A_T)] = \ln(A_t) + (\alpha - \delta - 0.5\sigma^2)(T - t)$$

Thus, the distance to default is the difference between $E[\ln(A_T)]$ and the bankruptcy level $\bar{B}$, normalized by the standard deviation:[2]

$$\begin{aligned} \text{Distance to default} &= \frac{E[\ln(A_T)] - \bar{B}}{\sigma\sqrt{T-t}} \\ &= \frac{\ln(A_t) + (\alpha - \delta - 0.5\sigma^2)(T - t) - \ln(\bar{B})}{\sigma\sqrt{T-t}} \end{aligned}$$

This is $\hat{d}_2$. The default probability is $N(-\text{distance to default})$.

The expected recovery rate, conditional on default, is

$$E(A_T|A_T < \bar{B}) = A_t e^{(\alpha-\delta)(T-t)} \frac{N\left[-\frac{\ln(A_t/\bar{B})+(\alpha-\delta+\frac{1}{2}\sigma^2)(T-t)}{\sigma\sqrt{T-t}}\right]}{N\left[-\frac{\ln(A_t/\bar{B})+(\alpha-\delta-\frac{1}{2}\sigma^2)(T-t)}{\sigma\sqrt{T-t}}\right]} \tag{8}$$

It is important to notice that the calculations in equations (7) and (8) are performed under the true probability measure (also sometimes called the *physical measure*). Thus, these equations provide estimates of the empirically observed default probability and recovery rate, but we cannot use them in pricing calculations. In order to compute the theoretical credit spread, for example, we replace the actual asset drift, α, with the risk-free rate in equations (7) and (8). This gives us

$$\Pr{}^*(A_T < \bar{B}; A_t) = N\left[-\frac{\ln(A_t/\bar{B}) + (r - \delta - \frac{1}{2}\sigma^2)(T - t)}{\sigma\sqrt{T-t}}\right] \tag{9}$$

and

$$E^*(A_T|A_T < \bar{B}) = A_t e^{(r-\delta)(T-t)} \frac{N\left[-\frac{\ln(A_t/\bar{B})+(r-\delta+\frac{1}{2}\sigma^2)(T-t)}{\sigma\sqrt{T-t}}\right]}{N\left[-\frac{\ln(A_t/\bar{B})+(r-\delta-\frac{1}{2}\sigma^2)(T-t)}{\sigma\sqrt{T-t}}\right]} \tag{10}$$

We can use these expressions to compute equation (5).

2. The Moody's KMV model uses the different expression $(A_t - \bar{B})/\sigma A_t$ as a measure of distance to default. See Crosbie and Bohn (2003) for a discussion.

Example 1. Suppose that $\overline{B} = \$100$, $A_0 = \$90$, $\alpha = 10\%$, $r = 6\%$, $\sigma = 25\%$, $\delta = 0$ (the firm makes no payouts), and $T = 5$ years. The theoretical debt value in this case is \$62.928, which implies a yield of 9.2635%.

Using equations (7) and (9), the true and risk-neutral default probabilities are 33.49% and 47.26%. Thus, over a 5-year horizon, we would expect to observe a default one-third of the time. Under the risk-neutral measure, however, defaults occur almost half the time. The greater risk-neutral default probability is due to the assets growing more slowly under the risk-neutral measure.

Using equations (8) and (10), the expected asset value conditional on default is \$71.867 under the true measure, and \$68.144 under the risk-neutral measure. Expected recovery rates are therefore

$$\text{E(Recovery rate)} = \frac{71.867}{100} = 0.71867$$

under the true measure, and

$$\text{E}^*\text{(Recovery rate)} = \frac{68.144}{100} = 0.68144$$

under the risk-neutral measure. Note that the risk-neutral expected loss given default is

$$\text{E}^*\text{(Loss given default)} = 1 - 0.68144 = 0.31866$$

Using the risk-neutral default probability and loss given default, we can compute the theoretical debt yield. From equation (5), the credit spread is

$$\frac{1}{5}\ln\left[\frac{1}{1 - 0.4726 \times 0.31866}\right] = 0.032635$$

This implies a debt yield to maturity of $0.060 + 0.032635 = 0.092635$, which is the same answer as that using the Black-Scholes formula to compute the theoretical debt value. ■

As the preceding example shows, historical data on *defaults* provides different information than historical data on *prices*. Historical default frequencies and recovery rates, which are observed under the true measure, correspond to equations (7) and (8). If we examine credit spreads, by contrast, we can infer the risk-neutral expected default frequency and recovery rate, which correspond to equations (9) and (10). Notice, however, that we would infer the same asset volatility from both sets of calculations.

Related Models

Suppose that the value of assets can jump to zero according to a Poisson process. Specifically, suppose that over an interval dt, the probability of a jump to zero is λdt, and that the occurrence of this jump is independent of the market and of other defaults. When a stock can independently jump to zero, the value of a European call is obtained by replacing the risk-free rate, r, with $r + \lambda$. As before, equity is a call option on the assets. If the firm makes no payouts, the value, B_t, of a single issue of zero-coupon debt maturing at time T is

$$B_t = A_t - \text{BSCall}(A_t, \bar{B}, \sigma, r + \lambda, T - t, 0) \quad (11)$$

The possibility that assets can jump to zero will raise the bond yield.[3]

There is a special case where the effect of the jump probability on the bond yield is particularly easy to interpret. When the bond is default-free except for the possibility of a jump, then the bond yield is $r + \lambda$: The yield increases one-for-one with the default probability.

Example 2. Suppose that a firm has a single issue of zero-coupon debt promising to pay \$10 in 5 years, and that $A_0 = \$90$, $\sigma = 30\%$, $r = 0.06$, and $\delta = 0$. From equation (11), when $\lambda = 0$, the value of the debt is

$$B_t = \$90 - \text{BSCall}(90, 10, 0.30, 0.06, 5, 0) = \$7.408$$

The yield on debt is $\ln(10/7.408)/5 = 0.06$. This bond is priced as if it were default-free.

When $\lambda = 0.02$, the price of the bond is

$$B_t = \$90 - \text{BSCall}(90, 10, 0.30, 0.06 + 0.02, 5, 0) = \$6.703$$

The yield is then $\ln(10/6.703)/5 = 0.08$: The yield increases by the default probability.

When a default is likely apart from jumps to zero, then the increase in the bond yield is less than λ. For example, when $\bar{B} = \$100$, the bond yield is 10.342% without jumps, and 11.588% with a 2% jump to zero. ■

The models we have discussed are relatively simple: There are no coupon payments and bankruptcy occurs only at maturity. In practice, firms typically have a mix of short-term and long-term coupon-paying debt, so that debt maturity is not well-defined and bankruptcy can occur at any time. One solution in this case is to approximate the bankruptcy trigger as the face value of short-term debt plus one-half the face value of long-term debt (Vassalou and Xing, 2004).

With barrier option pricing formulas, binomial valuation, Monte Carlo, or other numerical methods, it is possible to create bankruptcy models that permit bankruptcy prior to a maturity date. The Black and Cox (1976) model is a variant of the Merton model in which bankruptcy occurs if assets fall to a predetermined level, $\underline{A}$, prior to maturity. This assumption mimics a debt covenant that triggers default if the firm's financial condition worsens sufficiently. Equity in this model is a call option that knocks out if $A_t \leq \underline{A}$.

3. By differentiating the expression for yield to maturity ($\ln[\bar{B}/B_t]/T$) with respect to λ, it is possible to show that the increase in yield from a 0.01 increase in λ is

$$\text{Yield increase} = \frac{\text{BSCallRho}(A_t, \bar{B}, \sigma, r + \lambda, T - t, \delta)}{\text{Bond price} \times T}$$

where "BSCallRho" is the formula for the rho (interest rate sensitivity) of a call.

3. BOND RATINGS AND DEFAULT EXPERIENCE

Bond ratings provide a measure of the credit risk for specific bonds. Such ratings, which are provided by third parties, attempt to measure the likelihood that a company will default on a bond. In the United States, the Securities and Exchange Commission (SEC) identifies specific credit-rating firms as Nationally Recognized Statistical Rating Organizations (NRSROs). The history and significance of this designation was explained by the chairman of the SEC in congressional testimony:[4]

> The Commission originally used the term "Nationally Recognized Statistical Rating Organization," or NRSRO, with respect to credit rating agencies in 1975 solely to differentiate between grades of debt securities held by broker-dealers as capital to meet Commission capital requirements. Since that time, ratings by NRSROs have become benchmarks in federal and state legislation, domestic and foreign financial regulations and privately negotiated financial contracts.

During the 1990s there were three NRSROs: Standard and Poor's, Moody's, and Fitch. As of early 2012, there were 10. The rating agencies were widely criticized for some of their ratings activity prior to the 2008 financial crisis. Agencies had granted high ratings to securities that paid investors based on the performance of mortgages. Many of these highly rated securities were downgraded significantly during the financial crisis. Rating agencies are paid by issuers of the rated securities, and critics charged that this created a conflict of interest for the agencies. Rating agencies are still predominatly paid by issuers, but the Dodd-Frank Act in 2010 changed some of the rules pertaining to agencies. Specifically, Section 932 of the act required among other things that the rating agencies increase transparency of their rating methods and improve their internal controls. References to ratings are to be removed from federal statutes. The effect of the changes remains to be seen.

Moody's rates bonds using the designations Aaa, Aa, A, Baa, Ba, B, Caa, Ca, and C. Within each ratings category (except for Aaa, Ca, and C), bonds may be further rated as a 1, 2, or 3, with 1 denoting the highest quality within a category. Standard and Poor's and Fitch have a similar rating system, using the designations AAA, AA, A, BBB, BB, B, CCC, CC, and C, with "+" and "−" used to denote within -grade differences.

The market distinguishes between "investment grade" (a rating of Baa/BBB or above) and "below-investment grade" or "speculative grade" (a rating below Baa/BBB) bonds. Some investors are permitted to hold only investment grade bonds, and some contracts have triggers based upon whether a company's bond rating is investment grade. For example, prior to Enron's bankruptcy, some of the company's deals contained clauses requiring that Enron make payments if Enron lost its investment grade status. Enron's financial difficulties were worsened when its rating fell below investment grade.

4. "Testimony Concerning The State of the Securities Industry," by William H. Donaldson Chairman, U.S. SEC, U.S. Senate Committee on Banking, Housing, and Urban Affairs, March 9, 2005.

TABLE 1 Standard and Poor's 1-year global corporate average credit rating transition rates, 1981–2010 (%). NR means "no longer rated."

From/to	AAA	AA	A	BBB	BB	B	CCC/C	D	NR
AAA	87.91	8.08	0.54	0.05	0.08	0.03	0.05	0.00	3.25
AA	0.57	86.48	8.17	0.53	0.06	0.08	0.02	0.02	4.06
A	0.04	1.90	87.29	5.37	0.38	0.17	0.02	0.08	4.75
BBB	0.01	0.13	3.70	84.55	3.98	0.66	0.15	0.25	6.56
BB	0.02	0.04	0.17	5.22	75.75	7.30	0.76	0.95	9.79
B	0.00	0.04	0.14	0.23	5.48	73.23	4.47	4.70	11.71
CCC/C	0.00	0.00	0.19	0.28	0.83	13.00	43.82	27.39	14.48

Source: Vazza et al. (2011, Table 21).

Rating Transitions

A company that goes bankrupt will typically have had ratings downgrades prior to bankruptcy. By looking at the frequency with which bonds experience a ratings change, it is possible to estimate the ultimate bankruptcy probability. A change in ratings is called a **ratings transition**.

Table 1 is a *ratings transition matrix*, reporting the probability that a firm in a given ratings category will switch to another ratings category over the course of a year.[5] Firms rated AAA, AA, or A all have about an 88% chance of retaining their rating over a 1-year horizon, and almost no chance of suffering a default over that time. They do, however, have some chance of experiencing a downgrade, after which bankruptcy becomes likelier: The default probability increases as the rating decreases.

Given certain assumptions, we can use a short-term ratings transition matrix to compute the ultimate probability that a firm with a given rating will go bankrupt. Specifically, suppose we believe that a ratings transition matrix is constant over time and that the probability of moving from one rating to another in a given year does not depend on the rating in a previous year. Then we can use the matrix to compute the probability that a firm that is A-rated (for example) will move to any other rating, and the subsequent probability that it will move from one of the new ratings to a different rating, and so forth.

The following simple example will illustrate how to interpret and use a ratings transition matrix. Suppose that securities can be in one of three categories: Good, Bad, and Ugly. The matrix in Table 2 displays the probability that a firm with a rating in the left-hand column will, over the course of a year, move to a rating in the top row. For example, there is a 90% probability that a firm rated Good will still be Good 1 year later. There is a 3% chance that the Good firm will become Ugly.

5. A rating can be withdrawn if the rated obligation has matured or if the ratings agency deems that there is insufficient information for a rating.

TABLE 2 Ratings transition matrix. The entry in the ith row and jth column is the probability that a firm will, over 1 year, move from type i to type j.

		To:		
		Good	Bad	Ugly
	Good	0.90	0.07	0.03
From:	Bad	0.15	0.75	0.10
	Ugly	0.06	0.14	0.80

Notice that each row sums to one. This means that after 1 year each firm must be in one of the three categories. By contrast, in Table 1, there is a "no longer rated" category, indicating that a firm has for some reason dropped out of S&P's rating universe.

We can use the transition matrix to compute the probability that a firm rated Good will still be Good 2 years from now. To perform this calculation, recognize that there are three different paths by which a firm that is now Good can still be Good in 2 years.

- There is a 90% chance that a Good firm remains Good over 1 year. There is therefore an 81% (0.9×0.9) probability that the firm will be Good for both years.
- There is a 7% probability that the firm will be Bad next year, in which case there is a 15% chance the firm will become Good the subsequent year. There is therefore a 1.05% (0.07×0.15) probability that the firm will go from Good to Bad and then back to Good.
- Finally, there is a 3% probability that the firm will become Ugly, and then a 6% probability that it will become Good again. There is therefore a 0.18% (0.03×0.06) probability that the firm will become Ugly and then Good.

The total probability that a Good firm will still be Good in 2 years is therefore 82.23%:

$$(0.90 \times 0.90) + (0.07 \times 0.15) + (0.03 \times 0.06) = 0.8223$$

In order to perform this calculation, it may at first seem necessary to enumerate the possible transitions. Notice, however, that the calculation entails multiplying each element of the first row of the transition matrix by the corresponding element of the first column, and then summing the results. It turns out that if we wish to know all possible transitions over a 2-year period, we can construct a new matrix from the 1-year transition matrix, where the element in the ith row and jth column of the new matrix is created by multiplying the ith row of the original matrix by the jth column of the original matrix and summing the results. This is a multiplication of the transition matrix by itself. Table 3 shows the result.

In order to compute the ratings distribution after 3 years, we can duplicate the procedure, only taking the 2-year matrix and multiplying it by the 1-year matrix. This is the same as multiplying the 1-year matrix by itself twice.

In general, let $p(i, t; j, t + s)$ denote the probability that, over an s-year horizon, a firm will move from the rating in row i to that in column j. The entries in Table 1 give us

TABLE 3 Ratings transition probabilities after 2 years.

		To		
		Good	Bad	Ugly
From:	Good	0.8223	0.1197	0.0580
	Bad	0.2535	0.5870	0.1595
	Ugly	0.1230	0.2212	0.6558

$p(i, t; j, t+1)$. Suppose there are n ratings. Over 2 years, the probability of moving from rating i to rating j is

$$p(i, t; j, t+2) = \sum_{k=1}^{n} p(i, t; k, t+1) \times p(k, t+1; j, t+2)$$

From the 2-year transitions we can go to 3 years, and then 4, and so on. Given the $s-1$-year transition probabilities, the s-year transition probability is

$$p(i, t; j, t+s) = \sum_{k=1}^{n} p(i, t; k, t+s-1) \times p(k, t+s-1; j, t+s) \qquad (12)$$

Thus, a transition probability matrix can be used to tell us the probability that a firm will go bankrupt after a given period of time.

The long-term experience of bonds with a given rating is reported in Table 4. Note that if a bond has a AAA rating, after 7 years there is a 0.1% chance it will have gone bankrupt. However, bonds issued by firms initially rated B accounted for 54.1% of defaults over the 30-year period in Table 4.

Recovery Rates

Table 5 displays historical average recovery rates for bonds with different levels of seniority. When we model debt with different priorities, we assume that in a default, junior debtholders received no payment if senior debt was not completely repaid. This rule for paying bondholders is called **absolute priority**. If the bankruptcy process respects absolute priority, more senior bonds will have higher recovery rates. Table 5 shows that bonds designated as more senior generally have higher average recovery rates. It is important to understand that the numbers in Table 5 are averages, and there is considerable variation in recovery rates across firms.[6]

Reduced Form Bankruptcy Models

The existence of data on corporate bond ratings changes, and defaults suggests that we could construct statistical pricing models designed to match the behavior of bond prices.

6. Hamilton et al. (2005) report, for example, that for senior subordinated bonds in 2004, the mean recovery rate was 44.4%, but realized recovery rates ranged between 8% and 90%, with a standard deviation of 25%.

TABLE 4 Cumulative default rates (in percent) by original rating of issuer, 1981–2010.

	% of Total Defaults per Time Frame						
	AAA	AA	A	BBB	BB	B	CCC/C
1 year	0.0	0.0	0.0	2.6	9.6	48.7	39.1
3 years	0.0	0.0	0.9	4.1	18.0	64.7	12.3
5 years	0.0	0.2	1.1	5.6	21.6	62.9	8.6
7 years	0.1	0.3	1.8	6.6	23.0	60.6	7.5
Total	0.3	1.3	4.2	9.0	25.1	54.1	6.0

Source: Vazza et al. (2011, Table 12).

TABLE 5 Value-weighted average recovery rates (per $100 of par value) in the default year, based on post-default trading prices.

	Recovery	
Priority	2010	1982–2010
First lien bank loan	72.3	59.6
Bonds		
Senior secured	54.7	49.1
Senior unsecured	63.8	37.4
Senior subordinated	39.4	25.3
Subordinated	32.2	24.2
Junior subordinated	N/A	17.1

Source: Ou (2011, Exhibit 7).

Such models are called *reduced form models*.[7] In order to price bonds we require risk-neutral probabilities, so we cannot directly use historical data.

To understand how reduced form models work, consider the simplest version of such a model. Suppose a T-year bond promises to pay B at maturity and there is a zero recovery rate in the event of default. The risk-free rate is r and constant over time. If default follows a Poisson process with the risk-neutral intensity λ, then the bond price depends only on time and on the occurrence of the jump. The partial differential equation for pricing the bond is

7. The reduced form approach was first used in Jarrow and Turnbull (1995). See Duffie and Singleton (2003) for a survey.

$$\frac{\partial B(t)}{\partial t} - \lambda B(t) = rB(t)$$

With the boundary condition that $B(T) = \bar{B}$, the bond price is[8]

$$B(t) = \bar{B}e^{-(r+\lambda)(T-t)} \tag{13}$$

Given our strong assumptions that recovery rate is zero and interest rates are nonstochastic, it would seem a simple matter to price this bond by observing r and inferring λ from data on defaults. The problem, however, is that equation (13) presumes that λ is a risk-neutral jump probability. Thus, we can infer λ from bond prices but not from historical default data.

To understand the issue, suppose that bond defaults are idiosyncratic. In this case an investor can diversify default risk. We then expect λ in equation (13) to equal the historically observed λ.

If defaults are correlated, however, then even a portfolio containing numerous bonds will encounter systematic losses from correlated defaults. Defaults occur when firms perform poorly—i.e., when equity returns are low. Investors require a positive risk premium to hold such bonds, and therefore the risk-neutral default probability in equation (13) will exceed the historical default probability.

A more general approach than that in equation (13) uses ratings transitions. Equation (13) does not take into account that default becomes more likely as ratings decline. With risk-neutral ratings transitions, it is possible to price bonds taking into account the various paths by which default can occur. Jarrow et al. (1997) show how to use observed bond prices and historical ratings transitions to infer risk-neutral ratings transition probabilities.

4. CREDIT DEFAULT SWAPS

The buyer of a bond acquires both interest rate risk and the credit risk of the issuer. An investor may wish to hold a different combination of these risks. Credit derivatives, which have existed since the early 1990s, are contracts that permit the trading and hedging of credit risk. In theory, credit derivatives permit institutions to hedge credit risk just as they might hedge the cost of oil. The outstanding notional principal covered by credit default swaps, which we discuss in this section, grew significantly between 2004 and 2010.

Single-Name Credit Default Swaps

A single-name credit default swap (CDS) is an insurance contract on a bond. The CDS seller pays the buyer when the reference entity (the "single name" that issued the insured bond) experiences a credit event—for example, the failure to make a bond payment. The buyer of the swap is the *protection buyer,* and the counterparty providing the credit insurance is the *swap writer* or *protection seller*. If a credit event occurs, the protection buyer receives

$$\text{Protection buyer payoff} = \text{Bond par value} - \text{Bond market value} \tag{14}$$

8. Note that this is the same bond price solution we obtain in equation (11) when $B < A$, and $\sigma = 0$.

It is common for CDS contracts to settle in cash, with the seller paying the buyer the amount in equation (14).[9] A corporate bondholder, for example, could buy a CDS for protection against the credit risk of a company. The CDS buyer and seller are typically unrelated to the reference entity. CDS contracts can have any maturity, but it is common to see quotes for 5- and 10-year maturities.

Payment conventions for CDS contracts can be confusing. The payment for a CDS can have two components: a lump sum payment at the initiation of the contract (the "upfront payment"), and an annual premium, which is paid quarterly until expiration or the occurrence of a credit event, whichever is earlier. Prior to 2009, there was no upfront payment for reasonably credit-worthy firms, so buyers of CDS contracts paid only the annual premium. This amount is known as the *conventional spread*. Since 2009, CDS prices have been quoted either as a conventional spread or as points upfront with an implied annual premium of 500 basis points.

Figure 1 illustrates the relationship among a protection buyer (the investor), a protection seller (the swap writer), and the reference entity (XYZ). The figure assumes that the buyer pays the seller a conventional spread of 40 basis points. A default swap typically specifies one or more XYZ debt issues, called the *reference assets* or *reference obligations*. The reference asset is important because bonds from the same issuer with different seniority levels will have different prices after a default. Generally, the protection buyer can deliver any bond with payment rights equal to that of the reference asset. Although the figure shows the protection buyer owning a bond, it is possible to buy a CDS without owning the bond. The CDS buyer in this case is effectively short the bond, because the position makes money when the bond defaults.

You might wonder who decides whether a credit event has occurred and how the bond market value in equation (14) is determined. The International Swaps and Derivatives Association (ISDA) plays a central role in the CDS market: ISDA provides the standard documentation for CDS, an ISDA determination committee pronounces the occurrence of a credit event, and ISDA controls the settlement auctions that determine the payout. The standard procedure calls for dealers to submit both bid and ask prices for the defaulted bonds. The resulting demand and supply schedules are used to determine net open interest for the bond, after which there is an auction for that amount. The auction price is used to settle the CDS. Settlement procedures have changed over time in response to problems during settlement and will likely continue to evolve over time.[10]

CDS contracts are quoted for different expirations. The set of prices with different maturities generates a *credit spread curve*, where, for example, you may observe that credit spreads are small at short horizons and larger over 5 years. With an array of different maturities it is possible to make sophisticated bets. For example, you could buy protection

9. Early CDS contracts called for the CDS buyer to deliver the physical bond, but cash settlement is now common. The requirement of physical delivery could create a situation where buyers would have to pay a large premium to acquire the bond. For example, when Delphi declared bankruptcy in 2005, the quantity of CDS contracts outstanding greatly exceeded the quantity of bonds.

10. Gupta and Sundaram (2012) and Chernov et al. (2011) study CDS auctions. Both papers find that in auctions conducted between 2008 and 2010, the bond is underpriced relative to pre- and post-auction prices.

FIGURE 1

Depiction of the cash flows in a credit default swap. The CDS buyer may or may not own the reference asset, which was issued by XYZ. The CDS buyer pays 40 basis points per year in exchange for the CDS seller's payment in the event of a default by XYZ.

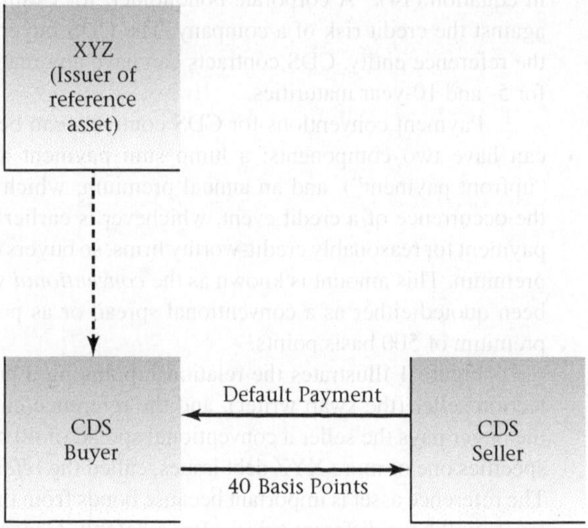

with a 4-year horizon and sell protection with a 5-year horizon; this is a bet that default will not occur in the fifth year.

Finally, recognize that both parties to a default swap face credit risk from the swap itself. The protection buyer may default on premium payments, and the protection seller could go bankrupt at the same time that a default occurs on the reference asset. This was a concern when AIG was rescued; see the box on the next page. Credit-linked notes, which we discuss below, are structured to eliminate counterparty credit risk.

Credit default premiums have become widely watched indicators of the likelihood of default for both firms and sovereigns, especially during times of financial stress. Figure 2 shows CDS prices (quoted as conventional spreads) for Morgan Stanley, Lehman Brothers, and Bank of America. It is easy to discern September 2008 in this figure. Lehman filed for bankruptcy on September 15, with its CDS contract having reached 688 the Friday before. Morgan Stanley survived, but its CDS premium reached 1260.90 on October 10, 2008. Bank of America fared more poorly following the crisis.

Figure 3 displays CDS premia for Germany, Greece, and Spain. All three countries had low credit spreads before late 2008. Greece defaulted in 2012, and investors had clearly become concerned about Spain. Germany maintained a relatively low CDS premium.

Pricing a Default Swap

An investor who buys a bond and a default swap on the bond owns a synthetic default-free bond. This observation suggests that the default swap premium should approximately equal the default premium on the bond. To make this more precise, suppose we simultaneously undertake the following set of transactions:

- Buy protection with a CDS on \$100 worth of senior bonds issued by XYZ. The default swap premium is ρ.

BOX 1: Standardizing CDS

Financial firms have many interlocking relationships stemming from lending and derivatives. A policy concern during the financial crisis was that, because of these linkages, the failure of one firm could trigger multiple other failures. To understand how this could happen, suppose that firms B, C, and D own the debt of firm X, and that they buy credit default swaps on X from firm A. If firms A and X were to fail simultaneously, firms B, C, and D would lose their insurance and also suffer losses on the debt of X. They could possibly fail. In September 2008, the Federal Reserve rescued AIG when the firm was unable to post collateral to cover losses on hundreds of billions of dollars of written credit default swaps. There is controversy about whether the rescue was necessary, but it likely reduced the chance of additional failures.

Following the crisis, both regulators and the financial industry sought to make the CDS market more standardized and transparent. On the regulatory front, the Dodd-Frank Wall Street Reform and Consumer Protection Act required that all standardized derivatives contracts be centrally cleared and margined. Had this requirement been in place before September 2008 and applied to credit default swaps, AIG would have had to post margin for its positions and would have been marked-to-market daily by a clearinghouse. The magnitude and risk of AIG's position would have been apparent to regulators. It is possible that with margin requirements, AIG would have written fewer CDSs in the first place.

The industry also worked to standardize CDS contracts. The "big bang" in April 2009 (Markit, 2009) created standard CDS coupons of 100 and 500 basis points, with standard payment dates. If the CDS premium on a firm would have been 40 basis points prior to the big bang (as in Figure 1), for a transaction after that date the CDS buyer would pay 100 basis points annually, and the seller would make an initial lump-sum payment ("points upfront") in order to compensate the buyer for the greater annual payment. Similarly, if the conventional spread would have been more than 100 basis points, the buyer would make an upfront payment to the seller, in addition to paying 100 basis points annually. For ease of interpretation, CDSs paying 100 basis points are quoted using the conventional spread. CDSs paying 500 basis points may be quoted as points upfront. One purpose of coupon standardization was to make CDS positions easier to trade and offset.

- Short-sell a \$100 default-free floating rate note paying r. (Such a note always sells at par.) Suppose that we can short-sell the bond costlessly.
- Buy XYZ senior floating-rate notes paying $c = r + a$, with par value \$100. The premium $a = c - r$ is constant over time.

The short-sale of the default-free note funds the purchase of the defaultable note. These transactions require no initial cash flow.

Each period prior to termination, the net cash flow on the position is $c - (r + \rho)$. XYZ either defaults or does not default prior to maturity of the CDS, so that the default swap terminates in either of two ways:

- If the CDS matures and XYZ has not defaulted, sell the XYZ floating rate bond and use the \$100 proceeds to buy the default-free floating rate note in order to close the

FIGURE 2

5-year credit default swap premia for Morgan Stanley, Lehman Brothers, and Bank of America, 2004-2012. Y-axis scales are different for each panel.

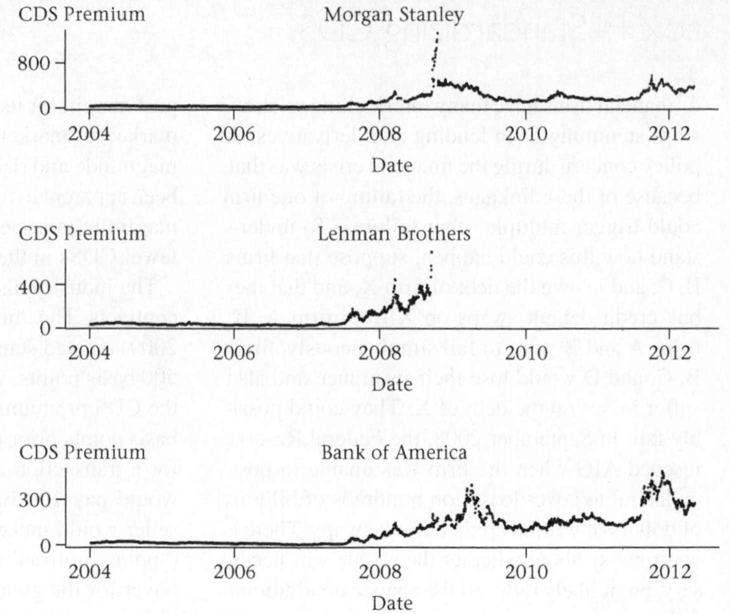

Source: Datastream and Bloomberg.

short sale. (By using floating rate notes, we ensure that both bonds are worth \$100 if there is no default.)

- If XYZ defaults, under the terms of the CDS, surrender the defaulted floating rate notes in exchange for \$100. Use the \$100 proceeds to buy the default-free floating rate note in order to close the short sale.

In either case, there is no net cash flow.

Since we can enter and close the position with no net cash flow, the interim cash flows should also equal zero, which implies that $c - (r + \rho) = 0$, or

$$\rho = c - r \tag{15}$$

In other words, the default swap premium equals the credit spread.

Notice that we made very strong assumptions to reach this conclusion, so we should not expect equation (15) to hold exactly.[11] In practice, we would need to take into account a variety of complications, including time variation in the credit spread, bonds having fixed

11. Blanco et al. (2005), using data from 2001 and 2002, find that the average difference between the CDS premium and the bond credit spread (the CDS-bond basis) is a positive 5.5 basis points, and that CDS prices reflect news before bond prices. (This calculation measures the bond credit spread as the bond yield less the credit rate.) Bai and Collin-Dufresne (2011) examine the CDS-bond basis during the financial crisis and find average a negative CDS-bond basis, with CDS premiums 250 basis points lower than credit

FIGURE 3

5-year credit default swap premia for Germany, Greece, and Spain, 2004–2012. Bloomberg does not provide data for Greek CDS after November 2011. Y-axis scales are different for each panel.

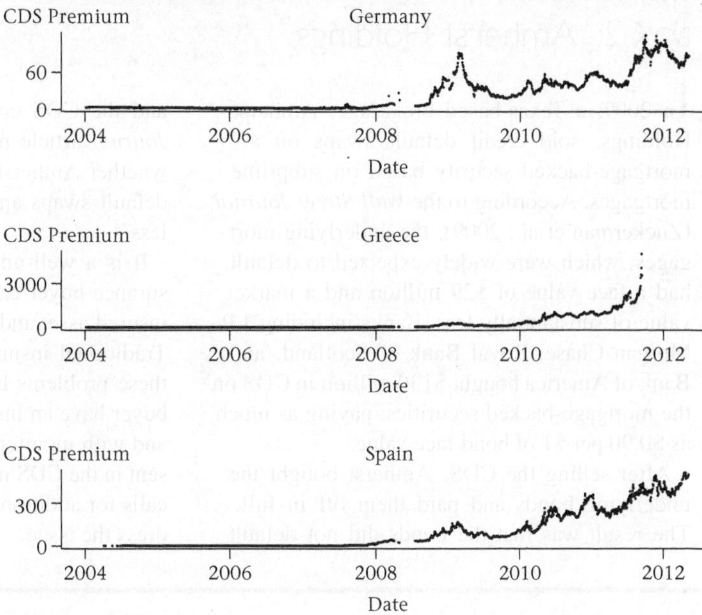

Source: Bloomberg.

coupons instead of being floating rate, and transaction costs (such as costs of short-selling). Duffie (1999) discusses the effects of many such complications.

A different set of issues is created by the possibility that a party to a CDS contract may be able to affect the value of the bonds, and thus affect the value of the CDS contract.

An important question implicitly raised by this discussion is the definition of an "otherwise equivalent default-free bond." It seems natural to use government bonds as a benchmark, but government bonds are unique in certain respects. Prices of government bonds include a liquidity premium and sometimes reflect special tax attributes (for example, in the United States, federal government bonds are exempt from state taxes). At the same time, yields on non-governmental bonds will reflect default risk.[12] Thus, the yield on an "equivalent default-free bond" is unlikely to be the government yield curve, and in fact may not be directly observable.

---

spreads. Given these prices, it would have been profitable to borrow at LIBOR, buy a bond, and buy the CDS. They attribute the mispricing to various market dislocations during the crisis.

12. Because of this issue, Blanco et al. (2005), when comparing bond yields to CDS quotes, compute the credit spread using both government bond yields and swap rates. Houweling and Vorst (2001) estimate a credit swap pricing model and find that, empirically, credit swap premiums are more related to the interest rate swap curve than to the government bond yield curve.

BOX 2: Amherst Holdings

In 2009, a Texas-based brokerage, Amherst Holdings, sold credit default swaps on a mortgage-backed security based on subprime mortgages. According to the *Wall Street Journal* (Zuckerman et al., 2009), the underlying mortgages, which were widely expected to default, had a face value of \$29 million and a market value of substantially less. Banks including J.P. Morgan Chase, Royal Bank of Scotland, and Bank of America bought \$130 million in CDS on the mortgage-backed securities, paying as much as \$0.90 per \$1 of bond face value.

After selling the CDS, Amherst bought the underlying bonds and paid them off in full. The result was that the bonds did not default and the CDS contracts were worthless. The *Journal* article noted, "Banks are questioning whether Amherst set them up by selling credit-default swaps and then rendering them worthless."

It is a well-understood problem that an insurance buyer cares less about the value of the insured asset and an insurance seller cares more. Traditional insurance contracts can deal with these problems by requiring that the insurance buyer have an insured interest, with deductibles, and with monitoring. These mechanisms are absent in the CDS market, although there have been calls for additional government regulation to address the issue.

CDS Indices

A CDS index is an average of the premiums on a set of individual CDSs. Thus, a CDS index provides a way to track credit for a market segment. The leading credit indices are the CDX indices for North American and emerging markets and iTraxx indices in the rest of the world. Leading CDX indices include the CDX.NA.IG (North American investment grade, equally weighted basket of 125 names), CDX.NA.HY (high yield, 100 names), CDX.NA.IG.HVOL (high volatility investment grade, 30 names), and CDX.EM (emerging markets, approximately 14 names). Leading iTraxx indices include iTraxx Europe (125 names), iTraxx Europe HiVol (30 names), and various sector indices. There are also credit indices for North America, Europe, Asia, Japan, and Australia (see Markit, 2008).[13]

Different contracts trade with different standard maturities. Most contracts are issued every 6 months. The CDX.NA.IG has standard maturities of 1, 2, 3, 5, 7, and 10 years.[14] The most recent 5 and 10-year contracts are the most heavily traded. The constituent firms can vary over time. Over the life of a contract, firms will drop out of an index due to bankruptcy or illiquidity, but otherwise the make-up of a given offering is set for the life of the offering. When a credit event occurs, the contract is reset with one fewer firm and a proportionally reduced notional principal.

13. See Duffie and Yurday (2004a) for an interesting account of the development of credit index products.

14. New contracts are issued every March and September, with expiration in June and December an appropriate number of years later. The actual maturity of 5.25 years gives a 5-year contract, for example, an average maturity of 5 years during the 6-month period when it is the on-the-run (i.e., the most recently issued) contract.

FIGURE 4

The structure of tranched CDX.NA.IG.

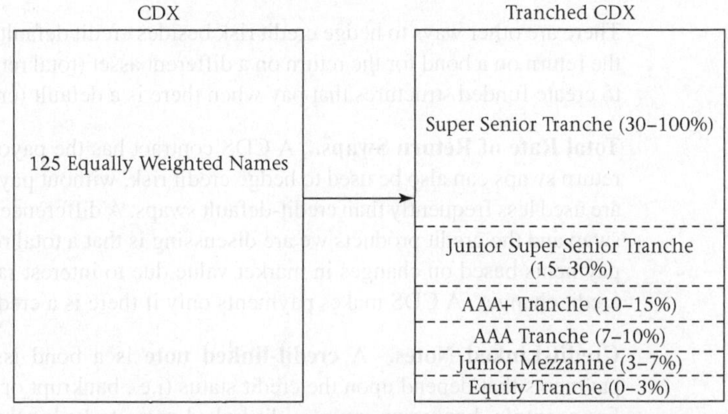

Source: Markit (2008).

The nomenclature for CDS indices specifies the issue date. For example, the CDX.NA.IG.9 was first traded on September 21, 2007, maturing on December 20, 2017.[15] The IG.10 contract was first traded in March 2008, and so forth.

To a first approximation, it is possible to replicate a CDS index by holding a pool of CDSs.[16] As with a single CDS, one party is a protection seller, receiving premium payments, and the other is a protection buyer, making the payments but receiving a payment from the seller if there is a credit event.

Variants of standard CDS indices trade:

- A CDS index can be funded or unfunded. The unfunded version is like a credit default swap, except that the underlying asset is a basket of firms. The funded index is a note linked to the index with a collateral arrangement in case the note buyer had to make a payment.
- The index contracts also trade based on tranches. We will discuss tranching and CDOs further in Section 5.
- The underlying assets can represent different countries, currencies, maturities, or industries.

Tranched investment grade CDX has a payoff structure illustrated in Figure 4. Products based on this structure can be either funded or unfunded. We discuss tranched structure below, and we will see that the pricing of the various tranches is sensitive to correlation. In fact, tranche pricing can be quoted using implied correlation in much the same way equity option premiums are quoted using implied volatility.

15. This is the CDS index contract made famous by J.P. Morgan Chase's hedging loss in early 2012 (Eavis and Craig, 2012).

16. The replication may not be exact, since a default index can define a credit event differently than a single-name CDS.

Other Credit-Linked Structures

There are other ways to hedge credit risk besides credit default swaps. It is possible to swap the return on a bond for the return on a different asset (total return swaps), and it is possible to create funded structures that pay when there is a default (credit-linked notes).

Total Rate of Return Swaps. A CDS contract has the payoff of an option. Total rate of return swaps can also be used to hedge credit risk, without paying a premium. These swaps are used less frequently than credit-default swaps. A difference between a total rate of return swap and the credit products we are discussing is that a total return swap for a bond makes payments based on changes in market value due to interest rate changes as well as due to credit changes. A CDS makes payments only if there is a credit event.

Credit-Linked Notes. A **credit-linked note** is a bond issued by one company with payments that depend upon the credit status (i.e., bankrupt or not) of a different company. For example, banks can issue credit-linked notes to hedge the credit risk of loans. To see how a credit-linked note works, suppose that bank ABC lends money to company XYZ. At the time of the loan, ABC creates a trust that issues notes: These are the credit-linked notes. The funds raised by the issuance of these notes are invested in bonds with a low probability of default (such as government bonds), which are held in the trust. If XYZ remains solvent, ABC is obligated to pay the notes in full. If XYZ goes bankrupt, the note-holders receive the XYZ loans and become creditors of XYZ. ABC takes possession of the securities in the trust. Thus, the credit-linked note is in effect a bond issued by ABC, which ABC does not need to repay in full if XYZ goes bankrupt. This structure eliminates a third-party insurance provider. Credit-linked notes can be rated and exchange-traded.

Because of the trust, the credit-linked notes can be paid in full even if ABC defaults. Thus, even though they are issued by ABC, the interest rate on the notes is determined by the credit risk of XYZ. An arrangement like this was used by Citigroup when it made loans to Enron in 2000 and 2001.[17] When Enron went bankrupt in late 2001, Citigroup avoided losses on over $1 billion in loans because it had hedged the loans by issuing credit-linked notes. (Citigroup was later sued over this transaction because it allegedly helped Enron misstate earnings.)

Credit Guarantees. If party A guarantees party B against default on a debt obligation, party A is said to have issued a *credit guarantee*. A credit guarantee is a put option on an obligation, with the option payable on a default or other credit event. Thus, a credit guarantee is effectively like a CDS. One consequence of the financial crisis is that the federal government in the United States has become a major provider of credit guarantees. Some of these are described in the box on the next page.

5. TRANCHED STRUCTURES

Financial institutions acquire assets that are difficult to resell individually, examples of which are auto loans, credit card receivables, home equity loans, and mortgages. A process called **securitization** provides a mechanism for reselling such assets by pooling together many of them and creating securities based on the pool. An **asset-backed security** (ABS)

17. See Daniel Altman, "How Citigroup Hedged Bets on Enron," *New York Times*, February 8, 2002, p. C1.

BOX 3: Government Credit Guarantees

The U.S. government is a major supplier of credit guarantees in a variety of financial activities. Some of the guarantees are front-page news: Federal debt guarantees for Chrysler in the 1980s and US Airways in 2002 are well-known examples. However, there are also a host of governmental and quasi-governmental insurance programs that many take for granted. Here is a partial list:

- The Federal Deposit Insurance Corporation (FDIC) guarantees bank deposits against default of the bank.
- The Pension Benefit Guarantee Corporation (PBGC) guarantees defined benefit pensioners against the failure of the firm to honor its pension obligations.
- The Federal National Mortgage Association (Fannie Mae) and the Federal Home Loan and Mortgage Corporation (Freddie Mac) buy mortgages that meet certain characteristics and resell them with a government-supported guarantee against default by the borrower.
- The federal government assumes the credit risk for most student loans.

As a result of the financial crisis, the United States government significantly increased its explicit exposure to credit risk, with Fannie Mae and Freddie Mac providing the most prominent example.* In 2010, traditional government debt outstanding was about \$13.5 trillion. In addition, direct loans and guarantees were about \$2.3 trillion, debt of Fannie Mae and Freddie Mac was about \$5 trillion, the FDIC insured about \$5.8 trillion in deposits, and the PBGC insured funds with liabilities in the vicinity of \$2.8 trillion (a 2007 estimate) (Lucas, 2011).

All told, the government has about 160 programs providing direct loans and loan guarantees (Office of Management and Budget, 2012). The accounting for these various programs is complex (Lucas, 2010), and it seems unlikely that government decision makers are fully aware of their true costs. Lucas and McDonald (2006, 2010) show, in the context of Fannie Mae and Freddie Mac, how a Merton approach could be used to provide estimates of the cost.

*To be precise, the government guarantees that Fannie Mae and Freddie Mac will have positive net worth, and thus remain able to meet their debt obligations (Jickling, 2008).

is a specific kind of structure used in securitizations. The regulatory definition of an ABS states in part that an ABS is "a security that is primarily serviced by the cash flows of a discrete pool of receivables or other financial assets, either fixed or revolving, that by their terms convert into cash within a finite time period."[18] In practice, the term "mortgage-backed security" (MBS) is used to refer to securitized mortgages, while ABS is used to refer to other kinds of securitized assets. The term **structured finance** is used generally to refer to the creation of new claims from existing assets. The box on the next page discusses the role of structured finance in the financial crisis.

When an asset pool is securitized, the cash flows can be passed directly through to investors, in which case the structure is a *pass-through*. An alternative is to reapportion the returns on the asset pool in such a way that different claims to the asset pool have differing priorities with respect to the cash flows. Such a structure is said to be *tranched*. Many

18. See 17 C.F.R. §229.1101(c)(1).

BOX 4: Structured Finance and the Financial Crisis

At the end of 1995, there was $257 billion of ABSs and $2.35 trillion of mortgage-related securities outstanding. ABSs and mortgage-related debt constituted about 23% of total outstanding debt in the United States (see sifma.org for data). By the end of 2007, there was $2.95 trillion of ABS and $8.16 trillion of mortgage-related debt, with the two categories constituting 34.6% of outstanding debt. This relative growth of structured products was fueled by the real estate boom and facilitated by credit rating agencies giving high ratings to new structured products.

The end result was that ABS and mortgage-related debt played a central role in the financial crisis. Many of the structured offerings were held by financial institutions: Benmelech and Dlugosz (2010) show that as of October 2008, financial institutions worldwide had reported $218 billion of writedowns related to ABS CDOs, with another $300 billion related to other products, including residential mortgage-backed securities.

These writedowns and losses were reflected in credit downgrades of these products. During the crisis there were significant downgrades of triple-A rated ABSs, CDOs, and similar products. Benmelech and Dlugosz (2010) find that between 1983 and 2008, 19% of products suffering a ratings downgrade of eight notches or more had originally had a rating of Aaa. (A downgrade from Aaa to Aa3, for example, would be three notches, bypassing Aa1 and Aa2.) Most such downgrades occurred in 2007 and 2008. The failure of so many highly rated structures led to widespread criticism of the credit rating agencies, and also to the new Dodd-Frank rules pertaining to credit rating agencies.

securitized structures have some degree of tranching. Our focus in this section will be on the effect of tranching.

Collateralized Debt Obligations

A **collateralized debt obligation** (CDO) is a financial structure that repackages the cash flows from a set of assets. You create a CDO by acquiring an asset pool and issuing tranched financial claims to finance the pool. The tranching makes it possible to take a pool of low-rated assets and create some tranches that are highly rated. Of course, the total risk of the pool is preserved, so other tranches will have low ratings. It is common for ABSs to be tranched, but for consistency we will refer to any tranched claim as a CDO.[19]

Given this general description, there are many different ways a CDO can be structured. First, the asset pool can be a fixed set of assets, in which case the CDO is *static*. If instead a

19. The terminology surrounding ABSs and CDOs can be confusing. When a group of home mortgages is pooled, the result is a residential mortgage-backed security (RMBS). Suppose the RMBS is tranched. If specific tranches of the RMBS are further pooled (for example, BBB tranches from multiple RMBSs are combined), and then tranched again, the result is an asset-backed security collateralized debt obligation, or ABS CDO. Finally, if tranches of the ABS CDO are again pooled and tranched, the result is a CDO squared, the returns of which are based on three layers of tranching. For a detailed description of securitization practices prior to the financial crisis, see Gorton (2010), especially Chapters 3 and 4. Gorton's Figure 3.8 illustrates a triply tranched transaction.

FIGURE 5

Structure of a CDO.

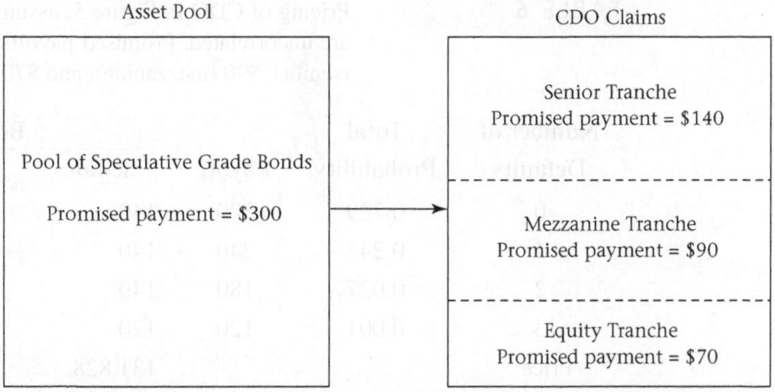

manager buys and sells assets during the life of the CDO, it is *managed*. Second, the CDO claims can directly receive the cash flows generated by the pool assets; this is a *cash flow* CDO. Alternatively, the CDO claims can receive payments based on cash flows and the gain or loss from asset sales; this is a *market value* CDO. Finally, a CDO can be created using credit default swaps or other unfunded claims; this is called a *synthetic* CDO.

There are at least two reasons for creating CDOs. First, financial institutions will sometimes want to securitize assets, effectively removing them from the institution's balance sheet by selling them to other investors.[20] A CDO can be used to accomplish this, in which case it is a *balance sheet CDO*. Second, a CDO can be created in response to institutional frictions. For example, some investors are permitted to hold only investment-grade bonds. As we will see below, CDOs can potentially be used to create investment-grade bonds from a pool of non-investment-grade bonds. This is called an *arbitrage CDO*.

A CDO with Independent Defaults. We will illustrate CDOs with a simple example. Suppose that there are three risky, speculative-grade bonds that each promise to pay $100 in 1 year. Defaults, which occur with a risk-neutral probability of 10%, are independent, and occur only at maturity of the bond. Each bond has a 40% recovery rate, and the risk-free rate is 6%. Using equation (2), the price of each bond is

$$e^{-0.06}\left[(1-0.1)\times \$100 + 0.1\times \$40\right] = \$88.526$$

The yield on each bond is $\ln(100/88.526) = 0.1219$.

Now suppose that among investors wishing to invest in bonds, some are happy to hold a speculative-grade bond, while others seek safer bonds. We can accommodate the different kinds of investors by creating a CDO to rearrange the cash flows from a pool of bonds. The structure of the CDO is illustrated in Figure 5. The total promised payoff on the three bonds is $300; the CDO apportions this payoff among three tranches of unequal size. The senior

20. There can be ambiguity about whether a transaction has actually removed an asset from a bank's balance sheet. See Acharya et al. (2012) for a discussion of such transactions in the context of the asset-backed commercial paper market during 2004–2007.

TABLE 6 Pricing of CDO in Figure 5, assuming that bond defaults are uncorrelated. Promised payoffs to the bonds are \$140 (senior), \$90 (mezzanine), and \$70 (equity).

Number of Defaults	Total Probability	Payoff	Bond Payoff Senior	Mezzanine	Equity
0	0.729	300	140	90	70
1	0.243	240	140	90	10
2	0.027	180	140	40	0
3	0.001	120	120	0	0
Price			131.828	83.403	50.347
Yield			6.010%	7.61%	32.96%
Default probability			0.0010	0.0280	0.2710
Average recovery rate			85.71%	42.86%	12.81%

tranche (\$140) receives first claim to the bond payments, the mezzanine tranche (\$90) has the next claim, and the equity tranche (\$70) receives whatever is left. For the bond that is ith in line, with a promised payment of $\bar{B}_i$, the payoff is

$$\text{Bond } i \text{ maturity payoff} = \min\left[\max\left(A_T - \sum_{j=1}^{i-1} \bar{B}_j, 0\right), \bar{B}_i\right] \tag{16}$$

where A_T is the maturity value of the asset pool.

To understand the pricing of the CDO claims, recognize that there are four possible outcomes: no defaults ($0.90^3 = 72.9\%$ probability), one bond defaults ($3 \times 0.90^2 \times 0.10 = 24.3\%$ probability), two bonds default ($3 \times 0.90 \times 0.10^2 = 2.71\%$ probability), and three bonds default ($0.10^3 = 0.1\%$ probability). To compute the price of a CDO tranche, we can compute the expected payoff of the tranche using the risk-neutral default probabilities.

The CDO pricing is illustrated in Table 6. Note that the senior tranche is almost risk-free. The only time the senior tranche is not fully paid is in the unlikely (0.1% probability) event that all three bonds default. In that case, the senior tranche receives \$120, a recovery rate of 85.7%. Since it is almost paid in full, investors will pay \$131.828 for the senior tranche, which is a yield of 6.02%.

The mezzanine tranche is fully paid if there is one default, but it is not fully paid if there are two or three defaults. The yield is 7.61% and the average recovery rate is $40/90 \times 0.027/0.028 = 0.4285$. Finally, the equity tranche receives less than full payment if there are any defaults. Consequently, it is priced to yield 32.96%. Note that the sum of the prices of the three tranches is \$265.58. As you would expect, this is the same as the price of the three bonds put into the asset pool.

A CDO with Correlated Defaults. In the preceding example we assumed that the bonds were uncorrelated. This is an important assumption. To illustrate the effects of correlation,

TABLE 7 Pricing of CDO in Figure 5, assuming that bond defaults are perfectly correlated. Promised payoffs to the bonds are $140 (senior), $90 (mezzanine), and $70 (equity).

Number of Defaults	Total Probability	Payoff	Bond Payoff Senior	Bond Payoff Mezzanine	Bond Payoff Equity
0	0.9	300	140	90	70
1	0	240	140	90	10
2	0	180	140	40	0
3	0.1	120	120	0	0
Price			129.963	76.283	59.331
Yield			7.4%	16.5%	16.5%
Default probability			0.1	0.1	0.1
Average recovery rate			85.71%	0	0

Table 7 shows how the CDO tranches are priced if the bonds are perfectly correlated—i.e., if at maturity, either all firms default or none do. A comparison of Tables 6 and 7 shows the importance of default correlation in the pricing of CDOs.

Given the structure of the CDO and the assumptions about the recovery rate, with perfect correlation of defaults, the mezzanine and equity tranches have the same yield. The senior tranche becomes riskier because the probability of three defaults—the only circumstance in which the senior tranche is not fully paid—is greater.

Suppose you had created a CDO where the tranches were priced and issued assuming zero correlation among the underlying assets, and then the market price of the tranches reflected an increase in correlations. You can see the effect by comparing the prices in Table 6 with that in Table 7. The senior and mezzanine tranches lose value, while the equity tranche increases in value. This is essentially what happened to many real estate–based CDOs during the period from 2006 to 2008, as it became apparent that the decline in real estate prices would be widespread rather than isolated to particular markets. Perceived correlations had increased.

Synthetic CDOs. A standard ABS or CDO is constructed by placing assets within a legal structure such as a trust or special purpose vehicle, which is funded by issuing tranched securities. If you own a tranche, you have a funded position. If you borrow to buy the tranche, you have a leveraged position in the tranche, which is equivalent to an unfunded position.

It is also possible to create a derivative that has the same payoff as an unfunded tranche position. This is called a **synthetic CDO**. Figure 4 illustrates tranched CDX, which is an example of a synthetic CDO. The holder of tranched CDX has a return depending upon the default experience of the names in the index, just as with a CDO.

The advantage of a synthetic CDO is that it is not necessary to create a physical position in assets. A disadvantage is that a synthetic position may have additional credit risk.

CDO-Squareds

A **CDO-squared** is a CDO comprised of CDOs.[21] Such a structure pools claims from the risky tranches of multiple CDOs and thereby creates a new CDO, the senior tranche of which can again (under certain assumptions) be highly rated.

A primary purpose of creating a CDO-squared is to transform low-rated bonds (e.g., mezzanine bonds) into highly rated bonds through pooling and tranching. Intuitively, this can only work if the risks in the different mezzanine bonds can be diversified by pooling. Moreover, if the CDO-squared is constructed under the belief that diversification is possible, and correlations then increase, you would expect the CDO-squared to suffer significant losses in all tranches, but primarily in the tranche that benefitted the most from diversification—namely, the senior tranche. (As a point of comparison, you can see from Tables 6 and 7 that the mezzanine tranche in the parent CDO is most harmed by an increase in correlation. The equity tranche benefits.) The box on the next page discusses several famous transactions in which CDOs were created from tranched securities.

We will examine the workings of a CDO-squared by building on the example in Table 6. We will see that the CDO-squared is more sensitive to a change in the assumed correlation than is the original CDO.

Suppose there are multiple CDOs consisting of three bonds, each with three tranches, as in Table 6. Consider creating a new CDO consisting of three mezzanine bonds, one from each of three CDOs. This structure is illustrated in Figure 6. For this new CDO, the par value of the three mezzanine bonds is \$270, so we will issue senior, mezzanine, and equity tranches with par values of \$150, \$80, and \$40.

In Table 6, each of the existing mezzanine bonds has *three* possible payoffs: a full payoff of \$90 (if the number of defaults in the originating CDO is zero or one), a partial payoff of \$40 (if there are two defaults), and a payoff of zero (if there are three defaults). Thus, for the new CDO each of the three bonds can make one of three payments, so there are 27 possible payoff states with 10 distinct asset values at maturity.

Table 8 presents the payoffs and associated probabilities for the CDO-squared. To understand the table, consider the second row, in which two of the three underlying mezzanine bonds pay in full, while one defaults. From Table 6, the total probability of exactly one full default is the probability of two full payments (which happens with zero or one default in the underlying CDO) times the probability of one zero payment (which happens with three defaults in the underlying CDO), and there are three ways this can happen. Thus, we have $(0.729 + 0.243)^2 \times 0.001 \times 3 = 0.00283$ as the probability in the second row. The payment in this case is \$180, which is apportioned across the three tranches using strict priority. Because there are 10 distinct outcomes, Table 8 is more complex than Table 6, but the logic is the same.

Table 9 presents the analysis for the case when the default correlation for the original bonds is 1 instead of 0. In this case, either no bonds default or all bonds default. With the original CDO, we saw in Table 7 that an increase in correlation harms the senior and mezzanine tranches, and increases the value of the equity tranche. The values of the underlying bonds do not change and the market value of the entire CDO does not change.

---

21. To be clear about terminology, the CDO-squared in the following example is doubly-tranched. In practice, the products called CDO-squareds are often triply tranched; see footnote 19.

BOX 5: Abacus and Magnetar

Publicly available data is scarce for the CDO and ABS markets. The transactions are complicated and difficult to document, but anecdotes have come to light as a result of regulatory action and investigative reporting. Two notable cases both hinge on the question of whether the party selecting assets for a CDO was simultaneously betting against it.

In 2010 the SEC brought a complaint against Goldman Sachs for a CDO named Abacus (U.S. Securities and Exchange Commission, 2010). According to the complaint, hedge fund manager John Paulson, who wished to bet against particular BBB-rated RMBS tranches, was permitted to help pick the specific securities that went into the deal. Abacus was structured as a synthetic CDO, so the investors in Abacus effectively sold a credit default swap with Paulson as counterparty. The transaction amounted to a bet between the two parties about the return on the assets. Paulson eventually earned $1 billion. Goldman ultimately settled the case, paying $550 million to the SEC. The Goldman employee in charge of Abacus was Fabrice Tourre, who was famously quoted in the SEC complaint: "More and more leverage in the system[. . .] The whole building is about to collapse anytime now . . . Only potential survivor, the fabulous Fab[rice Tourre] . . . standing in the middle of all these complex, highly leveraged, exotic trades he created without necessarily understanding all of the implications of those monstruosities[sic]!!!"

Eisinger and Bernstein (2010) reported extensively on the actions of a hedge fund named Magnetar, which profited during the crisis by again betting against CDOs. According to the articles, one twist is that Magnetar bought the equity tranches of CDOs, which facilitated their creation, and then bet against more senior tranches using credit default swaps. One CDO that Magnetar supposedly helped create was titled "Squared," as it consisted of tranches of other CDOs in which Magnetar had been involved. In a further twist, Magnetar in 2007 bundled its *equity* CDO positions and sold these as a new CDO, Tigris. Both Standard and Poor's and Fitch gave portions of Tigris a triple-A rating, but Moody's refused to rate it. Magnetar reportedly sold its interest for $450 million. Less than a year later, the CDO defaulted. Magnetar's activities came to light because of *Pro Publica's* reporting, but in May 2012, the *Wall Street Journal* reported that the SEC was investigating Magnetar (Eaglesham, 2012). The *Journal* reported that the SEC was investigating the same issue that arose with Abacus: Did Magnetar have inappropriate influence in selecting assets in certain CDOs?

With the CDO-squared, when correlation increases the value of the underlying mezzanine bonds declines, so the entire CDO is worth less. In addition, while all tranches decline in value—all are priced to yield 16.53%—the equity tranche has the lowest percentage decline. Thus, the CDO-squared has different sensitivity to correlation than does the original CDO.

Many CDOs are constructed from ABS and MBS bonds that are tranched, so in practice these CDOs resemble the CDO-squared in this example. Given this, it is no surprise that investors holding senior CDO tranches during the financial crisis suffered significant losses as housing prices fell nationwide.

FIGURE 6

Structure of a CDO-squared, created by pooling and tranching mezzanine bonds from CDOs A, B, and C.

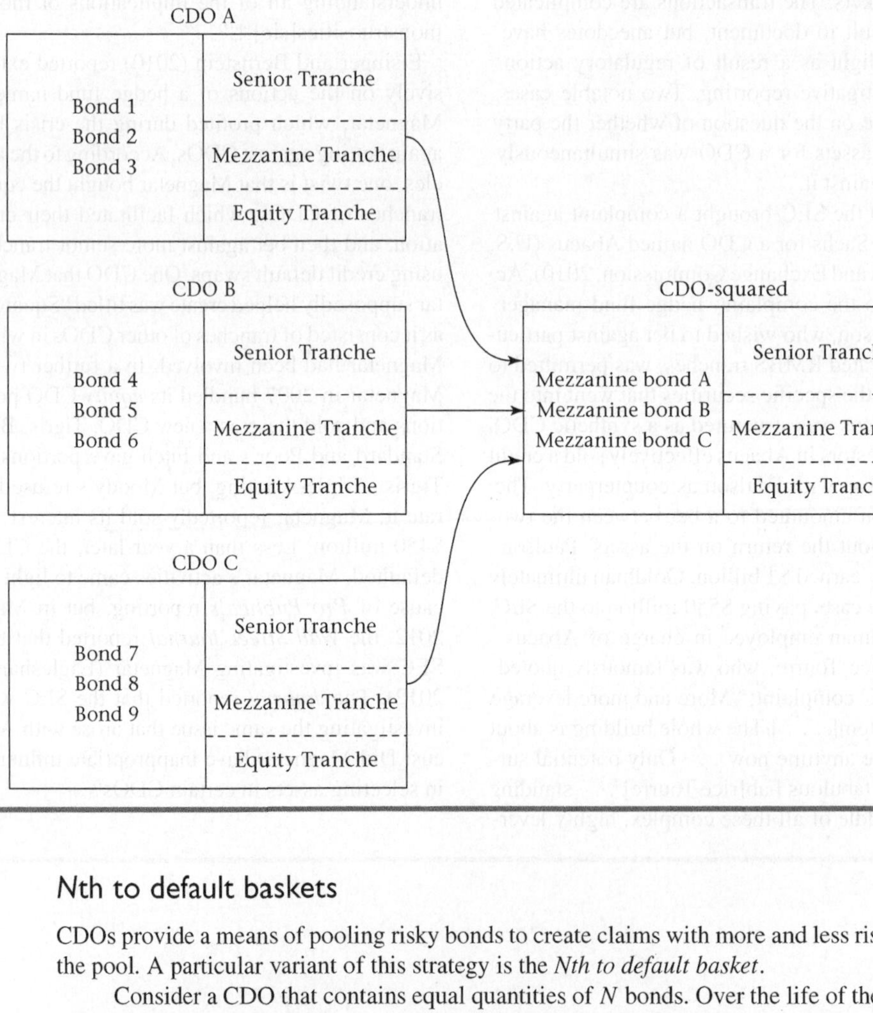

Nth to default baskets

CDOs provide a means of pooling risky bonds to create claims with more and less risk than the pool. A particular variant of this strategy is the *Nth to default basket*.

Consider a CDO that contains equal quantities of N bonds. Over the life of the CDO there can be anywhere between 0 and N defaults. It is possible to create tranches where particular bondholders bear the consequences of a particular default.

The owner of the first-to-default tranche bears the most risk: If any of the bonds in the asset pool default, the first-to-default owner bears the loss from this default. The owner of the last-to-default generally bears the least risk, since all bonds must default in order for this claim to bear a loss.

Table 10 shows the pricing that results from this structure, assuming that the defaults are uncorrelated and occur only at time T. By comparing Table 10 with Table 6, you can observe a similarity between the equity tranche and the first-to-default on the one hand, and on the other, the senior tranche and the third-to-default.

TABLE 8 Possible payoffs for a CDO constructed from mezzanine CDOs from Table 6, assuming that defaults on the underlying asset are uncorrelated. The count column is the number of events corresponding to the configuration of defaults, and the probability column is the total probability of this payoff.

Mezzanine Bond Payoff						Tranche		
$90	$40	$0	Count	Assets	Probability	Senior	Mezzanine	Equity
3	0	0	1	270	0.91833	150	80	40
2	0	1	3	180	0.00283	150	30	0
1	0	2	3	90	0.00000	90	0	0
0	0	3	1	0	0.00000	0	0	0
2	1	0	3	220	0.07653	150	70	0
1	1	1	6	130	0.00016	130	0	0
0	1	2	3	40	0.00000	40	0	0
1	2	0	3	170	0.00213	150	20	0
0	2	1	3	80	0.00000	80	0	0
0	3	0	1	120	0.00002	120	0	0
Price						141.26	74.35	34.59
Yield						6.003%	7.320%	14.520%
Default probability						0.0002	0.0817	0.0817
Average recovery rate						85.09%	83.94%	0

Figure 7 illustrates the pricing of *N*th to default bonds for a 10-bond pool assuming default correlations of 0, 0.25, and 1.[22] Again, we assume defaults occur only at time T. The result for a default correlation of 1 is like that in Table 11: When one bond defaults, all bonds default, so all claims have the same yield. The graphs for correlations of 0 and 0.25 show

22. How do we generate a default correlation of 0.25 among 10 bonds? We can generate 10 independent normally distributed random variables and create correlated normal random variables, z_i, using the Cholesky decomposition (equation 18). Following this procedure, each *pairwise* correlation is 0.25. Assuming a 10% unconditional default probability, a firm defaults if $z_i < -1.2816$. Note that once we use this method, we can also let z_i determine *when in time* the default occurs; we simply interpret a smaller z_i to mean that default occurs earlier. It is then necessary to specify a distribution for default times. For example, suppose default occurs with a constant Poisson intensity. Then the time to default is exponentially distributed, so that

$$\Pr(\text{default} < t) = 1 - e^{-ht}$$

Given this assumption, the default time is then $\tau = -\ln[N(z_i)]/h$. See Duffie and Yurday (2004b), Li (1999), and Watkinson and Roosevelt (2004) for a discussion of pricing credit tranches with default correlations modeled in this fashion.

TABLE 9 Possible payoffs for a CDO constructed from mezzanine CDOs from Table 7, assuming that defaults on the underlying asset are perfectly correlated. Column headings have the same meaning as in Table 8.

Mezzanine Bond Payoff						Tranche		
$90	$40	$0	Count	Assets	Probability	Senior	Mezzanine	Equity
3	0	0	1	270	0.90	150	80	40
0	0	3	1	0	0.10	0	0	0
Price						127.14	67.81	33.90
Yield						16.53%	16.53%	16.53%
Default probability						0.10	0.10	0.10
Average recovery rate						0	0	0

TABLE 10 Pricing of *N*th to default bonds. Assumes the bonds owned as assets have uncorrelated defaults.

Default	Probability	Probability N or More	Payoffs Default	Payoffs No Default	Expected Payoff	Price	Yield
First	0.243	0.271	40	100	83.74	78.863	0.237
Second	0.027	0.028	40	100	98.32	92.594	0.077
Third	0.001	0.001	40	100	99.94	94.120	0.061

significant differences for yields for low numbers of defaults. The first-to-default tranche, for example, has a yield of 16.02% when defaults are uncorrelated and 13.51% when the default correlation is 0.25. This again illustrates that *N*th to default baskets are a way to speculate on default correlations.

CHAPTER SUMMARY

A party to a contract may fail to make a required future payment. The possibility of this event, which is called default, gives rise to credit risk. Credit risk is an important consideration in valuing corporate bonds, where two key inputs are the probability of default and the expected payoff to the bond if the firm does default. The Merton model uses option pricing to value debt subject to default. Some credit rating firms are designated by the SEC as Nationally Recognized Statistical Ratings Organizations (NRSROs). Credit agencies assign

FIGURE 7

Pricing of an *N*th to default basket containing equal quantities of 10 bonds, each with a 10% probability of default.

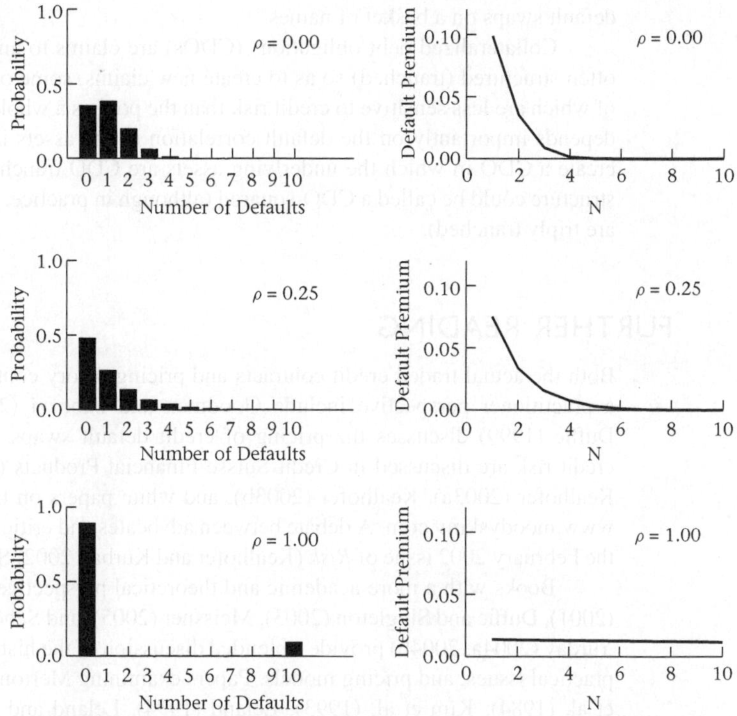

TABLE 11 Pricing of *N*th to default bonds. Assumes the bonds owned as assets have perfectly correlated defaults.

Default	Probability	Probability N or More	Payoffs Default	Payoffs No Default	Expected Payoff	Price	Yield
First	0.100	0.100	40	100	94.000	88.526	0.122
Second	0.100	0.100	40	100	94.000	88.526	0.122
Third	0.100	0.100	40	100	94.000	88.526	0.122

debt ratings to firms; these are designed to measure the probability of bankruptcy in the future.

There are various financial vehicles that permit the trading of credit risk. A single-name credit default swap pays to the protection buyer the loss on a corporate or government bond when there is a credit event. In exchange, the protection buyer makes a periodic premium payment to the seller. There are also credit default swap indices, which are credit default swaps on a basket of names.

Collateralized debt obligations (CDOs) are claims to an asset pool. The claims are often structured (tranched) so as to create new claims, some of which are more and some of which are less sensitive to credit risk than the pool as a whole. The value of these claims depends importantly on the default correlation of the assets in the pool. It is possible to create a CDO in which the underlying assets are CDO tranches. Such a doubly tranched structure could be called a CDO-squared (although in practice, claims called CDO-squared are triply tranched).

FURTHER READING

Both the actual traded credit contracts and pricing theory continue to evolve. Books with a practitioner perspective include Goodman and Fabozzi (2002) and Tavakoli (2001). Duffie (1999) discusses the pricing of credit default swaps. Frameworks for analyzing credit risk are discussed in Credit Suisse Financial Products (1997), J.P. Morgan (1997), Kealhofer (2003a), Kealhofer (2003b), and white papers on the Moody's KMV website, www.moodyskmv.com. A debate between advocates and critics of the KMV approach is in the February 2002 issue of *Risk* (Kealhofer and Kurbat, 2002; Sobehart and Keenan, 2002).

Books with a more academic and theoretical perspective include Cossin and Pirotte (2001), Duffie and Singleton (2003), Meissner (2005), and Schönbucher (2003). Duffie and Yurday (2004a, 2004b) provide a blended discussion of the history of some of the products, practical issues, and pricing models. Papers examining Merton-style models include Jones et al. (1984), Kim et al. (1993), Leland (1994), Leland and Toft (1996), and Longstaff and Schwartz (1995). Empirical studies of Merton-style models include Anderson and Sundaresan (2000), Bharath and Shumway (2004), and Eom et al. (2004). Shumway (2001) estimates hazard models of bankruptcy. Johnson and Stulz (1987), Hull and White (1995), and Klein (1996) consider how it affects prices of derivatives.

Gorton (2010) provides a valuable, detailed look at the functioning of the banking system before and during the crisis, including a look at structured products. Benmelech and Dlugosz (2010) and Benmelech and Dlugosz (2009) examine CDOs.

PROBLEMS

For the first eight problems, assume that a firm has assets of \$100, with $\sigma = 40\%$, $\alpha = 15\%$, and $\delta = 0$. The risk-free rate is 8%.

1. The firm has a single outstanding debt issue with a promised maturity payment of \$120 in 5 years. What is the probability of bankruptcy? What is the credit spread?

2. Suppose the firm issues a single zero-coupon bond with maturity value \$100.

   a. Compute the yield, probability of default, and expected loss given default for times to maturity of 1, 2, 3, 4, 5, 10, and 20 years.

   b. For each time to maturity compute the approximation for the yield:

$$\rho = r + \frac{1}{T} \times \text{Pr(default)} \times \text{Expected loss given default}$$

How accurate is the approximation?

3. Suppose the firm issues a single zero-coupon bond with time to maturity 3 years and maturity value $110.

a. Compute the price, yield to maturity, default probability, and expected recovery (E[B_T|Default]).

b. Verify that equation (5) holds.

4. Suppose the firm issues a single zero-coupon bond.

a. Suppose the maturity value of the bond is $80. Compute the yield and default probability for times to maturity of 1, 2, 3, 4, 5, 10, and 20 years.

b. Repeat part (a), only supposing the maturity value is $120.

c. Does default probability increase or decrease with debt maturity? Explain.

5. Repeat the previous problem, only compute the expected recovery value instead of the default probability. How does the expected recovery value change as time to maturity changes?

6. Suppose that there is a 3% per year chance that the firm's asset value can jump to zero. Assume that the firm issues 5-year zero-coupon debt with a promised payment of $110. Using the Merton jump model, compute the debt price and yield, and compare to the results you obtain when the jump probability is zero.

7. Suppose the firm has a single outstanding debt issue with a promised maturity payment of $120 in 5 years. Assume that bankruptcy is triggered by assets (which are observable) falling below $40 in value at any time over the life of the bond—in which case the bondholder receives $40 at that time—or by assets being worth less than $120 at maturity, in which case the bondholder receives the asset value. What is the probability of bankruptcy over the life of the bond? What is the credit spread?

8. Repeat the previous problem, except that the time to maturity can be 1, 2, 3, 4, 5, 10, or 20 years. How does the bond yield change with time to maturity?

For the next two problems, use this information on credit ratings. Suppose there are three credit ratings, F (first-rate), FF (future failure?), and FFF (fading, forlorn, and forsaken). The transition matrix between ratings looks like this:

	Rating to:		
Rating from:	**F**	**FF**	**FFF**
F	0.9	0.07	0.03
FF	0.15	0.80	0.05
FFF	0.10	0.30	0.6

9. Consider a firm with an F rating.

a. What is the probability that after 4 years it will still have an F rating?

b. What is the probability that after 4 years it will have an FF or FFF rating?

c. From examining the transition matrix, are firms tending over time to become rated more or less highly? Why?

10. Consider two firms, one with an FF rating and one with an FFF rating. What is the probability that after 4 years each will have retained its rating? What is the probability that each will have moved to one of the other two ratings?

11. Suppose that in Figure 6 the tranches have promised payments of \$160 (senior), \$50 (mezzanine), and \$90 (subordinated). Reproduce the table for this case, assuming zero default correlation.

12. Repeat the previous problem, only assuming that defaults are perfectly correlated.

13. Using Monte Carlo simulation, reproduce Tables 10 and 11. Produce a similar table assuming a default correlation of 25%.

14. Following Table 10, compute the prices of first, second, and Nth-to-default bonds assuming that defaults are uncorrelated and that there are 5, 10, 20, and 50 bonds in the portfolio. How are the *N*th-to-default yields affected by the size of the portfolio?

15. Repeat the previous problem, assuming that default correlations are 0.25.

Appendix: Continuous Compounding

Effective annual interest rates and continuously compounded interest rates are simply different conventions for expressing the same idea: If you invest \$1 today, how much will you have after 1 year? One simple unambiguous way to answer this question is using zero-coupon bonds. If you invest \$1 in zero-coupon bonds costing $P(0, T)$ for a \$1 maturity payoff at time T, then at time T you will have $1/P(0, T)$ dollars. However, it is more common to answer the question using interest rates rather than zero-coupon bond prices.

Interest rates measure the rate of appreciation of an investment, but there are innumerable ways of quoting interest rates. Continuous compounding turns out to provide a particularly simple quoting convention, though it may not seem so simple at first. Since in practice option pricing formulas and other financial formulas make use of continuous compounding, it is important to be comfortable with it.

You might think that continuous compounding is not much used in the real world and, hence, there is no point in using it when studying derivatives. It is true that an auto dealer is likely to give you a blank stare if you inquire about the continuously compounded loan rate for your new car. However, continuous compounding does have advantages, and it is not often appreciated that almost *all* interest rate quoting conventions are complicated, some devilishly so.

1. THE LANGUAGE OF INTEREST RATES

We begin with definitions. There are two terms that we will use often to refer to interest rates:

Effective annual rate. If r is quoted as an **effective annual rate**, this means that if you invest \$1, n years later you will have $(1 + r)^n$. If you invest x_0 and earn x_n n years later, then the implied effective annual rate is $\left(x_n/x_0\right)^{1/n} - 1$.

Continuously compounded rate. If r is quoted as an annualized **continuously compounded rate**, this means that if you invest \$1, n years later you will have e^{rn}. If you invest x_0 and earn x_n n years later, then the implied annual continuously compounded rate is $\ln\left(x_n/x_0\right)/n$.

Let's look at this definition in more detail.

From Appendix B of *Derivatives Markets*, Third Edition, Robert McDonald. Copyright © 2013 by Pearson Education, Inc. Published by Pearson Prentice Hall. All rights reserved.

2. THE LOGARITHMIC AND EXPONENTIAL FUNCTIONS

Interest rates are typically quoted as "$r\%$ per year, compounded n times per year." As every beginning finance student learns, this has the interpretation that you will earn an interest rate of r/n per period for n periods. Thus, if you invest \$1 today, in 1 year you will have

$$\left(1+\frac{r}{n}\right)^n$$

In T years you will have

$$\left(1+\frac{r}{n}\right)^{nT} \tag{1}$$

What happens if we let n get very large, that is, if interest is compounded many times a year (even daily or hourly)? If, for example, the interest rate is 10%, after 3 years we will have

- $(\$1+0.1)^3=\$1.331$ with annual compounding,
- $(\$1+0.1/12)^{36}=\$1.3482$ with monthly compounding,
- $(\$1+0.1/365)^{1095}=\$1.34980$ with daily compounding, and
- $(\$1+0.1/8760)^{26,280}=\$1.349856$ with hourly compounding.

The exponential function is e^x, where e is a constant approximately equal to 2.71828. If compounding is *continuous*—that is, if interest accrues every instant—then we can use the exponential function to compute future values. For example, with a 10% continuously compounded rate, after 3 years we will have a future value of

$$e^{0.1\times 3}=\$1.349859$$

Notice that assuming continuous compounding gives us a result very close to that assuming daily compounding. In Excel, we compute continuously compounded results using the built-in exponential function.

The above example is computed as $\exp(0.1\times 3)$.

Why does the exponential function work? The number e is *defined* as

$$e^{rT}\equiv \lim_{n\to\infty}\left(1+\frac{r}{n}\right)^{nT} \tag{2}$$

Thus, the expression defining e is the same expression used for interest compounding calculations, equation (1)! By using e, you can compute a future value.

If you know how much you have earned from a \$1 investment, you can determine the continuously compounded rate of return by using the natural logarithm, ln. The function ln is the *inverse* of the exponential function in that it takes a dollar amount and gives you a rate of return. In other words, if you apply the logarithmic function to the exponential function, you compute the original argument to the exponential function. Here is an example:

$$\ln(e^{rt})=rt$$

Example 1. Suppose you have a zero-coupon bond that matures in 5 years. The price today is \$62.092 for a bond that pays \$100. The annually compounded rate of return is

$$(\$100/\$62.092)^{1/5}-1=0.10$$

The continuously compounded rate of return is

$$\frac{\ln(\$100/\$62.092)}{5} = \frac{0.47655}{5} = 0.09531$$

The continuously compounded rate of return of 9.53% corresponds to the annually compounded rate of return of 10%. To verify this, observe that

$$e^{0.0953} = 1.10$$

Finally, note that

$$\ln(1.10) = \ln(e^{0.0953}) = 0.0953 \blacksquare$$

Changing Interest Rates

When we multiply exponentials, exponents add. So we have

$$e^x e^y = e^{x+y}$$

Suppose you can invest for 4 years, earning a continuously compounded return of 5% the first 2 years and 6% the second 2 years. If you invest \$1 today, after 4 years you will have

$$e^{2\times0.05}e^{2\times0.06} = e^{0.10+0.12} = \$1.2461$$

We could of course do the same calculation using effective annual rates. For the first 2 years, we earn $e^{0.05} - 1 = 5.127\%$, and for the second 2 years, $e^{0.06} = 6.184\%$. The future value of \$1 is

$$1.05127^2 1.06184^2 = \$1.2461$$

This calculation gives us the same answer.

What is the average annual rate earned over the 4 years? The average annual continuously compounded rate is

$$\frac{1}{4}\ln(1.24608) = 0.055$$

which is the average of 5% and 6%.

However, if we express the answer in terms of effective annual rates, we get

$$1.24608^{0.25} - 1 = 5.6541\%$$

This is *not* the average of 5.127% and 6.184%, which is 5.6555. This makes calculations with continuous compounding easier.

Symmetry for Increases and Decreases

On March 4, 1999, the NASDAQ composite index closed at 2292.89. On March 10, 2000, the index closed at 5048.62. On January 2, 2001, the index closed at 2291.86, essentially the same level as in March 1999. The percentage increase from March 1999 to March 2000 was

$$\frac{5048.62}{2292.89} - 1 = 120.19\%$$

The subsequent decrease was

$$\frac{2291.86}{5048.62} - 1 = -54.60\%$$

When computing simple rates of return, a price can have an increase exceeding 100%, but its decrease can never be greater than 100%.

We can do the same calculations using continuous compounding. The continuously compounded increase from March 1999 to March 2000 was

$$\ln(5048.62/2292.89) = 78.93\%$$

while the subsequent decrease was

$$\ln(2291.86/5048.62) = -78.97\%$$

When using continuous compounding, increases and decreases are symmetric.

Moreover, if the index dropped to 1000, the continuously compounded return from the peak would be

$$\ln(1000/5048.62) = -161.91\%$$

Continuously compounded returns can be less than -100%.

PROBLEMS

1. a. A bond costs $67,032 today and pays $100,000 in 5 years. What is its continuously compounded rate of return?

   b. A bond costs $50 today, pays $100 at maturity, and has a continuously compounded annual return of 10%. In how many years does it mature?

   c. An investment of $5 today pays a continuously compounded rate of 7.5% per year. How much money will you have after 7 years?

   d. A stock selling for $100 is worth $5 1 year later. What is the continuously compounded return over the year? What if the stock price is $4? $3? $2? What would the stock price after 1 year have to be in order for the continuously compounded return to be -500%?

2. Suppose that over 1 year a stock price increases from $100 to $200. Over the subsequent year it falls back to $100.

   a. What is the arithmetic return (i.e., $(S_{t+1} - S_t)/S_t$) over the first year? What is the continuously compounded return (i.e., $\ln(S_{t+1}/S_t)$)?

   b. What is the arithmetic return over the second year? The continuously compounded return?

   c. What do you notice when you compare the first- and second-year returns computed arithmetically and continuously?

3. Here are stock prices on 6 consecutive days: $100, $47, $88, $153, $212, $100. Note that the cumulative return over the 6 days is 0.

a. What are the arithmetic returns from the first to the second day, the second to the third, and so forth?

b. What are the continuously compounded returns from the first to the second day, the second to the third, and so forth?

c. Suppose you want to compute the cumulative return over the 6 days. Suppose you don't know the prices, but only your answers to parts (a) and (b). How would you compute the cumulative return (which is 0) using arithmetic returns and continuously compounded returns?

APPENDIX

Appendix: Jensen's Inequality

The purpose of this appendix is to understand Jensen's inequality. Suppose that x is a random variable with mean $E(x)$, and $f(x)$ is a convex function of x.

Proposition 1 Jensen's inequality states that if $f(x)$ is convex, then for any probability distribution for x,

$$\mathrm{E}[f(x)] \geq f\,[\mathrm{E}(x)] \tag{1}$$

If $f(x)$ is concave, the inequality is reversed.

In order to understand this result we first need some definitions. A function is convex if it is curved like the cross-section of a bowl; a function is concave if it is curved like the cross-section of an upside-down bowl.[1] We will provide some examples illustrating Jensen's inequality, and then we will provide a proof (including a more precise definition of convexity).

1. EXAMPLE: THE EXPONENTIAL FUNCTION

Figure 1 shows a graph of the exponential function, $f(x) = e^x$. Note that e^x is convex. Let $x \sim \text{Binomial}(-1, 1; 0.5)$. We have

$$\mathrm{E}(x) = (0.5 \times -1) + (0.5 \times 1) = 0$$

We also have

$$f(1) = e^1 = 2.7183$$
$$f(-1) = e^{-1} = 0.3679$$

Thus,

1. A way to remember this is that a con**vex** function has the shape of a "v" while a con**cave** function has the curvature of a **cave**.

From Appendix C of *Derivatives Markets*, Third Edition, Robert McDonald. Copyright © 2013 by Pearson Education, Inc. Published by Pearson Prentice Hall. All rights reserved.

FIGURE 1

Graph of e^x showing that it is convex, and that $[(0.5 \times f(-1)) + (0.5 \times f(1))] > f(0)$.

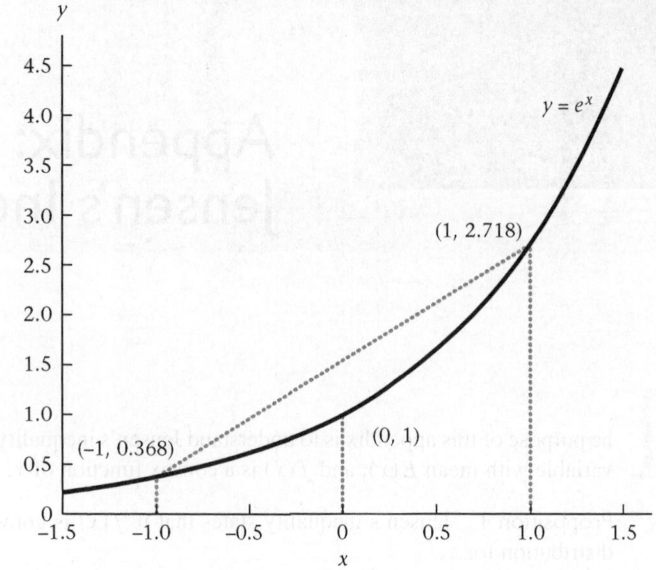

$$f[\mathrm{E}(x)] = e^{\mathrm{E}(x)}$$
$$= e^0$$
$$= 1$$

and

$$\mathrm{E}\left[f(x)\right] = (0.5 \times e^1) + (0.5 \times e^{-1})$$
$$= 1.5431$$

which is consistent with Jensen's inequality.

Graphically, the average of $f(1)$ and $f(-1)$ lies on the chord connecting those points, which is the straight line in Figure 1. $f(0)$ is below the chord, which is what Jensen's inequality states.

2. EXAMPLE: THE PRICE OF A CALL

Here is an example of Jensen's inequality. Consider a call option with a strike price of \$40. Suppose that x is the stock price, and that $x \sim$ Binomial(35, 45; 0.5). Then

$$\mathrm{E}(x) = (0.5 \times 35) + (0.5 \times 45) = 40.$$

Now let $f(x)$ be the value of the call at expiration:

$$f(x) = \max(x - K, 0)$$

When we evaluate the call price at the expected stock price, $f[\mathrm{E}(x)]$, we have

FIGURE 2

Illustration of Jensen's inequality with a call option. The line labeled $f(x)$ depicts the call payoff at expiration. The option evaluated at the expected stock price lies on this line. The expected value of the call, on the other hand, lies on the line connecting the points labeled (35, 0) and (45, 5). That line is always above the call payoff at expiration.

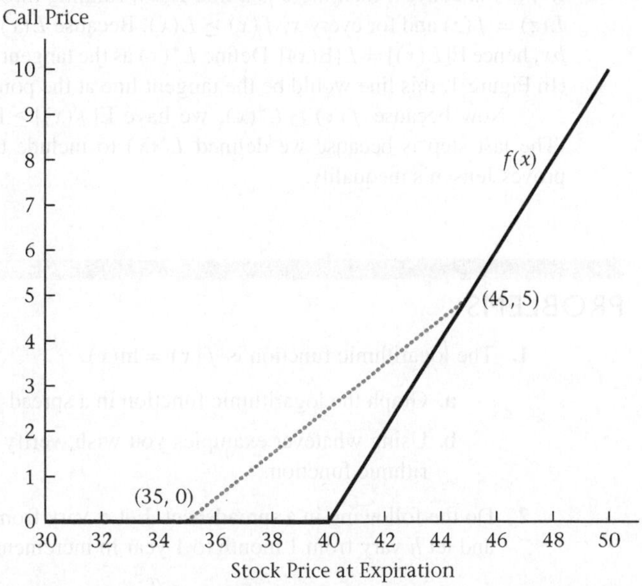

$$f[\mathrm{E}(x)] = \max[\mathrm{E}(x) - 40, 0]$$
$$= 0$$

And when we evaluate the expected value of the call, $\mathrm{E}\left[f(x)\right]$, we have

$$\begin{aligned}\mathrm{E}\left[f(x)\right] &= 0.5 \times f(45) + 0.5 \times f(35)\\ &= 0.5 \times \max(45-40, 0) + 0.5 \times \max(35-40, 0)\\ &= 0.5 \times 5 + 0 = 2.5\end{aligned}$$

Since $2.5 > 0$, $\mathrm{E}\left[f(x)\right] \geq f[\mathrm{E}(x)]$, in accord with Jensen's inequality.

Figure 2 displays this example graphically. The straight line connecting $f(35)$ and $f(45)$ represents $\mathrm{E}\left[f(x)\right]$; this line always exceeds the payoff to the call option. This example illustrates in a purely mechanical fashion why uncertainty makes an option more valuable.

3. PROOF OF JENSEN'S INEQUALITY[2]

A mathematical way to state the definition of convexity is that $f(x)$ is convex if for any two points x and y, $0 \leq \lambda \leq 1$, and $z = \lambda x + (1-\lambda)y$,

$$f(z) \leq \lambda f(x) + (1-\lambda) f(y) \tag{2}$$

2. This proof is from Mood et al. (1974).

If $f(x)$ is convex, then there is a line $L(x)$, running through the point $[z, f(z)]$ such that $L(z) = f(z)$ and for every x, $f(x) \geq L(x)$. Because $L(x)$ is a line, it can be written as $a + bx$, hence $\mathrm{E}[L(x)] = L[\mathrm{E}(x)]$. Define $L^*(x)$ as the tangent line at the point $\{\mathrm{E}(x), f[\mathrm{E}(x)]\}$. (In Figure 1, this line would be the tangent line at the point $x = 0$.)

Now because $f(x) \geq L^*(x)$, we have $\mathrm{E}[f(x)] \geq \mathrm{E}[L^*(x)] = L^*[\mathrm{E}(x)] = f[\mathrm{E}(x)]$. (The last step is because we defined $L^*(x)$ to include the point $\{\mathrm{E}(x), f[\mathrm{E}(x)]\}$.) This proves Jensen's inequality.

PROBLEMS

1. The logarithmic function is $f(x) = \ln(x)$.
   a. Graph the logarithmic function in a spreadsheet. Observe that it is concave.
   b. Using whatever examples you wish, verify Jensen's inequality for the logarithmic function.
2. Do the following in a spreadsheet. Let σ vary from 0.05 to 1 in increments of 0.05, and let h vary from 1 month to 1 year in increments of 1 month.
   a. Compute $0.5(e^{\sigma\sqrt{h}} + e^{-\sigma\sqrt{h}})$
   b. Compute $0.5(e^{-0.5\sigma^2 h+\sigma\sqrt{h}} + e^{-0.5\sigma^2 h-\sigma\sqrt{h}})$
3. Let $x \sim \text{Binomial}(-a, a; 0.5)$. Using a spreadsheet, evaluate $\mathrm{E}(e^{x-0.5a^2})$, for a's ranging from 0.025 to 1, in increments of 0.025.
4. Let $x \sim \text{Binomial}(-1, 2; 0.67)$. Verify Jensen's inequality for $f(x) = e^x$.
5. For the example of the call option in Section 2, verify with a numerical example that the value of the call is increasing in the spread of the prices around the mean of $40.
6. Using the numerical example in Section 2, verify Jensen's inequality for a put option.

References

Acerbi, C., 2002, "Spectral Measures of Risk: A Coherent Representation of Subjective Risk Aversion," *Journal of Banking and Finance*, 26(7), 1505–1518.

Acerbi, C. and Tasche, D., 2002, "On the Coherence of Expected Shortfall," *Journal of Banking and Finance*, 26(7), 1487–1503.

Acharya, V., John, K., and Sundaram, R. K., 2000, "On the Optimality of Resetting Executive Stock Options," *Journal of Financial Economics*, 57(1), 65–101.

Acharya, V., Schnabl, P., and Suarez, G., 2012, "Securitization without Risk Transfer," *Journal of Financial Economics*, forthcoming.

Admati, A. R., DeMarzo, P. M., Hellwig, M. F., and Pfleiderer, P., 2010, "Fallacies, Irrelevant Facts, and Myths in the Discussion of Capital Regulation: Why Bank Equity is Not Expensive," Working Paper, Stanford University.

Alexander, C., 2001, *Market Models*, Wiley, Chichester, England.

Allayannis, G., Brown, G., and Klapper, L. F., 2003, "Capital Structure and Financial Risk: Evidence from Foreign Debt Use in East Asia," *Journal of Finance*, 58, 2667–2709.

Allayannis, G., Lel, U., and Miller, D., 2004, "Corporate Governance and the Hedging Premium around the World," Working Paper, Darden School, University of Virginia.

Allayannis, G. and Weston, J., 2001, "The Use of Foreign Currency Derivatives and Firm Market Value," *Review of Financial Studies*, 14(1), 243–276.

Andersen, T., Benzoni, L., and Lund, J., 2002, "An Empirical Investigation of Continuous-Time Equity Return Models," *Journal of Finance*, 57(3), 1239–1284.

Andersen, T. G., Bollerslev, T., Diebold, F. X., and Labysd, P., 2003, "Modeling and Forecasting Realized Volatility," *Econometrica*, 71(2), 579–625.

Andersen, T. G., Bollerslev, T., Frederiksen, P. H., and Nielsen, M., 2005, "Jumps in Financial Markets," unpublished, Kellogg School, Northwestern University.

Anderson, J., 2006, "Betting on the Weather and Taking an Ice-Cold Bath," *The New York Times*

Anderson, R. and Sundaresan, S., 2000, "A Comparative Study of Structural Models of Corporate Bond Yields: An Exploratory Investigation," *Journal of Banking and Finance*, 24(1–2), 255–269.

Arnason, S. T. and Jagannathan, R., 1994, "Evaluating Executive Stock Options Using the Binomial Option Pricing Model," Working Paper, Carlson School of Management, University of Minnesota.

Artzner, P., Delbaen, F., Eber, J.-M., and Heath, D., 1999, "Coherent Measures of Risk," *Mathematical Finance*, 9(3), 203–228.

Arzac, E. R., 1997, "PERCs, DECs, and Other Mandatory Convertibles," *Journal of Applied Corporate Finance*, 10(1), 54–63.

Asquith, P., 1995, "Convertible Bonds Are Not Called Late," *Journal of Finance*, 50(4), 1275–1289.

From *Derivatives Markets*, Third Edition, Robert McDonald. Copyright © 2013 by Pearson Education, Inc. Published by Pearson Prentice Hall. All rights reserved.

Bai, J. and Collin-Dufresne, P., 2011, "The CDS-Bond Basis During the Financial Crisis of 2007-2009," unpublished, Federal Reserve Bank of New York.

Bakshi, G., Cao, C., and Chen, Z., 1997, "Empirical Performance of Alternative Option Pricing Models," *Journal of Finance*, 52(5), 2003–2049.

Bakshi, G. and Kapadia, N., 2003a, "Delta-Hedged Gains and the Negative Market Volatility Risk Premium," *Review of Financial Studies*, 16(2), 527–566.

Bakshi, G. and Kapadia, N., 2003b, "Volatility Risk Premium Embedded in Individual Options: Some New Insights," *Journal of Derivatives*, 45–54.

Bartram, S. M., 2008, "What Lies Beneath: Foreign Exchange Rate Exposure, Hedging and Cash Flows," *Journal of Banking and Finance*, 32(8), 1508–1521.

Bartram, S. M., Brown, G. W., and Fehle, F. R., 2004, "International Evidence on Financial Derivatives Use," Working Paper, University of North Carolina.

Bartram, S. M., Brown, G. W., and Fehle, F. R., 2009, "International Evidence on Financial Derivatives Use," *Financial Management*, 38(1), 136–206.

Bates, D. S., 2000, "Post-'87 Crash Fears the S&P 500 Futures Option Market," *Journal of Econometrics*, 94, 181–238.

Bates, D. S., 2003, "Empirical Option Pricing: A Retrospection," *Journal of Econometrics*, 116(1–2), 387–404.

Baubonis, C., Gastineau, G., and Purcell, D., 1993, "The Banker's Guide to Equity-Linked Certificates of Deposit," *Journal of Derivatives*, 1(2), 87–95.

Baxter, M. and Rennie, A., 1996, *Financial Calculus: An Introduction to Derivative Pricing*, Cambridge University Press, Cambridge, England.

Benmelech, E. and Dlugosz, J., 2009, "The Alchemy of CDO Credit Ratings," *Journal of Monetary Economics*, 56(5), 617–634.

Benmelech, E. and Dlugosz, J., 2010, "The Credit Ratings Crisis," *NBER Macroeconomics Annual*, 24(1), 161–208.

Bennhold, K. and Clark, N., 2008, "Police Report Says Société Générale Was Unaware of Rogue Trades," *The New York Times*, August 1 2008.

Benzoni, L., 2001, "Pricing Options under Stochastic Volatility: An Empirical Investigation," unpublished, University of Minnesota.

Bernard, C. and Boyle, P., 2009, "Mr. Madoff's Amazing Returns: An Analysis of the Split-Strike Conversion Strategy," unpublished, University of Waterloo.

Bernstein, P. L., 1992, *Capital Ideas: The Improbable Origins of Modern Wall Street*, Free Press, New York.

Bernstein, P. L., 1996, *Against the Gods: The Remarkable Story of Risk*, John Wiley & Sons, New York.

Bettis, J. C., Bizjak, J. M., and Kalpathy, S. L., 2010, "Why Do Insiders Hedge Their Ownership? An Empirical Examination," unpublished, SSRN-id1714039.

Bettis, J. C., Bizjak, J. M., and Lemmon, M. L., 2001, "Managerial Ownership, Incentive Contracting, and the Use of Zero-Cost Collars and Equity Swaps by Corporate Insiders," *Journal of Financial and Quantitative Analysis*, 36(3), 345–370.

Bharath, S. T. and Shumway, T., 2004, "Forecasting Default with the KMV-Merton Model," Working Paper, University of Michigan.

BIS, 1996, *Amendment to the Capital Accord to Incorporate Market Risks*, Technical Report, Basel Committee on Banking Supervision, Bank for International Settlements.

BIS, 2009, *Revisions to the Basel II Market Risk Framework*, Technical Report, Basel Committee on Banking Supervision, BIS.

Black, F., 1976a, "The Pricing of Commodity Contracts," *Journal of Financial Economics*, 3(1/2), 167–179.

Black, F., 1976b, "Studies of Stock Price Volatility Changes," *Proceedings of the 1976 Meetings of the American Statistical Association, Business and Economics Statistics Section*, 177–181.

Black, F., 1989, "How We Came Up with the Option Pricing Formula," *Journal of Portfolio Management*, 15(2), 4–8.

Black, F. and Cox, J., 1976, "Valuing Corporate Securities: Some Effects of Bond Indenture Provisions," *Journal of Finance*, 31, 351–367.

Black, F., Derman, E., and Toy, W., 1990, "A One-Factor Model of Interest Rates and Its Application to Treasury Bond Options," *Financial Analysts Journal*, 46(1), 33–39.

Black, F. and Karasinski, P., 1991, "Bond and Option Pricing When Short Rates Are Lognormal," *Financial Analysts Journal*, 47, 52–59.

Black, F. and Scholes, M., 1973, "The Pricing of Options and Corporate Liabilities," *Journal of Political Economy*, 81, 637–659.

Blanco, R., Brennan, S., and Marsh, I. W., 2005, "An Empirical Analysis of the Dynamic Relationship between Investment-Grade Bonds and Credit Default Swaps," *Journal of Finance*, 60(5), 2255–2281.

Blas, J., 2009, "Mexico's Big Gamble on Oil Pays Off," *Financial Times*.

Blas, J. and Thomson, A., 2008, "Mexico hedges almost all of its oil exports," *Financial Times*.

Bliss, R. R., 1997, "Movements in the Term Structure of Interest Rates," *Federal Reserve Bank of Atlanta Economic Review*, 82(4), 16–33.

Bodie, Z., 1995, "On the Risk of Stocks in the Long Run," *Financial Analysts Journal*, 51(3), 18–22.

Bodie, Z. and Crane, D., 1999, "The Design and Production of New Retirement Savings Products," *Journal of Portfolio Management*, 25(2), 77–82.

Bodie, Z., Kaplan, R. S., and Merton, R. C., 2003, "For the Last Time: Stock Options Are an Expense," *Harvard Business Review*, 81(3), 3–11, March 2003.

Bodie, Z. and Rosansky, V. I., 1980, "Risk and Return in Commodity Futures," *Financial Analysts Journal*, 36(3), 27–39.

Bodnar, G. M., Hayt, G. S., and Marston, R. C., 1998, "1998 Wharton Survey of Financial Risk Management by US Non-Financial Firms," *Financial Management*, 27(4), 70–91.

Bollerslev, T., 1986, "Generalized Autoregressive Conditional Heteroskedasticity," *Journal of Econometrics*, 31, 307–327.

Bollerslev, T., 1987, "A Conditional Heteroskedastic Time Series Model for Speculative Prices and Rates of Return," *Review of Economics and Statistics*, 69, 542–547.

Bollerslev, T., Engle, R. F., and Nelson, D. B., 1994, "ARCH Models," in R. F. Engle and D. L. McFadden (eds.), "Handbook of Econometrics," volume 4 of *Handbooks in Economics*, chapter 49, 2959–3038, Elsevier Science, Amsterdam.

Boyle, P. P., 1977, "Options: A Monte Carlo Approach," *Journal of Financial Economics*, 4(3), 323–338.

Boyle, P. P., Broadie, M., and Glasserman, P., 1997, "Monte Carlo Methods for Security Pricing," *Journal of Economic Dynamics and Control*, 21(8–9), 1267–1322.

Boyle, P. P. and Emanuel, D., 1980, "Discretely Adjusted Option Hedges," *Journal of Financial Economics*, 8(3), 259–282.

Boyle, P. P., Evnine, J., and Gibbs, S., 1989, "Numerical Evaluation of Multivariate Contingent Claims," *Review of Financial Studies*, 2(2), 241–250.

Brace, A., Gatarek, D., and Musiela, M., 1997, "The Market Model of Interest Rate Dynamics," *Mathematical Finance*, 7(2), 127–155.

Brealey, R., Myers, S., and Allen, F., 2011, *Principles of Corporate Finance*, Irwin McGraw-Hill, Burr Ridge, IL, 10th edition.

Brennan, M. and Schwartz, E., 1985, "Evaluating Natural Resource Investments," *Journal of Business*, 58, 135–157.

Brennan, M. J., 1991, "The Price of Convenience and the Evaluation of Commodity Contingent Claims," in D. Lund and B. Øksendal (eds.), "Stochastic Models and Option Values: Applications to Resources, Environment and Investment Problems," Contributions to Economic Analysis, 33–71, North-Holland, Amsterdam.

Brennan, M. J., 2000, "Real Options: Development and New Contributions," in Brennan and Trigeorgis (2000), chapter 1, 1–10.

Brennan, M. J. and Schwartz, E. S., 1977, "Convertible Bonds: Valuation and Optimal Strategies for Call and Conversion," *Journal of Finance*, 32(5), 1699–1715.

Brennan, M. J. and Schwartz, E. S., 1990, "Arbitrage in Stock Index Futures," *Journal of Business*, 63(1), S7–31.

Brennan, M. J. and Solanki, R., 1981, "Optimal Portfolio Insurance," *Journal of Financial and Quantitative Analysis*, 16(3), 279–300.

Brennan, M. J. and Trigeorgis, L., (eds.), 2000, *Project Flexibility, Agency, and Competition: New Developments in the Theory and Application of Real Options*, Oxford University Press, London.

Briys, E. and Bellala, M., 1998, *Options, Futures and Exotic Derivatives: Theory, Application and Practice*, Wiley Frontiers in Finance, John Wiley & Sons, Chichester, England.

Broadie, M., Chernov, M., and Johannes, M., 2004, "Model Specification and Risk Premiums: The Evidence from the Futures Options," Working Paper, Columbia University.

Broadie, M., Chernov, M., and Johannes, M., 2007, "Model Specification and Risk Premia: The Evidence from Futures Options," *Journal of Finance*, 62(3), 1453–1490.

Broadie, M. and Detemple, J., 1996, "American Option Valuation: New Bounds, Approximations, and a Comparison of Existing Methods," *Review of Financial Studies*, 9(4), 1211–1250.

Broadie, M. and Glasserman, P., 1997, "Pricing American Style Securities by Simulation," *Journal of Economic Dynamics and Control*, 21, 1323–1352.

Broadie, M., Glasserman, P., and Kou, S. G., 1997, "A Continuity Correction for Discrete Barrier Options," *Mathematical Finance*, 7(4), 325–349.

Brown, G. W., 2001, "Managing Foreign Exchange Risk With Derivatives," *Journal of Financial Economics*, 60(2–3), 401–448.

Brown, G. W., Crabb, P. R., and Haushalter, D., 2003, "Are Firms Successful at Selectively Hedging?" Working Paper, University of North Carolina.

Buffett, W., 2009, "Letter to the Shareholders of Berkshire Hathaway, Inc."

Bulow, J. and Shoven, J. B., 2005, "Accounting for Stock Options," *Journal of Economic Perspectives*, 19(4), 115–134.

Burghardt, G. and Hoskins, W., 1995, "The Convexity Bias in Eurodollar Futures," *Risk*, 8(3), 63–70.

Burnside, A. C., Eichenbaum, M., Kleshchelski, I., and Rebelo, S. T., 2008, "Do Peso Problems Explain the Returns to the Carry Trade?" Working Paper, Northwestern University.

Campbell, J. Y., Lo, A. W., and MacKinlay, A. C., 1997, *The Econometrics of Financial Markets*, Princeton University Press, Princeton, NJ.

Campello, M., Lin, C., Ma, Y., and Zou, H., 2010, "The Real and Financial Implications of Corporate Hedging," unpublished, University of Illinois.

Carr, P. and Madan, D., 1998, "Towards a Theory of Volatility Trading," in R. Jarrow (ed.), "Volatility," 417–427, Risk Publications.

Carr, P. and Wu, L., 2003, "What Type of Process Underlies Options? A Simple Robust Test," *Journal of Finance*, 58(6), 2581–2610.

Carter, D., Rogers, D., and Simkins, B., 2004, "Fuel Hedging in the Airline Industry: The Case of Southwest Airlines," unpublished, SSRN ID 578663.

Carter, D. A., Rogers, D. A., and Simkins, B. J., 2006, "Does Hedging Affect Firm Value? Evidence from the US Airline Industry," *Financial Management*, 35(1), 53–86.

Casella, G. and Berger, R. L., 2002, *Statistical Inference*, Duxbury, Pacific Grove, CA, 2nd edition.

Chance, D. M., Kumar, R., and Todd, R. B., 2000, "The 'Repricing' of Executive Stock Options," *Journal of Financial Economics*, 57(1), 129–154.

Chazan, G., 2010, "Oil Stockpile on Ships Shrinks," *Wall Street Journal*, p. C1.

Chen, S.-S., few Lee, C., and Shrestha, K., 2003, "Futures Hedge Ratios: A Review," *The Quarterly Review of Economics and Finance*, 43, 433–465.

Chernov, M., Gorbenko, A. S., and Makarov, I., 2011, "CDS Auctions," unpublished, London Business School.

Chicago Board Options Exchange, 2003, *VIX: CBOE Volatility Index*, Technical Report, Chicago Board Options Exchange.

Christie, A. A., 1982, "The Stochastic Behavior of Common Stock Variances," *Journal of Financial Economics*, 10(4), 407–432.

Cicero, D. C., 2009, "The Manipulation of Executive Stock Option Exercise Strategies: Information Timing and Backdating," *Journal of Finance*, 64(6), 2627–2663.

Cochrane, J. H., 2001, *Asset Pricing*, Princeton University Press, Princeton, NJ.

Cohan, W. D., 2009, *House of Cards: A Tale of Hubris and Wretched Excess on Wall Street*, Doubleday.

Collin-Dufresne, P. and Solnik, B., 2001, "On the Term Structure of Default Premia in the Swap and LIBOR Markets," *Journal of Finance*, 56(3), 1095–1115.

Constantinides, G. M., 1978, "Market Risk Adjustment in Project Valuation," *Journal of Finance*, 33(2), 603–616.

Constantinides, G. M., 1984, "Warrant Exercise and Bond Conversion in Competitive Markets," *Journal of Financial Economics*, 13(3), 371–397.

Cooper, L., 2000, "Caution Reigns," *Risk*, 13(6), 12–14, South Africa Special Report.

Core, J. E. and Guay, W. R., 2001, "Stock Option Plans for Non-Executive Employees," *Journal of Financial Economics*, 61(2), 253–287.

Cornell, B. and French, K. R., 1983, "Taxes and the Pricing of Stock Index Futures," *Journal of Finance*, 38(3), 675–694.

Cornell, B. and Shapiro, A. C., 1989, "The Mispricing of US Treasury Bonds: A Case Study," *Review of Financial Studies*, 2(3), 297–310.

Cossin, D. and Pirotte, H., 2001, *Advanced Credit Risk Analysis*, Wiley, Chichester, UK.

Coval, J. D. and Shumway, T., 2001, "Expected Option Returns," *Journal of Finance*, 56(3), 983–1009.

Cox, D. and Miller, H. D., 1965, *The Theory of Stochastic Processes*, Chapman and Hall, London.

Cox, J. C., 1975, "Notes on Option Pricing I: Constant Elasticity of Variance Diffusions," Working Paper, Stanford University (reprinted in *Journal of Portfolio Management* 1996, 22, 15–17).

Cox, J. C., 1996, "The Constant Elasticity of Variance Option Pricing Model," *Journal of Portfolio Management*, (22), 15–17.

Cox, J. C., Ingersoll, J. E., Jr., and Ross, S. A., 1981, "The Relation Between Forward Prices and Futures Prices," *Journal of Financial Economics*, 9(4), 321–346.

Cox, J. C., Ingersoll, J. E., Jr., and Ross, S. A., 1985a, "An Intertemporal General Equilibrium Model of Asset Prices," *Econometrica*, 53(2), 363–384.

Cox, J. C., Ingersoll, J. E., Jr., and Ross, S. A., 1985b, "A Theory of the Term Structure of Interest Rates," *Econometrica*, 53(2), 385–408.

Cox, J. C. and Ross, S. A., 1976, "The Valuation of Options for Alternative Stochastic Processes," *Journal of Financial Economics*, 3(1/2), 145–166.

Cox, J. C., Ross, S. A., and Rubinstein, M., 1979, "Option Pricing: A Simplified Approach," *Journal of Financial Economics*, 7(3), 229–263.

Cox, J. C. and Rubinstein, M., 1985, *Options Markets*, Prentice-Hall, Englewood Cliffs, NJ.

Crabbe, L. E. and Argilagos, J. D., 1994, "Anatomy of the Structured Note Market," *Journal of Applied Corporate Finance*, 7(3), 85–98.

Credit Suisse Financial Products, 1997, *CreditRisk+*, Technical Report, Credit Suisse First Boston, London.

Crosbie, P. and Bohn, J., 2003, *Modeling Default Risk*, White Paper, Moody's KMV.

Culp, C. L. and Miller, M. H., 1995, "Metallgesellschaft and the Economics of Synthetic Storage," *Journal of Applied Corporate Finance*, 7(4), 62–76.

Dai, Q. and Singleton, K. J., 2000, "Specification Analysis of Affine Term Structure Models," *Journal of Finance*, 55(5), 1943–1978.

Davydov, D. and Linetsky, V., 2001, "Pricing and Hedging Path-Dependent Options under the CEV Process," *Management Science*, 47(7), 949–965.

Debreu, G., 1959, *Theory of Value*, Yale University Press.

DeGroot, M. H., 1975, *Probability and Statistics*, Addison-Wesley, Reading, MA.

Demeterfi, K., Derman, E., Kamal, M., and Zou, J., 1999, "A Guide to Volatility and Variance Swaps," *Journal of Derivatives*, 6(4), 9–32.

Derman, E. and Kani, I., 1993, "The Ins and Outs of Barrier Options," Goldman Sachs Quantitative Strategies Research Notes.

Diebold, F. X., 2004, "The Nobel Memorial Prize for Robert F. Engle," NBER Working Paper 10423.

Dixit, A., 1989, "Entry and Exit Decisions under Uncertainty," *Journal of Political Economy*, 97, 620–638.

Dixit, A. K. and Pindyck, R. S., 1994, *Investment under Uncertainty*, Princeton University Press, Princeton, NJ.

Dubinsky, A. and Johannes, M., 2004, "Earnings Announcements and Equity Options," unpublished, Columbia Graduate School of Business.

Duffie, D., 1996, *Dynamic Asset Pricing Theory*, Princeton University Press, Princeton, NJ, 2nd edition.

Duffie, D., 1999, "Credit Swap Valuation," *Financial Analysts Journal*, 55(1), 73–87.

Duffie, D., 2001, *Dynamic Asset Pricing Theory*, Princeton University Press, Princeton, NJ, 3rd edition.

Duffie, D. and Huang, C.-f., 1985, "Implementing Arrow-Debreu Equilibria by Continuous Trading of Few Long-Lived Securities," *Econometrica*, 53(6), 1337–1356.

Duffie, D. and Kan, R., 1996, "A Yield-Factor Model of Interest Rates," *Mathematical Finance*, 6(4), 379–406.

Duffie, D., Pan, J., and Singleton, K., 2000, "Transform Analysis and Asset Pricing for Affine Jump-Diffusions," *Econometrica*, 68(6), 1343–1376.

Duffie, D. and Singleton, K. J., 2003, *Credit Risk*, Princton University Press, Princeton, NJ.

Duffie, D. and Yurday, E. C., 2004a, *TRAC-X Derivatives: Structured Credit Index Products and Default Correlation*, Case F-269, Stanford Graduate School of Business.

Duffie, D. and Yurday, E. C., 2004b, *TRAC-X: Emergence of Default Swap Index Products*, Case F-268, Stanford Graduate School of Business.

Duffie, D. and Zhu, H., 2011, "Does a Central Clearing Counterparty Reduce Counterparty Risk?" *The Review of Asset Pricing Studies*, 1(1).

Eaglesham, J., 2012, "SEC Probes Role of Hedge Fund in CDOs," *Wall Street Journal*, p. C1.

Eavis, P. and Craig, S., 2012, "The Bet That Blew Up for JPMorgan Chase," *The New York Times*, p. B1.

Eberhart, A. C., 2005, "Employee Stock Options as Warrants," *Journal of Banking and Finance*, 29(10), 2409–2433.

Edwards, F. R. and Canter, M. S., 1995, "The Collapse of Metallgesellschaft: Unhedgeable Risks, Poor Hedging Strategy, or Just Bad Luck?" *Journal of Applied Corporate Finance*, 8(1), 86–105.

Edwards, F. R. and Ma, C. W., 1992, *Futures and Options*, McGraw-Hill, New York.

Eisinger, J. and Bernstein, J., 2010, "The Magnetar Trade: How One Hedge Fund Helped Keep the Bubble Going," *Pro Publica*, http://goo.gl/bZGhW.

Emanuel, D. C., 1983, "Warrant Valuation and Exercise Strategy," *Journal of Financial Economics*, 12(2), 211–235.

Emanuel, D. C. and MacBeth, J. D., 1982, "Further Results on the Constant Elasticity of Variance Call Option Pricing Model," *Journal of Financial and Quantitative Analysis*, 17(4), 533–554.

Engle, R. F., 1982, "Autoregressive Conditional Heterodskedasticity with Estimates of the Variance of U.K. Inflation," *Econometrica*, 50, 987–1008.

Eom, Y. H., Helwege, J., and Huang, J.-Z., 2004, "Structural Models of Corporate Bond Pricing: An Empirical Analysis," *Review of Financial Studies*, 17(2), 499–544.

Eraker, B., 2001, "Do Stock Prices and Volatility Jump? Reconciling Evidence from Spot and Option Prices," unpublished, Duke University.

Fama, E. F., 1965, "The Behavior of Stock Prices," *Journal of Business*, 38(1), 34–105.

Faulkender, M., 2005, "Hedging or Market Timing? Selecting the Interest Rate Exposure of Corporate Debt," *Journal of Finance*, 60(2), 931–962.

Federal Reserve Bank of New York, 2010, *Tri-Party Repo Infrastructure Reform*, Technical Report, Federal Reserve Bank of New York.

Flannery, M. J., 2005, "No Pain, No Gain? Effecting Market Discipline via Reverse Convertible Debentures," in H. S. Scott (ed.), "Capital Adequacy beyond Basel: Banking, Securities, and Insurance," chapter 5, 171–196, Oxford University Press, USA.

Fleming, I., 1997, *Goldfinger*, Fine Communications, New York.

Fleming, M. J. and Garbade, K. D., 2002, "When the Back Office Moved to the Front Burner: Settlement Fails in the Treasury Market After 9/11," *FRBNY Economic Policy Review*, 8(2), 35–57.

Fleming, M. J. and Garbade, K. D., 2003, "The Repurchase Agreement Refined: GCF Repo," *Current Issues in Economics and Finance*, 9(6), 1–7.

Fleming, M. J. and Garbade, K. D., 2004, "Repurchase Agreements with Negative Interest Rates," *Current Issues in Economics and Finance*, 10(5), 1–7.

Forster, D. M., 1996, "The State of the Law after *Procter & Gamble v. Banker's Trust*," *Derivatives Quarterly*, 3(2), 8–17.

French, K. R., 1983, "A Comparison of Futures and Forward Prices," *Journal of Financial Economics*, 12(3), 311–342.

French, K. R. and Roll, R., 1986, "Stock Return Variances: The Arrival of Information and the Reaction of Traders," *Journal of Financial Economics*, 17(1), 5–26.

Froot, K., Scharfstein, D., and Stein, J., 1994, "A Framework for Risk Management," *Journal of Applied Corporate Finance*, 7(3), 22–32.

Fuller, K. P., 2003, "Why Some Firms Use Collar Offers in Mergers," *Financial Review*, 38(1), 127–150.

Galai, D. and Masulis, R. W., 1976, "The Option Pricing Model and the Risk Factor of Stock," *Journal of Financial Economics*, 3(1/2), 53–81.

Garman, M. B. and Kohlhagen, S. W., 1983, "Foreign Currency Option Values," *Journal of International Money and Finance*, 2(3), 231–237.

Gastineau, G. L., Smith, D. J., and Todd, R., 2001, *Risk Management, Derivatives, and Financial Analysis under SFAS No. 133*, The Research Foundation of AIMR and Blackwell Series in Finance.

Géczy, C., Minton, B. A., and Schrand, C., 1997, "Why Firms Use Currency Derivatives," *Journal of Finance*, 52(4), 1323–1354.

Geman, H., 2005, *Commodities and Commodity Derivatives*, John Wiley & Sons, Chichester, England.

Geman, H., Karoui, N. E., and Rochet, J.-C., 1995, "Changes of Numeraire, Changes of Probability Measure and Option Pricing," *Journal of Applied Probability*, 32, 443–458.

Geske, R., 1979, "The Valuation of Compound Options," *Journal of Financial Economics*, 7, 63–81.

Glasserman, P., 2004, *Monte Carlo Methods in Financial Engineering*, number 53 in Applications of Mathematics, Springer-Verlag, New York.

Goldman, B. M., Sosin, H. B., and Gatto, M. A., 1979a, "Path Dependent Options: Buy at the Low, Sell at the High," *Journal of Finance*, 34(5), 1111–1127.

Goldman, B. M., Sosin, H. B., and Shepp, L. A., 1979b, "On Contingent Claims That Insure Ex-Post Optimal Stock Market Timing," *Journal of Finance*, 34(2), 401–413.

Goodman, L. S. and Fabozzi, F. J., 2002, *Collateralized Debt Obligations: Structures and Analysis*, Wiley.

Gorton, G. and Metrick, A., 2009, "Haircuts," Yale ICF Working Paper No. 09-15.

Gorton, G. and Metrick, A., 2010, "Regulating the Shadow Banking System," unpublished, Yale University.

Gorton, G. and Rouwenhorst, K. G., 2004, "Facts and Fantasies about Commodity Futures," NBER Working Paper 10595.

Gorton, G. B., 2010, *Slapped by the Invisible Hand: The Panic of 2007*, Oxford University Press.

Graham, J. R. and Rogers, D. A., 2002, "Do Firms Hedge in Response to Tax Incentives?" *Journal of Finance*, 57, 815–839.

Graham, J. R. and Smith, C. W., Jr., 1999, "Tax Incentives to Hedge," *Journal of Finance*, 54(6), 2241–2262.

Gray, A., 2012, "Disasters Expose Flaws in Assumptions," *Financial Times*, 1, Special Report, Risk Management: Supply Chain.

Grenadier, S. R., 1996, "The Strategic Exercise of Options: Development Cascades and Overbuilding in Real Estate Markets," *Journal of Finance*, 51(5), 1653–1679.

Grenadier, S. R., 1999, "Information Revelation through Option Exercise," *Review of Financial Studies*, 12(1), 95–129.

Grinblatt, M. and Longstaff, F. A., 2000, "Financial Innovation and the Role of Derivative Securities: An Empirical Analysis of the Treasury STRIPS Program," *Journal of Finance*, 55(3), 1415–1436.

Grossman, S. J. and Stiglitz, J. E., 1980, "On the Impossibility of Informationally Efficient Markets," *American Economic Review*, 70(3), 393–408.

Guay, W. and Kothari, S. P., 2003, "How Much Do Firms Hedge with Derivatives?" *Journal of Financial Economics*, 70, 423–462.

Güntay, L., Prabhala, N., and Unal, H., 2004, "Callable Bonds, Interest Rate Risk, and the Supply Side of Hedging," Working Paper, University of Maryland, Smith School of Business.

Gupta, A. and Subrahmanyam, M. G., 2000, "An Empirical Examination of the Convexity Bias in the Pricing of Interest Rate Swaps," *Journal of Financial Economics*, 55(2), 239–279.

Gupta, S. and Sundaram, R. K., 2012, "CDS Auctions and Informative Biases in CDS Recovery Rates," Working Paper, NYU.

Hakannson, N. H., 1976, "The Purchasing Power Fund: A New Kind of Financial Intermediary," *Financial Analysts Journal*, 32(6), 49–59.

Hamilton, D., Varma, P., Ou, S., and Cantor, R., 2005, *Default and Recovery Rates of Corporate Bond Issuers: A Statistical Review of Moody's Ratings Performance 1920–2004*, Technical Report, Moody's Investor's Services.

Hanweck, G. A., 1994, *Essays on Interest-Rate Volatility and the Pricing of Interest-Rate Derivative Assets*, Ph.D. thesis, Department of Managerial Economics and Decision Sciences, Kellogg School, Northwestern University.

Harris, M. and Raviv, A., 1985, "A Sequential Signalling Model of Convertible Debt Call Policy," *Journal of Finance*, 40(5), 1263–1281.

Harrison, J. M. and Kreps, D. M., 1979, "Martingales and Arbitrage in Multiperiod Securities Markets," *Journal of Economic Theory*, 20, 381–408.

Haug, E. G., 1998, *The Complete Guide to Option Pricing Formulas*, McGraw Hill, New York.

Haushalter, G. D., 2000, "Financing Policy, Basis Risk, and Corporate Hedging: Evidence from Oil and Gas Producers," *Journal of Finance*, 55(1), 107–152.

Heath, D., Jarrow, R., and Morton, A., 1992, "Bond Pricing and the Term Structure of Interest Rates: A New Methodology for Contingent Claims Valuation," *Econometrica*, 60(1), 77–105.

Henderson, B. J. and Pearson, N. D., 2011, "The Dark Side of Financial Innovation: A Case Study of the Pricing of a Retail Financial Product," *Journal of Financial Economics*, 100(2), 227–247.

Hendricks, D., 1996, "Estimation of Value-at-Risk Models Using Historical Data," *Federal Reserve Bank of New York Economic Policy Review*, 2(1), 39–69.

Henriques, D. B., 1997, "The Wealthy Find New Ways to Escape Tax on Profits," *The New York Times*, Dec. 1, C1.

Heron, R. A. and Lie, E., 2007, "Does Backdating Explain the Stock Price Pattern around Executive Stock Option Grants?" *Journal of Financial Economics*, 83(2), 271–295.

Heston, S. L., 1993, "A Closed-Form Solution for Options with Stochastic Volatility with Applications to Bonds and Currency Options," *Review of Financial Studies*, 6(2), 327–343.

Ho, T. S. Y. and Lee, S.-B., 1986, "Term Structure Movements and Pricing Interest Rate Contingent Claims," *Journal of Finance*, 41(4), 1011–1029.

Hördahl, P. and King, M., 2008, "Developments in Repo Markets During the Financial Turmoil," *BIS Quarterly Review*, 37–53, Bank for International Settlements.

Horowitz, J., 2001, "The Bootstrap," in J. J. Heckman and E. Leamer (eds.), "Handbook of Econometrics," volume 5, 3159–3228, Elsevier Science, Amsterdam.

Horwitz, D. L., 1996, "*P&G v. Banker's Trust*: What's All the Fuss?" *Derivatives Quarterly*, 3(2), 18–23.

Houweling, P. and Vorst, T., 2001, "An Empirical Comparison of Default Swap Pricing Models," Erasmus University Working Paper.

Hsu, H., 1997, "Surprised Parties," *Risk*, 10(4), 27–29.

Huang, C. and Litzenberger, R., 1988, *Foundations for Financial Economics*, Elsevier Science, New York.

Huddart, S., 1998, "Patterns of Stock Option Exercise in the United States," in J. Carpenter and D. Yermack (eds.), "Executive Compensation and Shareholder Value," chapter 8, 115–142, Kluwer Academic Publishers, Norwell, MA.

Hull, J. and White, A., 1987, "The Pricing of Options on Assets with Stochastic Volatilities," *Journal of Finance*, 42(2), 281–300.

Hull, J. and White, A., 1990, "Pricing Interest-Rate-Derivative Securities," *Review of Financial Studies*, 3(4), 573–592.

Hull, J. and White, A., 1994, "Numerical Procedures for Implementing Term Structure Models I: Single Factor Models," *Journal of Derivatives*, 2(1), 7–16.

Hull, J. C., 2000, *Options, Futures, and Other Derivatives*, Prentice-Hall, Upper Saddle River, NJ, 4th edition.

Hull, J. C. and White, A., 1995, "The Impact of Default Risk on the Prices of Options and Other Derivative Securities," *Journal of Banking and Finance*, 19, 299–322.

Humphreys, T. A., 2010, *U.S. Tax Court Holds Prepaid Variable Forward Plus a Stock Loan is a Sale for Federal Income Tax Purposes in Long-Awaited Anschutz Decision*, Technical Report, Morrison & Foerster LLP, client alert.

Ingersoll, J. E., Jr., 1977, "A Contingent-Claims Valuation of Convertible Securities," *Journal of Financial Economics*, 4(3), 289–322.

Ingersoll, J. E., Jr., 2000, "Digital Contracts: Simple Tools for Pricing Complex Derivatives," *Journal of Business*, 73(1), 67–88.

J.P. Morgan, 1997, *CreditMetrics–Technical Document*, Technical Report, J.P. Morgan & Co., New York.

J.P. Morgan/Reuters, 1996, *RiskMetrics–Technical Document*, Technical Report, J.P. Morgan & Co., New York, 4th edn.

Jagolinzer, A. D., Matsunaga, S. R., and Yeung, E., 2007, "An Analysis of Insiders' Use of Prepaid Variable Forward Transactions," *Journal of Accounting Research*, 45(5), 1055–1079.

James, J. and Webber, N., 2001, *Interest Rate Modeling*, Wiley, Chichester, England.

Jamshidian, F., 1989, "An Exact Bond Option Formula," *Journal of Finance*, 44(1), 205–209.

Jarrow, R. A., 1996, *Modeling Fixed Income Securities and Interest Rate Options*, McGraw-Hill, New York.

Jarrow, R. A., Lando, D., and Turnbull, S. M., 1997, "A Markov Model for the Term Structure of Credit Risk Spreads," *Review of Financial Studies*, 10(2), 481–523.

Jarrow, R. A. and Oldfield, G. S., 1981, "Forward Contracts and Futures Contracts," *Journal of Financial Economics*, 9(4), 373–382.

Jarrow, R. A. and Rudd, A., 1983, *Option Pricing*, Richard D. Irwin, Homewood, Illinois.

Jarrow, R. A. and Turnbull, S. M., 1995, "Pricing Derivatives on Financial Securities Subject to Credit Risk," *Journal of Finance*, 50(1), 53–85.

Jickling, M., 2008, *Fannie Mae and Freddie Mac in Conservatorship*, Technical Report, Congressional Research Service, Library of Congress.

Jin, Y. and Jorion, P., 2006, "Firm Value and Hedging: Evidence from U.S. Oil and Gas Producers," *Journal of Finance*, 61(2), 893–919.

Jobst, A. A. and Solé, J., 2012, "Operative Principles of Islamic Derivatives—Towards a Coherent Theory," IMF Working Paper WP/12/63.

Johnson, H. and Stulz, R., 1987, "The Pricing of Options with Default Risk," *Journal of Finance*, 42(2), 267–280.

Johnson, S. A. and Tian, Y. S., 2000a, "Indexed Executive Stock Options," *Journal of Financial Economics*, 57(1), 35–64.

Johnson, S. A. and Tian, Y. S., 2000b, "The Value and Incentive Effects of Nontraditional Executive Stock Option Plans," *Journal of Financial Economics*, 57(1), 3–34.

Jones, E. P., Mason, S. P., and Rosenfeld, E., 1984, "Contingent Claims Analysis of Corporate Capital Structures: An Empirical Investigation," *Journal of Finance*, 39(3), 611–25.

Jorion, P., 1995, *Big Bets Gone Bad: Derivatives and Bankruptcy in Orange County*, Academic Press, San Diego, CA.

Jorion, P., 2001, *Value at Risk*, McGraw-Hill, New York, 2nd edition.

Jorion, P., 2006, *Value at Risk*, McGraw-Hill, New York, 3rd edition.

Judd, K. L., 1998, *Numerical Methods in Economics*, MIT Press, Cambridge, MA.

Karatzas, I. and Shreve, S. E., 1991, *Brownian Motion and Stochastic Calculus*, Springer-Verlag, New York, 2nd edition.

Karatzas, I. and Shreve, S. E., 1998, *Methods of Mathematical Finance*, number 39 in Applications of Mathematics: Stochastic Modelling and Applied Probability, Springer-Verlag, New York.

Karlin, S. and Taylor, H. M., 1981, *A Second Course in Stochastic Processes*, Academic Press, New York.

Kealhofer, S., 2003a, "Quantifying Credit Risk I: Default Prediction," *Financial Analysts Journal*, 59(1), 30–44.

Kealhofer, S., 2003b, "Quantifying Credit Risk II: Default Prediction," *Financial Analysts Journal*, 59(3), 78–92.

Kealhofer, S. and Kurbat, M., 2002, "Predictive Merton Models," *Risk*, 15(2), 67–71.

Kemna, A. G. Z. and Vorst, A. C. F., 1990, "A Pricing Method for Options Based on Average Asset Values," *Journal of Banking and Finance*, 14, 113–129.

Kim, I. J., Ramaswamy, K., and Sundaresan, S., 1993, "Does Default Risk in Coupons Affect the Valuation Of Corporate Bonds?: A Contingent Claims Model," *Financial Management*, 22(3), 117–31.

Klein, P., 1996, "Pricing Black-Scholes Options with Correlated Credit Risk," *Journal of Banking and Finance*, 20, 1211–1229.

Krishnamurthy, A., 2002, "The Bond/Old-Bond Spread," *Journal of Financial Economics*, 66(2-3), 463–506.

Kulatilaka, N. and Marcus, A. J., 1994, "Valuing Employee Stock Options," *Financial Analysts Journal*, 50, 46–56.

Leland, H. E., 1980, "Who Should Buy Portfolio Insurance?" *Journal of Finance*, XXXV(2), 581–594.

Leland, H. E., 1994, "Corporate Debt Value, Bond Covenants, and Optimal Capital Structure," *Journal of Finance*, 49(4), 1213–1252.

Leland, H. E. and Toft, K. B., 1996, "Optimal Capital Structure, Endogenous Bankruptcy, and the Term Structure of Credit Spreads," *Journal of Finance*, 51(3), 987–1019.

Lewis, M., 1989, *Liar's Poker*, Penguin, New York.

Lewis, M., 2011, *The Big Short: Inside the Doomsday Machine*, W. W. Norton.

Li, D. X., 1999, "On Default Correlation: A Copula Function Approach," RiskMetrics Group.

Lie, E., 2005, "On the Timing of CEO Stock Option Awards," *Management Science*, 51(5), 802–812.

Litterman, R. and Scheinkman, J., 1991, "Common Factors Affecting Bond Returns," *Journal of Fixed Income*, 1(1), 54–61.

Litzenberger, R. H., 1992, "Swaps: Plain and Fanciful," *Journal of Finance*, 47(3), 831–850.

Lo, A., 2012, "Reading about the Financial Crisis: A Twenty-One-Book Review," *Journal of Economic Literature*, 50(1), 151–178.

Longstaff, F. and Schwartz, E., 1995, "A Simple Approach to Valuing Risky Fixed and Floating Rate Debt," *Journal of Finance*, 50(3), 789–819.

Longstaff, F. A. and Schwartz, E. S., 2001, "Valuing American Options by Simulation: A Least Squares Approach," *Review of Financial Studies*, 14(1), 113–147.

Lowenstein, R., 2000, *When Genius Failed: The Rise and Fall of Long-Term Capital Management*, Random House, New York.

Lucas, D. J. (ed.), 2010, *Measuring and Managing Federal Financial Risk*, University of Chicago Press.

Lucas, D. J., 2011, "Credit Policy as Fiscal Policy," unpublished, MIT.

Lucas, D. J. and McDonald, R. L., 2006, "An Options-Based Approach to Evaluating the Risk of Fannie Mae and Freddie Mac," *Journal of Monetary Economics*, 53(1), 155–176.

Lucas, D. J. and McDonald, R. L., 2010, "Valuing Government Guarantees: Fannie and Freddie Revisited," in D. J. Lucas, (ed.) "Measuring and Managing Federal Financial Risk," chapter 6, 131–161, University of Chicago Press.

Lux, H., 1992, "LOR's Big Gamble on SuperShares," *Investment Dealer's Digest*, 58(48), 12, 30.

Macaulay, F. R., 1938, *The Movement of Interest Rates, Bond Yields and Stock Prices in the United States Since 1856*, National Bureau of Economic Research.

MacKay, P. and Moeller, S. B., 2007, "The Value of Corporate Risk Management," *Journal of Finance*, 62(3), 1379–1419.

Margrabe, W., 1978, "The Value of an Option to Exchange One Asset for Another," *Journal of Finance*, 33(1), 177–186.

Markit, 2008, *Markit Credit Indices: A Primer*, Technical Report, Markit Group Limited.

Markit, 2009, *The CDS Big Bang: Understanding the Changes to the Global CDS Contract and North American Conventions*, Technical Report, Markit Group Limited.

Masters, B., Jenkins, P., and Baer, J., 2011, "Banks Served LIBOR Subpoenas," *Financial Times*, 15.

Masters, M., 2008, "Testimony of Michael W. Masters before the Committeee on Homeland Security and Governmental Affairs, United States Senate," http://hsgac.senate.gov/public/_files/052008Masters.pdf.

McConnell, J. J. and Schwartz, E. S., 1992, "The Origin of LYONs: A Case Study in Financial Innovation," *Journal of Applied Corporate Finance*, 4(4), 40–47.

McDonald, R. L., 2000, "Real Options and Rules of Thumb in Capital Budgeting," in Brennan and Trigeorgis (2000), chapter 2, 13–33.

McDonald, R. L., 2003, "Is It Optimal to Accelerate the Payment of Income Tax on Share-Based Compensation?" unpublished, Northwestern University.

McDonald, R. L., 2004, "The Tax (Dis)Advantage of a Firm Issuing Options on Its Own Stock," *Journal of Public Economics*, 88(5), 925–955.

McDonald, R. L., 2012, "Contingent Capital with a Dual Price Trigger," *Journal of Financial Stability*, forthcoming.

McDonald, R. L. and Siegel, D., 1986, "The Value of Waiting to Invest," *Quarterly Journal of Economics*, 101(4), 707–727.

McDonald, R. L. and Siegel, D. R., 1984, "Option Pricing When the Underlying Asset Earns a Below-Equilibrium Rate of Return: A Note," *Journal of Finance*, 39(1), 261–265.

McDonald, R. L. and Siegel, D. R., 1985, "Investment and the Valuation of Firms When There Is an Option to Shut Down," *International Economic Review*, 26(2), 331–349.

McMillan, L. G., 1992, *Options as a Strategic Investment*, New York Institute of Finance, New York, 3rd edition.

McMurray, S., 2001, "Ka-Ching around the Collar: "Costless Collars" Can Cut Execs' Stock Risk. But Are They Good for Shareholders?" http://www.business2.com/b2/web/articles/0,17863,513180,00.html.

Meissner, G., 2005, *Credit Derivatives*, Blackwell Publishing, Malden, MA.

Mello, A. S. and Parsons, J. E., 1995, "Maturity Structure of a Hedge Matters: Lessons from the Metallgesellschaft Debacle," *Journal of Applied Corporate Finance*, 8(1), 106–120.

Merton, R. C., 1973a, "The Relationship between Put and Call Option Prices: Comment," *Journal of Finance*, 28(1), 183–184.

Merton, R. C., 1973b, "Theory of Rational Option Pricing," *Bell Journal of Economics and Management Science*, 4(1), 141–183.

Merton, R. C., 1974, "On the Pricing of Corporate Debt: The Risk Structure of Interest Rates," *Journal of Finance*, 29(2), 449–470.

Merton, R. C., 1976, "Option Pricing When Underlying Stock Returns Are Discontinuous," *Journal of Financial Economics*, 3(1), 125–144.

Merton, R. C., 1977, "On the Pricing of Contingent Claims and the Modigliani-Miller Theorem," *Journal of Financial Economics*, 5(2), 241–249.

Merton, R. C., 1990, "On the Mathematics and Economics Assumptions of Continuous-Time Models," in R. C. Merton (ed.), "Continuous-Time Finance," chapter 3, 57–93, Basil Blackwell, Cambridge, MA.

Merton, R. C., 1999, "Finance Theory and Future Trends: The Shift to Integration," *Risk*, 11(7), 48–51.

Miller, M. H., 1986, "Financial Innovation: The Last Twenty Years and the Next," *Journal of Financial and Quantitative Analysis*, 21(4), 459–471.

Miltersen, K. R., Sandmann, K., and Sondermann, D., 1997, "Closed Form Solutions for Term Structure Derivatives with Lognormal Interest Rates," *Journal of Finance*, 52(1), 409–430.

Mitchell, M. and Pulvino, T., 2001, "Characteristics of Risk and Return in Risk Arbitrage," *Journal of Finance*, 56(6), 2135–2175.

Modest, D. M. and Sundaresan, M., 1983, "The Relationship between Spot and Futures Prices in Stock Index Futures Markets: Some Preliminary Evidence," *Journal of Futures Markets*, 3(1), 15–41.

Modigliani, F. and Miller, M., 1958, "The Cost of Capital, Corporation Finance, and the Theory of Investment," *American Economic Review*, 48(3), 261–297.

Mollenkamp, C., 2008, "Libor Surges after Scrutiny Does, Too," *Wall Street Journal*.

Mood, A. M., Graybill, F. A., and Boes, D. C., 1974, *Introduction to the Theory of Statistics*, McGraw-Hill, New York, 3rd edition.

Morgenson, G., 1998, "Trimming Stock Options' Sails: Accounting Proposal Would Lift the Cost of Repricing," *The New York Times*, August 20, D1.

Mou, Y., 2010, "Limits to Arbitrage and Commodity Index Investment: Front-Running the Goldman Roll," unpublished, Columbia University.

Murphy, K. J., forthcoming, "Executive Compensation: Where We Are, and How We Got There," in M. Harris, R. Stulz, and G. Constantinides (eds.), "Handbook of the Economics of Finance," Elsevier.

Myers, S. C., 1977, "Determinants of Corporate Borrowing," *Journal of Financial Economics*, 5(2), 147–175.

Naik, V. and Lee, M., 1990, "General Equilibrium Pricing of Options on the Market Portfolio with Discontinuous Returns," *Review of Financial Studies*, 3(4), 493–521.

Neftci, S. N., 2000, *An Introduction to the Mathematics of Financial Derivatives*, Academic Press, San Diego, CA, 2nd edition.

Nelson, D. B., 1991, "Conditional Heterskedasticity in Asset Returns: A New Approach," *Econometrica*, 59, 347–370.

Neuberger, A., 1994, "The Log Contract," *Journal of Portfolio Management*, 20(2), 74–80.

Office of Management and Budget, 2012, *Federal Credit Supplement, Budget of the U.S. Government, Fiscal Year 2012*, Technical report, United States Government.

Ou, S., 2011, *Corporate Default and Recovery Rates, 1920–2010*, Technical Report, Moody's Investor's Service.

Paddock, J. L., Siegel, D. R., and Smith, J. L., 1988, "Option Valuation of Claims on Real Assets: The Case of Offshore Petroleum Leases," *Quarterly Journal of Economics*, 103(3), 479–508.

Pan, J., 2002, "The Jump-Risk Premia Implicit in Options: Evidence from an Integrated Time-Series Study," *Journal of Financial Economics*, 63(1), 3–50.

Patell, J. M. and Wolfson, M. A., 1979, "Anticipated Information Releases Reflected in Call Option Prices," *Journal of Accounting and Economics*, 1(2), 117–140, August 1979.

Patell, J. M. and Wolfson, M. A., 1981, "The Ex Ante and Ex Post Price Effects of Quarterly Earnings Announcements Reflected in Option and Stock Prices," *Journal of Accounting Research*, 434–458, Autumn 1981.

Pearson, N. D., 2002, *Risk Budgeting: Portfolio Problem Solving with Value-at-Risk*, John Wiley & Sons, Inc.

Perrow, C., 1999, *Normal Accidents: Living with High-Risk Technologies*, Princeton University Press, Princeton, NJ.

Petersen, M. A. and Thiagarajan, S. R., 2000, "Risk Measurement and Hedging: With and without Derivatives," *Financial Management*, 29(4), 5–29.

Petrie, K. N., 2000, "Why Some Firms Use Collar Offers in Mergers," Working Paper, Terry College of Business, University of Georgia.

Philips, M., 2012, "Stock Trading Is About to Get 5.2 Milliseconds Faster," *BloombergBusinessweek*, http://goo.gl/8FNoH.

Pindyck, R. S., 1993a, "Investments of Uncertain Cost," *Journal of Financial Economics*, 34(1), 53–76.

Pindyck, R. S., 1993b, "The Present Value Model of Rational Commodity Pricing," *The Economic Journal*, 103(418), 511–530.

Pindyck, R. S., 1994, "Inventories and the Short-Run Dynamics of Commodity Prices," *Rand Journal of Economics*, 25(1), 141–159.

Rapoport, M., 2010, "BofA, Citi Made 'Repos' Errors," *Wall Street Journal*, p. C1.

Rebonato, R., 1996, *Interest Rate Option Models*, Wiley, Chichester, England, 2nd edition.

Reiner, E., 1992, "Quanto Mechanics," *Risk*, 5(3), 59–63.

Reinganum, M. R., 1986, "Is Time Travel Impossible? A Financial Proof," *Journal of Portfolio Management*, 13(1), 10–12.

Rendleman, R. J., Jr. and Bartter, B. J., 1979, "Two-State Option Pricing," *Journal of Finance*, 34(5), 1093–1110.

Rendleman, R. J., Jr. and Bartter, B. J., 1980, "The Pricing of Options on Debt Securities," *Journal of Financial and Quantitative Analysis*, XV(1), 11–24.

Richard, S. F. and Sundaresan, M., 1981, "A Continuous Time Equilibrium Model of Forward Prices and Futures Prices in a Multigood Economy," *Journal of Financial Economics*, 9(4), 347–371.

Ronn, A. G. and Ronn, E. I., 1989, "The Box Spread Arbitrage Conditions: Theory, Tests, and Investment Strategies," *Review of Financial Studies*, 2(1), 91–108.

Routledge, B. R., Seppi, D. J., and Spatt, C. S., 2000, "Equilibrium Forward Curves for Commodities," *Journal of Finance*, 55(3), 1297–1338.

Royal Swedish Academy of Sciences, 2003, *Time-Series Econometrics: Cointegration and Autoregressive Conditional Heteroskedasticity*, Technical Report, Royal Swedish Academy of Sciences.

Rubinstein, M., 1991a, "Double Trouble," *Risk*, 5(1), 73.

Rubinstein, M., 1991b, "One for Another," *Risk*, 4(7), 30–32.

Rubinstein, M., 1991c, "Somewhere over the Rainbow," *Risk*, 4(10), 63–66.

Rubinstein, M., 1994, "Return to Oz," *Risk*, 7(11), 67–71.

Rubinstein, M. and Reiner, E., 1991a, "Breaking Down the Barrier," *Risk*, 4(8), 28–35.

Rubinstein, M. and Reiner, E., 1991b, "Unscrambling the Binary Code," *Risk*, 4(9), 75–83.

Ryan, M. D. and Granovsky, R. J., 2000, "Nikkei 225 Put Warrants," in J. C. Francis, W. W. Toy, and J. G. Whittaker (eds.), "The Handbook of Equity Derivatives," chapter 17, 368–394, Wiley, New York, revised edition.

Saly, P. J., Jagannathan, R., and Huddart, S. J., 1999, "Valuing the Reload Features of Executive Stock Options," *Accounting Horizons*, 13(3), 219–240.

Samuelson, P. A., 1965, "Proof that Properly Anticipated Prices Fluctuate Randomly," *Industrial Management Review*, 6(2), 41–49.

Schönbucher, P., 2003, *Credit Derivatives Pricing Models*, Wiley.

Schroder, M., 1988, "Adapting the Binomial Model to Value Options on Assets with Fixed-Cash Payouts," *Financial Analysts Journal*, 44(6), 54–62.

Schroder, M., 1989, "Computing the Constant Elasticity of Variance Option Pricing Formula," *Journal of Finance*, 44(1), 211–219.

Schroder, M., 1999, "Changes of Numeraire for Pricing Futures, Forwards, and Options," *Review of Financial Studies*, 12(5), 1143–1163.

Schwartz, E. S., 1997, "The Stochastic Behavior of Commodity Prices: Implications for Valuation and Hedging," *Journal of Finance*, 52(3), 923–973.

Schwartz, E. S. and Moon, M., 2000, "Rational Valuation of Internet Companies," *Financial Analysts Journal*, 56(3), 62–75.

Scott, L. O., 1987, "Option Pricing When the Variance Changes Randomly: Theory, Estimation, and an Application," *Journal of Financial and Quantitative Analysis*, 22(4), 419–438.

Shao, J. and Tu, D., 1995, *The Jackknife and Bootstrap*, Springer-Verlag, New York.

Sharpe, W. F., 1976, "Corporate Pension Funding Policy," *Journal of Financial Economics*, 3(3), 183–193.

Sharpe, W. F., 1978, *Investments*, Prentice-Hall, Englewood Cliffs, NJ.

Shiller, R. J., 2003, *The New Financial Order: Risk in the 21st Century*, Princeton University Press, Princeton, New Jersey.

Shumway, T., 2001, "Forecasting Bankruptcy More Accurately: A Simple Hazard Model," *Journal of Business*, 74(1), 101–124.

Siegel, D. and Siegel, D., 1990, *Futures Markets*, Dryden Press, Chicago.

Siegel, J. J., 1998, *Stocks for the Long Run*, McGraw-Hill, 2nd edition.

Smith, C. W. and Stulz, R. M., 1985, "The Determinants of Firms' Hedging Policies," *Journal of Financial and Quantitative Analysis*, 20(4), 391–405.

Smith, D., 2002, "Two Common Textbook Misstatements about Bond Prices and Yields," unpublished, Boston University School of Management.

Smith, D. J., 1997, "Aggressive Corporate Finance: A Close Look at the Procter & Gamble-Bankers Trust Leveraged Swap," *Journal of Derivatives*, 4(4), 67–79.

Sobehart, J. and Keenan, S., 2002, "The Need for Hybrid Models," *Risk*, 15(2), 73–77.

Sorkin, A. R., 2010, *Too Big to Fail: The Inside Story of How Wall Street and Washington Fought to Save the FinancialSystem–and Themselves*, Penguin.

Spatt, C. S. and Sterbenz, F. P., 1988, "Warrant Exercise, Dividends, and Reinvestment Policy," *Journal of Finance*, 43(2), 493–506.

Srivastava, S., 1998, "Value at Risk Analysis of a Leveraged Swap," Working Paper, Carnegie-Mellon University.

Steele, J. M., 2010, *Stochastic Calculus and Financial Applications*, Springer.

Stein, J. C., 1992, "Convertible Bonds as Backdoor Equity Financing," *Journal of Financial Economics*, 32(1), 3–21.

Stigum, M., 1990, *The Money Market*, McGraw-Hill, New York, 3rd edition.

Stigum, M. and Robinson, F. L., 1996, *Money Market & Bond Calculations*, Richard D. Irwin, Inc., Chicago, IL.

Stoll, H. R., 1969, "The Relationship between Put and Call Option Prices," *Journal of Finance*, 24(5), 801–824.

Stoll, H. R., 1973, "The Relationship between Put and Call Option Prices: Reply," *Journal of Finance*, 28(1), 185–187.

Stulz, R., 1982, "Options on the Minimum or the Maximum of Two Risky Assets," *Journal of Financial Economics*, 10(2), 161–185.

Stulz, R., 1996, "Rethinking Risk Management," *Journal of Applied Corporate Finance*, 9(3), 8–24.

Stutzer, M., 2010, "How Students Can Backtest Madoff's Claims," *Journal of Financial Education*, 8(1), 2010.

Sundaresan, S., 2009, *Fixed Income Markets and Their Derivatives*, Academic Press, 3rd edition.

Taleb, N. N., 2010, *The Black Swan*, Random House, 2nd edition.

Tan, K. S. and Boyle, P. P., 2000, "Applications of Randomized Low Discrepancy Sequences to the Valuation of Complex Securitie," *Journal of Economic Dynamics and Control*, 24(11-12), 1747–1782.

Tavakoli, J. M., 1998, *Credit Derivatives: A Guide to Instruments and Applications*, Wiley, New York.

Tavakoli, J. M., 2001, *Credit Derivatives & Synthetic Structures: A Guide to Instruments and Applications*, Wiley, New York, 2nd edition.

Taylor, J. B. and Williams, J. C., 2009, "A Black Swan in the Money Market," *American Economic Journal: Macroeconomics*, 1(1), 58–83.

Tett, G., 2010, *Fool's Gold: The Inside Story of J.P. Morgan and How Wall St. Greed Corrupted Its Bold Dream and Created a Financial Catastrophe*, Free Press.

Thatcher, K. L., Flynn, T., Ehrlinger, J., and Reel, M., 1994, *Equity Put Warrants: Reducing the Costs and Risks of a Stock Repurchase Program*, Technical Report, Salomon Brothers, New York.

Titman, S., 1985, "Urban Land Prices under Uncertainty," *American Economic Review*, 75(3), 505–514.

Todorov, V., 2010, "Variance Risk-Premium Dynamics: The Role of Jumps," *Review of Financial Studies*, 23(1), 345–383.

Triantis, A. and Borison, A., 2001, "Real Options: State of the Practice," *Journal of Applied Corporate Finance*, 14(2), 8–24.

Trigeorgis, L., 1996, *Real Options: Managerial Flexibility and Strategy in Resource Allocation*, MIT Press, Cambridge, MA.

Tsiveriotis, K. and Fernandes, C., 1998, "Valuing Convertible Bonds with Credit Risk," *Journal of Fixed Income*, 8(2), 95–102.

Tuckman, B., 1995, *Fixed Income Securities*, Wiley, New York.

Tuckman, B. and Serrat, A., 2012, *Fixed Income Securities: Tools for Today's Markets*, Wiley Finance, 3rd edition.

Tufano, P., 1996, "Who Manages Risk? An Empirical Analysis of Risk Management Practices in the Gold Mining Industry," *Journal of Finance*, 51(4), 1097–1138.

Tufano, P., 1998, "The Determinants of Stock Price Exposure: Financial Engineering and the Gold Mining Industry," *Journal of Finance*, 53(3), 1015–1052.

Turnbull, S. M., 1987, "Swaps: Zero Sum Game?" *Financial Management*, 16(1), 15–21.

U.S. Securities and Exchange Commission, 2010, "SECURITIES AND EXCHANGE COMMISSION, Plaintiff, v. GOLDMAN SACHS & CO. and FABRICE TOURRE, Defendants," http://www.sec.gov/litigation/complaints/2010/comp21489.pdf.

Valukas, A. R., 2010, *In re: Lehman Brothers Holdings Inc., et al., Debtors: Chapter 11 Case No. 08-13555 (JMP) (Jointly Administered). Report Of Anton R. Valukas, Examiner*, Technical Report, United States Bankruptcy Court, Southern District Of New York.

van Binsbergen, J. H., Brandt, M. W., and Koijen, R. S., forthcoming, "On the Timing and Pricing of Dividends," *American Economic Review*.

van Binsbergen, J. H., Hueskes, W., Koijen, R. S., and Vrugt, E. B., 2011, "A Term Structure of Growth," Working Paper, Northwestern University.

Vasicek, O., 1977, "An Equilibrium Characterization of the Term Structure," *Journal of Financial Economics*, 5(2), 177–188.

Vassalou, M. and Xing, Y., 2004, "Default Risk in Equity Returns," *Journal of Finance*, 59(2), 831–868.

Vazza, D., Kraemer, N., Khan, R., and Richhariya, N. M., 2011, *2010 Annual Global Corporate Default Study And Rating Transitions*, Technical Report, Standard and Poors, http://tinyurl.com/87yzenv.

Veronesi, P., 2010, *Fixed Income Securities: Valuation, Risk, and Risk Management*, Wiley.

Watkinson, L. and Roosevelt, D., 2004, *Correlation: The Layman's Guide to Implied Correlation*, Product Note, Morgan Stanley Fixed Income, New York.

Wiggins, J. B., 1987, "Option Values Under Stochastic Volatilities," *Journal of Financial Economics*, 19, 351–372.

Williams, S., 2009, "Mexico Hedges 2010 Oil Price Exposure at $57 a Barrel," *FOWeek*.

Wilmott, P., 1998, *Derivatives: The Theory and Practice of Financial Engineering*, John Wiley & Sons, Chichester, England.

WuDunn, S., 1996, "Sumitomo Increases Size of Copper-Trade Loss to $2.6 Billion," *The New York Times*.

Yermack, D., 1997, "Good Timing: CEO Stock Option Awards and Company News Announcements," *Journal of Finance*, 52(2), 449–476.

Zhang, P. G., 1998, *Exotic Options: A Guide to Second Generation Options*, World Scientific, Singapore, 2nd edition.

Zuckerman, G., Ng, S., and Rappaport, L., 2009, "A Daring Trade Has Wall Street Seething," *Wall Street Journal*, p. C1.

Zwick, S. and Collins, D. P., 2004, "One Year In and the Jury is Still Out," *Futures*, 33(1), 66.

Index